# Costa Rica

### Rob Rachowiecki

**LONELY PLANET PUBLICATIONS**
Melbourne • Oakland • London • Paris

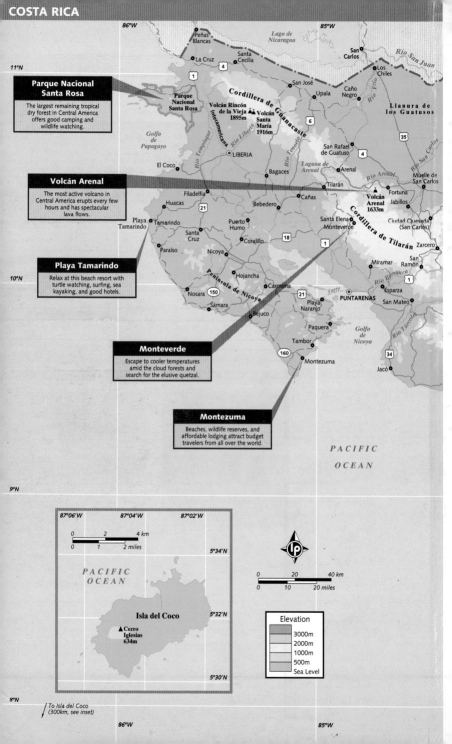

# COSTA RICA

**Parque Nacional Santa Rosa**
The largest remaining tropical dry forest in Central America offers good camping and wildlife watching.

**Volcán Arenal**
The most active volcano in Central America erupts every few hours and has spectacular lava flows.

**Playa Tamarindo**
Relax at this beach resort with turtle watching, surfing, sea kayaking, and good hotels.

**Monteverde**
Escape to cooler temperatures amid the cloud forests and search for the elusive quetzal.

**Montezuma**
Beaches, wildlife reserves, and affordable lodging attract budget travelers from all over the world.

Peñas Blancas
La Cruz
Santa Cecilia
San José
San Carlos
Los Chiles
Río San Juan
Lago de Nicaragua

Parque Nacional Santa Rosa
Volcán Rincón de la Vieja 1895m
Volcán Santa María 1916m
Upala
Caño Negro
Río Frío
Llanura de los Guatusos

Cordillera de Guanacaste
Golfo de Papagayo
LIBERIA
Bagaces
San Rafael de Guatuso
Laguna de Arenal
Arenal
Muelle de San Carlos

El Coco
Filadelfia
Cañas
Tilarán
Volcán Arenal 1633m
Fortuna
Jabillos

Huacas
Bebedero
Santa Elena
Monteverde
Ciudad Quesada (San Carlos)
Zarcero

Playa Tamarindo
Tamarindo
Puerto Humo
Cordillera de Tilarán

Santa Cruz
Coralillo
Miramar
San Ramón

Paraíso
Nicoya
Esparza
San Mateo

Hojancha
Carmona
Río Barranca

Nosara
Península de Nicoya
Playa Naranjo
PUNTARENAS
Ferry

Sámara
Bejuco
Golfo de Nicoya

Paquera
Tambor
Montezuma
Jacó

PACIFIC OCEAN

87°06'W  87°04'W  87°02'W
0    2    4 km
0    1    2 miles

PACIFIC OCEAN

5°34'N

Isla del Coco

5°32'N

▲ Cerro Iglesias 634m

5°30'N

0    20    40 km
0    10    20 miles

**Elevation**
3000m
2000m
1000m
500m
Sea Level

To Isla del Coco (300km, see inset)

86°W  85°W  11°N  10°N  9°N  8°N

NICARAGUA

CARIBBEAN
SEA

84°W

83°W

11°N

**Barra del Colorado**

World-class tarpon- and snook-
fishing trips leave from lodges
surrounded by a wildlife refuge.

Boca
Tapada

Barra del Colorado

**Tortuguero**

This Caribbean village is reached
by inland waterways through a
monkey-filled rainforest.

Llanura de
San Carlos

Río Toro

Río Chirripó

Llanura de
Tortuguero

Tortuguero

Pital

Puerto Viejo
de Sarapiquí

Río Tortuguero

Cariari

**Parque Nacional
Volcán Poás**

A short walk from the summit
parking area takes you to the
rim of the steaming crater.

Parque
Nacional
Volcán Poás

San
Miguel

Llanura de
Santa Clara

Río Sucio

Río Chirripó

Volcán ▲
Poás
2704m

Cordillera Central

4

Guápiles

Guácimo

Siquirres

32

PUERTO
LIMÓN

10°N

ALAJUELA

HEREDIA

Volcán ▲
Irazú
3432m

Lajas

32

**Puerto Viejo de
Talamanca**

This laid-back destination has
an intriguing mix of Bribri Indian
and black Caribbean cultures.

Ciudad
Colón

SAN JOSÉ

Pácayas

10

Río Pacuare

36

Santiago de
Puriscal

CARTAGO

Turrialba

Moravia

Pandora

Cahuita

San Ignacio
de Acosta

Paraíso

Tapantí

Río Chirripó Atlántico

Puerto Viejo
de Talamanca

San Marcos
de Tarrazú

Río Pirrís

Santa María
de Dota

Río Estrella

Shiroles

Bribri

Río Sixaola

Sixaola

Valle de
Parrita

Parque
Nacional
Chirripó

Río Telire

Amubri

Río Lari

Guabito
Changuinola

Parrita

▲ Cerro
Chirripó
3820m

Quepos

2

Rivas

San Isidro
de El General

Cordillera de Talamanca

Almirante

Savegre

Ujarrás

Dominical

Río General

Buenos
Aires

Uvita

Valle del
General

Potrero
Grande

Río Cotón

9°N

**Parque Nacional Chirripó**

A sleeping bag, warm clothes,
and strong legs are all you need
to climb Chirripó, the country's
highest peak.

34

Palmar
Norte

Paso Real

Valle de
Cóto Brus

Santa
Elena

PANAMA

Ciudad Cortés

Interamericana

Fila Costeña

Sabalito

Boquete

Sierpe

San
Vito

Río Sereno

Bahía
Drake

2

Agua
Buena

Isla del
Caño

Rincón

Golfo
Dulce

Golfito

Río
Claro

Neily

Parque
Nacional
Corcovado

Península
de Osa

Paso
Canoas

David

**Parque Nacional
Corcovado**

Visitors backpack and camp in
pristine rainforest with Costa
Rica's largest colonies of
scarlet macaws.

Laguna
Corcovado

Puerto
Jiménez

Playa
Zancudo

Valle de
Coto Colorado

Ferry

Carate

**Wilson Botanical Garden**

The country's best botanical
garden has comfortable
lodge accommodations.

Puerto
Armuelles

8°N

84°W

83°W

Costa Rica
5th edition – October 2002
First published – September 1991

Published by
Lonely Planet Publications Pty Ltd  ABN 36 005 607 983
90 Maribyrnong St, Footscray, Victoria 3011, Australia

Lonely Planet Offices
Australia Locked Bag 1, Footscray, Victoria 3011
USA 150 Linden St, Oakland, CA 94607
UK 10a Spring Place, London NW5 3BH
France 1 rue du Dahomey, 75011 Paris

Photographs
Many of the images in this guide are available for licensing from
Lonely Planet Images.
W www.lonelyplanetimages.com

Front cover photograph
Young white-faced capuchin monkeys playing
in tree (Catherine Kelliher/Getty Images)

ISBN 1 74059 118 6

text & maps © Lonely Planet Publications Pty Ltd 2002
photos © photographers as indicated 2002

Printed through Colorcraft Ltd, Hong Kong
Printed in China

# Contents

## INTRODUCTION 9

## FACTS ABOUT COSTA RICA 11

History . . . . . . . . . . . . . . 11
Geography . . . . . . . . . . . 15
Geology . . . . . . . . . . . . . . 16
Climate . . . . . . . . . . . . . . 16
Ecology & Environment . . . 16
Flora & Fauna . . . . . . . . . . 20
Government & Politics . . . . 24
Economy . . . . . . . . . . . . . 25
Population & People . . . . . . 26
Education . . . . . . . . . . . . . 26
Arts . . . . . . . . . . . . . . . . . 27
Society & Conduct . . . . . . . 28
Religion . . . . . . . . . . . . . . 30
Language . . . . . . . . . . . . . 30

## FACTS FOR THE VISITOR 32

Highlights . . . . . . . . . . . . . 32
Planning . . . . . . . . . . . . . . 32
Tourist Offices . . . . . . . . . . 34
Visas & Documents . . . . . . 35
Embassies & Consulates . . . 36
Customs . . . . . . . . . . . . . . 37
Money . . . . . . . . . . . . . . . 37
Post & Communications . . . 40
Internet Resources . . . . . . . 42
Books . . . . . . . . . . . . . . . . 42
Newspapers & Magazines . . 44
Radio & TV . . . . . . . . . . . . 44
Photography & Video . . . . . 44
Time . . . . . . . . . . . . . . . . 45
Electricity . . . . . . . . . . . . . 45
Weights & Measures . . . . . 45
Laundry . . . . . . . . . . . . . . 45
Toilets . . . . . . . . . . . . . . . 45
Health . . . . . . . . . . . . . . . 45
Women Travelers . . . . . . . . 51
Gay & Lesbian Travelers . . . 52
Disabled Travelers . . . . . . . 53
Senior Travelers . . . . . . . . . 54
Travel with Children . . . . . . 54
Useful Organizations . . . . . 54
Dangers & Annoyances . . . . 55
Emergency . . . . . . . . . . . . 56
Legal Matters . . . . . . . . . . 56
Business Hours . . . . . . . . . 57
Public Holidays &
Special Events . . . . . . . . . . 57
Activities . . . . . . . . . . . . . 58
Language Courses . . . . . . . 65
Work . . . . . . . . . . . . . . . . 65
Accommodations . . . . . . . 65
Food . . . . . . . . . . . . . . . . 67
Drinks . . . . . . . . . . . . . . . 69
Entertainment . . . . . . . . . 70
Spectator Sports . . . . . . . . 70
Shopping . . . . . . . . . . . . . 70

## GETTING THERE & AWAY 72

Air . . . . . . . . . . . . . . . . . . 72
Land . . . . . . . . . . . . . . . . 76
Sea . . . . . . . . . . . . . . . . . 80
Organized Tours . . . . . . . . 81

## GETTING AROUND 84

Air . . . . . . . . . . . . . . . . . . 84
Bus . . . . . . . . . . . . . . . . . 86
Train . . . . . . . . . . . . . . . . 87
Car & Motorcycle . . . . . . . 87
Taxi . . . . . . . . . . . . . . . . . 90
Bicycle . . . . . . . . . . . . . . . 91
Hitchhiking . . . . . . . . . . . . 91
Boat . . . . . . . . . . . . . . . . 91
Local Transportation . . . . . 92
Organized Tours . . . . . . . . 92

## SAN JOSÉ 96

Orientation . . . . . . . . . . . . 96
Information . . . . . . . . . . . 101
Things to See & Do . . . . . 108
Activities . . . . . . . . . . . . 112
Language Courses . . . . . . 113
Organized Tours . . . . . . . 114
Places to Stay . . . . . . . . . 115
Places to Stay –
In the City . . . . . . . . . . . 116
Places to Stay – Escazú . . . 125
Places to Stay –
Other Areas . . . . . . . . . . 127
Places to Eat . . . . . . . . . . 128
Entertainment . . . . . . . . . 136
Spectator Sports . . . . . . . 140
Shopping . . . . . . . . . . . . 140
Getting There & Away . . . 141
Getting Around . . . . . . . . 146

## CENTRAL VALLEY & SURROUNDING HIGHLANDS 149

Alajuela Area . . . . . . . . . 152
Alajuela . . . . . . . . . . . . . 152
Ojo de Agua . . . . . . . . . . 156
Butterfly Farm . . . . . . . . 157
West to Atenas . . . . . . . . 157
Northwest to Zarcero . . . . 158
Parque Nacional Juan
Castro Blanco . . . . . . . . . 163
Laguna Fraijanes Area . . . 163
Parque Nacional
Volcán Poás . . . . . . . . . . 163
Los Jardines de la
Catarata La Paz . . . . . . . 165
Heredia Area . . . . . . . . . 167

Heredia . . . . . . . . . . . . . . 167
Around Heredia . . . . . . . . 170
Parque Nacional
Braulio Carrillo . . . . . . . . 173
Moravia . . . . . . . . . . . . . 176
Coronado . . . . . . . . . . . . 177
Rancho Redondo . . . . . . . 177
Cartago Area . . . . . . . . . . 177
Cartago . . . . . . . . . . . . . . 177
Parque Nacional
Volcán Irazú . . . . . . . . . . 179
Lankester Gardens . . . . . . 181
Río Orosi Valley . . . . . . . . 181
Orosi . . . . . . . . . . . . . . . 182

Parque Nacional Tapantí-
Macizo Cerro
de la Muerte . . . . . . . . . . 184
Turrialba Area . . . . . . . . . 184
Río Reventazón . . . . . . . . 184
Turrialba . . . . . . . . . . . . . 185
Around Turrialba . . . . . . . 188
Monumento Nacional
Guayabo . . . . . . . . . . . . . 188
Parque Nacional
Volcán Turrialba . . . . . . . . 189
Rancho Naturalista . . . . . . 190
Río Pacuare . . . . . . . . . . . 191

## NORTHWESTERN COSTA RICA 193

Interamericana Norte . . . . 196
Refugio Nacional de Fauna
Silvestre Peñas Blancas . . . 196
Reserva Biológica
Isla Pájaros . . . . . . . . . . . 197
Monteverde & Santa Elena 197
Reserva Biológica Bosque
Nuboso Monteverde . . . . 212
Reserva Santa Elena . . . . . 215
Ecolodge San Luis &
Biological Station . . . . . . . 216
Juntas . . . . . . . . . . . . . . . 217
Tempisque Ferry . . . . . . . . 217
Cañas . . . . . . . . . . . . . . : . 217

Volcán Tenorio Area . . . . . 220
Volcán Miravalles Area . . . 221
Bagaces . . . . . . . . . . . . . . 222
Parque Nacional
Palo Verde . . . . . . . . . . . . 222
Reserva Biológica
Lomas de Bárbudal . . . . . . 223
Liberia . . . . . . . . . . . . . . . 224
Parque Nacional Rincón
de la Vieja . . . . . . . . . . . . 229
Parque Nacional
Santa Rosa . . . . . . . . . . . . 233
Refugio Nacional de Vida
Silvestre Bahía Junquillal . . 236

Parque Nacional
Guanacaste . . . . . . . . . . . 237
La Cruz . . . . . . . . . . . . . . 239
Bahía Salinas . . . . . . . . : . . 240
Peñas Blancas . . . . . . . . . . 241
Arenal Route . . . . . . . . . . 241
Ciudad Quesada
(San Carlos) . . . . . . . . . . . 241
Fortuna . . . . . . . . . . . . . . 243
Parque Nacional
Volcán Arenal . . . . . . . . . . 250
Laguna de Arenal Area . . . 252
Tilarán . . . . . . . . . . . . . . . 257

## PENÍNSULA DE NICOYA 259

Playa del Coco . . . . . . . . 262
Playa Hermosa . . . . . . . . . 267
Playa Panamá & the
Papagayo Project . . . . . . . 268
Playa Ocotal . . . . . . . . . . . 268
Accessing Beaches South
of Playa Ocotal . . . . . . . . 269
Filadelfia . . . . . . . . . . . . . 270
Playa Brasilito . . . . . . . . . 270
Playa Conchal . . . . . . . . . . 271
Playa Flamingo . . . . . . . . . 271
Bahía Potrero . . . . . . . . . . 272
Playa Pan de Azúcar . . . . . 273
Playa Tamarindo . . . . . . . . 274
Parque Nacional Marino Las
Baulas de Guanacaste . . . . 280

Playas Negra & Avellana . . 281
Playa Junquillal . . . . . . . . . 282
Santa Cruz . . . . . . . . . . . . 284
Accessing Beaches South
of Playa Junquillal . . . . . . 285
Nicoya . . . . . . . . . . . . . . . 286
Parque Nacional
Barra Honda . . . . . . . . . . . 288
Tempisque Ferry . . . . . . . . 289
Playa Nosara . . . . . . . . . . 290
Refugio Nacional de Fauna
Silvestre Ostional . . . . . . . 293
Playa Sámara . . . . . . . . . . 294
Playa Carrillo . . . . . . . . . . 297
Islita & Beyond . . . . . . . . 298
Southeast Corner . . . . . . . 299

Playa Naranjo . . . . . . . . . 299
Bahía Gigante . . . . . . . . . . 300
Islands near Bahía Gigante 300
Paquera . . . . . . . . . . . . . . 301
Refugio Nacional de Vida
Silvestre Curú . . . . . . . . . 302
Playas Pochote & Tambor 302
Cóbano . . . . . . . . . . . . . . 303
Montezuma . . . . . . . . . . . 303
Mal País . . . . . . . . . . . . . . 308
Cabuya . . . . . . . . . . . . . . 309
Reserva Natural Absoluta
Cabo Blanco . . . . . . . . . . 310

# NORTHERN LOWLANDS

Caño Negro Area . . . . . . . 313
Muelle de San Carlos . . . . 313
San Rafael de
Guatuso Area . . . . . . . . . 314
Upala . . . . . . . . . . . . . . 315
Refugio Nacional de Vida
Silvestre Caño Negro . . . . 316
Los Chiles . . . . . . . . . . . . 318

La Laguna del
Lagarto Lodge . . . . . . . . 320
San José to Puerto Viejo
de Sarapiquí . . . . . . . . . . 320
Western Route . . . . . . . . 321
Eastern Route . . . . . . . . . 322
Puerto Viejo de Sarapiquí  323

West of Puerto Viejo
de Sarapiquí . . . . . . . . . . 325
North of Puerto Viejo
de Sarapiquí . . . . . . . . . . 328
South of Puerto Viejo
de Sarapiquí . . . . . . . . . . 329

# CARIBBEAN LOWLANDS

San José to Puerto Limón  333
Guápiles & Environs . . . . . 333
Guácimo . . . . . . . . . . . . . 336
Siquirres . . . . . . . . . . . . . 336
Puerto Limón . . . . . . . . . 337
Around Puerto Limón . . . . 341
Northern Caribbean . . . . . 343
Parismina . . . . . . . . . . . . 343
Parque Nacional
Tortuguero . . . . . . . . . . . 344

Tortuguero Area . . . . . . . . 346
Barra del Colorado Area . . 352
Southern Caribbean . . . . . 357
Conselvatur . . . . . . . . . . 358
Aviarios del Caribe . . . . . . 359
Valle de La Estrella . . . . . . 359
Reserva Biológica
Hitoy Cerere . . . . . . . . . . 359
Cahuita . . . . . . . . . . . . . 360
Parque Nacional Cahuita  366

Puerto Viejo de Talamanca  368
East of Puerto Viejo
de Talamanca . . . . . . . . . 376
Manzanillo . . . . . . . . . . . 379
Refugio Nacional
de Vida Silvestre
Gandoca-Manzanillo . . . . 379
Bribri . . . . . . . . . . . . . . . 381
Sixaola. . . . . . . . . . . . . . . 381

# SOUTHERN COSTA RICA

Ruta de los Santos . . . . . . 383
Genesis II. . . . . . . . . . . . . 386
Mirador de Quetzales . . . . 387
San Gerardo de Dota . . . . 387
Cerro de la Muerte . . . . . . 388
Avalon Reserva Privada . . 388
San Isidro de El General . . 389

San Gerardo de Rivas . . . . 393
Parque Nacional Chirripó  394
Buenos Aires . . . . . . . . . . 397
Reserva Biológica Durika  397
Reserva Indígena Boruca  398
Palmar Norte & Palmar Sur 398
Palmar Norte to Neily . . . . 400

Neily . . . . . . . . . . . . . . . 400
Paso Canoas . . . . . . . . . . 402
San Vito . . . . . . . . . . . . . 404
Wilson Botanical Garden . . 406
Parque Internacional
La Amistad . . . . . . . . . . . 407

# PENÍNSULA DE OSA & GOLFO DULCE

To Corcovado via
Bahía Drake . . . . . . . . . . 410
Sierpe . . . . . . . . . . . . . . 410
Bahía Drake . . . . . . . . . . 413
From Bahía Drake
to Corcovado . . . . . . . . . 418
Reserva Biológica
Isla del Caño . . . . . . . . . . 420
Parque Nacional
Corcovado . . . . . . . . . . . 420

To Corcovado via
Puerto Jiménez . . . . . . . . 425
From the Interamericana to
Puerto Jiménez . . . . . . . . 425
Puerto Jiménez . . . . . . . . 425
South of Puerto Jiménez . . 429
Carate . . . . . . . . . . . . . . 431
Corcovado Lodge
Tent Camp . . . . . . . . . . . 432
Northern Golfo
Dulce Area . . . . . . . . . . . 433

Golfito . . . . . . . . . . . . . . 433
Playa Cacao . . . . . . . . . . 439
Refugio Nacional de Fauna
Silvestre Golfito . . . . . . . . 439
North along the
Golfo Dulce . . . . . . . . . . 440
Southern Golfo Dulce Area 442
Playa Zancudo . . . . . . . . 442
Pavones . . . . . . . . . . . . . 445
Tiskita Jungle Lodge . . . . . 446

## CENTRAL PACIFIC COAST                                                447

Puntarenas . . . . . . . . . . . . 447
Iguana Park . . . . . . . . . . 454
From Puntarenas to Parque
Nacional Carara . . . . . . . . 454
Parque Nacional Carara . . 455
Tárcoles Area . . . . . . . . . . 456
Punta Leona Area . . . . . . . 457
Playa Herradura . . . . . . . . 458
Jacó Area . . . . . . . . . . . . 459

Jacó to Quepos . . . . . . . . 466
Quepos . . . . . . . . . . . . . 466
Quepos to
Manuel Antonio . . . . . . . 472
Manuel Antonio . . . . . . . . 478
Parque Nacional Manuel
Antonio . . . . . . . . . . . . . 479
Manuel Antonio
to Dominical . . . . . . . . . . 483

Hacienda Barú . . . . . . . . 484
Dominical . . . . . . . . . . . . 486
Southeast of Dominical . . . 488
Uvita . . . . . . . . . . . . . . . 490
Parque Nacional
Màrino Ballena . . . . . . . . 491
Southeast of Uvita . . . . . . 492

## LANGUAGE                                                              494

## GLOSSARY                                                              502

## COSTA RICAN WILDLIFE GUIDE                                            505

## THANKS                                                                541

## INDEX                                                                 549

## MAP LEGEND                                                            560

# COSTA RICA MAP INDEX

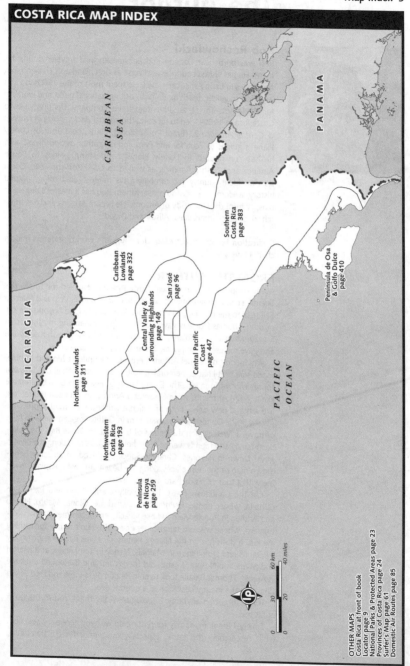

PANAMA

CARIBBEAN SEA

Southern Costa Rica
page 383

Caribbean Lowlands
page 332

San José
page 96

Peninsula de Osa & Golfo Dulce
page 410

NICARAGUA

Central Valley & Surrounding Highlands
page 149

Northern Lowlands
page 311

Central Pacific Coast
page 447

PACIFIC OCEAN

Northwestern Costa Rica
page 193

Peninsula de Nicoya
page 259

0  30  60 km
0  20  40 miles

OTHER MAPS
Costa Rica at front of book
Locator page 9
National Parks & Protected Areas page 23
Provinces of Costa Rica page 24
Surfer's Map page 61
Domestic Air Routes page 85

# The Author

## Rob Rachowiecki

Rob was born near London and became an avid traveler during his teens. He has visited countries as diverse as Greenland and Thailand, but specializes in Latin American travel. He spent most of the 1980s in Latin America, traveling, teaching English, visiting national parks and working for Wilderness Travel, an adventure travel company. His first visits to Costa Rica in 1980–1 led to his co-authorship of *Backpacking in Mexico & Central America 2*, (Bradt Publications). He is the author of Lonely Planet's guides to Ecuador and Peru and co-author of *Southwest*, and he has contributed to Lonely Planet's shoestring guides to South America and Central America, as well as to *USA*. Rob considers Costa Rica an ideal country for combining his interests in birding, natural history, wilderness areas and conservation. Rob has a master's degree in biology from the University of Arizona. He lives in Arizona and has three school-aged children, Julia, Alison and David.

**Dedication** For my sweet Alison Junebug, the world's greatest middle child. I love you.

## FROM THE AUTHOR

Many people showed me 'their' Costa Rica and enabled me to see this beautiful country with different view points. In San José, Vern and Marcela Bell treated me to their gallo pinto breakfast and helped beyond the call of duty. Thomas Douglas gave loads of support planning my travels. In Escazú, Michael and Yolanda Kaye turned over their guesthouse to me and gave me use of the phone, helping in innumerable ways.

My friends in Manuel Antonio, especially Jennifer, Chip and Robbie, made sure that I had a memorable visit. In San Isidro, Noel Ureña was a fountain of information. The Ewing family at Hacienda Barú treated me like a long-lost friend, while Susan and Andrew in Zancudo treated me like a brand new one – both of which a writer on the road appreciates greatly. Katie Duncan and partner Tom in Golfito regaled me with tales of travel as well as plentiful details of the area. In Drake Bay, the Kalmbach family and friends were a huge help – thanks for taking me diving, guys! Down in Pavones, Candyce Speck produced an amazing hand-drawn map of the best places along the beach, and John Aspinall awed me with a tour of his orchard around Tiskita.

On the Caribbean coast, I especially thank Pierre and Patricia in Cahuita, whose gentle, loving vibes relaxed me; Gloria, Mauro, Hilario and Andrea in Puerto Viejo, whose vivacity energized me; Daryl in Tortuguero, whose wisdom taught me; and Buttercup's family for turning me into a sloth fan. In the Nicoya Peninsula, I was helped enormously by Daniel and Dominique in Malpaís, Nancy in Tamarindo, and Marcel and Myriam in Nosara. Inland, old friends Jeff and Bill looked after me in Arenal, Thomas Batalla took over in Rincón de la Vieja and Don Efraín Chacón gave me my best look at a quetzal ever.

If I've forgotten anybody, I apologize. A big thank you to the team at LP, too.

Finally, I thank my family for putting up with my necessary absences while researching this book, especially my wonderful children, Julia,

Alison and Davy, whom I miss so much when I am on the road and whom I love so dearly.

# This Book

This 5th edition was written by Rob Rachowiecki. Some general information was drawn from the 1st edition of Scott Doggett's *Panama*.

## FROM THE PUBLISHER

The 5th edition of *Costa Rica* was produced by an immensely skilled, conscientious crew at Lonely Planet's Oakland office. Rachel Bernstein was the lead editor, receiving much-appreciated assistance from Elaine Merrill and Erin Corrigan. Senior editor Maria Donohoe's grace and clear thinking can't be topped. Don Root and Suki Gear proofed the text with the diligence and humor that only true pros can muster. When she stepped in to guide the book through layout, Rebecca Northen made unspeakable contributions. Kate Hoffman's support was, as always, welcomed.

Vigilant lead cartographer Stephanie Sims remained committed to the project even as the desks around her were slowly evacuated. She, with Justin Colgan, Gina Gillich, Molly Green, Brad Lodge, Laurie Mikkelson, Graham Neale, Carole Nuttall, Patrick Phelan, Herman So, John Spelman, Kat Smith and Ed Turley, created the maps, all with the support of senior cartos Sean Brandt and Annette Olson. Alex Guilbert oversaw all the cartographic work.

Lora Santiago designed the cutest cover in the world, and Tracey Croom produced it. Margaret Livingston laid out the fabulous Wildlife Guide and color wraps. Justin Marler earned superhero status when he drew the illustrations in the Wildlife Guide in no time at all; other illustrations were drawn by Justin, Hannah Reineck, Wendy Yanagihara, Hugh D'Andrade, Hayden Foell and Rini Keagy. Emily Douglas laid out *Costa Rica* without a hitch; Lora Santiago and Joshua Schefers chipped in. While providing moral and technical support, Ruth Askevold exhibited her usual hilarity and wisdom at all the right moments. Tracey Croom held all the pieces together during layout. Ken DellaPenta created the handy index. Susan Rimerman offered ongoing guidance.

Gianormous thanks go to all the Oakland LP publishing staff for providing inspiration and laughter – rock on, guys.

# Foreword

## ABOUT LONELY PLANET GUIDEBOOKS

The story begins with a classic travel adventure: Tony and Maureen Wheeler's 1972 journey across Europe and Asia to Australia. There was no useful information about the overland trail then, so Tony and Maureen published the first Lonely Planet guidebook to meet a growing need.

From a kitchen table, Lonely Planet has grown to become the largest independent travel publisher in the world, with offices in Melbourne (Australia), Oakland (USA), London (UK) and Paris (France).

Today Lonely Planet guidebooks cover the globe. There is an ever-growing list of books and information in a variety of media. Some things haven't changed. The main aim is still to make it possible for adventurous travelers to get out there – to explore and better understand the world.

At Lonely Planet we believe travelers can make a positive contribution to the countries they visit – if they respect their host communities and spend their money wisely. Since 1986 a percentage of the income from each book has been donated to aid projects and human rights campaigns, and, more recently, to wildlife conservation.

> Although inclusion in a guidebook usually implies a recommendation, we cannot list every good place. Exclusion does not necessarily imply criticism. In fact, there are a number of reasons why we might exclude a place – sometimes it is simply inappropriate to encourage an influx of travelers.

## UPDATES & READER FEEDBACK

Things change – prices go up, schedules change, good places go bad and bad places go bankrupt. Nothing stays the same. So, if you find things better or worse, recently opened or long-since closed, please tell us and help make the next edition even more accurate and useful.

Lonely Planet thoroughly updates each guidebook as often as possible – usually every two years, although for some destinations the gap can be longer. Between editions, up-to-date information is available in our free, quarterly *Planet Talk* newsletter and monthly email bulletin *Comet*. The *Upgrades* section of our website (W www.lonelyplanet.com) is also regularly updated by Lonely Planet authors, and the site's *Scoop* section covers news and current affairs relevant to travelers. Lastly, the *Thorn Tree* bulletin board and *Postcards* section carry unverified, but fascinating, reports from travelers.

**Tell us about it!** We genuinely value your feedback. A well-traveled team at Lonely Planet reads and acknowledges every email and letter we receive and ensures that every morsel of information finds its way to the relevant authors, editors and cartographers.

Everyone who writes to us will find their name listed in the next edition of the appropriate guidebook and will receive the latest issue of *Comet* or *Planet Talk*. The very best contributions will be rewarded with a free guidebook.

We may edit, reproduce and incorporate your comments in Lonely Planet products such as guidebooks, websites and digital products, so let us know if you don't want your comments reproduced or your name acknowledged.

**How to contact Lonely Planet:**
**Online:** e talk2us@lonelyplanet.com.au, W www.lonelyplanet.com
**Australia:** Locked Bag 1, Footscray, Victoria 3011
**UK:** 10a Spring Place, London NW5 3BH
**USA:** 150 Linden St, Oakland, CA 94607

# Introduction

Travelers today are increasingly turning toward the tropics as an exciting, adventurous, and exotic destination. Of the many attractive tropical countries to choose from, Costa Rica stands out as one of the most delightful in the world. There are not only tropical rainforests and beautiful beaches, but also some surprises – active volcanoes and windswept mountaintops. So although Costa Rica is a small country, many tropical habitats are found within it – and they are protected by the best-developed conservation program in Latin America.

Costa Rica is famous for its enlightened approach to conservation. Almost 26% of the country's land area is protected by the government in one form or another, and more than 12% is within the country's 25 national parks. In addition, there are numerous marine parks as well as privately owned preserves. The variety and density of wildlife in the preserved areas attract people whose

dream is to see monkeys, sloths, caimans, sea turtles, and exotic birds in their natural habitats. And see them you will! Many other animals can be seen, and, with luck, you'll glimpse even such rare and elusive animals as jaguars, tapirs, and harpy eagles.

With both Pacific and Caribbean coasts, there's no shortage of beaches in Costa Rica. Some have been developed for tourism, while others are remote and rarely visited. For a relaxing seaside vacation, you can stay in a luxurious hotel or you can camp – the choice is yours. And wherever you stay, you're likely to find a preserved area within driving distance where you will find monkeys in the trees by the ocean's edge.

Active volcanoes are surely one of the most dramatic natural sights, and few visitors to Costa Rica can resist the opportunity to peer into the crater of a smoking giant. Whether you want to take a guided bus tour to a volcanic summit or hike up

through the rainforest and camp out amid a landscape of boiling mud pools and steaming vents, the information you need is within this book.

Apart from hiking and camping in rainforests and mountains and on beaches, you can snorkel on tropical reefs, surf the best waves in Central America, and raft some of the most thrilling white water in the tropics. Pristine rivers tumble down the lower slopes of the mountains, and the riverbanks are clothed with curtains of rainforest – a truly unique white-water experience. The rivers and lakes offer a beautiful setting for fishing, and the ocean fishing is definitely world-class.

In addition to this natural beauty and outdoor excitement, there's the added attraction of a country that has long had the most stable political climate in Latin America. Costa Rica has had democratic elections since the 19th century and is one of the most peaceful nations in the world. The armed forces were abolished after the 1948 civil war, and Costa Rica has avoided the despotic dictatorships, frequent military coups, terrorism, and internal strife that have torn apart other countries in the region. Costa Rica is the safest country to visit in Latin America.

But it's not only safe – it's friendly. Costa Ricans delight in showing off their lovely country to visitors, and wherever you go, you'll find the locals to be a constant source of help, smiles, and information. The transportation system is inexpensive and covers the whole country, so Costa Rica, one of the most beautiful tropical countries, is also one of the easiest in which to travel.

# Facts about Costa Rica

## HISTORY
### Pre-Conquest

Of all the Central American countries, Costa Rica has been most influenced by the Spanish conquest, and there are relatively few signs of pre-Columbian cultures. The well-known Mexican and northern Central American civilizations, such as the Aztecs, Olmecs, and Mayas, did not reach as far south as Costa Rica. Those peoples who did exist in Costa Rica were few in number and relatively poorly organized. They offered slight resistance to the Spanish, left us little in the way of ancient archaeological monuments, and had no written language.

This is not to say that Costa Rica's pre-Columbian peoples were uncivilized. A visit to San José's Museo de Jade (Jade Museum) or Museo de Oro Precolombino (Pre-Columbian Gold Museum) will awe the visitor. The Museo de Jade has the world's largest collection of pre-Columbian jade – and most of it comes from the Costa Rican area. The Museo de Oro has approximately 2000 pieces on display. Unfortunately, not a great deal is known about the cultures that produced these treasures.

The Greater Nicoya area (consisting of Costa Rica's Península de Nicoya and reaching north along the Pacific coast into Nicaragua) continues to be the focus of archaeological study. In this area, still noteworthy for its pottery, workers have found a wealth of ceramics, stonework, and jade, which has provided excellent insight into the pre-Columbian peoples who lived here. Although it's almost certain that people were living in Central America prior to 20,000 BC, the first definite evidence (in the form of ceramics) is dated to about 2000 BC, which corresponds to what is called 'Period III' by archaeologists.

Period IV, from 1000 BC to AD 500, was characterized by the establishment of villages and of social hierarchies, and the development of jade production. Ceramics and jade from Mayan areas indicate the influence of other peoples through trade. Skill in making pottery improved during Period V (AD 500–1000), and by Period VI (AD 1000–1520) society had developed into a number of settlements, some with populations of about 20,000 ruled by a chief. Most of these settlements were quickly destroyed by the Spanish conquest and its aftermath. Today, the few remaining Indian groups are often known by the name of their last chief, as noted by the Spanish chroniclers. Particularly important in the Greater Nicoya area are the Chorotegas.

The Nicoya area had a dry season and a wet season; this led to a greater development in ceramics there than on the Caribbean side, where water was easier to obtain and rarely had to be stored or transported long distances. In addition, the many bays and safe anchorages of the Península de Nicoya area fostered trading, so it is not surprising that the Greater Nicoya area has left archaeologists with more artifacts than has the Caribbean coast.

The major archaeological site in Costa Rica is the Monumento Nacional Guayabo, about 85km east of the capital, San José. Guayabo is currently under investigation and is thought to have been inhabited from about 1000 BC to AD 1400. Streets, aqueducts, and causeways can be seen, though most of the buildings have collapsed and have not yet been restored. Gold and stone artifacts have been discovered there. Archaeologists believe Guayabo was an important religious and cultural center, although minor compared to Aztec, Inca, or Maya sites.

Of all the existing remnants of pre-Columbian culture, none are more mysterious than the stone spheres of the Diquís region, which covers the southern half of Costa Rica. Dotted throughout the area are perfectly shaped spheres of granite, some as tall as a person and others as small as a grapefruit. They can be seen in the Museo Nacional and various parks and gardens in San José, as well as throughout the Diquís region. Some, undisturbed for centuries, have been found on Isla del Caño, 20km west of the southern Pacific coast. Who carved these enigmatic orbs? What was their purpose? How did they get to Isla del Caño? No one has the answers to these questions. The puzzling granite spheres of southern

Costa Rica underscore how little we know of the region's pre-Columbian cultures.

## Spanish Conquest

Because of the lack of a large and rich indigenous empire at the time of the arrival of the Spaniards, the conquest of Costa Rica is euphemistically called a 'settlement' by some writers. In reality, the Spanish arrival was accompanied by diseases to which the Indians had no resistance, and they died of sickness as much as by the sword. Although the Indians did try to fight the Spanish, the small numbers of natives were unable to stop the ever larger groups of Spaniards that arrived every few years attempting to colonize the land.

The first arrival was Christopher Columbus himself, who landed near present-day Puerto Limón on September 18, 1502, during his fourth and last voyage to the Americas. He was treated well by the coastal Indians during his stay of 17 days, and he noted that some of the native people wore gold decorations. Because of this, the area was dubbed 'costa rica' (rich coast) by the Spaniards, who imagined that a rich empire must lie farther inland.

Spanish King Ferdinand appointed Diego de Nicuesa governor of the region and sent him to colonize it in 1506. This time the Indians did not provide a friendly welcome – perhaps they had become aware of the deadly diseases that accompanied the Europeans. The colonizers were hampered by the jungle, tropical diseases, and the small bands of Indians who used guerrilla tactics to fight off the invaders. About half the colonizers died and the rest returned home, unsuccessful.

Further expeditions followed. The most successful, from the Spaniards' point of view, was a 1522 expedition to the Golfo de Nicoya area led by Gil González Dávila. This was a bloodthirsty affair, with large numbers of the indigenous inhabitants killed or tortured for minor reasons. Although the expedition returned home with a hoard of gold and other treasures and claimed to have converted tens of thousands of Indians to Catholicism, it was unable to form a permanent colony and many expedition members died of hunger and disease.

By the 1560s, the Spanish had unsuccessfully attempted colonization several more times. By this time, indigenous resistance, such as it was, had been worn down; many Indians had died or were dying of disease and others had simply moved on to more inhospitable terrain, which was unattractive to the invaders.

In 1562, Juan Vásquez de Coronado arrived as governor and decided that the best place to found a colony, Cartago, was in the central highlands. This was an unusual move; the Spanish were a seafaring people and had naturally tried to colonize the coastal areas where they could build ports and maintain contact with Spain, but they realized that this was problematic because the coastal areas harbored disease. When Coronado founded Cartago in 1563, his followers encountered a healthy climate and fertile volcanic soil, and the colony survived.

Cartago was quite different from Spanish colonies in other parts of the New World. There were few Indians, so the Spanish did not have a huge workforce available, nor did they intermarry with indigenous people to form the *mestizo* culture prevalent in many other parts of Latin America. The imagined riches of Costa Rica turned out to be very little and were quickly plundered. The small highland colony soon became removed from the mainstream of Spanish influence.

For the next century and a half, the colony remained a forgotten backwater, isolated from the coast and major trading routes. It survived only by dint of hard work and the generosity and friendliness that have become the hallmarks of contemporary Costa Rican character.

In the 18th century, the colony began to spread and change. Settlements became established throughout the fertile plains of the central highlands (now known as the *meseta central*). Heredia was founded in 1706, San José in 1737, and Alajuela in 1782, although at the times of their founding the cities had different names.

Much of Cartago was destroyed in an eruption of Volcán Irazú in 1723, but the survivors rebuilt the town. This expansion reflected slow growth from within Costa Rica, but the colony remained one of the poorest and most isolated in the Spanish empire.

## Independence

Central America became independent from Spain on September 15, 1821, although

Costa Rica was not aware of this situation until at least a month later. It briefly became part of the Mexican empire, then a state within the Central American United Provinces. The first elected head of state was Juan Mora Fernández, who governed from 1824 to 1833. During his time in office, export of coffee, introduced in 1808 from Cuba, began in modest amounts.

The rest of the 19th century saw a steady increase in coffee exports, and this turned Costa Rica from an extremely poor and struggling country into a more successful and worldly one. Inevitably, some of the coffee growers became relatively rich, and a class structure began to emerge. In 1849, a successful coffee grower, Juan Rafael Mora, became president and governed for 10 years.

Mora's presidency is remembered both for economic and cultural growth, and for a somewhat bizarre military incident that has earned a place in every Costa Rican child's history books. In June 1855, the US filibuster William Walker arrived in Nicaragua with the aim of conquering Central America and converting it into slaving territory, then using the slaves to build a Nicaraguan canal to join the Atlantic and Pacific Oceans. Walker defeated the Nicaraguans and marched on to Costa Rica, which he entered more or less unopposed, reaching a hacienda at Santa Rosa (now a national park in northwestern Costa Rica).

Costa Rica had no army, so Mora organized 9000 civilians to gather what arms they could and march north in February 1856. In a short but determined battle, the Costa Ricans defeated Walker, who retreated to Rivas, Nicaragua, followed by the victorious Costa Ricans. Walker and his soldiers made a stand in a wooden fort, and Juan Santamaría, a drummer boy from Alajuela, volunteered to torch the building, thus forcing Walker to flee. Santamaría was killed in this action and is now remembered as one of Costa Rica's favorite national heroes.

Despite his defeat, Walker returned unsuccessfully to Central America several more times before finally being shot in Honduras in 1860. Meanwhile, Mora lost favor in his country – he and his army were thought to have brought back the cholera that caused a massive epidemic in Costa Rica. He was deposed in 1859, led a failed coup in 1860, and was executed in the same year that Walker died.

## Democracy

The next three decades were characterized by power struggles among members of the coffee-growing elite. In 1869, a free and compulsory elementary education system was established – though, inevitably, families in more remote areas were not able to send children to schools. In 1889, the first democratic elections were held, with the poor *campesinos* (peasants) as well as the rich coffee growers able to vote, although women and blacks had not yet received that right.

Democracy has been a hallmark of Costa Rican politics since then, and there have been few lapses. One occurred between 1917 and 1919, when the Minister of War, Federico Tinoco, overthrew the democratically elected president and formed a dictatorship. This ended in Tinoco's exile after opposition from the rest of Costa Rica and from the US government.

In 1940, Rafael Angel Calderón Guardia became president. His presidency was marked by reforms that were supported by the poor but criticized by the rich. These reforms included workers' rights to organize, minimum wages, and social security. To further widen his power base, Calderón allied himself, strangely, with both the Catholic church and the Communist party to form a Christian Socialist group. This alienated him even more from the conservatives, intellectuals, and the upper classes.

Calderón was succeeded in 1944 by the Christian Socialist Teodoro Picado, who was a supporter of Calderón's policies, but the conservative opposition claimed the elections were a fraud. In 1948, Calderón again ran for the presidency, against Otilio Ulate. Ulate won the election, but Calderón claimed fraud because some of the ballots had been destroyed. Picado's government did not recognize Ulate's victory, and the tense situation escalated into civil war.

Calderón and Picado were opposed by José (Don Pepe) Figueres Ferrer. After several weeks of civil warfare, in which more than 2000 people were killed, Figueres emerged victorious. He took over an interim government and in 1949 handed the presidency to Otilio Ulate.

That year marked the formation of the Costa Rican constitution, which is still in effect. Women and blacks finally received the vote, presidents were not allowed to run for successive terms, and a neutral electoral tribunal was established to guarantee free and fair elections. Voting in elections, held every four years, was made mandatory for all citizens over the age of 18. Although voter turnout is higher than in most Western countries, the mandatory vote is not legally enforced. But the constitutional dissolution of the armed forces is the act that has had the most long-lasting impact on the nation. Today, half a century later, Costa Rica is known as 'the country that doesn't have an army.'

Although there are well over a dozen political parties, since 1949 the Partido de Liberación Nacional (PLN; National Liberation Party), formed by Don Pepe Figueres, has dominated, usually being elected every other four years. Figueres continued to be popular and was returned to two more terms of office, in 1953 and 1970. He died in 1990. Another famous PLN president was Oscar Arias, who governed from 1986 to 1990. For his work in attempting to spread peace from Costa Rica to all of Central America, Arias received the Nobel Peace Prize in 1987.

In recent years, the Christian Socialists have continued to be the favored party of the poor and working classes, and Calderón's son, Rafael Angel Calderón Fournier, has played a large role in that party, running for president three times. After two losses, he was finally elected president in 1990, succeeding Oscar Arias.

During 1993, six PLN politicians vied for their party's candidacy for the 1994 presidential elections. They included Margarita Penon, who was the first woman to reach such an advanced position in a presidential race in Costa Rica. Penon is the wife of ex-president Oscar Arias. The winner of the PLN candidacy, however, was José María Figueres, Don Pepe's son.

PLN's Figueres was opposed by the Partido Unidad Social Cristiana (PUSC; Social Christian Unity Party). The PUSC pre-candidates for the 1994 presidential elections included Juan José Trejos, the son of ex-president José Juaquin Trejos (1966–70), and economist Miguel Angel Rodríguez, who became the PUSC candidate. There were also some presidential candidates from other minor parties.

Clearly, the history of politics in Costa Rica is strongly influenced by a handful of families, as shown by the father-son, husband-wife associations mentioned above. In fact, 75% of the 44 presidents of Costa Rica prior to 1970 were descended from just three original colonizers.

The winner of the 1994 election was Figueres, who received 49.6% of the vote, closely followed by Rodríguez with 47.6%. Figueres had campaigned on a populist platform, promising improved health care and education, but his presidency was unpopular, marked by price hikes, tax increases, bank closures, and strikes by teachers and other groups.

In 1998, Miguel Angel Rodríguez again represented the PUSC party in the election on February 1. He was opposed by PLN candidate José Miguel Corrales (incumbents are not allowed to run) and 11 others, including the country's first black candidate, and the first all-female ticket. Also for the first time, the two front-runners had women running in both vice-presidential positions.

Election results favored Rodríguez with 46.6% of the vote, barely 2% more than Corrales and much closer than expected. Rodríguez's term was not marked by major changes. Increases in tourism, high-tech products, and the traditional coffee and banana exports buoyed the president's attempts to fix the economy during the first two years of his administration, but his attempts to privatize state companies led to major street demonstrations. The economic downturn in the high-tech and agricultural sectors after 2000 resulted in a faltering economy and 'business as usual.'

Thirteen different parties put forward candidates for the 2002 elections, but by the February election there were only three serious contenders. These were PUSC's Abel Pacheco, 68, a psychiatrist and former TV commentator, PLN's Rolando Araya, 54, a chemical engineer and longtime PLN politician, and a surprising third choice in a traditionally two-party race, Ottón Solís of the Citizen Action Party. The fact that Solís, with his stance against corruption and ineffectual government, was a serious contender in itself spoke of the public's readiness for change.

With three contenders in the running, Costa Ricans were unable to decide whom they wanted for president, and 31% failed to vote at all. Pacheco led with 39%, just short of the 40% needed for election, followed by Araya with 31% and Solís with a sizeable 26% – enough to cause a runoff election between the two top candidates for the first time since the redrafting of the constitution in 1949.

The runoff between Pacheco and Araya was held in April 2002. The public's frustration with the conservative status quo led to the highest voter abstention ever, with more than 39% of eligible Costa Ricans not voting (they were led by Ottón Solís, who showed up at the polls only to cast a blank ballot). Pacheco won with 58% of the vote, due partly to his being well-known to Costa Ricans through his TV programs. Both candidates campaigned on an economic platform, but with the public against privatization of state companies and with a stagnant worldwide economy, Pacheco will have a hard time pleasing ticos once his honeymoon is over.

Other noteworthy events of recent years include several natural disasters that caused widespread flooding, road damage, and destruction of homes. The ill-famed Hurricane Mitch of November 1998 caused substantial damage to Costa Rica, but the most catastrophic events occurred in the countries to the north, especially Honduras, Nicaragua, and El Salvador. Rains associated with Hurricane Michelle in November 2001 let loose mudslides that closed many highways on the Pacific slopes (including the Interamericana) for several weeks, resulting in the several towns being stranded and some deaths.

On a positive note, Costa Rica's men's soccer squad was one of 32 countries to qualify for the prestigious World Cup tournament in mid-2002. This was only the second time that the tiny, soccer-crazy country has qualified.

## GEOGRAPHY

Costa Rica is bordered to the north by Nicaragua, to the northeast by the Caribbean Sea, to the southeast by Panama, and to the west and southwest by the Pacific Ocean. This tropical country lies between latitudes 11°13'N and 8°N and longitudes 82°33'W and 85°58'W. In addition, Costa Rica claims Isla del Coco (25 sq km), at about 5°30'N and 87°05'W.

Costa Rica is an extremely varied country despite its tiny size, which, at 51,100 sq km, is almost half the size of the state of Kentucky in the USA, two-thirds the size of Scotland, or three-quarters the size of Tasmania in Australia.

A series of volcanic mountain chains run from the Nicaraguan border in the northwest to the Panamanian border in the southeast, splitting the country in two. The northwesternmost range is the Cordillera de Guanacaste, consisting of a spectacular chain of volcanoes that can be appreciated by the traveler heading south from the Nicaraguan border along the Carretera Interamericana. These include Volcán Orosí (1487m) in Parque Nacional Guanacaste, the gently steaming Volcán Rincón de la Vieja (1895m) and Volcán Santa María (1916m), both in Parque Nacional Rincón de la Vieja, as well as Volcán Miravalles (2026m) and Volcán Tenorio (1916m).

Farther to the southeast is the Cordillera de Tilarán, which includes the renowned Monteverde cloud forest reserve and, just north of the main massif, the continually exploding Volcán Arenal (1633m), the most active volcano in Costa Rica.

The Cordillera de Tilarán runs into the Cordillera Central, which includes the famous Volcán Poás (2704m) and Volcán Irazú (3432m), both of which are active volcanoes lying at the center of national parks that are named after them, and Volcán Barva (2906m), which is in Parque Nacional Braulio Carrillo.

The southeasternmost mountains are associated with the Cordillera de Talamanca, which is higher, geologically older, more remote, and more rugged than the other ranges. About 16 separate peaks reach in excess of 3000m, the highest being Cerro Chirripó (3820m). Changing altitudes play an important part in determining geographical, climatic, and ecological variation. Many different ecological habitats are found, corresponding with altitudinal changes up the mountains.

In the center of the highlands lies the meseta central, which is surrounded by mountains (the Cordillera Central to the north and east, the Cordillera de Talamanca to the south). It is this central plain, between about 1000m and 1500m above sea level, that contains four of Costa Rica's five largest cities, including San José, the capital. Over half of the population lives on this plain, which contains fertile volcanic soil.

On either side of the volcanic central highlands lie coastal lowlands, which differ greatly in form. The smooth Caribbean coastline is 212km long and is characterized by year-round rain, mangroves, swamps, an intracoastal waterway, sandy beaches, and small tides. The Pacific coast is much more rugged and rocky. The tortuous coastline is 1016km long, with various gulfs and peninsulas. It is bordered by tropical dry forests that receive almost no rain for several months each year, as well as by mangroves, swamps, and beaches. Tidal variation is quite large and there are many offshore islands.

The two most important peninsulas are the Nicoya, separated from the mainland by a gulf of the same name, and the Osa, separated from the mainland by the Golfo Dulce. The Península de Nicoya is hilly, dry, and dusty for much of the year. It's known for its cattle farming and beach resorts. The Península de Osa contains Parque Nacional Corcovado, which is one of Costa Rica's protected rainforests.

## GEOLOGY

Geologists believe that the surface of the earth is covered with a number of huge tectonic plates that move slowly over millions of years, causing the earth's surface to change constantly. Like most of Central America, Costa Rica's geological history can be traced back to the impact of the Cocos Plate moving northeast and crashing into the Caribbean Plate at a rate of about 10cm every year – quite fast by geological standards. The point of impact is called a 'subduction zone,' in which the Cocos Plate forces the edge of the Caribbean Plate to break up and become uplifted. This is not a smooth process, and hence Central America is an area prone to earthquakes and volcanic activity (see Dangers & Annoyances in the Facts for the Visitor chapter).

This process began underwater and has been going on for about five million years. Most of Costa Rica itself is about three million years old, with the exception of the Península de Nicoya, which is many millions of years older. Most of the mountain ranges

in Costa Rica are volcanic; the exception is the massive Cordillera de Talamanca in the south, the largest range in Costa Rica. This is a granite batholith, or intruded igneous rock that formed under great pressure below the surface of the earth and was uplifted.

## CLIMATE

Like many tropical countries, Costa Rica experiences two seasons, the wet and the dry, rather than the four seasons of temperate regions. The dry season, *verano* (summer), lasts from about late December to April. The rest of the year tends to be wet and is called *invierno* (winter).

In the highlands, the dry season really is dry, with only one or two rainy days per month. It can, however, rain up to 20 days per month in the wet season. The north and central Pacific coastal regions have rain patterns similar to the highlands, while the southern Pacific coast can experience rain year-round, though less so in the dry season.

The Caribbean coastal region is rainy year-round, with September, October, February, and March having the least rainfall. The drier months are characterized by fewer rainy days and spells of fine weather sometimes lasting a week or more. Rain tends to be torrential, usually lasting a few hours rather than all day.

Temperatures vary little from season to season, and the main influencing factor is altitude. San José, at 1150m, has a climate the locals refer to as 'eternal spring.' Lows average a mild 15°C year-round, while highs are a pleasant 26°C. The coasts are much hotter – the Caribbean averages 21°C at night and over 30°C during the day; the Pacific is 2°C or 3°C warmer. Visitors used to a more temperate climate may find the high heat and humidity of the coastal areas oppressive, but most acclimatize after a few days.

## ECOLOGY & ENVIRONMENT
### Life Zones

Ecologists define 12 tropical life zones in Costa Rica, which are named according to forest type and altitude in a system devised by and named after LR Holdridge. Thus, there are dry, moist, wet, and rain forests in tropical, premontane, lower montane, montane, and subalpine areas.

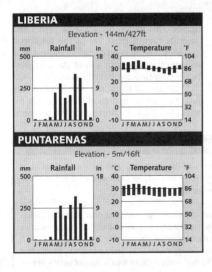

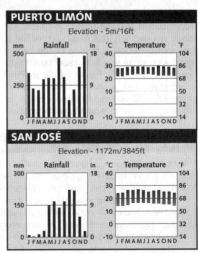

Within a life zone, several types of habitat may occur. Much of Parque Nacional Santa Rosa, for example, is tropical dry forest, but types of vegetation within this zone include deciduous forest, evergreen forest, mangrove swamp, and littoral woodland. Thus Costa Rica has a huge variety of habitats, each with particular associations of plants and animals. The country's extensive and ambitious national park system is an attempt to protect them all.

## Major Environmental Problems

Despite Costa Rica's national park system (see National Parks & Protected Areas, later in this chapter), the major problem facing the nation's environment is deforestation. Costa Rica's natural vegetation was originally almost all forest, but most of this has been cleared, mainly for pasture or agriculture. The UN Food and Agriculture Organization estimates that between 1973 and 1989, Costa Rica's forests were being lost at an average rate of 2.3% each year. The situation has improved over the past decade, however: Tree plantations are being developed, and the availability of commercially grown timber means there is less pressure to log the natural forests. Nevertheless, deforestation continues at a high rate and there is now very little natural forest outside the protected areas. Even within national parks, some of the more remote areas have

been logged illegally because there is not enough money to hire park guards to enforce the law throughout the parks.

Apart from the direct loss of tropical forests and the plants and animals that depend on them (see Conservation, below), deforestation has led directly or indirectly to other severe environmental problems. The first and greatest issue is soil erosion. Forests protect the soil beneath them from the ravages of tropical rainstorms, and after deforestation much of the topsoil is washed away, lowering the productivity of the land and silting up watersheds. Some deforested lands are planted with Costa Rica's main agricultural product, bananas, the production of which entails the use of pesticides and blue plastic bags to protect the fruit. Both the pesticides and the plastic bags end up polluting the environment.

## Conservation

The loss of key habitats, particularly tropical forests, is a pressing problem. Deforestation is happening at such a rate that most of Costa Rica's (and the world's) tropical forests will have disappeared by the first decades of the 21st century; loss of other habitats is a less publicized but equally pressing concern. With this in mind, two important questions arise: Why are habitats such as the tropical rainforests so important, and what can be done to prevent their loss?

Much of Costa Rica's remaining natural vegetation is tropical forest, and there are many reasons why this particular habitat is important. Almost a million of the known species on earth live in tropical rainforests; scientists predict that most of the millions more plant and animal species that await discovery will be found in the world's remaining rainforests, which have the greatest biodiversity of all the habitats known on the planet. This incredible array of plants and animals cannot exist unless the rainforest that they inhabit is protected – deforestation will result not only in loss of the rainforest but in countless extinctions as well.

The value of tropical plants is more than just the habitat and food they provide for animals, and it is more than the aesthetic

## Ecotourism

Costa Rica has so much to offer the wildlife enthusiast that it is small wonder that ecotourism is growing in the country. More than 70% of foreign travelers visit one or more nature destinations, and half of these visitors come specifically to see Costa Rica's wildlife.

During the past few years, the natural wonders of Costa Rica have been discovered. From the late 1980s to the mid-1990s, the annual number of visitors doubled, and now almost a million foreign tourists visit every year. Tourism recently surpassed bananas and coffee as the nation's biggest industry, and prices for the traveler have risen substantially.

The financial bonanza generated by the tourism boom means that new operations are starting up all the time – many are good, some are not. The big word in Costa Rica is 'ecotourism' – everyone wants to jump on the green bandwagon. There are 'ecological' car rental agencies and 'ecological' menus in restaurants.

Taking advantage of Costa Rica's 'green' image, some developers are promoting mass tourism and are building large hotels with accompanying environmental problems. Apart from the immediate impacts, such as cutting down vegetation, diverting or damming rivers, and driving away wildlife, there are secondary impacts like erosion, lack of adequate waste treatment facilities for a huge hotel in an area away from sewerage lines, and the building of socially, environmentally, and economically inadequate 'shanty towns' to house the maids, waiters, cooks, cleaners, and many other employees needed. We recommend staying in smaller hotels that have a positive attitude about the environment rather than the large, mass-tourism destinations.

At first, the growth in tourism took the nation by surprise – there was no overall development plan and growth was poorly controlled. Some people wanted to cash in on the short term with little thought for the future. Many developers are foreigners – they say that they are giving the local people jobs, but locals don't want to spend their lives being waiters and maids while watching the big money go out of the country.

Traditionally, tourism in Costa Rica has been on a small and intimate scale. The great majority of the country's hotels are small (fewer than 50 rooms), and friendly local people have worked closely with tourists, to the benefit of both. This intimacy and friendliness was a hallmark of a visit to Costa Rica, but this is changing.

The developers of a project to build a 402-room hotel (the first of a chain) on a remote Pacific beach were sued for causing environmental damage and treating employees unfairly. Although the government agreed that laws were broken, the Spanish-owned hotel opened in 1992 and sparked off a spirited controversy within Costa Rica (see the boxed text 'Clamor in Tambor' in the Península de Nicoya chapter).

The big question is whether future tourism developments should continue to focus on the traditional small-hotel, ecotourism approach, or turn to mass tourism, with planeloads of visitors accommodated in 'mega-resorts' like the ones in Cancún, Mexico. From the top levels of government on down, the debate has been fierce. Local and international tour operators and travel agents, journalists, developers, airline operators, hotel owners, writers, environmentalists, and politicians have all been vocal in their support of either ecotourism or mass tourism. Many believe that the country is too small to handle both forms of tourism properly.

value of the plants themselves. Many types of medicines have been extracted from forest trees, shrubs, and flowers. These range from anesthetics to antibiotics, from contraceptives to cures for heart disease, malaria, and various other illnesses. Many medicinal uses of plants are known only to the indigenous inhabitants of the forest. Other pharmaceutical treasures remain locked up in tropical forests, unknown to anybody. They may never be discovered if the forests are destroyed.

Costa Rica's Instituto Nacional de Biodiversidad (INBio) has signed contracts with pharmaceutical companies such as Merck & Company of the USA, the world's largest pharmaceutical company. Funding from the companies is used to support INBio's efforts to protect the rainforests by training locals to make plant and animal collections in the field and to make detailed inventories. Simple preliminary studies are carried out to identify those species that may have medical significance. Thus, local people are involved at a grassroots level, and pharmaceutical companies receive selections of species that may lead to vital medical breakthroughs. The deal doesn't stop there, however. The contracts earmark a percentage of the profits for conservation and preservation efforts. Also see the boxed text 'INBio' in the Central Valley and the Surrounding Highlands chapter.

Deforestation leads not only to species extinction but also to loss of the genetic diversity that could help certain species adapt to a changing world. Many crops are monocultures that suffer from a lack of genetic diversity. In other words, all the plants are almost identical because agriculturists have bred strains that are high yielding, easy to harvest, good tasting, etc. If monocultures are attacked by a new disease or pest epidemic, they could be wiped out because the resistant strains may have been bred out of the population. Plants such as bananas, an important part of Costa Rica's economy, are found in tropical forests, so in the event of an epidemic scientists could look for disease-resistant wild strains to breed into the commercially raised crops.

While biodiversity for aesthetic, medicinal, and genetic reasons may be important to us, it is even more important to the local indigenous peoples who still survive in tropical rainforests. In Costa Rica, Bribri Indian groups still live in the rainforest in a more or less traditional manner. Some remaining Cabecar Indians still practice shifting agriculture, hunting, and gathering. About half of Costa Rica's remaining Indian people are protected in the Área de Conservación La Amistad Caribe y Pacífico, which comprises three national parks and a host of indigenous, biological, and other reserves in the Talamanca region on the Costa Rica–Panama border. Various international agencies are working with the Costa Rican authorities to protect this area and the cultural and anthropological treasures within it.

Rainforests are important on a global scale because they moderate global climatic patterns. Scientists have determined that the destruction of the rainforests is a major contributing factor to global warming, which would lead to disastrous changes to our world. These changes include the melting of ice caps, causing rising ocean levels and flooding of major coastal cities, many of which are only a scant few meters above the present sea level. Global warming would also make many of the world's 'breadbasket' regions unsuitable for crop production.

All these are good reasons why the rainforest and other habitats should be preserved and protected, but the reality of the economic importance of forest exploitation by the developing nations that own tropical forests must also be considered. It is undeniably true that the rainforest provides resources in the way of timber, pasture, and possible mineral wealth, but this is a short-sighted view.

The rainforest's long-term importance, both from a global view and as a resource of biodiversity, genetic variation, and pharmaceutical wealth, is becoming recognized by the countries that contain forest as well as other nations of the world that will be affected by the destruction of these rainforests. Efforts are now underway to show that the economic value of the standing rainforest is greater than the wealth realized by deforestation.

One important way to make the tropical forest an economically productive resource without cutting it down is to protect it in national parks and preserves and make it accessible to visitors. This type of ecotourism has become extremely important to the economy of Costa Rica and other nations with similar natural resources. More people are likely to visit Costa Rica to see monkeys in the forest than to see cows in a pasture. The visitors spend money on hotels, transport, tours, food, and souvenirs. In addition, many people who spend time in the tropics gain a better understanding of the natural beauty within forests, and the importance of preserving them. The result is that when the visitors return home, they become goodwill ambassadors for tropical forests.

The fundamental concept of ecotourism is excellent, and it has been very successful – so successful that there have been inevitable problems and abuses (see the boxed text 'Ecotourism'). Apart from ecotourism, other innovative projects for sustainable development of tropical forests are being developed. Many of these developments are on private reserves such as Monteverde and Rara Avis. Here, individuals not connected with the government are showing how forests can be preserved and yield a higher economic return than if they were cut down for a one-time sale of lumber and the land then turned into low-yield pasture.

## FLORA & FAUNA

Costa Rica is a small country, but its range of habitats gives it an incredibly rich diversity of flora and fauna. The World Resources Institute, in a chart published in 1995, shows that Costa Rica has the most varied fauna of any country on the planet. A huge tropical country like Brazil will have more species than tiny Costa Rica, so the biodiversity (variety of species) is measured in terms of different species per unit area rather than per country. Counting all birds and mammals per every 10,000 sq km, Costa Rica comes out on top with 615 species (and neighboring Panama has a noteworthy 581 species). In comparison, the highest-ranked African countries are Rwanda and Gambia, with 596 and 574 species. The USA has just 104 species of birds and mammals per 10,000 sq km. Costa Rica's leading level of biodiversity attracts nature lovers from all over the world.

## Flora

The floral biodiversity is also high; well over 10,000 species of vascular plants have been described, and more are being added to the list every year. Orchids alone account for about 1300 species, the most famous of which is the March-blooming *Cattleya skinneri* (or *guaria morada* in Spanish), Costa Rica's national flower.

The tropical forest is very different from the temperate forests of North America or Europe. Temperate forests, such as the coniferous forests of the far north or the deciduous woodlands of milder regions, tend to have little variety. There are pines, pines, and more pines, or endless tracts of oaks, beech, and birch.

Tropical forests, on the other hand, have great variety; almost 2000 tree species have been recorded in Costa Rica. If you stand in one spot and look around, you'll see scores of different species of trees, but often you'll have to walk several hundred meters to find another example of any particular species.

This variety then generates biodiversity in the animals that live within the forests. There are several dozen species of fig trees in Costa Rica, for example, and the fruit of each species is the home of one particular wasp species. The wasp benefits by obtaining food and protection; when it flies to another fig tree, the fig benefits because the wasp carries pollen on its body. Many trees and plants of the forest provide fruit, seeds, or nectar for insects, birds, and bats. They rely upon these visitors to carry pollen across several hundred meters of forest to fertilize another member of the appropriate plant species.

These complex interrelationships and the high biodiversity are among the reasons why biologists and conservationists are calling for a halt to the destruction of tropical forests. It is a sobering thought that three-quarters of Costa Rica was forested in the late 1940s; by the early 1990s, less than a quarter of the country remained covered by forest. To try to control this deforestation and protect its wildlife, Costa Rica has instigated the most progressive national park system in Latin America; this has slowed deforestation substantially and the planting of lumber crops has taken some of the pressure off logging the rainforest.

## Fauna

The primary attractions for many naturalists are the birds, of which some 850 species have been recorded in the country. This is far more than what is found in any one of the continents of North America, Australia, or

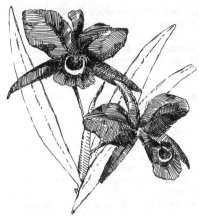

National flower *Cattleya skinneri*

Europe. Also, according to figures from INBio, there are more than 260 mammal species (including marine mammals), at least 65,000 classified insect species (with many thousands more remaining to be described), about 180 species of amphibians, 235 species of reptiles (of which more than half are snakes, 18 venomous), and 835 species of fish, of which about 700 are saltwater. (See the Wildlife Guide at the end of the book and the 'INBio' boxed text in the Central Valley chapter for more information.)

## Endangered Species

According to INBio, the Convention on International Trade in Endangered Species (CITES) reports that Costa Rica is home to many threatened and endangered species, including 16 bird species, 13 mammal species, eight reptile species, two amphibians, and dozens of plants. These are the most extremely endangered cases. In addition, Costa Rican laws passed in 1992 protect many more species from hunting, capturing, or trafficking. Locally, 87 birds, 27 mammals, 36 amphibians, 16 reptiles, all species of orchids, cacti, and tree ferns, and some palms are listed as endangered under Costa Rican law.

## Watching Wildlife

The best places to see wildlife usually are in the many national parks and private preserves in the country. While the forest in these protected areas supports a great deal of wildlife, it is often not very easy to observe it. The main reason for this is the forest itself – you could be 30m away from a jaguar and never know it because of the dense vegetation. Wildlife observation in the rainforest is much more difficult than in the open plains of East Africa, for example.

You can strategically increase your chances of seeing wildlife. The best ideas are to hire a guide or go on a guided tour. Local guides often know where the animals in their area are hanging out and also have a great eye for the tiny movement that can give away an animal's presence. Animals tend to be the most active and visible in the hours after dawn and just before dusk; it is more difficult to see an animal asleep in the middle of the day. Turn your thoughts away from the exotic but rarely seen large mammals, such as jaguars and tapirs, and concentrate instead on smaller things that are relatively easy to observe, such as the marching columns of leaf-cutter ants in most rainforests or bright red poison-arrow frogs hopping around many parts of the Caribbean slopes.

Look for wildlife using more than just your eyes. Some guides can smell a herd of peccaries before they see them. Everyone should use their ears, especially for birding. A walk through the cloud forest is often made eerie by the penetrating whistles and ventriloqual 'bonk!' calls of the three-wattled bellbird, a member of the cotinga family.

### Bird Extinction

Some Costa Rican birds are recent arrivals from other areas but have now become increasingly common here. This has occurred because of dramatic changes in Costa Rica's countryside in recent decades. As forests are replaced with pastures and agricultural land, the original fauna is put under pressure, and new species, better adapted at living in disturbed and more open land, move in and take over. Examples of recent arrivals are the cattle egret and black-shouldered kite, both of which were first recorded in Costa Rica in the 1950s and are now common (see the Wildlife Guide). Meanwhile, a famous species that has become almost extinct because of deforestation is the spectacular harpy eagle.

The haunting notes sound so loud that they can easily be heard half a kilometer away. Spotting this large, chestnut-brown bird, with its pure white head and neck decorated with three black wormlike wattles, is another matter. They call from display perches at the tops of the highest trees and are heard more often than seen. The male howler monkeys are heard as often as they are seen; their eerie vocalizations carry long distances and have been likened to a baby crying or the wind moaning through the trees. Many visitors are unable to believe they are hearing a monkey when they first hear the mournful sound.

Don't ignore areas outside the parks and preserves; often, small hotels in rural areas boast a fine menagerie of local 'guests.' Birds, monkeys, raccoons, and lizards are frequent visitors to hotel gardens.

## National Parks & Protected Areas

The national park system began in the 1960s, and now there are about 26 national parks, comprising about 11% of the country. In addition, there are scores of wildlife refuges, biological and forest reserves, monuments, and other protected areas in Costa Rica. These comprise more than 14% of the total land area, and the Costa Rican authorities enjoy their claim that over 25% of the country has been set aside for conservation. In addition, there are various buffer zones, such as Indian reservations, that boost the total area of 'protected' land to about 27%. These buffer zones still allow farming, logging, and other exploitation, however, so the environment within them is not totally protected.

In addition to the national park system, there are hundreds of small, privately owned lodges, reserves, and haciendas that have been set up to protect the land, and these are well worth visiting.

Although the national park system appears wonderful on paper, a report from the national system of conservation areas (SINAC; Sistema Nacional de Areas de Conservación) amplifies the fact that many of the parks are, in fact, paper tigers. The government doesn't own the parks – almost half of the areas are in private ownership and there isn't a budget to buy these lands. Technically, the private lands are protected from development, but many landowners

are finding loopholes in the restrictions and selling or developing their properties.

SINAC is a branch of the oddly paired environmental and energy ministry (MINAE; Ministerio del Ambiente y Energía). The agency has developed a project to link geographically close groups of national parks and reserves, private preserves, and national forests into 11 conservation areas that cover the country. The system will have two major effects. First, larger areas of wildlife habitats will be protected in blocks, allowing greater numbers of species and individuals to exist. Second, the administration of the national parks will be delegated to regional offices, allowing a more individualized management approach for each area. Each conservation area has regional and sub-regional offices delegated to provide education, enforcement, research, and management of it, although some regional offices play what appear to be obscure bureaucratic roles rather than providing necessary management and guidance.

Most of the national park system has been created in order to protect the different habitats and wildlife of Costa Rica. A few parks are designed to preserve other valued areas, such as the country's best pre-Columbian ruins, at Monumento Nacional Guayabo; an important cave system at Parque Nacional Barra Honda; and a series of geologically active and inactive volcanoes in several parks and reserves.

SINAC has a toll-free number (☎ 192 in Costa Rica) that can provide up-to-date admission and other information from 7am to 5pm weekdays. For specific parks, call the numbers given in the regional chapters.

Most national parks can be entered without permits, but a few of the biological reserves do require a permit that can be obtained by applying to the public information office (see Tourist Offices in the Facts for the Visitor chapter). The entrance fee to most parks is US$6 per day for foreigners, plus an additional US$2 for overnight camping where it is permitted.

Many national parks are in remote areas and are rarely visited – they suffer from a lack of rangers and protection. Others are extremely – and deservedly – popular for their world-class scenic and natural beauty, as well as their wildlife. In the idyllic Parque Nacional Manuel Antonio, a tiny park on

## NATIONAL PARKS & PROTECTED AREAS

1 Refugio Nacional de Vida Silvestre Bahía Junquillal
2 Parque Nacional Guanacaste
3 Parque Nacional Santa Rosa
4 Estación Experimental Horizontes
5 Parque Nacional Rincón de la Vieja
6 Refugio Nacional de Vida Silvestre Caño Negro
7 Parque Nacional Volcán Tenorio
8 Reserva Indígena Guatuso
9 Refugio Nacional de Vida Silvestre Barra del Colorado
10 Parque Nacional Tortuguero
11 Parque National Marino Las Baulas de Guanacaste
12 Reserva Biológica Lomas de Barbudal
13 Parque Nacional Volcán Arenal
14 Estación Biológica La Selva
15 Refugio Nacional de Vida Silvestre Ostional
16 Reserva Indígena Matambú
17 Parque Nacional Barra Honda
18 Parque Nacional Palo Verde
19 Reserva Biológica Isla de los Pájaros
20 Reserva Biológica Bosque Nuboso Monteverde
21 Refugio Silvestre de Peñas Blancas
22 Parque Nacional Juan Castro Blanco
23 Parque Nacional Volcán Poás
24 Parque Nacional Braulio Carrillo
25 Reserva Natural Absoluta Cabo Blanco
26 Refugio Nacional de Vida Silvestre Curú
27 Reserva Biológica Isla Guayabo
28 Reserva Biológica Islas Negritos
29 Parque Nacional Carara
30 Reserva Indígena Quitirrisí
31 Reserva Indígena Zapatón
32 Parque Nacional Volcán Irazú
33 Parque Nacional Volcán Turrialba
34 Monumento Nacional Guayabo
35 Reserva Indígena Barbilla
36 Parque Nacional Barbilla
37 Reserva Indígena Alto y Bajo Chirripó
38 Parque Nacional Tapantí-Macizo Cerro de la Muerte
39 Parque Nacional Manuel Antonio
40 Parque Nacional Chirripó
41 Reserva Indígena Telire
42 Reserva Indígena Tayní
43 Reserva Biológica Hitoy-Cerere
44 Reserva Indígena Talamanca-Cabécar
45 Reserva Indígena Talamanca Bribri
46 Parque Nacional Cahuita
47 Reserva Indígena Cocles/KéköLdi
48 Refugio Nacional de Vida Silvestre Gandoca-Manzanillo
49 Parque Nacional Marino Ballena
50 Parque Internacional La Amistad
51 Reserva Indígena Ujarrás
52 Reserva Indígena Salitre
53 Reserva Indígena Cabagra
54 Reserva Indígena Térraba
55 Reserva Indígena Boruca
56 Reserva Indígena Curré
57 Parque Nacional Chirripó
58 Zona Protectora Las Tablas
59 Reserva Biológica Isla del Caño
60 Humedal Nacional Térraba-Sierpe
61 Reserva Indígena Guaymí Coto Brus
62 Parque Nacional Corcovado
63 Reserva Indígena Guaymí de Osa
64 Parque Nacional Corcovado (Piedras Blancas Sector)
65 Refugio Nacional de Vida Silvestre Golfito
66 Reserva Indígena Abrojo-Montezuma
67 Reserva Indígena Conte Burica
68 Parque Nacional Isla del Coco

the Pacific coast, the number of visitors has reached 1000 per day in the high season. Annual visitation rocketed from about 36,000 visitors in 1982 to more than 150,000 by 1991. This number of visitors threatened to ruin the diminutive area by driving away the wildlife, polluting the beaches, and replacing wilderness with hotel development. In response, park visitation has been limited to 600 people a day, and the park is closed on Mondays to allow it a brief respite from the onslaught.

Costa Rica has a world-famous reputation for the excellence and far-sightedness of its national park system – but lack of funds, concentrated visitor use, and sometimes fuzzy leadership have shown that there are problems in paradise.

A further problem is that the Costa Rican government changes every four years and results in new political entities being formed and replacing previous ones, so there's a lack of cohesive, standard operation plans.

## GOVERNMENT & POLITICS

The government is based on the Constitution of November 9, 1949 (see History, earlier in this chapter). The president, who is both the head of government and head of state, wields executive power, assisted by two vice presidents and a cabinet of 12 ministers. (Previous governments had 18 ministers; in 1998, the president downsized the cabinet and added a team of eight advisors.) The presidential elections are held every four years, and an incumbent cannot be re-elected.

The country is divided into the seven provinces of San José, Alajuela, Cartago, Heredia, Guanacaste, Puntarenas, and Limón. Each province has a governor who is appointed by the president. The provinces are divided into 81 *cantones* (counties) and subdivided into 429 districts. For about every 30,000 people in each province, a *diputado/a* (congressman/woman) is elected every four years to the Legislative Assembly, or Congress, which totals 57 diputados in all (a number that will increase following the 2002 elections). This is where much of the power of government lies. Incumbents, however, cannot serve successive terms, which creates a lack of continuity: Whatever one congressperson does politically is liable to be reversed by his or her successor.

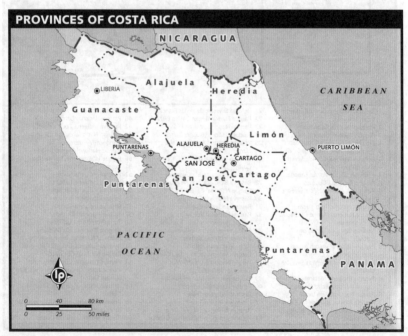

PROVINCES OF COSTA RICA

The Legislative Assembly appoints 22 Supreme Court magistrates for minimum terms of eight years, and these judges select judges for the lower courts. The idea behind these three power structures is to prevent any one person or group from having too much control, thus ensuring a real democracy. There is also an Electoral Tribunal that is responsible for supervising elections and ensuring that the electoral process is fair and democratic. Known as the 'fourth power,' the Electoral Tribunal consists of three magistrates and six substitutes who are independent of the government.

There is no army in Costa Rica. Instead, there's a Fuerza Publica, a form of an armed police force.

Although there are about 30 political parties, only two groups have been in power since 1949: the National Liberation Party (PLN) and the Social Christian Unity Party (PUSC). From 1998 to 2002, the PUSC has been in power, under the presidency of Miguel Angel Rodríguez. The elections of April 7, 2002, resulted in a win for Abel Pacheco of the ruling PUSC. He took office on May 8 for his four-year term.

The vote is officially mandatory for all citizens over 18 years old. An up-to-date and validated electoral card must be carried by all Costa Ricans as identification and is needed for anything from opening a bank account to getting a job.

Election day is very upbeat in Costa Rica – everyone treats it like a patriotic holiday, with flag waving, car-horn honking, and general euphoria. Still, voter apathy has been increasing in recent years, and almost 39% of eligible voters declined to vote in the 2002 elections. Citizens who didn't vote can get around the validated electoral card problem either by paying a fine or by going to a polling place to validate their card but then spoiling their ballot.

## ECONOMY

Until the middle of the 19th century, Costa Rica was a very poor country with an economy based on subsistence agriculture. Then the introduction of coffee began to provide a product suitable for export. This was followed by bananas, and today these two crops continue to be the most important in the country. Other important traditional exports include meat and sugar.

In the early 1990s, nontraditional export items such as ornamental plants and flowers, seafood, pineapples, pharmaceutical products, textiles and clothing, tires, furniture, and many other products began to rival the traditional exports. Also during the early 1990s, tourism experienced an unprecedented boom in Costa Rica. Numbers of foreign tourists visiting the country rose from 376,000 in 1989 to almost 1 million at present. The annual value of revenues from tourism soon rose to overtake the traditional banana and coffee exports during the mid 1990s. In 2000, revenues from tourism reached almost $1 billion, with 1,088,075 visitors. In 2001, a record-breaking 1,131,598 visitors were recorded, of which over 430,000 were US citizens, about the same as in 2000. There was a slight decrease in European and Canadian visitors to Costa Rica, and about a 10% increase from Latin American visitors.

In the late 1990s, the electronics sector showed a strong growth. Intel, the multinational manufacturer of computer chips, opened factories in Costa Rica. Their influence fueled the electronics industry to become Costa Rica's top dollar earner in 1998, bringing the country US$1.2 billion, of which about 78% was attributed to Intel. However, a drop in world demand for microchips resulted in much lower exports from Intel in succeeding years. The textile industry continues to show a strong growth.

In 2000, a world glut of bananas caused a drop in the value of Costa Rican banana exports from $667.5 million in 1998 to $546.5 million in 2000. Coffee, selling at over $140 per 100lb sack in 1998, brought in $409 million in that year. The average price of coffee dropped to about $95 a sack in 2000, bringing the country only $272 million in 2000. In 2001, with coffee dropping in value to a disastrous low of under $50 a sack, many coffee growers were forced to dump their produce and coffee exports were the lowest in many years. Costa Rican coffee growers claim that they need to make $92 a sack to break even.

The USA is by far the most important export destination, followed by Europe, especially Germany. The USA is also the main supplier of imports, distantly followed by Mexico, Europe, and Japan.

In 2001, devaluation of the colón against the US dollar was almost 7%, and inflation was over 11%, up from 10.3% in 2000. Recent unemployment figures (2000 estimate) were 5.2%, but there is considerable underemployment. As with the rest of the world, Costa Rica's economy was slowed after the World Trade Center attacks on September 11, 2001.

## POPULATION & PEOPLE

The last census was in July 2000, when 3,810,179 inhabitants were counted. About 60% of the people live in the highlands. The annual population growth rate is about 2%, and about 33% of the population is under 15. About 95% of those over age 15 are literate – this is among the highest literacy rates in Latin America.

The population density is almost 75 people per square kilometer, the third highest in Central America, after El Salvador and Guatemala. This is just over a quarter of the population density of the UK, but about two and a half times higher than that of the USA.

The vast majority of the people are white, mainly of Spanish descent. About 1.9% of the population is black, concentrated in the thinly populated Caribbean province of Limón, where almost 75% of the country's Afro–Costa Ricans live, tracing their ancestry mainly to the immigrant laborers from Jamaica who built the railways and worked the banana plantations in the late 19th century. As with other Caribbean blacks, many of them speak a lively dialect of English. They were actively discriminated against in the early 20th century, not even being allowed to spend a night in the highlands, but since the 1949 constitution they have had equal rights legally.

A small number of Indians remain, making up about 1.7% of the population. (Note that one translation of Indian is *indio,* which is an insulting term to Costa Rica's indigenous inhabitants. They prefer the alternate term *indígena,* which means 'Indian' or 'native inhabitant.') Until the latest census, estimates of the Indian population were up to 40,000 at most, and census-takers and indigenous leaders alike were surprised at the current figure, 63,876, of which almost 40% live in Limón province. Some Indians have integrated to the extent that they are more or less indistinguishable from other Costa Ricans, but over 46,000 live in or near the country's Indigenous Reserves, most of which are not easy to visit. The largest populations of culturally distinct tribes include 11,174 Bribris from the Talamanca area near the southeastern coast and Panamanian border; 10,016 Cabécares, in a remote area inland from the Bribris; 3934 Borucas in the southern Pacific coastal areas; and other smaller groups including the Guaymí, who straddle the Panamanian border, and Huetares, Malekus, Chorotegas, and Térrabas.

There are 22 Indigenous Reserves in Costa Rica, but, for the most part, these are of little interest to travelers, who often may not even know they are within a reserve. A few reserves discourage visitation, and a few have perhaps a store selling some local crafts, along with the usual country-store items like cans of sardines and bottles of soft drinks.

Finally, 0.2%, or about 7800 people, claim Chinese ancestry.

The Costa Rican people call themselves *ticos* and *ticas* (male and female). This supposedly stems from their love of the use of diminutives; *chico* (small) becomes *chiquito* and *chiquitito* or *chiquitico.* You don't hear the *tico* ending as much as before, though don't be surprised if a waiter in a café tells you he'll be with you in a *momentico.*

This author finds most ticos to be consistently friendly, polite, and helpful. Visitors are constantly surprised at the warmth of the Costa Rican people. This is still a very family-oriented society, however, and the friendliness and politeness tend to form somewhat of a shell over their true personalities. It is easy to make friends with a tico, but it is much more difficult to form deeper relationships.

## EDUCATION

About 20% of the national budget goes toward education. With the highest literacy rate in Latin America (95.2% of the population aged 10 and over, according to the 2000 census) and compulsory education going through ninth grade (age 14), the education system appears to be in good shape. Appearances can be deceptive, however, and there are certainly problems that don't show up in the official picture.

A Ministry of Public Education study, reported in the Costa Rican press in mid-1996, indicates that there are six times more dropouts from secondary school than there are students in the ninth grade – the final year of legally mandated study. This is blamed on various factors, including the need for conveniently located secondary schools, lack of student interest, lack of encouragement from parents, and a desire to enter the work force.

## ARTS

Costa Rica is famous for its natural beauty and friendly people rather than for its culture. Because of the overwhelmingly European population, there is very little indigenous cultural influence. And because the country was a poor subsistence-agriculture nation until the middle of the 19th century, cultural and artistic activities have only really developed since the late 19th century. Ticos consider San José to be the cultural center of the country, and it is here that the most important museums are found.

## Performing Arts

Theater is one of the favorite cultural activities in Costa Rica, and San José is the center of a thriving acting community. Plays are produced mainly in Spanish, but the Little Theater Group is well known for its English-language performances. (See the San José chapter for details.)

The most famous theater in the country is the Teatro Nacional, built between 1890 and 1897. The story goes that a noted European opera company, featuring the talented singer Adelina Patti, was on a Latin American tour but declined to perform in Costa Rica for lack of a suitable hall. Immediately, the coffee elite put a special cultural tax on coffee exports for the construction of a world-class theater.

The Teatro Nacional, in the heart of San José, is now the venue for plays, opera, performances by the National Symphony Orchestra, ballet, poetry readings, and other cultural events. It also is an architectural work in its own right and a landmark in any city tour of San José.

The National Symphony Orchestra is perhaps the most cosmopolitan of Costa Rica's performing arts groups. It has toured the USA, Eastern Europe, Spain, Asia, and other countries in recent years and has a high standard. International guest artists often perform with the orchestra, and tickets are inexpensive.

## Festivals

Costa Rica's biggest cultural event is the International Arts Festival, held annually in San José for about two weeks in March. The festival features theater, music, dance, film, and a variety of art shows with participants from many countries. Also important is the annual Monteverde Music Festival, held around February, concurrently with the South Caribbean Music Festival, held in Puerto Viejo.

## Literature

Carmen Naranjo (born 1930) is the one contemporary Costa Rican writer who has risen to international acclaim. She is a novelist, poet, and short-story writer who also served in the 1970s as ambassador to India and as the Minister of Culture. In 1996, she was awarded the prestigious Gabriela Mistral medal from the Chilean government. (Gabriela Mistral, a Chilean, won the 1945 Nobel Prize for Literature.) Naranjo's works have been translated into several languages, including English. Two of her short stories are found in *Costa Rica – A Traveler's Literary Companion,* which is the best introduction to Costa Rican literature (see Books in the Facts for the Visitor chapter).

Carmen Naranjo

## Crafts

Many crafts are available in Costa Rica, ranging from balsa birds to jungle-seed jewelry. Most of these are similar to crafts available in other tropical Latin American countries, but a few of them have a special Costa Rican niche.

A few decades ago, the *carretas* (gaily painted wooden carts drawn by oxen) were the common form of transportation in the countryside. Although carretas are rarely seen in use today (you'll occasionally see one in the most rural areas or during a fiesta), they have become something of a traditional craft form, both a symbol of agricultural Costa Rica and a souvenir peculiar to Costa Rica. They come in all sizes, from table-top models to nearly life-size replicas that double as liquor cabinets. They all fold down for transport. Sarchí is the main center for carreta construction (see the Central Valley chapter).

Wooden bowls sound like a humble art form, yet they have been elevated to international art status by Barry Biesanz, working in Escazú, San José. Biesanz's handcrafted wooden bowls are light and luminous, almost defying the definition of wooden. His best pieces sell for up to US$2000, and some of his bowls have been presented to US presidents. Biesanz also makes boxes with exposed joinery and other wooden objects – he signs each of his pieces. Numerous other woodcarvers have tried to imitate his work; some look quite similar at first glance but close examination will reveal inferior technique and lack of his signature.

The village of Guaitil on the Península de Nicoya is famed for its pottery. The attractive pots are made from local clays and use natural colors in the pre-Columbian Chorotega Indian style. They come in a variety of shapes and sizes – many of the huge pots seen decorating houses and hotels in Guanacaste come from here. Other distinctive, boldly painted ceramics are made by Cecilia Facio Pecas Figueres, the sister-in-law of President Figueres (1994–98). Her work is often identifiable by the painted initials PF.

Coffee and bananas have long been associated with Costa Rica, and now artisans have developed various crafts based on these crops. The most interesting is banana

paper (and, to a lesser extent, coffee paper), which is made into stationery, greeting cards, and notebooks. The gnarly roots and trunks of coffee trees yield mysteriously twisted sculptures and keepsakes.

## SOCIETY & CONDUCT

Costa Rican society is the least diverse of any Central American nation. As indicated under Population & People, above, most of the population is white. The majority are of Latin descent and practice Roman Catholicism. Traditionally, Costa Ricans have prided themselves on being a classless society.

Despite the apparent homogeneity, societal differences clearly exist. Historically, a small noble class *(hidalgos)* led the colony's affairs, and since Costa Rica became independent the descendants of three hidalgo families have provided the country with most of its presidents and congressional representatives. Nevertheless, politicians from the president down take pride in mingling with the public and maintaining some semblance of a classless society. The distribution of land and wealth is clearly uneven, but much less so than in other Central American countries.

Until 1949, the small black minority (many of whom are descendants of Jamaican workers hired to build the railway in the 1870s and 1880s) was actively discriminated against. Blacks did not have Costa Rican citizenship and were not allowed to vote or to travel into the highlands away from their Caribbean coastal homes. This was changed by the new (and current) constitution of 1949. Now racism is officially a thing of the past and black travelers are unlikely to encounter problems in the main cities and on the Caribbean coast, although some racist attitudes might still be encountered off the beaten path. One reader reported indifferent unfriendliness in San Vito, but most black foreign travelers with whom I have talked have not reported problems. Lonely Planet welcomes any feedback travelers may have.

Other minority groups are even smaller in number than the black population. The few remaining indigenous groups are but a tiny fraction of the population present when the Europeans arrived. There are far fewer Indians here than in any other Central American country, and their lot is a poor one. Although Indians do have reserves designed to enable them to live in a traditional manner, enforcing the boundaries and integrity of the reserves against loggers, plantations, colonists, mineral prospectors, and others has not been entirely successful. Indigenous people, with very few exceptions, remain a marginal element of Costa Rican society, and little is being done to change this.

Other ethnic groups include small but reasonably successful Chinese and Jewish communities. Although Costa Ricans claim that these are well integrated into the culture, anti-Semitic statements are occasionally made by ticos. In 1999, a false report that Chinese restaurants served rats led to a surprisingly strong wave of anti-Chinese sentiment. This motivated the president to make a publicized visit to a Chinese restaurant in an attempt to improve their unfairly tarnished image. (This book recommends Chinese restaurants.)

The San Vito area in southern Costa Rica is known for its Italian community, and the Monteverde area has a Quaker community that dates back to the arrival of a Quaker group from the USA about half a century ago. A new influx of citizens from the USA has occurred in recent decades – tens of thousands of retirees have decided that the year-round warmth and easygoing nature of Costa Rica are preferable to life in the States. Both the capital region and many of the coastal villages in the Península de Nicoya have large enclaves of US *pensionados*, as the retirees are called. Also in recent decades, there has been a surge of people from other Central American countries trying to avoid the conflicts there.

## Prostitution

Prostitution is legal in Costa Rica for women over 18. Professional prostitutes carry a health card showing how recently they had a medical check-up. Be aware, however, that some women don't bother with these cards. Also, some sexually transmitted diseases can take several days or weeks before they can be detected, so even an up-to-date health card doesn't guarantee that a prostitute is disease-free. AIDS is a growing problem in Costa Rica (see the Health and Gay & Lesbian Travelers sections in the Facts for the Visitor chapter).

An estimated 2000 children work as prostitutes in San José, hired both by foreign tourists and Costa Ricans. This is definitely illegal. Online publications promoting Costa Rica as a 'sex destination' partly because of legal prostitution and partly for pedophiles are discouraged by government officials, who do not consider legal sex for money to be a tourist attraction. Many of the children working as prostitutes have drug problems and no family to turn to. One of the few resources available to them is the Fundación Oratorio Don Bosco de Sor María Romero, a shelter for homeless street kids in San José. The Oratorio also provides food and counseling for addicted and abused kids. The shelter is funded by UNICEF and private donations. You can help by depositing money in their account at the Banco Nacional de Costa Rica No 174282-4 (in colones) or No 608592-2 (in US dollars) or calling the shelter (☎ 257-4470) for information about how to donate.

In 1999, the Costa Rican tourist board, encouraged by the Catholic church, attempted to link sex tourism with gay tourism. This is a clearly unfounded claim, as gay and straight tourists alike usually come here with partners or friends looking for a tropical vacation, and aren't interested in underage prostitutes. After protests from both straight and gay travelers and travel agencies, the official position was that sex tourism was discouraged, activity with underage prostitutes was illegal, and gay tourism remained in its usual limbo – it's legal but folks don't want to talk about it.

Appearances are important to Costa Ricans. As they say, they want to *quedar bien,* which translates more or less into leaving a good impression. They do this by dressing both conservatively and as well as they can (and sometimes can't) afford, and by acting in an agreeable and friendly manner, a hallmark of tico culture. Despite their conservatism, they can certainly loosen up in certain settings. Flirtation and public displays of affection, such as kissing, are unremarkable sights in the streets (but also see the section on Women Travelers in Facts for the Visitor).

Conservative dress is appropriate in the cities, and few Costa Ricans wear shorts in the highlands (except in athletic or exercise settings) – though once you get down to the coast, shorts are fine in the beach resorts and beachwear may be quite skimpy. Nudity or female toplessness is definitely considered inappropriate, however.

Costa Ricans, like most Latin Americans, consider greetings important. In all situations, politeness is a valued habit. A certain degree of formality and floweriness is often used in conversation – friends may say *'Buenos días, cómo amaneció?'* (Good morning, how did you awake?). An appropriate response is *'Muy bien, por dicha, y usted?'* (Very well, fortunately, and you?). Strangers conducting business will, at the minimum, exchange a cordial *'Buenos días, cómo está?'* before launching into whatever they are doing. Male friends and casual acquaintances meeting one another in the street shake hands at the beginning and end of even a short meeting; women kiss one another on the cheek in greeting and farewell. Men often kiss women decorously on the cheek, except in a business setting, where a handshake is more appropriate.

Family is a central part of Costa Rican life, and conversation will often include inquiries about your family. Strangers will ask if you are married and how many children you have, which is a fairly normal conversational gambit that's not meant to seem overly inquisitive. Conversations are frequently laced with local colloquialisms (see the Language section at the back of the book). References to a person's appearance are practical endearments and are not meant to give offense, though non-tico recipients may find them tiresome. These include *chino* (a person with an Asian appearance), *flaco* (a skinny person), *gordo* (a plump person), and *negro* (a black person). They may be made more affectionate by adding a diminutive (eg, *la gordita).*

The concept of smoking being a hazard to one's health is not very big in Costa Rica compared to the USA. Nonsmoking areas are infrequent, and some restaurants allow diners to smoke wherever they please.

## RELIGION

This can be summed up in one word: Catholicism. Depending on which statistics you read, about 70% to 90% of the population is Roman Catholic, at least in principle. In practice, many people tend to go to church only at the time of birth, marriage, and death, but they consider themselves Catholic nevertheless. Religious processions on holy days are generally less fervent or colorful than those found in other Latin American countries. Holy Week (the week before Easter) is a national holiday; everything, including buses, stops operating at lunchtime on Maundy Thursday and doesn't start up again 'til Holy Saturday.

The blacks on the Caribbean coast tend to be Protestant, though some traditional African and Caribbean beliefs persist. Most other denominations have a church in or around San José. Various fundamentalist and evangelist groups, as well as Mormons, are slowly gaining some adherents. There is a small Jewish community with a B'Nai Israel temple and a synagogue, and a sprinkling of people hold Middle Eastern and Asian religious beliefs, including Buddhists, Hindus, and Muslims.

## LANGUAGE

Spanish is the official language and is the main language for the traveler. English is understood in the better hotels, airline offices, and tourist agencies, as well as along much of the Caribbean coast.

Indian languages, primarily Bribri and Cabécar, are spoken in isolated areas. These languages are understood by an estimated 18,000 people living on both sides of the Cordillera de Talamanca.

If you don't speak Spanish, take heart. It is an easy language to learn. Courses are available in San José as well as in other towns (many are listed throughout this book), or you can study books, records, and tapes before your trip. These study aids are often available free from many public libraries, or you might want to consider taking an evening or college course. Once you have learned the basics, you'll find it possible to travel all over Latin America because, apart from Brazil, which is Portuguese-speaking, most of the countries use Spanish.

Spanish is easy to learn for several reasons. It uses Roman script and, with few exceptions, the language is written phonetically. Imagine trying to explain to someone learning English that there are seven different ways of pronouncing 'ough.' This isn't a problem in Spanish. Also, many words in Spanish are similar enough to English that you can figure them out by guesswork. 'Instituto Geográfico Nacional' means the National Geographical Institute, for example.

Even if you don't have time to take a course, at least bring a phrasebook (Lonely Planet's *Costa Rica Spanish phrasebook* is a good choice) and dictionary. Don't dispense with the dictionary, because the phrasebook won't help you translate local newspapers. For a quick reference to vocabulary and pronunciation, see the Language section near the back of this guidebook.

# Facts for the Visitor

## HIGHLIGHTS

Costa Rica's greatest attractions are natural. Rainforests, active volcanoes, and prolific birdlife are certainly at the top of the list because they are more accessible in Costa Rica than in most other countries with similar attractions. The national park system is the best in Central America and provides visitors with memorable experiences: You can safely peer into a smoking volcanic crater one day and photograph a flock of scarlet macaws flying over a coastal rainforest the next.

The most accessible volcanoes are Poás and Irazú, both of which have roads reaching overlooks of their active craters, and Arenal, which is one of the most active volcanoes in the world and best viewed from afar (head to the town of Fortuna for a good look). For rainforest, the national park at Corcovado is the wildest (though comfortable lodges are nearby), and Manuel Antonio is the prettiest. Tortuguero is excellent for wildlife, and Caño Negro is the least well known but is superb for birding.

Birders find Costa Rica offers exceptional opportunities almost anywhere they go. Vacations specifically designed to yield numerous excellent sightings every day are offered by tour companies that specialize in birding.

Outdoor enthusiasts also find top-notch surfing, white-water rafting, windsurfing, and fishing. Beaches at Puerto Viejo de Talamanca on the Caribbean coast and at Pavones, Dominical, Jacó, and Tamarindo on the Pacific coast are all favorite surfers' hangouts. River running through the rainforests on the Pacuare or Reventazón Rivers is offered daily by outfitters in San José and Turrialba, and overnight trips with riverside camping are also available. Windsurfers consider Laguna de Arenal to be among the best windsurfing spots in the world. Anglers routinely hook (and release) world-class tarpon and sailfish on both coasts, and first-class fishing resorts and experienced boat skippers provide all the necessary expertise. On the Caribbean, Barra del Colorado is excellent; on the Pacific, there are several other choices.

Combining outdoor adventure with the rainforest brings you to places where you can climb into the canopy and spend time on platforms gazing out over the tropical treetops. Some of these places are good for looking at birds or monkeys; others are geared more to fun rappelling and zip-lining through the forest; and yet others are a mix of the two. For wildlife, Corcovado Lodge Tent Camp, on the Península de Osa, and Hacienda Barú, on the central Pacific coast, are good choices. For zip-lining, the Canopy Tour in Monteverde is among the most experienced.

Many other interests are catered to but aren't as noteworthy as the above because, well, you can find equally good or better options in other places. But you can certainly laze on beaches, go scuba diving or snorkeling, try to pay for your vacation at a casino, go mountain biking or hiking, or visit museums and art galleries.

Your itinerary will depend on your interests. Many visitors go to Costa Rica specifically to practice a hobby such as surfing, fishing, or birding. Others rent a car and strike out on their own, or join a tour and visit the highlights. Budget travelers can use the public bus system to get around. Those wishing to relax can spend a week in one of the many wilderness lodges or in a charming B&B or comfortable hotel by the beach. The choice is yours.

## PLANNING

If this is your first trip to Latin America, you might want to check out Lonely Planet's *Read This First: Central & South America*. It's full of useful predeparture information on planning, buying tickets, visa applications, health issues, and what to expect from the region. It also includes a country profile section. See Books, later in this chapter, for other useful titles.

### When to Go

The late December to mid-April dry season is traditionally the best time to visit Costa Rica. During this time, beach resorts tend to be busy and often full on weekends and holidays; Easter week is booked months ahead. Schoolchildren have their main vacations from December to February.

Starting in late April, when the rains begin, many of the dirt roads in the backcountry require 4WD vehicles (which can be rented). However, travel in the wet season also means smaller crowds and lower hotel prices. Bring your umbrella and take advantage of it!

To travel in the least crowded months, try late April and May and from mid-October to mid-December.

## Maps

If you want a good map of Costa Rica before you go, the best choice is the very detailed 1:500,000 sheet with a 1:250,000 *Environs of San José* inset, published by and available from ITMB (W www.itmb.com), 530 W Broadway, Vancouver, BC, V5Z 1E, Canada. ITMB also publishes an excellent regional map, *Traveller's Reference Map of Central America*. These provide road, rail, topography, national park, and private reserve information.

Once you arrive in Costa Rica, there are several choices. The Instituto Costarricense de Turismo (ICT) publishes a 1:700,000 *Costa Rica* map with a 1:12,500 *Central San José* map on the reverse. This is free at the downtown San José ICT office, subject to availability, and sold for US$2 elsewhere.

The Instituto Geográfico Nacional de Costa Rica (IGN) publishes four kinds of maps that can be bought at the IGN in San José (☎ 257-7798 ext 2630), Avenida 20, Calles 9 & 11, or in major bookstores in the capital. There is a single-sheet 1:500,000 map of Costa Rica, which is very good but not as detailed as the ITMB map, and there is a nine-sheet 1:200,000 map covering the country in detail. Unfortunately, several sheets are out of print. However, the same maps are used in Wilberth's *Mapa-Guía de la Naturaleza – Costa Rica* (see Books, later in this chapter). Most of the country is covered by 1:50,000 scale topographical maps, useful for hiking and backpacking, and some of the

---

## Responsible Tourism

The term 'ecotourism' has been used and abused more than any other word in the huge growth of the tourism industry Costa Rica has experienced since the late 1980s. Some developers, hotel owners, and tour operators have jumped on the ecotourism bandwagon, offering a packaged glimpse of nature without making any positive impact on the country. Other operators and hoteliers have arrived at a series of guidelines designed to minimize negative impacts of tourism and to emphasize sustainable development of the industry at all levels. These guidelines enable the traveler to make enlightened choices when visiting Costa Rica, and can generally be applied to countries worldwide. There are two main themes in the guidelines: conservation and cultural sensitivity.

**1. Waste Disposal** Don't litter. Patronize hotels with recycling programs. Some hotels will provide towel or sheet changes on request, rather than daily, to minimize unnecessary use of soap and water. Travel with tour operators who provide and use waste receptacles aboard buses and boats and who dispose of trash properly.

**2. Wildlife** Don't disturb animals or damage plants. Stay on trails. Observe wildlife from a distance with binoculars. Follow the instructions of trained naturalist guides. Never feed wild animals. Do not collect or buy endangered animals or plants.

**3. Local Communities** Allow the small communities at your destination to benefit from tourism. Use local guides. Patronize locally owned and operated restaurants and hotels. Buy locally made crafts and souvenirs (though never those made from endangered species such as turtles or black coral).

**4. Cultural Sensitivity** Interact with local people. Speak as much Spanish as you can. Appreciate and learn from the different cultural traditions of the areas you visit.

**5. Education** Learn about wildlife and local conservation, environmental, and cultural issues both before your trip and during your visit. Ask questions.

**6. Sustainability** Avoid overcrowded areas unless you really want to see them. Support tourism companies with conservation initiatives and long-term management plans.

cities and urban areas are covered by a variety of 1:10,000 and 1:5000 maps. All of these maps provide physical as well as political detail and are well produced, but many are outdated or out of print.

Many private publishers in Costa Rica have produced country maps, available in bookstores in the country. Most are 1:500,000. The Fundación Neotropica has published a 1:500,000 map of the country showing all the national parks and other protected areas. These maps are available by mail order from Treaty Oak (☎ 512-326-4141, fax 512-443-0973, Ⓦ www.treatyoak.com), PO Box 50295, Austin, TX 78763-0295, USA. This company specializes in Latin American maps.

In Europe, the best source for maps is Stanfords (☎ 020-7836-1321, fax 020-7836-0189, Ⓦ www.stanfords.co.uk), 12-14 Long Acre, London WC2E 9LP, UK.

## What to Bring

The best advice is to travel as lightly as possible; don't bring things you can do without. Traveling on buses and trains is bound to make you slightly grubby, so bring one or two changes of dark clothes that don't show the dirt, rather than seven changes of smart clothes for a six-week trip. On the other hand, if you are going to spend a lot of time in the lowlands, dark clothes definitely feel hotter than light-colored ones. Bring clothes that wash and dry easily. (Jeans take forever to dry.)

The highlands can be cool, so bring a windproof jacket and a warm layer to wear underneath. A hat is indispensable. A collapsible umbrella is great protection against rain and sun as well, and is indispensable during the rainy season. In tropical rainforests, rainwear often makes you sweat, so many travelers prefer an umbrella.

You can buy clothes of almost any size if you need them, but shoes in large sizes are difficult to find. Most stores don't sell shoes larger than US size 11. (Limón is the one city where the author found a few size 12 shoes.) If you're planning a trip to the rainforest, remember that it will often be muddy even during the dry season, and very wet at other times, so bring a pair of shoes that you are prepared to get repeatedly wet and muddy. Long sleeves and pants are recommended for sun and insect protection in the tropics.

Shorts and skirts are fine on the beaches but less useful in the rainforests. See also Society & Conduct in the Facts about Costa Rica chapter for dress-code etiquette.

Other items you should consider bringing are binoculars (7x35 are recommended) for wildlife observation, a pocket flashlight (torch), a few meters of cord (useful for clothesline and spare shoelaces), toilet paper (sometimes missing in cheaper hotels and restaurants), earplugs to aid sleeping in noisy hotels, a Spanish-English dictionary and phrasebook, and a small padlock.

Hard traveling is notoriously wearing on your luggage, and if you bring a backpack, one with an internal frame is suggested. External frames snag on bus doors, luggage racks, and airline baggage belts, and are prone to getting twisted, cracked, or broken.

A good idea once you're in San José is to divide your gear into two piles. One is what you need for the next section of your trip; the rest you can stash in the storage room at your hotel (most hotels have one). Costa Rica is a small country, so you can use San José as a base and divide your traveling into, say, coastal, highland, and jungle portions, easily returning to the capital between sections.

## TOURIST OFFICES

Also see Useful Organizations, later in this chapter.

### Local Tourist Offices

In San José, the Instituto Costarricense de Turismo (ICT) answers questions (in English!) and sometimes provides maps at its public information office (☎ 222-1090, fax 223-1090, Ⓦ www.tourism-costarica.com). It's on the Plaza de la Cultura at Calle 5 and Avenida Central, next to the Museo de Oro, open 9am to 5pm Monday to Friday, with a flexible lunch hour. It also has an information center at the airport. ICT has a toll-free number in Costa Rica, ☎ 800-012-3456.

In other towns, there is sometimes a locally run information center. These are mentioned in the text where appropriate.

### Tourist Offices Abroad

Roughly 30% of all foreign visitors to Costa Rica come from the USA, where you can call ☎ 800-343-6332 for ICT brochures or information.

Citizens of other countries can ask the local Costa Rican consulate for tourist information, or email the Instituto Costarricense de Turismo via its website.

## VISAS & DOCUMENTS
### Passport

Citizens of all nations are required to have at least a passport to enter Costa Rica. Passports should be valid for at least six months beyond the dates of your trip.

Passport-carrying nationals of the following countries are allowed 90 days' stay with no visa: most western European countries, Argentina, Brazil, Canada, Israel, Japan, Panama, Paraguay, Romania, South Korea, Trinidad & Tobago, the UK, Uruguay, and the USA.

Passport-carrying nationals of the following countries are allowed 30 days' stay with no visa: most eastern European countries, Australia, Bolivia, Chile, Colombia, El Salvador, Guatemala, Honduras, Iceland, India, Ireland, Mexico, New Zealand, Russia, South Africa, Venezuela, and some others. The 30-day stay may be extended for another 60 days. Note that these lists are subject to change; see W www.rree.go.cr/visa-ingreso for recent information.

Officially, adult Canadians and US citizens can enter the country for up to 90 days with a birth certificate and photo ID such as a driver's license. Instead of a passport stamp upon arrival, you receive a tourist card for US$2. Costa Rican entry requirements change frequently, so it's worth checking at a consulate before your trip, especially if you want to stay more than 30 days.

When you arrive, your passport will be stamped. During your stay, the law requires that you carry your passport at all times (or a tourist card). A photocopy of the pages bearing your photo, passport number, and entry stamp will suffice when walking around town, but the passport should at least be in the hotel where you are staying, not locked up in San José.

### Visas

Most other nationalities are required to have a visa, which can be obtained from a Costa Rican consulate for US$20. At this time, Nicaraguan, Ecuadorian, and Peruvian citizens are among those that require visas before arriving in Costa Rica. Many coun-

tries are restricted by political problems, and citizens may have difficulty obtaining a visa for tourism.

**Visa Extensions** If you overstay your allotted 30 or 90 days, you will need a bureaucratically time-consuming exit visa, and the rules change often. Don't overstay your allotted time without checking locally about the current situation. Many travel agents will be able to get an exit visa for you for a small fee. The cost varies, depending on how long you overstay, but usually starts at about US$45. A better alternative is to leave the country for 72 hours (perhaps by visiting Panama or Nicaragua) and then return. Requirements change regularly; check with Migración (☎ 223-7555, 220-0355, 223-9465, fax 221-2066, 256-1650) before you decide whether to stay, leave, or visit another country for 72 hours.

The Migración office for visa extensions or exit visas is in San José opposite the Hospital Mexico, about 4km north of Parque La Sabana. Any Alajuela bus will drop you nearby. Hours are 8am to 4pm weekdays, and lines can be long. Some travel agencies will do the paperwork for you and charge a small processing fee; Tikal Tours is recommended.

### Onward Tickets

Travelers officially need a ticket out of the country before being allowed to enter, although this is often not asked for at the airport in San José because most airlines will not let you board their planes unless you have a return or onward ticket, or an MCO (miscellaneous charge order). Those travelers arriving without a passport (see the Passport section, earlier) do need onward tickets.

Travelers arriving by land may need an exit ticket, but the rules change and are enforced erratically. The easiest way for overland travelers to solve this requirement is to buy a ticket from the TICA Bus company, which has offices in both Managua (Nicaragua) and Panama City. (Ask other travelers, who can beat any guidebook for up-to-the-minute information.) Sometimes a show of cash is required to cross land borders – US$400 per month should be sufficient.

### Travel Insurance

No matter how you're traveling, make sure you take out travel insurance. This should cover you not only for medical expenses and luggage theft or loss, but also for unavoidable cancellation or delays in your travel arrangements. It should also cover the worst possible case, such as an accident that requires hospital treatment and a flight home. Coverage depends on your insurance and type of ticket, so ask both your insurer and your ticket-issuing agency to explain the finer points. Ticket loss is also covered by travel insurance. Make sure you have a separate record of all your ticket details – or, better still, a photocopy of it. Also make a copy of your policy in case the original is lost.

Buy travel insurance as early as possible. If you buy it the week before you fly, you may find, for instance, that you're not covered for delays to your flight caused by strikes or other industrial action that may have been in force before you took out the insurance.

### Driver's License & Permits

If you plan to rent a car, your driver's license from your home country is normally accepted. If you plan to drive down to Costa Rica from North America, you will need all the usual insurance and ownership papers. In addition, you have to buy additional Costa Rican insurance at the border (about US$20 a month) and pay a US$10 road tax. You can stay in the country for up to 90 days before you are required to get a Costa Rican driver's license. You are not allowed to sell the car in Costa Rica. If you need to leave the country without the car, you must leave the car in a customs warehouse in San José.

### Other Documents

International health cards are not needed to enter Costa Rica.

There is a small network of youth hostels in Costa Rica that will give you a discount if you have a youth hostel card from your home country. Student cards are of limited use in Costa Rica and are accepted only if they have a photograph.

### Photocopies

The cheapest insurance policy is keeping copies of your most important documents. Photocopy the pages of your passport containing your photograph and passport number. On the back, write the numbers of traveler's checks, airline tickets, credit card contact telephone numbers (in case of loss), health insurance contact telephone numbers, and anything else that may be important. Then photocopy this again; leave a copy at home and carry another copy separate from other documents.

## EMBASSIES & CONSULATES

Some of the most important embassies are listed below; also see W www.rree.go.cr.

### Costa Rican Embassies & Consulates

**Australia** (☎ 02-9261-1177, fax 02-9261-2953, ℮ perezdls@ozemail.com.au) 30 Clarence St, 11th floor, Sydney, NSW 2000

**Canada** (☎ 613-562-2855, fax 613-562-2582, ℮ embcrica@travel-net.com) 325 Dalhousie St, suite 407, Ottawa, ONT K1N 5TA

**France** (☎ 01 45 78 96 96, fax 01 45 78 99 66, ℮ embcr@wanadoo.fr) 78 avenue Emile Zola, 75015 Paris

**Germany** (☎ 49 30 26398990, fax 49 30 26557210, ℮ emb-costa-rica@t-online.de) Dessauerstr 2829, D-10963 Berlín

**Israel** (☎ 02-256-6197, fax 02-256-3259, ℮ emcri@netmedia.net.il) 13 Diskin St, No 1, Jerusalem 91012

**Italy** (☎ 06-4425-1046, fax 06-4425-1048, ℮ embcosta@tiscalinet.it) Via Bartolomeo Eustachio 22, Interno 6, Rome 00161

**Japan** (☎ 03-3486-1812, fax 3486-1813, ℮ rsembcrj @kty3.3web.ne.jp) Kowa Building No 38 Floor 12-24 Nishi-Azabu 4, Chome Minato-Ku, Tokyo, 106-0031

**Netherlands** (☎ 070-354-0780, 358-4754, fax 070-358-4754, ℮ embajada@embacrica.demon.nl) Laan Copes VanCattenburg 46,2585 GB Den Haag

**Nicaragua** (☎ 02-66-2404, 66-3986, fax 02-68-1479, ℮ embcr@ibw.com.ni) De la Estatua de Montoya, dos cuadras al lado y media cuadra arriba (Callejón Zelaya), Managua

**Panama** (☎ 264-2980, 264-2937, fax 264-4057) Calle Samuel Lewis, Edificio Plaza Omega 3 piso, contiguo Santuario Nacional, Panama City

**Spain** (☎ 91-345-9622, fax 91-353-3709, ℮ emba jada@embcr.org) Paseo de la Castellana 164, No 17A, 28046 Madrid

**UK** (☎ 020-7706-8844, fax 020-7706-8655, ℮ general@embcrlon.demon.co.uk) Flat 1, 14 Lancaster Gate, London W2 3LH

**USA** (☎ 202-234-2945, 234-2946, fax 202-265-4795, ℮ ambassador@costarica-embassy.org) 2114 S St NW, Washington, DC 20008

## Embassies & Consulates in Costa Rica

The following countries have embassies or consulates in the San José area. Call ahead to confirm locations and get directions. Embassies tend to be open in the mornings more often than in the afternoons. Australia and New Zealand do not have consular representation but do have embassies in Mexico City.

**Canada** (☎ 296-4149, fax 296-4270, e canadacr@racsa.co.cr) Oficentro Ejecutivo La Sabana, Edificio 5, 3rd floor, detrás La Contraloría, Sabana Sur

**France** (☎ 225-0733, 225-0933, 225-0058, fax 253-7027, e sjfrance@racsa.co.cr) 200m south, 25m west of the Indoor Club, Carretera a Curridabat

**Germany** (☎ 232-5533, 232-5450, fax 231-6403) 200m north, 75m east of the Casa de Dr Oscar Arias, Rohrmoser

**Israel** (☎ 221-6011, 221-6444, fax 257-0867, e embofisr@racsa.co.cr) Edificio Centro Colón, 11th floor, Paseo Colón, Calles 38 & 40

**Italy** (☎ 224-6574, 234-2326, fax 225-8200, e ambitcr@racsa.co.cr) Calle 33, Avenidas 8 & 10, quinta entrada de Los Yoses, casa blanca esquinera

**Netherlands** (☎ 296-1490, fax 296-2933, e nethemb@racsa.co.cr) Oficentro Ejecutivo La Sabana, Edificio 3, 3rd floor, detrás La Contraloría, Sabana Sur

**Nicaragua** (☎ 222-2373, 233-3479, 233-8747, fax 221-5481, e embanic@racsa.co.cr) Avenida Central, Calles 25 & 27, Barrio La California

**Panama** (☎ 257-3241, 256-5169, fax 257-4864) Calle 38, Avenidas 5 & 7

**Spain** (☎ 222-1933, 221-7005, 222-5745, fax 222-4180) Calle 32, Paseo Colón & Avenida 2

**Switzerland** (☎ 221-4829, 222-3229, fax 525-283, e swiemsj@racsa.co.cr) Edificio Centro Colón, 10th floor, Paseo Colón, Calles 38 & 40

**UK** (☎ 258-2025, fax 233-9938, e britemb@racsa.co.cr) Edificio Centro Colón, 11th floor, Paseo Colón, Calles 38 & 40

**USA** (☎ 220-3939, fax 220-2305, e hdssjo@usia.gov) Carretera Pavas, in front of the Centro Commercial

## Your Own Embassy

As a tourist, it's important to realize what your own embassy can and can't do.

Generally speaking, it won't be much help in emergencies if the trouble you're in is remotely your own fault. Remember you are bound by the laws of the country you are in. Your embassy will not be sympathetic if you end up in jail after committing a crime locally, even if such actions are legal in your own country.

In genuine emergencies, you might get some assistance, but only if other channels have been exhausted. For example, if you need to get home urgently, a free ticket home is unlikely – the embassy would expect you to have insurance. If you have all your money and documents stolen, it should assist in getting a new passport, but a loan for onward travel is out of the question.

Embassies used to keep letters for travelers or have a small reading room with home newspapers, but these days the mail-holding service has been stopped, and newspapers tend to be out of date.

## CUSTOMS

Costa Rica is less restrictive than many countries and allows 500 cigarettes or 500g of tobacco, and 3 liters of wine or spirits for each adult.

Camera gear, binoculars, and camping, snorkeling, and other sporting equipment are readily allowed into the country. Officially, you are limited to six rolls of film, but this is rarely checked or enforced. Generally, if you are bringing in items for personal use, there's no problem. If you are trying to bring in new items that you want to sell, you may be asked to pay duty.

## MONEY
### Currency

The Costa Rican currency is the *colón* (plural *colones*), named after Cristóbal Colón (Christopher Columbus). Colones are normally written as ¢.

Bills come in 50, 100, 500, 1000, 2000, 5000, and 10,000 colones, though the 50 and 100 colones bills are being phased out. Coins come in one (rarely), five, 10, 20, 25, 50, and 100 colones; older ones are silver, and newer ones are gold-colored.

### Exchange Rates

During the past years, the colón has fallen slowly against the US dollar at a rate of about two colones a month.

Prices in this book are quoted in US dollars, and the exchange rate is expected to reach 350 colones to US$1 by late 2002. Other currencies are rarely accepted; therefore exchange rates aren't given for them.

Euros are now readily exchanged in banks, and a few travel agencies are beginning to accept them as well, but US dollars are still preferred.

## Exchanging Money

A few banks in the capital will change a handful of non-US currencies, but rates are generally very poor. Outside of San José, US dollars are the only way to go. Non-US travelers should buy US dollars before they arrive in Costa Rica. There is occasional talk of linking the colón to the US dollar, and you can change cash US dollars almost anywhere.

Banks tend to be slow in changing money, especially the four state-run institutions (Banco Nacional, Banco Central, Banco de Costa Rica and Banco Popular), where it can sometimes take almost an hour. Private banks (Banex, Banco Interfin, Banco Scotiabank, and many others) tend to be faster.

Banking hours are 9am to 3pm weekdays, though in San José the banks often open by 8:30am and may remain open 'til 4pm. Carry your passport when changing money.

Hotels and travel agencies sometimes give the same rate as the banks, and are much faster and more convenient. Most allow only guests and customers to use their services, although some places will serve outsiders – it's worth trying. Another drawback is that they have limited cash resources and sometimes don't have enough colones. Some hotels charge a 'commission.'

Changing money on the streets is not recommended, except possibly at land borders where you have no other choice. Street changers don't give better rates, and scammers abound. A favorite scam is for the changer to say that the police are coming, and give you back your dollars – except that the dollars are counterfeit. Always count your colones carefully before handing over your dollars.

Try not to leave the country with many excess colones; it's difficult to buy back more than US$50 at the border or airport.

**Cash** US cash dollars with tears or in worn condition are not accepted by banks or anyone else. Make sure your bills are undamaged – Costa Rican banks are very picky about this.

You can use small-denomination bills (US$20 and less) to pay for almost anything from groceries in a corner store to cab fare. Larger bills can be used for more expensive purchases like tours, car rentals, and air tickets. Change some money into colones, as you'll need them for small expenses like a snack, budget hotel, or bus fare.

**Traveler's Checks** Major brands of traveler's checks in US dollars are readily exchanged into colones, but the rate is usually 1% or 2% lower than cash. Some banks will accept one kind of check but not another. Because they can be replaced in the event of loss, traveler's checks are safe. American Express checks are the easiest to replace quickly in Costa Rica. If your American Express traveler's checks are lost or stolen, call AmEx toll-free at ☎ 0-800-012-0039. It's worth having some US cash for use when banks are closed.

**ATMs** Banco Popular, ATH (A Todo Hora – 'at all hours'), and Credomatic have the biggest ATM networks, though there are others. The ATH machines have a large sun/moon symbol that looks like a capital O, and the OATH signs are distinctive. Most machines are in small, well-lit 24-hour booths accessed only with a credit/debit card, making it easy to obtain money around the clock.

Visa cards (on the Plus or Star networks) are by far the most useful, though MasterCard (on the Cirrus network) works in some machines as well, but some readers report difficulties in obtaining cash. You can find ATMs in cities and in most smaller towns, especially those that have a developed tourism industry. If you use a credit card in an ATM, you will begin paying very high interest from the moment you make a cash withdrawal, so either overpay your bill before you travel to have a positive balance or use a debit card that is connected with your checking account (again, with a positive balance) back home.

**Credit & Debit Cards** Holders of credit and debit cards can buy cash colones (and cash US dollars) in some banks. See ATMs, above, for tips about avoiding high interest payments.

Cards can also be used at the more expensive hotels, restaurants, travel and car rental agencies, and stores. MasterCard and Visa are both widely accepted (especially Visa), you are charged at close to the normal bank rates, and commissions are low. American Express cards are less readily accepted. Although this is now illegal, some places still charge up to a 7% commission for card use (be sure to ask). The legal loophole is that a 7% 'discount' is given for cash.

Before leaving for Costa Rica, card holders should call customer service for their credit/debit card–issuing bank to find out the most current numbers to dial in the case of loss or other problems with credit cards in Costa Rica. Often, you are told to dial your home country collect to report a lost card rather than calling a number in Costa Rica. An exception is American Express. Call AmEx toll-free at ☎ 0-800-011-0216 to report lost cards.

Users of credit cards linked to a currency other than the US dollar get poor rates for cash withdrawal of colones; get around this by withdrawing cash dollars for better rates.

**International Transfers** The main branches of several banks in San José will accept cash transfers but charge a commission. Shop around for the best deal. Allow several days and plenty of bureaucracy for a bank transfer. Western Union arranges international cash transfers more quickly than does a bank, but its commission is much higher. Transferring money internationally should be only a last resort.

### Security

Pickpockets prey on easy targets, and unsuspecting tourists are a prime choice. Avoid losing your money by following a few basic precautions: Carry money in inside pockets, money belts, or pouches beneath your clothes. Don't carry a wallet in a trousers or jacket pocket, as this is the first thing pickpockets look for. Divide your money among several places so if someone pickpockets you, you won't lose all your cash.

### Costs

Costa Rica is pricier than many Central or South American countries, although usually cheaper than the USA and Europe. Generally speaking, San José and the most popular tourist areas (Monteverde, Jacó,

Manuel Antonio, Guanacaste beaches) are more expensive than the rest of the country. The dry season (from December to April) is the high season and more expensive. Imported goods are also expensive.

Travelers on a tight budget will find the cheapest basic hotels start at about US$4 per person for four walls and a bed. Fairly decent but still quite basic rooms with private bathroom, hot water, and maybe air-conditioning start at around US$10 per person, depending on the area. First-class hotels charge well over US$100 for a single room, but there are plenty of good ones for less than that.

Meals cost from about US$2 to US$30, depending on the quality of the restaurant. Budget travelers should stick to the cheaper set lunches offered in many restaurants, which usually cost about US$2. Cafés or lunch counters, called *sodas,* are cheap places for meals. Beer costs from US70¢ to US$3, depending on how fancy the restaurant or bar is. National parks have a standard fee of US$6 per person per day.

Public transportation is quite cheap: The longest bus journeys, from San José to the Panamanian or Nicaraguan borders, cost under US$7. Domestic airfares are also relatively cheap, ranging from US$43 to US$84 one way with SANSA or Travelair. Round trips cost twice the one-way fare, and more expensive chartered flights are available. A taxi, particularly when you're in a group, isn't expensive and usually costs US$1 to US$2 for short rides. Car rental is expensive, however – figure on almost US$300 per week for the cheapest cars, including the mandatory insurance.

A budget traveler economizing hard can get by on US$12 to US$20 per day, especially if you are traveling with someone, because single rooms are more expensive. (Some readers have written to say that it's impossible to get by on US$12 a day – their definition of budget travel must be higher than rock-bottom.) If you want some basic comforts, such as rooms with private baths, meals other than set meals, and occasional flights, expect to pay about US$25 to US$50 per day. Travelers wanting to be comfortable can spend from US$50 to over US$150 per day, depending on your definition of comfort. The best tours cost from US$200 to US$400 per day, but these include flights and first-class accommodations and services. Cheaper tours are available.

## Taxes & Tipping

Better hotels add a 16.39% tax to room prices; this tax is included in the prices in the book, but always ask. Most restaurants automatically add a 13% tax and 10% tip to the bill, which is legally correct. Cheaper restaurants might add only the tip and the cheapest may not add anything. Tipping above the included amount is not necessary (ticos rarely do), but adding a few percent for excellent service is OK.

Tip bellhops in the better hotels about US50¢ to US$1 per bag. The person who cleans your hotel room deserves US50¢ to US$1 or more a day, except in the cheapest hotels, where they don't expect a tip.

Taxi drivers are not normally tipped, unless some special service is provided. Drivers tip boys and adults about US$1 (less for a short period) to watch their cars when parked on the street. The guardians take no responsibility for problems, but do keep thieves away.

On guided tours, tip the guide about US$1 to US$5 per person per day, depending on how good the guide is. (Tip more if the group is very small, less or nothing if the guide doesn't meet your expectations.) Tip the tour driver about half of what you tip the guide, unless, of course, the driver is great and the guide is poor!

## POST & COMMUNICATIONS

### Sending Mail

The better hotels provide stamps for your letters and postcards and will mail them for you; otherwise, go to the main post office in each town. There are no mailboxes. Mailing a postcard costs about US30¢ to the USA or Europe; a letter to the USA is less than US40¢. Faxes can also be sent from main post offices starting at about US25¢ a page nationally and US50¢ internationally. Sending parcels is expensive.

In addresses, *apartado* means 'PO Box'; it is not a street or apartment address.

### Receiving Mail

Unless you have a contact in Costa Rica, you can receive mail at the Correo Central (Main Post Office) of major towns. San José is the most efficient, and letters usually arrive within a week from North America, a little longer from more distant places. Post offices charge about US15¢ per letter received, and you need to show your passport to receive your mail – you can't pick up other people's.

Mail is filed alphabetically, but if it's addressed to John Gillis Payson, it could well be filed under 'G' or 'J' instead of 'P.' For San José, it should be addressed as in this example: John PAYSON, Lista de Correos, Correo Central, San José, Costa Rica. Ask your correspondents to clearly print your last name and avoid appending witticisms such as 'World Traveler Extraordinaire' to your name.

Avoid having parcels sent to you, as they are held in customs and cannot be retrieved until you have paid a usually exorbitant customs fee and gone through a time-consuming bureaucratic process. This is true of even small packages.

## Telephone

Generally, the telephone system is quite good, although systems sometimes get congested and some areas can be cut off temporarily due to weather conditions.

Public telephones are found all over Costa Rica and are of three kinds. They accept coins or one of two kinds of cards, but they are not set up to work with all systems. In larger towns, there are rows of public phones with different kinds of machines. The coin phones accept the older silver 10 and 20 colones coins; these phones are slowly being phased out. If you plan on calling often, it's best to buy one of each of the following types of cards.

The CHIP telephone cards are so called because of the metallic chip, visibly embedded in the card, which keeps track of the amount of time/money you have left. These cards are available in 1000 or 2000 colones values and are used in blue phones labeled CHIP. Push the card into the phone and follow instructions on the screen in Spanish or English. The digital CHIP phones can now be found even in small villages.

Telephone cards that work on any touch-tone phone by dialing a toll-free number (either ☎ 197 or 199) are also available. These cards have a scratch-off account number that is dialed first, followed by the number you wish to dial. The ☎ 197 cards are for in-country use and come in 300, 500 and 1000 colones values. Instructions are given in Spanish. The ☎ 199 cards are for international use and come in 3000 or 10,000 colones and US$10 or US$20 values. Instructions are given in English. Both CHIP and toll-free number cards can be purchased in many grocery stores, pharmacies, street stands, and other places.

**Local Calls** There are no area codes; just dial the seven-digit number. Calls are inexpensive, except for operator-assisted calls from hotels – the fancier the hotel, the more it seems to charge.

In remote areas of the country, look for the telephone symbol in even the most unlikely places. General stores in tiny villages often have a phone for public use.

For directory information, call ☎ 113.

**Pagers** Hotel owners and other businesses in remote areas sometimes receive messages on pagers, which are called 'beepers' in Costa Rica.

**International Calls** Calling internationally is quite straightforward, though not cheap. The cheapest calls are direct-dialed using a phone card. For collect (reverse charge) calls, dial ☎ 116 on any public phone to get an English-speaking international operator. The party you call can ring you back at many public telephones. Countries with reciprocal agreements with Costa Rica will accept collect calls, including the USA and many others.

To call directly to a foreign country, dial ☎ 00 + country code + area code (if there is one) + phone number. Country codes are the same as those dialed worldwide (eg, 1 for USA, 44 for UK, 61 for Australia, etc).

Many countries have a direct number that can be dialed from any Costa Rican phone to reach foreign operators. These numbers are listed under 'País Directo' in the White Pages of the Costa Rica telephone directory. After reaching the foreign operator, you can either call collect or charge the call to your calling-card number – you can get through in less than a minute. These methods are convenient but expensive; ask the operator for costs or find out from your home country before you travel.

To call Costa Rica from abroad, use the international code (☎ 506) before the seven-digit Costa Rican telephone number. Remember Costa Rica has no area codes.

### Fax
Radiográfica (RACSA) and main post offices have fax machines (see the regional chapters for office locations). They will also accept and hold fax messages. If you are faxing to Costa Rica, make sure you put your return fax number on the document; some machines in Costa Rica won't do this automatically.

### Email & Internet Access
It's not difficult to stay connected to your email account in Costa Rica. The main post office in San José and other major cities have public Internet access. These post offices have a 'punto.com' sign. RACSA offices also have Internet access in some cities.

Cybercafés are popular and are popping up all over San José and in most other towns; see listings in the regional chapters of this book. Rates are low (about US$1 for 30 minutes) and dropping. If one isn't listed or is closed, ask around.

Travelers with a laptop and modem will find that hotels and some other locales (friends' houses and offices) have RJ-11 phone jacks similar to those used in the USA.

If you are traveling in Costa Rica frequently or for a long time, you can set up a

---

### Communicating with Costa Rica

Readers and travelers have commented that phone messages, faxes, and emails sent to Costa Rica can remain unanswered for a week or more. The reason is simply that the remote location of many of the hotels and lodges there means that someone must go into the nearest town to recover their messages (which might happen only once or twice a week) and then answer later. Some places rely on public Internet cabins and don't have a computer on their desk. So don't get discouraged if your communication doesn't get answered right away, and allow extra time for this when possible.

local account. See the San José chapter for suggestions.

## INTERNET RESOURCES

The World Wide Web is a rich resource for travelers. You can research your trip, hunt down bargain airfares, book hotels, check on weather conditions, or chat with locals and other travelers about the best places to visit (or avoid!).

Try the Lonely Planet website (W www .lonelyplanet.com) for summaries on traveling to most places on earth, postcards from other travelers, and the Thorn Tree bulletin board, where you can ask questions before you go or dispense advice when you return. You can also find travel news and updates to some of our guidebooks, and the site's subWWWay section links you to useful travel resources elsewhere on the Web.

A useful background site on many aspects of Costa Rica (not much on travel, though) is W http://lanic.utexas.edu/la/ca/cr. A useful general site is W www.infocosta rica.com. Numerous travel-oriented sites specialize mainly in the higher end of the market, including the better hotels, domestic air service, car rentals, etc. A good one is W www.centralamerica.com, and there are many others. Other websites are mentioned throughout this guide.

## BOOKS

Some books are published in different editions by different publishers in different countries. As a result, a book might be rare in one country yet readily available in another. Bookstores and libraries can search by title or author, so your local bookstore or library is the best place to find out about the availability of the following.

Many of the books listed below are available outside Costa Rica in good bookstores or catalogs specializing in travel and wildlife. A few bookstores in San José and a few other places carry some titles, especially those published in Costa Rica. These bookstores are listed in the regional chapters. Books published outside the country are more expensive in Costa Rica.

### Lonely Planet

Lonely Planet's *Central America on a shoestring* is useful for travelers visiting several Central American countries on a tight budget. There are many useful maps. LP's *Watching Wildlife Central America* covers the wildlife of Belize, Costa Rica, and Panama. It has hundreds of color photos and is a great tool for birders.

In *Green Dreams: Travels in Central America,* author Stephen Benz questions the impact visitors are having on the region and its people.

Lonely Planet's *Costa Rica Spanish phrasebook* will come in handy for travelers who want to try out the local lingo.

If you are a first-time visitor to Central America, also see the Planning section, earlier in this chapter.

### Guidebooks

Costa Rica has changed greatly over the past few years, and the tourism boom is one of the greatest changes of all. When choosing travel guidebooks, get a recent edition – older ones may be cheap, but the travel information is way out of date.

If you're driving to Costa Rica from the United States, there's *Driving the Pan-American Highway to Mexico and Central America,* by Audrey Pritchard et al.

*Mapa-Guía de la Naturaleza – Costa Rica,* by Herrera S Wilberth, is a book of maps based upon the Costa Rican IGN 1:200,000 topo series. All natural areas are highlighted and described in Spanish and English, with good color photographs. This guide is a cross between Boza's park book (described below) and the IGN maps.

*The Essential Road Guide for Costa Rica,* by Bill Baker, is a useful kilometer-by-kilometer guide for driving along the major roads of the country; it also has good maps and background information on bus terminals, getting around, and driving in Costa Rica, though the most recent edition is 1995.

*Choose Costa Rica for Retirement,* by John Howells, is perhaps the best of the 'how to retire in Costa Rica' books, although some folks prefer *The New Golden Door to Retirement and Living in Costa Rica,* by Christopher Howard. In either case, get the most recent edition, as the retirement laws have changed recently. Also useful is *Living Overseas Costa Rica,* edited by Robert Lawrence Johnston.

*Vern Bell's Walking Tour of Downtown San José,* subtitled 'with some glimpses of history, anecdotes, and a chuckle or two,' is a fun-to-read, 48-page booklet available from long-time resident Vernon Bell. Call ☎ 225-4752, fax 224-5884 in San José, or send US$6.50 to Vernon Bell, Dept 1432, PO Box 025216, Miami, FL 33102, USA. It's recommended if you have a day to walk around San José.

## Adventure Travel

*Backpacking in Central America,* by Tim Burford, has plenty to keep the hiker busy. *Adventuring in Central America,* by David Rains Wallace, has lots of conservation-related background.

*The Rivers of Costa Rica: A Canoeing, Kayaking, and Rafting Guide,* by Michael W Mayfield et al, is just the ticket for river runners. *Costa Rica's National Parks and Preserves – A Visitor's Guide,* by Joseph Franke, provides useful maps and background on the parks.

## Nature & Wildlife

*Parques Nacionales Costa Rica* by Mario Boza, the former Costa Rican Vice-Minister of Natural Resources, is a coffee-table book with beautiful photographs and Spanish and English text describing the national parks; it's readily available in San José. A slimmer but no less beautiful book is *Costa Rica: The Forests of Eden,* by Kevin Schafer and Alvaro Ugalde, which concentrates on the tropical forests.

*Costa Rican Natural History,* by Daniel H Janzen (with 174 contributors), is an excellent, if weighty (almost 2kg and more than 800 large pages) introduction for the biologist.

The entertaining and readable *Tropical Nature,* by Adrian Forsyth and Ken Miyata, is recommended for the layperson interested in biology, particularly that of the rainforest. *A Neotropical Companion,* by John C Kricher and Mark Plotkin, is a readable book subtitled 'An Introduction to the Animals, Plants, and Ecosystems of the New World Tropics' – which tells you all you need to know.

*Sarapiquí Chronicle,* by Allen M Young, is subtitled 'A Naturalist in Costa Rica.' The book tells the story of the invertebrate zoologist's quarter century of expeditions to the rainforests near the Río Sarapiquí. It's a good read.

## Field Guides

*Costa Rica: The Ecotravellers' Wildlife Guide,* by Les Beletsky, is the best wildlife guide if you want just one book for everything.

*A Guide to the Birds of Costa Rica,* by F Gary Stiles and Alexander F Skutch, is an excellent and thorough book and the only one recommended for birding. *Site Guides: Costa Rica & Panama – A Guide to the Best Birding Locations,* by Dennis W Rogers, is useful for finding out where to bird.

*Neotropical Rainforest Mammals – A Field Guide,* by Louise H Emmons, is also recommended. It's a detailed and portable book, with almost 300 mammal species described and illustrated. Although some of the mammals included are found only in other Neotropical countries, most of Costa Rica's mammals, and certainly all the rainforest ones, are found within the book's pages.

*Butterflies of Costa Rica and Their Natural History,* by Philip J DeVries, is a detailed two-volume guide for lepidopterists.

*A Field Guide to the Orchids of Costa Rica and Panama,* by Robert Dressler, has 240 photos and almost as many drawings of orchids within its 274 pages. Several other plant guides for the specialist can be found in Costa Rica.

## People & Politics

*The Costa Ricans,* by Richard Biesanz et al, is a recommended book with a historical perspective on politics and social change in Costa Rica and many insights into the tico character. *The Ticos: Culture and Social Change in Costa Rica,* by Mavis Biesanz, is a more recent (1998) resource. Both are available in Costa Rica at Biesanz Woodworks (see Shopping in the San José chapter).

*What Happen: A Folk History of Costa Rica's Talamanca Coast* and *Wa'apin Man* are both written by former Peace Corps volunteer and sociologist Paula Palmer and are about the people of the south Caribbean coast of Costa Rica. *Taking Care of Sibö's Gifts,* by Paula Palmer, Juanita Sánchez, and Gloria Mayorga, is subtitled 'An Environmental Treatise from Costa Rica's KéköLdi Indigenous Reserve' and is an excellent booklet discussing the traditional Bribri lifestyle, focusing on the environment in which they now live.

## Fiction

*Costa Rica – A Traveler's Literary Companion,* edited by Barbara Ras, is an excellent compendium of 26 short stories by 20th-century Costa Rican writers. The selections offer a satisfying variety of Costa Rican writing that reveals special glimpses of tico life. The stories are grouped by geographical location, hence the title of the anthology.

*When New Flowers Bloomed: Short Stories by Women Writers from Costa Rica and Panama,* edited by Enrique Jaramillo Levi (Latin American Literary Review Press, 1991), is a little harder to get ahold of than the previous book, and a few stories are found in both. If you like the first one, look for the second.

*Jurassic Park,* by Michael Crichton – unless your interest in Hollywood blockbuster movies is zero, you've heard of it – is the novel that gave rise to the movie, and the dino-action is based in Costa Rica. Locals don't appreciate the references to the Costa Rican Air Force (there is no military force here) and 'ticans' (it should be 'ticos'), but it beats *War and Peace* for those lazy moments of your trip (apologies to dedicated Tolstoy readers).

## NEWSPAPERS & MAGAZINES

The best-established daily newspaper in San José is *La Nación* (Ⓦ www.nacion.co.cr), which was founded in 1936. It has thorough but fairly right-wing coverage of tico news and the most important international news, and is the most widely distributed paper in Costa Rica. You can read the main headlines on the Internet. Its main competitor is *La República,* founded in 1950 and also quite conservative. For a more left-wing slant on the day's events, read *La Prensa Libre,* San José's only afternoon daily and also its oldest, having been published for more than a century. There are several other tabloids. *Esta Semana* is the best local weekly news magazine.

An English-language newspaper appearing every Friday is the *Tico Times* (Ⓦ www.ticotimes.net), published since the 1950s. It costs about US$1 and is a recommended source of information about things going on in Costa Rica. It publishes an annual tourism edition that is available in local bookstores or directly from the newspaper. Foreign subscriptions are available for one year for US$61 (USA), US$96 (Canada and other Western Hemisphere countries, Europe, and the Middle East), and US$139 (Africa, Asia, and the Far East). Write to Apartado 4632-1000, San José, Costa Rica (fax 233-6378, Ⓔ ttcirc@racsa.co.cr). US residents can write to SJO 717, PO Box 025216, Miami, FL 33102-5216.

*Costa Rica Outdoors* is a slim but colorful bimonthly magazine on sportfishing, adventure sports, golf, and tico culture, with an emphasis on fishing. Written in English, it's available in Costa Rica for US$2.50 a copy, or by subscription in Central and North America for US$20 a year and in other countries for US$40 a year. To subscribe, write or call Costa Rica Outdoors (☎ 800-308-3394, Ⓔ jruhlow@racsa.co.cr, Ⓦ www.costaricaoutdoors.com), Dept SJO 2316, PO Box 025216, Miami, FL 33102-5216, USA.

Major bookstores in San José carry some North American and other newspapers as well as magazines such as *Time* and *Newsweek.* The international edition of the *Miami Herald* is usually the most up-to-date of the foreign newspapers.

## RADIO & TV

There are several local TV stations (programming is poor), but many of the better hotels also receive international cable TV.

There are over 100 local radio stations, some of which broadcast in English. Radio 2 (99.5 FM) has news, pop-rock favorites, and a US-style morning show from 5am to 9am, Monday to Friday, with trivia contests and telephone calls. For classical music, there's Radio Universidad (96.7 FM). Rock (107.5 FM) plays rock of the past four decades while Punto Cinco (103.5 FM) concentrates on oldies of the 1960s and '70s. Super-radio (102.3 FM) also plays US and British rock classics. 95.5 FM has good jazz.

If you have a portable shortwave radio, you can listen to the BBC World Service and Voice of America, among many others.

## PHOTOGRAPHY & VIDEO

Film is easily developed in Costa Rica, but professionals prefer to bring their film home to their favorite processing lab. Don't carry around exposed rolls for months – that's asking for washed-out results. Camera gear is expensive in Costa Rica and film choice is limited.

Note that the international airport in San José has a vicious X-ray machine. On one trip in the mid-1990s, my film came home with a grayish cast to it, and two friends who were there later reported the same thing. Carry all your film separately. I have received a report that the X-ray machine can also damage computer disks, although I can't figure out how.

Costa Rican videos are compatible with the US video system NTSC, and don't work on European and Australian systems. Some tourist-oriented videos are made in European and/or Australasian systems; check.

Tropical shadows are very strong and come out almost black on photographs. Often a bright but hazy day makes for better photographs than a very sunny one. Photography in open shade or using fill-in flash will help. The best time for shooting is when the sun is low – the first and last two hours of the day. If you are heading into the rainforest, you will need high-speed film, flash, a tripod, or a combination of these if you want to take photographs within the jungle. The amount of light penetrating the layers of vegetation is, surprisingly, very low.

Most people resent having a camera thrust in their faces, so ask permission with a smile or a joke, and if this is refused (rarely), don't be offended. Be aware and sensitive of people's feelings – it is not worth upsetting someone to get a photograph.

## TIME

Costa Rica is six hours behind Greenwich Mean Time (GMT), which means that Costa Rican time is equivalent to Central Time in North America. There is no daylight saving time.

## ELECTRICITY

Costa Rica's electricity supply is 110 V AC at 60 Hz (same as the USA). Bring a voltage converter to use 240/250 V AC-powered items. Most outlets accept two-pronged plugs with flat prongs of the kind used in the USA. Three-pronged outlets are occasionally found (but these also accept two-pronged plugs).

## WEIGHTS & MEASURES

Costa Rica uses the metric system. There is a conversion table at the back of this book.

## LAUNDRY

There are few self-service laundries in Costa Rica, mainly in San José. This means you have to find someone to wash your clothes for you or wash them yourself.

Many hotels will have someone to do your laundry; this can cost very little in the cheaper hotels (about a dollar for a change of clothes). The problem is that you might not see your clothes again for two or three days, particularly if it is raining and they can't be dried. Better hotels have dryers but charge more. A few upscale coastal fishing lodges are now offering free laundry service because the charter flight to reach the lodges permits only a 25lb baggage allowance per person.

You can handwash your clothes; some cheaper hotels have sinks in which to do this.

## TOILETS

Costa Rican plumbing is often poor and has very low pressure in all but the best hotels and buildings. Often, putting toilet paper into the bowl clogs up the system, so a waste receptacle is provided for the used paper. This may not seem particularly sanitary, but it's much better than clogged bowls and toilet water overflowing onto the floor. A well-run hotel, even if it is cheap, will ensure that the receptacle is emptied and the toilet cleaned every day. The same applies to restaurants and other public toilets. The better hotels have adequate flushing capabilities. In places where toilet paper baskets are provided, travelers are urged to use them.

Public toilets are limited mainly to bus terminals, airports, and restaurants. Lavatories are called *servicios higiénicos* and may be marked 'SS.HH' – a little confusing until you learn the abbreviation. People needing to use the lavatory can go into a restaurant and ask to use the *baño;* toilet paper is occasionally not available, so the experienced traveler learns to carry a personal supply.

## HEALTH

It's true that most people traveling for any length of time in Latin America are likely to have an occasional mild stomach upset. It's also true that if you take the appropriate precautions before, during, and after your trip, it's unlikely that you will become seriously ill.

Dengue fever, a mosquito-spread disease, is on the rise. There have been several hundred recent cases of malaria in low-lying regions. Both diseases are most common on the Caribbean coast, although malaria has been reported on the Península de Osa. Despite this, Costa Rica has one of the highest standards of health care and hygiene in Latin America.

## Predeparture Preparations

The Costa Rican authorities do not, at present, require that anyone have an up-to-date international vaccination card to enter the country, though you should make sure that all your normal vaccinations are up to date. Pregnant women should consult their doctors before taking any vaccinations. Occasionally, if a widespread cholera or malaria outbreak is occurring, travelers (especially those arriving overland) may be subject to cholera jabs or asked to show they have anti-malarials.

However fit and healthy you are, *do* take out travel insurance, preferably with provisions for flying you home in the event of a medical emergency. Even if you don't get sick, you might be involved in an accident.

You should put together a first-aid kit. How large or small your first-aid kit should be depends on your knowledge of first-aid procedures, where and how far off the beaten track you are going, how long you will need the kit for, and how many people will share it. A convenient way of carrying your first-aid kit so that it doesn't get crushed is in a small plastic container with a sealing lid, such as Tupperware.

If you wear prescription glasses, make sure you have a spare pair and a copy of the prescription. The tropical sun is strong, so prescription sunglasses are a good idea. Ensure that you have an adequate supply of any prescription medicines you use regularly. If you haven't had a dental examination for a long time, you should have one rather than risk a dental problem on your trip.

## Water & Food

Water is usually safe in San José and the major towns, though it is a good idea to boil, filter, or purify it in out-of-the-way places. The lowlands are the most likely places to find unsafe drinking water. When in doubt, ask: Some better hotels may be able to show you a certificate of water purity. Bottled mineral water, soft drinks, and beer are readily available alternatives.

Some places have had problems with contaminated ice. Try to avoid ice if you're unsure of its safety. Uncooked foods (such as salads and fruits) are best avoided unless they can be peeled.

## Medical Problems & Treatment

**Diarrhea** The drastic change in diet experienced by travelers means you are often susceptible to minor stomach ailments, such as diarrhea. After you've been traveling in Latin America for a while, you seem to build up some immunity. If this is your first trip to the area, take heart. Costa Rica has one of the better health-care systems in Latin America. Many people get minor stomach problems, but a simple nonprescription medicine such as Pepto-Bismol usually takes care of the discomfort quickly. Note that Lomotil or Imodium will temporarily stop the symptoms of diarrhea but will not cure the problem.

**Dysentery** If your diarrhea continues for days and is accompanied by nausea, severe abdominal pain, and fever, and you find blood in your stools, you may have contracted dysentery, which is uncommon in Costa Rica. If you contract dysentery, you should seek medical advice.

**Hepatitis** Hepatitis A infection occurs when you ingest contaminated food or water. Salads, uncooked or unpeeled fruit, and unboiled drinks are the worst offenders. Infection risks are minimized by using bottled drinks, except in major towns or places where you know the water has been purified; washing your own fruits and vegetables with purified water; and paying scrupulous attention to your toilet habits.

Hepatitis sufferers' skin and especially the whites of their eyes turn yellow, and they feel so tired that it literally takes all of their energy to go to the toilet. There is no cure except rest for a few weeks. Protection can be provided with the antibody gamma globulin or with a newer vaccine called Havrix, also known as hepatitis A vaccine.

The incidence of hepatitis A is low in Costa Rica, so many travelers opt not to bother with these shots.

**Cholera** Very few cholera cases are reported from Costa Rica, and the chance of a tourist contracting this illness is almost nil.

**Malaria** Malarial mosquitoes aren't a problem in the highlands, but some cases of malaria are reported in the lowlands. Be particularly careful in the south Caribbean coastal area near the Panama border and the Península de Osa, although there is a risk in any lowland area. If you plan on visiting the lowlands, purchase anti-malarial pills in advance, because they should be taken from two weeks before until six weeks after your visit. Dosage and frequency of administration vary from brand to brand, so check this carefully.

Chloroquine (known as Aralen in Costa Rica) is recommended for short-term protection. The usual dose is 500mg once a week. Long-term use of chloroquine *may* cause side effects, and travelers planning a long trip into the lowlands should discuss this risk against the value of protection with their doctor. Pregnant women are at a higher risk when taking anti-malarials. Fansidar is now known to cause dangerous side effects, so this drug should be used only under medical supervision.

People who plan to spend a lot of time in tropical lowlands and prefer not to take anti-malarial pills on a semipermanent basis should remember that malarial mosquitoes bite mostly at night. Wear long-sleeved shirts and long trousers from dusk 'til dawn, use frequent applications of insect repellent, and sleep under a mosquito net. Sleeping with a fan on is also effective; mosquitoes don't like wind.

Changing into a skirt or dress, or changing clothes right before dinner, is not a good idea in mosquito-prone areas, because dusk is a particularly bad time for mosquitoes and that dressy skirt does nothing to keep the insects away. Keep the long pants and bug repellent on.

Note that only some *Anopheles* species carry the disease, and they generally bite standing on their heads with their back legs up – mosquitoes that bite in a position horizontal to the skin are not malarial mosquitoes.

**Dengue Fever** No prophylactic is available for this mosquito-spread disease; the main preventative measure is to avoid mosquito bites (see Malaria, above). The carrier is *Aedes aegypti* – a different species from that which carries the malarial parasite, but it is avoided in the same way.

A sudden onset of fever, headaches, and severe joint and muscle pains is the first sign, before a pink rash starts on the trunk of the body and spreads to the limbs and face. After about three or four days, the fever will subside and recovery will begin. A shorter, less severe second bout may occur about a day later. There is no treatment except for bed rest and painkillers. Aspirin should not be taken. Drink plenty of liquids to stay hydrated.

Serious complications are uncommon, but full recovery can take several weeks. Quite common in some Latin American countries, dengue fever is less common in Costa Rica, though a few hundred cases are reported every year. Less than 3% of cases in the Americas are of the more dangerous hemorrhagic dengue fever, which may be lethal. It's not easy to tell the difference, so seek medical help.

**Leishmaniasis** This disease is caused by some sand-fly bites. Sand flies are about one-third the size of mosquitoes and bite mainly at night; they are found in rural areas. There is no prophylactic available, so prevention is by avoiding bites (see Malaria, above). Leishmaniasis is not common in Costa Rica, and you are unlikely to get it, especially if you follow the malaria prevention techniques. Symptoms show up months or even years after you're bitten and include skin sores that don't heal or anemia accompanied by enlargement of the spleen and liver.

**Insect Problems** Insect repellents go a long way in preventing bites, but if you do get bitten, avoid scratching. Unfortunately, this is easier said than done.

To alleviate itching, try applying hydrocortisone cream, calamine lotion, or some other kind of anti-itch cream, or soaking in baking soda. Scratching will quickly open bites and cause them to become infected. Skin infections are slow to heal in the heat of the tropics, and all infected bites as well as cuts and grazes should be kept scrupulously clean, treated with antiseptic creams, and covered with dressings on a daily basis.

## Insect Repellent

The most effective ingredient in insect repellent is diethyl-metatoluamide, also known as Deet. You can buy repellent with 90% or more of this ingredient; many brands (including those available in Costa Rica) contain less than 15%. I find that the rub-on lotions are the most effective, and pump sprays are good for spraying clothes, especially at the neck, wrist, waist, and ankle openings.

Some people find that Deet is irritating to the skin – they should use lower strengths. Research indicates that 30% strength works about as well as the stronger stuff, and doctors discourage use of 90% Deet for medical reasons. Everyone should avoid getting Deet in the eyes, on the lips, and on other sensitive regions. This stuff can dissolve plastic, so keep it off plastic lenses, etc. I know of someone who put plenty of Deet onto his face and forehead, then began sweating and got Deet-laden sweat in his eyes, resulting not only in eye irritation but clouding his plastic contact lenses!

Deet is toxic to children and shouldn't be used on their skin. Instead, try Avon's Skin So Soft, which has insect-repellent properties and is not toxic – get the oil, not the lotion. Camping stores sometimes sell insect repellents with names such as 'Green Ban' – these are made with natural products and are not toxic, but I find them less effective than repellents with Deet.

Mosquito spirals (coils) can sometimes be bought in Costa Rica. They work like incense sticks and are fairly effective at keeping mosquitoes away.

---

A reader writes that rubbing lime or lemon juice on mosquito bites makes them itch like crazy for a short while, but then they stop itching entirely and heal more quickly.

Another insect problem is infestation with lice (including crabs) and scabies. Lice and crabs crawl around in your body hair and make you itch. To get rid of them, wash with a shampoo containing benzene hexachloride or shave the affected area. To avoid being reinfected, wash all your clothes and bedding in hot water and the shampoo; it's probably best to throw away your underwear. Lice thrive on body warmth; those beasties lurking in clothes will die in about 72 hours if the clothing isn't worn.

Chiggers are mites that burrow into your skin and cause it to become red and itchy. The irritation lasts for weeks, but you don't feel the bites until it's too late. The recommended prevention is to sprinkle sulfur powder on socks, shoes, and lower legs when walking through grass. Liberal application of insect repellent works reasonably well.

Scorpions and spiders can give severely painful – but rarely fatal – stings or bites. A common way to get bitten is to put on your clothes and shoes in the morning without checking them first. Develop the habit of shaking out your clothing before putting it on, especially in the lowlands. Check your bedding before going to sleep. Don't walk barefoot, and look where you place your hands when reaching to a shelf or branch. It's unlikely that you will get stung, so don't worry too much about it, but take the precautions outlined above.

**Snakebites** These are also extremely unlikely. Should you be bitten, the snake may be a nonvenomous one (try to identify the offending creature). Do not try the slash-and-suck routine on the bite.

The venom of most dangerous snakes does its nasty work via the lymph system, not the bloodstream, so treatment aimed at reducing the flow of blood or removing venom from the bloodstream is likely to be futile. Aim to immobilize the bitten limb and bandage it tightly and completely (but don't make a tourniquet – that's now considered too dangerous and not particularly effective). Then, with a minimum of disturbance, particularly of the bound limb, get the victim to medical attention as soon as possible. Keep calm and reassure the victim.

One of the world's deadliest snakes is the fer-de-lance, and it has an anticoagulating agent in its venom. If you're bitten by a fer-de-lance, your blood coagulates twice as slowly as the average hemophiliac's, so slashing at the wound with a razor is a good way to help yourself bleed to death. The slash-and-suck routine does work in some cases, but this should be done only by people who know what they are doing. Even the deadly fer-de-lance succeeds in killing only a small percentage of its victims.

**Sexually Transmitted Diseases** Prostitution is legal in Costa Rica, and female prostitutes are required to be registered and receive regular medical checkups (see the boxed text 'Prostitution' in the Facts about Costa Rica chapter). Nevertheless, incidence of sexually transmitted diseases, including HIV/AIDS, is increasing among Costa Rican prostitutes. In addition, male prostitutes, including transvestites, are unlikely to receive the required medical checkups. Travelers are strongly advised against sex with prostitutes. Having sex with a person other than a prostitute may be somewhat safer, but it's still far from risk-free. The use of condoms minimizes, but does not eliminate, the chances of contracting an STD. Condoms *(preservativos)*, including some imported brands, are available in Costa Rican pharmacies.

Diseases such as syphilis and gonorrhea are marked by rashes or sores in the genital area and burning pain during urination. Women's symptoms may be less obvious than men's. These diseases can be cured relatively easily by antibiotics. If untreated, they can become dormant, only to emerge in much more difficult-to-treat forms a few months or years later. Costa Rican doctors

know how to treat most STDs – if you have a rash, discharge, or pain, see a doctor. Herpes and AIDS are incurable as of this writing. Herpes is not fatal.

**HIV/AIDS** The human immunodeficiency virus (HIV) may develop into AIDS, acquired immune deficiency syndrome *(SIDA* in Spanish). HIV is a significant problem in all Latin American countries, particularly among prostitutes of both sexes. Any exposure to infected blood, blood products, or bodily fluids may put the individual at risk. Transmission in Costa Rica is predominantly through homosexual male sexual activity, with about 70% of cases reported in men who have sex with men. However, many of these men also have sex with women, and the disease is spreading among heterosexual women, too.

HIV/AIDS can also be spread through infected blood transfusions; if you need a transfusion, go to the best clinic available and make sure they screen blood used for transfusions. It can also be spread by dirty needles – vaccinations, acupuncture, tattooing, and body piercing can be as dangerous as intravenous drug use if the equipment is not clean. If you do need an injection, ask to see the syringe unwrapped in front of you, or buy a needle and syringe pack from a pharmacy if you have any doubt about the sterility of the needle.

Apart from abstinence, the most effective way to prevent sexual transmission of HIV is to always practice safe sex using latex barriers such as condoms, gloves, and dams. Condoms are available in Costa Rican pharmacies. It is impossible to detect the HIV status of a healthy-looking person without a blood test.

Figures from 1999 give estimates that 0.5% of Costa Rican adults are HIV+. This figure rises to over 1% of sex workers and 3% to 6% of gay males. Unfortunately, many of them don't know they are infected and continue to be sexually active, so the virus is spreading. Information about safe sex and condoms – indeed, any kind of sex education – lags in Costa Rica because sex education is opposed by the powerful Roman Catholic church. Other problems are cultural and have to do with *machismo* – a 'real' man doesn't need to use a condom. Also, it is widely thought that HIV+ people look sick,

## Healthcare Tourism

Medical care in Costa Rica is generally much less expensive than it is in most Western countries, although the standards in San José are high. Costa Rica is experiencing a boom in dental, cosmetic, and plastic surgery. Foreigners come here specifically to have these nonessential medical procedures done at lower cost than at home. One couple wrote that they had what would have been US$10,000 worth of dental work (in the USA) done in Costa Rica for a third of the cost – the savings more than paid for their trip! Check with the Costa Rican Surgeons and Dentists Association (☎/fax 256-3100, ⓔ dentista@racsa.co.cr) for lists of qualified dentists.

Many surgeons have received medical training in the USA, speak English, and are well qualified. You can get lists of plastic surgeons and other information from the Costa Rican Doctors and Surgeons Association (☎ 232-3433, fax 232-2406, ⓔ medicos@racsa.co.cr) or Costa Rican Plastic Surgery Association (☎ 232-6547, fax 231-6161, ⓔ mchaconb@racsa.co.cr).

Holistic health retreats and resorts are also springing up in Costa Rica; several are listed in appropriate parts of the text.

---

when the reality is that HIV+ people are likely to look and act completely healthy for several years after infection, all the time carrying and perhaps spreading the disease.

Fear of HIV infection should never preclude treatment for serious medical conditions. Although there may be a risk of infection, it is very small indeed.

**Altitude Sickness** This may occur when you ascend to high altitude quickly, for example, when you fly into the highlands. This is not a problem in San José (1150m), which is not high enough to cause altitude problems.

If you are planning on driving up one of the volcanoes such as Poás (2704m) or Irazú (3432m), you may experience some shortness of breath and headache. Overnight stays are not allowed on these volcanoes, so you will be able to descend quickly if you feel unwell. Heading south from San José on the Interamericana, the road crosses the continental divide at 3335m, 95km south of the capital. Again, you will probably be going down again before you get sick.

If you climb Chirripó (3819m, the highest mountain in Costa Rica and southern Central America), you may experience much more severe symptoms, including vomiting, fatigue, insomnia, loss of appetite, a rapid pulse, and irregular (or Cheyne-Stokes) breathing during sleep.

The best thing you can do to avoid altitude sickness is to climb gradually. Consider taking two days for the Chirripó ascent

rather than one. If you feel sick, the best treatment is rest, deep breathing, an adequate fluid intake, and a mild painkiller such as Tylenol to alleviate headaches. If symptoms are very severe, the only effective cure is to descend to a lower elevation.

**Heat & Sun** The heat and humidity of the coastal tropics make you sweat profusely and can also make you feel apathetic. It is important to maintain a high fluid intake and ensure that your food is well salted. If fluids lost through perspiration are not replaced, heat exhaustion and cramps may result. The feeling of apathy that some people experience usually fades after a week or two.

If you're arriving in the tropics with a great desire to improve your tan, you've certainly come to the right place. The tropical sun will not only improve your tan but also burn you to a crisp. Travelers may enjoy the sun for an afternoon, and then spend the next couple of days with severe sunburn. An effective way of immobilizing yourself is to cover yourself with sunblock, walk down to the beach, remove your shoes, and badly burn your feet, which you forgot to put lotion on and which are especially untanned.

The power of the tropical sun cannot be overemphasized. Don't spoil your trip by trying to tan too quickly; use strong sunblock lotion frequently and put it on all exposed skin. Wearing a wide-brimmed sun hat is also a good idea.

**Rabies** Rabid dogs are more common in Latin America than in more developed nations. If you are bitten by a dog, try to have it captured for tests. If you are unable to test the dog, you must assume that you have rabies, which is invariably fatal if untreated, so you cannot take the risk of hoping that the dog was not infected. Treatment consists of a series of injections. Rabies takes from five days (exceptionally) to several months to develop, so if you are bitten, don't panic. You've got plenty of time to get treated. Ensure that any bite or scratch is cleaned thoroughly with soap and running water or swabbed with alcohol to prevent potential infections or tetanus.

Rabies is also carried by vampire bats, which actually prefer to bite the toes of their sleeping human victims rather than necks, as popular folklore suggests. Don't stick your toes out from your mosquito net or blanket if you're sleeping in an area where there are bats. Other carriers are monkeys, cats…in fact, many mammals. A rabies vaccine is available and should be considered if you are in a high-risk category (for example, if you intend to explore caves with bats or work with animals).

## Medical Services
If you've taken the precautions mentioned in the previous sections, you can look forward to a generally healthy trip. Should something go wrong, you can get good medical advice and treatment in San José.

The social security hospitals provide free emergency services to everyone, including foreigners. Private clinics are also available and are listed under San José and other main towns in this book. Their services are

### A Terrific Tumor

Costa Rican surgeons were amazed several years ago when they discovered a huge abdominal tumor in a 52-year-old patient. After extraction, they found that the tumor was a record-breaking 46lb, over three times heavier than the previously recorded largest tumor of this type. Five days after surgery, the much lighter patient was able to return to work.

normally of a higher standard than the social security hospitals.

An emergency phone number worth knowing is the Red Cross (Cruz Roja; ☎ 128, no coin needed) for ambulances in the San José area. In remote areas, in can take hours for an ambulance to arrive and, in emergencies, it may be faster to ask around for someone with a car. Outside San José, the Cruz Roja can be reached either by dialing ☎ 911 nationwide (see the Emergency section), or at a different number in each province:

| | |
|---|---|
| Alajuela | ☎ 441-3939 |
| Cartago | ☎ 551-0421 |
| Guanacaste | ☎ 666-0994 |
| Heredia | ☎ 237-1115 |
| Puerto Limón | ☎ 758-0125 |
| Puntarenas | ☎ 661-0184 |

Most prescription drugs are available in Costa Rica; some are sold over the counter. For minor ailments and illnesses, pharmacists will often advise and prescribe for you.

If you have insurance to cover medical emergencies, note that many doctors expect to be paid up front; then you have to claim from the insurance company to get reimbursed.

## WOMEN TRAVELERS
### Attitudes Toward Women
Generally, women travelers find Costa Rica safe and pleasant to visit. Women are traditionally respected in Costa Rica (Mother's Day is a national holiday), and women have made gains in the workplace. A woman vice president, Victoria Garrón, was elected in 1986, and another woman, Margarita Penon, ran as a presidential candidate in 1993. Both vice presidents (Costa Rica has two) elected in 1998 were women, Astrid Fischel and Elizabeth Odio. Women routinely occupy roles in the political, legal, scientific, and medical fields – professions that used to be overpoweringly dominated by men.

This is not to say that machismo is a thing of the past. On the contrary, it is very much alive and practiced. Costa Rican men generally consider *gringas* to have looser morals and to be easier 'conquests' than ticas. They often make flirtatious comments to or stare at unaccompanied women, both local and foreign. A couple of women traveling together are not exempt from this attention; women traveling with men are less likely to receive attention.

Comments are rarely blatantly rude; the usual thing is a smiling '*Mi amor*' or an appreciative hiss. The best way to deal with this is to do what the ticas do – ignore the comments completely and do not look at the man making them.

Women travelers will meet pleasant and friendly Costa Rican men. It is worth remembering, though, that gentle seduction is a sport, a challenge, even a way of life for many Costa Rican men, particularly in San José. Men may conveniently forget to mention that they are married, and declarations of undying love might mean little in this Catholic society where divorce is frowned upon.

Women who firmly resist unwanted verbal advances from men are normally treated with respect. But there are always a small number of men who insist on trying to hold hands or give a 'friendly' hug or kiss – if the feeling is not mutual, turn them down firmly and explicitly. Some women find that wearing a cheap 'wedding' ring helps – though, of course, you have to be ready to answer the inevitable 'Where is your husband?'

There have been reports of some cab drivers making inappropriate advances to women – women alone may want to use cabs from a hotel rather than a cab on the street. Pirate cabs (without the insignia of a cab company) are more likely to present a problem. Lone women might avoid those, especially after dark if going for a long ride.

## What to Wear

Costa Ricans are generally quite conservative, and that applies to dress. Women travelers are advised to follow suit to avoid calling unnecessary attention to themselves. On the beach, skimpy bathing costumes are quite acceptable, although topless bathing and nudity are not. Some women travelers, especially Europeans, tend to think that what they do on the Mediterranean they can do in Costa Rican beach areas. Going topless is seen in Costa Rica as insensitive, rude, and generally unacceptable.

## Organizations

The Centro Feminista de Información y Acción (CEFEMINA; ☎ 224-3986), in San Pedro, is the main Costa Rican feminist organization. It publishes a newsletter and can provide information and assistance to women travelers.

Newsletters aimed specifically at advising women travelers are of a general nature and not specifically about Costa Rica. *Journeywoman* is an online magazine, at **w** www.journeywoman.com, with many useful links.

## GAY & LESBIAN TRAVELERS

Although Costa Rica is known for its good human rights record, the situation for gays and lesbians is still poor (though better than in most Central American countries). Legally, homosexuality is not singled out as a criminal offense (except when an adult is with a minor under 18 of any gender), and most Costa Ricans are tolerant of gay and lesbian people – as long as they don't show affection for one another in public. Which means that homosexual life is pretty low-key in Costa Rica.

The tolerance of gay people only goes as far as a 'Don't ask; don't tell' philosophy. Despite the legal protection and theoretical equal rights of all Costa Ricans, gay or straight, police harassment in gay clubs and other locales has resulted in a string of human rights violations. People who come out publicly are often discriminated against by their employers and families. This results in a high level of depression, drug and alcohol abuse, and other psychological problems within the gay community.

In 1992, Triángulo Rosa (Pink Triangle), the first legally recognized gay group in Central America, was founded to support human rights for all members of the gay, lesbian, and bisexual community, despite opposition from the political and religious establishment. Triángulo Rosa works in various fields, including AIDS and safe sex education, struggling against discrimination, supporting HIV+ people and those with AIDS, operating a community center, forging positive relationships within the gay community and with the straight community, and providing information. Travelers will find that Triángulo Rosa can recommend gay-friendly hotels, bars, and meeting places in Costa Rica (especially in San José).

Leaders of Triángulo Rosa write that the situation with the gay rights movement in

San José is about where it was in the non-urban USA in the 1960s. In addition, the culture of machismo makes life 'a veritable hell for gays and lesbians,' according to a local psychologist who treats HIV+ patients. The Triángulo Rosa is staffed by about 20 volunteers and is supported mainly by local donations with some international funding. The volunteers say that their main aim is to save lives through education. For more on the AIDS situation in Costa Rica, see the Health section, earlier in this chapter.

In 1998, a gay and lesbian festival that had been planned in San José was canceled following comments from the Roman Catholic clergy that promoted heavy opposition to gay rights. The church has continued to lead homophobic sentiment in Costa Rica, forcing the cancellation of a gay and lesbian tour to Manuel Antonio and encouraging the blockade of a coastal hotel hosting a group of North American gays. The situation took an embarrassing turn in 1999, when the president of the ICT said that Costa Rica should not be a destination for sex tourism or gay men and lesbians. The gay community made it clear that it was against sex tourism, and that the linking of gay tourism with sex tourism was both untrue and defamatory. The official position in Costa Rica shifted toward stating that gay tourism was neither discriminated against nor encouraged.

However, the bottom line remains that discreet gay couples generally enjoy their vacations, and harassment is not a problem if ticos are unaware of your sexual orientation.

## Organizations

You can contact Triángulo Rosa (☎ 234-2411 English, ☎ 258-0214 Spanish, ✉ atrirosa@racsa.co.cr) for information or to make a donation.

A useful website is Ⓦ www.gaycostarica.com; it includes a calendar of events.

Instituto Latinoamericano de Prevención y Educación en Salud (ILPES; ☎ 253-8662, 257-9187, ✉ ilpes@racsa.co.cr) gives support to people living with or at risk for HIV/AIDS.

The International Gay & Lesbian Travel Association (IGLTA) has a list of hundreds of travel agents, tour operators, and tourism industry professionals all over the world. Browse its home page at Ⓦ www.iglta.org.

The local gay magazine, *Gente 10,* is available at some of the hotels listed below and in some of the bars listed under Gay & Lesbian Venues in the Entertainment section of the San José chapter.

## Meeting Places

Some gay-friendly hotels, described later in this book, are the Hotel Kekoldi, Joluva Guesthouse, Colors, and Apartamentos Scotland in San José, and the Hotel Casa Blanca, Villas Nicolas and the Hotel Mariposa in Manuel Antonio. Manuel Antonio also has a nude beach for gay people – one of the few places in the country where a blind eye is turned to nudity.

There is a good number of gay and lesbian nightclubs, especially in San José. These range from slightly dangerous meat markets to raving dance clubs to quiet places for a drink and talk. The main street action is in the blocks south of the Parque Central, but some blocks (though not all) are somewhat dangerous at night, so don't go around alone unless you know how to look after yourself or have good local information. There are also clubs in other areas. See the San José chapter for details.

## DISABLED TRAVELERS

Although there is an Equal Opportunities for Disabled Persons Law, its provisions are much less strict than those of similar laws in first world countries. Still, it is a small move in the right direction for disabled people.

Unfortunately, the law only applies to new or newly remodeled businesses (including hotels and restaurants), so older businesses (built prior to the mid-1990s) are exempt. New businesses are required to have a barrier-free entrance for disabled people.

Realistically, independent travel is difficult for disabled people. For example, very few hotels and restaurants, except for the newest, have features specifically suited to wheelchair use. Many don't even have the basic minimum of a wheelchair ramp and room or bathroom doors wide enough to accommodate a wheelchair. Special phones for hearing-impaired people or signs in Braille for blind people are very rare.

Outside the buildings, streets and sidewalks are potholed and poorly paved, often making wheelchair use frustrating at best.

Public buses don't have provisions to carry wheelchairs.

Most national parks and outdoor tourist attractions have trails not suited to wheelchair use. Notable exceptions include Volcán Poás, which has a wheelchair-accessible path up to the crater viewing area, and the Rainforest Aerial Tram, also wheelchair accessible.

## Organizations

In Costa Rica, Vaya con Silla de Ruedas (☎ 391-5045 cellular, fax 454-2810, ⓔ vayacon@racsa.co.cr, ⓦ www.gowith wheelchairs.com) has a van especially designed to transport travelers in wheelchairs; equipment meets international accessibility standards, and up to three wheelchairs can be transported. It can help with other arrangements such as bilingual guides, hotel reservations, and tours lasting from a few hours to a few days.

La Fundacion Kosta Roda (☎/fax 771-7482, ⓔ chabote@racsa.co.cr) in San Isidro is a nonprofit organization working with the ICT to list accessible sites of interest to disabled travelers.

## SENIOR TRAVELERS

Though many seniors travel in Costa Rica, no special in-country discounts are available to them. Seniors normally pay the regular fares, hotel costs, museum entrances, etc. However, international airlines flying into Costa Rica may offer discounted tickets.

Elderhostel (☎ 877-426-8056, 978-323-4141, fax 877-426-2166, 617-426-0701, ⓦ www.elderhostel.org), 11 Avenue de Lafayette, Boston, MA 02111, USA, is one of the best agencies for learning vacations for those 55 and older. See also the earlier Books section for titles about retiring in Costa Rica.

## TRAVEL WITH CHILDREN

Children pay full fare on buses if they occupy a seat, but often ride for free if they sit on a parent's knee. Children under 12 pay a discounted fare (variable) on domestic airline flights and get a seat, while infants under two pay 10% of the fare but don't get a seat. Children's car seats are not always available in Costa Rican car rental agencies, so bring one if you plan on driving.

In hotels, the general rule is simply to bargain, except in top-end hotels, where discounts are normally posted. Children should never have to pay as much as an adult, but whether they stay for half price or free is open to discussion. A few hotels don't allow children under a certain age in order to maintain a quiet atmosphere.

While 'kids' meals' (small portions at small prices) are not normally offered in restaurants, it is perfectly acceptable to order a meal to split between two children or an adult and a child.

Foreigners traveling with children will meet with extra, generally friendly, attention and interest. For more suggestions, see Lonely Planet's *Travel with Children*.

## USEFUL ORGANIZATIONS

In addition to the specific groups listed above, others of a more general nature are given here.

### The South American Explorers

The SAE (☎ 607-277-0488, fax 607-277-6122, ⓦ www.samexplo.org) is at 126 Indian Creek Rd, Ithaca, NY 14850, USA. The club is an information center for travelers, has clubhouses in Peru and Ecuador, and provides information for travelers to Central America as well.

The club has books, maps, and trip reports left by other travelers. Maps and books are sold through a print and online catalog. This is a membership-supported nonprofit organization. Membership costs US$50 and gets you four quarterly issues of the informative *South American Explorer* magazine. Members can make use of the clubhouses (if heading on to Peru or Ecuador) as well as the extensive information facilities and books, available by mail, before you go.

### Latin American Travel Advisor

You can get up-to-date information on safety, political and economic situations, health risks, costs, etc, for all the Latin American countries (including Costa Rica) from the *Latin American Travel Advisor*. This impartial, 16-page quarterly newsletter is published in Ecuador. Four issues are US$39, the most recent issue is US$15, and back issues are US$7.50, sent by airmail. The Latin American Travel Advisor (fax 888-215-9511 in the USA, fax 02-562-566 in Ecuador, ⓦ www.amerispan.com/lata) is reachable at PO Box 17-17-908, Quito, Ecuador.

## DANGERS & ANNOYANCES
### Thefts & Muggings
Locals and frequent visitors have noted an increase in tourist-oriented crime in recent years – likely precipitated by the increase in tourism. Although rip-offs are a fact of life when traveling anywhere, you'll find Costa Rica is still less prone to theft than many countries. You should, nevertheless, take some simple precautions to avoid being robbed.

Armed robbery is rare, but sneak theft is more common, and you should remember that crowded places are the haunts of pickpockets – places such as badly lit bus stations or bustling streets around market areas.

Occasionally, a couple of women may try to physically harass a man – one tries lasciviously to gain your attention while the other tries to pull your wallet. Other scams include being squirted with mustard or some other noxious substance; 'Samaritans' offering to help wipe you off are lifting your wallet at the same time. Alertness helps – don't allow yourself to be distracted. If you are used to dealing with big-city hassles, you should have no great problem.

Thieves look for easy targets. Tourists carrying a wallet or passport in a hip pocket are asking for trouble. Leave your wallet at home; it's an easy mark for a pickpocket. Carrying a small roll of bills loosely wadded under a handkerchief in your front pocket is as safe a way as any of carrying your daily spending money. The rest should be hidden. Always use at least an inside pocket or preferably a body pouch, money belt, or leg pouch to protect your money and passport. Separate your money into different places.

Carry some of your money as traveler's checks or credit cards. The former can be refunded if lost or stolen; the latter can be canceled and reissued. Carry an emergency packet somewhere separate from all your other valuables. It should contain a photocopy of your papers (see Photocopies under the Visas & Documents section, earlier). Also, keep one high-denomination bill in with this emergency stash. You will probably never have to use it, but it's a good idea not to put all your eggs in one basket.

Take out travelers' luggage insurance if you're carrying valuable gear such as a good camera. But don't get paranoid: Costa Rica is still a reasonably safe country.

If you are robbed, make a police report as soon as possible. This is a requirement for any insurance claims, although it is unlikely that the police will be able to recover the property. Police reports should be filed with the Organismo de Investigación Judicial (OIJ) in the Corte Suprema de Justicia (Supreme Court, ☎ 222-1365) complex at Avenida 6, Calles 17 & 19, in San José. If you don't speak Spanish, bring a translator. Outside of San José, call ☎ 911 to report a robbery and find out where the nearest OIJ is. In addition, travelers who have suffered crimes or price-gouging can write to the Costa Rican Tourist Board, Apartado 777-1000, San José. By Costa Rican law, the tourist board is obliged to represent foreign tourists who are victims of tourist-related crimes in court cases if necessary, thus allowing the tourist to go elsewhere (like home).

Costa Rica has a long history of business-related crimes – real estate and investment scams have occurred frequently over the years. If you want to sink money into any kind of Costa Rican business, make sure you both know what you are doing and check it out thoroughly.

### Ocean Hazards
The tourist brochures, with their enticing photographs of tropical paradises, do not mention that approximately 200 drownings a year occur in Costa Rican waters. Of these, an estimated 90% are caused by riptides.

A riptide is a strong current that pulls the swimmer out to sea. It can occur in waist-deep water. It is most important to remember that riptides will pull you *out but not under*. Many deaths are caused by panicked swimmers struggling to the point of exhaustion.

If you are caught in a riptide, float. Do not struggle. Let the riptide carry you out beyond the breakers. If you swim, do so parallel to the beach, not directly back in. Go with the flow of the current. You are very unlikely to be able to swim against a riptide and will only exhaust yourself. When you are carried out beyond the breakers, you will find that the riptide will dissipate – it won't carry you out for miles. Then you can swim back to shore. Swim at a 45° angle to the shore to avoid being caught by the current again.

If you feel a riptide while you are wading, try to come back in sideways, thus offering less body surface to the current. Also remember to walk parallel to the beach if you cannot make headway, so you can get out of the riptide. Some riptides are permanent; others come and go or move along a beach. Beaches with a reputation for rips are Playa Bonita near Limón; the area at the entrance of Parque Nacional Cahuita; Playa Doña Ana and Playa Barranca near Puntarenas; Dominical; and Playa Espadilla at Parque Nacional Manuel Antonio.

Other swimming problems are occasional huge waves that can knock waders over – stay within your limits and remember that few beaches have lifeguards. Follow all signs, swim within sight of the lifeguards if there are any and, if you get into trouble, swim out beyond the breakers and wave for help.

Some beaches are polluted by litter, or worse, sewage and other contamination, which can pose a health hazard. Beaches are now checked by the local authorities, and the cleanest are marked with a blue flag.

## Hiking Hazards

Many visitors like to hike in the national parks and wilderness areas. Hikers should be adequately prepared for their trips. Always carry plenty of water, even on short trips. In 1993, two German hikers going for a short 90-minute hike in Parque Nacional Barra Honda got lost and died of heat prostration and thirst. Hikers have been known to get lost in rainforests. Carry maps and extra food, and let someone know where you are going to narrow the search area in the event of an emergency (for more information on hiking, see Hiking & Backpacking under Activities, later in this chapter).

## Earthquakes

It comes as no surprise that Costa Rica, with its mountain chains of active volcanoes, should be earthquake prone. Recent major quakes occurred on March 25, 1990 (7.1 on the Richter scale), and on April 22, 1991 (7.4 on the Richter scale, killing over 50 people in Costa Rica and about 30 more in Panama). Smaller quakes and tremors happen quite often.

If you are caught in a quake, make sure you are not standing under heavy objects that could fall and injure you. The best

places to take shelter if you are in a building are in a door frame or under a sturdy table. If you are in the open, don't stand near walls, telephone poles, or anything that could collapse on you.

## Racial Discrimination

Despite Costa Rica's apparently friendly, democratic image, racism does exist, though many ticos will deny it. The predominantly white (or mestizo) population of the highlands tends to act as if they are the only ones living there. Racism is rarely overt (it is illegal), but racist attitudes are encountered.

One black traveler says that he felt reasonably comfortable most of the time but occasionally encountered cold stares in some smaller highland towns.

Anti-Semitic statements and 'jokes' are also encountered; however, most Jewish travelers in Western clothing are treated like other Americans or Europeans. In 1999, a false report that a Chinese restaurant was serving rat meat disguised as shrimp made newspaper headlines, and the Asian population noted a drastic decline of patronage in their restaurants and unkind 'jokes' about 'latoncitos flitos' (flied lats). Asian ticos noted that they have constantly been the subject of immature jokes. Matters came to a head when the president ate a well-publicized meal in a Chinese restaurant in an attempt to improve the tico image.

## EMERGENCY

The general emergency number (☎ 911) is available throughout the country. In major cities, 911 may be staffed by English-speaking operators. Dialing 911 enables you to connect with medical, ambulance, police, and fire services.

## LEGAL MATTERS

If you get into legal trouble and are jailed, your embassy can offer only limited assistance. This may include an occasional visit from an embassy staff member to make sure your human rights have not been violated, letting your family know where you are, and putting you in contact with a Costa Rican lawyer, whom you must pay yourself. Embassy officials will not bail you out, and you are subject to Costa Rican laws, not to the laws of your home country.

Penalties in Costa Rica for possession of even small amounts of illegal drugs are much stricter than in the USA or Europe. Defendants often spend many months in jail before they are brought to trial and, if convicted (as is usually the case), can expect sentences of several years in jail.

Drivers should carry their passport as well as driver's license. In the event of an accident, leave the vehicles where they are until the police arrive and make a report. This is essential for all insurance claims. While waiting for the police, keep your eye on the vehicle to protect it from theft or vandalism. After the police have made the report, you can move the car. Call the rental company to find out where they want the car taken for repairs or who they want to tow it if it isn't driveable. If the accident results in injury or death, you may be prevented from leaving the country until all legalities are handled. Drive as defensively as you can.

## BUSINESS HOURS

Banks are open 9am to 3pm weekdays (Monday to Friday), with a few exceptions in San José. Government offices are supposedly open 8am to 4pm weekdays, but often close for lunch between about 11:30am and 1pm. Stores are open 8am to 6pm or 7pm Monday to Saturday, but a two-hour lunch break is not uncommon, especially outside San José.

## PUBLIC HOLIDAYS & SPECIAL EVENTS

National holidays (días feriados) are taken seriously in Costa Rica, and banks, public offices, and many stores close. There are no buses at all on the Thursday afternoon and Friday before Easter, and many businesses are closed for the entire week before Easter. From Thursday to Easter Sunday, all bars are closed and locked and alcohol sales are prohibited. Beach hotels are usually booked weeks ahead for this week, though a limited choice of rooms is often available. Public transport tends to be tight on all holidays and the days immediately preceding or following them, so book tickets ahead.

The week between Christmas and New Year's Day is an unofficial holiday, especially in San José. In addition, various towns have celebrations for their own particular day. These other holidays and special events are not official public holidays, and banks, etc,

remain open. All of the official national holidays plus the most important other events are listed below. Those marked with an asterisk (*) are official national holidays when banks and businesses are closed throughout the country. See the regional chapters for details on events.

### January

**New Year's Day\*** – the 1st

**Fiesta de Santa Cruz** – mid-January; this town on the Península de Nicoya features a religious procession, rodeo, bullfight, music, and dancing.

### February

**Fiesta de los Diablitos** – dates vary; one of the few indigenous festivals, it features masked dancing held on the Reserva Indígena Boruca near Curré.

### March

**Día del Boyero** – second Sunday; in honor of ox-cart drivers, this festival held in Escazú features a colorful ox-cart parade and associated events.

**Día de San José (St Joseph's Day)** – the 19th; honors the patron saint of the capital; a former national holiday.

**Semana Santa (Holy Week)\*** – March or April; the Thursday and Friday before Easter are both national public holidays when everything stops nationwide.

### April

**Día de Juan Santamaría\*** – the 11th; honors the national hero who fought at the Battle of Rivas against William Walker in 1856. Major events (dances, parades, etc) are held in Alajuela, his hometown.

### May

**Labor Day\*** – the 1st; especially colorful around Puerto Limón, where there are dances and cricket matches.

### June

**Día de San Pedro & San Pablo (St Peter & St Paul Day)** – the 29th; a former national holiday; some religious processions are held in villages of those names.

### July

**Fiesta de La Virgen del Mar (Fiesta of the Virgin of the Sea)** – mid-July; held in Puntarenas and Playa del Coco, with a colorful regatta and boat parade in addition to many land-based festivities.

**Día de Guanacaste\*** – the 25th; the annexation of Guanacaste Province, which was formerly part of Nicaragua, is celebrated with a nationwide holiday and many events in Guanacaste towns.

**August**

**Virgen de Los Angeles\*** – the 2nd; the patron saint of Costa Rica is celebrated with a particularly important religious parade from San José to Cartago.

**Día del Madre (Mother's Day)\*** – the 15th; coincides with the annual Catholic feast of the Assumption.

**September**

**Independence Day\*** – the 15th; children march in evening lantern-lit parades.

**October**

**Día de la Raza\*** – the 12th; the local name for Columbus Day (discovery of the Americas), celebrated especially near Puerto Limón with a carnival-like fiesta.

**November**

**Día de los Muertos (All Souls' Day)** – the 2nd; celebrated, as in most of Latin America, with family visits to graveyards and religious parades.

**December**

**Immaculate Conception** – the 8th; a former national holiday.

**Christmas Day\*** – the 25th; the 24th is often an (unofficial) holiday as well.

**Last week in December** – the last week in December (the 25th to the 31st) is a nonstop holiday in San José, with bullfights, equestrian processions and events, and a dance on New Year's Eve.

---

### National Holidays

Until 1996, there were 15 official national holidays, but in that year four holidays lost their official status in a governmental reform of the work code. Older books may, therefore, show more official holidays than the 11 indicated in this section.

Of these 11, all but two (August 2 and October 12) require that employees get paid if they take the day off, or receive double pay if they must work. Previously, only six holidays had obligatory pay, so although there are fewer total official holidays, employees who take them are entitled to more pay than previously.

---

## ACTIVITIES

San José is the cultural center of Costa Rica, with good restaurants, the Teatro Nacional (which puts on theater, dance, symphony, and other musical performances), cinemas, art galleries, museums, and shopping centers. But many of Costa Rica's greatest attractions are found away from the capital.

Costa Rica's conservationist attitude and activities are the most developed in Latin America. The wonderful array of national parks and private preserves and their attendant wildlife and scenery draw travelers from all over the world. Visitors can enjoy an intimate look at habitats and environments ranging from tropical rainforest to highland *páramo*, from active volcanoes to beautiful beaches, and from white-water rivers to mountain ranges. The wildlife and vegetation are magnificent and accessible. No wonder most visitors travel to at least one park or preserve, and that the primary focus of many trips is natural history, especially birding, which is among the best in the world.

Outdoor enthusiasts will find much to their liking. From running some of the best white water in Central America to just relaxing on palm-fringed beaches, from backpacking through the rainforest to horseback riding, from camping on mountaintops to record-breaking deep-sea sportfishing, from snorkeling to world-class surfing, many adventures are possible.

The more sedentary visitor can enjoy leisurely drives through the pretty countryside, perhaps visiting a coffee *finca* (farm) or villages known for handicrafts. Luxurious lunch or dinner cruises on elegant boats in the Golfo de Nicoya on the Pacific coast are also popular activities, as are day trips to peer into the crater of one of Costa Rica's many volcanoes.

See the Getting There & Away and Getting Around chapters for some suggested international and local tour operators that can arrange activities.

### Warning

Lack of regulation in adventure activities has led to three river-rafting fatalities and the death of one person in a canopy tour in 2001.

The government is actively working on a bill that will regulate adventure outfitters and increase safety. Meanwhile, travelers are advised to use the most reputable outfitters possible.

## Wildlife Watching

Scarlet macaws, marine turtles, hummingbirds, sloths, leaf-cutter ants, quetzals, marine toads, monkeys, blue morpho butterflies, tanagers, poison-arrow frogs, crocodiles, toucans, bats, iguanas, parrots – the list of Costa Rican wildlife seems endless, and there are many opportunities to see these animals. An overview of the most important, interesting, and frequently seen species is provided in the Wildlife Guide in this book. Unless you spend your entire time in San José, you cannot fail to see some tropical wildlife in Costa Rica. Many people come specifically to spend their days watching wildlife or birds, and many companies arrange guided natural history tours.

Tours aren't cheap and will be beyond the pocketbooks of shoestring travelers. Here are some tips for budget travelers who want to view as much wildlife as possible (though travelers on an expensive tour should also follow these suggestions). The national parks and preserves are all good places for observation, but private areas such as gardens around rural hotels can also yield a good number of birds, insects, reptiles, and even monkeys. Always be alert for these possibilities. Early morning and late afternoon are the best times to watch for wildlife activity anywhere; the hot and bright middle of the day is when many animals rest. Carry binoculars. An inexpensive lightweight pair brought from home will improve wildlife observation tremendously; they don't have to be the most expensive.

Have realistic expectations. Wildlife is plentiful in the fantastic rainforest environment, but it is hard to see because the vegetation is so thick. You could be 15m from a jaguar and not even know it is there. Don't expect to see jaguars, ocelots, tapirs, and many other mammals, which are shy, well camouflaged, and often rare. Concentrate on things that are easier to observe and enjoy them – most of the animals listed at the beginning of this section can be seen fairly easily if you visit different parts of the country. Walk slowly and quietly; listen as well as look.

The single best area for wildlife watching, in my opinion, is the Península de Osa. This is also one of the most difficult areas to get to, which is perhaps why the animals have remained relatively undisturbed. Other excellent places are the national parks, especially Santa Rosa, Tortuguero, and Caño Negro, although all of them are good. Of these, Santa Rosa is the easiest to get to on a tight budget (a bus from San José passes the park entrance; then you can walk in). But they are all definitely worthwhile.

## Fishing

Sportfishing of the 'catch and release' variety (though a small number of fish are kept to eat or mount as trophies) is a tremendously popular activity despite the very high costs involved. People on fishing vacations routinely spend several hundred dollars a day to fish, and the most exclusive all-inclusive fishing packages can cost over US$1000 a day. This doesn't stop 12% of foreign tourists from saying that one of the reasons they are here is to fish. They say it's worth it because the fishing is world-class and several of the fish caught in Costa Rican waters have broken world records. Local anglers say that a bad day of fishing in Costa Rica is often better than a good day of fishing in most other places.

To help protect this resource, local skippers, guides, and anglers adhere to the 'catch and release' philosophy – if they didn't, the excellent fishing would become endangered.

The most popular fishing areas are on the coast, rather than inland. People often stay at coastal fishing lodges and go out to sea on a daily basis in modern boats outfitted with state-of-the-art fishing and navigation equipment. Some people prefer to spend their entire time living aboard a boat, and this option is also available. Further information is given in the chapters on the Caribbean Lowlands, Southern Costa Rica, Central Pacific Coast, Península de Osa, and Península de Nicoya. The best places to look for fishing lodges and boats are in Parismina, Tortuguero, and (especially) Barra del Colorado on the Caribbean side and in the Golfito and Quepos areas and many parts of the Península de Nicoya on the Pacific side, though there certainly are other places.

Note that while most of the fishing lodges described in the book provide tackle, inveterate anglers may prefer to bring their own.

Lures and other essentials are sold by the lodges but, because of import duties, are more expensive than at home. Lures are not included in the packages. The lodges will be happy to advise you about all aspects of fishing equipment if you make a reservation with them.

Inland, trout fishing in rivers and lake fishing are also popular, though not as much as the coastal fishing. Particularly recommended are the Río Savegre near San Gerardo de Dota for trout fishing and Laguna de Arenal for *guapote* or rainbow bass, although you can fish almost anywhere you have a mind to.

You can fish almost any time. Laguna de Arenal has a closed season from October to December and certain rivers may have closed seasons sometimes – check with local operators. The ocean is always open and, if you are prepared to fish on either coast and accept what species are biting, there is fishing year-round. Some books and brochures provide month-by-month breakdowns of what fish to catch where. Having looked at several of these, all I can say is that anglers love to tell stories – and each one is different! Certainly, fishing varies from season to season. As a general rule, the Pacific coast is slowest from September to November, though you'll get better fishing if you are on the south coast in those months, and the Caribbean can be fished year-round, though June and July are the slowest months.

The fish most sought after by anglers are tarpon and snook on the Caribbean side and sailfish and black marlin on the Pacific side.

Fishing licenses are required but are cheap and included in outfitters' packages and tours. *Costa Rica Outdoors* (see Newspapers & Magazines, earlier in this chapter) has news about fishing in Costa Rica.

## Surfing

Point and beach breaks, lefts and rights, reefs and river mouths, warm water and waves year-round make Costa Rica a favorite surfers' destination. Some beaches may be hard to get to but are totally uncrowded (sometimes you'll be the only one surfing there all day), and even the easily accessible ones tend to be much less crowded than the beaches of Hawaii, southern California, and Sydney.

The waves are often quite big, though not as huge as the almost mythical ones in Hawaii. But they make up for this in length, with fast kilometer-long waves at Pavones on the south Pacific coast giving rides of two or three minutes. It's an athletic challenge to stay upright on such a long wave.

Dedicated surfers bring their own boards from home. Most airlines accept a surfboard (properly packed in a padded bag designed for surfboards) as one of the two pieces of checked luggage. However, once in Costa Rica, the two domestic airlines either don't allow them or charge extra for them, and many surfers prefer to rent a Jeep to give themselves mobility. SANSA airline will not accept boards longer than 7 feet, 2 inches. At the end of your trip, you can easily sell the board in Costa Rica.

A few places rent equipment. These are mainly in the popular coastal towns and villages such as Jacó, Quepos, Tamarindo, and Puerto Viejo de Talamanca. In the San José area, there is the Mango Surf Shop (☎ 225-1067), near the Banco Popular in the San Pedro suburb, or Tsunami (☎ 280-0278), 100m east of the Iglesia San Pedro.

There are dozens of surfing areas, and some of the best are shown on the accompanying surfing map. Further details are given in the text. Most of the north Caribbean coast has wonderful waves, but few surfers ride them because of riptides, heavy surf, and shark reports, especially near the river mouths. Also surf the Web at ⓦ www .crsurf.com and ⓦ www.surf.co.cr for tides and surf reports.

## River Running

Rivers tumbling from the central mountains down to the coast afford good white-water rafting possibilities, and several tour operators provide rafts, paddles, life jackets, helmets, and guides for these adventures. One-day trips include roundtrip bus transportation from San José and lunch. These start around US$69 per person. Multiday trips can also be arranged. Most river-running companies offer kayak rental or at least provide information on it, and sometimes you can accompany a rafting trip in a kayak if you have the requisite experience. Thousands of tourists enjoy running a river each year, and the vast majority have a memorable and enjoyable adventure.

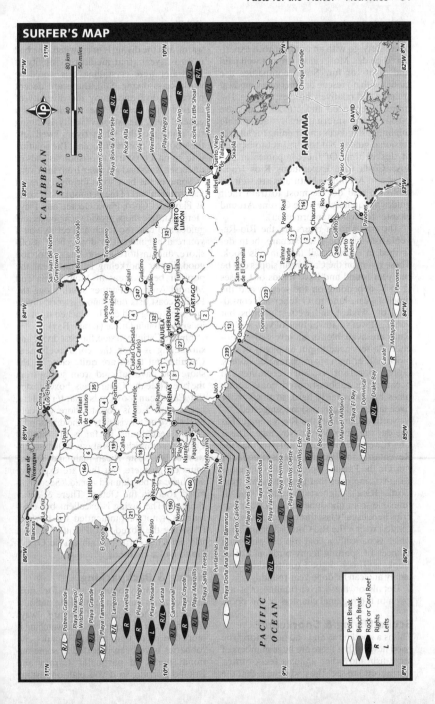

**SURFER'S MAP**

CARIBBEAN SEA

PACIFIC OCEAN

NICARAGUA

PANAMA

Point Break
Beach Break
Rock or Coral Reef
**R** Rights
**L** Lefts

However, river-running companies are not regulated in Costa Rica, so, for your own safety, go with an outfitter with experienced guides. Most guides are not well paid and do it for fun. Some companies use guides with no rescue or emergency medical training and relatively little experience. The more experienced and ethical guides are pushing for internationally acceptable minimum standards and training for all professional guides, but this had yet to happen at this writing. Of the companies in San José, Costa Rica Expeditions, Ríos Tropicales, and Aventuras Naturales are well established and do the most to train their guides adequately (see the Getting Around chapter for contact information).

The best-known rivers are the Río Reventazón and the Río Pacuare, both described in more detail later in this book. These rivers on the Caribbean slopes can be run year-round and have rapids of Classes II to V, depending on the section and the time of year. June to October are considered the wildest and wettest months, but you'll get wet whatever time of year you go. Runs are available for all levels of experience. Rafters need to put on plenty of sunblock and bring a spare change of clothes. Going barefoot is not recommended because the rubber-floored boats sometimes hit rocks fairly hard, so sneakers or river sandals (like Tevas) are suggested.

North of San José, the Río Sarapiquí has one-day runs from May to November. This is a narrower and more technical river than the Reventazón and Pacuare, and less frequently run. On the Pacific slope, the Río Chirripó is a big-volume river that tumbles down from Costa Rica's highest mountain and is runnable from mid-June to mid-December. Trips here usually last three or four days. The gentlest river is the Río Corobicí, near Cañas, which is basically a float trip but with good chances of spotting many birds and often monkeys. This is a good trip for the whole family and can be done year-round.

Details on these river-running trips are given in the regional chapters of this book.

## Scuba Diving & Snorkeling
This is a good news and bad news story. The good news is that there are huge numbers of large fish and other animals (eels, turtles, starfish, etc) to see. The bad news is that the

visibility is poor to adequate, but never excellent. The good news is that the water is warm, and the diving is uncrowded. The bad news is…yeah, that mediocre visibility. If the water were crystalline, this would be world-class diving. Still, there are decent places to dive and enjoy the diversity of marine life, despite the visibility. As a general rule, the worst visibility is during the rainy months, when rivers swell and their outflow clouds the ocean. The solution is to go on a boat trip to offshore islands or undersea walls and get away from the rivers.

Some of the best areas for diving are off the northern part of the Península de Nicoya; at Playa del Coco, Playa Ocotal, and Playa Hermosa, dive shops provide gear, boats, and guides and can also teach and certify you if you're a beginner. The diving here is offshore, and inshore snorkeling is not too good. Better snorkeling is found near the popular beach areas at Montezuma and Manuel Antonio. Farther south along the Pacific coast, Isla del Caño has good diving and snorkeling and can be reached from the lodges on Bahía Drake (Drake Bay).

On the Caribbean side, the best diving and snorkeling is over the coral reefs near Cahuita, but these are quite close to the shore and have suffered from silting from the rivers (see the 'Coral Reefs' boxed text in the Caribbean Lowlands chapter). Here, because the reef is close to shore, you definitely have better visibility in the dry months.

The best diving by far is off Isla del Coco – but this island is about 500km southwest of the Costa Rican mainland. Diving tours do go there, but they are expensive and have to be planned ahead. (See Organized Tours in the Getting There & Away chapter.) The diving is excellent but challenging – not recommended for novices. (Also see the boxed text 'Parque Nacional Isla del Coco' in the Península de Osa & Golfo Dulce chapter.)

## Hiking & Backpacking
There are many opportunities for short hikes of a few hours in most of the national parks and other reserves. There are always short nature trails where wildlife watching is more the point than hiking. Assaults and robberies have been reported in some national parks, in particular Carara and Braulio Carrillo, so if you plan on visiting

these areas, go with a group or a guided tour and seek local information. Other parks don't seem to have this bad reputation. However short your hike, always remember to carry plenty of water (bring extra in case you get lost), insect repellent, and sun protection when hiking in the tropics.

For longer distance and overnight hiking, there are several good choices. If you've always wanted to try backpacking in the rainforest, then Parque Nacional Corcovado offers some adventurous opportunities. If you prefer to get away from the heat and humidity, try a climb of Chirripó, Costa Rica's highest peak, located in the national park of the same name. Other good hiking trips include a visit to Parque Nacional Santa Rosa, where you hike through tropical dry forest down to the beach and camp. The hike from the Arenal area to Monteverde, which can be done in one long day, has recently become popular. More details are given in the text for the appropriate places. See the Dangers & Annoyances section, earlier, for advice on hiking safety.

### Mountain Biking
Some cyclists claim that the steep, narrow, winding, and potholed roads and aggressive Costa Rican drivers add up to a generally poor cycling experience. This may be true of the main roads, but there are numerous less-trafficked roads that offer good adventures. Local outfitters and tour companies from the USA arrange guided bike trips, which let you avoid the hassle of finding the best roads. Because of the poor condition of the roads, mountain bikes are a better option than road bikes.

Most airlines will fly your bike as one of your pieces of checked baggage if you box it. However, boxing the bike gives baggage handlers little clue to the contents and the box is liable to be roughly handled, possibly damaging the bike. An alternative is wrapping it in heavy-duty plastic or bubble wrap – baggage handlers are less likely to drop or throw the bike in this case. Airlines' bicycle-carrying policies do vary a lot, so shop around. It is also possible to cycle down from the USA through Central America, and a handful of people do that every year.

There are several tour operators and bicycle outfitters who can rent you a bike and give you a map or provide you with a complete tour package with bike, guide, and support vehicle. These packages cost about US$50 to US$75 a day. Unless you are really dedicated and insist on your own bike, there is no reason to bring your own, as you can rent a decent mountain bike with helmet and water bottle for about US$15 to US$30 a day.

### Windsurfing
Laguna de Arenal, Costa Rica's largest lake, is the nation's undisputed windsurfing center and, from December to March, is considered one of the three best windsurfing spots in the world. Winds are often strong and steady, especially at the western end during the dry season. The lake has a year-round water temperature of 18°C to 21°C with 1m-high swells and winds averaging 20 knots in the dry season, a little less in the wet. May, June, September, and October are the least windy months; December to February are the most windy. Maximum winds often go over 30 knots, and windless days are a rarity. These consistently high winds attract experienced windsurfers – beginners will require expert instruction.

Complete windsurfing equipment is available for rent in several hotels at the west end of the lake. Of these, the Hotel Tilawa has the best selection and location, is open year-round, and has reliable, experienced instructors.

Puerto Soley, on the far northern Pacific coast, has also developed windsurfing schools and resorts.

### Horseback Riding
Riding horses has been part of rural Costa Rican life for as long as anyone can remember. Wherever you go, you are sure to find someone renting a horse. Most of the resort and tourist areas have horses available for rides along the beaches or up into the mountains. Guides are available to lead you to scenic waterfalls and views. Rates vary from about US$40 to US$100 a day, and shorter (two-hour) or overnight trips can also be arranged.

Some areas have become very popular for horse treks, and the increased demand for rides has led to unscrupulous 'outfitters' cashing in on the popularity by providing undernourished and overworked horses for

## Claudia Poll's Gold

Costa Rican swimmer Claudia Poll won a gold medal at the 1996 Atlanta Olympics in the women's 200m freestyle event. This was the first ever Olympic gold for the country. Poll continues to dominate the world swimming circuit with gold medals in many major meets and is still among the best female swimmers in the world.

She added to her 1996 Olympic medal with bronze medals in both the women's 200m and 400m freestyle events at Sydney 2000, the only medals that Costa Rica won at those games. Poll, then aged 27, said Sydney was her last Olympiad. Though she has spoken of retiring from competitive swimming, she managed to win two golds and two silvers in the January 2002 swimming World Cup event in Imperia, Italy.

rides. The worst area recently has been the popular Arenal to Monteverde (or vice versa) ride, where a number of outfitters cut costs by overworking their horses. Numerous readers wrote to say that they have witnessed guides beating horses, emaciated animals with sores, and even horses dying on this trail, which is steep, often muddy, and difficult for horses. Taking the cheapest tour is not in the best interest of the horses. Riders weighing over 100kg cannot expect the small local horses to carry them very far. Since the last edition of this book, efforts have been made to improve conditions for the horses. (For more, see the 'To Ride or Not to Ride?' boxed text in the Northwestern Costa Rica chapter.)

Horseback riding is a pleasure if it's done right. It's certainly part of the tico culture. I welcome further feedback from readers about caring (or otherwise) outfitters.

### Rainforest Canopy Tours

Until recently, most visitors to the rainforest had to make do with either walking through it or traveling by boat. You could see what was around you, but seeing the top of the canopy was not easy. Since the late 1980s, several ways of exploring the rainforest canopy have been devised.

At the most simple level are tree platforms, where you are winched up on a rope and scramble out onto a platform some 20m or more above the ground. Sitting in a platform, you wait, hoping that a flock of birds or troop of monkeys will come close – which, often, they do. Good places for sitting on a platform are at Hacienda Barú (see the Central Pacific Coast chapter) and Corcovado Lodge Tent

Camp (see the Península de Osa & Golfo Dulce chapter).

Another system consists of a series of platforms joined by cables. You climb or are winched up to the first platform, then slide (in a sling) along the cable to the next platform. This rather adventurous activity is offered in several places by Canopy Tour (see Organized Tours in the Getting Around chapter). These tours are exciting but rarely offer many opportunities for observing wildlife.

The most technologically advanced is the Rainforest Aerial Tram (see the Central Valley & the Surrounding Highlands chapter). This is like a ski lift stretching for 1.6km through various levels of the canopy just east of Parque Nacional Braulio Carrillo. Passengers ride in open gondolas carrying five visitors plus a guide. This is the easiest way see the canopy.

Safety is the most important concern in these operations. The ones mentioned here have properly trained staff and use high-quality equipment. There are numerous spin-off rainforest canopy tours, not all of which maintain the most rigorous safety conditions.

### Sea Kayaking

This is still a small but growing activity in Costa Rica. Sea kayaks range from inflatable toys to slim, elegant craft with foot rudders that can be paddled by one or two people and used on overnight kayaking/beach-camping trips. It's easy enough to learn at least the basics of getting around, so this could be a good activity for beginners as well as experienced people.

Kayakers at Bahía Drake tell of expeditions up jungle rivers where they were able to glide noiselessly up to wildlife (in one case, a tapir) without disturbing the animals. Combining ease of learning with an enhanced chance of spotting wildlife, a coastal kayaking trip is a great experience – no wonder sea kayaking is such a growing sport. Many places along the coast rent sea kayaks.

## Hot-Air Ballooning

This is a fledgling activity in Costa Rica. Contact Serendipity Adventures for more information (see Organized Tours in the Getting There & Away chapter).

## Bungee Jumping

Yes, finally in Costa Rica you can safely make a head-first, screaming plunge off a bridge to which you are safely attached with a 60m elastic rope. After safely bouncing around for a while, you are hauled back up to the bridge. Highly trained jump masters guarantee your safety. I prefer playing chess.

For further information, contact Tropical Bungee (☎ 248-2212, 383-9724 cellular, W www.bungee.co.cr). They do jumps off the Río Colorado bridge near the Grecia turnoff from the Interamericana. The first jump costs US$50, and you can do it again for US$25. If you just want to watch the jumpers from the safety of solid ground (or bridge), contact them anyway. They'll provide transportation for spectators as well as jumpers.

## LANGUAGE COURSES

Spanish language courses are offered mainly in San José but also in Alajuela, Manuel Antonio, and a few other places. These are popular ways for travelers to visit the country, learn the language, and become aware of tico lifestyle and culture. Language schools are listed under San José and other appropriate parts of the text.

## WORK

It is difficult, but not impossible, to find work in Costa Rica. The most likely source of paid employment is as an English teacher in language institutes in San José, which advertise courses in the local newspapers. Word of mouth from other travelers is another way to find out about this kind of work.

Writers can occasionally sell work to the English-language weekly, the *Tico Times*. Naturalists or river guides may be able to find work with the private lodges or adventure travel operators. Don't expect to make more than survival wages from these jobs, and don't arrive in Costa Rica expecting to get a job easily and immediately. Getting a bona fide job requires a work permit, which is a bureaucratic, time-consuming, and difficult process.

## Volunteer Work

Volunteer work in nature preserves or national parks is sometimes possible. Volunteers usually provide their own transport to Costa Rica, pay US$10 to US$12 per day for living expenses and live with park rangers in ranger stations. They help with a variety of jobs ranging from providing visitor information to constructing trails or buildings to office work or surveys. Spanish communication skills are required. Some volunteers are needed in the San José headquarters as well as in remote areas – efforts are made to match volunteers' interests and skills with the projects available. A minimum commitment of 15 days is requested, and volunteers work six days a week. Several hundred volunteers are used each year; almost half of them are foreign and the rest are Costa Rican.

If you are interested in working in the national parks, there are two programs: Programa de Voluntariado Internacional, SINAC (☎/fax 233-4989, e asvo89@racsa .co.cr) and Voluntarios para la Conservación del Ambiente (PROVAC; ☎ 395-0412, ☎/fax 222-7549, e mam271@racsa.co.cr or cecimesen@yahoo.com), Calle 21, Avenidas 8 & 10, San José. Contact both organizations for more information and an application. Many people apply, but few actually end up volunteering. Some travelers report that you can just show up at the park of your choice and ask to volunteer.

A few private lodges and organizations need English-speaking volunteers – see Caribbean Conservation Corporation, and ANAI in the Caribbean Lowlands chapter; Genesis II in Southern Costa Rica; the Reserva Biológica Bosque Nuboso Monteverde in Northwestern Costa Rica; and others mentioned in the text.

## ACCOMMODATIONS
## Youth Hostels & Camping

There is a small Hostelling International youth hostel system, and the charge for a night in a hostel varies from about US$10 to US$40, depending on the hostel. The more expensive hostels are usually good hotels or lodges giving a discount to youth hostel members. The San José hostel is the headquarters for the network of Costa Rican youth hostels, and information and reservations for the others can be made there. Budget travelers will find cheaper rooms in basic hotels.

There are rarely campsites in the towns; the constant availability of cheap hotels makes town campsites unnecessary.

Cheap camping facilities are available in many of the national parks. The handful of campgrounds suitable for trailers (caravans) or for motorhomes are mentioned in the text.

## B&Bs

Almost unknown in Costa Rica in the 1980s, the B&B phenomenon has swept the country in the past years. B&B places vary from mid-range to top end in price, and have been generally well received and recommended by travelers.

## Hotels

There is great variety and no shortage of places to stay in Costa Rica. It is rare to arrive in a town and be unable to find somewhere to sleep, but during Easter week or weekends in the dry season, the beach hotels can be full. Indeed, most beach hotels are booked several weeks in advance for Easter week. Hotel accommodations can also be tight if a special event is going on in a particular town. Private lodges and expensive hotels in remote areas should always be reserved in advance if you want specific dates. However, the cheapest hotels are more likely to have a room available at any time. In the low season, you can often find rooms in most hotels on the day you arrive. Note that reservations made abroad will always be at the highest rates, and discounts can be obtained in-country.

Some travelers prefer to make advance reservations everywhere – this is possible even in the cheapest hotels and recommended in the better places. Faxes and emails are being used increasingly to make reservations, as they are cheaper than phone calls and solve the problem of language difficulties – they can be translated readily enough. Mail is slow. Note that most hotels will give rainy season (charmingly dubbed the Green Season) discounts (from about late April to mid-December). If you are already in Costa Rica, a telephone call a day or two ahead will often yield a reservation.

Sometimes it's a little difficult to find single rooms, and you may get a room with two beds. In most cases, though, you will be charged the single rate. The single rate is rarely half of the double rate, except in a few of the cheapest hotels. In a few hotels, single and double rates are the same. If you are economizing, travel with someone and share a room.

Before accepting a room, look around the hotel if possible. The same prices are often charged for rooms of widely differing quality. Even in the US$4-a-night cheapies, it's worth looking around. If you get shown into a horrible airless box with just a bed and a bare lightbulb, you can ask to see a better room without giving offense. You'll often be amazed at the results. At the other end of the scale, hotels may want to rent you their most expensive suites – ask if they have more economical rooms if you don't want the suite.

Note that many hotels in Costa Rica are called *cabinas*. These aren't literally 'cabins.' They are usually large rooms, often but not always with several beds (suitable for a family) and with a private bath. Cabinas aren't necessarily separated into individual units but are often duplexes or rows of rooms adjoining one another. This style of hotel tends to the budget end of the market.

**Hotel Categories** Budget hotels are certainly the cheapest but not necessarily the worst. Although they are sometimes very basic, with just a bed and four walls, they can nevertheless be well looked after, very clean, and amazing value for the money. They are often good places to meet other budget travelers, both Costa Rican and foreign.

Prices in the budget section begin at about US$4 per person and go up to the US$20s for a double room. Almost every town (except exclusive tourist resorts) has hotels in this price range. Although you'll usually have to use communal bathrooms in the cheapest hotels, you can sometimes find rooms with a private bathroom for as low as US$12 a double.

Hotels in the mid-range category usually charge from about US$30 to US$80 for a double room, but the cheaper ones are not always better than the best hotels in the budget price range. On the whole, you can find some very decent hotels here. Even if you're traveling on a budget, there may be occasions when you feel like indulging in comparative luxury for a day or two.

Top-end hotels charge over US$100 a double and can ask over twice that in San José, the beach resorts, and some of the upscale lodges. The prices and services compare favorably with international standards in the best places.

Apartotels are like a cross between an apartment and a hotel and can be rented for extended stays. They are mostly found in San José, and occasionally elsewhere. See the San José chapter for a detailed description.

**Hotel Tax** A 16.39% tax is currently added to hotel prices. The hotel tax situation changes from government to government and year to year, but expect to pay a tax percentage somewhere in the teens. Some hotels give prices including tax, others give prices without tax, so always clarify this point when asking about room rates. This book attempts to give full prices, including taxes, for the 2002 high season. Some hotel prices have risen dramatically with the tourism boom of the past few years, and you should not be surprised by further increases. However, some hotels may lower prices to attract guests during tourism slumps.

**Bathrooms** In the cheaper hotels, bathroom facilities are rarely what you may be used to at home. The cheapest hotels don't always have hot water. Even if they do, it might not work or it may be turned on only at certain hours of the day.

An intriguing device to know about is the electric shower: a cold-water showerhead hooked up to an electric heating element that is switched on when you want a hot (more likely tepid) shower. They work best when heating a small amount of water, so if you turn the water on all the way, you'll get a fairly cold flow, but if you turn it on just enough to be able to wash with, the water will be warmer. These showers are found in some budget hotels and lower mid-range; more expensive hotels rarely use them.

Despite sounding scary, they are very common and, when properly installed and grounded, pose no hazard.

Flushing a toilet in the cheaper hotels may create an overflow. See the Toilets section for details on that problem.

**Security** Although hotels give you room keys, carrying your own padlock is a good idea if you plan on staying in the most basic hotels.

Once in a while, you'll find that a room doesn't look very secure – perhaps there's a window that doesn't close or the wall doesn't come to the ceiling and can be climbed over. It's worth finding another room. This is another reason why it's good to look at a room before you rent it.

You should never leave valuables lying around the room; it's just too tempting for someone who makes less than US$1 an hour for their work. Money and passport should be in a secure body pouch; other valuables can usually be kept in the hotel strongbox, although some cheaper hotels might not want to take this responsibility. In this case, keep your valuables locked in your bag and not in plain sight. Beware of local 'fishermen' – people who poke sticks with hooks on them through openable windows to fish out whatever they can get. If you do use a hotel strongbox, insist on a signed receipt; occasional pilfering is reported.

### Homestays
The option of staying with a family is also possible, mainly in San José. See the San José chapter for details.

### FOOD
If you're on a tight budget, food is the most important part of your expenses. You can stay in rock-bottom hotels, travel by bus, and never consider buying a souvenir, but you've got to eat well. This doesn't mean expensively, but it does mean that you want to avoid spending half your trip sitting on the toilet.

The worst culprits for making you sick are salads and unpeeled fruit. With the fruit, stick to bananas, oranges, pineapples, and other fruit you can peel yourself. With unpeeled fruit or salad vegetables, wash them yourself in water you can trust (see the Health section, earlier). Many hotels provide tropical fruit for breakfast; if the hotel is well run, the fruit is usually clean.

As long as you take heed of the salad warning, you'll find plenty of good things to eat at reasonable prices. You certainly don't have to eat at a fancy restaurant – their kitchen facilities may not be as clean as their white tablecloths. A good sign for any restaurant is that the locals eat there – restaurants aren't empty if the food is delicious and healthy.

If you're on a tight budget, eat the set meal offered in most restaurants at lunchtime. It's usually filling and cheap. Also try the cheap luncheon counters called *sodas*. The sodas in the central markets of most towns are locally popular and usually very cheap. Eat at one that is frequented by ticos and you'll probably find that the food is good and clean. There are reasonably priced Chinese and Italian restaurants in most towns.

A good range of restaurants at all price levels are given throughout this book. Remember that a combined 25% in taxes and services is added to restaurant bills in all but the cheapest sodas. Further tipping is not necessary unless you want to. Where approximate prices are given for restaurant meals in this book, taxes are included for a main course. Drinks and desserts are usually extra unless specified.

## What to Order

Most restaurants serve *bistek* (beef), *pollo* (chicken), and *pescado* (fish) dishes. *Carne* literally means meat, but in Costa Rica it tends to refer to beef. Chicken, *puerco* (pork), and *chivo* (goat) aren't necessarily included, so specifically ask for *vegetariano* if you want something without any meat. Many visitors from North America, used to spicy Mexican food capable of burning out taste buds, mistakenly assume that Costa Rican food is very spicy too. Generally, it's not.

Of course, internationally popular food is available: pizzas, spaghetti, hamburgers, sandwiches, Chinese rice dishes, steaks, etc. However, Costa Rican specialties include the following:

*gallo pinto* – literally 'spotted rooster,' a mixture of rice and black beans that is traditionally served for breakfast, sometimes with *natilla* (something like a cross between sour cream and custard) or *huevos fritos/revueltos* (fried/scrambled eggs).

This dish is lightly seasoned with herbs and is filling and tasty.

*tortillas* – either Mexican-style corn pancakes or omelets, depending on what kind of meal you're having.

*casado* – a set meal that is often filling and always economical. It normally contains *arroz* (rice), *frijoles* (black beans), *platano* (fried plantain), beef, chopped *repollo* (cabbage), and maybe an egg or an avocado.

*olla de carne* – a soup (enough for a full meal) containing beef and vegetables such as potatoes, corn, squash, plantains, and a local tuber, *yuca*.

*palmitos* – hearts of palm, usually served in a salad with vinegar dressing; *pejibaye* is a rather starchy-tasting palm fruit also eaten as a salad.

*arroz con pollo* – a basic dish of rice and chicken.

*elote* – corn on the cob served boiled *(elote cocinado)* or roasted *(elote asado)*.

Desserts *(postres)* include the following:

*mazamorra* – a pudding made from cornstarch.

*queque seco* – simply a pound cake.

*dulce de leche* – milk and sugar boiled to make a thick syrup that may be used in a layered cake called *torta chilena*.

*cajeta* – similar to dulce de leche, but thicker still, like a fudge.

*flan* – a cold caramel custard.

These snacks are often obtained in sodas:

*arreglados* – little puff pastries stuffed with beef, chicken, or cheese; this term might also be used for sandwiches.

*enchiladas* – heavier pastries stuffed with potatoes and cheese and maybe meat.

*empanadas* – Chilean-style turnovers stuffed with meat or cheese and raisins.

*pupusas* – El Salvadoran–style fried corn and cheese cakes.

*gallos* – traditionally, a snack of leftovers from a previous meal. Sodas sell gallos of a tortilla with various toppings – meats, beans, or chopped, cooked veggies.

*ceviche* – seafood marinated with lemon, onion, garlic, sweet red peppers, and coriander. Also made with *corvina* (a white sea bass), or occasionally with *langostinos* (shrimp) or *conchas* (shellfish).

*patacones* – a coastal specialty, especially on the Caribbean side, consisting of slices of plantain deep-fried like french-fried potatoes – delicious.

*tamales* – boiled cornmeal pies (pasties), usually wrapped in a banana leaf (you don't eat the leaf). At Christmas they traditionally come stuffed with chicken or pork; at other times of year they may come stuffed with corn and wrapped in a corn leaf. *Tamales asado* are sweet cornmeal cakes.

Many bars serve *bocas,* also known as *boquitas.* These are little savory side dishes such as black beans, ceviche, chicken stew, potato chips, and sausages, and are designed to make your drink more pleasurable – maybe you'll have another one! If you have several rounds, you could eat enough bocas to make a very light meal. Many of the cheaper bars have free bocas, some charge a small amount extra for them, and some don't have them at all. Some bars specialize in bocas and have a wide variety, usually costing about US$1 each.

Occasionally, a boca might be a turtle egg. These used to be common, but now that marine turtles are endangered, their eggs are less frequently offered as bar bocas. Although, technically, it is still possible to harvest marine turtle eggs legally, poaching goes on as well. It is very difficult to establish whether turtle eggs have been taken legally, and a large number have not. Until turtles recover, travelers are urged to refrain from eating turtle eggs.

## DRINKS
### Nonalcoholic Drinks
Coffee is traditionally served strong and mixed with hot milk to taste, but increasingly fewer establishments insist on serving it this way. Perhaps this is just as well, because the hot milk tends to form a skin, which some drinkers find quite unappetizing. Strong, tasty, and black is a good option. Tea (including herb tea) is also available. Milk is pasteurized and safe to drink.

The usual brands of soft drinks are available, although many people prefer *refrescos* – fruit drinks made either *con agua* (with water) or *con leche* (with milk). Possible fruit drinks to sample are mango, papaya, *piña* (pineapple), *sandía* (watermelon), *melón* (cantaloupe), *mora* (blackberry), *zanahoria* (carrot), *cebada* (barley), or *tamarindo* (a slightly tart but refreshing drink made from the fruit of the tamarind tree). Be careful where you buy these to avoid getting sick.

Tropical is a good bottled fruit drink sold in many stores and restaurants. The most common flavors are mora, piña, *cas* (a tart local fruit), and *frutas mixtas.*

*Pipas* are green coconuts that have a hole macheted into the top of them and a straw stuck in so you can drink the coconut 'milk' – a slightly astringent but refreshing and filling drink.

*Agua dulce* is simply boiled water mixed with brown sugar, and *horchata* is a cornmeal drink flavored with cinnamon.

### Alcoholic Drinks
Costa Ricans like to drink, but they don't like drunks. Most restaurants serve a good variety of alcoholic drinks. Imported drinks are expensive; local ones are quite cheap.

There are several brands of local beer. Pilsen and Imperial are both good, popular beers; Imperial is the largest-selling beer in the country and its nickname is *una águila* for the black eagle on the label. Bavaria has a gold foil around the cap and is a little more expensive and supposedly more full-bodied than the first two, though it's hard to tell the difference. Also, a local version of Heineken is made, which costs about the same as Bavaria. Most of these are 4% or 4.5% alcohol. Rock Ice, with a 4.7% alcohol content, has a slightly more bitter taste. Other beers are imported and expensive.

Local beers cost about US60¢ in the very cheapest bars, about US$1.25 in average bars and restaurants, and almost US$3 in some of the fancy tourist lodges, restaurants, hotels, and resorts.

Most Costa Rican wines are cheap, taste cheap, and provide a memorable hangover. Recently, 'La Casa de Garita,' produced locally by an Italian vintner, has been reviewed as an acceptable table wine, though it isn't easy to find. Good imported wines are available but expensive. Chilean brands are your best bet for a palatable wine at an affordable price.

Sugarcane is grown in Costa Rica, so liquor made from this is cheap. The cheapest is *guaro,* which is the local firewater,

### Drinkers Beware

No alcohol can be served or sold on election days and from the Thursday to Saturday before Easter. This applies to stores, bars, and restaurants, so plan ahead.

drunk by the shot. Also inexpensive and good is local rum, usually drunk as a *cuba libre* (rum and cola). Premixed cans of cuba libre are available.

Local vodka and gin aren't bad, but whisky is poor. Expensive imported liquors are available, as are imported liqueurs. One locally made liqueur is Café Rica, which, predictably, is based on coffee and tastes like the better-known Mexican Kahlua.

## ENTERTAINMENT

San José has the best selection of entertainment, though it is modest compared to many other capital cities. Traditionally, family get-togethers are what ticos do to entertain themselves. There are plenty of cinemas, theaters, and nightclubs in San José (see details in that chapter) but relatively few elsewhere. Costa Rica is a poor destination for travelers looking for entertainment of the nightlife variety.

## SPECTATOR SPORTS

*Fútbol* (soccer) is by far the most important spectator sport. It is almost a national passion, especially for men (although girls and women do play and show some interest). Costa Rica's most memorable soccer appearance was at the 1990 Men's World Cup in Italy, when the national team made the quarterfinals. The second time that the national team qualified for the World Cup was in the 2002 games held in Japan/Korea.

The regular season is from August to May, and the games are played at 11am on Sunday mornings, and sometimes on Wednesday evenings. Competition is fierce, and fan rivalry does not support the notion that ticos are friendly. They can get really wild during games!

There are 12 teams in the First Division. At the end of each season, the 12th team is relegated to the Second Division while the top team in the Second Division is promoted to the First Division. In addition, the 11th team in the First Division has to play against the runner-up in the Second Division to determine which of these plays in the First Division the next season. The top teams in the regular season then play another championship in June or July, so there are matches almost year-round.

At the ends of both the 1999–2000 and 2000–2001 seasons, La Liga, the team from Alajuela, won the championship. In 2001, Heredia finished second and Saprissa, the San José team, finished third. La Liga and Saprissa have finished at or near the top of the league for most of the past years. You can watch Saprissa play at home in the suburb of Tibas (any cab driver knows it). Tickets cost about US$20 and are usually available on the day of the game. The more expensive tickets give you seats in the shade *(sombra)* with a more sedate crowd; the cheapest tickets are in direct sun *(sol)* with a wilder crowd of fans.

Other popular spectator sports (though not even close rivals to soccer) are basketball and bullfighting. In Costa Rica, the bull is not killed, so international matadors don't bother to come here. Local bullfights are held at various times of year; in San José the main season is from Christmas to just after New Year's Day. The popular Latin American sport of cockfighting is illegal.

## SHOPPING
### Coffee

Coffee is excellent; many visitors bring a bag of freshly roasted coffee beans back home. Gift stores sell expensive, elegantly wrapped packages of coffee beans for export, but you can also shop ordinary grocery stores. The national coffee liqueur, Café Rica, is also a popular buy.

### Handicrafts

The things to buy are wood and leather items, which are well made and inexpensive. Wood items include salad bowls, plates, carving boards and other useful kitchen utensils, jewelry boxes, and a variety of carvings and ornaments. Furniture is also made but is hard to bring home, and having it shipped is expensive. Leatherwork includes the usual wallets and purses, handbags, and briefcases, and is usually cheaper than at home.

Interesting wood/leather combinations are the rocking chairs seen in many tourist lodges and better hotels in the country. Because of their leather seats and backs, they can be folded for transport and are usually packed two to a carton. If you're not bringing too much else back, you could check a pair of them in your airline baggage.

There are plenty of excellent souvenir shops in San José. Many people, however, opt to visit a village such as Sarchí where many souvenirs are made, especially wood-work, and where you can watch artisans at work. Although it is undeniably touristy, Sarchí is the center for making the colorfully painted replicas of the ox carts *(carretas)* that were traditionally used for hauling produce and people in the countryside – and still are in some remote regions. These ox carts are, as much as anything else, a typical souvenir peculiar to Costa Rica. They come in all sizes, from table-top models to nearly life-size replicas that double as drink cabinets. They all fold down for transport.

Ceramics and jewelry are also popular souvenirs. Some ceramics are replicas of pre-Columbian artifacts. Colorful posters and T-shirts with wildlife, national park, and ecological themes are also very popular, attractive, and reasonably priced. Some of the profits from these go to con-servation organizations in Costa Rica. Indian handicrafts from Costa Rica, as well as Guatemala and Panama, are also avail-able. Masks are popular.

A recent addition to the list is items made of banana paper – notebooks, sta-tionery and the like.

# Getting There & Away

Costa Rica can be reached by air, land, and sea. However, few people use the ocean route (unless stopping briefly on a cruise) because it is less convenient and usually more expensive than flying.

## AIR
### Airports & Airlines

Juan Santamaría International Airport, 17km outside San José, is where almost all international flights to Costa Rica arrive. The airport in Liberia, 217km northwest of San José on the Carretera Interamericana (Interamerican Hwy), is the backup international airport. It is little used except during the high season, when it receives a few direct charter flights from Miami and Canada for travelers wanting to go to the Península de Nicoya without stopping in San José.

Usually, going through immigration, baggage pickup, and customs at the main airport is fairly straightforward and takes about 30 minutes to an hour, occasionally longer if several international flights land at almost the same time.

Most airlines serving Costa Rica fly from the USA. These include American Airlines, Continental, Delta, and United, all based in the USA; Lacsa, the international Costa Rican carrier (part of the TACA Central American airline group, which includes Aviateca of Guatemala, Taca of El Salvador, Taca International of Honduras, and Nica of Nicaragua); and Mexicana.

From Europe, most airlines connect with flights from Miami; those airlines that do fly to Costa Rica may stop in the Caribbean instead. Carriers from Europe change every year. Recently, Martinair (a KLM subsidiary) from the Netherlands and Iberia from Spain offered service to Costa Rica. See the San José chapter for a list of airline offices in that city.

## Buying Tickets

The ordinary tourist or full economy-class fare is not the most economical way to go. It is convenient, however, because it enables you to fly on the next plane out and your ticket is valid for 12 months. If you want to economize further, there are several options.

(For information on travel seasons in Costa Rica, see When to Go in the Facts for the Visitor chapter.)

**Youth & Student Fares** Students with international student ID cards and anyone under 26 years of age can get discounts with most airlines. Although youth and student airfares can be arranged through most travel agents and airlines, it is a good idea to go through agents that specialize in student travel – several are listed in the regional sections later in this chapter. Note that student fares are not only cheap but often include free stopovers, don't require advance purchase, and may be valid for up to a year – a great deal if you are a student.

In Costa Rica, OTEC (☎ 256-0633, 257-0166, fax 233-8678), Calle 3, Avenida 3, in San José, specializes in student and youth fares and works closely with most of the student travel specialists listed in the following sections.

**Airline Deals** Whatever your age, if you purchase your ticket in advance it costs approximately 30% or 40% less than the full economy fare. These are often called APEX, excursion, or promotional fares, depending on the country you fly from and the rules and fare structures that apply there.

Often, the following restrictions apply: You must purchase your ticket at least 21 days (sometimes more or fewer days) in advance; you must stay a minimum period (about 14 days on average); and you must return within 180 days (sometimes fewer). Individual airlines have different requirements and these can change from time to time. Most of these tickets do not allow stopovers, and there are extra charges if you change your itinerary or dates of travel. These tickets may sell out well in advance, so try to book early.

You can also use the Internet to hunt for low fares. Most airlines have their own websites with online ticket sales, often discounted for online customers. The airlines may sell seats by auction, offer last-minute specials, or simply cut prices to reflect the reduced cost of electronic selling. To purchase a ticket via the Web, you'll need to use a credit card – this is straightforward and secure, as card details are encrypted. Commercial reservation networks offer airline ticketing as well as information and bookings for hotels, car rental, and other services.

**Discounted Tickets** Another cheap way to go is through consolidators (also called 'bucket shops,' though this term is less in vogue these days) that are allowed to sell discounted tickets to help airlines fill their flights. These tickets are often the cheapest of all, particularly in the low season, but they may sell out fast and you may be limited to only a few available dates.

While youth and student fares, economy fares, and discounted tickets are available direct from the airlines or from a travel agency (there is no extra charge for any of these tickets if you buy them from an agent rather than direct from the airline), consolidated discount tickets are available only from the discount ticket agencies themselves. Most of them are good, reputable, bonded companies, but once in a while a fly-by-night operator comes along, taking your money for a supercheap flight and giving you an invalid or unusable ticket. Carefully check what you are buying before handing over your money.

Discount ticket agencies often advertise in Sunday newspapers and travel-oriented magazines; there is much competition and a variety of fares and schedules are available. Fares to Latin America are traditionally quite expensive, but discount ticket agencies have recently been able to offer increasingly economical fares.

**Courier Flights** If you are flexible with travel dates and can get by with minimal luggage, you can fly to Costa Rica as a courier. (This is most practical from the USA.) Couriers are hired by companies that need to have packages delivered to Costa Rica (and many other international destinations). The company will give the courier exceptionally cheap tickets in return for the use of his or her checked-baggage allowance. The traveler can bring carry-on luggage only. These are legitimate operations – all baggage you are to deliver is completely legal. And it is amazing how much you can fit in your carry-on luggage!

Remember, you can buy things like T-shirts, a towel, and soap after you arrive at your destination, so traveling with just carry-on luggage is certainly feasible.

Courier flights are more common from the United States than Europe. Most courier flights to San José originate in Miami, Los Angeles, and New York, though not many are offered. For up-to-date information, contact the International Association of Air Travel Couriers (IAATC; ☎ 352-475-1584, fax 352-475-5326, Ⓦ www.courier.org), PO Box 980, Keystone Heights, FL 32656, USA. Another option is taking a courier flight to Panama City and continuing overland by bus.

**Other Considerations** Roundtrip fares are always much cheaper than two one-way tickets. They are also cheaper than 'open-jaw' tickets, which enable you to fly into one city (say San José) and leave via another (say Panama City). However, a few agencies can offer good fares on open-jaw tickets, which are suitable for someone who wants to do a little overland travel in Central America, so it pays to shop around before making your decision.

If, because of a late flight (but not a rescheduled one), you miss a connection or

**Warning**

The information in this chapter is particularly vulnerable to change: Prices for international travel are volatile, routes are introduced and canceled, schedules change, special deals come and go, and rules and visa requirements are amended. Airlines and governments often seem to make price structures and regulations as complicated as possible. You should check directly with the airline or a travel agent to make sure you understand how a fare (and any ticket you may buy) works. In addition, the travel industry is highly competitive and there are many hidden costs and benefits.

The upshot of this is that you should get opinions, quotes, and advice from as many airlines and travel agents as possible before you part with your hard-earned cash. The details given in this chapter should be regarded as pointers and are not a substitute for your own careful, up-to-date research.

are forced to stay overnight, the carrier is responsible for providing you with help in making the earliest possible connection and paying for a room in a hotel of its choice. The airline should also provide you with meal vouchers. If you are seriously delayed on an international flight, ask for these services.

Travelers are sometimes confused about the meaning of the term 'direct flight.' A direct flight goes from your departure point to San José and does not require that you get off the plane. However, unless it is specifically called a nonstop direct flight, the plane can stop in several cities en route to its final destination.

## Baggage & Other Restrictions

These vary depending on the airline and the class of service you have chosen. The airline or your travel agent will be able to explain restrictions to you. At minimum, you will be allowed two pieces of luggage totaling 20kg, plus a carry-on bag that fits under the seat in front of you. On some airlines or in business and 1st-class, you will be allowed more.

Restrictions on cheaper tickets usually mean you cannot get a refund, and if you change your dates of travel, you must pay an additional charge.

## Travelers with Special Needs

Most airlines can accommodate travelers with special needs, but only if such services are requested some days in advance. On flights with meals, a variety of special cuisines can be ordered in advance at no extra charge.

Airlines can easily accommodate travelers requiring physical assistance. Wheelchairs designed to fit in aircraft aisles, plus an employee to push the chair if necessary, are available with advance notice. Passengers can check their own wheelchairs as luggage. Blind passengers can request that an employee take them through the check-in procedure and all the way to their seats. Again, if you have special needs, ask – airlines usually work to oblige.

## Departure Tax

A US$17 departure tax is payable at the international airport by all foreign passengers departing on international flights (ticos pay more). Payment can be in cash US dollars or colones.

## The USA

The Sunday travel sections in the major newspapers advertise cheap fares to Central America, although these are sometimes no cheaper than the APEX fares offered by one of the several airlines serving Costa Rica.

Any reputable travel agent can help you find a reasonably priced ticket to Costa Rica. Students and people under 26 years of age should try one of the following experts in student travel – they also deal with regular fares and can help with things like international student ID cards, guidebooks, and youth hostel memberships.

A travel agent that can find you the best deal is Council Travel, a subsidiary of the Council on International Educational Exchange (CIEE). You can find its office locations and phone numbers in the telephone directories of more than 70 US cities, particularly those with universities, as well as 200 worldwide. Contact them at ☎ 800-226-8624 or Ⓦ www.counciltravel.com. Council Travel works with all age groups.

Also good for cheap airfares, mainly for students, is STA Travel (☎ 800-781-4040, Ⓦ www.statravel.com), with office locations worldwide. The toll-free numbers automatically connect you to the nearest office.

Another excellent contact is Tico Travel (☎ 800-493-8426, Ⓦ www.ticotravel.com), which offers discounted airfares from US gateway cities to anywhere in Central America and can provide connecting flights from all major US cities, as well as good rates on car rentals, etc, inside Costa Rica.

Another excellent source of cheap tickets is eXito Latin America Travel Specialists (☎ 800-655-4053, fax 510-655-4566, Ⓦ www.exitotravel.com). It specializes in Latin America exclusively and can arrange both short- and long-term tickets with multiple stopovers if desired.

APEX fares vary wildly depending on whether there's a price war going on, which airline you fly with, and when and how long you travel. Note that the lowest fares are usually available from consolidators; fares under US$300 are sometimes available from Miami. More frequently, fares from Miami range from US$400 to US$600. The cheapest days to fly are Monday to Thursday. Other gateway cities include Los Angeles, New York, Houston, New Orleans, Dallas–Fort Worth, San Francisco, and Washington, DC.

You should be able to get a ticket for US$700 or less from all of these places.

Because of the bewildering number of possibilities for air travel between the USA and Costa Rica, booking through a reputable agent is a good idea.

Courier travel is another possibility; see Buying Tickets, earlier in this chapter, for details.

Also see the Organized Tours section at the end of this chapter. Note that 'tours' doesn't necessarily mean a tour group – there are companies that will customize a tour for just a couple of people.

## Canada

Most travelers to Costa Rica must connect through one of the US gateway cities, though there may be direct charters.

Travel CUTS (☎ 866-246-9762, 🅆 www.travelcuts.com) is a good choice for student, youth, and budget airfares. Travel CUTS has dozens of offices throughout Canada.

Also see the entries under the USA, earlier; these companies can arrange discounted fares from Canada.

Canadians will find that various companies arrange inexpensive winter getaway charters to Costa Rica. These normally include several days of hotel accommodations in San José and/or a beach resort but are a good value for the money if the hotels happen to be to your liking. It's easiest to go through a travel agent, as charter companies don't always sell tickets directly to the public.

## Latin America

Central American airlines of the TACA group (🅆 www.grupotaca.com), which includes the Costa Rican carrier, Lacsa, provide services between all the Central American capitals and San José. In addition, Copa (Panama) provides services to San José.

For South America, you'll find that the TACA group flies to/from all countries except Paraguay, Uruguay, and the Guianas. American Airlines, Continental, Delta, and United all have connections to several Latin American countries. A few South American national airlines fly to Costa Rica, but routes change often.

Flights from Latin America are expensive because most Latin American countries tax airfares heavily (usually over 10%), and the number of APEX fares is limited. Consolidators aren't found easily. If you plan on traveling from outside the region to several Latin American countries by air, it is better to book tickets from home in advance rather than pay as you go. You can save hundreds of dollars this way, but the downside is that by booking in advance, you lose flexibility with your travel dates.

## The UK & Ireland

Discount ticket agencies ('bucket shops') generally provide the cheapest fares from Europe to Latin America. Fares from London, where competition is fiercest, are often cheaper than from other European cities. It may be cheaper to fly via London than direct from elsewhere.

Agencies advertise in newspaper classifieds. I have heard consistently good reports about Journey Latin America (JLA; ☎ 020-8747-8315 for tours, ☎ 020-8747-3108 for flights, fax 020-8742-1312, 🅆 www.journeylatinamerica.co.uk), 12 & 13 Heathfield Terrace, Chiswick, London W4 4JE. There is also an office in Manchester. JLA specializes in cheap fares to most Latin American countries and arranges itineraries for both independent and escorted travel. Ask for its free magazine, *Papagaio*, which offers helpful information. JLA agents will make arrangements for you over the phone or by fax.

Another reputable budget travel agency in the UK is Trailfinders (☎ 020-7937-5400, 🅆 www.trailfinder.co.uk), 215 Kensington High St, London W8 6BD. Trailfinders also has branches in several other British cities (see website) and at 4/5 Dawson St, Dublin 2, Ireland (☎ 01-677-7888). Its useful travel publication, *Trailfinder Magazine*, is available free from the agency.

Flightbookers (☎ 0870-010-7000 in UK, ☎ 44-20-7757-2626 outside UK, fax 020-7489-2200, 🅆 www.flightbookers.net), 177 Tottenham Court Rd, London W1P OLX, also offers cheap flights from the UK, Ireland, and 10 European cities.

Agencies specializing in student fares and youth discounts include STA Travel (☎ 020-7581-4132, fax 020-7368-0075, 🅆 www.statravel.co.uk), 86 Old Brompton Rd, London, SW7 3LQ, with over a dozen other addresses in London, as well as offices in 25 cities in the UK (all listed on its website).

The typical advance-purchase roundtrip fares from London to San José range from about UK£500 to UK£700. The variation in fares depends on how long you want to stay (longer stays are more expensive), which airline you choose, and when you travel. You need to go through a professional discount agent to get these fares, however. Note that the high season for air travel is the northern summer and December, which doesn't coincide with the Costa Rican high season of December to April.

## Continental Europe

Some airlines from Europe will take you to Miami, where you connect with other flights to Costa Rica. Airlines that may fly direct to San José (with stops in either Miami or the Caribbean) are Martinair (a KLM subsidiary) from the Netherlands and Iberia from Spain. Fares, routes, and low/high seasons change frequently; the best information to be had is from travel professionals.

STA Travel (see the USA section) has offices in the following European countries:

Austria (W www.oekista.at)
Denmark (☎ 33-14-15-01, W www.statravel.dk)
Finland (☎ 09-6812-7710, W www.statravel.fi)
Germany (W www.statravel.de)
Norway (☎ 815-59-905, W www.statravel.no)
Sweden (☎ 020-611010, W www.statravel.se)
Switzerland (☎ 1297-1111, W www.ssr.ch)

## South Africa

STA (W www.statravel.co.za) has several offices, including in Cape Town (☎ 021-685-1808) and Pretoria (☎ 012-342-5292).

## Australia & New Zealand

Travelers coming from Australia's east coast will usually fly to Costa Rica via the USA or Mexico. Most major airlines fly to Los Angeles, where you can get connecting flights to Costa Rica. Economy advance-purchase fares range from A$2200 to over A$3000 (though most should be under A$3000), so it pays to shop around. The low season in terms of fares is February and March (high season in Costa Rica) and mid-October to mid-November. The high season is mid-June to the end of July (mid- to low-season in Costa Rica) and mid-December to mid-January.

Qantas, Air New Zealand, and other trans-Pacific carriers fly to Los Angeles via Auckland, Nadi, or Honolulu, usually with one stopover allowed on the roundtrip, and connect with various carriers onward to San José. Also consider the overland route through Mexico as a cheaper alternative.

Fares from New Zealand via the Pacific will be somewhat lower than those from Australia's east coast. Routes via Asia are impractical.

Students and travelers under age 26 (though travelers of all ages can buy tickets) would do well to contact STA Travel in Australia (☎ 1300-733-035, W www.statravel.com.au) or New Zealand (☎ 0508-782-872, W www.statravel.co.nz). Both countries have dozens of offices in the major cities.

Trailfinders also has several Australian offices including one (☎ 02-9247-7666, fax 02-9247-6566, W www.trailfinders.com.au) at 8 Spring St, Sydney, NSW 2000.

## Asia

There is very little choice of direct flights between Asia and Latin America apart from Japan, and there certainly won't be any bargains there. The cheapest way is to travel to the US West Coast and connect with flights to Costa Rica from there.

STA Travel has several offices in Asia:

Japan (☎ 03-5269-0757, 06-6266-7927, W www.statravel.co.jp)
Malaysia (☎ 603-2148-9800, W www.statravel.com.my)
Singapore (☎ 65-737-7188, fax 65-737-2591, W www.statravel.com.sg), 33A Cuppage Rd, Cuppage Terrace, Singapore 229458; also at the Singapore Polytechnic and National University of Singapore
Thailand (☎ 2-236-0262, fax 2-237-6005, W www.statravel.co.th), Wall Street Tower, No 1406, 33/70 Surawong Rd, Bangrak, Bangkok 10500

## LAND

If you live in North or Central America, it is possible to travel overland to Costa Rica. The nearest US town to San José is Brownsville, Texas, on the border with Mexico. From there it is about 4000km by road to San José, half of which traverses Mexico; the rest is through Guatemala, Honduras, Nicaragua, and Costa Rica. It is possible, though not necessary, to travel through El Salvador and Belize. Costa Rica has land borders with Nicaragua to the north and Panama to the south.

You can drive your own car, but the costs of insurance, fuel, border permits, food, and accommodations will be higher than that of an airline ticket. Many people fly down and rent a car in San José.

If you drive down, consider the following: Driving even major Central American roads at night isn't recommended – they are narrow, unlit, rarely painted with a center stripe, often potholed, and subject to hazards such as cattle and pedestrians in rural areas. Traveling by day, allowing for time-consuming and bureaucratic border crossings, will take about a week from the US-Mexico border, or more to enjoy some of the sights (ruins, villages, markets, volcanoes, etc) en route. But it can certainly be done – get good insurance, be prepared for border bureaucracy, have your papers in impeccable order, and never leave your car unattended except in guarded parking areas. Don't leave anything of value in the car unless you are with it, and don't travel with fancy hubcaps, mirrors, etc, which are liable to be stolen. (US license plates are attractive to thieves, so display these inside the car.) Note that unleaded gas is not always available in Central America.

The American Automobile Association (AAA) publishes a map of Mexico and Central America (free to AAA members) that highlights the Carretera Interamericana and major side roads. AAA sells insurance for driving in Mexico, but not in Central America. For insurance coverage in Mexico and Central America, call Sanborn's (☎ 800-222-0158, 956-686-3601, fax 956-686-0732, ⓦ www.sanbornsinsurance.com), 2009 S 10th St, McAllen, TX 78503. Sanborn's also has offices in other cities near the US-Mexico border in Texas, Arizona, and California. For auto insurance details specific to travel within Costa Rica, see the Driver's License & Permits section in the Facts for the Visitor chapter.

A series of public buses will take you from the USA to San José. Bus travel is slow and cramped, but cheap and interesting. See Lonely Planet's *Mexico* and *Central America on a shoestring* for details on bus travel and accommodations en route. Direct buses from San José to the capitals of several Central American countries will cost you more than taking local buses to the borders and changing. Regardless of which buses you travel on, adding the cost of bus tickets to food and (budget) hotels, you'll pay as much as the airfare. You will, however, see and experience far more – it depends on your schedule.

The Carretera Interamericana continues as far south as Panama, then peters out in the Darién Gap, an area of roadless rainforest. It is possible to drive on to South America; vehicles must be transported by ferry (or be airfreighted) from Panama to Colombia.

It is possible to ship a car from Miami to Costa Rica for about US$450 and up, depending on the car. For specifics, contact Latii Express International (☎ 800-590-3789 in the USA, ☎ 877-270-3006 Canada, ☎ 296-1146, 296-0806, fax 231-7957, ⓦ www.latii express.com).

## Nicaragua

The one major crossing point between Nicaragua and Costa Rica is at Peñas Blancas, on the Carretera Interamericana. Almost all international overland travelers from Nicaragua enter Costa Rica through here.

**Peñas Blancas** This is the main border post, not a town, and so there is nowhere to stay.

The border is open from 6am to 8pm daily on both the Costa Rican and Nicaraguan sides, though bus traffic stops in the afternoon. The earlier in the day you get there, the better. The Costa Rican and Nicaraguan immigration offices are almost 1km apart – most passengers are traveling through by bus or private car. Travelers without a through bus will find golf carts (!) running between the borders for a few cents, or walking is not a problem. The Nicaraguan offices, complete with an air-conditioned bank and duty-free shop, are new as of this writing and some construction is still ongoing; it may be that transport services between the Nica and Tico offices will improve in the future.

On the Costa Rican side, the Migración office is in the immigration building. Inside is the Restaurant La Frontera, which serves adequate food, and the BanCrédito, which deals with colones but not cordobas. US cash dollars and AmEx traveler's checks can be exchanged into colones. The border bank is open from 8am to 5pm weekdays and 8am to noon Saturday. There is also a tiny Costa Rican tourist information office. Opposite the immigration building, a Transportes Deldu bus office sells tickets for departures to San José and Liberia; there are seven buses a day to San José, departing between 5am and 3:30pm. The trip takes 5½ hours and costs about US$6. Try to arrive early if you plan on taking a bus. There are also white mini-buses that go to La Cruz (30 minutes) at irregular times. Taxis are always an option.

If you are entering Costa Rica, sometimes an onward or exit ticket out of Costa Rica is requested – if you don't have one, you can buy a round-trip bus ticket to San José and back to the border from the bus office. This is acceptable to the Costa Rican authorities, who are generally helpful as long as your documents are in order. (Reports indicate that onward tickets, while legally required, are rarely asked for if you are carrying a passport that doesn't need a visa.)

If you are leaving Costa Rica, no special permit is required if you haven't overstayed the time allocated in your passport. If your time has expired, you need an exit visa, which you can pay for at the border (though you are less likely to encounter delays if you get your documents in order in San José).

International travelers between San José and Managua (or vice versa) on Sirca or TICA buses will find that the bus will wait for all passengers to be processed. This is time-consuming, and delays of up to eight hours have been reported (though two or three hours is more likely). To avoid the crowds, take local buses to the border post, walk (or find a golf cart) to the other border post, and then continue on another bus – but cross as early in the day as possible. Several travelers have reported that luggage placed on the roofs of buses in Nicaragua has been pilfered, sometimes when only a bus employee has been allowed on the roof. Stolen objects are often mundane items such as deodorant or clothing. If you can't lock your luggage, try wrapping it in a large sack with a lock on that (primitive but it deters pilferers). Carry your luggage aboard the bus if possible. Note that poverty in Nicaragua is worse than in Costa Rica, and therefore thefts from buses are much more frequent. Watch your gear very carefully.

Nicaragua charges a US$2 departure or entry tax between 8am and 5pm Monday to Friday. At other times, the tax is US$4, apparently because you are crossing outside normal office hours. They want cash dollars, not cordobas or colones. The Nicaraguan Bancentro, at the border, changes cordobas to cash dollars and vice versa during office hours. At other times, money changers (cambistas) hang around the borders and give rates almost as good as the banks. Be careful to count money very carefully as 'mistakes' occur with frequency. Changers will also change colones into cordobas on request, but rates are at a greater loss than dealing with US dollars. Try to arrive at the border with as little local money as possible.

The first (or last) Nicaraguan city of any size is Rivas, 37km north of the border, with several cheap hotels. There are frequent buses from the border to Rivas until 5pm; get to the border by early afternoon to make sure you get on a bus. Alternatively, colectivos (buses, minivans, or cars operating as shared taxis) charge twice as much as a bus and leave more often. From Rivas, you can continue to the cities of Granada and Managua by bus, or across Lago de Nicaragua by boat.

Nicaraguan visa regulations change frequently, so check in with the Nicaraguan embassy in San José or in your home country. Recently, citizens of the USA, UK, and a few European nations were allowed to enter Nicaragua for up to 90 days with a passport, which must be valid for at least six months after the date of entry. Citizens of Canada, Australia, New Zealand, and some European nations were only allowed 30 days with a valid passport. In most cases a tourist card is also required; the card costs US$5 and can be obtained at the border. Nationals of other countries mostly require a visa of one kind or another.

**Los Chiles** Non-Nicaraguan and non-Costa Rican travelers rarely use this route, though it's possible for other nationals to cross here with the usual documents. Note that some nationals may require a visa; many don't.

Heading north from Costa Rica, a very rough road (a taxi with 4WD is essential) traverses the 14km from Los Chiles to near the Nicaraguan town of San Carlos, on the southeastern corner of Lago de Nicaragua at the beginning of the Río San Juan. At this time, there are no border crossing facilities here. However, the newly paved road from Muelle de San Carlos to Los Chiles is slated to continue to this border point, a bridge is planned and this will become the main border crossing, according to local immigration officials. When will this happen? The officials shrugged, grinned and said 'some year.' This will eventually become a major route to Managua from northeastern Costa Rica, avoiding having to traverse San José.

Meanwhile passenger boats on the Río Frío go from Los Chiles to San Carlos about three times a day (11am, 1pm, and 4pm recently, but subject to change according to demand). The one-hour ride costs US$6.

San Carlos has basic *pensiones* and a couple of slightly better hotels. There is regular boat service twice weekly (recently 2pm Tuesday and Friday, US$3, 14 hours) to Granada, a major Nicaraguan town on the northwestern corner of Lago de Nicaragua. This boat is usually full, so you should buy a ticket the day before if possible. Alternately, four daily buses go via Juigalpa to Managua (US$5.50, 9 hours) or you can fly to Managua every morning.

The Costa Rican Migración office (☎ 471-1223) has an office by the dock and on the main road (ask anyone for directions). The Nicaraguan consul is Sra Julieta Gómez (☎ 471-1166). The border crossing should be hassle-free if your papers are in order.

## Panama

There are three road border crossings between Costa Rica and Panama. Note that Panama's time is one hour ahead of Costa Rica's.

**Paso Canoas** This border crossing on the Carretera Interamericana is by far the most frequently used entry and exit point with Panama.

Border hours are currently 24 hours if crossing by private vehicle. Other travelers should arrive during the day because buses stop running soon after nightfall.

If you are entering Panama from Costa Rica, you may need a visa or tourist card in addition to your passport. Visitors from the UK, some western European countries, some Central American countries, and a

few others need only a passport. Citizens of Australia, Canada, New Zealand, the USA, some western European countries, and others can buy a tourist card for US$5, which allows for a 30-day stay. Longer stays require a visa. Visas typically cost up to about US$20, depending on your nationality. Visas are not obtainable at the border.

Tourist cards are officially available, but the immigration office on the border has been known to run out, so get your visa or tourist card in advance if you need one. Panamanian officials often require that you have an onward ticket out of Panama before you are allowed to enter. If you don't have one, a roundtrip bus ticket to David can be purchased at the border and should suffice. Officials may also require that you have the equivalent of US$500 as proof of sufficient funds, though this isn't usually asked for if you look reasonably prosperous.

Regulations are subject to change, so you should check at the Panamanian consulate in San José about current requirements.

Once you are in Panama, there is a Panamanian bus terminal in front of the border post. The nearest town of any size and with decent hotels is David, about 1½ hours away by bus (US$1.50). There are buses to David many times throughout the day; the last one leaves the border about 8:30pm. If you want to travel on to Panama City, you can either fly or catch a bus from David. The last regular bus (about US$11, seven hours) leaves David at 8pm. Express buses (about $15, six hours) leave at 10pm and midnight. David is also the hub of an extensive bus network throughout northern Panama (see Lonely Planet's *Panama*).

If you are entering Costa Rica, you may be required to show a ticket out of the country and US$500. If you don't have a ticket, buy a TRACOPA bus ticket in David

### Crossing Borders

When crossing borders, sometimes a show of cash is required – US$400 per month should be sufficient. Costa Ricans are sensitive to appearances; putting on your most presentable clothes and avoiding unusual fashions will make entrance procedures easier.

for the roundtrip between David and Paso Canoas; this is acceptable to the Costa Rican authorities. Apparently, purchasing just the Paso Canoas–David section at the border isn't considered sufficient proof of intent to exit the country.

There are Costa Rican consulates in David and in Panama City.

People of most nationalities require only a passport and exit ticket to enter Costa Rica. See Visas & Documents in the Facts for the Visitor chapter for additional details. The border crossing in either direction is generally straightforward if your documents are in order.

**Sixaola/Guabito** This crossing is on the Caribbean coast, and the continuation of Sixaola on the Panama side is called Guabito. There are no banks, but stores in Guabito will accept colones, Panamanian *balboas*, or US dollars. The border is open from 7am to 5pm daily in Costa Rica (8am to 6pm in Panama). Occasionally, immigration guards take a siesta – ask anyone at the border office to tell you where they are.

Procedures here are mainly geared to Costa Ricans popping down to Panama to spend a short vacation in the nearby pretty islands and pleasant beaches around Bocas del Toro. The Bocas del Toro area is becoming a popular destination, and people who have traveled this way say it is attractive and worth seeing (see Lonely Planet's *Panama*). Non-ticos should ensure that they get all the proper stamps in their passports and not just breeze through with a vacationing group of ticos. There are minibuses and taxis from near the border crossing to Changuinola, 16km into Panama.

In Changuinola, there is a bank, immigration office (where you may need to go if you don't already have a tourist card) and an airport with daily flights to David. There are several moderately priced hotels, including the Hotel Changuinola (☎ 758-8678, fax 758-8681) near the airport.

From Changuinola, frequent buses travel the 22km to Almirante, where there are cheap public launches (US$3, 30 minutes) departing at least every hour from 6am to 6pm to Bocas del Toro, where there are dozens of hotels. Also from Almirante, a new road goes to Chiriquí Grande, where there are hotels. From here, a road goes to

David and the rest of Panama. There are two or three buses a day from Almirante to Panama City (about US$25, 10 hours).

**Río Sereno** The road transiting this border crossing goes east from San Vito, through the border post by Río Sereno (a village on the Panamanian side), and on to the village of Volcán near the Parque Nacional Volcán Barú, the highest part of Panama. This is a remote and rarely used route with great scenery.

Panamanian immigration officials will require a return ticket to your country of origin, plus at least US$500 to show you are solvent, as well as the usual passport with a visa or tourist card (if you need one). However, the US$500 is rarely asked for if you have a passport from a first-world country and appear reasonably affluent, and the return ticket can be out of San José. The immigration station is beside the police station. The Costa Rican officials require the usual visas and documents as described in the Facts for the Visitor chapter. The border crossings are open 8am to 6pm daily, but remember Panama is an hour ahead of Costa Rica.

There is a decent hotel in Río Sereno on the Panama side, but the banking facilities at the border do not deal with foreign exchange. However, you can pay for anything you need with small US bills.

Buses from Río Sereno travel to Concepción and David (in Panama); the last bus leaves the village at 5pm daily. On the Costa Rica side there are no facilities, but four buses a day travel from San Vito at 7am, 10am, 2pm, and 4pm, returning from the border an hour later.

## SEA

Cruise lines stop in Costa Rican ports and enable passengers to make a quick foray into the country. Most cruises are, however, geared to shipboard life and ocean travel, so passengers can expect no more than a brief glimpse of Costa Rica – perhaps a day or so. Typically, cruise ships dock at either the Pacific port of Caldera (near Puntarenas) or the Caribbean port of Moín (near Puerto Limón). Passengers at Caldera get a chance to do a day trip to San José and the Central Valley or perhaps visit Parque Nacional Carara. Passengers at Moín may take a trip up the canals toward Parque Nacional Tortuguero or go on a river-rafting excursion. Other options are often possible – talk to your onboard excursion director.

Freighters also arrive in Costa Rica, but most are for cargo only. A few may accept a small number of passengers. Private yachts cruise down the Pacific coast from North America.

## ORGANIZED TOURS

Scores of tour operators in North America and Europe run tours to Costa Rica. It is beyond the scope of this book to list them all (about three dozen tour operators in California alone run Costa Rica tours!). In contrast, there are few operators in other parts of the world.

Typical tours combine nature and adventure. Travelers visit one or more national parks and reserves, with overnight accommodations in comfortable lodges and hotels. Apart from birding and wildlife observation, and guided cloud or rainforest walks, other activities include river running, snorkeling, kayaking, deep-sea or freshwater fishing, horseback riding, bicycling, hiking, touring the countryside, and just plain relaxing.

Many tours in Costa Rica are 1st-class and expensive, and costs for the best trips can easily exceed US$200 per person per day, plus airfare to San José. The best tours usually provide an experienced bilingual guide, the best accommodations available, all transport, and most meals. If you are shopping for a cheaper tour, ask about the guide. Is the guide fluent in English? What are the guide's particular interests and qualifications? Will they accompany you throughout the trip or will there be different guides for different portions? Here are some other questions to consider: How big will the tour group be? How many meals are included? What kind of lodging is used? Can I talk to past clients?

The advantage of a tour is you have everything taken care of from the time you arrive 'til the time you leave. You don't have to worry about speaking Spanish, figuring out itineraries, finding bus stations, haggling with cab drivers, locating hotels with available rooms, or translating restaurant menus. Tours are often preferred by people who have a short vacation period and enough money to afford being taken care of. People on tours can have activities scheduled for every day of their trip and don't need to spend time figuring out what to do and how to do it once they get to San José.

Travelers who like these advantages but hate the idea of traveling with a tour group are served by several companies that arrange custom itineraries. These are not cheap, but neither are they necessarily super-expensive. Ask for moderate hotels and try to travel with a small group of friends and family to share the cost of a guide.

The following tour operators are reputable, but there are scores of others. Most are upscale, although some cheaper outfits are suggested as well. Most have a sliding price scale (a group of four on a two-week trip might pay about US$300 per person more than a group of 14, for example). Prices are based on double occupancy, and single travelers may pay several hundred dollars more. The ones listed below operate from outside of Costa Rica.

For information on Costa Rican companies (some of which also have a US address or contact phone number), see the Getting Around chapter.

### The USA

**General & Natural History** These companies emphasize general sightseeing and natural history tours based in hotels, but may have other offerings.

**Abercrombie & Kent** (☎ 630-954-2944, 800-323-7308, fax 630-954-3324, W www.abercrombie kent.com), 1520 Kensington Rd, Oak Brook, IL 60523-2141. Among the most deluxe general tours.

**Adventure Center** (☎ 510-654-1879, 800-227-8747, fax 510-654-4200, W www.adventurecenter.com), 1311 63rd St, suite 200, Emeryville, CA 94608. Represents several different companies.

**Ecotour Expeditions** (☎ 401-423-3377, 800-688-1822, fax 401-423-9630, W www.naturetours.com), PO Box 128, Jamestown, RI 02835-0128. Offers five- to 10-day natural history and highlights tours.

**Elderhostel** (☎ 978-323-4141, 877-426-8056, fax 617-426-0701, 877-426-2166, W www.elderhostel .org), 11 Avenue de Lafayette, Boston, MA 02111-1746. Excellent educational tours for travelers over 55 (younger companions permitted).

**International Expeditions** (☎ 205-428-1700, 800-633-4734, fax 205-428-1714, W www.international expeditions.com), 1 Environs Park, Helena, AL 35080. High-quality natural history tours include excellent guides and accommodations; eight- to 10-day tours from Miami from US$2400, including air; custom itineraries are also available.

**Wilderness Travel** (☎ 510-558-2488, 800-368-2794, fax 510-558-2489, W www.wildernesstravel.com), 1102 9th St, Berkeley, CA 94710. Ten- to 12-day comprehensive natural history adventures guided by bilingual local experts; comfortable lodge accommodations. The 10-day tours start at US$2300 plus airfare.

**Wildland Adventures** (☎ 206-365-0686, 800-345-4453, fax 206-363-6615, W www.wildland.com), 3516 NE 155th St, Seattle, WA 98155. Wide selection of seven- to 10-day tours, including some designed for families; costs range from US$1250 to US$2700 plus airfare.

## Sportfishing
For more information on fishing, see Activities in the Facts for the Visitor chapter.

**JD's Watersports** (☎ 970-356-1028, 800-477-8971, fax 970-352-6324, W www.jdwatersports.com), 1115 11th Ave, Greeley, CO 80631. Fishing from Hotel Punta Leona (near Jacó, but you don't have to stay there); also diving, kayaking, boogie boarding, river, and sunset cruises. See the entry under Punta Leona Area in the Central Pacific Coast chapter for local contact information.

**Rod & Reel Adventures** (☎ 800-356-6982, fax 541-242-0742, W www.rodreeladventures.com), 2294 Oakmont Way, Eugene, OR 97401. Well known, represents several of the best lodges and boats. Four-night/three-day ocean-fishing packages from about US$1000 to US$2000, depending on accommodations and boats used; longer trips available. It also arranges freshwater trips on Laguna de Arenal.

## Surfing
For more information on surfing, see Activities in the Facts for the Visitor chapter.

**Tico Travel** (☎ 800-493-8426, W www.ticotravel.com). Cheap-fare specialist with plenty of surfing information; offers sportfishing as well.

## Diving
For more information on diving, see the Facts for the Visitor chapter.

**JD's Watersports** (see Sportfishing, above). PADI-certified trips at the Hotel Punta Leona, resort courses (mini-courses for beginners to determine whether they like diving), and certification courses are offered.

**Okeanos Aggressor** (☎ 985-385-2628, 800-348-2628, fax 985-384-0817, W www.aggressor.com), PO Box 1470, Morgan City, LA 70381. Runs dive trips to Isla del Coco for experienced divers.

## Other Activities
These companies usually offer some specialized activities in addition to general and natural history tours.

**Backroads** (☎ 510-527-1555, 800-462-2848, fax 510-527-1555, W www.backroads.com), 801 Cedar St, Berkeley, CA 94710. Seven- or eight-day easy walking or mountain-biking adventures based in excellent hotels. Walk 4km to 10km a day, ride 16km to 70km a day, with river rafting and jungle hiking available. Tours only in dry season; expensive but reputable.

**BattenKill Canoe Ltd** (☎ 802-362-2800, 800-421-5268, fax 802-362-0159, W www.battenkill.com), PO Box 65, Historic Rte 7a, Arlington, VT 05250. Eleven-day trips with an emphasis on canoeing – no experience needed. Cost is about US$2000 plus airfare; custom itineraries or add-on days can be arranged.

**Earthwatch** (☎ 978-461-0081, 800-776-0188, fax 978-461-2332, W www.earthwatch.org), 3 Clock Tower Place, suite 100, Box 75, Maynard, MA 01754. Ten-day turtle-tagging projects; 'volunteers' pay about US$1800 to assist scientists carrying out research; work at night and sleep by day. Longer and cheaper projects involving caterpillar studies, octopus investigations, tropical forest research, and other trips are offered; all are tax deductible.

**Mountain Travel/Sobek** (☎ 510-527-8100, 888-687-6235, fax 510-525-7710, W www.mtsobek.com), 6420 Fairmount Ave, El Cerrito, CA 94530. Offers sea kayaking, river rafting, hiking, and natural history tours. Costs are US$1500 to US$2500 on 10-day trips.

**Serendipity Adventures** (☎ 734-995-0111, 800-635-2325, 558-1000 in Costa Rica, fax 734-426-5026, W www.serendipityadventures.com), PO Box 2325, Ann Arbor, MI 48106. All kinds of adventures, ranging from hot-air ballooning (US$900 for six people) to nine-day/eight-night cross-country biking trips (US$1900 per person in high season). Other activities include rafting, climbing, kayaking, snorkeling, tree-climbing, hiking, horseback riding, and camping, as well as the usual natural history; novices welcomed.

## Customized Itineraries
These companies will find a group tour or arrange a customized itinerary to suit your interests.

**Costa Rica Connection** (☎ 805-543-8823, 800-345-7422, fax 805-543-3626, W www.crconnect.com), 1124 Nipomo St, suite C, San Luis Obispo, CA 93401. Wide variety of itineraries at US$120 to US$300 per day, plus air.

**Costa Rica Experts** (☎ 773-935-1009, 800-827-9046, fax 773-935-9252, W www.costaricaexperts.com), 3166 N Lincoln Ave, suite 424, Chicago, IL 60657. Specializes in Costa Rica and the best lodging options at upper-middle to top-end budgets. Many different activities.

**Holbrook Travel** (☎ 352-377-7111, 800-451-7111, fax 352-371-3710, ⓦ www.holbrooktravel.com), 3540 NW 13th St, Gainesville, FL 32609-2196. Owns and operates the Selva Verde Lodge (listed in the Northern Lowlands chapter) and arranges various other trips from US$100 to over US$200 per day.

**Preferred Adventures** (☎ 651-222-8131, 800-840-8687, fax 651-222-4221, ⓦ www.preferred adventures.com), 1 W Water St, suite 300, St Paul, MN 55107. Well-recommended, experienced, environmentally sensitive adventure and nature travel with cheap airfares with any land package.

**Tread Lightly** (☎ 860-868-1710, 800-643-0060, fax 860-868-1718, ⓦ www.treadlightly.com), 37 Juniper Meadow Rd, Washington Depot, CT 06794. Personal attention and an environmentally friendly approach.

## Canada

**Adventures Abroad** (☎ 604-303-1099, 800-665-3998, fax 604-303-1076, ⓦ www.adventures abroad.com), 20800 Westminster Hwy, suite 2148, Richmond, BC V6V 2W3. Moderately priced one- and two-week escorted bus tours; maximum of 20 participants.

**Gulf Islands Kayaking** (☎/fax 250-539-2442, ⓦ www.seakayak.bc.ca/tour), S-24, C-34, Galiano Island, BC V0N 1P0. Has seven-day/six-night kayaking trips out of Drake Bay. Fifteen years of experience paddling Costa Rica.

**Trek Holidays** (☎ 780-439-9118, 800-661-7265, fax 780-433-5494, ⓦ www.trekholidays.com). Has several locations.

## The UK

**Adventures Abroad** (☎ 0114-247-3400, fax 0114-251-3210), H/04 Staniforth Estates, Main St, Hackenthorpe, Sheffield S12 4LB. See Canada, above.

**Condor Journeys and Adventures** (☎ 01700-841-318, fax 01700-841-398, ⓦ www.condor journeys-adventures.com), 2 Ferry Bank, Colintraive, Argyll PA22 3AR. Independent and group tours all over Latin America.

**Journey Latin America** (JLA; ☎ 020-8747-8315, fax 020-8742-1312, ⓦ www.journeylatinamerica

.co.uk), 12 & 13 Heathfield Terrace, Chiswick, London W4 4JE. Also an office in Manchester. Recommended flight, tour, and custom-itinerary specialists to Latin America, with many years of experience.

**Last Frontiers Limited** (☎ 01296-653000, fax 01296-658651, ⓦ www.lastfrontiers.co.uk), Fleet Marston Farm, Aylesbury, Buckinghamshire HP18 0QT. Tours and tailor-made itineraries all over Latin America.

**Sunvil Holidays** (☎ 020-8758-4774, fax 020-8568-8330, ⓦ www.sunvil.co.uk), Sunvil House, 7-8 Upper Square, Old Isleworth, Middlesex TW7 7BJ. Arranges independent travel, including hotel reservations and car rentals, with some organized tours.

## Australia & New Zealand

No companies from this part of the world specialize in Costa Rica; the following have some Costa Rican itineraries. Most travelers from Australia and New Zealand arrange tours through Costa Rican or North American outfitters via the Internet.

**Adventure Associates** (☎ 02-9389-7466, fax 02-9369-1853, ⓦ www.adventureassociates.com), 197 Oxford St, Bondi Junction, Sydney, NSW 2022. Standard one-week tours in addition to independent travel arrangements.

**Adventure Travel Company** (☎ 03-9696-8400, fax 03-9696-8600, ⓦ www.adventure-travel.com.au), South Melbourne, Australia. Contact them for brochures from several international companies doing trips to Costa Rica.

**Adventure World** (☎ 02-8913-0755, fax 02-9956-7707, ⓦ www.adventureworld.com.au), 73 Walker St, Sydney, NSW 2060. Has information about all Central America, including Costa Rica.

**Adventures Abroad** (☎ 09-273-9366, 0-800-800-434, fax 09-273-3265), 6 Glassonby Rd, Howick, Auckland 1705, New Zealand. See Canada, earlier.

**Contours** (☎ 03-9670-6900, fax 03-9670-7558, ⓔ contours@contourstravel.com.au), Level 6, 310 King St, Melbourne, VIC 3000. Good variety of Latin American tours at mid-range to lower top-end prices.

# Getting Around

The population distribution of Costa Rica dictates how its public transport works. Roughly one quarter of the country's almost four million inhabitants live in the greater San José area, and roughly two-thirds live in the Central Valley, one of the most densely populated regions in Central America. This means that there are a lot of roads and buses in the center of the country. As you go farther afield, there are generally fewer roads, particularly paved ones, and less public transport.

To get to most regions, you have to start from San José, which is the main center for public transport. It is often easier to go to one region and then return to San José to find transport to another area.

The majority of Costa Ricans do not own cars. Therefore, public transport is quite well developed and you can get buses to almost any part of the country. Remote or small towns may be served by only one bus a day, but you can get there.

## AIR

Costa Rica's two domestic airlines are SANSA (Servicios Aéreos Nacionales SA; ☎ 221-9414, W www.taca.com, www.fly sansa.com) and Travelair (☎ 220-3054, W www.travelair-costarica.com).

SANSA is now linked with Grupo TACA, and you can buy tickets through any travel agent. It has upgraded its fleet, services, and reservation system, though flights are still subject to delays and occasional cancellations. Services are with small Cessna Caravans (14 passengers) and similar aircraft. Flights leave from the domestic terminal of Juan Santamaría International Airport, 17km from the center of San José. Demand for seats is high, so try to book as far in advance as possible. Because the aircraft are small, baggage allowance is limited to 12kg (about 26lb).

Travelair is the newer domestic airline and is slightly more expensive than SANSA. Travelair has a reputation for better on-time service and fewer canceled flights than SANSA, but since the latter became part of Grupo TACA, service has improved. Travelair works with Adobe Rent a Car to provide free pickup and dropoff at any of the destinations listed in the table below.

Travelair flies from the smaller Tobías Bolaños Airport in Pavas, about 5km from the center of San José. Service is with nine-passenger Britten Islanders, 15-passenger Britten Trislanders, and similar planes. Again, book as far in advance as possible and remember to limit your luggage to 12kg.

Fares given are for high-season one-way/roundtrip flights from San José and are subject to change. Most flights are daily; some are more frequent. Destinations served can change from season to season. Low-season fares are slightly cheaper.

| destination | Travelair | SANSA |
|---|---|---|
| Barra del Colorado | US$60/118 | US$55/110 |
| Carate | US$96/186 | - |
| Carrillo – see Sámara | | |
| Drake Bay | US$85/165 | - |
| Golfito | US$76/147 | US$66/132 |
| Liberia | US$73/141 | US$66/132 |
| Neily/Coto 47 | - | US$66/132 |
| Palmar Sur | US$66/128 | US$66/132 |
| Playa Nosara | US$73/141 | US$66/132 |
| Playa Tamarindo | US$73/141 | US$66/132 |
| Puerto Jiménez | US$76/147 | US$66/132 |
| Punta Islita | US$73/141 | US$66/132 |
| Quepos | US$45/87 | US$44/88 |
| Sámara/Carrillo | US$73/141 | US$66/132 |
| Tambor | US$60/118 | US$55/110 |
| Tortuguero | US$60/118 | US$55/110 |

Intermediate fares are available for some flights between towns outside of San José. These change often and are subject to passenger demand, so ask. If all else fails, small aircraft can be chartered between any airports (see below).

Oversize items (surfboards, bicycles) cost an extra US$15.

As a general rule, the most popular destinations are Playa Tamarindo, Quepos, Palmar Sur, and Puerto Jiménez, so you should book as far ahead as possible for those destinations if you want to fly on a particular day. Barra del Colorado and Tortuguero are also fairly popular. Both airlines suggest you not book a flight to connect with an international flight the same day because if the domestic flight has to be canceled (which happens a few times each season), you will probably miss your international flight, and nobody wants to be responsible.

The head offices of SANSA and Travelair are in San José, though any travel agent can book your flight. Remember that reservations with SANSA must be prepaid in full before they can be confirmed. Most agents, especially if you are calling from outside Costa Rica, add a booking fee of a few dollars. Details of other offices are given under the appropriate towns in the regional chapters of this book.

## Charters

Tobías Bolaños Airport also caters to small single- and twin-engined aircraft that can be chartered to just about anywhere in the country where there is an airport. Fares start at about US$300 per hour for the smaller planes, and it takes 40 to 90 minutes to fly to most destinations. You also have to pay for the return flight, unless you can co-ordinate with the company to fly you out on a day when they are picking up somebody else. If a group of you fills up the plane (three, five, or seven passengers in most cases), the fare is not prohibitive, but luggage space is very limited.

Aero Costa Sol (☎ 441-1444, fax 441-2671, ⓔ flyacs@racsa.co.cr) has five- and seven-passenger aircraft flying out of Juan Santamaría International Airport. Slightly cheaper charters fly out of Tobía Bolaños Airport and include Aerobell (☎ 290-0000, fax 296-0460, ⓔ aerobell@racsa.co.cr) and Pitts Aviation (☎ 296-3600, fax 296-1429, ⓔ skytours@racsa.co.cr). Alfa Romeo Aero Taxi (☎ 775-1515 in Golfito, ☎ 735-5178 in Puerto Jiménez) flies to and from the southern parts of Costa Rica.

Many towns that have an airport will have light aircraft available for charter; those of particular interest to the traveler are mentioned in the text.

You can arrange flights directly by going to Tobías Bolaños Airport, or you can book ahead by phone or email. Many tour agencies will charter planes for you if you take one of their tours.

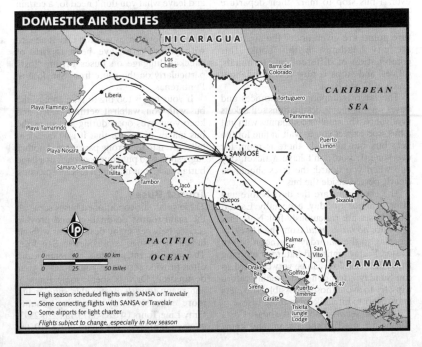

**DOMESTIC AIR ROUTES**

— High season scheduled flights with SANSA or Travelair
- - Some connecting flights with SANSA or Travelair
o  Some airports for light charter
*Flights subject to change, especially in low season*

## BUS

The ICT tourist office in San José (see Tourist Offices in the Facts for the Visitor chapter) has a (usually) up-to-date listing of many bus departure points and the destinations they serve. Other places to find bus timetables are Ecole Travel in San José (see Organized Tours, below) and at some hotels.

### Standard Buses

San José is the center of the country's bus network, and buses depart from the capital for just about anywhere in the country. See the San José chapter for details.

There are few central bus terminals. In San José, some bus companies leave from what used to be the old Coca-Cola bottling plant in San José – the area is still known as 'La Coca-Cola.' A few blocks north, the Atlántico Norte terminal serves some northern destinations, and the Caribbean area is served by the Caribe terminal, in another location (see the San José chapter).

Other companies leave from their own offices elsewhere in the city. Still others leave from bus stops on the street, and some leave from street corners without even a bus stop to mark their departure point. The addresses or street intersections of bus companies, bus stops, or bus departure points are given under the appropriate city headings in this book. This combination of different bus terminals, offices, and stops is how it is throughout much of Costa Rica.

The larger companies with offices and buses serving major destinations sell tickets in advance. The smaller companies with just a bus stop expect you to wait in line for the next bus, but normally there is room for everyone. If you don't have a ticket, buy one when you board; the fares should be clearly posted inside the bus.

The exceptions are the days before and after a major holiday, especially Easter, when buses are ridiculously full. Note that there are *no buses at all* from the Thursday morning to the Saturday afternoon before Easter. Friday night and Saturday morning trips out of San José can be very crowded, as can Sunday afternoon and evening return trips; try to avoid those if possible. Travelers may resort to hitchhiking in these cases.

If this all seems chaotic, take heart. Costa Ricans are used to the system and know where buses depart – just ask. Alternatively, take a tourist bus.

Fares are generally cheap, with even the longest and most expensive run out of San José costing under US$7.

Long-distance buses are of two types, *directo* and *normal* (or *corriente*). The direct buses are a little faster and more expensive. Travelers on a budget can save as much as a quarter of the direct bus fare by taking a normal bus, which stops on demand at various intermediate points and usually takes an hour or two longer.

Roads are narrow and winding and sometimes unpaved; normal buses are rather old, so comfort is not one of the things that the bus journeys are known for, particularly those to smaller and more remote destinations served by battered old Bluebird school buses. But they get you there. Trips longer than four hours have a rest stop, and no trips are scheduled to take longer than about nine hours. If you want reasonable comfort, take the more expensive direct buses.

Luggage space is limited, so you could break your Costa Rica stay into sections and leave what you don't need for a certain section in San José. A small bag is certainly much easier to travel with and easier to keep your eye on, as you can take it aboard with you. There have been reports of checked luggage on buses getting 'lost,' particularly on the route from San José to Puntarenas.

If your bag is too big to take aboard the bus with you, watch it getting loaded and keep your eyes open during any stops the bus makes to ensure that it isn't 'accidentally' given to the wrong passenger. Another suggestion is to put your backpack in a large burlap sack, thus making it less conspicuous.

### Tourist Buses

These small, air-conditioned buses serve all the main tourist destinations and provide service between many destinations without having to change companies in San José. They are efficient, punctual, convenient, and often provide service to your hotel at your destination. Drivers speak some English, and many tourists prefer this simpler but more expensive way of getting around. Gray Line Tours (☎ 283-5573, fax 220-2393, Ⓦ www.fantasy.co.cr) charges US$19 for most trips, and Interbus (☎ 283-5573, fax 283-7655, 🌐 www.costaricapass.com) is a few dollars more but serves more destinations. Contact details for local offices of these companies are given in the appropriate city sections.

## TRAIN
The railway lines in Costa Rica were severely damaged in the 1991 earthquake and have been closed since then. They were running at a financial deficit before the closure, so despite occasional talk of privatizing the system with foreign money, it is unlikely that the system will be repaired or reopened. This is a shame, because the run from San José to the Caribbean coast was a famous and well-loved ride.

## CAR & MOTORCYCLE
Few people drive to Costa Rica in their own vehicle, though it is certainly possible (see the Getting There & Away chapter for

details). Renting a car after arrival, on the other hand, is something many travelers do for part of their trip. Some rent motorcycles, though this is not such a popular option and is expensive.

### Road Rules
San José is notorious for its narrow streets, complicated one-way system, heavy traffic, and thefts from cars. Driving a rental car around San José is not recommended, except to get out of the city.

Once out of San José, the roads vary from barely passable to very good. But even the good ones can suffer from landslides and thick fog, so you should always be prepared for the unexpected. Most roads are single-lane, lack hard shoulders, and are very winding, so defensive driving is recommended. Always be prepared for cyclists, pedestrians, a broken-down vehicle, heavily laden, slow-moving trucks, or even an ox cart around the next bend. Potholes of

---

## Traffic Signs

Traffic signs are in Spanish and don't always have an internationally recognized symbol. Drivers should be aware of the following to help prevent accidents.

One of the most important signs is found at one-lane bridges (of which there are many). On one side of the bridge there will normally be a Cede el Paso sign, which means 'Yield' or 'Give Way.' The driver who has this sign must stop for oncoming traffic – it is not the first car to enter the bridge that has the right of way. Other important signs to know are the following:

| | |
|---|---|
| Adelante | Ahead |
| Alto | Stop |
| Cede el Paso | Yield; Give Way |
| Curva Peligrosa | Dangerous Curve |
| Derrumbes en la Vía | Landslides or Rockfalls in the Highway |
| Despacio | Slow |
| Desvío | Detour; Alternate Route |
| Hundimiento | Dip |
| Mantenga Su Derecha | Keep to the Right |
| No Adelantar | No Passing |
| No Estacionar | No Parking |
| No Hay Paso | No Entrance |
| Peligro | Danger |
| Puente | Bridge |
| Trabajos en la Vía | Road Work |
| Transito Entrando | Traffic Entering the Highway |

Know, and take seriously, these signs. An hundimiento can be an axle-breaking sinkhole that needs to be negotiated in first gear. A puente might be a one-lane bridge just after a blind curve, with no guardrails. Be prepared!

varying sizes and depths are an unfortunately frequent occurrence (and a grim national joke).

After major hurricanes or earthquakes, the Interamericana may be closed for weeks, so always be prepared for delays. During the June to November wet months, sudden heavy storms can cause landslides and flooding, which can close roads or render them passable only to 4WD vehicles. This can happen locally at any time.

Some roads have a reputation for being particularly dangerous. The Cerro de la Muerte area on the Interamericana between Cartago and San Isidro de El General (the highest section of the Interamericana) suffers from frequent landslides and dense fog at any time of day or night. The busy San José-to-Puntarenas road is steep, narrow, and tortuously winding, but local drivers familiar with the road drive it very fast. The section between San Ramón and Esparza is especially notorious: There is one area that suffers from permanent earth subsidence, and the road sometimes goes over a chassis-breaking drop – be careful. The road from San José to Guápiles goes through Parque Nacional Braulio Carrillo and is subject to landslides and heavy fog, especially later in the day. Similarly, the stretch of the Interamericana from Palmar Norte to Buenos Aires is subject to frequent rockfalls and landslides. The Pacific coastal highways, especially between Quepos and Jacó, are deceivingly well paved and maintained in places, changing suddenly to slick, bumpy, and unguarded one-way bridges with little warning. Don't drive this road too fast, especially at night (which is generally not recommended anyway).

If you are involved in an accident, you should not move the car until the police get there. Injured people should not be taken from the scene until the Red Cross ambulance arrives. Try to make a note or sketch of what happened, and don't make statements except to authorized people.

Because of difficult driving conditions, there are speed limits of 100km/h or less on all primary roads and 60km/h or less on secondary roads. Traffic police use radar, and speed limits are enforced with speeding tickets. You can also get a traffic ticket for not wearing a seat belt. All rental cars have seat belts. It is illegal to enter an intersection unless you can also leave it, and it is illegal to make a right turn on a red light unless a sign indicates that a turn is permitted. At unmarked intersections, yield to the car on your right. Driving in Costa Rica is on the right, and passing is allowed only on the left.

If you are given a ticket, you have to pay the fine at a bank; instructions are given on the ticket. If you are driving a rental car, the rental company may be able to arrange your payment for you – the amount of the fine should be on the ticket. A 30% tax is added to the fine; it goes to a children's charity.

Fines can be expensive: up to US$150 for driving 40km/h over the speed limit, US$70 for running a red light, and US$15 for not wearing a seat belt. Police have no right to ask for money under any circumstances. Police have no right to confiscate a car unless the driver cannot produce a license and ownership papers, the car lacks license plates, or the driver is drunk or has

## Police Corruption

The problem of police corruption has diminished dramatically in recent years. Government officials now have a low tolerance for it, instead of turning a blind eye as they used to. Still, isolated incidents do occur.

In 1999, while I was driving to the Nicaraguan border on the Interamericana, a uniformed police officer pulled me over for speeding. Following some suggestive and heartfelt banter about his desire to help me out, the officer indicated that rather than pay an official ticket of US$80, I could drop US$20 through the open window of his car onto the backseat.

After a moment or two of temptation (during which I wondered whether he might take my US$20 and still give me the ticket), I ruefully expressed my preference for the official channels. The official ticket turned out to be only US$25, and we parted ways amicably.

Always remember that an officer does not have the right to take money directly. Tickets are often turned in and paid at a bank. I was able to pay this speeding ticket through the rental company when dropping off the car – simple, cheap, and legal.

**– John Thompson**

been involved in an accident causing serious injury.

If you are driving and see oncoming cars with headlights flashing at you, it often means that there is some kind of road problem or a radar speed-trap ahead. Slow down immediately. Also watch for a branch on the side of the road: This often means that a vehicle is broken down just ahead. Police cars are blue with white doors and have a small red light on the roof – they can be small sedans or pickups. White or red police motorcycles are also in use.

Many foreign drivers complain that the roads are inadequately signed. This is often true, though more signs have been placed in the last few years. Still, you should get a decent road map and ask locals when you are not sure of directions. They are nearly always able and willing to give assistance.

## Rental

There are plenty of car rental agencies in San José but few in other cities. Several agencies also have offices at the Juan Santamaría International Airport.

Car rental is popular because a car can get you places you can't get to by public transport. It also gives you the freedom to travel where you want and to stop wherever you like. Because buses to remote areas are not very frequent, you can cover more ground in a shorter time with a car.

Realize that car rental is not very cheap. Discounts are available if you rent by the week, but expect to pay close to US$300 per week for a subcompact car in the high season. You may be able to get a small discount by renting through your hotel, or by searching the Internet and booking in advance if you know your dates. Almost all cars now come with air-conditioning and a cassette/radio, so bring a few of your favorite tapes. The cost includes (mandatory) insurance and unlimited mileage (or *kilometraje*, as they call it).

The insurance accounts for at least US$12 per day of your cost (up to US$20 for larger vehicles); rental companies won't let you rent a car without it because they say your policy at home will not be valid in Costa Rica in case of an accident or theft of the car. Even if you use a gold or platinum credit card, which will often provide free insurance in many countries, you'll find that

Costa Rican car rental companies won't accept their insurance coverage (though there is a discount if you use a gold card). Perhaps this is because of the terrible condition of many Costa Rican highways – cars often come back damaged from hitting a pothole at a fast speed. Even with insurance, there is a high deductible (as much as US$1500 in some cases), but you can pay an extra fee (US$8 to US$10 per day) to waive this. And even with the extra fee, you are still held accountable for damage if you are deemed to have been negligent, so don't drive off a bridge!

If you want more than a subcompact car, expect to pay about US$400 per week for a medium-size car or sports Jeep, and about US$500 to US$700 for a van or larger 4WD vehicle. All rates include free kilometers and insurance. (These are in-country high-season rates.)

For travel during the rainy season, many rental agencies insist you rent a 4WD vehicle if you are going to places where you need to drive on dirt roads – the Península de Nicoya, for example. The rainy season is also the low season, and discounted rates may apply, but it's still not cheap.

Many of the major car rental companies, such as Avis, Budget, Dollar, Hertz, and National, have offices worldwide, so you can rent a car in advance from home. Normally, you need to book a car at least 14 days in advance, and the rate when booked at home is often a little cheaper than it is in San José, though you should check that no extra fees will be charged after you arrive. You can also book through the Internet.

To hire a car you need a valid driver's license, a major credit card, and your passport. If you don't have a major credit card, some companies may allow you to make a cash deposit of about US$1000. Your driver's license from home is acceptable for up to three months if you are a tourist; you don't need an international driving permit.

The minimum age for car rental is 21 years, though most companies prefer to rent to drivers over 25. One reader wrote in to report that the maximum age for car rental in Costa Rica is 70. While this has not been confirmed, senior travelers should plan ahead.

Dozens of car rental companies are listed in the San José yellow pages – most are

## Driving Accidents

If you are involved in an accident while driving, call the Red Cross to help injured parties. Also call the Instituto Nacional de Seguros (National Insurance Institute; ☎ 800-835-3467) as soon as possible. Then call the transit police or Guardia Civil to make a report for insurance purposes. Note that the following numbers were correct at the time of this writing but are liable to change.

| province | all emergencies | Red Cross | Transit Police | Guardia Civil |
|---|---|---|---|---|
| San José | 911 | 128 | 222-9330 | 911 |
| Alajuela | 911 | 441-3939 | 911 | 441-6346 |
| Cartago | 911 | 551-0421 | 911 | 551-0455 |
| Heredia | 911 | 237-1115 | 911 | 237-0011 |
| Guanacaste | 911 | 666-0994 | 911 | 666-5193 (La Cruz 666-3755) |
| Limón | 911 | 758-0125 | 911 | 758-0365 |
| Puntarenas | 911 | 661-0184 | 911 | 661-0640 |

Note that ☎ 911 is now used nationwide for all emergencies (police, fire, ambulance, road accidents), but the local numbers given above may sometimes get a faster response in remote areas.

fairly reputable. However, a few readers have reported that their rental company added surcharges for damage after the vehicle was turned in, or provided shoddy vehicles in the first place, or otherwise was unreliable. One solution is to rent a vehicle (if you can) through a reputable hotel or travel agent in San José. They pass a fair volume of travelers on to the car rental companies, and in the case of a problem, you are more likely to receive the benefit of the doubt if you go through a hotel or travel agent.

When you rent a car, carefully inspect it for minor dents and scratches, missing radio antennae or hubcaps, and anything else that makes the car look less than brand new. (Minor nicks are acceptable.) These damages must be noted on your rental agreement; otherwise, you may be charged for them when you return the car. The insurance won't cover it, because of the deductible. This can be a problem in Costa Rica, because rental vehicles typically see well over 50,000km of driving before they are sold, unlike, say, in the USA, where rental vehicles are renewed almost every year.

If your car breaks down, call the rental company. Don't attempt to get the car fixed yourself, because most companies won't reimburse you for your expenses without prior authorization from them.

Thieves can recognize rental cars, and there have been many thefts from them. You should never leave valuables in sight when you are away from the car, and you should remove luggage from the trunk when checking into a hotel overnight. Many hotels will provide parking areas for cars. It is better to park the car in a guarded parking lot than on the street. This cannot be overemphasized – don't leave valuables in the car.

Small mopeds and dirt bikes can be rented in a few places along the coast but aren't much cheaper than compact cars. In San José, expensive large bikes (including Harleys) are available.

The price of gas (petrol) is about US50¢ per liter of regular (about US$1.90 per US gallon or US$2.30 for an imperial gallon), although it has varied a bit. Most stations sell regular and diesel; unleaded and super are available in larger towns. Most rental cars take regular. The price of gas is the same at all stations nationwide, so gas up wherever you want.

## TAXI

It may come as a surprise to most people that taxis are considered a form of public transport outside urban areas. Taxis can be hired by the hour, the half day, or the day. Meters are not used on long trips, so arrange the fare with the driver beforehand.

There are various occasions when you may want to consider using a taxi. Visiting some of the national parks by public transport is not possible. Your alternatives are to take a tour, rent a car, hitch a ride, walk, cycle, or catch a taxi.

The roundtrip journey from San José to Volcán Poás, for example, is about 110km. A half-day excursion allowing a couple of hours at the volcano and photo stops along the way costs around US$50 to US$70, depending on the taxi driver and your bargaining ability. That's not a bad deal, and it's cheaper than a tour if you share your cab with other travelers. Of course, if you get an English-speaking cab driver through an agency, you'll probably pay more.

When you are out in the country, you may need to take a taxi to a remote destination on a bad road. During the rainy season, 4WD may be required. Many taxis are 4WD Jeeps and can get you just about anywhere.

## BICYCLE

All the warnings under the Road Rules section, above, apply here – but even more so. There are no bike lanes and traffic can be hazardous on the narrow, steep, winding roads. Cycling is a possibility, however, and long-distance cyclists report that locals tend to be very friendly toward them. It is possible to cycle all the way from the USA, or you can fly your bicycle down as luggage. Check with airlines for regulations – on some a bicycle may be carried free of charge if it is properly packed and doesn't exceed luggage size and weight requirements (see Mountain Biking in the Facts for the Visitor chapter).

A few companies rent bikes and/or arrange escorted tours; some are listed in the Organized Tours section, later; some in the Getting There & Away chapter; and others in the San José chapter.

## HITCHHIKING

Hitchhiking is never entirely safe in any country, and Lonely Planet doesn't recommend it. Travelers who hitchhike should understand that they are taking a small but potentially serious risk. People who do hitchhike will be safer if they travel in pairs and let someone know where they are planning to go.

On the main roads, the frequency of inexpensive buses makes hitchhiking unusual, except during the holiday periods when buses may be full. If you do get a ride, offer to pay for it when you arrive: '¿Cuánto le

debo?' ('How much do I owe you?') is the standard way of doing this. Often, your offer will be waved aside; sometimes you'll be asked to help with gas costs. If you're driving, picking up hitchhikers in the countryside is normally no problem and often gets you into some interesting conversations.

Tico hitchhikers are more often seen on minor rural roads. If you hitch, imitate the locals. They don't simply stand there with their thumbs out. Vehicles may pass only a few times per hour and ticos try to wave them down in a friendly fashion, then chat with the driver about where they're going and how lousy the bus service is. (This gives you a chance to size up the driver and car occupants; if you don't feel comfortable, don't take the ride.)

## BOAT

There are various passenger and car ferries in operation. Three cheap ferries operate out of Puntarenas across the Golfo de Nicoya. One is a car ferry that leaves several times a day for Playa Naranjo (a 1½-hour trip). The others are a car ferry and a small passenger-only ferry that crosses to Paquera two or three times a day, taking about 1½ hours. Buses meet the ferries at Paquera to transport you onward into the Península de Nicoya. Complete details are given in the appropriate town sections in this book.

There is also a car ferry operating across the mouth of the Río Tempisque, which cuts two or three hours off the road trip to the Península de Nicoya – if you can time the ferry crossing just right. The ferry runs every hour from 5am to 8pm; see the Northwestern Costa Rica chapter for details. Note that a bridge over the Rió Tempisque is under construction and will replace the ferry. It is slated to open by 2003; check locally for details.

A daily passenger ferry links Golfito with Puerto Jiménez on the Península de Osa; the trip takes about 1½ hours. This ferry is subject to occasional cancellation. Puerto Jiménez is the nearest town of any size to Parque Nacional Corcovado.

A small ferry carrying three vehicles crosses the Río Coto Colorado on demand on the Golfito–Playa Zancudo road. It runs during daylight hours and may stop at the lowest tides.

Motorized dugout canoes ply the Río Sarapiquí once a day on a scheduled basis and more frequently on demand. See Puerto Viejo de Sarapiquí in the Northern Lowlands chapter for more details. Daily motorboats also go to Tortuguero (see the Tortuguero Area section in the Caribbean Lowlands chapter).

Other boat trips can be made, but these are tours rather than rides on scheduled ferries. These include canal boats up the inland waterway from Moín (near Puerto Limón) to Parque Nacional Tortuguero and Refugio Nacional de Fauna Silvestre Barra del Colorado.

Boats can be hired at Puerto Viejo de Sarapiquí down the Río Sarapiquí to the Río San Juan, the south bank of which forms much of the Costa Rica–Nicaragua border. It's possible to travel along the border down the Río San Juan as far as its mouth, and then down into the Refugio Nacional de Fauna Silvestre Barra del Colorado. This is not a regularly scheduled trip, but it can be arranged – see the sections on Puerto Viejo de Sarapiquí in the Northern Lowlands chapter or Barra del Colorado in the Caribbean Lowlands chapter for further information.

People staying in the Bahía Drake area (see the Península de Osa & Golfo Dulce chapter) often arrive or leave via an exciting boat trip on the Río Sierpe.

For adventurous types, river running or floats down Ríos Pacuare, Reventazón, Corobicí, Chirripó, and Sarapiquí for one or more days is one option – see Organized Tours, later in this chapter, for further information. Fishing trips, either on Laguna de Arenal or offshore, are another option.

One-day sailing trips in the Golfo de Nicoya can be booked on various boats, the best known of which is the yacht *Calypso* (see Organized Tours); others can be arranged with travel agents in San José.

## LOCAL TRANSPORTATION
### Bus
Local buses serve urban and suburban areas, but services and routes can be difficult to figure out. Many towns are small enough that getting around on foot is easy. Some local bus details are provided in the Getting There & Away sections for major towns in this book.

Local people are usually very friendly, and this includes bus drivers, who will often

be able to tell you where to wait for a particular bus.

### Taxi
In San José, taxis have meters, called *marías*, but these might not be used, particularly for foreigners who can't speak Spanish. (It is illegal not to use the meter.) Outside San José, taxis don't have meters and so fares are agreed upon in advance; bargaining is acceptable. In rural areas, 4WD Jeeps are used as taxis.

Within San José, a short ride should cost about US$1. A ride across town will cost around US$2, and it's about US$4 to suburbs. Rates are comparable in other parts of the country. Taxi drivers are not normally tipped. Taxi cabs are red and have a small sticker in the windshield identifying them as a 'TAXI.'

## ORGANIZED TOURS
Over 200 tour operators are recognized by the Costa Rican Tourist Board, with the majority in San José.

Many companies specialize in nature tours, with visits to the national parks and wilderness lodges. They can provide entire guided itineraries (with English-speaking guides) and private transport to any part of the country, especially the nature destinations. Many of these nature-tour companies also specialize in adventure tourism, such as river running or mountain biking. Almost all agencies also provide services such as day trips around the Central Valley, San José city tours, hotel reservations, and airport transfers.

Prices vary depending on the services you require. Two people wishing to travel with a private English-speaking guide and a private vehicle will obviously pay a lot more than two people who are prepared to join a group and/or can understand a Spanish-speaking guide. Note that although these companies are in Costa Rica, most will happily take advance reservations from abroad. For detailed information on operators that arrange tours of Costa Rica from abroad, see the Organized Tours section in the Getting There & Away chapter.

For an overview of things to do on tours, see the Activities section in the Facts for the Visitor chapter. For more on fishing trips, see the coastal chapters.

Most companies in Costa Rica don't specialize in just one type of tour and can arrange whatever kind or combination of tours you'd like. Therefore the following subdivisions are for rough guidance only.

## Natural History

The oldest (since 1978) and biggest nature/adventure-tour company is *Costa Rica Expeditions* (☎ 257-0766, 222-0333, fax 257-1665, e *costarica@expeditions.co.cr*, W *www.costaricaexpeditions.com, Calle Central, Avenida 3)*. It pioneered adventure and nature tourism in Costa Rica and has received awards for both its work and its environmental awareness, including honorable mentions in the *Condé Nast Traveler* Ecotourism Awards in 1995 and 1996 and the *Travel and Leisure* Critics' Choice Award in 1999. The top guides are well-qualified naturalists or ornithologists – all the staff is very professional and the company is highly recommended. It specializes in natural history tours, particularly to Parque Nacional Tortuguero and Reserva Biológica Monteverde (where it has its own luxurious lodges) and Parque Nacional Corcovado (where it has a tent camp and a rainforest canopy platform). Some tours are designed for families. It also does adventure tours including river rafting (it is the oldest rafting company in Costa Rica) and other multisport trips (mountain-biking, rafting, hydrobiking, kayaking). The standard of services is excellent (its motto is 'legendary service…unforgettable memories'), and the trips are priced accordingly. The mailing address is Dept 235, PO Box 025216, Miami, FL 33102-5216, USA.

Another highly recommended nature-tour company is *Horizontes* (☎ 222-2022, fax 255-4513, e *horizont@racsa.co.cr, info@horizontes.com*, W *www.horizontes.com, Calle 28, Avenidas 1 & 3)*. It has been arranging nature and adventure tours for 18 years and has built up an excellent reputation. Some of the tours are recommended for families with children over five. Wheelchair-accessible itineraries can also be suggested. Horizontes is Costa Rica Expeditions' biggest competitor, but it speaks well for both companies that they regard themselves as colleagues in running environmentally and socially responsible operations.

*Costa Rica Sun Tours* (☎ 296-7757, fax 296-4307, e *info@crsuntours.com*, W *www.crsuntours.com)*. Run by the Aspinall family, ticos who have a long history in the country's tourism industry, this company does all the normal nature tours and fishing trips. It also operates the Arenal Observatory Lodge at Volcán Arenal, where fishing trips on large Laguna de Arenal can also be undertaken, and is connected with Tiskita Jungle Lodge, which is on a private reserve on the far southern Pacific coast. The company is recommended. As with the above two companies, they can arrange an independent itinerary to suit your own group, be it two or 22 people.

## Activities

Several companies specialize in river rafting (but will arrange other tours as well). Especially recommended is *Ríos Tropicales* (☎ 233-6455, fax 255-4354, W *www.riostro.com, Calle 38, Paseo Colón)*, which has river-rafting and kayaking trips and sea-kayaking expeditions. It has a lodge on the Río Pacuare for overnight trips. Owned and operated by Costa Rican kayaking champions, this is an excellent organization that does much to improve the sport and protect the rivers in Costa Rica.

*Aventuras Naturales* (☎ 225-3939, 224-0303, 800-514-0411 in the USA, fax 253-6934, e *avenat@racsa.co.cr*, W *www.toenjoynature.com, Avenida Central, Calles 33 & 35)* also has hiking and cycling tours. You can combine tours and stay overnight at its Río Pacuare Lodge.

*Coast to Coast Adventures* (☎ 296-7757, fax 225-6055, e *info@ctocadventures.com*, W *www.ctocadventures.com)* goes coast to coast in 14 days using bikes, rafts, or kayaks, and on foot. They also do shorter trips and have a kayaking school.

*Ocarina Expeditions* (☎ 221-5322, fax 221-5031, e *ocarina@racsa.co.cr*, W *www.ocarinaexpeditions.com)* specializes in hiking expeditions, including ascents of Chirripó, Rincón de la Vieja, and Tenorio, and jungle hiking. They also arrange rafting and horseback tours.

*Safaris Corobicí* (☎/fax 669-6091, e *safaris@racsa.co.cr*, W *www.nicoya.com)* specializes in Río Corobicí float trips.

*Sarapiquí Aguas Bravas* (☎ 292-2072, fax 229-4837, e *info@aguas-bravas.co.cr*,

W *www.aguas-bravas.co.cr)* rafts the Río Sarapiquí and offers biking trips.

Also check out Costa Rica Expeditions (see Natural History, earlier).

## General Tourism

*Ecole Travel* (☎ 223-2240, fax 223-4128, ᴇ *info@ecoletravel.com,* W *www.travel costarica.net, Calle 7, Avenidas Central & 1)* specializes in budget travel, especially to Tortuguero and Corcovado, but also to other destinations. Budget tours mean you might stay in rock-bottom-priced hotels and meals might not be included, but they get you there. Some tours are more costly but include meals or better lodging. They also do more upscale tours.

*OTEC Viajes* (☎ 257-0166, fax 257-7671, ᴇ *otec@gotec.com,* W *www.gotec.com, 275m north of the Teatro Nacional, San José)* is for students, issues International Student Cards, and arranges student discounts on tours. They also do general tours for other age groups.

*Green Tropical Tours* (☎ 229-4192, ☎/fax 292-5003, 380-1536 cellular, ᴇ *information@ greentropical.com,* W *www.greentropical .com)* does trips all over the country, specializing in trips in the central and northern parts of Costa Rica, including to Monumento Nacional Guayabo, which not many companies visit. It also offers bilingual driver/guides (one person who drives and guides) with vans for nine, 15, or 22 passengers (see W www.coachcostarica.com). Owner Juan Carlos Ramos does a great job and sometimes accompanies groups himself. Recommended by several readers.

*Expediciones Tropicales* (☎ 257-4171, 257-4133, fax 257-4124, ᴇ *sales@expedicion estropicales.com, expetrop@racsa.co.cr,* W *www.costaricainfo.com, Calle 3 bis, Avenidas 11 & 13)* has a vast array of day tours and makes reservations for hotels, flights, car rentals, and Spanish schools.

Readers have recommended *Cosmos Tours* (☎ 234-0607, fax 253-4707, ᴇ *cosmos@ racsa.co.cr, 600m west of Taco Bell, San Pedro)*, good for airline reservations and hotel and tour bookings. Other agencies that readers have recommended for general travel and tours include *Central American Tours* (☎ 255-4111, fax 255-4216), with an office in the Cariari Hotel (☎ 239-0281) and a friendly staff.

## Boat Cruises

One of the most famous boat trips is an all-day yacht cruise through the Golfo de Nicoya to Isla Tortuga – excellent food and good swimming opportunities. The longest-running of these cruises is by *Calypso Tours* (☎ 256-2727, fax 256-6767, ᴇ *info@calypso tours.com,* W *www.calypsotours.com, Edificio Las Arcadas, Avenida 2, Calles 1 & 3)*. It uses a luxurious and fast catamaran, the *Manta Ray,* and does other cruises; see the Islands Near Bahía Gigante section in the Península de Nicoya chapter for more details.

There are cruises along the Caribbean canals to Tortuguero, too. These usually involve one or two nights at lodges in either Parque Nacional Tortuguero or Barra del Colorado, and can be combined with bus or airplane returns, wildlife watching, and fishing trips, depending on your time and budget. These companies are listed under the Tortuguero Area section in the Caribbean Lowlands chapter.

## Other Tours

There are many fishing lodges and boats on both coasts.

*Costa Rica Travel Advisors* (☎ 223-4331, fax 221-0096, ᴇ *fishing@racsa.co.cr, Avenida 1, Calle 9, San José)*, with an office in the lobby of the Hotel del Rey, can advise you about these and arrange a customized itinerary to fit your needs. Also see lodges and companies listed in Barra del Colorado (Caribbean Lowlands chapter) and Quepos (Central Pacific Coast chapter).

*Canopy Tour* (☎/fax 257-5149, 256-7626, ᴇ *canopy@canopytour.com,* W *www.canopy tour.com)* has pioneered adventurous rainforest canopy tours that involve a rope ascent or a rope traverse to a platform built in a tall tree, followed by traverses to other platforms. This is not recommended for someone who is afraid of heights! The first platform/rope systems were constructed near Monteverde and at Iguana Park near Orotina. Others were put up at Volcán Rincón de la Vieja, Drake Bay, near Fortuna, and near Ciudad Quesada. The Canadian founders' objective is to provide an adventurous ecological experience while helping to preserve the rainforest through direct financial support. There are many other canopy tours – these are the original ones with a higher safety standard than most.

***Costa Rica Rainforest Outward Bound*** (☎/fax 777-1222, 777-0052, 800-676-2018 in the USA, 🌐 www.crrobs.org) has an 85-day adventure course that visits Costa Rica and surrounding countries, with academic credit available. The course fees are from US$1695 to US$7900 for 10- to 85-day

multi-activity courses that include kayaking, surfing, and Spanish language. Some are suitable for 14-year-olds and others are for older students.

Other agencies that serve just a local area are mentioned in the appropriate sections of the regional chapters.

# San José

Compared to other Central American capitals, San José is more cosmopolitan, even North Americanized. There are department stores and shopping malls, fast-food chain restaurants, and blue jeans.

It takes a day or two to start getting the real *tico* feeling of the city. Perhaps the first sign of being in Costa Rica is the friendli-

## Highlights

- Visiting the world's finest collection of pre-Columbian jade at the Museo de Jade
- Enjoying a cultural event from a Victorian-style box in the Teatro Nacional
- Pushing past handcrafted saddles, piles of coffee beans, and sides of beef in the bustling Mercado Central
- Marveling at the almost priceless collection in the Museo de Oro Precolombino
- Savoring a cup of Costa Rican coffee in one of the capital's cafés

OTHER MAPS
Map 1 San José & Environs
page 97

Map 5 Escazú
pages 104–105 ●

Map 2 San José
pages 98–99
Map 3 Central San José
pages 100–101
Map 4 Coca-Cola Bus
Terminal Area
page 102

ness of the people. Asking someone the way will often result in a smile and a genuine attempt to help you out – a refreshing change from many other capital cities.

Although the city was founded in 1737, little remains from the colonial era. Indeed, until the Teatro Nacional was built in the 1890s, San José was a small, largely forgotten city. Today, the capital boasts several excellent museums, good restaurants, and a fine climate – the main attractions for visitors. But most visitors have a quick look at the museums, then go on to the national parks, rainforests, and beaches – tasty food and an agreeable climate can be found elsewhere in the country. Because Costa Rica's public transport and road system radiates from San José, the capital is often used as a base from which to visit the country's many attractions.

Although Costa Rica is known for trying to preserve the environment with one of the best national park systems in Latin America, the environmental effort is less evident in urban areas. In the late '90s, the phasing out of leaded fuel and the introduction of a vehicle emissions program (Ecomarchamo) were followed by a slight decrease in lead and carbon monoxide levels. However, air pollution, mainly from street traffic, remains a definite problem in the city. Central pedestrian areas and large parks make a welcome break from vehicle traffic.

The population of the city itself is about a third of a million, but the surrounding suburbs boost the number to about a million. The population of the whole province is about 1.35 million, or 35% of the country. Inhabitants of San José are sometimes referred to as *josefinos*.

## ORIENTATION

The city stands at an elevation of 1150m and is set in a wide and fertile valley known throughout Costa Rica as the Valle Central (Central Valley).

The city center, where many visitors spend much of their time, is arranged in a grid. All the streets are numbered in a logical fashion, and it is important to learn the system because all street directions

## MAP 1  SAN JOSÉ & ENVIRONS

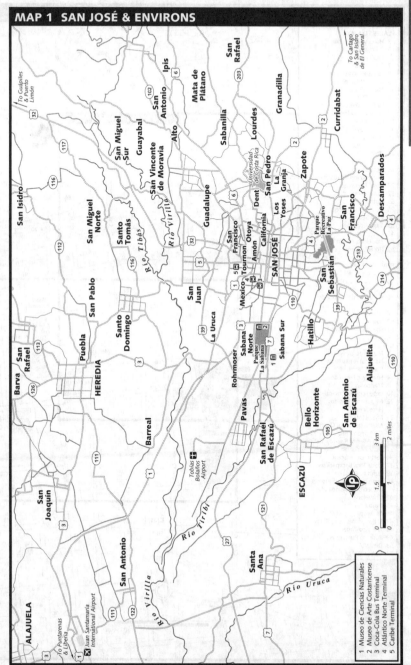

1 Museo de Ciencias Naturales
2 Museo de Arte Costaricense
3 Coca-Cola Bus Terminal
4 Atlántico Norte Terminal
5 Caribe Terminal

SAN JOSÉ

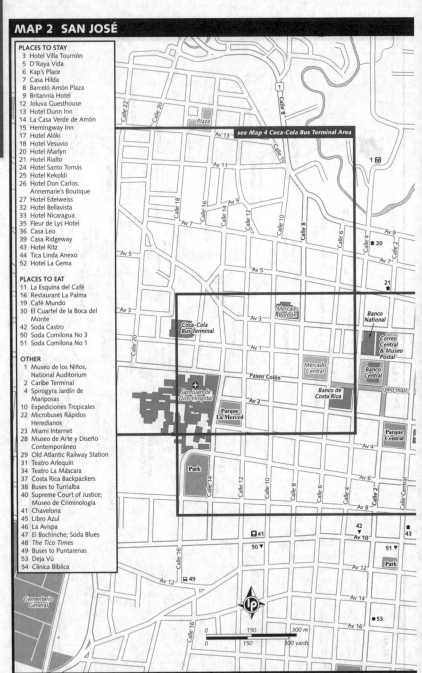

## MAP 2 SAN JOSÉ

**PLACES TO STAY**
3  Hotel Villa Tournón
5  D'Raya Vida
6  Kap's Place
7  Casa Hilda
8  Barceló Amón Plaza
9  Britannia Hotel
12  Joluva Guesthouse
13  Hotel Dunn Inn
14  La Casa Verde de Amón
15  Hemingway Inn
17  Hotel Alóki
18  Hotel Vesuvio
20  Hotel Marlyn
21  Hotel Rialto
24  Hotel Santo Tomás
25  Hotel Kekoldi
26  Hotel Don Carlos;
    Annemarie's Boutique
27  Hotel Edelweiss
32  Hotel Bellavista
33  Hotel Nicaragua
35  Fleur de Lys Hotel
36  Casa Leo
39  Casa Ridgeway
43  Hotel Ritz
44  Tica Linda Anexo
52  Hotel La Gema

**PLACES TO EAT**
11  La Esquina del Café
16  Restaurant La Palma
19  Café Mundo
30  El Cuartel de la Boca del
    Monte
42  Soda Castro
50  Soda Comilona No 3
51  Soda Comilona No 1

**OTHER**
1  Museo de los Niños,
   National Auditorium
2  Caribe Terminal
4  Spirogyra Jardín de
   Mariposas
10  Expediciones Tropicales
22  Microbuses Rápidos
    Heredianos
23  Miami Internet
28  Museo de Arte y Diseño
    Contemporáneo
29  Old Atlantic Railway Station
31  Teatro Arlequin
34  Teatro La Máscara
37  Costa Rica Backpackers
40  Supreme Court of Justice;
    Museo de Criminología
41  Chavelona
45  Libro Azul
46  La Avispa
47  El Bochinche; Soda Blues
48  *The Tico Times*
49  Buses to Puntarenas
53  Deja Vú
54  Clínica Bíblica

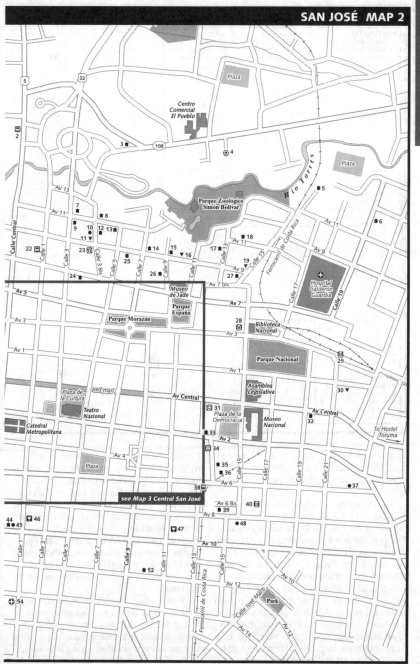

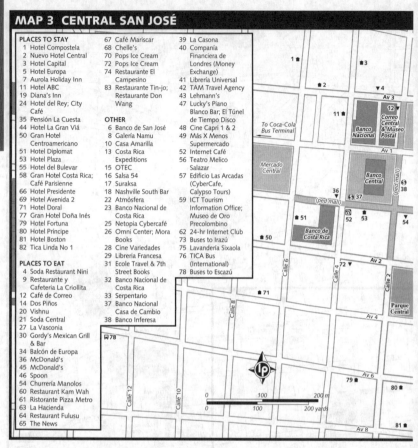

## MAP 3  CENTRAL SAN JOSÉ

**PLACES TO STAY**
1 Hotel Compostela
2 Nuevo Hotel Central
3 Hotel Capital
5 Hotel Europa
7 Aurola Holiday Inn
11 Hotel ABC
19 Diana's Inn
24 Hotel del Rey; City
   Café
35 Pensión La Cuesta
44 Hotel La Gran Viá
50 Gran Hotel
   Centroamericano
51 Hotel Diplomat
53 Hotel Plaza
55 Hotel del Bulevar
58 Gran Hotel Costa Rica;
   Café Parisienne
66 Hotel Presidente
69 Hotel Avenida 2
71 Hotel Doral
77 Gran Hotel Doña Inés
79 Hotel Fortuna
80 Hotel Príncipe
81 Hotel Boston
82 Tica Linda No 1

**PLACES TO EAT**
4 Soda Restaurant Nini
9 Restaurante y
   Cafetería La Criollita
12 Café de Correo
14 Dos Piños
20 Vishnu
21 Soda Central
27 La Vasconia
30 Gordy's Mexican Grill
   & Bar
34 Balcón de Europa
36 McDonald's
45 McDonald's
46 Spoon
54 Churrería Manolos
60 Restaurant Kam Wah
61 Ristorante Pizza Metro
63 La Hacienda
64 Restaurant Fulusu
65 The News

67 Café Mariscar
68 Chelle's
70 Pops Ice Cream
72 Pops Ice Cream
74 Restaurante El
   Campesino
83 Restaurante Tin-jo;
   Restaurante Don
   Wang

**OTHER**
6 Banco de San José
8 Galería Namu
10 Casa Amarilla
13 Costa Rica
   Expeditions
15 OTEC
16 Salsa 54
17 Suraksa
18 Nashville South Bar
22 Atmósfera
23 Banco Nacional de
   Costa Rica
25 Netopia Cybercafé
26 Omni Center; Mora
   Books
28 Cine Variedades
29 Librería Francesa
31 Ecole Travel & 7th
   Street Books
32 Banco Nacional de
   Costa Rica
33 Serpentario
37 Banco Nacional
   Casa de Cambio
38 Banco Inferesa

39 La Casona
40 Compañía
   Financiera de
   Londres (Money
   Exchange)
41 Librería Universal
42 TAM Travel Agency
43 Lehmann's
47 Lucky's Piano
   Blanco Bar; El Túnel
   de Tiempo Disco
48 Cine Capri 1 & 2
49 Más X Menos
   Supermercado
52 Internet Café
56 Teatro Melico
   Salazar
57 Edificio Las Arcadas
   (CyberCafe,
   Calypso Tours)
59 ICT Tourism
   Information Office;
   Museo de Oro
   Precolombino
62 24-hr Internet Club
73 Buses to Irazú
75 Lavandería Sixaola
76 TICA Bus
   (International)
78 Buses to Escazú

and addresses rely on it (see the boxed text 'Costa Rican Street Addresses'). This system is also applied in many other Costa Rican towns.

The center has several districts, or *barrios* (see Map 1). These are rather loosely defined, but they are well known to josefinos. Perhaps the most interesting to downtown visitors is Barrio Amón, northeast of Avenida 5 and Calle 1, which has the best concentration of historical buildings, most of which tend to be residential or small commercial structures rather than major public edifices. East of Amón is Barrio Otoya, a less trendy version of Amón. East of downtown is the semiresidential barrio of Los Yoses, with an increasing number of first-class restaurants and hotels, followed by San

Pedro, which is a major suburb in its own right and is where the main university is found, with the accompanying university-area ambience. Heading east on Avenida Central from central San José through Los Yoses, the traveler passes a traffic circle with a huge fountain – the Fuente de la Hispanidad and a local landmark. San Pedro begins beyond the fountain, and about 300m east of the fountain along Avenida Central is the San Pedro church, another important landmark.

West of the center is La Sabana, named after the biggest park in San José. Northwest of La Sabana lies Rohrmoser, which has many elegant addresses, including several ambassadors' residences. In the hills several kilometers southeast of La Sabana is the

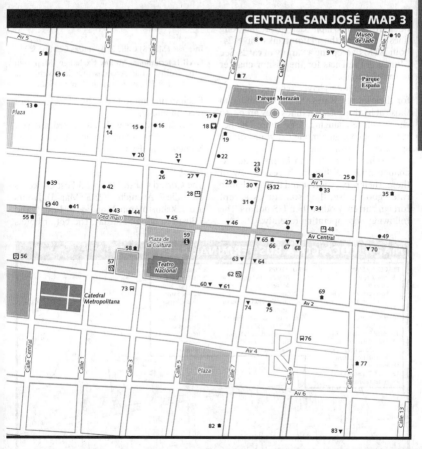

suburb of Escazú, with many B&Bs offering fine views of central San José.

## INFORMATION

The friendliness of the Costa Ricans has already been mentioned – but it really is one of the outstanding features of this country. The local people can often be your best source of information.

### Tourist Offices

The main tourist office of the Instituto Costarricense de Turismo (ICT; ☎ 222-1090, 222-1733 ext 277, fax 223-1090, W www .tourism-costarica.com) is on the Plaza de la Cultura (Map 3) at Calle 5 & Avenida Central, next to the Museo de Oro. It's open 9am to 5pm weekdays, with a flexible 45-minute lunch break. There is also a small ICT office at the airport to greet arriving travelers, which is open for longer hours.

### Money

Any bank will change foreign currency into colones, but US dollars by far are the most accepted currency. The commissions, when charged, should be small – never more than 1% of the transaction; otherwise, go elsewhere. The four state banks are often slow; over 20 private banks tend to give the fastest service. Each has many branches; some are shown on the maps. Most banks in the capital are open 8:30am to 3:30pm weekdays. A few banks are open longer than normal hours or on weekends. One to try is the small kiosk of the Banco Nacional at Avenida Central, Calle 4 (Map 3) which is open 10:30am to 6pm daily (but has long lines). Most of the major banks have 24-hour ATMs, accepting a variety of cards. See Money in the Facts for the Visitor chapter for more details.

The better hotels have exchange windows for their guests. Rates should be similar to those at banks, but sometimes they aren't, so check before changing large sums. The advantage of changing money at your hotel is speed and convenience.

Another alternative to banks is an exchange house, although there are few of these. Their service is fast and their exchange rates good. Also, they sometimes accept foreign currency other than US dollars. The following were operating recently:

**Compañía Financiera de Londres** (Map 3; ☎ 222-8155, fax 221-2003) Calle Central & Avenida Central

**Inferesa** (Map 3) Calle 2, Avenidas Central & 1

**GAB International Money Exchange** (Map 3) in the Edificio Las Arcadas arcade, Avenida 2, Calles 1 & 3; open 8:15am to 4pm weekdays

Exchanging money on the streets is not recommended.

Credit cards are widely accepted, and you can use them to buy colones in banks (see Money in the Facts for the Visitor chapter).

## Post

The Correo Central (Central Post Office) is on Calle 2, Avenidas 1 & 3 (Map 3). Hours are 7:30am to 6pm Monday to Friday and 7:30am to noon Saturday. The better hotels

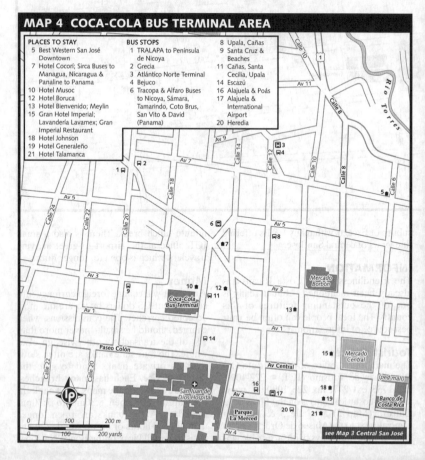

**MAP 4  COCA-COLA BUS TERMINAL AREA**

**PLACES TO STAY**
5  Best Western San José Downtown
7  Hotel Cocorí; Sirca Buses to Managua, Nicaragua & Panaline to Panama
10 Hotel Musoc
12 Hotel Boruca
13 Hotel Bienvenido; Meylin
15 Gran Hotel Imperial; Lavandería Lavamex; Gran Imperial Restaurant
18 Hotel Johnson
19 Hotel Generaleño
21 Hotel Talamanca

**BUS STOPS**
1  TRALAPA to Península de Nicoya
2  Grecia
3  Atlántico Norte Terminal
4  Bejuco
6  Tracopa & Alfaro Buses to Nicoya, Sámara, Tamarindo, Coto Brus, San Vito & David (Panama)
8  Upala, Cañas
9  Santa Cruz & Beaches
11 Cañas, Santa Cecilia, Upala
14 Escazú
16 Alajuela & Poás
17 Alajuela & International Airport
20 Heredia

## Costa Rican Street Addresses

Few addresses in Costa Rica have the street and number system that many visitors are used to. Instead, addresses are traditionally given from nearby street intersections or from local landmarks. The system is described here and uses San José for specific examples, but it is similar in other Costa Rican towns.

The streets running east-west are avenidas, and the streets running north-south are calles. Avenida Central runs east-west through the middle of the city; avenidas north of Avenida Central are odd-numbered, with Avenida 1 running parallel and one block north of Avenida Central, followed by Avenida 3, and so on. The avenidas south of Avenida Central are even-numbered. Similarly, Calle Central runs north-south through the heart of downtown, and calles east of Calle Central are odd-numbered and calles west of Calle Central are even-numbered.

If you ask a passerby for directions, they will probably instruct you to, for example, go seven blocks west and four blocks north ('Siete cuadras al oeste y cuatro cuadras al norte'). Often, 100m is used to mean a city block, so you may be told, 'Setecientos metros al oeste y cuatrocientos metros al norte.' This does not literally mean 700m west and 400m north; it refers to city blocks. 'Cincuenta metros' (50m) means half a block. Perhaps one reason for this method of giving directions is the lack of street signs, especially away from downtown.

Street addresses in San José are rarely given by the building number (although some numbers do exist). Instead, the nearest street intersection is given. Thus, the address of the Museo Nacional is Calle 17, Avenidas Central & 2. This means it's on Calle 17 between Avenida Central & Avenida 2 ('y' means 'and' in Spanish). This is often abbreviated in telephone directories or other literature to C17, A Ctl/2, or occasionally C17, A 0/2, with 0 replacing the Central. If an address is on or near a corner, just the street intersection is given.

Note that San José's Avenida Central becomes Paseo Colón west of Calle 14. The building on the north side of Paseo Colón, Calles 38 & 40, is known as 'Centro Colón' and is a local landmark.

Many ticos use local landmarks to give directions, or even addresses in smaller towns. Thus, an address may be 200m south and 150m east of a church, a radio station, a restaurant, or even a pulpería (corner grocery store). Sometimes, the landmark may no longer exist, but because it has been used for so long, its position is known by all the locals.

A good example is La Coca-Cola, which is a bus terminal in San José where a Coca-Cola bottling plant used to be for many years. Everyone knows this, except for the first-time visitor! This can get confusing, but persevere; the friendly ticos will usually help you out. Note that taxi drivers especially like to know the landmark address. Drivers will sometimes say they don't understand where you want to go until you explain your destination in terms of landmarks. It pays to use them – cab drivers are unlikely to overcharge you if you look like you know where you're going.

Street signs in central San José are plentiful, but there is a dearth of them away from the center and in many towns. Although the city maps in this book show the official names of the streets, beware of the fact that very few streets have their names posted at every corner. Many locals don't know street addresses and will be much more likely to use local landmarks. Many hotels have business cards with landmark addresses rather than street addresses.

To have mail delivered, many places have a post office box (apartado), so if you see an apartado or 'apdo' address, don't look for it on the map.

have mailboxes and sell stamps. Most people use the post office to mail their letters. (Most ticos also use the post office to receive their mail at a PO box, or apartado, because of the lack of precise street addresses.)

You can receive mail addressed to you c/o Lista de Correos, Correo Central, San José, Costa Rica. They are extremely strict about whom they give mail to. You must produce identification (usually your passport) before they will even look for your mail. They will not give mail to friends or family members; you must get it in person. There is a US15¢ fee per piece of mail received. Mail is held for a month before being returned to sender.

# MAP 5 ESCAZÚ

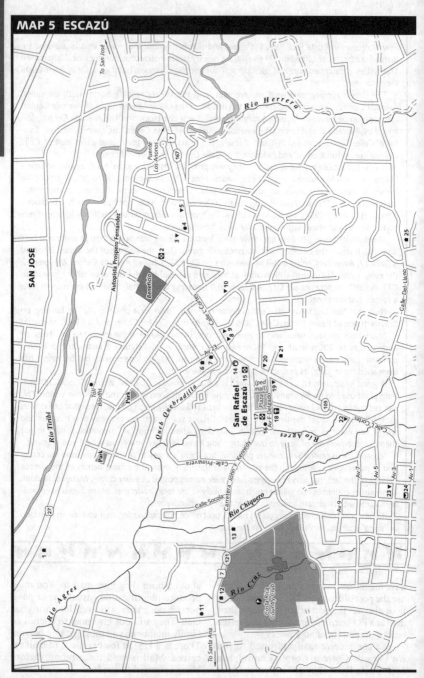

# ESCAZÚ  MAP 5

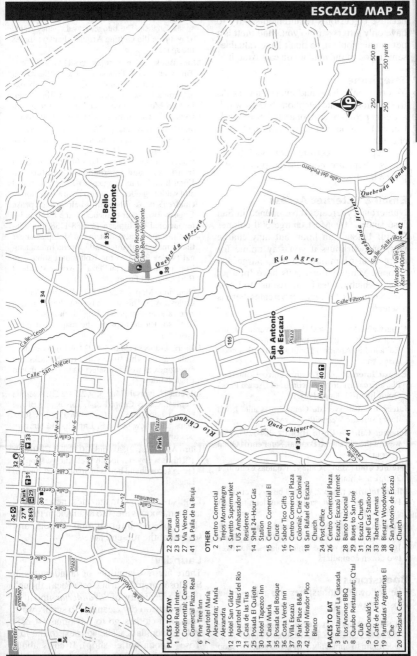

500 m
500 yards
250
250
0
0

**PLACES TO STAY**
1  Hotel Real Inter-
   Continental; Centro
   Comercial Plaza Real
6  Pine Tree Inn
7  Apartotel María
   Alexandra; María
   Alexandra
12 Hotel San Gildar
13 Apartotel Villas del Rio
21 Casa de las Tías
25 Posada El Quijote
30 Hotel Tapezco Inn
34 Casa María
35 Posada del Bosque
36 Costa Verde Inn
37 Villa Escazú
39 Park Place B&B
42 Hotel Mirador Pico
   Blanco

**PLACES TO EAT**
3  Restaurant La Cascada
5  Los Anonos BBQ
8  Quiubo Restaurant; Q'tal
   Club
9  McDonald's
10 Café de Artistes
19 Parrilladas Argentinas El
   Che
20 Hostaria Cerutti

22 Samurai
23 La Casona
27 Via Veneto
41 La Paila de la Bruja

**OTHER**
2  Centro Comercial
   Trejos Montealegre
4  Saretto Supermarket
11 US Ambassador's
   Residence
14 Shell 24-Hour Gas
   Station
15 Centro Comercial El
   Cruce
16 Sabor Tico Gifts
17 Centro Comercial Plaza
   Colonial; Cine Colonial
18 San Rafael de Escazú
   Church
24 Post Office
26 Centro Comercial Plaza
   Escazú; Escazú Internet
28 Banco Nacional
29 Buses to San José
31 Escazú Church
32 Shell Gas Station
33 Taberna Arenas
38 Biesanz Woodworks
40 San Antonio de Escazú
   Church

Receiving packages can be problematic because of customs requirements – try to have only letters sent to you. Mail theft is a perennial problem, so don't have valuables sent to you in the mail if you can avoid it.

## Telephone

You can make local and international calls from various public telephone booths, which are either coin- or card-operated. See Post & Communications in the Facts for the Visitor chapter.

Telephone directories are available in hotels. There are none in the public telephone booths.

## Email & Internet Access

Numerous cybercafés have opened in San José since 2000. Most charge 300 colones (about US86¢) an hour, but may charge you for two hours if you stay online for more than 61 minutes. Some charge 400 colones. Many better hotels have Internet access, which ranges from free use to US$1 for 15 minutes. Of many cybercafés, here is a selection:

**CyberCafe** (Map 3; ☎ 233-3310, Avenida 2 just west of the Teatro Nacional, downstairs in the Edificio Las Arcadas) Popular, and with a good snack bar.

**Escazú Internet** (Map 5; in Centro Comercial Plaza Escazú, northwest corner of Escazú Park) Open 10am-11:30pm daily.

**Internet Cafe** (Avenida Central at Calle 4, 4th floor) Surf the Web with a city view.

**Internet Cafe de Costa Rica** (☎ 224-7295, 75m west of the old Banco Popular, San Pedro) Open 24 hours.

**Internet Club** (Map 3; Calle 7, Avenidas Central & 2) Open 24 hours.

**Miami Internet** (Map 2; Calle 3 bis at Avenida 9) Popular with gay cybernauts – but definitely not exclusively so.

**Netopia Cybercafe** (Map 3; Avenida 1 at Calle 11, upstairs) Open 9am-midnight Mon-Sat, 10am-10pm Sun. One of the largest places, with over two dozen computers.

## Bookstores

The following bookstores are among the most noteworthy:

**7th Street Books** (aka Chispas Books; Map 3; ☎ 256-8251), Calle 7, Avenidas Central & 1. Open 9am to 6pm daily. This is an attractive shop with new and used books in English and other languages as well as wildlife guides, guidebooks, magazines, and newspapers. The helpful owners speak English. The budget travel agency Ecole Travel (see the Getting Around chapter) shares the space.

**Mora Books** (Map 3; ☎/fax 255-4136, 383-8385) This secondhand bookstore, next to the Omni Center, has books mainly in English; guidebooks and comic books are also a specialty. The owner, Darren Mora, is a cool, well-traveled tico with flawless English who will gladly give you advice.

**Librería Internacional** (☎ 253-9553, fax 280-5473), in Barrio Dent behind the San Pedro Mall, 300m west of Taco Bell. This store offers new books from Latin American authors (in Spanish and in translation) and international literature (in English and other languages) as well as travel and wildlife guides. They also have a selection of children's books. The staff is helpful and speaks English. Two other branches: in the Librería Internacional Multiplaza (☎ 288-1138, fax 288-1139), in the Escazú area, in the Multiplaza near the Camino Real hotel; and Libreria Internacional (☎ 259-9553), in the Rohrmoser suburb, in front of the Comercial Plaza Mayor, west side of Restaurant El Fogoncito.

**Lehmann's** (Map 3; ☎ 223-1212), Avenida Central, Calles 1 & 3. This shop has some books, magazines, and newspapers in English and a selection of Costa Rican maps (in the map department upstairs).

**Librería Francesa** (Map 3; ☎ 223-7979), Avenida 1, Calles 5 & 7. This store sells French books and magazines, as well as a selection of German and English titles.

**Librería Universal** (Map 3; ☎ 222-2222), Avenida Central, Calles Central & 1. This is one of the biggest bookstores in Costa Rica. It has IGM maps and a few books in English, and tends to be crowded.

**Libro Azul** (Map 2), Avenida 10, Calles Central & 1. This is a tiny but locally well-known shop offering secondhand books in Spanish and some in English.

English-language magazines, newspapers, and some books are also available in the gift shops of the international airport and several of the top-end hotels.

## Laundry

There are few laundries or launderettes in San José (or, indeed, in Costa Rica), though there are plenty of *lavanderías,* most of which only do dry cleaning. To simply wash your own clothes, go to Lava-más (☎ 225-1645), Avenida 8, Calle 45 (next to the Los Yoses Spoon coffee shop). It costs about US$4.50 per load to wash and dry, self-

SAN JOSÉ

service. Hours are 9am to 5pm Monday to Friday, 9am to 3pm Saturday. Lavandería Lavamex (☎ 258-2303), Calle 8, Avenidas Central & 1 (across from the Mercado Central), will wash and dry your clothes in about two to three hours for US$5.50 per load; they are open 8am to 6pm Monday to Friday, to 5pm Saturday.

Burbujas (☎ 224-9822), 50m west and 25m south of Más x Menos Supermercado in San Pedro, is open 8am to 6pm weekdays and 8:30am to 4:30pm Saturday. They have coin-operated machines charging US$6 total for wash and dry.

Downtown, the Lavandería Sixaola (☎ 221-2111), Avenida 2, Calles 7 & 9 (Map 3), charges US$4.50 a load (wash and dry) and has same-day service. They claim to have been scrubbing since 1912. Also, there's Sol y Fiesta, Avenida 8, Calles 7 & 9, which charges US$5 a load, including soap.

Most hotels will arrange for your laundry to be washed, but beware that the top-end hotels charge as much for a couple of items as you'd pay to get a whole load washed elsewhere.

## Medical Services

The most central social security (free) hospital is Hospital San Juan de Dios (Map 2; ☎ 257-6282) at Paseo Colón, Calle 14.

If you can afford to pay for medical attention (costs are much cheaper than in the USA or Europe, for example), go to the well-recommended Clínica Bíblica (Map 2; ☎ 257-5252, 257-0466 in an emergency, ☎ 800-911-0800, Ⓦ www.clinicabiblica.com) on Avenida 14, Calles Central & 1. They have some English-speaking staff and are open 24 hours for emergencies. They will carry out laboratory tests (stool, urine, blood samples, etc) and recommend specialists if necessary. They also have a full range of other medical services, including a 24-hour pharmacy.

Also recommended are the Clínica Católica (☎ 283-6616) in the suburb of Guadalupe, and the new (in 2001) and very modern Hospital CIMA (☎ 208-1000) in the suburb of Guachipelín de Escazú. Both of these have 24-hour pharmacies. There are plenty of other pharmacies in San José.

Your embassy is a good source of references for specialists if you need one.

Embassy staff get sick too – and they usually know the best doctors, dentists, etc.

## Emergency

Call ☎ 911 for all emergencies. Call ☎ 128 for a Cruz Roja (Red Cross) ambulance, ☎ 118 for the Bomberos (fire department), ☎ 222-9330 for the Policía de Transito (Traffic Police), and ☎ 800-800-8000 for traffic accidents.

## Dangers & Annoyances

There has been a noticeable increase in street crime over the past few years. That doesn't make San José as dangerous as some other Latin American capitals, or parts of many North American and European cities, but you should exercise basic precautions.

Sneak theft is much more likely than getting mugged – the generally peaceful outlook of ticos seems to extend even to street crime. Pickpockets and bag snatchers abound, so carry your money in an inside pocket, and carry bags firmly attached to your body with a strap rather than letting them dangle loosely over your shoulder. Keep day packs in front of you rather than on your back, where they can be unzipped and pilfered in a crowd. Don't wear expensive jewelry and watches downtown – they can be snatched off.

In recent years, most thefts from travelers, including a number of muggings, happened in the area west of the Mercado Central, especially around the Coca-Cola bus terminal, so be careful in this area. The lively, popular area around Avenida 2 and the Parque Central has been the scene of many pickpocketing attempts, particularly late at night. Muggings have been reported after dark – so keep alert. This is also the

### Kissing Parks

Many ticos live with their families until they get married, which puts a premium on good public locales for romancing. This gives travelers a way of gauging the safety of city parks after dark – if you see more than two couples smooching, chances are it's a safe area.

– John Thompson

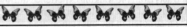

heart of the tourist area, with many budget hotels nearby and high-quality hotels on the edges. Many people walk these streets by night and rarely have a problem; nevertheless, take the precautions you would when traveling to any large city with typical crime problems – don't carry valuables, keep money hidden, and keep your eyes open.

Don't leave cars parked on the streets – find a guarded parking lot. Don't leave any packages inside the car, even in a guarded lot, as they invite window smashing and theft. Men should beware of friendly prostitutes – they may pair up with you on quiet streets and pickpocket you while distracting you. Prostitutes are known for their abilities to take more than their customers bargained for, including lifting wallets during a sexual encounter. Another occasional scam is getting sprayed with ketchup and robbed by the person who steps in to help 'clean up.' Yet another is being invited out by a well-dressed stranger (both male or female) for an evening that ends with too many stiff drinks and missing belongings. Women traveling alone have complained of being harassed by cab drivers at night – certainly, you should firmly discourage a macho driver at the first sign of an inappropriate comment, or ask to be dropped off immediately in a central area if you feel uncomfortable. (None of this happens very frequently.)

The best way to prevent problems is to first find out (from your hotel or other travelers) about the area you are going to, and, especially if bar-hopping at night, to go with a friend. The following neighborhoods are reportedly unsafe at night and dodgy during the day (although few of these are on the travelers' trail): Leon XIII, 15 de Septiembre, Cuba, Cristo Rey, Sagrada Familia, Coca Cola, Méxixo, Bajo Piuses, Los Cuadros, Torremolinos.

Finally, noise and smog are unavoidable components of the San José experience. Most central hotels have some street noise, and some are very noisy indeed. Even the best hotels are liable to suffer from some street noise, which might not be a problem if you live in a major city and are used to traffic. Using earplugs to sleep is one solution. There is a fair amount of smog, which detracts from the walking experience during the day and may create a problem in some cheaper hotels in the bus station area.

Also, watch out for open gutters and potholes in the sidewalks, some of which are big enough to swallow a dog (a big dog).

## THINGS TO SEE & DO

The downtown area is small and congested with heavy traffic. Driving is not recommended, parking is very difficult, and sightseeing is best done on foot. The cluster of parks northeast of the center, and the neighborhoods between them, offer the most pleasant walking – particularly Barrio Amón, northeast of Avenida 5 and Calle 1, which has the best concentration of historical buildings.

East of Amón is Barrio Otoya, a less-trendy version of Amón. Eight blocks of the Avenida Central, from the Mercado Central through the Plaza de la Cultura to Calle 9, are a pedestrian mall that makes a good urban walk. The Plaza de la Democracia is just below the Museo Nacional and the Parque Nacional and offers decent views of the mountains surrounding the city. It will be fairly easy for you to find a route to join some of the sites of interest described below.

Author Vernon Bell of Bell's Home Hospitality (see Books in the Facts for the Visitor chapter and Places to Stay, later) has produced a useful booklet describing suggested walks. Avenida 2 carries the main flow of traffic from west to east. Many downtown streets are one-way.

**Museum Hours & Admission** Opening hours sometimes fluctuate, especially at the smaller museums; before making a long trek, call ahead to ensure that the museum will be open when you arrive. Ticos often pay less than foreign visitors; the non-tico admission fees are given in this book.

### Museo de Jade

This is perhaps Costa Rica's most famous museum and is located on the 11th floor of the Instituto Nacional de Seguros *(Map 3; INS; ☎ 287-6034, 223-5800 ext 2584, Avenida 7, Calles 9 & 11; admission US$2, children 11 & under free; open 8:30am-3pm Mon-Fri).* Remodeled in 2001 and reopened in 2002, the museum houses the world's largest collection of American jade, and hundreds of pieces are on display. Many pieces are mounted with a backlight so the exquisite translucent quality of this gemstone can be fully appreciated. There are also archaeological exhibits of ceramics, stonework, and gold, arranged by cultural regions.

The 11th-floor vantage point offers a good view of the city – bring your camera. There's an interesting metal building to the southwest. It was designed in France and shipped over in prefabricated sections (it's now a school). With the city view and world-class jade collection, this museum is at the top of most visitors' lists of places to see.

Note that 'jade' is written the same as in English but is pronounced 'HA-day' in Spanish.

## Museo Nacional

The popular National Museum is housed in the Bellavista Fortress, the old army headquarters *(Map 2; ☎ 257-1433, Calle 17, Avenidas Central & 2; admission US$1, students with ID & child under 10 yrs free; open 8:30am-4:30pm Tues-Sun)*. The small museum displays Costa Rican archaeology, some jade and gold, colonial furniture and costumes, colonial and religious art, and historical exhibits. Some pieces are labeled in English as well as Spanish. There is a small garden with cannons, and some of the walls are pockmarked with bullet holes from the 1948 civil war. There is also a gift shop here.

## Museo de Oro Precolombino

This museum, in the basement of the Plaza de la Cultura complex, under the tourist information office *(Map 3; ☎ 243-4202, Calle 5, Avenidas Central & 2; adult/student US$4.50/1; open 10am-4:30pm Tues-Sun)*, houses a dazzling collection of over 2000 pre-Columbian gold pieces and is well worth seeing. There is also a small numismatic museum and a changing display of Costa Rican art.

The museum is owned by Banco Central and security is tight: You must leave your bags at the door.

## Museo de Arte Costarricense

This small museum of Costa Rican art *(Map 1; ☎ 222-7155, just off Calle 42, Paseo Colón & Avenida 2; admission about US$1.50, students with ID & children half-price, free Sun; open 10am-4pm Tues-Sat, 10am-2pm Sun)* contains a collection of local paintings and sculpture from the 19th and 20th centuries. The sculptures are

especially worth a look. There are also changing shows of local artists.

The museum is in Parque La Sabana, which was San José's airport until 1955, and the collection is housed in the old airport terminal.

## Museo de Arte y Diseño Contemporáneo

The Museum of Contemporary Art and Design *(Map 2; ☎ 257-7202, Avenida 3, Calles 15 & 17; admission US$1, students US50¢; open 10am-5pm Tues-Sat)* houses changing shows. It is next to the Biblioteca Nacional (National Library) in the former National Liquor Factory, which is now the Centro Nacional de Arte y Cultura (National Cultural and Arts Center). The museum itself is a large space, and the changing exhibits of working Costa Rican as well as international artists are well presented, crisply lit, and always worth a look. The center presents occasional lectures and avant-garde theatrical and dance performances.

## Serpentario

This is a small but unusual collection of live snakes and other reptiles housed in the center of San José *(Map 3; ☎ 255-4210, Avenida 1, Calles 9 & 11; admission US$4.50, children 3-14 US$1.50; open 9am-6pm Mon-Fri, 10am-5pm Sat & Sun)*. Anyone interested in reptile or amphibian identification will benefit from a visit to this live display of many of Costa Rica's exotic species.

A bilingual biologist is sometimes available to explain the collection, and there is a tiny gift shop.

## Museo de los Niños

The Children's Museum is in the old *penitenciaría (Map 2; ☎ 258-4929, Calle 4, north of Avenida 9; adult/child US$2.50/1; open 8am-3pm Tues-Fri, 10am-4pm Sat & Sun)*. The hands-on and interactive displays allow children to learn and experience science, music, geography, and other subjects. Part of the old jail can still be visited. There are exhibits about children in Costa Rica, children's rights, and so on. It's a big place and there's lots to do!

## Museo de Ciencias Naturales

The Natural History Museum is housed in the old Colegio (high school) La Salle near the southwest corner of Parque La Sabana *(Map 1; ☎ 232-1306, Parque La Sabana; adult/student US$1.50/1; open 7:30am-4pm Mon-Sun)*. Basically, this is a large collection of stuffed animals and mounted butterflies, a resource for those wishing to identify some of the species they may see in the wild. There are also exhibits on paleontology and archaeology.

Most cab drivers know the Colegio La Salle and charge less than US$2 to get there. A Sabana-Estadio or Sabana-Cementario city bus from Parque Central will take you there for a few colones – ask the driver to let you know where the museum is.

### Museo de Insectos

Also known as the Museo de Entomología, this is a fine collection of insects curated by the Facultad de Agronomía at the Universidad de Costa Rica and housed (surprisingly) in the basement of the Artes Musicales building on campus *(Map 1; ☎ 207-5318, 207-5647; admission US$2.25, students half-price; open 1pm-5pm Mon-Fri)*. It is claimed that this is the only insect museum of its size in Central America – the collection is certainly extensive, and many splendid and exotic insects can be seen.

The museum is signposted, or you can ask for directions. Ring the bell to gain admission. A cab to the university (in San Pedro) costs about US$2, or take a San Pedro bus along Avenida 2 from Calle 5.

### Parque Zoológico Simón Bolívar

This small national zoo is in Parque Simón Bolívar *(Map 2; ☎ 233-6701, Avenida 11, Calles 7 & 9; admission US$2; open 8am-3:30pm Mon-Fri, 9am-4:30pm Sat & Sun)*. You can see many of Costa Rica's animals, along with a small sprinkling of exotics. Unfortunately, as in many Latin American countries, the cages are too small, although not as bad as in some zoos.

There are also dozens of labeled Costa Rican plants on the grounds, and a brochure describing them is available. The zoo is popular with josefinos on weekends. Go north on Calle 7 and east on Avenida 11 to get there.

### Spirogyra Jardín de Mariposas

Not to be confused with the large butterfly farm in La Guacima, this smaller version offers close-up looks at Costa Rican butterflies in a garden setting close to downtown *(Map 2; ☎ 222-2937; adults/children US$6/3; open 8am-4pm)*. The garden is 100m east and 150m south of Centro Comercial El Pueblo and can be reached on foot (about a half hour from downtown), by taxi, or by bus to El Pueblo (where there is a sign).

### Museo Postal, Telegráfico y Filatélico de Costa Rica

This postal, telegraphic, and stamp-collecting museum is upstairs in the central post office *(Map 3; ☎ 223-6918, 223-9766 ext 269, Calle 2, Avenidas 1 & 3; admission free; open 9am-5pm Mon-Fri)*.

### Museo de Criminología

The stated objective of this museum, which is in the Supreme Court of Justice *(Map 2; ☎ 295-3850, 223-0666 ext 2378, Calle 17, Avenidas 6 & 8; open 7:30am-noon, 1pm-4pm Mon-Fri)*, is the prevention of crime through the presentation of exhibits of criminal acts. It reportedly contains such niceties as limbs that have been separated from their rightful owners by machete-wielding criminals.

### Teatro Nacional

The National Theater *(Map 3; ☎ 221-1329, 233-6354, Calles 3 & 5, Avenidas Central & 2; admission US$2; open 9am-5pm Mon-Sat)* is one of San José's most impressive public buildings. Built in the 1890s (see Arts in the Facts about Costa Rica chapter), the Teatro Nacional is the center of Costa Rican culture and stands on the south side of the Plaza de la Cultura. The outside is elegant, though not particularly impressive, with statues of Beethoven and Calderón de la Barca, a 17th-century Spanish dramatist, flanking the entrance, and a columned façade.

The more interesting interior holds paintings of Costa Rica, the most famous of which is a huge canvas showing coffee harvesting and export. It was painted in Italy in the late 19th century and was reproduced on the five-colón note. (This note is now out of circulation, but can sometimes be obtained in banks – or by paying about US$1 to one of the street vendors outside.) The marble staircases, gilded ceilings, and parquet floors made of local hardwoods are worth seeing.

There are regular performances in the theater, and seeing a show is the best way to see the splendid public areas inside the building. The private box seats are certainly a treat – bring your opera glasses and a fan. There is a coffee shop to the left of the theater lobby, with changing shows by local artists, good coffee, and a quiet atmosphere in which to write postcards – though it gets very crowded at lunchtime. Café hours are 9am to 6pm Monday to Saturday.

## Mercado Central

This market *(Map 3; Avenidas Central & 1, Calles 6 & 8)* is interesting to visit if you've never been to a Latin American market, although it is a little tame compared to the markets of many other countries. Nevertheless, it is crowded and bustling and has a variety of produce and other goods ranging from live turkeys to leatherwork for sale. Some of the cheapest meals in town are served here.

A block away at Avenida 3, Calle 8, is the similar **Mercado Borbón**. The streets surrounding the markets are jam-packed with vendors. Beware of pickpockets in these areas and definitely dress down – leave the Rolex and gold chain at home.

## Parque Nacional

This is a pleasant and shady park *(Map 2; Avenidas 1 & 3, Calles 15 & 19)*. In the center of the park is the Monumento Nacional, showing the Central American nations driving out William Walker (see History in the Facts about Costa Rica chapter). In the gardens of the Asamblea Legislativa, across from the park's southwest corner, is a statue of national hero Juan Santamaría.

Important buildings surrounding the park include the Asamblea Legislativa (Legislative Assembly or Congress Building) to the south, the Biblioteca Nacional (National Library) to the north, and the Fábrica Nacional de Licores (National Liquor Factory, founded in 1856 and now housing the Museo de Arte y Diseño Contemporáneo) to the northwest.

## Parque España

This small park seems to have some of the tallest trees in San José *(Map 3; Avenidas 3 & 7, Calles 9 & 11)*. It is a riot of birdsong just before sunset, and a riot of color on Sunday, when there is an outdoor art market.

To the north of the park is the INS building, housing the Jade Museum and fronted by a huge statue. To the west is the famous iron building (now a school), designed in

### Kids' Stuff

Apart from the kid-oriented **Museo de los Niños**, other museums that are often a hit with children are the **Serpentario** (Map 3) – my kids certainly like looking at live snakes and lizards – and, for those into nature, the butterflies at the **Spirogyra Jardín de Mariposas** (Map 2).

The gruesome exhibits at the **Museo de Criminología** (Map 2) may also be of interest. Teenagers check one another out and meet at the **Plaza de la Cultura** (Map 3), near which, on Avenida Central, are several fast-food joints (including the ubiquitous McDonald's, which some kids love but others wouldn't be caught dead in!) and ice cream bars. All these places are described in this chapter.

A few kilometers west of town is **Water Land** – great for the whole family. See the Alajuela Area section of the Central Valley chapter for details.

The *Tico Times* (see Newspapers & Magazines in the Facts for the Visitor chapter) has a page for children, and it sometimes reviews plays and movies (many in English) that will appeal to children. The **Teatro Eugene O'Neill** (see the Theater section in Entertainment, later in this chapter) has a Children's Theater group; seeing a performance might be a fun Spanish lesson. Movies screened at cinemas include G-rated ones suitable for the whole family, and in original English (with Spanish subtitles).

Most kids, though, will probably want to get out of San José as fast as possible to experience the adventures of the rainforests, beaches, exploding volcanoes, and national parks. I encourage families traveling with kids to write me with your 'Kids' Stuff' recommendations for future editions.

France, shipped from Belgium in parts, and welded together in Costa Rica during the 1890s; to the east is the old liquor factory; and to the northeast is the Casa Amarilla (Yellow House), which is Costa Rica's Ministry of Foreign Affairs.

### Parque Morazán

This park (Map 3) intersects at four city blocks at Calle 7 and Avenida 3, and is graced in the center by a dome-roofed structure, the so-called Templo de Música. There are several other statues and monuments, as well as many stone benches for a quick respite from sightseeing.

### Plaza de la Cultura

This plaza (Map 3) is not particularly prepossessing, but it is the site of the Teatro Nacional, Museo de Oro Precolombino, and ICT office. Young people hang out here and check out what everyone else is doing – it's a good place to people watch.

### Parque Central

This park is the place to catch many local city buses (Map 3; Avenidas 2 & 4, Calles Central & 2). These streets are very busy (especially Avenida 2) and pickpockets hover to prey on the unwary. To the east is the fairly modern and not very interesting Catedral Metropolitana. To the north is the well-known Teatro Melico Salazar.

### Plaza de la Democracia

Situated below the Museo Nacional, this mostly bare plaza (Map 2) has a few interesting sculptures and, on its western side, an open-air arts and crafts market. It gets busy just before Christmas and around other holidays, although there is often plenty of stuff for sale at any time of year. There are decent views of the mountains surrounding San José.

### Parque La Sabana

This park (Map 1), at the western end of the Paseo Colón, is home to both the museum of Costa Rican art and the national stadium, where international and division one soccer matches are played. It is a spacious park, with a lagoon, fountain, and a variety of sports facilities (see below). It's a good place for a daytime stroll or a picnic beneath the trees, and offers relief from the congestion of downtown. Don't wander the grounds after dark.

## ACTIVITIES

**Parque La Sabana** has a variety of sporting facilities. There are tennis courts, volleyball, basketball, and baseball areas, jogging paths, and an Olympic-size swimming pool, but it costs about US$3 to swim, and it is open only noon to 2pm. Many ticos prefer the excursion to the **Ojo de Agua pool** (near Alajuela, frequent buses), where swimming is available all day.

The **Cariari Country Club** (☎ 293-3211, 239-2455, 239-0022, e cariari@racsa.co.cr) has an 18-hole championship golf course (6590 yards, par 71), Costa Rica's oldest 18-hole course and considered by many the best in Central America. Rates are US$40 per day plus a US$10 caddie fee; club rental (US$15) and golf carts (US$25) are available. Although only guests of the country club can play, guests of top-end hotels can get greens privileges on a space-available basis – ask your concierge. Reservations can be made in the USA through Costa Rica Golf Adventures (☎ 877-258-2688, W www.golfcr.com). The country club also has 11 tennis courts (most are lighted), a pro shop, an Olympic-size swimming pool, and a gym.

The **Valle del Sol** (☎ 282-9222), in the Santa Ana suburb, is a new 18-hole, par 35, 6542-yard public golf course. Greens fees are about US$50 and golf carts another US$25.

The **Costa Rica Country Club** (☎ 228-9333/4/5/6/7/8, e country@racsa.co.cr, Escazú) has a nine-hole course.

Tennis is also available at the **Costa Rica Tennis Club** (☎ 232-1266) on the south side of La Sabana, though the courts aren't top quality.

You can join a local gym for about US$20 a month or use the facilities in the best hotels if you happen to be staying in one. Gyms are listed under 'Gimnasios' in the yellow pages telephone directory.

If you're interested in knocking down some pins, near the North American–Costa Rican Cultural Center you'll find the **Compañia de Bolinche** (☎ 253-5745, Avenida Central, Calle 23), where you can rent bowling shoes for US$1.50 per person and bowl for US$11 per hour.

## LANGUAGE COURSES

There are some excellent Spanish-language schools in and near San José, but they are not particularly cheap. (Readers looking for cheaper options might consider Guatemala.) Lessons are usually intensive, with class sizes varying from two to five pupils per teacher. Individual tutoring is also available. Classes usually last for several hours every weekday. Most students are encouraged to stay with a Costa Rican family to immerse themselves in the language. Family homestays are arranged by the schools, as are the necessary visa extensions. Cheaper classes usually involve larger group sizes and/or fewer hours. Short and long courses are available.

Spending a month learning Spanish in Costa Rica is an excellent and recommended way to see and learn about the country. Most schools offer more than just language courses. Lectures, discussions, field trips, dance lessons and other activities may be available – topics include the environment, women's issues, human rights, social studies, economics, politics studies, agriculture, culture, and travel.

Many language schools advertise in the *Tico Times* every week. If you want to arrange classes in advance, write to or call the schools in the following list for details. There are dozens of existing schools – noninclusion here does not mean that a school is not good. The schools listed meet one or both of the following criteria: They have been operating for at least five years, or they have received several reader recommendations. Most schools are in San José, but those in nearby suburbs are also included. Also see Language Courses in the Central Valley chapter and the Central Pacific Coast chapter.

Brief descriptions give an idea of price – most schools also have longer or shorter programs than those described and will tailor a program to fit your needs. Also, you can arrange more or fewer hours of class time. Note that if you opt for the language course only, rather than staying with a local family, this can be arranged at much cheaper rates (though you'll probably end up paying more to stay in a hotel and pay for your own meals).

**Amerispan Unlimited** (in the USA ☎ 215-829-0418, 800-879-6640, ⓦ www.amerispan.com)
This US-based organization arranges classes with schools throughout Latin America in Costa Rica, Mexico, Guatemala, Panama, and several South American countries.

**Academia Latinoamericano de Español** (☎ 224-9917, fax 225-8125, ⓔ espalesa@racsa.co.cr, Avenida 8, Calles 31 & 33) This school offers 20 hours of classes a week for US$165, plus family homestay for another US$145 a week.

**Centro Lingüístico Conversa** (☎ 221-7649, in the USA ☎ 800-367-7726, fax 233-2418, ⓦ www.conversa.net) There are two locations: Paseo Colón, Calles 38 & 40 in San José, and a Santa Ana suburb. Cheap classes without homestays and for short periods of time are available in San José. Classes in Santa Ana are intensive and include homestays and cultural programs – they start at US$650 per week and go up to US$2500 per month.

**Costa Rican International Language Academy** (☎ 233-8914, 233-8938, in the USA ☎ 800-854-6057, 866-253-5672, fax 233-8670, ⓦ www.telecomcr.com/crlang) In the San Pedro suburb, this academy gives students a chance to learn about Costa Rican culture through optional lessons in music, cooking, dancing, and customs. Prices are US$10 per hour for lessons, US$100 (or less depending on program) per week for homestay. Four-week courses include two long-distance excursions.

**Forester Instituto Internacional** (☎ 225-3155, 225-1649, 225-0135, fax 225-9236, ⓦ www.forest.com,

### Dance Schools

Do you speak Spanish and want to meet some locals? Dance classes are offered not for tourists but for ticos, but travelers who speak Spanish are welcome. Latin dancing – salsa, cha-cha, merengue, bolero, tango, etc – as well as the latest local dance crazes are taught. Classes are inexpensive; around US$20 a month gives you two hours of group classes per week. Private lessons cost US$7 to US$14 per hour. Travelers can also find dance classes through many language schools.

**Academia de Bailes Latinos** (☎ 233-8938) Avenida Central, Calles 25 & 27

**Malecón** (☎/fax 222-3214) Avenida 2, Calles 17 & 19

**Merecumbe** (☎ 224-3531, 228-6253, fax 283-0106) Escazú and other suburbs

**Kurubandé** (☎ 234-0682) Guadalupe and other suburbs

about 75m south of the Automercado, Los Yoses) The school charges about US$1360 for four weeks of classes (20 hours a week), including homestays, excursions, Internet access, and free Latin dance classes. Private lessons at US$18 an hour are available.

**Institute for Central American Development Studies** (ICADS; ☎ 234-1381, fax 234-1337, W www.icadscr.com) This school, in the suburb of San Pedro, offers intensive 30-day programs (4½ hours daily, four students maximum) for US$1600, including homestay and meals. It offers extra lectures and activities on environmental, women's, and human rights issues, and will also place you in local volunteer positions. 'Semester abroad' programs for college credit are also offered.

**Central American Institute for International Affairs** (ICAI; ☎ 233-8571, fax 221-5238, W www.educaturs.com) In a residential area 10 minutes from the heart of San José, this program offers one- to four-week programs with homestays, lectures, dance lessons, and travel information for US$500 to US$1500. Private lessons are US$16.

**Instituto Latinoamericano de Idiomas** (ILISA; ☎ 280-0700, in the USA ☎ 800-454-7248, fax 225-4665, W www.ilisa.com) About 400m south and 50m east of the San Pedro church. It offers small groups, intensive studies (four to six hours a day), family homestays, and a Central American history and culture program. A four-week course including homestays costs from US$1700.

**Instituto Británico** (☎ 234-9054, fax 253-1894, W www.institutobritanico.co.cr) About 75m south of the Subaru dealership in Los Yoses. This one emphasizes homestays and cultural activities. Registration is $50; individual classes US$19 per hour; group classes US$390 for 40 hours over two weeks; homestays with meals US$125 per week.

**Instituto Universal de Idiomas** (☎ 257-0441, 223-9662, fax 223-9917, W www.universal-edu.com, Calle 9, Avenida 2, 2nd floor) Centrally located, this school advertises a free trial lesson! It offers classes with a six-student maximum, ranging from three-day crash courses (six hours a day, US$140) to economy packages (four weeks, three hours per day, homestay with meals, textbook, and airport pickup, US$940). Individual instruction is available for US$14 per hour.

**Intensa** (☎ 224-6353, in the USA ☎ 866-277-1352, fax 253-8912, W www.intensa.com, Calle 33, Avenidas 1 & 3) Intensa offers a variety of programs, the most expensive being a four-week program, six lessons a day, with homestay for US$1466.

**Institute for Spanish Language Studies** (ISLS; ☎ 258-5111, in the USA ☎ 800-765-0025, 626-441-3507, W www.isls.com, 2130 Huntington Dr No 201, South Pasadena, CA 91030) This company represents many schools throughout the country.

**Universidad Veritas** (☎ 283-4747, fax 225-2907, W www.uveritas.ac.cr, in the Edificio ITAN, Carretera a Zapote) A 20-minute walk southeast of San José, this school has a wide range of levels and courses.

## ORGANIZED TOURS

The following is a list of the most popular tours offered in, around, and out of San José. Approximate prices per person are provided, but be sure to look around for bargains, such as two people for the price of one.

Many hotels will arrange tours for you. The more expensive hotels seem to charge more than the budget hotels for the very same tour – partly because the cheaper hotels will accept smaller commissions and partly because some tour companies will give a favorable rate to budget hotels because they know that these clients are economizing.

Day tours normally include lunch and pickup and return from your San José hotel; multiday tours normally include accommodations, meals, and transport. Bilingual guides, usually fluent in English, accompany most tours. Good guides deserve a tip.

For information on tour operators in Costa Rica, see the Organized Tours section in the Getting Around chapter.

**Half-day city tour** – US$20 to US$25.

**Half-day tours** to one or two of the following: Volcán Irazú, Volcán Poás, ox-cart factory at Sarchí, Lankester Gardens and the Valle de Orosi, La Paz Waterfall and butterfly garden, coffee tour, butterfly farm – US$25 to US$55.

**Full-day tour** combining two or more of the above – US$65 to US$100.

**Full-day 4-in-1 tour** offering Poás, La Paz Waterfall and Butterfly Garden, Ri'o Sarapiquí jungle river cruise, Braulio Carillo National Park drive through (this is a full and busy day which is becoming increasingly popular) – about US$79

**Full-day tour** to one of the following: Rainforest Aerial Tram, Jungle Train with Parque Nacional Braulio Carrillo, Volcán Arenal, Volcán Barva, Reserva Biológica Carara with Playa Jacó, Cerro de la Muerte, Parque Nacional Tapantí, Colonia Virgen del Socorro, Golfo de Nicoya cruise to Isla Tortuga, horseback riding, white-water rafting trip on one of the Ríos Reventazón, Pacuare, Sarapiquí, or Corobicí – US$55 to US$110. (Note: One-day tours from San José to Manuel

Antonio, Tortuguero, Caño Negro, or Monteverde are offered from about US$100, but these generally involve too much travel to be comfortable one-day trips. Volcán Arenal is also pushing it a bit in one day.)

**Two days/one night tour** river rafting and camping or river lodge – US$250 to US$320 (usually the Río Pacuare; four passengers is the minimum).

**Three days/two nights at Tortuguero** – per person, double occupancy, US$235 and up depending on transport, accommodations, and guides desired.

**Three days/two nights at Monteverde** – per person, double occupancy, US$360 and up. (Note that cheaper options for the last two may lack good hotels, meals, or naturalist guides.)

## PLACES TO STAY

There are more than 200 hotels of all types in San José, but accommodations may be tight in some of the better ones during the high season (December to May) and especially in the week before and after Christmas and the week before Easter. If you want to stay in a particular hotel at these times, you should make reservations – as much as three months in advance for Christmas and Easter. Reservations should be prepaid, or they will sometimes be ignored. If you have no reservations, you can still find rooms, but your choices are limited.

Although there is a large choice of hotels, accommodations are generally lackluster, especially downtown. Many hotels, although clean and secure, tend to suffer from musty carpets, street noise, and unappealing decor (though there are exceptions – especially the smaller hotels, which are often in beautifully restored older houses).

For people staying a while, *apartotels* offer furnished rooms with kitchens at mid-range hotel rates; also look in the newspapers for apartments to rent. Those advertised in the Spanish-language *La Nación* are generally a little cheaper than those advertised in the English-language *Tico Times*. The most luxurious hotels are good, but not many travelers want to pay well over US$100 for a place to sleep. Budget rooms are usually grim and noisy little boxes, but at least they are fairly cheap. There is also one youth hostel associated with Hostelling International.

Since the early 1990s, a large number of small bed & breakfast hotels have appeared on the scene that offer a reasonably priced alternative to traditional top-end hotels. B&Bs offer more than just breakfast – they also tend to provide a family-like atmosphere in a house rather than a more impersonal hotel. There are several outlying suburbs with mid-range to top-end hotels and B&Bs. People stay there to get out of the hustle and bustle of San José, or to be closer to the airport (17km away), or because of the rural atmosphere. These areas are served by local buses, described in the Getting Around section later in this chapter.

Prices given here (and in the rest of the book) are current high-season rates, including the 16.39% government and tourist tax. Rates are subject to demand and may change substantially (both up and down) over the life of this book.

Note there are many B&Bs and hotels (especially mid-range to top-end ones) in Escazú and on the way to the international airport, both west of San José. These are listed in the Escazú and Other Areas sections that follow the Places to Stay – In the City listings.

### Making Reservations

Some of the budget, many of the mid-range, and all of the top-end hotels accept reservations by phone, fax, email, or snail-mail. Some have US telephone numbers (occasionally toll free). A reservation deposit is normally required. A good travel agent can help you make reservations from home.

Local phone numbers and street addresses are given below, and, for those hotels that accept reservations from abroad, email and postal addresses (apartados) and/or US phone numbers are also given. Email is fast becoming the most common way to make reservations, and hotels are rushing to get online; if a hotel below doesn't have an email address listed, it is worth a quick call to see if it has added one since this writing. If you are making mail reservations, allow several months – letters can be very slow. Phoning, faxing, emailing, or using a travel agent are the best ways to make reservations.

Pat Bliss (☎ 228-8726, ✉ crnow@amnet .co.cr) is a long-time resident of San José and founded 'B&Bs in Costa Rica.' She can arrange B&B accommodations throughout Costa Rica, with an emphasis on the San José area.

Budget hotels may not accept reservations, but the phone numbers will at least enable you to find out whether they have rooms available.

## Homestays

This is an alternative to staying at a hotel or B&B. You stay with a local family (most are ticos, a few are foreign residents) that provides a room (or perhaps two) for one to three guests per room. Thus, you or your small group will be the only guests, and you'll receive a more in-depth look at Costa Rica, often participating in family activities. Host families may or may not speak English, smoke, have children or pets, have private showers for guests – each is unique.

A well-recommended agency is run by Vernon Bell (a Kansan who has lived in Costa Rica for 30 years) and his tica wife, Marcela. They have some 70 homes available, each of which has been personally inspected to maintain their high standards of cleanliness and wholesomeness. All are close to public transportation, and readers have sent only positive comments about these places. The Bells will also help arrange car rental and other reservations and will help plan guests' itineraries.

Rates are US$30/45 single/double, including breakfast, or an extra US$5 with private bath; dinners can be arranged and discounts are usually available for stays over two weeks. Contact Bell's Home Hospitality (☎ 225-4752, fax 224-5884, ℮ homestay@ racsa.co.cr, ⓦ www.homestay.thebells.org).

## PLACES TO STAY – IN THE CITY
## Budget

There are dozens of cheap places to spend the night.

**Hostels** A little over a kilometer east of downtown is *Hostel Toruma* (☎ 234-8186, ☎/fax 224-4085, Avenida Central, Calles 29 & 31). Dorm beds US$11/13 HI members/ nonmembers. This clean but slightly worn place is the only youth hostel associated with Hostelling International. There are 100 bunk beds (with railway compartment–like shutters) in segregated dormitories, and hot water is available at times. Although a little pricey for a hard bunk bed, it's a popular place and sometimes booked up in advance. Laundry facilities are available in the afternoons, and there is a spacious lounge and a message board.

The hostel is also headquarters for the network of Costa Rican youth hostels, and information and reservations for the others can be made here. Note that the San José hostel is the cheapest – the others offer private rather than dormitory rooms.

*Costa Rica Backpackers* (Map 2; ☎ 221-6191, fax 222-0588, ℮ costarica@backpackers .com, ⓦ www.costaricabackpackers.com, Avenida 6, Calles 21 & 23). Dorm beds US$9, double rooms US$20. This independent hostel boasts a swimming pool, garden hammocks, free 24-hour Internet access, kitchen privileges with free tea and coffee, laundry facilities, book exchange, lounge with cable TV, and numerous bathrooms with hot water. In early 2002, a special Internet rate of US$7 in dorms and US$17 a double was offered, so check to see what's available. The 10 double rooms go fast; other travelers sleep in dorms of four to six beds. This place is popular with budget travelers trying to avoid the grungy feel of older places.

*Buccaneers Hostel* (☎ 221-1992, 396-0364 cellular, fax 240-1026, ℮ buccaneers@ vacationmail.com, ⓦ www.angelfire.com/ns/ buccaneershostel/home.htm, Avenida 13 at Calle 3 bis). Beds from US$8. Calling itself 'the coolest freaking hostel in Costa Rica,' this 18-bed place attracts a young crowd and includes breakfast and Internet access in its rates. Showers are hot and kitchen privileges and a TV lounge are available in this converted older house in historic Barrio Amon.

*Casa Ridgeway* (Map 2; ☎ 222-1400, ☎/ fax 233-6168, ℮ friends@racsa.co.cr, Calle 15, Avenida 6 bis) Dorm beds US$10 per person, doubles US$24. This interesting small hostel was formerly known as the Peace Center and continues to be affiliated with and operated by Quakers. It is a useful place for information and discussion on peace issues. There is a small library, and the center is staffed mainly by volunteers. Dorm accommodations are in four clean, small rooms with four bunk beds and individual lockers. There are five double rooms, and all nine rooms share five bathrooms with hot showers. Kitchen and laundry facilities (US$5 per load) are offered; quiet hours are from 10pm to 7am.

**Hotels** Many cheap hotels are found west of Calle Central. There have been reports of occasional thefts and muggings in the area around the Coca-Cola bus terminal, Mercado Central, and Parque Central – keep your eyes open and use taxis if arriving at night. Certainly, unless you're a die-hard fan of grunge and bustle, this is one of San José's less pleasant neighborhoods.

**Gran Hotel Imperial** *(Map 4;* ☎ *222-8463,* ☎*/fax 256-9650,* e *granhimp@sol .racsa.co.cr, Calle 8, Avenidas Central & 1)* Rooms US$4.50 per person. Many shoe-string travelers head for this basic hotel. Fronted by an unassuming chained iron door leading into a bare stairwell, this cavernous hotel provides all the basic necessities – security, reasonably clean beds, communal showers with spasmodic hot water, and one of the best-value restaurants in town, with a balcony where you can sip a beer while watching the busy market action below. There are few single rooms here and the place is full of international backpackers. The hotel will hold a room for you until the afternoon if you call ahead.

**Tica Linda Anexo** *(Map 2;* ☎ *221-3120,* e *charour@hotmail.com, Avenida 10, Calles Central & 1, next to Libro Azul)* Rooms US$4 per person or US$5 single. Ten basic rooms sleep 23 people and share two bathrooms with hot showers. A sink for clothes washing, a small patio, kitchen privileges, storage area and friendly staff make this a recommended option for shoe-stringers, especially young travelers on the 'gringo trail.' The place is somewhat cramped and noisy but friendly and secure. Its main attraction is as a place to meet other budget travelers.

**Tica Linda No 1** *(Map 3;* ☎*/fax 222-4402, Calle 7, Avenidas 6 & 8)* Rates are the same as at Tica Linda Anexo, and Charo at the Anexo can pass email messages to José Luis at the No 1. This place has 36 beds in a variety of rooms, two bathrooms with hot showers, and also offers kitchen and storage facilities.

**Hotel Nicaragua** *(Map 2;* ☎ *223-0292, Avenida 2, Calle 13)* Rooms US$3 per person. This small, family-run hotel is reasonably clean and secure and is a good basic place. There are only cold-water showers, and the hotel is often full of travelers from other Central American countries. Gringos report that the owners try and charge them more than Latin travelers and that the 10am check-out is rigidly enforced.

**Hotel Avenida 2** *(Map 3;* ☎ *222-0260, fax 223-9732, Avenida 2, Calles 9 & 11)* Singles/doubles US$7.50/12. Close by is this basic but clean hotel, which has hot communal showers. There are other basic cheap hotels on the same block. Unfortunately, Avenida 2 is very noisy.

**Hotel Rialto** *(Map 2;* ☎ *221-7456, Calle 2, Avenida 5)* Singles/doubles without bath US$6/10, with bath US$11.50. This is another reasonable, decent cheapie, which has hot water in the mornings.

**Hotel Marlyn** *(Map 2;* ☎ *233-3212, Calle 4, Avenidas 7 & 9)* Singles without bath US$7, with bath & hot water US$14. This is another cheap place, and it's very secure – the entrance is always locked and the owners let you in.

**Hotel ABC** *(Map 3;* ☎ *221-5007, Calle 4, Avenidas 1 & 3)* Singles/doubles with bath, fans, US$9/15. There is a public lounge area with a TV and phone.

**Hotel Generaleño** *(Map 4;* ☎ *233-7877, Avenida 2, Calles 8 & 10)* Rooms without bath US$6/9. This place is stuffy and basic, with spartan rooms. Shared showers are cold.

**Hotel Boruca** *(Map 4;* ☎ *223-0016, fax 232-0107, Calle 14, Avenidas 1 & 3)* Rooms US$5/7.50. Rooms here are small but it's convenient to buses, although some rooms are rather noisy because of them and the bar below. It is open 24 hours, but it's family-run, friendly, secure, clean, and has hot water some of the time.

**Hotel Boston** *(Map 3;* ☎ *221-0563, fax 257-5063, Avenida 8, Calles Central & 2)* Singles/doubles with bath US$10/15. This hotel has large rooms with private baths and tepid water. The management is friendly; some rooms are noisy, but inside rooms are reasonably quiet. A block away, Calle 2 has a seedy red-light district.

**Hotel Príncipe** *(Map 3;* ☎ *222-7983, fax 223-1589, Avenida 6, Calles Central & 2)* Singles/doubles with bath US$12/17. This place is secure and has decent rooms with private warm showers.

**Hotel Compostela** *(Map 3;* ☎ *257-1514, Calle 6, Avenidas 3 & 5)* Doubles without bath US$14, singles/doubles with bath US$16. This is a secure place. There is a private hot bath for some of the very clean single or double rooms, but you have to cross the corridor to reach it. There also are double rooms with communal hot showers and some small rooms with communal cold showers.

*Nuevo Hotel Central (Map 3; ☎ 222-3509, 221-2767, fax 223-4069, Avenida 3, Calles 4 & 6)* Singles/doubles with hot bath US$12.50/17. This is a reasonable choice and has large clean rooms. Four people can share a room for US$23. The upstairs rooms are the nicest.

*Hotel Musoc (Map 4; ☎ 222-9437, fax 255-0031, Calle 16, Avenidas 1 & 3)* Singles/doubles without bath US$8/13, with hot bath US$9.50/15. Hotel Musoc is a large building (with some noisy rooms) close to the Coca-Cola bus terminal. The hotel is clean, has some English-speaking staff, and accepts credit cards.

*Hotel Cocorí (Map 4; ☎ 233-0081, 233-2188, Calle 16, Avenida 3)* Singles/doubles with hot bath US$12/18. Rooms here are adequate, but be careful at night around the nearby bus terminal areas.

*Casa Leo (Map 2; ☎ 222-9725, Avenida 6 bis, Calles 13 & 15)* Dorm beds US$10, singles/doubles without bath US$12/22, with bath US$15/25. Bathrooms here have hot showers, the dormitories are very clean and laundry and kitchen privileges are available. The owners are friendly and helpful with tourist information, and the place attracts budget travelers.

*Hotel Johnson (Map 4; ☎ 223-7633, 223-7827, fax 222-3683, Calle 8, Avenidas Central & 2)* Rooms with bath US$14, single or double. Hotel Johnson accepts credit cards and reservations, has hot water in the private showers, and offers 60 reasonably sized rooms with telephones and use of the fax. This makes it popular with Central Americans in town on business. The quiet inside rooms are a bit on the dark side, and the beds have seen better days – but you can't expect the Hilton for these prices. There is a mid-priced restaurant and bar on the premises, with music on Friday night. Some 'suites' with TVs, which can accommodate up to six people, cost about US$24.

The friendly *Hotel Capital (Map 3; ☎ 221-8497, fax 221-8583, Calle 4, Avenidas 3 & 5)* Singles/doubles with bath US$15/17. Rooms here are simple but clean with hot water, fans, and TV. The outside rooms are noisy (par for the course throughout the city center); some interior rooms are quieter, though darker.

*Hotel Bellavista (Map 2; ☎ 223-0095, in the USA ☎ 800-637-0899, Avenida Central, Calles 19 & 21)* Singles/doubles with bath US$23/28. This friendly and clean place has pleasant rooms with hot water. Some readers complain that the walls are thin. Welcome to Central America!

*Gran Hotel Centroamericano (Map 3; ☎ 221-3362, fax 221-3714, Avenida 2, Calles 6 & 8)* Singles with bath US$18. Rooms here are clean, though rather small, and have private electric showers and telephones. It costs about US$5 more for each additional person (up to six people). Its main attraction is the central location; the management is friendly and laundry service is available.

*Hotel Bienvenido (Map 4; ☎ 233-2161, fax 221-1872, ℮ hotel_bienvenidocr@hotmail.com, Calle 10, Avenidas 1 & 3)* Singles/doubles US$18, US$9 for additional people. Credit cards accepted. This secure place has helpful, knowledgeable staff and about 50 good, clean rooms with hot water (sometimes). There is a restaurant, open at 7am, with cheap tico food.

## Mid-Range

**B&Bs** The B&B phenomenon has swept San José, from a couple of places in the 1980s to dozens today. Places listed here are mid-priced – see under Top End and Escazú for more options.

*Pensión La Cuesta (Map 3; ☎ 256-7946, ☎/fax 255-2896, ℮ ggmnber@racsa.co.cr, ☒ www.suntoursandfun.com/lacuesta, Avenida 1, Calles 11 & 15)* Singles without bath US$17-23; extra person about US$10. This place is on a little *cuesta* (hill) behind the Asamblea Legislativa. It's an attractive 1920s house with plenty of artwork and a living room for hanging out. There are eight clean and pleasant bedrooms sharing three communal hot-water baths. Management offers discounts for cash and longer stays and has a travel agency that arranges coastal trips. The place has continental breakfasts, 24-hour security, kitchen and laundry facilities, a cable TV lounge, and English- and Italian-speaking management.

*Kalexma Inn (☎ 232-0115, 290-2624, fax 231-0638, ℮ frontdesk@kalexma.com, ☒ www.kalexma.com, 50m west, 25m south of John Paul II traffic circle, La Uruca)* Single/double shared bath US$18/25, private bath US$25/35. About 5km west of downtown (near a bus stop), in a quiet neighborhood offering restaurants, a bank and an Internet café, this B&B doubles as a Spanish school. English is spoken. Six rooms have private bath; six do not. Water is hot, and there are two TV lounges.

*Hotel Aranjuez* (☎ 256-1825, fax 223-3528, e info@hotelaranjuez.com, w www .hotelaranjuez.com, Calle 19, Avenidas 11 & 13) Singles/doubles without bath US$21/22, with bath US$26/33 or US$28/36. The more expensive rooms have a larger bathroom and TV; all rates include breakfast. All rooms have phones with free local calls and the showers are hot. The place is run by a friendly Costa Rican family (English and German are spoken) that enjoys international guests. There is plenty of parking.

*Joluva Guesthouse* (Map 2; ☎ 223-7961, fax 257-7668, e joluva@racsa.co.cr, w www .joluva.com, Calle 3 bis, Avenidas 9 & 11) Singles/doubles with bath and TV US$35/50. This small gay-run guesthouse is a clean, well-run place in a historical barrio. Double gates ensure security. Management speaks English and can inform you about the local gay scene and suggest travel arrangements. Old-fashioned public areas are the most attractive feature; the seven rooms are fairly small, nonsmoking, and include cable TV. Six have private baths, and one has a separate bath (US$25). Internet service, VCR rental, and a continental breakfast are available.

*Ara Macao Inn* (☎ 233-2742, fax 257-6228, e aramacao@hotels.co.cr, w www .hotels.co.cr/aramacao.html, Calle 27, Avenidas Central & 2) Singles/doubles/triples with bath US$40/50/60. This is a nice place in a quiet area about four blocks east of the Museo Nacional (tell cab drivers it's 50m south of the Pizza Hut in Barrio California). Eight rooms all have private bathrooms, fans, clock radios, and cable TV; some rooms have kitchenettes. The staff is bilingual and friendly, and there is a pleasant outdoor courtyard for dining and barbecuing. Continental breakfast and laundry services are included.

*Diana's Inn* (Map 3; ☎/fax 223-6542, 223-6498, e dianas@racsa.co.cr, Calle 5, Avenida 3) Singles/doubles with bath US$28/38. This is an attractive clapboard house overlooking the Parque Morazán, near the center of town. Rooms are pleasant, spacious, and air-conditioned and include TV and phones. The staff is friendly and helpful; one drawback is that all rooms overlook a busy street.

*Hemingway Inn* (Map 2; ☎/fax 221-1804, e hemingway@hemingwayinn.com, w www .hemingwayinn.com, Calle 9, Avenida 9) Singles US$42-53, doubles US$53-65. This inn is in a solid-looking 1930s house in the traditional Barrio Amón. About 17 old-fashioned rooms each bear the name of a (male) 20th-century writer and offer comfortable beds, ceiling fans, cable TV, clock radios, telephones (free calls within Costa Rica), and electric hot showers. The hotel is attractive, though some rooms are small, which is reflected in the cheapest rates. There is a hot tub. An additional 10% fee is charged for credit card use. Breakfast is served in a plant-filled patio.

*Hotel Kekoldi* (Map 2; ☎ 248-0804, fax 248-0767, e kekoldi@racsa.co.cr, w www .kekoldi.com, Avenida 9, Calles 5 & 7) Singles/doubles/triples US$51/65/80. The Kekoldi is in a fabulously light and airy art-deco building in traditional Barrio Amón. This hotel is gay-friendly and also popular with younger travelers wanting to stay in the barrio. All rooms have private hot baths and telephones; there is cable TV in the lobby. The 'master queen' room features a garden view, two queen-size beds, and a larger bathroom and rents for US$75 single or double and US$93 triple. Note that singles are limited in high season. Rates include a healthy breakfast served in a grassy, hilly garden. Luggage storage and tour arrangements are available, and English, German, and Italian are spoken.

*La Casa Verde de Amón* (Map 2; ☎/fax 223-0969, e casaverd@racsa.co.cr, Calle 7, Avenida 9) Doubles US$53-75, suites and family rooms sleeping four US$87-110, with breakfast. This is a mint-green clapboard house dating from 1910. It received Costa Rica's 1994 Best Restoration Award and is now a National Historic Site, in the heart of Barrio Amón. There are eight rooms and suites, all with queen- and king-size beds, TV, telephones, radios, fans, and private baths. A sitting room with a grand piano and a garden patio are available, and the staff speaks English. Decor is Victorian throughout, and this is one of San José's best-looking small hotels; a glassed-in patio has been added to dampen the traffic noise, and a couple of inside rooms are quieter.

There are discounts for single occupancy. Buffet breakfast is served on the patio, and smoking is allowed outside only.

**Hotels** Guests all want to return to *Kap's Place* (☎ 221-1169, 390-0971 cellular, fax 256-4850, ℮ isabel@racsa.co.cr, ⓦ www.kaps place.com, Calle 19, Avenidas 11 & 13) Singles/doubles US$23/35 with bath, apartment US$50, US$5 less May & June and Sept-Nov. Weekly and monthly rates offered. Very personably run by spirited Karla Arias, a single mother who speaks perfect English and good French, this tiny hotel in a house offers two singles, three doubles, one triple, and one apartment sleeping four, all with good, hot, private showers, comfortable beds, cable TV, phones, and eclectic furnishings. Two other singles share a bath. Guests gather in the kitchen-dining-sitting area and free coffee and tea is provided, as is use of the kitchen, laundry, and luggage storage. Internet access is available. Karla prides herself on her clean rooms, personalized service, Costa Rica information, and travel reservations. She has an annex across the street with two doubles and a quadruple room, with a separate kitchen.

*Hotel Ritz* (Map 2; ☎ 222-4103, 233-1731, fax 222-8849, ℮ ritzcr@racsa.co.cr, Calle Central, Avenidas 8 & 10) Singles/doubles without bath US$18/24, with bath & hot water US$24/29. The tico staff make you feel at home; the hotel is clean and quiet in this central area. At the time of research, the rooms were old and worn, though renovations were being planned. Breakfast is available for US$2.

*Hotel Fortuna* (Map 3; ☎ 223-5344, fax 221-2466, Avenida 6, Calles 2 & 4) Singles/doubles with bath US$22/28. This is a clean, quiet choice that has decent though smallish rooms with good beds and hot water. Rooms have phones but lack TV and fans. The neighborhood is close to the Calle 2 red-light district.

*Hotel Diplomat* (Map 3; ☎ 221-8133, 221-8744, fax 233-7474, Calle 6, Avenidas Central & 2) Singles/doubles with bath US$21/28. Standard, small but clean rooms come with TV and private hot showers and are a fair deal for a central location. This hotel has a decent restaurant.

*Casa Hilda* (Map 2; ☎ 221-0037, fax 221-2881, ℮ c1hilda@racsa.co.cr, Avenida 11, Calles 3 & 3 bis) Singles/doubles with bath US$28/38. Casa Hilda has nice rooms, with hot water. The owners are friendly and tour services are available nearby.

*Hotel del Bulevar* (Map 3; ☎ 257-0022/23, fax 257-1517, Calle Central, Avenidas Central & 2) Singles/doubles US$30/35. There's a balcony overlooking the avenue, a good restaurant, and quiet, pleasant rooms with air-conditioning, TV, and telephones. This one is a good value for standard rooms downtown.

*Hotel Petit Victoria* (☎/fax 221-0953, 255-8488, 385-5849 cellular, ℮ victoria@ amnet.co.cr, Calle 28, Avenida 2) Singles/doubles with bath US$30/40. Another small hotel in a refurbished century-old wooden house, the original tiled floors here are attractive. Management claims that former President Oscar Arias lived here. The 15 fairly simple rooms are a bit dark (because of the wood throughout) but have large bathrooms and rates include breakfast, parking, Internet access, and laundry service. Unfortunately, the rooms at the front are close to the street and somewhat noisy.

*Hotel Doral* (Map 3; ☎ 233-9410, fax 233-4827, ℮ hdoral@racsa.co.cr, ⓦ www.hotels .co.cr/doral.html, Avenida 4, Calles 6 & 8) Rooms with bath US$37/54/67. Hotel Doral has 42 nice rooms with TV, radios, telephones, and hot showers, and rates include breakfast. There is a bar and restaurant, which is closed in the low season.

*Hotel La Gema* (Map 2; ☎ 257-2524, fax 222-1074, Avenida 12, Calles 9 & 11) Singles/doubles US$32/41. This hotel has pleasant rooms with fans, hot water, TV, and telephones. Smaller, noisier rooms facing the street start at US$15 single. There is a decent restaurant and bar on the premises.

*Hotel Plaza* (Map 3; ☎ 222-5533, 257-1896, fax 222-2641, ℮ hotplaza@racsa.co.cr, Avenida Central, Calles 2 & 4) Singles/doubles/triples US$36/43/56. This place has 40 nice if worn rooms in the heart of downtown and rates include breakfast. TV, telephone, and in-room fans .

*Hotel Talamanca* (Map 4; ☎ 233-5033, fax 233-5420, ℮ hoteltalamanca@racsa.co.cr, Avenida 2, Calles 8 & 10) Rooms US$40. Although the rooms are cramped, they do have fans, TV, and telephone. The hotel's best feature is a 9th-floor bar that opens at 4pm and has a fine city view. There's also a restaurant, room service, and safe parking.

***Hotel Cacts*** *(☎ 233-0486, 221-6546, 221-2928, fax 221-8616, 222-9708, ⓔ hcacts@sol.racsa.co.cr, Avenida 3 bis, Calles 28 & 30)* Standard singles/doubles US$37/42, deluxe singles/doubles with bath US$47/59. A little out of the way, this small but popular hotel is, consequently, quiet. Helpful management, clean and spacious rooms with TVs and phones, hot water in the private baths, and buffet breakfast are included in the price. The cheaper, standard rooms lack TV and telephone, but still include breakfast. There is also a pool, Jacuzzi, TV lounge, rooftop terrace (where breakfast is served), and a travel agency. Discounts for multi-night stays can be arranged, and English, German, and French are spoken.

***Gran Hotel Doña Inés*** *(Map 3; ☎ 222-7443, 222-7553, fax 223-5426, ⓔ notadea@racsa.co.cr, ⓦ www.amerisol.com/costarica/lodging/ines, Calle 11, Avenidas 2 & 6)* Singles/doubles/triples with bath US$40/50/60. In an older house converted into a small hotel, the quaint rooms here are set around a pretty courtyard. Continental breakfast is included, and American breakfast is US$3. Most rooms are off the street. All come with TV, radios, phones, and private hot bath, and there is parking (US$3) and 24-hour security. The staff speaks English, Spanish, and Italian and helps with travel arrangements. The hotel is popular with Europeans and North Americans.

***Hotel Vesuvio*** *(Map 2; ☎ 221-8325, 256-1616, ☎/fax 221-7586, ⓔ info@hotelvesuvio.com, ⓦ www.hotelvesuvio.com, Avenida 11, Calles 13 & 15)* Singles/doubles with bath US$41/47. This family-owned and managed hotel is on a quiet street. The hotel is one long corridor with a total of 20 rooms on either side, but, because the corridor angles away from the street, it is one of the quietest hotels near downtown. The carpeted rooms are smallish but clean and feature cable TV, telephones, fans, and small bathrooms with private showers. Hairdryers are provided on request and email service is available. Tropical breakfast is included. There is a terrace and private parking.

***Hotel Edelweiss*** *(Map 2; ☎ 221-9702, fax 222-1241, ⓔ info@edelweisshotel.com, ⓦ www.edelweisshotel.com, Calle 15, Avenida 9)* Singles/doubles/triples US$47/58/70. Hotel Edelweiss has a simple elegance and is located in Barrio Otoya in a quiet area near the Parque Nacional. It is across the street from the romantic restaurant Café Mundo. The 27 tastefully decorated rooms feature TV, telephone, and fans. Airport pickup can be arranged, continental breakfast is included, and English and German are spoken.

***Hotel La Gran Vía*** *(Map 3; ☎ 222-7737, 222-7706, fax 222-7205, ⓔ hgranvia@racsa.co.cr, ⓦ www.granvia.co.cr/gran/via.html, Avenida Central, Calles 1 & 3)* Singles/doubles US$50/65. This hotel has some attractive rooms with balconies facing the street, which is a pedestrian zone so traffic noise is minimized, and even quieter inside rooms. The 32 modern, carpeted rooms feature direct dial phones, cable TV, refrigerators on request, and either two queen beds or one bed and a desk area. It has a reasonably priced restaurant, and breakfast is included from Monday to Saturday, December through April.

***Hotel Dunn Inn*** *(Map 2; ☎ 222-3232, 222-3426, fax 221-4596, ⓔ willpa@racsa.co.cr, Calle 5, Avenida 11)* Singles/doubles US$60. This 24-room hotel is in an attractive late-19th-century house. Unfortunately, some rooms face the noisy street; some newer rooms added onto the back are quiet but have ugly plywood walls, but do offer TVs, radios, fans, and phones. The hotel attracts a faithful clientele of anglers. There is a plant-filled restaurant, courtyard, and bar, and a guarded parking lot. A suite is US$120.

***Hotel Ambassador*** *(☎ 221-8155, 221-8205, 221-8311, fax 255-3396, ⓔ info@hotelambassador.co.cr, ⓦ www.hotelambassador.co.cr, Paseo Colón, Calles 26 & 28)* Singles/doubles with bath US$58/70, suites with bath US$95. This modern hotel has over 70 rooms, including some top-floor suites with good views. As their website says, they have 'all the adequate elements' – cable TV, telephone, air-conditioning, and breakfast. Group discounts are available, and children under 12 years stay free in the same room as their parents. The hotel is not special but is popular especially with business travelers.

***Best Western San José Downtown*** *(Map 2; ☎ 255-4766, fax 255-4613, ⓔ garden@racsa.co.cr, ⓦ www.bestwestern.co.cr, Avenida 7, Calle 6)* Singles/doubles with bath US$62/73. This hotel has a pool, tour information, guarded parking, bar, and restaurant. Rooms are air-conditioned and have TV, telephones, and hot water. The room rate includes continental breakfast, free local calls, coffee, an evening cocktail hour, and a transfer back to the airport. This is a fair value – but the neighborhood is not the best. Take a taxi and then ask the desk to show you the safest walking route.

**Hotel Don Carlos** *(Map 2;* ☎ *221-6707, fax 255-0828,* ⓔ *hotel@doncarlos.co.cr,* Ⓦ *www.doncarlos.co.cr, Calle 9, Avenidas 7 & 9)* Singles US$58-70, doubles US$70-81. A popular hotel in this price category, this place is in a beautifully remodeled mansion, and each of the 33 rooms is different but comfortable (some more than others). All have cable TV, telephone with free calls within Costa Rica, and bathrooms featuring hot showers and hairdryers. Two rooms have connecting doors to form a family room sleeping four (US$104). Rates include tropical breakfast and a welcome cocktail. Children 12 and under are free with their parents. The excellent gift shop (open 9am to 7pm daily) is one of the best in town; they have a tour desk and, occasionally, live marimba music. The hotel's attorney (grandson of the original Don Carlos) provides a complementary consultation for guests; ask for details. There are two computers with free 24-hour Internet access for guests. You'll find an attractive indoor patio and pre-Columbian-themed garden with sundeck and a Jacuzzi; covered parking is available.

**Hotel Don Fadrique** *(*☎ *225-8166, 224-7583, fax 224-9746,* ⓔ *fadrique@intercentro .net, Calle 37, Avenida 8, second entrance to Los Yoses)* Singles/doubles with bath US$64/76, with continental breakfast. This is a family-run hotel decorated with a fine private collection of contemporary Central American and Costa Rican art, and it features a large plant-filled patio with a fountain. There are 20 rooms with hardwood floors and comfortable furnishings, all with TV, fans, telephones, and baths. There is a decent restaurant (open for breakfast daily and 6pm to 10pm dinner from Monday to Saturday) and bar. They provide transport to or from the airport for US$15 and arrange a variety of adventure tours, including mountain biking and river rafting.

**Gran Hotel Costa Rica** *(Map 3;* ☎ *221-4000, fax 221-3501,* ⓔ *granhcr@racsa.co.cr,* *Calle 3, Avenidas Central & 2)* Singles/ doubles: US$52/64 small standards, US$63/83 larger superior standards, US$80/98 junior suites, US$98/115 suites. Dating from 1930 as the city's first prominent hotel, this place does have a certain old-world charm in its 105 rooms. Though the rooms have all modern necessities such as cable TV, telephones, and 24-hour room service, many of them show their age. The 24-hour pavement café outside the lobby is good for breakfast as well as meals and drinks throughout the day, and, with its view of the Teatro Nacional, is downtown's prime people-watching spot. This alone brings guests back time and time again. There is also a full-service restaurant and a 24-hour casino. Discounts aren't hard to get if the hotel isn't full.

**Hotel del Rey** *(Map 3;* ☎ *257-7800, fax 221-0096,* ⓔ *info@hoteldelrey.com,* Ⓦ *www .hoteldelrey.com, cnr Avenida 1 & Calle 9)* Standard singles/doubles/triples with bath US$64/79/87. Deluxe rooms US$99 (one or two people). This is a shocking-pink, five-story, renovated neoclassical building with 105 rooms. It is popular with anglers and gamblers and has one of San José's liveliest 24-hour bars, known for its flirtatious atmosphere. The casino starts with US$2 roulette bets. There's also a good restaurant and a deli. The reception area has a tour and fishing desk staffed by people who know Costa Rican waters like the backs of their hands. They also set up car rentals and ecotourism. All rooms come with TV, telephones, private showers, carpeting, and either fans or air-conditioning. Some interior rooms lack windows, but are very quiet.

**Hotel Milvia** *(*☎ *225-4543, fax 225-7801,* ⓔ *hmilvia@racsa.co.cr, Avenida Central, San Pedro)* Singles/doubles with bath US$76/82, with continental breakfast. This is one of the best small hotels in San Pedro, on a quiet street a short bus ride away from the center of San José. It is housed in the 1930 home of Ricardo Fernández Peralta, an artillery colonel who fought in Costa Rica's last war (the 1948 civil war). The home was lovingly restored to its original architecture and interior ambience by the colonel's grandson, Mauricio Jurado Fernández, who named the hotel for his wife. Now the hotel is operated by Costa Rica Sun Tours. Nine spacious and charming rooms come with TV, phone, minibar, fan, and a large bathroom with oodles of hot water in the shower. A small library, with games, chess, backgammon, maps, and novels, opens out onto an upstairs terrace overlooking a garden. A bar provides guests with a 4pm to 6pm happy hour. The receptionists will help with travel arrangements; breakfast is served as early (or late) as you need it. Lunch and dinner are available noon to 8pm, and there is free coffee or tea at any time. Guarded parking and a free security box are available. The hotel is 50m north and 200m east of the Supermercado Muñoz y Nanne, a landmark known to all cab drivers, on Avenida Central.

**Hotel Santo Tomás** (*Map 2;* ☎ 255-0448, *fax 222-3950,* e *info@hotelsantotomas.com,* w *www.hotelsantotomas.com, Avenida 7, Calles 3 & 5)* Singles/doubles with bath: standard (one double bed) US$58/75, superior (one queen bed) US$75/84, deluxe (two queen beds) US$93-104. English is spoken and a tropical breakfast is included in rates. This excellent downtown choice features 20 rooms with tiled or wood floors and 4m-high ceilings in a refurbished early-20th-century coffee-plantation house. Antique pieces and Persian rugs add to the elegance of the public areas and rooms, all of which have private hot showers, cable TV, and telephones. A major feature is a small garden thoughtfully designed to provide guests with a solar-heated swimming pool (lit at night), raised Jacuzzi with water slide, rock waterfall, lawn with deck chairs and ornamental plants – a real oasis in the heart of San José. Staff, along with affable North Carolinian owner Thomas Douglas, go out of their way to arrange hotel reservations, car rentals, and tours for you. (Thomas' tica wife is a real estate lawyer; foreign guests interested in buying property or opening a business receive an initial consultation at no charge.) Guests also have Internet access, with 30 minutes free each day. There is a small bar and a restaurant (tico and international food) that has received good reviews. The hotel has a locked gate, and the rooms are set back from the busy street.

**Fleur de Lys Hotel** (*Map 2;* ☎ 233-1206, *257-2621, fax 257-3637,* e *florlys@racsa .co.cr,* w *www.hotelfleurdelys.com, Calle 13, Avenidas 2 & 6)* Singles/doubles US$76/87, suites US$104-157. Housed in a beautifully restored 1926 building, this fine hotel features 31 individually decorated rooms, each named after a native flower and all with cable TV, telephones, sparkling private baths, hairdryers, and including breakfast. The six suites are more spacious and three feature a Jacuzzi. Both public areas and private rooms feature Costa Rican art and attractive furnishings; woodwork is beautifully polished. The hotel is owned by the tour company Aventuras Naturales, which has a tour desk at reception. The hotel restaurant is good, and Costa Ricans regularly come in for the *plato del día.*

**Hotel Europa** (*Map 3;* ☎ 222-1222, *fax 221-3976,* e *europa@racsa.co.cr, Calle Central, Avenidas 3 & 5)* Singles/doubles with bath US$70/81. This central hotel has a pool, a pricey restaurant, and a car rental and tour agency. The rooms are spacious and air-conditioned. Cheaper rooms overlooking the street are available, but they are pretty noisy. This hotel is popular with business travelers.

**Hotel Presidente** (*Map 3;* ☎ 222-3022, *256-1175, fax 221-1205,* e *info@hotel presidente.com,* w *www.hotel-presidente.com, Avenida Central, Calles 7 & 9)* Singles/doubles US$70/81, junior suites US$87/99, suites US$110/122. This modern 102-room hotel has spacious air-conditioned rooms with cable TV and direct-dial phones, a casino, business center, Jacuzzi, sauna, a decent restaurant with room service, and a café. American breakfast is included.

**Best Western Irazú** (☎ 232-4811, *fax 232-4549,* e *bestwestern@irazu.co.cr,* w *www .bestwestern.co.cr)* Singles/doubles US$87/98, superior rooms US$104/115. Hotel Irazú is about 5km west of downtown, just off the freeway to the airport. With 325 rooms, this is the largest hotel in the city and a slice of Americana – a small shopping mall, 24-hour Denny's restaurant, Burger King or Pizza Hut room service, tennis court, swimming pool and sauna, exercise room, casino, bar, Internet service, and airport transfers. The hotel is used by charter tour groups escaping the North American winter and, with the facilities available, some guests don't leave the hotel! Too bad – there's nothing especially Costa Rican about it. If you do want to get away, there is a travel desk and car rental office, and shuttle buses leave daily to the Best Western Jaco Beach. Rates include TV and telephones; the superior rooms have two queen or a king-size bed and private balconies overlooking the pool or garden.

## Top End

**B&Bs** Ask for weekly/monthly/low-season discounts at **D'Raya Vida** *(Map 2; ☎ 223-4168, 223-4157, e rayavida@costarica.net)* Singles/doubles US$94/110, with full breakfast & airport pickup. This hotel is 100m north of Hospital Calderón Guardia on Calle 17, then 50m west on Avenida 11, where a sign directs you 50m north to the hotel (tell this to your cab driver). This elegant Costa Rican house is described as an 'antebellum estate' (alluding to the years preceding the Costa Rican, not the US, civil war; the architecture is, however, reminiscent of the USA's Deep South). The bedrooms and dining and sitting areas reflect the owner's interest in art, antiques, and decorating. Stained glass, hardwood floors, a patio with fountain, a fireplace, and a small garden make this a nice place to spend a few days. Owner Michael Long will help with car rental and reservations elsewhere in the country; he knows most of Costa Rica's B&Bs. The four bedrooms all have private baths and cable TV.

**Colours** *(☎ 296-1880, in the USA ☎ 877-932-6652, fax 296-1597, W www.colours.net, Boulevard Rohrmoser, northwest of 'El Triangulo')* A variety of double rooms and suites US$92-173. This large, gay-run B&B is in the quiet, elegant, residential Rohrmoser district; call for directions. 'Colours' refers to the rainbow flag, and this charming B&B welcomes gay and lesbian couples. A lovely garden with a pool, Jacuzzi, and sunbathing area is surrounded by Spanish-colonial style architecture. Rooms have all modern amenities and are spacious and bright.

**Hotels** There are 35 rooms and suites at **Hotel Grano de Oro** *(☎ 255-3322, fax 221-2782, e granoro@racsa.co.cr, W www.hotel granodeoro.com, Calle 30, Avenidas 2 & 4)* Singles/doubles: standard US$93/99, superior US$111/116, deluxe US$128/134; 2-person suites US$157-279 (plus US$5.80 for extra people). This attractive hotel was an early-20th-century mansion (check out the old photos in the hallways). Standard rooms have a queen-size bed. The deluxe rooms are somewhat larger with two beds. Suites feature a private spa and a miniature garden

or panoramic view. All rooms are nonsmoking, have cable TV and telephones, and are furnished with Victorian-style pieces, brass accents, and hairdryers in the bathrooms. No two rooms are alike. The hotel has a courtyard, serves delicious meals in a sunny restaurant (which attracts locals as well as hotel guests). The staff provides a comfortable stay and makes travel arrangements for guests, many of whom are North American.

**Hotel Le Bergerac** *(☎ 234-7850, fax 225-9103, e bergerac@racsa.co.cr, W www .bergerac.co.cr, Calle 35, 50m south of Avenida Central, Los Yoses)* Singles US$68-91, doubles US$79-102, with full breakfast. This 19-room hotel has a decidedly French flair in its dining room and artwork. Rooms are elegant and have cable TV, direct-dial telephones, ceiling fans, hairdryers and private baths; some also boast private patios or a balcony. A honeymoon suite has a mountain view from its balcony. A conference room with computer hookup, slide and video screen, fax machine, and concierge services is available. The French restaurant is excellent.

**Hotel Alóki** *(Map 2; ☎ 223-1598, 222-6702, fax 221-2533, e aloki@tropical costarica.com, W www.tropicalcostarica.com, Calle 13, Avenidas 9 & 11)* Singles/doubles US$81/104, suite US$128/162, with breakfast, including homemade bread & jam. This century-old Spanish-style house, furnished with antiques, has been turned into an elegant and tastefully apportioned six-room boutique hotel. The rooms (plus a presidential suite) are arranged around the lovely central courtyard that doubles as a Spanish-Italian restaurant-pub, known for its lunch specials. The presidential suite, with its huge Victorian tiled bathroom floor, sitting room, and inviting bedroom is one of the nicest rooms in San José. All the rooms have large bathrooms with biodegradable soaps and solar-powered hot showers, as well as modern essentials such as cable TV and coffeemakers. The staff is hard-working and friendly.

**Hotel Occidental Torremolinos** *(☎ 222-5266, 222-9129, fax 255-3167, e torrehtl@ racsa.co.cr, W www.occidentaltorremolinos .com, Calle 40, Avenida 5 bis)* Singles/doubles US$81 with bath, suites US$105 with bath. Featuring a pool and garden, this clean 84-room hotel is in a quiet neighborhood.

Carpeted rooms are smallish but clean and have TV, radios, telephones, and hairdryers. Larger suites feature air-conditioning, minifridges, and terraces. There is a restaurant and bar; parking is available.

**Britannia Hotel** (*Map 2;* ☎ *223-6667, in the USA* ☎ *800-263-2618, 888-535-8832, fax 223-6411,* ⓔ *britania@racsa.co.cr,* ⓦ *www .centralamerica.com/cr/hotel/britania.htm, Calle 3, Avenida 11*) Singles/doubles with breakfast: standard US$90/104, deluxe US$108/122, suites US$123/136. This is a small but elegant hotel in a renovated 1910 mansion in the heart of Barrio Amón. It is one of the loveliest hotels in the area, its spacious, gracious lobby an inviting place to relax. There is a good restaurant, bar, and equipped conference room, and the hotel has 24 attractive rooms. The 14 standard rooms are a little on the small side, so you should opt for the better-value deluxe rooms if you can. Standard rooms have direct-dial phones, TV, fans, and good-size bathrooms. Five much larger deluxe rooms have air-conditioning, hairdryers in the bathrooms, and writing desks. There are five junior suites. Children under 10 years stay free.

**Quality Hotel** (☎ *257-2580, in the USA* ☎ *800-228-5151, fax 257-2582,* ⓔ *info@hotel centrocolon.com,* ⓦ *www.hotelcentrocolon .com, Avenida 3, Calles 38 & 40*) Singles/ doubles with bath: standard US$87, superior rooms US$99, junior suites US$105, plus US$12 for additional people. This establishment is a member of the Quality Hotel chain in the USA. The 126 rooms and suites with air-conditioning, TV, hairdryers, phones, and private baths meet the standards you would expect from this chain (ie, fairly high but rather bland). There is a 24-hour cafeteria and room service, a bar, and a casino.

**Hotel Villa Tournón** (*Map 2;* ☎ *233-6622, fax 222-5211,* ⓔ *hvillas@racsa.co.cr,* ⓦ *www .costarica-hotelvillatournon.com*) Singles US$82-95, doubles US$81-101. You'll find this modern hotel about 750m north of downtown and across the Río Torres. There is a decent restaurant, pool, spa, tour office, and a spacious feel, and the popular Centro Comercial El Pueblo is nearby. Cab drivers know it as 300m east of the *República* newspaper office. Rooms have air-conditioning, bathtubs, and TV.

**Melía Confort Corobicí** (☎ *232-8122, in the USA* ☎ *800-227-4274, fax 231-5834,* ⓔ *corobici@sol.racsa.co.cr,* ⓦ *www.solmelia .es, Calle 42, 200m north of Parque La Sabana*) Standard singles/doubles US$145, executive rooms US$170, junior suites US$190 (some with a whirlpool bath), other suites US$200-500. Off-season discounts can be substantial – book online for rates as low as US$75. The cavernous architecture is interesting to look at, but the huge lobby echoes into some bedrooms. On the other hand, the air-conditioned rooms are spacious and comfortable, and the restaurants, although expensive, serve excellent food and provide 24-hour room service. There are over 200 air-conditioned rooms and suites with TV, telephones, minibars, and large bathrooms. There is an executive floor for business travelers, a casino, spa, sauna, a disappointing pool, massage services, and a gym.

**Aurola Holiday Inn** (*Map 3;* ☎ *233-7233, in the USA* ☎ *800-465-4329, fax 222-2621,* ⓔ *aurola@sol.racsa.co.cr, Calle 5, Avenida 5*) Singles/doubles US$87-164 (depending on availability), presidential suite US$550. You'll find this luxurious, 17-story building, topped with a fancy restaurant, right downtown. It's a San José landmark – ticos and cab drivers know it as Hotel Aurola. This is the most convenient large luxury hotel to downtown, and it has all the amenities you might expect, including a pool and parking. Rooms range from luxury standard, and are more expensive on the executive floor; there are even more expensive suites available, including the presidential suite. Children under 12 years stay free in their parents' rooms.

## PLACES TO STAY – ESCAZÚ

The Escazú suburb has a variety of accommodations, as well as some elegant residential areas that are popular with foreign residents. San Rafael de Escazú, about 7km west of downtown San José, and San Antonio de Escazú, about 1.5km south of San Rafael, are the central areas (see the Escazú map), but around them are several other districts with delightful rural accommodations with urban amenities.

### B&Bs

These are really popular in the suburbs of San José, especially in the Escazú area. Most are within walking distance of a bus line or are a 15-minute cab ride from San José. Many are owned by North American expats who can't imagine a better place to live than Escazú, and they show a genuine pride in their properties, many of which are very attractive or have great views (or both). Street addresses aren't given here – refer to the map or call the hotel for directions. Most B&Bs will give low-season or long-stay discounts.

**Park Place B&B** (☎ 228-9200, Interlink 358, PO Box 025635, Miami, FL 33102) Singles/doubles US$40/45. This is a small but friendly place run by Barry Needman, who can hook you up with reasonably priced tours run by locals. Park Place is an attractive alpine-style house with four guest bedrooms sharing two bathrooms and kitchen privileges. Weekly and monthly rates are available. Buses to San José stop just outside several times an hour. This place is a good value.

**Villa Escazú** (☎/fax 289-7971, e vescazu@ hotels.co.cr, W www.hotels.co.cr/vescazu .html) Rooms US$30-60, with breakfast. This is a Swiss chalet-type building surrounded by terraced gardens and fruit trees. A verandah is good for watching birds and eating the full gourmet breakfast. Six rooms share three bathrooms. Rooms feature wood paneling, bookshelves, sofas, and artwork. A stone fireplace dominates the central area. There is also a studio apartment with equipped small kitchen, cable TV, and good-size tiled bathroom for US$250/week, which is an excellent deal. A sitting room with a fireplace invites you to relax in this tranquil getaway. English is spoken.

**Costa Verde Inn** (☎ 228-4080, fax 289-8591, e costai@racsa.co.cr, W www.costa verdeinn.com) Singles/doubles US$52/64, apartments US$76. This is an attractive country inn with hot tub, lighted tennis court, small pool, Jacuzzi, sundeck, barbecue area, and fireplace. Rooms have fans, king-size beds, cable TV, and private hot showers, while the two apartments have balconies. All include full breakfast served on an outdoor terrace. Low-season and weekly discounts are available.

**Casa María** (☎ 228-0190, fax 228-0015, e costarica@costarica.org, W www.costarica .org) Singles US$63, doubles US$80-103, with full breakfast. Casa María is a seven-room hotel, and room rates vary depending

on the room (some share baths, others don't.) There is a pool, and lunches and dinners are provided on request. Maps, books, and travel information are available to help guests plan their trips. Decor includes walls covered with psychedelic murals and traditional art prints that combine to…well, look and decide for yourself.

**Casa de las Tías** (☎ 289-5517, fax 289-7353, e casatias@kitcom.net, W www.hotels .co.cr/casatias.html) Singles US$63, doubles US$76-90, triples US$87-101. In a quiet area of San Rafael de Escazú, this house is decorated with art and crafts from all over Latin America. The tico owners provide generous breakfasts and other meals on request, and English, French, and Hebrew are spoken. The five rooms all have ceiling fans and private bathrooms. Smoking is allowed outside only, children are accepted with advance notice, and free airport pickup is available if you have a reservation.

**Posada El Quijote** (Map 5; ☎ 289-8401, fax 289-8729, e quijote@racsa.co.cr, W www .quijote.co.cr) Singles US$64-87, doubles US$76-99, with full breakfast. Posada El Quijote is a splendid B&B on the east side of Escazú, in the Bello Horizonte district. The sumptuously appointed living room has a magnificent view down onto the Central Valley, and the well-chosen artwork found in the living room continues throughout the house. Rooms are bright and spacious, with cable TV, telephones, and modern bathrooms with excellent showers. Two bedrooms are designated for nonsmokers. Breakfast is served in the plant-filled breakfast-bar area. Outside is a garden and terrace with lounge chairs. Two apartments are for long-term rentals (US$850 or US$950 monthly). Air conditioning is available for US$5. If you like small, elegant B&Bs, this one is hard to match for top quality at a fair price; discounts are given for weeklong stays or in the low season. Airport pickup and tours can be arranged by the American owners, who also speak French and Spanish.

**Posada del Bosque** (Map 5; ☎ 228-1164, fax 228-2006, e posada@amerisol.com) Doubles US$69, with full breakfast. This country inn is set in pleasant gardens. The helpful tico owners will cook for you on request and enjoy chatting in English with their international guests. There are eight rooms with private baths in this nonsmoking inn. There is a fireplace, laundry service, and a barbecue area. A swimming pool, tennis court, and horseback-riding trails are nearby. Children are invited. Airport pickup is available.

## Hotels & Apartotels

*Apartotel María Alexandra* (☎ 228-1507, fax 289-5192, ℮ matour@ racsa.co.cr, ☒ www .mariaalexandra.com, Calle 3, Avenida 23, San Rafael de Escazú) Apartments US$93-116. This is a clean and quiet apartotel, with a pool, sauna, parking, VCR rentals, and laundry facilities. The restaurant (☎ 289-4876) is medium priced and well recommended – people come from the city to eat. This is one of the most comfortable apartotels and is usually booked up several months ahead, especially for the dry season. Apartments with one bedroom and bathroom cost US$93 for two people. Apartments with two bedrooms sleeping four people cost US$105, and apartments with two bedrooms, two bathrooms, and a studio sleeping up to five cost US$116. All apartments have fully equipped kitchenettes, dining areas, air-conditioned bedrooms, TV, clock radios, and direct telephones. Maid service is included. Discounts of 10% or 20% for a week or month are available. The apartotel is also home to Harley Davidson motorbike tours and rentals.

*Pine Tree Inn* (☎ 289-7405, fax 228-2180, ℮ pinetree@racsa.co.cr) Singles/doubles US$58/64, with breakfast (additional people US$10). Just beyond the apartotel is this place with 15 rooms, with ceiling fans, cable TV, telephones, and private hot baths. There is a swimming pool and snack bar.

*Hotel Tapezco Inn* (☎ 228-1084, fax 289-7026) Singles/doubles US$45/55, with breakfast. Near the Escazú church, this hotel has a Jacuzzi, sauna, and small restaurant-bar looking out over the valley. The management is friendly and the rooms are simple but nice enough; bathrooms are private. It's a short walk from a San José bus stop and the cafés around the town park.

*Hotel San Gildar* (☎ 289-8843, fax 228-6454, ℮ info@hotelsangildar.com, ☒ www .hotelsangildar.com) Singles/doubles US$114, with breakfast (additional people US$17). This hotel is on the northwest side of Escazú. A pool set in a pretty garden is surrounded by the modern hacienda-style

building, which houses 27 comfortable rooms. The management is helpful, and the flute of champagne presented to guests upon arrival is a classy welcome. The restaurant and bar attract diners from outside the hotel. Spacious, air-conditioned rooms have cable TV and phones in both the bedroom and bathroom.

*Apartotel Villas del Río* (☎ 289-8833, fax 289-8835, ℮ info@villasdelrio.com) Apartments US$100-350. Near the San Gildar is this exclusive-looking place, where there are 40 modern, air-conditioned apartments. It has a pool, sauna, playground, gym, bar, travel agency, and sundries shop. Villas del Río aims at long-term clients, and monthly rates are about US$2000 to US$4000.

*Hotel Real Inter-Continental* (☎ 289-7000, fax 289-8930, ℮ sanjose@interconti .com, ☒ www.interconti.com) Rooms about US$250; suites up to US$1000. About 2km northwest of Escazú, not far from Hwy 27/Autopista Prospero Fernandez, is this posh place. The five-story building has 260 deluxe air-conditioned rooms with cable TV, minibars, direct-dial phones with voice mail, clock radios, and hairdryers. It also houses a pool, spa, gym, casino, three restaurants, two bars, a convention and business center, concierge services including baby-sitting, and a small shopping lobby. There are a few more expensive suites available. The country's largest shopping mall, the Multiplaza, is close by.

*Hotel Mirador Pico Blanco* (☎ 228-1908, 289-6197, fax 289-5189, ℮ pblanco@costarica .net) Singles US$41-54, doubles US$54-76, cottages US$76-89. This is a pleasant 15-room countryside hotel in the hills about 3km southeast of central Escazú. There are balconies with views of the mountains and of San José below, and a restaurant and bar. Rooms are spacious, with prettily painted rock walls, queen-size beds, and private hot showers. Many rooms have great views and some have refrigerators. Three cottages (which lack views) sleep up to six. You're pretty high in the hills here, and the driveway leading up to the hotel is steep and narrow. You can call for a pickup from the airport, or from Escazú or San José.

## PLACES TO STAY – OTHER AREAS

The two suburbs of Santa Ana (several kilometers west of Escazú) and San Antonio de Belén (en route to the international airport in Alajuela) have several good places to stay. Beyond that, see the Central Valley & Surrounding Highlands chapter.

Remember that the city of Alajuela is much closer to the international airport than San José is and therefore is more convenient for travelers needing to overnight after or before an international flight.

## Camping

There is a full-service *campground* in San Antonio de Belén, 2km west of the San Antonio–Heredia intersection with the Interamericana, near the Cariari Hotel.

**Belén Trailer Park** (☎ 239-0421, 239-0731, fax 239-1613, ⓔ lasutter@racsa.co.cr) Tents and small vehicles US$8, larger motorhomes US$13. There are signs for this campground in San Antonio. There are full hookups for camper vehicles, as well as safe, grassy tenting areas for backpackers. Hot showers, laundry facilities, public phone, local information, and nearby public buses to San José are all available.

## Hotels & Apartotels

There are two luxury hotels near the Cariari Country Club, about 9km northwest of San José on the way to the international airport. Both hotels have country club privileges. (For information about golf at the Cariari Country Club, see the Activities section, earlier in this chapter.)

**Melía Cariari Hotel** (☎ 239-0022, 231-6442, in the USA ☎ 888-535-8832, 800-948-3770, fax 239-2803, 220-1914, ⓔ cariari@centralamerica.com, ⓦ www.centralamerica.com/cr/hotel/cariari.htm) Rooms from US$200, presidential suite US$550. This luxurious hotel has a suite that actually is used by presidents of many countries. The hotel has three pools, sauna, children's play area, casino, shopping mall, restaurants (24-hour room service), and bars, in addition to guest privileges at the neighboring country club. The 220 rooms and suites all come with air-conditioning, cable TV, telephones, and minibars, and many have a private balcony.

**Hotel Herradura** (☎ 239-0033, fax 239-2292, ⓔ hherradu@racsa.co.cr, ⓦ www.hotelherradura.com) Single/double rooms US$151/163, suites US$268-925. This place also has privileges at the neighboring Cariari Country Club and has convention

facilities. A travel desk will make arrangements for fishing charters and other tours. The hotel features 234 rooms and suites, three pools including one with waterfalls and a swim-up bar, five Jacuzzis, a 24-hour casino, sauna, and concierge services. There are four restaurants and two bars. Shuttle service to downtown is available.

**Marriott Hotel** (☎ 298-0000, in the USA ☎ 800-228-9290, fax 298-0011, ⓔ marriott@racsa.co.cr, ⓦ www.marriotthotels.com) Rooms US$243-278, suites US$520. Still closer to the airport is this hotel, part of the international Marriott chain. It's in the village of San Antonio de Belén, 5km south of the airport. The hotel features a pool, tennis courts, gym, sauna, nearby spa, golfing privileges, and a game room. There are five restaurants and bars, 248 rooms, and seven suites. Conference and banquet rooms are available. Free airport transportation is offered.

## PLACES TO EAT

Cosmopolitan San José has a wide variety of restaurants – something to satisfy most tastes and budgets. You'll find Peruvian and Middle Eastern restaurants, as well as the old standbys, Italian, Chinese, and French. American chain restaurants are also popular if you need a fast-food fix. And, of course, there are tico specialties. This section is broken down into restaurants in and around the city, and places in Escazú.

Remember that most restaurants, apart from the very cheapest, automatically add a 13% tax plus a 10% service charge to your bill. Many of the better restaurants can get quite busy, so a telephoned reservation may help you avoid a wait. (Telephone numbers are given here only for the finer restaurants.) Where approximate prices are given as a guide, bear in mind that anything with shrimp, lobster, or crab will be more expensive.

Note that the Centro Comercial El Pueblo *(Map 2)* has a variety of restaurants, bars, and nightspots as well as shops, and is about 1.5km north of downtown. Several of the restaurants and bars listed below are found here, and it is a good place to go for a wide variety in a small area.

Some of the popular bars also have good food; see the Entertainment section later in this chapter.

In and around the lively but untouristy Caribbean town of Puerto Limón

An impromptu soccer game, Puerto Limón

Preparing bananas for market

San José's Museo Nacional, in the 19th-century Bellavista Fortress

Milkman pushing his cart, San José

The capital's Teatro Nacional, built in the 1890s

Fruit vendor on the streets of San José

## In the City

**Budget Restaurants** Shoestring travelers trying to economize may find San José a somewhat expensive city in which to eat. Apart from the sodas (see below), here are some suggestions. The *Mercado Central (Map 3)*, at Avenidas Central & 1, Calles 6 & 8, has a variety of cheap sodas and restaurants inside. It's a great place to eat elbow-to-elbow with local ticos – plenty of atmosphere. There are several other cheap places to eat near the market, especially on the Avenida 1 side. The area around the market is not dangerous, but it is a little rough. There are pickpockets, too. Don't wander around with cameras and cash bursting out of your pockets, and leave that diamond-studded gold tennis bracelet at home.

*Restaurante El Campesino (Map 3; Calle 7, Avenida 2)* Open 11am-11pm daily. US$2-4. This is a pleasant place with booth seating and a homey atmosphere. It serves a few Chinese dishes and chicken roasted over a wood fire (not fried) – the latter is about US$2 for a quarter chicken with tortillas or mashed potatoes and a drink. There is take-out as well.

*La Vasconia (Map 3; ☎ 223-4857, Avenida 1, Calle 5)* Set lunch US$2; other dishes US$1.50-6. Open 7am-midnight daily. La Vasconia is a cheap, basic but decent place with plenty of local atmosphere, a largely tico clientele, and a wide variety of food on the chalkboard menu. A *pinto con huevo* breakfast (rice and beans with an egg) is about US$1, and they have set *casado* (cheap meal of the day) lunches from about US$2. Some nights, musicians stroll in and play a while.

*Café Mariscar (Map 3, Avenida Central, Calles 7 & 9)* Dishes US$2-4. This popular grilled-chicken place has an open-air bar in the back with loud music. It's popular with young ticos and budget travelers who enjoy the raucous bohemian atmosphere.

*Dos Piños (Map 3; Calle 1, Avenida 1 & 3)* Dishes US$2-4. Open for lunch and dinner Monday to Friday, this is a locally popular place with vegetarian as well as meat meals.

Most restaurants offer a casado for lunch at a price well below eating à la carte. These fixed-price meals can cost from US$1 in the cheapest places to US$5 in the fancier restaurants, where the meal may be called an *almuerzo ejecutivo* (business lunch), and are often a good value.

The *Meylin (Map 4)*, adjoining the Hotel Bienvenido at Calle 10, Avenidas 1 & 3, is open 10am to 8pm Monday to Saturday, 8am to 4pm Sunday. The *Gran Imperial Restaurant (Map 4)*, is in the hotel of that name at Calle 8, Avenidas Central & 1; both are inexpensive (US$1 to US$3) and popular.

*Restaurante y Cafeteria La Criollita (Map 3; ☎ 256-6511, Avenida 7, Calle 11)* Open 7am-6pm daily. Meals US$4-7. A recommended eatery in Barrio Amón, 50m west of INS, La Criollita serves full American or tico breakfasts, with coffee and juice included, for about US$4, with free refills on coffee and fast, friendly service. Set lunches (11am to 3pm Monday to Friday) here are about US$4.50, include a soup, salad, and drink, and offer a small choice of entrees including a vegetarian one. These attract huge crowds of in-the-know office workers from about noon to 1pm, when it is crowded and crashingly noisy; eat at 2pm for a quiet meal.

**Sodas** These luncheonette-type snack bars are usually cheap and are a good choice for the budget traveler, particularly for breakfast or lunch, when you can have a light meal for as little as US$1. Most are featureless and not fancy, but are popular with ticos. They cater to students and working people, and some close on weekends. There are dozens of sodas in San José, so what follows is just a selection.

*Soda Central (Map 3; Avenida 1, Calles 3 & 5)* This is an inexpensive place, where the *empanadas* are good and you can have *gallo pinto con huevo* for US$2.50 or a casado for US$3.

*Soda Restaurant Nini (Map 3; Avenida 3, Calles 2 & 4)* Dishes US$1-4. Open 10:30am-10pm daily. This cheap, brightly lit, self-service place serves large portions of both tico and Chinese food.

*Soda Magaly (Avenida Central, Calle 23)* Dishes under US$2. This place has a good variety of cheap meals and is close to the Hostel Toruma. There are several other sodas near here. *Soda Pulpería La Luz (Avenida Central, Calle 33)* is a local landmark and is also close to the hostel. The menu is limited to cheap, tasty local snacks and meals.

*Chelle's* *(Map 3; Avenida Central, Calle 9)* Open 24 hrs. It is quieter than the others and has similar prices to Soda Pulpería La Luz and a full bar. Some ticos say you haven't really experienced San José until you've had a wee-hours breakfast here after a night of drinking.

Other 24-hour options are *Soda Comilona No 1* and *Soda Comilona No 3* *(Map 2)*, five blocks away from each other on Avenida 10, at Calle Central and Calle 10 respectively, in an area of town where a taxi is advisable late at night. In fact, a lot of taxi drivers hang out at these places.

*Soda Castro* *(Map 2; Avenida 10, Calles 2 & 4)*. An old-fashioned tico family spot – check out the sign prohibiting public displays of romance. This place serves desserts and fruit salads.

*Soda Tapia* *(Calle 42, Avenida 2)* If you're out by Parque La Sabana, stop by this locally popular place for sandwiches or set meals. It's a tad pricier than the others.

**Cafés & Coffee Shops** These are very popular among Costa Ricans, who have a sweet tooth for pastries and cakes. They are often good places for travelers to catch up on journal or letter writing. Prices are not necessarily cheap, but you don't have to buy much and can sit for hours.

*Café Parisienne* *(Map 3; Calle 3, Avenida 2)* Main courses US$6-12. Open 24 hrs. A favorite people-watching place is this pavement café of the Gran Hotel Costa Rica, where you get a good view of the comings and goings in the Plaza de la Cultura. Anything from coffees to full meals is served here.

*Café Ruiseñor* *(Map 3)* Open 9am-6pm Mon-Sat. In the Plaza de la Cultura is the Teatro Nacional, within which you'll find this elegant café. It is popular and always full at lunchtime – come early and people watch. Changing art displays are on the walls. It's not cheap, but it serves some of the best coffee in Costa Rica. It stays open later if there's a show.

*Café de Correo* *(Map 3; Calle 2 near Avenida 3)* Open 9am-7pm Mon-Fri, 9am-5pm Sat. Charmingly located in the Correo Central, this is an excellent place to read and write letters over a good cup of coffee or espresso and a pastry or cake. Both hot and iced drinks are available and there is a small selection of pasta dishes for the hungry.

*City Café* *(Map 3)* Open 24 hrs. This café is part of the Hotel del Rey downtown, but with a separate entrance. It serves excellent huge sandwiches (about US$6) as well as pies, coffee, and full meals. Often, blues or jazz plays in the background, and an all-night guard makes this a safe place to eat in the wee hours, if you don't mind the prostitutes sizing you up.

*Churrería Manolos* *(Map 3; Avenida Central, Calles Central & 2)* Open 24 hrs. US$1-7. Famous for its cream-filled *churros* (hollow doughnut tubes), Manolos serves other desserts and light or full meals as well. Set lunches are US$3. From the 2nd floor you can watch the people going by on the pedestrian-only street below. It's a popular breakfast spot.

*La Esquina del Café* *(Map 2; ☎ 257-9868, Avenida 9, Calle 3 bis)* Open 9am-8:30pm daily. Meals US$5-11. The cheapest meal is the set lunch, including coffee, served from 11:30am to 2:30pm Monday to Friday. At other times, well-presented á la carte food, both tico and international, is more expensive, but the main reason to come here is the fine selection of Costa Rican coffees. Enjoy an espresso in a century-old traditional building in Barrio Amón, and learn a little about the nation's signature product.

*The News* *(Map 3; ☎ 222-3022)* Open 6am-10pm daily. On the ground floor of the Hotel Presidente, the News is a central, modern coffee shop with newspapers and jazz. Sandwiches are also served.

*Bagelmans Bagel* *(☎ 224-2432, Avenida Central, Calle 33, Los Yoses)* Bagels US50¢, sandwiches US$3-5. This place is usually crowded.

Ice-cream eaters craving a cone on the go should look for *Pops*, an ice-cream chain with several locations in San José and outside the capital.

**Vegetarian** Although vegetarianism still isn't big in Costa Rica, there are several vegetarian restaurants, most of them fairly inexpensive. In addition , remember that the many Chinese and Italian restaurants have vegetarian plates.

*Vishnu* *(Map 3; ☎ 222-2549, Avenida 1, Calles 1 & 3)* Set meals US$3. A popular cafeteria-style restaurant, Vishnu specializes in vegetarian dishes. Try the veggie burger and fruit drink combo. Read carefully when ordering their fruit salads, or you may end up with something more like an ice-cream sundae than a healthy meal. There are other Vishnu restaurants scattered around the suburbs.

*Restaurant Ovo Lácteo Vegetariano* (☎ 224-1163, 100m north of San Pedro church) Dishes US$2-4. Open 10am-6pm Mon-Fri. Close to the university, this place is a hit with students. Weirdest thing on the menu? Seafood ceviche.

*La Mazorca* (☎ 224-1163, 234-8516, 100m north & 200m east of San Pedro church) US$1-5. Closed Sun. This is a more upmarket macrobiotic-vegetarian restaurant, also popular with students. In a funky older house, La Mazorca has been dishing out healthful food since 1978. It has a store selling health-food products as well as freshly baked macrobiotic breads and desserts.

**Fast Food** US-style fast-food restaurants in Costa Rica serve food similar in taste and price to what you get in the USA (about US$3 for a medium-size meal, less for just a small burger). They are liked by ticos, especially the younger ones. More fast-food joints open every year.

*McDonald's* (Map 3), at Calle 4, Avenidas Central & 1, and also on the north side of the Plaza de la Cultura at Avenida Central, Calles 3 & 5, and elsewhere, has been recommended for its clean bathrooms. (Note that McDonald's restaurants are found in a few other Costa Rican towns, where they are used as landmarks.)

*Archi's* Also on the north side of the Plaza de la Cultura is this Costa Rican version of US fast food serving both hamburgers and chicken.

*Kentucky Fried Chicken* (Pollo Kentucky; branches: Paseo Colón, Calles 32 & 34; Avenida Central, Calle 31 in Los Yoses) Both these places are local landmarks. Tell a cab driver that you want to go 125m north of the Pollo Kentucky on Paseo Colón and you'll be taken there directly and probably charged the same fare as a local! (This is actually the address of the Machu Picchu restaurant, described later.)

There's also a *Taco Bell* and a *Burger King*, both on Calle 5, Avenidas Central & 2 (Map 3).

Parents of small children note that the *McDonald's* and *Kentucky Fried Chicken* opposite the Plaza del Sol Mall at the west end of San Pedro both have huge kiddie playgrounds .

**Costa Rican** Apart from beans and rice, which exemplifies thrifty country cooking, Costa Rican food doesn't have a strong character. As much as anything else, national specialties include steak and seafood, so most of the restaurants in the next section can also be thought of as Costa Rican. Although there isn't a strong typical culinary tradition in Costa Rica, a few restaurants serve tico country cooking, and the food is quite good.

*La Cocina de Leña* (Map 2; ☎ 223-3704, 255-1360, Centro Comercial El Pueblo) Dishes US$8-14. Open 11:30am-11pm daily, to midnight Fri & Sat. One of the best-known places, the restaurant's name means 'the wood stove.' The owners have had so much success, however, that they moved to bigger premises, which has detracted from the homey feel somewhat, and their prices are no longer 'country kitchen.' Still, it's a nice enough place, with strings of onions hanging from the wood beams. The food is well prepared, and they continue their tradition of printing the menu on a brown paper bag. A selection of typical dishes includes corn soup with pork, black bean soup with eggs, tamales, beef casado, gallo pinto with meat and eggs, stuffed peppers, oxtail served with yucca and plantain, and, of course, steak and fish. They also serve local desserts and alcoholic concoctions, including the tico firewater, *guaro*. A band or dance group may perform on busy nights in the high season.

*El Cuartel de la Boca del Monte* (Map 2; ☎ 221-0327, Avenida 1, Calles 21 & 23) Open 11:30am-2pm, 6pm-10pm daily. Main courses US$3-7.50. Also worth trying, this is a coffee house and restaurant during the day, serving some Costa Rican dishes – casually elegant and moderately priced – and a bar at night. Meals range from soups and salads to meaty main courses. The Cuartel's unique architectural blend of red brickwork, worn wooden floors, iron grillwork, cross-beamed ceiling, and mosaic table tops attracts an equally diverse middle-class tico crowd which keeps it busy at lunch. It gets livelier in the evening when bands play (which is not every night so check ahead) when it's loud with young people and live bands.

If you come right down to it, the **Mercado Central** is as good a place as any for a plate of pinto beans with sour cream or a couple of banana-leaf-wrapped tamales. It'll be your cheapest option.

**Steak & Seafood** Some of these restaurants are for dedicated carnivores; side salads are usually available, but otherwise the meals are very meaty. Many have a good selection of both meat and seafood dishes, while others have seafood only. Note that in most restaurants plates with lobster or jumbo shrimp will cost about US$10 more than the main courses listed below.

*La Hacienda (Map 3; ☎ 223-5493, 222-5992, Calle 7, Avenidas Central & 2)* Lunch specials US$3, main courses US$7-20. Noon-10pm daily. This wood-beamed place is quiet and unpretentious and has very good steaks, from around US$10. Pasta and seafood dishes are also on the menu. On Saturday and Sunday, an 'all-you-can-eat' pork-rib lunch for US$4.50 is featured.

*El Chicote (☎ 232-0936)* Appetizers US$4-8, main courses US$8-15. Open 11am-3pm & 6pm-11pm Mon-Fri, 11am-11pm Sat & Sun. This good steakhouse is on the north side of La Sabana, 400m west of the ICE building. It includes pricier seafood on its menu but the steaks are the best reason to eat here; they are cooked on a grill in the middle of the restaurant and served tropical style with black beans and fried banana slices, as well as a baked potato. A small pavement patio is available, and the large interior is flower-filled. You can get to the north side of the Parque La Sabana on the Sabana Estadio bus, which goes out along Paseo Colón.

*Lukas (Map 2; ☎ 233-2309, 233-8145, in Centro Comercial El Pueblo)* US$7-12. Open 11am-2am daily. Lukas has a good mid-priced selection of standard meat and seafood entrees, as well as Italian plates and sandwiches. It's locally recommended for good steaks at reasonable prices. The weekday 'almuerzo ejecutivo,' served from noon to 2pm, is a good deal at US$5.

*La Estancia (Map 2; ☎ 221-1482, in Centro Comercial El Pueblo)* US$14. Open 11am-2pm Mon-Sat & 6pm-midnight daily,

to 2am Fri & Sat. At meat-lover's delight, choose your cut from a selection of T-bones, ribs, filets, chops, or chicken breasts and have it grilled just the way you like it.

*Rías Bajas (Map 2; ☎ 221-7123, in Centro Comercial El Pueblo)* Most entrees US$10-20. Open noon-3pm & 6pm-11:30pm Mon-Sat. This is an elegant place that specializes in seafood but also has meat dishes. The shrimp and lobster entrees carry a US$30 to US$45 price tag.

**Asian** Chinese restaurants are found all over the Americas from Alaska to Argentina, and San José has its fair share (a *Tico Times* reporter claims there are over 250 in San José and the Central Valley area). Most are good and medium priced. Some excellent Japanese restaurants are found in the top hotels and tend to be pricey, though the food is good. A handful of restaurants combine their Chinese offerings with Indian or Thai curries.

*Restaurant Fulusu (Map 3; ☎ 223-7568, Calle 7, Avenidas Central & 2)* Meals US$3-8, open 11am-11pm daily. This is a good choice for spicy Szechuan and Mandarin food.

*Restaurant Kam Wah (Map 3; ☎ 222-4714, 222-9415, Avenida 2, Calles 5 & 7)* Meals US$2.50-8. Open 11am-midnight daily. Especially popular at lunchtime, when local workers crowd the place for the inexpensive set lunch (US$2.50), this is a good choice at any time.

*Ave Fénix (☎ 225-3362, 283-1201, 175m west of the San Pedro church)*. Meals US$3-10. This well-known spot has been serving Szechuan meals for over three decades and is a local favorite.

*Restaurante Tin-jo (Map 3; ☎ 221-7605, 257-3622, Calle 11, Avenidas 6 & 8)* Dishes US$8-12. The best downtown place is this recommended one, which has expanded its seating and added Thai and Indian cuisine to its Chinese menu. Vegetarian curries are featured. The restaurant is attractive and cozy, and the waitstaff is gracious.

*Restaurante Don Wang (Map 3; ☎ 223-5925, Calle 11, Avenidas 6 & 8)* Dishes US$1-12. Almost next door to Tin-jo, the Don Wang specializes in dim sum as well as an extensive menu of vegetarian and other Chinese dishes.

*Sakura (☎ 239-0033)* Open Tues-Sun. One of the city's best places is in the Hotel

Herradura (see Places to Stay – Other Areas, earlier). It serves authentic Japanese food and may be closed on Monday.

*Fuji* Open Mon-Sat. Another recommended Japanese restaurant, Fuji is in the Melía Confort Corobicí (see Places to Stay – Top End, earlier).

*Arirang* (☎ 223-2838, Paseo Colón, Calles 38 & 40, Edificio Centro Colón, 2nd floor) Open 11:30am-3pm, 5:30pm-10pm Mon-Fri, 11:30am-11pm Sat & holidays. Arirang serves moderately priced Japanese and Korean food.

**Mexican** There are mariachis on Friday and Saturday night at *Los Antojitos* (☎ 225-9525, Avenida Central, 50m west of the Fuente de Hispanidad, Los Yoses) Dishes US$3-13. Open 11am-11pm Mon-Thur, 11am-12:30am Fri & Sat, 11am-10:30pm Sun. Although this place has several locally popular locations, the best known is this one in Los Yoses. The food is inexpensive, though not as authentic as some might like (they call it 'Mexican-tico'). Choices range from a couple of tacos to a full-blown plate of beef fajitas, with seafood dishes as well.

*La Hacienda de Pancho's* (☎ 224-8261) Open daily. Featuring weekend mariachis, this place has more authentic Mexican cuisine than Los Antojitos and is 200m east of the rotunda to Zapote (south of San Pedro).

*Huaraches* (Avenida 22, Calles 5 & 7) Open 11am-11pm. South of the center, this place is run by Don Ernesto, who used to make his living in Mexico as a dolphin trainer. He's expanded and upscaled a bit, but the place still gets crowded.

*Gordy's Mexican Grill & Bar* (Map 3; ☎ 222-4642, Calle 7, Avenida 1) Dishes US$3-11. Open daily. With its downtown location and a menu featuring a photograph of every dish, this place draws in everybody who isn't sure what Mexican food is all about. It's vaguely Tex-Mex rather than pure Mexican, but the food tastes good.

Also see the Entertainment section, later in this chapter, for other suggestions.

**Spanish** The service is excellent and the surroundings attractive at *La Masía de Triquell* (☎ 296-3528, Edificio Casa España, Sabana Norte; ☎ 232-3584, 100m east, 175m north of ICE, Rohrmoser) Main courses US$10-20. Closed Sun. This is one of the longest-running Spanish restaurants here (though it has moved a couple of times and added the branch at Rohrmoser). It specializes in Catalan cuisine and is expensive but worth the splurge.

*Marbella* (☎ 224-9452, Centro Comercial Calle Real, San Pedro) Open 11:30am-3pm & 6:30pm-10:30pm Tue-Fri, noon-3pm & 7pm-11:30pm Sat, noon-5pm Sun. About 75m east of the Banco Popular, this prize-winning restaurant's Spanish chef claims to make the best paella in Costa Rica (though Francisco, at La Masía, might well disagree!).

**French** There are several French restaurants in San José, most of them expensive (at least by Costa Rican standards), and all recommended by and for lovers of French cuisine.

*La Bastille* (☎ 255-4994, Paseo Colón, Calle 22) Mains US$13-18. Open 11:30am-2pm Mon-Fri, 6:30pm-11pm Mon-Sat. Out along Paseo Colón is this cheerfully elegant place, with excellent main courses at relatively cheap prices. La Bastille is one of San José's longest-standing French restaurants and continues to fill up with discerning diners.

*Le Chandelier* (☎ 225-3980) Mains US$10-40. Open Mon-Sat. The best French restaurant in town is in Los Yoses. Tell the cab driver to go to the Los Yoses ICE building, then 100m west and 100m south. The restaurant is lovely, with dining in a choice of outdoor patios, indoor areas next to a fireplace, or larger and smaller private rooms.

*Restaurant L'Ile de France* (☎ 283-5812, in Hotel Le Bergerac). This hotel/restaurant regularly attracts locals as well as guests.

**Italian** Pizzas and pastas vie with Chinese cuisine and US-style hamburgers for the most widespread foreign cuisine prize in Costa Rica.

*Balcón de Europa* (Map 3; ☎ 221-4841, Calle 9, Avenidas Central & 1) Dishes US$6-10. Open 11:30am-10pm Sun-Fri. One of San José's most popular, this restaurant has been in the city (though not always in the same location) since 1909 and claims to be the oldest eatery in Costa Rica. The late Italian chef Franco Piatti took over the restaurant in 1984, fired all but one of the staff, and retrained the new employees to his own specifications. The restaurant became an enormous success, is usually packed with both ticos and visitors, and continues to be a local culinary landmark. Unusually, it is closed on Saturday.

*La Piazetta* (☎ 222-7896, *Paseo Colón near Calle 40*) Dishes US$7-18. Closed Sun. This place has a mouth-watering menu of creative Italian food served on silver platters – locals call this the most elegant Italian restaurant in San José.

*Il Ponte Vecchio* (☎ 283-1810, *150m east of La Fuente de Hispanidad & 10m north, San Pedro*) Dishes US$6-15. Closed Sun. Another elegant Italian place vying for the title of 'best Italian' is at the other end of town, in San Pedro. The chef survived 18 years of preparing Italian food in New York, and his work is recommended so much that the restaurant was named one of the 100 best in Central America. Call for open hours, which vary.

*Fellini* (☎ 222-3520, *Avenida 4, Calle 36*) Open noon-2:30pm Mon-Fri, 6:30pm-11pm Mon-Sat, noon-4:30pm & 6:30pm-10pm Sun. Also on the upscale Italian scene is this place, 200m south of the Toyota dealership on Paseo Colón. It has good food and a decor that gives more than a nod to its namesake film director. Live music serenades diners on Friday and Saturday evening.

*Ristorante Pizza Metro* (*Map 3;* ☎ 223-0306, *Avenida 2, Calles 5 & 7*) Dishes US$7-12. Open noon-3pm & 6pm-10:30pm daily. This eatery serves pizzas and pastas.

*Pizzería Il Pomodoro* (☎ 224-0966, *60m north of San Pedro church*) Students like to grab a pizza at this lively place, near the Universidad de Costa Rica. Locals claim it's the best pizza in town.

*Pizza Hut* (☎ 223-0244, *Calle 4, Avenidas Central & 2;* ☎ 255-1122, *Paseo Colón, Calle 28*) There is a salad bar at these locations, and there are many other branches.

**Continental** Several restaurants serve food with a European flair.

*La Galería* (☎ 234-0850, *125m west of the ICE building in Los Yoses*) Open noon-2:30pm Mon-Fri, 7pm-11pm Mon-Sat. This restaurant (behind Apartotel Los Yoses) has long been popular for its well-prepared and reasonably priced food, which shows a stron German influence and is served in a

classical setting. Many main courses are priced under US$10.

*Café Mundo* (*Map 2;* ☎ 222-6190, *Avenida 9, Calle 15*) Dishes US$6-15. Open 11am-11pm Mon-Thur, 11am-midnight Fri, 5pm-midnight Sat. This continually popular restaurant with a romantic ambience is set in a lovely older house, and diners have a choice of several dining rooms, gardens, or balconies. A nice selection of international dishes include some with a Costa Rican flavor, as well as pizzas, pastas, meats, and large salads. This is also a nice place for a dessert and espresso.

*Zermatt* (☎ 222-0604, *Avenida 11, Calle 23*) Dishes US$11-16. Open noon-2pm Mon-Fri, 6:30pm-11pm Mon-Sat. A fancy place for fondues (US$25 for two people) and other Swiss delights, this place is 100m north and 25m east of the Santa Teresita church.

Several hotels offer fine continental dining and are open to the public:

*Fleur de Lys* (*Map 2;* ☎ 233-1206, 257-2621, *fax 257-3637, Calle 13, Avenidas 2 & 6*) (see Places to Stay – Mid-Range, earlier) This hotel restaurant has a good Swiss-influenced menu.

*El Oasis* (*Map 2;* ☎ 255-0448, *fax 222-3950, Avenida 7, Calles 3 & 5*) Most main courses US$8-15. Open 11:30am-3pm & 6pm-11pm Mon-Fri, 5pm-11pm Sat. El Oasis, which is in the Hotel Santo Tomas (see Places to Stay – Mid-Range, earlier in this chapter), makes a playful nod to the all-time favorite in Latin America, rice and chicken, but serves chiefly Italian pastas and an international meat and seafood menu.

*Grano de Oro* (☎ 255-3322, *fax 221-2782, Calle 30, Avenidas 2 & 4*) (see Places to Stay – Top End, later) Most dinner entrees US$10-20. Open 6am-10pm daily. Foremost among small hotel-restaurants is Grano de Oro, which has received good reviews both for its attractive dining area and its international food. Guests can have it delivered to their rooms at no additional charge.

**Other Cuisines** There is a host of other international restaurants, with food from several countries.

*Machu Picchu* (☎ 222-7384, 255-1717, *Calle 32, Avenidas 1 & 3*) Ceviches US$4-6, main courses US$6-10. Open 11am-3pm & 6pm-10pm Mon-Sat. This favorite is 125m north of the Pollo Kentucky. It serves authentic Peruvian cuisine, especially seafood, at moderate prices. It also makes *pisco* sours (the Peruvian national cocktail). Opposite is *Nuestros Mares* (☎ 222-6419), with fairly similar prices and food, but closed on Monday and open Sunday.

*Restaurant La Palma* (Map 2; ☎ 258-4541, Avenida 9, Calles 9 & 11) US$9-18. Open 5pm-11pm Tues-Sun. An elegant wood-paneled interior plus garden seating draws diners looking for a choice of Peruvian or Italian food.

*Restaurant/Bar Libanes Lubnán* (☎ 257-6071, Paseo Colón, Calles 22 & 24) Open Tues-Sun. This is the place to go for good Lebanese food.

*Ambrosia* (☎ 253-8012, in the Centro Comercial de la Calle Real in San Pedro, opposite the new Banco Popular) Main courses US$8-14. Open 11:30am-3pm & 6pm-10:30pm Mon-Sat, 11:30am-4pm Sun. Ambrosia has an unconventional and indefinable menu, with many adventurous recipes. Expect pastas, crepes, salads, chicken and other meats, and seafood.

## Escazú

*Tiquicia* (☎ 289-5839, 228-0468) For Costa Rican food, this is upmarket price-wise, with a rustic setting. Set in a farmhouse up in the hills of Escazú, this restaurant gives diners great views and sometimes has live local music. Hours are erratic but it's usually open late for dinner – call first and ask for directions. After rain, you might need a 4WD to get there.

*La Paila de la Bruja* (☎ 228-1850) Dishes US$2-4. Open 4pm-midnight Mon-Thur, noon-midnight Fri-Sun. In San Antonio de Escazú and much easier to reach and cheaper than Tiquicia, this restaurant also offers views from its terrace. It often has marimba players on weekend evenings, and the food is definitely country tico. Don't be put off by the name, which translates into 'Witches Cauldron.'

*Mirador Valle Azul* (☎ 254-6281, 700m south & 700m west from Hotel Mirador Pico Blanco) Meals about US$10. Closed Mon. Another tough steep drive takes you to the aptly named Mirador Valle Azul, from where the views of the San José valley are breathtaking. Get there before sunset. Food is pretty good, too, with a wide selection of

the usual pastas, meats, and seafood, accompanied by live music on Saturdays and Sundays.

*La Casona* (☎ 289-8734) Dishes US$2-5. Open 11am-midnight. In the center of Escazú, this is a small, typical restaurant-bar selling tico food and snacks.

*Via Veneto* This is a nice bakery-coffee shop on the central plaza.

*Quiubo Restaurant* Dishes US$5-15. There's nothing special but nothing bad, either, in this extensive menu of tico, vegetarian dishes, salads, snacks, sandwiches, meats, and seafood.

*Café de Artistas* (☎ 228-6045, W *www.cafe artistas.com*) Dishes US$4-9. Open for breakfast, lunch & dinner. A great selection of local art (some for sale) graces the walls and shelves, and the snacks, sandwiches, light meals (reminiscent of California cuisine), and coffees are good, too. The menu varies so often that they have a website to reflect weekly changes. They often have live music on Sundays.

*Los Anonos BBQ* (☎ 228-0180) Dishes US$7-18. Open Tues-Sun. Out on the road approaching Escazú is this well-known place, which has served barbecued steaks and other food for three decades. Prices are very reasonable for the quality.

*Restaurant La Cascada* (☎ 228-0906, 228-9393) Close to Los Anonos BBQ, this is another longtime favorite, with a good selection of seafood as well as grilled steaks and other meats.

*Parrilladas Argentinas El Che* (Map 5; ☎ 228-1598) Burgers US$3-6, steaks US$10-13. Open 11:30am-10pm daily. A small outdoor patio fronts a lively pub, and Argentine-style steaks sizzle on the outdoor grills. Don't come without a carnivorous appetite – they have excellent hamburgers and tender steaks, but not much else.

*Orale* (☎ 228-6437) Situated in the Centro Comercial Trejos Montealegre (Map 5), Orale serves pretty good Mexican food.

*Hostaría Cerutti* (☎ 228-4511, 228-9954) Dishes US$10-20. Open noon-2:30pm, 6:30pm-11pm Wed-Mon. This is a recommended Italian restaurant with authentic Italian dishes. From the clients to the chef, you'll hear a lot of Italian spoken in this upscale eatery.

*Samurai* (☎ 228-4124) US$5-25. Open noon-3pm & 6:30pm-11pm Mon-Fri, noon-

11pm Sat, noon-10pm Sun. This is the genuine article – an elegant Japanese restaurant with Japan-trained chefs. Diners choose between sitting on the floor at traditional low tables or on chairs at regular tables. The cheaper end of the menu (US$4.50 to US$12) features fresh sushi, sashimi, hosomaki, temaki, and tofu tempura; meat, fish, and seafood grills, teppanyaki style if you like, are in the US$18 to US$25 range.

*María Alexandra* Dishes US$9-15. Open Mon-Sat. In the apartotel of the same name in Escazú, this is a small and locally recommended restaurant. The story goes that when John F Kennedy visited Costa Rica in 1963, he was accompanied by his personal chef, Hans Van Endel. The chef liked Costa Rica so much that he gave up his job cooking for the president and stayed in Costa Rica to work in the María Alexandra, where he supervises a Dutch-influenced continental menu. It is closed on Sunday.

Note that many shopping centers in Escazú have several decent restaurants each.

## ENTERTAINMENT

Stop by the ICT information center in the Plaza de la Cultura for leaflets on live music and nightclub acts. Of San José's newspapers, *La Nación* has the best listing (in Spanish) of clubs, theaters, cinemas, etc, in its 'Viva' section. The *Tico Times* has a 'Weekend' section that tends to cover more theater, music, and cultural events, though it will occasionally profile a local band or nightclub.

### Music Scene

Area bands and musicians are locally popular but haven't made much impact outside of Costa Rica. Having said that, there are some good Costa Rican acts that will get you listening or dancing – especially dancing, which ticos love to do. Occasionally, a famous foreign touring band will come through. Street musicians and mariachi bands looking for tips wander in and out of many downtown bars (see Bars & Dance Clubs, below).

Some groups have been together for a decade or more and are institutions on the tico music scene. Marfil, founded in Limón in 1974, is a band with a constantly evolving lineup that gets audiences jumping with standard Latin rhythm – salsa, merengue, and Carlos Santana covers. Los Garbanzos

and El Guato are recommended rock/pop bands. Rock, jazz, and *nueva trova* (modern Latin folk music, often with a political, anti-establishment, human rights, social, etc, theme) bands are also popular. A local music guru is Darren Mora of Mora Books (see Bookstores, earlier in this chapter), who helped start a number of radio stations in the country and knows the latest on what's going on.

There are usually a number of concerts on the beach (mostly rock and reggae), some with bus caravans leaving from San José; look for signs around town. (See the Monteverde & Santa Elena section in the Northwestern Costa Rica chapter for information on the Monteverde Music Festival, and the Puerto Viejo de Talamanca section in the Caribbean Lowlands chapter for the South Caribbean Music Festival.)

### Bars & Dance Clubs

Although there are some bars you go to just to drink and some nightclubs you go to just to dance, ticos delight in mixing the two, and they are also mixed together in this section. Places that have withstood the test of time are emphasized. There are a few new listings, but the scene is a bit sparser than it was in the mid-1990s. In the late '90s, a crackdown on after-hours drinking (previously something of a tradition in San José) led to a number of popular places being shut down. Most close by 10pm or 11pm except on weekends, when things may go until 1am or 2am. New places open and close every year, and the most changeable and happening scene is, predictably, in San Pedro, home to the Universidad de Costa Rica and plenty of student hangouts. Also see the Gay & Lesbian Venues section, below.

The Centro Comercial El Pueblo *(Map 2)* has a good variety of restaurants and nightspots – most are rather pricey. Wander around on Friday or Saturday nights and take your pick; some spots are cheaper than others.

*El Cuartel de la Boca del Monte (Map 2; ☎ 221-0327, Avenida 1, Calles 21 & 23)* A restaurant by day, it transforms at night into one of the capital's busiest and most popular nightspots for young people. The music is sometimes recorded and sometimes live, but always loud, and it's elbow-room only in the back room, where there is a small dance floor. In front, it's less frenzied but still crowded. Monday nights are traditionally busy, as are weekends. This is a good place to meet young ticos.

**Bar Tango Che Molinari** (☎ 226-6904, in El Pueblo) This is an Argentine bar featuring live tango for a small cover charge. It's open 9pm 'til late Tuesday to Saturday.

**Bar Los Balcones** (☎ 223-3704, in El Pueblo) This small bar features folk or acoustic musicians and no cover charge. Nearby **Café Boruca** is similar, and open 8pm to 2am nightly.

Other bars in El Pueblo may feature jazz or reggae; still others are just quiet places to have a drink without any music. The selection of live music lessens midweek, but there's usually something going on. Several discos here charge US$2 to US$4 to get in – and then may ask you to buy at least US$4 worth of drinks.

**Infinito** (☎ 221-9134, in El Pueblo) Perhaps the best known of the discos in the area, Infinito has three separate dance areas, one with Caribbean sounds like salsa and reggae, another with rock and pop music, including US and European hits, and a third with romantic music. One cover gets you into all three. This place attracts a wide variety of people, but the person flirting with you may be on the job.

**Coco Loco** (☎ 222-8782 ext 18, 257-9995 ext 18) This is another popular dance club in El Pueblo.

**La Plaza** (☎ 233-5516) You'll find this place opposite El Pueblo.

Dance clubs downtown include the following, all of which have cover charges of US$2 to US$4.

**El Túnel de Tiempo Disco** (Map 3; Avenida Central, Calles 7 & 9) This place has the usual flashing lights and disco music.

**Dynasty** and **Partenón**, both in the Centro Comercial del Sur, near the old Puntarenas railway station (around Calles Central & 4, Avenidas 20 & 24), play soul, reggae, calypso, and rap music.

**Salsa 54** (Map 3; Calle 3, Avenidas 1 & 3) This is one of the cheaper places (US$2 cover), with Latin music, especially salsa. The local dancers here are expert *salseros*.

**Lucky's Piano Blanco Bar** (Map 3; Avenida Central, Calles 7 & 9) This is a US-style bar that tends to be frequented by travelers from the US and other English-

speaking foreigners. It features videos of North American sports events and an occasional piano player.

**Nashville South Bar** (Map 3; ☎ 221-7374, Calle 5, Avenidas 1 & 3) This has country music and good hamburgers, chili dogs, and other bar meals.

**Río Bar & Restaurant** (☎ 225-8371, Avenida Central, Calle 39, Los Yoses) Close to the university, this place attracts a younger crowd, which spills over onto the outdoor verandah on weekends; there may be a live band, and the place gets really packed.

**Sand Rock Bar** (Avenida Central, Los Yoses) Opposite the San Pedro Mall, just west of the Fuente de Hispanidad, this is the loudest and most popular dancing place for the latest rock and heavy metal. In the same complex is the **All Star Bar & Grill**, a big, friendly sports bar with a large-screen TV and a variety of beers on tap. Occasionally, there is also live music and dancing. The crowd here is a mix of ticos, students, and travelers.

**The Shakespeare Bar** (☎ 257-1288, Avenida 2, Calle 28) Open 3pm-midnight. So called because it's next to a couple of small theaters, this is the place to go before or after a show. It has a dartboard, piano bar, and occasional live jazz.

**México Bar** (☎ 221-8461, Avenida 13, Calle 16) An interesting and somewhat upscale bar with delicious bocas and great mariachi music some nights, this bar is next to the Barrio México church. The beer is kind of pricey, but the free bocas that come with it are excellent. The bar itself is good, although the neighborhood leading to it is a poor one; you'd be best off taking a cab.

**Chelle's** (Map 3; ☎ 221-1369, Avenida Central, Calle 9) Open 24 hrs. This seven-days-a-week downtown bar has been here for decades and become a local landmark. It serves simple, medium-priced meals and snacks, and, of course, beer and other drinks, but its main attraction is that it's always open. You never know who may come wandering into this harshly lit bar.

**Chavelona Bar** (Map 2; Avenida 10, Calles 10 & 12) Open 'til 1am. This is a fun place in a mainly deserted neighborhood south of the center; take a taxi. It is frequented by radio and theater workers, ranging from DJs and actors to producers and wannabes.

*Jazz Café* (☎ 253-8933, *opposite Banco Popular in San Pedro*) With different live bands every night, this is a popular and upscale bar.

There are many other bars in San José; this is just a selection to start with.

*Q'Tal Club* (*Map 5; ☎ 228-4091*) This bar is associated with Quiubo Restaurant and has upscale dinner and dance shows with live bands, as well as live jazz in the evenings. Cover varies depending on who's playing, but isn't cheap.

*Taberna Arenas* (*Map 5; ☎ 289-8256, diagonal from the Shell Station*) A delightful, old-fashioned little tico bar with yummy bocas (US$1). Owner Don Israel is a real gentleman and has photos of himself with various heads of state on the walls, mixed in with the agricultural implements that are de-riguer in any decent country bar.

## Gay & Lesbian Venues

There are a good number of gay and lesbian nightclubs in San José. These range from slightly dangerous meat markets to raving dance clubs to quiet places for a drink and talk. The main street action is in the blocks south of the Parque Central, but some blocks (though not all) have higher-than-typical crime rates, so don't go around alone at night. There are also clubs in other areas. Clubs may close on some nights (especially Mondays) and may have women-only or men-only nights, so call before you go.

The following listings are among the most established gay places. The first three clubs listed charge a cover on most nights – about US$2 to US$6, depending on what's happening.

*La Avispa* (*Map 2; ☎ 223-5343, Calle 1, Avenidas 8 & 10*) This black-and-yellow building (*avispa* means 'wasp') is a popular gay and lesbian dance club; Sunday and Tuesday are big nights. There's also a pool table and big-screen TV upstairs.

*Deja Vú* (*Map 2; ☎ 223-3758, Calle 2, Avenidas 14 & 16*) This one is best known for spectacular shows and plenty of dancing, especially by men. Although the clientele are elegantly dressed, the area is not always safe, so take a taxi.

*El Bochinche* (*Map 2; ☎ 221-0500, Calle 11, Avenidas 8 & 10*) This is a more upscale drinks bar that is popular among young professional ticos out for a night of wearing fancy clothes and flirting.

Contact Triángulo Rosa (Pink Triangle; ☎ 234-2411 in English, ☎ 258-0214 in Spanish, ℮ atirosa@sol.racsa.co.cr), an organization founded to support human rights for all members of the gay and bisexual community, for information on at least another dozen places, some of which may have just opened in the fast-changing world of gay nightlife.

See the Gay & Lesbian Travelers section in the Facts for the Visitor chapter for additional information and resources.

## Theater

Theaters advertise in the local newspapers, including the *Tico Times*. Although many performances are in Spanish, prices are so moderate that you'll probably enjoy yourself even if you don't understand Spanish all that well. A few performances are in English.

*Teatro Nacional* (*Map 3; ☎ 221-5341, 221-1329, 233-6354, 257-0863, Avenida 2, Calles 3 & 5*) This is the city's most important theater, which stages plays, dance, opera, symphony, Latin American music, and other cultural events. The season is from March to November, although less-frequent performances occur during other months. Tickets start as low as US$4. The National Symphony Orchestra plays here and is of a high standard.

*Little Theater Group* (*☎ 289-3910*) This English-language theater group presents several plays a year. The LTG is always on the lookout for actors, so if you plan on being around for a few months and like to act, give them a call.

*Teatro Melico Salazar* (*Map 3; ☎ 233-5172, 221-4952, Avenida 2, Calles Central & 2*) The restored 1920s theater has a variety of performances, including music and dance, as well as drama. Every Tuesday evening there's a folkloric dance performance aimed at foreign tourists.

*Teatro de la Aduana* (*☎ 225-4563, 257-8305, Calle 25, Avenidas 3 & 5*) This is where the National Theater Company performs.

*Teatro La Máscara* (*☎ 255-4250, 222-4574, Calle 13, Avenidas 2 & 6*) This theater has dance performances, as well as alternative theater.

*Teatro Carpa* (*☎ 234-2866, Avenida 1, Calles 29 & 33*) This place is known for alternative and outdoor theater, as well as performances by the Little Theater Group, which also performs at the *1887 Theater* (☎ *222-2974, Avenidas 5 & 7, Calles 11 & 13*).

*Teatro Laurence Olivier* (☎ *223-1960, 222-1034, Calle 28, Avenida 2*) The LTG also performs at this place, which is a small theater, coffee shop, and gallery, where anything from jazz to film to theater may be showcased.

*Teatro del Angel* (☎ *222-8258, Avenida Central, Calles 13 & 15*) This is the comedy venue.

*Teatro Sala Vargas Calvo* (☎ *222-1875, Avenida 2, Calles 3 & 5*) Performances of theater-in-the-round can be seen here.

*Teatro Arlequin* (☎ *222-0792, 221-5485, Calle 13, Avenidas Central & 2*) A theater showcasing original works.

*Teatro Eugene O'Neill* (☎ *225-9433, 253-5527, Avenida Central, Calle 37*) This theater is for performances sponsored by the North American–Costa Rican Cultural Center.

Most theaters are not very large, performances are popular, and ticket prices are very reasonable. This adds up to sold-out performances, so get tickets as early as possible. Theaters rarely have performances on Mondays.

Other important theaters are *Teatro de la Comedia* (☎ *255-3255, Avenida Central, Calles 13 & 15*); *Teatro Moliére* (☎ *223-5420, 255-2694, Calle 13, Avenida 2 & 6*); *Teatro Lucho Barahona* (☎ *223-5972, Calle 11, Avenida 6 & 8*) and *Teatro Bellas Artes* (☎ *207-4327*) on the east side of the Universidad de Costa Rica campus in San Pedro.

## Cinemas

Many cinemas show recent US films with Spanish subtitles and the original English soundtrack. Occasionally, films are dubbed over in Spanish *(hablado en Español)* rather than subtitled; ask before buying a ticket. Most have two screens; the Cine San Pedro has 10 screens. The Teatro Sala Garbo offers international films tending toward the avant-garde. You'll also find more independent films at Variedades. Movies cost about US$3 per screening. Cinemas advertise in the *Tico Times* and in other local newspapers. The following are some of the best cinemas:

**Bellavista** (☎ 221-0909, Avenida Central, Calles 17 & 19)

**Capri 1 & 2** (☎ 223-0264, Avenida Central, Calle 9)

**Cine San Pedro** (☎ 283-5715/6, Planet Mall, San Pedro)

**Colonial 1 & 2** (☎ 289-9000, Plaza Colonial, Escazú)

**Magaly** (☎ 223-0085, Calle 23, Avenidas Central & 1)

**Omni** (☎ 221-7903, Calle 3, Avenidas Central & 1)

**Teatro Sala Garbo** (☎ 222-1034, Avenida 2, Calle 28)

**Cine Variedades** (☎ 222-6108, Calle 5, Avenidas Central & 1)

## Casinos

Gamblers will find casinos in several of the larger and more expensive hotels, including the Aurola Holiday Inn, Barceló Amón Plaza, Camino Real, Cariari, Corobicí, del Rey, el Bulevar, Gran Hotel Costa Rica, Herradura, Irazú, Presidente, Quality, Royal Dutch, and San José Palacio (see the Places to Stay section, earlier in this chapter, for addresses). These are fairly informal places, and dress codes are neat but casual, especially in

### Gambling Tico-Style

The most popular game is 21, which is similar to Las Vegas–style blackjack but with tico rules. You get two cards, and then ask for another card ('carta') or stay put with the two you have ('me quedo').

As in blackjack, the idea is to get as close to 21 points as possible without going over, with face cards counting as 10 points and aces counting as one or 11. If your first three cards are the same number (eg, three kings) or a straight flush (eg, five, six, seven of the same suit), you have a 'rummy' and you are paid double. And if your three-of-a-kind happen to be three sevens (which equal 21), you get an even higher bonus. If you get 21 with two cards or get five cards without breaking 21, there's no double bonus as you get in many international casinos. Splitting pairs is allowed.

Other games played include roulette, where the numbers are drawn from a lottery tumbler rather than spun on a roulette wheel, and electric slot machines. There are also other, uniquely tico, card games you'll need to learn before you can play!

the non-luxury hotels. One of the most popular and casual is in the Hotel del Rey.

Minimum bets in most places are 500 colones (about US$1.50), though you can also play with US cash in some places (US$5 minimum).

## SPECTATOR SPORTS

The national sport is soccer (see the Facts for the Visitor chapter for more details). International and national games are played in the Estadio Nacional in Parque La Sabana. (See Things to See & Do, earlier in this chapter.)

## SHOPPING

If you have the time and the inclination you can find wide selections of well-priced items in the suburb of Moravia, about 8km northeast of downtown, or by taking a day trip to the village of Sarchí, where many of Costa Rica's handicraft items are produced. (Both villages are described in the Central Valley & Surrounding Highlands chapter.) Also see Bookstores under Information, earlier in this chapter.

*Annemarie's Boutique* (Map 2; ☎ 221-66707, Hotel Don Carlos, Calle 9, Avenida 9) This recommended souvenir shop is not just the usual hotel gift store with a limited selection of overpriced gift items for guests with little time to shop around. The public is welcome and both the prices and selection are very good.

*Galería Namu* (Map 3; ☎ 256-3412, Avenida 7, Calles 5 & 7) See the boxed text 'Indigenous Art.' English is spoken.

*Sol Maya* (☎ 221-0864, Avenida Central, Calles 16 & 18) This shop sells handicrafts

A carver at work in Escazú

with a Mayan theme, mostly made from Guatemalan textiles.

*La Casona* (Map 3; Calle Central, Avenidas Central & 1) This is a large complex of many stalls, with a wide selection of items, including imports from other Central American countries.

*Malety* (☎ 221-1670, Avenida 1, Calles 1 & 3; ☎ 223-0070, Calle 1, Avenidas Central & 2) These two shops specialize in leather goods.

Some galleries carry top-quality work that is excellent but expensive (though this doesn't necessarily mean overpriced). If you are looking for top quality and are prepared to pay for it, try one of the shops from the following selection.

*Suraksa* (☎ 221-0129, Calle 5, Avenida 3) Suraksa has a good selection of gold work in pre-Columbian style, and fine ceramicware.

*Atmósfera* (☎ 222-4322, Calle 5, Avenidas 1 & 3) This gallery has a wide selection of paintings, wall hangings, and Indian work. It's one of the few stores to carry Barry Biesanz's splendid woodwork and is one of the best arts stores in the city.

*Biesanz Woodworks* (Map 5; ☎ 289-4337, fax 228-6164, e woodwork@biesanz.com, w www.biesanz.com) Biesanz's showroom, in Bello Horizonte, is open from 8am to 5pm on weekdays and weekends by appointment. See the Arts section in the Facts about Costa Rica chapter for more information about his work. Interested shoppers can take a tour of the Biesanz workshop and learn about how the craftsman selects, ages, and prepares the wood for years before he even begins to cut it. A lake, botanical garden, and native hardwood nursery are on the property and, at the time of research, a café was in the works.

*Sabor Tico Gifts* (Map 5; ☎ 289-5270, one block west of the Centro Comercial Plaza Colonial in San Rafael de Escazú) Sabor Tico has a small but exquisite selection of colorful tico crafts; closed Sunday. You can also buy local art at *Café de Artistas* (see Places to Eat earlier in this chapter).

The *Plaza de la Democracia* (Map 2) doubles as an impromptu arts market, with everything from T-shirts to carvings to paintings to inexpensive jewelry. The *Mercado Central* (Central San José; Avenidas Central & 1, Calles 6 & 8) has a small selection of handicrafts (leatherwork, sandals, clothing, wooden toys).

Also look for *Café Rica*, the local liquor that looks and tastes rather like the better-known Kahlua. And, of course, bring home a 500g bag of local coffee beans – the country's most traditional export.

Heading east on Avenida Central beyond San Pedro, look for the huge *indoor arts and crafts market* on the south side of the road in the suburb of Curridabat. It has the largest collection of crafts and souvenirs for sale in San José.

Also shop in nearby Moravia near Heredia (see the Central Valley & the Surrounding Highlands chapter).

## GETTING THERE & AWAY

San José is not only the capital and the geographical heart of Costa Rica, it is also the hub of all transportation around the country.

Unfortunately, the transport system is rather bewildering to the first-time visitor. Most people get around by bus, but there is no central bus terminal. Instead, there are dozens of bus stops and terminals scattered around the city, all serving different destinations. Efforts have been made to consolidate bus services, and the Atlántico Norte and Caribe terminals definitely helped the situation. There are also two airports.

Fortunately, the tourist office does pretty well keeping up with what goes where and when, so check with them if you get stuck. The friendliness of the Costa Rican people also goes a long way toward easing transport difficulties – if you need directions, ask.

### Air

**Airports** The two airports serving San José are Juan Santamaría International Airport (☎ 443-2942), in Alajuela, and Tobías Bolaños International Airport (☎ 232-2820), in Pavas. The latter is officially called an 'international airport' because you can charter flights out of the country, but there are no *scheduled* international departures from this small airport.

The Juan Santamaría Airport, as of 2002, is continuing extensive and (some say) long-overdue renovations; a brand new terminal has been added, and a more facilities to deal with expected increases in tourism are being implemented. There's still quite a bit to do; at the time of research there was no restaurant open in the main part of the airport in the early morning, for example.

**Domestic Airlines** SANSA and Travelair are the two domestic airlines with scheduled flights. San José is the hub for both of them. In addition, air taxis provide charter services to a host of airstrips all over the country. For details, see the Getting Around chapter.

SANSA will check you in at its office downtown and provide transportation to Juan Santamaría International Airport's domestic terminal, which is a few hundred meters to the right of the international terminal. Remember that reservations with SANSA must be prepaid to SANSA in full before they can be confirmed. You should also reconfirm in advance, preferably several times.

Travelair, the newer domestic airline, flies from Tobías Bolaños Airport in Pavas. You can buy Travelair tickets from any travel agent, or from the Travelair desk at the airport. There are no buses to Tobías Bolaños – a taxi costs about US$3 from downtown.

SANSA, Travelair, and a number of air-taxi companies provide reasonably priced charters with small (most often three- to five-passenger) aircraft to many airstrips in Costa Rica:

**Aéro Costa Sol** (☎ 441-1444, 441-0922, fax 441-2671, e flyacs@sol.racsa.co.cr, w www.costa sol.co.cr), Juan Santamaría Airport

**Aerobell** (☎ 290-0000, fax 296-0460, e aerobell@racsa.co.cr)

**Aerolíneas Turísticas de America** (ATA; ☎ 232-1125, fax 232-5802), Tobías Bolaños Airport

**Aviones Taxi Aéreo SA** (☎ 441-1626, fax 441-2713), Juan Santamaría Airport

**Helicópteros del Norte** (☎ 232-7534), Tobías Bolaños Airport

**Pitts Aviation** (☎ 296-3600, fax 296-1429, w www .pitts-aviation.com)

**SANSA** (☎ 221-9414, 233-3258, 233-4179, fax 255-2176, e reservations@flysansa.com, w www.fly sansa.com, www.grupotaca.com), Calle 24, Paseo Colón & Avenida 1 (☎ 441-8035), Juan Santamaría Airport

**Travelair** (☎ 220-3054, 232-7883, fax 220-0413, e reservations@travelair-costarica.com, w www .travelair-costarica.com), Tobías Bolaños Airport

**Viajes Especial Aéreos SA** (VEASA; ☎ 232-1010, 232-8043, fax 232-7934), Tobías Bolaños Airport

**International Airlines** International carriers that serve Costa Rica or have offices in San José are listed here, with their country of origin in parentheses (where it isn't obvious). Airlines serving Costa Rica directly are marked with an asterisk; they also have desks at the airport.

**Air France** (☎ 280-0069, fax 280-9707), Curridabat suburb

**Alitalia** (Italy; ☎ 295-6820, fax 295-6824), Calle 24, Paseo Colón

**American Airlines**\*(USA; ☎ 257-1266), Avenida 5 bis, Calles 40 & 42

**Avianca** (Colombia; see SAM, below)

**British Airways** (☎ 257-6912), Barrio Otoya

**Continental Airlines**\* (USA; ☎ 296-4911, 296-5554, fax 296-4920)

**COPA**\* (Panama; ☎ 222-6640, fax 221-6798), Calle 1, Avenida 5

**Cubana de Aviación**\* (☎ 221-7625, 221-5881), Avenida Central, Calle 1, Edificio Lux, 5th floor

**Delta**\* (USA; ☎ 257-4141), Calle 32, Avenidas Central & 2

**Grupo Taca**\* (Guatemala, Honduras, El Salvador, Costa Rica; ☎ 257-9444, 257-0408, 296-9353), Sabana Este

**Iberia**\* (Spain; ☎ 257-8266, fax 223-1055), Paseo Colón, Calle 40

**Japan Air Lines** (257-4646, 257-4023, fax 258-3203), Calle 42, Avenidas 2 & 4

**KLM**\* (Netherlands; ☎ 220-4111, fax 220-3092), Sabana Sur

**LTU** (Germany; ☎ 234-9292, fax 234-8442), Barrio Dent

**Lufthansa** (Germany; ☎ 256-6161, fax 233-9485)

**Mexicana**\* (☎ 295-6969, fax 257-6338), Calle 28, Paseo Colón

**SAM** (Avianca)\* (Colombia; ☎ 233-3066), Centro Colón

**United**\* (USA; ☎ 220-4844, fax 220-4855), Sabana Sur

**Varig**\* (Brazil; ☎ 290-5222, fax 290-0200), Avenida 5, Calles 3 & 5

## Bus

Read the general information in the Getting Around chapter about Costa Rican bus travel before you begin taking buses around the country. This section lists the addresses and some phone numbers for the long-distance public bus companies. However, at bus offices there may be no clear evidence of a particular company – bus offices are more often identified by destination than by company (with the exception of international bus companies). Many companies have no more than a bus stop; some have a tiny office with a window opening onto the street; some operate out of a terminal.

In addition to the public bus companies used by ticos to get around the country, there are two tourist bus companies that have scheduled departures around the country specifically designed for international travelers. These companies, Interbus and Fantasy Bus-Gray Line, charge several times more than the regular public buses but are air-conditioned, more comfortable, and easier to locate than the complicated system that ticos blithely use.

The ICT information office at the Plaza de la Cultura has up-to-date bus information and will provide you with a detailed brochure of bus services and times upon request. Also useful is a brochure titled *Hop on the Bus,* found in tourist offices, hotels, and places where tourists gather – this focuses mainly on destinations of interest to tourists. Both Interbus and Fantasy Bus-Gray Line publish their own schedules, available from many hotels and travel agents.

Calling bus companies themselves is usually more frustrating than helpful unless you are fluent in Spanish; the most reliable way to find out about routes and schedules is to go in person to the bus stop and ask for information. Talk to the ticket seller, if there is one, or the bus conductor. Bus departure points and general terminals are shown on this book's city maps.

Try to avoid leaving San José on Friday night or Saturday morning, when the buses are full of josefinos off for the weekend. If you must travel then, try to book ahead. Buses during Christmas and Easter are very crowded indeed.

In addition to the old Coca-Cola terminal, named after a Coca-Cola bottling plant that existed on the site many years ago, San José has two general bus terminals. The Coca-Cola terminal (Map 4) is between Calles 16 & 18, north of Avenida 1, and is one of the best-known landmarks in San José. The Caribe terminal (Map 2), north of Avenida 13 on Calle Central, serves the Caribbean coast. The Atlántico Norte terminal (Map 4), at Avenida 9, Calle 12, serves northern destinations, including Monteverde, the Arenal area, and Puerto Viejo de Sarapiquí.

Several companies serve a number of different towns from in and around the Coca-Cola terminal. There are a few small signs in the terminal and it seems bewildering at first, but just ask someone to show you where your bus is; everyone seems to know where each bus leaves from. Several other companies have buses leaving from within three or four blocks of the Coca-Cola terminal, so this is an area to know. It's not the best part of town, so watch for pickpockets and use common sense. The area is generally safe during the day, though after dark you might take a taxi rather than walking, particularly if you are a solo woman traveler. Some travelers suggest that you take a cab at any time.

The Atlántico Norte terminal is in the same neighborhood, but is better organized and often has a guard on duty.

The Caribe terminal is a longish walk from downtown through a somewhat deserted area that is considered safer than the Coca-Cola area; a taxi is certainly the easiest way to go. The terminal itself is modern and bursting with amenities – restaurants, shops, bathrooms, and phones. For general information about either the Atlántico Norte or Caribe terminals, call ☎ 256-8129.

Bus fares (in US dollar terms) tend to stay fairly stable for internal routes over time, but schedules change more often. Try calling, or go by the bus stop for the latest departure times.

**Fantasy Bus-Gray Line** Call ☎ 800-326-8279 for reservations and departure information. English is spoken. They have buses every morning (departures between 7am and 8:30am) from San José to the tourist destinations of Tamarindo, Playa Hermosa, Liberia, Fortuna, Jaco, Cahuita, Puerto Viejo de Talamanca, and Manuel Antonio. The set fee is US$19 anywhere the bus goes. They also do intermediate trips such as Tamarindo to Jaco; call for details.

**Interbus** Call ☎ 283-5573 or check W www.interbusonline.com for reservations and departure information. English is spoken. This company essentially does the same as Fantasy Bus-Gray Line but has more routes, more buses, and fares vary according to destination (most are US$25 to US$38). Passengers can arrange pickups and dropoffs at hotels if desired. They also do Flexipasses (from US$110 for four trips to US$200 for 10 trips) valid for any trips within a month. These are popular with travelers who don't want to bother with the regular tico buses.

**To Nicaragua** See the Getting There & Away chapter for details of what to expect when taking international buses. TICA Bus (☎ 221-8954), Calle 9, Avenidas 2 & 4, has buses to Managua daily at 6am (there may be a second bus at 7:30am, or fewer buses, depending on demand, so check locally). The trip takes 11 hours and costs about US$10 from San José (it varies from year to year depending on exchange rates). These buses continue to San Salvador (US$32) or Tegucigalpa (US$30) and Guatemala City (US$38, 2½ days; passengers sleep in hotels in Managua and San Salvador). Buses to San José leave Managua at 6am.

A similarly priced but less reliable service to Managua is provided by Sirca (☎ 256-9072), Calle 16, Avenidas 3 & 5. Departures for Managua are at 4:30am daily. Sirca recommends that you buy tickets three days in advance. Fares from Managua are rarely the same as from San José because of differences in currency regulations.

Remember to bring your passport when buying international tickets.

**To Panama** TICA Bus has a daily service to Panama City at 10pm (US$20, 18 hours). It leaves Panama City at 11am for the return to San José. Buses have onboard bathrooms and video. Buy tickets in advance. This company will also sell you a ticket to David, the first major town in Panama. Another company with buses to David is TRACOPA (☎ 222-2666), Calle 14, Avenidas 3 & 5, with direct buses at 7:30am daily (US$9, nine hours) and at midday if there is enough demand.

A company with fairly comfortable express bus service to Panama City is Panaline (☎ 256-8721, 255-1205), near the Hotel Cocorí at Calle 16, Avenida 3. The trip costs US$20 and takes 16 hours, with daily departures at 1pm. Buses to San José leave Panama City at 2pm as well.

Note that fares from Panama City are usually higher than from San José because of differences in currency regulations.

**To Southern Costa Rica** TRACOPA and Empresa Alfaro share a terminal (☎ 222-2666), Calle 14, Avenidas 3 & 5. TRACOPA has six daily buses to Neily and on to the Panamanian border at Paso Canoas. It is about seven hours to Neily, eight hours to the border. Fares are US$6/7 to Neily/Paso Canoas direct, or a little cheaper on the normal route. TRACOPA also has seven daily buses to Palmar Norte (US$5.50, five hours) and three daily buses to Golfito (US$7, eight hours). TRACOPA buses to Coto Brus, en route to San Vito (US$6.75, seven hours), leave four times a day.

Buses to Puerto Jiménez in the Península de Osa (US$7, eight hours) leave at 6am and noon with Autotransportes Blanco (☎ 257-4121) from the office at Calle 14, Avenida 9 & 11.

Buses to San Isidro de El General (US$3, three hours) depart from a terminal (☎ 222-2422, 771-0414, 223-0686) at Calle Central and Avenida 22, about every hour during the day.

Buses for Santa María de Dota (and the Ruta de los Santos) depart several times a day with Autotransportes Los Santos

(☎ 223-1002, 546-6248); they leave from Avenida 16, Calles 19 & 21. The fare is about US$2 for the 2½-hour trip.

**To the Central Valley** Buses to Cartago leave several times an hour from the SACSA station (☎ 233-5350) at Calle 5, Avenida 18. The trip takes almost an hour, depending on traffic, and costs about US40¢. Some of these buses continue to Turrialba, but more Turrialba buses leave from the TRANSTUSA station (☎ 556-0073, 591-4145), Avenida 6, Calle 13. The two-hour ride costs just over US$1.

Microbuses to Heredia leave several times an hour between 5am and midnight and every half hour between midnight and 4am from Calle 1, Avenidas 7 & 9; the half-hour trip costs about US40¢. Microbuses to Heredia also leave from the south side of Avenida 2, Calles 10 & 12 (across from the Alajuela bus stop), every 15 minutes between 6am and 8pm. Microbuses Rápidos Heredianos (☎ 233-8392, 261-0506) also leave from Calle Central, Avenidas 7 & 9.

Buses to Alajuela leave every few minutes from the TUASA terminal (☎ 222-5325) at Avenida 2, Calle 12. There are two terminals on the north side of Avenida 2, both east and west of Avenida 2. Most of these buses stop at the international airport.

Buses to Grecia (US40¢, one hour) and continuing on 7km to Sarchí (☎ 494-2139, US50¢, 90 minutes) leave hourly from the Coca-Cola terminal. It is often easier to go to Alajuela and change. The Coca-Cola is the place for frequent buses to several small central valley towns such as Atenas, Naranjo, and Orotina; see the Central Valley chapter for bus information to other small towns.

**To the Pacific Coast** Buses to Quepos and Manuel Antonio leave from the Coca-Cola terminal with Transportes Morales (☎ 223-5567). Direct buses to Manuel Antonio, with reserved seats, leave at 6am, noon, 6pm, and 7:30pm, and cost US$5 for the 3½-hour trip. Slower and cheaper buses to Quepos leave five times a day. Other Transportes Morales buses (☎ 232-1829, 223-1109) go to Jacó at 7:30am, 10:30am, and 3:30pm from the Coca-Cola terminal. The 2½-hour journey costs about US$2.

Buses to Puntarenas leave every 40 minutes from 6am to 7pm from a terminal at Calle 16, Avenida 12, with Empresarios Unidos de Puntarenas (☎ 222-0064, 233-2610, 221-5749). The two-hour trip costs about US$2.50.

Although traditionally most services to Dominical and Uvita are via San Isidro de El General and change buses, the opening of a new paved road from Dominical to Cuidad Cortés (near Palmar Norte) has led to a new service from San José with Alfaro (☎ 222-2666), Calle 14, Avenidas 3 & 5, to Ciudad Cortés (eight hours) stopping at Dominical and Uvita. Buses leave at 8:30am and 2:30pm. Look for more buses on this route in the future.

**To the Península de Nicoya** Buses to the Península de Nicoya and its popular beaches have to negotiate the Golfo de Nicoya, a formidable body of water. Buses either cross the Río Tempisque (at the northwestern end of the Golfo de Nicoya) on the ferry between the mainland and peninsula highways, which leaves about every hour, or take the longer overland route through Liberia. Thus, bus times can vary considerably depending on the route chosen and, if using the ferry, whether you have to spend a long time waiting for it – it leaves about every hour. A bridge is being built north of the current ferry crossing, which, when completed, will make this route quicker. At the time of research, completion was slated for late 2002. The car ferry from Puntarenas does not normally take buses.

Empresa Alfaro (☎ 258-4716, 222-2666), Calle 14, Avenidas 3 & 5, has eight daily buses to Nicoya (US$6, six hours), some going to Santa Cruz and Filadelfia. More interestingly, they also have daily buses to beaches at Sámara (12:30pm daily, 5:45pm Thur-Sat, US$6, six hours) and Tamarindo (3:30pm, US$6, five hours), as well as a bus to Quebrada Honda, Mansión, and Hojancha (2:30pm).

On Calle 12, Avenidas 7 & 9, is a small office (☎ 257-1835, 258-3883) with 6am and 3:30pm buses to Jicaral and the beaches at Bejuco and Islita (US$5.50, five hours).

TRALAPA (☎ 221-7201/2), at Calle 20, Avenida 5, has daily buses to Playa Flamingo (8am, 11am, 3pm, US$8), Playa Panamá (3:25pm, US$5.50, 4½ hours), Junquillal (2pm, US$8), and Santa Cruz (nine daily, US$5.25).

The Pulmitan station (☎ 222-1650), Calle 24, Avenida 5, has two buses to Playa del Coco, at 8am and 2pm daily (US$5).

These schedules are for the dry season, when people go to the beach – during the wet season, services may be curtailed. Beach resorts are very popular among Costa Ricans and buses tend to be booked up ahead of time, especially during dry-season weekends. Buses are booked up days and weeks ahead for Easter week. Reserve a seat if possible.

**To Northern & Northwestern Costa Rica** Unless otherwise noted, the following buses leave from the Atlántico Norte terminal (☎ 222-3854), Avenida 9, Calle 12. (Many taxi drivers call this the San Carlos terminal.) Express buses to Monteverde (☎ 645-5159, 695-5611) leave at 6:30am and 2:30pm daily for the four-hour trip, which costs about US$5. It is worth getting tickets the day before, because the buses get booked up quickly; the ticket office is closed from 12:30pm to 2pm. Buses to Tilarán (US$3.50) leave at 7:30am, 9:30am, 12:45pm, 3:45pm, and 6:30pm.

Buses to Ciudad Quesada (☎ 256-8914, 460-5032, US$2.50, three hours) via Zarcero (one hour) leave at least every hour; a few buses are express to Ciudad Quesada. (Note that Ciudad Quesada is also known as San Carlos.) From Ciudad Quesada you can take buses west to Fortuna, Volcán Arenal, and on to Tilarán, or east toward Puerto Viejo de Sarapiquí and Río Frío. There are also direct buses to Fortuna (☎ 256-8914) at 6:15am, 8:40am, and 11:30am (US$4, 4½ hours). Buses to Los Chiles (☎ 460-5032, US$4, five hours) leave at 5:30am and 3:30pm.

Direct buses to Puerto Viejo de Sarapiquí (☎ 257-6859), not to be confused with Puerto Viejo de Talamanca on the southeastern Caribbean coast, leave eight times a day between 6:30am and 6pm and cost about US$3. (Note that these buses are slated to move offices for the Terminal Caribe – see below – so call and check). Most of these buses go via Río Frío and Horquetas (for Rara Avis) and return to San José via Varablanca and Heredia; a few do the route in reverse. If going to Horquetas, make sure you go via the Río Frío route or you will get stuck on the bus for four hours instead of 2½ hours. The Heredia/Varablanca route is more scenic. Check departures with the bus stop or the ICT – they tend to change frequently.

The following buses do not leave from the Atlántico Norte terminal.

Buses to Cañas with TUASUR (☎ 222-3006) leave six times a day from Calle 16, Avenidas 1 & 3, opposite the Coca-Cola terminal. The trip takes about 3½ hours and costs about US$2.50. There also is one bus to La Cruz (near the Nicaraguan border), continuing to Santa Cecilia, at 2:45pm. A bus to Upala leaves at 6:30am daily (6am on Saturdays). Buses to Upala also leave from Calle 12, Avenidas 3 & 5, at 3pm and 3:45pm daily.

Buses to the Nicaraguan border at Peñas Blancas, with stops at the entrance to Parque Nacional Santa Rosa and La Cruz, leave from behind the Hotel Cocorí, Calle 14, Avenidas 3 & 5, with Transportes Deldu (☎ 256-9072). There are five buses daily, and the cost is about US$5.50 for the six-hour trip to the border.

Buses to Liberia (US$4, 4½ hours) leave 10 times a day from Pulmitan (☎ 256-9552), Calle 24, Avenida 5.

**To the Caribbean Coast** The following buses all leave from the Caribe terminal (☎ 257-8129). Buses to Guápiles (☎ 222-0610) leave about every half hour between 6am and 9pm. Buses to Sixaola that stop at Cahuita and Puerto Viejo de Talamanca leave at 6am and 10am and 1:30pm and 3:30pm. Tickets cost about US$5; the trip to Cahuita takes about four hours, to Puerto Viejo about 4½ to five hours, and to Sixaola about six hours. Direct buses to Puerto Limón (☎ 221-2596) leave hourly from 5:30am to 7pm; the trip takes almost three hours and costs about US$4. From Limón there are frequent buses southeast along the coast.

### Train

The railway was severely damaged in the 1991 earthquake, causing all services to be canceled, and it is highly unlikely that the services from San José to Puerto Limón or to Puntarenas will resume. The famous and attractive route to Puerto Limón was known as the 'banana train.' Ask at the ICT in the Plaza de la Cultura about day tours on old trains for parts of this route.

## GETTING AROUND

Downtown San José is very busy and relatively small. The narrow streets, heavy traffic, and complicated one-way system often mean that it is quicker to walk than to take the bus. The same applies to driving: If you rent a car, don't drive in downtown – it's a nightmare! If you're in a hurry to get somewhere that is more than a kilometer away, take a taxi.

### To/From the Airport

For the main international airport (Juan Santamaría) there is no airport bus as such, but most buses to Alajuela will stop at the international airport. Look for a sign in the bus window, or ask before boarding ('¿aeropuerto?'). Alajuela buses leave every few minutes from Avenida 2, Calle 12, and cost about US40¢, whether you go to the airport or Alajuela. (From midnight to 5am, buses go about every hour.)

Heading into San José from the airport, you'll find the bus stop outside the international terminal, behind the car rental agencies. This is several blocks away, and sharing a taxi is definitely more convenient if you have a bunch of baggage. During the rush hour, the Alajuela to San José buses may be full when they come by, and you may have to wait for some time.

Airport taxis are orange, and the fare to or from the airport is a set US$12 – though some budget hotels may be able to negotiate a US$10 fare. Cab drivers at the airport may try to hustle you, either by trying to charge more than US$12 or by asking you to share the cab with another passenger into San José, and then charging each of you US$12. Don't start a cab journey without establishing the fare first.

The Interbus service charges US$5 for a hotel to airport ride (6am to 10pm) or US$10 late at night. Make reservations ahead of time.

There are no direct buses to the local airport at Tobías Bolaños. Your best bet is to take a taxi – about US$3.

### Bus

Local buses are useful to get you into the suburbs and surrounding villages, or to the airport. They have set routes and leave regularly from particular bus stops downtown. Buses run from about 5am to 10pm and cost from US15¢ to US50¢.

Buses from Parque La Sabana head into town on Paseo Colón, then go over to Avenida 2 at the San Juan de Dios hospital. They then go three different ways through town before eventually heading back to La Sabana. Buses are marked Sabana-Cementario, Sabana-Estadio, or Cementario-Estadio. These buses are a good bet for a cheap city tour. Buses going east to Los Yoses and San Pedro go back and forth along Avenida 2, going over to Avenida Central at Calle 29 outbound. They start at Avenida 2, Calle 7, near the Restaurante El Campesino.

Buses to the following outlying suburbs and towns begin from bus stops at the indicated blocks (though they pick up passengers at other stops along the way, which you'll figure out by asking or doing the journey once from the beginning). Some places have more than one stop – only the main one is listed here. If you need buses to other suburbs, inquire at the tourist office.

**Escazú** Calle 16, Avenidas Central & 1

**Guadalupe** Avenida 3, Calles Central & 1

**Moravia** Avenida 3, Calles 3 & 5

**Pavas** Avenida 1, Calle 18

**Santa Ana** Calle 16, Avenidas 1 & 3 (at the back of the Coca-Cola terminal)

**Santo Domingo** Avenida 5, Calles Central & 2

### Electric Trams

Trams were the main form of city transport in the early 1900s but stopped running in 1950. Plans to reopen a section of track have yet to materialize.

### Car

There are more than 50 car rental agencies in San José. Look in the newspaper or the yellow pages under *Alquiler de Automóviles* for a comprehensive listing. The *Tico Times* often carries ads for those companies that are having specials. However, car rental is quite expensive, at least by North American standards. Review the Car & Motorcycle section in the Getting Around chapter before venturing onto the roads. As long as you're careful, you can have fun with a car in Costa Rica.

Car rental rates vary by about 10% among companies, so shop around.

### Motorcycle

Given the narrow roads and difficult driving conditions, riding a motorcycle is not recommended, especially for people without much experience. However, if you are an experienced and careful biker, renting a motorcycle is an option. Rentals start about US$30 to US$40 per day including unlimited mileage, insurance, and one (or two) helmets. Weekly discounts are available. Rental bikes are usually small, in the 185cc to 350cc range. Larger bikes are very expensive.

A few motorcycle rental companies have come and gone over the years. Try Wild Rider (☎/fax 258-4604, Ⓦ www.ritmo-del-caribe.com), Paseo Colón, Calle 32, opposite Kentucky Fried Chicken. They start at US$180/week for a Suzuki DR 250 and do guided tours as well. Much more expensive is Harley Davidsons Rentals (☎ 289-5552, fax 289-5551) in Escazú. Others advertise occasionally in the newspapers (but may not be in the yellow pages).

### Taxi

San José taxis are red, with the exception of airport cabs, which are orange. Downtown, meters *(marías)* are supposed to be used, but some drivers will pretend they are broken and try to charge you more – particularly if you are a tourist who doesn't speak Spanish. Driving with a broken maría is illegal. Always make sure that the maría is working when you get in – if it isn't, you can get out and hail another taxi or negotiate a fare to avoid being grossly overcharged at your destination.

Short rides downtown should cost around US$1, longer rides around US$2, and a cab to Escazú about US$3 to US$4. There is a 20% surcharge after 10pm, which may not appear on the maría. Waiting time has to be negotiated – about US$5 an hour is reasonable. San José cab drivers are the toughest in Costa Rica; on the other hand, they are a lot more friendly than cab drivers in many other countries.

You can hire a taxi and driver for half a day or longer if you want to do some touring around the Central Valley. Around US$40 is reasonable for half a day, depending on how far you want to go. Cabs will take three or four passengers. To hire a cab, either ask your hotel to help arrange it or flag one down on the street. Alternatively, talk to drivers at any taxi stand. There are cab stands at the Parque Nacional, Parque Central, near the Teatro Nacional, and in front of several of the better hotels. Taxi drivers are not normally tipped in Costa Rica.

You can have a taxi pick you up if you are going to the airport or have a lot of luggage. The most difficult time to flag down a taxi is when it's raining (especially afternoons in the May to November wet months).

### Bicycle
Most bike shops in San José will sell bikes and parts, but are reluctant to rent them. Call the shops listed under *Bicicletas* in the yellow pages and see if you can find something. Trek of Costa Rica (☎ 296-3383, 280-3580, fax 289-7013) in Rohrmoser has good bikes from US$20 a day.

# Central Valley & Surrounding Highlands

The 'Central Valley' is the popular English name for the region in the center of Costa Rica around San José. It is not really a valley, and a more appropriate name would be the 'central plateau' or 'central tableland.' This is, in fact, the literal translation of the Costa Rican name for the area, Meseta Central.

This region is both historically and geographically the heart of Costa Rica. To the north and east, the Central Valley is bounded by the mountain range known as the Cordillera Central, which contains several volcanoes, including the famous Volcán Poás and Volcán Irazú.

To the south, the region is bounded by the north end of the Cordillera de Talamanca and a short mountainous projection called the Fila de Bustamente. Between the Cordilleras Central and Talamanca is the beautiful Río Reventazón valley, which gives San José its historical access to the Caribbean. To the west, the plateau falls off into the Pacific lowlands.

This chapter covers the Central Valley (except San José) and, additionally, the upper Río Reventazón valley and the volcanoes of the Cordillera Central. Although not geographically part of the Central Valley, these surrounding highlands are usually visited on day trips from San José.

About two-thirds of Costa Rica's population live in the Central Valley. The region's fertile volcanic soil and pleasant climate attracted the first successful Spanish settlers. Before the arrival of the Spaniards, the region was an important agricultural zone, inhabited by thousands of Indian farmers, most of whom were wiped out by diseases brought by the Europeans. The first colonial capital city was at Cartago.

Today, four of Costa Rica's seven provinces have fingers of land within the Central Valley, and all four have their political capitals there. Thus, we see an unusual situation in which three provincial capitals are within a scant 25km of San José, which itself is the capital of San José Province. The others are the cities of Cartago, Alajuela, and Heredia, all capitals of provinces of the same names.

Despite their provincial capital status, the cities of the Central Valley do not have a

## Highlights

- Whooping it up on whitewater descents of the Reventazón and Pacuare Rivers
- Gazing into the active craters of Irazú or Poás volcanoes
- Hiking past numerous cascades at Los Jardines de la Catarata la Paz
- Visiting quintessential highland villages and the country's oldest churches in the Orosi valley
- Learning lots about lepidopterology at the Butterfly Garden
- Strolling around the peculiarly trimmed hedges in Zarcero's topiary plaza
- 'Cupping' coffee – learning about varieties and flavors at Café Britt

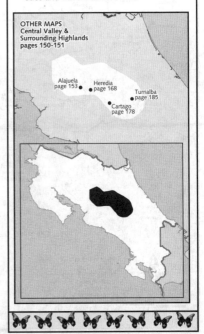

OTHER MAPS
Central Valley &
Surrounding Highlands
pages 150-151

Alajuela
page 153

Heredia
page 168

Turrialba
page 185

Cartago
page 178

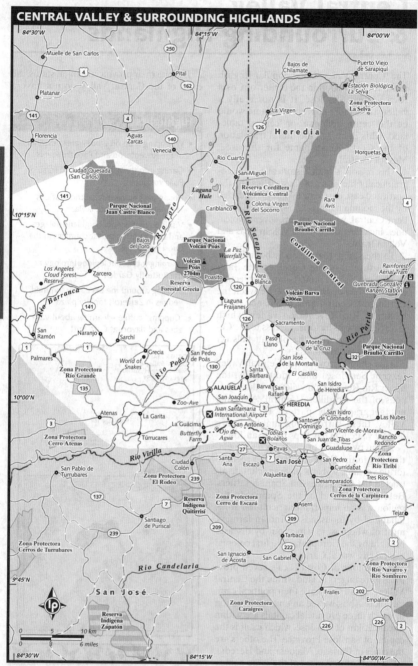

# CENTRAL VALLEY & SURROUNDING HIGHLANDS

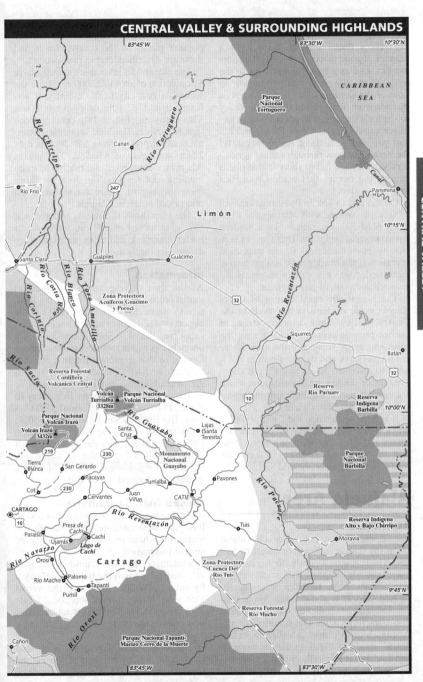

## CENTRAL VALLEY & SURROUNDING HIGHLANDS

well-developed hotel infrastructure, with the exception of Alajuela, which, close to the international airport, does have a number of good places to stay. Most visitors use San José as a base for day trips to the other cities, as well as many other attractions of the Central Valley region. A public bus ride from San José out to Central Valley towns for a day trip is as good a way as any to see some of rural Costa Rica – and it'll cost you next to nothing. As visitors travel the area, they pass through rolling agricultural countryside full of shiny-leafed plants bearing the berries that made Costa Rica famous – coffee.

On the way to Volcán Poás, huge areas of hillside are covered with what appear to be black plastic sheets, rather like a modern environmental sculpture. These are, in fact, *viveros* (plant nurseries). Closer inspection reveals that the black plastic is a protective mesh under which a variety of plants are grown before sale to greenhouses.

The essentially rural nature of Costa Rica is made evident by the roads of the Central Valley. Thin, winding strips of tarmac provide tenuous links among the cities and many villages of the area. There are no freeways, and the road system is difficult to navigate unless you keep a sharp eye out for the few small road signs, which are easy to miss. It's quite confusing unless you've been here for a while.

It is hard to arrange the Central Valley into a logical sequence that follows obvious routes and cities. For want of a better solution, this chapter is arranged in a roughly west-to-east sequence, around San José.

# Alajuela Area

## ALAJUELA

The provincial capital of Alajuela lies about 18km (as the crow flies) northwest of San José. The city is on a gently sloping hill that has an altitude of 920m on the southwestern side of town, rising to 970m on the northeastern side. It is about 200m lower than San José and has a slightly warmer climate, thus attracting *josefinos* on summer outings. Alajuela's town center is a slightly scaled-down version of the busy market areas in San José, but it generally enjoys a more unhurried pace of than the nearby capital.

Several nearby villages and other attractions (the Butterfly Farm and Zoo Ave) are popular places on the tourist circuit, and these are described later in this section.

The city and its immediate suburbs have a population of about 223,000, making it the second-largest city in the country. It was founded in 1782 (the original name was Villa Hermosa), but no 18th-century architecture survives. The Juan Santamaría International Airport, serving San José, is only 2.5km southeast of Alajuela. This makes Alajuela a convenient alternative to more bustling and smoggy San José for those using the airport. There are several good mid-priced hotels in Alajuela.

The map shows the streets and avenues, but, as in most Costa Rican towns, locals prefer landmark addresses, and street addresses are rarely used.

### Information

At the time of research, a talked-about tourist office had yet to appear; try the Instituto Costarricense de Turismo (ICT) at the airport (☎ 442-1820) or at the Hotel Los Volcanes (see Places to Stay). There are half a dozen banks within two blocks of the Parque Central to change money. Internet access is available at SAEC, which is open 7am to 9pm weekdays and 7am to 7pm Saturday, or at Tropicafé Internet, open from 8am to 10pm daily. They charge about US$1 an hour. The Hospital San Rafael (☎ 441-5011) provides basic medical services at Avenida 9, Calles Central & 1, and the 24-hour Clínica Norza (☎ 441-3572), Avenida 4, Calles 2 & 4, has some English-speaking staff. Most sick travelers get treated in San José.

### Museo Juan Santamaría

Alajuela's main claim to fame is that it's the birthplace of the national hero, Juan Santamaría, for whom the nearby international airport was named.

Santamaría was the drummer boy who volunteered to torch the building defended by filibuster William Walker in the war of 1856 (see History in the Facts about Costa Rica chapter). He died in this action and is now commemorated by the museum and a park in Alajuela.

The Museo Juan Santamaría is in what used to be a jail, northwest of the Parque Central (☎ 441-4775, Calle 2, Avenida 3;

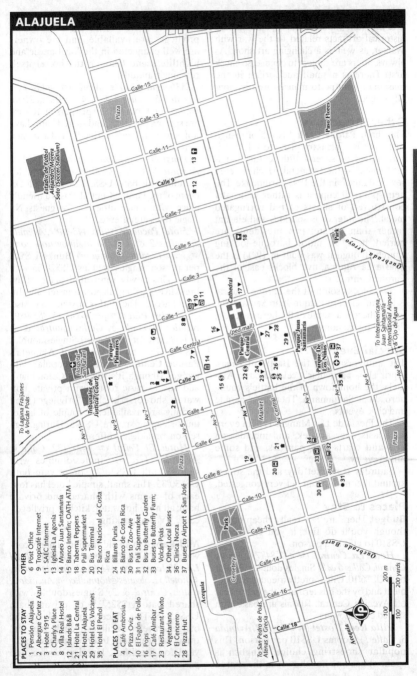

CENTRAL VALLEY

**ALAJUELA**

PLACES TO STAY
1 Pensión Alajuela
2 Albergue Cortez Azul
3 Hotel 1915
5 Charly's Place
8 Villa Real Hostel
12 Islands B&B
21 Hotel La Central
26 Hotel Alajuela
29 Hotel Los Volcanes
35 Hotel El Peñol

PLACES TO EAT
4 Café Ambrosia
7 Pizza Oviz
10 El Fogón de Pollo
16 Pops
17 Café Almibar
23 Restaurant Mixto
   Vegetariano
27 El Cencerro
28 Pizza Hut

OTHER
6 Post Office
9 Tropicafé Internet
11 SAEC Internet
13 Iglesia La Agonia
14 Museo Juan Santamaría
15 Banco Interfin; OATH ATM
18 Taberna Peppers
19 Pali Supermarket
20 Bus Terminal
22 Banco Nacional de Costa
   Rica
24 Billares Punis
25 Banco de Costa Rica
30 Bus to Zoo-Ave
31 Pali Supermarket
32 Buses to Butterfly Garden
33 Buses to Butterfly Farm;
   Volcán Poás
34 Other Local Buses
36 Clínica Norza
37 Buses to Airport & San José

*admission free; open 10am-6pm Tues-Sun).*
The museum contains maps, paintings, and
historical artifacts related to the war with
Walker, as well as a changing art show. As
always, hours are subject to change, so check
first. There is a small auditorium in the
museum where performances are occasionally staged.

## Other Attractions

The shady **Parque Central** is full of mango
trees and is a pleasant place to relax. It is
surrounded by several 19th-century buildings, including the **cathedral**, which suffered
severe damage in the 1991 earthquake. The
hemispherical cupola is rather unusually
constructed of sheets of red corrugated
metal. The interior is spacious and elegant
rather than ornate; two presidents are
buried here. A more baroque-looking
church (though it was built in 1941) is the
**Iglesia La Agonía**, five blocks east of the
Parque Central.

Two blocks south of the Parque Central
is the rather bare **Parque Juan Santamaría**,
where there is a statue of the hero in action,
flanked by cannons.

## Special Events

The anniversary of the Battle of Rivas,
April 11, is particularly celebrated in Alajuela, the hometown of the battle's young
hero, Juan Santamaría. There is a parade
and civic events.

The Fiesta de Los Mangos is held every
July, lasts over a week, and includes an
arts and crafts fair, parades, and some
mild revelry.

Saturday is market day, and the streets
around the market can get very congested.

## Places to Stay

**Budget** There are few really cheap hotels,
though you'll do fine if you can spend
US$10 to US$15 a person.

*Hotel La Central* (☎ 443-8437, Avenida
Central, Calles 6 & 8) Singles/doubles without
bath US$6/10. Under pretty friendly manage-
ment and by the bus terminal, the entrance is
off Avenida Central. Rooms are basic with
shared cold showers.

*Villa Real Hostel* (☎ 441-4022, Avenida
3, Calle 1) Rooms US$10 per person. This
popular shoestring choice (English is
spoken) has one hot shower in the shared

bathroom, a funky sitting area showing
movies on cable TV, and a porch. Kitchen
privileges are available, and the owners
are well connected in the local music and
nightlife scene (though the hostel itself
remains tranquil).

*Albergue Corte Azul* (☎ 443-6145,
Avenida 5, Calles 2 & 4, ℮ corteazul@latin
mail.com). From US$10 per person. Rooms
are spartan but clean, and shared baths have
hot water. The staff is friendly and a kitchen
is available.

*Pensión Alajuela* (☎/fax 441-6251,
Avenida 9, Calles Central & 2) Doubles
without/with bath US$20/28. Four blocks
north of the Parque Central, this is a friendly
place with a nice little bar for guests. No
single rates are offered.

*Hotel Pacande* (☎/fax 443-8481, Avenida
5, Calles 2 & 4, ℮ joslozano@uole.com,
ⓦ www.hotelpacande.com) Bunks US$12
per person, singles/doubles US$20/35 with
bath. This newly renovated place offers
breakfast, parking, airport transfer, and Internet access. The staff is anxious to please.

*Charly's Place* (☎/fax 441-0115, 385-9891
cellular, Avenida 5, Calles Central & 2,
℮ lilyhotel@latinmail.com) Singles/doubles
US$30. Two blocks north of Alajuela's
Parque Central, Charly's is popular with
gringos (though it's run by a Colombian),
and has 13 basic rooms with private hot-
water showers; kitchen privileges and
parking are available. A couple of larger
units sleeping six are US$45. During high
season, breakfast is offered.

*Hotel El Peñol* (☎ 442-2132, Calle 4,
Avenidas 4 & 6) Singles/doubles with
shared bath US$20/25, or private bath
US$30/35. This small, simple hotel has four
each of rooms with shared and private
bath; all have hot water, kitchen privileges,
cable TV, and parking.

**Mid-Range** In an old-fashioned home converted into a small six-room B&B is **Hotel
Los Volcanes** (☎ 441-0525, fax 440-8006,
℮ hotellosvolcanes@hotmail.com, Avenida 2,
Calles Central & 2) Singles/doubles with
shared bath US$25/35, or private bath
US$35/45. This place aims to please the
budget traveler. Facilities include tour and
travel information, Internet access, courtyard for breakfast, laundry service, and
parking. Rooms, while not big, do have two

beds, TV, and telephone. Two rooms have private baths and all showers are heated.

**Hotel Alajuela** (☎ 441-1241, 441-6595, fax 441-7912, Calle 2, Avenidas Central & 2) Singles/doubles with bath US$30/40. Just south of the Parque Central, this old-fashioned building has 50 rather dark rooms with fans and private electric showers. The hotel is well run, and is often full during high season because of its proximity to the international airport. Long-stay discounts are available.

**Islands B&B** (☎ 442-0573, 383-8258 cellular, fax 442-2909, e islandsbb@hotmail.com, Avenida 1, Calles 7 & 9) Singles/doubles with bath US$35/40, with continental breakfast. Islands is 50m west of Iglesia La Agonía and has 10 clean rooms with hot water and two beds. A living room has cable TV and parking and airport pickup are available.

**Hotel Brilla Sol** (☎ 442-5129, ☎/fax 443-5326, e florelo@racsa.co.cr, w www.hotel brillasol.com) Singles/doubles US$34/45. This reader-recommended hotel is 4km west of the airport in the village of El Roble. It's a modern place with a pool; rates include breakfast.

**Hotel 1915** (☎/fax 441-0495, Calle 2, Avenida 5 & 7) Doubles with bath US$53, with breakfast. This place has unaffected, nice rooms, with private hot showers surrounding a courtyard in an elegant house. Breakfast is served outside, rooms feature cable TV, and parking is available.

**Tuetal Lodge** (☎ 442-1804, e back96@ racsa.co.cr, w www.islandnet.com/~tuetal/ tuetal.html) Cabins US$42 per double, cabins with kitchenettes US$47. This Canadian-run lodge is about 4km north of the center (see Getting There & Away, later in this section, for buses; you could also take a taxi). There are six clean and roomy cabins. The gardens have a pool and a patio restaurant-bar that serves homestyle meals; the lodge is in a nice location fairly close to the airport, and pickup can be arranged.

**Hampton Inn** (☎ 443-0043, toll free in Costa Rica ☎ 0800-426-7866, in the USA ☎ 800-426-7866, fax 442-9532, e hampton@ hamptonhotel.co.cr, w www.hamptonhotel .co.cr) Singles/doubles US$107/114, US$8 per extra bed. Continental breakfast, airport transfers, and 24-hour coffee are included. Hampton Inn is 1.5km east of the airport

and is the easiest hotel to reach from there. It is a clean and modern American-style hotel with spacious air-conditioned rooms with cable TV, free local calls, and free airport pickup. There is a pool. This hotel will ease the culture shock between the USA and Costa Rica.

**Las Orquideas Inn** (☎ 433-9346, fax 433-9740, e info@orquideas.com, w www.hotels .co.cr/orquideas.html) Singles with bath US$57-91, doubles US$68-103, suites US$139-151. About 5km west of Alajuela on the road to San Pedro de Poás (call for precise directions) is this attractive US-owned, Spanish-style mansion with a pool and spacious, airy rooms with wood parquet floors. Air-conditioned rooms vary in price depending on the room; more expensive ones feature mountain or garden views with two double beds. There is a restaurant and bar: The first is excellent for breakfast, served from 8am to 9am (included in rates), and the second is famous for its Marilyn Monroe paraphernalia (presided over by a cat named Marilyn, of course). No children under 10 are allowed in either hotel or bar.

**Hotel Buena Vista** (☎ 442-8595, fax 442-8701, e bvista@racsa.co.cr, w www.arweb .com/buenavista) Standard singles/doubles US$75/81, deluxe doubles US$99, suites US$122-134. Rates include breakfast and airport transfer. This hotel is run by the friendly Ed Pratt, who has 'retired' to Costa Rica from Florida. It is 5km north of Alajuela on the road to Poás and has good views of the Central Valley and nearby volcanoes. There is a swimming pool, gift shop, restaurant, and bar. The more expensive rooms have balcony views of the volcanoes.

**Top End** Set in a coffee plantation overlooking the Central Valley about 6km north of Alajuela is **Xandari Resort Hotel & Spa** (☎ 443-2020, fax 442-4847, e paradise@ xandari.com, w www.xandari.com) Villa singles/doubles US$163/186, ultra-villas US$239/262. This lovely, relaxed resort has great views, waterfalls, and 3km of walking trails. Many comforts are available, including a library, a video room, two swimming pools, heated Jacuzzi, spa services, and gourmet dining room with healthful meals – vegetarian plates always available. Rates for the 17 spacious, individually decorated villas include breakfast (on your private terrace or

CENTRAL VALLEY

balcony) and airport pickup. The larger villas have kitchenettes and sitting rooms. Physical fitness and special spa programs are offered on daily and weekly basis.

## Places to Eat
*Café Ambrosia* (☎ 442-1768, 442-5985, Calle 2, Avenida 5) US75¢-US$3. Open 9:30am-5:30pm Mon-Sat. With a street corner patio, this is a popular café with a selection of coffees, pastries, sandwiches, and light meals. Set lunch is US$3, and lasagna or fettuccine are also available.

*Café Almibar* (Avenida Central, Calles 1 & 3) Coffee and a variety of yummy desserts are the standbys at this café. They do a casado for US$2.50 from noon to 2pm Monday to Friday.

*Restaurant Mixto Vegetariano* (Avenida Central, Calles 2 & 4) US$1.75-3. Open 7:30am-6pm Mon-Sat. This has self-service cafeteria some vegetarian soy dishes and some meat dishes as well; it's a good value.

*El Fogón de Pollo* (Calle 1, Avenidas 1 & 3) US$2-4. This is the standard Costa Rican roasted chicken joint.

*El Cencerro* (☎ 441-2414, Avenida Central, south side of Parque Central) Dishes US$8-15. Open 11am-10pm. The name of this place translates to 'the cowbell' – it serves steaks as the house specialty, although it serves other food as well.

Pizza lovers have the choice of the locally owned *Pizza Oviz* or the international chain *Pizza Hut* (with a salad bar), both on Calle Central. There are other Italian places on this block.

At the northeast corner of the park is *Pops*, a favorite for ice cream and snacks. The *Plaza de Estación* is a small mall with several pleasant little eateries.

## Entertainment
A nice place for a drink is *Taberna Peppers*, a friendly little corner bar that has good *bocas*.

On Calle 4, a few blocks south of the center, *Monkey Shot* is a favorite among young people wanting to listen to live music, which plays most nights. Taxi drivers will know where to drop you off. Nearby is *Pub 99* (Calle 4, south of Avenida 10), near the Shell gas station, with the *Spectros* disco on the 2nd floor.

At *Billares Punis*, a small, upscale pool hall (air-conditioning!) that overlooks the Parque Central, you can't drink beer, but staff can give you suggestions about other good nightspots farther out from the center. There are five good tables, which rent for US$3.50 per hour, and an unobtrusive cable TV.

The perennial Costa Rican soccer champions, Alajuela's own La Liga, play at the stadium at the northeast end of town on Sunday during soccer season.

## Getting There & Away
TUASA buses for Alajuela (US40¢) leave San José from Avenida 2 and Calle 12 every 10 minutes between 5:30am and 7pm. From 7pm 'til midnight, buses leave at 15- or 20-minute intervals. Late-night buses are also available at less frequent intervals from Calle 2, Avenida 2. The return buses from Alajuela to San José leave from the stop at Avenida 4, Calles 2 & 4.

To get to the airport, either take a San José bus and get off at the airport (make sure that the bus stops there) or take a bus from Avenida 4, Calles 2 & 4, or take a taxi. Taxis to the airport are available from the Parque Central (west side) at any hour of the day or night. The fare is about US$2 during the day, more at night. A taxi to San José costs about US$12.50.

For other destinations, it's more complicated and travelers should ask carefully at their hotels or from locals for details. The Alajuela bus terminal, Calle 8, Avenidas Central & 1, is the departure point for buses to some towns. Another area of bus departures for many local destinations is along Avenida 2, around Calles 8 & 10. Look for buses to the Butterfly Garden, Zoo Ave, and Volcán Poás. (The bus to Poás leaves from in front of the Restaurant El Cencerro on Saturday and Sunday mornings). To reach the Tuetal Lodge, take a Tuetal Norte bus (leaving every hour) and watch for lodge signs.

Buses to Puntarenas (connecting with buses to Monteverde) and to La Fortuna leave from 'La Radial' on Calle 4, about 100m south of Avenida 10.

## OJO DE AGUA
About 6km south of Alajuela are the Ojo de Agua springs (☎ 441-2808), a favorite resort

for working-class people from both San José and Alajuela. Twenty thousand liters of water gush out from the spring each minute. This fills swimming pools and an artificial boating lake before being piped down to Puntarenas, for which it is a major water supply.

The recreational complex can be very crowded when picnicking locals flock there on weekends; it's quieter midweek. Hours are 8am to 5pm daily. Entrance to the complex costs about US$1.20, and there are places to eat, game courts, and a small gym. The end of the dry season is the least impressive time to visit, because water levels are low, partly due to local deforestation.

Another water park in the Alajuela area is the more upscale **Water Land** *(☎ 293-3009, 293-2773)*, which has several pools (including children's pools) with a variety of water slides, as well as underwater caves, a wave machine, an artificial river for float trips, and water volleyball. Lifeguards are on duty. In addition, there is a miniature golf course and a go-cart track (US$3 each), a video arcade, a picnic area, and a restaurant. It's closed for maintenance on Monday and has some days for members only and others for the general public (US$6). Call for directions and more information.

### Getting There & Away

Buses leave from the terminal in Alajuela. Buses also leave every hour (more frequently on weekends) from Avenida 1, Calle 20, in San José.

Drivers from San José should take the San Antonio de Belén exit off the Interamericana (in front of the Hotel Cariari) and go through San Antonio to Ojo de Agua.

## BUTTERFLY FARM

Yes, they farm butterflies in Costa Rica, and it's a fascinating process. The Butterfly Farm *(☎ 438-0400, fax 438-0300, ⓔ info@butterflyfarm.co.cr, Ⓦ www.butterflyfarm.co.cr, adult/student/child 5-12 yrs US$15/9/7, child under 5 yrs free; open 8:30am-5pm daily)* opened in 1983 and was the first commercial butterfly farm in Latin America. Informative guided tours will take you through tropical gardens filled with hundreds of butterflies of many species. You can see and learn about all the stages of the complex butterfly life cycle as well as find out about the importance of butterflies in nature. Every Monday, and on Thursday from March to August, visitors can watch thousands of pupae being packed for export all over the world. Sunny weather (mornings in the rainy season) is usually the best time to see activity.

There are also traditional ox-cart rides, a bee garden, and tropical birds that abound. Bring your camera.

Guided butterfly tours in English, Spanish, French, and German last two hours and run continuously from 8:30am to 3pm. Once your tour is over, you can stay as long as you want. A restaurant serves snacks.

The Butterfly Farm also offers complete tour packages from San José with hotel pickups at 7:20am, 10am, and 2pm; the cost is US$25/15 for adults/children. In addition, staff can arrange a tour (for two people minimum) with lunch combined with the Coffeetour at Café Britt Finca (see Around Heredia, later in this chapter) for US$60/45, with hotel pickups beginning at 8am; this combined tour includes lunch. With a six-person minimum, a similarly priced combination with Zoo Ave (see West to Atenas, below) is available.

### Getting There & Away

The farm is almost in front of El Club Campestre Los Reyes (a country club) in the village of La Guácima, 12km southwest of Alajuela. Buses to La Guácima leave San José at 11am and 2pm daily from a stop marked 'San Antonio/Ojo de Agua' at Avenida 1, Calles 20 & 22. The bus returns to San José at 3:15pm.

There are also buses from Alajuela at 6:30am, 9am, 11am, and 1pm, leaving from Calle 8, Avenida 2; ask locals, as the stop is poorly marked. Make sure your bus goes to La Guácima Abajo. The last bus departs for Alajuela at 5:45pm.

Drivers coming from San José should take the San Antonio de Belén exit off the Interamericana by the Hotel Cariari and drive through San Antonio to La Guácima. There are blue butterfly signs as you get close to the farm. Tours are available from San José travel agencies as well as direct from the farm.

## WEST TO ATENAS

West of Alajuela is a road that leads to Atenas, a small village about 25km away. En route to Atenas you pass Zoo Ave and

La Garita. **Zoo Ave** (☎ 433-8989, fax 433-9140, ✆ info@zooave.org, ☒ www.zooave.org; foreign adult/tico or child US$9/1; open 9am-5pm daily, closed Christmas) is about 10km west of Alajuela and has a collection of tropical birds, including over 80 Costa Rican species, displayed in a parklike setting. There is a program to breed endangered native species and reintroduce them into the wild, including the endangered macaws. There are also a few mammals (including all four species of Costa Rican monkeys) and reptiles, but the birds are certainly the highlight.

If you are driving west from San José or Alajuela on the Interamericana, at the Atenas exit go 3km east to Zoo Ave. Buses between Alajuela and La Garita pass by the entrance every half hour.

A few kilometers beyond Zoo Ave is **La Garita**, with an unusual restaurant that serves every dish you could imagine – as long as it is made from *maize* (corn). **La Fiesta del Maíz** (☎ 487-7057) is open 8am to 9pm Friday to Sunday. The restaurant is open additional days during the high season.

The area is famous for its *viveros*, where local flora are grown and sold for use within Costa Rica.

### Places to Stay & Eat

There are a few small hotels in the area.

***Ana's Place*** (☎ 446-5019, fax 446-6975) Doubles US$40, with breakfast. Ana's has seven decent rooms, some with private baths, around a quiet backyard populated by a few large, exotic birds. Ana's Place is near the Atenas bus station and about four blocks southwest of the Atenas Parque Central.

***Vista Atenas B&B*** (☎/fax 380-3252, ✆ vistaatenas@hotmail.com, ☒ www.vista atenas.com) Singles/doubles/triples US$45/50/55, cabins US$60 with breakfast. Just south of Atenas and reachable only by car, this B&B has a few modern rooms, a small pool, and views over the Central Valley. The cabins include a kitchenette. English and French are spoken and local excursions can be arranged.

***Hotel Colinas del Sol*** (☎ 446-4244, fax 446-7582, ✆ info@hotelcolinasdelsol.com, ☒ www.hotelcolinasdelsol.com) Units US$53. About 4km from Atenas, this place has modern bungalows scattered around a hilly and tranquil six-hectare property

surrounded by farmland; the airport is only 20 minutes away and pickup can be arranged. Each unit has a kitchenette, terrace, and private hot bath. There is a large pool, bar, coffee shop, and 24-hour security. The hotel is just 25 minutes from the Juan Santamaria International Airport. If driving, take the Interamericana toward San Ramon, take the Atenas exit, turn left and go about 14km, following signs to the hotel.

***El Cafetal Inn B&B*** (☎ 446-5785, 446-7361, fax 446-7028, ✆ cafetal@racsa.co.cr, ☒ www.cafetal.com) Singles/doubles with bath US$70/87, including big buffet breakfast. This friendly and clean place is about 5km north of Atenas (in Santa Eulalia de Atenas) – there are plenty of signs. There's a large garden (with two easy trails to waterfalls), a pool, and 10 attractive rooms with plenty of light and great country views. One, the tower room, offers exceptional vistas and goes for US$99, and a casita with kitchenette is US$120 for a family of four. The property is on a coffee plantation, and the owners recently opened the ***Mirador del Cafetal*** (☎ 446-7361) on the outskirts of Atenas. This lovely coffee shop, which sells its own brand of *La Negrita* coffee, is named Mirador ('lookout') for good reason. Javaphiles will be in heaven with 19 types of cappuccino on the menu, and there is also a variety of snacks and meals. Souvenirs from all over the country are sold here. Other restaurants are nearby. Airport pickup is US$25 per group, and rental cars can be arranged directly at the inn so you don't have to drive from the airport.

### Getting There & Away

Buses go to Atenas from the San José Coca-Cola terminal several times a day, but they do not pass Zoo Ave. To get to Zoo Ave and La Garita, take one of the buses from Alajuela's bus terminal to La Garita, which leave about every half hour. Call Coopetransatenas (☎ 446-5767) for bus information.

## NORTHWEST TO ZARCERO

Northwest of Alajuela are the villages of Grecia (22km), Sarchí (29km), Naranjo (35km), and Zarcero (52km). They all have colorful churches typical of the Costa Rican countryside.

All of these small towns can be reached by buses that depart either from the Coca-Cola terminal in San José or the bus terminal in Alajuela. The drive to Zarcero is along a narrow, winding, and hilly road with pretty views of the coffee *fincas* (farms) that cover the Central Valley hillsides.

## Grecia

Grecia is an agricultural center (pineapples and sugarcane) and is known for its red church, a local landmark. There is a small regional museum in the **Casa de Cultura** *(☎ 444-6767)*, open sporadically during the week, which also features a tiny insect museum.

The best-known attraction in the Grecia area, located about 2km south of the town center, is the **World of Snakes** *(☎/fax 494-3700,* e *snakes@sol.racsa.co.cr; admission adult/children over 7 yrs US$11/6; open 8am-4pm),* an open-air public exhibit with a commitment to research and to breeding endangered species. Some 150 snakes, representing over 40 species of snakes (as well as some frogs and reptiles, including baby caimans and crocodiles), are on display in cages simulating the species' home environments. The snakes are from all over the world, with an emphasis on Costa Rica. Informative tours in English, German, or Spanish last a minimum of 45 minutes; if there's time, guides will talk to you for as long as you're interested – and even let you handle the snakes. Any bus to or from Grecia can drop you at the entrance.

Also on the south side of town, about 4km from the center, is an 18th-century rock bridge connecting the hamlets of Puente de Piedra with Rincón de Salas (ask any local for directions). Grecians say that the only other rock bridge like this is in China, and the superstitious claim it was built by the devil! In 1994, it was declared a National Site of Historical Interest.

About 5km southwest of Grecia, near Tacares, a spring falls out of a mountainside forming a popular area of bathing pools and picnic sites. (There's a small restaurant here as well).

Otherwise, Grecia's main importance for the traveler is as a place to change buses to continue to Sarchí (although there are also direct buses to Sarchí from the Coca-Cola terminal in San José).

The citizens pride themselves that Grecia was once voted 'the cleanest little town in Latin America!'

**Places to Stay** *Pensión Familiar (☎ 444-5097)* Run by the Quíros family, this is one of the cheapest digs near the town center.

*Healthy Day Country Inn (☎ 444-5903, fax 494-7357,* e *healthyday@racsa.co.cr)* Doubles US$48, including continental breakfast. A suite with kitchenette is US$80. A mid-range option, this place is 800m northeast of the red church, on the main road out of town. Here a loosely organized variety of health services are available (homeopathic therapies, massage, macrobiotic meals), as well as a tennis court, gym, and Jacuzzi. The rooms are cute and a decent value; ceiling fans, telephone, and cable TV are featured.

*Vista del Valle Plantation Inn (☎/fax 450-0800, 450-0900, 451-1165,* e *mibrejo@ racsa.co.cr,* w *www.vistadelvalle.com)* Singles/doubles US$85/100, suites US$135-160, breakfast included (additional people US$20). This critically acclaimed place is the best for miles around. It is in the village of Rosario, about 7km southwest of Grecia as the parrot flies, and borders the small Zona Protectora Río Grande, a cloud forest reserve at about 800m, as well as coffee fincas and fruit orchards.

The Plantation has extensive grounds, which include an orchard and a botanical garden. Trails lead into the adjoining reserve past a 90m-high waterfall, and a pool and Jacuzzi are on the hotel grounds. Massage therapy (by appointment) and horseback tours (for experienced riders) are available. The rooms are lovely and airy, with balconies and views; a few are in garden cottages with kitchenettes. Meals, airport pickup (20 minutes away, about US$30 roundtrip, US$20 one way if before 6am or after 10pm), tour and travel information are available from the owners, one of whom was a US Peace Corps volunteer here in the 1960s and knows the country intimately. From different parts of the property it is possible to get views of volcanoes and of San José city lights. Meals can be eaten in a common area or privately. There are 10 suites of varying sizes with kitchens or kitchenettes and two rooms in the main house.

## Sarchí

This small town is Costa Rica's most famous crafts center, and tour buses and locals stop here to buy crafts, particularly woodwork. It is, of course, commercial, but in a charmingly understated Costa Rican way. Although some would qualify it as a tourist trap, there is no pressure to buy anything, and there is the opportunity to see crafts being made. Unfortunately, the shopping is mainly in the modern area, away from the older and nicer part of town.

Among the best-known crafts are the *carretas* (see Arts in the Facts about Costa Rica chapter), which are often used nowadays to decorate people's gardens; scaled-down versions are used as indoor tables, sideboards, and bars. Miniature models are available for use as indoor sculptures. All sizes come apart and fold down for transport.

You can see carretas being made in a couple of *fábricas de carretas* (cart factories); the most interesting part is watching local artisans paint colorful mandala designs onto the carts. The oldest and best-known factory is Fábrica de Carretas Joaquín Chaverri (see below).

The bright paintwork is also used to decorate wooden trays, plates, and other souvenirs. Unpainted woodwork, such as salad bowls, kitchen cutting boards, serving dishes, jewelry boxes, letter openers, statuettes, toy cars and planes, and a variety of other utilitarian knickknacks, are also sold.

There are also furniture factories in Sarchí. While the elegantly carved headboards and bedsteads, tables and chairs, and sitting room furniture are mainly designed for local sale and use, some travelers buy the leather and wood rocking chairs – these come apart and fold down for transport.

Whatever you do, leave a shopping trip to Sarchí until the end of your trip. Thus, you won't be encumbered by presents while you are traveling around the country. And shop around – there are plenty of factories and stores to choose from in Sarchí. Note that almost everything here is also available in San José.

**Orientation & Information** Sarchí is divided by the Río Trojas into Sarchí Norte and Sarchí Sur and is rather spread out, straggling for several kilometers along the main road from Grecia to Naranjo.

At the Plaza de la Artesanía, in Sarchí Sur, is an information booth with sketch maps of Sarchí.

In Sarchí Norte, you'll find the main plaza with the twin-towered typical church, a hotel, and some restaurants. There is also a Banco Nacional (☎ 454-4262), open 8:30am to 3pm weekdays; it cashes traveler's checks and dollars.

**Crafts** In Sarchí Sur is *Plaza de la Artesanía* (☎ 454-4271), a shopping mall with over 30 souvenir stores and restaurants, as well as local musicians playing marimbas. (Locals say that there is a disco upstairs on weekend nights.) Nearby on the main road are several *factories* specializing in rocking chairs and other furniture, including *Los Rodríguez* (☎ 454-4097), *La Sarchiseña* (☎ 454-4062), and *El Artesano* (☎ 454-4304).

*Fábrica de Carretas Joaquín Chaverri* (☎ 454-4411, fax 454-4944) is the oldest and best-known carretas factory in Sarchí Sur.

There are more factories and stores, including *Taller Lalo Alfaro*, Sarchí's oldest workshop, at the far north end of town, and *Artesanía Sarchí* (☎ 454-4267), at the south end of Sarchí Norte, specializing in typical Costa Rican clothing.

By the main plaza, *Pidesa Souvenirs* (☎ 454-4540) specializes in handpainting all local souvenirs, including full-size milk cans. Get a couple for that person in your life who already has everything.

**Places to Stay & Eat** Few people stay here, since most visitors come on day trips.

*Hotel Daniel Zamora* (☎ 454-4596, fax 454-3029) Doubles with bath US$30. On a quiet street just east of the soccer field, this is a friendly, decent budget option, with clean rooms including ceiling fans and cable TV. Ask the owners about their newer, better place on the outskirts, with air-conditioned rooms for US$40.

*Hotel Cabinas Sarchí* (☎ 454-4425) If you get stuck, try this fairly decent place on the noisy main road next to the Banco Nacional.

*Restaurante Típico La Finca* At the north end of Sarchí Norte, this place overlooks a tranquil garden – a nice break from the hurly-burly of shopping.

There are also restaurants in *Plaza de la Artesanía* in Sarchí Sur and at the *Fabrica de Carretas Joaquín Chaverri*.

**Getting There & Around** Buses to Sarchí leave the Coca-Cola terminal in San

Picture-perfect beach near Puerto Limón

Volcán Arenal, active almost daily since 1968

One of the lake-filled craters at Volcán Irazú

Bubbling, steaming Volcán Poás, active since at least the early 19th century

Hiking through mountain oaks, PN Chirripó

Río Colorado, PN Rincón de la Vieja

Tropical rainforest of Golfo Dulce

LUKE HUNTER

LUKE HUNTER

RALPH LEE HOPKINS

José at 12:15pm and 5:30pm Monday to Friday. Apart from these buses, the quickest way to get to Sarchí from San José is to take one of the frequent buses to Grecia from the Coca-Cola terminal and then connect with an Alajuela-Sarchí bus going through Grecia.

Driving, you can take the unpaved road northeast from Sarchí to Bajos del Toro and on through Colonia del Toro to the northern lowlands at Río Cuarto. The main attraction of this route is the beautiful waterfall north of Bajos del Toro. Look for local signs for the 'Catarata.'

Taxis Sarchí (☎ 454-4028) will shuttle you from Sarchí Norte to Sarchí Sur and drive you to any workshop you wish to visit.

## Palmares

Driving west along the Interamericana (Hwy 1) between the turnoffs for Naranjo and San Ramón (see below), you'll see a turnoff to Palmares, a village that is a few kilometers south of the highway. Palmares' main claim to fame is the annual fiesta, held for 10 days in the middle of January. This country fair attracts ticos from all over the Central Valley and has events for the whole family, including carnival rides, bullfights (the bull is not killed in Costa Rican fights), food, beer stands, and a variety of unusual sideshows. One year the fair featured robot ponies and snake caves.

## San Ramón

From Sarchí, the road continues west to Naranjo, where it divides. You can then continue 13km south and west to San Ramón or 17km north to Zarcero.

San Ramón is a pleasant small town about halfway between San José and Puntarenas, just off the Interamericana, which joins the capital with the Pacific coast. The town is known locally as the 'city of presidents and poets,' because several of them were born or lived here. Ex-president Rodrigo Carazo lives a few kilometers to the north and owns a tourist lodge surrounded by the Los Angeles Cloud Forest. A museum in town has further information about famous native sons and daughters of San Ramón. The Saturday farmers' market is a big one, with lots of locals and few tourists. There are smaller markets on Wednesday and Sunday.

Buses to San Ramón (☎ 222-8231) leave San José from Calle 16, Avenidas 10 & 12, about every hour from 5:15am to 7pm; the trip takes an hour.

**Museo de San Ramón** This museum (☎ 445-5533; admission free; closed Sun), on the north side of the Parque Central, has interesting exhibits on local history and culture. It's well worth a look but museum hours tend to be a bit erratic.

**Places to Stay** There are some cheap and basic places in town. Close to the center, try *Hotel Gran* (☎ 445-6363); *Hotel El Viajero* (☎ 445-5580); *Hotel Nuevo Jardín* (☎ 445-5620); or *Hotel Washington* (☎ 445-7349), reportedly the worst.

*La Posada B&B* (☎ 445-7349, 445-7359) Singles/doubles/triples US$25/40/52, with breakfast. This place, 100m south and 50m east of the hospital, is the nicest hotel in central San Ramón. Rooms have cable TV; English is spoken.

## San Ramón to La Tigra

A paved road links San Ramón with La Tigra and Fortuna (see the Northwestern Costa Rica chapter). This road goes north from San Ramón, across the central highlands, and down to Fortuna, and it could also be placed in the next chapter. The road goes through cloud forest and coffee fincas, but it is steep, narrow, and winding and there are few landmarks or pull-offs for the driver.

**Los Angeles Cloud Forest Reserve** This private reserve is about 20km north of San Ramón; look for signs along the highway. The last few kilometers are on an unpaved but good road to the west of the paved highway.

The reserve is centered around a dairy ranch owned by ex-president Rodrigo Carazo and his wife. Some 800 hectares of primary forest have a short boardwalk trail and longer horse and foot trails leading to waterfalls and cloud forest vistas. Bilingual naturalist guides are available to lead hikes, and the birding is good. Horse rentals are US$12 per hour and guided hikes cost US$24 (unguided hikes cost US$15). A canopy tour costs US$39. Tours of the reserve are arranged through the Hotel Villablanca (see below). There are relatively few tourists in this cloud forest, which has a good variety of species, some of which, however, are hard to see.

**Places to Stay & Eat** ***Hotel Villablanca*** *(☎ 228-4603, fax 228-4004, ⓔ info@villablanca-costarica.com, Ⓦ www.villablanca-costarica.com)* Singles/doubles US$92/115. This hotel has a large main lodge and restaurant with about 30 whitewashed, red-tiled, rustic adobe cabins scattered around, all surrounded by the cloud forest. 'Rustic' describes the ambiance but not the amenities – the comfortable cabins have refrigerators, hot water, bathtubs, fireplaces, and even electric kettles. Meals (buffet-style country cooking) are served in the main lodge for about US$15 (US$8 breakfast). Call the hotel about day trips from San José, including transportation and a choice of a guided horseback ride, canopy tour, or hike; lunch at the hotel; and snacks, all for US$72.50. Ask about programs and discounts for students and groups, who stay in a dormitory style building.

***Valle Escondido Lodge*** *(☎ 231-0906, fax 232-9591, ⓔ info@valleescondido.com, Ⓦ www.valleescondido.com)* Singles/doubles/triples US$70/93/105. About halfway between the Hotel Villablanca and the village of La Tigra is this lodge, on a working farm that grows ornamental plants and citrus fruits. With over 100 hectares of preserved forest, this whole place is good for birding. Guided horseback rides cost US$30 for two hours, or you can hike the trails yourself (US$8 trail fee for nonguests). There is a pool, Jacuzzi, and a locally popular restaurant with Italian specialties. Tours to various parts of the country and special 'green season' packages can be arranged. Two dozen spacious and attractive rooms are available. Meals cost about US$15 (US$8 for breakfast, US$7 for a boxed lunch).

## Zarcero

North of Naranjo, the main road climbs about 20km to Zarcero, a town at 1736m at the western end of the Cordillera Central. The town is famous for its topiary garden in front of the town church. The bushes and shrubs have been cut into a variety of animal and human shapes and the effect is very pretty. (Look to your right if you're traveling northbound by bus from San José.)

The surrounding countryside is mountainous and attractive, and the climate cool and refreshing. The area is also well known for peach jam, homemade cheese,

ALFREDO MAIQUEZ

Zarcero is famous for the 'playground' of bushes fronting the town church.

CENTRAL VALLEY

and organic vegetables, all of which are for sale in town.

**Places to Stay & Eat** On the north side of the town church is the clean and pleasant *Hotel Don Beto* (☎ 463-3137, 463-2509) Doubles US$25-30. It has eight rooms of varying size, four sharing two baths and four others with private baths. Breakfast is available, the owner has lots of local information, and tours, rafting, horseback riding, and airport transfers can be arranged.

There are a number of simple *restaurants* around Zarcero's main square.

### Getting There & Away

Buses for Ciudad Quesada (San Carlos) via Zarcero leave San José's Atlántico Norte terminal frequently. There are also buses from Alajuela. From San José to Zarcero, it takes almost two hours, and from Alajuela a little less.

Buses from Zarcero leave from the red bus stands at the northwest corner of the park (the church plaza with the topiary art). Northbound buses continue over the Cordillera Central and down to Ciudad Quesada, 35km away. Southbound buses go to San José every hour; some of them will drop you in Alajuela. Because Zarcero is on the busy San José-to-Ciudad Quesada run, buses may be full when they come through, especially on weekends.

### PARQUE NACIONAL JUAN CASTRO BLANCO

This 14,285-hectare park was created in 1992 to protect the slopes of Volcán Platanar (2183m) and Volcán Porvenir (2267m) from logging. This is an important watershed area for several rivers that would have been severely damaged by the erosion caused by logging. Now, the premontane rainforest and montane cloud forest shelter a great variety of flora and fauna and safeguard the quality of the watershed.

This national park has almost no infrastructure for visitors. You can enter the edge of it by driving north from Sarchí for about 18km to the village of Bajos del Toro at the edge of the park. Alternately, a shorter road to Bajos del Toro goes east from Zarcero, but is in worse shape. From Bajos del Toro, footpaths and 4WD tracks

travel a short way into the park as they follow along the Río Toro, which was dammed in 1995. There are several waterfalls near here, some of which are now dry because of the hydroelectric project. You can also approach the park from the north (see West of San Miguel in the Northern Lowlands chapter).

### LAGUNA FRAIJANES AREA

This small lake (☎ 482-2166 *information; open 9am-3:30pm Tues-Sun*) is surrounded by trails, play areas, and picnic sites, and is a stopping place en route to Volcán Poás. Laguna Fraijanes is 15km north of Alajuela on Rte 130. Admission is US60¢. A few simple cabins with bunks and kitchenette sleep up to six people and cost US$25. Bring everything, including bedding or sleeping bag.

### PARQUE NACIONAL VOLCÁN POÁS

This 6506-hectare park *(admission for non-residents US$6; open 8am-3:30pm daily)* lies about 37km north of Alajuela by road and is a popular destination for locals and visitors alike. It is one of the oldest and best-known national parks in Costa Rica.

The centerpiece of the park is, of course, Volcán Poás (2704m), which has been active since well before records were started in 1828. There have been three major periods of recorded activity, from 1888 to 1895, 1903 to 1912, and 1952 to 1954.

The volcano continues to be active to varying extents with different levels of danger. The park was briefly closed after a minor eruption in May 1989 sent volcanic ash spouting more than a kilometer into the

*CENTRAL VALLEY*

air. Lesser activity closed the park intermittently in 1995.

Now, the crater is a bubbling and steaming cauldron, but it doesn't pose an imminent threat, and the park is steadily open. This volcanic activity, though, has resulted in acid rain that has damaged the area coffee and berry crops. Rangers don't recommend drinking water in the park; buy bottled water. Occasionally, when the wind and rain conditions are just right, the fumes from the crater can cause acidic moisture that closes the park briefly.

The mountain is made of composite basalt. The huge crater is 1.5km across and 300m deep. Geyser-type eruptions take place periodically, with peaceful interludes lasting minutes or weeks, depending on the degree of activity within the volcano. Because of toxic sulfuric acid fumes, visitors are prohibited from descending into the crater, but the view down from the top is very impressive. This park is a must for anyone interested in seeing an active volcano.

Apart from Volcán Poás itself, there's a dwarf cloud forest near the crater, one of the best examples of this kind of habitat in the national park system. Here you can wander around looking at the bromeliads, lichens, and mosses clinging to the curiously shaped and twisted trees growing in the volcanic soil.

Birds abound, especially the magnificent fiery-throated hummingbird, a high-altitude specialty of Costa Rica. Other highland specialties to look for include the sooty robin and the quetzal, which has been reported here.

A nature trail leads through this cloud forest to another crater nearby (this one extinct), which forms the pretty Laguna Botos. This trail was closed for maintenance at time of research, but should reopen by the end of 2002.

## Information

The park is crowded on Sunday, and the annual number of visitors is around 250,000. The visitor center has a coffee shop, gift shop, and video shows every hour from 9am to 3pm. A small **museum** offers explanations in both Spanish and English.

The best time to go is in the dry season, especially early in the morning before the clouds roll in and obscure the view. Nevertheless, even in late afternoon and during

the rainy season, you may be lucky enough to catch a great view. If it's clouded in, don't despair! Winds may blow the clouds away, so walk around the cloud forest and keep checking back on the crater.

Overnight temperatures can drop below freezing, and it may be windy and cold during the day, particularly in the morning, so dress accordingly. Poás receives almost 4m of rain a year, so be prepared for it.

There are well-marked trails in the park. It's an easy walk (about 1km) to the active crater lookout for spectacular views; the trails through the cloud forest are somewhat steeper but still not very difficult or long. The route to the crater is a paved road that is shut to cars, but anybody who is unable to negotiate it on foot can request permission to drive to the rim. This is normally OK early in the day at midweek but difficult on Sunday, when the road is crowded with pedestrians.

There's a parking lot where rangers on patrol look after your car during your visit. Parking costs vary slightly, depending on the size of your vehicle.

## Organized Tours

Numerous companies advertise tours that depart from San José just about every day. Typically, they cost US$20 to US$70 per person, and you arrive at the volcano by about 10am or a little later. Some tours spend very little time at the crater, so check before you fork out your hard-earned cash. The cheaper tours are large group affairs providing only transportation, park entrance, and limited time at the crater. The more expensive tours feature smaller group size, bilingual naturalist guides, and lunch. There are now daily buses to the park from San José (see Getting There & Away, later in this section), which offer the cheapest way to visit.

## Places to Stay & Eat

The coffee shop has a limited menu, so bringing your own food is a good idea. There are picnicking areas, but it's best to bring your own drinking water; you can buy bottles at the café, but it may run out.

There are no overnight accommodations within the park, and camping is prohibited. There are several places to stay outside the park. The following are described in the order you encounter them after leaving the park.

**La Providencia Reserva Ecológica** (☎ 232-2498, 380-6315, fax 231-2204) Doubles with bath US$40, with breakfast; cabins US$17 per person (sleep 4-10 people). This place is high up on the southwestern flanks of the volcano, reached by taking a 2.5km dirt road (normally passable to cars) leaving from the paved highway about 2km after the national park entrance/exit. The 572-hectare property adjoins the national park and is a working dairy ranch with about 200 hectares of primary forest and much secondary forest.

There are four small rustic guest cabins with private bath, some of which are quite isolated. Electricity and hot showers have been added to some; alcohol is not allowed. One cabin sleeps four, and one sleeps 10 people; the per person rate with the cabins does not include breakfast. Three-hour horseback tours with a resident biologist guide are sometimes available for US$25. There are several trails; some are good for birding (quetzals have been seen) and others for views. Reportedly, both oceans, Lago de Nicaragua, and San José – plus a wee glimpse of Arenal – can be seen from here if it's clear. The decidedly rustic restaurant (dirt floor, wood stove, wooden stools) is open to the general public and serves breakfast, lunch, and dinner, though it's best to call ahead to arrange meals.

**Lagunillas Lodge** (☎ 389-5842) Singles with bath US$20 (additional people US$5). About 3.5km from the park exit, a sign indicates this lodge, which is reached by a steep 1km dirt road (you may need 4WD to get out – call ahead). This small lodge (which is recommended by the park rangers) offers five rooms with baths (hot water available on request), and they can accommodate up to four extra people. Typical meals cost US$4 to US$7, and horse rental costs US$8 per hour; staff say they'll take you to the Poás crater. Quetzals have been seen on the property from June to October.

**Lo Que Tu Quieres Lodge** (☎ 482-2092) Cabins with bath US$20. Just over 5km from the park entrance, the name of this place translates to 'Whatever You Want Lodge.' It has three basic little cabins, with private hot showers, that sleep up to three people. There is a small restaurant and sweeping views of

the valley; the owners are friendly and will allow camping for a nominal fee.

**Poás Volcano Lodge** (☎/fax 482-2194, e poasvl@racsa.co.cr, w www.poasvolcano lodge.com) Singles/doubles without bath US$40/53, with bath US$53/75; junior suites US$64/93; master suite US$70/116; all with breakfast. This lodge is about 16km east of the volcano near Varablanca. It's in a dairy farm at 1900m, and has good mountain views (though none of the rooms have views of the volcano). The attractive stone building blends rural architectural influences from Wales, England, and Costa Rica (the original owners were English farmers), and this is the nicest lodge in the Poás area. Trails surround it, and common areas include a billiard room ('pool' doesn't do it justice) and a sitting area with a sunken fireplace and books and board games to while away a stormy night. There are six large comfortable rooms ('junior suites') and a master suite with a fireplace and French doors that open onto a garden. There are also a couple of smaller rooms with shared baths. Lunch (or box lunch) is US$10 and dinner costs around US$10 to US$20. The hotel offers Internet access from its office and free local calls.

### Getting There & Away
From San José, a bus leaves from Avenida 2, Calles 12 & 14, at 8:30am daily, sometimes followed by a second bus if there is passenger demand. Get there early (especially in the high season) to get onto the first bus, and when you get to the volcano, make a beeline for the crater to have the best chance of seeing it before the clouds roll in. The fare is about US$4 (roundtrip), the journey takes almost two hours, and the return bus leaves at 2:30pm. This bus also stops in Alajuela. A taxi from Alajuela costs about US$35, including a couple of hours at the park; it costs twice that from San José.

### LOS JARDINES DE LA CATARATA LA PAZ
La Paz Waterfall Gardens (☎ 482-2720, fax 482-2722, e wgardens@racsa.co.cr, w www .waterfallgardens.com; entrance US$16/8 adults/students over 5 yrs; open 7am-5pm Mon-Sat, 9am-5pm Sun) feature not only a series of waterfalls reached by a fine trail system, but also Costa Rica's largest (at

time of writing) butterfly garden, botanical and birding exhibits, and a restaurant with a fine view. The restaurant is open 11:30am to 4pm and features a filling buffet of Costa Rican food for US$8/4 for adults/children.

The Río La Paz cascades almost 1400m down the flanks of Volcán Poás' in less than 8km, culminating in a dramatic series of waterfalls. The lowest, whose name means 'Peace Waterfall,' is perhaps the most famous in Costa Rica. This is partly for its impressive size and partly because it is just off the highway, about 8km north of Varablanca.

Visitors, many on tours from San José, enter through a visitor center containing a gift shop, auditorium, and restaurant. A visit often begins with a short video to describe facilities at the 30-hectare gardens. Then 3.5km of trails wind through the

huge butterfly gardens (50ft high and the length of a football field), continuing through hummingbird gardens, an orchid exhibit, and a fern trail (with more birding opportunities) before plunging steeply down alongside five waterfalls. (Various shortcuts allow for shorter loops.) The trails are well-maintained and graveled or paved, and wooden hiking staffs are provided. A shuttle bus meets hikers at the bottom of the falls and drives back up to the visitor center. Small children, city slickers, and active seniors won't have any problems with this adventure, and the views of the waterfalls are excellent (and damp with spray).

The lunch is good and the restaurant provides fine views of the rainforest from the patio. In the event of a rainy day, diners

La Paz Waterfall Gardens also has Costa Rica's largest butterfly observatory.

gather upstairs where a huge fireplace provides welcome respite from the weather.

# Heredia Area

## HEREDIA

This small but historic city is the capital of the province of Heredia and lies about 11km north of San José. It has a population about half that of nearby Alajuela and retains more of a small-town colonial air than the neighboring capitals.

The elevation is 1150m above sea level, about the same as San José. The Universidad Nacional is on the east side of town, and there is a sizable student population. Despite this, there is little nightlife, and most people head into San José to party.

### Information

There is no tourist office. Several banks in the town center change money. Banco Interfin (☎ 238-3633), Avenida 4, Calles Central & 2, and Banco Popular (☎ 261-0536), Avenida Central, Calles 1 & 3, are usually faster than most; others are shown on the map. The Internet Center on the west side of the Parque Central and the Internet Café near the university are both open from 8am to 10pm and charge about US$1 an hour. The Hospital San Vicente de Paul (☎ 261-0091) is at Calle 14, Avenida 8, or call the Red Cross Ambulance (☎ 911, 237-1115). Most sick people get treated in nearby San José.

### Things to See & Do

The city was founded in 1706, and its colonial character is the main reason to visit. The **Parque Central** is the best place to see the older buildings. To the east of the park is the church of **La Inmaculada Concepción**, built in 1797 and still in use. Opposite the church steps, you can take a break and watch old men playing checkers at the park tables while weddings and funerals come and go. The church's thick-walled, squat construction is attractive in an ugly sort of way – rather like Volkswagen Beetles are attractive to many people. The solid shape has withstood the earthquakes that have damaged or destroyed almost all the other buildings in Costa Rica that date from this time.

To the north of the park is a colonial tower called simply **El Fortín** (the small fortress). This area is a national historic site. At the park's northeast corner is the **Casa de la Cultura**, formerly the residence of President Alfredo González Flores (1913–7), now housing art and historical exhibits. The center of the park has a covered bandstand where there are occasional performances.

Uphill and north from the center is a somewhat untended park that offers views across stretches of the valley and the mountains to the south.

A visit to the Universidad Nacional campus is of interest. The marine biology department has a **Museo Zoomarino** (☎ 277-3240; admission free; open 8am-4pm Mon-Fri), where almost 2000 displayed specimens give an overview of Costa Rica's marine diversity.

The countryside surrounding Heredia is almost completely dedicated to growing coffee. Tour companies in San José sometimes arrange visits to the coffee fincas. The countryside is attractive and has several points of interest and good hotels. See the Around Heredia section, later in this chapter, for details.

### Language Courses

The following seem to do a good job. These are fine choices if you'd like to stay near San José without actually being in the capital.

**Centro Panamericano de Idiomas** (☎ 265-6213, in the USA ☎ 888-682-0054, fax 265-6866, [e] info@cpi-edu.com, [w] www.cpi-edu.com/heredia.html) In a suburb about 10 minutes by bus from Heredia, this school offers four weeks of classes (5½ hours/day) for about US$1100, including family homestay, all meals, and field trips. Classes average two or three students (four maximum). This center has been recommended by several students.

**Interculturae Lenguaje Pura Vida** (☎/fax 237-0387, [e] info@costaricaspanish.com, Avenida 3, Calles 8 & 10) Courses cost US$320 to US$370 a week, all with family homestay, meals, four hours of class a day, and extracurricular activities and tours every afternoon; extra tutoring is available for US$16 per hour. Courses without homestay cost US$230 a week. Classes for seven- to 13-year-olds are also available.

**Instituto Profesional de Educación** (☎ 238-3608, fax 238-0621, [e] ipedcr@racsa.co.cr, [w] www.learnspanishcostarica.com) Classes for a maximum of six students (most smaller) are

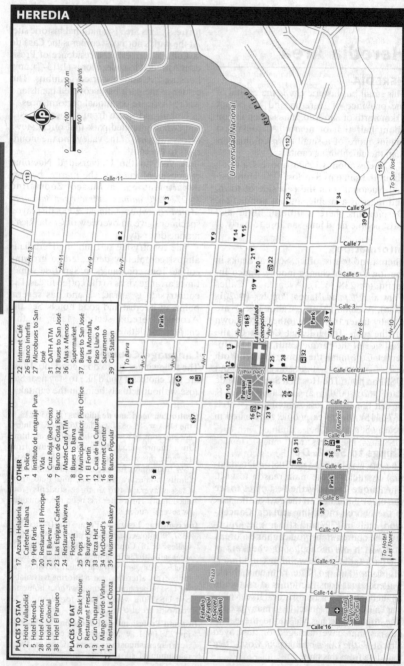

# HEREDIA

**PLACES TO STAY**
2 Hotel Valladolid
5 Hotel Heredia
28 Hotel America
30 Hotel Colonial
38 Hotel El Parqueo

**PLACES TO EAT**
3 Cowboy Steak House
9 Restaurant Fresas
13 Gran Chaparral
14 Mango Verde Vishnu
15 Restaurant La Choza
17 Azzura Heladería y
   Cafetería Italiana
19 Petit Paris
20 Restaurant El Príncipe
21 El Bulevar
23 Las Espigas Cafetería
24 Restaurant Nueva
   Floresta
25 Pops
29 Burger King
33 Pizza Hut
34 McDonald's
35 Musmanni Bakery

**OTHER**
1 Police
4 Instituto de Lenguaje Pura
   Vida
6 Cruz Roja (Red Cross)
7 Banco de Costa Rica;
   MasterCard ATM
8 Buses to Barva
10 Municipal Palace; Post Office
11 El Fortín
12 Casa de la Cultura
16 Internet Center
18 Banco Popular
22 Internet Café
26 Banco Interfín
27 Microbuses to San
   José
31 OATH ATM
32 Buses to San José
36 Mas x Menos
   Supermarket
37 Buses to San José
   de la Montaña,
   Paso Llano &
   Sacramento
39 Gas Station

Universidad Nacional

Río Pirro

Parque
Central

La Immaculada
Concepción

Estadio
de Fútbol
(Soccer
Stadium)

Plaza

Hospital
San Vicente
de Paúl

Market

CENTRAL VALLEY

held in central Heredia. Rates are US$320 to US$1940 for one to eight weeks with homestay, US$225 to US$1290 without homestay. Private lessons cost US$12 per hour.

**Intercultura** (☎ 260-8480, ☎/fax 260-9243, in the USA ☎ 800-205-0642, e info@intercultura costarica.com, w www.spanish-intercultura.com) Classes are held near central Heredia. Rates are US$350 to US$1125 for one to four weeks with homestay, or US$250 to US$725 without homestay. Classes are in small groups for four hours a day. Students can also take free daily Latin dance classes and weekly cooking or music classes. Private classes are US$17 per hour.

## Places to Stay

With San José so close, most travelers stay in the capital, though some elect to stay here because it's quieter. There are quite a few hotels in Heredia, however, partly to cater to the student population of the nearby university. Cheap hotels may give monthly discounts to students, but they are also used for short-term rentals – the walls are often thin.

**Hotel El Parqueo** (☎ 238-2882, Calle 4, Avenidas 6 & 8) Rooms US$5 per person with shared bath, doubles US$15 with private bath. This basic place is friendly and clean enough but lacks hot water.

**Hotel Colonial** (☎ 237-5258, Avenida 4, Calles 4 & 6) Singles/doubles without bath US$7.50/12.50. This place is reasonably clean and family-run, rooms have fans, and there's hot water in the shared baths.

**Hotel Heredia** (☎/fax 238-0880, Calle 6, Avenidas 3 & 5) Singles/doubles with bath US$14/24. The rooms aren't much to look at but the beds are clean and there's hot water; also, this hotel will change US dollars. Meals are available.

**Hotel Las Flores** (☎ 261-8147, 260-8147, Avenida 12, Calles 12 & 14) Singles/doubles with bath US$13/20. Slightly away from the center, this is a family-run place, with private parking and rooms with clean hot showers.

**Hotel America** (☎ 260-9292, fax 260-9293, Calle Central, Avenidas 2 & 4) Singles/doubles with bath US$29/41, including continental breakfast. The 36 rooms here are light, modern, reasonably sized, and have hot water and cable TV. There is a 24-hour restaurant and bar. Airport transfers are available.

**Apartotel Vargas** (☎ 237-8526, fax 260-4698) Doubles US$45. On the northwest side of Heredia (head north on Calle 12 about 1km), this establishment has good apartments with kitchenettes, hot-water showers, TVs, and laundry facilities.

**Hotel Valladolid** (☎ 260-2905, fax 260-2912, e valladol@racsa.co.cr, Calle 7, Avenida 7) Singles/doubles/triples with bath US$66/75/84 including continental breakfast. The best hotel in town is this five-story building, which features a sauna/Jacuzzi/solarium on the top floor with good views of the surrounding area. The 12 rooms are attractive, air-conditioned, and feature minibars, cable TVs, telephones, and hot water. A good restaurant and bar are on the premises.

There are a number of mid-range and top-end hotels in the countryside surrounding Heredia (see Around Heredia, later in this chapter).

## Places to Eat

**Gran Chaparral** (☎ 237-1010, Avenida Central, Calles Central & 1) Dishes US$4-6. Open 11am-11pm. Near the Parque Central, this is a locally popular place serving Chinese meals as well as steak and seafood.

There are some student bars and cafés close to the university; **El Bulevar** and **Restaurant La Choza** have been recommended, but several others nearby look equally good.

**Restaurant Fresas** (☎ 262-5555, Avenida 1, Calle 7) Dishes US$4-9. Open 8am-midnight. Near the university, this place serves good, fairly typical meals and has an outdoor dining area. Cheaper snacks, desserts, and fruit drinks are available.

**Mango Verde Vishnu** (☎ 237-2526, Calle 7, Avenidas Central & 1) Dishes US$2-4. Open 9am-6pm Mon-Sat. Just down the street from Fresas, this branch of the San José–area Vishnu chain has good vegetarian food; try the veggie burger and fruit shake combo.

**Cowboy Steak House** (Calle 9, Avenidas 3 & 5) Dishes US$2-8. Open 4pm-2am. Carnivores can try this place, a few blocks away. Food ranges from snacks and sandwiches to seafood and steaks – not bad.

**Restaurant El Principe** (☎ 238-1894, Calle 5, Avenidas Central & 2) Dishes US$4-9. Open 'til midnight, this locally popular place has a mixed menu: Chinese plates, curries, seafood, and meats. Take-out is available.

Some students prefer *Pizza Hut*, *McDonald's*, or *Burger King* in the university area. (McDonald's and the super-huge Burger King signs have become landmarks used by cab drivers.) There are clean *sodas* in the market for inexpensive meals.

*Restaurant Nueva Floresta* (☎ 237-0336) For something slightly less basic, this is a good choice, overlooking the south side of Parque Central. They serve Chinese food – decent chop suey with shrimp costs about US$4.

*Petit Paris* (☎ 262-2564, Calle 5, Avenidas Central & 2) US$5-9. Open 11am-10pm Mon-Sat. A good place for French-influenced food, starting with the specialty crepes (US$5). Indoors, a café atmosphere is enhanced by pictures of 'gay Paree'; outdoors, there's a dining patio.

For good ice cream, deluxe coffee, or light snacks, the best places are *Azzura Heladería y Cafetería Italiana*, on the southwest side of the Parque Central, or *Las Espigas Cafeteria* directly across the street. There is also a *Pops* ice-cream parlor and a *Musmanni* bakery.

## Entertainment

Ask around the university area for currently popular nightspots. Both *La Choza* and *El Bulevar* restaurants are good places to hang out over a drink. The *Restaurant Viena* in the Hotel America has karaoke or live music and dancing on weekends. You can always go into San José for nightlife, too.

## Getting There & Away

Minibuses leave San José for Heredia every 15 minutes from 6am to 10pm, from Avenida 2, Calles 10 & 12.

In Heredia, there is no central terminal, and buses leave from bus stops near the Parque Central and market areas. Destinations, departure points, and approximate frequency are as follows:

**Barva** – by the Cruz Roja (Red Cross), Calle Central, Avenidas 1 & 3, every 30 minutes

**Paso Llano (Porrosatí) & Sacramento (for Volcán Barva in Parque Nacional Braulio Carrillo)** – Calle 4, across from the market, at 6:30am, 11am, and 4pm

**San José** – Calle Central, Avenida 4; and Avenida 4, Calles Central & 1, every few minutes

**San José de la Montaña** – Calle 4, across from the market, every hour

Ask around the market for information on other destinations.

A taxi ride to San José costs about US$5; a ride to the airport costs about US$8.

## AROUND HEREDIA

The small colonial town of **Barva**, 2.5km north of Heredia, was founded in 1561 and is a national historic monument. Its church and surrounding houses date from the 1700s. Although there is no particular building to see, the town as a whole has a pleasant old-world ambiance and is fun to stroll around in.

A short distance south of Barva is the famous **Café Britt Finca** (☎ 261-0707, 260-2748, fax 238-1848, e info@cafebritt.com, coffeetour@cafebritt.com, w www.cafebritt.com; tours US$20; tours at 9am & 11am year-round, 3pm in high season), which does 'coffeetours.' These begin with a visit to the coffee finca and continue with a bilingual (Spanish-English) multimedia presentation using actors to describe the historical importance of coffee to Costa Rica. The tour also shows parts of the production process. The presentation finishes with coffee-tasting sessions led by experienced coffee cuppers (as the tasters are called). It's a real eye-opening experience! Then you can buy as much coffee as you want, along with coffee paraphernalia, at the Café Britt gift shop.

'Coffeetours' are held year-round and cost a little more if you go from San José. The Café Britt bus will pick you up from major San José hotels – call for a reservation. If you drive or take the bus, you can't miss the signs between Heredia and Barva.

Other tour choices include combining a 'coffeetour' with the Butterfly Farm (see that entry in the Alajuela Area section earlier in this chapter) or with a visit to the **Museo de Cultura Popular** (☎ 260-1619; admission US$1.50; open 8am-4pm daily) in Santa Lucía de Barva, about 1.5km southeast of Barva. The museum is housed in a century-old farmhouse that is restored with period pieces and gives a look at late 19th-century life in rural Costa Rica. A 3pm combined Café Britt/museum tour runs from December to May and costs US$25 from San José. From mid-November to mid-March, a full-day tour visiting Volcán Poás, an organic coffee farm (where you can pick coffee), and a working coffee mill, and including a typical lunch, costs about US$80 from San José. The all-day tours are led by an agronomist guide and go with a minimum of four people.

West and then north of Barva, buses go to **San Pedro de Barva** (where there is a coffee research station) and on to **Santa Bárbara** (where there is an exclusive hotel – see Places to Stay).

About 1km north of Barva, the road forks. The right fork continues to the village of **San José de la Montaña**, about 5km north of Barva. The village is pleasantly located at about 1550m on the south slopes of Volcán Barva. The higher elevation gives a fresh nip to the air, and you should bring some warm clothes, particularly if you're staying overnight in one of the country inns north of the village. From San José de la Montaña, three buses a day continue toward **Sacramento**, and this is the route to the trails up Volcán Barva, part of Parque Nacional Braulio Carrillo.

Three kilometers northeast of Heredia is San Rafael de Heredia, where a road leads about 8km north to **Monte de la Cruz** and its inexpensive restaurant that serves local food. Here are great views of the mountains, the Central Valley, and San José. There is pleasant hiking in the area. Places that locals recommend for trails include Bosque de la Hoja, El Chopipe, Cerro Dantas, and Jaguarundi private reserves. Ask locally about these.

A couple of kilometers before you get to Monte de la Cruz is the **Club Campestre El Castillo** (☎ *267-7111, 267-7115, fax 267-7114,* e *castillo@racsa.co.cr*). You can use this country club's facilities for a few dollars. Among the attractions are a pool, sauna, ice-skating rink (in the tropics!), and go-carts. There is a restaurant, bar, and picnic area, and camping is allowed for members.

Some 5km east of San Rafael is San Isidro de Heredia, which has a couple of B&B hotels (see Places to Stay).

## INBio

Tiny Costa Rica is world-famous for its biodiversity, but an approximate 84% of its species are unknown to science. A private, not-for-profit organization named El Instituto Nacional de Bioversidad (National Bioversity Institute; w www.inbio.ac.cr) was formed in 1989 with the goal of promoting local awareness of the country's biodiversity and thereby ensuring its conservation. The innovative formation of INBio differed radically from conservation organizations in other tropical nations, in that the institute hired and trained local workers to research and do an inventory of the country's species, to spread this information into the world's databanks, and to find sustainable ways to conserve the biodiveristy. Of particular interest are the 'parataxonomists,' who are often local rural dwellers trained to specialize in one type of organism (beetles or mollusks, for example) and then hired to make collections and inventory those species in biologically rich sections of the country. Parataxonomists collect and isolate many new species; similar to paramedics, their job is to do the essential work of data collection and stabilization quickly and inexpensively before passing the information on to the experts.

This and other fascinating stories are told at INBioparque (☎ 244-4730, fax 244-4790, e inbioparque@inbio.ac.cr), a new facility opened in Santo Domingo de Heredia and easily visited from either San José or Heredia. The park is modeled after a US National Park visitor center, with an introductory video, state-of-the-art computerized interactive audiovisual demonstrations, maps of the entire Costa Rican national park system, exhibits of plants and insects, and three well-signed wheelchair-accessible trails totaling 2km and passing a lake and representations of different Costa Rican ecosystems. A restaurant and gift shop are on the premises, as is a library and research room where visitors are able to use a photocopier and the Internet. The center is an excellent introduction to the country's biodiversity and national parks. Some visitors feel that the price is a bit steep (nonresident adults/students/children 5-12 yrs US$15/12/8, parking US$3), but admission includes a guided tour in Spanish or English and the profits do go to a worthwhile cause. Hours are 7:30am to 4pm year-round.

**CENTRAL VALLEY**

## Places to Stay

**Santa Bárbara** Just before Santa Bárbara is *Finca Rosa Blanca* (☎ 269-9392, fax 269-9555, ⓔ info@FincaRosaBlanca.com, ⓦ www.fincarosablanca.com) Singles US$175-274, doubles US$198-297, additional people US$35 each; all with breakfast. Kids three to 12 pay half-price. This is one of the most exclusive small country hotels in Costa Rica. It has only nine suites (two are two-bedroom garden villas). The property contains walking and jogging trails leading to a waterfall. A hot tub and horseback riding are available.

The most expensive room is surreal: a tower with a 360° view reached by a winding staircase made of a single tree trunk. The bathroom is painted like a tropical rainforest, which is complemented by an artificial waterfall – not your run-of-the-mill hotel bathroom. The hotel's other rooms, all different, are also intriguing and feature murals, handmade furniture, and modern architecture. All rooms have a private patio or deck.

There is a lovely outdoor pool, a game room, a library, and a restaurant and bar for the guests. A top-notch four- or five-course dinner (about US$35) may be reserved in advance. The owners and staff are gracious and helpful with varied tour reservations and airport pickups; they provide free Internet access for guests.

**San José de la Montaña** A few kilometers north of San José de la Montaña (and at a higher elevation) are several comfortable country hotels, all known for their attractive settings. Walking and birding are the main activities. Although three buses a day (from Heredia to Sacramento) come close to the hotels, they will provide you with courtesy pickup. Alternatively, get a taxi from San José de la Montaña. The hotels are small and sometimes close temporarily midweek if there is no demand. During the weekends, they may well be full with locals, so you should call first to make reservations, get precise directions, or arrange to be picked up.

*Las Ardillas Resort* (☎/fax 260-2172) Doubles US$60, with breakfast. This place has seven cabins, each with its own fireplace, kitchen area, and accommodations for two to four people, and another seven cabins nearby in its Cabañas Las Milenas annex. There is a spa and a restaurant. A massage with a US-trained physical therapist costs US$30, and mud treatments cost US$20. Ask about long-stay discounts.

*Hotel El Cypresal* (☎ 237-4466, fax 237-7232) Singles/doubles with bath US$40/50. This hotel has two dozen standard rooms, with terraces, fireplaces, TV, and hot showers. There's a small swimming pool, a sauna, horse rental, and a restaurant.

*Hotel El Pórtico* (☎ 266-1000, 262-4669, fax 266-1002) Doubles US$40. Popular with ticos, this place has 18 heated rooms, a restaurant, sauna, and pool. You can rent horses.

**Monte de la Cruz** Between Monte de la Cruz and Club Campestre El Castillo, you'll find this recommended small country hotel, *Hotel Chalet Tirol* (☎ 267-6222, fax 267-6229, ⓔ info@chalet-tirol.com, ⓦ www.chalet-tirol.com/tirol/home.htm) Doubles from US$90. It has a variety of 24 comfortable suites and is set at 1800m in the foothills of the Cordillera Central. There is a good French restaurant and tennis courts. Trails head into the cloud forest on the grounds and beyond, and horses are available for rent. Trout fishing and birding are other activities. The rate varies, depending on the suite. The staff will pick you up from San José or the airport for an extra US$15; reservations are recommended.

*Hotel La Condesa* (☎ 267-6000, fax 267-6200, ⓔ condesam@racsa.co.cr) Rooms & villas US$130-160. A member of the Spanish Occidental Hotels & Resorts chain (ⓦ www.occidental-hoteles.com), this luxurious modern hotel has large rooms, several restaurants, a pool, Jacuzzi, and sauna. It's also close to the El Castillo country club.

**Santo Domingo de Heredia** Another good country hotel in Santo Domingo de Heredia, about halfway between Heredia and San José, is *Bougainvillea Santo Domingo* (☎ 244-1414, fax 244-1313, ⓔ info@bougainvillea.com, ⓦ www.bougainvillea.co.cr) Singles/doubles US$79/88, junior suites US$116. This place is close enough to the capital that many visitors stay here instead of San José. There are orchards on the extensive grounds, and there is a restaurant, pool, and tennis court. Free shuttle buses run to San José and tours and car rental can be arranged. The 83 rooms and suites have balconies with views either of the mountains or San José in the distance, sitting rooms, cable TV, and direct dial phones. Six of the rooms are handicapped accessible.

## PARQUE NACIONAL BRAULIO CARRILLO

This national park is a success story for both conservationists and developers. Until the 1970s, San José's links with the Caribbean coast at Puerto Limón were limited to the (now defunct) railway and a slow, narrow highway. A fast, paved, modern highway was proposed as an important step in advancing Costa Rica's ability to transport goods, services, and people between the capital and the Caribbean coast.

This development was certainly to Costa Rica's economic advantage, but the most feasible route lay through a low pass between Volcán Barva and Volcán Irazú to the northwest of the Central Valley. In the 1970s, this region was virgin rainforest and conservationists were deeply concerned that the development would lead to accompanying colonization, logging, and loss of habitat, as well as damage to the watershed that is the single greatest source of water for the San José area.

A compromise was reached by declaring the region a national park and allowing this one single major highway to bisect it. This effectively cuts the region into two smaller preserved areas, but it is considered one national park.

Parque Nacional Braulio Carrillo (named after Costa Rica's third chief of state) was established in 1978. The San José-to-Guápiles highway was completed in 1987, and 47,583 hectares have been protected from further development. The pristine areas to either side of the highway are large enough to support and protect a great and varied number of plant and animal species, and San José has its much-needed modern connection with the Caribbean coast.

Most people see the park by simply riding through it on one of the frequent buses traveling the new highway between San José and Guápiles or Limón. The difference between this highway and other roads in the Central Valley is marked: instead of small villages and large coffee plantations, the panorama is one of rolling hillsides or roadside cliffs clothed with thick montane rain-forest. About 75% of Costa Rica was rain-forest in the 1940s; now less than a quarter of the country retains its natural vegetative cover, and it is through parks such as Braulio Carrillo that the biodiversity represented by the remaining rainforest is protected.

The buses traveling the new highway rarely stop, and most passengers just gaze out of the window and admire the thick vegetation covered with epiphytes (air plants) such as bromeliads and mosses. On the steepest roadside slopes are stands of the distinctive huge-leafed *Gunnera* plants, which quickly colonize steep and newly exposed parts of the montane rainforest. The large leaves can protect a person from a sudden tropical downpour – hence the plant's nickname is 'poor folks' umbrella.' A walk into the forest will give you a chance to see the incredible variety of orchids, ferns, palms, and other plant life, although the lushness of the vegetation makes viewing the many species of tropical animals something of a challenge. You will certainly hear and see plenty of birds, but the mammals are more elusive.

Part of the reason there is such a variety of plant and animal life in Braulio Carrillo is that it encompasses a wide spread of altitudinal zones. Elevations within the park range from 2906m at the top of Volcán Barva to less than 50m in the Caribbean lowlands. Five of the Holdridge Life Zones are represented, and the differences in elevation create many different habitats.

A visit to the park can consist of anything from sightseeing from a bus crossing the park to a difficult and adventurous trip of several days, climbing Volcán Barva and perhaps the nearby Volcán Cacho Negro (2150m) before descending to the lowlands on foot. The observant naturalist may see Costa Rica's most famous bird, the resplendent quetzal, as well as umbrella birds, toucans, trogons, guans, eagles, and a host of other avifauna.

Mammals living in the park include cats such as the jaguar, puma, and ocelot, and also tapirs and sloths, all of which are difficult to see. More likely sightings include peccaries or any one of the three species of monkeys present in the park.

### Orientation & Information

There are two main ways to access the park. One is from the new highway; the second is from the road north of San José de la Montaña toward Sacramento (see Getting There & Away, later in this section). On both these routes are ranger stations where you can get further information, though the station on the second route doesn't keep regular hours. A third route is along a minor road with no ranger stations.

The park entrance on the new highway is about 20km northeast of San José. From the highway toll booth (US60¢ for cars), continue on the new highway almost 2km to the Puesto Zurquí ranger station on the right, (where there are no visitor facilities). Less than 1km past the station, the road goes through the 600m-long Túnel Zurquí. Along the highway, there are occasional unmarked dirt pullouts with views. About 22km beyond the tunnel is the Quebrada González ranger station, on the right – keep your eyes peeled or you'll miss it. (Coming from Puerto Limón, this ranger station is on the left

almost immediately after the sign announcing the park boundary.) Some rangers live here, and there is a guarded parking lot, toilets, and three **walking trails** *(admission US$6 per person; open 8am to 3:30pm)*. The gate isn't normally locked, so if you arrive before 8am, you can open the gate, park, hike, and pay the national park fee when you return. The three trails are 1.6km, 2km, and 2.5km long. Two of them pass a viewpoint and another passes a waterfall; ask the rangers for details.

Note there is no fee to drive through the park. Also note that, although there are numerous restaurants along the highway out of San José, they peter out completely by the time you reach the toll booth and there are none for many kilometers. It's possible to get to the park by public bus, but it's not recommended because on the way back you have to walk 2km along the highway to reach a stop at a restaurant; a vulnerable position (see Warning).

## Rainforest Aerial Tram

The intricate Rainforest Aerial Tram is the brainchild of biologist Don Perry, one of the pioneers of rainforest canopy research. He started exploring the canopy using rope-climbing techniques in 1974 and began stringing ropes together into a canopy-exploration web in 1979 (see the June 1980 *Smithsonian* magazine). In 1984, he started work on an Automated Web for Canopy Exploration (AWCE) in Rara Avis (see the Northern Lowlands chapter), and in 1992 he began construction of the Rainforest Aerial Tram. It opened in late 1994 and is located just past the northeastern exit from Parque Nacional Braulio Carrillo (on the right coming from San José).

The 2.6km aerial tram has 22 cars, which each take five passengers and a naturalist guide. The ride is designed to go silently through and just over the rainforest canopy and takes 40 minutes each way, thus affording riders a unique view of the rainforest and unusual plant and birding opportunities. Although there are platforms, ropes, and walkways in the rainforest canopy in Costa Rica and other countries, this is the first time (that I know of) that a canopy project of this scale has been accessible to the general public anywhere in the tropics.

Amazingly, the whole project was constructed with almost no impact on the rainforest. A narrow footpath follows the tram and all the 250,000kg of construction material was carried in on foot or by a cable system to avoid erosion, with the exception of the 12 towers supporting the tram that were helicoptered in by the Nicaraguan Air Force (Costa Rica has no armed forces!). The pilot involved in the project called it 'the best work' he had ever done.

There is a 400-hectare reserve around the tram, and visitors often go for a guided introductory hike (about an hour) before embarking on the tram. Three kilometers of the reserve boundary is contiguous with Parque Nacional Braulio Carrillo. This is not a zoo and the numbers of animals seen will not be high, although many have been recorded in the area – about 118 species of reptiles and amphibians, 300 species of birds, 85 species of bats, and about 50 other mammals.

The sheer density of the vegetation makes observing animals difficult. Mammals are spotted only very occasionally, though there are fairly good opportunities to get close to rainforest birds. The best time to go is first thing in the morning, though most tours arrive later. When I went at

**Warning** Unfortunately, there have been many reports over the last few years of thefts from cars parked at entrances to some trails (though not from the three walking trails mentioned above), as well as armed robbers accosting tourists hiking on the trails or walking along the highway. Readers have reported hearing shots fired on the trails, and hitchhikers have reported being told it is a dangerous area. Don't leave your car parked anywhere along the main highway unless there is a park ranger on duty, such as at Quebrada González.

Unfortunately, the Servicio de Parques Nacionales (SPN) doesn't have the money to patrol most of the park. An alternative is to go with an organized tour. This situation may improve in the near future, but exercise extra caution in the meantime.

## Climbing Volcán Barva

Use the park entrance via San José de la Montaña if you plan to climb this volcano.

From the road, foot trails go to the summit of Barva, which is climbable in about four or five hours roundtrip at a leisurely pace. A trail goes from Paso Llano (Porrosatí) to the summit of Barva (about 9km) and returns to Sacramento. However, at last check the trail from Paso Llano was reported to be badly overgrown and poorly maintained. Most people go from Sacramento, about 5km beyond Paso Llano. There is a guard post near Sacramento, open at erratic hours. Sometimes the rangers will take you to the top: about 4km one way.

The trail up Barva from Sacramento is fairly obvious, and it's marked by a sign. On the park border, near the guard post, is a small cabin; to arrange accommodations call ☎ 283-5906, and someone will contact the rangers by radio. If you wish to continue from Barva north into the lowlands, you will find that the trails are not marked and not as obvious. It is possible, regardless, to follow northbound 'trails' (overgrown and

### Rainforest Aerial Tram

about 9am, I had the opportunity to glimpse an unusual white bat as well as get a nice close view of a pair of toucans. The most lasting impression, though, is of silently swooping through the different layers of rainforest, sometimes just a meter above the ground and at other times 30m above a chasm clothed in trees. Certainly, riding the tram was a memorable experience and one that I would recommend.

It doesn't come cheaply, however, and several budget travelers have complained to me that it's too expensive. Personally, I think the experience is unique enough to warrant the cost, but you'll have to decide for yourself.

The Rainforest Aerial Tram (in San José ☎ 257-5961, fax 257-6053, e reservas@rainforest.co.cr, w www.rainforesttram.com) is open 6:30am to 4pm every day of the year. (The tram stays open until dusk.) Note that on Mondays no trams run until 9am (for maintenance), although you can enter and walk around. There is a guarded parking lot at the entrance where tickets are sold, and it's worth getting tickets in advance to save time. The San José office is at Avenida 7, Calles 5 & 7, and is staffed 6am to 9pm, or you can buy tickets through a travel agent. Tickets cost US$49 (half-price for students and five- to 18-year-olds; children under five are not permitted). From the parking lot, a truck takes you about 3km to the tram loading area, where there is a small exhibit/information area (there was a live pit viper there once – on a log, not in a cage!) and a restaurant and gift shop. Here, you can see an orientation video, and there are short hiking trails that you can use for as long as you want. Tram riders should be prepared for rain – although the cars have tarpaulin roofs, the sides are open to the elements.

If you are not driving, you can take a bus to Guápiles (under US$2, every 30 minutes, from the Caribe terminal in San José) and ask the driver to drop you at the entrance. The people at the entrance will help you flag down a return bus. Alternately, you can arrange a tour with a bus pickup from major San José hotels to the tram and return, including lunch (US$78.50/53.75 adults/students & five- to 18-year-olds; children under five not permitted). Allow about six hours for this.

unmaintained) all the way through the park to La Selva near Puerto Viejo de Sarapiquí. A tico who has done it reported that it took him four days and it is a bushwhacking adventure only for those used to roughing it and able to use a map and compass.

The slopes of Barva are one of the best places in the park to see the quetzal. Near the summit are several lakes; the biggest are Lagos Danta, Barva, and Copey, with diameters of 500m, 70m, and 40m, respectively. Camping is allowed anywhere you can pitch a tent, but no facilities are provided so you must be self-sufficient. The rangers have built two platforms, one on the crater edge and one near Lago Barva. These could be used for pitching a tent.

There is plenty of water (the park receives between 3m and 6m of rain per year depending on locality), and there are innumerable lakes, streams, and waterfalls. This means that trails are often muddy and that you should be prepared for rain at any time of year.

The best time to go is the supposedly 'dry' season (from December to April), but it is liable to rain then, too, though less than in the other months. If you're going on a day trip, leave as early as possible, as the mornings tend to be clear and the afternoons cloudy. The nighttime temperatures can drop to several degrees below freezing.

### Getting There & Away

**Via the New Highway** It is possible to get one of the buses going through the park to Guápiles along the new highway and get off where you want (the Quebrada González ranger station is the suggested place). However, taking a public bus is not recommended, as you will have to flag one down from the highway when you want to leave – this is a problem in part because buses are often full and don't want to stop (especially on weekends), but mainly because it can be dangerous; see the Warning earlier in this section about visiting this area. Hitchhiking is also, for the same reason, not a good idea. Unfortunately for budget travelers, the best options are to go on a tour or hire a car.

**Via San José de la Montaña** For the entrance via San José de la Montaña, three buses a day (at the time of research, at 6:30am, 11am, and 4pm) leave Heredia for Paso Llano ('Porrosatí' on some maps) and Sacramento. Ask the driver to drop you at the track leading to Volcán Barva. During the wet season, the bus might not make it up to Sacramento, when 4WD may be necessary. The bus returns at 5pm. It's about 13km from San José de la Montaña to the park entrance.

**Via Alto Palma** From San Juan de Tibás in northern San José, take this little-used, locally known road through Guayabal, Paracito, San Jerónimo, and Alto Palma to Bajo Honduras. This was the main ox-cart trail to Puerto Limón in the mid 19th century, and it parallels and the main highway on the east; some maps show it as Hwy 220. It is paved almost to Alto Palma. Bajo Honduras is near the park entrance, and the dirt road continues a few kilometers into the park. Local guides are available.

## MORAVIA

This village is named San Vicente de Moravia or San Vicente on many maps, but is known as Moravia by the local inhabitants. It's about 7km northeast of San José and used to be the center for the area's coffee fincas. Today, the village is famous for its handicrafts, especially leather, but also ceramics, jewelry, and the ubiquitous wood.

Around and nearby the spacious and attractive Parque Central are several stores. Some started as a saddle shops but now sell a variety of leather and other goods. Look for *La Rueda* (home to an odd pair of the world's largest birds), *Artesanía Bribri* (which sells work made by the Bribri Indians of the Caribbean slope), and many others.

*Mercado de Artesanías Las Garzas* (☎ 236-0037) Open 8:30am-6pm Mon-Sat, 9am-4pm Sun. This complex holds arts and crafts stores, simple restaurants serving tico food, and clean toilet facilities. It's 100m south and 75m east of the *municipio* (town hall). Shoppers who are planning a spree should note that some stores are closed on Sunday, especially in the low season.

There are frequent buses (Nos 40, 40A, and 42) from Avenida 3, Calles 3 & 5, in San José to (San Vicente de) Moravia. A taxi from San José costs about US$2.

## CORONADO

This is the general name for several villages centered on San Isidro de Coronado, about 6km east of Moravia. About 1km before San Isidro de Coronado is San Antonio de Coronado, and close to this is Dulce Nombre de Coronado.

San Isidro de Coronado is 1383m above sea level, 200m higher than San José. It is a popular destination during the dry season for josefinos looking for an escape from the city. There are some simple restaurants but no accommodations. The village has an annual fiesta on May 15.

### Instituto Clodomiro Picado

The main reason to visit Coronado is to see the snake 'farm' at Instituto Clodomiro Picado at Dulce Nombre (☎ 229-0344; admission free; call for hours).

The institute is run by the University of Costa Rica and has a selection of local poisonous snakes on display. Once a week, visitors can see the snakes being 'milked' for their poison, which is then used to make antivenin. At other times, callers can view the snakes, learn about the serum-making process, or buy some serum.

### Getting There & Away

Take a bus from Avenida 3, Calles 3 & 5, in San José. From San Isidro, it is 1km or so back to the snake institute – ask the bus driver for directions. It's a pleasant downhill walk back to Moravia, about 6km away.

## RANCHO REDONDO

This little community is a 16km drive east of San José. The road climbs slowly to about 2000m, allowing you picturesque views of the agricultural countryside and of San José.

*Hacienda San Miguel* (☎ 229-5058, 229-4792, fax 229-1097, e *hotelhsm@racsa.co.cr*) Doubles US$33-44, with breakfast included on weekends only. This is a country lodge with spa, Jacuzzi, and a recreation area with a fireplace. The hacienda operates horseback tours (US$10, 90 minutes) through rainforest on the 400-hectare property, a working cattle ranch.

Most people drive here, but buses for Rancho Redondo (Rte 47) leave San José from Avenida 5, Calles Central & 2.

# Cartago Area

## CARTAGO

This is the fourth provincial capital of the Central Valley, and the most historic one. The city was founded in 1563 and was the capital of the country until 1823. Unfortunately, an eruption of Volcán Irazú in 1723 and major earthquakes in 1841 and 1910 ruined almost all the old buildings, and there is not a great deal of architecture left to see; it is the least visually interesting of the provincial capitals.

Cartago was built at an elevation of 1435m in the valley between the Cordillera Central and the Cordillera de Talamanca; Volcán Irazú looms nearby.

The metropolitan area, including the densely settled suburbs, has a population of about 132,000 and is the nation's third-largest urban area. It's 22km southeast of San José and the two cities are connected by a good road and frequent buses.

### Information

There is no tourist office. Several banks in the town center change money; Banco Interfin (☎ 591-1000), Avenida 2, Calle 2, is usually faster than most and has a 24-hour OATH ATM. Several Bancréditos have 24-hour ATMs. The Café Internet, in the Edificio Rosalina next to the Pizza Hut on Avenida 4, is open 9am to 10pm Monday to Friday, 'til 9pm Saturday, and closed on Sunday. The Hospital Max Peralta (☎ 550-1999) is at Calle 5, Avenidas 1 & 3, though most sick travelers head to San José.

### Churches

The most interesting sights in Cartago are churches. The church at Avenida 2, Calle 2, was destroyed by an earthquake in 1910. Las Ruinas (The Ruins) was never repaired, and the solid walls of the church now house a pretty garden. Las Ruinas is a major landmark of downtown Cartago, and is a pleasant spot to sit on a park bench and watch people go about their business.

East of the downtown area at Avenida 2, Calle 16, the Basílica de Nuestra Señora de los Angeles is the most famous church of the Central Valley, if not of all Costa Rica. The Basilica was destroyed in the 1926 earthquake and rebuilt in Byzantine style. It has an airy spaciousness with fine stained-glass windows.

**CARTAGO**

0    150    300 m
0    150    300 yards

| PLACES TO STAY & EAT | | 12 Bancrédito ATM |
| 1 Hotel Dinastia | | 13 Bancrédito ATM |
| 5 Pops | | 14 Soda Apolo; Cine Teatro |
| 7 Pizza Hut | |    Apolo |
| 9 La Puerta del Sol; Los | | 15 Taxi Stand |
|    Angeles Lodge | | 16 Las Ruinas (Ruined |
| 10 Pizza Hut | |    Church) |
| | | 17 Buses to Paraíso & Volcán |
| **OTHER** | |    Irazú |
| 2 Buses to Tierra Blanca | | 18 Buses to Orosi |
| 3 Banco de Costa Rica | | 19 Buses to Presa de Cachí |
| 4 Gas Station | | 20 Tribunales de Justicia |
| 6 Buses to San José | | 21 Buses to Aguacaliente |
| 8 Café Internet | | 22 San Francisco Church |
| 11 Banco Interfin OATH ATM | | 23 Buses to Turrialba |

The story goes that a statue of the Virgin was discovered on the site on August 2, 1635, and miraculously reappeared on the site after being removed. A shrine was built on the spot, and today the statue, known as La Negrita, is a pilgrimage destination. The Virgin associated with the statue is the patron saint of Costa Rica.

Miraculous healing powers are attributed to La Negrita, and pilgrims from all over Central America come to the Basilica to worship every August 2. There is a procession on foot from San José, 22km away. Inside the Basilica is a chapel dedicated to La Negrita, where gifts from cured pilgrims can be seen. The gifts are predominantly metal (including gold) models of parts of the human body that have been miraculously healed. A staircase descends into a small room where the rock where La Negrita reappeared can be seen – this place is absolutely jammed during pilgrimages and holy days.

## Other Attractions

A few kilometers out of the city are several interesting sights, the most famous of which is Volcán Irazú (see Parque Nacional Volcán

Irazú, later in this chapter). A favorite trip for locals is to the suburb of Aguacaliente, about 5km south of Cartago. Here are natural hot springs that have been dammed to form a swimming pool; it's a popular picnic spot.

## Special Events

The annual August 2 pilgrimage to La Negrita at La Basílica de Nuestra Señora de los Angeles is a major Costa Rican event. Pilgrims enter the church on their knees and shuffle forward in a show of faith, piety, and humility.

## Places to Stay & Eat

Most visitors stay in nearby San José or continue to the prettily placed village of Orosi (see the Orosi section, later in this chapter). There are only a couple of decent places in Cartago.

*Los Angeles Lodge* (☎ 551-0957, 591-4169, fax 591-2218) Singles/doubles/triples with bath US$20/25/30, with full breakfast. On the north side of the Plaza de la Basílica, this clean, older six-room B&B has hot water and cable TV.

*Hotel Dinastia* (☎ *551-7057*) Singles/
doubles without bath US$9/12, with bath
US$15. The 22 rooms here are nothing
special but they are clean, the water is hot,
and laundry service and parking are available. You'll find this family-run place 25m
north of the market.

There are no outstanding restaurants, but
there are several reasonable places where
you can get a meal. Just stroll along the
main streets of Avenida 2 and Avenida 4
downtown and take your choice. A few suggestions are marked on the map: *La Puerta
del Sol*, open from 8am to midnight, is probably the best, with a full menu of tico food
(US$3 to US$6). The *Soda Apolo*, opposite
the park, is open 24 hours and has atmosphere. Or take a picnic lunch to one of the
scenic spots in the Cartago area.

## Getting There & Away

SACSA (☎ 233-5350) buses leave San José
several times an hour from Calle 5, Avenida
18. Services run from about 5am to midnight, the journey takes almost an hour depending on the traffic, and the fare is US55¢.
There are also hourly night buses.

Buses arriving in Cartago from San José
come in on Avenida 2 from the west and
head east, stopping every few blocks, until
reaching the Basilica, the last stop. Buses
from Cartago back to San José (☎ 551-0225)
leave from Avenida 4, Calles 2 & 4.

You can also take a *colectivo* (shared) taxi
from Avenida Central, Calles 11 & 13, in San
José. They charge almost US$2 per person
and leave when they have five passengers.

To continue from Cartago to Turrialba
(1½ hours, under US$1), take a TRANS-
TUSA bus (☎ 591-5145, 556-0073) from
Avenida 3, Calles 8 & 10 (in front of the Tri-
bunales de Justicia). Buses leave every 30
minutes from 6am to 10:30am and every
hour from 10:30am to 10:30pm. Some buses
originate in San José and come through
town on Avenida 3. Space may be limited on
these buses.

Local destinations are served from a
variety of bus stops; if what you need isn't
listed here or if the stop you're looking for
has moved, ask locals for directions. For
Paraíso (and the turnoff for Lankester
Gardens), the bus leaves from Avenida 1,
Calles 2 & 4. For Orosi, the bus leaves from
Calle 6 near Avenida 1. For Aguacaliente,

the bus leaves from the corner of Calle 1,
Avenida 3. For the Presa de Cachí (Cachí
Dam), the bus leaves from Calle 6 and
Avenida 3. All of these buses are cheap
and leave at least every hour.

Buses to Tierra Blanca (a village 18km
before Volcán Irazú) leave from Calle 4,
Avenidas 6 & 8. Buses leave Cartago at
7am, 9am, and 1pm Monday to Friday for
Tierra Blanca, from where you could walk
or hitch to the volcano (ask the driver to set
you down at the right turnoff, a few kilometers before the village). Walkers should
remember that the altitude will make the
hike a breathlessly difficult one and hitch-
ers will find few cars midweek.

There is no daily bus service to Volcán
Irazú. The weekend bus from San José stops
in Cartago at 8:30am outside Las Ruinas *if*
seats are available; it's not a reliable option.

Hire cabs from a taxi stand on the west
side of the Parque Central to any of the
local destinations. A cab to Irazú costs
about US$25 (bargain hard), including a
short wait at the crater.

## PARQUE NACIONAL VOLCÁN IRAZÚ

The centerpiece of this national park is the
highest active volcano in Costa Rica, Volcán
Irazú, at 3432m. This and other volcanoes'
eruptions have made the soil of the Central
Valley quite fertile. Eruptions have been
recorded since 1723, when the governor of
the then Province of Costa Rica, Diego de
la Haya Fernández, reported the event. His
name is now given to one of the two main
craters at the summit.

The last major eruption of Irazú was a
memorable one; it occurred on March 19,
1963, the day that US President John F
Kennedy arrived on a state visit. San José,
Cartago, and most of the Central Valley
were covered with several centimeters of
volcanic ash – it piled up to a depth of over
half a meter in some places. The agricultural
lands northeast of the volcano were temporarily uninhabitable due to the rocks and
boulders that came hurling out of the crater.
Since that explosive eruption, Volcán
Irazú's activity has been limited to gently
smoking *fumaroles* that can be observed by
the curious visitor.

The national park was established in
1955 to protect 2309 hectares in a roughly

circular shape around the volcano. The summit is a bare landscape of volcanic ash and craters. The Principal Crater is 1050m in diameter and 300m deep, while the Diego de la Haya Crater is 690m in diameter and 100m deep and contains a small lake.

There are two smaller craters, one of which also contains a lake. In addition, there is a pyroclastic cone, formed of rocks fragmented by volcanic activity. A few low plants have begun slowly to colonize the landscape – if it weren't for these, you might feel that you were on a different planet. A few high-altitude bird species, such as the volcano junco, hop around. A 1km trail goes from the parking lot to a lookout over the craters. A longer, steeper trail leaves from behind the bathrooms and gets you closer to the craters. Trails are marked by blue and white pedestrian symbols – other 'trails' that are marked by a sign saying *'Paso Restringido'* (Restricted Access) are precarious and should be avoided.

From the summit, it is possible to see both the Pacific and the Caribbean, but it is rarely clear enough.. The best chances for a clear view are in the very early morning during the dry season (from January to April). It tends to be cold, windy, and cloudy on the summit, with temperatures ranging from -3°C to 17°C and an annual rainfall of 2160mm. Come prepared with warm and rainproof clothes as well as food.

Below the summit is a thicker cloud forest vegetation, with oak and *madroño* trees covered with epiphytic plants. The lower you get, the lusher the vegetation. As you emerge from the edge of the park, the land is agricultural, with much cattle and dairy farming.

## Information

A paved road leads to near the summit, where there's a parking lot, small information center, mobile soda wagon with snacks and simple meals during dry-season weekends, but no overnight accommodations or camping facilities. The main gate is open 8am to 3:30pm, but you can enter any time. The entrance fee is US$6 per person when the gate is open.

## Organized Tours

Tours from San José cost about US$22 to US$40 for a half-day tour, or up to US$60 for a full day combined with visits to Lankester Gardens and the Río Orosi valley. Many companies will arrange this; see Organized Tours in the Getting Around chapter for recommendations.

Tours from hotels in Orosi (US$18 to US$40) are also offered; these may include lunch, visits to the Basilica in Cartago, or visits to some sites around the Río Orosi valley.

## Places to Stay & Eat

*Hotel Gestoría Irazú* (☎ 253-0827, fax 225 9647, ℮ gestoria@racsa.co.cr) Rooms with bath US$20. If you insist on staying on the volcano, there's this place, about 11km below the summit. Basic, cold rooms have heated showers (which the management admits are only lukewarm) and the restaurant is not always open. Call ahead.

*Restaurant Linda Vista* Claiming to be the highest restaurant in Costa Rica and decorated with license plates and business cards from all over the world, this is perhaps the best place to eat. It's a few kilometers below the summit on your right as you descend.

## Getting There & Away

**Bus** The company Buses Metrópoli (☎ 272-0651, 591-1138) operates a weekend bus to the national park. The bus leaves San José from Avenida 2, Calles 1 & 3, at 8am on Saturday, Sunday, and holidays (and sometimes on a weekday during the high season). The bus stop is across the street from the front of the Gran Hotel Costa Rica, and the roundtrip fare is US$5. The bus (if seats are available) stops on Avenida 2 in front of (Las Ruinas) in Cartago. The return bus leaves the summit parking lot at 1pm, allowing a little over three hours at the top.

You can also take an early-morning bus from Cartago to Tierra Blanca (see the Cartago section, earlier in this chapter) and walk.

**Car** The road occasionally has signs, but not at every turn. Leave Cartago from the northeast corner of the Basilica on Hwy 8, which goes all the way to the summit. If there is no sign at road forks, either take the more major-looking road or avoid signs for highways other than Hwy 8 (you will intersect with Hwys 233, 230, 227, and 6 on the way up). It's not difficult to find your way.

## LANKESTER GARDENS

This is a botanical garden run by the University of Costa Rica (☎ 552-3247, ☎/fax 552-3151; admission adults/students/children 5-10 yrs US$5/3.50/1; open 8:30am-3:30pm daily). Originally a private garden run by British orchid enthusiast Charles Lankester, it's now open to the public and is frequently visited by plant lovers. The gardens are about 6km east of Cartago.

You can visit the gardens year-round, but the best time for orchids in bloom is February to April (though there are always some in bloom). In addition, lush areas of bromeliads, palms, secondary tropical forest, heliconias, and other tropical plants are seen from the paved trails winding through the gardens. This trip is recommended to all interested in plants. Although the collection is large, the number of labels is small, so you see many species without knowing what they are.

To get there, catch a Paraíso bus and ask the driver to let you off at the turnoff for Lankester Gardens. From the turnoff, it is 0.75km farther on foot to the entrance; there is a sign.

A taxi costs about US$2 from Cartago. Tours from San José often stop by the gardens on the way to either Irazú or the Río Orosi.

## RÍO OROSI VALLEY

This river valley southeast of Cartago is famous for its beautiful views, two colonial churches (one in ruins), hot springs, coffee fincas, the lake formed by a hydroelectric damming project, and a wild national park. Numerous waterfalls and trails can keep you occupied for days if you have an adventurous spirit. Most people visit the valley briefly by taking a tour from San José or by driving their own cars, but many parts are easily accessible by public bus; overnight options are available.

The first bustling little town you come to is **Paraíso**, 8km east of Cartago. Here, you can eat at the recommended *Bar Restaurant Continental* (as you drive in from Cartago; it gets loud with music at night) and other restaurants, which have decent food.

Beyond Paraíso, you have the choice of going east to Ujarrás and the lake formed by the Presa de Cachí (Cachí Dam) or south to Orosi.

From Cartago, buses go to both the village of Orosi and the Presa de Cachí. The two roads are linked by a gravel road. You can drive this road, which is often used by some of the tour groups, in your own car. However, if you are traveling by public bus, you'll have to do one leg of the trip and then backtrack in order to do the other. This is in an attractive, rural, and not over-touched area.

### East of Paraíso

The Cachí bus will drop you off at the entrance to **Ujarrás**, about 7km east of Paraíso. A few kilometers above and before Ujarrás is a good lookout point for the artificial **Lago de Cachí**. The hydroelectric dam itself is at the northeastern corner of the lake.

Driving, you'll find Ujarrás at the flat bottom of a long, steep hill – a couple of stores with the word 'Ujarrás' tell you that you've arrived. Turn right at a sign for Restaurant La Pipiola to head toward the old village (about 1km), which was damaged by the flood of 1833 and abandoned. The waters have since receded and the interesting ruin of the 17th-century church is in a parklike setting. Every year, usually the Sunday closest to April 14, there is a procession early in the morning from Paraíso to the ruins, mass is said, and food and music celebrate the day of La Virgen de Ujarrás, who, legend has it, helped locals defeat a group of marauding British pirates in 1666. The church's grassy grounds are a popular picnicking spot on Sunday afternoon.

About 2km south of the Cachí Dam is the *Casa del Soñador (Dreamer's House;* ☎ 577-1186, 577-1047; ⓔ miguelqb@latinmail.com; open 8am-6pm daily; admission free), a whimsical house designed and built by the renowned tico carver Macedonio Quesada and now, since his death in 1995, run by his sons. Miguel speaks some English. The house, built completely of coffee branches and other wood, is filled with carvings of local campesinos and religious figures. Many are life-size and carved from the gnarled and twisted roots of the coffee tree, others are made from the trunk and branches; and a selection is available for sale.

*La Casona del Cafetal Restaurant* (☎ 577-1414, 577-1515) Main courses US$5-15. Open 11am-6pm daily. Situated about

3km southeast of the dam, this place serves international and tico food and features coffee from its plantation. Apart from drinks, there are various coffee-flavored desserts and, from November to March, the chance to watch coffee-picking. It's popular on Sunday, when tico families hang out and the kids go for short horseback or horse-drawn cart rides.

## South of Paraíso

*Linda Vista B&B* (☎ 574-5534, 574-5497) Doubles without bath US$36, with breakfast. At the beginning of the road to Orosi, a gravel road leads a short way to this B&B, where showers are hot, and guests have kitchen privileges.

*Mirador Sanchirí* (☎ 533-3210, fax 533-3873, e sanchiri@racsa.co.cr, w www.sanchiri .com) Doubles with hot bath US$45, with breakfast. About 2km south of Paraíso is this tourist center with an excellent view of the Río Orosi Valley; there's also a restaurant and picnic area, and a few rather dark wooden cabins for rent. All have private hot-water bathrooms, telephones, and balconies. This area has some of the best views of the entire valley. There are trails and horses can be rented.

*Mirador Orosi* A little farther, this ICT-run place has parking and good views.

The bus goes on to the village of Orosi (see below), about 6km farther south. The Orosi bus usually continues about 4km south of Orosi, through the villages of **Río Macho** and **Palomo**. Río Macho has a power plant on the river of that name, and there is good fishing here.

*Hotel Río Palomo* (☎ 533-3128, ☎/fax 533-3057) Cabins with bath US$25 double, with kitchen US$40 for four people. Near the end of the bus run, just after crossing a large river bridge, look on the left for this hotel. It has an adequate restaurant, open 8am to 6pm daily, and a big swimming pool.

About 5km east of the Río Palomo on the road to Cachí is the *Casa del Soñador* (described above under East of Paraíso).

*Kiri Lodge* (☎ 592-0638, 551-3746, fax 591-2839) Doubles with bath US$30. About 2km or 3km beyond Purisil is this friendly place, the closest lodging to Parque Nacional Tapantí (see below). Its 50-hectare property has six cabins with hot showers, and rates include breakfast. There's a trout-fishing

pond (US$5 per kilo) and a restaurant-bar (sandwiches and simple meals US$3 to US$6). It has access to free trails behind the property leading into the Río Macho Forest Preserve, adjacent to Tapantí, with much of the same wildlife.

## OROSI

This town was named after a Huetar Indian chief who lived here at the time of the conquest. Orosi and its surrounding district have a population of about 9000 people. The main product is coffee, and a nearby finca offers tours.

This is one of the few colonial towns to survive Costa Rica's frequent earthquakes. It boasts an attractive church built in the first half of the 18th century – probably the oldest church still in use in Costa Rica and boasting a fine altar. It's on the west side of town. There is a small religious **art museum** adjacent to the church (☎ 533-3051; admission US80¢; open 9am-noon, 2pm-5pm Tues-Fri, 9am-5pm Sat-Sun). Call ahead before going, as hours change.

Hot springs and swimming pools include **Los Balnearios** (☎ 533-2156; admission US$1.80; open 7:30am-4pm) on the southwest side of town next to the Orosi Lodge. There's another set of hot springs, called **Los Patios** (☎ 533-3009; admission US$1.60; open 8am-4pm), about 1km south of town. Both claim to have the hottest water, but they're about the same temperature: warm, but not super hot. It's a small town – ask anyone for directions.

Ask around about hikes to waterfalls or lookout points.

## Information

A clothing store next to the Supermercado Anita 2, on the main street, doubles as an information center and rents clunky bikes for US$1 an hour. Opposite is an Internet place (US$1.25 per hour). Another Internet place is run by English-speaking Luis, two blocks from Montaña Linda hostel (see below); the hostel also is a great source of information. Also see Orosi Lodge (below) for bike, horse, and canoe rental.

## Organized Tours

Most travel agencies in San José offer day tours to this area; see Organized Tours in the Getting Around chapter. The Montaña

Linda hostel and Orosi Lodge organize tours throughout the valley.

## Language School
Montaña Linda runs a small, inexpensive language school. Maximum class size is three and teachers live in the village, so even without homestay (which can be arranged), part of the appeal is getting involved with the local community. A basic package of five three-hour classes including breakfast, dinner, and accommodations for six days costs US$120; shorter and longer packages are available, and accommodations at places other than the hostel can be arranged.

## Parque Purisil
About 10 km southeast of Orosi, en route to Parque Nacional Tapantí-Macizo Cerro de la Muerte (described below) is this pleasant new park (☎ 228-6630, 381-3895, W www .purisilpark.org; admission US$3/2 for adults/children; closed Mon. This park is an easy and comfortable introduction to the Tapantí forests, with barbecue pits, artificial fishing ponds, short trails to a waterfall, and a restaurant (US$10 three-course lunch or cheaper individual plates, open 10am to 4pm). If you catch a trout in the well-stocked pond, they'll fillet and cook it for you for US$5/kg.

## Places to Stay & Eat
*Montaña Linda* (☎ 533-3640, fax 533-2153, e info@montanalinda.com, W www .montanalinda.com) Campsites with/without own tent US$2.50/3.50, dorm beds US$6, singles/doubles US$9/14, doubles with bath US$29. This place is two blocks south and three blocks west of the bus stop, by the soccer field (where you get off from Cartago). It has a fun hostel environment and accommodations are mainly in dormitories, but there are a few doubles for couples. There are hot showers and kitchen privileges, and cheap meals are available. Helpful owners Toine and Sara are a good source of local information and organize tours in the valley. Day trips to Volcán Irazú and Monumento Nacional Guayabo cost US$12 and US$25 per person, respectively, and white-water rafting costs US$70. This is a simple but enjoyable place.

*Media Libra Cabinas* (☎ 533-3838, fax 533-3737) Rooms with bath US$30. Six clean and well-maintained rooms sleep one to three people. Each unit has hot water, and three have cable TV or refrigerator. Parking is available.

*Orosi Lodge* (☎/fax 533-3578, e ccneck@ racsa.co.cr, W www.orosilodge.com) US$40/53 doubles/triples. This small, comfortable hotel, well-signed and just a few blocks from the bus route from Cartago, has six rooms with excellent views of Orosi and volcanoes beyond. Rooms include a private hot shower, a wet bar with mini-fridge and coffeemaker, and a shared balcony or patio. A small garden separates the rooms from the reception area in the Cafeteria Orosi, where guests have Internet access. The entrance to Los Balnearios hot springs is just a few steps away.

*Cafeteria Orosi* (in the Orosi Lodge) Dishes US$1-3. Open 7am-7pm or later if clients are there. This cool little café has a great selection of coffees that can be accompanied by apple strudels, cakes, croissants, minipizzas or bagels. Big breakfasts (US$4.50) and ice-cream dishes are also served. Admire the old working jukebox with classic tico tunes (plus a Sinatra song), enjoy the local art gracing the walls (for sale), play a game of Scrabble or foozball or relax on the little balcony overlooking Orosi while world music plays in the background.

*Restaurant Coto* (☎ 533-3032, 533-3868) Main courses US$3-8. Open 8am-11pm. Right by the central park, which doubles as a soccer field, this clean place has both indoor and outdoor dining and offers a variety of food. It's the best option in Orosi center. Nearby, some inexpensive but good and friendly sodas include *Soda Luz*, a block north of the church, and *Soda Cisco*, a block south of the church.

*Rancho Rios Perlas*, about 2km north of Orosi, is a new four-star resort/spa that was still under construction at the time of research.

## Getting There & Away
Buses run between Cartago and Rio Macho, stopping at Orosi about twice an hour between 5:30am and 10pm, or 7am and 10pm on Sunday (US30¢ to US45¢, depending on the bus). In Orosi, bus stops are simply marked by a stripe of yellow paint on the main street.

## PARQUE NACIONAL TAPANTÍ-MACIZO CERRO DE LA MUERTE

This park with the unwieldy name was greatly expanded in 2000 and now covers 58,323 hectares, but the main access continues to be from a few kilometers south of Orosi. The park covers the wild and wet country on the rainforested slopes of the Cordillera de Talamanca and contains many hundreds of rivers, which gives an indication of the area's wetness. Waterfalls and trees abound, and the wildlife is prolific, though not easy to reach because the terrain is rugged and the trails are few. Reportedly, rainfall is about 2700mm in the lower sections but reaches over 7000mm in some of the highest parts of the park – maybe you should pack an umbrella. Nevertheless, Tapantí (as it remains locally known) is a popular destination for dedicated birders, and opens at 6am to accommodate them.

Quetzals are said to nest on the western slopes of the valley, where the park information center is located. Well over 200 other bird species have been recorded, including eagles and hummingbirds, parrots and toucans, and difficult-to-see forest floor inhabitants such as tinamous and antbirds.

There is a large variety of other animals: amphibians, reptiles, mammals, and butterflies. The rare jaguar, ocelot, jaguarundi, and little-known margay and oncilla cats have been recorded here, but more usual sightings include squirrels, monkeys, raccoons, and agoutis. Tapirs are occasionally spotted.

A well-graded dirt road runs through a northern section of the park and is quite popular with mountain bikers.

### Information

The park is open 6am to 4pm daily. Admission costs US$6 per person. There is an information center near the park entrance and a couple of trails leading to various attractions, including a picnic area, a swimming hole, and a viewpoint with great views of a waterfall. Fishing is allowed in season (from April to October; permit required), but the dry season (from January to April) is generally considered the best time to visit the refuge, although you should be prepared with rain gear even then. Camping may be allowed with a permit, and you may be able to arrange to sleep in the ranger station or for a ranger to show you around. (See the National Parks & Protected Areas section in the Facts about Costa Rica chapter for general contact information.)

### Getting There & Away

If you have your own car, you can take a gravel road (passable year-round) from Orosi through Río Macho and Purisil to the park entrance. Most buses from Cartago to Orosi go as far as Río Palomo, which is a 9km walk from the park (or hire a taxi).

There is a daily early-morning bus from Cartago to Orosi going as far as Purisil, from where it is a 5km walk. A taxi from Orosi costs US$5 to US$10 one way. Several tour companies in San José do day trips. Some of the best are with bilingual naturalist guides from Costa Rica Expeditions or Horizontes, which charge US$99 per person including lunch and entrance fees (four-person minimum). See Organized Tours in the Getting Around chapter for contact information. Cheaper tours are available in Orosi; see that section, earlier in this chapter.

# Turrialba Area

## RÍO REVENTAZÓN

From the northeast end of Laguna Cachí flows one of the more scenic and exciting rivers in Costa Rica, the Río Reventazón. (In fact, the Cachí Dam across the Río Reventazón created the artificial lake Lago de Cachí.) The river tumbles from the lake at 1000m above sea level and down the eastern slopes of the mountains to the Caribbean lowlands. It is a favorite river for rafters and kayakers; some sections offer Class III and IV white water, while others are relatively flat and placid. Four sections are normally run between the dam and the finish, below Siquirres. The sections vary in difficulty and the second one is considered the most difficult. The last section, 'La Florida,' is mainly Class III and is the most frequently run because of the ease of take out just below Siquirres. Water levels stay fairly constant year-round because of releases from the dam. Note that there are no water releases from the dam on Sunday and, although the river is runnable, this is considered the worst day. Minimum age for rafters is usually nine.

Single- and multiday river trips are offered by several agencies in San José, including Costa Rica Expeditions, which is the oldest and best-known company. Ríos Tropicales, Horizontes, and Aventuras Naturales are also all reputable (see Organized Tours in the Getting Around chapter). A day trip costs about US$69 to US$85, depending on which section of the river you want to run, and includes the following: roundtrip bus transportation from San José, a breakfast stop in a country restaurant, all river equipment and life jackets, a gourmet picnic lunch on the river, and several hours of guided fun on the thrilling white water. All the guides speak English.

## TURRIALBA

This small town is attractively perched on the Caribbean slope of the Cordillera Central at an elevation of 650m above sea level. It is on the banks of the Río Turrialba, which flows into the Reventazón, 4km to the east.

The town used to be the major stopping point on the old highway from San José to Puerto Limón, but since the opening of the highway via Guápiles, Turrialba has been bypassed by travelers heading to the coast and has suffered economically. Nevertheless, it's a pleasant town and makes a good base for several nearby excursions, so tourism, while still very low-key, is increasingly important.

With the surge of interest in river running during the 1980s, the town became somewhat of a center for kayakers and rafters. Turrialba is also an excellent base for visits to the archaeological site at Guayabo, as well as for climbing Volcán Turrialba – all these are described later in this section.

Turrialba is a minor agricultural center for the coffee fincas in the highlands around the town and the sugarcane and banana plantations in the lowlands to the east. The town's population is about 32,000.

### Information

Change money at the Banco Popular (☎ 556-6098), Banco de Costa Rica (☎ 556-0422), or Banco Nacional (☎ 556-1211). Café Internet, at the end of a small alley off Calle 2, Avenidas 2 & 4, charges about US$1 per hour and is open 9am to noon, 1pm to 9pm

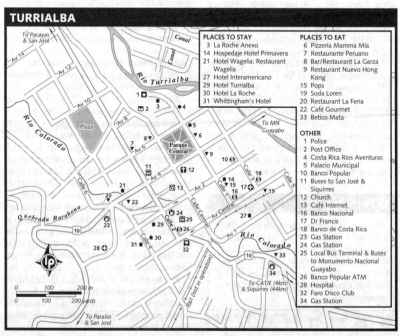

**TURRIALBA**

PLACES TO STAY
3  La Roche Anexo
14 Hospedaje Hotel Primavera
21 Hotel Wagelia; Restaurant Wagelia
27 Hotel Interamericano
29 Hotel Turrialba
30 Hotel La Roche
31 Whittingham's Hotel

PLACES TO EAT
6  Pizzería Mamma Mía
7  Restaurante Peruano
8  Bar/Restaurant La Garza
9  Restaurant Nuevo Hong Kong
15 Pops
19 Soda Loren
20 Restaurant La Feria
22 Café Gourmet
33 Betico Mata

OTHER
1  Police
2  Post Office
4  Costa Rica Rios Aventuras
5  Palacio Municipal
10 Banco Popular
11 Buses to San José & Siquirres
12 Church
13 Café Internet
16 Banco Nacional
17 Dr Francis
18 Banco de Costa Rica
23 Gas Station
24 Gas Station
25 Local Bus Terminal & Buses to Monumento Nacional Guayabo
26 Banco Popular ATM
28 Hospital
32 Faro Disco Club
34 Gas Station

Monday to Friday, and 1pm to 7pm on Saturday. The William Allen Hospital (☎ 556-1133) is at the end of Calle 6. There are also several clinics, pharmacies, and private doctors in the center; Dr Francis at Avenida Central and Calle 3 is bilingual and has been recommended. See the Río Pacuare section, at the end of this chapter, for details of river running companies.

## Places to Stay

**In Town** On the south side of the old railway tracks is *Hotel Interamericano* (☎ 556-0142, fax 556-7790, e hotelint@racsa.co.cr, W www .hotelinteramericano.com) Singles/doubles/ triples/quads US$10/18/27/35 with shared bath, US$20/30/40/50 with private bath. This is the best of the budget places, and is clean and friendly. Rooms are simple and basic but brightly painted. A popular place with river runners, it is run by a mother and daughter who trade time between Turrialba and New York (the global village in action). There is a snack bar with TV and Internet service on the premises. Laundry service and luggage storage are available. The nearby *Hotel Central* and *Hospedaje Chamango* are just a couple of dollars cheaper but are not recommended.

*Hotel La Roche* (☎ 556-1624) This small place is basic but clean, with shared showers and rates similar to the Interamericano's.

*La Roche Anexo* (☎ 556-7915) has basic doubles with cold bath for US$15.

*Whittingham's Hotel* (☎ 556-8822, 556-6013, 550-8927) Doubles with hot bath US$12.50. Another popular cheapie to try, Whittingham's has large but rather dark and dismal rooms (though frequent groups of athletic river types brighten the atmosphere). It can be hard to find someone to open the hotel and provide a key.

### Where Am I?

Note that most of the maps throughout this book give official street names, but the locals rarely use them, preferring the tico landmark system instead. Read the boxed text 'Costa Rican Street Addresses' in the San José chapter for a full discussion of this phenomenon.

*Hospedaje Hotel Primavera* Rooms US$5 per person. This very basic but friendly place has shared baths.

*Hotel Turrialba* (☎ 556-6654, 556-6396) Singles/doubles with bath US$13/19. The 11 clean rooms come with TVs, fans, and private hot showers, but are somewhat noisy.

*Hotel Wagelia* (☎ 556-1566, fax 556-1596, e hotelwagelia@racsa.co.cr, Avenida 4, Calles 2 & 4) Singles/doubles with bath US$41/53. This is the best hotel in town – it's clean and set in a landscaped garden. The 14 standard rooms offer fans, TV, and hot water. Five rooms have air-conditioning but cost the same. If you reserve in advance, prices are often US$10 or US$20 higher; although it's cheaper to just show up, the hotel is often full. The management will arrange one-day Reventazón river-running excursions and other local trips.

*Hotel Geliwa* (☎ 556-1142, ☎/fax 556-1029) This hotel is run by the Hotel Wagelia, has the same prices, and includes breakfast. It's 1km north of town en route to Santa Rosa. There are 26 modern but unexciting rooms, all with showers and fans, half with TV. A restaurant (breakfast and dinner only) and small pool are on the premises. The hotel takes the overflow from the Wagelia when it's full, and serves as an alternative for travelers not wanting to stay in the town center.

**Out of Town** There are several small but pleasant country hotels several kilometers east of Turrialba.

*Turrialtico* (☎ 538-111, 538-1414, fax 538-1575, e info@turrialtico.com, W www .turrialtico.com) Singles/doubles with bath US$40/50, including breakfast. About 8km away, on the road to Siquirres and Limón, is this place, known for the good tico meals served in its restaurant (open 7am to 10pm) and favored by river runners. There are 14 rustic rooms in a nice older building; the wooden floors can be loud for light sleepers. Meals range from US$5 for breakfast to US$8 for dinner. Outside, there's a tiny kids' playground. The hotel is set on a little hill and has great views. Management arranges river-running trips.

*Pochotel* (☎ 538-1010, 538-1515, fax 538-1212, e pochotel@racsa.co.cr) Singles/ doubles with hot bath US$40/46 (additional people US$17) including breakfast. About 11km away from Turrialba, also on the road to Limón, this is a favorite of local river guides. The hotel is above the village of Pavones, and there is a sign for the hotel in the village. A very steep 1.5km dirt road reaches the hotel, which has great views. There is also a tico-style restaurant here (breakfast costs about US$5, other meals about US$7), a lookout tower to admire the Irazú and Turrialba volcanoes above, and a dam and new lake below, and a small playground for kids. The 10 rooms have hot electric showers, some also have tubs and clock radios. Reservations are recommended.

Both hotels can help arrange nearby excursions or river-running trips. If you call in advance, staff will pick you up in Turrialba, or you can get off the Turrialba-Siquirres bus at the appropriate spot. Both are well recommended.

**Casa Turire Hotel** (☎ 531-1111, fax 531-1075, e turire@racsa.co.cr, w www.hotel casaturire.com) Rooms US$140, suites US$163-256. About 8km southeast of Turrialba, this elegant three-story building features wide, shady verandahs and is set in well-landscaped grounds with sugarcane, coffee, and macadamia nut plantations nearby. There is a swimming pool, tennis court, and a game room with a pool table. Children under 16 years old are not accepted. The spacious rooms, most with private balconies, have hot water, telephones, and cable TVs, and four suites have refrigerators and king-size beds. The most expensive suite has two floors, a balcony that takes up the whole side of the building, and a spa. Full breakfast (US$10), lunch (US$22), and dinner (US$25) are served. Horse and mountain-bike rental and guided walks in the rainforest and plantations are available. This is about as nice as hotels get in Costa Rica.

Other country hotels are found near Monumento Nacional Guayabo and at the Rancho Naturalista, described later in this chapter.

## Places to Eat

The hotels **Wagelia**, **Turrialtico**, **Pochotel**, and **Casa Turire** all have good restaurants. The one at Hotel Wagelia is one of the best in town and has meals in the US$5 to US$11 range; prepare to relax and enjoy it because service is slow.

**Bar/Restaurant La Garza** US$3-6. Open 10am-10pm. This eatery has been here for years and offers a good variety of seafood, chicken, and other meat dishes.

**Restaurant Nuevo Hong Kong** This budget restaurant serves slightly cheaper Chinese food than La Garza.

**Café Gourmet** (☎ 556-9689) US$1-3. Open 7am-7pm Mon-Sat. This cute little café sells Turrialba's best coffee, as well as various snacks and pastries. What's available depends largely on what the friendly owner has in stock – go with her suggestions and you can't go wrong.

**Restaurant La Feria** (☎ 556-5550, 556-0386, 373-0031 cellular) Sandwiches US$1.50, meals US$3-6. Open 10am-10pm daily, until 3pm Tues. This charming little eatery is operated by trained chef Roberto Barahona who, locals say, is the best cook in town. Food includes casados, spaghettis, and a variety of meat and fish dishes accompanied by fresh vegetables.

**Restaurante Peruano** (☎ 556-5151, 643-3771) US$4-8. Open 11am-3pm & 6pm-10pm Mon-Sun, closed Tues. Newly opened when this book was being researched, the Peruvian food cooked by Peruvian chef/manager Freddy Conde is authentic and good.

**Soda Loren** US$2-4. Of many sodas in the center, this one, in the old railway station, has the most character and serves food as good as anywhere.

**Pizzería Mamma Mia** US$3-5. A popular place with local young folk, this place stays open late.

**Betico Mata** (☎ 556-8640) US75¢-$3. At the south end of town, this clean and well known hole-in-the-wall specializes in small plates of grilled meat, most served with a tortilla and going down well with a cold beer. Grab a few to make a meal. This is a great place to hang out in the evenings.

**Restaurant Kingston** (☎ 556-1613) Dishes US$3-10. On the outskirts of town on the road to Puerto Limón, this has a long good reputation in Turrialba and has meals mostly at the higher end of the price range. The locally well-known chef is Jamaican-trained, and this shows in some of the meals.

For ice cream, there's the ubiquitous **Pops**.

**CENTRAL VALLEY**

## Entertainment

Turrialba doesn't have much in the way of entertainment. Try *Faro Disco Club* for weekend dances.

## Getting There & Away

TRANSTUSA (☎ 556-4233) buses from San José to Turrialba leave hourly from Calle 13, Avenidas 6 & 8, and take about two hours. The cost is US$1.25 direct or US$1 with stops. The route runs through Cartago and then either through Pacayas or through Paraíso to Turrialba.

There are two main bus terminals in Turrialba. The main stop on Avenida 4 near Calle 2 serves San José (you can get off at Cartago) with hourly buses. From this stop you can also go to Siquirres (connecting for Puerto Limón), with buses about every hour from 6am to 7pm.

The other terminal is between Avenidas Central & 2 and Calles Central & 2. This terminal has buses serving local communities such as La Suiza and Tuis every hour, and Santa Cruz three times a day. Buses to Santa Teresita (also known as Lajas) travel within 4km of Monumento Nacional Guayabo and leave a few times a day. Other local communities served include Juan Viñas, Pejibaye, Tucurrique, and Pavones.

Buses to Monumento Nacional Guayabo (☎ 556-0583) also leave from here; at last check scheduled departures were at 11am and 5:15pm Monday to Saturday and 9am on Sunday, allowing several hours at the ruins. Alternately, take the first morning bus to Santa Teresita, walk 4km, and return from Guayabo on buses that leave there at 12:30pm and 5pm Monday to Saturday, or 4pm on Sunday. These are subject to change, so ask locally.

## AROUND TURRIALBA

The Centro Agronómico Tropical de Investigación y Enseñanza, known throughout Costa Rica by its acronym of **CATIE** (which is just as well), is comprised of about 1000 hectares dedicated to tropical agricultural research and education. Agronomists from all over the world recognize CATIE (☎ 558-2000, fax 556-1533, ℮ catie@catie.ac.cr) as one of the most important agricultural stations in the tropics.

The attractively landscaped grounds of CATIE lie just to the left of the main road to Siquirres, about 4km east of Turrialba. Visitors are allowed to walk around the grounds from about 8am to 4pm Monday to Friday (definitely subject to change), and birders will enjoy a visit to the small lake on the site where waterbirds such as the purple gallinule are a specialty. Another good birding area is the short but steep trail descending from behind the administration building to the Río Reventazón.

Those with a serious interest in tropical agriculture (not tourists) can visit the facilities, including one of the most extensive libraries of tropical agricultural literature anywhere in the world, a teaching and research facility with student and faculty accommodations, laboratories, greenhouses, a dairy, an herbarium, a seed bank, and experimental fruit, vegetable, and forest plots.

About 10km east of Turrialba, in the village of Pavones (500m east of the cemetery) is **Parque Viborana** (☎ 538-1510, 381-4781), known for its serpentarium. Here, you can see a variety of Costa Rican snakes, including some unusual albino specimens and several boas, one of which weighs as much as a good-size person. The serpentarium has a rustic visitors' area with educational exhibits. Stop by if you're driving east of Turrialba.

## MONUMENTO NACIONAL GUAYABO

Guayabo lies 20km northeast of Turrialba and contains the largest and most important archaeological site in the country. Although interesting, it does not come close to comparing with the Mayan and Aztec archaeological sites of Honduras, Belize, Guatemala, and Mexico to the north. Nevertheless, excavations have revealed a number of cobbled roads, stone aqueducts, mounds, retaining walls, and petroglyphs that interested visitors can examine. Some pottery and gold artifacts have been found and are exhibited at the Museo Nacional in San José.

Archaeologists are still unclear about the prehistory and significance of the site. It seems to have been inhabited perhaps as far back as 1000 BC and reached the pinnacle of its development around AD 800, when some 10,000 people are thought to have lived in the area.

Guayabo is considered an important cultural, religious, and political center, but more precise details still remain to be unearthed. The site was abandoned by AD 1400, and the Spanish conquistadors, explorers, and settlers left us no record of having found the ruins.

The area was rediscovered in the late 19th century by Anastasio Alfaro, a local naturalist and explorer, who began some preliminary excavations and found a few pieces that are now in the Museo Nacional.

In 1968, Carlos Aguilar Piedra, an archaeologist with the University of Costa Rica, began the first systematic excavations. As the importance of the site became evident, it was obviously necessary to protect it, and it became a national monument in 1973, with further protection decreed in 1980. The latest round of excavations began in 1989 and is still underway.

The monument is small, some 232 hectares, and the archaeological site itself is thought to comprise no more than 10% of the total. Most of these ruins are yet to be excavated. The remaining 90% of the monument is premontane rainforest. The monument is important because it protects some of the last remaining rainforest of this type in the province of Cartago. However, because of its small area, there aren't many animals to be seen. The few that do live in this rainforest, though, are interesting.

Particularly noteworthy among the avifauna are the oropendolas, which colonize the monument by building sacklike nests in the trees. Other birds include toucans and brown jays – the latter are unique among jays in that they have a small, inflatable sac in the chest, which causes the popping sound that is heard at the beginning of their loud and raucous calls. Mammals include squirrels, armadillos, and coatis, among others.

## Information

The archaeological site is being worked on during the week, and sections may be closed to visitors. Opening hours are 8am to 3pm; park rangers or trained guides are available to take you around for a nominal fee. This is as much to protect the site as to give you a cheap tour, but it's a good deal anyway!

There is an information center near the monument entrance where you pay the US$6 national park admission fee. There is a small interpretive display and maps are available. Within the monument are trails, picnic areas, latrines, and running water. Camping is allowed. You can visit the park midweek if you just want to visit the rainforest, bird-watch, picnic, or camp.

The average annual rainfall is about 3500mm, and the best time to go is during the January to April dry season (though it might still rain).

## Places to Stay & Eat

Apart from camping in the monument, visitors can stay in the one nearby country hotel.

*Albergue La Calzada* (☎ 559-0437 after 5pm, ☎ 556-0465 information only) Rooms from about US$10 per person. Less than 1km from the entrance to the monument, this is a small place with a few rooms, without and with private baths. There is also a fun kids' playground with bicycle-powered swings and boats, as well as a café. Calling ahead for reservations is recommended – the friendly owners will help you with current bus information from Turrialba and pick you up from the bus stop nearest to the hotel.

## Getting There & Away

There are buses from Turrialba to Guayabo (the community at the north entrance to the monument), but check the schedule in Turrialba, as it changes often.

There are also buses from Turrialba to Santa Teresita (marked as 'Lajas' on just about every map you'll see) that pass the turnoff to the southern entrance of the monument; it's a 4km walk to the monument from this entrance. You could try hitchhiking or hire a taxi from Turrialba (about US$15 one way). Once you've sussed out the constantly changing bus schedules, your best bet might be to take a taxi in the early morning and return by bus later.

Tours to the monument can be arranged with travel agencies in San José for about US$75 including lunch in Turrialba, and can be combined with visits to Irazú, Cartago, or Lankester Gardens. Green Tropical Tours specializes in this area; see Organized Tours in the Getting Around chapter for details.

## PARQUE NACIONAL VOLCÁN TURRIALBA

This newly created national park highlights a 3329m-high (some sources say 3339m) active volcano that is actually part of the

Irazú volcanic massif, but it is more remote and difficult to get to than Irazú. The name of the volcano was coined by early Spanish settlers, who named it Torre Alba, or 'white tower,' for the plumes of smoke pouring from its summit in early colonial days. The volcano is only about 15km northwest of Turrialba as the crow flies, but over twice as far by car and continuing on foot.

The last eruption was in 1866. Although the volcano lies dormant today, it's likely that the tranquil farmlands on Turrialba's fertile soils will again be disturbed by earth-shattering explosions sometime in the future.

The summit has three craters, of which the middle one is the largest. This is the only one that still shows signs of activity with fumaroles of steam and sulfur. Below the summit is a montane rain and cloud forest, dripping with moisture and mosses, full of ferns, bromeliads, and even stands of bamboo.

To climb Turrialba, take a bus to Santa Cruz, from where an 18km road climbs to the summit. The road is paved for the first 10km, then becomes increasingly rough and a 4WD vehicle is necessary to reach the summit. There is a picnic table, and a trail part of the way around the crater. There are signs along the way, and this is the official route into the national park. At time of writing, there was neither ranger station nor admission fee, but this may change.

Another approach is to take a bus from Cartago to the village of San Gerardo on the southern slopes of Volcán Irazú. From here, a rough road continues to Volcán Turrialba – it's farther than from Santa Cruz, but San Gerardo, at 2400m, is a higher starting point than Santa Cruz is at 1500m. The rough road goes about 25km, then there are a few kilometers of walking, but this route is unsigned.

## Places to Stay

**Volcán Turrialba Lodge** (☎ 273-4335, 273-0194, 383-6084 cellular, fax 273-0703, e volturri@racsa.co.cr, w www.volcan turrialbalodge.com) Rooms about US$40 per person, with all meals. About 14km northwest of Santa Cruz is this lodge, which is accessible by 4WD only (the first 10km are paved; call for directions or they'll pick you up if you have a reservation). The lodge is high up between the Turrialba and Irazú volcanoes and has great views and interesting, well-guided tours including horseback rides to Volcán Turrialba. The lodge is a working cattle ranch and 24 horses are available for riding. Friendly owner Tony Lachner speaks English and his staff speak very patient and slow Spanish. The rustic hotel has a blazing wood stove in the bar-restaurant and sitting room (with TV and board games). The cozy rooms have electric heaters; some have wood stoves. Food is served buffet-style and tends toward tico with an international flair. It definitely gets cold and wet up here, but the place is recommended for travelers looking for some cool highland adventure. Quetzals nest on the property from February to April.

## RANCHO NATURALISTA

This 48-hectare ranch is about 20km southeast of Turrialba just past the village of Tuis (4WD needed). The ranch has the following lodge, which is popular with birders and naturalists.

**Albergue de Montaña** (☎ 297-4134, fax 297-4135, e jkerb@racsa.co.cr, w www .ranchonaturalista.com; in the USA Costa Rica Gateway, ☎ 888-246-8513) Rooms per person US$135/877 per night/week, with all meals. The ranch has a Spanish-style five-bedroom lodge plus six duplex cottages, which are popular with birders and naturalists. The North American owners are avid birders who have recorded over 400 species of birds in the area (over 200 species have been recorded from their balcony alone). Hundreds of species of butterflies can be found on the grounds as well. The ranch lies at 900m above sea level in montane rain and wet forest and there is a trail system. This is a recommended destination for people who would like some quiet days of birding and nature study in a tranquil environment (which the owners call 'Eden-like').

Costs here are not cheap, but once you decide to go you'll find almost everything is included. Because the owners wish to maintain a relaxed atmosphere, they ask guests to book for a minimum of three days to enjoy and explore their surroundings at a leisurely pace. Many guests stay for a week. Discounts for groups or longer stays are available.

The prices include taxes, three home-cooked meals a day, maid service, guided birding trips, horseback riding, and (with stays of a week or more) roundtrip transportation from San José and a day trip to another area. About the only things not included are bottled or canned drinks.

Nine of the comfortable rooms have private baths and hot water, two share a bath if the lodge is full. Most rooms have very good or excellent views, one room lacks a view, and two have only fair-to-good views, so check which room you are reserving. Reservations can be made with owners Kathy and John Erb or with their travel agency, Costa Rica Gateway. They'll be happy to help you plan your trip.

## RÍO PACUARE

The Río Pacuare is the next major river valley east of the Reventazón. It is arguably the most scenic rafting river in Costa Rica and one of the world's classic white-water experiences. The river plunges down the Caribbean slope through a series of spectacular canyons clothed in virgin rainforest. The Class IV rapids are exciting and separated by calm stretches that enable you to stare at the near-vertical green walls towering hundreds of meters above the river – a magnificent and unique river trip.

The Pacuare is relatively remote and inaccessible, and two-day trips are done often, with nights spent camping on the riverbank or staying in a riverside lodge. (One-day trips are also available – the run is 28km.) On longer trips, stops are made for swimming and exploring the beautiful tributaries of the main river. Some of these tributaries arrive at the Pacuare in a plunging cascade from the vertical walls of the canyon, and your raft may pass directly beneath the falls.

The highest water is from October to December, when the river runs very fast with huge waves. In March and April, the river is at its lowest and, though waves aren't big, the river is very rocky and technical. Either time, rapids occasionally reach Class V. (The class depends not only on the difficulty of the river, but the difficulty of swimming should a paddler fall out. This river should not be run by young children, non-swimmers, and folks who aren't reasonably fit.)

The usual agencies in San José do this trip. *Costa Rica Expeditions* provides excellent service. *Ríos Tropicales*, *Horizontes*, and *Aventuras Naturales* are other options. See Organized Tours in the Getting Around chapter for details. The river can be run year-round, though June to October are considered the best months. One-day trips cost US$89, and two-day trips cost about US$250 per person, with seven passengers. Three-day trips cost US$305 per person. Costs are more per person in smaller groups, but you can often join another group to cut costs. Combined tours with other rivers are also available.

Overnights are in wilderness tent camps with permanent bathroom, toilet, and restaurant facilities (Costa Rica Expeditions); in the Pacuare Lodge with comfortable but slightly incongruous riverside rooms (Rios Tropicales); or the Aventuras Naturales lodge (with a pretty waterfall forming a riverside swimming hole). All are good and travelers can choose where they want to stay, irrespective of whom they book with.

Another option is to look for signs in Turrialba; a number of smaller companies advertise around town, offering the possibility of more personalized service and lower prices. One such company is the tico-owned *Tico's River Adventures* (☎ 556-1231, 394-4479 cellular, ⓔ info@ticoriver.com, ⓦ www.ticoriver.com), which has English-speaking guides and offers day trips for US$70, as well as longer raft trips.

*Costa Rica Rios Aventuras* (☎ 556-9617, cel 371-9936, fax 556-6362, ⓔ RMcLain@racsa.co.cr, ⓦ www.costaricarios.com), also based in Turrialba (look for signs just northeast of the Parque Central), offers raft and kayak trips (they have more than 50 kayaks). Owner Ray McLain writes a regular column for *The Tico Times* and is a personable and enthusiastic guide. Lessons and trips all around the country can also be arranged.

Also based near Turrialba are *Rain Forest World* (☎ 556-2678, ⓦ www.rforestw.com) and *Jungla Expeditions* (☎ 556-2639, fax 556-6225, ⓦ www.junglaexpeditions.com), both of which offer rafting and other adventures, such as kayaking, biking, and horseback riding. Also see Serendipity Adventures in the Organized Tours section of the Getting There & Away chapter. Their Costa Rica base is just outside Turrialba.

In 1986, the Pacuare was declared a 'wild and scenic river,' and protected status was conferred upon it by the government – the first river to be so protected in Central America. Despite this, the National Electric Company began an 'exploratory feasibility study' for a hydroelectric dam. It's not clear whether or not the dam would be successful in generating electricity, but it would certainly ruin the Río Pacuare valley by flooding it, thus destroying the most beautiful tropical river valley in Costa Rica, and one of the most beautiful and unique in the world. At the time of writing, plans to build a dam were on hold, but still being discussed.

# Northwestern Costa Rica

Costa Rica's spectacular central highlands stretch out to the Nicaragua border. To the northwest of the Cordillera Central lie two more mountain chains: the Cordillera de Tilarán and the Cordillera de Guanacaste.

The Cordillera de Tilarán is characterized by rolling mountains that used to be covered with cloud forest. The famous cloud forest reserve at Monteverde is an important and popular destination for those wishing to see something of this tropical habitat.

Separating the Cordillera de Tilarán and Cordillera de Guanacaste are Laguna de Arenal and the nearby Volcán Arenal, currently the most active volcano in Costa Rica and one of the most active volcanoes in the world. It is also the centerpiece of Parque Nacional Volcán Arenal. The spectacular sights and sounds of the eruptions draw visitors to the nearby town of Fortuna.

The Cordillera de Guanacaste is a spectacular string of dormant or gently active volcanoes, five of which are protected in Parque Nacional Rincón de la Vieja, Parque Nacional Guanacaste, and Parque Nacional Volcán Tenorio. To the west of the Cordillera de Guanacaste, shortly before the Nicaragua border, is the Península Santa Elena, which contains a rare dry tropical forest habitat descending down to remote Pacific beaches. The dry forest and coastline are preserved in the beautiful and historic Parque Nacional Santa Rosa, which is well worth a visit. All in all, this is a very scenic part of Costa Rica and, apart from the Monteverde and Arenal areas, one that is not much visited by foreign tourists.

The Interamericana Norte section describes the towns, parks, reserves, and mountains found along the northwestern section of the Carretera Interamericana, while the Arenal Route section deals with a route on minor roads around the northeast side of the mountains, past the explosive Volcán Arenal, and connecting eventually with the Interamericana at Cañas. If you have the time, consider taking the rougher back route. Otherwise, the well-paved Interamericana will quickly take you through this spectacular part of Costa Rica.

## Highlights

- Searching for beautiful but elusive quetzals in the cloud forests of Monteverde and Santa Elena
- Taking a hike up Rincón de la Vieja, one of the few active volcanoes safe to climb
- Shopping at Toad Hall and Lucky Bug – two quirky and unique stores on Lake Arenal
- Windsurfing on Lake Arenal or Bahía Salinas – with some of the world's best wind
- Looking at and listening to the explosively exciting Volcán Arenal
- Camping and watching wildlife in tropical dry forest at Santa Rosa

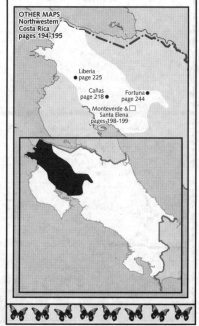

OTHER MAPS
Northwestern
Costa Rica
pages 194-195

Liberia
● page 225

Cañas
page 218 ●

Fortuna ●
page 244

Monteverde & □
Santa Elena
pages 198-199

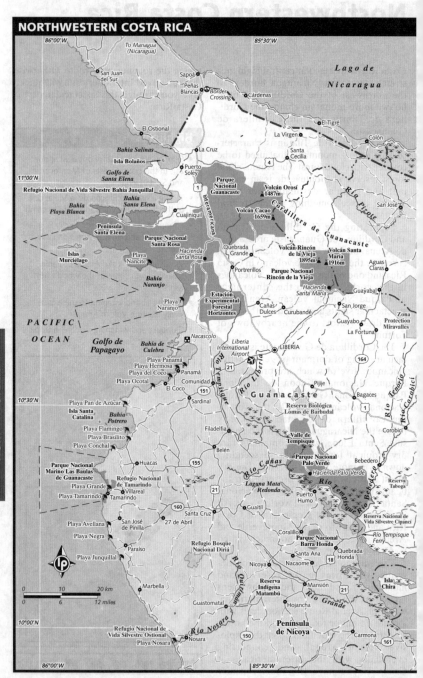

# NORTHWESTERN COSTA RICA

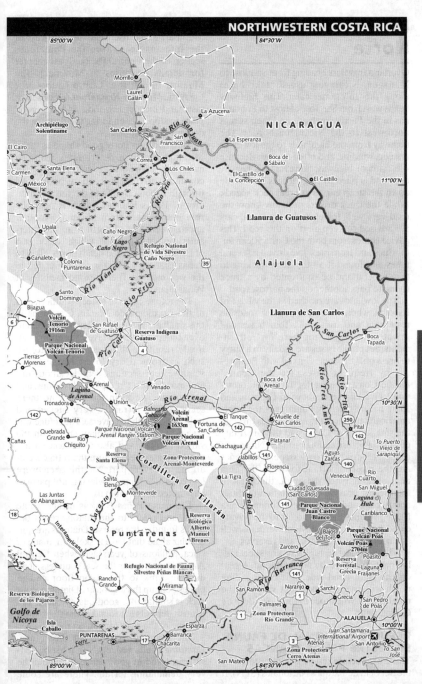

# Interamericana Norte

Overland travelers heading from San José to Managua, Nicaragua, usually take buses along the Interamericana. This highway heads west from San José almost to Puntarenas in the Pacific lowlands and then swings northwest to the Nicaragua border. The highway from the highlands to the lowlands is steep, winding, and often narrow. Because it is a major highway, however, it is heavily used and is plied by large trucks that hurtle down the steep curves at breakneck speeds. While the truck drivers probably know the road very well, travelers driving rental cars are advised to keep alert on this road. This advice comes from both the Costa Rican authorities and from me – I've driven it several times and found it a little nerve-racking to take a bend and be confronted by a truck trying to pass another on the narrow road.

The lowlands are reached at the village of Esparza, where there is a popular roadside restaurant and fruit stalls. Tour buses and private cars often stop here for refreshments, but public buses are usually in a hurry to press on. (Esparza is linked with Puntarenas by frequent buses; see the Central Pacific Coast chapter for further information.) Five kilometers beyond Esparza, and 15km before reaching Puntarenas, the Interamericana turns northwest. It heads through the small town of Cañas and the larger city of Liberia before ending up at the Nicaragua border. Liberia and, to a lesser extent, Cañas are the most important towns in the area and, although not major destinations in themselves, provide transportation facilities and accommodations. The Interamericana Norte provides the best access to the private cloud forest reserve at Monteverde as well as a host of national parks and reserves.

Views from the highway are spectacular, particularly at the northern end. A seat on the right-hand side of a bus heading north will give you excellent views of the magnificent volcanoes in the Cordillera de Guanacaste.

## REFUGIO NACIONAL DE FAUNA SILVESTRE PEÑAS BLANCAS

This 2400-hectare refuge is administered by the Servicio de Parques Nacionales (SPN). It lies about 6km northeast of the village of Miramar, which itself is 8km northeast of the Interamericana (see the Puntarenas section of the Central Pacific Coast chapter for details on buses to Miramar). The Miramar turnoff is at Cuatro Cruces near the rustic *Miramar Restaurant*, which serves tasty and inexpensive food and is a good place to stop after enduring the rigors of the descent from San José.

The road is in fairly good shape as far as Miramar but then deteriorates. You can either hike 6km northeast into the refuge or continue driving east on a poor road through Sabana Bonita to the tiny community of Peñas Blancas, which is near the refuge and 14km from Miramar. Another approach is to head north from the Interamericana at Macacona, which is 3km east of Esparza. A dirt road heads north 20km to Peñas Blancas – 4WD is recommended in the wet months. There are no facilities at Peñas Blancas.

The refuge clings to a steep southern arm of the Cordillera de Tilarán. Elevations in this small area range from less than 600m to over 1400m above sea level. Variation in altitude results in different types of forest, such as tropical dry forest in the lower southwestern sections, semideciduous dry and moist forests in middle elevations, and premontane forest in the higher northern sections. The terrain is very rugged and trails are difficult to traverse. The refuge was created to protect the plant species in the varied habitats and also to protect an important watershed. Before the refuge's creation, however, parts of the area were logged, which is partly why it is not particularly noted for its animals.

The name Peñas Blancas means 'white cliffs' and refers to the diatomaceous deposits found in the reserve. Diatoms are unicellular algae that have a 'skeleton' made of silica. Millions of years ago, when Central America was under the sea, countless dead diatoms sank to the ocean floor and in places built up thick deposits. Diatomaceous rock is similar to a good-quality chalk. The whitish deposits are found in the steep walls of some of the river canyons in the refuge.

There are no facilities at the refuge. *Camping* is allowed, but you must be self-sufficient and in good shape to handle the very demanding terrain. There are some hiking trails. The dry season (from January to early April) is the best time to go – it's not likely that you'll see anyone else there.

## RESERVA BIOLÓGICA ISLA PÁJAROS

Isla Pájaros (Bird Island) lies less than a kilometer off the coast at Punta Morales, about 15km northwest of Puntarenas. There are no facilities on the 3.8-hectare islet, which has a small colony of nesting seabirds. The predominant vegetation is wild guava. Generally speaking, biological reserves were created to protect flora and fauna, and in the more fragile areas part of the protection consists of not encouraging visitors. This is a case in point.

## MONTEVERDE & SANTA ELENA

Monteverde is one of the more interesting places in Costa Rica and is one of the most popular destinations for both foreign and local visitors. The name 'Monteverde' refers to a small but spread-out community founded by North American Quakers in 1951 and to the cloud forest reserve that lies adjacent to the community. The entrance point for this area is the village of Santa Elena, a *tico* settlement that, in response to Monteverde's popularity, is developing a tourism infrastructure of its own.

### Orientation

Driving from the Interamericana, you will arrive first at Santa Elena. This is where you'll find the public bus stop and ticket office (☎ 695-5611, 645-5159), as well as the cheapest pensiones and restaurants. The community of Monteverde is spread out along an unpaved road running roughly southeast from Santa Elena. At the end of this road, about 6km from Santa Elena, are the entrance to the Monteverde cloud forest reserve and the visitor center. In between, about 4km from the reserve, is a district locally called Cerro Plano. Hotels of various price levels are strung out along and just off this road.

Five kilometers northeast of Santa Elena is the Reserva Santa Elena. Both this and

## The Quakers of Monteverde

The story of the founding of Monteverde is an unusual one that deserves to be retold. It begins in Alabama with four Quakers (a pacifist religious group also known as the 'Friends') who were jailed in 1949 for refusing to register for the draft in the USA.

After their release from jail, they, along with other Quakers, began to search for a place to settle where they could live peacefully. After searching for land in Canada, Mexico, and Central America, they decided on Costa Rica; its peaceful policies and lack of army matched their philosophies. They chose the Monteverde area because of its pleasant climate and fertile land, and because it was far enough away from San José to be (at that time) a relatively cheap place to buy land.

Forty-four original settlers (men, women, and children from 11 families) arrived in Monteverde in 1951. Many flew to San José. They loaded their belongings onto trucks, and a few drove from Alabama to Monteverde, a journey that took three months. If you think the roads to Monteverde are bad now, imagine what they must have been like over five decades ago! In 1951, the road was an ox-cart trail, and it took weeks of work to make it barely passable for larger vehicles.

The Quakers bought about 1500 hectares and began dairy farming and cheese production. Early cheese production was about 10kg per day; today, Monteverde's modern cheese factory produces over 1000kg of cheese daily, which is sold throughout Costa Rica. The cheese factory is now in the middle of the Monteverde community and can be visited by those interested in the process.

There has been talk of paving the really rough road from the Interamericana to Monteverde. Many locals don't want this to happen, though, rightly concerned that a paved road would dramatically change the area for the worse.

Note that due to the Quaker influence and the high level of tourism, much of the local population speaks English, and many local places are named in English as well as Spanish. Also remember that there were a few rural Costa Rican families in the area before the Quakers arrived – Geovanny Arguedas (of the Hotel El Sapo Dorado) had grandparents who were among the first *tico* farmers here.

NORTHWESTERN

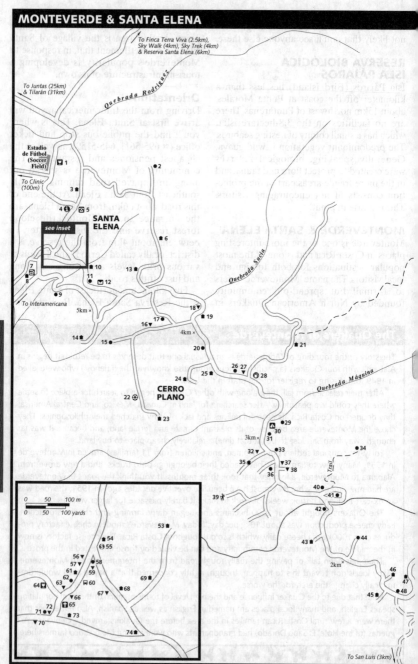

**MONTEVERDE & SANTA ELENA**

To Finca Terra Viva (2.5km),
Sky Walk (4km), Sky Trek (4km)
& Reserva Santa Elena (6km)

*Quebrada Rodrigues*

To Juntas (25km)
& Tilarán (31km)

Estadio
de Fútbol
(Soccer
Field)

To Clinic
(100m)

**SANTA
ELENA**

see inset

To Interamericana

5km ×

*Quebrada Sucia*

*Quebrada Máquina*

**CERRO
PLANO**

4km ×

3km ×

*Trail*

2km ×

0     50     100 m
0     50     100 yards

To San Luis (3km)

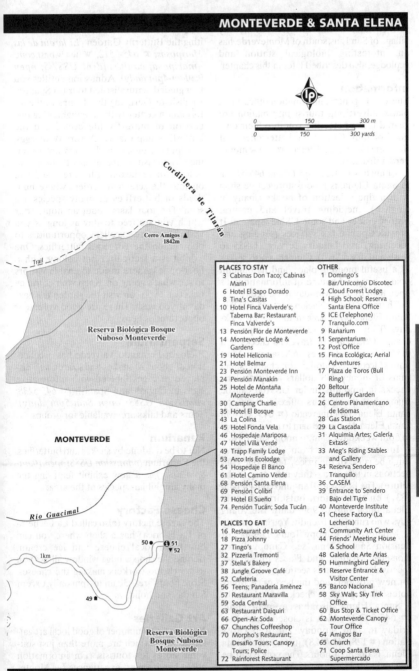

## MONTEVERDE & SANTA ELENA

NORTHWESTERN

**PLACES TO STAY**
3 Cabinas Don Taco; Cabinas Marín
6 Hotel El Sapo Dorado
8 Tina's Casitas
10 Hotel Finca Valverde's; Taberna Bar; Restaurant Finca Valverde's
13 Pensión Flor de Monteverde
14 Monteverde Lodge & Gardens
19 Hotel Heliconia
21 Hotel Belmar
23 Pensión Monteverde Inn
24 Pensión Manakín
25 Hotel de Montaña Monteverde
30 Camping Charlie
35 Hotel El Bosque
43 La Colina
45 Hotel Fonda Vela
46 Hospedaje Mariposa
47 Hotel Villa Verde
49 Trapp Family Lodge
53 Arco Iris Ecolodge
54 Hospedaje El Banco
61 Hotel Camino Verde
68 Pensión Santa Elena
69 Pensión Colibrí
73 Hotel El Sueño
74 Pensión Tucán; Soda Tucán

**PLACES TO EAT**
16 Restaurant de Lucia
18 Pizza Johnny
27 Tingo's
32 Pizzería Tremonti
35 Stella's Bakery
38 Jungle Groove Café
52 Cafetería
56 Teens; Panadería Jiménez
57 Restaurant Maravilla
59 Soda Central
63 Restaurant Daiquiri
66 Open-Air Soda
67 Chunches Coffeeshop
70 Morpho's Restaurant; Desafío Tours; Canopy Tours; Police
72 Rainforest Restaurant

**OTHER**
1 Domingo's Bar/Unicornio Discotec
2 Cloud Forest Lodge
4 High School; Reserva Santa Elena Office
5 ICE (Telephone)
7 Tranquilo.com
9 Ranarium
11 Serpentarium
12 Post Office
15 Finca Ecológica; Aerial Adventures
17 Plaza de Toros (Bull Ring)
20 Beltour
22 Butterfly Garden
26 Centro Panamericano de Idiomas
28 Gas Station
29 La Cascada
31 Alquimia Artes; Galería Extasis
33 Meg's Riding Stables and Gallery
34 Reserva Sendero Tranquilo
36 CASEM
39 Entrance to Sendero Bajo del Tigre
40 Monteverde Institute
41 Cheese Factory (La Lechería)
42 Community Art Center
44 Friends' Meeting House & School
48 Galería de Arte Arias
50 Hummingbird Gallery
51 Reserve Entrance & Visitor Center
55 Banco Nacional
58 Sky Walk; Sky Trek Office
60 Bus Stop & Ticket Office
62 Monteverde Canopy Tour Office
64 Amigos Bar
65 Church
71 Coop Santa Elena Supermercado

Cordillera de Tilarán

Cerro Amigos
1842m

Trail

Reserva Biológica Bosque
Nuboso Monteverde

**MONTEVERDE**

Río Guacimal

Reserva Biológica
Bosque Nuboso
Monteverde

the Monteverde cloud forest reserve are described later in this chapter. The nearby village of San Luis, south of Monteverde, has an interesting biological station and ecolodge, also described later in this chapter.

## Information

There is no general information office; most places advertising tourist information are geared toward steering you into their own hotel or tour. One of the better ones is at the Pensión Santa Elena (W www.monte verdeinfo.com).

Chunches Coffeeshop (☎/fax 645-5147), in Santa Elena, is a bookstore/coffee shop with a fine selection of books (many in English), including travel and natural history guides and some US newspapers. It provides public fax services (sending and receiving) and laundry service (US$5 to wash and dry a load). Chunches also serves as a useful meeting place, and its bulletin board is a good source of information; it's open 8am to 6pm Monday to Saturday.

There is a Banco Nacional (☎ 645-5027) in Santa Elena, open 8:30am to 3:45pm weekdays. They want to see your passport to change US dollars or traveler's checks, and they give cash advances on Visa cards. Most hotels accept US dollars or change small sums of money. US dollars and traveler's checks in amounts under US$100 can be changed at the upstairs office of the Coop Santa Elena Supermercado (☎ 645-5006) in Santa Elena. Hours are 8am to noon and 1pm to 5pm weekdays, 8am to noon Saturday.

Internet access is from US$3 an hour (high because of the pricey telephone connections in this area – they may drop in the future). The best is at Tranquilo.com (☎ 645-5831) on the western outskirts of Santa Elena, open 9am to 9pm daily. The young guys who run it are friendly. You can also try at Monteverde Canopy Tours, Desafío, or Pensión Santa Elena (see Canopy Tours, Horseback Riding, and Places to Stay, respectively, later in this section); ask around for new providers and the best price. Many hotels allow guests to check or send email.

Santa Elena also has a small clinic (☎ 645-5076), which is closed from 3pm Friday to 7am Monday. The Red Cross station (☎ 128, 645-6128), just north of Santa Elena, is open 24 hours. The police can be reached at ☎ 117 or ☎ 645-5127.

## Butterfly Garden

One of the most interesting activities is visiting the Butterfly Garden (El Jardín de las Mariposas; ☎ 645-5512, W www.best.com/ ~mariposa; adult/student US$7/5; open 9:30am-4pm daily). Admission entitles you to a guided, naturalist-led tour (in Spanish, English, or German) that begins in the information center with an enlightening discussion of butterfly life cycles and the butterfly's importance. A variety of eggs, caterpillars, pupae, and adults are examined. Then visitors are taken into the greenhouses, where the butterflies are raised, and on into the screened garden, where hundreds of butterflies of many species are seen. The tour lasts about an hour, after which you are free to stay as long as you wish. There are excellent opportunities to photograph the gorgeous butterflies. One exhibit is a leaf-cutter ant colony with a fiber-optic camera inside to enable visitors to see what's going on. Keep your entrance ticket and you can visit the garden the next day if you wish. There are good volunteer opportunities here.

## Serpentarium

Biologist Fernando Valverde has a collection of about 20 snakes and lizards well displayed in cages labeled with informative signs in English and Spanish (☎ 645-5238; admission US$3; open 8am-5pm daily). Tours and talks are available for groups.

## Ranarium

Not to be outdone by snakes and butterflies, the Ranarium (admission US$8; open 10am-8pm daily) is a new exhibit featuring the many amphibian species of the area.

## Cheese Factory

The cheese factory (also called La Lechería or La Fábrica) has a shop where you can buy fresh local cheese and ice cream. Behind the shop, a huge window allows you to watch the workers making the cheeses. Store hours are 7:30am to 4pm daily, except Sunday and holidays.

## Art Galleries

You can visit a number of good local art galleries, all of which are more than just souvenir stores for tourists. (For information about hands-on art experiences, see Monteverde Studios of the Arts under Courses, later in this section.)

**CASEM** *(☎ 645-5190; open 8am-5pm Mon-Sat, 10am-4pm Sun in the high season)* is a local women's arts and crafts cooperative that sells embroidered and hand-painted blouses and handmade clothing as well as other souvenirs and crafts. Profits benefit the local artists and community.

**The Hummingbird Gallery** *(☎ 645-5030; open 7:30am-4:30pm daily)*, just outside the cloud forest reserve entrance, has feeders that constantly attract several species of hummingbird, including the violet sabrewing (Costa Rica's largest hummer) and the coppery-headed emerald, one of only three mainland birds endemic to Costa Rica. Great photo opportunities! An identification board shows the nine species that are seen here. Inside, slides and photographs by the renowned British wildlife photographers Michael and Patricia Fogden are on display and for sale. At the time of writing, a botanical garden was being added on the premises.

**Galería Extasis** *(☎ 645-5548; open 9am-5pm daily)*, off the main road between the reserve and Santa Elena, specializes in woodwork. Many artists from all over Costa Rica exhibit here, and the quaint

multilevel building that houses the gallery is an exhibit in itself.

New in 2002, **Alquimia Artes** *(☎ 645-5518)* showcases many talents, including local Indian craftspeople, sculptor/jeweler Tarcicio Castillo from the Ecuadorian Andes, painter Marianela Moreyra, and many others.

Other places on the main road include the **Community Art Center**, which specializes in pottery; **Meg's Gallery**, next to Stella's Bakery, which showcases a variety of work by Meg of the Riding Stables; and **Galería de Arte Arias**.

## Trails & Hiking

The 22,000-hectare **Bosque Eterno de los Niños** *(Children's Eternal Rainforest; day-use fee US$5/4 adult/child & student with ID; trail open 7:30am-5:30pm daily)* is a preserve largely funded by school groups from all over the world. Its 3.5km Sendero Bajo del Tigre (Jaguar Canyon Trail) offers more open vistas than do those in the cloud forest, so spotting birds tends to be easier. Parking is available. The preserve is managed by Monteverde Conservation League (MCL; ☎ 645-5003, 645-5305, fax 645-5104, ⓔ acmmcl@racsa.co.cr). You can join the MCL for US$25 – this entitles you

### Who Has Seen the Golden Toad?

One animal you used to be able to see so often that it almost became a Monteverde mascot was the golden toad *(Bufo periglenes)*. Monteverde was the only place in the world where this exotic little toad appeared. The gold-colored amphibian used to be frequently seen scrambling along the muddy trails of the cloud forest, adding a bright splash to the surroundings. Unfortunately, no one has seen this once-common toad since 1989, and what happened to it is a mystery.

During an international conference of herpetologists (scientists who study reptiles and amphibians), it was noted that the same puzzling story was occurring with other frog and toad species all over the world. Amphibians once common are now severely depleted or simply not found at all. The scientists were unable to agree upon a reason for the sudden demise of so many amphibian species in so many different habitats.

One of several theories holds that degenerating worldwide air quality is the culprit. Amphibians breathe both with primitive lungs and through their perpetually moist skin, and they're more susceptible to airborne toxins because of the gas exchange through their skin. Another theory is that deforestation and global warming pushed the frogs ever higher, until there was no higher altitude for them to go. Yet another theory is that their skin gives little protection against UV light, and increasing UV light levels in recent years have proven deadly to amphibians. Perhaps they are like the canaries miners used in the old days to warn them of toxic air in the mines. When the canary keeled over, it was time for the miners to get out!

Are our dying frogs and toads a symptom of a planet that is becoming too polluted?

to a subscription to the organization's quarterly publication, *Tapir Tracks*.

The **Finca Ecológica** *(Ecological Farm;* ☎ *645-5363; adult/student with ID/child US$7/6/4; open 7am-5pm daily)* is a private property with four loop trails (the longest takes about 2½ hours at a slow pace) offering hikes of varying lengths through premontane forest, secondary forest, and a small area of coffee and banana plantations, and past a couple of waterfalls and lookout points. Coatis, agoutis, and sloths are seen on most days, and monkeys, porcupines, and other animals are sometimes seen as well. Birding is good and a bird list is available. Some of these animals are seen at feeders, but they are wild. There is an information booth where you can find out where animals are being seen and get help with identification.

Another small private reserve with trails is the **Reserva Sendero Tranquilo** (Quiet Path Reserve), which limits visitation to two groups at any one time, with just two to six people per group. Visitation is permitted with a trail guide only, and the average hike lasts three to four hours – you see no one outside your group. Information is available from Hotel El Sapo Dorado (☎ 645-5015, 645-5010). The guided hike costs US$20 per person.

The **Hidden Valley Trail** is behind the Pensión Monteverde Inn (see Places to Stay, later). This is free to inn guests and US$5 to others.

The **Sky Walk** *(☎ 645-5238, fax 645-5796,* e *info@skywalk.co.cr,* w *www.skywalk.co.cr; adult/student with ID/child US$15/12/6; open 7am-4pm daily)*, as a way of getting up among the trees, is a serene alternative to the zip-wire tours offered by Monteverde Canopy Tours and Sky Trek (see below) or a fine complement to a Sky Trek tour. For an additional US$12, a guided walk is provided at 8am and 1pm. Seven suspension bridges, some as long as 300m, stretch high across valleys. Swaying gently on the bridges and gazing down through green layers of cloud forest is akin to snorkeling among reefs in deep water. Quetzals have been seen along the walk, as have monkeys, and it is a treat for birders to see their quarry dart by beneath them. Transportation from the Santa Elena bank costs US$2 per person (US$4 from hotels along the Monteverde road). The Sky

Walk is only 2km from the entrance to the Reserva Santa Elena, so a combined day trip is easy to arrange. The Sky Walk/Sky Trek office is in Santa Elena. Hiking and nature trails in the Monteverde and Santa Elena reserves are described later in this chapter.

A free hiking option is the trail up to **Cerro Amigos** (1842m). This hill has good views of the surrounding rainforest and, on a clear day, of Volcán Arenal, 20km away to the northeast. The trail leaves Monteverde from behind the Hotel Belmar and ascends roughly 300m in 3km; from the hotel, take the dirt road going downhill, then the next left. Near the end of the trail are a couple of TV/radio antennae, so the route is easy to follow.

## Canopy Tours

**Monteverde Canopy Tours** *(☎ 645-5243; adult/student/child US$45/35/30)* leave four or five times a day. The Original Canopy Tour opened its first site here, on the grounds of Cloud Forest Lodge. They also have an information office in Santa Elena.

The tour begins with a short guided hike through the forest to a series of five platforms between 20m and 33m up in the trees. The first platform is reached by a rope

Monteverde's tranquil Sky Walk

ladder that goes up the inside of a giant hollow fig tree; then you whiz across on a pulley harness attached to fixed ropes to the other platforms, and finally make a rappel descent to the ground. All participants are harnessed to safety equipment throughout the tour, which lasts about 2½ hours. See Organized Tours in the Getting Around chapter for more details.

An alternative to the Canopy Tour is the **Sky Trek**, which offers a similar ride through the treetops. Sky Trek also operates the Sky Walk (see Trails & Hiking, earlier, for contact details). Sky Trek features four zip lines, each approximately 100m long, and costs US$35/28 for adults/students, or US$40/34 in combination with the Sky Walk. Sky Trek tours are offered at 7:30am, 9:30am, 11:30am, 1:30pm, and 2pm; reservations are needed. Recent travelers' reports have given favorable reviews of this trip.

Neither of these tours is particularly about wildlife observation; the thrill of the ride (which produces the high-spirited yells that scare off most wildlife) is more the point.

Off the road to Finca Ecológica, **Aerial Adventures** (☎ 645-5960, e wmvargas@racsa.co.cr; ticket US$12; open 7am-6pm daily) offers a much more sedate ride through the trees. Essentially a ski lift, the tour offers a 1.5km journey in electrically propelled gondola chairs along rails attached to towers; heights range from near ground level to 12m up. The ride lasts between one and 1½ hours; you have the option of pausing your car briefly to look around. Lacking the thrills offered by the zip-line tours, this quieter tour offers similar views and probably a better chance of seeing birds and wildlife. Tickets include the loan of tree and bird identification guides, and the opening hours make dawn and dusk visits possible. Ask about night visits.

## Horseback Riding

Another option is horseback tours. There are plenty of outfitters in the area, and your hotel can arrange a tour for you. Average rates are US$10 per hour (more for just an hour, less for day rides). Some outfitters may charge less but aren't reliable.

One well-recommended outfitter is **Meg's Riding Stables** (☎ 645-5052, or call Stella's Bakery, listed in Places to Eat, later), which takes you on private trails. Their horses are well looked after, and this is the longest-established operation in Monteverde. It's also among the priciest at about US$20 an hour (less for groups or long rides). **Caballeriza La Estrella** (☎ 645-5075) has also been recommended.

Also check with **Sabine's Smiling Horses** (at Pensión Santa Elena; w www.horseback-riding-tour.com). Sabine speaks English, French, Spanish, and German and offers multiday horseback trips as well as US$10/hour local trips. **Desafío** (☎ 645-5874, w www.desafiocostarica.com), in Santa Elena, arranges short and long rides (as well as nonlocal rafting trips). Another outfitter that has been suggested is **Toucan Valley Tour** (☎ 645-5479); ask for Kattya Corales or Celimo Saraya. Apart from forest tours, day treks can be arranged to viewpoints from which Volcán Arenal can be seen (see the boxed text 'To Ride or Not to Ride?' for information about horse trips to Fortuna).

## Viewing Volcán Arenal

A rough road goes 8km or 9km nnorth of Santa Elena, past the turnoff to the Reserva Santa Elena, to an area where there are great views (if it's clear) of the volcano exploding away about 15km to the northeast. You could drive, bike, or hike along this road for the views. There are a couple of places to stay out here. The lookout tower at the Reserva Santa Elena (see later in this chapter) and Cerro Amigos (see Trails & Hiking, earlier) also offer volcano-viewing opportunities.

## Organic Farming

There is a fair amount of organic farming in the area, and visitors can learn about how it's done. Information about volunteering on Finca La Bella, which gives locals an opportunity to learn organic coffee-farming methods, is available through the Monteverde Institute (see Courses, below). Behind Stella's Bakery, Rigo Alvarado oversees a well-developed organic garden; produce goes to Stella's and comes back again as compost. Rigo can be reached through Meg Wallace (Stella's daughter and operator of Meg's Riding Stables; see Horseback Riding, above); he can tell you about other organic farming projects in the area.

## Courses

Organized by the enterprising Sybil Terres Gilmar, the new *Monteverde Studios of*

## To Ride or Not to Ride?

The fascinating Arenal area's active volcano and cloud forests attract ecotourists from all over the world. The only towns with a tourism infrastructure here are Fortuna and Monteverde; they're just a few kilometers apart, but thanks to this region's rugged terrain, it takes a day of hard driving over rough roads to get from one to the other.

Local entrepreneurs discovered that ecotourists were interested in visiting both Fortuna and Monteverde and began providing horseback-riding tours that joined the towns. The catchphrase they used was 'The shortest and most convenient connection,' and it proved successful and popular, with many 'outfitters' jumping on the horseback-tour bandwagon. Tourists thought that riding a horse from Fortuna to Monteverde or vice versa was a good way to cover the route and see some of the countryside. Demand for horseback rides rose and competition became fierce to earn the tourists' dollars.

The result was cutthroat competition and severe price-cutting in order to attract tourists, who often looked for the best prices. Unfortunately, this led to unethical practices such as buying cheap old horses for a few hundred dollars and literally working them to death. The trails between Fortuna and Monteverde are steep, slippery, and often very muddy, and the horses were sometimes forced to work without adequate rest breaks or days off. There were a few cases of horses dying on the trail; more often they were worked until they couldn't carry a rider and then sold to a butcher.

In the late 1990s, many travelers wrote to let me know that they were saddened and, in some cases, outraged to see their tour horses treated so poorly. I received repeated reports of animals that were old, thin, worn out, plagued by sores, underfed, and beaten by the guides to make them move faster. Because some owners bought the horses as a short-term investment, the animals didn't receive the necessary veterinary care.

After I wrote about this in the last edition, a number of outfitters were angered by my description, saying that I was destroying their business and that my job was to write a guidebook, not harass them. Some outfitters went out of business. Travelers began to ask questions about the problems I described. Today, tours have improved overall, horses are generally treated better, and the costs have gone up. However, this isn't to say that horseback tours are recommended here and throughout the country. Unfortunately, some people continue to mistreat animals, without realizing, perhaps, that there are other options.

Some companies have responded in positive ways. They encourage tourists to ask hard questions, provide health certificates for their horses on request, rotate their horses to give them days off after a hard ride, and provide the horses with extra food if necessary. Clearly, horses provide pleasurable transportation for tourists. Equally clearly, tourists should make every effort to ensure that animals are not treated as expendable sources of short-term profit. And if this raises the cost of the tours, so be it.

**the Arts** (☎ 645-5434, in the USA ☎ 800-370-3331, ✉ mstudios@racsa.co.cr, 🖥 www.mvstudios.com) offers visitors the wonderful opportunity of taking classes with artists from the Monteverde community. Held in local homes and studios, the classes include woodworking, photography, stained-glass design, painting and drawing, paper and textile work, cooking, and storytelling. Most classes last a week and cost about US$235, with additional materials fees in some cases; ask about shorter classes. Food and lodging with private bath can be arranged for about US$360/285/220 per person singles/doubles/triples for six nights.

**Monteverde Institute** (☎ 645-5053, fax 645-5219, 🖥 www.mvinstitute.org) is a nonprofit educational institute founded in 1986. The institute offers interdisciplinary courses in tropical biology, agroecology, conservation, sustainable development, local culture, Spanish, and women's studies. These are occasionally open to the general public – check their website. There is also a volunteer-placement program for people who wish to teach in local schools or work in reforestation programs.

The Institute's short courses (10 to 14 days) give high school and college students and adults the opportunity to learn about conservation and land use in the Monteverde area. Costs are US$700 to US$1500, all-inclusive from San José. Long courses (eight to 10 weeks) are university-accredited programs for undergraduates and emphasize tropical community ecology. Costs are about US$4000. Graduate students interested in doing thesis research in the area can apply for office space and housing through the institute; the application fee is US$25.

*Centro Panamericano de Idiomas* (☎/fax 645-5448, in the USA ☎ 888-682-0054, e info@cpi-edu.com, w www.cpi-edu.com/monteverde.htm) has opened a Spanish-language program in Monteverde, with homestays available. (Also see the entry under Heredia in the Central Valley & Surrounding Highlands chapter.)

## Monteverde Music Festival

The Monteverde Music Festival is held annually on variable dates from late January to early April and has gained a well-deserved reputation as one of the top music festivals in Central America. Music is mainly classical, jazz, and Latin, with an oc-casional experimental group to spice things up. Concerts are held on Thursday, Friday, and Saturday, with a different group each weekend. Tickets are US$10. Ask locally for venues.

## Places to Stay

During Christmas and Easter, many hotels are booked up weeks in advance. During the January-to-April busy season, and also in July, hotels tend to be full often enough that you should telephone before arriving to ensure yourself a room in the hotel you want. You may have to book well in advance to get the dates and hotel of your choice. If you're flexible, you can almost always find somewhere to stay. The Santa Elena bus stop is one of the few places in Costa Rica where you're likely to be besieged on arrival by people trying to offer you a place to sleep.

**Budget** In an attractive riverside location is *Camping Charlie* (☎ 645-5799) Campsites US$2.50 per person. This is a small, loosely organized spot; bathrooms are basic. *La Colina Lodge* (see Mid-Range, below) also allows camping (US$5 per person) and offers hot showers.

## Responsible Tourism

Monteverde started as a Quaker community founded by peaceful people who wanted to live in a quiet and friendly environment. This has changed drastically in the past two decades with the large influx of visitors. There is a limit to the number of visitors Monteverde can handle before losing its special atmosphere, and there is a limit to the number of people who can visit the Monteverde reserve without causing too much damage.

Quakers have traditionally been adept at peaceful resolution of problems, and they have handled their status as a tourist attraction with grace and common sense. The income from tourism is important, but preserving their own lifestyle and surroundings is equally, if not more, important to the inhabitants. Monteverde is a special but fragile place – visitors are very welcome but should remember that they are visiting a peaceful community and a cloud forest reserve.

One way that the canny Quakers have preserved the area is by *not* making requests for improved vehicular access. Unlike most other towns and villages, who frequently petition the authorities and government for improved roads, the Monteverdians are happy to keep the status quo. Rough rocky roads keep out the biggest tourist buses, and visitors are forced to spend at least one if not two nights in the area, instead of day-tripping through.

Most visitors are delighted with their stay, but a few complain about how muddy the trails are (you have to expect mud in a cloud forest), how boring the nightlife is (Quakers traditionally don't do much nightclubbing), or how difficult it is to see the quetzal (this is not a zoo). Monteverde is not for everybody – if clouds and Quakers, cheese and quetzals do not sound like your idea of fun, head for a resort more to your liking.

Many, though not all, of the cheapest hotels are in Santa Elena, about 5km to 6km from the reserve.

**Hotel El Sueño** (☎ 645-5021) Quads from US$5 per person. This is a family-run place with basic quadruple rooms, as well as slightly better rooms with private bath for about twice as much. There is hot water, and they will cook for you on request.

**Pensión Santa Elena** (☎ 645-5051, fax 645-6060, e pension@monteverdeinfo.com) Rooms US$6-9 per person. A friendly and popular place, Pensión Santa Elena offers about 24 small rooms, including some with private bath and nonelectric hot shower (!). There are electric showers in the communal bathrooms. You can get wine, beer, and Internet access; there is a communal kitchen and an attractive eating area. They also own two houses next door with nicer, larger rooms with bath for US$20 to US$40 for a double. Multilingual owner Jacques is a frenzied and busy source of information.

**Pensión Colibrí** (☎ 645-5682) Rooms without bath US$5 per person, doubles with bath US$20. Near Pensión Santa Elena, this small, clean, and friendly place offers basic rooms with shared bathroom and electric hot shower, or other rooms with private bath. Some rooms have sunny windows, and there is a little balcony; the place as a whole feels perched among the trees. The staff will cook for you on request (US$3.50 for a *casado*), and horse rental is available – a day trip to Reserva Santa Elena is US$20 per person.

**Hospedaje El Banco** (☎ 645-5204) Rooms without bath US$7 per person. Behind the bank, this place is basic but friendly. The shared electric showers are warm, and laundry service and meals are available on request.

**Hotel Camino Verde** (☎/fax 645-5916) Rooms without/with bath US$5/8 per person. This hotel has laundry service, will change small amounts of money, and has clean basic rooms; one reader reports poor service.

**Cabinas Don Taco** (☎/fax 645-5263, e cabdontaco@racsa.co.cr) Rooms without bath US$6 per person. Cabins with bath US$20 double. About a half kilometer north of Santa Elena, past the school and radio tower, this quiet place has clean rooms with bunk beds, communal bath, and hot showers. Some rooms have balcony access. Breakfast costs US$4.

**Cabinas Marín** (☎ 645-5279) Doubles without/with bath US$14/20. Near Don Taco's, this place is clean, quiet, and friendly, with good-size rooms (though the wooden walls make them look a bit dark). Some rooms have views.

**Pensión Tucán** (☎ 645-5017) Rooms without/with bath US$7/10 per person. This pensión has 14 small but clean double rooms with hot water. Seven rooms have shared bathrooms and seven others have private bath. The pensión will rent cabins with kitchenettes from US$125 a month. Meals are available, and the helpful owner is a good cook.

**Tina's Casitas** (☎ 645-5641, e tinas_casitas@hotmail.com) Singles US$10-12, doubles US$12-14 with shared bath; singles US$15-20, doubles US$25-30 with private bath. This good budget place, just outside the village to the southwest, has three little houses set around an outdoor terrace, from which the Golfo de Nicoya is visible. Room rates vary depending on size. Showers are hot, and a kitchen is available. One casita sleeps four for US$40. The owner speaks German and English. From behind the Santa Elena supermarket, it's about a 200m walk down a dirt road and up a small hill; there are signs. The cabins are simple but nicely built, and a little restaurant is next door.

**Pensión Flor de Monteverde** (☎/fax 645-5236, e flormonteverde@racsa.co.cr) Rooms without/with hot bath US$7/10 per person. Farther out than the others, this is a small, clean, friendly, family-run, and helpful place. Owner Eduardo Venegas Castro has worked at both the Monteverde and Santa Elena reserves and was director of the latter. He offers three meals a day for another US$15 on top of room rates. Tours and transportation can be arranged, a number of wildlife guides are available to guests, and there is laundry service.

**Pensión Manakín** (☎ 645-5080, fax 645-5517, e manakin@racsa.co.cr) Rooms without bath US$10 per person, doubles with bath US$30. In Cerro Plano, this 11-room place is simple but friendly and has hot water. Good breakfasts cost US$2 to US$5, depending on what you want to eat. The pensión also offers Internet access, picnic lunches, laundry service, and basic kitchen privileges, and it can arrange local tours and transportation. The doubles with bath have received reader recommendations. The owners are knowledgeable about what's going on in the area.

**Pensión Monteverde Inn** (☎ 645-5156, fax 645-5945) Singles/doubles with bath US$10/18. In a remote part of Cerro Plano is this friendly place, from which the Hidden Valley Trail goes into a deep canyon and through an 11-hectare reserve. The owners' daughters, Lisetta and Vanessa, are fun and enjoy guiding folks along the trail. The rooms are spartan but adequate and have private hot showers; breakfast is available on request for US$5, and the owners can pick you up at the bus stop if you have a reservation. The remote and very quiet location is the main attraction here.

**Monte Los Olivos Ecotourist Lodge** (☎ 661-8126, 286-4203) Singles/doubles without bath US$15/20, singles/doubles/triples/quads with bath US$22/30/38/45. About 3km or 4km northwest of Santa Elena on the road to Tilarán, this is a community project supported by the Arenal Conservation Area, the Canadian World Wildlife Fund, and the Canadian International Development Agency. The project is intended to develop grassroots ecotourism that protects forests and directly benefits small communities such as this one. Two similar lodges have opened in northwestern Costa Rica (see the Volcán Tenorio Area, later in this chapter). This one has nine rustic but clean cabins with hot water. Five of the cabins share bathrooms, and the remaining four have private bath. Breakfasts (US$2) and other meals (US$5) are served. You can arrange guided hikes and horseback rides with the locals.

**Mid-Range** **La Colina** (☎/fax 645-5009, e lacolina@racsa.co.cr, w www.lacolina .com) Singles/doubles without bath US$29/34, with bath US$34/45; US$11.60 for extra people. Full breakfast is included. This is the former 'Flor Mar' opened in 1977 by Marvin Rockwell, one of the original Quakers in the area, who was jailed for refusing to sign up for the draft and then spent three months driving down from Alabama. The new owners have renovated the rooms, some of which have balconies and all of which have cozy Central American bedspreads and other touches. Six rooms have private baths, and five others share two bathrooms. The private restaurant (perhaps it'll go public soon) features Mediterranean cuisine with Spanish, Italian, North African, and vegetarian influences. A full meal, including dessert and coffee, is US$10. The owners speak English and German and offer a book exchange and a TV room.

**Hospedaje Mariposa** (☎ 645-5013) Singles/doubles/triples with private bath US$20/25/30. This friendly family-run place has just three simple but clean rooms, each with a double and single bed and private warm shower. Its best feature is that it is only 1.5km from the Monteverde reserve. Rates include a Costa Rican breakfast. Other meals can be arranged.

**Sunset Hotel** (☎ 645-5228, fax 645-5344) Singles/doubles/triples with private bath US$26/38/48. About 1.5km out of Santa Elena toward Reserva Santa Elena, this is a small, well-kept place with a quiet location and great views. The seven rooms have hot water, and rates include breakfast. Readers have reported substantial wet-season discounts and have enjoyed their stays here. German and English are spoken.

**Finca Terra Viva** (☎ 645-5454, fax 645-5208, e reptiles@racsa.co.cr) Rooms US$30. About 3km out on the road toward Reserva Santa Elena, this is a 135-hectare *finca*, of which 60% is forest and the rest is pasture slowly returning to forest. The finca has cattle, pigs, goats, horses, chickens – a typical Costa Rican rural experience. Each of the four rustic wooden rooms has a private hot shower and sleeps up to four. Guests share a large fully equipped kitchen and a dining room with Internet access. Owner Montse will cook three meals (international menu) for US$20 per person, or you can use the kitchen yourself for US$5 per person per stay. Discounts are offered for groups larger than 10 people. Co-owner Federico (Montse's husband) is a well-known naturalist guide who has long envisioned living in a finca that combines education, conservation, and farming – this is the result. Horseback riding can be arranged, and you can watch/help/learn milking and cheese making.

**Arco Iris Ecolodge** (☎ 645-5067, fax 645-5022, e arcoiris@racsa.co.cr, w www .arcoirislodge.com) Doubles US$30-55. This small place is on a little hill overlooking Santa Elena and the surrounding forests.

NORTHWESTERN

The multilingual owners are generally helpful. The quiet hotel has a large garden that produces some of the organic vegetables served in the restaurant, which currently offers only breakfast to guests (US$6.50) but may reopen to the public for other meals. The lodge has 10 pleasant cabins, most with private hot shower. The prices vary depending on room size and view, and low-season discounts are substantial here. All the local tours are organized quickly. Trails have been developed on the mountain behind the lodge.

*Hotel El Bosque* (☎ 645-5221, 645-5158, ☎/fax 645-5129, e elbosque@racsa.co.cr) Singles/doubles with bath US$30/40. This hotel is behind the popular Tremonti restaurant. The 28 rooms are simple but clean, bright, and spacious and have private hot showers – good for the money.

*Swiss Hotel Miramontes* (☎ 645-5152, fax 645-5297, e miramontes@racsa.co.cr, w www.swisshotelmiramontes.com) Doubles with bath US$40-55. Just outside Santa Elena on the road to Juntas is this pleasantly situated place with eight rooms of varying size, all with private hot bath. Four languages are spoken, the hotel is well run, and the restaurant offers a well-reviewed, mainly Swiss menu.

*Delucia Inn* (☎ 645-5976, fax 645-5537, e delucia@racsa.co.cr) Singles/doubles US$46/58, including breakfast. Next to the fine restaurant of the same name and with the same owners, the Delucia Inn is a large house with a dozen spacious rooms. Each room has a double and a single bed and a private bathroom with hot showers. A large balcony is available to guests.

*Hotel Finca Valverde's* (☎ 645-5157, fax 645-5216, e info@monteverde.co.cr, w www.monteverde.co.cr) Singles/doubles US$46/64, suites US$68/82 (US$12 for additional people). Outside Santa Elena, this is a working coffee farm. There are five cabins, each with two clean and spacious (if rather bare) units with private bathtubs and hot water, an upstairs loft, and a balcony. Note that three of the cabins are a short (20m to 50m) but very steep hike up from the parking lot. There are also eight standard rooms and two junior suites. Discounts are available for student groups. A simple but pleasant restaurant, open to the public, serves Costa Rican food, and the attached

bar is locally popular. Restaurant hours are 7am to 9pm.

*Hotel Villa Verde* (☎ 645-5025, fax 645-5115, e estefany@racsa.co.cr) Singles/doubles/triples with bath US$43/65/81, suites US$89, including breakfast. Just over a kilometer away from the reserve, this attractive stone-and-wood building is popular with groups and can get noisy. There are 18 standard rooms with hot bath and five suites with kitchenette and fireplace that sleep up to seven people. Amenities include a reasonable restaurant-bar, a conference room, and laundry service. All local tours are quickly arranged. They advertise low-season, student, and long-stay discounts.

*Trapp Family Lodge* (☎ 645-5858, fax 645-5990, e trappfam@racsa.co.cr, w www.trappfam.com) Singles/doubles/triples with bath US$64/76/87. This is now the closest lodge to the reserve entrance (slightly less than a kilometer away). Newly finished, it has 20 spacious rooms with high wooden ceilings, big bathrooms, and fabulous views from the picture windows overlooking either gardens or cloud forest. The corner room with two entire walls made of glass is incredible. The homey restaurant serves breakfast (US$8.60), lunch, and dinner (US$14.75) for guests only; a bar and sitting room with cable TV is open 'til 10pm. The friendly owners can arrange tours and transportation.

**Top End** Four kilometers from the reserve is *Hotel Heliconia* (☎ 645-5109, 223-3869, fax 645-5007, e heliconi@racsa.co.cr) Singles/doubles US$74/80, junior suites US$80/85, suites US$100/106. The attractive wooden family-run lodge and bungalows behind it offer 32 good-size if rather bare rooms, each with private bath (and tub) with hot water. A separate building houses a spa, and there is a nice-looking restaurant and bar. Full breakfasts or boxed lunches cost US$10.50; other meals cost US$17. The restaurant specializes in Italian food and has received recommendations. Behind the hotel is a private, 4km trail system, and rubber boots are loaned on request.

*Hotel Fonda Vela* (☎ 645-5125, 645-5114, fax 645-5119, e fondavel@racsa.co.cr, w www.fondavela.com) Singles/doubles US$88/98, junior suites US$98/110, master suites US$108/120, US$11 for additional people. This is the closest top-end place to the reserve, just over 1.5km away. Trails through the 14-hectare grounds offer good birding possibilities, and on-site stables mean there's no wait to rent a horse. The restaurant is in a beautiful building; the owners' father, Paul Smith, is a well-known local artist whose work, along with others', graces the walls. A smaller restaurant features a fireplace.

Nine separate structures house a total of 20 standard rooms, 18 junior suites, and two master suites. The standard rooms are spacious and light, with wood accents and large windows. Each suite is well equipped with a sitting room, minibar, bathtub, balcony, cable TV, and loft. All rooms have telephones, private hot showers, and two queen-size beds, and some have great views. Many rooms are wheelchair accessible. The *restaurant* is open to the public. Set meals are served from 6:15am to 9am, noon to 2pm, and 6:30pm to 8:30pm. Breakfast costs US$9.50, lunch costs US$15, and dinner costs US$20 – the food is good. Readers wrote to recommend this place.

*Hotel Belmar* (☎ 645-5201, fax 645-5135, e belmar@racsa.co.cr, W www.hotel belmar.com) Singles US$76-93, doubles US$81-98, US$12-15 for additional people. Also recommended, this is a beautiful wooden hotel on a hill almost 4km from the reserve. Its two Alpine-looking buildings have 34 rooms. The road up to the hotel is steep and slippery for the last 300m, and cars don't always make it in heavy rain. But once you get there, you're rewarded with superb views of the Golfo de Nicoya when the weather is clear. Most of the attractive spacious rooms have balconies. Breakfast costs about US$10, lunch US$16, dinner US$19, and the food is a good international menu with tico touches. The restaurant adjoins a bar with a pool table. Horseback rides and the usual tours are arranged.

*Hotel de Montaña Monteverde* (☎ 645-5046, 645-5338, fax 645-5320, e monteverde@ ticonet.co.cr, W www.ticonet.co.cr/monteverde /info.htm) Doubles standard/superior/deluxe US$67/88/109. Opened in 1978 as the first top-end hotel in Monteverde, this place has 16 standard, 13 superior, and 12 deluxe rooms, some of which have been recently renovated and others newly added. All have private hot showers, and some have mini-bars, hair dryers, tubs, balconies, and views. There is a good restaurant featuring tico food, as well as a cozy adjoining bar and a TV lounge. The spacious gardens and forests of the 15-hectare property are pleasant to walk around. A sauna and Jacuzzi can be used for US$1 per hour by reservation (for privacy) from 4pm to 9pm. All the local tours and activities are arranged.

*Hotel El Sapo Dorado* (☎ 645-5010, fax 645-5180, e elsapo@racsa.co.cr, W www.sapo dorado.com) Singles/doubles/triples/quads: mountain suites US$89/103/118/133, terrace suites US$95/115/132/150. This hotel is owned by longtime residents Geovanny Arguedas and Hannah Lowther, a tico-Quaker couple who met as children in school at Monteverde. They are active in the community, promoting sustainable tourism and other values. The private forest behind the hotel has trails, and the restaurant-bar serves excellent and healthy meals, with gourmet vegetarian main courses always among the choices. They occasionally have live music and a musically accompanied slide show by noted area photographer and naturalist Richard Laval. The restaurant is open to the public 7am to 10am, noon to 3pm, and 6pm to 9pm. The bar is open 7am to 10pm and serves snacks. Professional massage services are available for US$29 per hour.

There are 30 spacious rooms mostly in duplex cabins. All have two queen-size beds, a table and chairs, and private hot-water showers. The 'mountain suites' have mountain views, a small balcony, and a fireplace. Each of the larger 'sunset terrace suites' has a minibar, fridge, and French doors that open to a private terrace with views down to the Golfo de Nicoya. Light sleepers should opt for the sunset terrace suites, which have thicker walls than the mountain suites.

*Monteverde Lodge & Gardens* (☎ 645-5057, fax 645-5126, e ecotur@expeditions .co.cr) Singles/doubles/triples US$96/115/133. The most upscale hotel in the Monteverde area, this place is 5km from the reserve. A progressive recycling strategy, a solar-energy system, and a policy that sheets and towels are changed only at a guest's request are among the hotel's noteworthy environmentally sound practices. The 27 rooms are larger than most and have picture windows with garden or forest views. Bathrooms feature

NORTHWESTERN

hair dryers, tubs, and showers. Apart from a smoking wing, most guestrooms and the restaurant are nonsmoking areas. The large lobby is graced by a huge fireplace. Adjoining the lobby, a huge solar-powered – but nice and hot – Jacuzzi allows up to 15 guests to soak away the stresses of hiking steep and muddy trails. A popular feature is the lodge's Internet café (US$4 per hour).

The grounds are attractively landscaped with a variety of native plants, emphasizing the ferns, bromeliads, and mosses of the cloud forest, and a short trail leads to a bluff with an observation platform. The bluff is at the height of the forest canopy, with good views of the forest and a river ravine. Children under five years old stay and eat for free; children from ages six to 10 stay for free (with their parents) and receive a 50% discount on meals. Meals are served à la carte and feature some of the best international cuisine in the area (about US$20 for dinner). Transportation to the Monteverde or Santa Elena reserve costs US$8 per person; to San José it's US$40. The staff will arrange guided reserve visits, horseback rides, and all other activities.

Reservations should be made with lodge owner/operator Costa Rica Expeditions (see Organized Tours in the Getting Around chapter). Complete tours that include transportation, meals, and accommodations are also available (for example, three days/two nights from San José, including a half day at the Monteverde reserve, costs US$349 per person, double occupancy).

## Places to Eat

Many people eat in their hotels, most of which provide meals and will also provide picnic lunches on request. Several hotel restaurants are open to the public. Other possibilities include the following.

*Pizza Johnny* (☎ 645-5066) Pizza pie US$4-9. Popular with both travelers and locals, this place serves other good Italian dishes as well as pizza. It's a pleasant place for a meal.

*Pizzería Tremonti* (☎ 645-6120, 694-4282) Dishes US$5-11. Open 11:30am-10pm Mon-Sat. This very pleasant and popular Italian place serves good pizzas, pastas, seafood, and meats for lunch and dinner. The spacious restaurant is nearly 3km from the reserve.

*Restaurant de Lucia* (☎ 645-5337) Open 11am-8:30pm daily. On the same road as the Butterfly Garden, this Chilean-owned place is one of Monteverde's best restaurants, though not very expensive at about US$20 for a meal for two people.

*Tingo's* (☎ 645-6034) Dishes US$6-8. Open 9am-10pm daily. The cook from the former Muelle 595 has taken his seafood dinners to this place near the Centro Panamericano de Idiomas. It may close in the low season (September to November).

There are cheap places to eat in Santa Elena, especially if you stick with basic plates like the casado, which can be had for under US$3. The *Soda Central* is popular. Next to the church, a small *open-air soda* is open early. *Chunches Coffeeshop* (see Information, earlier in this chapter) has espresso coffee and delicious homemade cookies and snacks.

*Morphos Restaurant* (☎ 645-5607, ☎/fax 645-5065) Breakfasts US$2-3, other meals US$4-7. Open 7am-9:30pm daily. This popular café in downtown Santa Elena features a good long menu with sandwiches, salads, pastas, casados, vegetarian plates, and the usual meat and seafood dishes. Portions are big.

*Rainforest Restaurant* (☎ 645-5818) Dishes US$3-17. Open 8am-10pm daily. This new, spacious restaurant with plants and picture windows at the corner of a major Santa Elena intersection provides a varied menu – from simple breakfasts and casados to soups, salads, and pizzas to meat and seafood dishes. They specialize in seafood, offering octopus, shrimp, lobster, ceviche, and more. This is Santa Elena's most upscale restaurant.

The friendly *Teens* has sandwiches, hamburgers, barbecued chicken, and ice cream – it's popular with a younger crowd. Below is *Panadería Jiménez* for baked goods. Nearby is *Restaurant Daiquiri*, which has dishes for US$5 to US$10 and tends to stay open late. Homey *Restaurant Maravilla* serves breakfast, lunch, and dinner in the US$1.50 to US$4 range.

*Jungle Groove Café* Open noon-late Dec-Aug. This place has *bocas,* Cuban meals and snacks, a small bar, and occasional live music on weekends. It's a popular hangout.

*Stella's Bakery* (☎ 645-5560) Prices US$2-5. Open 6am-6pm daily. Stella's has fresh salads, soups, and sandwiches (many of the ingredients are grown organically behind the bakery), coffee drinks, and a variety of delicious pastries, homemade breads, and rolls – all of which make for good picnic lunches.

Opposite Stella's, there is a **grocery store** next to CASEM. **La Lechería** (the cheese factory) sells fresh cheese and ice cream. In Santa Elena, stop by the **supermarket**.

There is a decent **cafeteria** just inside the entrance of the Monteverde reserve.

## Entertainment

**La Cascada** Open 9pm-1am Thur-Sun. This is a popular dance club in Cerro Plano; there may be a cover charge.

**Domingo's Bar/Unicornio Discotec** The locals go to this place, next to the soccer field at the north end of Santa Elena.

Popular bars are **Amigos Bar** in Santa Elena, which has a pool table, and the **Taberna Bar** by the Hotel Finca Valverde's, which has a small dance floor. Several of the better hotels have **slide shows** and bars for evening entertainment. Also see the Monteverde Music Festival, earlier in this chapter.

## Getting There & Away

**Bus** After stopping in Santa Elena, most buses to the Monteverde area continue on to La Lechería, about 2.5km before the reserve. Ask to be dropped off anywhere before that point, near the hotel of your choice. These buses also begin the return trip from La Lechería, stopping at several points, including the bus office (☎ 645-5159, 645-5644) next to the Soda Central in Santa Elena, before continuing. Departure times from La Lechería for buses on this route are 5:30am for Las Juntas, 5:45am for Puntarenas, and 6:30am and 2:30pm for San José – these buses pick up passengers at the Santa Elena bus office about 10 minutes later.

Buses to the Monteverde area leave from Las Juntas at 2:30pm, from Puntarenas at 2pm (US$2.50, about three hours), and at 6:30am and 2:30pm from San José (US$5, about four to five hours). During the high season, a 1pm departure from Puntarenas may also be offered.

The bus to Tilarán leaves at 7am from the church in Santa Elena; the departure from Tilarán (☎ 222-3854) to Santa Elena is at 12:30pm (US$2, about three hours). Try

to buy tickets for all buses a day in advance, especially in the high season. Several hotels arrange private transportation to or from San José.

Beltour (☎ 645-5978) has faster air-conditioned minibuses to San José (US$30) and to Manuel Antonio or Tamarindo (US$35). These prices vary by a few dollars depending on season and demand. Buses normally leave around 9am; they may run in conjunction with Interbus. Most hotels in Monteverde can make reservations.

**Car** Drivers will find all the roads to Monteverde in poor condition, and 4WD may be necessary in the rainy season. Many car rental agencies will refuse to rent you an ordinary car during the wet season if you state that you are going to Monteverde. Ordinary cars are OK in the dry months, but it is a slow and bumpy ride during which cars occasionally break down or sustain damage to the undercarriage – drive with care.

There are four roads from the Interamericana to Santa Elena and Monteverde. Coming from the south, the first turnoff is at Rancho Grande, 18km northwest of the turnoff for Puntarenas. All there is at Rancho Grande is the Bar Rancho Grande and a sign for 'Sardinal, Guacimal, Monteverde,' both on the right (north) side of the highway. The second turnoff is at the Río Lagarto bridge (just past Km 149, and roughly 15km northwest of Rancho Grande). Here there is another not very obvious sign: 'Guacimal, Santa Elena, Monteverde.' These two roads join one another about a third of the way to Monteverde and then follow the same route. Both routes are steep, winding, and scenic dirt roads with plenty of potholes and rocks to ensure that the driver, at least, is kept from admiring the scenery. (There is good birding en route.) These are the roads most frequently used.

A third road goes via Juntas (see that section, later in this chapter). This begins as a paved road until a few kilometers past Juntas, then becomes unpaved and just as rough as the first two. Finally, if coming from the north, drivers could take the paved road from Cañas via Tilarán (both towns are described later in this chapter) and then take the rough, unpaved road from Tilarán to Santa Elena.

Which road should you take? Good question. The first two are about the same distance (35km from the Interamericana to Santa Elena). The Rancho Grande road is reached more quickly from San José, and many bus drivers prefer it for that reason, but the Río Lagarto road seems to be favored by local drivers and may be in marginally better condition. If you're driving, talk to everyone you can about current conditions and weigh the (invariably conflicting) advice received – once you are thoroughly confused, you can begin your journey!

The roads from Juntas or Tilarán are just as bad (some people say they're worse – a point that is debated by road warriors having an evening drink in the hotel bars). All are drivable in an ordinary car during the dry season, at least – drive carefully.

**Jeep & Boat** When leaving from Fortuna, it's possible to take a 4WD jeep taxi to Río Chiquito, then a boat across Laguna de Arenal, and be met by a taxi on the other side to continue to Fortuna. This takes about five hours and the whole package costs US$25 per person with Beltour (☎ 645-5978), which sometimes offers US$19 discounted trips – ask. Several hotels advertise the same route – ask them for the best time/price. Both morning and afternoon departures are available.

**Horse** A number of people offer horseback rides between Monteverde and Fortuna, but this option is not recommended as the trip is very hard on the horses – there have even been reports of horses dying on the trail (see the boxed text 'To Ride or Not to Ride?'). Instead, take one of the shorter horse-jeep-boat combos that are offered. These go part of the same route as the jeep and boat transfers described above, but they have the added adventure of spending three or four hours of the trip on horseback. The cost is US$65 per person.

## RESERVA BIOLÓGICA BOSQUE NUBOSO MONTEVERDE

When the Quaker settlers first arrived, they decided to preserve about a third of their property in order to protect the watershed above Monteverde. In 1972, with the help of organizations such as the Nature Conservancy and the World Wildlife Fund (WWF),

more land was purchased adjoining the already preserved area. This was called the Reserva Biológica Bosque Nuboso Monteverde (Monteverde Cloud Forest Biological Reserve), which the Centro Científico Tropical (Tropical Science Center) of San José bought and operated. Gradually, more land was acquired and added to the reserve.

In 1986, the Monteverde Conservation League (MCL) was formed, and it continues to buy land to expand the reserve. In 1988, the MCL launched the International Children's Rainforest project, whereby children and school groups from all over the world raise money to buy and save tropical rainforest adjacent to the reserve. This project does more than ask children to raise money for rainforest preservation – it's an educational program as well.

The most striking aspect of this project is that it is a private enterprise rather than a national park administered by the government. Governments worldwide must begin to count conservation as a key issue for the continued well-being of their citizens, but it is interesting to see what a positive effect ordinary people can have on preserving their environment. This preservation relies partly on donations from the public, which can be made at the reserve. Donations to the Children's Rainforest project and to aid educational work and sustainable development in the local community can also be sent to Monteverde Conservation League (W www.acmonteverde.com), Apartado 10581-1000, San José.

Visitors should note that some of the walking trails are very muddy, and even during the dry season (from late December to early May) the cloud forest tends to drip. Therefore, rainwear and suitable boots are recommended if you plan on going a long distance. (Rubber boots can be rented at the entrance for about US$1.50 – bring your own footwear for the best fit.) Many of the trails have been stabilized with concrete blocks or wooden boards and are easier to walk. During the wet season, the unpaved trails turn into quagmires, but there are usually fewer visitors then. The annual rainfall here is about 3000mm, though parts of the reserve reportedly get twice as much. It's usually cool (high temperatures around 18°C/65°F), so wear appropriate clothing. Dry-season visitors who plan to stay on the main trails really don't need rubber boots – I've seen sweaty-footed hikers looking elegant in their personal pink rubber boots with barely a splash of mud on them. Binoculars rent for US$10 per day.

Because of the fragile environment, the reserve will allow in a maximum of 120 people at any given time. During the dry season it can be busy in the morning, though the 120-person limit is not often reached. It is usually less crowded in the afternoon. The least busy months are May, June, September, October, and November. If you are traveling in the dry season, consider going to the less-crowded Reserva Santa Elena, described later in this chapter.

It's important to remember that the cloud forest is often cloudy and the vegetation is thick. This combination cuts down on sounds as well as visibility.

I have received several letters from readers who have been disappointed with the lack of wildlife sightings in the cloud forest, and they have asked me not to raise people's expectations with enthusiastic descriptions of the fauna. I find the cloud forest exhilarating and mysterious even on those cloudy and stormy days when the forest reveals few of its animal secrets – but I do emphasize that, for many people, the secretive wildlife is a disappointment. If your expectations are not met, I am sorry – but, please, don't blame me for that!

## Information

The information office (☎ 645-5122, 645-5112, fax 645-5034, ⓔ montever@racsa .co.cr, ⓦ www.cct.or.cr/monte_in.htm) and gift store at the entrance of the reserve, and the reserve itself, are open 7am to 4pm daily. Entrance to the reserve costs US$10 per day, or US$5.50 for children over 11 and students with ID. Younger children are admitted free.

You can get information and buy trail guides, bird and mammal lists, and maps here. The gift shop also sells T-shirts, beautiful color slides by Richard Laval, postcards, books, posters, and a variety of other souvenirs.

## Tours & Guides

Although you can hike around the reserve on your own, you'll have a better chance of seeing a quetzal or other wildlife if you hire a guide.

The reserve offers guided natural history tours every morning at 8am, and on busy days at 7:30am and 8:30am as well. Call ☎ 645-5112 the day before to make a reservation. Tours are usually limited to about 10 participants and cost US$15 per person, plus the cost of entrance to the reserve. Participants meet at the Hummingbird Gallery, where a short 10-minute orientation is given, followed by a 30-minute slide show (the slides are by renowned wildlife photographers Michael and Patricia Fogden), followed by a 2½- to three-hour walk. The guides all speak English and are trained naturalists. Once your tour is over, you can return to the reserve on your own, as your ticket is valid for the entire day. Proceeds from the tours benefit environmental-education programs in 16 local schools.

The reserve also offers tours at 7:30pm nightly. These are by flashlight (bring your own for the best visibility) and led by guides who know about nocturnal wildlife. The night tour costs US$13 and lasts 2½ hours; reservations are not required.

Guided birding tours in English are available with one-day advance reservation. Various options are available. A morning tour beginning at Stella's Bakery at 6am usually sights over 40 species. This costs about US$29 per person, including reserve admission, with a minimum of three and maximum of six participants (US$39 per person with two participants). Longer tours go on by request into the afternoon at a higher fee, and usually over 60 species are seen. All-day tours begin at 5:30am with a hotel pickup and visit both the Monteverde reserve and the San Luis Biological Station (described later in this chapter) and include breakfast, lunch, and transportation. The cost is US$55 per person, four minimum and six maximum, including reserve admission. Normally, over 80 species are seen. Profits from all these tours and entrance fees go directly to the reserve.

Most hotels will be able to arrange for a local to guide you either within the reserve or in some of the nearby surrounding areas.

You can also hire a guide for a private tour. Costs vary depending on the season, the guide, and where you want to go, but average about US$30 to US$65 for a half-day tour. Entrance costs may be extra, especially for the cheaper tours. Full-day tours are also available. The size of the group is up to you – go alone or split the cost with a group of friends.

The following guides all work for the reserve and, as such, are recommended. All of them have good general natural history knowledge. They can be contacted through the reserve or personally.

| | |
|---|---|
| Samuel Arguedas | ☎ 645-5554, 387-2926 cellular, ☎/fax 645-5142 |
| Eric or Geovanny Bello | ☎ 645-5291 |
| Gary Diller | ☎ 645-5045 |
| Ricky Guindon | ☎ 645-5085 |
| Melvin Leiton | ☎ 645-5995, 645-5198 |
| Adrian Mendez | ☎ 645-5282 |
| Jorge Quesada | ☎ 645-5546, 645-5543 |
| Danilo Brenes Ramírez | ☎ 645-5483 |
| Sergio Vega | ☎ 645-6054 |
| Mark Wainwright | ☎ 645-5598 |

Other guides are available. Because of the historical Quaker presence, many locals and most guides speak English as well as Spanish.

## Trails & Hiking

Inside the reserve are various marked and maintained trails; a free trail map is provided with your entrance fee. The most popular paths are found in a roughly triangular area ('El Triángulo') to the east of the reserve entrance – these are all suitable for day hikes. There are seven trails, which vary from 200m to 2km one-way. The 1.75km-long **Chomogo Trail** climbs 150m to reach 1680m above sea level, the highest point in the triangle.

Longer trails stretch out east across the reserve and down the Peñas Blancas river valley (it's not connected with the Peñas Blancas refuge) to lowlands north of the Cordillera de Tilarán. Some of these trails enter the Children's Rainforest. These longer trails have shelters (see Places to Stay & Eat, below). Ask at the reserve about hiking through to the northern lowlands.

The bird list includes over 400 species that have been recorded in the area, but the one most visitors want to see is the resplendent quetzal (see the Wildlife Guide at the back of this book). The best time to see the quetzal is when it is nesting in March and April, but you could get lucky anytime of year.

There is a host of other things to observe. A walk along the **Sendero Bosque Nuboso** (Cloud Forest Trail; see the boxed text 'A Hike on the Sendero Bosque Nuboso') will take you on a 2km (one-way) interpretive walk through the cloud forest to the conti-

## A Hike on the Sendero Bosque Nuboso

When I walked this trail, the clouds were low over the forest and the gnarled old oak trees, festooned with vines and bromeliads, looked mysterious and slightly foreboding. Palm trees and bamboos bent menacingly over the trail, and I felt as if I were walking through a Grimm fairy tale – a wicked witch or grinning goblin would not be out of place.

Suddenly the cold, clammy mist was rent by the weirdest metallic *bonk!*, followed by an eerie high-pitched whistle such as I had never heard before. I stopped dead in my tracks.

For a full minute I listened and heard nothing but the sighing of the faintest of breezes and a lone insect circling my ear. Then again, the strange *bonk!* and whistle were repeated, louder and high overhead. I craned my neck and searched the treetops with my binoculars.

Finally, after several more extremely loud *bonk!* sounds and whistles, I spied an odd-looking large brown bird with snow-white head and shoulders just visible on a high snag.

At first, I thought the bird was eating a lizard or small snake – through my binoculars I could clearly see the wormlike objects hanging from the bill. But then the beak gaped wide open and, instead of seeing a reptile wriggling away, I heard another *bonk!* and whistle. Finally, I realized that I was watching the aptly named three-wattled bellbird.

The three black, wormy-looking wattles hanging from the bill were fully 6cm long – about a fifth of the length of the entire bird. The metallic *bonk!* did sound rather bell-like, but it traveled over an incredible distance. It seemed to be flooding the forest with sound, but the bird itself was probably 100m away or more, barely visible in the top of the cloud forest.

nental divide. The US$1.50 trail guide (with numbers matching discrete markers on the trail) describes plants, weather patterns, animal tracks, insects, and ecosystems that you'll see along the way.

## Places to Stay & Eat

Almost all visitors stay in one of the many hotels, pensiones, and lodges in either the Monteverde community or Santa Elena; see details earlier in this chapter. But the reserve also has its own limited accommodations.

Near the park entrance are *dormitory-style accommodations* holding 39 bunks (US$10 per person). These are often used by researchers and student groups but are sometimes available to tourists – call the information office for details. The dorms have shared bathrooms, and full board can be arranged in advance.

Backpackers can stay in one of three basic *shelters* on the reserve. Each has at least 10 bunks (US$3.50 to US$5 per person), drinking water, a shower, electricity, a stove, and cooking utensils. You need to carry a sleeping bag and food. The shelters are about two, three, and six hours' hike (6km, 8km, and 13km) from the entrance along muddy and challenging trails. Each shelter is locked, but you can get a key from the reserve office after making a reservation. Usually, you can head out on the trails the day after making a reservation (your reservation may not be confirmed until fairly late in the day, too late to set out). You'll also have to pay the usual daily entrance fee; the farthest-in shelter costs US$5 per person and has room for 22 people.

There is a small *cafeteria* by the park entrance, open 'til 4pm. It has a small and inexpensive selection of snacks and meals. Otherwise, carry your own lunch on day hikes in the reserve.

## Getting There & Away

The entrance to the reserve is uphill from all the hotels. There are two public buses, leaving Santa Elena at 6am and 1pm, which can be flagged down anywhere along the road. Ask your hotel what time the buses usually pass its doorstep; return trips leave the reserve at noon and 4pm. The one-way fare is about US$1. The better hotels can arrange a vehicle to take you up to the reserve, or you can take your own vehicle

to the small parking lot by the entrance. A taxi from Santa Elena will cost about US$5 to US$6.

You can also walk – look for paths that run parallel to the road. There are views all along the way, and many visitors remark that some of the best birding is on the open road leading up to the reserve entrance, especially the final 2km.

## RESERVA SANTA ELENA

This cloud forest reserve was created in 1989 and opened to the public shortly thereafter. It is now managed by the high-school board and bears the quite unwieldy official name of Reserva del Bosque Nuboso del Colegio Técnico Profesional de Santa Elena (☎/fax 645-5390, e rbnctpse@racsa.co.cr). You can visit the reserve office at the high school.

The reserve provides a welcome alternative to the more visited one in Monteverde. The Reserva Santa Elena is about 6km northeast of the village of Santa Elena. The cloud forest in the reserve is slightly higher than, but otherwise similar to, Monteverde, and you can see quetzals here too – I did. Within an hour or two of hiking from the entrance, you reach lookouts from which you can see Volcán Arenal exploding in the distance – I didn't. I reached the lookouts, but it was too cloudy; the 20m visibility just didn't quite make it. Rule No 407 of cloud forest travel: It's often cloudy.

The Reserva Santa Elena is less visited than Monteverde yet has a good (though not 'concrete blocked') trail system. It offers a good look at the Costa Rican cloud forest, despite lacking the cachet conferred by the Monteverde name.

Over 12km of trails are currently open, and expansion of the reserve is planned. Currently, four circular trails offer walks of varying difficulty and length, from 45 minutes to 3½ hours (1.4km to 4.8km). There is a program of cloud forest study for both local and international students. Projects for volunteers (minimum age 16) are also available, with housing provided, though volunteers must contribute toward food and other expenses. Contact the reserve office in Santa Elena (see above) for information about studying or volunteering. Donations are gladly accepted.

**NORTHWESTERN**

## Information

The reserve is open 7am to 4pm daily. There is an information center at the entrance where you can see a small exhibit, obtain trail maps and information, and pay the entry fee of US$8 (US$4.50 for students with ID). Rubber boots can be rented here; bring your own for a better fit. Guided tours (2½ hours) can be arranged for US$15. These normally leave at 7:30am and 11:30am with two people minimum, six maximum. Night tours leaving at 7pm are available by reservation at the Santa Elena office. Also at the entrance are a small gift shop and a coffee shop. All proceeds go toward managing the reserve and to environmental-education programs in local schools.

## Getting There & Away

The reserve can be reached by bus, by car, or on foot; head north from Santa Elena and follow the signs. Buses leave the Santa Elena Banco Nacional at 6:45am and 11am, returning at 10:30am and 3:30pm. The fare is US$2. A taxi from Santa Elena costs about US$6 each way; at the reserve entrance they can radio for a return taxi. Sky Trek (see the Canopy Tours section, earlier in this chapter) is nearby; following a tour there, you could walk the 2km to this reserve.

## ECOLODGE SAN LUIS & BIOLOGICAL STATION

Formerly just a tropical biology research station, this facility now integrates research with ecotourism and education. It is directed by on-site tropical biologists and has hosted many researchers and university courses. The addition of comfortable accommodations has made this a station to rival better-known places, like La Selva, as a great place to stay for travelers interested in learning about the cloud forest environment and experiencing a bit of traditional rural Costa Rica.

The 70-hectare site is on the Río San Luis and adjoins the southern part of the Monteverde reserve. Its average elevation of 1100m makes it a tad lower and warmer than Monteverde, and birders discover that this is a good place to find species that prefer slightly lower elevations. About 230 species have been recorded in this small protected area, and the list will grow. Many mammals have been sighted as well, and visitors have a good chance of spotting coatis, kinkajous, tayras, sloths, monkeys, and others. There are a number of trails into primary and secondary forest, and there's also a working farm with tropical fruit orchards and a coffee harvest from November to March.

Activities include day and night hikes guided by biologists, horseback rides, excellent birding, farm activities, seminars and slide shows, research and cultural programs, and relaxing by swimming in the river or swinging in a hammock.

## Places to Stay

Reservations can be made at the **Ecolodge San Luis** (☎ 645-5890, 645-5364, ☎/fax 380-3255, ✉ liebermv@racsa.co.cr, ⒲ www.eco lodgesanluis.com). Dorm beds without bath US$58, rooms with bath US$68-97 per person including meals, children 7-13 yrs US$36 with adult. Three types of lodging are available. Near the center's dining room, lecture hall, and library are four bunkhouse rooms with a total of 30 beds and shared segregated bathrooms with hot water. Four rooms nearby have private baths and sleep up to five. Finally, 12 larger cabins (the most expensive) have private hot bath, two double beds, a balcony, and a view from porches overlooking the Río San Luis. These are about 400m from the central area. Rates include three meals a day (tico home cooking served family style), guided hikes, slide shows, and participation in seminars, research activities, etc. Horseback riding costs US$10 an hour. Discounts can be arranged for students, researchers, large groups, and long stays. Ask about the week-long rainforest-ecology course. A minimum of two nights' stay is recommended so you can enjoy at least one full day at the station.

## Getting There & Away

From Santa Elena, take a 4WD taxi or walk down on the dirt road from Monteverde (see the Monteverde & Santa Elena map) for about 3km. If driving from the Interamericana, about 12km before Santa Elena look for an orange bus shelter. Here, a sign points right to San Luis and the ecolodge, approximately 8km away. A full description of the route, and an introduction to Costa Rica and to the area around the lodge, are available on the lodge website.

## JUNTAS

Although marked only as 'Juntas' on some Costa Rican maps, the full name of this town is Las Juntas de Abangares. This small town on the Río Abangares used to be a major gold-mining center in the late 19th and early 20th centuries, attracting fortune seekers and entrepreneurs from all over the world. The gold boom is now over, but a museum opened in 1991 and a small tourist industry is beginning in this sleepy Costa Rican town. It makes an interesting side trip for travelers wishing to get away from the tourist hordes.

Five kilometers beyond Juntas is **Ecomuseo de las Minas de Abangares** *(admission US$1.50; open 7am-3pm Tues-Fri, 7am-5pm Sat, Sun & holidays)*. This small museum has a few photographs and models depicting the old mining practices of the area. On the grounds outside the museum are a picnic area and children's play area; trails above the museum lead to mine artifacts, such as bits of railway. There's good birding along these trails – it's very quiet here and the birds are rarely disturbed. The area is several hundred meters above the coastal lowlands and attracts some different species.

### Places to Stay & Eat

*Cabinas Las Juntas* (☎ 662-0153) Rooms with cold bath US$6 per person, doubles with hot bath US$20. All rooms are airconditioned, and the more expensive doubles have TVs.

*Hospedaje El Encanto* (☎/fax 662-1016) US$7.50 per person. This place has a small restaurant-bar and a pool, which attracts locals on weekends. It's 75m behind El Caballo Blanco. Fourteen basic rooms offer fans and private cold showers.

There are several other places to eat – try the *Soda La Amiga* by the bus terminal and the restaurant on the Parque Central.

On the way out of town toward the museum, you pass the ramshackle *El Caballo Blanco* bar, which is an interesting place full of mining artifacts and colorful characters.

### Getting There & Away

**Bus** There are buses from Cañas to Juntas at 9:30am and 2:50pm. There are also buses from the Puntarenas terminal in San José at 11am and 5pm. From Santa Elena, there is a

bus at 5am. There are no buses to the Ecomuseo, though 4WD taxis can be hired to take you there.

Buses leave Juntas for San José at 6am and 11am, for Cañas at 6:30am and 12:30pm, and for Monteverde and Santa Elena at 2:30pm.

**Car** The turnoff from the Interamericana is 27km south of Cañas and is reasonably well signed: 'Las Juntas 6km, Ecomuseo 11km.' (There is a locally popular restaurant called *La Irma* at this intersection.) The road is paved through Juntas and a few kilometers beyond. To get to the Ecomuseo, follow the paved road for 100m past the Parque Central, turn left, cross a bridge and pass the Caballo Blanco on your left, then turn right; you'll see a sign indicating 'Ecomuseo 4km.' A couple of kilometers past Juntas, the road forks – a sign indicates a road going left to Monteverde (30km), rarely used by tourists but passable with 4WD (the first few kilometers are paved), and to the right to the Ecomuseo (3km). In the small community of La Sierra, the road forks – take the right fork to the museum.

### TEMPISQUE FERRY

About 23km south of Cañas on the Interamericana is a turnoff to the Tempisque ferry, 25km to the west. Drivers heading from San José to the Península de Nicoya will save some 110km of driving by taking this ferry as compared to driving through Liberia. Some buses from San José to the Península de Nicoya beaches come this way – ask about the route in the San José bus offices. Note that bus passengers must get off, buy a passenger ferry ticket, and board the ferry on foot – don't miss the boat, because the bus won't wait.

The ferry runs every hour from 5am to 8pm (westbound) and 5:30am to 8:30pm (eastbound). The crossing takes 20 minutes and costs US$3 per car and US25¢ for foot passengers. Drivers may have to wait for the next ferry at peak times, especially Sunday afternoons returning to the mainland.

A bridge is being built north of here – it is projected to open in late 2002.

### CAÑAS

This small agricultural center serves about 30,000 people in the surrounding area. If you're coming from the south, this is the first town of any size in Costa Rica's driest and dustiest province, Guanacaste, known for its cattle ranches and folk dances. You'll see an occasional cowboy hat and swagger on the streets of this little town. It's 90m above sea level (hot!) and about 180km from San José along the Interamericana. There is a small MINAE/ACT office (☎/fax 669-0533, 669-2200) here that has limited information about nearby national parks and reserves. Cañas is also the beginning or end point for the Arenal backroads route, described later in this chapter.

Internet Ciberc@ñas is open 8am to 9pm Monday to Saturday, 2pm to 9pm Sunday. Rates are US$1.50 per hour.

## Things to See & Do

There is not much to do in Cañas itself, but travelers use it as a base for visits to the nearby Parque Nacional Palo Verde and other reserves, the Ecomuseo in Juntas, and for Corobicí River trips.

**Church** While in town, stroll over to the Parque Central, where the modern church is distinguished by huge colorful mosaic murals decorating the outside. It's unique in Costa Rica.

**River Trips** The nearby Río Corobicí offers gentle rafting trips.

**Safaris Corobicí** (☎/fax 669-6091, ℮ safaris@racsa.co.cr, ⓦ www.nicoya.com) books raft trips from its office on the Inter-

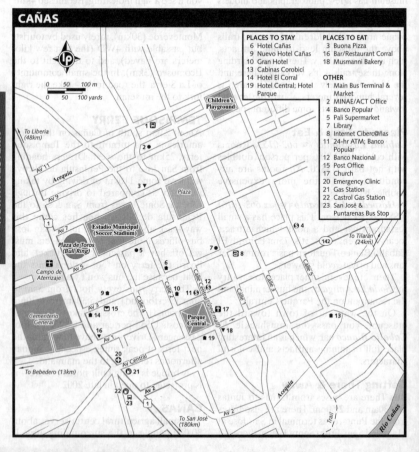

**CAÑAS**

| PLACES TO STAY | PLACES TO EAT |
|---|---|
| 6 Hotel Cañas | 3 Buona Pizza |
| 9 Nuevo Hotel Cañas | 16 Bar/Restaurant Corral |
| 10 Gran Hotel | 18 Musmanni Bakery |
| 13 Cabinas Corobicí | |
| 14 Hotel El Corral | **OTHER** |
| 19 Hotel Central; Hotel Parque | 1 Main Bus Terminal & Market |
| | 2 MINAE/ACT Office |
| | 4 Banco Popular |
| | 5 Pali Supermarket |
| | 7 Library |
| | 8 Internet Ciberc@ñas |
| | 11 24-hr ATM; Banco Popular |
| | 12 Banco Nacional |
| | 15 Post Office |
| | 17 Church |
| | 20 Emergency Clinic |
| | 21 Gas Station |
| | 22 Castrol Gas Station |
| | 23 San José & Puntarenas Bus Stop |

0    50    100 m
0    50    100 yards

To Liberia (48km)

Av 11
Acequia
Av 9

Children's Playground

Plaza

Estadio Municipal (Soccer Stadium)
Av 7

Plaza de Toros (Bull Ring)
Campo de Aterrizaje
Av 5

Cementerio General

Av 3
Av 1

Parque Central

To Bebedero (13km)

Av Central

Av 2
Av 2

To San José (180m)

To Tilarán (24km)
142

Río Cañas
Trail
Acequia
Calle Central (main)
Calle 2
Calle 3
Calle 5

americana about 4.5km north of Cañas. The emphasis of these trips is wildlife observation rather than exciting white water. The river is Class I to II – in other words, pretty flat – but families and nature-lovers enjoy these trips. Swimming holes are found along the river.

Safaris Corobicí offers departures on the Río Corobicí from 7am to 3pm daily. A two-hour float costs US$37 per person, a three-hour birding float covering 12km costs US$45 per person, and a half-day 18km float including lunch costs US$60 per person. All prices are based on a two-person minimum; children under 14 accompanying adults receive a 50% discount, and large groups can ask for a better rate, depending on group size.

**Las Pumas** Safaris Corobicí also has access to Las Pumas, a wild-animal shelter directly behind its office. Started in the 1960s by Lilly Hagnauer, a Swiss woman, it is said to be the largest shelter of its kind in Latin America. The emphasis, as the name suggests, is on cats – you may get to see pumas, jaguars, ocelots, and margays, plus peccaries and a few birds. The animals were either orphaned or injured, and it has clearly been a labor of love to save and raise them. Although the cages aren't large, the animals are well looked after and are certainly much better off than if they'd been left to die. Unfortunately, Lilly herself died in 2001, and now Safaris Corobicí is running Las Pumas. Admission is by donation; Las Pumas is not officially funded and contributions help offset the high costs of maintaining the shelter.

**Refugio de Vida Silvestre Cipanci** New in 2001, this small wildlife refuge is at the confluence of the Ríos Tempisque and Bebedero, at the south end of Parque Nacional Palo Verde. Local fishers have a 20-passenger boat available for tours on these two rivers. A three-hour guided tour costs US$20 per person (US$140 minimum). Further information is available from the MINAE/ACT office in Cañas, or from boat captain Oscar Gutiérrez Fernández (☎ 661-8106, leave a message). The boat leaves from the Níspero dock, just north of the Tempisque Ferry and reached by that road.

## Places to Stay

Cañas is a cheaper place to stay than Liberia, which may be why so many long-haul truck drivers spend the night here. Get in by midafternoon for the best choice of rooms.

Two basic but adequate hotels on the southeastern side of the Parque Central are the **Hotel Central** (☎ 669-0070) and the grottier **Hotel Parque**, both with balconies overlooking the park, cold shared showers, and rates of about US$3.50 per person. The Central also has four rooms with private bath for US$6/11 singles/doubles.

**Gran Hotel** *(no phone)* On the northwestern side of the park, this rundown cold-water flophouse offers basic rooms for US$4.50 per person, or doubles with private bath for US$11.

**Cabinas Corobicí** *(☎ 669-0241, Avenida 2 near Calle 5)* Rooms with cold shower US$7 per person. At the southeastern end of town, this is a better budget option.

**Hotel Cañas** *(☎/fax 669-0039, ⓔ hotel canas@racsa.co.cr, Calle 2 & Avenida 3)* Singles/doubles with cold bath & fan US$14/21, or with air-conditioning & TV US$21/30. The best-established place in downtown Cañas, this hotel has simple rooms and a good *restaurant*. It's very popular – the air-conditioned rooms go fast.

**Nuevo Hotel Cañas** *(☎ 669-5118, 669-5511, fax 669-1319, ⓔ hotelcanas@racsa .co.cr)* Rooms US$25/40. A block away from Hotel Cañas, this hotel takes Cañas' overflow. It has 20 newer air-conditioned rooms with cable TV and hot showers. There's a pool and Jacuzzi (available to nonguests for a small fee).

**Hotel El Corral** *(☎ 669-1467, 669-0622, fax 669-1722)* Rooms with bath & air-con US$15-30 per person. Right on the Interamericana, this is the most expensive place in town and has 28 plain rooms. About 20 have cable TV and only three have hot water. There is a cheap restaurant.

**Hotel Capazuri** *(☎ 669-6280, 399-8363 cellular, fax 669-0580, ⓔ capazuri@racsa.co.cr)* Campsites US$3 per person, singles/doubles with bath US$25/44. This place is 3km northwest of Cañas on the Interamericana. The 18 rooms have fans, TVs, and private showers, and rates include a full breakfast. The spacious grounds have a pool and offer many shade trees and hammocks.

## Places to Eat

**Hotel Cañas** Meals US$2-5. Open 6am-9:30pm daily. The hotel restaurant is good;

its breakfast attracts some of the town's important people to sit around and plan the day's events.

**Bar/Restaurant Corral** (☎ 669-0367) Sandwiches & meals US$2-5. Open 6am-10pm daily. In the Hotel Corral, this restaurant sells pizzas, as well as casados and other meals. There's also **Buona Pizza**, near the stadium on Avenida 7.

Around and near the park are some typical *sodas* as well as a few unremarkable *Chinese restaurants* with adequate meals in the US$2 to US$5 range. The **Musmanni Bakery** provides baked goods from 5am to 9pm daily.

**Hotel Capazuri** Snacks & meals US$2-4. Open 6am-9pm daily. On weekends, this spacious, simple restaurant attracts locals who enjoy using the hotel pool.

**Hacienda La Pacífica** (☎ 669-6050, 669-6055). Dishes US$7-12. Open 7am-9pm daily. Once a working hacienda, nature reserve, and elegant country hotel 5km north of Cañas on the Interamericana, La Pacífica is now a private hotel for researchers. Their elegant, spacious, and plant-filled international restaurant remains open to the public and is the most upscale eatery in the Cañas area.

**Rincón Corobicí** (☎ 669-1234, 669-0303, fax 669-2121) Snacks US$2, dishes US$5-9. Open 8am-7pm daily (after 7pm with advance notice). This attractive Swiss-run restaurant, affiliated with Safaris Corobicí, provides travelers with a welcome break from the highway; it's on the Interamericana, 5.5km north of Cañas on the banks of the Río Corobicí. A terrace provides pretty river and garden views, and a short trail follows the river bank (people swim off the rocks). English, French, and German are spoken.

## Getting There & Away

Buses for Cañas leave San José six times a day from Calle 16, Avenidas 1 & 3, opposite the Coca-Cola terminal. There are also TRALAPA buses from Calle 20 & Avenida 3. The trip takes about 3½ hours and costs about US$2.50.

Cañas has two bus stops. The main bus terminal is at Calle 1 & Avenida 11 – most buses leave from here. In addition, many San José- and Puntarenas-bound buses can be flagged down outside the Castrol gas station (see map). Call Transportes La Cañera (☎ 669-0145) for departure times.

The terminal has about seven daily buses to Liberia, seven to Tilarán, two to Juntas (at 9am and 2pm, but this may change, so check), six to Bebedero (near Parque Nacional Palo Verde), seven to Upala, and seven to Puntarenas. Not all buses originate in Cañas – many just stop here, such as the Liberia-Cañas-Puntarenas bus. Ask whether it would be faster to wait on the highway for these buses.

## VOLCÁN TENORIO AREA

The 58km paved highway to Upala goes north from the Interamericana about 6km northwest of Cañas. This road passes in between Volcán Miravalles (2028m) to the west (see below) and Volcán Tenorio (1916m) to the east. Tenorio is an active volcano, though activity is limited to fumaroles, hot springs, and mud pots, with none of the spectacular activity of Volcán Arenal.

Tenorio is part of **Parque Nacional Volcán Tenorio** (☎/fax 466-8610), one of Costa Rica's newest national parks and part of the Area de Conservación Arenal (ACA). Services at this park are pretty rudimentary as of this writing. The park boasts five life zones, and the virgin forests near the volcano's summit are the haunts of tapirs and pumas. At the summit is a small lake surrounded by epiphyte-laden cloud forests. On the northeastern flanks of the volcano, the **Río Celeste**, notable for the blue created by many minerals dissolved in its waters, is a famous though infrequently visited scenic attraction. Its thermal headwaters contain springs and boiling mud pots – take great care not to scald yourself when you're exploring the area. Because of these dangers, it's recommended that you go with a guide. A locally recommended guide is Pedro Alvarado; he works as a park ranger and can be contacted through Cabinas Tío Henry in Guatuso (see the Northern Lowlands chapter). He can take climbers to the volcano's summit, which is normally a two-day trip. Alternately, the lodges mentioned below can arrange tours.

About 33km north of the Interamericana and 25km south of Upala is the community of **Bijagua**. Here you'll find the **Heliconia Ecotourist Lodge** (☎ 259-3605 reservations, ☎ 286-4203, 466-8483, fax 259-

9430, e cooprena@racsa.co.cr) Singles/doubles/triples US$35/45/55. This lodge, sponsored by the Canadian WWF and ACA and operated by an association of local families, is 3km east of Bijagua on a bumpy, unpaved road. Surrounding the lodge are a few trails, including a short walk to a canopy platform that gives a bird's-eye view of the rainforest and valley. Guests can visit local farms or go on locally guided hikes and horseback rides to waterfalls, hot springs, and rivers in Parque Nacional Volcán Tenorio. Tours cost US$10 to US$25 per person. The adventurous can get information about where to hike and camp on the volcano without guides.

The lodge has six simple, comfortable cabins with private hot showers. A *restaurant* with sweeping views of the valley, Volcán Miravalles, and (on a clear day) Lago de Nicaragua serves breakfast (US$2) and other meals (US$5). If you speak Spanish, you can leave a message at the public phone near the lodge (☎ 470-0622) or ask if the lodge's direct line has been installed. The signed turnoff to the lodge is by Bijagua's Banco Nacional, where you can change money.

*La Carolina Lodge* (☎ 380-1656, e info@lacarolinalodge.com, w www.lacarolinalodge.com) Room & board US$75 per person. Six kilometers north of Bijagua, a sign points east to this lodge, about 7km east of the highway toward the village of San Miguel. A taxi from Bijagua costs about US$12. This is a rustic country farm offering double rooms, a dorm, and shared bathrooms with hot showers. Horseback and hiking tours onto neighboring Volcán Tenorio are offered, and other tours may also be available. Rates include a bed, three home-cooked meals, a guided horseback ride, and a guided hike. They can get you up to see Río Celeste. Recommendations have been received about this place, and some folks spend a week (ask for long-stay discounts).

## VOLCÁN MIRAVALLES AREA

Volcán Miravalles (2028m) is the highest volcano in the Cordillera de Guanacaste. It's afforded a modicum of protection by being within the Zona Protectora Miravalles. Although the main crater is dormant, there is some geothermal activity at Las Hornillas (a few bubbling mud pools and steam vents), at about 700m above sea level on the south slopes of the volcano.

Volcán Miravalles is 27km north-northeast of Bagaces and can be approached by a paved road that leads north of Bagaces through the communities of Salitral, La Ese, Guayabo, and on to Aguas Claras. A parallel paved road to the east avoids La Ese and Guayabo – instead, it goes through Salitral and then the community of La Fortuna before rejoining the first road just north of Guayabo. The road beyond Aguas Claras is a rough one continuing to Upala. North of La Fortuna is the government-run Proyecto Geotérmico Miravalles, a project (open for visits) that generates electrical power from geothermal energy. A few bright steel tubes from the plant snake along the flanks of the volcano, adding an eerie touch to the remote landscape. There are small signs for both the project and Las Hornillas along the road. There are no guardrails around the vents and mud pools – stay away from their edges, which occasionally collapse. Four kilometers north of the plant is **Yoko Hot Springs** (admission US$4), a small locally owned resort where you can buy a drink and relax in the thermal waters. Call the Miravalles Lodge (see below) to ask about opening hours.

The village of **Guayabo** is about 30km north of Bagaces in the saddle between Parque Nacional Rincón de la Vieja and Volcán Miravalles. In the village are a couple of *sodas*; if you ask around, you could probably find somewhere to stay in someone's home.

*Cabinas Las Brisas* (☎ 673-0333) Singles/doubles US$8/14. A couple of kilometers north of Guayabo is this place, run by Armando Rodríguez, who cooks up good, simple Cuban cuisine and offers basic rooms with hot showers.

*Miravalles Lodge* (☎ 673-0823, fax 673-0350, e volctour@racsa.co.cr, w www.costa-rica-volcano-adventures.com) Doubles with bath US$45. About 5km farther north is this attractive lodge where the rooms feature high ceilings, wood paneling, air-conditioning, and great views of the volcano. There is a spacious restaurant-bar and a swimming pool, tours are available, and the owners speak English. A short path leads from the lodge through a neighbor's farm to a small hot spring in a cool brook; there are other trails nearby. Dan Stasiuk, Canadian foreman of a nearby cattle ranch, can be contacted through the lodge for horse tours; he is a friendly, experienced horseman whose enthusiasm and respect for Guanacaste culture make him an enjoyable guide.

In La Fortuna, near the soccer field, is the basic, friendly *Cabinas Jesse*, with small rooms for about US$3 per person.

A daily bus goes from Liberia to Aguas Claras, leaving at 1:30pm; from Bagaces, there are four buses a day for Aguas Claras, which can drop you near any of the places to stay described above. Several buses a day go from Bagaces through La Fortuna and can drop you at the power plant or hot springs.

## BAGACES

This small town is about 22km northwest of Cañas on the Interamericana. The main reason to stop here is to visit the national park and reserve offices.

The headquarters of the Area de Conservación Tempisque (ACT; ☎ 671-1290, 671-1455, ☎/fax 671-1062), which administers Parque Nacional Palo Verde, Reserva Biológica Lomas de Barbudal, and several smaller and less-known protected areas, is in Bagaces on the Interamericana opposite the main entry road into Parque Nacional Palo Verde (which is signed). The office is mainly an administrative one, though sometimes rangers are available. The staff is friendly and will try to help – you can ask them to call Palo Verde to get information directly from the rangers. Office hours are 8am to 4pm weekdays.

### Places to Stay & Eat

There aren't many places to stay in this small town.

*Albergue Bagaces* (☎ 671-1267, fax 666-2021) Singles/doubles US$12/20. This is the best place in town, on the Interamericana opposite the ACT office. Rooms are clean and have fans and private bath. The town's best *restaurant* is also here, open 9am to 10pm (though sometimes it shuts down for the day if business is slow). There's a good, cheap roadside *soda* by the gas station. There are a couple of cheap and basic *pensiones* in town; ask around to see which one is currently the best maintained.

### Getting There & Away

The bus terminal here is a block north of the village park; ask for directions from the highway. Most buses going to Liberia or Cañas can drop you on the Interamericana at the entrance to town. Everything is within a few blocks of the highway. See the Volcán Miravalles Area section (above) for information on buses from Bagaces to that area.

## PARQUE NACIONAL PALO VERDE

The 18,417-hectare Parque Nacional Palo Verde lies on the northeastern banks of the mouth of Río Tempisque at the head of the Golfo de Nicoya, some 30km west of Cañas and 30km south of Bagaces. It's a major sanctuary for resident and migrating waterfowl as well as forest birds. A large number of different habitats are represented, ranging from mangrove swamps, marshes, and lagoons to a variety of seasonal grasslands and forests. Some 150 tree species have been recorded in the park. A number of low limestone hills provide lookout points over the park. The dry season, from December to March, is very marked, and much of the forest dries out. During the wet months, large portions of the area are flooded.

Palo Verde is a magnet for birders, who come to see the large flocks of herons (including the country's largest nesting colony of black-crowned night herons, on Isla de Los Pájaros), storks (including the only Costa Rican nesting site of the locally endangered jabiru stork), spoonbills, egrets, ibis, grebes, and ducks. Inland, birds such as scarlet macaws, great curassows, keel-billed toucans, and parrots may be seen. Approximately 300 bird species have been recorded in the park. Other possible sightings include crocodiles (reportedly up to 5m in length), iguanas, deer, coatis, monkeys, and peccaries.

The recommended time for a visit is September to March because of the huge influx of migratory and endemic birds. This is one of the greatest concentrations of waterfowl and shorebirds in Central America. December to February are the best months. September and October are very wet, and access may be limited. When the dry season begins, the birds tend to congregate in the remaining lakes and marshes. Trees lose their leaves and the massed flocks of birds become easier to observe. In addition, there are far fewer insects in the dry season, the roads and trails are more passable, and mammals are seen around the water holes. Take binoculars or a spotting scope if possible.

## Information

Admission to the park is US$6 a day, which you pay at the park entrance. Optional guided half-/full-day visits are available for US$15/30 adults, US$10/20 children; make reservations through the Hacienda Palo Verde Research Station (see Places to Stay & Eat, below).

The research station is 8km from the park entrance; several trails lead from the station area into the national park. There is also an observation tower in the area. A couple of kilometers farther into the park, you will reach the park headquarters and ranger station.

The ACT office in Bagaces can be contacted for information about the park (see Bagaces, above), but the research station is the best source of information.

## Places to Stay & Eat

Both the research station and ranger station provide accommodations and food that should be reserved in advance. Overnight and day visitors alike must pay the US$6 park fee in addition to the rates given below.

**Hacienda Palo Verde Research Station** (☎ 240-6696, fax 240-6783, ⓔ reservas@ ns.ots.ac.cr, ⓦ www.ots.ac.cr) Singles/doubles US$55/100 adults; discounts for students & children. The research station is run by the Organization of Tropical Studies (OTS), which conducts tropical research and teaches university graduate-level classes. Researchers and those taking OTS courses get preference for accommodations, which are mostly in dormitory rooms with shared bathrooms. A few two- and four-bed rooms with shared bathrooms are also available. Rates include three meals, which are US$7 each for day visitors.

**Palo Verde Ranger Station** (call ACT, in Bagaces, for information about the ranger station or to pass on a message to rangers) Rooms US$15 per person. Fans, mosquito nets, and showers are provided in six rooms, each with six beds. These may be occupied by tico student groups, so call ahead. Meals are available here for about US$6, preferably by advance arrangement.

**Camping** Campsites US$2 per person. Camping is permitted near the Palo Verde ranger station, where toilets and shower facilities are available to campers.

## Getting There & Away

There are several routes into the park, but it's difficult to get there unless you have your own transportation, are on a tour, hire a taxi, or walk. If you call in advance, park rangers may be able to pick you up in Bagaces; try the ACT office in Bagaces (see above).

The most frequently used route begins in Bagaces, where there is a signed turnoff from the Interamericana. From here, follow signs for the national park. At times, the graveled road forks – if in doubt, take the fork that looks more used. If you can't decide which is the main fork, take the road that has a power line running along it. After about 28km, you reach the park entrance station, where you pay admission fees. Another 8km brings you to the limestone hill, Cerro Guayacán, from which there are good views of the park. This is where the OTS research station is found; a couple of kilometers farther are the Palo Verde park headquarters and ranger station.

The road is supposedly passable to ordinary cars year-round, but get up-to-date information if you are traveling in the rainy season. Note that the road from the Interamericana to Reserva Biológica Lomas de Barbudal, which skirts the edge of the reserve, eventually joins the Bagaces–Palo Verde road near the park entrance. Therefore, both these areas can be visited without having to return to the Interamericana.

Boats go into the park via the Cipanci refuge (see Cañas, earlier). Major tour companies in San José also offer tours, but they're not cheap.

## RESERVA BIOLÓGICA LOMAS DE BARBUDAL

The 2646-hectare Lomas de Barbudal reserve is separated from the northern edge of Palo Verde by a narrow strip of privately owned land. About 70% of the area is deciduous forest that contains several species of endangered trees, such as mahogany and rosewood, as well as the common and quite spectacular *Tabebuia ochracea* (it's locally called the *corteza amarilla* or yellow cortez). This tree is what biologists call a 'big bang reproducer' – all the yellow cortezes in the forest burst into bloom on the same day, and for about four days the forest is an incredible mass of yellow-flowered trees. This usually occurs late in the dry season, about four days after an unseasonal rain shower.

During the dry season, many of the trees shed their leaves just as they do in autumn in temperate lands. This kind of forest, known as tropical dry forest, was once common in many parts of the Pacific slopes of Central America, but very little of it now remains. In addition to tropical dry forests, there are riparian forests along the Río Cabuyo (which flows through the reserve year-round) and small areas of other types of forest.

Lomas de Barbudal is also locally famous for its abundant and varied insects. There are about 250 different species of bee in this fairly small reserve – this represents about a quarter of the world's bee species. Bees here (and in nearby Palo Verde) include the Africanized 'killer' bees – if you suffer from bee allergies, this is one area where you really don't want to forget your bee-sting kit. Wasps, butterflies, and moths are also locally abundant.

There are well over 200 bird species, including the great curassow, a chickenlike bird that is hunted for food and is endangered. Other endangered species found locally are the king vulture, scarlet macaw, and jabiru stork. Mammals you may see include white-tailed deer, peccaries, coatis, and howler and white-faced monkeys.

## Orientation & Information

At the reserve entrance, there's a small local museum and information center. The actual reserve is on the other side of the Río Cabuyo, behind the museum, but the river is not passable to vehicles, so you have to wade across at this point. Alternatively, you can drive to the right toward San Ramón de Bagaces (2km) and continue along the edge of the reserve by vehicle, making short incursions at various points. It's difficult to drive into the reserve because of the river, but hikes are certainly possible. This road eventually joins up with the road between Bagaces and Palo Verde.

The biological reserve is administered by MINAE and is part of the ACT; information can be obtained from the ACT office in Bagaces.

Depending on whom you talk to, entrance to the reserve is by donation or free or costs

US$1 or US$6. Camping is allowed. The dry season is from December to April, and it can get very hot then – temperatures of 38°C (100°F) are sometimes reached. During the rainy season it is a little cooler, but insects are more abundant; bring repellent.

## Getting There & Away

The turnoff to Lomas de Barbudal from the Interamericana is near the small community of Pijije, 14km southeast of Liberia or 12km northwest of Bagaces. The road to the reserve is signed – it says '6km,' but it's actually just over 7km to the entrance to the reserve. The road is unpaved but open all year – some steep sections may require 4WD during and after heavy rains. Even during the dry season, it's barely passable to cars.

## LIBERIA

This is Costa Rica's most northerly town of any importance. It's the capital of the province of Guanacaste but has a population of only 40,000. This is an indication of how rural most of Costa Rica is once you leave the Central Valley.

The city is 140m above sea level and surrounded by ranches, making it a center for the cattle industry. It's also a fairly important transportation center, lying on the Interamericana at the intersection with the road to the west, which is the main entry route into the Península de Nicoya. Liberia is also a good base for visiting Parques Nacionales Santa Rosa, Guanacaste, and Rincón de la Vieja, all to the north, as well as Parque Nacional Palo Verde and Reserva Biológica Lomas de Barbudal to the south.

## Orientation & Information

Note that though streets are labeled on the map, very few of them are signed, especially once you get away from Parque Central.

There is a tourist information office (☎ 665-0135) in a historic mid-19th-century house at the corner of Avenida 6 and Calle 1. (The office may be moving to La Gobernación, by the Parque Central, in 2003.) It's open from 8am to noon and from 1:30pm or 2pm to 5pm. The staff is helpful with local details about hotels, bus schedules, national parks information, etc, and has a large-scale map for reference. It helps if you speak Spanish.

# LIBERIA

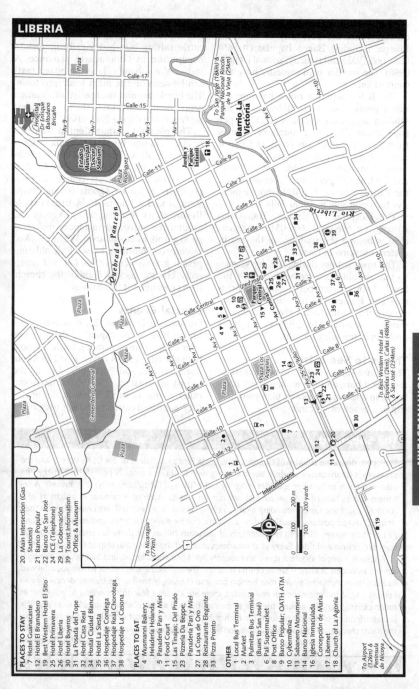

**PLACES TO STAY**
7   Hotel Guanacaste
12  Hotel El Bramadero
19  Best Western Hotel El Sitio
25  Hotel Primavera
26  Hotel Liberia
30  Hotel Boyeros
31  La Posada del Tope
32  Hotel Casa Real
34  Hostal Ciudad Blanca
35  Hotel La Siesta
36  Hospedaje Condega
37  Hospedaje Real Chorotega
38  Hospedaje La Casona

**PLACES TO EAT**
4   Musmanni Bakery;
    Heladería Holanda
5   Panadería Pan y Miel
11  Food Court
15  Las Tinajas; Del Prado
23  Pizzeria Da Beppe;
    Panadería Pan y Miel
27  La Copa de Oro
28  Restaurante Elegante
33  Pizza Pronto

**OTHER**
1   Local Bus Terminal
2   Market
3   Pulmitan Bus Terminal
    (Buses to San José)
6   Pali Supermarket
9   Post Office
10  Banco Popular; OATH ATM
10  Cybermanía
13  Sabanero Monument
14  Banco Nacional
16  Iglesia Inmaculada
    Concepción de María
17  Libernet
18  Church of La Agonía
20  Main Intersection (Gas
    Stations)
21  Banco Popular
22  Banco de San José
24  ICE (Telephone)
29  La Gobernación
39  Tourist Information
    Office & Museum

**NORTHWESTERN**

Most of the better hotels will accept US dollars. There are currently 13 banks in Liberia, including Banco Popular (☎ 666-0158, 666-1932) and Banco Nacional (☎ 666-0996). The smaller banks usually have the shortest lines.

The ICE telephone office has international phone and fax facilities – you can send an urgent fax overseas (US$1.20 per page to the USA) in a couple of minutes from here. Libernet, on Avenida Central east of Parque Central, provides Internet access from 8am to 9pm Monday to Saturday, for US$1.50 per hour. Cyberm@nia, on the Parque Central, is a little more expensive but open 8am to 10pm daily.

The Hospital Dr Enrique Baltodano Briceño (☎ 666-0011, 666-0318 emergencies) is behind the stadium on the northeastern outskirts of town.

The town is busy during the dry season, so you should make reservations for the hotel of your choice, particularly at Christmas and Easter and on weekends. Conversely, the better hotels give discounts in the wet season. Mosquitoes can be a problem in the rainy months.

### Things to See & Do

There are a number of good hotels, restaurants, and bars, and the main activity is relaxing in one of them as you plan your next trip to a beach or volcano.

The tourist information center has a tiny **museum** of local ranching artifacts – cattle raising is a historically important occupation in Guanacaste province. A statue of a *sabanero* (see the boxed text) can be seen on the main road into town. The blocks around the tourist information center contain several of the town's oldest houses, many dating back about 150 years.

The pleasant **Parque Central** frames a modern church, Iglesia Inmaculada Concepción de María. Walking six blocks northeast of the park along Avenida Central brings you to the oldest church in town, popularly called **La Agonía** (though maps show it as La Iglesia de la Ermita de la Resurrección). Strolling to La Agonía and around the surrounding blocks makes as good a walk as any in town. When I walked by early one morning, I saw a little old campesino gravely remove his hat and reverently kiss the locked door of the church, then cross himself three times.

### Special Events

Guanacaste Day, July 25, is actively celebrated here in the capital of the province with a *tope* (horse parade), cattle auction, bullfight (the bull is never killed in Costa Rica), music, and rural fair. Ask at the tourist information office about topes and other events in small towns in the area – they happen frequently though irregularly.

### The Sabanero

The open, dry cattle country of Guanacaste is Costa Rica's equivalent of the USA's West – and the *sabanero* is Guanacaste's cowboy. But in keeping with Costa Rica's mainly peaceful self-image, the sabanero tends to be a figure of steely dignity rather than of fist-fighting rambunctiousness. A sabanero carries himself with an air that will remind you as much of a samurai or knight as of a cowboy. You'll see sabaneros riding along roads in Guanacaste, and will recognize them by their straight-backed posture, casual hand on the reins, holster-slung machetes, and the high-stepping gait of their horses. This gait is a signature of sabanero culture – it demands endurance and skill from both horse and rider. Every year sabaneros show off their horsemanship at the local *tope*.

A tope is a mix of Western rodeo and country fair. Food stalls, music, and bull-riding – the bulls are not wounded or killed – are all central features. The bull-riding spectacle is where violent wild oats are sown. A macho young man turning pale and crossing himself as the bullring door is thrown open is a sight to remember. For comic relief, there are always a few drunks willing to volunteer as rodeo clowns, dancing around the ring to distract the bull as fallen riders scramble to safety. The horseback riding of the sabaneros is the high point of the day. Almost every little town has a tope; the dates change, so ask locally in any region you're visiting about when the next one will be held.

– John Thompson

## Places to Stay

**Budget** Cheap and basic places to try in the US$3 to US$4 range include *Hospedaje Real Chorotega* (☎ 666-0898) and *Hospedaje Condega* (☎ 666-1165).

*La Posada del Tope* (☎/fax 666-3876, e hottope@racsa.co.cr) Rooms US$5-6 per person. This is a mid-19th-century house with an attractive front and lobby. Six basic but clean rooms with fans share one shower. The staff is friendly and guests can use the kitchen. There is a private parking area, and tourist information is available. English is spoken, and inexpensive transport to Rincón de la Vieja can be arranged. Opposite is the *Hotel Casa Real*, under the same ownership. Here, 10 rooms have shared baths and four rooms have private cold showers and TV. There is a small courtyard, and they plan to open an outdoor café for guests of both hotels. This is a good budget-traveler choice.

*Hospedaje La Casona* (☎/fax 666-2971) Rooms US$5 per person. La Casona offers seven basic rooms with fans. The rooms share three bathrooms, and there's a TV lounge.

*Hotel Liberia* (☎/fax 666-0161, e maicero@racsa.co.cr) Singles/doubles without bath US$8/12, with cold bath US$12/22. This solid-looking turn-of-the-20th-century house just south of the park holds basic and rather dark little rooms with fans. A 20% discount is offered to holders of ISIC international student cards.

*Hotel Guanacaste* (☎ 666-0085, fax 666-2287, e htlguana@racsa.co.cr, Avenida 3) Singles/doubles/triples with shower US$15/28/39. This hotel is affiliated with Hostelling International and has a small dorm for HI members for US$8 per person. A few of the 30 rooms are air-conditioned, but it's otherwise quite basic. A restaurant with outdoor patio is attached. This is a stopping place and agency for Nicabus (☎ 666-0085) with buses to Managua. The hotel is a block off the Interamericana and popular with Costa Rican truck drivers and families, so it's often full. Check in early for the best rooms. Internet access is available to guests. The hotel has a guarded parking lot and a laundry. It will change US dollars and can arrange numerous tours all over the region.

**Mid-Range** The Tica Bus agency is at the *Hotel El Bramadero* (☎ 666-0371, fax 666-

0203, e bramdero@racsa.co.cr) Singles/doubles/triples US$29/37/43. This hotel is near the intersection of the Interamericana and the main road into town (Avenida Central). Plain, clean rooms have private bath, cable TV, and air-conditioning. There is an adequate restaurant (open 6am to 10pm) and swimming pool.

*Hotel Primavera* (☎ 666-0464, fax 666-2271) Singles/doubles US$20/26. On the Parque Central, this hotel has 30 clean and modern rooms with TV, fans, private cold baths, and parking. Rates are slightly more for air-conditioning if the hotel is full.

*Hotel La Siesta* (☎ 666-0678, 666-2950, fax 666-2532, e ropeflo@hotmail.com, Calle 4, Avenidas 4 & 6) Singles/doubles with cold bath & air-con US$25/38, including breakfast. On a quiet street, this place is nothing fancy, but it does offer a good night's sleep and 18 clean rooms. Some rooms have TV. There is a small restaurant-bar and a tiny swimming pool.

*Hostal Ciudad Blanca* (☎/fax 666-3962, fax 666-4382) Singles/doubles US$30/50 in the high season. This small hotel – one of Liberia's most attractive – occupies a mansion. The 12 guestrooms have air-conditioning, fans, cable TVs, nice furnishings, and private (hot) baths. There is a charming little restaurant-bar.

*Hotel Boyeros* (☎ 666-0995, 666-0809, fax 666-2529, e hboyeros@racsa.co.cr) Singles/doubles/triples with hot bath US$37/44/50. Near the intersection of the Interamericana and the main road into Liberia, this place is distinguished by a handsome life-size statue of a *boyero* (a man leading an ox cart) outside the hotel. It's the largest place in town, with about 70 air-conditioned rooms with cable TV and small balconies or patios. Ask for one of the upstairs balcony rooms. Amenities include a 24-hour restaurant, adults' and kids' swimming pools, a water slide, and dancing on weekends – get a room away from the music if you are looking for an early night.

**Top End** Many hotels (especially the more expensive ones) give substantial discounts in the low (rainy) season, except in late July for Guanacaste Day.

*Best Western Hotel Las Espuelas* (☎ 666-0144, fax 666-2441, e espuelas@racsa.co.cr) Singles/doubles with private bath US$56/69, including continental breakfast. This hotel is on the east side of the Interamericana, about 2km south of the main road into Liberia. It has pleasant grounds, a pool, restaurant-bar, casino, and gift shop. There are over 40 rooms with private bath, TV, telephone, and air-conditioning.

*Best Western Hotel El Sitio* (☎ *666-1211, fax 666-2059,* e *htlsitio@racsa.co.cr)* Singles/doubles US$58/75 in the high season, US$12 for additional people. On the road to Nicoya about 250m west of the Interamericana, this hotel has 52 spacious air-conditioned rooms with TVs and private hot baths. The hotel is attractively decorated with original art. Pre-Columbian motifs and sabanero scenes predominate, and there are various *guanacasteco* touches. It has a decent restaurant-bar, a spa, and adults' and kids' pools. The hotel arranges horseback rides, car rental, and tours to beaches and national parks.

## Places to Eat
The better hotels in Liberia have reasonable restaurants.

*Las Tinajas* Dishes US$2-7. Open 10am-10pm daily. On the southwest side of the Parque Central, this is a good place to sit outside with a cold drink and watch the un-energetic goings-on in the park. Sandwiches, hamburgers, snacks, and light meals are the main offerings.

Several Chinese restaurants (*Restaurante Elegante* and *La Copa de Oro* as good as any) are near the Parque Central, with meals in the US$2 to US$6 range. Several sodas are nearby.

There are a few Italian places in town. *Pizza Pronto (Calle 1 & Avenida 4).* This pizzeria is in a 19th-century house and is a nice place, with a wood-burning pizza oven, outdoor patio with a kids' play area, and small art gallery.

*Pizzería Da Beppe (Avenida Central & Calle 10)* Breakfasts US$2-6. Dishes US$5-7. This is another good place for pastas and other meals.

*Restaurant Paso Real* Dishes US$4-10. Open 11am-10pm daily. At the southeast corner of the park, this is a cheerful, modern place with a balcony and views of the cathedral. A large TV shows international sports. This is the most popular place to hang out in the center.

For delicious pastries, there are two branches of *Panadería Pan y Miel*. The larger one next to Pizzería Da Beppe serves cheap breakfasts and lunches (US$1 to US$3) and is open from 7am to 6pm weekdays, 7am to 2pm Saturday and Sunday. A smaller one is a block north of Parque Central. There's also a *Musmanni Bakery*, open 5am to 9pm daily for pastries.

For ice cream, good choices include *Heladería Holanda*, on Calle 2, a couple of blocks north of the park, and *Del Prado*, next to Las Tinajas.

For fast food, a *food mall*, conveniently on the Interamericana at the main entrance to town, features Burger King hamburgers, Churches fried chicken, and Papa John's pizza.

## Entertainment
*Las Tinajas* has traditional music shows at 7pm on Thursday and Sunday. Dancing at the *Hotel El Sitio* is another possibility.

## Getting There & Away
**Air** The airport is about 12km west of town. Since early 1993, it has served as Costa Rica's second international airport, which allows sun-starved North American tourists trying to escape harsh winters to fly almost directly to Costa Rica's Pacific beach resorts. Most international traffic here consists of charters originating in Canada during the high season; there are also some from Germany and the USA. From mid-November to mid-April, an average of two international flights arrive per day. There is a modern terminal (with pleasant air-conditioning!), but this is not a busy airport. Immigration and customs are here for those coming from abroad.

SANSA (☎ 668-1047) and Travelair both fly San José–Liberia one or more times a day, and may continue to Tamarindo or other destinations. Schedules to Liberia seem to change more often than they do anywhere else in Costa Rica; there have been flights via Tambor and Nosara in the past. Tickets for both airlines can be bought at the airport, or call the San José offices (SANSA ☎ 221-9414; Travelair ☎ 220-3054) for information.

A taxi to the airport will cost a few dollars. Or take any of the buses headed to Nicoya or the Playa del Coco region and ask to be let off at the entrance road – note that you'll have to walk about 1.6km from the main road to the airport terminal, so this is only an option for travelers willing to carry their luggage that far.

**Bus** Most visitors arrive by bus (or car). Pulmitan buses leave San José (US$4, 4½ hours) 10 times daily from Calle 24 & Avenida 5. From the Liberia Pulmitan terminal (☎ 666-0458), on Avenida 5, buses for San José leave 11 times a day between 4am and 6pm (a few of them may originate in Playa del Coco).

The bus terminal on Avenida 7, a block from the Interamericana, has departures for local and provincial destinations. Two companies service Filadelfia, Santa Cruz, and Nicoya (about US$2), with buses leaving roughly every hour from 5am to 8pm. Buses for Playa del Coco leave six times a day. Buses for Playa Hermosa and Playa Panamá leave at 7:30am, 11:30am, 3:30pm, 5:30pm, and 7pm. These last three destinations are the closest beach resorts to Liberia (see the Península de Nicoya chapter), but bus services may be curtailed in the rainy season.

Buses for La Cruz and Peñas Blancas (on the Nicaragua border) leave about every hour during the day – some buses stop en route from San José, but seats are usually available. These are the buses to take if you want to get dropped off at the entrance to Parque Nacional Santa Rosa. Other northbound destinations include Cuajiniquil (north side of Santa Rosa) at 3:30pm, Santa Cecilia (passing Hacienda Los Inocentes) at 7pm, Quebrada Grande at 3pm, and several buses for the nearby towns of Colorado and Cañas Dulces.

Transnica buses to Managua (US$12.50) pass through at 7am, 8am, and 9am (depending on demand). Buy tickets at the Hotel Guanacaste one day ahead for a seat; otherwise show up and stand.

Southbound buses go to Bagaces and Cañas at 5:45am, 1:30pm, and 4:30pm, and to Puntarenas at 5am, 8:30am, 10am, 11:15am, and 3:15pm. All these schedules are liable to change, but they give you an idea.

**Car** From Liberia, the Interamericana heads south to Cañas (48km) and San José (234km). Northbound, the highway reaches the Nicaragua border at Peñas Blancas

(77km). A paved highway to the west is the major road into the Península de Nicoya, which is famous for its good beaches and surfing, cattle ranches, terrible roads, and friendly inhabitants. A poor road to the east leads to Parque Nacional Rincón de la Vieja.

Rental cars are available – you should check their condition here even more than in San José. However, with more international flights arriving, car rental agencies have improved their services. Travelair can arrange for Adobe Rent a Car to meet you at the airport. In Liberia, shop around for the best deal. Ada (☎ 668-1122), Dollar (☎ 668-1061), Elegante (☎ 668-1054), National (☎ 666-5595), and Toyota Rent a Car (☎ 666-8190) rent cars at prices similar to those in San José. Cars can be picked up at the airport or in the center. La Posada de Tope (see Places to Stay, earlier) arranges the cheapest car rental in Liberia.

**Taxi** There is a taxi stand at the northwest corner of the Parque Central. These cabs will take you to the beaches if you can't wait for a bus. They will also take you to Parque Nacional Santa Rosa (US$15 to US$20 per cab) and up the rough road to Parque Nacional Rincón de la Vieja (US$30 to US$40 per cab). Most cab drivers consider four passengers their limit. During the wet season, 4WD taxis are used to get to Rincón de la Vieja.

## PARQUE NACIONAL RINCÓN DE LA VIEJA

This 14,161-hectare national park is named after the active Volcán Rincón de la Vieja (1895m), which is the main attraction. In the same volcanic massif are several other peaks, of which Volcán Santa María (1916m) is the highest. The numerous cones, craters, and lagoons in the summit area can be visited on horseback and foot.

Volcanic activity has occurred many times since the late 1960s, with the most recent eruption of steam and ash in 1997, but at the moment the volcano is gently active and does not present any danger from eruption (ask locally to be sure). There are fumaroles and boiling mud pools, steam vents, and sulfurous springs to explore.

Thirty-two rivers and streams have their sources within the park, an important water catchment area. It was to protect this watershed that the park was created in 1973.

**NORTHWESTERN**

Forests protect the rivers from evaporation in the dry season and from flooding in the wet season.

Elevations in the park range from less than 600m to 1916m, and the changes in altitude result in four life zones. Visitors pass through a variety of different habitats as they ascend the volcanoes. Many tree species are found in the forests. And the area has the country's highest density of Costa Rica's national flower, the purple orchid *(Cattleya skinneri)*, locally called *guaria morada*.

Because of its relative remoteness, the park is not heavily visited, but several lodges just outside the park provide access, and transportation is easy to arrange from Liberia. Rincón de la Vieja is the most accessible of the volcanoes in the Cordillera de Guanacaste.

### Orientation & Information

Admission to the park costs US$6 per day, and camping costs US$2 per person. The park is part of the Area de Conservación Guanacaste (ACG), which also includes the parks of Santa Rosa and Guanacaste as well as other protected areas. The ACG has its headquarters in Parque Nacional Santa Rosa (☎ 666-5051, fax 666-5020), where you can get information. The ranger station at Las Pailas (☎ 661-8139) also has information.

There are two entrances to the park, with a park ranger station and camping area at each. Las Pailas, with trails past various volcanic features and waterfalls and up to the summit, is the most visited. At the Santa María ranger station is the Casona Santa María, a 19th-century ranch house with a small public exhibit that was reputedly once owned by US President Lyndon Johnson. This station is the closest to the hot springs (which are 6km from Las Pailas) and also has an observation tower and a nearby waterfall.

### Wildlife Watching

The wildlife of the park is extremely varied. Almost 300 species of bird have been recorded here, including curassows, quetzals, bellbirds, parrots, toucans, hummingbirds, owls, woodpeckers, tanagers, motmots, doves, and eagles – to name just a few.

Insects range from beautiful butterflies to annoying ticks. Be especially prepared for ticks in grassy areas such as the meadow in front of the ranger station – long trousers

tucked into boots and long-sleeve shirts offer some protection. A particularly interesting insect is a highland cicada that burrows into the ground and croaks like a frog, to the bewilderment of naturalists.

Mammals are equally varied; deer, armadillos, peccaries, skunks, squirrels, coatis, and three species of monkey are frequently seen. Tapir tracks are often found around the lagoons near the summit, and you may be lucky enough to catch a glimpse of this large but elusive mammal as it crashes away like a tank through the undergrowth.

Several of the wild cat species have been recorded here, including the jaguar, puma, ocelot, and margay, but you'll need a large amount of patience and good fortune to observe one of these.

### Trails & Hiking

Trails to the summit and the most interesting volcanic features begin at Las Pailas. Sign in at the ranger station when you arrive and they will give you maps.

A circular trail east of the ranger station (about 8km in total) takes you past the boiling mud pools (Las Pailas), sulfurous fumaroles, and a miniature volcano (which may subside at any time).

North, trails lead 8km (one-way) to the summit area. Below the summit is the Laguna de Jilgueros, which is reportedly where you may see tapirs – or more likely their footprints, if you are observant. About 700m west of the ranger station is a swimming hole. Farther away are several waterfalls – the largest, Catarata La Cangreja, 5km west, is a classic, dropping straight from a cliff into a small lagoon where you can swim. Dissolved copper salts give the fall a deep blue color. This trail winds through forest, then comes out onto open grassland on the volcano's flanks, where you can get views as far as the Golfo de Nicoya. The Cangreja Trail is among the best-recommended on the mountain. The slightly smaller Cataratas Escondidas (hidden waterfalls) are 4.3km west on a different trail; there are cliff views and swimming.

From the Santa María ranger station, a trail leads 2.8km west through a forest (nicknamed the 'enchanted forest') and past a waterfall to sulfurous hot springs with supposedly therapeutic properties. You should not soak in them for more than about half an hour (some people suggest much less) without taking a dip in one of the nearby cold springs to cool off. An observation point is 450m east of the station. Though the hikes here are shorter than at Las Pailas, you should still check in with the rangers to let them know where you're going.

## Places to Stay

**Inside the Park** Both ranger stations have *camping* for US$2 per person. Each campground has water, pit toilets, showers, tables, and grills. There is no fuel available, so bring wood, charcoal, or a camping stove. Mosquito nets or insect repellent are needed in the wet season. In the past, meals could be arranged; while this is currently not available, call ahead to see if this has changed.

Camping is allowed in most places within the park, but you should be self-sufficient and prepared for cold and foggy weather in the highlands – a compass is very useful. Beware of ticks in the grassy areas. The wet season is very wet (October is the rainiest month), and there are plenty of mosquitoes then. Dry-season camping is much better. December, March, and April are recommended; January and February are prone to strong winds.

**Outside the Park** Note that all of these places are a long way from a restaurant, so you're stuck with paying for meals at the hotel restaurant.

*Rinconcito Lodge (in Liberia ☎ 666-2764, fax 666-4527, or ☎ 224-2400 to leave a message in English for 'Rinconcito'; at the lodge ☎ 380-8193 cellular; ℮ rinconcito@ racsa.co.cr)* Doubles US$20. This place is just outside the Santa María sector of the park, near the village of San Jorge, and is very rustic but friendly. It is the cheapest of the lodges near the park. The five cabins share a couple of cold-water bathrooms. Rural tico breakfasts cost US$3; other meals cost US$5. Guides and horses can be hired for US$15, and both the Rincón de la Vieja and Miravalles volcanoes can be visited on tours. Make reservations and get directions from the owners, Gerardo and María Inés Badilla, at the Liberia phone and fax numbers listed above. They offer transport to the lodge for about US$35 roundtrip and will take up to six people for that price.

Two lodges – the Hacienda Lodge Guachipelín and Rincón de la Vieja Mountain Lodge – lie near the Las Pailas sector at the park's southwest corner and are reached by the gravel road described in Getting There & Away, below. Both require a US$2 entrance fee because the road crosses private property with a toll booth.

*Hacienda Lodge Guachipelín (☎ 442-2818, 442-2695, 384-2049, fax 442-1910, ℮ info@guachipelin.com, ₩ www .guachipelin.com)* Singles/doubles/triples US$37/56/72, children under 10 yrs free. This lodge is on the site of a 19th-century ranch, parts of which are incorporated into the current building. The hacienda has some 1200 hectares, part primary forest, part secondary forest, and part a working cattle ranch. Most accommodations are in 30 spacious, light duplex cabins with large private bathrooms (hot water) and porches. Six older rooms have doubles for US$35, but these will be phased out. A restaurant serves breakfast and boxed lunches for US$5, and a three-course hot lunch or dinner plus coffee for US$10. The menu allows for three meal choices. A large rustic barn acts as a reception area, bar, and relaxation room, behind which is a swimming pool.

The lodge's canopy tour is called Kazm Canyon and is unique in that parts of it are on zip-lines through a rocky canyon. A little wall-climbing and a 'Tarzan swing' get you through the canyon; the guides appear well-trained and safety conscious. This canopy tour is US$45/35/28 for adults/youth 13-17 yrs/children. Various horseback tours to different destinations are US$15 to US$30, plus US$6 park entrance for the more expensive (and longer) tours. A day combo, including Kazm Canyon, a horse ride into the national park, and lunch, is US$70/57/42, plus entrance fees. Guided hiking and mountain-biking is also available on request. The lodge can provide transportation from Liberia for about US$10 roundtrip per person (larger groups get discounts). They also arrange three-day/two-night tours from San José, including transport, meals, accommodations, Kazm Canyon tour, and two horseback rides for US$249 per person.

*Rincón de la Vieja Mountain Lodge (☎ 200-5133 cellular, ☎/fax 661-8198, ℮ info@ rincondelaviejalodge.com, ₩ www .rincondelaviejalodge.com)* Standard singles/

doubles/triples US$46/59/82, standard-plus doubles/triples US$78/101, US$17 for additional people. Five kilometers past Hacienda Lodge Guachipelín is this lodge. It's closest to the park and is therefore popular. There are 40 rooms, of which nine are older, smaller, darker wooden standard rooms (these are quite a good value). The standard-plus rooms consist of 21 newer, larger units, some with wildly painted walls or rustic beamed roofs. In addition, 10 cabins have balconies and are larger still. All have private, nicely tiled hot showers. There's 24-hour electricity, and the rooms are screened – insects are abundant in the wettest months and the screens do help. Amenities include a small pool, Internet access, a small lending library, butterfly garden, and a canopy tour. The lodge is about 2km from the mud pools and 5km from the fumaroles described earlier. Meals are available at the lodge; breakfast is US$9, a boxed lunch is US$7.50, and a sit-down lunch and dinner are both US$12.

Various tours are offered, including a scary wild canopy tour with 16 platforms joined by steel cables (US$49.50, or US$82 at night, or US$110 overnight on a platform). Local guides (US$30), naturalist guides (US$60), horses (US$20 a half day), mountain bikes (US$30 all day), and transportation from Liberia are all available, as are multiday packages – call the lodge for details.

**Buenavista Lodge** (☎/fax 661-8158, e buenavistalodge@altavista.net, W www .buenavistalodge.net) Singles/doubles/triples US$41/55/60. On a different road via Cañas Dulces, this lodge is set on an 1800-hectare farm. It offers horseback tours (US$30) and hiking tours into Rincón de la Vieja (it takes about five hours to the park), private natural mud and steam pools (US$15), and a swimming pool with a 420m water slide that takes about 1½ minutes to descend (US$15). A canopy tour is available for US$30 – there are 11 platforms, 10 zip-lines, and scary-looking photos on their website. Interestingly enough, helmets are provided for the water slide but not for the canopy tour. Recently expanded, this lodge now has over 70 large wooden (some stone) rooms, all with private bath and hot water. There is a bar and restaurant offering breakfast (US$7.50), lunch (US$12.50), and dinner (US$10) served buffet-style. A combo tour

including lunch, canopy, mud spa, and water slide costs US$60.

**Hotel Borinquen** (☎ 666-0363, fax 666-2931, W www.borinquenresort.com) Singles/doubles US$117/129, extra people US$35. This new resort and spa has lovely, air-conditioned bungalows spaced out on a hillside on the lower slopes of Rincón de la Vieja. Each comes with huge glassed double doors and large windows, a spacious deck, satellite TV, and attractive furniture. Rates include a continental breakfast and a full-body mud pack in their natural hot springs spa. A large pool was under construction in 2002. You get around the somewhat far-flung resort buildings by golf carts, though the steepness of the roads linking the buildings looks scary – walking is probably safer in wet conditions.

## Getting There & Away

**To Las Pailas** Almost 5km north of Liberia on the Interamericana is a signed turnoff to the northeast onto a gravel road; from here, it is just over 20km from the Interamericana to the station at Las Pailas. Most hotels (or the tourist office) in Liberia can arrange transport from about US$12 roundtrip (four people minimum).

The road passes through the grounds of the Hacienda Lodge Guachipelín (there are signs for the lodge along the way). There is a guarded gate (open during daylight hours) and a US$2 per person vehicle fee for use of what is now a private road. This is reimbursed if you stay at the Hacienda Lodge Guachipelín, but if you continue to the Rincón de la Vieja Mountain Lodge, there is no refund. The Hacienda Lodge Guachipelín is 3km beyond the gate, and the Mountain Lodge is 5km farther still.

Alternatively, you can walk about 8km from the Santa María ranger station to Las Pailas or the Rincón de la Vieja Mountain Lodge.

**To Santa María** The park is 25km northeast of Liberia by a poor road that often requires 4WD in the rainy season but is passable in ordinary cars in the dry. To get to the Santa María ranger station, drive, walk, or take a taxi (US$30 to US$40) on the road that heads northeast out of Liberia through the Barrio La Victoria suburb. After about 18km, the road passes the village of San

Jorge and then continues as far as Santa María. Sometimes a ride from Liberia can be arranged when a park service vehicle is in town. Most people drive or arrange a ride with the lodge where they are staying.

**To Buenavista Lodge** This is reached from the Interamericana by driving 12km north from Liberia and turning right on the signed road. The 5km drive from this point to Cañas Dulces is paved (there are buses to Cañas Dulces from Liberia); the additional 13km drive to the Buenavista Lodge is on unpaved road.

## PARQUE NACIONAL SANTA ROSA

This national park is one of the oldest (established 1971) and biggest (38,674 hectares) in Costa Rica and has one of the best-developed, though still simple, camping facilities of the nation's parks.

Santa Rosa covers most of the Península Santa Elena, which juts out into the Pacific at the far northwestern corner of the country. The park is named after the Hacienda Santa Rosa, where a historic battle was fought on March 20, 1856, between a hastily assembled amateur army of Costa Ricans and the invading forces of the North American filibuster William Walker. In fact, it was mainly historical and patriotic reasons that brought about the establishment of this national park in the first place. It is almost a coincidence that the park has also become extremely important to biologists.

Santa Rosa protects the largest remaining stand of tropical dry forest in Central America, and it also protects some of the most important nesting sites of several species of sea turtle, including endangered ones. Wildlife is often seen, especially during the dry season when animals congregate around the remaining water and the trees lose their leaves. So for historians and biologists, campers and hikers, beach and wilderness lovers, this park is a great attraction.

One of the most innovative features of Parque Nacional Santa Rosa is that local people have been involved in preserving and expanding the park. Through a campaign of both education and employment, locals have learned the importance of conservation and have been able to put it to their own use by working as research assistants, park rangers, or other staff, and also by using conservation techniques to improve their own land use on the surrounding

---

### Research at Santa Rosa

Santa Rosa is a mecca for scientists, particularly tropical ecologists. Near the park headquarters are simple accommodations for researchers and students, many of whom spend a great deal of time both studying the ecology of the area and devising better means to protect the remaining tropical forests of Costa Rica.

Tropical ecologist Dr Daniel H Janzen has spent much of his research time in Santa Rosa and has been instrumental in creating the conservation-area system that is making protection of all the national parks more effective. He has been very vocal about how the needs of local people must be addressed in order for conservation to become truly effective on a long-term basis. Most recently, Janzen has been involved in the INBio project to catalog as many species as possible and to screen them for potential pharmaceutical value.

Janzen has also done much solid research on the tropics and is noted for a plethora of scientific papers. The titles of these range from the whimsical ('How to Be a Fig' in *Annual Review of Ecology & Systematics*, vol 10, 1979) to the matter-of-fact ('Why Fruits Rot, Seeds Mold, and Meat Spoils' in *American Naturalist*, vol 111, 1977) to the downright bewildering ('Allelopathy by Myrmecophytes: The Ant *Azteca* as an Allelopathic Agent of *Cecropia*' in *Ecology*, vol 50, 1969). But perhaps Janzen's strangest claim to fame, among students of ecology at least, is his experiment on tropical seeds. He studied how seed germination is affected by the seeds being eaten and passed through the digestive systems of a variety of animals. Facing a lack of suitable animal volunteers, Janzen systematically ate the seeds himself, then recovered the seeds and tried to germinate them. Tropical ecology can be a messy business!

farms and ranches. This attitude of cultural involvement has made the relationship between the national park authorities and the local people one that benefits everybody. It stands as a model for the future integration of preservation and local people's interests in other parts of Costa Rica and in other countries.

The best season is the dry season, when there are fewer biting insects, the roads are more passable, and the animals tend to congregate around water holes, making them easier to see. But this is also the 'busy' season when, particularly on weekends, the park is popular with Costa Ricans wanting to see some of their history. It is less busy midweek, but it's always fairly quiet compared to parks like Volcán Poás or Manuel Antonio. In the wet months, you can observe the sea turtles nesting and often have the rest of the park virtually to yourself. The best months for sea turtles are September and October, though you are likely to see some from July to December as well. An increase in large tour groups wanting to see the turtles nesting prompted a closure of Playa Nancite (the best-known turtle-nesting beach) to large groups, though individuals and small groups can sometimes obtain a permit to see the nesting. Visitation during turtle season is limited to 25 people per night, and you should make a reservation with the park headquarters (☎ 666-5051, fax 666-5020).

## Orientation

Parque Nacional Santa Rosa's entrance is on the west side of the Interamericana, 35km north of Liberia and 45km south of the Nicaragua border. From the entrance, a 7km paved road leads to the main center of the park. Here there are administrative offices, scientists' quarters, an information center, campground, museum, and nature trail.

From this complex, a 4WD trail leads down to the coast, 12km away. It's impassable and closed from May to November (wet season). Horses and walkers can use the road all year. About a third of the way down this trail are two lookout points with views of the ocean. There are several beaches, and a camping area lies at the southern end of Playa Naranjo, though you need permits from the park rangers to camp on the

beach, and camping may be prohibited during turtle-nesting months. There are also other jeep, foot, and horse trails that leave the main visitor complex and head out into the tropical dry forest and other habitats.

The park's Sector Murciélago (Bat Sector) encompasses the wild northern coastline of the Península Santa Elena. A ranger station and camping area are here; a short trail leads to a water hole where swimming is reportedly pleasant. The story is that this area was once owned by Nicaraguan dictator Anastasio Somoza – after he was deposed, the area became part of the national park. You can't get there from the main body of the park. To reach the Sector Murciélago, you need to return to the Interamericana and travel farther north, as described in Getting There & Away, below.

The Interamericana forms the eastern border of Santa Rosa and also the western border of Parque Nacional Guanacaste – the two parks are contiguous.

## Information

The park entrance station (just off the Interamericana) is open 8am to 4:30pm daily (though walkers can get in anytime). At the entrance booth you pay the US$6 park admission and, if you plan on camping, an extra US$2 per person. Unlike many parks, the US$6 entrance is per stay, not per day. Maps of the park are sometimes for sale here.

It is another 7km to the park's headquarters (☎ 666-5051, fax 666-5020) and campground. There are no buses, so you must walk or hitch if you don't have a car. Rangers may allow travelers to accompany them on their rounds of the park. Note that the park headquarters also administers the Area de Conservación Guanacaste (ACG) and has information about (and maintains radio/phone contact with) Parque Nacional Rincón de la Vieja, Parque Nacional Guanacaste, and other protected areas.

Several of the park rangers have been trained as naturalist guides and will accompany you on tours of Santa Rosa and other areas within the ACG.

## La Casona

The historic La Casona (the main building of the old Hacienda Santa Rosa) was destroyed by arson in May 2001 and rebuilt in 2002 using historic photos and local timber.

The battle of 1856 was fought around this building, and the military action is described in documents, paintings, maps, and diagrams, some of which were destroyed in the fire. Other battles were fought in this area in 1919 and 1955.

The arson was set by a local father-son team of poachers who were disgruntled by being banned from hunting here by park rangers. They were caught and sentenced to 20 years of prison for torching a building of national cultural and historical value.

The newly reconstructed La Casona was finished at the time of writing, and plans were to reopen it as a museum interpreting the historical, cultural, ecological, and biological significance of the park.

Behind La Casona, a short trail leads up to the Monumento a Los Héroes and a lookout platform.

## Wildlife Watching

Near La Casona is a short nature trail with signs interpreting the ecological relationships among the plants, animals, and weather patterns of Santa Rosa. The trail is named **El Sendero Indio Desnudo** after the common tree whose peeling orange-red bark can photosynthesize during the dry season, when the tree's leaves are dry and dry. The reddish bark is supposed to represent a naked Indian, though local guides suggest that 'sunburned tourist' might be a better name. The tree is also called gumbo limbo. Also seen along the trail is the national tree of Costa Rica, the guanacaste *(Enterolobium cyclocarpum)*. The province is named after this very large tree species, which is found along the Pacific coastal lowlands. Although the Indio Desnudo nature trail is short (a little over 1km roundtrip), you will certainly see a variety of plants and birds and probably, if you move slowly and keep your eyes and ears open, monkeys, snakes, iguanas, and other animals. Markers along the trail explain what you see – also look out for the petroglyphs (probably pre-Columbian) etched into some of the rocks on the trail.

The wildlife is certainly both varied and prolific. Over 250 bird species have been recorded. One highly visible bird, common in Santa Rosa and frequently seen and heard around the park campground, is the white-throated magpie jay. This raucous blue-and-white jay is unmistakable with its long crest of maniacally curled feathers. The forests contain parrots and parakeets, trogons and tanagers, and as you head down to the coast, you will be rewarded by sightings of a variety of coastal birds.

At dusk, the flying animals you see probably won't be birds. Bats are very common; about 50 or 60 different species have been identified in Santa Rosa. Other mammals you have a reasonable chance of seeing include deer, coatis, peccaries, armadillos, coyotes, raccoons, three kinds of monkey, and a variety of other species – about 115 in all. There are many thousands of insect species, including about 4000 moths and butterflies.

There are also many reptiles – lizards, iguanas, snakes, crocodiles, and four species of sea turtle. The olive ridley sea turtle is the most numerous, and during the July to December nesting season, tens of thousands of turtles make their nests on Santa Rosa's beaches. The most popular beach is Playa Nancite, where, during September and October especially, it is possible to see as many as 8000 of these 40kg turtles on the beach at the same time! The turtles are disturbed by light, so flash photography and flashlights are not permitted. Avoid the nights around a full moon – they're too bright. After nesting, the olive ridleys range all over the tropical eastern Pacific, from the waters of Mexico to Peru. Playa Nancite is strictly protected and restricted, but permission can be obtained from park headquarters (☎ 666-5051, fax 666-5020) to observe this spectacle.

The variety of wildlife reflects the variety of habitat protected within the boundaries of the park. Apart from the largest remaining stand of tropical dry forest in Central America, habitats including

Costa Rica's national tree, the guanacaste

savanna woodland, oak forest, deciduous forest, evergreen forest, riparian forest, mangrove swamp, and coastal woodland.

## Surfing

Playa Naranjo, the next major beach south of Playa Nancite, is near the southern end of the national park's coastline. The surfing here is reportedly good, especially near Witches Rock. This is a popular place to camp and surf, but you'll need to pack everything in – surfboards, tents, food, and drinking water (though brackish water is available for washing off after a day in the waves). The hike in takes several hours. Surfing and boat tours to Witches Rock are offered from Playa del Coco and Playa Tamarindo (see the Península de Nicoya chapter).

## Places to Stay & Eat

**Campgrounds** Campsites US$2 per person. There's a campground at the park headquarters. Facilities are not fancy but do include drinking water, picnic benches, grills, flushing toilets, cold-water showers, and garbage cans. Large fig trees provide shade. The campsites on the coast, when open, have pit toilets but no showers. Ask the rangers whether drinking water is available; you may need to pack in your own. The Playa Naranjo campground has basic facilities and limited drinking water – ask at the ranger station about current supplies, but be prepared to pack in your own.

**Research station** (☎ 666-5051, fax 666-5020) Beds US$20 per person. This station at the park headquarters has eight rooms, each sleeping up to eight people. Showers are shared. Researchers and students stay here, but there may be room for travelers, who should call ahead. The cost does not include meals, about US$3 to US$6 each. Make arrangements for accommodations and meals in advance with the ranger station.

A **snack bar** sells soft drinks and a few snacks. Occasionally, simple meals may be available (when rangers or guests haven't eaten all the food!) and they may rustle up lunch with a couple of hours' notice.

## Getting There & Away

To get to the main park entrance by public transport, take any bus between Liberia and the Nicaragua border and ask the driver to set you down at the park entrance. When you are ready to leave, you can ask the ranger on duty for a timetable of passing buses. There are about 12 buses a day heading to the border and about six each to Liberia and San José. If you are driving from the south, watch for the kilometer posts on the side of the road – the park entrance is about 300m south of Km 270.

To get to the northern Sector Murciélago of the park, go 10km farther north along the Interamericana, then turn left to the village of Cuajiniquil, 8km away by paved road. There are passport controls both at the turnoff and in Cuajiniquil itself, so don't have your passport buried. Buses go here once or twice a day from La Cruz, and buses from the main park entrance go here at 4pm and 5:30pm (subject to change). You could also hitch or walk the 8km. Cuajiniquil has a basic soda and *pulpería* but no accommodations. (The paved road continues beyond Cuajiniquil and dead-ends at a marine port, 4km away – this isn't the way to the Sector Murciélago but goes toward Refugio Nacional de Vida Silvestre Bahía Junquillal.) Park rangers say it's about 8km beyond Cuajiniquil to the Murciélago ranger station by poor road – 4WD is advised in the wet season, though you might make it in an ordinary vehicle if you drive carefully. At the Murciélago ranger station, you can camp and, if you advise the Santa Rosa headquarters in advance, eat meals. The dirt road continues beyond the ranger station for about 10km or 12km, reaching the remote bays and beaches of Bahía Santa Elena and Bahía Playa Blanca. This road may be impassable in the wet season.

## REFUGIO NACIONAL DE VIDA SILVESTRE BAHÍA JUNQUILLAL

This 505-hectare wildlife refuge is part of the Area de Conservación Guanacaste, administered from the park headquarters at Santa Rosa. The quiet bay and protected beach provide gentle swimming, boating, and snorkeling opportunities, and there is some tropical dry forest and mangrove swamp. Short trails take the visitor to a lookout for marine birding and to the mangroves. Pelicans and frigatebirds are seen, and turtles nest here seasonally. Volcán Orosí can be seen in the distance.

## Information

There is a ranger station (☎ 679-9692) in telephone and radio contact with Santa Rosa. Entrance here costs US$6 (and also allows entrance to Santa Rosa), although if you aren't going to Santa Rosa you may be charged much less. Camping is US$2 per person. During the dry season especially, water is at a premium and is turned on for only one hour a day. There are pit latrines.

## Getting There & Away

From Cuajiniquil (see Parque Nacional Santa Rosa, above), continue for 2km along the paved road and then turn right onto a signed dirt road (the sign may say 'Playa Cuajiniquil,' but it's the correct turn). Continuing 4km along the dirt road (passable to ordinary cars) brings you to the entrance to Bahía Junquillal, which is open from 7am to 7pm. From here, a poorer 700m dirt road leads to the beach, ranger station, and camping area.

## PARQUE NACIONAL GUANACASTE

This newest part of the ACG was created on July 25 (Guanacaste Day), 1989. The park is adjacent to Parque Nacional Santa Rosa, separated from it by the Interamericana, and is only about 5km northwest of Parque Nacional Rincón de la Vieja.

The 34,651 hectares of Parque Nacional Guanacaste are much more than a continuation of the dry tropical forest and other lowland habitats found in Santa Rosa. In its lower western reaches, the park is an extension of Santa Rosa's habitats, but the terrain soon begins to climb toward two volcanoes: Volcán Orosí (1487m) and Volcán Cacao (1659m). Thus it enables animals to range from the coast to the highlands, just as many of them have always done.

Scientists have come to realize that many animal species need a variety of different habitats at different times of year, or at different stages of their life cycles, and if habitats are preserved singly, the animals within them may not thrive. If a series of adjoining habitats is preserved, however, the survival of many species can be improved. This is one of the main reasons for the formation of conservation areas such as the ACG.

Not all the preserved areas are natural forest. Indeed, large portions of the ACG

are ranch land. But researchers have found that if the pasture is carefully managed (and much of this management involves just letting nature take its course), the natural forest will reinstate itself in its old territory. Thus, crucial habitats are not just preserved, but in some cases they are also expanded.

For information on this park, contact the ACG headquarters in Parque Nacional Santa Rosa (☎ 666-5051, fax 666-5020).

## Research Stations

Research is an important part of Guanacaste, and there are no less than three biological stations within its borders. They are all in good areas for wildlife observation or hiking.

**Maritza Biological Station** This is the newest station and has a modern laboratory. To get there, turn east off the Interamericana opposite the turnoff for Cuajiniquil (see Parque Nacional Santa Rosa, earlier). The station is about 17km east of the highway along a dirt road that may require a 4WD vehicle, especially in the wet season. The main problem with driving the road is entering it from the Interamericana – there is a very steep curb – but once you've negotiated that, the going gets better.

From the station, at 600m above sea level, rough trails run to the summits of Volcán Orosí and Volcán Cacao (about five to six hours). There is also a better trail to a site where several hundred Indian petroglyphs have been found, about two hours away. Reportedly, another trail goes to Cacao Biological Station.

**Cacao Biological Station** This station is high on the slopes of Volcán Cacao at an elevation of about 1060m above sea level. The station is reached from the southern side of the park. At Potrerillos, about 9km south of the Santa Rosa park entrance on the Interamericana, head east for about 7km on a paved road to the small community of Quebrada Grande (marked 'Garcia Flamenco' on many maps). A daily bus leaves Liberia at 3pm for Quebrada Grande. From the village square, a 4WD road heads north toward the station, about 10km away. Contact the ACG headquarters in Parque Nacional Santa Rosa (☎ 666-5051, fax 666-5020) to find out if the road is passable.

From the station, rough trails lead to the summit of Volcán Cacao and to the Maritza Biological Station.

**Pitilla Biological Station** This station is a surprise – it lies on the northeast side of Volcán Orosí in forest more like that found on the Caribbean slopes than on the Pacific, although the Pacific is only 30km to the west while the Caribbean is 180km to the east. Because the station is on the eastern side of the continental divide, the rivers flow into the Caribbean and the climate and vegetation are influenced by the Caribbean.

To get to the station, turn east off of the Interamericana about 12km north of the Cuajiniquil turnoff, or 3km before reaching the small town of La Cruz. Follow the paved eastbound road for about 28km to the community of Santa Cecilia. From there, ask about the poor dirt road heading 10km or 12km south to the station – you'll probably need 4WD. (Don't continue on the unpaved road heading farther east – that goes over 50km farther to the small town of Upala.)

## Places to Stay & Eat
**Inside the Park** Since the creation of the national park in Guanacaste, the biological research stations are sometimes available for tourist accommodations.

*Maritza* or *Cacao* (☎ 666-5051, fax 666-5020) Beds US$25. These two stations are where you are most likely to be allowed to stay – Pitilla is the province of research biologists and students. The stations are all quite rustic, with dormitory-style accommodations for about 30 people and shared cold-water bathrooms. Rates include a bed and three meals, only if arranged in advance.

Permission to *camp* near the stations may also be obtained; the fee is about US$2 per night although there is no campground as such. To stay in the stations, make arrangements with the Santa Rosa headquarters (details listed above). Research personnel and students always get preference. Park personnel in Santa Rosa may be able to arrange transport from that park's headquarters to the biological stations for about US$10 to US$20, depending on where you go.

**Outside the Park** There are two lodges within a few kilometers of the park boundaries – one on the south side and one on the north. Either can be used as a base to explore the national park.

*Santa Clara Lodge* (☎ 391-876, 691-8062, fax 666-4047) Rooms US$10 per person, US$27 with meals. On the south side of the park, this is a small, rustic, friendly, family-run lodge in a working dairy farm on the banks of the Río Los Ahogados ('River of the Drowned' – a not-very-reassuring name!). A cold-water mineral spring near the lodge is channeled into a dip pool; the locals claim the water is good for the skin. Rooms are clean but very small and simple. Electricity is available from 6pm to 10pm; otherwise, candles are provided. Showers are cold, and there may be noise in the early morning because of the farm animals. Most rooms have shared baths.

The lodge is about 7km due south of Parque Nacional Guanacaste and 9km west of Parque Nacional Rincón de la Vieja. Horseback and taxi tours are available around the ranch and to local waterfalls and thermal springs; to Santa Rosa, Rincón de la Vieja, and Junquillal; and, on weekends only, to **Sutton Ostrich Farm** (unique in Costa Rica as of this writing), which is on the western outskirts of the nearby village of Quebrada Grande. Tours cost US$20 to US$65 and usually require a minimum of three participants. Ask about visiting other places.

The lodge is reached by heading 4km south of Quebrada Grande on a dirt road (see Cacao Biological Station, above, for information about reaching Quebrada Grande).

*Hacienda Los Inocentes* (☎ 679-9190, 679-9294, fax 265-4385, 679-9224, e orosina@racsa.co.cr) Rooms US$58-74 per person with meals. This is a ranch on the north side of Parque Nacional Guanacaste. The owners are interested in wildlife and conservation as well as ranching; they promote recycling and solar energy and host scientists engaged in environmental research. The hacienda building itself is a very attractive century-old wooden house converted into a comfortable country lodge owned and operated by the Viquez family, who have been here for generations. Current owner Jaime Viquez embodies the graciousness and confidence of traditional Guanacaste. The setting below Volcán Orosí is quite spectacular. About two-thirds of the 1000-hectare ranch is forested (mainly with secondary forest), and bird- and animal-watching opportunities abound. You might see howler monkeys on foot trails by the nearby Río Sábalo, as well as a variety of parrots in the forest and king vultures overhead.

Trips into Parque Nacional Guanacaste can be arranged, and you can climb Volcán Orosí, looming high on the horizon about 7km to the south. Naturally, horses are available (by this stage in the chapter, you probably realize that horses are an important way of getting around rural Costa Rica). The lodge building has 11 spacious wooden bedrooms upstairs – each room has a private bathroom with electric shower on the ground floor, so though you never have to share a bathroom, you do have to walk downstairs to reach it. The upper floor is surrounded by the beautiful shaded wooden verandah with hammocks and volcano views – a good spot for sunset and moonrise. A dozen new cabins with private bath are near the main lodge. The food is good here. You can wander around at will, or take a dip in the small pool or Jacuzzi. Guided tours are extra, though very reasonably priced at US$27.50 for a two-hour horseback ride. These are popular with guests from other hotels – the lodge owns over 100 horses to deal with the demand.

Reach the hacienda by driving 15km east from the Interamericana on the paved road to Santa Cecilia. It is just over half a kilometer from the entrance gate to the lodge itself. Buses from San José to Santa Cecilia pass the lodge entrance at about 7:30pm, and buses from Santa Cecilia returning to San José pass the lodge around 5:15am. More frequent buses join La Cruz with Santa Cecilia and can drop you at the hacienda entrance. Taxis from La Cruz charge about US$10 for the 20km ride.

In **Santa Cecilia** itself, you'll find a *soda*, *pulpería*, and several basic *pensiones* where you can find lodging for about US$4 per person; two of them are right next to where the bus stops. Ask around for others; it's a remote but friendly little place. About 3km out of Santa Cecilia, on a poor dirt road that passes by orange groves on the way to the village of La Virgen, you can get views of the islands in Lago de Nicaragua.

## LA CRUZ

This is the first and last settlement of any size you'll encounter before reaching the

Nicaragua border at Peñas Blancas, 20km farther north on the Interamericana. It's a small and slightly desperate town, with few places to eat, poor bus services, and only one working phone on the central plaza. Its best feature is the location on a small hill overlooking Bahía Salinas in the distance – there are sweeping views of the coast.

## Information

The Banco Nacional (☎ 679-9296, ☎/fax 679-9110) is at the junction of the short road into the center and the Interamericana. The Banco Popular (☎ 679-9352) is in the center. Changing money is slow. There is a small clinic (☎ 679-9116) and police station (☎ 679-9197).

## Places to Stay

*Cabinas Maryfel* (☎ 679-8072) Doubles US$9. Opposite the bus station, this place rarely has rooms, as they are usually taken by long-term migrant workers.

*Hotel El Faro* Doubles US$9. An even more basic choice than Cabinas Maryfel, this hotel is on the road leading into town from the Interamericana.

*Cabinas Santa Rita* (☎ 679-9062, ☎/fax 679-9305) Rooms US$5-10 per person. A couple of blocks south of the Parque Central, this hotel has about 30 clean rooms. It is popular and often full, especially in the dry season. Rates vary depending on facilities – some rooms have private baths, fans, TV, air-conditioning, or combinations thereof.

*Hostal de Julia* (☎/fax 679-9084) Singles/doubles US$24/35. North of the gas station on the road going into town from the Interamericana, this place has a dozen clean motel-like rooms (with fans and private hot bath) around a whitewashed courtyard.

*Amalia's Inn* (☎/fax 679-9181) Doubles US$35. This is a seven-room inn with private hot showers, a small pool, and secure parking. It's on a coastal bluff with good sea views. Amalia, the elderly tica owner, has filled the house with paintings by her late North American husband. She locks up at 10pm – and the phone rarely works for incoming calls!

*Hotel Colinas del Norte* (☎/fax 679-9132) Doubles US$55. About 6km north of La Cruz is this attractive ranch that arranges local tours. Children are welcome, and there is a small miniature-golf course on the back lawn. You can rent a horse for US$15 per hour, and discounts are given for longer stays. They have hot showers, a pool, tennis court, restaurant, and bar, which functions as a disco on some weekends.

## Places to Eat

Most close soon after dark.

*Restaurant Las Orquideas* Meals US$3-10. One (and perhaps the only) place that is open late is this truck stop next to the gas station on the Interamericana. Dismal ambience with adequate but overpriced food doesn't encourage lingering. Another choice is a *chicken take-out* place at the corner of the central plaza.

*Bar y Restaurante Thelma* (☎ 679-9150) This central eatery serves decent lunches in a friendly atmosphere.

Just past the park is the hole-in-the-wall *Soda Santa Marta*, which serves cheap local breakfasts and meals. There are a handful of other sodas.

## Getting There & Away

La Cruz has bus connections with San José, Liberia, and the Nicaragua border. Buses come through on the way to Liberia and San José seven times a day, and to the border nine times a day.

In La Cruz, the bus station is a couple of blocks from the center. There is no place to buy tickets, and timetable information is grudgingly imparted by the lady who cleans the bathrooms. Many of the southbound buses begin at the border, and locals complain that it's sometimes difficult to board by the time the bus comes through La Cruz. If this is the case, you could try backtracking 20km to the border and catching a bus there – though many of the buses to the border originate in Liberia or San José and may also be full as they come through La Cruz. Catch-22.

Local buses leave La Cruz for Santa Cecilia (passing Hacienda Los Inocentes) about six times a day. In Santa Cecilia, there are basic pensiones and connections with buses on to Upala in the northern lowlands. There are also local buses from La Cruz to Puerto Soley at 5am and 1pm and to Cuajiniquil at 12:30pm. (See Parque Nacional Guanacaste, earlier, for more information on Santa Cecilia.)

A taxi to the border runs about US$6.

## BAHÍA SALINAS

A dirt road (normally passable to ordinary cars) leads down from the lookout point in La Cruz past the small coastal fishing community of Puerto Soley and out along the curve of the bay to where there are a couple of newer resorts. Boats can be rented here to visit Isla Bolaños (you can't land, but you can approach and view the nesting seabird colonies) and other places; horse rental is also available. The bay is becoming something of a windsurfing spot, and there is a windsurfing school where you can rent boards and get lessons.

## Windsurfing

This is the second-best place in Costa Rica (after Lake Arenal) to practice this sport. The strongest and steadiest winds blow from December through March, but windsurfing is pretty good year-round, they say. The shape of the hills surrounding the bay funnels the winds into a predictable pattern, and the sandy protected beaches make this a safe place for beginners and experienced board riders alike. Rentals and lessons are available from the two resorts below.

## Places to Stay & Eat

*Restaurant/Bar Salinas* (☎ 382-2989) Campsites US$6 per person, seafood meals US$8. In Puerto Soley, this place provides tents and bathrooms and is a cheap alternative to the resorts below.

*Hotel Ecoplaya* (☎ 679-9380, fax 666-4683, ℮ ecoplaya@racsa.co.cr, ☒ www .ecoplaya.com) Singles/doubles US$68/136; more expensive villas and suites available. About 16km from La Cruz, this beachside resort includes three meals and all drinks (including domestic alcoholic beverages) in its rates. The hotel rents mountain bikes (US$4 per hour) and kayaks (US$8 per hour), and arranges a variety of tours and activities (fishing, windsurfing, boat cruises, horseback riding, diving). There's a pool, Jacuzzi, and games room.

*Hotel Three Corners Bolaños Bay Resort* (☎ 289-5561, fax 228-4205, ℮ 3cornco@racsa.co.cr, ☒ www.3corners bolanosbay.com) Singles/doubles US$75/130. Continuing on the road beyond Puerto Soley along the coast, you come to this all-inclusive resort set on an attractive, windy point overlooking the bay. The 72 air-conditioned bungalows all have telephones, terraces, and private hot showers. Rates include three daily buffet-style meals, domestic alcoholic beverages, and use of mountain bikes and kayaks. There are adults' and children's pools, a spacious bar-restaurant, dancing lessons in the evenings, and a variety of activities, tours, and rentals. Windsurfing is US$45 per day, and horseback riding, scuba diving, and canopy tours are quickly arranged for extra cost.

At Puerto Soley is a rustic *beachfront restaurant* where you can have good, cheap, fresh fish and cold beer; ask about renting a boat to visit the Isla Bolaños refuge. Expect to pay about US$20 per hour for a boat that will hold eight or 10 passengers.

### Getting There & Away
Two buses a day from La Cruz can drop you at any of the places described above; current departure times are 10:30am and 1:30pm, but ask at the La Cruz bus station. A taxi to one of the resorts costs about US$8.

### PEÑAS BLANCAS
On the border with Nicaragua, Peñas Blancas is a border post, not a town. There isn't anywhere to stay, although meals and money-changing are available.

See the Getting There & Away chapter for border-crossing details.

# Arenal Route

The route described here goes from San José in a northwesterly direction through Ciudad Quesada (San Carlos), Fortuna, Arenal, and Tilarán, joining with the Interamericana at Cañas. From Cañas, you could head north toward Liberia and Nicaragua, or turn south along the Interamericana and thus make a loop trip back to San José. Fortuna makes a good base for visiting the active Volcán Arenal, and there are adequate bus connections. Drivers can do the complete circuit on paved roads, though some are badly potholed. It is also possible to connect with Monteverde, although the roads are in poor shape, and with the northern lowlands of Costa Rica.

## CIUDAD QUESADA (SAN CARLOS)
The official name of this small city is Ciudad Quesada (sometimes abbreviated to 'Quesada'), but all the locals know it as San Carlos, and local buses often list San Carlos as the destination. The town lies 650m above sea level on the northwestern slopes of the Cordillera Central, overlooking the Llanura de San Carlos (San Carlos Plains) stretching off to Nicaragua. The population is about 35,000.

Roads north and east of the city take the traveler into the northern lowlands. Roads to the northwest lead to Fortuna and the spectacular Volcán Arenal, and over the mountains to the Interamericana.

Ciudad Quesada is a convenient place to spend the night if you like to travel slowly and want to see one of Costa Rica's smaller cities. It's an important agricultural and ranching center, and the Feria del Ganado, or cattle fair and auction, held every April, is the biggest such event in the country. The fair is accompanied by the usual carnival rides and a *tope* (horse parade). If you're interested in horses, check out the *talabarterías,* or saddle shops, found near the town center. They make and sell some of the most intricately crafted leather saddles in Costa Rica; a top-quality saddle can cost US$1000. Just walking into a talabartería and smelling all the leatherwork is a memorable olfactory experience.

The town's focal point is the large **Parque Central**, with shade trees and benches. Almost everything of importance is either on this square or within a few blocks of it.

### Information
Tourist information offices have been open intermittently.

Banco de Costa Rica (with an ATM) is on the southwest corner of the Parque Central, and Banco de San José is a block north of the park's northwest corner.

Internet access is available from Avenida 1, Calles Central & 1, 1½ blocks northwest of the park.

Emergency medical attention is available at the Hospital de San Carlos (☎ 460-1176) and Clínica Monte Sinai (☎ 460-1080).

### Places to Stay
**Budget** Three blocks northeast of the park is *Hotel del Norte* (☎ 460-1959, 460-1758,

*Calle 1 & Avenida 3)* Rooms without bath US$4.50, singles/doubles with bath US$9/15. This is a clean budget place with hot showers and TVs.

There are several budget hotels on or just off Calle 2, such as the *Hotel Cristal* (☎ 460-0541), *Hotel Diana* (☎ 460-3319), *Hotel del Valle* (☎ 460-0718), and *Hotel Axel* (☎ 460-1423). Some of these have hot water, and rooms with either shared or private bathrooms go for US$3 to US$6 per person.

*Hotel El Retiro* (☎ 460-0463) Singles/doubles with bath US$10/15. On the Parque Central, rooms here are basic but clean and have private baths with electric showers. There is a parking lot.

**Mid-Range** Just 600m south of the park is *Hotel Conquistador* (☎/fax 460-0546, 460-1877, *Calle Central)* Singles/doubles with hot bath US$17/22. It has 46 clean and adequate rooms with TVs. There is a restaurant for early breakfast and a parking lot.

*Hotel Don Goyo* (☎ 460-1780, ☎/fax 460-6383) Singles/doubles US$16/21. A block south of the Parque Central, this hotel has 20 small but very clean and pleasant rooms with fans and private hot showers. There is a guarded parking area and a restaurant. The hotel reception is closed on weekends unless you call ahead.

*Hotel La Central* (☎ 460-0301, 460-0766, fax 460-0391) Singles/doubles with bath US$15/25. On the park, this place has 50 small and clean but older rooms with fans, TV, and hot water. There is a restaurant, public fax service, and a tiny casino. The hotel is popular with local businesspeople.

*Balneario San Carlos* (☎ 460-6857, fax 460-2145) Doubles with bath US$18. On the northwestern outskirts of town, these 10 basic cabins are in a complex that includes a swimming pool, restaurant, and bar. There's dancing on weekends.

**Top End** Look for the large white gate at *El Tucano Resort & Thermal Spa* (☎ 460-6000, fax 460-1692, ℮ tucano@central america.com, Ⓦ www.occidentaltucano .com) Standard doubles US$105, deluxe rooms US$157, suites US$221. This relaxing Mediterranean-style resort is 8km northeast of Ciudad Quesada on the left-hand side of the road leading to Aguas Zarcas. Facilities include a recommended

Italian restaurant, swimming pool, Jacuzzi, and sauna, and various sports facilities ranging from tennis courts to miniature golf. Nearby thermal springs are tapped into three small hot pools where you can soak away your ills. The thermal waters are said to have medicinal and therapeutic properties. A spa provides massages, mud baths, and more. Horse, boat, and vehicle excursions can be arranged to anywhere in the region. The whole complex is well run and popular, and the 182-hectare resort offers 90 spacious rooms with large beds, cable TVs, and fans.

The full high-season rates that are given above include breakfast. Day visitors are charged about US$3 Monday to Thursday and US$9 on weekends to use the pools and facilities.

Outside the hotel is a public park and recreation area named **Aguas Termales de la Marina** – popularly referred to as 'El Tucanito' by the locals – through which flows the same hot river used in the hotel. You can bathe directly in the hot springs for US$2.

Both the hotel and hot springs can be reached from Quesada by taxi or by a variety of buses to Puerto Viejo, Pital, Venecia, Río Frío, etc.

Several other good hotels are found to the north in or near Muelle de San Carlos, as described in the Northern Lowlands chapter.

**Places to Eat**
There aren't many fine restaurants, but you certainly won't starve. Apart from the *hotel restaurants*, there are several places to eat on or near the park and budget travelers can stroll along the first two blocks of Calle 2, north of the northwest corner of Parque Central, to the produce market. There's a bunch of cheap eateries at the bus terminal.

*Restaurant Coca Loca* (☎ 460-3208) This is cattle country, and Coca Loca, on the west side of the park, is perhaps the town's best steakhouse. Also on this side of the park are *Pollos Jeffry* (☎ 460-3351) for chicken, *Pops* for ice cream, and *Pizza Hut*. Half a block east of the northeast corner is a *Musmanni Bakery* with the usual selection of baked goods. *La Terraza*, an upstairs restaurant on Calle Central three blocks north of the park, is locally popular.

## Entertainment

There's a three-screen cinema in the Plaza San Carlos, a new shopping center 1km north of the center.

## Getting There & Away

Buses to Ciudad Quesada leave San José from the Atlántico Norte terminal about every hour from 5am to 7:30pm. The journey costs about US$2.50 and is an attractive ride over the western flanks of the Cordillera Central, reaching 1850m at Laguna, just beyond Zarcero. Then begins the long and pretty descent to Quesada at 650m. The bus makes many stops and takes three hours, unless you get a direct one all the way to Quesada (2¼ hours).

The bus terminal in Quesada is in the Plaza San Carlos, about 1km north of the center. Autotransportes San Carlos has buses to San José about every hour from 5am to 6:15pm. Buses to Fortuna take just over an hour, leaving at 6am, 10:30am, 1pm, 3:30pm, and 5:15pm; there are several routes, so ask at the station. Buses to Tilarán take four or five hours and leave at 6am and 4pm, stopping in Fortuna. At other times, buses from other towns to Fortuna come through here; seats may be available.

Eastbound buses leave for Puerto Viejo de Sarapiquí via Venecia eight times a day from 4:40am to 8pm – the 6am, 10am, and 3pm departures continue to Río Frío. Buses north to Los Chiles leave 13 times a day from 5am to 5pm; and northwest to San Rafael de Guatuso, buses leave three times a day. Ask at the bus terminal for other local destinations.

## FORTUNA

Officially called La Fortuna de San Carlos, this small town (population about 7500) is the nearest to the spectacular Volcán Arenal. Fortuna is 250m above sea level and has excellent views of the 1633m volcano only 6km to the west. The volcano attracts many visitors, and Fortuna's tourist industry has expanded greatly in recent years, so you'll see many other travelers here. It's a friendly town with various local attractions, including a lovely waterfall, hot springs, a lake, the inevitable canopy tour, horseback rides, and tours to caves and the nearby Caño Negro wildlife refuge (described in the Northern Lowlands chapter).

## Orientation & Information

The map doesn't show street names because there are no street signs in Fortuna, although there are plans to erect some. Even if street signs appear, locals will continue to use landmarks instead. The central soccer field is slowly being rebuilt into a park, with a bandstand in the southeast corner next to the bus stop.

There's no impartial tourist office, though tour offices give tourist information (see Organized Tours, below). Most of the hotels provide tourist information, too.

Banco Popular, Banco de Costa Rica, and Banco Nacional change money, with the first giving the fastest service. Both the Banco Popular and Banco de Costa Rica have Visa-Plus ATMs.

Internet access is available at the matter-of-factly named Internet, open 8am to 10pm daily and charging US90¢ for 30 minutes. Also check many of the tourist agencies and hotels; those that also charge under US$1 for 30 minutes include La Posada Inn, Hotel Las Colinas, Aguas Bravas, and Desafio Tours, among others.

The clinic, police station, and post office are shown on the Fortuna map. Masajes Serendipity offers to treat weary muscles for US$20. The laundry on the main street is open 8am to 9pm Monday to Saturday and charges US$5.75 to wash and dry a small (4kg) load.

## La Catarata de La Fortuna

A visit to this long and narrow waterfall is one of the area's most popular excursions, after the obligatory visits to the Arenal volcano and lake. It is easy to visit the falls from town – you don't need a guide unless you want one.

A signed road runs from the south side of the church (the sign claims it is 5.5km to the falls). After almost 1km, the paved road becomes dirt and makes several twists and turns; each one of these is marked, though the signs are sometimes hard to see. It makes a pleasant walk through agricultural countryside. Alternately, ride a horse or drive, though you'll need 4WD in the rainy months. Early risers will find good birding along this road.

At the overlook to the falls, you must park; snacks and sodas are sold here. A good view of the ribbonlike falls cascading

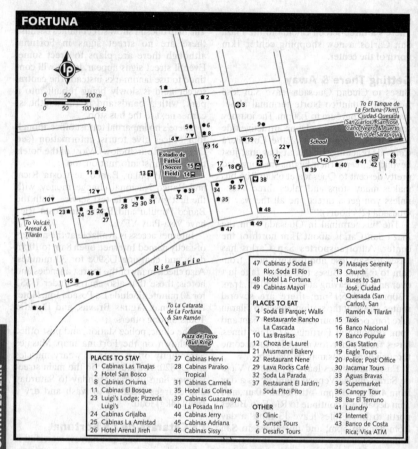

## FORTUNA

0   50   100 m
0   50   100 yards

To El Tanque de
La Fortuna (7km),
Ciudad Quesada
(San Carlos), San José,
Caño Negro & Puerto
Viejo de Sarapiquí

Estadio de
Fútbol
(Soccer
Field)

School

To Volcán
Arenal &
Tilarán

Río Burío

To La Catarata
de La Fortuna
& San Ramón

Plaza de Toros
(Bull Ring)

**PLACES TO STAY**
1  Cabinas Las Tinajas
2  Hotel San Bosco
8  Cabinas Oriuma
11 Cabinas El Bosque
23 Luigi's Lodge; Pizzería
   Luigi's
24 Cabinas Grijalba
25 Cabinas La Amistad
26 Hotel Arenal Jireh
27 Cabinas Hervi
28 Cabinas Paraíso
   Tropical
31 Cabinas Carmela
35 Hotel Las Colinas
39 Cabinas Guacamaya
40 La Posada Inn
44 Cabinas Jerry
45 Cabinas Adriana
46 Cabinas Sissy

47 Cabinas y Soda El
   Río; Soda El Río
48 Hotel La Fortuna
49 Cabinas Mayol

**PLACES TO EAT**
4  Soda El Parque; Walls
7  Restaurante Rancho
   La Cascada
10 Las Brasitas
12 Choza de Laurel
21 Musmanni Bakery
22 Restaurant Nene
29 Lava Rocks Café
32 Soda La Parada
37 Restaurant El Jardín;
   Soda Pito Pito

**OTHER**
3  Clinic
5  Sunset Tours
6  Desafío Tours

9  Masajes Serenity
13 Church
14 Buses to San
   José, Ciudad
   Quesada (San
   Carlos), San
   Ramón & Tilarán
15 Taxis
16 Banco Nacional
17 Banco Popular
18 Gas Station
19 Eagle Tours
20 Police; Post Office
30 Jacamar Tours
33 Aguas Bravas
34 Supermarket
36 Canopy Tour
38 Bar El Terruno
41 Laundry
42 Internet
43 Banco de Costa
   Rica; Visa ATM

---

down the far side of a very steep forested canyon is enough for some people. A US$3 fee allows you to continue down an extremely steep trail to the base of the falls. People swim there, though it can get pretty wild after heavy rains, so take care and don't swim under the falls themselves, which is very dangerous. Remember that the hike out afterward is steep uphill! The admission fees have been used to stabilize the trail and build steps in the steepest sections. Allow several hours roundtrip if you are walking, and bring a picnic lunch.

### Organized Tours

A number of tour operators have sprung up in the past few years. Many operate out of hotels. Prices and quality of tours can vary substantially, so shop around and try to talk to someone who has just been on a tour to see what's good.

Tour touts meet tourists arriving on buses or talk to travelers on the streets. These folks aren't reliable and may either steer you to an agency in return for a commission or take you on a tour with inferior service. Touts are best avoided; if you must use them, don't pay any money up front. It's best to use one of the many agencies in hotels or with their own offices.

The most popular tour is a visit to Volcán Arenal. You can go by day or night, though an increasingly popular option is a mid-afternoon departure to take a short hike in daylight, watch the sunset, and observe nocturnal volcanic activity. If the weather is clear, red-hot lava around the distant crater can be seen at night. (Note that tours can't get close to the crater because it's extremely dangerous.) If it is cloudy in late afternoon, it is unlikely that you will see the lava, and there is no refund if you don't see anything. You may hear the explosions in the distance. Many tours allow time for a soak in the Tabacón hot springs, which becomes a sort of second prize on cloudy nights, but this is at extra cost. (Both the volcano and Balneario Tabacón are described in detail later in this chapter.) Night tours leave daily and cost US$20 to US$30 per person – shop around. Discounts are sometimes available if you buy the tour through the hotel where you are staying. The cheapest tours are more crowded, and some offer a dip in some free hot springs. The pricier tours include national park entrance and better guides and vehicles. Always check to see which hot springs might be part of the tour and whether the entry fee is included or extra.

Tours are also available to La Catarata de La Fortuna waterfall (see earlier) by horseback (half day, US$22 per person), Caño Negro by bus and boat (from US$45 for a full day), the caves at Venado, fishing on Laguna de Arenal (US$135/250 for a half/full day per boat, which takes two anglers), and other local places on request. The Caño Negro tour is one of the most popular, and Fortuna is as good a base as any from which to do this trip. Note that these prices vary; the cheaper tours aren't necessarily better value.

Other tours include white-water rafting on the Ríos Toro and Peñas Blancas. Tours range from 1½ to 3½ hours of river time, with Class III and IV rapids. The trips vary depending on local conditions and cost US$40 to US$70 per person.

Of the several tour operators, **Sunset Tours** (☎ 479-9800, 479-9801, ☎/fax 479-9415, fax 479-9099, ✉ mcastro@racsa.co.cr) is one of the best established and most helpful. Apart from tours, the staff will help with flight reconfirmation, international phone and fax messages, and local information. **Desafío Tours** (☎ 479-9464, fax 479-9463, ✉ desafio@racsa.co.cr) has been recommended by readers for adventure tours and specializes in local river rafting. **Arenal Adventures** (☎ 479-9133, 479-9300, fax 479-9295, ✉ avarenal@racsa.co.cr, ⊛ www.arenal

adventures.com) offers mountain biking, fishing, Caño Negro, and other tours. **Aguas Bravas** (☎ 292-2072, 479-9025, fax 229-4837, ✉ info@aguas-bravas.co.cr, ⊛ www.aguas-bravas.co.cr) has river trips. **Eagle Tours** (☎/fax 479-9091, 479-9485) and **Jacamar Tours** (☎/fax 479-9456, ✉ jacamar@racsa.co.cr) also appear reputable.

## Places to Stay – In Town

Fortuna is popular with both ticos and foreign travelers interested in seeing the famous exploding volcano. On weekends, especially in holiday periods, the cheaper hotels can be full, so try to arrive early or make an advance reservation if possible. Prices tend to be a little higher during holiday weekends and lower when the town isn't full; listed here are approximate busy-weekend rates.

A number of small, family-run places, each with just a few simple rooms with private bath and electric showers or shared showers, provide cheapish lodging. Some aren't well signed, and you may hear about them through word of mouth. These places will help arrange local tours and are a good way to help locals cash in on the tourism boom. Hotel touts meet the buses and are a little more aggressive with their wares than in most of Costa Rica; not all are trustworthy.

Note that hotels beyond the town center are listed separately here (see the additional Places to Stay sections below).

**Budget** Bathroom and kitchen facilities are available for campers at **Cabinas Sissy** (☎ 479-9256, 479-9356) Campsites US$2 per person, singles/doubles US$7/12. The 12 rooms are basic but clean and have fans and electric showers. Guests have kitchen privileges.

**La Posada Inn** (☎/fax 479-9793) Rooms without bath US$5. This basic but clean and friendly place has four rooms with shared hot showers and is popular with young backpackers.

**Cabinas Adriana** (☎ 479-9474) Rooms US$3 per person. This rundown hotel has cramped rooms with fans and shared baths; thefts have been reported.

**Cabinas Jerry** (☎ 479-9707) Rooms with shared bath US$5 per person, singles/doubles US$10/12. Three small rooms sleep two, three and four people and share a shower. Six better rooms have private bathrooms and fans. Travelers have given mixed reports about the security of this place.

**Hotel Dorothy** (e *noelsamuels@usa.net*) Rooms US$6 per person. Readers have recommended this new hotel, 200m south and 25m east of the church (just off the map). Rooms have private hot showers, and the owner, Noel, from Limón, is knowledgeable, helpful, and speaks English.

**Cabinas El Bosque** (☎ 479-9365) Rooms with shared bath US$7 per person, singles/doubles with private bath US$9/15. Friendly and family run, this tranquil place has a garden and hot showers, and it's away from the bustling center.

**Cabinas y Soda El Río** (☎ 479-9341) Singles/doubles US$10/14. This tiny place is next to a popular little restaurant. Rooms have fans and hot showers.

**Cabinas Carmela** (☎/fax 479-9010, e/mail *cabinascarmela@racsa.co.cr*) Singles/doubles US$15/20. This clean place has 13 fairly large rooms with private hot-water bath and fan. Mattresses are good and firm. Some rooms have minifridges, and one has a kitchenette. Parking is available.

**Cabinas La Amistad** (☎ 479-9390, 479-9364, fax 479-9342) Rooms US$10 per person. Thirteen standard rooms offer fans and private hot showers. Four more rooms with kitchenette and bath are US$30/double. Parking is available.

**Cabinas Grijalba** (☎/fax 479-9129) Rooms US$10 per person. All rooms have private hot showers, and some have TV.

**Hotel La Fortuna** (☎/fax 479-9197) Singles/doubles with hot bath US$12/20. This decent place has 13 rooms and a soda.

**Cabinas Hervi** (☎ 479-9430, 479-9100) Singles/doubles without bath US$10/13, with bath US$15/20. This reader-recommended place has good-size rooms with bath and fan, and smaller, dingy rooms sharing two baths and a kitchen.

**Cabinas Oriuma** (☎/fax 479-9111) Rooms US$10 per person. This is a family-run place (the office is in the hardware store downstairs) with six rooms, most with a queen and two single beds and private hot shower. They advertise US$10 per person, but this is usually for three or four people; singles and doubles have to be negotiated according to demand.

**Mid-Range** A swimming pool is featured at **Cabinas Mayol** (☎ 479-9110) Singles/doubles US$15/25, new rooms US$35. The rooms have fans and are clean if spartan. The four new rooms have TV, minifridge, coffeemaker, and two double beds.

**Cabinas Las Tinajas** (☎ 479-9308, fax 479-9099) Doubles with bath US$30. Here you'll find four clean and spacious rooms with fans and hot water, on a quiet street.

**Hotel Las Colinas** (☎ 479-9305, ☎/fax 479-9107, e *hcolinas@racsa.co.cr*) Rooms US$15 per person, including breakfast. This place is clean and good with 19 rooms, all with fan, private bath, and hot water. Management is friendly and helpful, and Internet access is available.

**Cabinas Guacamaya** (☎ 479-9393, ☎/fax 479-9087, e *info@cabinasguacamaya.com*, W *www.cabinasguacamaya.com*) Singles/doubles/triples/quads US$41/47/58/69. The nine light, good-size, air-conditioned but spartan rooms have refrigerator, private bath, and hot water. There is a patio with volcano views; a parking area; and a small breakfast room.

**Cabinas Paraíso Tropical** (☎ 479-9222, ☎/fax 479-8239) Doubles US$35-50. This place offers 12 pleasant, spacious, air-conditioned rooms, all with private bath and hot water. Some rooms have cable TV, a minifridge, and kitchenette.

**Hotel Arenal Jireh** (☎ 479-9004, ☎/fax 479-9236, e *jimmyv@racsa.co.cr*) Singles/doubles US$35/41. Rooms here are air-conditioned and come with TV and refrigerator. Bathrooms have hot water, and three have a tub/shower combo. There's a small pool.

**Hotel San Bosco** (☎ 479-9050, fax 479-9109, e *fortuna@racsa.co.cr*, W *www.arenal-volcano.com*) Singles/doubles/triples with bath & fan US$35/40/45, with bath & air-con US$45/50/55. This hotel has balcony views of Arenal, a garden with a pool and Jacuzzi, and a guarded parking lot. It can arrange tours. There are eight pleasant fan-equipped rooms and 19 air-conditioned, more spacious rooms. However, few single rooms are available. Some rooms sleep four or five. Two furnished houses, each with kitchen and fans, cost US$80 (six beds, one bathroom, maximum eight people) and US$100 (10 beds, two bathrooms, maximum 14 people).

*Luigi's Lodge* (☎ 479-9909, 479-9636, ☎/ fax 479-9898, ⓔ luigis@racsa.co.cr, ⓦ www .luigislodge.com) Singles/doubles/triples US$59/70/83, including breakfast. Twenty-four carpeted, air-conditioned rooms have ceiling fans, refrigerators, and shower/tub bathrooms with hair dryers. Some rooms have TV, and many open onto an upstairs balcony with good volcano views (though Fortuna is not the side with the most lava). There's a good-size swimming pool and a gym (free for guests, US$4.50 a day, US$14 a month for the public). A good Italian restaurant is attached.

## Places to Stay – East of Town
*Cabinas Villa Fortuna* (☎/fax 479-9139) Doubles with bath US$40-46. Almost 1km east of town, this place is set in pleasant gardens that have chili-pepper plants and uncaged pet toucans. The rooms are clean, and each has a fridge and private hot shower. Some rooms have air-conditioning, and most have views of the volcano.

*Hotel Las Cabañitas* (☎/fax 479-9400, 479-9408, ⓔ cabanita@racsa.co.cr) Doubles US$80 (US$12 for additional people). Almost 1.5km east of Fortuna, this resort has two pools, a tour desk, restaurant, bar, and 30 spacious individual cabins, all with ceiling fans and porches and many with great volcano views; no TVs or telephones are in the rooms.

*Hotel Rancho Corcovado* (☎ 479-9300, ☎/fax 479-9090) Rooms US$55/65. In the village of El Tanque de La Fortuna, 7km east of Fortuna, is this clean, comfortable, and helpful place, which has a swimming pool and restaurant and arranges local tours and horse rental.

Beyond El Tanque, the road continues to Muelle de San Carlos and the excellent Tilajari Resort Hotel, 20km from Fortuna and described in the Northern Lowlands chapter.

## Places to Stay – South of Town
*Arenal Country Inn* (☎ 479-9670, 479-9669, fax 479-9433, ⓔ info@costaricainn.com, ⓦ www.costaricainn.com) Singles/doubles US$88/95. The paved road to San Ramón passes this place, which is about 1km south of town. Here you'll find 20 spacious, modern, air-conditioned rooms, all with two queen-size beds and private patio; some rooms are wheelchair-accessible. Rates

include full breakfast. The restaurant-bar is an interesting open-air affair, housed in a restored cattle corral. Spacious grounds include adults' and children's pools, volcano views, and a river running through the property. This is a quiet and relaxing hotel, with friendly, helpful staff.

*Chachagua Rainforest Lodge* (☎ 231-0356, fax 290-6506, ⓔ chachagua@novanet .co.cr, ⓦ www.novanet.co.cr/chachagua) Singles/doubles with bath US$84/98. This lodge is about 12km south of Fortuna, 2km off the main highway to San Ramón. The rough final stretch into the lodge may require 4WD after rains. It's a working cattle and horse ranch adjacent to the Children's Eternal Rainforest reserve; horseback rides are available, and the wildlife watching is reportedly excellent. Accommodations are available in two dozen comfortable wooden bungalows with spacious baths and ceiling fans; each has a porch or terrace. You can watch birds and horses from the open-air restaurant.

## Places to Stay – West of Town
Several hotels are nearby on the road that heads west toward the volcano.

*Hotel Arenal Rossi* (☎ 479-9023, fax 479-9414, ⓔ contactus@hotelarenalrossi.com, ⓦ www.hotelarenalrossi.com) Singles/ doubles with fan US$38/47, with air-con US$47/55 and up. Two kilometers west of town, this hotel offers 25 rooms, all with private hot bath, TV, and minifridge. The 16 air-conditioned rooms vary in size and go up to US$68 double; some sleep up to five for US$89. There is a gift shop, swimming pool, and small kids' playground. A restaurant specializing in steaks is on the premises.

*Cabinas Las Flores* (☎ 479-9307) Singles/doubles with hot bath US$20. Close to Hotel Arenal Rossi, this friendly place has clean rooms, and the helpful owner often gives discounts if things are slow. Camping is allowed for US$3 per person.

*La Catarata Ecotourist Lodge* (☎ 479-9612, 479-9522, fax 479-9168, ⓔ cooprena@ racsa.co.cr) Singles/doubles/triples with hot bath US$30/48/66. This place is on a side road almost 2km south of Cabinas Las Flores. It is another of the ecotourism projects run by local communities and funded by the Canadian WWF, ACA, and other agencies (see the Volcán Tenorio Area and Monteverde &

Santa Elena sections, earlier in this chapter, for similar projects). As such, it is well worth supporting. Great volcano views and tours led by locals are highlights. There are nine cabins, and rates include full breakfast. A simple restaurant serves casados (US$6) for the other meals. A butterfly garden, orchid house, and paca-breeding house can be visited (US$1 for nonguests).

*Jungla & Senderos Los Lagos* (☎ 479-8000, 479-9126, fax 479-8009) Singles US$62-72, US$10 per extra person. About 6km west of Fortuna, this place has a nicely landscaped garden with two swimming pools (one heated), scary concrete water slides, a swim-up bar, a restaurant, gift shop, and pleasant air-conditioned rooms and cabins (for one to five people) with cable TVs, phones, minifridges, and private hot showers. From the entrance area, a dirt road with scenic views climbs steeply to two lakes in the foothills of the volcano, about 3km away from the entrance. Above here, two tourists and their guide were caught in a gaseous eruption in August 2000; only one person survived. Some of the upper trails are now closed, and the lower area, where the hotel is, lies in a valley that might be covered by deadly gaseous or volcanic flows in the event of a major eruption. The danger isn't imminent, but the situation could change for the worse very quickly at any time.

*Volcano Lodge* (☎ 460-6080, 460-6022, fax 460-6020, e volcanolodge@racsa.co.cr, w www.costaricavolcanolodge.com) Doubles US$90, including continental breakfast. With about two dozen modern rooms, this new hotel gets extra points for its excellent volcano views from both patios and picture windows. Each room has two double beds and a hot shower, as well as rocking chairs to relax in while gazing at Arenal. A restaurant, large pool, and Jacuzzi are available.

*Hotel Arenal Paraiso* (☎ 460-5333, fax 460-5343, e arenalpa@racsa.co.cr, w www .arenalparaiso.decostarica.co.cr) Doubles with fans/air-conditioning US$69/101, extra people about US$20. Full breakfast is included. Eight kilometers west of Fortuna, on the north side of the volcano, this newly expanded place now has 12 clean standard cabins with ceiling fans, refrigerators, cable TVs, telephones, private baths, hot water, and patios with volcano views. It also has 25 larger, air-conditioned, deluxe wooden cabins, a few of which are wheelchair-accessible. These have larger, glassed-in porches. Guests can use a Jacuzzi or one of two pools (one is for kids) and a swim-up bar; there is a restaurant. Short walking trails behind the hotel go to a private waterfall.

*Montaña de Fuego Inn* (☎ 460-1220, 479-9579, 460-6720, fax 460-1455, e monfuego@ racsa.co.cr, w www.montanadefuego.com) Standard/deluxe doubles US$95/121, US$25 for additional people. Rates include breakfast buffet. Nine kilometers west of town, this inn has 16 older standard and 24 deluxe rooms, mostly in wooden duplex cabins, each with a patio and picture windows facing the volcano. The deluxe rooms are larger and of lighter construction; they have both front and back decks, with the back one giving views of the forested hillside (and of other cabins!). More rooms are planned. All rooms sleep up to four and have views, fans, and hot showers, and some have air-conditioning. Amenities include a pool with swim-up bar; a Jacuzzi; and a spa with sauna, massage rooms, mud baths, and a small gym. Lunches and dinners are pricey at about US$20. Horseback riding and other local excursions can be arranged.

*Tabacón Resort* (☎ 256-1500, fax 221-3075, e sales@tabacon.com, w www .tabacon.com) Doubles/junior suites US$151/203, with breakfast buffet. Rates include unlimited access to their Tabacón Hot Springs spa, across the road and 400m away. The hotel is 12km from Fortuna and offers 73 modern, large, but uninspired air-conditioned rooms with cable TV, hair dryers, coffeemakers, and private patio or balcony, most with volcano views; nine larger junior suites are available. There is a tour desk, and mountain bikes are available for rent.

The Tabacón Resort's well-known, upscale, and undeniably lovely **Tabacón Hot Springs** features hot tubs, a water slide, swim-up bar, waterfalls, and 12 cold and hot swimming and soaking pools all set in a lovely green garden. Temperatures vary from 22°C to 41°C. The area is open 9am to 10pm daily, and there is a US$17 admission fee (US$9 for children) – the place is extremely popular with visitors from other hotels. Within the hot springs complex, the **Iskandria Spa** offers a multitude of treatments such as massages, volcanic mud masks, manicures, and aromatherapy, ranging from US$25 to US$70 and lasting 20 to 75 minutes. Treatment packages cost US$90 to US$130 and last 1½ to 2½ hours.

Admission is free to just visit the bar, café, and restaurant, from which you can watch either the bathers bathing or Arenal exploding, depending on where you sit. The views are good, especially on a clear night when your dinner is enhanced by periodic volcanic fireworks to liven up what could be called a hot date. One hopes that it doesn't get too hot – the spa is on the site where a volcanic eruption ripped through in 1975, killing one local (there weren't any tourists here in those days). In the event of an eruption, the management has installed an evacuation plan that visitors should be familiar with. Considering that a pyroclastic flow of superheated gases can travel at 100km/h, there may not be enough time to evacuate all spa-goers – then again, there probably won't be an eruption when you visit. The hotel itself, on the other side of the road and up a hill, is out of the danger area.

Farther west you pass the entrance to Parque Nacional Volcán Arenal; there are more places to stay beyond the volcano and around Laguna de Arenal, described later in this chapter.

## Places to Eat
*Soda La Parada* (☎ 479-9547) Snacks US$1-2. This soda is cheap, popular for snacks, and a good place to while away a wait for the bus. Other good inexpensive sodas include *Soda El Río*, with good, reasonably priced food in a simple setting, and *Soda El Parque*, on the north side of the soccer field.

*Musmanni Bakery* Open 5am-9pm. This bakery has the best selection of breads, etc, for a picnic. There's also a *Walls*, adjoining Soda El Parque, for ice-cream lovers.

*Lava Rocks Café* (☎ 479-9222) Dishes US$2-6. Open 7am-10pm daily. This inexpensive and popular café offers espresso and cappuccino thoughout the day in a light, modern setting. Breakfasts are US$2 to US$4; hamburgers and sandwiches are about US$2; casados, spaghetti, and meaty dinners are US$4 to US$6.

*Restaurant El Jardín* (☎ 479-9360) Meals US$4-9. Somewhat overpriced, this place is popular with tourists because of its central location. Locals eat at the outside window counter, called *Soda Pito Pito*, where prices are reasonable though selection is limited.

*Restaurante Rancho La Cascada* (☎ 479-9145, 479-9351) Sandwiches US$3, meals US$5-9. If you want more than the basic casado, this attractive, thatched-roof restaurant, at the corner of the soccer field, has average food, with both Italian and tico specialties.

*Restaurant Nene* (☎ 479-9192) Dishes US$5-8. Open 10am-11:30pm daily. This is one of the nicest places in town, though very reasonably priced. A big steak costs about US$7, and there are plenty of cheaper options.

*Choza de Laurel* (☎ 479-9231) Breakfasts US$2-4, dishes US$4-9. Open 6:30am-10pm daily. At the west end of town, this rustic place has good casados, grills, and tico food. They serve espresso and cappuccino.

*Pizzería Luigi's* (☎ 479-9909, 479-9636) Dishes US$8-14. Open 6am-11pm daily. In the hotel of the same name, this is Fortuna's best Italian restaurant. It features calzones, fettuccines, pizzas, and other pastas at the lower end of the price range, and tico and international food as well.

*Las Brasitas* (☎ 479-9819) Dishes US$5-15. Open 11am-11pm daily. At the west end of town, this is a new Mexican restaurant in a large open-air structure that has gone through several incarnations. Perhaps this one will stick.

*La Vaca Muca* (☎ 479-9186) Dishes US$6-14. Open Tues-Sun. Just under 2km west of town on the road to the volcano, this recommended place is an attractive tico-style country restaurant with good food.

## Entertainment
*Restaurante Rancho La Cascada* You can dance in the nightclub over this restaurant, but it is usually empty except on weekends. They show videos here sometimes. Otherwise, there's not much in the way of entertainment in Fortuna apart from hanging out with other travelers or locals over a beer. *Bar El Terruño* is a basic local drunks' bar that serves bocas.

*Volcán Look* (☎ 479-9690/1) About 5km west of town, this is supposedly the biggest discotheque in Costa Rica outside of San José. It's usually dead except on weekends and holidays.

## Getting There & Away

**Air** Flights stopped in September 2000 (after a plane crashed into Volcán Arenal due to pilot error). Ask locally about when they might resume.

**Bus** Direct buses from San José to Fortuna leave the Atlántico Norte terminal at 6:15am, 8:40am, and 11:30am. Alternatively, take one of the frequent buses to Ciudad Quesada and connect there with an afternoon bus. There are also buses from Tilarán.

In Fortuna, buses stop on the southeast end of the park/soccer field. There is a bus shelter here with a timetable, but it's best to check locally as the timetable doesn't get updated every time a schedule changes. Buses for San José (US$2.50, 4½ hours) leave at 12:45pm and 2:45pm. Buses for Ciudad Quesada leave 10 times a day. Some of these connect in Ciudad Quesada with a San José bus. Buses for Tilarán leave at 8am and 5:15pm. Buses for San Ramón leave at 5:30am, 9am, 1pm, and 4pm. For most other northern destinations, ask locally; you'll usually be told to go to Ciudad Quesada and change buses.

Most hotels will make reservations for Interbus, which goes to San José at 8am and 1:30pm for US$25. There are also daily morning departures (usually at 8:30am or 9am) from Fortuna to Monteverde, Liberia, Puerto Viejo de Sarapiquí, and several Pacific beach towns for US$25 to US$38.

## PARQUE NACIONAL VOLCÁN ARENAL

This park was created in 1995. Along with Tenorio, Miravalles, the Monteverde cloud forest reserve, and other areas, it is part of the Area de Conservación Arenal, which protects most of the Cordillera de Tilarán. This area is rugged and varied, and the biodiversity is high; roughly half the species of land-dwelling vertebrates (birds, mammals, reptiles, and amphibians) known in Costa Rica can be found here.

Obviously, the centerpiece of this park is the volcano. Arenal was dormant from about AD 1500 until July 29, 1968, when huge explosions triggered lava flows that destroyed two villages and killed about 80 people and 45,000 cattle. Despite this massive eruption, the volcano retained its almost perfect conical shape, which, combined with its continuing activity, makes Arenal everyone's image of a typical volcano. Occasionally, the activity quiets down for a few weeks or even months, but generally Arenal has been producing menacing ash columns, massive explosions, and glowing red lava flows almost daily since 1968.

Every once in a while, perhaps lulled into a sense of false security by a temporary pause in the activity, someone tries to climb to the crater and peer within it. This is very dangerous – climbers have been killed and maimed by explosions. The problem is not so much getting killed (that's a risk the foolhardy insist is their own decision) but rather risking the lives of Costa Rican rescuers.

The best nighttime views of the volcano are usually from its north side, although activity can sometimes be seen from any direction. Still, most visitors drive or take a tour around to the north side in hope of catching these most impressive views. The degree of activity varies from year to year and week to week – even day to day. Sometimes it can be a spectacular display of flowing red-hot lava and incandescent rocks flying through the air; at other times the volcano subsides to a gentle glow. During the day, the glowing lava isn't easy to see, but you might still see a great cloud of ash thrown up by a massive explosion. Between 1998 and 2000, the volcano was particularly active (which is when many of those spectacular photos you see in tourist brochures were taken). In 2001 and early 2002, the volcano was less active, but you can still expect to see some lava glowing on a clear night. It could well be really rambunctious by the time you read this.

Be aware that clouds can cover the volcano at any time, and tours don't guarantee a view (though sometimes you can hear explosions). Also be aware that on cloudy, rainy days, a tour can be a miserably cold affair, and that staying in your (sometimes expensive) hotel room can be rather miserable as well!

## Orientation & Information

The ranger station/information center (☎ 461-8499) is on the west side of the volcano and is reached by driving west of Fortuna for 15km, then turning left at a 'Parque Nacional' sign and taking a 2km dirt road to the entrance, open 7am to

10pm. Here you pay the US$6 park fee. There is a restroom here. A road continues 1.4km toward the volcano, where there is a parking lot. From here, a 2km trail continues toward the volcano. Rangers will tell you how far you are allowed to go. Currently, this area is not in a danger zone.

It should be noted that this route gets you close to the volcano, but as a result, the view is foreshortened. Many visitors prefer more distant views from some of the lodges west of the volcano or from Laguna de Arenal. However, the explosions do sound loud from here!

## Places to Stay

**Inside the Park** No camping is allowed inside the park, though people have camped (no facilities) off some of the unpaved roads west of the volcano by the shores of the lake.

There are plenty of places to stay in Fortuna (see earlier) and outside of the park around Laguna de Arenal (see below), but only the following lodge is within the park itself.

**Arenal Observatory Lodge** (☎ 695-5033, e info@arenal-observatory.co.cr, w www.arenal-observatory.co.cr) Rooms US$52-149. This lodge is operated by Costa Rica Sun Tours (☎ 296-7757, fax 296-4307, e info@crsuntours.com, w www.crsuntours.com). Originally a private observatory, it was established in 1987 on a macadamia nut farm on the south side of Volcán Arenal. The site was chosen both for its proximity to the volcano and for its safe location on a ridge. Volcanologists from all over the world, including researchers from the Smithsonian Institution in Washington, DC, have come to study the active volcano. A seismograph operates around the clock.

The lodge has 30 rooms and is a good base for exploring the nearby countryside. It's set on a ridge just over 2km from the volcano, and volcano views and sounds of eruptions are excellent, although most lava flows are on the north side while the hotel is on the west. Laguna de Arenal is visible in the other direction. Four rooms, the new pool, and a paved trail through the property are wheelchair-accessible. A Jacuzzi and a massage therapist are on the property. You can hike to a nearby waterfall (short hike); to see recent lava flows (2½ hours); to see old lava flows (three hours); or to climb Arenal's

dormant partner, Volcán Chato, which is 1100m high and only 3km southeast of Volcán Arenal (four hours). There is a lake in Chato's summit crater, and canoes and paddles are provided for those who can't resist the chance to boat out on a volcano. For the best nighttime views, a guided hike is suggested. Maps and local English-speaking guides are available for these hikes.

You can wander around the macadamia nut farm or through the primary forest that makes up about half of the 347-hectare site. Horse rental costs US$7 per hour. There's good birding, and there are good volcano views. Full-day Caño Negro tours cost US$70 per person, and Venado cave tours cost US$55.

The lodge is spread around the property. The **Observatory Block** is where the observatory was built and now houses the office, a newly remodeled restaurant-bar, and standard rooms, most with volcano view. Rates are US$73/95/109/127 for one to four people. (The wheelchair-accessible rooms are in this block but are new and are priced at the Smithsonian rate). About 200m away is the **Smithsonian Block**, reached on foot by a suspension bridge over a forested ravine – quite dramatic. The 10 newer, spacious rooms here have picture windows with volcano views and rent for US$102/128/138/149 for one to four people. A viewing deck, conference room, and seismograph are here. All the rooms have private hot showers.

**La Casona** is about a half kilometer away in the original farmhouse. It now houses four rustic double rooms sharing two bathrooms; there are volcano views from the house porch. Rates here are US$52/67/85/103. All quoted rates are for the high season and include buffet breakfast and one guided hike to the waterfall and to a lava flow (US$6 per-person park fee is extra). Lunch (US$16) and dinner (US$19) are available.

The **White Hawk Villa** is a hilltop house with two bedrooms, two bathrooms, a kitchen, sitting room, cable TV, stereo, and great views. It rents for US$350. Day use of the grounds and trails costs US$3.50 for nonguests.

Various multiday packages are available that include transport from San José or Fortuna. Otherwise, take a bus to Fortuna and hire a taxi to the lodge. Drivers from

Fortuna should turn left on the road toward Parque Nacional Arenal and drive about 9km to the lodge. There's only one major fork (after about 5.5km) where you go left – there are several signs.

**Outside the Park** If you follow the road past the ranger station to the fork described above and turn right (instead of left to the Arenal Observatory Lodge), you'll come to two other hotels.

*Linda Vista del Norte* (☎ 380-0847, fax 479-9443, ✉ info@lindavistadelnorte.com, 🖳 www.lindavistadelnorte.com) Singles/ doubles/triples US$47/65/75. Two 'suites' are US$62/91/110. Just over 3km beyond the fork, after you have forded two rivers (high clearance needed in the wet months, though bridges are planned), you reach this lodge. It has 11 simple but clean rooms with fans and private hot showers, and rates include breakfast. Set up on a ridge, the rooms have good forest and lake views, but only two have volcano views. However, the restaurant-bar has a huge picture window and outdoor terrace with super volcano views. They offer all the usual local tours at competitive prices.

About 2.5km farther, after you've forded yet another river and gone through the tiny communities of El Castillo and Pueblo Nuevo, you come to the next hotel. *Arenal Vista Lodge* (☎ 221-0965, 221-2389, 382-2565, fax 221-6230, ✉ arenalvi@racsa.co.cr, 🖳 www.arenalvistalodge.com) Singles US$76 (US$12 for additional people up to four). This attractive place has 25 spacious rooms, all with fan, private hot shower, balcony, and volcano views. There's a restaurant (breakfast US$7.50, lunch US$10, dinner US$12.50), a conference room, pool, and a volcano-viewing room. Horseback rides to a waterfall and lava flow (US$20) and other places are offered, and fishing and other excursions can be arranged.

## LAGUNA DE ARENAL AREA

It's about an 18km drive west from Fortuna, past Tabacón and the national park road, to the dam that marks the beginning of the lake. The dam is crossed by a 750m-long causeway, and the road continues around the north and west shores of the lake, past the village of Arenal, to the small town of Tilarán. Along the way are frequent splen-

did lake and volcano views. Many small hotels and other establishments have been built along this road, and they are described here in the order that you'll pass them as you drive west around the lake. Distances given are from the dam. Mostly, these are mid-range to top-end places, except in the village of Arenal.

The 88-sq-km lake is an artificial body of water formed when the dam was built in 1974, flooding small towns such as Arenal and Tronadora. Laguna de Arenal is Costa Rica's largest lake and now supplies water for Guanacaste and hydroelectricity for the region. Winds are usually strong and steady, especially at the western end during the dry season, and the lake is recommended for sailing and windsurfing. (See the Activities section of the Facts for the Visitor chapter and the 'World-Class Windsurfing' boxed text.)

Rainbow bass (locally called *guapote*) weighing up to 4kg are reported by anglers, who consider this a premier fishing spot; 10 species of fish are now found here. Boats and guides can be hired for fishing expeditions – ask at any of the major hotels in the area.

While most of the road is supposedly paved, repairs have been infrequent, and there are some huge potholes. Some of the paved road is passable to cars only with care. Don't expect to drive this stretch quickly.

## Arenal

This small village, sometimes called Nuevo Arenal, replaced the earlier Arenal and other villages that were flooded by the lake formed after 1974. The old Arenal is now 27m underwater; 3500 people were displaced. The new Arenal is 29km west of the dam and is the only town between Fortuna and Tilarán.

Arenal has a gas station, a bank, a few simple places to stay and eat, and a bus stop near the park. It also offers a disco and live Costa Rican music and dancing on weekends.

## Arenal Botanical Gardens

These gardens (☎ 694-4273, 694-4305, 385-4557 cellular, fax 694-4086, 🖳 www.jungle gold.com; admission US$8, US$6 in bad weather; open 9am-5pm daily) are 25km beyond the dam and 4km southeast of

Arenal village. They were founded in 1991 as a reserve and living library of tropical and subtropical plants. Well-laid-out trails lead past 1200 varieties of tropical plants from Costa Rica and all over the world, and guide booklets in English, German, and Spanish describe what you see. Plenty of birds and butterflies are attracted to the gardens, which feature a butterfly farm and trails through primary forest. Michael LeMay is the helpful and knowledgeable English-speaking owner.

## Places to Stay & Eat

The following listings start from the dam and work west. These places can look wonderful in sunshine and dreary in the rain – it's cloud forest scenery.

*Arenal Lodge* (☎ 228-3189, 228-7387, fax 289-6798, Ⓔ *arenal@racsa.co.cr*, Ⓦ *www.arenallodge.com*) Singles/doubles US$73/80, junior suites US$130/136, chalets US$134/143, suites US$165/171, US$23 additional people. About 400m west of the dam, a paved but incredibly steep road rises

---

### World-Class Windsurfing

Some of the world's most consistent winds blow across northwestern Costa Rica, and this consistency attracts windsurfers from all over the world. Lake Arenal is rated one of the three best windsurfing spots in the world, mainly because of the predictability of the winds. From December to April, the winds reliably provide great rides for board sailors who gather on the southwest corner of Lake Arenal for long days of fun on the water. Windsurfing is possible in other months, too, but avoid September and October, which are considered the worst.

The best company for windsurfing is **Tico Wind** (☎ 692-2002, Ⓔ *info@ticowind.com*, Ⓦ *www.ticowind.com*), which sets up a camp every year during the December 1 to April 15 season. They have state-of-the-art boards and sails that are replaced every year; rentals cost US$35 for a half day or US$65 for a full day, including lunch. They have 50 sails to allow for differing wind conditions, experience, and people's weights, but rent only 12 at a time so that surfers can pick and choose during the day as conditions change – a class act. They'll arrange nearby hotel accommodations. Serious surfers book boards weeks ahead of time; newbies and those wishing to improve their skills can take lessons.

The Hotel Tilawa (see Places to Stay & Eat in the Laguna de Arenal Area section) also has an excellent selection of sailboards that rent at comparable rates. The hotel has a windsurfing school. Lessons during the first day begin on land with stationary boards so you can learn what to do before going out on the water.

Some folks think that the high winds, waves, and world-class conditions are too much for a beginner to handle. The folks at Tilawa disagree, and say that if you don't enjoy your first day of lessons and can't get at least a short ride by the end of the day, they'll refund your money. After the first day, lessons become more expensive and cater to all skill levels – once you've learned the basics, self-motivated practice with short instructional periods is the best way to learn.

It gets a little chilly on Lake Arenal, and rentals usually include wet suits, as well as harnesses and helmets (serious boarders bring their own for the best fit, just renting the board and sail). For a warm change, head down to Bahía Salinas on Costa Rica's far northwestern coast. Resorts here offer windsurfing year-round, and though the wind may not be quite as world-class as at Lake Arenal, it comes pretty close. The seasons are the same as for the lake.

2.5km to the right to this lodge. There are exceptionally fine volcano views, and the forests surrounding the attractive grounds provide wildlife-watching opportunities. The lodge has a Jacuzzi with a volcano view, a billiards room, a pricey restaurant (most main courses US$11 to US$15), and a variety of accommodations. There are six economy rooms that sleep two and lack volcano views. There are 16 spacious tiled junior suites with wicker furniture, a good-size bathroom (hot water) and a picture window or balcony with volcano views; four junior suites have kitchenettes. Ten chalets sleep four and have kitchenettes and good views. Three larger suites sleeping up to five are available. Look for big low-season discounts here. Breakfast is included in the rates, as is use of mountain bikes, a horseback ride around the property, and transfers to Tabacón Hot Springs. The staff arranges all tours and has experienced fishing guides on hand.

*Hotel Los Heroes* (☎ 692-8012/3, ☎/fax 692-8014, ✉ heroes@racsa.co.cr, W *www.hotel losheroes.com*) Doubles without/with balcony US$55/65, apartments US$115. Just over 14km west of the dam is this unmistakable and slightly incongruous Alpine-style building with wooden balconies and window shutters. The volcano is visible from some parts of the grounds. Facilities include a cold whirlpool, swimming pool, chapel, and good European-style restaurant with a heavy Swiss influence; it's popular with European tourists. Meals seem a fair value in the US$4 to US$11 range (fondue's at the higher end). There's a poolside bar with a cheerful fireplace. Thirteen large rooms have private hot bath, and three apartments with huge bathrooms and balconies sleep up to six. Breakfast is included in the rates. Credit cards and personal checks are *not* accepted. They also run a two-deck Swiss-style tour bus from San José, leaving from the Gran Hotel Costa Rica at 8am on Tuesday, Thursday, and Saturday. Rates are US$57 per person roundtrip, including lunch and dinner with wine, cocktail, overnight accommodations, breakfast, and an Arenal volcano visit. This seems like a good deal if you don't mind traveling with a group of mainly European visitors. They have recently installed a miniature train that gives daily one-hour tours at 9am, 11am, and 1:30pm for US$3.

*Toad Hall* (☎ 692-8020, fax 692-8001, W *www.toadhall-gallery.com*) Breakfasts US$3 5, lunch US$7-8. Open 8am-5pm daily. A little over 2km farther west in the tiny community of Unión is Toad Hall, a great place to stop for a coffee (espresso drinks or regular), fruit drink, and a home-made snack or meal. Their macadamia chocolate brownies are Costa Rica's best! The restaurant overlooks the forest and serves a short but interesting and tasty menu for breakfast and lunch. While there, you can browse the art gallery, which has a small but very high-quality collection of local and indigenous art and jewelry, as well as a bookstore (travel and wildlife guides in English) and a pulpería-type general store where local farmers stop for sundries.

Just beyond Toad Hall, a dirt road to the right goes to **Venado** and on into the northern lowlands. Near Venado are caves that can be explored with guides (see San Rafael de Guatuso in the Northern Lowlands chapter).

*La Mansion Inn Arenal* (☎ 692-8018, fax 692-8019, ✉ info@lamansionarenal.com, W *www.lamansionarenal.com*) Cottages US$175, deluxe cottages US$228, suites US$291. Rates for double occupancy include a fruit basket, welcome cocktail, and full champagne breakfast. Immediately past the Venado turnoff is this inn, which is close to the lake and has a dock just over a kilometer away from the hotel. Rowing boats or canoes are available for guest use at no charge. An ornamental garden features Chorotega Indian pottery and a negative-edge swimming pool that appears to flow into the lake. The Belgian/Italian owners speak several European languages. The inn has a good if pricey restaurant (a full four-course Italian/Belgian dinner with cocktails and wine is US$61.50), a pool table, and a cozy bar – shaped like the prow of a ship – that invites lingering. The 12 huge split-level rooms, each with private terrace and lake view, feature high ceilings, Italianate painted walls, and louvered arched bathroom doors. These are lovely rooms, though the bathrooms are a tad small for the price. The deluxe cottages also have a TV and minibar with free drinks. The two spacious suites have kitchens (and bigger bathrooms). Fishing trips on the lake cost US$100 per half day for two people, and other excursions are arranged.

*Complejo Turístico La Alondra* (☎ 384-5575) Doubles with bath US$30. Two kilometers farther west is this small tico-owned place offering 10 standard rooms with private bath. Each room has a small terrace and lake view. There is a *restaurant*, open 7am to 10pm, and hiking trails are behind the property.

A kilometer beyond is *Restaurante Sabor Italiano*, a tiny place in the owner's house. Excellent wood-oven pizzas and pastas cost about US$5. The new Argentine owners may soon expand the menu.

*La Ceiba Tree Lodge* (☎/fax 692-8050, ☎ 385-1540 cellular, ☺ ceibaldg@racsa.co.cr, ☒ www.ceibatree-lodge.com) Singles/doubles with hot bath US$39/64, including breakfast. Continuing almost 4km farther brings you to this place, which has five spacious, cross-ventilated rooms and one apartment (US$99), all with attractive decor. Mountain bikes are available and tours can be arranged. Lake views from the huge ceiba tree by the house are pretty, and the grounds have a collection of 70 local orchids and good birding possibilities. The friendly owners will cook dinner for you by advance request. English and German are spoken.

Continuing west, you pass the Botanical Gardens described above and, 3km beyond La Ceiba, arrive at the next recommended place.

*Villa Decary B&B* (☎ 383-3012 cellular, fax 694-4330, ☺ info@villadecary.com, ☒ www.villadecary.com) Singles/doubles US$80/90, doubles with kitchen US$135, US$15 for additional people. This place is an all-around winner with bright, spacious, well-furnished rooms, delicious full breakfasts included, and fantastic hosts. Five rooms have private hot showers, a queen and a double bed, bright Latin American bedspreads and artwork, and balconies with excellent views of woodland immediately below (good birding from your room!) and of the lake just beyond. There are also three separate casitas with a kitchenette. Credit cards are not accepted. Paths into the woods behind the house give good opportunities for watching wildlife, including howler monkeys that might wake you in the morning (though rooms have clock radios as well). Guests can borrow binoculars and a bird guide to identify what they see. Jeff, one of the US owners, has gotten the bird

bug and can help out with identification. His partner, Bill, is a botanist specializing in palms (Decary was a French botanist who discovered a new palm). They are very enthusiastic about the area and enjoy accompanying guests into nearby Arenal on weekends to listen to tico music and introduce you to the locals. They know all the best places to eat and visit.

Arenal village is just a few kilometers beyond the Villa Decary B&B, on the left side of the highway from this direction.

*Aurora Inn* (☎ 694-4245, 694-4071, fax 694-4262, ☺ aurorainn@hotmail.com) Singles/doubles US$41/54, with breakfast. On the shoreline and next to the soccer field, this inn has a swimming pool, Jacuzzi, restaurant, bar, and 10 rooms. Fishing trips on the lake can be arranged.

*Cabinas Rodríguez* Rooms without/with bath US$5/10 per person. This friendly place, close to the Aurora, is the cheapest in the village.

*Restaurant Típico Arenal* (☎ 694-4159) Dishes US$3-6. In between the Aurora and Cabinas Rodríguez, this tico place is a good choice for budget travelers.

*Pizzeria e Ristorante Tramonti* (☎ 694-4282) Dishes US$5-8. Open 11:30am-3pm & 5pm-10pm Tues-Sun. Also in Arenal, this pizzeria is a classy Italian-run place with a wood-burning pizza oven, attractive outdoor patio, and good-value Italian meals.

*Chalet Nicholas* (☎/fax 694-4041, ☺ nicholas@racsa.co.cr) Singles/doubles US$45/69, with breakfast. Two kilometers northwest of Arenal, Chalet Nicholas is an attractive little place. Owners Catherine and John Nicholas are helpful and knowledgeable hosts; their co-owners are Great Danes (don't be alarmed when they come bounding out to greet you). The two downstairs rooms have private baths; the upstairs loft has two linked bedrooms sharing a downstairs bathroom. On clear days, all rooms have views of the volcano at the end of the lake, 25km away as the parrot flaps. The owners enjoy natural history and have a living collection of dozens of orchids. Birding is good too – one guest reported seeing 80 bird species in four days. Smoking is not allowed, and credit cards aren't accepted. This place has many repeat guests.

*Caballo Negro Restaurant* (☎ 694-4515, fax 694-4074) Lunch & dinner US$5-12.

Hours 8am-8pm daily. Three kilometers west of Arenal, the Caballo Negro (Black Horse) serves recommended vegetarian and European fare handcrafted by owner Monica, who speaks English and German. The restaurant has forest and lake views, and a canoe can be rented for paddling on the lake, which is stocked with fish. Look for iguanas, turtles, and birds while you are dining. Also here is the fabulously quirky **Lucky Bug Gallery**, which features high-quality work from local and national artisans, not least of whom are Monica's teenage triplets, Kathryn, Alexandra, and Sabrina Krauskopf. The talented girls turn the profits of their work toward an animal-rescue project – the whole family is passionate about animals, their gallery, and their restaurant. Stop here and buy a bug!

Four or five kilometers west of Arenal is a sign for the next establishment.

**Lago Coter Ecolodge** (☎ 440-6768, fax 440-6725, e ecolodge@racsa.co.cr, w www .ecolodgecostarica.com) Singles/doubles/triples: rooms US$48/56/66, cabins US$56/77/87. A 3km unpaved but OK road leads to the lodge, which is near Lago Coter. The emphasis is on natural history and adventure – amenities include naturalist guides for hiking and birding, canoes (US$15 per half day), kayaks (US$25 per half day), and horses (US$20 per half day). There are trails through the nearby cloud forest, and birding is promising – the lodge brochure claims that over 350 bird species have been recorded in the area. Guided hikes (US$20), canopy tours (US$45), and fishing (US$75 per day) are offered, and a variety of nearby excursions are available. The handsome wood-and-stone lodge has a large fireplace and a relaxation area with billiards, TV, and a small library. Food is buffet-style and plentiful and costs about US$7.50 for breakfast and US$15 for lunch or dinner. The 23 small but comfortable standard rooms are in the main lodge. A few hundred meters away, 14 larger cabins with coffeemakers and hot showers feature a mix of red-tiled and carpeted floors, white walls and paneled windows, and good lake views, though some gaze down on metal cabin roofs. Many visitors come on complete packages that include lodging, all meals, rental equipment, and activities led by naturalist guides.

**Rock River Lodge** (☎/fax 695-5644, e info@rokriverlodge.com, w www.rock riverlodge.com) Doubles US$52, bungalows US$76, US$12 for additional people. This place has six rooms in a long, rustic-looking wooden building with a porch and lake/volcano views. Eight separate bungalows have larger rooms and private terraces. The staff specializes in arranging mountain biking (rental US$40 a day with guide) and windsurfing (rental US$35 a day), with discounts to lodge guests, and can arrange other excursions. They tend to close down the windsurfing outside of the December-to-April high-wind season. There is a good **restaurant** open to the public; breakfasts cost US$7.50 and dinners cost US$15 (no lunch).

**Equus Bar/Restaurant** Meals average US$9. Four kilometers beyond Rock River is a popular bar-eatery specializing in barbecued meats. There's live music some nights – ask at your hotel.

A few hundred meters west, at the northwest end of the lake, a signed road goes to Tierras Morenas, 7km away. (It continues to Bijagua, 36km away on the flanks of Volcán Tenorio.) Four hundred meters farther up this road is the next resort.

**Mystica Resort** (☎ 692-1001, fax 692-1002, e mystica@racsa.co.cr) Singles/doubles US$41/58, with breakfast. This place has great views of the 30km-long Laguna de Arenal and the volcano puffing away just beyond the end of it. The friendly Italian owner runs a good pizzeria (open 7am to 9pm, US$5 to US$10) with a wood-burning oven on the premises, and the bar-restaurant is cozy and has a fireplace. Each of the six comfortable, uniquely decorated, good-size rooms has hot showers and opens up onto a long shared balcony with garden and lake views. The bright decor features charming light fixtures and cheerful prints on the walls. All the usual sporting and touring options can be arranged.

Almost 6km beyond the Tierras Morenas turnoff and 9km north of Tilarán, a sign points to the Hotel Tilawa.

**Hotel Tilawa** (☎ 695-5050, fax 695-5766, e tilawa@racsa.co.cr, w www.hotel-tilawa .com) Singles/doubles US$44/56 garden view, US$56/67 lake view, US$90 with kitchenette. With frescoes, columns, and architecture reminiscent of the Palace of Knossos in

Crete, this place is certainly a change from the wooden cabins found elsewhere, but some rooms could do with a little refurbishing. It is 400m off the main road and has good lake and volcano views from its hillside location. There are two dozen spacious rooms with two queen-size beds and four suites with kitchenettes. The hotel has a windsurfing school (see the 'World-Class Windsurfing' boxed text) and a 12m yacht for up to 20 passengers. Sailing tours go to Tabacón (five hours, US$49, includes entry to baths). Other local tours are offered, and mountain bikes are rented (US$10 per half day). The hotel has a swimming pool, tennis court, horse rentals, and a basic restaurant.

### Getting There & Away

**Bus** These places along Laguna de Arenal can be reached by buses between Tilarán and Fortuna or Ciudad Quesada. Also, there are buses from Tilarán to Arenal village (1¼ hours) several times a day.

There is an afternoon bus from Arenal to San Rafael de Guatuso – the bus is simply marked 'Guatuso' and goes to several other small villages in the northern lowlands.

**Car** Most of the road is narrow and winding, and although it is mostly paved there are badly potholed sections. Although it is only 60km from Tilarán around the lake to the dam at the eastern end, allow about two hours to drive.

### TILARÁN

This is a small, quiet market town 550m above sea level near the northern end of the Cordillera de Tilarán. For most foreign visitors, Laguna de Arenal (5km away) is the principal attraction, though the power-generating windmills – over 200 of them – lining the hilltops will certainly draw attention. Cattle farming is important in the area, and there is a rodeo and fiesta (Días Cívicas) on the last weekend in April that is very popular with tico visitors; hotels are often full at that time. There is another fiesta on June 13.

The pleasant climate, rural atmosphere, annual rodeo, and proximity of Laguna de Arenal have brought about the development of a small tourist industry. A local leaflet proclaims Tilarán 'the city of broad streets, fertile rains, and healthful winds, in which friendship and progress is cultivated.' I have no quibbles with that.

Cafe Internet, opposite the bus station, is open 9am to 11pm weekdays, 10am to noon, 1pm to 5:30pm, and 6:30pm to 10pm Saturday and Sunday. Rates are US$1.80 per hour.

### Places to Stay

**Hotel y Restaurant Mary** (☎/fax 695-5758) Rooms US$7/10 per person with shared/private bath. This friendly, remodeled hotel on the south side of the park is good, clean, and pleasant, and has a reasonably priced restaurant attached. There are about 18 rooms with private hot showers and fans; four rooms share a bath.

**Hotel Central** (☎ 695-5363) Rooms US$6 per person, cabins with bath US$18. This hotel is near the southeast corner of the town church, 50m from the park and 350m south of the principal road into town. Rooms are basic but clean and some have shared baths. Cabins will sleep up to four people.

**Hotel Tilarán** (☎ 695-5043) Rooms US$6 per person with shared bath, doubles US$15 with private bath. This basic 33-room hotel received a bright new coat of paint in 2002. The downstairs rooms are dark and noisy; the upstairs rooms are brighter and have TVs, but cost US$1.50 more.

**Hotel Naralit** (☎ 695-5393, fax 695-6767) Singles/doubles from US$14/21. Opposite the church, the Naralit ('Tilarán,' reversed!) has two dozen clean rooms with fans, private baths, and hot water; some have cable TVs and minifridges. Upstairs rooms are slightly bigger and cost about US$1.50 per person more.

**Hotel El Sueño** (☎/fax 695-5347) Singles/doubles with bath US$15/25. This friendly, clean place is a block from the bus terminal and the Parque Central and has free coffee and tea. (A restaurant downstairs is convenient but not part of the hotel.) A balcony has views of the Tenorio and Miravalles volcanoes, and parking is available. Twelve rooms with private baths, pretty bedspreads, warm water, ceiling fans, and cable TVs surround an indoor courtyard with a fountain. Three nicer, larger rooms with a minifridge and more TV channels are US$20/30. Three downstairs rooms without TV and sharing a bath are US$8/15. The owners are helpful.

**Hotel Guadalupe** (☎ 695-5943, fax 695-5387) Doubles US$30. This good hotel is a

NORTHWESTERN

block south and a block east of the cathedral. It has about 20 pleasant rooms, each with private bath, hot water, and TV.

*La Carreta* (☎ 695-6593, fax 695-6654) Singles/doubles US$30/55. This small six-room B&B behind the cathedral is new in 2002. The rooms are larger than others in town, and breakfast is served in the adjoining restaurant. There's a souvenir shop, Jacuzzi, small orchid garden, and a rooftop view of Tilarán and volcanoes in the distance.

## Places to Eat

*El Parque* Dishes US$3-5. This restaurant, under the Cabinas El Sueño, serves tico and Chinese food as well as sandwiches.

*La Carreta* Dishes US$5-11. Open 7am-10pm daily. In front of the hotel of the same name, this restaurant has a pleasant terrace (dine in or out) and does the best food in town. The menu is long and varied, with a selection of salads, sandwiches, pizzas, pastas, and meat and fish dishes.

## Getting There & Away

**Bus** Autotransportes Tilarán (☎ 695-5611 in Tilarán, ☎ 222-3854 in San José) buses from the Atlántico Norte terminal in San José cost about US$3.50 and take 3½ hours. They leave at 7:30am, 9:30am, 12:45pm, 3:45pm, and 6:30pm. Buses from Puntarenas leave at 11:30am and 4:30pm. Buses from Ciudad Quesada (San Carlos) via Fortuna leave at 6am and 4pm. There are several buses a day from Cañas.

Buses leave Tilarán from the bus terminal, half a block from the Parque Central as you head away from the cathedral. Buses to San José on Sunday afternoon may be sold out by Saturday. Buses between Tilarán and San José travel via Cañas and the Interamericana, not the Arenal-Fortuna-Ciudad Quesada route.

Tilatur Info (☎ 695-8520), next to the bus terminal, watches luggage (US30¢) and sells tickets to Santa Elena (Monteverde). They also sell tours, but you don't have to go on one to use their baggage and bus-ticket services.

As of this writing, the timetable (subject to change) for departures from Tilarán is as follows:

Arenal – 5am, 6am, 10am, 12:30pm, 4:30pm; 1¼ hours

Cañas – 6am, 7:30am, 8am, 8:40am, 10am, 11:30am, 3:30pm, 5pm; 45 minutes

Ciudad Quesada (via Fortuna) – 7am, 12:30pm; 4 hours

Puntarenas – 6am, 1pm; 2 hours

San José – 5am, 7am, 7:45am, 2pm, 4:45pm; 3½ hours

Santa Elena – 12:30pm; 3 hours

The travel times given in the preceding table are minimum advertised times, and buses often take longer. A few other local villages are also served by bus from Tilarán; inquire at the terminal for details.

**Car** Tilarán is 24km by paved road from the Interamericana at Cañas. The route to Santa Elena and Monteverde is unpaved and rough, though ordinary cars can get through with care in the dry season.

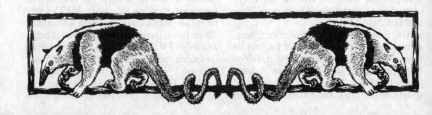

# Península de Nicoya

This peninsula jutting south from the northwestern corner of Costa Rica is over 100km long, by far the country's largest. Despite its size, it has few paved roads – most are gravel or dirt. Some of Costa Rica's major beach resorts – sometimes remote and difficult to get to – are here, offering beaches and sun rather than villages, arts, or wildlife. Most visitors come for the beaches, and if all you want to do is swim, surf, sunbathe, and relax, you'll probably enjoy a few days on part of the beautiful shoreline of the peninsula. Otherwise, you could become bored very quickly. An adventurous traveler, however, may still discover remote beaches and villages where a conversation with a smiling local could be more memorable than a hammock on the beach.

Several small wildlife reserves and a national park on the peninsula are worth visiting. In 1940, about half of the peninsula was covered with rainforest; this was mostly cut down by the 1960s. Much of the peninsula has been turned over to cattle raising, which, along with tourism, is the main industry.

The main highway through the peninsula begins at Liberia (see the Northwestern Costa Rica chapter) and follows the center of the peninsula through the small towns of Filadelfia and Santa Cruz to Nicoya, the largest town in the area (which, nevertheless, is still a small town). From Nicoya, the main road heads east to the Río Tempisque ferry (soon to be replaced by a nearby bridge) or southeast to Playa Naranjo, from where the ferry to Puntarenas leaves several times a day. These roads are good, and, for the most part, paved. Many drivers arrive from the main part of Costa Rica by taking the car ferry from Puntarenas (to Playa Naranjo or Paquera) or the car ferry across the Río Tempisque. In this chapter, however, the peninsula is covered from north to south.

From the main central highway, side roads branch out to a long series of beaches stretching along the Pacific coastline of the peninsula. Many of these roads are gravel or dirt and may be in poor condition. Once you get to the beach area of your choice, you're usually stuck there and cannot con-tinue north or south along the coast for any long distance because there's no paved coastal road. If you have a 4WD vehicle, it's possible to more or less follow the coast on the poor dirt roads. But if you're traveling

## Highlights

- Diving with massive manta rays near Playa del Coco
- Surfing, surfing, and more surfing – almost anywhere along the Pacific coast
- Buying beautiful ceramics direct from the artists at Guaitil
- Day-hiking past cliffs and ocean views while enjoying the wildlife of Cabo Blanco
- Delving deep into Costa Rica's caves at Parque Nacional Barra Honda
- Marveling at thousands of massive sea turtles arriving simultaneously at beaches to lay eggs

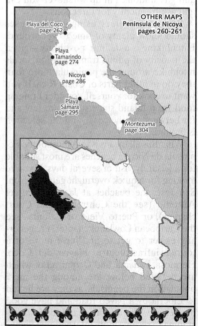

OTHER MAPS
Península de Nicoya
pages 260-261

Playa del Coco page 262
Playa Tamarindo page 274
Nicoya page 286
Playa Sámara page 295
Montezuma page 304

PENÍNSULA DE NICOYA

by bus or in an ordinary car to the next set of beaches, you often need to backtrack to the main central highway and then come back again on another road. Some beaches have a hotel but no village, and bus service may be nonexistent. If there's a small village, bus service is often limited to one per day. Many visitors come by car rather than relying on the bus, though there's no problem using buses if you have plenty of time and patience. Note that bus service may be reduced during the wet season, when few *ticos* go to the beach.

The beaches at Tamarindo, Nosara, Sámara, and Tambor have regularly scheduled flights from San José with SANSA or Travelair. This avoids the difficult road travel but limits your visit to just one beach. Some people rent a car (4WD is useful in the dry season and recommended in the wet – many car rental companies won't allow you to rent an ordinary car to go to the Península de Nicoya in the wet season), but this is an expensive option if you're going to park your car by the beach for a few days. If you decide to rent a car, be prepared for a frustrating lack of road signs and gas stations. Fill up whenever you can and ask frequently for directions.

Budget travelers using public buses should allow plenty of time to get around. Hitchhiking is a definite possibility – given the paucity of public transportation, locals hitchhike around the peninsula more than they do in other parts of Costa Rica. If you want to cook for yourself, consider bringing food from inland since stores are few and far between on the coast, and the selection is limited.

What this all means is that most of the Península de Nicoya beaches are most suitable for a leisurely visit of several days. If you're looking for a quick overnight getaway from San José, the beaches at Jacó or Manuel Antonio (see the Central Pacific Coast chapter), or Puerto Viejo or Cahuita (see the Caribbean Lowlands chapter) are generally easier to get to and have more of a tourist infrastructure. Playas del Coco, Hermosa, Panamá, and Ocotal, all of which are detailed below, are among the most popular on the peninsula, as they are linked to Liberia by a paved road and have good bus service. The airport near Liberia is beginning to receive more international flights,

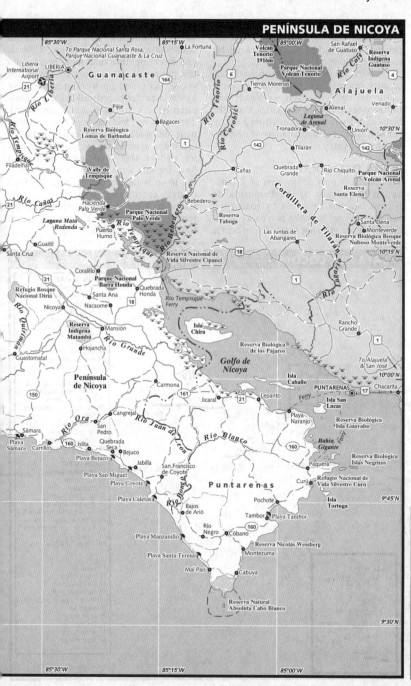

PENÍNSULA DE NICOYA

mainly serving visitors to 'all-inclusive' beach resorts in the northern part of the peninsula and surfers heading straight for the more renowned beaches.

As with beach areas throughout the country, reservations are a good idea, especially during dry-season weekends and Easter week. Prices in this chapter are the high- and dry-season prices (from December to Easter). Substantial rainy-season discounts are usually given.

## PLAYA DEL COCO

This beach is only 35km west of Liberia and is the easiest of the Península de Nicoya beaches to access by road from San José. It's set between two rocky headlands and is a growing scuba diving center (see Activities, below). Here you'll find a number of hotels, a small village, good bus connections from San José and Liberia, and more nightlife than most beaches on the peninsula. It's a popular resort for young ticos, and on weekends the town has a cheerful boardwalk beach atmosphere (think young Bruce Springsteen). The town has had garbage bins installed near the beach and organized an antilitter campaign to minimize the impact of partying visitors. Many buildings around town have for-sale signs up; this is not because the town is fading, but because longtime owners are hoping to strike it rich by selling to a big developer. However, this remains one of the less expensive beach towns on the peninsula.

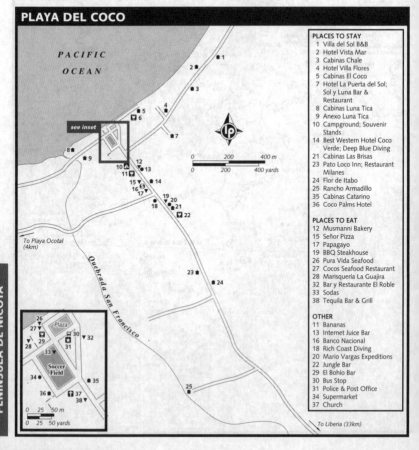

**PLAYA DEL COCO**

PACIFIC OCEAN

see inset

To Playa Ocotal (4km)

Quebrada San Francisco

To Liberia (33km)

Plaza
Soccer Field

0    25   50 m
0    25   50 yards

0    200    400 m
0    200    400 yards

**PLACES TO STAY**
1  Villa del Sol B&B
2  Hotel Vista Mar
3  Cabinas Chale
4  Hotel Villa Flores
5  Cabinas El Coco
7  Hotel La Puerta del Sol; Sol y Luna Bar & Restaurant
8  Cabinas Luna Tica
9  Anexo Luna Tica
10 Campground; Souvenir Stands
14 Best Western Hotel Coco Verde; Deep Blue Diving
21 Cabinas Las Brisas
23 Pato Loco Inn; Restaurant Milanes
24 Flor de Itabo
25 Rancho Armadillo
35 Cabinas Catarino
36 Coco Palms Hotel

**PLACES TO EAT**
12 Musmanni Bakery
15 Señor Pizza
17 Papagayo
19 BBQ Steakhouse
26 Pura Vida Seafood
27 Cocos Seafood Restaurant
28 Marisquería La Guajira
32 Bar y Restaurante El Roble
33 Sodas
38 Tequila Bar & Grill

**OTHER**
11 Bananas
13 Internet Juice Bar
16 Banco Nacional
18 Rich Coast Diving
20 Mario Vargas Expeditions
22 Jungle Bar
29 El Bohío Bar
30 Bus Stop
31 Police & Post Office
34 Supermarket
37 Church

PENÍNSULA DE NICOYA

## Information

The police station and post office are both on the southeast side of the plaza by the beach. The few people arriving at Playa del Coco by boat will find the immigration service in the police station. The Banco Nacional will change US dollars and traveler's checks. The Internet Juice Bar and Cabinas Catarina have Internet access for US$3 an hour. Note that some maps combine this beach with a neighboring one and call them Playas del Coco.

## Activities

The Playa del Coco area has the best scuba diving in Costa Rica; see the boxed text 'Scuba Diving' for details on various sites in the area. The surrounding beaches have several dive shops offering offshore **scuba diving**, and most can arrange **snorkeling** and other water sports.

Most of the dive shops are competitively priced. Typical rates start at US$50 for two dives including all gear. Trips out to Isla Catalina or the Islas Murciélago are more expensive and for experienced divers. Rates are about US$85 or US$115 for two dives here. Nondivers can go on snorkeling trips from the boat for US$25 with gear, and boats should have divemasters or instructors aboard. Instruction is offered, ranging from certification for beginners to advanced courses teaching night diving and other specialties. A complete certification course costs about US$300. People who have never dived can take an introductory lesson for about US$75, which includes a guided dive to see if they like it before shelling out for complete certification. Hotel and dive packages are also available. Always ask for low-season or multiday or group discounts.

**Sailing** is also offered. A five-hour sunset cruise with open bar costs about US$50, for example, and a full day of sailing costs about US$85 with lunch. Other cruises can be arranged.

**Surfing** is popular in the area. Surfers can hire a boat for about US$175 to take up to six people to Witches Rock, which is within Parque Nacional Santa Rosa and difficult to reach by land. This has one of the best beach breaks in the area from December to March. Potrero Grande, a surfing beach farther north, can be reached only by sea (US$200).

Power boats are available for **sportfishing** (from US$35 an hour) and **water-skiing** (from US$45 an hour). Larger boats for offshore fishing may range up to US$850 a day.

**Sea kayaking** is a great way to explore local waters. Kayaks can be rented for US$8 to US$10 a day. Irritatingly noisy and polluting, **Jet Skiing** has recently been added to the list of activities, though not without local detractors.

The following is a list of outfitters, for scuba diving and other water activities, in Playa del Coco and nearby Playa Hermosa:

**Bill Beard's Diving Safaris** (☎ 672-0012, fax 672-0213; in the USA ☎ 877-853-0538, 954-453-5044, fax 954-351-9740; ⓔ costarica@diveres.com, ⓦ www.billbeardcostarica.com, Sol Playa Hermosa Resort, Playa Hermosa) These folks have been scuba diving and snorkeling here since 1970 and are very experienced. They also do Nitrox courses and dives and can arrange extended nationwide adventure tours as well as resort packages.

**Deep Blue Diving** (☎ 670-1004, ⓔ deepblue@racsa.co.cr, ⓦ www.deepblue-diving.com, in the Best Western Playa Coco Verde on the main street of Playa del Coco) One of the newer and cheaper outfitters, they have received several reader recommendations (they have no connection with Lonely Planet whatsoever, despite their offer of a discount to carriers of this book).

**El Ocotal Resort** (☎ 670-0323, fax 670-0083, ⓔ elocotal@racsa.co.cr, ⓦ www.ocotalresort.com) This resort, overlooking Playa Ocotal, has a dive shop that can handle large groups of up to 40 divers. It also does fishing charters (it has six boats) and offers kayak rentals. Complete resort packages are offered.

**Hotel El Velero** (☎ 672-0036, ☎/fax 672-0016, ⓦ www.costaricahotel.net, Playa Hermosa) El velero means 'sailboat' in Spanish; the hotel owns a yacht and offers daily sunset cruises.

**Mario Vargas Expeditions** (☎/fax 670-0351, ⓔ divexpeditions@yahoo.com, ⓦ www.divexpeditions.com, on the main street of Playa del Coco) Tico Mario Vargas is the country's best-known divemaster and has taken ex-president Figueres diving, but not many tourists get to dive with the man himself, and their other guides aren't as good as he is. Spanish, English, French, and Italian are spoken.

**Rich Coast Diving** (☎/fax 670-0176, in the USA ☎ 800-434-8464, ⓔ dive@richcoastdiving.com, ⓦ www.richcoastdiving.com, on the main street of Playa del Coco, just past the Playa Ocotal turnoff) This young, enthusiastic company has been well reviewed by readers. It has a trimaran for sailing and overnight diving trips, and *pangas* (light boats) for fishing, water-skiing, and surfing trips. Not all divemasters speak English.

**Spanish Dancer** (☎ 670-0332, e *dancer@racsa.co.cr)* This 36-foot catamaran offers sunset and other cruises for US$35 to US$55 per person.

## Places to Stay

**Budget** There's a *campground* just off the main road (behind a bunch of souvenir stands) with basic bathrooms and showers. Camping is about US$3 per person per night.

*Cabinas Catarino* (☎ 670-0156, fax 670-0168, e *cabinascatarino@hotmail.com)* Rooms US$10 per person. This place is on the main road fairly close to the beach. It's friendly and clean, but its eight rooms (for three, four, or five people) are cramped. Each room has a fan and private cold bath. An Internet café is here. Other than this place, bottom-end hotels are

pricier around here than in most areas of Costa Rica.

*Cabinas El Coco* (☎ 670-0110, fax 670-0167, e *cocomar@racsa.co.cr)* Rooms with fan US$12-18 per person, doubles with air-con US$39. This place is to the right as you arrive on the beach and is one of the cheaper hotels. It's fairly popular, though not because the rooms are anything special. The cheapest rooms are at the back of the hotel and are dark and dingy. The better rooms are at the front and have sea views. Twelve rooms are air-conditioned and often full. There's a decent mid-priced restaurant on the premises and a disco next door. All rooms have private showers.

*Cabinas Luna Tica* (☎ 670-0127) Rooms US$13 per person. These *cabinas* have rather stuffy rooms with private baths, fans, and double beds, and not all have hot water.

## Scuba Diving

Scuba diving is the main attraction, and Playa del Coco is the best place for it in the country. There's no good beach diving in this area, so dives are around volcanic rock pinnacles near the coast, or from a boat farther off at Isla Santa Catalina (about 20km to the southwest) or Islas Murciélago (40km to the northwest near the tip of Península Santa Elena).

The diving is mediocre from a visibility standpoint (6m to 24m visibility, though it's usually well under 20m) but pretty good in other aspects. The water is warm – around 26°C at the surface, with a thermocline at around 20m below the surface, where it drops to 23°C. This means you can skin dive (no wet suit) if you want to. The best feature is the abundant marine life – you might sight manta rays with 4m to 6m fin spans, other rays, sharks, huge schools of fish, and plenty of coral-reef life. Most of the dive sites are less than 25m deep, allowing three dives a day. This is a relatively little-known area, still being explored by divers.

The so-called Papagayo winds blow from early December to late March, and they make the water choppy and cooler, cutting down on visibility, especially for the four days around the full moon. June and July are usually the best months for visibility. Manta rays are frequently reported around Isla Catalina from late December to late April. The Islas Murciélago (Bat Islands) take almost two hours to reach from shore, but divers are rewarded with excellent diving – they may see huge bull sharks or big fish such as jewfish and groupers, as well as schools of innumerable smaller fish. Narizones is known as a good deep dive (about 27m). Note that the Bat Islands are definitely best in the wet season – it gets really cold and choppy in the dry season. For inexperienced divers, Punta Gorda is considered one of the easier descents.

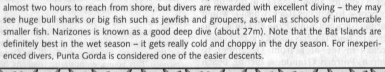

There's a decent restaurant, and breakfast is included in the low season.

**Anexo Luna Tica** (☎ 670-0459) Across the street from Cabinas Luna Tica and similarly priced, the rooms here seem breezier and better. These are probably the best of the budget options. The reception area is in the cabinas.

**Cabinas Las Brisas** (☎ 670-0155) Doubles with bath US$26. These basic rooms have small fans that don't seem to move the air very much.

**Cabinas Chale** (☎ 670-0036) Doubles with bath US$34. About 100m from the beach and a 600m walk from town, this simple place is to the right as you arrive (there are signs). The 25 air-conditioned rooms are clean but unexciting; some have a fridge, and there's a big pool. Some rooms sleep five or six people, and you can negotiate good rates for these at not much above the double rate – a good deal.

**Mid-Range** Clean, spacious rooms have fans and hot water at **Coco Palms Hotel** (☎ 670-0367, fax 670-0117, e hotelcoco palm@racsa.co.cr) Rooms with bath US$18 per person, with breakfast. A larger room that sleeps six costs US$73. The attached bar is popular with Europeans, and a large 'German Embassy' sign welcomes beer drinkers. There's a good restaurant here.

**Pato Loco Inn** (☎/fax 670-0145, e patoloco@racsa.co.cr, w www.costarica info.com/patoloco.html) Doubles/triples with bath US$40/50, US$10 more with aircon. This is a small, European-style hotel owned by a Dutch/Italian couple who also speak English, French, and Spanish. Their small inn has three triple rooms and one double, each with a desk, fan, cross ventilation, and hot-water bathroom; two rooms have air-conditioning. They also have two apartments for long-term rental. All local activities can be arranged for you. The L'Angoletto di Roma restaurant is here, too.

**Hotel Vista Mar** (☎ 670-0753, e hvista mar@racsa.co.cr) Singles/doubles US$35/52 with fan, US$41/64 with air-con. This secluded place is on a shady, grassy beachfront lot north of town. The nine rooms are spacious and have hot showers. Breakfast is included, and discounts are available for longer stays.

**Villa del Sol B&B** (☎/fax 670-0085, in the USA and Canada ☎ 866-815-8902, e info@ villadelsol.com, w www.villadelsol.com) Double rooms US$46-64, with breakfast, double villas US$70-87. This quiet French Canadian-run place is about a kilometer north of the main road and offers seven large and very clean rooms with private baths. All rooms have hot water, and three are air-conditioned. Six villas include a kitchen. The hotel is about 100m from the beach, which is little visited at this end. There's a pool and a balcony with ocean view, and a French-Italian restaurant that opens intermittently – usually by client demand. Long-term vacation rentals and all local activities can be arranged. Room rates are at least US$12 less in the wet season. French, English, and German are spoken.

**Hotel Villa Flores** (☎ 670-0787, ☎/fax 670-0269) Doubles US$54-68, with breakfast. This Italian-run place is about 300m from the main road. There's an open-air restaurant, TV lounge, swimming pool and Jacuzzi. The owner is a scuba diver who loves to arrange dives for his guests (and go along with them when he can). Each of the eight simple, clean rooms has fans and a private bath; some have air-conditioning.

**Top End** Apart from the hotels listed here, also see the choices under Playa Ocotal (4km to the south) and Playa Hermosa (7km to the north) described later in this chapter.

**Best Western Hotel Coco Verde** (☎ 670-0494, 670-0544, fax 670-0555, e cocoverd@ racsa.co.cr, w www.costa-rica-beach-hotels .com) Singles/doubles with bath US$64/80, including breakfast. This hotel has 33 big, modern, air-conditioned rooms with cable TV and telephone. There's a pool, and the attractive restaurant is open 6am to 10pm daily. A sports bar picks up US sports events on cable TV, and there's a small casino. Fishing and diving packages are offered. Rates are over 20% less in low season.

**Flor de Itabo** (☎ 670-0011, 670-0292, 670-0455, fax 670-0003, e info@florde itabo.com, w www.flordeitabo.com) Bungalows with fan US$45, singles/doubles with air-con US$55/70, deluxe rooms US$80/100 for 4/6 people, apartments with kitchens US$120/140 for 4/6 people. This low-key place is 1.5km before the beach, on the right-hand side as you arrive. The hotel gardens attract monkeys and birds and surround a large pool with swim-up bar. A good restaurant has Italian and international food, a casino, and a bar with a reputation for attracting anglers. The Italian owners will help arrange fishing and diving excursions, and there are horses for rent. Italian, English, French, and German are spoken.

*Hotel La Puerta del Sol* (☎ 670-0195, fax 670-0650, e hotelsol@racsa.co.cr, w www .lapuertadelsol.com) Singles/doubles US$78/92, suites US$128, including continental breakfast, extra people US$29. Only a five-minute walk from 'town' but in a quiet area, this comfortable small hotel offers eight spacious, brightly pastel-painted, modern rooms, each with a small sitting area, cable TV, telephone, air-conditioning, ceiling fan, and private bathroom with hair dryer and hot water. The 'suites' are larger and add a refrigerator, coffeemaker, and balcony. The grounds boast a putting green, along with a pool and minigym, and the hotel's Sol y Luna Bar & Restaurant serves excellent Italian food. Multiday diving packages in combination with Rich Coast Diving are available.

*Rancho Armadillo* (☎ 670-0108, fax 670-0441, e info@ranchoarmadillo.com, w www .ranchoarmadillo.com) Singles/doubles US$93/105, suites US$148, with breakfast. Near the entrance to town, this place is an entrancing hotel on a hillside about 600m off the main road. The view from the common areas is the best in town, and the five comfortable air-conditioned rooms and two suites are all light, spacious, and decorated with paintings by talented US artist John English. Units have coffeemakers, minifridges, individually crafted pieces of furniture, plenty of closet space for long-stay guests, and large bathrooms with attractive toiletries and great showers. There's a swimming pool, gym equipment, and, of course, plenty of decorative armadillos. The owners, who are from the US, are helpful with arranging fishing, sailing, diving, and surfing trips. Guests into gourmet cooking will enjoy comparing recipes with owner Rick Vogel, a chef himself, and using the fully equipped professional kitchen (the owners do the dishes!) The suites will sleep four or six people; some have two bathrooms and two entrances. The entire hotel can be rented for groups, family gatherings,

or conferences for US$5570 per week in the high season, US$2500 in the low season.

## Places to Eat

Italian food is big in Playa del Coco; most Italian restaurants are linked with hotels. The following serve main courses for US$6 to US$12.

*Sol y Luna Restaurant & Bar* Inside the Hotel Puerto del Sol, this is considered the best Italian restaurant among a bunch of good contenders. Also worth a try are the *Flor de Itabo Pizzería* and the *L'Angoletto di Roma*, associated with the Pato Loco Inn. Next door to the Pato Loco Inn is *Restaurant Milanes*, another Italian choice.

*Señor Pizza* Dishes US$3-10. For pizza, many folks say this is your best bet. Other Italian plates are also available.

Closer still to the beach are a bunch of inexpensive *sodas* at the northeast corner of the soccer field. Almost opposite, *Bar y Restaurante El Roble* is mainly a bar serving tico food. Around the small plaza, you can eat seafood at *Cocos Seafood Restaurant* (which serves pizza as well) and at *Pura Vida Seafood* (US$6 to US$10), which has the best view in town. Just off the plaza, *Marisquería La Guajira* is a local seafood place, and *CocoMar Bar* is popular with ticos on vacation. CocoMar serves a variety of food, and most tables are far enough away from the adjacent disco that you can hear yourself speak. All these places are almost on top of one another, so walk around and choose what's best for you.

*Papagayo* Dishes average US$10. This is the best seafood restaurant in town; go for the food, not the ambience, which is that of a noisy roadside diner. You can choose from four kinds of fish prepared 10 different ways, including some delightfully prepared Cajun sauces. (The owner is a divemaster, and the fish is as fresh as can be.) The chef, trained in Cajun-style cooking, plans to open another, air-conditioned, restaurant on the same block, so look for competition.

*Tequila Bar & Grill* Dishes US$6-11. Mexican food is the specialty here, and the place has been well reviewed by locals who enjoy a change from seafood. This is a popular bar as well as restaurant.

*BBQ Steakhouse* Steaks US$7-14. This place has the best steaks in town, served in a rustic, semi-open-air setting.

## Entertainment

Beach party life doesn't tend to be about lasting commitments, and hip spots come and go. A quick walk around will let you know what's in vogue.

**CocoMar Disco** This loud place, for those into dancing, is right in the middle of the beachfront scene, adjacent to the Coco-Mar Bar restaurant.

**Bananas** Farther inland on the main road, Bananas also has dancing and is popular with visiting foreigners. You can play pool here or catch a breeze on the balcony bar, which is currently the happening place in the evening.

**Jungle Bar** This place gets going with the dancing crowd later at night, when people might drift over from Bananas.

The restaurants around the plaza double as bars; **El Bohío Bar** is something of a favorite.

**Tequila Bar & Grill** is another hot spot, while the **Flor de Itabo** hotel has a small casino and is popular with anglers.

## Getting There & Away

The main bus stop in Playa del Coco is on the plaza in front of the police station. Buses overnight at a depot next to the Pato Loco Inn, but buses don't leave from there (this could change).

The San José Pulmitan station (☎ 222-1650), Calle 24 & Avenida 5, has two buses daily to Playa del Coco, at 8am and 2pm (US$5), plus a 4pm departure in the high season. The return bus leaves Playa del Coco at 4am, 8am, and 2pm.

Buses leave Liberia for Playa del Coco eight times daily from 5:30am to 6:30pm during the high season, returning from Playa del Coco nine times a day from 5:30am to 6pm. There are fewer departures in the wet season.

A taxi from Liberia costs US$12 to US$15. Note that there's no gas station in town; the nearest one is in Sardinal, about 9km before Playa del Coco.

## PLAYA HERMOSA

This gently curving and relatively safe beach is about 7km (by road) north of Coco. At the moment, it's quieter and less crowded, although the ongoing development of the so-called Papagayo Project beginning at the next beach (see Playa Panamá, later) may

change this dramatically. See Activities under Playa del Coco, above, for a list of activities in the area and outfitters in Playa Hermosa.

## Places to Stay & Eat

Many ticos camp for free near the beach; there are some good, shady spots.

**Hotel Playa Hermosa** (☎/fax 672-0046) Singles/doubles with bath US$25/40. Near the south end of the beach, this is a quiet hotel. Clean beachfront rooms have fans, private baths, and electric showers. There's an Italian restaurant on the premises. Several cheaper oceanfront restaurants serve fresh fish on this part of the beach.

**Cabinas y MiniSuper El Cenizaro** (☎ 672-0186, fax 282-7359) Doubles with bath US$30. Rooms are basic and have fans. Groceries are available.

**Cabinas La Casona** (☎ 672-0025) Doubles without/with kitchenette from US$24/28. This friendly place, opposite the Hotel El Velero (see below), has basic beach cabins; ask for a room with cross breezes. A room sleeping five costs US$31.

**Iguana Inn** (☎ 672-0065) Singles/doubles US$17/20, apartments US$50. Set 100m back along the north entrance to the beach, this is an eco-surfer kind of place with about 10 simple, rather beat-up rooms with private baths. The newer apartments have a kitchen, two bedrooms, and a foldout sofa and sleep up to six.

**Villa Huetares** (☎ 672-0081, 672-0052, fax 672-0051) Rooms US$40-90. This well-maintained place has 15 small apartments with air-conditioning, kitchenettes, dining areas, and private baths. Some rooms sleep up to six people. Rates vary depending on the number of people and season, with some discounts for longer stays. There's a pool and a TV lounge.

**Hotel El Velero** (☎ 672-0036, 672-1017, ☎/fax 672-0016, e elvelerocr@yahoo.com, elvelero@costarica.net, w www.costarica hotel.net) Doubles with air-con US$84-96. Just steps from the beach, this place has 22 spacious, light rooms with coffeemakers and two double beds. Colorful bedspreads liven up the otherwise plain rooms. There's a pool and restaurant. The hotel yacht provides guests and others with a variety of cruises (roughly US$55 per person including meals) for snorkeling or just enjoying the sunset with an open bar.

***Restaurant Pescado Loco*** (☎ 672-0017)
Almost opposite the Hotel El Velero, this restaurant has received several recommendations.

***Sol Playa Hermosa Resort*** (☎ 672-0001, fax 672-0212, e hermosol@racsa.co.cr, w www.solmelia.com) Doubles US$154, villas US$300-340. Operated by the Sol Melia group, this resort is proud to offer the quiet and insulation of a gated community. It's a condominium complex with over 100 units; each villa has a kitchenette, cable TV, hot water, and air-conditioning. Some units have their own small swimming pool! The modern rooms lack the kitchenette. On the grounds there are tennis courts, a pool, discotheque, restaurant, and bar; off-site diving, snorkeling, fishing, kayaking, boating, and horseback riding can be arranged. Bill Beard's Diving Safaris operates out of this resort.

### Getting There & Away
Empresa Esquivel (☎ 666-1249) buses leave Liberia for Playa Hermosa at 7:30am, 11:30am, 3:30pm, 5:30pm, and 7pm, returning at 5am, 6am, 10am, 4pm, and 5pm. Some of these may not go all the way to Playa Panamá – ask locally. An express bus leaves San José from Calle 20 & Avenida 5, at 3:25pm and takes about five hours, stopping first at Playa Hermosa and then at Playa Panamá. It returns from Playa Panamá at 5am. A taxi from Liberia costs about US$12 to US$15, and a taxi from Coco costs about US$4.

If you're driving from Liberia, take the signed turnoff to Playa Nosara about 3km or 4km before reaching Playa del Coco.

## PLAYA PANAMÁ & THE PAPAGAYO PROJECT
This protected dark-sand beach is one of the best swimming beaches in the area. About 3km north of Playa Hermosa, this social rural beach, scattered with campers and toddlers splashing in the shallows, used to be the end of the road. But now, facing it from across the bay are the beginnings of a massive condo colonization – the huge and controversial Papagayo Project, which aims to put a large number of luxury hotels, condominiums, and villas in the hitherto almost deserted area surrounding Bahía de Culebra, the most protected large bay on

the peninsula. As many as 15,000 rooms, plus golf courses, are planned in this development, which has drawn attacks from those who feel the project is a blatant misuse of the area. The tropical dry forest (see the Parque Nacional Santa Rosa section in the Northwestern Costa Rica chapter) that surrounds the bay is being bulldozed, and the few local mangrove swamps have been destroyed, to provide what the Mexican developer claims is an ecologically sensitive tourism project. No environmental impact studies were done. Go figure!

In 1995, several lawsuits were brought, charging, among other things, embezzlement and corruption among top-level government tourism officials, including the former Minister of Tourism. The project is rolling on despite the legal wrangling.

Tourists visiting Papagayo Project hotels will be selling themselves short, in that they will not really be seeing Costa Rica, but just a big, self-contained megaresort plunked down on top of (not within) an area of tropical forest. You could be almost anywhere. Parallels with soulless Cancún have been frequently drawn. Curious locals hanging around outside gates manned by officious guards, through which busloads of foreigners on package trips occasionally pass, give the whole thing a somewhat feudal air. The intimacy and amiability that characterize most interactions between tourists and ticos are lost here.

Several large and luxurious ***resort hotels*** are already operating here. They offer air-conditioned rooms, suites and villas, restaurants, bars, casinos, pools, tennis courts, sports, saunas, spas, ocean views, and activities. Further information is easily obtained from travel agencies.

## PLAYA OCOTAL
This attractive but small beach is 3km or 4km southwest of Coco by unpaved road (there are plans to pave it for the 2003 high season). It's the cleanest, quietest beach in the area, offering good swimming and snorkeling. Scuba diving is available, and nearby Isla Catalina is a recommended diving spot; it's the best place to see huge schools of rays, including the giant manta ray. Accommodations are good but not cheap. Camping is possible but not that common; be discreet and you'll have a better time.

The south end of the beach is recommended for snorkeling.

## Places to Stay

*Villa Casa Blanca* (☎ 670-0518, ☎/fax 670-0448, e vcblanca@racsa.co.cr, w http://costa-rica-hotels-travel.com) Rooms US$80-110, condos US$116. Between Playa del Coco and Playa Ocotal, this attractive villa is in a pleasant hilltop location a few minutes' walk from the beach. Rates include a huge and varied buffet breakfast served on a balcony with views that make departure difficult. This small B&B has about 10 pleasant rooms, some with romantic canopy beds, and each with private bath, ceiling fan, and air-conditioning. Rooms are beautifully decorated; some have Victorian decor and four-poster beds, others are more modern, and all are delightful. Three honeymoon suites are somewhat larger and feature a step-up bathtub and ocean views, and two fully equipped condos with kitchens are available. The hotel entrance is through a small garden that attracts birds and artfully takes advantage of every square meter. The pool is crossed by a garden bridge and has a swim-up bar. The lobby has a souvenir shop with an English-language-book exchange. The owner's husband is a fountain of information about living in Costa Rica, and prospective retirees or entrepreneurs often stay for a few days just to pick his brain! Free transport to the restaurant at El Ocotal Resort is available. This is a recommended and relaxing place to stay.

*El Ocotal Resort* (☎ 670-0321, 670-0323, fax 670-0083, e elocotal@racsa.co.cr, w www.ocotalresort.com) Singles/doubles/triples with bath US$99/113/130, bungalows US$160, suites US$201. Perched on an oceanside cliff with spectacular views, rooms are stacked in three levels, while bungalows are spread along a road. Rooms have air-conditioning, cable TV, direct-dial phones, ceiling fans, coffeemakers, and huge picture windows opening onto a private terrace with ocean view. Bathrooms have hair dryers and hot showers, but they look a bit small and old-fashioned compared to the crisp modern rooms. There are roomier bungalows and large ocean-view suites as well, some with Jacuzzi tubs and sitting rooms. There are four swimming pools, a tennis court, and a Jacuzzi. A restaurant showcases the cliff

views and offers a full American breakfast (US$11) or all three meals (US$57). A fully equipped dive shop offers complete packages including boat dives (you don't have to dive every day), overnight accommodations, and breakfast only or all meals. Nitrox is available, and equipment and transportation from San José can be included. Prices vary tremendously depending on services required – contact them for rates. If you don't want to go as part of a package, you can rent all the gear, get instruction, and do day dives. Sportfishing is also available, either as an all-inclusive package or for daily rates if the boats are not booked for packages. Sea kayaks and mountain bikes can be rented.

*Bahía Pez Vela Villas Hotel Club* (☎ 670-0129, e bahiapez@racsa.co.cr, w www.costa-rica-travel-hotels.com) Condos US$150-250. This luxury condo complex features 29 fully equipped air-conditioned villas sleeping three to eight people. Like them? Individual units are for sale. The complex includes three pools.

## Places to Eat

*Father Rooster Restaurant* Dishes average US$5. Apart from the hotels (where the food is pricey), there's the Rooster, adjacent to El Ocotal Resort down near the beach. Inexpensive and fun, this place serves snacks and burgers, plus seafood dinners. They make a good margarita.

## ACCESSING BEACHES SOUTH OF PLAYA OCOTAL

It's possible to reach the set of beaches farther south by taking a poor dirt road from Sardinal to Potrero. This requires 4WD in all but the very best conditions. Ask locally about how good this road is. The first 9km stretch, named the Congo Trail, ends at yet another **canopy tour** (☎ 666-4422; US$35). After that, the road deteriorates.

Otherwise, to visit beaches south of Ocotal, return to the main peninsula highway at Comunidad. Then head south for 12km through the little town of Filadelfia, the community of Belén (18km), and the small town of Santa Cruz (35km south of Comunidad).

A paved road heads 25km west from Belén to the small community of Huacas, where shorter paved roads radiate to a number of popular beach areas. From Santa Cruz, a 16km paved road heads west to the tiny community of 27 de Abril, where unpaved roads also radiate to a number of beaches. It's possible to drive from 27 de Abril to Huacas; thus, all the beaches described in this section are accessible from Santa Cruz.

Filadelfia and the beaches near Huacas are described first, then Santa Cruz and the beaches reached via 27 de Abril.

## FILADELFIA

Filadelfia is about 32km from Liberia. The population of Filadelfia and the surrounding district is about 7100.

There's an inexpensive hotel here, the *Cabinas Amelia* (☎ 688-8087, ☎/fax 688-9172), three blocks from the central park. Also try the basic *Cabinas Tita* (☎ 688-8073) nearby. A couple of local places to eat are around or near the park.

The bus terminal, half a block from the park, has several buses a day to San José, and hourly buses pass through en route to Nicoya or Liberia.

## PLAYA BRASILITO

The road from Huacas hits the ocean at the village of Brasilito, which has a few small stores and restaurants and the cheapest accommodations in the area. There's a beach, but other beaches nearby are better. On weekends, buses from the capital roll in, the beach fills up, and accommodations prices rise.

At the entrance of town are several pizzerías, a cybercafé, and a SANSA office.

## Activities & Organized Tours

**Brasilito Excursiones** (☎ 654-4237) operates out of the Hotel Brasilito and offers horseback riding, sailing, and scuba diving. An hour-long beach ride costs US$25, guide included; a two-hour guided ride to Playa Grande costs US$35. A two-hour sailing trip to Isla Catalina costs US$45, or US$75 with diving included. You can rent bikes.

## Places to Stay & Eat

*Brasilito Lodge* (☎/fax 654-4452, e brasil ito@racsa.co.cr, w www.brasilito-conchal .com) Campsites US$3 per person, rooms US$9 per person. Run by a German family, this place is just off the beach, about 200m from the Brasilito Plaza in the direction of Playa Conchal. Showers and shade trees are available for campers. Basic cabins

have kitchenettes, fans, and private cold showers. Long-stay and low-season discounts are offered.

*Cabinas Ojos Azules* (☎ 654-4346) Doubles without/with hot water US$14/20. This somewhat ramshackle place is a couple hundred meters south along the main road and has big, comfy beds complete with mirrored headboards. A supermarket is nearby, and there's a communal kitchen.

*Cabinas El Caracol* (☎ 654-4073, fax 654-4374) Doubles from US$25. This nicer cheapie is a bit farther down and has clean, roomy doubles, most with cold showers but a few with hot water. Its restaurant is open daily.

*Hotel Brasilito* (☎ 654-4237, fax 654-4247, e hotel@brasilito.com, w www.brasilito .com) Doubles/triples/quads with bath US$30/35/40. On the beach side of the plaza in Brasilito, this hotel has simple, clean, screened rooms with fans and private cold showers; it's US$5 more for a sea-view room. Staff speak German and English and will help arrange tours. A restaurant is attached.

*Restaurant Happy Snapper* (☎ 654-4413) Meals US$6-10. Near the Hotel Brasilito on the beach side of the plaza, this cheerful restaurant serves steaks and seafood and has occasional live music. Several other cheap eateries lie around the plaza.

*Cabinas Nany* (☎/fax 654-4320, e cab nany@racsa.co.cr, w www.flamingo beachonline.com) Doubles US$32. Between Playas Brasilito and Conchal, this small hotel has a pool and communal outdoor cooking area. Rooms come with ceiling fans, cold-water bathroom, cable TV, and minifridge.

*Restaurante y Bar Camarón Dorado* (☎ 654-4028) This large beachfront place, a couple of blocks north of the school, is reputedly the best place to eat.

*La Boca de La Iguana* (☎ 654-4861) Literally, 'the mouth of the iguana' – ever tried iguana? It tastes like chicken! Which is exactly what you'll get at this fried-chicken restaurant.

*Il Forno* (☎ 654-4125) Of several Italian pizza and pasta joints, this one comes locally recommended.

## Getting There & Away

TRALAPA in Brasilito (☎ 654-4628) has return buses starting from Flamingo and swinging through Potrero and Brasilito on the way to San José at 8:45am and 2pm daily, 3am weekdays, and 10am on Sunday. See Playa Flamingo, below, for more details on travel in the area.

## PLAYA CONCHAL

Playa Conchal, so called for the many *conchas* (shells) that pile up on the beach, is the most common name given to a pretty sweep of bay beginning about 2km south of Brasilito. The clear water makes for nice snorkeling. A huge hotel has been built on the northern stretch of the beach, which makes beach access difficult unless you are staying there.

### Places to Stay & Eat

*Condor Lodge & Beach Resort* (☎ 654-4050, fax 654-4044, e condorlodge@cs.com, w www.condorlodge.com) Doubles US$91-102. Rates include breakfast; rooms have two queen-size beds or a king and a single. At the far south end of the beach, accessible from the main road, this hotel was remodeled in 2000 and has 30 rooms with air-conditioning, ceiling fans, minifridges, cable TVs with VCRs, and private hot baths. There's a restaurant, bar, two pools, and a tennis court, all with good views.

*Hotel Melia Playa Conchal* (☎ 654-4123, fax 654-4181, e mconchal@racsa.co.cr, w www.meliaplayaconchal.com) Doubles US$288. This enormous new resort development extends its walls up to the edge of the beach but is, nonetheless, relatively unobtrusive from the road. In addition to all the usual amenities, the resort has a championship golf course and the country's largest free-form swimming pool. There are over 300 suites and 11 restaurants and bars; more condos are being built and a second golf course is planned, which will make this a megaresort community. Detractors point out that Guanacaste is dry for five months of the year, and the water needed for the golf courses and luxurious resort is being diverted away from the nearby town of Santa Cruz and surrounding villages, which will suffer from increased aridity.

### Getting There & Away

See Playa Flamingo, below, for details. Note that the gas station between Playa Brasilito and Playa Flamingo is the only one in the area.

## PLAYA FLAMINGO

Three or 4km north of Brasilito, the road comes to Playa Flamingo, a beautiful white-sand beach. It has been developed for sportfishing and boating and is one of the better-known beaches in Costa Rica. Many maps mark the beach with its original name, Playa Blanca, but it's now known as Playa Flamingo after the famous Flamingo Beach Hotel. (There are no flamingos in Costa Rica.) It's the country's original upscale beach resort and has a large fleet of sportfishing boats.

There are many luxurious private houses and villas (many owned by well-heeled North Americans), but there's no village as such here, so if you're looking for life outside of the hotels, forget it unless you want to go to Brasilito or Potrero. But if you want luxury with comfortable hotels, a pretty beach, and first-class boating facilities, then this popular place will make a good destination.

A Banco de Costa Rica (☎ 654-4984, fax 654-4986) recently opened. It has an ATM and changes dollars.

### Activities, Organized Tours & Courses

*The Edge Adventure Company* (☎/fax 654-4946, e theedge@racsa.co.cr) offers a full range of rentals and tours. It's at the entrance to Flamingo Beach and acts as an ad hoc information center. A two-tank dive costs US$65, snorkels and bikes rent for US$5 per hour, body boards for US$2; boat trips for diving or snorkeling and sunset sails start at about US$40 per person.

*Samonique III* (☎ 394-4152, 388-7870) is a 52-foot ketch available for sunset cruises beginning at 2pm for US$60 per person, four minimum. Overnight tours are available by arrangement.

*Centro Panamericano de Idiomas* (☎ 645-5441, w www.cpi-edu.com) has a Spanish school here; it's a branch of the school described under Heredia in the Central Valley & the Surrounding Highlands chapter, and under Monteverde in the Northwestern Costa Rica chapter.

### Places to Stay & Eat

There are no budget places here.

*Guanacaste Lodge* (☎ 654-4494) Doubles US$45-70. At the edge of town, this hotel with eight rooms and a pool is among the cheapest. Rooms are air-conditioned.

*Mariner Inn* (☎ 654-4081, fax 654-4024, e mariner@costarica.net) Doubles US$50-70. This inn has a dozen clean and spacious air-conditioned rooms with hot water and TVs. There's a restaurant and bar, and all the local water activities are easily arranged.

*Flamingo Marina Resort* (☎ 654-4141, fax 654-4035, e tickledpink@flamingomarina .com, W www.flamingomarina.com) Double rooms/suites US$128/169 including breakfast, quads with kitchens US$210-326. This hotel is up on a hill and has good ocean views. The 22 rooms have air-conditioning, ceiling fans, minibars, satellite TVs, telephones, and views from terraces or balconies. The suites have kitchenettes and Jacuzzi tubs. Fully equipped condo and bungalow apartments have one or two bedrooms. There are four pools, a Jacuzzi, lighted tennis court, dive shop, restaurant, bar, tour agency, and the nearby marina with all the sportfishing boats you could possibly want. The hotel's restaurant and bar attract diners who aren't staying here and are among the best in town.

*Flamingo Beach Resort* (☎ 654-4070, in the USA ☎ 800-500-9090, e flamingobeach resort@yahoo.com, W www.flamingo-beach .com) Rooms US$140/163, suites US$272. The more expensive rooms are poolside in this 91-room complex on the beach. The hotel features several pools and all the activities you can handle, including horseback riding and mountain biking, as well as all the usual water-based activities. It has two restaurants and two bars.

Apart from the hotel restaurants, there are a few other places to eat.

*Marie's* (☎ 654-4136) Open 6:30am-9:30pm daily. This is one of the longest-established eateries in town and offers a variety of snacks and full meals. Their breakfast pancakes are locally famous, and this is the best place in town for a big hamburger.

*Amberes* (☎ 654-4001) This classy dinner place has a casino, disco, and live music on occasion.

## Getting There & Away
**Air** The Flamingo Beach Resort has a private airstrip where plane charters are possible. Alternatively, you can fly to Tamarindo, the nearest airstrip with scheduled flights. The airstrip is about 20km from Playa Flamingo and, if you have hotel reservations, you can arrange with the hotel to be picked up.

**Bus** TRALAPA in Santa Cruz (☎ 680-0392) has buses for Playas Conchal, Brasilito, Flamingo, and Potrero at 6am and 3pm, returning from Potrero at 9am and 5pm; the schedule changes often. See the Santa Cruz section, later in this chapter, for details.

TRALAPA in San José (☎ 221-7201/2), at Calle 20 & Avenida 5, has daily express buses to Playa Flamingo (8am, 11am, 3pm; US$8).

## BAHÍA POTRERO
This stretch of bay is 6km or 7km north of Brasilito and is separated from Playa Flamingo by a rocky headland. There's a small community at Potrero, just beyond the north end of the beach. This is where the bus line ends, and the beaches here don't get the weekend rush found at Brasilito. Though upscale Playa Flamingo is visible across the bay, this is still an area where monkeys can be heard in the trees and oxen come down to the shore to lick salt out of the water.

Several beaches are strung along the bay. The black-sand beach is Playa Prieta, the white-sand beach is Playa Penca, and Playa Potrero, the biggest, is somewhere in between – these names, it should be noted, are used loosely. Hotels on the beaches rent water-sports equipment. The rocky islet 10km due west of Playa Pan de Azúcar is **Isla Catalina**, a popular diving spot (see Playa del Coco, earlier in this chapter).

## Places to Stay
**Budget** You can camp near the beach. *Mayra's* (☎ 654-4213, 654-4472) Campsites US$3 per person, rustic rooms with bath US$25. At the far south end of the beach, this friendly place has a shady camping area, with beach showers and a small soda available. There are also a few rooms with baths and fans. Mayra's companion, Álvaro Chinchilla, is a retired journalist and is well stocked with stories.

*Cabinas Isolina* (☎/fax 654-4333, e admin@isolinabeach.com, W www .isolinabeach.com) Doubles/triples/quads US$25/30/40, with kitchen US$10 extra. Set back from the north end of the beach, but with easy beach access through a garden,

Cabinas Isolina has 11 nice, simple rooms surrounded by hibiscus. Each room has a double bed and bunk bed, small tiled hot shower, and ceiling fan. Some have a kitchenette. Italian and English are spoken.

**Mid-Range** About 700m away from the sea near the north end is *Cabinas Cristina* (☎ 654-4006, fax 654-4128, ⓔ info@cabinas cristina.com, ⓦ www.cabinascristina.com) Cabins US$35-93. This place has a small pool and friendly management. Local tours and boat rentals can be arranged. Rooms vary from simple doubles with fans and bathroom to fully equipped quads with air-conditioning and kitchenette. The more expensive rate is for five people.

*Bahia Esmeralda* (☎ 654-4480, fax 654-4479, ⓔ bahiaesmeralda@racsa.co.cr, ⓦ www .hotelbahiaesmeralda.com) Doubles/triples/quads US$41/47/54, apartments US$85, villas US$110. About 50m east of the village center, this new place has clean, comfortable rooms with heated water and fans. Air-conditioning in the four standard rooms costs an extra US$6. Apartments sleep up to four and villas sleep up to six; all have kitchenettes, terraces, and ceiling fans, and cost an extra US$11.50 with air-conditioning. Low-season and long-stay discounts can be negotiated. A pool and an Italian restaurant are on the premises. English and Italian are spoken and all local tour activities can be arranged.

*Casa Sunset B&B* (☎/fax 654-4265) Doubles US$50 including breakfast, US$10 extra people. Here you'll find seven nice cabins on a lush hillside north of the village, with views over the bay. Monkeys and birds are often seen on the grounds, and a nearby estuary provides good birding in the wet season. Each cabin has fans and a private bath; a shared open-air kitchen with fridge and ice machine is available. Discounts are given for longer stays.

*Puesta del Sol Catalina B&B* (☎/fax 654-5005, ⓔ dane_vickie@racsa.co.cr) Doubles US$50-80, depending on season and number of nights. This small new B&B has five bright rooms with kitchenettes, cable TV, queen-size beds, ceiling fans, and bathrooms nicely tiled in blue and white. There's also an outdoor kitchen area for guest use and immediate access to the beach. You'll have nice views of the protected and calm waters – ideal for swimming for all ages. There's a small library of English books, and a mini-market is a few minutes' walk away.

## Places to Eat

Aside from the hotel restaurants mentioned above, there are several options.

*Hardens Gardens & Bakery* (☎ 654-4495) Fifty meters inland from the Bahía Potrero Resort, this place serves pizzas, pastries, and sandwiches.

*Las Brisas Bar & Grill* (☎ 654-4424) At the far end of the bay past the village, this place claims to be the oldest bar in Guanacaste. Texan Bill Enell came to the area some 20 years ago and serves up big Texas-style *bocas* and tall tales. The pool table is popular with ticos from the village, and the open-air bar is a great place to watch the sunset while lights come on in yachts moored across the bay.

## Getting There & Away

See Playa Flamingo, earlier, for details.

## PLAYA PAN DE AZÚCAR

This small white-sand beach is 2km or 3km north of Potrero and is the last beach reachable by road. The waters are protected by rocky headlands at either end of the beach and offer good snorkeling.

*Hotel Sugar Beach* (☎ 654-4242, in North America ☎ 800-458-4735, fax 654-4239, ⓔ sugarb@racsa.co.cr, ⓦ www.sugar-beach .com) Doubles from US$128, suites US$192-221, beach houses US$410-525. This is a small, lovely hotel on rambling grounds above Playa Pan de Azúcar. A long-established hotel with excellent service, it's the only choice here. About 22 good rooms, each with an individually carved wooden door, have air-conditioning, private baths, telephone, and hot water. The more expensive ones have cable TV, minibars, and ocean views. There are also four suites and one beach house (with two or three bedrooms sleeping up to 10) available. The restaurant is good and has a great view. There's some forest in the area, and you can watch monkeys and birds near the hotel. Boat charters are available for fishing, diving, and snorkeling, and horse and sailboard rentals are also offered.

The nearest bus goes to Playa Potrero, from where you'll have to walk or drive on a rough road.

## PLAYA TAMARINDO

Instead of turning north from Huacas to Brasilito and Flamingo, you can head south to Tamarindo on a mostly paved road that's in decent shape. The village of Tamarindo is spread along the last 1.5km. Both commercial fishing and tourism are of economic importance here, though you'll see far more surfers than fishers wandering around the village.

Both surfing and windsurfing are good, and there's a wildlife refuge and marine national park nearby. The beach is large enough that nonsurfers can still find quiet stretches. Parts of the beach have rip currents or barely submerged rocks, so make local inquiries before swimming. This beach has better access by public transport than

most of the beaches in the area and is bustling with small-scale development. During the dry months, especially February, winds can make the beach a bit gritty.

Tamarindo's combination of attractions is well served with accommodations, restaurants, and equipment rentals, all of interest to nonsurfers here to enjoy village beach life or the nearby refuges. However, Tamarindo is definitely a surfer town. Except for the global village flavor of the tattoos and the smaller, sharper boards, you might think you'd walked into California in the 1950s. There are good waves at the river estuary north of town and at Playa Grande across the estuary. There's some surfing right off Playa Tamarindo, but the rocks make for limited space. Playa Langosta, a couple of kilometers south

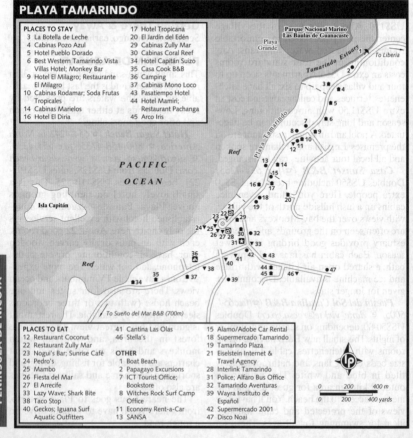

**PLAYA TAMARINDO**

PLACES TO STAY
3  La Botella de Leche
4  Cabinas Pozo Azul
5  Hotel Pueblo Dorado
6  Best Western Tamarindo Vista Villas Hotel; Monkey Bar
9  Hotel El Milagro; Restaurante El Milagro
10 Cabinas Rodamar; Soda Frutas Tropicales
14 Cabinas Marielos
16 Hotel El Diria
17 Hotel Tropicana
20 El Jardín del Edén
29 Cabinas Zully Mar
30 Cabinas Coral Reef
34 Hotel Capitán Suizo
35 Casa Cook B&B
36 Camping
37 Cabinas Mono Loco
43 Pasatiempo Hotel
44 Hotel Mamiri; Restaurant Pachanga
45 Arco Iris

Parque Nacional Marino Las Baulas de Guanacaste
Playa Grande
Tamarindo Estuary
To Liberia

PACIFIC OCEAN

Isla Capitán

Reef

Reef

To Sueño del Mar B&B (700m)

PLACES TO EAT
12 Restaurant Coconut
22 Restaurant Zully Mar
23 Nogui's Bar; Sunrise Café
24 Pedro's
25 Mambo
26 Fiesta del Mar
27 El Arrecife
33 Lazy Wave; Shark Bite
38 Taco Stop
40 Geckos; Iguana Surf Aquatic Outfitters
41 Cantina Las Olas
46 Stella's

OTHER
1  Boat Beach
2  Papagayo Excursions
7  ICT Tourist Office; Bookstore
8  Witches Rock Surf Camp Office
11 Economy Rent-a-Car
13 SANSA
15 Alamo/Adobe Car Rental
18 Supermercado Tamarindo
19 Tamarindo Plaza
21 Eiselstein Internet & Travel Agency
28 Interlink Tamarindo
31 Police; Alfaro Bus Office
32 Tamarindo Aventuras
39 Wayra Instituto de Español
42 Supermercado 2001
47 Disco Noai

0    200    400 m
0    200    400 yards

of Tamarindo, is a favorite uninhabited surfing beach. About 6km or 7km farther south is Playa Avellana, described later in this section. Sea kayaking is also good.

### Information

There's an Instituto Costarricense de Turismo (ICT) office (see map), though information tends toward brochures rather than hard facts. Tourist information is available from any of the equipment outfitters (see below); this is also an easy town in which to ask around.

There are a number of public CHIP phones (see Post & Communications in the Facts for the Visitor chapter for information) on the road circle at the south end of town. This is also where you'll find Internet cafés open from 9am to 9pm daily and charging about US$2.50 per hour.

Banco Nacional (☎ 653-0366) changes US cash and traveler's checks, but it's open only from 8:30am to 3:30pm weekdays and doesn't give cash advances against credit cards. Hotels can help get you a doctor in case of emergency. Don't leave anything in your unguarded car – break-ins are common.

### Activities & Organized Tours

A passport or credit card may be necessary for some rentals. Look for fliers at hotels and cafés for people offering services like group transport to surf beaches.

The well-run **Iguana Surf Aquatic Outfitters** (☎/fax 653-0148) rents kayaks, surfboards, body boards, snorkeling gear, and other sports equipment at reasonable prices, and it sells many other things you need on the beach. It also offers local tours and surfing or kayaking lessons. Typical rental rates for a full day are US$20/25 for a short/longboard, US$12.50 for snorkeling gear or a body board, and US$45 for an ocean kayak, with hourly rates available. Surf taxi service is also available – US$10 to Playa Grande, or US$25 to Playa Negra, minimum two passengers.

**Papagayo Excursions** (☎ 653-0254, fax 653-0227), near the entrance to town, is one of the longest-running outfitters and arranges excursions such as boat tours, scuba diving, snorkeling, sportfishing, horseback riding, and visits to turtle nesting areas on Playa Grande in Parque Nacional Marino Las Baulas de Guanacaste. With varying

amounts of luck, you can see turtles nesting year-round, but the best months are December to March.

**Tamarindo Aventuras** (☎ 653-0108, fax 653-0640) rents scooters (US$32 per day), mountain bikes (US$16), dirt bikes (US$43), and water-sports equipment. Weekly rentals cost the equivalent of five days. It also offers surfing lessons and ATV and kayak tours.

**Witch's Rock Surf Camp** (☎ 670-1138, 670-1175, 395-7152, e witchsrock@hotmail.com, w www.witchsrocksurfcamp.com) is perched right in front of one of Tamarindo's best breaks. They arrange overnight tours to the famed Witch's Rock near Parque Nacional Santa Rosa. Board rentals and lessons are available, and they have a café and a few basic rooms for surfers. They also run shuttles to Playa del Coco and other local surfing beaches.

Many people offer sportfishing charters. Among the cheapest options is to hire a panga for around US$45 an hour; ask for **Capt Brian King** at Cantina Las Olas. **Capullo Sportfishing** (☎ 653-0048) has a 36-foot Topaz and a 22-foot Boston Whaler. Both inshore and offshore fishing are available for a half day (US$275 to US$500) and full day (US$400 to US$900). Other boats include the following:

**Rainbow Runner** (☎ 653-0048) This 22-foot Boston Whaler takes three anglers for a full day for US$375.

**Lone Star** (☎ 653-0101, 653-0254) This 30-foot Palm Beach is available for US$650 for a full day. Ask for Capt Gaylord Townley.

**Osprey** (☎ 653-0162, fax 653-0254) This 31-foot Rampage is available for US$750 a day. Capt Brock Menking is well known and respected locally.

**Agua Rica Diving Center** (☎ 653-0094) has moved several times but is now in the Tamarindo Plaza next to the Banco Nacional. A four-day PADI certification course for beginners costs US$300; two-tank dives from a boat cost US$65.

**Mandingo Sailing** (☎ 653-0623, 653-0276) has a gaff-rigged schooner available for snorkel sails, sunset sails, and combinations. Prices are US$45 to US$60 per person.

**Tamarindo Long Lines** (☎/fax 653-0597) operates a new eight-cable zip-line canopy tour on the outskirts of Tamarindo. They didn't use helmets on recent inspection.

## Places to Stay

**Budget** There's much more of a price selection here than in most of the towns on this coast, but it's almost impossible to get cheap single rooms during the high season, so budget travelers need to find a buddy.

Camping areas have recently been shut down, citing a law that camping isn't allowed on Costa Rican beaches. One *campsite* (US$3 per person) remains, but it may close.

*La Botella de Leche* (☎ 653-0544) Rooms US$8 per person. This 22-bed hostel is the best bet for impecunious surfers. The owner is an Argentine lady and the guests are young surfers from all over the world. English, French, and Italian are spoken. Beds are scattered in a variety of different doubles and quads with shared cold showers. Guests have kitchen privileges, Internet access, a TV room, a patio and balcony with a view of the river mouth, and individual lockers to stash their stuff. Board rentals are available.

*Cabinas Rodamar* (☎ 653-0109) Doubles US$11. These six basic, airy rooms have private showers. There's an open-air kitchen, and you can camp in the backyard for US$2 per person.

*Cabinas Coral Reef* (☎ 653-0291) Doubles US$15. These cabinas are a bit disheveled, but the owner is cheery and small doubles are offered.

*Hotel Mamiri* (☎/fax 653-0079, @ hotel mamiri@hotmail.com) Rooms with bath US$30. This peaceful, charming place has 10 different rooms with attractively painted walls in Asian motifs. Showers are hot and there's a relaxing garden. The excellent Restaurant Pachanga is attached.

*Cabinas Pozo Azul* (☎/fax 653-0280) Doubles with bath US$24-33. This place is

rather spartan-looking, with 17 basic but large rooms on bare grounds. All have private cold baths and shaded patios, with a choice of fans or air-conditioning. Most rooms have a kitchenette and refrigerator, and there's a pool.

*Cabinas Mono Loco* (☎ 653-0238) Doubles US$32. This place, colorfully renovated in 2001, has spacious rooms with private showers and fans. A communal kitchen is available.

*Cabinas Marielos* (☎/fax 653-0141) Doubles with bath US$35-40. This pleasant place provides slightly larger rooms with fans; the pricier rooms have hot water. Air-conditioning is available for an extra US$5.

*Cabinas Zully Mar* (☎ 653-0140, 226-4732 cellular, fax 653-0028, @ zullymar@ racsa.co.cr, W www.tr506.com/zullymar) Doubles US$40-58. At the end of the road is this reasonably priced favorite. Basic rooms with private baths and fans are the cheapest, though not a very good value. Better-value rooms with refrigerators cost US$12 more. The best and most expensive rooms are air-conditioned and have refrigerators and electric warm showers. There are 42 rooms in all, along with a small streetside swimming pool, guarded parking, and currency exchange.

**Mid-Range** A cluster of four pretty hillside cabinas make up *Arco Iris* (☎/fax 653-0330) Doubles with bath US$45. This Italian-owned place is imaginatively decorated and quite romantic. Prices are open to negotiation if times are slow. An open-air kitchen is available, as are shiatsu massage (US$25 per hour), a karate dojo, and impressive tattoo artists.

*Hotel Tropicana* (☎ 653-0503, ☎/fax 653-0261, @ info@tropicanacr.com, W www .tropicanacr.com) Singles/doubles/triples US$70/80/90. This large building has about 40 clean, simply decorated rooms, all with phones, fans, writing desks, and private hot baths. Some rooms are air-conditioned (US$10 extra). US$20 discounts are available for groups of seven or more people paying in advance. There's a big pool, Jacuzzi, and a tower that gives a view of the sea. Their restaurant charges US$8 for breakfast and US$18 for a full lunch or dinner. Rooms lack TVs (though management claims that they'll soon be added), but there's one in the restaurant. English and Italian are spoken.

***Pasatiempo Hotel*** (☎ 653-0096, fax 653-0275, ⒠ passtime@racsa.co.cr, ⒲ www.hotel pasatiempo.com) Doubles US$59, suites US$79, US$12 additional people. Rates include coffee and pastries for breakfast. This small hotel has a great reputation. The 12 rooms have comfortable beds, hot baths, fans, and air-conditioning. Walls are prettily painted in pastels with murals depicting local beaches, and each room has a little patio with a hammock. Each of the two suites has a living room with foldout couches – good for families. There's a pool, and the popular bar has satellite TV and live music jams once or twice a week. The accompanying restaurant is good and reasonably priced. English is spoken.

***Hotel El Milagro*** (☎ 653-0042, fax 653-0050, ⒠ elmilagro@elmilagro.com, ⒲ www .elmilagro.com) Doubles US$98, US$12 for additional people. The 32 rooms are a bit close together, but the grounds are nice, and each air-conditioned room has its own little patio and private bath with hot water. Breakfast is included. There's a small pool, restaurant, and bar. Local tours of all kinds are arranged.

***Hotel Pueblo Dorado*** (☎ 653-0008, fax 653-0013) Singles/doubles with bath & aircon US$70/77. This place is very clean and has a pre-Columbian motif throughout. There's a small pool and restaurant. Sport-fishing and touring can be arranged. Rooms are pleasantly bright with hot showers.

***Casa Cook B&B*** (☎ 653-0125, fax 653-0753, ⒠ casacook@racsa.co.cr) Cabina doubles US$140, US$10 additional people or air-conditioning. This pretty, well-kept little inn in a private house is owned by a hospitable US couple. Four cabinas feature completely equipped kitchens, ceiling fans, and cable TV. A sitting room has foldout couches for extra guests. There's a pool, and a garden leads to the beach, where hammocks hang and body boards are available to guests.

**Top End** On a hill overlooking Tamarindo is ***El Jardín del Edén*** (☎ 653-0137, ☎/fax 653-0111, ⒠ frontdesk@jardindeleden.com, ⒲ www.jardindeleden.com) Singles US$82-104, doubles US$116-128, apartments US$140, US$23/18 additional adult/child. This elegant, luxurious, Italian-run hotel has

18 beautiful rooms, each with a private patio or balcony (and some of Tamarindo's best views) and a sitting area. All rooms have fans and air-conditioning, refrigerators, cable TV, telephones, and private baths with hot water and hair dryers. All rates include breakfast. Rooms vary in size and prices reflect this. There are also two apartments with kitchenettes. Kids under five stay free. There's a Jacuzzi, a restaurant, and a lovely big pool with a swim-up bar. All the usual local tours can be arranged, and a professional massage therapist/acupuncturist is available. Although not right on the beach, the hotel enjoys the advantages of being high on a hill: good views and ocean breezes. The pool and grounds of the hotel are very inviting, and it takes only a few minutes to walk to the beach. The recommended restaurant specializes in French and Italian seafood dishes (most mains US$12 to US$25), which vary from night to night. The hotel can arrange a private bus to and from San José (US$25 per person, four minimum). Various low-season, long-stay, and package discounts can be arranged.

***Hotel El Diria*** (☎ 653-0031, fax 653-0208; in San José ☎ 258-4224/5, fax 258-4226; ⒠ tnodiria@racsa.co.cr, ⒲ www.tamarindo diria.co.cr) Doubles US$130-170. In town next to the beach, this large place is popular with German-speaking tourists (Spanish and English are also spoken). This is Tamarindo's first luxury hotel and has a faithful older clientele. Regular face-lifts and expansions have kept it in pretty good shape. It has two pools set in plant-filled tropical gardens and a good restaurant and bar. Staff can make all tour arrangements. There are 123 air-conditioned rooms with fans, cable TV, phones, and hot-water bathrooms. Most rooms are standard; the ocean- and sunset-view rooms cost US$150 and US$170. One reader writes that, during the wet season, the management brings mosquito repellent around to the diners at its outdoor restaurant! (Indoor seating is available as well.)

***Hotel Capitán Suizo*** (☎ 683-0075, fax 653-0292, ⒠ capsuizo@racsa.co.cr, ⒲ www.hotel capitansuizo.com) Doubles with fan/air-conditioning US$134/157, bungalows US$186, including continental breakfast, US$23 additional people. Right on the beach at the far south end, this Swiss-run hotel has a cheerful plant- and bird-filled garden and an expert staff. Its beautiful spacious rooms have bigger bathrooms than anywhere else. The large free-form pool is right next to the beach, so you can choose a freshwater float or a salty swim. There's a good restaurant and bar, kayaks and horses are available for rent, and other tours can be arranged. It's a bit far away from the center of things, but if you prefer peace and quiet you'll be delighted with this. There are 22 rooms on two levels; the lower 11 are air-conditioned, and the upper 11 have fans and are designed with cross-breezes in mind. All have a minifridge, a telephone, a sitting area with a futon, and a terrace or balcony. There are also eight bungalows, which are larger still, with huge sunken bathtubs and fans but no air-conditioning. The rates listed are for the high season and they go up US$10 to US$20 during Christmas, New Year, and Easter, and drop US$20 to US$30 in the low season. There's also a five-bedroom apartment sleeping up to eight for US$338, with no breakfast.

South of the hotel, the road continues about a kilometer to Playa Langosta.

***Sueño del Mar B&B*** (☎/fax 653-0284, e *innkeeper@sueno-del-mar.com*, w *www.sueno-del-mar.com*) Doubles US$163, cottage (2-4 people) US$175-198, honeymoon suite US$204. This memorable place, with thick, cool walls in Spanish posada style, is at Playa Langosta. There are three rooms in the beautifully and eclectically decorated house, a small cottage with kitchen and loft alongside, and a honeymoon suite. The rooms feature four-poster beds, artfully placed crafts from all over the world, unique tiling, and relaxing open-air (but private) showers. The honeymoon suite has a wraparound window with a fine sea view. A delicious breakfast is included, served in a roofed patio next to a refreshing plunge pool. A colorful splash of garden separates the pool from the beach, which has some sandy areas and rocky tide pools that invite investigation. Handcrafted rocking chairs, colorful hammocks, and a living room with board games provide a relaxing environment. All the usual activities can be arranged.

***Best Western Tamarindo Vista Villas Hotel*** (☎ 653-0114, fax 653-0115, e *tamvv@racsa.co.cr*, w *www.bestofcostaricahotels.com*) Doubles US$104-127, suites US$150-243, with continental breakfast. Radically remodeled by Best Western, the 33 rooms and suites are all air-conditioned and have telephones, cable TVs, VCRs, coffeemakers, and hair dryers. Perched up on a hill overlooking the entrance to Tamarindo, some have ocean views. The suites have well-equipped kitchens with dining areas, patios or balconies, and living rooms with two foldout futons. Up to four people can be accommodated. Larger two-bedroom units have two bathrooms and can sleep up to eight people. These are well designed, modern, and very comfortable. The hotel boasts a pool with swim-up bar, the popular Monkey Bar & Grill (a happening place in the evenings), a dive shop, car rental, surfing lessons and rentals, and a tour desk that arranges all activities.

## Places to Eat

There's a good selection of restaurants in Tamarindo, and more seem to open every year.

***Soda Frutas Tropicales*** (☎ 653-0041) Snacks US$1.50-4. This is a tourist-friendly soda with good fruit drinks.

***Restaurant Coconut*** Main courses US$6-12. Open from 3pm daily. This place serves Mexican and international food. The dining is upstairs in a tropical bamboo setting – rather romantic.

There are several places to eat at the road circle at the southwest end of the road into town.

***Mambo*** You can get real cappuccinos here, and there are good sandwiches and salads starting at US$2.50. There's a small pool table in back.

***Restaurant Zully Mar*** Dishes US$5-10. Open 7am-10pm. This more-or-less open-air place has good sea views, which is the best reason to dine here – the food is OK but not memorable.

***Nogui's Bar*** (☎ 653-0029) Main courses US$6-11. Also right on the beach, this is a superpopular little place for beer, salads, grilled food, and seafood. Come early for dinner or you might wait an hour for a table. In the morning, the same place is renamed the ***Sunrise Café*** (both signs are there if you look hard) and is a good spot for breakfasts as early as 6am.

***Pedro's*** Whole fish US$4.50. Barely 100m behind Nogui's Bar, walking along the beach, you'll find this place, which doesn't look like much. Appearances deceive – if you just want a fresh fish, this is a good place to eat well and inexpensively.

*Fiesta del Mar* Dishes US$6-12. This large, high-roofed, and attractive place is the most upscale in this area and serves good steaks, seafood, and tropical cocktails, though it has been upstaged by Nogui's as of late.

*El Arrecife* Dishes US$3.50-6. This is the best tico joint in the area, with inexpensive *casados* and chicken-and-rice dishes drawing a local clientele.

Heading away from the main road are several places worth seeking out.

*Lazy Wave* (☎ 653-0737) Breakfasts from US$2.50, lunches US$4.50, dinner appetizers US$4-5, main courses US$8-15. Gringos crowd in for the pancake breakfasts. At night, a chalkboard announces nouvelle cuisine expertly prepared by Canadian chef Derek Furlani; the menu changes from night to night, but you can rely on various versions of braised meats, seared ahi tuna, and other fresh seafood. Appetizers include sushi, ceviche, and heart of palm. The outdoor patio built around a huge tree attracts many dedicated diners who come away happy.

*Shark Bite* (☎ 653-0453) Snacks, pastries & sandwiches US$2-4. This cool little deli in front of the Lazy Wave serves excellent sandwiches made to order, as well as espressos and cappuccinos. It has a book exchange and feisty staff.

*Cantina Las Olas* Dishes average US$5. Open 6pm daily, closed Sun. This is a popular Mexican-food restaurant and bar.

*Taco Stop* Tacos from US$3. This is a great place for Mexican tacos, and they do good take-out (which is just as well, because the seating area is very small).

*Geckos* Average US$6. Inside the Iguana Surf Aquatic Outfitter complex, this popular eatery serves a variety of Italian and international plates and is a good value.

*Stella's* (☎ 653-0217) Main courses US$13-23, individual pizzas US$6-11. Closed Sun. This is Tamarindo's most elegant restaurant, with white tablecloths and sparkling glassware in a semirustic building. Seafood and Italian are the specialties here, though there are plenty of other choices. The pizza is wood-oven baked.

*Restaurant Pachanga* (☎ 653-0021) Appetizers US$5-7, main courses US$11-17. Open 6pm-10pm Tues-Sat. This mellow little place was considered the top of the

bunch by Tamarindo foodies when we went to press. The small menu features fabulously prepared seafood with an Asian twist – look for Thai curry, shrimp in coconut sauce, sashimi, and other delights. Meat entrées are usually offered as well.

Don't forget the recommended restaurants in the more upscale hotels.

## Entertainment

There's usually live or recorded dance music happening at one or more of the road-circle restaurants on weekends. The *Monkey Bar* in the Best Western hotel is a popular spot.

There are live music jams once or twice a week at *Pasatiempo Hotel*, and *Disco Noai* also has live music some nights.

Ask around – there's always something going on in an impromptu fashion.

## Getting There & Away

**Air** The Tamarindo airstrip is about 2.5km from the north end of the village; a hotel bus is usually on hand to pick up arriving passengers. SANSA (☎ 653-0012, 653-0357, fax 653-0001) has an office on the main road, and the Hotel Pueblo Dorado is the Travelair agent. Both airlines have flights to and from San José; the trip takes about an hour, and return flights leave Tamarindo immediately following arrival. In the high season, SANSA has six daily departures from San José. In the high season, Travelair offers five daily flights from San José. Some of these may stop in Liberia, Nosara, or Sámara. Check locally for the ever-changing schedules. One-way/roundtrip fares from San José are US$66/132 with SANSA and US$73/141 with Travelair.

**Bus** The Empresa Alfaro office in Tamarindo is next to the police station (there isn't a working phone there). Empresa Alfaro (☎ 258-4716, 222-2666), at Calle 14, Avenidas 3 & 5, San José, has a daily bus at 3:30pm. Its bus returns from Tamarindo direct to San José at 5:45am, with an extra bus at noon on Sunday. Several buses leave Santa Cruz daily for Tamarindo. Buses to Santa Cruz leave Tamarindo at 6am, 7am, 9am, noon, and 4pm. Buses to Liberia leave at 8:40am and 4:30pm.

Eiselstein Travel Agency sells tickets for Interbus and Gray Line services.

**Car & Taxi** If you're driving to Tamarindo, the better road is from Belén to Huacas and south. It's also possible to drive from Santa Cruz 17km to 27 de Abril on a paved road and then northwest on a dirt road for 19km to Tamarindo; this route is rougher, though still passable to ordinary cars. A taxi from Santa Cruz should cost about US$12 to US$15. Allow twice that from Liberia.

## Getting Around

Many people arrive in rental cars. If you get here by air or bus, you can rent bicycles and motorbikes (see Activities & Organized Tours, earlier) or cars from Economy Rent-a-Car (☎ 653-0728) or Alamo/Adobe (☎ 653-0727). Travelair passengers can arrange for a rental car to be waiting at the airport. However, there seems to be a different car rental agent in town almost every year, so things will probably have changed by the time you arrive. There isn't a gas station, though you can buy expensive gas from drums in a shack near the entrance of town. Fill up in Santa Cruz.

## PARQUE NACIONAL MARINO LAS BAULAS DE GUANACASTE

Formerly a national wildlife refuge, this national marine park was created in 1991 and covers about 379 hectares on the north side of the Río Matapalo estuary, just north of Tamarindo village. In addition, 22,000 hectares of ocean are also protected. Most of the land is mangrove swamp containing all six of the mangrove species found in Costa Rica – two species of black mangrove

Twists and turns of swamp life

as well as tea, white, red, and buttonwood. This creates a great habitat for caimans and crocodiles, as well as numerous bird species, including the beautiful roseate spoonbill.

But the main attraction and raison d'être of the park is undoubtedly **Playa Grande**, the country's important nesting site for the *baula* (leatherback turtle), briefly described in the Wildlife Guide at the back of this book. Its nesting season is from October to March (especially November to January), and more than 100 of the reptiles may be seen laying their eggs on Playa Grande during the course of a night (dark nights are best); about 2500 nests are made each season. Other species are occasionally seen in other months.

Playa Grande is also a favored surfing beach, its break touted as the most consistent in Costa Rica. So far, surfers and turtles have coexisted within the national park with few problems. The park was created more to control unregulated tourism and to protect the nests from poaching.

Until the formation of the park, tourists arrived by the boatload and harassed the animals by using flash photography, touching them, and generally acting like yahoos. Now turtle-watchers pay a US$6 entry fee to the park and must stay in specified viewing areas. You must be accompanied by a guide or ranger, and no flash photography or lights are allowed, as they disturb the egg-laying process.

Other creatures to look for when visiting this reserve are howler monkeys, raccoons, coatis, otters, and a variety of crabs.

The park office (☎/fax 653-0470) is by the northern entrance and is open 9am to 6pm. Maps and brochures about park wildlife are available. The US$6 entrance fee is generally charged only for the nighttime turtle-watching tours.

## Turtle Watching

Tamarindo hotels and agencies will organize turtle-watching tours in season. Some of these are by boat. Tours cost about US$20 to US$35, depending on the size of the group, where you start from, the quality of the guide, etc. A limited number of visitors are allowed in the park at any given time, and seeing a turtle is never guaranteed; don't pressure your guide to break the rules!

A recommended way to begin your tour is with a visit to **El Mundo de la Tortuga** (☎/fax 653-0470/1; admission US$5; open 2pm-early morning during the laying season, 2pm-6pm rest of year), an excellent exhibit about leatherback turtles near the north end of the park. The exhibit is a self-guided introduction to the life of a leatherback turtle, narrated over headphones in English, French, German, or Spanish and accompanied by beautiful photographs. A visit here will make your turtle-watching tour much more rewarding. Most of the tours offered from the exhibit itself are guided by re-formed poachers who know the turtles well. The museum has tours running all night. Show up early to put your name on the tour list; when turtles arrive, small groups are led out to the beach in the order that they signed up. A full tour costs US$18, but this includes the US$5 entrance fee to the exhibit. Transport to and from Tamarindo can be arranged for an additional US$7.

## Places to Stay & Eat

Most people stay in Tamarindo, just south of the park. At the north end of Playa Grande (at the north end of the park) are a few small hotels.

*Centro Vacacional Playa Grande* (☎ 237-2552 in Heredia, ☎ 384-7661 cellular) Campsites US$2 per person, rooms from US$6 per person. A few hundred meters back from the beach on the main road, this place is popular with vacationing tico families and surfers. Basic rooms have fans and cold showers, and some have kitchenettes. There's a restaurant and pool.

*Villa Baula* (☎ 653-0493, 653-0650, fax 653-0459, e hotelvb@racsa.co.cr, w www .hotelvillabaula.com) Doubles US$70, bungalows US$116-145. At the southern end of the park just across the estuary from Tamarindo, this pleasantly rustic beachfront complex has 25 family cabins sleeping one to five people. All have private showers, but not all have hot water. The more expensive bungalows have a kitchenette and air-conditioning. There's a pool, and surfboards, body boards, kayaks, and bikes are available. Ask about exploring the estuary, where birds, monkeys, and caimans can be seen.

*Hotel Cantarana* (☎ 653-0486, fax 653-0491, e cantarana@hotmail.com) Singles/doubles US$53/76 with breakfast, US$71/104

with breakfast & dinner. This hotel near the estuary has 10 air-conditioned rooms with private hot showers and fans. It has a good European restaurant, offers massage and kayak rental, and has a pool. The restaurant draws diners from outside the hotel. The German owners also speak French and English.

*Hotel Las Tortugas* (☎ 653-0423, ☎/fax 653-0458, e surfegg@cool.co.cr, w www.cool .co.cr/usr/turtles) Doubles US$95. The 11 spacious air-conditioned rooms here have private hot baths, thick walls, and small windows to enable daytime sleep after a night of turtle-watching. Discounts of 40% are given in low season. There's a pool, Jacuzzi, and restaurant, and tours to the national park and elsewhere can be arranged. The owner, Louis Wilson, was instrumental in organizing protection for the turtles and designed the hotel so that the lights, which are quite dim, shine away from the beach area, even though the hotel is right on the beach. Surfboards, body boards, sea kayaks, snorkels, and horses are rented. Ask about renting apartments or houses near the beach.

## Getting There & Away

There are no buses to Playa Grande. You can drive to Huacas and then take the paved road to Matapalo and then a 6km dirt road to Playa Grande. If you're staying at one of the hotels on Playa Grande, ask them to pick you up from the Matapalo turnoff (where the bus from San José can drop you off). It's also possible to take day tours to the reserve from Tamarindo, or get a local boat captain to take you across the estuary from Tamarindo to the southern end of Playa Grande (see the Playa Tamarindo section, earlier).

## PLAYAS NEGRA & AVELLANA

These popular surfing beaches offer both left and right breaks. Avellana is a long stretch of white sand about 15km south of Tamarindo by road (unpaved south of Villareal), but closer to 10km if you walk in along the beaches. Negra, a few kilometers farther south, is a darker beach broken up by rocky outcrops that offer exciting surfing. If you're not coming from Tamarindo, head west on the paved highway from Santa Cruz, through 27 de Abril to Paraíso, then follow signs or ask locals. The last section is unpaved. Either way, the road is rough and may require 4WD in the wet season, so get local updates. The relatively difficult access means that these beaches are frequented by those who appreciate them, mainly surfers, some of whom have written to complain that there are too many surfers!

The following places to stay and eat are very spread out and are listed approximately from north to south.

**Cabinas Las Olas** (☎ 382-4366) Singles/doubles/triples/quads US$45/55/65/75. Set on spacious grounds, the 10 airy individual cabins here have porches and hammocks. Boardwalk trails lead through mangroves down to Playa Avellana; there are very few surfers at this end of the beach.

**Cabinas El León** (☎ 381-1361) Singles/doubles US$24/38, including breakfast. About 250m from the beach, this popular place has bright clean rooms with private hot showers. Italian and English are spoken.

**Rasta Mike's** (no phone) Campsites US$5 per person, rooms US$15 per person, including breakfast. This place, about a 15-minute walk from the beach, is popular with the budget crowd. Facilities include a shared kitchen, a variety of cabins and rooms, and a restaurant (dinner about US$5).

**Las Hermanas Restaurant** Lunches & snacks under US$5. This place is opposite Rasta Mike's.

**Mono Congo Lodge** (☎/fax 382-6926) Rooms US$35 per person. More or less between Playas Avellana and Negra, this large open-air ranch building is surrounded by monkey-filled trees. There's a comfortable common living room and a star-watching deck. This place was recently for sale.

A bit closer to Playa Negra are a variety of surfer-oriented places.

**Aloha Amigos** and **Juanitos Ranchitos** (☎ 680-0280) Rooms US$10 per person. These basic side-by-side places share a phone and charge the same rates. Kitchen and laundry facilities, bikes, and transport to Paraíso are available.

**Hotel Playa Negra** (☎ 382-1301, fax 382-1302, ⓔ info@playanegra.com) Singles/doubles US$50/60, US$10 additional people. On the beach, this hotel offers spacious, circular bungalows. Tours and rentals are available.

**Pablo's Picasso** (☎ 382-0411, fax 680-0280) Doubles US$40. Another classic

surfers' hangout, Pablo's is 400m from the beach. It features hamburgers 'as big as your head,' huge surfing murals, laundry facilities, TV, and cabins and dorms. Some rooms have kitchens and air-conditioning. This place was also for sale in 2002.

## PLAYA JUNQUILLAL

This wide and wild beach has high surf, strong rip currents, and few people. It's 2km long and has tide pools and pleasant walking. Locals go surf-fishing here.

Junquillal is about midway between Las Baulas de Guanacaste and Ostional. Ridley sea turtles nest here in December and January, but in smaller numbers than at the refuges. There's no village as such (the nearest is **Paraíso**, about 4km inland), but there are several nice places to stay near the coast. Because of the length of the beach and the lack of a village, the beach is uncrowded, and there's a pleasant away-from-it-all feel. Some hotels don't even have phones, and those that do suffer from occasional cuts in service. Hotels lower their rates by 20% to 40% outside the mid-December to mid-April high season.

### Places to Stay & Eat

**Hotel Iguanazul** (☎ 658-8124, ☎/fax 658-8123, ⓔ info@iguanazul.com, ⓦ www.iguanazul.com) Singles US$70-92, doubles US$82-105. This recommended Canadian-run hotel is elegant and secluded, but friendly and fun. Amenities include a pool; a game room with a pool table, darts, and table tennis; volleyball; a small souvenir shop with a well-chosen selection of gifts; and a recommended restaurant and bar with a good view of the beach, just a short walk away by trail. Snorkeling gear (US$5 a half day) and horse rental (US$15 for the first hour, US$10 for each additional hour) are available. Sportfishing, diving, and local tours can be arranged. High-season rates are listed for the 24 tiled rooms with fans and hot showers. Multiday activity packages are available.

**Campground** There's an excellent campground near the hotel on a shady hillside overlooking the ocean; look for signs. Campers are sometimes allowed to use the hotel facilities.

**Beach apartment** Rates US$70-100. The Iguanazul also has information about renting a two-room apartment with a hot-water bathroom, fans, a kitchen, dining area, and balcony. One room has a double bed; the second room has two double beds. High-season rates are about US$120 for the whole apartment and US$80 for the apartment without the second room. You can use all the hotel facilities.

*Hotel El Castillo Divertido* (☎/fax 658-8428) Doubles US$40. On a hilltop about half a kilometer beyond the Iguanazul entrance is this small, seven-room, German/tica-owned hotel, which looks like a little white castle. It has a panoramic view from the rooftop bar – a breezy place to laze in a hammock and watch the sunset. The tower bedroom faces the ocean. This is a place only a dreamer could build, and the owners are enthusiastic hosts. Good meals are available, and it's well under a kilometer from the beach itself. Rooms aren't huge, but all have private hot showers and fans; some have balconies.

*Guacamaya Lodge* (☎ 658-8431, fax 658-8164, e info@guacamayalodge.com, w www.guacamayalodge.com) Singles/doubles US$53/58, villa for 4 US$140. A short way beyond El Castillo is this quiet little Swiss-run place with six bungalows with fans and private hot-water baths, and a two-bedroom villa with kitchen. There's a pool and restaurant-bar. The owners speak six (!) languages.

*Hotel Tatanka* (☎ 658-8426) Rooms US$45-65. Another half kilometer along brings you to this hotel, which is a row of motel-like rooms; readers write that the Italian management is friendly and that the restaurant is good.

*El Malinche* Campsites US$3 per person. A few hundred meters beyond Tatanka, this campground has bathrooms and good views.

*Hotel Playa Junquillal* (☎ 658-8432, in the USA ☎ 888-666-2322, e info@playa-junquillal.com, w www.playa-junquillal.com) Singles/doubles with bath & fan US$26/36. Although US-owned, this place is run by friendly locals Bernardo and Senjia Sánchez, who speak some English and are very helpful. Four beach cabins have fans and hot showers and are often full in the dry season. Hammocks and body boards are available. The restaurant-bar is popular with locals, serves good tico meals, and has live marimba music on Saturday night. You

could ask to camp here, or you could probably camp almost anywhere along the beach if you have your own food and water.

*Hotel Hibiscus* (☎/fax 658-8437) Doubles with bath US$48. Almost opposite Hotel Playa Junquillal, this tico/French-run hotel has five pleasant rooms with fans, and rates include breakfast. It serves French-inspired cuisine and has a flower garden.

*El Lugarcito* (☎/fax 658-8436, e ellugarcito@racsa.co.cr) Doubles US$50. This Dutch-run three-room B&B rents snorkeling gear and offers scuba diving and PADI courses. The owner is a divemaster.

*Hotel Villa Serena* (☎/fax 658-8430, e serenaho@racsa.co.cr, w www.land-ho.com) Doubles with bath US$70-100. About half a kilometer beyond the Hibiscus, 12 modern bungalows spread around a small pool where open-air musical aerobics classes are held. Palm trees abound, and there's a sauna, tennis court, and horses for rent. A health and beauty spa is on the premises. Spacious doubles have fans, private hot-water bathrooms, and (in some cases) patios facing the beach. Some rooms are air-conditioned and some sleep up to six. The restaurant has a good ocean view.

*Hotel Antumalal* (☎/fax 658-8425/6, e antumal@racsa.co.cr) Singles/doubles US$85/100, suites US$120. At the end of the road almost a kilometer beyond the other places, this hotel is on spacious grounds frequently visited by wild monkeys. The 30 attractive cabins have private hot baths, fans, and terraces. Amenities include a pool and a kids' pool, a tennis court, good restaurant, and two bars. Horses are available for rent (cheap rates, and nonguests are welcome), boats are available for fishing and diving, and PADI certification courses can be arranged from the hotel's dive shop. German and English are spoken.

Apart from the hotels, there's nowhere to eat unless you return 4km to the village of Paraíso, where there are a few simple local restaurants, sodas, and bars.

## Getting There & Away

**Bus** TRALAPA (☎ 221-7201/2), in San José at Calle 20 & Avenida 5, has a daily bus to Playa Junquillal at 2pm, taking about five hours. The return bus leaves Junquillal at 5am. There's also a daily TRALAPA bus from Santa Cruz at 6:30pm, returning at

5am. The bus may go only as far as Paraíso, 4km by foot or taxi from the beach.

**Car & Taxi** If you're driving, it's about 16km by paved road from Santa Cruz to 27 de Abril, and another 17km by unpaved road via Paraíso to Junquillal.

From Junquillal, you can head south by taking a turnoff about 3km east of Paraíso. This road is marked 'Reserva Ostional' and is passable in ordinary cars, at least during the dry season. Most people visiting the beaches south of Junquillal reach them from Nicoya. Expect to have to ford some rivers (especially if it's been raining), and carry spare everything. There are no gas stations on this coastal dirt road, and it carries little traffic.

A taxi from San José costs about US$125 to US$150; from Santa Cruz, it's about US$20.

## SANTA CRUZ

This small town is on the main peninsula highway 25km south of Filadelfia, 57km south of Liberia, and 23km north of Nicoya. A paved road leads 16km west to 27 de Abril, from where dirt roads continue to Playa Tamarindo, Playa Junquillal, and other beaches. Santa Cruz is a possible overnight stop when you're visiting the peninsula – it gives the visitor a chance to experience Costa Rican life in a small country town. It also has some of the cheapest places to stay on the peninsula.

About three city blocks in the center of town were burned to the ground in a devas-

tating fire in 1993. A major town landmark, the **Plaza de Los Mangos**, a large grassy square named after the three mango trees growing on the north side, is now not much more than a vacant lot. However, many town addresses are still given from that plaza. The attractive and shady **Parque Bernabela Ramos**, a new park with folklore-themed statues, has opened 400m south of here. Across from a ruined clock tower and a modern church with interesting stained glass windows, the new park is a nice place to soak in Santa Cruz life.

There's an annual rodeo and fiesta during the second week in January, with plenty of Guanacasteco dancing, marimba music, and traditional food. Another fiesta is held in late July. Santa Cruz is considered the folklore center of the region, if not the entire country, although not much seems to happen here outside of fiesta time. Nearby villages (see the boxed text 'Guaitil') are famous as Chorotega pottery centers. The population of Santa Cruz and the surrounding district is about 17,500.

You can change money at the Banco de Costa Rica (☎ 680-3253), three blocks north of the Plaza de Los Mangos.

## Places to Stay

**Budget** Rooms are basic but OK at *Pensión Isabel* (☎ 680-0173) Rooms US$5 per person. It's about 400m south and 50m east of the Plaza de Los Mangos.

*Hotel Anatolia* (☎ 680-0333) Rooms US$4-6 per person. Basic wooden boxes are

---

### Guaitil

An interesting excursion from Santa Cruz is the 12km drive by paved road to the small pottery-making community of Guaitil. Get there by taking the main highway toward Nicoya and then taking the signed Guaitil road to the left, about 1.5km out of Santa Cruz. This road is lined by trees and is very attractive in April when all the trees are in bloom. The road used to be the main highway to Nicoya and passes the small town of Santa Bárbara before reaching Guaitil, where you can see people making pots outside their houses. There are local buses from Santa Cruz.

The attractive pots are made from local clays, using natural colors in the pre-Columbian Chorotega Indian style. They come in a variety of shapes and sizes – many of the huge pots decorating houses and hotels in Guanacaste come from here. Ceramics are for sale outside the potters' houses in Guaitil and also in San Vicente, 2km beyond Guaitil by unpaved road. If you ask, you can watch part of the potting process. Many of the approximately 100 families engaged in this industry are descendants of the Chorotega Indians who once inhabited the area but who have now been largely assimilated into Costa Rican culture.

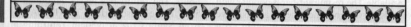

available at this boardinghouse-like place, 100m west and 200m south of the Plaza de Los Mangos. Look for the cute paintwork on the outside. There's a restaurant.

**Pensión Amadita** This is another cheapie, 250m north of the plaza.

**Cabinas Tauro** (☎ 680-0289) Rooms US$10. This friendly place offers a row of decent rooms in a family garden, 100m north and 100m west of the Plaza de Los Mangos. Room rates are for two or three people.

**Mid-Range** One hundred meters west of the Plaza de Los Mangos is **Hotel La Estancia** (☎ 680-0476, 680-1033, fax 680-0348) Singles/doubles/triples US$12/24/29. This hotel has 16 clean rooms with fans, TVs, and private baths.

**Hotel Plazza** (☎ 680-0169) Singles/doubles US$13/20. On the west side of the Plaza de Los Mangos, the 13 clean, simple rooms here have fans and private showers.

**Hotel La Pampa** (☎ 680-0586) Singles/doubles with fan US$16/24, with air-con US$25/34. Hotel La Pampa is 50m west of the Plaza de Los Mangos and has 20 simple but clean modern rooms with private baths.

**Hotel Diria** (☎ 680-0080, 680-0402, fax 680-0442, e hoteldiria@hotmail.com) Singles/doubles with bath US$30/46. On the northern outskirts of town, at the intersection with the main peninsula highway and about 500m north of the Plaza de Los Mangos, this is the best hotel in town. It has a pool, restaurant, and 50 air-conditioned rooms with TVs and telephones. Occasionally, the hotel may host entertainment on weekends – live marimba music or recorded dance music are both possibilities. (Marimbas are wooden xylophone-like instruments of African origin, although some musicologists claim that the Central American version is of Guatemalan Indian origin.)

## Places to Eat

**Coopetortillas** Open 5am-6:30pm daily. Check out this place, also known as La Fábrica de Tortillas (Tortilla Factory), on a side street 700m south of the Plaza de Los Mangos (250m south of Parque Ramos). It's a huge corrugated-metal barn that looks like a factory. Inside are plain wooden tables, and you eat whatever's available – always homemade Costa Rican food cooked right in front of you in the wood-stove kitchen. It's interesting, and the food is tasty and inexpensive.

**Restaurant La Luna**, at the northeast corner of Parque Ramos, looks like a nice place serving large and inexpensive portions of Chinese food.

**Restaurant Barbará** (☎ 680-0646) is a simple restaurant-bar with a Guanacaste cowboy ambience.

## Getting There & Away

There are two bus terminals and some other bus stops. Check all departure points carefully. Unscheduled services to the beaches west of here crop up frequently; ask around. Folklórico, a little company in a wooden building 100m south and 25m west of the plaza, is worth checking. Transportes La Pampa buses (☎ 680-0382) leave the terminal on the north side of the Plaza de Los Mangos for Nicoya 17 times a day from 6am to 9:30pm, and for Liberia 16 times a day from 5:30am to 7:30pm.

The main terminal is 400m east of the center. TRALAPA (in San José ☎ 221-7201/2, in Santa Cruz ☎ 680-0111) has buses leaving Calle 20 & Avenida 5, in San José nine times a day for Santa Cruz (five hours, US$5.25). Buses to San José leave Santa Cruz at 3am, 4:30am, 5am, 6:30am, 8:30am, 10:15am, 11:30am, 1pm, and 5pm. Expect one or two buses fewer in the wet season. Alfaro buses between San José and Nicoya also go through Santa Cruz. Buses to Puntarenas leave at 6:20am and 3:20pm. Buses to Liberia leave at 5:30am and 7:30pm. Various local villages are also served, including Guaitil about six times a day.

Buses for the beach also leave from the main terminal. There are buses for Playas Conchal, Brasilito, Flamingo, and Potrero four times a day during the dry season – fewer in the wet. Some TRALAPA beach buses also go via Santa Cruz. A bus leaves for Junquillal at 6:30am and for Tamarindo at 6:45am and 8:30pm.

## ACCESSING BEACHES SOUTH OF PLAYA JUNQUILLAL

To visit any of the beaches south of Junquillal, many people return to the main peninsula highway and go through Nicoya, 23km south of Santa Cruz. Dirt roads to the southwest reach the attractive beaches at Playas Nosara, Garza, Sámara, and Carrillo, and the wildlife refuge at Ostional. There are airstrips with scheduled flights at Nosara and Sámara/Carrillo. Paved roads east of Nicoya pass the national park at Barra Honda en route to the Tempisque car ferry, which crosses over to the main part of Costa Rica. Paved and unpaved roads to the southeast lead to Playa Naranjo and the Puntarenas car ferry. Travelers using public buses will find it difficult to continue farther south to the popular beach at Montezuma and other areas – you'll need to return to Puntarenas and take the passenger ferry back to Paquera.

## NICOYA

This is the most important town on the peninsula and has a population of about 21,000 (including the surrounding district). The town is named after the Chorotega Indian chief Nicoya, who welcomed the Spanish conquistador Gil González Dávila in 1523. The Indians presented the Spaniard with rich gifts, part of the reason why the country became known as Costa Rica. The Chorotegas were the dominant Indian group in the area at the time of the conquest, and many of the local inhabitants are at least partly of Indian descent.

In the Parque Central, a major town landmark is the attractive white colonial **Church of San Blas**, which dates back to the mid-1600s. The church, whose mosaic tiles are crumbling, has been under restoration for some years but can be visited. It holds a small collection of colonial religious artifacts; more are on display at the Banco Nacional de Costa Rica. The park is an inviting spot to

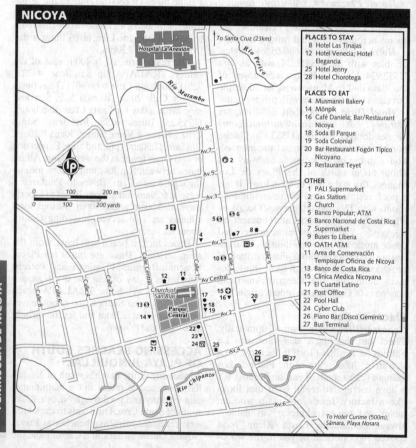

**NICOYA**

To Santa Cruz (23km)

Hospital La Anexión

Río Perico

Río Matambo

Río Chipanzo

To Hotel Curime (500m),
Sámara, Playa Nosara

PLACES TO STAY
8 Hotel Las Tinajas
12 Hotel Venecia; Hotel Elegancia
25 Hotel Jenny
28 Hotel Chorotega

PLACES TO EAT
4 Musmanni Bakery
14 Mönpik
16 Café Daniela; Bar/Restaurant Nicoya
18 Soda El Parque
19 Soda Colonial
20 Bar Restaurant Fogón Típico Nicoyano
23 Restaurant Teyet

OTHER
1 PALI Supermarket
2 Gas Station
3 Church
5 Banco Popular; ATM
6 Banco Nacional de Costa Rica
7 Supermarket
9 Buses to Liberia
10 OATH ATM
11 Area de Conservación Tempisque Oficina de Nicoya
13 Banco de Costa Rica
15 Clínica Medica Nicoyana
17 El Cuartel Latino
21 Post Office
22 Pool Hall
24 Cyber Club
26 Piano Bar (Disco Geminis)
27 Bus Terminal

Church of San Blas

Parque Central

stroll and people-watch, and the wooden-beamed church is appealingly peaceful. To minimize wear on the antique building, a new church was built a block north.

Nicoya is now the commercial center of the cattle industry as well as the political capital and transportation hub of the peninsula.

## Information

US dollars can be exchanged at any of the several banks in town (see the Nicoya map). The Cyber Club, half a block south of the Parque Central, is open from 9am to 9pm Monday to Saturday and charges US$1.50 an hour for Internet access. The main hospital on the peninsula is the Hospital La Anexión (☎ 685-5066), north of town. Emergency care is available at the Clínica Médica Nicoyana (☎ 685-5138). The **Area de Conservación Tempisque Oficina de Nicoya** (☎ 686-6760, 685-5267, ☎/fax 685-5667) has some information about wildlife in the region and can make reservations for camping, accommodations, or cave exploration at Parque Nacional Barra Honda (see below). The office is open 8am to 4pm weekdays.

## Places to Stay

**Budget** On the north side of the park is *Hotel Venecia* (☎ 685-5325) Singles/doubles without bath US$5/8, doubles with bath US$12. Basic, clean rooms have shared cold showers; for a little more money you can get a private shower. The hotel was being renovated at time of writing.

*Hotel Elegancia* (☎ 685-5159) Doubles US$9/12 without/with bath. Next to Hotel Venecia, this place is adequate.

*Hotel Chorotega* (☎ 685-5245) Rooms without/with bath US$4/5 per person. Often full, the town's best cheap hotel is two blocks south of the park. All rooms have fans, and some have private showers.

**Mid-Range** Two hundred meters west and 100m north of the park is *Hotel Las Tinajas* (☎/fax 685-5081) Singles/doubles/triples with bath US$11.50/15.50/22. Twenty-eight clean though aging rooms have fans and cold showers. Larger rooms with private baths sleep up to seven people for US$40. Reception is open 24 hours.

*Hotel Jenny* (☎ 685-5050, fax 686-6471) Singles/doubles with bath US$15/24. One

hundred meters south of the park, these 24 clean, air-conditioned rooms have private baths and TVs. Good luck getting in! This is among the best values in town and fills up early.

*Cabinas Nicoya* (☎ 686-6331) Doubles US$30-45. Five hundred meters east of the Banco Nacional de Costa Rica, this small place has clean air-conditioned rooms with TVs and hot showers. Amenities include parking and a tiny pool. The staff are welcoming.

*Hotel Curime* (☎ 685-5238, fax 685-5530) Singles/doubles with fan US$32/42, with air-con US$45/54, including breakfast. This rustic resort complex about half a kilometer south of town on the road to Playa Sámara is the best place in town. It offers a pool and basic restaurant, tennis and volleyball courts, and horses. Rooms have TVs, refrigerators, and private hot showers (which don't always work, according to one reader).

## Places to Eat & Drink

The several Chinese restaurants in the town center are among the best cheap places to eat. A good one is the *Restaurant Teyet*, which has three tables in a little outdoor patio (as well as more tables in the air-conditioned interior). There are several others on this block, probably equally good.

*Café Daniela* (☎ 686-6148) Meals US$1-5. Open 7am-9:30pm Mon-Sat, 7am-5pm Sun. A block east of the park, this squeaky-clean café serves breakfasts, casados, burgers, pizzas, cakes, shakes, and snacks and is a local favorite.

*Bar/Restaurant Nicoya* Meals US$3-8. Next to Café Daniela, this Chinese-run place is good for standard meals in a slightly upscale setting.

*Bar Restaurant Fogón Típico Nicoyano* Meals US$7-10. This is your best bet for steak, served in a barnlike setting.

Cheap snacks are available from several stands and sodas around the park. The *Soda Colonial* has cheap local food, and the *Soda El Parque* is popular. Ice cream is served at *Mönpik*, and pastries are available at *Musmanni Bakery*.

## Entertainment

*El Cuartel Latino* This discotheque on the Parque Central draws a teenage crowd. Older folks go for a drink at the *Piano Bar*, which morphs into the Disco Geminis on some nights.

There are a couple of pool halls, frequented mainly by young men.

## Getting There & Away

The bus terminal at the south end of Calle 5 is where most buses depart. An antique bus on display here was the first bus to make the San José to Nicoya run, on December 11, 1958.

Alfaro (in Nicoya ☎ 685-5032, in San José ☎ 222-2666), at Calle 14, Avenidas 3 & 5, San José, has eight buses a day to Nicoya (six hours, US$6). Most of these go through Liberia, Filadelfia, and Santa Cruz – a few cross on the Río Tempisque ferry. Buses from Nicoya to San José leave eight to 10 times a day between 4am and 5pm. Buses to Playa Naranjo leave at 5:15am and 1pm, connecting with the ferry from Naranjo to Puntarenas. A 1pm bus leaves for Playa Nosara; four daily buses head to Playa Sámara (fewer in the wet season); buses depart at 10am and 3pm to go to Quebrada Honda; and one or two buses a day go to a variety of other nearby villages.

Departures for Liberia (US$1.35) leave 24 times a day between 4am and 7pm from Transportes La Pampa (☎ 685-5313) at Avenida 1 and Calle 5. These buses go through Santa Cruz and Filadelfia.

Taxis Unidos de Nicoya (☎ 686-6857) provides 24-hour service.

The gas stations in town accept Visa but not MasterCard.

## PARQUE NACIONAL BARRA HONDA

This 2295-hectare national park is unique in that it was created to protect an area of great geological and speleological interest rather than to conserve a particular habitat.

The park lies roughly midway between Nicoya and the mouth of the Río Tempisque in a limestone area that has been uplifted into coastal hills over 400m in height. A combination of rainfall and erosion has created a series of deep caves, some more than 200m deep. Nineteen caves have been explored, which is about half of the cave system estimated to be there, so Barra Honda is of special interest to speleologists looking for something new.

The caves are complete with stalagmites, stalactites, and a host of beautiful and (to the nonspeleologist) lesser-known formations with intriguing names such as fried eggs, organs, soda straws, popcorn, curtains, columns, pearls, flowers, and shark's teeth. Cave creatures, including bats, sightless salamanders, fish in the streams running through the caves, and a variety of invertebrates, live in the underground system. Pre-Columbian human skeletons have also been discovered, although who these people were and how they got into the caves remains a mystery.

The 62m-deep Terciopelo (Velvet) Cave is the only one with regular access to the public. Visitors may be required to get permits from the Servicio de Parques Nacionales to enter some of the other caves. These include Santa Ana, the deepest (249m); Trampa (Trap), 110m deep with a vertical 52m drop; Nicoya, where human remains were found; and Pozo Hediondo (Stinkpot), which has a large bat colony. In all cases, a guide is required (see the Proyecto Nacaome section, below).

Above the ground, the Barra Honda hills have trails and are covered with the deciduous vegetation of a tropical dry forest. The top of Cerro Barra Honda boasts a lookout with a view that takes in the Río Tempisque and Golfo de Nicoya. There are waterfalls (adorned with calcium formations) in the rainy season and animals year-round. Howler and white-faced monkeys, armadillos, coatis, and white-tailed deer are sometimes seen and certainly heard. Striped hog-nosed skunks and anteaters are frequently sighted.

### Information

The dry season is the best time for caving; entering the caves is dangerous and discouraged during the rainy months. However, you can come anytime to climb the hills, admire the views, and observe the wildlife. If you come in the dry season, however, be sure to carry several liters of water and let someone know where you are going. Two German hikers died at Barra Honda in 1993; they planned a short hike of about 90 minutes and didn't want to hire a local guide. They got lost, had no water, and died of dehydration.

You can get maps and information at a ranger station in the southwest corner of the park. Park entry is US$6 per day. Near the station is an area with bathrooms and showers where camping is permitted for about US$2 per day. Trails from the ranger station lead to the top of Cerro Barra Honda – allow about half a day roundtrip. These trails can be hiked using only a map, but, again, take lots of water and tell the rangers where you are going.

The park is part of the Area de Conservación Tempisque, with administrative headquarters in Nicoya (☎/fax 685-5667, Spanish only). You should obtain permits from this office if you wish to explore the cave system. You can also reserve guides and accommodations. The park is open from 7am to 4pm daily, and the Terciopelo Cave is open from 7am to 1pm daily.

### Proyecto Nacaome

This locally run project is administered through the park and provides a basic tourist infrastructure as well as work for local residents. It offers food, accommodations, and information at the park entrance. Guides from the area come here looking for clients. It has proven an excellent way to involve locals in conserving the area, and a visit here is grassroots ecotourism at its best.

*Camping* costs US$2 per person and *cabins* are US$5 per person. There are three small cabins, each with a shower and six beds. A simple *restaurant* serves typical local meals for about US$3 each; it's best to arrange meals in advance. A guide service is available for hiking the trails within the park and also for descending into the most popular caves. A guide charges about US$22 for a group of up to four cavers. Equipment rental is an additional US$12 per person. The descent involves using ladders and ropes, so you should be reasonably fit.

To make reservations for accommodations or guide service, call the park office in Nicoya (☎/fax 685-5667, Spanish only), which contacts the park by radio. There's no phone at the park. The guides speak only Spanish, though a few of the rangers at the park itself speak some English and can help with arrangements.

### Getting There & Away

Getting to the park is somewhat confusing, because a map shows two ways to

---

### The Earthquake

Nicoya has a history of being hit by an earthquake about every 50 years, and starting in 1999, residents of the area have been waiting for the next one. No one knows for sure if it will happen, but people certainly have opinions about the subject! For more information on earthquakes in Costa Rica and safety tips, see the Facts for the Visitor chapter.

– John Thompson

---

enter. Barra Honda is shaped like a U; at the east end is the village of Quebrada Honda, with a dirt road leading north from it into the park. This is not the best way to enter the park.

The west arm of the U is the way to the ranger station. If you are driving from the Tempisque ferry, you will see a sign on the right-hand side for 'Barra Honda' about 16km after leaving the ferry and 1.5km before you reach the main peninsula highway between Nicoya and Carmona. If you're driving from the peninsula highway, take the turnoff for the Tempisque ferry and look for the Barra Honda road to your left after 1.5km – there's no sign when you're coming this way. From the turnoff, the road goes 4km to the small community of Nacaome, where a signed dirt road goes another 6km into the park. The community of Santa Ana is passed en route. This road has some steep and rough stretches that may require 4WD in the rainy season.

No buses go to the park, but you can get a bus from Nicoya to Santa Ana and walk the last kilometer. A daily bus leaves Nicoya for Santa Ana at 12:30pm, costs less than US$1, and takes about 30 minutes, with the return bus leaving Santa Ana at around 1pm. There may also be an early morning bus. A taxi from Nicoya to the park entrance costs about US$10.

### TEMPISQUE FERRY

The car-and-passenger ferry crossing is 17.5km from the main peninsula road. See the description of the Tempisque ferry in the Northwestern Costa Rica chapter for more details.

## PLAYA NOSARA

This attractive white-sand beach is backed by a pocket of luxuriant vegetation that attracts birds and wildlife. The area has seen little logging, partly because of the nearby wildlife refuge and partly because of real-estate development – an unlikely sounding combination.

Many houses and condominiums here are lived in year-round, and others can be rented by the week or month. The permanent occupants are mainly foreign (especially North American) retirees. The expatriate community is interested in protecting some of the forest, which makes Nosara an attractive area to live in, and you can see parrots, toucans, armadillos, and monkeys just a few meters away from the beach. So far, there's been a reasonable balance between developing the area and preserving enough habitat to support wildlife. The residents' association has been winning legal battles to keep out large-scale development. The hotels and other places to stay are spread out along the coast and a little inland, set unobtrusively into the forest and mixed in with private houses, condos, and a cosmopolitan selection of restaurants.

Note that the village and airport of Nosara are 5km inland from the beach, and food supplies and gas are available in the village. There are three distinct beaches. The southernmost is **Playa Guiones**, a long calm stretch of white sand with corals and the best snorkeling opportunities; **Playa Pelada**, in the middle, is a small crescent with shady trees and a simple restaurant near which you can camp; **Playa Nosara**, north of the river and hardest to access, has surf. Thus the Nosara area (three beaches, airport, and village) is very spread out. There are many unidentified little roads. This makes it hard to get around if you don't know the place – look for hotel and restaurant signs and ask for help.

## Information

The post office, police, and Red Cross are all together by the soccer field in the village center. There's no bank. The Super La Paloma supermarket, midway between the village and the beach, acts as a Banco Popular agent on Monday and Friday and will change US dollars and traveler's checks. MasterCard is not accepted in Nosara, but Visa sometimes is.

## Activities & Organized Tours

Most hotels and cabinas offer tours or can hook you up with one. Going to Ostional is the most popular tour; see the Refugio Nacional de Fauna Silvestre Ostional section, later in this chapter. Another good trip is to the private **Reserva Biológica Nosara**; see the Lagarta Lodge entry in the Places to Stay & Eat – Near the Beaches section, below. By the soccer field in the village, the Dutch-run **Tuanis** (☎/fax 682-0249) has bike rentals (US$8 per day), tour information, a notice board, a good selection of local crafts, books, a book exchange, and Internet access, and it helps arrange conversation groups for those interested in practicing Spanish and meeting locals. They speak English and can tell you about **La Madrugada** (about 1km away), where roller skates can be rented; they have a half pipe for skateboarders. The **Nosara Surf Shop** (☎ 682-0186, ⓦ www.nosarasurfshop.com) repair surfboards and rents snorkeling gear. They also give surf lessons and arrange surfing tours. The **Nosara Retreat** (☎/fax 682-0071) offers yoga classes and massage.

## Places to Stay & Eat – Near the Village

The cheapest accommodations are in the village, inland.

**Cabinas Chorotega** (☎ 682-0129) Doubles without/with bath US$15/35 per person. This place has a pleasant courtyard balcony and has recently been refurbished. All rooms have fans, and six share baths. Four have a private shower and air-conditioning, and these rooms may soon get cable TV. Next door is a restaurant-bar that may have entertainment, including karaoke, at night.

**Cabinas Agnel** (☎ 682-0142) Rooms US$5 per person. A bit closer to the village center, this row of basic blue cabins is cheaper but not as well maintained.

**Casa Rio Nosara** (☎ 682-0117, fax 682-0182, ⓔ carinos@racsa.co.cr, ⓦ www.tropicalholiday.com) Rooms US$10 per person, dorm beds US$5. Between the beaches and the village, this place has six rustic rooms by the river. Basic but adequate, the rooms have private hot showers. A 10-person dorm serves shoestring travelers. Determinedly downscale, this place is run by Germans Toni and Beate Kast, who organize all kinds of tours, on water and horseback, for US$20 to US$80 per person, including guide and lunch. Their philosophy is that Costa Rica is to be actively enjoyed by everyone, and if budget travelers can save money on accommodations they can afford more of an adventure. Good idea! Readers have written to recommend them. Breakfast is available.

**Sodita Vannessa** Lunches US$3. On the main road by the public phone, Vannessa is locally popular for breakfast and lunch. There are other sodas and restaurants around the soccer field.

**Rancho Tico** Main courses US$5-9. On the western outskirts, this is the best choice for dinner in the village, though it seems rather overpriced.

**La Casona** Main courses US$4-8. Beyond the airport, west of the village, this is probably the best budget place. It serves pizzas and tico food.

## Places to Stay & Eat – Near the Beaches

**Blew Dog's Surf Club** (☎ 682-0080, e jake@ blewdogs.com, W www.blewdogs.com) Doubles US$35-45. A five-minute walk from Playa Guiones, this surf lodge has four small cabins with a double bed and hot shower, and three larger cabins with two beds and a kitchenette. There's also the charmingly named 'flop house' with four beds at US$10 each. A restaurant-bar serves American-style food – burgers, pizzas, and, of course, fish. The lively bar has dart boards, games, and surf videos.

**Casa de los Vagabundos** (☎ 682-0531, e penguin@racsa.co.cr) Rooms from US$7 per person. Just off the main road between Playas Guiones and Pelada, this new place offers basic rooms and cabins for budget travelers, students, and groups. A kitchen, hot shower, satellite TV, and Internet access are available. British hosts Patrick and Joan do educational and specialty tours (☎ 682-0309) to watch sea turtles, go birding, visit remote Guanacaste communities, and learn about local wildlife and habitats. Horses, kayaks, bicycles, and 4WD vehicles are used.

**Almost Paradise** (☎ 682-0173) Singles/ doubles with bath US$40/45, including breakfast. This old wooden building, high on a hill overlooking Playa Pelada, has plenty of character. Its five pleasant rooms are decorated with tico crafts, a balcony gives fine ocean views, and there's a good new restaurant-bar that brings in diners wanting to eat and drink with a view.

**Rancho Suizo Lodge** (☎ 682-0057, fax 682-0055, e rsuizo@infoweb.co.cr, W www .nosara.ch) Singles with bath US$30, doubles with bath US$50-68. A few minutes' walk from Playa Pelada, this place is run by René and Ruth, a Swiss couple. The lodge provides 11 pleasant bungalows with fans and five larger, newer units. There's a small pool, whirlpool, and restaurant (make advance reservations for dinner), and horse rental and tours can be arranged on request. A 'pirate bar' has been installed near the beach – you can barbecue.

**Estancia Nosara** (☎/fax 682-0178, e estangis@racsa.co.cr) Doubles/quads from US$50/60. This Italian/Swiss-run place is about 1km away from the beach at the south end of the Nosara area. Rooms have refrigerators, kitchenettes, private electric showers, and fans; some are air-conditioned. There's a pool and plenty of trees, and rentals and tours are available.

**Lagarta Lodge** (☎ 682-0035, fax 682-0135, e lagarta@racsa.co.cr, W www.lagarta .com) Singles/doubles/triples US$70/75/80. This seven-room hotel is a repeatedly recommended choice. High on a steep hill above the private 50-hectare **Reserva Biológica Nosara**, it offers stunning views over the estuary, reserve, and beach. Trails lead directly from the lodge through the reserve and down to the river and beach; entrance to the reserve costs US$5 (free to guests). Ask at the hotel for a trail map. Birding is good here – watch from the comfort of the hotel balcony or see many more species on hikes through the reserve. Rooms at this relaxing retreat aren't large but have high airy ceilings, cool whitewashed rock, fans, hot showers, and a small private patio or balcony. There's Internet access, a pool and massages, and tours can be arranged. Their balcony restaurant is worth a sunset visit; indeed, guests from other hotels make dinner reservations here on a regular basis. Weekend dinner specials include a seafood fondue on Friday, a Chinese fondue (meat) on Saturday, and a mixed barbecue and salad bar on Sunday. Other nights have a small changing menu of steak, fish, and chicken dishes. Dinners average US$12, lunches US$6, and breakfast buffet US$6.

*Hotel Villas Taype* (☎ 682-0333, 682-0280, fax 682-0187, ⒺⒾ info@villataype.com, Ⓦ www.villataype.com) Singles/doubles US$41/52 with fans, US$58/80 with air-con, suites & bungalows US$116-128, including breakfast buffet. This is the largest hotel in town; its six luxury bungalows and suites have pretty tiled bathrooms, cable TV, and minifridge. There are two pools, one with a swim-up bar, as well as a tennis court, Internet service, a games room, and restaurant. English and German are spoken.

*Hotel Playas Nosara* (☎ 682-0121, fax 682-0123, Ⓦ www.nosarabeachhotel.com) Doubles with cold/hot bath from US$40/50. With its incomplete minaret-like tower, this is the most unusual and most visible of Nosara's hotels. On an attractive hilltop between Playas Pelada and Guiones, the hotel has been here for 20 years and has a *1001 Nights* feel – fanciful and apparently eternally under construction. The balconied rooms offer beautiful beach views. There's a restaurant and pool. The North American owners speak many languages and will help organize local tours. Rooms have fans.

*Casa Romantica* (☎/fax 682-0019, Ⓔ casroma@racsa.co.cr, Ⓦ www.hotelcasaromantica.com) Singles/doubles US$58/68, apartments with kitchen US$68/79, air-con US$10 extra. Rates include breakfast. Down beside Playa Guiones, this private home has been converted into a small hotel with about 10 spacious modern rooms and a couple of apartments. Swiss owners Rolf Sommer and Angela Schmid run the place with professionalism and grace and speak English, German, Italian, and French. Their international restaurant (main courses average US$12, closed Sunday) is popular with local residents, and the poolside garden and bar are a nice respite from the beach, which is a short walk away. Wellness services – yoga, massage, fitness and nutrition counseling, stress reduction, etc – can be arranged.

*Café de Paris* (☎ 682-0087, fax 682-0089, Ⓔ info@cafedeparis.com, Ⓦ www.cafedeparis.net) Doubles without/with kitchen US$57/68, bungalows US$115, villas US$139, extra people US$12. Continental breakfast is included. Farther south, back out on the main road, this place began as the town's best bakery/café but is now a hotel and restaurant as well. You can have a good meal followed by an espresso or drink at the bar, and they'll let you take a dip in the pool. All rooms are modern, spacious, very clean, air-conditioned, and have hot showers.

*Marlin Bill's* (☎ 682-0548) Near the Café de Paris, this popular local bar also serves seafood dinners.

*Rancho Congo* (☎/fax 682-0078, Ⓔ rcongo@racsa.co.cr) Doubles/triples US$30/40, including breakfast. There are just two spacious rooms here, both with fans and big bathrooms with hot water. Set in pleasant gardens, they seem like a good value. German and English are spoken.

*Giardino Tropicale* (☎ 682-0258, Ⓦ www.giardinotropicale.com) Doubles US$50 with bath. Four cool white-walled cabins with fans, writing desk, and hot showers look out on a lawn shaded by a huge tree. On the same property, a rambling, rustic thatched *restaurant* has both indoor and outdoor decks for dining. Its wood-burning stove produces the best pizza in town: pizzas start from US$5, and pastas and Italian meals are US$7 to US$9.

*Gilded Iguana Bar & Restaurant* (☎ 682-0259, Ⓔ pattydoe@gildediguana.com, Ⓦ www.gildediguana.com) Singles/doubles/triples US$40/50/60. This place is popular with fishers and has four spacious rooms with fans, coffeemakers, refrigerators, and toasters, but no hot plates. Showers are hot, and two larger suites are planned. Fishing charters can be arranged. Kayaking, snorkeling and nature-watching is offered by Joe (☎ 682-0450, Ⓔ joe@gildediguana.com), who speaks English. The restaurant serves breakfast, lunch, and dinner (they'll grill your catch for you), and the bar is a popular US hangout with cable sports TV, bocce ball, and plenty of beer. From the main road, follow the signs to Olas Grandes.

*La Dolce Vita* (☎ 682-0107) Meals US$7-14. Open for dinner Tues-Sun. This is a good, upscale Italian restaurant.

*Olga's Bar & Restaurant* This popular tico-owned place is down on Playa Pelada. Grab a casado for just US$3, or get a fish dinner for about US$6.

## Getting There & Away

**Air** Both SANSA and Travelair have daily late-morning flights from San José for about US$70. Some flights may continue to Sámara before returning to San José. The

SANSA office (☎/fax 682-0168) is just west of the soccer field in the village.

Paula White (☎ 682-0070, ℮ paula@ nosaratravel.com, ⓦ www.nosaratravel .com) is the local travel agent and can arrange charter flights from San José for about US$80 per person with two people minimum. She can also arrange car rentals and hotel reservations.

**Bus** There's a daily bus from Nicoya's main bus terminal at 1pm, returning to Nicoya at 6am. The journey usually lasts about 2½ hours, but it can take much longer depending on road conditions. As we go to press, a new company, Traroc (☎ 685-5352), is announcing three buses a day between Nicoya and Nosara. There's a daily bus (about six hours) from San José with Empresa Alfaro (☎ 258-4716, 222-2666), Calle 14, Avenidas 3 & 5, San José, at 6am, returning from Nosara at 12:45pm.

**Car** The 35km dirt road from Nosara to Nicoya (via Guastomatal) is a poor one – locals say it's passable only to 4WD vehicles, and there are no signs. Most people take the longer paved road from Nicoya toward Playa Sámara. You turn off about 5km before Sámara (there's a sign). The last 25km stretch to Nosara has many sudden dips and washboarded areas, and there may be rivers to ford, especially in the wet season. Nevertheless, this is the way the bus comes, though even it occasionally doesn't get through! You may have some difficulty getting through in an ordinary car during the rainy season. It's also possible to continue north, past Ostional, to Paraíso and Junquillal, though you'll have to ford some small rivers and will need 4WD in the rainy season.

Gas up in Nicoya. The gas station in Nosara is a tank and a five-gallon Jerry can.

## REFUGIO NACIONAL DE FAUNA SILVESTRE OSTIONAL

This coastal refuge includes the beaches of Playa Nosara and Playa Ostional, the mouth of the Río Nosara, and the beachside village of Ostional.

The reserve is a narrow strip about 8km long but only a few hundred meters wide. The protected land area is 352 hectares; 587 hectares of adjoining sea are also protected.

The main attraction and reason for the creation of the refuge is the annual nesting of the olive ridley sea turtle on Playa Ostional. This beach and Playa Nancite in Parque Nacional Santa Rosa are the most important nesting grounds for the olive ridley in Costa Rica (see Parque Nacional Santa Rosa in the Northwestern Costa Rica chapter for more information). The nesting season lasts from July to November, and August to October are peak months.

The turtles tend to arrive in large groups of hundreds or even thousands – these mass arrivals, or *arribadas*, occur every three or four weeks and last for about a week, usually on the dark nights preceding a new moon. However, you can see turtles in lesser numbers almost any night you go during the nesting season. Villagers will guide you to the best places.

Coastal residents used to harvest both eggs and turtles indiscriminately, and this made the creation of a protected area essential for the turtles' continued well-being. An imaginative conservation plan has allowed the inhabitants of Ostional to continue to harvest the eggs from early layings. Most turtles return to the beach several times to lay new clutches, and earlier eggs may be trampled or damaged by later layings. Thus, it seems reasonable that locals harvest the first batches and sell them – they're popular snacks in bars throughout the country.

The leatherback and Pacific green turtle also nest here in smaller numbers. Apart from the turtles, there are iguanas, crabs, howler monkeys, coatis, and many birds. Some of the best birding is at the southeast end of the refuge, near the mouth of the Río Nosara, where there's a small mangrove swamp.

The rocky Punta India at the northwest end of the refuge has many tide pools that abound with marine creatures such as sea anemones, sea urchins, starfish, shellfish, and fish-fish. Along the beach are thousands of almost transparent ghost crabs, bright red Sally Lightfoot crabs, and a variety of lizards. The vegetation behind the beach is sparse and consists mainly of deciduous trees such as frangipani and stands of cacti.

The rainy season lasts from May to December, and the annual rainfall is about 2000mm. The best time to see the turtles is the rainy season, so be prepared. The average daytime temperature is 28°C. There's a Universidad de Costa Rica research station, and the villagers of Ostional are helpful with information and will guide you to the best areas.

Ostional has a small *pulpería* where you can get basic food supplies. Beware of very strong currents off the beach – it's not suitable for swimming.

## Places to Stay & Eat

*Camping* is permitted on the ocean side of the soccer field, but there are no facilities.

*Hospedaje Guacamaya* Rooms with bath US$4.50 per person. Next to the Ostional pulpería, this place advertises four rooms. It's usually full during the best turtle-nesting nights. Next door, the *Salon Brisas del Pacífico* bar may have very loud music on weekends, precluding sleep.

*Cabinas Ostional* (☎ 682-0428) Rooms US$5-6 per person. Near Hospedaje Guacamaya, Cabinas Ostional offers six rooms with hot showers in a pleasant family backyard.

*Restaurant Mirador Las Lomas* Up a hill at the south end of Ostional, about 200m before reaching Cabinas Ostional, this place has views and the best dinners in town, though it's not always open.

*Soda Surfo* This cheap soda is at the corner of the soccer field.

## Getting There & Away

The refuge begins at Playa Nosara; Ostional village is about 8km northwest of Nosara village. This unpaved road is passable, but some minor rivers need to be forded and 4WD is necessary in the wet season. From the road joining Nosara beach and village, turn north just before the Supermercado La Paloma. After 0.4km, take the right fork and continue another 0.4km, across a new bridge over the Río Nosara. After the bridge, there's a T-junction; take the right fork and continue another 1.2km to a T-junction where you take the left fork. From here, continue on the main road north to Ostional, about 6km away. The road from Santa Cruz to just before Paraíso and south along the coast to Ostional is in similar condition – passable to an ordinary car in the dry season, but with some small rivers to ford; in the rainy season 4WD is necessary. The rivers have firm bottoms; walk across to

find the shallowest route, then roar through in low gear.

During the dry months, there are two daily buses from Santa Cruz – these may or may not run during the wet season, depending on road conditions. Hitchhiking from Nosara is reportedly easy. Many of the better hotels in the region offer tours to Ostional during egg-laying periods.

Drivers arriving at Ostional should slow down; three of the most vicious speed bumps in the country greet you at the entrance of town.

## PLAYA SÁMARA

This beach is 16km southeast of Bahía Garza and about 35km southwest of Nicoya. Sámara has a beautiful, gentle, white-sand beach that has been called one of the safest and prettiest in Costa Rica. Former president Oscar Arias had a vacation house near here, as do many other wealthy ticos. It's also a favorite beach for tourists and has good bus and air service. One drawback is the relative lack of forest, which means there's less wildlife and shade than at other Nicoya beaches.

The village has a few stores and discos and several hotels, restaurants, and bars. Things are a little spread out – ask for directions to places away from the center. Local inhabitants (other than retirees) do a little farming and fishing.

Playa Sámara is still a fairly tranquil place, but development has picked up since the paved road arrived in 1996. There's a fair amount of construction going on in the village center, and new places continue to open.

### Information

The Super Sámara Market has Internet access and tourist information and sells Travelair Tickets. There's no bank.

### Activities & Organized Tours

**Capt Rick Ruhlow**, a well-known local skipper, has a boat for sportfishing here. Ask at any hotel to get in touch with him. **Capt Rob Gordon** (☎ 656-0170) offers his boat, the *Kitty Cat*, for sportfishing.

**Ciclo Mora**, in a soda about 100m west of Cabinas Arenas, rents bicycles. Horse rentals can be arranged through several of the hotels, as mentioned below.

**Popos** *(☎ 656-0086, fax 656-0092,* e *info@ poposcostarica.com,* w *www.poposcostarica .com),* based in Playa Carrillo and run by Tad Cantrell, offers exciting, well-orchestrated, and reasonably priced kayak tours, including a few designed especially for families.

**The Flying Crocodile** *(☎ 383-0471, fax 656-0196,* e *flycroco@racsa.co.cr),* several kilometers west along the road to Nosara, offers ultralight flights (about 15 minutes for US$70). **Wingnuts** *(☎/fax 656-0153)* offers canopy tours for US$39.

## Places to Stay

**Budget** Just behind the sign for *Coco's Camping* are several places to camp for about US$3 per person; ask around for the best price.

*Hotel Playa Sámara (☎ 656-0190)* Rooms US$5.50 per person. This is a cheap, grungy place to stay. It's usually full with tico beachgoers on weekends. It's not well maintained; check to see if the water is working. The Tutti Frutti Discotheque is nearby.

*Cabinas Magaly* Rooms US$8 per person. Another cheap place, this one has a few rooms with musty baths.

*Bar/Cabinas Los Mangos (☎ 656-0356)* Rooms US$5 per person. About 1km south of town, Los Mangos is a straight-up place with shared showers. It's casually managed and doesn't have firm prices – bargain.

*Cabinas El Ancla (☎ 656-0254)* Doubles/ triples US$15/18. This place has simple, clean rooms with shared cold baths by the beach. There's a restaurant and cheerful bar.

**Mid-Range** Rooms are adequate at *Cabinas Arenas (☎ 656-0320)* Doubles US$30. You get private baths and fans – and a room for US$15/single if there's space.

*Casa Valeria B&B (☎ 656-0511, fax 656-0317,* e *casavaleria_af@hotmail.com)* Singles/doubles/triples with bath US$20/25/35, bungalows doubles/triples/ quads US$40/45/55. In the village, this place has a grove of trees and hammocks by the beach. The three rooms and four bungalows are clean and have hot water and fans. A communal kitchen is available. The owners arrange some tours.

*Hotel Giada (☎ 656-0132, fax 656-0131,* e *info@hotelgiada.net,* w *www.hotel giada.net)* Singles/doubles/triples/quads

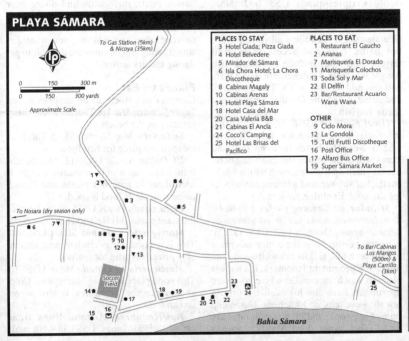

**PLAYA SÁMARA**

To Gas Station (5km)
& Nicoya (35km)

0   150   300 m
0   150   300 yards
*Approximate Scale*

To Nosara (dry season only)

Soccer Field

To Bar/Cabinas Los Mangos (500m) & Playa Carrillo (3km)

*Bahía Sámara*

**PLACES TO STAY**
3 Hotel Giada; Pizza Giada
4 Hotel Belvedere
5 Mirador de Sámara
6 Isla Chora Hotel; La Chora Discotheque
8 Cabinas Magaly
10 Cabinas Arenas
14 Hotel Playa Sámara
18 Hotel Casa del Mar
20 Casa Valeria B&B
21 Cabinas El Ancla
24 Coco's Camping
25 Hotel Las Brisas del Pacífico

**PLACES TO EAT**
1 Restaurant El Gaucho
2 Ananas
7 Marisquería El Dorado
11 Marisquería Colochos
13 Soda Sol y Mar
22 El Delfín
23 Bar/Restaurant Acuario Wana Wana

**OTHER**
9 Ciclo Mora
12 La Gondola
15 Tutti Frutti Discotheque
16 Post Office
17 Alfaro Bus Office
19 Super Sámara Market

PENÍNSULA DE NICOYA

US$29/44/56/65. On the main road down to the beach, the Giada is one of the nicest places in this price range. Plants and bamboo give it a tropical feel, and there's a pool and Jacuzzi. The 13 large rooms have balconies or patios, private hot baths, and fans, and breakfast is included. The hotel can arrange horse rental and all local tours, and it has a bar, laundry service, and tourist information. The SANSA agent has an office in the lobby. A good pizza restaurant is on the premises. Italian, English, and German are spoken.

*Hotel Casa del Mar* (☎ 656-0264, fax 656-0129) Singles/doubles/triples with shared bath US$35/41/47, rooms with bath US$47-104 for 1-6 people, air-con US$11.50 extra. Continental breakfast is included. This place is next to the Super Sámara Market close to the beach and has spacious, very clean, pleasant rooms with fans. Eleven rooms have private bathrooms; six share. There's a Jacuzzi and small restaurant. The French-Canadian owners speak French and English.

*Hotel Belvedere* (☎/fax 656-0213, e belvedere@samarabeach.com) Singles/doubles/triples/quads US$27/42/53/58, doubles with kitchen US$58. Hotel Belvedere is set in a breezy garden with nice views. The 10 rooms all have private hot baths, fans, and access to a small terrace, and rates include breakfast. Two bungalows have a kitchenette. For US$6, you can add air-con or TV. There's a pool and Jacuzzi, and the German owners also speak English.

*Hotel Fenix* (☎ 656-0158, fax 656-0162, e fenix@samarabeach.com) Doubles US$75. Near the beach between 1km and 2km south of the center, this charming hotel has six small apartments, each with a kitchenette, hot shower, and a balcony overlooking the pool. English is spoken.

*Mirador de Sámara* (☎/fax 656-0044, e mdsamara@racsa.co.cr, w www.mirador desamara.com) Doubles US$104, US$11.50 per extra person. Near the center, this place is built on a hill, and its tall white-and-blue tower is a prominent landmark. It's a great place to watch for monkeys. Five good-size apartments have airy high ceilings, private hot showers, fans, and kitchens. They sleep up to five people and high-season rates are listed. The owner, Max Mahlich, speaks German and English, and he'll take guests on van tours anywhere they want to go.

*Isla Chora Hotel* (☎ 656-0174/5, fax 656-0173, e hechombosol@racsa.co.cr) Doubles US$93, apartments with kitchenettes US$140, US$11.50 per extra person. At the west end of town, this attractive place has 10 air-conditioned rooms in five two-story buildings around a large central pool, plus four apartments. The rooms each have private balconies or patios, large modern hot-water bathrooms, fans, two queen-size beds, and free safe-deposit boxes. The restaurant has an Italian menu, and there's a genuine Italian ice-cream parlor (they imported the ice-cream maker and make their own – it's delicious). During high-season weekends, there's a discotheque and occasional live bands, and pool aerobics and Latin American dance lessons may be offered. This place attracts upper-class ticos.

*Hotel Las Brisas del Pacífico* (☎ 656-0250, fax 656-0076, e brisasdelpacifico@ racsa.co.cr, w www.brisas.net) Doubles US$64-104, US$17 per extra person. Hotel Las Brisas has two pools, a spa, and a good restaurant. The hotel has a gift shop, and horses, boats, surfboards, and diving gear are available for rent. The 34 rooms all have private hot showers; rates vary depending on room size and whether you want air-conditioning. Single rates are difficult to get during the dry season.

## Places to Eat
Campers can stock up on supplies at the *Super Sámara Market*. There are also cheap eateries on the beach.

*Soda Sol y Mar* Meals US$3-5. This is an inexpensive place for tico food.

*El Delfín* Meals US$6-12. This beachfront restaurant is quite romantic at night. It specializes in gourmet pizzas and French dishes, but all its food is good.

*Pizza Giada* Pizzas US$5. In the hotel of the same name, this is a good place for pizza.

*Marisquería Colochos* Meals US$5-10. This is a good, long-standing, and reasonably priced favorite for seafood.

*Marisquería El Dorado* Meals US$5-10. This good place is giving Marisquería Colochos a run for its money. It also serves Italian food.

*Bar/Restaurant Acuario Wana Wana* (☎ 655-0595) Tapas US$3.50-4.50, main courses US$8-20. Near the coast, this Spanish restaurant has excellent seafood, attentive service, and live music on weekends.

**Restaurant El Gaucho** (☎ 656-0124) Meals US$5-9. Up on the hill as you enter town, this place offers more meaty dishes.

**Ananas** (☎ 656-0491) Dishes US$1.50-4. Open 7am-5pm. Next to El Gaucho, this is a good little place for sandwiches, cake, fast food, ice cream, fruit salad, and shakes.

### Entertainment

**La Gondola** This is a fun nightspot, with pool, darts, Ping-Pong, and an unlikely mural of Venice.

**Tutti Frutti Discotheque** This disco operates most weekends of the year.

**La Chora Discotheque** In the Isla Chora Hotel, this disco operates during high-season weekends and is classier than Tutti Frutti.

### Getting There & Away

**Air** The airport is between Playa Sámara and Playa Carrillo (actually a bit closer to the latter) and serves both communities. Sometimes the airport is referred to as Carrillo. The SANSA agent is at the Hotel Giada, and Travelair is at the airport.

SANSA has flights from San José every morning; Travelair has daily flights around noon. Some flights stop at Nosara or Punta Islita. Itineraries and routes change often, depending on demand. Fares are about US$70 one-way.

**Bus** Empresa Alfaro (☎ 656-0269, in San José ☎ 258-4716, 222-2666) has a daily bus to Sámara at 12:30pm (six hours), continuing on to Playa Carrillo and costing US$6. The bus returns to San José (starting from Carrillo) at 4:30am, or at 1pm on Sunday.

Buses from Nicoya leave several times a day, take about two hours, and cost US$1.25. Most buses continue to Playa Carrillo. Call the new bus company, Trararoc (☎ 685-5352), for information.

### PLAYA CARRILLO

This beach begins 3km or 4km southeast of Sámara and is a smaller, quieter version of it. With its clean sand, rocky headlands, and curving boulevard of palm trees, Carrillo is a postcard-perfect tropical beach. Over holiday periods like New Year's and Easter, the beach has traditionally been popular with ticos. A recent prohibition on camping cut down on the number of visitors and is a source of some controversy – some complain that big developers are trying to restrict the beach to only the wealthy. The signs are still up but are sometimes ignored. The two beaches are separated by the narrow Punta Indio and thus are almost, but not quite, contiguous. See the Playa Sámara section, earlier, for activities.

### Places to Stay & Eat

**Victorio's** Just off the beach, Victorio's offers basic **camping** facilities. Nearby, **Villa Palma** reportedly offers camping and cheap rooms.

**Casa Pericos** (☎/fax 656-0061) Dorm beds US$9, doubles with bath US$24. This laid-back place is to the left up a steep hill as you arrive in Playa Carrillo. It has four dorm beds and two double rooms with ocean views, private baths, and fans. There's a verandah, living room, and communal kitchen. You can also camp here. The welcoming owners speak German and English and offer scuba courses and dive or fishing trips. There are a couple of other unsigned places in this area that sometimes offer cheap cabins – ask around.

**Cabinas El Tucan** (☎ 656-0305) Rooms US$24. Up the hill off the main road, these clean, bamboo-bedecked rooms sleep up to four people, and rates include breakfast. There's a *pizzeria*, and the staff will drive you down to the beach or airport.

Farther into the village, **El Mirador** is an OK restaurant with good views of the bay. Nearby, **Restaurant El Yate** is a good, inexpensive seafood place – sea bass in garlic costs US$4.

**Cabinas El Colibrí** (☎ 656-0656) Doubles US$25-30, including breakfast. This Argentine-run place has six cabins with fans, private baths, and hot water; five have kitchenettes. A restaurant-bakery is attached. Though a bit hard to find, it's a good value and worth searching out. It's about a five-minute walk to the beach.

**Popo's Cabinas** (☎ 656-0086, fax 656-0092) Doubles US$25-35. Opposite Cabinas El Colibrí, this place is also home to Popos (see Activities & Organized Tours under Playa Sámara). These rustic A-frame cabins opened in 2002 and feature fans, decks, and private cold baths. Breakfast is included.

*Hotel Esperanza B&B* (☎ 656-0564, e esperanz@racsa.co.cr) Doubles US$30-45, including full breakfast. The brightly painted rooms at this seven-room B&B have fans and private hot showers, and they sleep up to six. There's a European restaurant, and the multilingual staff can arrange tours.

*Guanamar Beach Resort* (☎ 656-0054, fax 656-0001, e info@guanamar.com, w www .guanamar.com) Rooms & suites US$120-200. This beachfront resort has changed management recently and should be newly renovated by now. Sportfishing is the name of the game here.

## Getting There & Away

See the Playa Sámara section, earlier, for transportation information.

## ISLITA & BEYOND

It's possible to continue southeast beyond Playa Carrillo, more or less paralleling the coast, to reach the southern tip of the peninsula. Although Punta Islita is less than 10km by road southeast of Playa Carrillo, the road is so bad that when a small luxury resort opened near there in the mid-1990s, Travelair began stopping at the small Punta Islita airstrip en route to Sámara and Nosara. The coast southeast of Playa Carrillo remains the most isolated stretch on the peninsula. There are various small communities and deserted beaches along this stretch of coast, but accommodations and public transportation are minimal.

## Places to Stay & Eat

You can *camp* in many places (usually without facilities) if you have a vehicle and are self-sufficient. Otherwise, the few hotels are listed in order heading southeast from Playa Carrillo.

*Hotel Punta Islita* (☎ 231-6122, fax 231-0715, e info@hotelpuntaislita.com, w www .hotelpuntaislita.com) Rooms, suites, villas with 1-3 bedrooms US$200-700. This hilltop hotel offers about 40 luxurious units, some with private outdoor Jacuzzis or pools, and all with views overlooking Playa Islita. Beach shuttles are provided. This is one of the best hotels in the region. It has a fine restaurant and a lovely pool and spa. You can rent equipment for snorkeling, mountain biking, tennis, boating, fishing, etc.

*Blue Pelican* (☎ 390-7203) Doubles with bath US$25. An attractive option by the beach is this place, where the romantic doubles have canopy beds and fans. Simpler rooms sleeping up to five also cost US$25. Good food and ice-cold beer are available.

*Hotel Arca de Noé* (☎/fax 656-0065, e arcanoe@racsa.co.cr) Doubles US$58, including breakfast. Inland from the beach, this pleasant complex has 10 attractive rooms, a pool, Italian restaurant, and bar. Horses and kayaks can be rented. They also have three 'surfer rooms' for US$20 per person.

In San Francisco de Coyote, a small village 4km inland from Playa Coyote, are a couple of *sodas* and *pulperías*.

*Soda Familiar* Rooms US$15. The folks at this soda offer clean cabins sleeping up to four people, as well as horse rental (US$5 per hour). The family-run *Rancho Loma Clara* is similarly priced. Both places prepare simple country meals. The *Centro Social Los Amigos* offers beer and pool.

*Bar/Cabinas Veranera* About 300m from Playa Coyote, this bar also offers cheap accommodations. Adventurous travelers may well come across other cheap cabinas along this coast.

## Getting There & Away

**Air** Travelair and SANSA fly to Punta Islita from San José daily.

**Bus** Arsa (☎ 257-1835) has a daily bus that crosses the Golfo de Nicoya on the Puntarenas ferry and continues through the villages of Jicaral, San Francisco de Coyote, and on to Playa San Miguel and Bejuco. The bus leaves San José at 6am and 3pm, passing through San Francisco de Coyote at 11:30am and 10pm and arriving at Playa San Miguel at noon and 10:30pm. The return bus leaves Bejuco at 2am and 12:30pm, passing through Playa San Miguel at 2:30am and 1pm, and San Francisco de Coyote at 3am and 2pm. This service may not run in the rainy season.

There don't seem to be buses from Nicoya, or any other bus services going south along this coast between Playa Coyote and Mal País. Mal País can be reached via Cóbano (see Mal País, later in this chapter).

**Car** It's about 70km by very rough road from Playa Carrillo to the town of Cóbano.

Allow about four hours for the trip if you have a 4WD vehicle and encounter no delays. Several rivers have to be forded, including the Río Ora about 5km east of Carrillo. This river can be impassable at high tide, even to 4WDs, so check the tides and water levels. If you time it right and are ready for adventurous driving, you can make it in an ordinary car in dry season.

A slightly easier route, if you're driving, is to head inland from Playa Carrillo through the communities of San Pedro, Soledad (also known as Cangrejal), and Bejuco and down to the coast at either Islita (to the northwest) or Jabilla (to the southeast). This loop is about 18km and is very steep in places – a regular car can just make it in the dry season, but you'll probably need 4WD in the wet.

Adventurous drivers with 4WD (or maybe a regular car in the dry season) can continue on past Playas Coyote, Caletas, Arío, and Manzanillo (camp at any of these places if you're self-sufficient) before heading inland via Río Negro to get to Cóbano, Mal País, Montezuma, and Cabo Blanco. There are several rivers to be crossed in this stretch as well. Be prepared to get lost and to ask directions frequently. These last three places are usually reached by the road that connects with the ferry from Puntarenas to Playa Naranjo and follows the southeastern part of the peninsula; they are described below.

## SOUTHEAST CORNER

From Nicoya, buses go southeast through Jicaral and Lepanto to the car-ferry terminal of Playa Naranjo, about a 72km drive. From Jicaral, you can get buses to Playas Coyote and San Miguel (see above). Otherwise, to travel beyond Playa Naranjo into the southern part of the peninsula, you need your own transportation – all buses either end at the car ferry or cross over to Puntarenas. In fact, Playa Naranjo and the southern end of the peninsula are part of the province of Puntarenas, even though it looks as if this area should belong to the province of Guanacaste, as does the north and central part of the peninsula described thus far in the chapter. If you want to go farther south from Playa Naranjo and don't have your own car, cross the Golfo de Nicoya on the car ferry to Puntarenas and then recross the

gulf on the Puntarenas-Paquera passenger ferry. Buses go from Paquera farther south.

**Jicaral** and **Lepanto** are two villages of note on the Nicoya–Playa Naranjo run. There are a couple of cheap and basic places to stay in Jicaral, and 4WD taxis are available to take you anywhere you want to go.

Near Lepanto, salt pans are visible from the road. This is a good place to stop and look for waders – you may see roseate spoonbills here, among other birds. Four kilometers before reaching Playa Naranjo, near the school of Cabo Blanco, is the new *Jardines del Golfo* project, with a restaurant and dry forest trails. Cabins are planned.

## PLAYA NARANJO

This tiny village is the terminal for the Puntarenas car ferry. The beach isn't very exciting. Most ferry passengers continue on to Nicoya by bus.

### Places to Stay & Eat

A few hotels offer lodging for those waiting for a ferry; they all can arrange horseback or water-based tours.

*Hotel Del Paso* (☎/fax 661-2610) Doubles US$40. This place has clean rooms with air-conditioning, TVs, and cold water. Amenities include a pool, hammocks, and a reasonable restaurant serving fresh seafood.

*Hotel Oasis del Pacífico* (☎/fax 661-1555) Singles/doubles with bath US$50/60. This is the nicest hotel and has a pool, tennis court, restaurant, and bar.

There are several simple *restaurants* and *sodas* near the ferry dock.

### Getting There & Away

All transportation is geared to the arrival and departure of the ferry. The hotels pick up ferry passengers if they know you're coming, but you could easily walk – it's not far.

Buses meet the ferry and take passengers to Nicoya, three to four hours away. There are no other public transportation options except for 4WD taxis, which can take you to Paquera for about US$25.

The ferry (☎ 661-1069 for information) leaves Playa Naranjo daily at 5:10am, 8:50am, 12:50pm, 5pm, and 9pm, and the crossing to Puntarenas takes an hour. (There may be more frequent departures on busy weekends and fewer in the rainy season, so plan accordingly.) Fares are about US$12 for car and driver, US$1.50 for adults, US75¢ for children, and US$2.50 for bicycles and motorbikes. Note that on most buses using the ferry, passengers have to get off the bus to buy a separate ticket – don't dally in the nearby sodas, as the bus may leave without you! If you're driving, you may need to show up a couple of hours early during holiday periods.

The road from Playa Naranjo to Paquera is in very poor shape (this is one of the bumpiest stretches of main road on the peninsula; 4WD may be essential in the rainy season), but it improves beyond Paquera.

## BAHÍA GIGANTE

This bay is about 9km southeast of Playa Naranjo.

*Hotel Bahía Luminosa Resort* (☎ 641-0386, fax 641-0387, e *tropics@racsa.co.cr*, w *www.bahialuminosa.com*) Doubles US$65. Overlooking the beach, this place is set on a little hill and is recently under new management. There's a marina with a variety of sailing and boating excursions, and a dive shop. A restaurant and pool are on the premises.

## ISLANDS NEAR BAHÍA GIGANTE

The waters in and around Bahía Gigante are studded with islands, 10 large enough to be mapped on the 1:200,000 map, and many smaller little rocks and islets. In fact, this area packs in more islands than anywhere on Costa Rica's coasts, and they attract a variety of sightseers and boat traffic.

The biggest of these islands is the 600-hectare **Isla San Lucas**, which is about 4km northeast of Bahía Gigante and 5km west of Puntarenas. The island used to hold a prison, which had a reputation for being the roughest jail in Costa Rica. The prison was closed in 1992, and now visitors can see the largely overgrown remains of the prison cells, some of which are over 100 years old (see Organized Tours, below).

A few hundred meters off the coast, **Isla Gitana** (shown on most maps as Isla Muertos because of the Indian burial sites found here) is smack in the middle of Bahía Gigante. The almost 10-hectare island is a sort of rustic resort, with trails through the forest, a nice beach, and a saltwater pool. There's a small *lodge* (☎/fax 661-2994) with a couple of simple cabins for US$50 per person. Rates include meals, or are less if you cook for yourself. Cabins are cooled by sea breezes and sleep up to six – no luxuries. The ramshackle *restaurant-bar* on the beach attracts the occasional boater, and the owners have various boats and kayaks, snorkeling gear, and windsurfers available for guests. This is an unusual place where you can get away from it all. Call for information and reservations and to arrange pickup from Puntarenas (US$50), Paquera (US$15), or Bahía Gigante. Remember to bring lots of spare batteries for your flashlight.

**Isla Guayabo** and **Islas Negritos** are well-known seabird sanctuaries but, for the protection of the birds, no land visitors are allowed except researchers with permission from the Servicio de Parques Nacionales. The reserves can be approached by boat, however, and you can observe many of the seabirds from the boats. The Paquera ferry is the cheapest way to get fairly close, and the Isla Tortuga trips and chartered boats are other ways to go.

Isla Guayabo is a 6.8-hectare cliff-bound rocky islet about 3km east of Punta Gigante (at the north end of Bahía Gigante). There's very little vegetation. Costa Rica's largest nesting colony of brown pelicans (200 to 300 birds) is found here, and peregrine falcons overwinter on the island. The Islas Negritos are two islands 10km southeast of Bahía Gigante and just a few hundred meters east of the easternmost point of the peninsula. They have a combined size of 80 hectares and are covered with more vegetation than is Guayabo. Frangipani, gumbo limbo, and spiny cedar are the dominant trees. Both Guayabo and the Negritos have colonies of magnificent frigatebirds and brown boobies.

The best-known island in the area is **Isla Tortuga**, which is actually two uninhabited islands about 5km southwest of Islas Negritos. They have beautiful beaches for snorkeling and swimming and can be reached by daily boat tours from Puntarenas (see Organized Tours, below).

### Organized Tours

The most well-known tour goes to Isla Tortuga. In 1975, **Calypso Tours** (see Organized Tours in the Getting Around chapter) began offering tours to the island aboard the yacht *Calypso*. The company has since built up a reputation for excellence in food and service. It has many repeat customers and has now added the luxurious 70-foot motorized catamaran *Manta Ray* to its fleet. This air-conditioned boat is built for fun and speed – there are even a couple of outdoor Jacuzzis and an underwater viewing window. Onboard freshwater showers are available as well.

The *Manta Ray* does tours to Isla Tortuga from San José. The tours cost US$99 per person (US$94 from Puntarenas) and include a dawn departure from San José; a private bus to Puntarenas with a continental breakfast; the boat trip to the islands; a delicious four-course picnic lunch and cocktails on the beach; plenty of time for swimming, snorkeling, and sunbathing; and transport back to San José, returning around 8pm. The two island biological reserves of Guayabo and Negritos are passed en route, with opportunities to see the bird colonies from the boat.

This is undoubtedly a classy trip, and several other companies offer similar tours (though none have a boat as sophisticated as the *Manta Ray*), which has led to complaints that Isla Tortuga is more crowded than it was in earlier years. Information on other tours to the island can be obtained from various local hotels and tour operators (see the Montezuma section, later in this chapter) in the southern Península de Nicoya. Better hotels in Puntarenas and San José and travel agents in San José can make reservations for you. Go midweek to avoid the crowds.

On Isla Tortuga, **Canopy Tours** (see Organized Tours in the Getting Around chapter) offers an adventurous canopy platform and ropes tour.

Isla Tortuga is not the only tour destination available. Partly in response to the competition, Calypso now offers a tour that stops at the prison island of **Isla San Lucas**, cruises by the various wildlife islands, and lands at Punta Coral, a private beach at the easternmost point on the peninsula. Guided nature walks, swimming, snorkeling, and sea kayaking are offered, along with the usual superb lunch. This full-day tour departs San José on Wednesday and Sunday.

The company also offers a night **astronomy cruise** through the islands aboard the *Manta Ray* every Friday, accompanied by a professional astronomer. A landfall is made for a barbecue dinner, and a telescope is set up for stargazing.

## PAQUERA

It's about 25km by road from Playa Naranjo to the village of Paquera, which is 4km from the Paquera ferry terminal. Most travelers pass straight through on their way to or from Montezuma – perhaps that's a good reason to stop here for a night and meet some locals. The village has a Banco de Costa Rica and an Internet café.

### Places to Stay & Eat

There are a couple of cheap hotels in the village of Paquera.

*Cabinas and Restaurant Ginana* (☎ 641-0119) Singles/doubles US$7/11 with fans, doubles US$20 with air-con. This is considered the best place, and rooms have private showers and fans. There's a decent restaurant.

*Cabinas Jardín* (☎ 641-0003) Doubles with fan/air-con US$10/20. Rooms here have private baths.

### Getting There & Away

**Boat** The Ferry Peninsular (☎ 641-0118, 641-0515, 661-8282) leaves Puntarenas for Paquera at 8:45am, 2pm, and 8:15pm and returns from Paquera to Puntarenas at 6am, 11:15am, and 6pm daily. The fare is US$1.50 for adults, US$1 for bicycles and children, US$3.20 for motorbikes, and US$12 for car and driver. Crossing time is about 90 minutes.

Naviera Tambor (☎ 661-2084) has car ferries from Puntarenas at 5am, 12:30pm, and 5pm. They return at 8am, 2:30pm, and 8:30pm. The fare is about the same as the Ferry Peninsular, except that this company offers an air-conditioned 1st-class cabin for US$2.50 (adults). Guests at the Hotel Playa Tambor have preference on this ferry; extra ferries may run on busy weekends.

**Bus, Car & Taxi** A crowded truck takes passengers into Paquera village. Most travelers take the bus from the ferry terminal to Montezuma (two hours, US$2.25). The bus can be crowded; try to get off the ferry early to get a seat.

The road from Paquera to Playa Tambor has been paved, but the rest remains unpaved. A 4WD taxi from Paquera to

Montezuma costs about US$30; taxis usually meet the ferry.

There are no northbound buses. A 4WD taxi to Playa Naranjo costs about US$25.

## REFUGIO NACIONAL DE VIDA SILVESTRE CURÚ

This small 70-hectare refuge is at the eastern end of the Península de Nicoya, about 5km south of Paquera village. Despite its small size, it holds a great variety of habitats. There are deciduous and semideciduous forests with large forest trees, mangrove swamps with five different mangrove species,beaches fringed by palm trees, and rocky headlands. The forested areas are the haunts of deer, monkeys, agoutis, and pacas, and three species of cats have been recorded. Iguanas, crabs, lobsters, chitons, shellfish, sea turtles, and other marine creatures are on the beaches and in the tide pools. The snorkeling and swimming are good. Birders have recorded about 200 species of birds, but there are probably more. For such a small place, it has a lot of wildlife.

The refuge is privately owned. The owners, Señora Julieta Schutz and her children (☎ 661-2392), provide tours, rustic *accommodations*, and home-cooked *meals* when arranged in advance. Keep in mind that the Schutzs also run a working ranch and are often busy; moreover, student groups often have priority. Most of the better hotels in the area will arrange guided day tours to Curú. The reserve is not signed and is down a dirt road (as is everything in this area). If you want to visit without a guide, call in advance to get directions and to make sure the gate is open.

## PLAYAS POCHOTE & TAMBOR

These two long beaches are protected by Bahía Ballena (Whale Bay), the largest bay on the southern peninsula coastline. The beaches begin 14km south of Paquera, at the tiny community of Pochote, and stretch for about 8km southwest to the village of Tambor – they're divided by the narrow and wadable estuary of the Río Pánica. The calm beaches are safe for swimming, and whales are sometimes sighted in the bay.

### Places to Stay

**Budget** At the south end of the bay in the village of Tambor is *Hotel Dos Lagartos*

(☎/fax 683-0236) Doubles without/with bath US$18/30. It's clean and pleasant and has beach views and a restaurant. A few rooms have private baths and fans, but most share bathrooms. Tours can be arranged to nearby areas.

*Cabinas Tambor Beach* (☎ 683-0057) and *Cabinas Cristina* (☎ 683-0028) both have cabins for about US$30 that sleep up to four people.

A *campsite* halfway between Tambor and the Bahía Ballena Yacht Club has basic cold showers and charges about US$2.50 per person.

**Top End** The most controversial hotel in the history of Costa Rican tourism is *Hotel Barceló Playa Tambor* (☎ 683-0303, fax 683-0304, W www.barcelo.com) Doubles US$200. See the boxed text, 'Clamor in Tambor.'

*Tango Mar Resort* (☎ 683-0001/2, in San José ☎ 222-4637, fax 683-0003, e info@tango mar.com, W www.tangomar.com) Double rooms & suites US$192, oceanfront suites US$244, villas US$465, extra person US$23. This resort is 3km south of Tambor village in an area unspoiled by big development. It's an attractive, romantic, and secluded beachfront resort and country club with two spring-fed pools, a 10-hole golf course, two lighted tennis courts, a soccer field, and a 1st-class international and seafood restaurant where lunch and dinner plans are US$19 and US$25. Tours are available, and you can rent 4WDs, horses, boats, and fishing and diving gear. Nature trails, a cliffside waterfall, natural pools, and a secluded beach are not the least of the attractions. Besides the extravagantly equipped rooms and suites, roomy villas feature two bedrooms and a kitchen. There's also a huge, four-bedroom, ocean-view Presidential Villa with its own pool for US$1455. Nonguests can play golf for US$35.

*Tambor Tropical* (☎ 683-0011, fax 683-0013; in the USA ☎ 503-365-2872, fax 503-371-2471; e info@tambortropical.com, W www.tambortropical.com) Doubles US$175-204. This is one of the newest resorts and offers 10 spacious rooms in five split-level cabins on the beach. Each room has a queen-size bed, a fully equipped kitchen, fans, a verandah, and a large hot-water bathroom. There's a pool, Jacuzzi, restaurant, and open-air bar. Guided horse-

## Clamor in Tambor

Grupo Barceló, the Spanish owner of Hotel Playa Tambor, was sued in 1992 for environmental violations during construction. The accusations included illegally filling in a swamp, taking massive amounts of sand off beaches and gravel from rivers (causing serious erosion), improperly treating sewage, and harassing passersby on the public beach. Some workers complained of inadequate health care and safety rules – two employees died in accidents in questionable circumstances.

The Costa Rican Supreme Court ordered the project halted and the Minister of Tourism commanded Grupo Barceló to stop building within 50m of the beach because, they said, necessary permits had not all been obtained. Despite this, the project proceeded as planned and opened in November 1992. This led to criticism that the government appeared unable to enforce the law, and boycotts of the hotel by tourism operators who felt that the highly touted 'environmentally sensitive ecotourism' image of Costa Rica was being destroyed. Nevertheless, enough tourists visited the place to make it economically possible to continue running it.

Grupo Barceló was fined the tiny sum of US$9000 for the unambiguously illegal act of destroying a mangrove swamp. As of 2002, other issues remain legally unresolved but the hotel is operating successfully.

back riding, snorkeling, parasailing, waterskiing, kayaking, windsurfing, boating, diving, and fishing trips are available at extra cost. Swimming off the beach in front of the cabins is safe. Rates are the same year-round and include breakfast. Children under 16 are not allowed.

Most hotels have their own restaurants. There are also some beachfront *sodas*.

### Getting There & Away

The airport is just north of the entrance to Hotel Playa Tambor. SANSA and Travelair have daily flights.

Paquera-Montezuma buses pass through here. A taxi to Montezuma reportedly is more expensive from here than from Paquera.

### CÓBANO

This small inland town is the most important community in the far south of the Península de Nicoya, though most people go on to Montezuma. There's a Banco Nacional (☎ 642-0210), a gas/service station (☎ 642-0072), a good 24-hour clinic called Emergencia 2000 (☎ 642-0630, 683-0338), a post office, shops, and other services.

There are a few cheap *sodas* and basic *pensiones*, including *Cabinas Grelmar* and *Hotel Caoba*. Both have restaurants. *Cabinas Sueño Feliz*, on the way out of the village toward Montezuma, looks a bit nicer than these two.

The Paquera-Montezuma bus comes through here. A 4WD taxi to Montezuma costs US$6. Buses to Mal País leave at 10:30am and 2:30pm.

### MONTEZUMA

This little village near the tip of the Península de Nicoya has beautiful beaches, welcoming residents, and plenty of hotels. It wasn't always like this, though.

Once a remote fishing village, Montezuma gained popularity in the 1980s and early 1990s with younger gringo travelers who enjoyed both the beautiful surroundings and the laid-back atmosphere. Accommodations were very cheap, and the village became a party beach on the Costa Rican part of the gringo trail. In fact, there now seem to be more gringos than locals in town (which one reader nicknamed 'Gringolandia').

Montezuma remains one of the most popular destinations on the coast, and many people like to stay for at least several days (which is a good way to get beyond the hippie-frat-party aspect of the place) to enjoy not only the beaches and village, but also the nearby nature reserves and various activities. Readers fall into two groups: those who absolutely love the place, and those who claim that there are too many tourists. If you want a remote little coastal village to get away from other travelers, this is not the place for you.

PENÍNSULA DE NICOYA

## Information

Aventuras in Montezuma (☎/fax 642-0059, e avenzuma@racsa.co.cr, w www.aventuras enmontezuma.com) is air-conditioned and provides local information and international faxing, phone, and Internet access (about US$1 for 15 minutes). They can arrange/confirm national and international flights, and they offer many tours. Christina is extremely helpful. Hours are 8am to 8pm daily in the high season.

Pizzanet charges about US$1 for 15 minutes of Internet access. There are no banks, but you can change your US cash or traveler's checks at Aventuras in Montezuma. You might also be able to change US cash at some restaurants – if they have enough colones available. There's a laundry

(see the Montezuma map for location details). Librería Topsy has a book exchange – mainly English books, but there are a few in other languages.

Montezuma is a small town, and parking can be a problem. Walking is the best way to get around.

## Activities & Organized Tours

Apart from Aventuras in Montezuma, there's Montezuma Ecotours (☎/fax 642-0467) for activities and tours, or ask at your hotel for information. Prices for daily **vehicle rentals** are around US$15 for bicycles, US$50 for motorbikes, and US$75 for ATVs. A half-day of **horseback riding** runs about US$25 – ask for Deanne at Montezuma Ecotours. **Snorkeling** gear and **body**

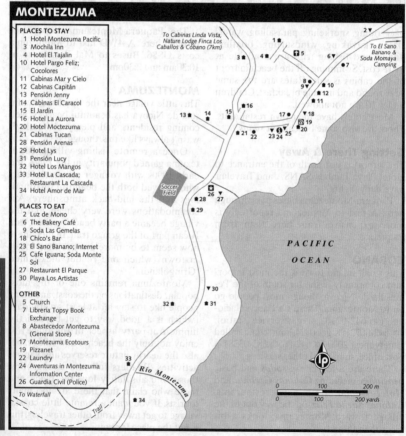

**MONTEZUMA**

**PLACES TO STAY**
1  Hotel Montezuma Pacific
3  Mochila Inn
4  Hotel El Tajalin
10 Hotel Pargo Feliz;
   Cocolores
11 Cabinas Mar y Cielo
12 Cabinas Capitán
13 Pensión Jenny
14 Cabinas El Caracol
15 El Jardín
16 Hotel La Aurora
20 Hotel Moctezuma
21 Cabinas Tucan
28 Pensión Arenas
29 Hotel Lys
31 Pensión Lucy
32 Hotel Los Mangos
33 Hotel La Cascada;
   Restaurant La Cascada
34 Hotel Amor de Mar

**PLACES TO EAT**
2  Luz de Mono
6  The Bakery Café
9  Soda Las Gemelas
18 Chico's Bar
23 El Sano Banano; Internet
25 Cafe Iguana; Soda Monte
   Sol
27 Restaurant El Parque
30 Playa Los Artistas

**OTHER**
5  Church
7  Librería Topsy Book
   Exchange
8  Abastecedor Montezuma
   (General Store)
17 Montezuma Ecotours
19 Pizzanet
22 Laundry
24 Aventuras in Montezuma
   Information Center
26 Guardia Civil (Police)

To Cabinas Linda Vista,
Nature Lodge Finca Los
Caballos & Cóbano (7km)

To El Sano
Banano &
Soda Momaya
Camping

Soccer
Field

PACIFIC
OCEAN

Río Montezuma

To Waterfall

Trail

0          100          200 m
0          100          200 yards

**boards** cost about US$10 per day, and a variety of tours with snorkeling opportunities are offered, starting at US$40.

A 20-minute stroll to the south takes you to a lovely **waterfall** with a **swimming hole**, reached by taking the trail to the right just after the bridge past the Hotel & Restaurant La Cascada. The waterfall can be climbed, but at your own risk – at least five visitors have fallen here and died. Since one such death here in 2001, a small warning sign has been erected, but family members say it's not enough for such a dangerous place. A second set of falls, which some consider even prettier, is farther upriver. There's a beautiful nature reserve a few kilometers to the south (see the Reserva Natural Absoluta Cabo Blanco section, later). Lovely **beaches** are strung out along the coast, separated by small rocky headlands and offering great beach-combing and tide-pool studying.

All-day **boat excursions** to Isla Tortuga (see the Islands Near Bahía Gigante section, earlier) cost US$40 a person. Lunch, fruit, and drinks are provided. It's 90 minutes to the island, where you can swim or snorkel (the boats carry snorkeling gear). Boats carry up to four passengers for fishing, snorkeling, or sightseeing. A half day of **fishing** with gear costs about US$160 per person; all day is US$300.

Tours to the Cabo Blanco reserve are available, though most people don't bother because it's easy enough to get around by yourself. However, a guide costs only US$5 per person, and you'll see more. Tours to other destinations may be offered if there's enough demand.

## Places to Stay – Montezuma

The high season (from December to April) and weekends occasionally get crowded, but you'll certainly find something even if you just show up. If you arrive on a Friday afternoon though, don't expect much choice! If you arrive midweek, first thing in the morning, you may need to wait a couple of hours for people to leave to catch the afternoon ferry for rooms to become available. As usual, low-season discounts are common, especially in the higher-priced places – high-season prices are listed here. Note that most hotels have a dozen rooms or fewer.

**Budget** Theft has been reported from a few places, so keep your stuff locked up. Camping in town itself is locally discouraged, and beach camping is either illegal or discouraged to keep the beaches clean.

**Soda Momaya Camping** (☎ 642-0048) Campsites US$3 per person. A short walk north along the beach, this campground has showers, lockers, laundry, and a soda.

**Pensión Jenny** Rooms US$5.50 per person. Up on a hill, this is the cheapest place in town – readers have described it as a dump.

**Cabinas El Caracol** (☎ 642-0194) Rooms without bath US$6 per person, doubles with bath US$16. Near Pensión Jenny, this place has bare but large rooms. A cheap restaurant is attached, though one reader reports being grossly overcharged here and another claims the bathrooms didn't work.

**Pensión Lucy** (☎ 642-0273) Singles/doubles without bath US$8/12. Verandahs overlook the ocean, the rooms are airy, and the better upper-level ones get cooling sea breezes. It's popular with backpackers.

**Cabinas Tucan** (☎ 642-0284) Singles/doubles without bath US$10/15. The decent little rooms here share cold showers.

**Pensión Arenas** (☎ 642-0308) Similarly priced to Cabinas Tucan, Pensión Arenas has rooms with private showers. It's in a good location right on the beach, and a family-run restaurant is attached.

**Hotel Lys** (☎ 642-0642, ☎/fax 642-0568) Singles/doubles US$10/15. Almost next to the Pensión Arenas, this newer option has been well received. Ten rooms, each with a double bed, share two clean showers and toilets. German, Italian, and English are spoken.

**Hotel Moctezuma** (☎ 642-0258, 642-0058) Singles/doubles/triples US$12/18/27. This place is right in the center and has a restaurant and popular bar with music. Light sleepers should bring earplugs. The 21 rooms are dark, but they're large, clean, and have fans and private cold showers. Rooms sleep two to six people.

**Cabinas Capitán** (☎ 642-0069) Singles without bath US$10, doubles with cold bath US$16. Some rooms here sleep six. The place has a party reputation.

**Cabinas Mar y Cielo** (☎/fax 642-0261) Doubles with bath US$25-40, depending on season. The rooms here are clean and have fans, and the ones upstairs are breezy with nice views. Some rooms accommodate up to six people. The place is set back from the street; ask at the store in front to see rooms.

*Hotel Pargo Feliz* (☎ 642-0064, ☎/fax 642-0065) Doubles with bath US$25-30. Next to a recommended restaurant, this hotel has well-kept rooms with fans. The four lower rooms are US$25; the four upper ones are US$30.

*Mochila Inn* (☎ 642-0030) Rooms from US$400 per month. This inn is on a quiet, lush hillside on the way into the village. Look for a path just past the ICE telephone sign. Each room has a bathroom and fridge, and there's a communal kitchen.

**Mid-Range** Up on the hill as you come into town is *Hotel La Aurora* (☎ 642-0051, fax 642-0025) Doubles US$20-50. In a vine-covered mansion are about 15 rooms with fans and mosquito nets; some have private hot baths and air-conditioning, which accounts for the variation in price. There are homey touches like a kitchen, free coffee and tea, a library, and nice areas to hang out in. One of Montezuma's first hotels, La Aurora has been here for over 20 years. It has a good local reputation for recycling and being involved in environmental issues.

*Hotel El Tajalin* (☎ 642-0061, fax 642-0527, ✉ tajalin@racsa.co.cr, ⓦ www.tajalin .com) Singles/doubles with bath US$18/31, with air-conditioning US$30/45. A dozen nice clean rooms have polished hardwood floors, fans, and private hot bath; some have air-conditioning and TVs. The owners speak English and Italian.

*Hotel Montezuma Pacific* (☎ 642-0204) Singles/doubles US$35/45. Almost next to Hotel El Tajalin, this quiet place has decent, simpler air-conditioned rooms with private hot-water bathrooms. Some rooms have balconies.

*El Jardín* (☎ 642-0548, ☎/fax 642-0074, ✉ jardin@racsa.co.cr, ⓦ www.hoteleljardin .com) Doubles US$40-60. Near the entrance to town, the 15 wooden cabinas here have private hot baths and fans; some have air-conditioning and balconies. There are nice ocean views. The Italian management also speaks French and English.

*Hotel La Cascada* (☎ 642-0056/7) Doubles with bath US$36. This hotel is in a nice location by the river en route to the

waterfalls. The rooms are clean and have fans, private cold baths, and ocean views. Some sleep up to six. The friendly tico owner will lower rates substantially (he said by over half!) in the low season.

*Hotel Los Mangos* (☎/fax 642-0076, ⓦ www.hotellosmangos.com) Doubles without/with bath US$35/60, bungalow doubles US$80. This lovely place has a good restaurant and Montezuma's first (and, as of this writing, only) swimming pool. The hotel has rooms in the main building and bungalows on the spacious grounds, which are filled with – you guessed it – mango trees. The hotel rooms are fairly big and have fans. Each of the cozy wooden bungalows has a thatched roof, a private hot shower, and a verandah with hammocks, chairs and ocean views.

*Hotel Amor de Mar* (☎/fax 642-0262, ✉ shoebox@racsa.co.cr) Doubles US$40-87. At the south end of town, this quiet place has pleasant grounds and a beautiful shorefront with a tide pool big enough to swim in. A 2nd-floor balcony area overlooks the sea. A restaurant serves breakfast 'til lunch time. Eleven rooms vary – some have cold or hot showers, a couple have shared showers, some have river or sea views.

## Places to Stay – Around Montezuma

*Cabinas Linda Vista* (☎ 642-0274, fax 642-0104) Doubles US$30. About 1.5km out of town toward Cóbano, the Linda Vista offers rooms with private cold showers and, yes, good views. Some have kitchenettes.

*Nature Lodge Finca Los Caballos* (☎/fax 642-0124, ✉ naturel@racsa.co.cr, ⓦ www .naturelodge.net) Doubles with bath US$60, bungalows US$80. Caballos is Spanish for 'horses,' and the Canadian owner prides herself on having the best-looked-after horses in the area. Apart from horse rentals, the lodge offers bike rentals, arranges tours, and has a swimming pool. Its eight pleasant rooms have private baths and patios, and there's a two-bedroom bungalow. A nice restaurant is on the premises. The place is about 3km north of town, just off the road to Cóbano.

*Cabinas Las Rocas* (☎ 642-0393) Doubles without bath US$25, apartments US$70. About 2.5km south on the road to Cabuya, this is a tranquil spot near rocky tide pools. One-bedroom apartments have private baths and kitchens. The mellow Swiss owner will pick you up in Montezuma if you call ahead.

*El Sano Banano* (☎ 642-0638, ☎/fax 642-0068, [e] elbanano@racsa.co.cr, [W] www .elbanano.com) Doubles US$73-83, bunga-lows US$89, apartments US$133, extra people US$10. The folks who run the El Sano Banano restaurant have 14 quiet rooms and bungalows next to a pretty beach about a 15-minute walk north of town (you can't drive there; they'll bring your baggage for you). The buildings are intriguingly shaped polygons or geodesic domes, all with private hot baths, fans, fridges, porches, and sea views. Some have kitchen facilities. There's a swimming pool.

## Places to Eat
*Chico's Bar* This is the traditional place to go for a beer and a simple meal. These days it's also popular for its loud music 'til about 11pm (a town rule to allow folks to sleep!). A number of other places have opened in recent years – they cater to tourists and may charge 23% tax on top of the bill: If you're on a budget, ask. Some places close down or have limited hours during the rainy months.

Cheap places that don't add tax include the typical *Soda Las Gemelas* (☎ 642-0612) and *Restaurant El Parque*. You can get a fish casado at these places for about US$3.50, perhaps a little less with chicken, or around US$5 for a fish dinner. They don't sell alcohol, but you can bring your own. These places offer the best budget values and are very popular with young travelers – you should go by about 6pm for the best choice of food and tables.

*Soda Monte Sol* Serving North American as well as typical Costa Rican meals, this place is reasonably priced.

*Cafe Iguana* Next to Soda Monte Sol, the Iguana is the place to come for juices, ice cream, and dessert.

*Cocolores* (☎ 642-0348) The specialty here is large portions of French-influenced food.

*Restaurant La Cascada* (☎ 642-0589) Meals US$4-10. This quiet place is next to a stream. Tico and Spanish food is served, and the paellas are noteworthy.

*Pizzanet* This inexpensive air-conditioned Internet café serves pizza whole or by the slice. It's next to the *Hotel Moctezuma*, which has a popular restaurant-bar.

*El Sano Banano* Main courses US$6-12. This place serves yogurt, juices, fruit salads, breakfasts, full vegetarian and seafood meals, and espressos. It also shows movies every night (US$5 minimum consumption). The owners are actively involved in community and environmental affairs, and Internet access is available.

*The Bakery Café* This café has a nice little verandah and good coffee and pastries.

*Luz de Mono* Sandwiches US$6, main courses US$10. Farther along the same road is this beautiful pyramid building with an elegant outdoor ambience. Food is international. They occasionally have live entertainment, including both music and dinner theater.

*Playa Los Artistas* Main courses US$10. Locally favored, this small, rustic restaurant is known as 'the Mediterranean place' and has a short, frequently changing menu. Excellent northern Italian and seafood dinners are served here.

## Shopping
To make your own picnic lunches, buy supplies at the *Abastecedor Montezuma*. Its selection is limited, but it's the best place. Some gringos report getting overcharged in the few Montezuma stores; it never hurts to stay alert and use your Spanish.

## Getting There & Away
**Ferry/Bus** The ferries from Puntarenas connect with the Paquera-Montezuma bus. Buses leave Montezuma for Paquera at 5am, 8am, 10am, noon, 2pm, and 4pm to connect with the ferries to Puntarenas. The fare is US$2.50 (US50¢ as far as Cóbano). Ask at Aventuras in Montezuma about where to buy bus tickets and where to catch the bus. Currently, the departure point is outside Pizzanet, but it's subject to change.

**Bus** Buses leave Montezuma for Cabo Blanco (US$1.20) at 8am, 9:50am, 2:10pm, and 6:30pm.

**Taxi** During the rainy season, the section to Cóbano may be impassable to 2WD vehicles. A 4WD taxi between Cóbano and Montezuma costs US$6. A 4WD taxi from Montezuma to Paquera costs about US$30, to Cabo Blanco about US$10, and to Mal País or the Tambor airport about US$25. There aren't many taxis around; reserve one at your hotel or at Aventuras in Montezuma.

**Boat** Depending on weather and tide conditions, it's possible to get boats to Jacó (US$30) or Playa Sámara (US$35). Those rates are per person, four minimum. Ask about other destinations.

## MAL PAÍS

This small village is on the west coast of the peninsula, about 4km north of Cabo Blanco, in an area that is increasingly popular with surfers. About 2km or 3km north of Mal País, next to the attractive Playa Santa Teresa, is a tiny community nicknamed Santa Teresita. The road from Cóbano meets the beach road between the two communities at Frank's Place (see Places to Stay & Eat, below), with Mal País to the south (left). The Mal País end of the beach is rockier, emptier, and good for tide-pool exploration; the Santa Teresa end is sandier and better for surfing. Horses can be rented for the 4km ride down to Cabo Blanco. This area has blossomed with new places to stay, and more are opening almost every month. A useful website is 🖥 www.malpais.net.

## Places to Stay & Eat

*Frank's Place* (☎ 640-0096, ☎/fax 640-0071, 🖅 frank5@racsa.co.cr, 🖥 www.frankplace .com) Doubles US$20, triples US$50 with hot shower & kitchenette. At the intersection of the Cóbano road and the beach road, this is a central landmark. Frank is a local who has become a pillar of the surfing community. An information booth has helpful maps, and a small store (cold beer!) will sometimes change US cash and traveler's checks. There's Internet access and a pool, and tours can be arranged. The popular restaurant here has satellite TV and serves breakfast and sandwiches (average US$3), casados (US$4) and other plates (US$7 to US$8).

If you walk straight to the beach 300m from Frank's, you'll find some surfers *camping* (though this is discouraged because of increasing numbers of people and no facilities as of yet) and the *Mambo Café*, which serves veggie burgers and smoothies (when there's ice). It has a shady verandah and a

bamboo rack where surfboards are stacked like horses tied up at a saloon. A flier board advertises the many temporary services a surfer community generates – massage, grocery delivery, photos of you surfing....

The following are all along the beach road south of Frank's, toward Mal País. Distances are from Frank's.

*Ritmo Tropical* (☎/fax 640-0174) 100m, doubles US$36. This series of new, bright white individual cabins features private hot showers and small patios.

*The Place* (☎/fax 640-0001, 🖅 theplace@ racsa.co.cr, 🖥 www.surftheplace.com) 200m, doubles US$50-60. Airy, light cabins are modeled after African, Asian, and Mediterranean motifs. All have private hot showers. A restaurant on the premises serves grilled and Mediterranean-style seafood. The Swiss owners are multilingual and can arrange a variety of local tours.

*Mal País Surf Camp & Resort* (☎/fax 640-0061, 🖅 surfcamp@racsa.co.cr, 🖥 www .malpaissurfcamp.com) 500m, campsites US$7, shared rooms US$11.50 per person, doubles with shared bath US$29, cabins & villas US$75. On 20 lush acres, the restaurant-bar is good, and the Ping-Pong and pool tables make it a popular hangout. Surfboard repairs and rentals, horseback riding, satellite TV, a pool, and surf videos are all available. Dude!

*Blue Jay Lodge* (☎ 640-0089, fax 640-0141, 🖥 www.bluejaylodgecostarica.com) 1km, doubles US$70. This tico-owned lodge has seven private bamboo bungalows, each with huge screened half-walls (protected with an awning), a fan, hot shower, two beds, and a large verandah with a view. Nice! Some bungalows are high in the forest and require a short walk. Rates include breakfast; a restaurant serves lunch and dinner and there is also a 'palapa' bar. Guided tours in Spanish, French, and English are available.

*Cabinas Bosque del Mar* (☎ 640-0074) 2.5km, singles/doubles with bath US$25/28. The big rooms have hot showers, and some rooms have kitchenettes for a few dollars more. There's a good Italian restaurant here.

*Mary's* 3.1km. Just before the road to Cabuya, this locally owned café serves good pizza. In the village itself are a few *sodas;* ask around about camping.

**Star Mountain Eco Resort** (☎ 640-0102, ☎/fax 640-0101, ℮ info@starmountaineco .com, ⓦ www.starmountaineco.com) 5.5km, singles/doubles US$55/75, including breakfast. This place is off the rough road between Mal País and Cabuya, about a kilometer from the beach road, alongside the Cabo Blanco reserve boundary (follow the small signs for the jungle lodge). A small river is crossed and 4WD is needed in wet months. The small resort was built without cutting down trees (on areas that had been previously logged) and the forest around is full of birds and monkeys. With its pool, Jacuzzi, and verandah restaurant, this is a tranquil retreat from the beach. It features a pretty row of four hillside rooms, each different and painted in cool tropical pastels. The 86-hectare property is half forested and half old pasture and has trails with good birding and a viewpoint overlooking both sides of the peninsula. Allow about 90 minutes to hike the trail circuit. The multilingual Belgian managers will prepare excellent suppers (about US$15) on request, something that most guests take advantage of. They'll also help with tours, reservations, etc.

The following are north of Frank's, toward Playa Santa Teresa, which stretches for about 6km.

**Tropico Latino Lodge** (☎/fax 642-0062, ℮ tropico@centralamerica.com) 800m, doubles US$65. A large pool and Jacuzzi sit next to the beach, and six thatched bungalows have king-size beds, fans, private hot-water bathrooms, and patios with hammocks. A restaurant serves Italian food and tours can be arranged.

**Rancho Itáuna** (☎ 640-0095) 1.6km, rooms US$55. Rancho Itáuna has four rooms in two octagonal towers, each with a double bed, bunk bed, private heated shower, and fridge. The restaurant serves Brazilian food and barbecue, and it prides itself on its music selection.

**Cabinas Higuerones** 2.2km. You'll find budget rooms and camping nearby. Next door is a surf shop that buys, sells, rents, and mends boards – a good place for surf information.

**Cabinas & Restaurant Santa Teresa** (☎/fax 640-0137) 2.8km, cabins US$25-30. This place has a sherbet-colored row of clean cabins, each sleeping four. Some have private showers.

**Cecilia's B&B** (☎ 640-0115) 3.9km, doubles US$55. Run by personable French-Canadians, this place has a few spotless rooms near the beach.

**Roca Mar** 4km. This camping area provides showers and surfboard rental. A soda is attached.

**Milarepa** (☎ 640-0023, ℮ milarepa@ mail.ticonet.co.cr, ⓦ www.ticonet.co.cr/ milarepa) 4.2km, doubles US$116-140. This beachfront hotel has elegant, spacious bamboo-and-wood bungalows in safari style. Each features attractive imported Indonesian teak furniture and a semi-outdoor bath. The French owners run a good restaurant.

**Hotel Flor Blanca** (☎/fax 640-0232, ℮ florblanca@expressmail.com) 6km, 1-bedroom villa US$437, 2-bedroom villa US$670, including gourmet breakfast. Brand new in 2002, this intimate, luxurious hotel was built by Susan Money, who owned the extremely successful Sueño del Mar B&B in Tamarindo and has many years of experience in upscale pampering. Ten large, romantic, air-conditioned villas are on seven acres of white-sand beach. Each villa has an ocean view and Susan's signature outdoor bath with sunken tub. Facilities include an open-air restaurant, yoga center, naturalist guide, gym, artwork, a music room… Wow!

## Getting There & Away

From Cóbano, there are buses at 10:30am and 2:30pm. From Mal País, there are buses to Cóbano at 7am and noon. A taxi from Cóbano costs US$15.

## CABUYA

This tiny village is about 9km south of Montezuma and 2km north of Cabo Blanco. An interesting feature is the local cemetery, which is on Isla Cabuya, just to the southeast. The cemetery can be reached only at low tide because the (otherwise uninhabited) island is cut off from the mainland at high tide.

**Ancla de Oro** (☎/fax 642-0369) Rooms US$10 per person, cabins with kitchen US$35. This restaurant-cum-cabinas is one of the original places to stay in the area. There are simple thatched-roof huts in a pleasant garden and rooms inside the house. The restaurant serves decent seafood, and the owners arrange boat, horse, and vehicle tours to local sites of interest. You can rent a horse for about US$20 a day.

*Hotel Cabo Blanco* (☎ *642-0332, fax 642-0369)* Rooms with fan/air-conditioning US$30/40. Close to Hotel Cabo Blanco, this place has spacious rooms with private baths and TVs.

*Hotel Celaje* (☎/*fax 642-0374,* e *celaje@ racsa.co.cr)* Singles/doubles/triples US$35/45/55, including breakfast. This hotel has air-conditioned rooms, a pool, and a restaurant.

More places may open as this village begins to take some of the overflow from Montezuma and cater to travelers who want to stay closer to the Cabo Blanco reserve.

## RESERVA NATURAL ABSOLUTA CABO BLANCO

This beautiful reserve encompasses 1272 hectares of land and 1700 hectares of surrounding ocean and includes the entire southern tip of the Península de Nicoya. The reserve was established in 1963 by the late Karen Morgenson and Olof Wessberg, who donated it to Costa Rica several years before a park system had even been created. Thus, it's the oldest protected area in Costa Rica.

Until the late 1980s, Cabo Blanco was called an 'absolute' nature reserve, because no visitors were permitted. Now there are trails and visits are allowed, but the recent upsurge in the popularity of the Montezuma area has led to greater visitation than expected. Accordingly, park directors have closed the reserve on Monday and Tuesday to minimize tourist impact.

### Information

Just inside the park, south of Cabuya, is a ranger station (☎/fax 642-0093) where you pay a US$6 entrance fee and can obtain a trail map. The reserve is open 8am to 4pm Wednesday through Sunday.

The average annual temperature is about 27°C and annual rainfall is some 2300mm at the tip of the park. The easiest months for visits are from December to April – the dry season.

Camping is not permitted. No food is available, so bring snacks and plenty of drinking water.

### Wildlife Watching

The reserve preserves an evergreen forest, a couple of attractive beaches, and a host of birds and animals. Several kilometers of trails are excellent for wildlife observation. Monkeys, squirrels, sloths, deer, agoutis, and raccoons are among the more common sightings – ocelots and margays have also been recorded, but you'd have to be very lucky to see one of these elusive wild cats. Armadillos, coatis, peccaries, and anteaters are also present.

The coastal area is known as an important nesting site for the brown booby. Some nest on the mainland, but most are found on Isla Cabo Blanco, 1.6km south of the mainland. The island supposedly gains its name (meaning 'white cape') from the guano encrusting the rocks. Other seabirds in the area include brown pelicans and magnificent frigatebirds. The beaches at the tip of the peninsula abound with the usual marine life – starfish, sea anemones, sea urchins, conchs, lobsters, crabs, and tropical fish are a few of the things to look for.

### Trails & Hiking

A trail (about 4.5km) leads from the ranger station south of Cabuya to the beaches at the tip of the peninsula. The hike takes a couple of hours and passes through lush forest before emerging at the coast – a great opportunity to see many different kinds of birds, ranging from parrots and trogons in the forest to pelicans and boobies on the coast. You can visit two beaches at the peninsula tip and then return by a different trail. The high point of the reserve is 375m, and parts of the trail are steep and strenuous.

Check with park rangers about trails and tides. The trail joining the two beaches at the tip of the reserve may be impassable at high tide.

### Getting There & Away

The reserve is about 11km south of Montezuma by a decent dirt road, though 4WD is needed for the last section in the rainy season. See the Montezuma section, earlier, for bus and taxi information.

# Northern Lowlands

The traveler heading north from San José, over the volcanic ridges of the Cordillera Central, soon arrives in the flat tropical lowlands stretching from just 40km north of the capital to the Nicaragua border and beyond. The northern halves of the provinces of Alajuela and Heredia both contain large tropical plains, called *llanuras*. The northern slopes of the central mountains (Cordillera Central) and the two llanuras beyond are described in this chapter.

The original vegetation of much of the northern lowlands is mixed tropical forest that becomes increasingly evergreen as one heads east to the Caribbean. The climate is generally wet and hot. The dry season is more pronounced in the western part of the northern lowlands, near the slopes of the Cordillera de Guanacaste. As one moves east toward the Caribbean, the dry season tends to be shorter and not entirely dry. Much of the original vegetation has been destroyed and replaced by pasture for raising cattle, which is the main industry in most of the northern lowlands.

In many of the more remote areas near the Nicaragua border, especially in the Llanura de los Guatusos and the Llanura de San Carlos, the pastureland floods extensively during the wet season, creating vast swamps and lakes. One such area has been protected in Refugio Nacional de Vida Silvestre Caño Negro – one of the more remote of Costa Rica's national wildlife refuges and parks. Other swamp areas have been utilized for rice cultivation.

The northern lowlands generally have a very low population density, with only a few small towns, mainly rough roads, poor public transportation, and relatively little in the way of tourist facilities. A major exception to this is in the northeastern lowlands around the small town of Puerto Viejo de Sarapiquí, which is well served by public buses. Here there are many hotels, and nearby are several tourist lodges and a biological station. The Puerto Viejo area is the destination of most visitors wanting to see some of the northern lowlands.

The Caño Negro area has seen an increase in visitors. Visitors traveling between Puerto Viejo and popular Volcán Arenal (see the Northwestern Costa Rica chapter) are starting to discover this area, which now has several hotels, the national wildlife

## Highlights

- Watching wildlife in the little-known Refugio Nacional de Vida Silvestre Caño Negro
- Cruising along the Río San Juan, the remote boundary between Costa Rica and Nicaragua
- Visiting Estación Biológica La Selva, one of the country's best-known tropical research stations
- Dangling in mid-air on the 269m-long suspension bridge between Centro Neotrópico Sarapiquís and Tirimbina Rainforest Center
- Examining, and perhaps buying, exquisite stained glass at Rancho Leona

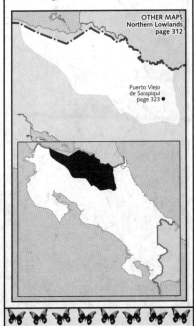

OTHER MAPS
Northern Lowlands
page 312

Puerto Viejo
de Sarapiquí
page 323 •

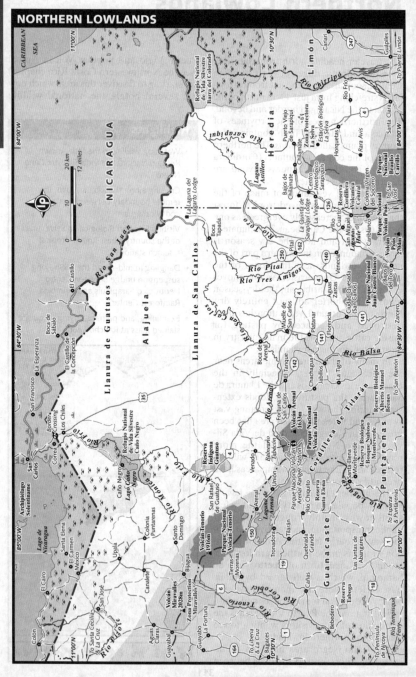

refuge with excellent birding, and a number of small towns that have not yet been much visited by gringos. Los Chiles, which provides the easiest access to the refuge, is often busy midday with tour buses making day trips from the Arenal area, but for the most part the Caño Negro area retains a remote and unvisited feel.

This may soon change. The Costa Rican government recently repaved the road to Los Chiles and there are plans to pave it all the way to the Nicaragua border. Costa Ricans expect their Nicaraguan counterparts to improve the road beyond the border and eventually, this will become a major road link between Managua and Caribbean Costa Rica, avoiding San José.

# Caño Negro Area

From Muelle de San Carlos, two paved roads head out across the northern lowlands. These are the road northwest to San Rafael and Upala and the road north to Los Chiles. The Caño Negro area is between these two roads.

## MUELLE DE SAN CARLOS

This small crossroads village is locally called Muelle, which means 'dock.' It's one of the first places from which the Río San Carlos is navigable. There is a 24-hour gas station at the main highway intersection. Unless you're staying at the comfortable Tilajari Resort Hotel, there's nothing to do here apart from deciding whether you want to go north, south, east, or west. The resort offers a variety of tours; see the entry in Places to Stay & Eat, below, for details.

### Places to Stay & Eat
The cheap-looking *Cabinas Violetas* is near the middle of the village (almost 2km north of the main road intersection).

*Tilajari Resort Hotel* (☎ *469-9091, fax 469-9095,* e *info@tilajari.com,* w *www.tilajari .com*) Singles/doubles US$95/107, junior suites US$107/117, US$12 additional people, including buffet breakfast. Most overnight visitors stay at this modern place, which is the most luxurious hotel in the area and a good base for exploring the surrounding attractions. One of the owner/managers is Jaime Hamilton, who came to the area with the

Peace Corps and has lived in Costa Rica since the 1960s. His business partner, Don Ricardo, is the consummate Costa Rican gentleman. The hotel used to be a country club, and it offers 74 spacious, air-conditioned rooms and suites. All come with private hot showers, ceiling fans, telephones, private patios or balconies, and two double beds; the suites have living rooms, TVs, refrigerators, and larger terraces. Two suites have a loft with three single beds, recommended for families with children. Children under 12 years old stay free (one child per adult). Some rooms and trails are wheelchair accessible. An attractive, open-sided restaurant serves excellent lunches and dinners for US$18. Multiday packages are a good deal (three nights for the price of two plus taxes).

There are two pools, a sauna, a spa, two racquetball courts, six lighted tennis courts (two indoor), a game room with pool table, and a small gift shop. The hotel is set on pleasantly landscaped grounds with good views of the Río San Carlos. There's an enclosed butterfly garden (US$3), and the grounds are surrounded by a 240-hectare working cattle ranch adjacent to a 400-hectare private rainforest preserve with several trails. The preserve is unusual in this area where most of the land has been deforested for cattle. It's about a 20-minute hike from the hotel to the preserve. Horseback riding is available.

Tours offered by the hotel are expensive unless you can join a group – with so many people staying at the hotel, this is reasonably feasible. The following prices are for day tours per person for groups of one, two, and three or more: to Volcán Arenal and the Tabacón Hot Springs (US$90/45/35), La Catarata de La Fortuna and jungle lakes (US$70/35/25), and the Venado Caves (US$90/45/30). Guided boat trips at Caño Negro, including transportation from the hotel and a box lunch, cost US$48 per person (two-person minimum). Boat and fishing tours are available from US$75 per person. A variety of rafting options are offered.

About 5km south of Muelle on the road to Ciudad Quesada (San Carlos) is the tiny community of Platanar. *La Quinta Lodge* (☎/fax 475-5260, 475-5921, 378-9656 cellular, e *la.quinta.lodge@hotmail.com*) Bunk beds US$11.50, rooms US$36, apartments US$60. Near Platanar, this rustic inn, with a pool and sauna, is run by the Ugaldes, a friendly *tico* couple who taught in the USA for years and speak excellent English. Birds have adopted the grounds as an aviary, and there's a small river behind the inn where fish and caimans can be seen. Breakfast is US$2.50.

*Hotel La Garza* (☎ 475-5222, fax 475-5015, in the USA fax 888-782-4293, e *information@hotel-lagarza-arenal.com*, w *www.hotel-lagarza-arenal.com*) Doubles with bath US$80. Also near Platanar, this attractive, more upscale place is a 600-hectare working dairy ranch/citrus plantation with views of the Río Platanar and far-off Volcán Arenal. The parking lot is on the bank of the river, and visitors enter the ranch via a graceful suspension footbridge. The hotel has 12 large, clean, polished wooden cabins with big porches, ceiling fans, telephones, and good-size private bathrooms. Tennis, basketball, and volleyball courts are available, as are a swimming pool and Jacuzzi. Meals are served in the adjoining farmhouse (US$7 for breakfast, US$13 for lunch and dinner). A number of tours are available, and horseback rides through the extensive grounds (US$25 to US$40 for two to four hours) are quickly arranged.

*Hotel Río San Carlos* (☎ 460-0766, 460-0301, 469-9194, fax 460-0391, 469-9179) Rooms US$26 per person, including breakfast. Nine kilometers north of Muelle is this small hotel, in the village of Boca de Arenal. Reservations can be made at the Hotel Central in Ciudad Quesada (San Carlos). There are five pleasant rooms with fans, air-conditioning, and private electric showers – two rooms have views of the Río San Carlos. The hotel is in pleasant gardens with a pool.

### Getting There & Away

Buses to and from San Rafael de Guatuso and Los Chiles pass through Muelle and can drop you off. (See the sections for those towns, later, for details.)

Drivers will find paved roads north to Los Chiles (74km); east to Aguas Zarcas (22km) and Puerto Viejo (55km); south to Ciudad Quesada (San Carlos; 21km) and on to San José (124km); west to Fortuna (28km) and Volcán Arenal; and northwest to San Rafael de Guatuso (58km). This is certainly a crossroads town.

## SAN RAFAEL DE GUATUSO AREA

Although marked on most maps as San Rafael, this small community is locally known as Guatuso. About 6600 people inhabit the town and the surrounding district. San Rafael is on the Río Frío, 19km northeast of (Nuevo) Arenal by poor dirt road or 40km northwest of Fortuna (de San Carlos) by paved road. This latter road gives good views of Volcán Arenal to the south. (In late 2001, a section of this road was closed because of subsidence, and now you have to make a detour on dirt roads, passable to ordinary cars. As of this writing, it's not known when repairs will be made.)

About 10km before San Rafael, a dirt road heads south for about 10km to Venado (which means 'deer'), visited mainly on day tours, though there are reportedly basic *cabinas* if you're stuck.

### Things to See & Do

Four kilometers south of Venado are **caves** that can be explored; there's an entry fee of about US$3. You should be prepared with several sources of light and with clothes that you don't mind getting wet and dirty. Bat roosts are found in the caves, so be prepared to see them. There are local guides in Venado, or you can take a tour from any of the larger hotels in the Caño Negro and Fortuna areas. There's an afternoon bus from Ciudad Quesada.

Just before reaching San Rafael, the road passes through the **Reserva Indígena Guatuso**, although nothing obviously demarcates the reserve.

From San Rafael, you may be able to hire a boat in the wet season to take you up the Río Frío to Refugio Nacional de Vida Silvestre Caño Negro.

Local guide Pedro Alvarado (☎ 296-2626 pager), who also works as a Tenorio park ranger, can be hired for visits to the Río Celeste and Volcán Tenorio. About 5km northwest of Guatuso, a road signed 'Los Teñidores' goes 10km to Río Celeste where he can meet you (or ask at Cabinas Tío Henry, see below).

### Places to Stay & Eat

*Cabinas Milagro* (☎ 464-0037) Singles/doubles with bath US$6/8. This quiet, family-run place on the edge of town is the most tranquil budget option in Guatuso. From the center, go past the church toward the Río Frío bridge and turn right just past the soccer field. Rooms have cold showers and fans.

**Cabinas Tío Henry** (*☎/fax 464-0344*) Singles/doubles with bath US$8/15, with shared bath US$6 per person. This place in the center of town has a small locked parking area. All rooms have air-conditioning and TV; eight have private bath and four share a bath. Tío Henry no longer runs the place but new owner Ignacio López Villalobos arranges local tours to Río Celeste, Volcán Tenorio, Caño Negro, and Venado caves.

**Cabinas El Bosque** (*☎/fax 464-0335, ☎ 464-0235 owner*) Singles/doubles US$6/10.50 with fan, US$9/13.50 with air-conditioning. Just north of town, this 10-room hotel has clean, simple rooms, some with cable TV, and a locked parking lot.

You'll find a few other cheaper and more basic places to stay in the center; one is **Hotel Las Brisas** (*☎ 464-2087*).

There are a handful of inexpensive eateries on the main street. **Restaurant El Turista** has good *casados* for US$2; the locally recommended **Soda La Macha** has a homey atmosphere and wood-fire cooking. **Rancho Ukurin** (*☎ 464-0308*), just past the Río Frío bridge en route to Upala, is an attractive, open-air, cone-roof affair that seems locally popular.

### Getting There & Away
Buses leave about every two hours for either Tilarán or Ciudad Quesada (some continue to San José). Ciudad Quesada is the most frequent destination.

A paved road leads 40km northwest to Upala.

### UPALA
This small town is 9km south of the Nicaragua border, in the far northwestern corner of the northern lowlands. About 12,400 people live in Upala and the surrounding district. Dirt roads lead up to and across the border, but these are not official entry points into either Costa Rica or Nicaragua. Sometimes there's a passport check by the bridge at the south end of town (coming from San Rafael de Guatuso) and another near Canalete (coming from the Carretera Interamericana on the paved road from Cañas).

Upala is the center for the cattle and rice industries of the area. A few remain-

### Dogs

You'll see many dogs running loose in Costa Rica; generally, they are not a cause for alarm. If dogs are a good barometer of local attitudes toward strangers, then the friendliness of strays in this country – dogs are rarely kept at home as pets – reflects the friendly, cosmopolitan attitude of most *ticos*. If you stop to ask for directions in a remote area, it's as unusual to get hassled by a dog as it is to get an unfriendly response from a person.

– John Thompson

ing Guatuso Indians live in the region. It has become increasingly important – the paved secondary road to Upala from the Interamericana opened in the 1980s, so there are good bus connections with San José. Few travelers come here, however, and those who do are mostly heading to or from the infrequently visited west side of Caño Negro. The trip to Upala and its surroundings is an interesting off-the-beaten-track experience.

### Places to Stay & Eat
Although few travelers come through, Upala is visited by a relatively large number of ticos, especially midweek when the hotels may be full of businesspeople. Call ahead and get there early in the week for the best choice of rooms.

**Cabinas Buenavista** (*☎ 470-0186*) Rooms US$7.50 per person. This is a popular place near the Super San Martín (the sign for the cabinas is under a large advertisement for Glidden paint). The rooms, with fans, private cold showers, and parking, are a bit stuffy, but the courtyard is nice and the owners are friendly – it's often full, especially midweek.

**Cabinas Maleku** (*☎ 470-0142*) Singles/doubles US$9/15. This is another adequate place, just off the open plaza behind the bus station. Rooms have private cold baths, fans, and TVs; a few air-conditioned doubles are US$21. A *soda* is attached.

**Hotel Restaurante Upala** (*☎ 470-0169*) Singles/doubles US$9/15. Also off the plaza, this hotel has basic, clean rooms with private cold showers, fans, and TV. The owner is nice, reception is open 24 hours, and there's a parking lot.

*Hotel Rosita* (☎ 470-0198) Rooms US$4-6 per person. Across from the bridge, this is another clean, cheap place to stay. Some rooms have a shared bath, and others have a private bath.

*Cabinas del Norte* (☎ 470-0061) Rooms US$4 per person. Right next to the bus station and market, this one is convenient but noisy.

*Rancho del Racio* One block off the main plaza, this eatery is locally popular for casados.

*Restaurante Buena Vista* This is in a pleasant, breezy location overlooking the river, just to the right after you cross the bridge entering town from the south.

### Getting There & Away

There are two or three buses a day from San José and an afternoon bus from Ciudad Quesada (San Carlos). The most frequent bus service is from Cañas, with seven departures a day.

From the Upala bus station, buses go to San José two to four times daily (US$4, five to six hours); to Ciudad Quesada once each morning; to Cañas six or seven times daily; to Santa Cecilia three times daily; to Caño Negro once or twice daily if the road is OK; and to various other small local destinations. Call Auto Transportes Upala (☎ 470-0061) in the Cabinas del Norte for schedule updates.

If you are driving to Upala, have documents accessible for passport controls on the outskirts.

### REFUGIO NACIONAL DE VIDA SILVESTRE CAÑO NEGRO

This 10,171-hectare refuge is of interest especially to birders, who come to see a variety of waterfowl, including anhingas, roseate spoonbills, storks, ducks, herons, and the largest Costa Rican colony of the olivaceous cormorant. The refuge is the only place in Costa Rica where the Nicaraguan grackle regularly nests. In addition, pumas, jaguars, and tapirs have been recorded here more often than in many of the other refuges. It certainly is in a remote and sparsely populated area that's conducive to these rare large mammals. Many smaller mammals have also been reported.

The Río Frío flows through the refuge and offers good birding and some wildlife spotting. During the wet season, the river breaks its banks and forms an 800-hectare lake. During the dry months of January to April, the lake shrinks and is no longer accessible by boating down the river; by April it has almost completely disappeared – until the May rains begin. During the dry season, the lake is accessible from the Caño Negro village, where you can rent boats. There are also some foot and horse trails, but the only way to go for most of the year is by boat. January to March is the best time for seeing large flocks of birds, though smaller flocks can be seen year-round.

Fishing is excellent during the July to March season.

### Orientation & Information

The refuge is part of the Area de Conservación Arenal-Huetar Norte. In the tiny community of Caño Negro, you'll find a ranger station (☎ 661-8464). Aside from administering the refuge, the rangers are contact points for a few community projects, including a butterfly garden put together by a local women's association (ASOMUCAN) and a turtle nursery. Admission officially costs US$6; camping is US$2, or you can stay in the rangers' house for US$6 if it's arranged in advance. There are cold showers, and meals can be arranged. Few people come here.

To arrange for local guides and boat transport or to contact the ranger station, call the Los Chiles subregional office (☎ 460-6484, ☎/fax 460-0644). Alternatively, ask at the places to stay when you arrive. Boats can be hired for about US$12 per hour (including driver) to take you on fishing and birding trips. There are about five local boat pilots – Carlos Sequera and Napoleon Sequera both speak English. Fishing is not allowed from April to June, but during the rest of the rainy season you can catch a variety of fish if you have a license, which you can buy at the station for US$30. Two local guides who have been recommended are Elgar Ulate and Vicente Mesa. Horse rental can also be arranged.

Most visitors come on guided tours either from one of the area's better hotels or, more cheaply, by arranging them in the town of Los Chiles. A few visitors arrange tours from the San Rafael de Guatuso or Upala areas.

## Organized Tours

Several hotels in this area arrange tours to Caño Negro (see Muelle de San Carlos, earlier in this chapter, and the Fortuna section in the Northwestern Costa Rica chapter), and a couple of tour operators are in Los Chiles (see that section, later). Travel agencies in Fortuna and San José also arrange tours. Horizontes, in San José, has some of the best tours, but they're not the cheapest (see the Organized Tours section in the Getting Around chapter).

## Places to Stay & Eat

Aside from the ranger station, accommodations in Caño Negro are few; this is definitely still an off-the-beaten-track place, although the recently built bridge between Caño Negro and Los Chiles may change things.

**Cabinas Arguedas** (☎ 224-2400 to leave a pager message in Spanish) Campsites US$3 per person, rooms US$4 per person. At the eastern edge of the community, just off the main road, this place has campsites plus a few basic rooms on spacious grounds. The rooms have fans, mosquito nets, and cold showers. Don Álvaro Arguedas has set up an information booth about the area at the cabins' entrance, and he rents boats and arranges trips on the river.

**Cabinas & Restaurante Machon** (no phone) Rooms US$5-7 per person. Near the center of the community (look for signs), this place is friendly and can feed or house you.

**Caño Negro Fishing Club** (☎ 656-0071, fax 656-0260, ℮ info@canonegro.com, Ⓦ www.canonegro.com) Rooms US$60 double, US$14 for additional people, including continental breakfast. This place has eight rooms in four duplex cabins, set in a lakeside orchard of mango and citrus trees. Rooms are clean and light, and each has two double beds, ceiling fan, and private hot shower. Staff can arrange fishing tours and rent you high-quality tackle for tarpon and rainbow bass, among other species. A 4.2m boat for two anglers costs US$300 a day including guide and fishing tackle; other rentals are available.

There's a small *soda* near the public phone and the bus stop, where you can get snacks and some meals. Other local people

in Caño Negro village may provide meals or a place to stay or camp; ask around.

**Caño Negro Natural Lodge** (☎ 265-6370, fax 265-4561, ℮ info@canonegrolodge.com, Ⓦ www.canonegrolodge.com) Singles/doubles/triples/quads US$88/100/111/123; prices increase with a variety of meal options. This new lodge is on the east side of the reserve and is more easily reached from the road to Los Chiles (see below). Perched on land that becomes a virtual island in the Río Frío during the high-water season, this family-run lodge has 10 rooms, each with private hot shower and ceiling fan. Their restaurant is open to the public, and anglers often stop for a beer or a bite. The lodge offers a swimming pool, Jacuzzi, and a games area with table tennis and board games. Mountain bikes are available. Three-day/two-night and four-day/three-night packages can be arranged including a boat trip to the reserve, mountain biking, a birding excursion, and a nature hike.

## Getting There & Away

The reserve can be reached by road from Upala and Los Chiles or by boat from Los Chiles or San Rafael de Guatuso. Buses to and from Caño Negro usually stop at the center of the community, near the public phone and the small soda. However, if you're leaving the area, ask locals about the best place to meet the bus.

**From Upala** A daily bus runs between Upala and Caño Negro, but it might not run when the road is bad. Call Auto Transportes Upala for updates (☎ 470-0061). Pickup trucks drive along this road a couple of times per day and will pick up people. If you're driving, take the road southeast toward San Rafael de Guatuso. After 11km, at the community of Colonia Puntarenas, there's a signed turnoff for Caño Negro. It is 26km away by very rough road, though the first half is in better shape. A normal car can just barely get through in the dry season (let's hope the car rental companies aren't reading this!), but you'll definitely need 4WD in the wet season.

**From Los Chiles** Access from Los Chiles is easier. There are fewer buses (the bus to Upala, leaving around 1pm on Monday, Wednesday, and Friday when conditions

**NORTHERN LOWLANDS**

permit, passes through Caño Negro), but many boats go down the Río Frío. These are day trips, described under the Los Chiles section, below. In the wet season, boats coming down the river can reach the lake in the center of the park, and these could leave you at the Caño Negro Natural Lodge or near the Caño Negro village and ranger station.

A bridge has been built over the Río Frío, so the road from Los Chiles to Caño Negro is now open. However, the road's condition varies from year to year depending on how bad the rainy season was – ask locally for information. Reportedly, the bridge was damaged and temporarily replaced by a car ferry; at this writing the bridge is open again.

The 19km unpaved road to the Caño Negro Natural Lodge leaves the Los Chiles–Muelle road about 10km south of Los Chiles. Call the lodge to determine whether you'll need 4WD.

## LOS CHILES

Los Chiles is about 70km north of Muelle by a paved road, with long green vistas underscored by the red soil typical of the northern regions. The small town is on the Río Frío, 3km before the Nicaragua border. About 10,000 people inhabit the Los Chiles

district. Although the town is midway between the Pacific and Caribbean coasts, its elevation is only 43m above sea level – it's not for nothing that this region is called the northern lowlands.

Los Chiles was originally built to service river traffic on the nearby Río San Juan; the south bank forms the Nicaragua–Costa Rica border for much of the river's length. A landing strip connects Los Chiles with the rest of the country. Since a road was built, there's no scheduled air service, although planes can be hired from San José (see information on air charters in the Getting Around chapter).

This is a small town, and you can ask almost anybody for directions to places mentioned below. Information is also available from Servitur and Ecodirecta (see Organized Tours, below).

In the 1980s, Los Chiles was on an important supply route for the Contras, which explains why the authorities were touchy about the border crossing here. In fact, until Violeta Chamorro became the Nicaraguan president in 1990, this crossing was closed except to ticos and Nicaraguans (nicas). This crossing is now open to all travelers with proper documents. Some nationals need a visa; many don't. See the Getting There & Away chapter for additional information.

### Sí a Paz

As a result of the Contra-Sandinista hostilities, many people living on or near the Río San Juan left for a safer area. Because the fighting that took place here was different from, for example, Vietnam, where defoliants and herbicides destroyed much of the countryside, most of the rainforest in the Río San Juan area has been protected from colonization and preserved in its virgin state. While forests were being cut for pasture in northern Costa Rica, the San Juan area remained free of farmers. Since the cessation of hostilities in 1990, colonists have been drifting back, though the discovery of un-exploded mines in the area has somewhat stemmed the tide of resettlement.

Meanwhile, environmentally aware Costa Rican authorities have worked with their Nicaraguan counterparts to establish an 'international' park – a national park that spans the border. The name of the park is Sí a Paz (literally, 'yes to peace'). It's hoped that it will eventually stretch north from the Caño Negro refuge to Lago de Nicaragua and east through a large tract of primary rainforest in southeastern Nicaragua, along the Río San Juan to the Caribbean coast, and join up there with the existing Barra del Colorado refuge.

The project is still in the planning stages, even though several international organizations have put financial support into the park and you may see a boat with 'Sí a Paz' emblazoned on its side patrolling the river. The idea has been accepted, but park boundaries and responsibilities are still on the table. Environmentally, this is a perfect region to preserve because it has been so little disturbed, but political, social, and economic factors have a way of making such projects difficult to realize.

## Organized Tours

From the main highway, you have to drive west through town to reach the Río Frío. Caño Negro tours are recommended if you enjoy watching wildlife; there are plenty of monkeys, caimans, sloths, turtles, lizards, and butterflies, as well as toucans, parrots, and other birds. Wildlife sightings are comparable to the more frequently visited Tortuguero (some readers say they saw more here than they did in Tortuguero). Tours are available year-round; guides almost always increase your chances of seeing wildlife.

Individual travelers looking to join a group and save money may find it easier to hook up with the tours that are offered in Fortuna, where there are many other travelers (see the Fortuna section in the Northwestern Costa Rica chapter). Los Chiles is a lot quieter – however, people who stay overnight here and take a locally organized morning tour (before lots of day visitors from Fortuna hit the river) usually see more wildlife. There are currently two tour operators in Los Chiles, and visits to the river are increasing.

*Servitur* (☎ 471-1496), run by the friendly Manfred Vargas Rojas, now operates out of Cabinas Jabirú. The company has been in the area for a while. In addition to the well-known Caño Negro trips, it runs tours to the nearby private reserve of Medio Queso, with horseback riding, the opportunity to observe traditional farming techniques, and a typical farm lunch – a chance to see some of rural Costa Rica not yet discovered by tourists. Other tours and guided camping trips go to the islands in Lago de Nicaragua (about US$65 per person, including food). A half-day tour to Caño Negro, including lunch, costs US$70 for two people and US$20 per person for groups over two.

*Ecodirecta* (☎/fax 471-1414) With an office in the new Rancho Ecodirecta, this is a Dutch-run reforestation company that has a tourism wing offering tours along the river and accommodations in town (see the Places to Stay section, below). Three-hour Caño Negro trips, not including lunch, cost US$60 for two people and US$20 per person for groups. Oscar Rojas is the helpful tico manager of the tours; the Dutch owners can provide details about how tourists can involve themselves with the reforestation investment project.

At the boat dock, you can also hire individual *boat captains* to take you up the Río Frío during the dry season and all the way into Lago Caño Negro during the rainy season. Boat rental costs about US$45 to US$80 for a trip lasting at least three or four hours, depending on the size and type of boat (a canopied boat is usually more expensive; it protects you somewhat from direct sun and rain but cuts down a little on your field of view). Note these prices are per boat taking several people.

It's also easy to arrange going upriver to San Carlos in Nicaragua; ask either a tour operator or at the public dock (sometimes a passenger boat there will make regular trips).

The MINAE subregional office (☎ 460-6484, ☎/fax 460-5615) is on the right side of the main highway coming into town.

## Places to Stay

The following two places are the rock-bottom options in town, but neither is particularly welcoming to travelers (this is a border town in a mainly agricultural area). *Hotel Onassis*, at the corner of the 'parque' (actually a soccer field), and the *Hotel Río Frío*, near the immigration office, have rooms with shared cold baths for about US$3 per person.

*Hotel Los Chiles* (☎ 471-1267) Singles/doubles US$4.50/7.50. This one is a better cheapie near the town center; it has basic rooms with shared showers, and some have skylights.

*Hotel Carolina* (☎ 471-1151) Rooms US$3-6 per person. Near the entrance of town, this basic choice has some rooms with private bath.

*Cabinas Jabirú* (☎ 471-1496) Doubles with bath US$12, plus air-con US$17.50. Easily the nicest budget option in town, this place has 12 simple but good-size and attractive units around a backyard garden. Each unit has a double and two single beds (separate little bedrooms), a private bath with hot shower, fans, and a small sitting room. There's a parking area. The Servitur office is currently located here.

*Rancho Ecodirecta* (☎/fax 471-1414, fax 442-8475, e ecolodge@racsa.co.cr) Singles/doubles US$22.50/28.50. This air-conditioned eight-room lodge, a few blocks from the docks and opposite the immigration police in central Los Chiles, is the best hotel in town. Rooms are large with private hot showers, and there's a restaurant and TV lounge. The Ecodirecta tour office is here.

## Places to Eat

**Restaurant El Parque** (☎ 471-1032, 471-1090) Open 6am-9pm. Serving pretty good tico food, this place near the park has a nice self-service coffee bar. Tour-bus groups eat lunch here, but breakfast and dinner tend to be a more private affair. The cheaper **Restaurant Central,** nearby, provides casados for locals.

**Rancho Ecodirecta** In the hotel (see earlier), this place is considered the best in town, although the menu is much more limited than at the El Parque.

**Heladería Fantasía** Serving ice cream, juices, and snacks, this place, not far from the Cabinas Jabirú, is locally popular; the owner also runs Servitur. **Los Petates** and, close to the police post on the main highway, the **Soda Sonia** are both good for simple local food.

## Getting There & Away

About a dozen buses a day run between Ciudad Quesada (San Carlos) and Los Chiles. Direct buses from San José leave for Los Chiles at 5:30am and 3:30pm from the Atlántico Norte station and return at 5am and 3pm. A bus to Upala, leaving around 1pm on Monday, Wednesday, and Friday, passes through Caño Negro if road conditions permit.

## LA LAGUNA DEL LAGARTO LODGE

One of the most isolated places in the country is **La Laguna del Lagarto Lodge** (☎ 289-8163, ☎/fax 289-5295, ℮ info@lagarto-lodge-costa-rica.com, ✆ www.lagarto-lodge-costa-rica.com). Singles/doubles/triples US$40/57/67 with shared bath, US$52/68/79 with private bath. The lodge has 18 screened rooms with private baths, fans, and large verandahs, and two more rooms with shared bath. Breakfast (US$5.50), lunch (US$7.50), and dinner (US$11) are available.

This is one of the few places where the increasingly rare great green macaw can be seen frequently. This macaw nests near the lodge, which is used as a base by researchers studying the bird. Many other birds have

been recorded – almost 300 species at last count. Monkeys, poison-arrow frogs, and caimans are routinely seen.

Most of the 500-hectare 'grounds' of the lodge is rainforest. Some of it is swampy, and there's a lagoon, but canoes are available to explore these parts. There are about 10km of foot trails, and horseback trips (US$15 for two hours) are offered. You can also take a boat tour down the Río San Carlos to the Río San Juan on the Nicaragua border (US$25, three hours).

To get to the lodge, drive on the paved road to Pital (north of Aguas Zarcas) and continue on a gravel road 29km to the tiny community of Boca Tapada, from where it's 7km farther to the lodge (there are signs). A 4WD vehicle is recommended, though not absolutely essential (call ahead to find out how the road is). Buses from Ciudad Quesada go to Pital several times a day. From Pital, there are two buses a day to Boca Tapada. There are also two buses daily (at 5:30am and 12:30pm) from the Coca-Cola bus terminal in San José that go to Pital and connect with a Pital–Boca Tapada bus. If you have a reservation, lodge staff will pick you up from Boca Tapada. A jeep taxi from Pital to the lodge costs about US$35. The lodge provides roundtrip transportation from San José for US$90 per person (two-person minimum).

Alternatively, the lodge offers complete three-day/two-night package tours that include transportation from San José, meals, a guided jungle hike, a four-hour boat tour, and unlimited canoeing and trail use for US$257 per person (two minimum).

# San José to Puerto Viejo de Sarapiquí

Puerto Viejo de Sarapiquí can be approached from San José from either the west or the east, so a roundtrip can be done without backtracking. The western route goes via Heredia, Varablanca, Catarata La Paz, San Miguel, La Virgen, and Chilamate. The eastern route goes via the highway through Parque Nacional Braulio Carrillo, then north through Horquetas to Puerto Viejo. Both routes are paved.

Playa Tamarindo on the Península de Nicoya

Swimming beneath waterfalls, Reserva Biológica Lomas Barbudal

Boating along a canal on the Caribbean coast

LUKE HUNTER

Fording a stream, Parque Nacional Chirripó

RALPH LEE HOPKINS

Reserva Biológica Bosque Nuboso Monteverde

LUKE HUNTER

The Pacific coast, Parque Nacional Corcovado

## WESTERN ROUTE
### San José to San Miguel

The western road is spectacular and a favorite of tour companies. The road leaves San José via Heredia and Barva and continues over a pass in the Cordillera Central between Volcán Poás to the west and Volcán Barva to the east (see the Central Valley & Surrounding Highlands chapter). The steep and winding mountain road climbs to over 2000m just before the tiny community of Varablanca.

A couple of kilometers past the highest point is a turnoff to Poasito and Volcán Poás; then a dizzying descent with beautiful views begins. People on tours or with their own vehicles can stop for photographs or for high- and middle-elevation birding. Travelers on public buses must be content with the excellent window gazing.

About 8km north of Varablanca, the Río La Paz is crossed by a bridge on a hairpin bend. On the left side of the bridge is an excellent view of the spectacular Catarata La Paz (see Los Jardines de la Catarata La Paz section in the Central Valley & Surrounding Highlands chapter). Several other waterfalls may be seen, particularly on the right-hand side (heading north) in the La Paz river valley, which soon joins with the Sarapiquí river valley.

About 6km or 7km beyond Catarata La Paz is a turnoff to the right on a dirt road leading to **Colonia Virgen del Socorro**, a small community several kilometers away across the river. This road (which may require 4WD) is famous among birders, who often spend several hours looking for unusual species along the quiet road; a forest, a river, clearings, and changes in elevation all contribute to species diversity in this one spot.

Barely a kilometer north of the turnoff for Virgen del Socorro, just past the community of Cariblanco (which has one of the only gas stations on this road), is a turnoff to the left that leads along a poor dirt road to the attractive **Laguna Hule**. The 9km road is just passable to ordinary cars in the dry season, but 4WD is advised during the wet season. The lagoon is the remnant of a volcanic crater and is set amid luxuriant rainforest – though away from the lake, most of the forest is gone. The lake is reputedly good for fishing.

About 7km north of the Virgen del Socorro turnoff, the road forks at the community of San Miguel. The westbound fork goes to Ciudad Quesada, about 35km away by paved road, and the north fork heads for Puerto Viejo de Sarapiquí to the northeast.

### West of San Miguel

The westbound road hugs the northern limits of the Cordillera Central, and there are occasional views of the northern lowlands. About 14km west of San Miguel along this road is the village of **Venecia**, where the basic *Hospedaje Torre Forte* has rooms. Halfway between San Miguel and Venecia is the hamlet of Río Cuarto, from which an unpaved road heads southeast past the beautiful waterfall near Bajos del Toro, through Parque Nacional Juan Castro Blanco, and on to Zarcero (see the Central Valley & Surrounding Highlands chapter).

A few kilometers north of Venecia is the pre-Columbian archaeological site called **Ciudad Cutris**, which can be reached by 4WD vehicle or on foot. The site has not been properly excavated, has no tourist facilities, and is on private land. You must inquire locally about permission to see it.

About 8km west of Venecia is the small town of **Aguas Zarcas**, which is the largest settlement between the Puerto Viejo and Caño Negro areas. It has a couple of cheap and basic places to stay.

### San Miguel to Puerto Viejo de Sarapiquí

The road north from San Miguel drops for 12km to the village of **La Virgen** (not Colonia Virgen del Socorro, mentioned previously), which is truly in the northern lowlands. The now-flat road goes through mainly agricultural country an additional 13km to **Bajos de Chilamate**, and then 6km on to Puerto Viejo de Sarapiquí. Several hotels and lodges along this stretch are described under West of Puerto Viejo de Sarapiquí, later in this chapter.

**Río Sarapiquí Trips** Some parts of the Sarapiquí are good for river running year-round, though May to November are considered the best. This river is a good one for families (minimum age nine). The put-in point is usually around La Virgen, where Class II and III rapids are encountered.

Alternatively, you can put in at Chilamate, where it's a more gentle float with mainly Class I and maybe a few Class II rapids. Check to ensure you are signing up for the level you want.

Tours run most days with one company or another and cost about US$69 per person. *Costa Rica Expeditions*, *Horizontes*, and *Ríos Tropicales* all run day trips that involve two hours of driving from San José, 2½ hours on the river, and two hours back to San José. Lunch and bilingual river guides are provided; see the Organized Tours section in the Getting Around chapter for contact information.

Other companies offering river rafting here include *Sarapiquí Aguas Bravas* (☎ 292-2072), next to Islas del Río Lodge near Chilamate; *Sarapiquí Outdoor Center* (☎/fax 761-1123, 297-1010 pager) in La Virgen, operated by the friendly David Duarte Soto; and *Aventuras del Sarapiquí* (☎ 766-6768, Ⓦ www.sarapiqui.com).

Another option is a kayak tour operated by Rancho Leona in La Virgen (see the Rancho Leona entry, later in this chapter).

## EASTERN ROUTE

After visiting the interesting Puerto Viejo de Sarapiquí area, you can return to San José via the eastern road. (You can also arrive in Puerto Viejo by the eastern road; buses go in both directions.)

About 4km southeast of Puerto Viejo, the road passes the entrance to Estación Biológica La Selva (described later in this chapter). About 15km farther is the village of **Horquetas**, from where it's 15km to the rainforest preservation project and lodge at Rara Avis (also described later in this chapter).

From Horquetas, the paved road continues about 17km through banana plantations to the main San José–Puerto Limón highway near the village of Santa Clara. Turn east for Guápiles and the Caribbean; turn west for San José. This route to San José takes you through the middle of Parque Nacional Braulio Carrillo.

About 2km south of Horquetas, an unpaved road goes east for 9km to the village of **Río Frío**, an important banana center. This used to be on the main road between Santa Clara and Horquetas, and some buses still go through here, even though it's about 9km farther and the road is not paved. Río Frío has an airstrip, and flights can be chartered to and from Tortuguero. There is a basic *hotel* where buses between San José and Puerto Viejo often stop for a meal break. You can catch buses several times a day from here to Puerto Viejo, San José, or Guápiles.

---

## Bananas

Around here, you'll see banana plants everywhere you look. Bunches of bananas are often covered with large blue plastic sacks while the fruit is still on the tree. The plastic keeps the plants warm (as in a miniature greenhouse) and also concentrates ethylene gas, which is produced by ripening fruit.

Strange-looking little tractor-trains pull wagons loaded with fruit to processing centers. In some plantations, bunches of bananas are hung on wire contraptions, which are pushed by workers into the processing area. The bananas are washed and sprayed to prevent molding and then shipped off in crates and boxes to the coast and the world.

The banana companies have been criticized for a multitude of ills over the decades. Rainforests have been replaced by plantations, blue plastic bags litter and clog the streams and rivers, and the insecticide and fungicide sprays used have caused health problems, including sterility, in thousands of workers.

These problems have been largely ignored, mainly because the plantations give workers minimum housing and a livelihood, and bananas have been, along with coffee, the main source of foreign income for Costa Rica.

Slowly, however, the health and environmental problems are being addressed. Though the damage already done cannot be easily reversed, some attempt is being made to minimize further biollution, degradation, and sickness. Most of this is 'too little, too late,' but it's better than nothing at all.

## PUERTO VIEJO DE SARAPIQUÍ

The locals simply refer to the town as Puerto Viejo, but its full name distinguishes it from another popular destination, Puerto Viejo de Talamanca on the Caribbean coast.

The town is at the confluence of the Río Puerto Viejo and the Río Sarapiquí. About 16,000 people live in the Puerto Viejo district, which, despite its ramshackle appearance, has an interesting history. It was an important port on the trade route to the Caribbean before the days of roads and railways. Boats plied the Sarapiquí as far as the Nicaragua border and then turned east on the Río San Juan to the sea. With the advent of roads and railways, Puerto Viejo lost its importance as a river port.

Despite its distance from Nicaragua, Puerto Viejo has something of the feel of a jungle border town – there's an immigration post near the small wooden dock, and emigrating Nicaraguans sometimes share the river with local fishers and visiting birders. Adventure-seeking travelers can still travel down the Sarapiquí in motorized dugout canoes.

This region is known for its nearly undisturbed premontane tropical wet forest, which extends from the northern arm of Parque Nacional Braulio Carrillo. A biological research station and several forest lodges nearby have made this habitat accessible to scientists and travelers. A new addition is an ambitious rainforest reserve, museum, and lodge called Centro Neotrópico Sarapiquís (see West of Puerto Viejo de Sarapiquí, later in this chapter).

Grassroots environmental activity is also strong in this area – a good contact for those interested in finding out about or contributing to local activity is local guide Alex Martínez, owner of the Posada Andrea Cristina B&B (see Places to Stay & Eat, below).

There is no dry season in this area, but late January to early May is the less wet season. A weather station at La Selva, just outside Puerto Viejo, records about 170mm of rain in February (the driest month) and close to 500mm in December, which is the wettest month. The drier season means fewer insects and less muddy trails, but it's never really dry.

Banco Popular has an ATM and changes money. Internet Sarapiquí, at the west end of town, is open from 8am to 10pm.

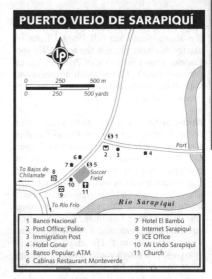

### PUERTO VIEJO DE SARAPIQUÍ

| | |
|---|---|
| 1 Banco Nacional | 7 Hotel El Bambú |
| 2 Post Office; Police | 8 Internet Sarapiquí |
| 3 Immigration Post | 9 ICE Office |
| 4 Hotel Gonar | 10 Mi Lindo Sarapiquí |
| 5 Banco Popular; ATM | 11 Church |
| 6 Cabinas Restaurant Monteverde | |

## Places to Stay & Eat

**Budget** Although most foreign visitors tend to stay in one of the more expensive lodges in the area, budget travelers will find a few cheap and basic hotels in Puerto Viejo itself. Most are along the one main street, so you won't have any difficulty finding them. The problem is, though, that the best cheap rooms are often full of local workers who use them on a long-term basis, so the choice of rooms may be limited. There are several inexpensive restaurants, bars, and sodas.

*Cabinas Restaurant Monteverde* (☎ 766-6236) Singles/doubles US$7.50/10. The six rooms are fairly basic and have private cold showers and table fans. The restaurant here is popular and reasonably priced.

*Hotel Gonar* (☎ 766-6055) Rooms US$4.50 per person. Above a hardware shop called Almacén y Ferretería Gonar (☎ 766-6196), this place has 18 bare rooms with beds and fans, sharing one basic cold shower. There's a US$6 deposit for the key.

*Mi Lindo Sarapiquí* (☎/fax 766-6281) Singles/doubles US$12/20. This place on the south side of the soccer field has the nicest budget rooms. There are only six of them, all simply decorated, but they're clean and have private hot showers and fans. Below the hotel is a decent, locally recommended *restaurant* open 9am to 10pm.

***Cabinas Yacaré*** Rooms US$6 per person, singles/doubles with bath US$8/14. If all of the above places are full, budget travelers can try this basic place in the small village of Guaria, almost 3km west of Puerto Viejo on the main road to Chilamate. It has six rooms with shared baths and four more rooms with private cold showers.

**Mid-Range** About 1km west of the center, on the road to Chilamate, is ***Posada Andrea Cristina B&B*** (✆/fax 766-6265) Cabins US$20 per person. This clean, family-run place has six quiet little cabins in its garden. Each cabin has a fan and a private hot bath. The rate includes a big home-cooked breakfast with some of Costa Rica's best coffee. The owner, Alex Martínez, is an excellent and charming guide and a passionate frontline conservationist. He arrived here 30 years ago as a tough young hunter exploring what was virgin forest, saw firsthand the rapid destruction of the forest, changed his philosophy, and is now a volunteer game warden – who will abandon a Saturday night soccer match to chase down poachers on the river. He helped found ABAS, a local environmental protection and education

agency. Alex speaks English and can tell you as much as you want to know about environmental issues of the area as well as help with transport and tour arrangements.

***Hotel Ara Ambigua*** (✆/fax 766-6971) Singles/doubles US$20/30. About 2km west of town, this small new hotel has a dozen clean cabins with fans and private hot-water bathrooms. They have a pool and a semi-outdoor *restaurant*.

***Hotel El Bambú*** (✆ 766-6359, fax 766-6132, ✉ info@elbambu.com, ⊞ www.el bambu.com) Singles/doubles US$53/64, including continental breakfast. On the west side of the soccer field, El Bambú has 16 spacious, air-conditioned rooms, all with fans, cable TVs, telephones, and hot water. Children under 12 years old stay free with their parents, and substantial discounts are offered in the wet season. The large and modern *dining room* is open 7am to 10pm and has meals in the US$4 to US$10 range. A balcony overlooks the street, and there's a pool and a parking lot.

### Getting There & Away
**Bus** Express buses from San José via Braulio Carrillo leave from the Atlántico

---

### Sailing to Nicaragua

Sailing down the Río Sarapiquí to the Río San Juan is a memorable trip. If the water is low, dozens of crocodiles can be seen sunning on the banks. If the water is high, river turtles climb out of the river to sun themselves on logs. Birds are everywhere. North of Puerto Viejo, much of the land is cattle pasture with few trees, but as you approach the Nicaragua border, more stands of forest are seen. In trees on the banks, you may see monkeys, iguanas, or maybe a snake draped over a branch.

On my trip, the boat captain suddenly cut the engine, so I turned around to see what was the matter. He grinned and yelled what sounded to me like 'Slow! Slow!' It was obvious that we were going slowly, and it took me a while to realize that he was saying 'Sloth!' It was not until the dugout had gently nosed into the bank beneath the tree, and the sloth raised a languid head to see what was going on, that I finally realized what we were stopping for. How he managed to make out the greenish-brown blob on a branch (the color is caused by the algae that grows in the fur of this lethargic animal) as a sloth is one of the mysteries of traveling with a sharp-eyed campesino.

We continued on down to the confluence of the Sarapiquí with the San Juan, where we stopped to visit an old Miskito Indian fisher named Leandro. He claimed to be 80 years old, but his wizened frame had the vitality of a man half his age. From the bulging woven-grass bag in the bottom of his fragile dugout, Leandro sold us fresh river lobster to accompany that evening's supper.

The official border between Nicaragua and Costa Rica is the south bank of the San Juan, not the middle of the river, so you are technically traveling in Nicaragua when on the San Juan. This river system is a historically important gateway from the Caribbean into the heart of Central America. Today, it remains off the beaten tourist track and is a worthwhile trip to see a combination of rainforest and ranches, wildlife and old war zones, and deforested areas and protected areas.

Norte terminal about eight times a day between 6:30am and 6pm (about 1½ hours). Three buses a day, at 6:30am, noon, and 3pm, take the scenic route via Heredia and Varablanca (four hours). There are also buses from Ciudad Quesada (San Carlos) and Guápiles. Note that arriving buses will continue down to the port (a five-minute walk) if you ask the driver.

Buses leave Puerto Viejo for San José on a similar schedule, from a bus stop on the main street – ask anyone. A nearby stop has buses for Ciudad Quesada and other destinations. About eight buses a day stop in Guápiles between 5:30am and 6pm.

**Boat** The port is small and not very busy. A few motorized dugouts are available for hire. A boat leaves at about noon daily for the Nicaragua border near Trinidad on the Río San Juan, returning the next morning at 4:30am – the fare is US$4 to Trinidad (see Trinidad Lodge under North of Puerto Viejo de Sarapiquí, later in this chapter). Boat departure times are very flexible, so check carefully and arrive early.

Local lodges can arrange transportation almost anywhere, for a price. Boat captains at the dock might be cheaper and will take you anywhere; short trips along the river cost about US$6 per hour for a group of four, US$20 per hour for a single person. Trips to Tortuguero and back cost about US$50 per person, with a minimum of four people. A larger boat holding 15 people costs about US$420.

**Taxi** There is a taxi sign on the main street of Puerto Viejo. If a taxi isn't there, wait by the stand and one will eventually cruise by. Taxis will take you to the nearby lodges and biological station for US$3 to US$6.

## WEST OF PUERTO VIEJO DE SARAPIQUÍ
### Selva Verde
In Chilamate, about 7km west of Puerto Viejo, a once-private *finca* has been turned into a tourist facility called Selva Verde (☎ 766-6800, fax 766-6011; in the USA ☎ 800-451-7111, 352-377-7111, fax 352-371-3710; ℮ selvaverde@holbrooktravel.com, ℗ www.selvaverde.com). Singles/doubles/triples/quads US$90/144/180/196, with full board. Children under 12 stay free with

adults; children over 12 sharing with adults pay US$37 each. Accommodations without meals are about US$30 less per person; meals are available separately at about US$10 each.

Well over half of Selva Verde's approximately 200 hectares are forested; the rest contain the lodge buildings on attractively landscaped grounds. The main lodge (the River Lodge) has 45 rustic but comfortable double rooms with private hot showers. Large communal verandahs have hammocks and forest views. A conference hall is often used by Elderhostel groups; slide shows, lectures, and discussions on a variety of topics are presented the nights that Elderhostel groups are staying there and at irregular intervals at other times. Meals are served buffet-style at set times. There's a small reference library for guests.

The lodge is owned and operated by Holbrook Travel (see Organized Tours in the Getting There & Away chapter). Because of the travel agency connection, the lodge is popular with tour groups.

**Things to See & Do** There are several kilometers of **walking trails** through the grounds and into the forest (premontane tropical wet forest); trail maps are available, or you can hire a bilingual guide from the lodge (US$15 per person, plus a customary tip, for a three-hour hike on the trails). There are plenty of birds and butterflies, and observant visitors may see mammals, frogs, and reptiles.

On one visit, I saw a pair of nesting sunbitterns on the banks of the Río Sarapiquí. Stiles and Skutch write in their authoritative *A Guide to the Birds of Costa Rica* that 'the sunbittern's nest has rarely been found, and the best available account of its breeding is that of a pair that nested in the gardens of the Zoological Society of London more than a century ago.' Seeing sunbitterns in a nest in the wild is not a bad way to start a day of birding.

There's also a **garden** of medicinal plants, as well as a **butterfly garden** (*admission US$5, free for lodge guests*) planted with flowers, shrubs, and trees designed to attract a variety of butterfly species. Explanatory tours are offered.

Various **boat tours** on the Río Sarapiquí are also available. You can rent a small boat, raft, or canoe with a guide for four or five hours for US$45 per person. Three-hour motorized boat trips on the Sarapiquí cost US$25 per person from the lodge. These trips give you a good chance of seeing a sloth in the trees, but only if you have a local guide – most tourists just can't spot them. Locally guided horseback rides (US$20 for two to three hours) can also be arranged.

The Holbrook family funds the nonprofit Sarapiquí Conservation Learning Center, nearby. Staffed by foreign volunteers, the center provides classes for the local community and visitors. English classes are the most popular, but computer, conservation, sports, and cultural interaction are also in the program. The town's only library is here. Guests at Selva Verde sometimes visit the center to buy their arts and crafts, chat with locals, and perhaps make a donation.

**Getting There & Away** Buses en route to or from Puerto Viejo will drop you off at Selve Verde's entrance – all the drivers know where it is. Taxis from Puerto Viejo to the lodge cost about US$4. If you call ahead, Selva Verde can arrange private transportation from San José.

## La Quinta de Sarapiquí Lodge

About 5km north of the village of La Virgen, a 1.3km-long gravel road to the west leads to La Quinta de Sarapiquí Lodge (☎ 761-1300, 761-1052, fax 761-1395, ✉ quinta@racsa.co.cr, ⓦ www.laquintasarapiqui.com). Singles/doubles/triples US$58/70/81. This pleasant family-run lodge on the banks of the Río Sardinal has 26 rooms in clean bungalows set in a garden. All rooms have terraces, ceiling fans, and private hot showers; four rooms are wheelchair accessible. Meals in the open-air *dining room* cost US$7.50 for breakfast, US$11 for lunch, and US$12.50 for dinner.

Friendly tico owner Beatriz Gámez is active in local environmental issues and is a good source of information on the area. She helps administer the Cámara de Turismo de Sarapiquí (CANTUSA), which works to promote a balance between conservation and tourism.

Activities at the lodge include swimming in the river (there's a good swimming hole near the lodge), horseback riding, fishing, boat trips, mountain biking, and birding, and you can spend time in the large butterfly garden or hike the 'frog land' trail where poison-dart frogs are commonly seen. Fishing and horseback rides are free to lodge guests. There's also a small swimming-hole-like pool overlooking the river, and an informal bar.

On the hotel grounds is the air-conditioned **Museo Joyas del Trópico Húmedo** *(Jewels of the Humid Tropics; admission US$8.50, free to lodge guests)*. The jewels are many thousands of insects, spiders, centipedes, and crustaceans that make up the lifetime collection of Richard Whitten, a North American biologist who now resides in Costa Rica. Some are displayed in biological research cases, well labeled in both Spanish and English, while others are crafted into stunningly beautiful works of art. Museum visits feature education, interpretive tours, and videos.

## Centro Neotrópico Sarapiquís

Two kilometers east of the village of La Virgen is an ecotourism complex called the Centro Neotrópico Sarapiquís (☎ 761-1004, fax 761-1415, ✉ magistra@racsa.co.cr, ⓦ www.sarapiquis.org). Standard singles/doubles US$76/90, deluxe singles/doubles US$84/99.

This unique project, declared by presidential decree to be a 'Project of National Interest' at its inception in 1997, features a lodge, museum, botanical garden, and archaeological site and is the gateway to the reserve at Tirimbina Rainforest Center (see below). The aim of the museum and lodge is to heighten visitors' awareness of both the cultural and natural history of the rainforest before they enter the reserve itself. This is done through a mixture of ambience and education. The center is the product of the passion and vision of designer/architect Jean Pierre Knockaert, president of the project's nonprofit developer, Landscape Foundation Belgium.

Cars are left near the highway, and visitors walk through orange groves and gardens to the lodge, which is modeled after a 15th-century pre-Columbian village. Four conical Palenque-style buildings with palm-thatch roofs house comfortable rooms decorated with pre-Columbian motifs. Three of them house eight spacious rooms each; every room has a large bathroom, ceiling fan, telephone, and private terrace. The 12 standard rooms are in another building attached to a library/research area and are designed for students. The main difference is that they're smaller and lack an individual terrace. The fourth building houses the reception area, restaurant, bar, and a fascinating display of century-old photographs depicting the area. The restaurant serves meals incorporating spices and edible flowers used in indigenous cuisine, as well as fresh fruits and vegetables from the surrounding gardens. Meals are US$6 for breakfast and US$12.50 for lunch or dinner buffets of vegetarian and Costa Rican food.

The **museum**, opened in 2002, chronicles the history of the rainforest (and of human interactions with it) through a mixture of displays, audio presentations, and animation. The tour is interactive and is 'led' by the 19th-century Costa Rican naturalists and explorers Anastasio Alfaro and José Cástulo Zeledon. Following the museum tour, visitors enter the Tirimbina reserve via a 267m suspension bridge.

The **archaeological site**, Alma Ata, has about a dozen Maleko Indian tombs excavated so far, with an estimated 70 more burial sites to be excavated over the next five years. Petroglyphs and pottery have been found here. Like other Costa Rican sites, Alma Ata is not a visually spectacular pyramid but rather a small site where guided tours create a more personalized experience. Admission is US$7.

The **botanical garden**, Chester's Field, combines displays of Costa Rican, New World, and Old World plants, many labeled with scientific and common names. A booklet is available to further explain 73 numbered plants in the gardens, which boast the largest scientific collection of medicinal plants in Costa Rica.

The entire project's wastewater is recycled through a natural biological wastewater treatment plant, which looks like a huge field of sugarcane and other vegetation. It's hard to tell it's there when looking directly at it from the lodge; ask for a visit. Solar energy is used for heating water, and cross-ventilation keeps rooms cool without air-conditioning.

The **Tirimbina Rainforest Center** (☎/fax 761-1418, ℮ tirimbin@racsa.co.cr, ☒ www .tirimbina.org) is a 300-hectare reserve that adjoins the center. Reached by two suspen-

sion bridges, 267m and 111m long, spanning the Río Sarapiquí, the reserve has over 6km of trails, some of which are paved or wood-blocked. The approach to the reserve is fabulous – you stand on a suspension bridge high over the river surrounded by rainforest, which means exceptional birding opportunities. Some visitors spend an hour or more just walking across the bridges. Halfway across, a spiral staircase drops down to a large island in the river. The reserve offers environmental and ecological courses, mainly for local students, and research opportunities for university students.

A four- to six-hour visit to the museum, botanical gardens, bridges, and rainforest reserve costs US$25 (US$12.50 for children under 12), including a naturalist guide. Fees are subject to change.

### Rancho Leona

In the village of La Virgen, 19km west of Puerto Viejo, is rustic Rancho Leona (☎/fax 761-1019, ℮ rleona@racsa.co.cr), primarily a day lodge with a restaurant-bar and art studio.

The lodge's American/tica owners, Ken and Leona, are artisans and musicians who provide a laid-back family atmosphere. Musicians are welcome to stop by and jam with Ken on the piano. The focus of their artwork is Tiffany-style stained glass made with a copper foil technique. Their studio/workshop is a dazzling display of windows, glass hangings, and especially, lampshades, all of which are custom-designed; they have done work for customers all over the world, working out sketches via fax, and many of the pieces hanging in the studio are also for sale. This artistic technique is a painstaking and time-consuming process; the results are exquisitely lovely but don't come cheap. They also sell T-shirts and tropical jewelry made from local seeds and beads that will meet the needs and pocketbooks of casual souvenir shoppers.

The *restaurant-bar* serves Italian food, salads, and sandwiches, all freshly made and moderately priced (US$3 to US$7). Stop by for lunch and, while you wait for your order to be prepared, take a tour of the studio.

Kayaking trips can also be arranged on an ad hoc basis. Visitors are welcome to hang out at the lodge, swim in the nearby river, or hike to riversides and a waterfall (about an hour's walk along roads and then through pasture and forest). Guides are available, and all the people who work here speak English.

Though this isn't really a hotel, bunks are available. Amenities include solar-heated showers, a sweat lodge, hot tub, and games/reading area.

## La Virgen

Although it's just a tiny community, La Virgen is the largest village on the road between Puerto Viejo and San Miguel. It also has one of the best budget lodging options in the area, the Outdoor Center.

*Sarapiquí Outdoor Center (☎/fax 761-1123, ☎ 297-1010 pager)* Campsites US$3 per person, rooms US$8 per person. The rooms are simple and a fair value with river views from some windows. There's a communal kitchen and a covered terrace in case of rain. Meals are available for guests. A white-water rafting day trip costs US$45, other boat trips cost US$30, and horseback trips can be arranged for US$25.

*Hotel Claribel (☎ 761-1190)* Singles/doubles US$10/16. Here you'll find simple, clean rooms with TVs and private showers.

*Restaurante y Cabinas Tía Rosita (☎ 761-1032, 761-1125)* Singles/doubles/triples US$7.50/13.50/18. Four cabins have private bath, hot water, TV, and fan. Slightly cheaper and simpler than Hotel Claribel, this place gets a lot of truckers. The restaurant's main courses cost US$3 to US$4.

*Restaurante Nuevo Cevi* This restaurant features a nice porch and its cook has a good local reputation; prices are slightly higher here.

*Restaurant & Bar Sansi (☎ 761-1163)* This friendly and popular eatery specializes in seafood. It's open until 2am on weekends, when it may have dancing.

## NORTH OF PUERTO VIEJO DE SARAPIQUÍ
### El Gavilán

About 4km northeast of Puerto Viejo are the lodge and private 100-hectare preserve of El Gavilán (*no lodge phone; San José reservations ☎ 234-9507, fax 253-6556; ⓔ gavilan@racsa.co.cr, Ⓦ www.gavilanlodge.com*). Singles/doubles US$53/58 with breakfast, US$29 for extra people. These are the officially advertised prices; if you just show up

and there's space, you can often get a discount. Day-trip and multinight packages are available. Reservations can be made in San José with Peace Rainbow Travel Agency at the phone/fax numbers listed above.

El Gavilán used to be a cattle hacienda and is surrounded by attractive gardens with large trees that are great for birding. The lodge has 12 simple but good-size rooms and cabins, each with a large private bathroom, hot shower, and fan. Three more rooms share two bathrooms. There's a nice outdoor Jacuzzi for relaxation. Full tico-style lunches (US$11) and dinners (US$15) are available. A variety of tropical fruit is harvested for meals. Note that the restaurant serves no alcohol – bring your own if you wish.

You can rent a horse or go hiking on 5km of trails. Three-hour guided hiking or horseback tours cost US$20 per person. Boat trips are also available. They range from short jaunts down the Río Sarapiquí for a couple of hours (US$20 per person), to day tours on the Río San Juan (US$75 per person, four minimum, lunch included), to multiday trips down the Sarapiquí to the San Juan and then on to the coast and down to Barra del Colorado or Tortuguero (US$400 one-way; several people can go for this price). Rafting and tours to Volcán Arenal are also offered.

Overnight packages for two people, including transportation from San José, accommodations, meals, and tours, start at US$380 for two days and one night and go to US$760 for five days and four nights. Day-trip packages from San José, including a ride on the Río Sarapiquí and lunch, cost US$70 per person.

El Gavilán can arrange transportation from San José for US$25 per person one-way (four-person minimum). Otherwise, take any Puerto Viejo de Sarapiquí bus, then a taxi for about US$2 or US$3. Boat captains from the Puerto Viejo dock (if you can find one readily available) will take you across the river to the lodge for about the same price. If you're driving, look for a sign to the right about 2km before Puerto Viejo coming from Horquetas; from the main road, it's about 1km to the lodge.

### Trinidad Lodge

In the village of Trinidad, at the confluence of Ríos Sarapiquí and San Juan, is Trinidad

Lodge (no lodge phone; in San José ☎ 213-0661, 259-1679). Doubles US$15; rates per person seem to change. This budget travelers' lodge, across from the Nicaragua border post, is also rather grandiloquently called Cabinas Paraíso de las Fronteras. It's a working ranch, and there are about six clean, spacious cabins with three beds and private baths. Reasonably priced and tasty home-cooked meals are available. Birding is good, and horse rentals and boat tours can be arranged. Trinidad is served by an 11am daily boat from Puerto Viejo, returning around 2pm.

## SOUTH OF PUERTO VIEJO DE SARAPIQUÍ
### Estación Biológica La Selva
Not to be confused with Selva Verde in Chilamate, the Estación Biológica La Selva (☎ 766-6565, fax 766-6335, ℮ laselva@sloth.ots.ac.cr) is a biological station, not a lodge, though you can stay here if you have an advance reservation. The biological station is the real thing, teeming with research scientists and graduate students using the well-equipped laboratories, experimental plots, herbarium, and library to investigate the ecological processes of the rainforest.

La Selva is operated by the Organization for Tropical Studies (OTS; ☎ 240-6696, fax 240-6783, ℮ reservas@ots.ac.cr, ☒ www.ots.ac.cr), a consortium founded in 1963 to provide leadership in the education, research, and wise use of tropical natural resources. Member organizations from the USA, Latin America, and Australia include 64 universities and research institutions.

Many well-known tropical ecologists have trained at La Selva. Twice a year, OTS offers an eight-week course open mainly to graduate students of ecology. The students visit several of the other OTS sites, but La Selva is the biggest and most frequently used. Course work is grueling, with classes, discussions, seminars, and field work running from dawn 'til dusk and into the evening. Various other courses and field trips are also offered. Many long-term experiments are underway at La Selva, and researchers come here year after year.

The area protected by La Selva is 1513 hectares of premontane wet tropical rainforest. Most of the land has not been disturbed. It's bordered to the south by the 47,583 hectares of Parque Nacional Braulio Carrillo, creating a protected area large enough to support a great diversity of species. Over 430 bird species have been recorded at La Selva, as well as 120 mammal species, 1900 species of vascular plants (especially from the orchid, philodendron, coffee, and legume families), and thousands of insect species. The list goes on and increases every year.

**Information** You can visit La Selva year-round, but with almost 200mm of rain falling in each of the months of February and March (the driest months), you should be prepared with rainwear or an umbrella.

Insect repellent, a water bottle, clothes that you don't mind getting dirty, and footwear that's suitable for muddy trails are also essential. The total annual rainfall is 4100mm, and high temperatures average 24°C but are often higher. The elevation is about 35m at the research station and goes up to about 150m by the time Braulio Carrillo is reached.

There's a small exhibit room and a gift shop that sells books, maps, posters, and T-shirts.

**Nature Trails & Hiking** Birding is excellent because of the well-developed trail system at La Selva. A few trails have a boardwalk for relatively easy access even during the wet season (though watch your footing – those wet boards can get very slick). The total length of trails, many of which are rough jungle paths, is about 60km. Guided hikes are offered daily, but unguided hiking is no longer allowed; the rising popularity of the research station with visitors led to a conflict with research interests. Now, guided 3½-hour hikes are offered at 8am and 1:30pm daily. These cost US$25 per person, or US$40 for both hikes. Children aged five to 12, accompanied by an adult, pay US$15 for one hike, or US$25 for both. Guided birding hikes are led at 6am and night hikes at 7pm, depending on demand. The hikes are mainly on cement or boardwalk trails, suitable for all abilities – some trails are wheelchair or walker accessible. You come here to learn, not to have a remote wilderness experience. Profits from these walks help to fund the research station. Mandatory reservations for guided hikes can be made directly with La Selva; see above for contact information.

**Places to Stay & Eat** You can come on a day trip or stay overnight (see below for rates). There are simple but comfortable bungalows with six bunks per room and a limited number of singles and doubles. Bathrooms are communal, but there are plenty of them. A dining room serves meals, although researchers and students always have priority. If there's room, tour groups (especially birding ones) and individual travelers can use the facilities, but reservations must be made in advance. There's usually space available if reservations are made a few weeks in advance, though during the popular dry season the place may be booked two or three months ahead. Reservations for overnight stays should be made with OTS (☎ 240-6696, fax 240-6783, e reservas@ots.ac.cr, w www.ots.ac.cr).

The overnight foreign tourist rates are US$75/130 singles/doubles, and US$20 for children (five to 12 years) sharing with adults, including three meals a day and one guided hike each day. Beer is available if ordered in advance; other alcohol is not available. Laundry machines are available in the afternoons only. The accommodations-only rates are US$55/92 singles/doubles; meals are available separately at US$7 each.

**Getting There & Away** The public bus to Puerto Viejo via the Río Frío and Horquetas route can drop you off at the entrance road to La Selva, about 3km before Puerto Viejo. From here it's almost 2km on a dirt road to the research station. Taxis from Puerto Viejo will take you there for about US$3.

OTS runs buses from San José (7am) to La Selva and back (3pm) on Monday. The fare is US$10 one-way, and reservations should be made when you arrange your visit. Researchers and students have priority.

OTS also runs a van service into Puerto Viejo and back several times a day (except Sunday, when there's only one trip).

## Sarapiquí Ecolodge

Run by the Murillo family, just outside of La Selva, this is an 80-hectare dairy ranch (☎ 766-6569, fax 236-8762). Rooms US$10 per person. Rustic accommodations are in bunks in the family ranch house; country-style meals cost US$5 to US$6. There are 18 beds in four rooms upstairs, and they share four bathrooms with hot showers downstairs. Behind the lodge, the Río Puerto Viejo (a tributary of the Sarapiquí) is good for swimming and boating. Horses can be rented, and boat tours are available. Get there by using the same entrance road as for La Selva (above) and then following a dirt road another kilometer to the left just before the La Selva gate.

## Rara Avis

This remote private preserve (☎ 764-3131, fax 764-4187, e raraavis@racsa.co.cr, w www .rara-avis.com) of 1335 hectares of tropical rainforest lies at elevations between 600m and 700m on the northeastern slopes of the Cordillera Central. The land borders the eastern edge of Parque Nacional Braulio Carrillo. Rara Avis was founded by Amos Bien, an American who came to Costa Rica as a biology student in 1977. There's a lodge, and visitors can use the trail system either alone or accompanied by guides. Rainforest birding is excellent, with over 350 species. Many mammals, including monkeys, coatis, anteaters, and pacas, are often seen.

Rara Avis can be visited year-round. It rains over 5000mm every year and there are no dry months, although from February to April is slightly less wet. This is definitely rainforest.

A short trail from the lodge leads to La Catarata – a 55m-high waterfall that cuts an impressive swath through the forest. With care, you can take a gloriously refreshing swim at the base of the falls, though you have to beware of flash floods, so ask the lodge staff for advice.

There have been complaints that the quality of the food, guiding, and accommodations has recently fallen. Amos admits that the lodge has had a couple of lean and mean years, but he says that a change in management and a large infusion of cash should bring it back in shape for the 2003 season.

**Places to Stay & Eat** Contact Amos Bien (see contact information above) to make the required reservations at any of the accommodations listed below.

*Casitas* Rooms US$45 per person. These are two-room, rustic cabins designed for students and budget travelers. Each room has two to four beds and each cabin has a cold-water bathroom. This place is at the edge of the preserve, 12km from Horquetas by a very bad road through farmland. (Horquetas itself is about 18km south of Puerto Viejo and 10km west of Río Frío.) Rates include meals.

*Waterfall Lodge* Singles/doubles/triples with bath US$90/160/210, including meals, guides, and transportation from Horquetas. Another 3km of bad road through the rainforest brings you to this lodge, named for the falls nearby. This rustic but attractive jungle lodge has 10 rooms with private showers and hot water, and balconies overlooking the rainforest. Even when it's pouring outside, you can watch birds from your private balcony. Because access is time consuming and difficult, a two-day minimum stay is recommended. There is no electricity, but kerosene lanterns are provided. The open-air dining room serves big meals. Children four to 16 years old sharing rooms with their parents are charged half price.

*River-Edge Cabin* This two-room cabin, with facilities similar to those at the Waterfall Lodge, is set in the rainforest about a half kilometer away from the dining room.

**Getting There & Away** First get a bus to Horquetas – you're given a schedule when you make your reservation. In Horquetas, you'll be met and transported to Rara Avis. The road climbs from Horquetas, at 75m, to the lodge, at 710m above sea level. En route, two rivers must be forded (there are footbridges).

The road is so bad that a tractor pulls a wagon (which has padded bench seats); Rara Avis asks that guests pack lightly, and it has a storage facility in Horquetas for extra luggage. The tractor leaves Horquetas every morning at 9am and returns from Rara Avis at 2pm. The 15km trip takes three to five hours. You can arrange to have a 4WD jeep take you the first 12km (up to the Casitas), taking under an hour, but then you must walk for the last 3km. Horses are available through Rara Avis.

# Caribbean Lowlands

The Caribbean and Pacific coasts of Costa Rica are very different. The Pacific coast is indented, resulting in a long and irregular coastline, while the Caribbean is a smooth, relatively short sweep of beaches, mangrove swamps, and coastal forest. The tidal variation on this smooth coastline is small. The Pacific has a dry season; the Caribbean can be wet year-round (though it's less rainy from February to March and September to October). About half of the Caribbean coastline is protected by two national parks and two national wildlife refuges, while less than 10% of the Pacific coastline is protected.

The entire Caribbean coast is part of Limón province, which covers 18% of Costa Rica but is home to only 8.9% of the population; among all the provinces it ranks next to last (above only Guanacaste) in both total population and population density. One-third of the province's 340,000 inhabitants are blacks of mostly Jamaican descent. Most of them live on or near the coast and many still speak English, albeit a dialect that sounds old-fashioned to most nonlocal ears. They provide a cultural diversity missing in the rest of Costa Rica. Also, several thousand indigenous Bribri and Cabecar people inhabit the southern part of the province.

Partly because of the small population of the region and partly because, until the development of the 1949 constitution, blacks were legally discriminated against, the Caribbean lowlands have been developed at a much slower rate than the Pacific. There are proportionately fewer roads, and there are more areas that can be reached only by boat or light aircraft. Limón province has less than 10% of the country's hotel rooms, while the Pacific coastal provinces of Guanacaste and Puntarenas have a combined total of over 40%. Traditionally, Costa Ricans from the populous Central Valley have vacationed on the Pacific, and even today the Caribbean is not a primary destination for most nationals. This has slowly begun to change since the 1987 opening of the San José–Puerto Limón highway, which cut driving time to the coast in half, but traditions die hard.

Foreign travelers, on the other hand, are more attracted to the Caribbean, partly for the romance associated with the word 'Caribbean' and partly for the cultural diversity found here. The main road from San José to the Caribbean ends at the provincial capital of Puerto Limón. From here there's just a single road heading south along the coast to the Panama border. Northbound travelers must depend on boats to take them up the

## Highlights

- Observing wildlife in Tortuguero – turtles, monkeys, and birds galore!
- Surfing the gnarly 'Salsa Brava' off Puerto Viejo
- Hanging out on the white-sand beach at Cahuita
- Tarpon fishing off Barra del Colorado
- Learning about and touring indigenous reserves with ATEC
- Supporting sloth rehabilitation and research at Aviarios del Caribe

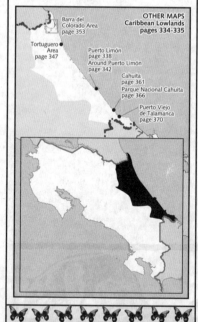

Barra del Colorado Area page 353

OTHER MAPS
Caribbean Lowlands
pages 334-335

Tortuguero Area page 347

Puerto Limón page 338
Around Puerto Limón page 342

Cahuita page 361
Parque Nacional Cahuita page 366

Puerto Viejo de Talamanca page 370

Intercoastal Waterway (a series of canals locally known as *los canales*), through wilderness areas, past remote fishing villages, and on to Nicaragua. Limited access to the region has helped its inhabitants maintain a sense of traditional values, making a Caribbean visit more culturally interesting than a trip to the Pacific beaches, though not as luxurious.

There are exceptions, of course. The Tortuguero and Barra del Colorado areas both have 1st-class lodges and fishing resorts in wilderness environments, and the hotel quality is improving in the south. But most of the Caribbean coast has a gentle, laid-back, unhurried feel to it.

# San José to Puerto Limón

## GUÁPILES & ENVIRONS

This town is the transport center for the Río Frío banana-growing region. It is in the northern foothills of the Cordillera Central, 62km northeast of San José, and is the first town of any size on the San José-Puerto Limón highway. The region is home to several small B&B-style hotels, which offer an excellent base for visiting the Rainforest Aerial Tram (only 20km west of Guápiles, described in the Central Valley & Surrounding Highlands chapter), some small local reserves (see Places to Stay & Eat, below), and the banana-growing region to the north. Most travelers speed through on

Hwy 32, which connects most of the places described in this section, but increasing numbers are finding a stop in the region worthwhile. There is a lively agricultural market on Saturday, but for the most part, there is little of interest in Guápiles itself.

### Jardín Botánico Las Cusingas

This is not your typical botanical garden (☎/*fax* 710-2652). The *tico* owners, Jane Segleau and Ulyses Blanco, emphasize education on a variety of subjects, including medicinal plants, rural Costa Rican life, conservation, the ethical use of plants for profit, and a variety of other nature-related subjects. They give interesting tours of the grounds (in English or Spanish) for US$5; tours last about two hours. Eighty medicinal-plant species, 80 orchid species, 30 bromeliad species, and over 100 bird species have been recorded on the 20-hectare grounds. The owners also work with neighbors to protect surrounding areas. Two trails go into the forest; the longer one is 1.5km and leads to a river, while a shorter loop is carefully graded to allow access for people of any age and fitness level (though not to wheelchair users). Various courses, research projects, and a library are all open to visitors and locals. Jane is a 2nd-degree practitioner of Reiki (a hands-on natural healing technique).

A rustic *cabin* has two rooms (US$30 for up to four people), along with a sitting room, a wood-burning stove, and kitchen equipment (no microwave!). You can eat with the owners' family, with advance notice. Hot

### Banana Trains

Bananas, Costa Rica's most important export, used to be loaded onto steam trains and hauled to the Caribbean coast. Today, trucks have superseded trains for transporting bananas, though small sections of track remain for hauling banana cargo in the Caribbean lowlands.

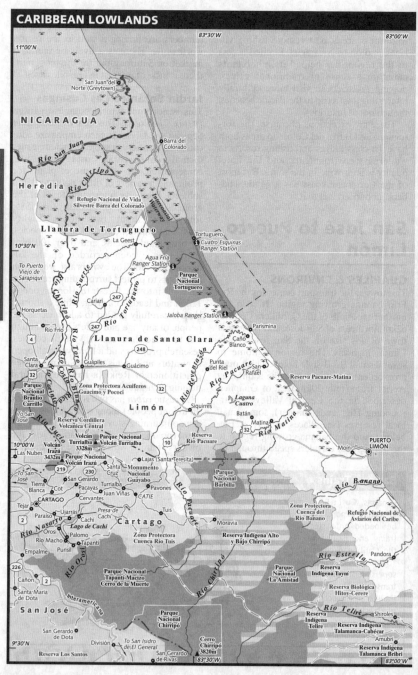

## CARIBBEAN LOWLANDS

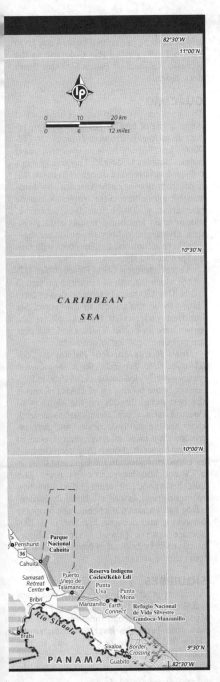

showers are available. This place is recommended for people who want to spend a few days studying natural history in a rustic setting. Reservations should be made for both the cabin and for guided tours.

Get to the garden by going 4km by paved road from the main highway (Hwy 32). The turn off for the road, which heads south, is near the Servicentro Santa Clara (gas station), on the eastern outskirts of Guápiles.

## La Danta Selvaje

Near a waterfall in a private 410-hectare rainforest reserve is the rustic lodge of La Danta Selvaje (*☎/fax 750-0012,* e *ladanta@ racsa.co.cr,* W *www.puertoviejo.net/ladanta/ ladantasalvaje.htm).* 4-day/3-night packages US$200 per person. On the Caribbean slope at 800m above sea level, this lodge is reached from Guápiles by a 4WD road, followed by a three-hour hike. There is no electricity, but there are flush toilets, hot showers, and a fireplace. The owners, David and Dalia Vaughan, live in Puerto Viejo de Talamanca and arrange guided visits to their remote reserve. Trips take place about twice a month, with a four-person minimum and eight-person maximum.

## Places to Stay & Eat

**In Town** There are no street signs, so you have to ask for these places. The first three lodgings listed below are clean, well run, and have TVs and fans. The fourth place is more upscale.

*Restaurant y Cabinas Madrigal (☎ 710-0520)* Singles/doubles US$8/12. This family-run place has eight windowless rooms with cold showers.

*Cabinas Irdama (☎ 710-7034, ☎/fax 710-7177)* Singles/doubles US$10/13, apartments US$17/300 per night/month. Here you'll find 21 decent and brighter rooms with cold showers. There's also a little restaurant. Ask the owners about the three apartments with two double beds, kitchenettes, and warm showers.

*Cabinas Car (☎ 710-0035)* Rooms US$12 per person. About 50m west of the Catholic church, this place has 10 rooms with private warm showers.

*Hotel Suerre (☎ 710-7551, fax 710-6376,* e *suerre@suerre.com,* W *www.suerre.com)* Singles/doubles US$70/87, suites US$120-150. The best hotel in town, this place has about 50 spacious, tiled, air-conditioned but bland rooms and suites with cable TV, telephones, and private hot showers. It also has a restaurant, Olympic-sized pool, two tennis courts, and a sauna and spa for guests. The hotel is 1.8km north of the Servicentro Santa Clara on the main highway, east of town.

**West of Town** Note that the phones don't work well in this area, so when calling the following establishments be patient or try a fax.

*Casa Río Blanco* (☎ 382-0957, fax 710-2264, e crblanco@racsa.co.cr) Singles/doubles/triples US$52/69/87. This small B&B and reserve, where local tours can be arranged, is friendly and environmentally conscious. Three cabins perch 20m above the Río Blanco, offering great rainforest canopy views and excellent birding and other wildlife watching; two rooms inside the main house have garden views. All rooms are fully screened, with private baths and hot water. Kerosene lanterns are used for lighting and there is solar electricity in the bathrooms. Rates include breakfast and a guided nature hike on private trails. Rubber boots for hiking and inner tubes for river floating are available. Volunteer positions in the reserve can be arranged.

The entrance road to the Casa Río Blanco is 5km west of Guápiles on the west side of the Río Blanco bridge. From here it's about 1.5km south to the site. If you're not driving, ask the bus driver to stop by the *Restaurant La Ponderosa* (☎ 710-7144), which is 300m west of the entrance road. Call from here and you can arrange to get picked up. The Ponderosa, which is complete with a photograph of Ben Cartwright and the boys from the TV show *Bonanza*, serves delicious *bocas* (US50¢ each or free with a beer), as well as sandwiches and steaks.

*Río Blanco Restaurant and B&B* (☎ 710-7857) Singles/doubles US$15/20. Just east of the Río Blanco bridge, this is another good place to eat. Behind the restaurant are a few motel rooms with fans, TV, and private hot bath. Rates include breakfast.

For another lodging option outside of Guápiles, see the Jardín Botánico Las Cusingas section, above.

**Getting There & Away**
Buses to San José (under US$2) or Puerto Limón leave about every hour. Buses to Río

Frío leave three or four times a day. There are also buses via paved road to Cariari, and from there one or two buses a day go to Puerto Lindo on the Río Colorado in the Refugio Nacional de Fauna Silvestre Barra del Colorado.

## GUÁCIMO
This small town is 12km east of Guápiles and is the home of **EARTH** *(Escuela de Agricultura de la Región Tropical Húmeda; ☎ 713-0000, fax 713-0001, w www.earth.ac.cr)* Singles/doubles US$40/55. This school has a college-level program designed to teach students from all over Latin America about sustainable agriculture in the tropics. A banana plantation, a 400-hectare forest reserve, nature trails, and horse rentals attract visitors. Overnight visitors (by prior arrangement) are accommodated in rooms with fans and private hot showers.

Also of interest is **Costa Flores** *(☎/fax 717-6439)*, which is north of Guácimo on signed roads. This 120-hectare tropical flower farm claims to be the largest in the world. Six hundred varieties of tropical plants are grown here for export. Visitors and shoppers are welcome – call for information.

*Hotel Restaurant Río Palmas* (☎ 760-0330, 760-0305, fax 760-0296, e riopalmas@racsa.co.cr) Singles/doubles US$45/50 in high season. Some 600m east of EARTH, this is the best motel directly on the highway to Puerto Limón. The 32 rooms are good-sized, clean, and pleasantly decorated, and the glass windows are more effective than screens in keeping bugs out, though they keep the heat in. Large fans alleviate the heat, and there is a TV and hot shower in every room. The hotel has a good restaurant and an attractive swimming pool, as well as a butterfly garden, a frog garden, and trails behind the property for hiking and horseback riding in a 200-hectare reserve (about US$6 per hour; horses must be booked in advance). Rafting tours can be arranged.

## SIQUIRRES
A railway junction until recently, this town is 25km southeast of Guácimo. It remains significant as the road junction of the old San José-Turrialba-Puerto Limón route (Hwy 10) with the new highway to the coast (Hwy 32). The old route is slower, but more scenic – good for those with a little

time on their hands. Siquirres is the last major town on the main highway before Puerto Limón, 58km farther east. Note that if you want to drive to Turrialba from here (on Hwy 10), you have to take a poorly signed overpass over the main highway. Most travelers go straight through or maybe stop at the small but bustling center, where there are a few interesting-looking buildings (see the round church), and a few cheap and basic *hotels*.

## PUERTO LIMÓN

This port is the capital of Limón province and ticos refer to the city as Limón. The mainly black population of Limón and the surrounding district is about 90,000, meaning some 27% of the province's inhabitants live in and around the provincial capital. Limón is quite lively, as ports tend to be, but is not considered a tourist town, although there are good hotels and something of a beach resort at Playa Bonita, 4km northwest of the town center. The presence of direct bus service from San José to the coastal villages south of Limón has decreased casual tourist traffic here.

### Orientation

Streets are poorly marked, and most do not have signs. Calles and avenidas go up one number at a time (Calle 1, Calle 2, etc) instead of going up in two's, as they do in most other towns. Locals get around by city landmarks such as the market, Radio Casino, and the *municipalidad* (town hall), on Parque Vargas. If you ask where the intersection of Calle 5 and Avenida 2 is, most people will have no idea. (It's 500m west of the municipalidad, or 100m west of the southwest corner of the market.)

Avenida 2 is one of the main streets – Parque Vargas, the municipalidad, the market, a couple of banks, the museum, and the main bus terminal are all on or just off this street.

Limón is on rocky Punta Piuta, a point that shelters the main port at Moín (about 6km or 7km west of Limón).

### Information

There is no tourist office. For information on tours, ask at some of the better hotels; for local information, asking locals is what ticos do.

House on stilts, Puerto Limón

ERIC L WHEATER

**Immigration** The Migración office is on Avenida 3, Calles 6 & 7. Visa extensions are normally given in San José.

**Money** Banco de Costa Rica (☎ 758-3166) and other banks, most of which have ATMs, will change money. The better hotels all take credit cards, and some will exchange US dollars. Exchange facilities are poor elsewhere along the coast (though the better lodges and hotels accept US dollars or even traveler's checks).

**Email & Internet Access** Edutec (☎ 798-5717), upstairs at the Plaza Caribe, is open 8am to 10pm daily.

**Medical Services** The Hospital Tony Facio (☎ 758-2222), on the coast at the north end of town, serves the entire province. The tiny Centro de Rehabilitación (☎ 798-5073) offers a half-hour upper-back massage for US$7.50; a full-hour therapeutic rub costs US$13. The Centro Médico Monterrey, with several private doctors, is opposite the cathedral.

**Dangers & Annoyances** People have been mugged in Limón, so stick to well-lit

# PUERTO LIMÓN

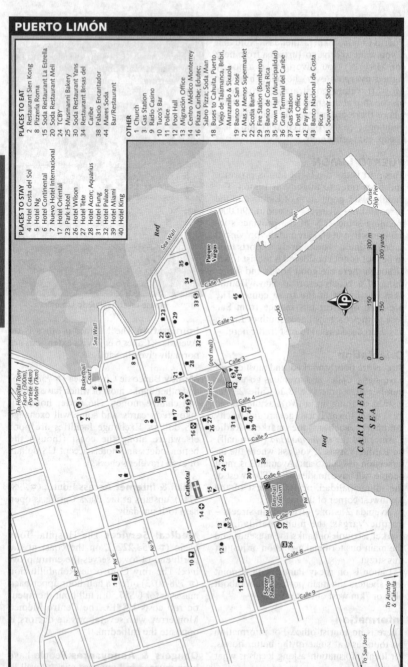

**PLACES TO STAY**
4 Hotel Costa del Sol
5 Hotel Ng
6 Hotel Continental
7 Nuevo Hotel Internacional
17 Hotel Oriental
23 Park Hotel
26 Hotel Wilson
27 Hotel Tete
28 Hotel Acon; Aquarius
31 Hotel Fung
32 Hotel Palace
39 Hotel Miami
40 Hotel King

**PLACES TO EAT**
2 Restaurant Sien Kong
8 Pizzería Roma
15 Soda Restaurant La Estrella
20 Soda Restaurant Meli
24 TCBY
25 Musmanni Bakery
30 Soda Restaurant Yans
34 Soda Restaurant Brisas del Caribe
38 Palacio Encantador
44 Mares Soda Bar/Restaurant

**OTHER**
1 Church
3 Gas Station
9 Radio Casino
10 Tuco's Bar
11 Police
12 Pool Hall
13 Migración Office
14 Centro Médico Monterrey
16 Plaza Caribe; Edutec;
 Sabro Pizza; Soda Man
18 Buses to Cahuita, Puerto Viejo de Talamanca, Bribri, Manzanillo & Sixaola
19 Banco de San José
21 Mas x Menos Supermarket
22 Scotia Bank
29 Fire Station (Bomberos)
33 Banco de Costa Rica
35 Town Hall (Municipalidad)
36 Gran Terminal del Caribe
37 Gas Station
41 Post Office
42 Pay Phones
43 Banco Nacional de Costa Rica
45 Souvenir Shops

main streets at night. Also watch out for pickpockets during the day. These are normal precautions for many port cities – Limón is not unusually dangerous.

Don't park anywhere after dark except in a guarded parking lot. Vehicle break-ins are common.

## Things to See & Do

The main attraction is the waterfront **Parque Vargas**, where you'll find tall palms and other tropical trees and flowers, and birds and sloths hanging out (literally) in the trees. It's not easy to see the sloths, but locals will help you spot one.

From the park it's a pleasant walk north along the **sea wall** of Puerto Limón, with views of the rocky headland upon which the city is built.

There are no beaches clean enough for swimming in Limón. At **Playa Bonita**, 4km northwest of town, there is a sandy beach with decent waves that is OK for swimming. There are picnic areas and places to eat, and the backdrop of tropical vegetation is attractive.

On his fourth and last transatlantic voyage, Columbus landed at **Isla Uvita**, which can be seen about 1km east of Limón. It is possible to hire boats to visit the island, and the better hotels can arrange tours there. Organized tours to Tortuguero, Cahuita, and other destinations of interest can also be arranged from all the better hotels (as well as in San José).

One focal point of the town is the colorful daily **central market**, which has a variety of cheap places to eat and plenty of bustling activity.

## Special Events

Columbus Day (October 12), locally known as El Día de la Raza, is celebrated here with more than the usual enthusiasm because of Columbus' historic landing on Isla Uvita. Tens of thousands of visitors, mainly ticos, stream into town for a *carnaval* of colorful street parades and dancing, music, singing, drinking, and general carrying-on that lasts four or five days. Hotels are booked well in advance of this event.

Labor Day is also especially colorful around Puerto Limón; people come up from the beach villages and there are dances and cricket matches.

## Places to Stay

Hotels all along the Caribbean coast are in demand on weekends during the San José holiday seasons (Christmas, Easter, and the months of January and February) and especially during the Columbus Day celebrations, when prices rise. Reserve ahead if possible during those periods.

Some hotels may operate on two price structures: one for locals and a higher one for visitors.

**Budget** The cheapest hotels can be dirty, a poor value, and used by prostitutes and their clients. While not salubrious, these places don't seem particularly dangerous, though solo women travelers may want to avoid them. Basically, they are places to crash for a night; the ones listed here are on the more wholesome end of the spectrum. This is a town where it's worth spending a little more for a better room.

*Hotel Oriental* (☎ 758-0117) Doubles without bath US$8. This is a decent, basic place with shared cold showers.

*Hotel Ng* (☎ 758-2134) Singles/doubles without bath US$5/8, with cold bath US$7/11. This hotel is filled with workers during the week but is usually less busy on weekends.

*Hotel Wilson* (☎ 758-5028) Singles/doubles with bath US$9/13. This hotel seems friendly and takes boarders, who often fill up the single rooms. The clacking of dominos and the drone of TVs create some noise. Rooms have fans.

*Hotel King* (☎ 758-1033) Rooms without bath US$4.50 per person, doubles with bath US$12. This clean, well-run and cheerful place is a good choice in this price range. Most rooms have fans, and private showers are cold.

*Hotel Fung* (☎ 758-3309) Singles/doubles without bath US$4/8, with bath US$6.50/10.50. This is a fair place, where most rooms have fans and some have sunny windows. All showers are cold.

*Hotel Costa del Sol* (☎ 798-0707, fax 758-4748) Rooms US$10-20. This place has parking, is open 24 hours, takes credit cards, and has clean, decent rooms, some with private baths and some with air-conditioning.

*Hotel Palace* (☎ 758-0419) Singles/doubles without bath US$6.50/10, doubles with bath US$13-16. Rooms with communal baths are basic and dark. Better doubles have private baths and a fan. The hotel is housed in an interesting-looking old building around a courtyard with flowers. Despite the 24-hour sign, this is not a place used for prostitution – the owner allows visitors only in the sitting area.

*Nuevo Hotel Internacional* (☎ 798-0545, 798-0532) Singles/doubles with fan US$7/11, with air-conditioning US$10/19. Rooms here are a fair value for Limón and are good and clean with private baths and hot water in the morning. Across the street is the similar *Hotel Continental*, owned by the same individual. The Continental has a parking lot.

**Mid-Range** All guestrooms have private cold showers at the clean *Hotel Miami* (☎/fax 758-0490) Singles/doubles with fan US$12.50/17.50, with air-conditioning US$18/24. The air-conditioned rooms have TV, and there's a café and parking.

*Hotel Tete* (☎ 758-1122, fax 758-0707) Singles/doubles with fan US$10/18, with air-conditioning US$18/24. This hotel has a nicer interior than exterior and is a good deal; rooms all have private hot showers.

*Hotel Acon* (☎ 758-1010, fax 758-2924) Singles/doubles with bath US$25/30. The decent rooms here have air-conditioning, TV, and phones. It has a reasonable restaurant and a popular dance club on the 2nd floor (see Entertainment, below). Major credit cards are accepted.

*Park Hotel* (☎ 798-0555, 758-3476, fax 758-4364) Doubles with bath US$40. The rooms here have TV, air-conditioning, and private baths with hot water. A few nicer rooms with sea views and little balconies cost US$5 more. Ask if cheaper single and double rooms with fans are still available. There is a parking lot and a simple but adequate restaurant. This is downtown Limón's best hotel.

There are also better hotels to be found northwest of Limón (see the Around Puerto Limón section, later in this chapter).

## Places to Eat

There are many snack bars and *sodas* around the market.

*Mares Soda Bar/Restaurant* Dishes US$3-7. More upscale, popular, and clean than most of the market eateries, this place is on the south side of the market. It offers a variety of snacks and meals for US$3 to US$7 and is a good spot for people watching.

*Soda Restaurant Meli* On the north side of the market, this is a Chinese restaurant that is cheap and popular with locals.

At the Plaza Caribe, *Sabro Pizza* and *Soda Man* have off-street courtyards and are relatively relaxing places for a meal or to have a coffee and write postcards.

*Soda Restaurant La Estrella* A block west, this soda is one of the cleaner cheap places you'll find in town, though the food is greasy. It's open until the wee hours.

*TCBY* (☎ 758-0044) Almost kitty-corner to La Estrella, this place is pricier but still pretty cheap – and it is air-conditioned. Snacks, breakfasts, ice cream, and burgers are sold here. Next door, *Musmanni* provides baked goods.

*Restaurant Brisas del Caribe* On the north side of Parque Vargas, this airy place is mid-priced.

*Pizzería Roma* Dishes from US$5. Open until 11pm daily. This upstairs Italian place is near the north end of the seawall.

*Restaurant Sien Kong* (☎ 758-0254) Dishes US$5-10. Farther from the center, this is the best Chinese restaurant in town.

*Palacio Encantador* (☎ 758-0163) US$3-9. A couple of blocks west of the market, this clean place offers decent Chinese food.

Within a block are a couple of sodas that have small menus but are popular among locals – one is *Soda Restaurant Yans* (US$1.25-4.50).

The better hotels (see above) have decent restaurants that are open to the public.

## Entertainment

Various bars by Parque Vargas and a few blocks west are popular hangouts for a variety of coastal characters: sailors, ladies of the night, entrepreneurs, boozers, losers, and the casually curious. These aren't places for a quiet drink and certainly aren't for solo women travelers. Go at your own risk!

*Tuco's Bar* This cozy place has good bocas, which come with the cheap beer. This is one bar where women can go. Nearby is a friendly *pool hall*, mainly frequented by young men.

*Aquarius* For dancing, check out this disco in the Hotel Acon (see Places to Stay, above). It's lively on weekends, with Latin music and a small cover charge.

## Getting There & Away

Limón is the transportation hub of the Caribbean coast, though its role has declined with the introduction of direct bus service between San José and the southern coast.

**Air** The airstrip is about 4km south of town, near the coast, but is little used for passenger traffic.

**Bus** Express buses from San José to Limón leave the Caribe terminal hourly from 5am to 6:30pm, returning to San José from the Gran Terminal del Caribe on Calle 2, near the soccer stadium. The fare is US$4 for the three-hour ride. From the same terminal there are buses to Siquirres and Guápiles many times a day.

Buses heading south leave from a block north of the market. Currently, buses from Limón to Cahuita (US80¢) leave seven times a day, from 5am to 6pm. Buses normally continue to Puerto Viejo de Talamanca (US$1.20). Some then go on to Bribri (US$1.40) and Sixaola (US$2, three hours); others go to Manzanillo instead. The buses are crowded, so try to get a ticket in advance and show up early. Advance tickets are sold next to the soda by the *parada* (bus stop). Note that buses from the south to San José don't go into central Limón.

Buses also leave from here to Penshurst and Pandora (Valle de La Estrella) several times a day. From Pandora you can go to the Reserva Biológica Hitoy Cerere.

**Car** If you are driving, take note that south of Limón there is only one gas station on the coast, at the crossroads just north of Cahuita. There is also one inland at Pandora, in the Valle de La Estrella. Last-ditch options are the roadside stands near some of the villages, which sell dirty gasoline out of drums.

**Boat** Limón is the country's major Caribbean port, and cruise ships or (more likely) cargo freighters occasionally dock at Moín, about 7km west of Limón, for a short visit. Boats to Tortuguero and points farther north leave from Moín. Cruise ships occasionally dock at the pier southeast of Limón

center; a few gift shops have opened where the passengers leave the dock for short land excursions.

**Taxi** A taxi to Cahuita costs about US$20 (though foreigners may get charged twice that – bargain hard). If you make this trip at night on a weekend, make an advance hotel reservation in Cahuita. Taxis to the good hotels around Portete, about 4km northwest of Limón, cost around US$3.

## AROUND PUERTO LIMÓN
### Portete & Playa Bonita

Portete and Playa Bonita both offer decent little beaches and a handful of pleasant accommodations; if you are staying in the area, these places make a nice break from downtown Puerto Limón. If you are driving on Hwy 32 toward Limón from the west, take the Moín turnoff to the left, about 6km before reaching Limón, to avoid downtown. If you go this way, 3km after turning off the main highway, just before the Moín dock, take a right for Portete and Playa Bonita, and follow the coast road east past the coastal hotels. This route eventually leads back to Limón itself. If you are not driving, take the Moín bus from downtown Limón, though this bus is often crowded; a taxi would be a better way to go.

**Places to Stay & Eat** About 4km out of Limón, and 2.5km from the Moín dock, is *Hotel Cocori* (☎ 758-2930, ☎/fax 798-1670) Doubles US$40-45. This hotel is on the small beach at Playa Bonita. It offers an open-air restaurant with an ocean view, and has cabins with kitchenettes, air-conditioning, and refrigerators. This is a good budget option outside of town.

*Hotel Matama* (☎ 758-1123, fax 758-4499, e matamasol.racsa.co.cr) Singles/doubles US$58/64. Across the street from the Hotel Cocori, this place is 300m to 400m from the beach at Playa Bonita. The Matama has a swimming pool, bar, and restaurant. The air-conditioned rooms are in a variety of bungalows and cabins – there are eight double rooms, four rooms sleeping four, and four rooms sleeping six. The buildings are set in hilly gardens of tropical vegetation; inside some of the bathrooms are miniature jungle gardens, making a nice change from all the other

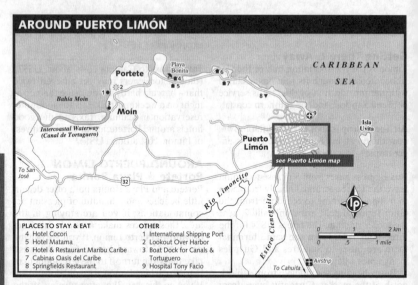

**AROUND PUERTO LIMÓN**

*CARIBBEAN*
*SEA*

Portete
Playa Bonita
■■4
★6
■5
★7

*Bahía Moín*
1●
❉2
8▽

**Moín**
3●

*Intercoastal Waterway*
*(Canal de Tortuguero)*

**Puerto Limón**

✚9

*Isla Uvita*

To San José
32

*Río Limoncito*

*see Puerto Limón map*

0        1        2 km
0      .5       1 mile

*Estero Cieneguita*

To Cahuita
✈ Airstrip

| PLACES TO STAY & EAT | OTHER |
|---|---|
| 4  Hotel Cocori | 1  International Shipping Port |
| 5  Hotel Matama | 2  Lookout Over Harbor |
| 6  Hotel & Restaurant Maribu Caribe | 3  Boat Dock for Canals & |
| 7  Cabinas Oasis del Caribe | Tortuguero |
| 8  Springfields Restaurant | 9  Hospital Tony Facio |

hotel bathrooms you may see during your trip. Rates, which are much less in the low season, include breakfast.

***Hotel Maribu Caribe*** (☎ 758-4010, 758-4543, fax 758-3541) Singles or doubles high season/low season US$85/50. This hotel is just over a kilometer east of the Matama, or about 3km northwest of Puerto Limón. It is on a small hill that catches ocean breezes and offers a good view, especially from the restaurant. There are two pools in addition to the restaurant and bar. Accommodations are in private, air-conditioned, thatched bungalows. Most of these top-end hotels will arrange local tours.

***Cabinas Oasis del Caribe*** (☎ 758-2024, fax 758-1731, @ moyso@racsa.co.cr) Singles/doubles US$15/25. About 200m east of the Maribu Caribe, this establishment has pleasant, quiet cabins and a restaurant on the premises. Showers are unheated.

***Springfields Restaurant*** (☎ 758-1203) A few hundred meters farther along, this place serves Caribbean food and is locally popular in the evenings.

### Moín

This port is about 7km west of Puerto Limón. The main reason to come here is to take a boat up the canals to Parque Nacional Tortuguero and on to Refugio Nacional de Fauna Silvestre Barra del Colo-

rado. (However, there are other ways, mentioned in the following sections, to reach those places – you don't have to travel via Moín.)

The canals are so called because they are not all natural. There used to be a series of natural waterways north of Limón as far as Barra del Colorado, but they were not fully connected. In 1974, canals linking the system were completed, eliminating the need for boats to go out to sea when traveling north from Moín. This inland waterway is safer than traveling up the coast offshore.

When sometimes the canals north of Moín are blocked by water hyacinths or logjams, the riverside village of Matina, on the Río Matina halfway between Puerto Limón and Siquirres, or other road-accessible ports are used until the blockage is cleared.

### Getting There & Away

**Bus** Buses to Moín depart from Limón several times an hour, starting at 6am. The buses leave either from in front of the cathedral or from the Gran Terminal Caribe.

**Boat** Most travelers get to the national parks on organized tours with prearranged boat or plane transport. These tours are usually good but not cheap, although it is possible to pay for just the travel portion and then stay in cheaper accommodations in the Tortuguero area. There are also some new, cheaper ways of getting to Tortuguero (see Boat under Getting There & Away in the Tortuguero Area section, later in this chapter).

To arrange transportation independently, go down to the Moín dock early and start asking around. The boat dock for Tortuguero is about 300m to the left of the main port, through a guarded gate. There are passenger and cargo boats leaving most days, but it takes a bit of asking around about schedules. Cargo boats are cheaper but are officially for cargo only, though you might persuade a captain to allow you aboard. The trip to Tortuguero can take from 2½ hours to all day, depending on the type of boat.

Most travelers take a private boat; boat operators offer the roundtrip to Tortuguero for US$45 per person with a three-person minimum, or less with large groups. There are often boaters hanging around the dock area in the early morning, and boats normally leave between 7am and 8am. The trip takes about five hours to Tortuguero (allowing for photography and wildlife viewing). After lunch and a brief visit to Tortuguero, the return trip is done in 2½ hours. Overnights and returns on the following day can be arranged. There is a locked and guarded parking area for those who drive to the dock area, but don't leave valuables in the car.

You can make arrangements for the trip in advance in San José (or in Cahuita), or with boat operators and agencies in Limón. With *Laura's Tours* (☎ 758-2410) it costs US$65 for roundtrip transport to Tortuguero, with up to two nights' stay between journeys. Alfred Brown Robinson of *Tortuguero Odysseys Tours* (☎ 758-0824) offers US$75 overnight tours, including a cheap hotel and meals, or a day tour for US$50. Ask about discounted trips, especially for groups. *Modesto Watson* (in San José ☎ 226-0986, e *fv watson@racsa.co.cr*, w *http://members .tripod.com/~Francescatours*) has been recommended and speaks good English. Other boat operators who have been recommended include *Willis Rankin* (☎ 798-1556), and *Mario Rivas*.

# Northern Caribbean

## PARISMINA

This village is at the mouth of the Río Parismina, about 50km northwest of Limón. It boasts some of the better fishing lodges on the Costa Rican Caribbean. Record-breaking Atlantic tarpon and snook are the fish to go for. Offshore reef fishing is also good. Traditionally, the tarpon season is from January to mid-May and the season for big snook is from September to November. However, all the locals will tell you that the fishing is good any month of the year, because these fish don't migrate. Parismina's proximity to the south end of Parque Nacional Tortuguero means that nature tours can also be enjoyed (see listings under Places to Stay & Eat, below). Unless you are into sportfishing, though, there's not much to do here and accommodations are expensive. Spouses accompanying anglers often go on a Tortuguero trip, which is cheaper than the fishing rates.

### Places to Stay & Eat

*Río Parismina Lodge* (☎ 229-7597, fax 292-1207; in the USA ☎ 800-338-5688, 210-824-4442; e *fish@riop.com*, w *www.riop.com*) Singles/doubles: three days of fishing US$2050/3700, seven days of fishing US$3250/5900. This is a comfortable lodge that also provides local nature tours on request. The lodge, on 20 hectares, has a pool, Jacuzzi, and nature trails and is the best place to fish in Parismina. Absolutely everything is provided in the lodge's all-inclusive fishing packages (except tips for fishing guides and lodge staff), which include a night in a 1st-class San José hotel at either end of your lodge stay, plus air or land transfers from San José. Extra days of fishing cost US$550 per person. Reduced rates are offered for nonfishers.

*Jungle Tarpon Lodge* (☎ 380-7636, in the USA ☎ 800-544-2261, e *greatalaska@ greatalaska.com*, w *www.jungletarpon.com*) Sportfishing from US$1200 for three days/two nights. This lodge is comfortable and specializes in small groups of up to 10 anglers at a time.

*Caribbean Expedition Lodge* (☎ 232-8118, in the USA ☎ 361-884-4277, e *lodge@*

*costaricasportfishing.com*, ⓦ *www.costarica sportfishing.com)* Packages from US$1400 for three days fishing, including air charters from San José. Another option, this lodge has six spacious cabins.

If you just want budget accommodations, there are a couple of cheap and pretty basic *cabinas*, which charge about US$20 for a double with shared cold shower or a bit more with private hot shower. Ask around – the **Thorny Rose Inn** is one.

### Getting There & Away

You pass Parismina on the canal boats to Tortuguero from points farther south; the dock at Caño Blanco, which is reached by bus, is only a few minutes by boat to the fishing lodges. Some visitors fly in to the local airstrip (charter flights only).

### PARQUE NACIONAL TORTUGUERO

This recently expanded 31,187-hectare coastal park (plus about 52,000 hectares of marine area) is the most important breeding ground for the green sea turtle in all of the Caribbean. There are eight species of marine turtles in the world; six nest in Costa Rica and of those, four are in Tortuguero (see the Wildlife Guide at the back of this book). The many turtles give the national park its name. The Tortuguero nesting population of the green turtle *(Chelonia mydas)*

Green sea turtle

has been continuously monitored since 1955 and is the most studied. Comparatively little is known about other marine turtles.

Parque Nacional Tortuguero is under extreme pressure. With only a handful of personnel to work in the three ranger stations, the protected area is being encroached upon by loggers, banana and oil-palm plantations, ranches, colonists, and some tourist developments. Arriving by air is frightening. If you fly in, you'll see nothing but plantations and cattle ranches until you reach the Caribbean. At the last possible moment, there is a narrow swath of coastal land that looks relatively undisturbed. Visitors arriving by boat are treated to rainforest views along the canal banks, but a few minutes' walk into the forest will reveal that these

---

### Pacuare Nature Reserve

This 800-hectare private reserve is near the mouth of the Río Pacuare, about 30km northwest of Puerto Limón. It is owned by the Endangered Wildlife Trust, which works to protect the area in partnership with the British charity Rainforest Concern. The highlight is a 6km-long beach that is used for nesting by giant leatherback turtles from March to June, and by green turtles from June to August.

Volunteers work at the reserve, patrolling the beaches, moving nests to safer areas, tagging turtles, and monitoring hatchlings from mid-March through July of each year. Rustic but comfortable accommodations and food are provided, and volunteers are requested to stay for at least one week and pay US$100 per week toward living expenses. In 1998, 133 volunteers from 17 countries worked on the reserve. If you're interested, contact Rainforest Concern (ⓔ info@rainforest concern.org, ⓦ www.rainforestconcern.org), 27 Lansdowne Crescent, London W11 2NS, England. In Costa Rica, contact La Reserva Pacuare (☎ 233-0451, fax 221-2820, ⓔ fdezlaw@ sol.racsa.co.cr), Avenidas 8 & 10, Calle 19, No 837, San José.

The reserve has a lodge with three double rooms and a kitchen available for rent; a cook is provided on request. Also, two cottages sleep larger groups (maximum 20). Contact the reserve about availability and rates. Minimum stays of one week are the norm. Trails from the lodge lead along the beach and into the forest, where a rich variety of bird life and various mammals can be observed.

views are cosmetic in many cases. The western parts of the national park are being eroded, and it has been difficult to stop this effectively. The recent addition of almost 12,000 hectares to the west and northwest sides of the park will help as a buffer against continued loss of habitat and illegal logging.

Devastatingly, the inhabitants of inland Caribbean-slope villages such as Cariari and towns such as Guápiles have illegally tried to push a road through the national park to Tortuguero village. The completion of such a road would change the tranquil nature of the village and encourage illegal logging and colonization, and the abundant wildlife would soon be forced away. You can show your support for maintaining the wilderness by discussing conservation issues with local boat and tour operators, and whomever else you come across on your journey.

Despite these problems, here you can still see more wildlife, especially birds, monkeys, sloths, and reptiles, than you can in many other parts of Central America. The park is home to about half the bird and reptile species found in Costa Rica.

## Orientation & Information

'Humid' is the driest word that could truthfully be used to describe Tortuguero. With annual rainfall of up to 6000mm in the northern part of the park, it is one of the wettest areas in the country. Rainwear is a must year-round and an umbrella is a good idea. There is no dry season, although it does rain less in February, March, and also September. The average temperature is 26°C (79°F), but it is often hotter during the middle of the day. Bring insect repellent – you'll use it.

There are two ranger stations visited by travelers. The Jalova station is on the canal at the south entrance to the national park. Here you'll find a short nature trail, a bathroom, and drinking water.

Most visitors go to the Cuatro Esquinas station (and park headquarters), which is at the north end of the park, along the canal. (The village of Tortuguero is a few minutes' walk away, just beyond the park boundary.) Information is available here. From the headquarters there is a 2km loop nature trail (returning along the beach) that is maintained but is often flooded or otherwise impassable during rainy months.

Although the beaches are extensive, they are not suitable for swimming. The surf is rough, the currents strong, and, if that's not enough to faze you, sharks regularly patrol the waters. Despite this, the occasional adventurous surfer has ridden some waves here; the surfing is good but the shark risk keeps most folks away.

**Fees** The entrance fee to the park is US$7 per day – most visitors pay the fee at the headquarters. In 1998, nocturnal boat visits into the park were prohibited because the bright lights, engine exhaust, and noise were impacting the wildlife. In 1999, a nine-month experimental program was initiated to allow a limited number of night tours, but only in boats with a maximum of 17 passengers and accompanied by a guide and park ranger, using quiet, electric motors and one light of 200,000 candlepower or less. This experimental program was unsuccessful, and night visits by boat are not currently allowed.

In season only, land tours at night to see turtles are permitted. Park fees for two-hour night tours are US$5, and several local lodges operate these tours (if there is a demand) at costs as high as US$30 per person. Local guides, who are knowledgeable, charge US$10.

For detailed information on organized tours of Parque Nacional Tortuguero, see the Tortuguero Area section, later in this chapter.

## Turtle Watching

Travelers are allowed to visit the nesting beaches at night and watch the turtles lay their eggs or observe the eggs hatching. However, camera flashes, video cameras, and flashlights are prohibited by law, as they disturb the egg-laying process and attract predators to the hatchlings. Night visits are allowed from February through November. The best season to visit the beaches is July to mid-October, when green turtles lay in large numbers; the highest numbers nest from late July to late August. Guides (available by asking anyone in the area) must accompany visitors to the viewing areas. Some of the nesting beaches are outside the park.

In the 1980s, scientists noted that anywhere from only a few hundred to over 3000 female green turtles came to the Tortuguero nesting beach during any given season, compared to tens of thousands in earlier decades. Because of conservation efforts, however, by the mid-1990s it was estimated that 15,000 to 20,000 were nesting here annually.

The story of the decline and return of the green turtle and the setting up of turtle conservation projects in the Caribbean is told in two popular books by Archie Carr, a herpetologist who did much work with turtles and played an important role in getting Tortuguero protected. The books are *The Windward Road: Adventures of a Naturalist on Remote Caribbean Shores* and *The Sea Turtle: So Excellent a Fishe.*

If you are unable to visit during the green turtle breeding season, the next best time is February to July, when leatherback turtles nest in small numbers (the peak is from mid-April to mid-May). Hawksbill turtles nest sporadically from March to October, and loggerhead turtles are also sometimes seen. Stragglers have been observed during every month of the year. Only the green turtle nests in large numbers; the other species tend to arrive singly.

## Watching Other Wildlife

Turtles are by no means the only attraction at Tortuguero. The national park offers great wildlife viewing and birding opportunities, both from the few trails within the park and on guided or paddle-yourself boat trips. All three of the local species of monkeys (howler, spider, and white-faced capuchin) are often seen. Sloths, anteaters, and kinkajous are also sighted. Manatees are protected but not often seen. Peccaries, tapirs, and various members of the cat family have also been recorded, but you have to be exceptionally lucky to see them.

Also of great interest are the area's reptiles and amphibians. Apart from the sea turtles, there are seven species of freshwater turtle. Look for them lined up on a log by the river bank, sunning themselves. As you see them, they see you, and one by one they plop off the log and into the protective river. You may also see lizards, caimans, crocodiles, and snakes, including the deadly fer-de-lance (a pit viper). A variety of colorful little frogs and toads hop around in the rainforest, including tiny poison-arrow frogs and large marine toads. About 60 species of amphibian have been recorded in the park.

More than 400 bird species have been recorded in the Tortuguero area. These include oceanic species, such as the magnificent frigatebird and royal tern; shorebirds such as plovers and sandpipers; river birds such as kingfishers, jacanas, and anhingas; and inland forest species such as hummingbirds and manakins.

Many migrant birds from North America pass through here, either on their way south from the North American winter or returning to the north for summer.

The variety of habitat within the park contributes to the diversity of birds. On just one boat ride near Tortuguero, I saw six species of heron, including the chestnut-bellied heron, which Stiles' and Skutch's *A Guide to the Birds of Costa Rica* describes as an uncommon-to-rare resident of the humid lowland forests of the Caribbean slopes.

More than 400 tree species and at least 2200 species of other plants have been recorded, but there are undoubtedly more to be identified.

## Places to Stay

*Camping* costs US$2 per person. There's a camping area at the park headquarters – just make sure your tent is waterproof. Drinking water, showers, and toilets are provided. However, in wet months (which is most of them) the camping area is subject to flooding and is not recommended.

Just outside the northern boundary of the park in the village of Tortuguero (see the following section), you can find basic, inexpensive accommodations, food, boats, and guides. Between 1km and 4km north of the village are several comfortable and more expensive jungle lodges.

## TORTUGUERO AREA

The 600 inhabitants of the sleepy little village of Tortuguero, just north of the national park, make most of their living from turtles and tourism. They work in the hotels and tour lodges, or as park rangers or researchers, or as guides and boat operators, and a few do a little farming and fishing. Generally, a good balance has been struck among the interests of the local people, visitors, and the turtles. This is mainly because access is limited to boats and planes.

Instead of harvesting the turtles, the people exploit them and the surrounding park in nondestructive yet economically satisfactory ways. The community takes pride in 'its' turtles and national park.

## Information

In the center of Tortuguero village is an informative kiosk explaining the natural history, cultural history, geography, and climate of the region.

Apart from the kiosk, several places offer local information. The **Tortuguero Information Center**, in front of the Catholic church (ask anyone), can recommend local guides and businesses catering to independent travelers. Local guides use dugout canoes or skiffs with electric motors to avoid disturbing wildlife while allowing tourists to get good views. Canadian biologist Daryl Loth, who has lived in the area for years, leads inexpensive local tours and knows the best local guides. He can be contacted at the Information Center or online at Ⓔsⓐfari@racsa.co.cr, Ⓦ http://tortuguero_s.tripod .com/. You can try phoning ☎ 392-3201, but phone service is erratic, so keep trying if you don't reach him first try.

Also ask in the Jungle Shop, which has handicrafts and souvenirs, and the Paraíso Tropical Store (☎ 710-0323), which has a wide selection of souvenirs and sundries, and sells Travelair tickets. A tiny park outside this store has towering bird statues and benches. The Super Morpho Pulpería, in the center of the village, has a public phone and the best food selection (though no alcohol). Booze is sold across the street in the rough La Culebra Bar.

Few places have phones – most listed are cellular phones, radiophones, or message phones. At the time of research, the telephone company, ICE, was slated to link Tortuguero up to the rest of the country by the end of 2002, so private phone lines should become available then. There is a small police post and a medical center – the latter has a doctor one day a week (currently Wednesday), so plan your illnesses with care.

## Caribbean Conservation Corporation

The Caribbean Conservation Corporation (*CCC;* ☎ *710-0547, in the USA* ☎ *800-678-7853,* Ⓔ *ccc@cccturtle.org,* Ⓦ *www.cccturtle .org; admission US$1; open 10am-12:30pm & 2pm-5pm Mon-Sat, 2pm-5pm Sun*) operates a research station about 1km north of Tortuguero village. The station has a small but well-run visitor center and museum explaining the turtle conservation and research work; an 18-minute video (in English or Spanish) about the history of local turtle conservation is shown on request. The research station teaches courses in various biological fields – contact the CCC for information. Visitors with a background or interest in biology may be able to stay in the CCC's *dorms* (four to six beds each) if they're not full.

From March through October, there are volunteer programs for people interested in assisting scientists with turtle tagging and research. Volunteers pay US$1360 to US$2180 for seven to 21 days, including transfers from San José, one night's lodging

**TORTUGUERO AREA**

Estación Biológica Caño Palma

Caño La Palma

Cerro Tortuguero 119m

Trail

0        1        2 km
0       .5       1 mile

To Barra del Colorado

Isla Chica

Laguna del Tortuguero

CARIBBEAN SEA

Tortuga Lodge & Gardens

Airstrip

Laguna Penitencia

**Parque Nacional Tortuguero**

■ Ilan Ilan Lodge

Caribbean Paradise Eco-Lodge

● Laguna Lodge

● Manati Lodge

Tortuguero Caribe Lodge

Jungle Lodge ■

Mawamba Lodge ■

Caribbean Conservation Corporation Research Station & Visitor Center

Pachira Lodge

Evergreen Lodge

Caño Chiquero

**Tortuguero Village**

Cuatro Esquinas Ranger Station (Park Headquarters & Entrance)

Trail

Isla Cuatro Esquinas

Caño Chiquero

**Parque Nacional Tortuguero**

Laguna del Tortuguero

Caño Mora

Río Tortuguero

To Moín

in San José at the beginning and end of the trip, and room and board in the research station dorms. (Air-conditioned rooms are available for an extra charge.) There are also bird-migration programs from March through May and August through October costing US$1210 to US$1975 for seven to 21 days. These are popular projects, and advance reservations must be made through the US office of the CCC.

## Canoeing & Kayaking

There are several signs in Tortuguero, just north of the entrance to the park, announcing boats for hire. You can paddle yourself in a dugout canoe for about US$2 per person per hour, or go with a guide for a little more. Miss Junie's and the Manati Lodge (see Places to Stay & Eat, below) have plastic kayaks for rent, as do other places – ask around.

## Hydrobiking

Mount a bicycle frame onto a catamaran-like set of pontoons and you get – a hydro-bike! Pedaling propels the craft forward, like a paddleboat; you steer by simply turning the handlebars, and the whole contraption is surprisingly stable (you can stand up with no wobbling). This is a silent way to glide around the canals; the hydrobikes include a basket for binoculars, a camera, and a water bottle. Rent them from the Paraíso Tropical Store for US$9 an hour. Tortuga Lodge & Gardens also has hydrobikes for its guests; they may rent to nonguests if more bikes are available. A tip: Ask for a ride in a motor boat to where you want to go, deep in the canals, and arrange to be picked up later.

## Hiking

Apart from visiting the waterways and beaches of the park, hikers can climb the 119m **Cerro Tortuguero**, about 6km north of the village. You need to hire a boat and guide to get there. Cerro Tortuguero is the highest point right on the coast anywhere north of Puerto Limón – it actually lies just within the southern border of Refugio Nacional de Fauna Silvestre Barra del Colorado. The path is steep and usually muddy, but it offers good views of the forest, canals, sea, birds, monkeys, and other wildlife.

## Organized Tours

Many travel agencies in San José and elsewhere offer tours of the Tortuguero area, but they normally end up subcontracting (at the same price) with the companies associated with the lodges listed under Places to Stay & Eat (see below).

Tours from San José include one-day and overnight options. For those with limited time, a rushed day trip is offered by **Caño Blanco Marina** (☎ 259-8216, 256-9444, 284-2017 cellular, fax 259-8229, e tucanti@racsa.co.cr). This tour includes a dawn flight from San José to Tortuguero, a park tour with a bilingual guide, breakfast and lunch in Tortuguero, a visit to the CCC museum (at the visitor center), a return along the canals by speedboat to Caño Blanco, continuing to San José by bus and arriving at 5:45pm. This costs US$89, plus US$7 park and US$1 museum fees.

Overnight options of one, two, or three nights are available, with the three-day/two-night option the most popular; it provides a reasonably good look at the area.

The cheaper three-day/two-night tours start with a drive from San José to one of several possible docks on the canals, where you board a boat for a two- to five-hour journey (depending on departure point and power of the boat) through the canals to Tortuguero. The journey itself is part of the adventure – the boat slows down for photographs, and a bilingual guide identifies what you see. On the second day, guided walking and boat tours of the area are provided (these may or may not be included in the price). A night visit to the beach is added during the turtle-nesting season, or a night canoe tour might be offered for an extra charge. You return by boat and bus on the third day. More expensive tours will utilize more comfortable lodges, offer better guides, and cut down on travel time by flying one-way (all those described in the following sections can be upgraded with a one-way or roundtrip flight at extra cost). During the low season, 'green season' discounts are offered – shop around in San José.

**Fran and Modesto Watson** (☎/fax 226-0986, e fvwatson@racsa.co.cr, w http://members.tripod.com/~Francescatours), who own and operate the riverboat *Francesca*, offer guided overnight tours that include transport from San José to Moín by van, a

## COTERC

The Canadian Organization for Tropical Education and Rainforest Conservation (COTERC) is a nonprofit organization with many local education, research, and conservation activities. COTERC operates the Estación Biológica Caño Palma in the Caño La Palma area just north of Cerro Tortuguero and about 7km north of Tortuguero village. Although the biological station is actually within the southern boundary of Refugio Nacional de Fauna Silvestre Barra del Colorado, access is easiest from Tortuguero.

The station accommodates researchers, student groups, and volunteers, who pay a nominal fee for food and board and help with the upkeep of the station and assist ongoing research projects. Other guests (nature tourists) are accepted when space is available. The buildings are 200m from the Caribbean, but separated from it by a river. Rivers, streams, and lagoons can be explored, and there is a trail system into the rainforest. Researchers, volunteers, and visitors stay in simple dormitories with bunks and bedding, and outdoor showers and bathrooms. There is also a covered area with four hammocks, a study area, and a kitchen and dining area. The rate is US$45 per person per day including three meals and use of the trails. Guided boat excursions can be arranged.

You can reach the station by hiring a boat from Tortuguero. If you make prior arrangements, the staff will pick you up either at Tortuguero airport or village for US$10.

COTERC relies on members and donors to run its programs. Members receive the quarterly newsletter, *Raphia*. For further information and reservations, contact COTERC (in Canada ☎ 905-831-8809, fax 905-831-4203, ℮ info@coterc.org, ⍵ www.coterc.org, PO Box 335, Pickering, ON L1V 2R6, Canada). Drop-in visitors can usually find space.

boat ride to Tortuguero, lodging at the Laguna Lodge (or other), a two-hour boat tour of the park, entry fees, and meals for US$170 to US$185 per person, inclusive. Their guiding services are knowledgeable and they can customize tours.

Budget or independent travelers can stay in Tortuguero village and hire local guides. See also the Moín section, earlier in this chapter, for tours from Puerto Limón.

### Places to Stay & Eat

**Tortuguero Village** Budget travelers normally stay in the village. You might be able to bargain the following prices down by US$1 to US$2 per person per day if you're staying for a few days or in the low season.

*Cabinas Mariscar (reservations in San José ☎ 290-2804, 296-2626 messages)* Rooms US$6 per person. This friendly, family-run place has small, basic but clean rooms with fans and shared baths. They also have a couple of more expensive rooms with private baths.

*Cabinas Sabina* Doubles/triples US$10/15. This place, near the ocean, is basic but clean and is the biggest in the village, with 31 rooms. However, the owner

is unfriendly (locals have been heard to say, 'fighting is what keeps her alive').

*Tropical Lodge* Rooms US$5 per person. This lodge, just north of the park entrance, has a few basic cabins.

*Cabinas Tortuguero* Rooms US$10 per person. This is a good, clean place.

*Cabinas Joruki (☎ 233-3333, leave message for Sherman Johnson)* Rooms US$10 per person. Rooms have private cold showers and are behind a riverfront restaurant, which serves reasonably priced meals.

Rooms with baths are found at *Cabinas Pancana* and the slightly better *Cabinas Aracari (☎ 798-3059)*, both with only a few rooms; the rate is about US$10 per person or less.

*Miss Junie's (☎ 710-0523)* Singles/doubles US$25/35. At the north end of the village is Miss Junie's, featuring 12 clean rooms with fans and private baths. Miss Junie is Tortuguero's best-known cook, and she (and now her daughter) prepares good Caribbean-style meals (such as fish in coconut sauce) for about US$5. You'll need to order a meal several hours in advance or even the day before.

*Casa Marbella (☎ 392-3201, ℮ safari@racsa.co.cr, ⍵ http://casamarbella.tripod.com)*

US$30/48 single/double. Across from the Catholic church, this four-room B&B features light, airy rooms with private solar-heated showers and a full breakfast. Some rooms can sleep up to four (in bunk beds). A common room offers board games. At the time of research, Internet access and satellite TV were scheduled for installation in 2003. The owners are biologist Daryl Loth and his wife.

Restaurants charge about US$3 per meal, and it is basic food. One of the best cheap places is *La Caribeña*, across from the Super Morpho Pulpería. Slightly more upscale are *La Casona*, by the soccer field, and Miss Junie's. *The Vine*, which is fairly new, serves pastries and also sandwiches. There are a few others.

**North of the Village** About 1km north of Tortuguero is *Mawamba Lodge* (☎/fax 710-7282; in San José ☎ 223-2421, fax 222-5463; W *www.grupomawamba.com*) 3-day/2-night package US$252, 2-day/1-night package US$201; rates are per person based on double occupancy. This place caters mainly to prearranged tours but will rent you a room if it is not full. There are 54 pleasant and spacious rooms with fans and private hot showers. Verandahs with hammocks and rocking chairs allow for relaxation. The lodge has a good restaurant and a second dining-bar area next to an attractive swimming pool, complete with a waterfall and a bridge to swim under. The food and tropical drinks are definitely tasty. There is a souvenir shop and the beach is 100m away (not suitable for swimming here or anywhere in the Tortuguero area). An air-conditioned conference room enables local guides to give natural history presentations. This is the best lodge within walking distance of the village. Its three-day/two-night package includes a breakfast stop at the company's Río Danta Restaurant, near Parque Nacional Braulio Carrillo, and begins the canal portion from a private dock at Matina.

*Laguna Lodge* (☎ 710-0355; in San José ☎ 225-3740, fax 283-8031) 3-day/2-night package US$234, 2-day/1-night package US$187; rates are per person based on double occupancy. This lodge is about 2km north of the village, and has about 50 attractive rooms with fans, hardwood floors, and tiled private bathrooms with hot water. The lodge's rustic restaurant serves good tico food, family style, and there's an attractive free-form pool. Guides speak decent English. Walk-in clients are accepted on a space-available basis.

**Other Areas** The remaining lodgings all require a boat ride to get to and from Tortuguero village, which means you are pretty much stuck in the lodge for meals and other activities, though you can arrange transportation to the village (at extra cost) if you want.

*Manati Lodge* (☎/fax 383-0330) Singles/doubles US$25/35, triples/quads US$15 per person. This friendly and *tranquilo* lodge has eight simple rooms (four doubles, three triples, and a quintuple), each with a warm private shower and fan. The rate includes breakfast. Lunches and dinners cost US$7 each. Trails lead to the canals on either side of the lodge. Kayaks are available for US$5 for two hours. The grounds are attractive, and meals feature good tico home cooking. This lodge is used as a base for research on the endangered manatee and is recommended for folks interested in conservation and local issues. **Ecole Travel** (☎ 223-2240, 255-4172, ☎/fax 223-4128, e *ecolecr@racsa.co.cr, Calle 7, Avenidas Central & 1*) arranges overnight tours here for US$95/125 for one/two nights per person, double occupancy. Tours start and end at the dock at Moín (Ecole gives you up-to-date instructions on how to get there by public transport) and do not include lunch or dinner, but do include breakfast and some local excursions. Ecole Travel also does the same trip using other lodges for a room upgrade.

*Ilan Ilan Lodge* 3-day/2-night package US$224 per person, double occupancy. This lodge has 24 medium-sized, plain but clean rooms with fans and cold private showers. The hotel sits on about 8 hectares of nicely landscaped grounds and has a swimming pool with Jacuzzi. Packages with mainly Spanish-speaking guides are arranged in advance with **Mitur Tours** (☎ 255-2031, 255-2262, fax 255-1946, e *mitour@racsa.co.cr, W www.mitour.com, Paseo Colón, Calles 20 & 22, San José*). Walk-ins can be accommodated on a space-available basis.

*Jungle Lodge* 3-day/2-night packages US$240 per person, double occupancy; 2-day/1-night packages about US$50 less. The

50 rooms here have hot showers and fans and are nicer than those at Ilan Ilan Lodge. The grounds have a small swimming pool, and several dozen trees are numbered so that you can identify the species using a list (which was unavailable when I stopped by). A *restaurant* serves buffet-style meals, and a separate bar features a small dance floor and free dance lessons (so the bartender tells me). As with others described above, this lodge accepts walk-ins but relies on its package-tour groups; packages are booked through **Cotur** (☎ 233-0133, fax 233-0778, e cotour@racsa.co.cr, Calle 38 & Paseo Colón, San José). This company often services large groups.

**Pachira Lodge** (☎ 221-7319, 376-0351 cellular, fax 257-3525, e pachira@ahcostarica .com) 3-day/2-night package from San José, including the usual services, US$239 per person, double occupancy, or US$313 for one person. This place has some of the prettiest rooms in the Tortuguero area, with pleasant pastels offering a break from the interminable wood. It has 44 airy rooms with good ventilation and hot water, and a spacious restaurant-bar area with good food. In addition, it operates the *Evergreen Lodge*, across the Laguna Penitencia. Walk-ins are often accommodated there.

**Caribbean Paradise Eco-Lodge** (☎ 221-4420, fax 221-4315, ☎/fax 290-7670, e caribbeanparadis@racsa.co.cr) Doubles US$60; 3-day/2-night package from San José about US$200 per person, double occupancy, or US$239 for one person. This lodge has 16 simple rooms with fans and hot showers, an attractive thatched restaurant, and a small swimming pool. The base rate includes breakfast. It will arrange a complete

**Tortuguero Caribe Lodge** (☎ 385-4676; in San José ☎ 259-0820, 259-1811) Rooms without/with bath US$14/24 per person, packages available. This rustic place just south of Caribbean Paradise Eco-Lodge offers nine simple cabins, two with private bath. Good home-cooked meals cost US$10 each (this includes a wide spread; you can eat more cheaply if you ask for a simple dish).

**Tortuga Lodge & Gardens** (☎ 710-6861) Singles/doubles/triples US$95/115/133, packages available. This was the first comfortable lodge built in the area and remains the cushiest place to stay. It offers superior rooms that are spacious, screened, and cross-

ventilated, and have ceiling fans and large tiled bathrooms with hot showers. Rocking chairs and hammocks wait invitingly in covered walkways outside all the rooms. An airy bar-restaurant is right on the riverside, and there's verandah dining next to the water. Rates here are for the high season. Large and delicious all-you-can-eat meals cost US$13 for breakfast, US$18 for lunch, and US$21 for dinner.

Beyond the restaurant, an inviting boulder-edged free-form swimming pool flows serenely by, mirroring the languid movement of the canals. The lodge has won numerous awards for supporting the local community through sustainable development, hiring locals, and supporting local conservation projects. The well-prepared food is plentiful, served family style, and includes plenty of vegetables and local specialties. The staff and guides are helpful and well trained, and many speak English. The lodge is on 20 hectares of landscaped gardens, with ornamental tropical trees, palms, shrubs, orchids, and other flowers that attract birds, lizards, and butterflies. A quiet pond often has a caiman floating lazily in it or a toad hiding nearby. The tropical rainforest begins beyond the gardens, and a troop of howler monkeys is usually heard and often seen near the bedrooms. You'll find red and black poison-arrow frogs in the forest behind the lodge.

Many guests come on packages with tours included. Tours that cost extra include night turtle walks in season (US$20 per person), two-hour dawn wildlife boat tours (US$15 per person), guided private boat rental (US$10 per hour per person, two people minimum) and various half-day excursions (US$45). Tortuga Lodge also provides fishing boats and guides, who often go up to the Barra del Colorado area (less than an hour away) if that's where the best fishing is. See the Barra del Colorado Area section, later in this chapter, for more fishing information. Boat rental for **fishing** (including guide and tackle) is US$45 per hour (minimum two hours, maximum two people) for local canal fishing; US$189 per person (two minimum) for a full day of inshore fishing; and US$219 per person (four minimum) or US$319 per person (two minimum) for deep-sea fishing with highly experienced guides. Fishing depends on weather and other local conditions.

Costa Rica Expeditions (see Organized Tours in the Getting Around chapter) owns the Tortuga Lodge and has the best-trained guides. A complete three-day/two-night package including roundtrip transport between the lodge and San José (by air one-way and by boat/bus the other), hotel transfers, a separate guided boat tour, meals, and park fee, costs US$379 per person, double occupancy. Extra days cost US$110, including three meals.

## Getting There & Away

**Air** The small airstrip is 4km north of Tortuguero village, across the canal from Tortuga Lodge & Gardens. Travelair and SANSA both have daily flights from San José, some connecting to Barra Colorado. The designated ticket-sales agent for Travelair in Tortuguero is the Paraíso Tropical Store (☎ 710-0323). SANSA has an office in Barra Colorado (☎ 710-7711). Hotels can often arrange scheduled flights out, and charters are available.

**Boat** See Organized Tours, earlier in this section, or the Moín section, earlier in this chapter, for details on transport by passenger boat.

At the time of writing, the cheapest way to arrive and leave from Tortuguero was to take a bus from the Atlántico Norte bus terminal in San José to Cariari (about US$2.50, two hours) first thing in the morning, then take a bus from Cariari to La Geest (about US$1.50, 90 minutes). La Geest is a dock in a banana plantation on the Río Suerte (locally called Caño Suerte). Here, you will be met by boat captains who run boats to Tortuguero for about US$10 per person. Some unscrupulous operators will tell you that you must buy a package tour to be sure of getting accommodations, park entry, return trip, etc. This is simply not true. The cheapest way to go is to pay for a one-way boat ride and then decide where you want to stay when you arrive in Tortuguero.

Once you are ready to return from Tortuguero, ask at one of the information centers or your hotel about a boat operator to take you back to La Geest.

## BARRA DEL COLORADO AREA

At 90,400 hectares (including the frontier zone with Nicaragua), Refugio Nacional de Fauna Silvestre Barra del Colorado (locally called Barra, which also refers to the neighboring village of Barra del Colorado) is the biggest national wildlife refuge in Costa Rica. It is virtually an extension of Parque Nacional Tortuguero, and the two combine to form a regional conservation unit.

There are several differences between Tortuguero and Barra del Colorado. Barra is more remote, more difficult to visit cheaply, and is not as famous for its marine turtles. (Although they are found in the reserve, they don't nest in large numbers.)

Despite being a national wildlife refuge, Barra has traditionally attracted visitors for sportfishing rather than for natural history tours, although this is not as true as it once was. Barra receives as much rainfall as Tortuguero, and has much of the same variety of wildlife, best seen from a boat. The birding is excellent, and visitors should get good looks at monkeys, sloths, caimans, and other wildlife. The rainforest and river scenery is lovely. Although fishing is still the bread and butter of most of the area's lodges, wildlife tours here are attracting increasing numbers of visitors and are less likely to encounter other tour groups than in Tortuguero. If you want to do a wildlife tour, let the lodge staff know in advance, as most guides are more oriented toward fishing (though many of the locals are adept at spotting wildlife).

The northern border of the refuge is the Río San Juan (also the border with Nicaragua). This area was politically sensitive during the 1980s, which contributed to the isolation of the reserve. Since the relaxing of Sandinista-Contra hostilities in 1990, it has become straightforward to journey north along the Río Sarapiquí and east along the San Juan to the reserve. This is an interesting trip (see Entering Nicaragua, later).

The western part of the refuge is less accessible, but that doesn't mean that no one goes there. Infrared satellite photography has shown large amounts of unauthorized logging and road construction at the western boundary of the refuge. Undoubtedly, illegal logging activity is going on within Barra del Colorado, but there aren't enough reserve wardens to police the area properly. The western part of the refuge is now accessible to vehicles and there is a daily bus (road and weather conditions

Península de Osa's tropical rainforests

Root buttress, Parque Nacional Corcovado

Reserva Biológica Bosque Nuboso Monteverde

Tropical oak forests on Cerro de la Muerte

RALPH LEE HOPKINS

ALFREDO MAIQUEZ

LUKE HUNTER

RALPH LEE HOPKINS

ROB RACHOWIECKI

Costa Rica's remarkable flora includes more than 10,000 vascular plant species.

allowing) to Puerto Lindo, on the Río Colorado, in the heart of the reserve. This road brings in loggers, ranchers, farmers, and colonists and does not bode well for the western part of Barra del Colorado, but the eastern sections (where the lodges are) are swampy and not conducive to logging; that area, at least, may be less vulnerable to change.

Surprisingly, there are over 2000 inhabitants in the area, and they want the rough road to Puerto Lindo to be improved; they've petitioned the government to make the road all-weather. However, this is not in the cards in the near future; in fact, the road was badly damaged by Hurricane Mitch in 1998, and Barra remains one of the most remote parts of Costa Rica.

## Orientation & Information

The village of Barra del Colorado lies near the mouth of the Río Colorado and is divided by the river into Barra del Norte and Barra del Sur. There are no roads. The airstrip is on the south side of the river, but more people live on the north side. The area outside the village is swampy and travel is almost exclusively by boat, though some walking is possible around some of the lodges scattered in the area.

The Servicio de Parques Nacionales (SPN) maintains a small ranger station on the south side of the Río Colorado near the village. However, there are no facilities here. Officially, US$6 is charged to enter the refuge, but this has not been enforced for some time.

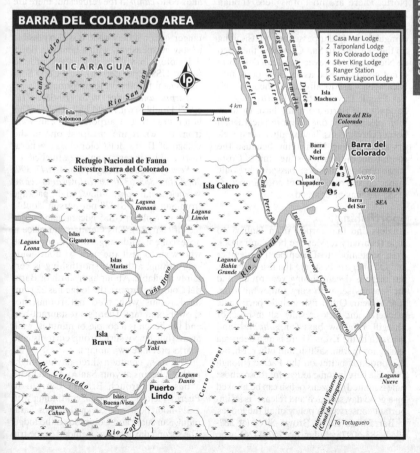

**BARRA DEL COLORADO AREA**

1 Casa Mar Lodge
2 Tarponland Lodge
3 Río Colorado Lodge
4 Silver King Lodge
5 Ranger Station
6 Samay Lagoon Lodge

CARIBBEAN LOWLANDS

From the airport, only the Tarponland and Río Colorado Lodges (see Places to Stay & Eat, below) are accessible on foot. All other lodges require a boat ride (a boat operator will be waiting for you at the airport if you have a reservation).

C&D Souvenirs (☎ 710-6592), close to the airport, has a public phone and fax and offers tourist information. There's a small grocery store about 100m away.

**Entering Nicaragua** Day trips along the Río San Juan and some offshore fishing trips enter Nicaraguan territory, but no special visa is required (though you should carry your passport for checkpoints along the San Juan). The Nicaraguan village at the mouth of the Río San Juan is San Juan del Norte. There are no hotels here, though lodging can be found with local families. San Juan del Norte is linked with the rest of Nicaragua by irregular passenger boats sailing up the San Juan to San Carlos, on the Lago de Nicaragua. However, San Juan del Norte is not normally used as an entry point into Nicaragua – ask locally about the possibilities. People traveling from Puerto Viejo de Sarapiquí to Barra normally have to show their passports at one or more Nicaraguan border checkpoints. Technically, river travelers are entering Nicaragua, because the south bank of the river is the limit of Costa Rican territory. However, passports are only inspected and recorded, but not stamped. A US$5 fee may be charged.

## Sportfishing

Anglers find that tarpon from January to June (February to May are best) and snook from September to December (September and October are best) are the fish of choice, but there is decent fishing year-round, and the seasons seem to vary somewhat from year to year. Other fish include barracuda, mackerel, and jack crevalle, all inshore; or bluegill, rainbow bass (or *guapote*), and *machaca* in the rivers. There is also deep-sea fishing for marlin, sailfish, and other fish, but this option is better on the Pacific (though available here in some lodges for those whose time is limited). Dozens of fish can be hooked on a good day, so 'catch and release' is an important conservation policy of all the lodges.

Barra-born Eddie Brown Silva (☎ 382-3350, 383-6097 cellular, fax 252-4426), who holds a world fishing record for cubera snapper, and other fishing records for Costa Rica, is well known and in great demand as a fishing captain. He rents his boat, the *Bullshark,* to anglers and arranges accommodations at various prices in local lodges. Eddie has a large following, and he is often booked up, but the other skippers available at the lodges are also knowledgeable.

## Places to Stay & Eat

**Budget & Mid-Range** Most visitors stay in one of several area lodges, which cater primarily to anglers but also to naturalists. Most of these are beyond the pocketbook of shoestring travelers, although there are a few moderately priced places.

Visitors to Barra del Colorado are allowed to *camp* in the refuge, but there are no facilities. The rangers at the station sometimes let visitors set up a tent in front of the ranger station if they want. It is also possible to stay inexpensively with a family in Barra del Colorado village if you ask around (about US$10 per person) – try C&D Souvenirs near the airport for information.

*Tarponland Lodge (☎/fax 710-6592, 710-6917)* Doubles with cold bath US$45. This hotel, next to the airport (you can walk from there), is the cheapest one in the village of Barra del Colorado. A general store and basic restaurant are attached.

*Samay Lagoon Lodge (☎ 384-7047, 390-9068, fax 383-6370, e info@samay.com, w www.samay.com)* 3-day/2-night package from San José US$278 per person, double occupancy, plus a US$5 Nicaraguan border fee (if charged). This German-run place is an excellent mid-range option for those who wish to visit the area without going sportfishing, although sportfishing is certainly available. About 8km south of Barra del Colorado airport, the lodge has 22 standard rooms with tiled bathrooms, hot showers, and fans. There's a restaurant-bar, and the beach is a couple of minutes' walk away (but heavy surf, strong currents, and sharks preclude swimming).

The most common three-day/two-night package begins at your San José hotel with a bus ride through Braulio Carrillo to Puerto Viejo de Sarapiquí, continuing with a 3½-hour boat ride down the Ríos Sarapiquí, San Juan, and Colorado to the lodge. The second day includes a guided canoe trip

## Sleeping in a Houseboat

The *Rain Goddess* is a 19.5m-long, 5.4m-wide air-conditioned houseboat that plies the waters of Tortuguero and Barra del Colorado, allowing guests to see the area in comfort. There are six spacious cabins, four with a queen-size and single bed, and two with a double bed (no bunks here!). Each cabin has its own sink, and there are three shared bathrooms, each with hot shower. There is an elegant dining salon and bar, and the chef does a first-class job. The owner, Alfredo Lopez, is an affable medical doctor who sometimes cruises along with the guests and offers free medical services to locals in the remote settlements visited, which means that the houseboat is a welcome sight to local residents.

Both sportfishing and natural history cruises are offered, with a minimum of six and maximum of 12 passengers for the fishing trips and a minimum of eight for the natural history tours. The latter are accompanied by bilingual naturalist guides. If you arrange your own minimum-sized group, you can rent the whole boat; otherwise, you can share with other travelers. Small boats are towed both for fishing and jungle exploration.

Three nights with three full days of fishing, plus a night in a San José hotel and flights to/from Barra, cost US$1750 per angler (US$850 for nonanglers), including all airport transfers, meals, and an open bar. Basic fishing tackle is provided. The same tour for five nights and five days of fishing costs US$2250/1070 per angler/nonangler. Extra days cost US$350/110. Three-day/two-night natural history tours leave San José by bus to Puerto Viejo de Sarapiquí, where an express boat connects guests with the *Rain Goddess* on the Río Colorado in early afternoon. On the second and third days, the boat cruises through the Barra area and back to Puerto Viejo, where passengers board an afternoon bus to San José. The cost is US$475 per person, all-inclusive.

For further information and reservations, contact Blue Wing International (☎ 231-4299, fax 231-3816, in the USA ☎ 877-258-9464, 🖳 www.bluwing.com).

---

and guided hike into the rainforest, and the third-day return takes you back the way you came. The package includes meals, lodging, transportation, and a tour. Extra days cost US$75 per day, including meals and canoe use. Budget travelers can arrange a similar tour for US$199, but they must make their own way to Puerto Viejo de Sarapiquí, and they'll only get one guided tour. You can fly one (or both) ways for extra cost.

Guided horseback riding, fishing, and other tours can be arranged. Anglers can set up fishing trips from US$295 per day, including lodging and meals, plus a one-time US$40 fishing-license fee, plus transportation. The lodge will also arrange combination tours to other areas.

**Top End** *Casa Mar Lodge (☎ 381-1380; for reservations in the USA ☎ 800-543-0282, 714-578-1881, fax 800-367-2299, 714-525-5783; 2634 W Orangethorpe No 6, Fullerton, CA 92833,* 🖳 *casamar@orbitcostarica.com,* 🖳 *www.orbitcostarica.com/casamar.htm)* Packages: singles/doubles US$3640/5530 for 7 days, US$1700/2650 for 3 days. This small

sportfishing lodge with six duplex cabins is set in a pleasant 2.8-hectare garden that attracts lots of birds; ecotourists stay here for that reason. Rooms all have fans and tiled hot showers; all-you-can-eat home-cooked meals are included in the rates. Casa Mar is open year-round. Its seven-day packages include transfers from the Barra del Colorado airport, all fishing, accommodations, meals, and an open bar. Trips of other lengths can be arranged. The lodge staff will make San José hotel reservations and SANSA or private air-charter arrangements (at additional cost) upon request.

***Río Colorado Lodge** (☎/fax 710-6879; in San José ☎ 231-5987, 232-4063; in the USA ☎ 800-243-9777, fax 813-933-3280;* 🖳 *tarpon@ riocoloradolodge.com,* 🖳 *www.riocolorado lodge.com)* Rooms US$100 per nonangler; fishing packages US$1667/2854 singles/doubles for 5 nights with 3 days fishing (other packages available). Built in 1971, this is the longest-established lodge on the Caribbean coast and is well known. The lodge also has an office in the Hotel Corobicí in San José. The rambling tropical-style buildings, near the mouth of the Río Colorado, are constructed on stilts, and the carpenter who erected the original buildings was still working on lodge upkeep 30 years later – a nice touch. Cages around the covered walkways house tropical birds and some small monkeys, and a tapir named Baby wanders around.

Although dated, all 18 rooms are well maintained, air-conditioned, have fans and hot showers, and are breezy and pleasant. Some rooms have extra touches (including a honeymoon suite with wicked ceiling mirrors), and two rooms have wheelchair access. The food is all-you-can-eat, served family style. For relaxation after a day of fishing, the lodge features a happy hour with free rum drinks, a lounging area with a pool table and other games, a breezy outdoor deck, and a video room with satellite TV.

This is the only upscale lodge from which you can walk to the airport. As its brochure states, villagers often drop by with their guitars in the evening, so it doesn't take much to get a party started. The Río Colorado is run by Mississippian Dan Wise, a colorful character who meets guests with a Belgian Malinois that responds only to commands in German. This place has a reputation for being a 'party lodge,' and it is.

Most guests are anglers, but nonfishing visitors can stay here. The daily rate includes meals. For those interested in natural history, the staff can arrange local rainforest tours or transportation by boat from Puerto Viejo de Sarapiquí to the lodge, returning to San José via Tortuguero. The lodge is open year-round, and the package rates include boats, bilingual guides, all meals, accommodations, air-transfers from San José, and first and last nights' hotel in San José. They'll take you fishing in Nicaragua on request for an extra charge.

***Silver King Lodge*** *(☎/fax 381-1403, 381-0849; in the USA ☎ 888-682-7766, 800-847-3474, fax 561-369-7912; ⓔ slvrkng@racsa .co.cr, Ⓦ www.silverkinglodge.com, Aerocasillas, Dept 1597, PO Box 025216, Miami, FL 33102)* Rooms US$130; 3-day package US$2320/3700 singles/doubles, 5-day package US$3289/4700, longer stays arranged. This is the best sportfishing lodge on this coast. About 1.5km southwest of the Barra del Colorado airport, it consists of 10 duplexes that have the largest rooms of any lodge. Each room has a coffeemaker

(complimentary coffee) and a big tiled bathroom with hot water.

There is a large indoor Jacuzzi, a small outdoor pool with waterfall (surrounded by loungers and hammocks), a dining room with excellent and varied all-you-can-eat meals (cooked by a top-notch chef and served buffet- or family style with complimentary wine), and a separate screened 24-hour bar with river views and a TV/VCR with videos. Soft drinks, local beer, and rum cocktails are free all day (and night), and all boats come with an ice chest well stocked with soft drinks and beer. Covered walkways link all the areas. A nice feature is the free daily laundry service. The lodge's fax/phone and email are available for client use.

Boats used for fishing include 6m unsinkable, self-bailing skiffs with 65hp engines, suitable for two anglers and a guide, and 13 new 7m, deep-V-hull boats with 150hp engines. There's also an offshore boat with two 150hp engines, downriggers, outriggers, radio, and sonar available. All guides are English-speaking local fishers. Rods and reels are provided for regular fishing, and a wide selection of lures is sold in the lodge's tackle shop. Loaner rods and reels are free, unless you lose or break them, in which case you are charged. Fly-fishing gear is also available for anglers wishing to try for a tarpon on a fly rod!

To see the wildlife, you can use one of the Silver King's 5m aluminum canoes, either on your own or with a guide. They'll give you a lift to a recommended area and then leave you to explore if you want, picking you up at a prearranged time. Multiday canoeing tours are available for those more interested in land-based wildlife, such as monkeys, birds, and caimans, than in snook and tarpon.

The lodge, which guarantees complete satisfaction, has developed a reputation as the best in the area. It is managed and owned by genial Ray Barry, who has a fund of wild stories to entertain you with, and smiling Shawn Feliciano-Barry, one of the few women anglers on the coast. If you aren't happy with the services, they'll transport you to another Barra lodge of your choice for the remainder of your trip. The staff and service are exceptional. The lodge is usually full during the busiest months (mid-January to mid-May); you should book several months in advance to get the dates you want. This lodge closes in July and December.

Package rates include full days of fishing, all lodge facilities, roundtrip air from San José, and luxury hotels in San José at either end if needed. The only extra fees are US$40 for a fishing license, plus gratuities, the cost of lures, imported liquors, and phone calls.

Canoeing tours cost about US$50 per day with a guide, depending on the number of clients.

### Getting There & Away
**Air** Most visitors arrive by air from San José. You can charter a light plane or take a regularly scheduled flight with SANSA (☎ 710-7711) or Travelair (see the Getting Around chapter for details).

**Boat** A few of the boats from Moín to Tortuguero continue to Barra, but there is no regular service. Boats can be hired in Tortuguero to take you to Barra for about US$50 (two hours); they'll take three to five passengers. If you don't have a group and have time on your hands, you could probably do it more cheaply by asking the locals and going with them.

Occasional passenger boats go from Barra to Puerto Viejo de Sarapiquí via the Ríos San Juan and Sarapiquí, or boats can be hired to make this trip anytime. Several lodges (especially the Samay Lagoon Lodge; see Places to Stay & Eat, earlier) arrange parts of their tours to include a boat ride from Puerto Viejo.

You can also hire a boat to take you from Barra to the small riverside community of Puerto Lindo, less than an hour by motorboat up the Río Colorado. From Puerto Lindo, vehicles go to the town of Cariari, from where there are buses to Guápiles. The road is often closed after heavy rains, but provides the cheapest link with San José for local inhabitants who share transportation. There used to be a bus service between Puerto Lindo and Cariari, but Hurricane Mitch damaged the road in 1998, and now you'll need to hire a taxi with 4WD. Ask in Barra or Cariari about possibilities. This road is the subject of much contention between developers and conservationists.

# Southern Caribbean

The road southeast of Puerto Limón approximately parallels the coast, first offering views of freighters scattered outside the port – near Isla Uvita, where Columbus made a landing – and then of miles of palm trees, waves, and empty beaches.

The inhabitants of this district are predominantly blacks of Jamaican descent who settled on the Costa Rica coast in the middle of the 19th century; many speak a Creole form of English. This can be confusing at first, because some words and phrases do not have the meanings that other speakers of English are accustomed to. For example, 'All right!' means 'Hello!' and 'Okay!' means 'Goodbye!'

These settlers have traditionally lived by small-time agriculture and fishing, although catering to tourists has become an industry of its own. The influx of tourist cash helps improve the standard of living, but at a cultural cost. Traditional ways slowly become eroded and, inevitably, local people have some difficulties in adjusting to the new – and sometimes demanding or obnoxious – tourist presence. Some of the younger locals have become demanding or obnoxious as well. Nevertheless, much of the Creole and indigenous culture remains for those who look for it, particularly in cooking, music, and local knowledge of medicinal plants.

The mixture of black and indigenous culture on this stretch of coast is interesting; you can buy Bribri handicrafts and listen to reggae or calypso music, take horseback rides into local indigenous reserves, go fishing with the locals, go surfing, snorkeling, and swimming, or just hang out with the old-timers and talk. There's plenty to do, but everything is very relaxed. Take your time and you'll discover a beautiful way of life.

The wet and dry seasons are not as clearly distinguished in this region as in other parts of the country; the relative warmth of the Caribbean Sea, combined with the proximity of the Cordillera de Talamanca and the cooler air pushing over from the Pacific side, means that rain is a possibility any time of year. In the wettest season, it can rain hard for days on end. However, sun is a year-round possibility as well – even during the rainiest months, cloud patterns often adopt a regular rhythm that will give you several predictable hours of sun a day. Come prepared for rain, but hope that the best of this microclimate will smile your way.

The high season is the usual late December through April (with extra-high rates at Christmas, New Year's, and Easter). In addition, because so many foreign travelers arrive in the northern summer, many hotels charge high-season rates in August as well.

Until the 1970s, this area was quite isolated from the rest of Costa Rica. A ride in an old bus on a dirt road, a river-crossing by wobbly canoe, and a train ride were required just to get from Cahuita to Puerto Limón – this journey could take half a day. The 1987 opening of the highway from Limón to San José means that the coast is now about three hours from the capital – and the paved road leading southeast from Limón has cut the journey to Cahuita to a 45-minute drive (under good conditions), with Puerto Viejo de Talamanca only another 20 minutes farther south. Since the 1991 earthquake, which pushed some reefs in the area a foot or two out of the water, this stretch of road is still in a state of upheaval; potholes will slow down those drivers interested in safety. Recently, direct bus service from San José to the coastal villages has eliminated the need for a bus change in Limón.

Despite increasing ease of access, the area retains much of its remote, provincial, and unhurried flavor. Most Costa Ricans still head to the Pacific coast for their beach vacations, and there are few luxury hotel developments on the Caribbean.

In addition to the reserves described below, a number of organic farm communities have sprung up in the area in recent years, many of them founded by immigrants from the USA and Europe interested in creating sustainable agriculture and in tapping into local knowledge of flora, fauna, and farming methods. Some of these communities can be contacted through tour agencies in the villages.

Just northeast of Puerto Viejo, the main road turns inland toward Bribri, then turns southeast again before reaching Sixaola, on the Panama border. This border is commonly used as a gateway to the Bocas del Toro islands in Panama.

The southern Caribbean has received, generally unfairly, a bad rap for danger, theft, and drugs. This is mainly because of a couple of murderous incidents over the last few years, which have spurred local hoteliers and tourism officials to work together to improve safety and provide the local police with a car. Take the usual precautions you would take in any tourist area. Keep your hotel room locked and the windows closed, never leave gear unattended on beaches when swimming, don't walk the beaches alone at night, and be prudent when entering local bars. Don't give money for a service in advance, as you might not see the person again, and always count your change.

Most residents are not happy with young travelers who come to the area in search of drugs. Remember that buying drugs is illegal as well as dangerous (dealers may be crooked or collaborating with the police).

Some solo women travelers have complained that local men can be too persistent in their advances. Women may feel that traveling with a friend is safer than traveling alone. Some local men have a reputation for trying aggressively to pick up female travelers (especially blonde ones).

Some people come to the beach villages looking for sexual flings. Caution is advised; as everywhere in the world, AIDS and other STDs are a danger here. If you can't resist the temptations the Caribbean offers, you should bring your own condoms.

Note that despite the casual atmosphere both here and in other coastal areas, nude or topless bathing is definitely not accepted. Also, wearing skimpy bathing clothes in the villages is frowned upon. Wearing at least a T-shirt and shorts is expected and appreciated.

If you're sensitive to bugs and staying in the cheapest hotels, bring insect repellent or mosquito coils.

## CONSELVATUR

This tour company owns a private 850-hectare reserve, one-third of which is a family farm; the remainder is rainforest preserved for tourism. Conselvatur (W www .conselvatur.com) arranges various tours in the area (and throughout the country, especially into La Amistad). You can reach the farm by driving almost 20km south of Limón, then turning west at the Río Bananito and heading up the river valley for about 15km. You'll need a 4WD for the last few kilometers, though staff can pick you up if you request it. Contact the lodge for information on combining the use of public transportation with getting picked up. Which bus the staff instructs you to take (ie, where they pick you up) depends on what they're up to at the time.

**Selva Bananito Lodge** (☎/fax 253-8118, fax 280-0820, in the USA ☎/fax 641-236-3894, e conselva@racsa.co.cr, w www.selva bananito.com) Singles/doubles/triples/quads US$120/200/258/344, including meals; 3-day/2-night package with transport from San José US$340/600 singles/doubles. On the farm, this is an 11-cabin lodge. Each cabin has a solar-heated, tiled shower, two double beds, a writing desk, a large deck with hammock and rainforest views, but no electricity (portable bedside lamps are available). Packages include three meals (there are discounts for kids under 12) and one or two tours for those staying two or three nights. Tour options include hiking to waterfalls, birding, rappelling, horseback riding and mountain biking. Bicycle rental costs US$12 per day.

## AVIARIOS DEL CARIBE

Thirty-one kilometers south of Limón, or about 1km north from where the coastal highway crosses the Río Estrella, is the small wildlife sanctuary, sloth research center, and B&B of Aviarios del Caribe (☎/fax 382-1335, e aviarios@costarica.net). Doubles US$80-105, with full breakfast. The sanctuary is an 88-hectare island in the delta of the Río Estrella, where the owners, Luis and Judy Arroyo, have recorded about 320 bird species – and are still counting. A variety of local nature-oriented excursions are offered. The most popular is the kayak tour (US$30) that lasts about three hours. A guide paddles you quietly through the Estrella delta, getting you close to a variety of birds and animals. Look for sloths, monkeys, caimans, and river otters.

The now-famous orphaned sloth named Buttercup reigns over the grounds. Buttercup's mother was killed by a car, and Luis and Judy raised the youngster, only about five weeks old when they found it. This gave rise to a passion for sloths, and now Aviarios del Caribe has a sloth rescue sanctuary that

doubles as a sloth research center. The owners' passion for sloths is palpable, and there are about 10 animals here at any one time. They also have all sorts of other interesting animals, as well as an ant house and a poison-arrow frog hatchery! Visits and informative guided tours (in English) of the sloth center are available for US$5. There is a volunteer program here – contact Luis and Judy for details.

Art by Mindy Lighthipe graces the walls of the B&B – her paintings of butterflies are stunning. A balcony provides a view of the garden and forest, and there is a library and a game room. Guestrooms are spacious, with fans, comfortable beds, restful decor, flower vases, and well-designed bathrooms with hot water. Rates given are for high season. If you call for reservations, keep trying; it can be difficult to get through on the phone.

Any bus to Cahuita will drop you off at the entrance to Aviarios del Caribe.

## VALLE DE LA ESTRELLA

The Río Estrella valley is a long-established banana- and cacao-growing area. There are plantations producing several other types of tropical fruit as well. Traveling south from Limón, the valley is reached by turning right (west) on the signed road just south of the bridge over the Río Estrella. This is the route to Reserva Biológica Hitoy Cerere. Buses from San José leave from the Caribe terminal at 3pm, returning at 6am the next day.

## RESERVA BIOLÓGICA HITOY CERERE

This 9950-hectare reserve is 60km south of Limón by road, but only half that distance as the vulture glides. Although not far from civilization, it is one of the most rugged and rarely visited reserves in the country. There is a ranger station, but there are no other facilities – no campsites, nature trails, or information booths. The reserve lies at elevations between about 100m and 1025m on the south side of the Río Estrella valley.

Though few people come to Hitoy Cerere, that is no reason to ignore it. The reserve is a fascinating place and, being so rarely visited, offers a great wilderness experience in an area that has been little explored. This may be the wettest reserve in the parks system; its dense evergreen forests typically get inundated with 4000mm to 6000mm of rain annually.

Hiking is permitted, but the steep and slippery terrain and dense vegetation make it a possibility only for the most fit and determined hikers. Heavy rainfall and broken terrain combine to produce many beautiful streams, rivers, and waterfalls. These often take several hours of difficult hiking to reach. Hiking along a streambed is the best way of getting through the dense vegetation. Reportedly, there is one more-or-less maintained trail leading south from the ranger station. The reserve is home to many different plants, birds, mammals, and other creatures, many of which have not yet been recorded because of the remoteness of the site.

### Information
Visitors should call ahead (☎ 758-5855, 798-3170 in Limón) to see if somebody will be at the ranger station when they arrive. You might be permitted to sleep at the ranger station for a small fee, but this is normally reserved for researchers only.

### Getting There & Away
Take a bus to Valle de la Estrella from Limón. From the end of the bus line it is an additional 10km to 15km to the reserve along a dirt road. There are 4WD taxis available to drive you there for about US$10 one-way. The drivers are reliable, and will come back to pick you up at a pre-arranged time. From Cahuita (about 30km away), 4WD taxis will take you to the reserve for about US$30. (Ordinary cars can get there during the drier months.)

## CAHUITA
This small village lies southeast of Puerto Limón, about 43km by road. It is known for the attractive beaches nearby (more suitable for snorkeling and swimming than for surfing), some of which are in Parque Nacional Cahuita, which adjoins the village to the south.

Cahuita is becoming a tourist destination, boasting a few fairly new hotels, restaurants and locally run tour companies. But the main street is still made of sand – more suited to horses and bicycles with clunky wheels than to the cars and 4WDs with which tourists send up clouds of choking dust. One local woman said that the tourists' vehicles were the biggest problem that tourism has caused. She could not even hang her laundry out to dry in front of her house because of the dust.

### Information
Tourist information is available from the places listed in the Organized Tours section, below.

**Money** US dollars are readily exchanged. Some hotels will change traveler's checks if they have enough colones, as will some of the tour operators; rates may vary significantly from place to place. Cabinas Safari changes other currencies and traveler's checks, but the commission is high.

**Email & Internet Access** Internet access is now sporadically available at some businesses and hotels for about US$3 an hour; ask around.

### Beaches
Three beaches are within walking distance of the village. At the northwest end of Cahuita is **Playa Negra**, a long, black-sand beach with good swimming. Some people think that the black-sand beach has better swimming than the white-sand beach at the eastern end of town, though ask about currents at both. This latter beach is in the national park, and a trail in the jungle behind the beach leads you to a third beach, about 6km away. These last two beaches are separated by a rocky headland with a coral reef offshore that is suitable for snorkeling (see the Parque Nacional Cahuita section, later in this chapter).

### Activities & Organized Tours
A number of places rent equipment and arrange tours. **Brigitte** (see Centro Turístico Brigitte in Places to Stay), a Swiss woman who has lived by Playa Negra for years, offers half-day guided horseback tours for US$30 to US$40. She rents bicycles at rates ranging from US$1.25 an hour to US$28 a week.

**Mister Big J Tourist Service** (☎ 755-0328) and **Roberto Tours** (☎/fax 755-0117) are both presided over by personable locals who cover all the standards and have individual specialties. Mister Big J has been

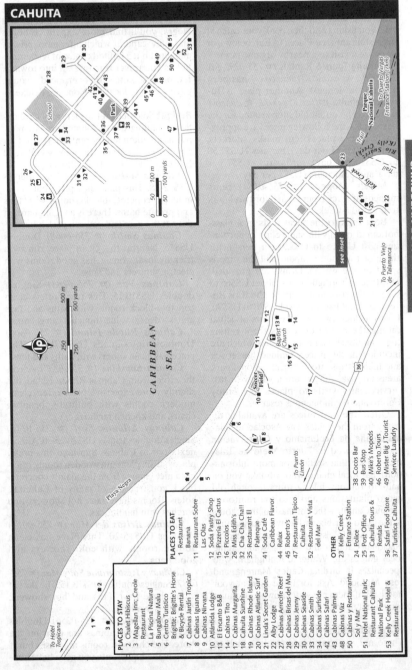

# CAHUITA

PLACES TO STAY
2 Chalet Hibiscus
3 Magellan Inn; Creole Restaurant
4 La Piscina Natural
5 Bungalow Malu
6 Centro Turístico Brigitte; Brigitte's Horse & Bicycle Rental
7 Cabinas Jardin Tropical
8 Cabinas Iguana
9 Cabinas Nirvana
10 Atlántida Lodge
13 El Encanto B&B
14 Cabinas Tito
17 Cabinas Margarita
18 Cahuita Sunshine
19 Cabinas Rhode Island
20 Cabinas Atlantic Surf
21 Linda's Secret Garden
22 Alby Lodge
27 Cabinas Arrecife Reef
28 Cabinas Brisas del Mar
29 Cabinas Jenny
30 Cabinas Seaside
33 Cabinas Smith
34 Cabinas Surfside
42 Cabinas Safari
43 Cabinas Palmer
48 Cabinas Vaz
50 Cabinas y Restaurante Sol y Mar
51 Hotel National Park; Restaurant Cahuita National Park
53 Kelly Creek Hotel & Restaurant

PLACES TO EAT
1 Restaurant Banana
11 Restaurant Sobre Las Olas
12 Soda Pastry Shop
15 Pizzería El Cactus
16 Piccolos
26 Miss Edith's
32 Cha Cha Chall
35 Restaurant El Palenque
41 Soda Café
44 Caribbean Flavor Relax
45 Roberto's
47 Restaurant Típico Cahuita
52 Restaurant Vista del Mar

OTHER
23 Kelly Creek Entrance Station
24 Police
25 Post Office
31 Cahuita Tours & Rentals
36 Safari Food Store
37 Turística Cahuita
38 Cocos Bar
39 Bus Stop
40 Mike's Mopeds
46 Roberto Tours
49 Mister Big J Tourist Service; Laundry

CARIBBEAN LOWLANDS

leading horse tours in the area for many years and does boat rentals; Roberto will take you fishing and then cook your catch at his restaurant (see Places to Eat, below), or organize a visit to a nearby organic farm.

**Cahuita Tours & Rentals** (☎ 755-0232, fax 755-0082, e exotica@racsa.co.cr) has been around the longest. Another place is **Turística Cahuita** (☎/fax 755-0071, e dltacb@racsa.co.cr). You should shop around for the best deals – the following prices are approximate. These places rent masks, snorkels, and fins (US$7 per day), bicycles (US$7.50 to US$10 per day), surfboards (US$7 per day), and binoculars (US$7 per day).

**Mike's Mopeds** (☎ 755-0184) rents mopeds at rates from US$10 for two hours to US$150 a week.

Boat trips to the local reefs in a glass-bottomed boat, with snorkeling opportunities, cost US$15 to US$20 per person for three or four hours (about half the time is spent on the water). Drinks are provided. Day trips to Tortuguero cost about US$65 to US$75. River-running trips on the Ríos Reventazón and Pacuare cost US$70 to US$90. (Trips include two or three hours of actual rafting; the rest of the day is spent getting there and back and eating meals, which are included in the price). Guided horseback and hiking trips into the local national park areas are available, as are a variety of taxi services and visits to places like Hitoy Cerere and the indigenous reserves.

Often, the best prices are available directly from the guides. The **Asociación Talamanqueña de Ecoturismo y Conservación** (ATEC), based in Puerto Viejo de Talamanca (see that section for more information), has local guides who will take you on half- to full-day hiking tours through old cacao plantations and into the rainforest around Cahuita – the emphasis of these tours is the Afro-Caribbean lifestyle plus natural history. ATEC also offers visits to Parque Nacional Cahuita and birding walks. Some local guides are **Walter Cunningham**, who specializes in birding, **Carlos Mairena**, and **José McCloud**. Ask for these men at your hotel; all of them are well known in Cahuita (you don't need to go through ATEC).

## Places to Stay

There are two possible areas in which to stay. In town, hotels are generally cheaper,

noisier, and close to restaurants and the national park. Northwest of town, along Playa Negra, you'll find more expensive hotels and a few cabinas, which offer more privacy and quiet but a limited choice of restaurants unless you travel 1km or 2km into town. A few of these hotels are overpriced – you're paying for the location. None are deluxe.

**Budget** Solo budget travelers may have difficulty finding cheap rooms because many rooms are intended for rental to two to four people. For *camping* options, see Parque Nacional Cahuita, later in this chapter.

**Cabinas Surfside** (☎ 755-0246) Doubles US$12-18. This place has plain but clean, modern, concrete-block rooms with fans and private baths. There is a night guard on duty at the gate and you can park here.

**Cabinas Smith** (☎ 755-0068) Doubles US$15. Nearby, this clean place, run by a friendly local woman, has good rooms with electric showers and fans.

**Cabinas Vaz** (☎ 755-0283) Singles/doubles US$10/15. This place offers clean concrete-block rooms with baths and fans and is a decent value, though it can get noisy.

**Cabinas Rhode Island** (☎ 755-0866) Doubles/triples/quads US$12/15/18. This place has clean rooms with baths and fans.

**Cahuita Sunshine** (☎ 755-0237) Across the street from Cabinas Rhode Island, this slightly more expensive place offers clean, modern rooms with bathtubs, beanbag chairs, and kitchen facilities.

**Cabinas Atlantic Surf** (☎ 755-0116) Singles/doubles/triples US$20/25/30. Almost next door to Cabinas Sunshine, this pretty place has six pleasant, wooden rooms, offering a nice change from the mainly concrete-block construction of many of Cahuita's hotels. Rooms have fans, hot showers, and porches with hammocks.

**Cabinas Brisas del Mar** (☎ 755-0011) Doubles US$15-20. This place has clean double rooms with cold showers and good beds.

**Cabinas y Restaurante Sol y Mar** (☎ 755-0237) Singles/doubles US$13/15. The decent rooms here have fans and hot showers. Parking is available.

**Cabinas Jenny** (☎ 755-0256) Doubles US$15-25. These cabinas are right on the shore. The cheapest rooms are basic, but if you pay the higher rate you get a better upstairs room with a private bath, or a spacious downstairs cabin that also has a porch and hammock – both offer more privacy and sea views. They are being remodeled, and prices may rise to US$30 to US$40 by 2003.

***Cabinas Seaside*** (☎ 755-0210, 755-0027, e spencer@racsa.co.cr) Doubles US$16-20. Next door to Cabinas Jenny, this pleasant place has a number of hammocks strung beneath the coconut palms – a good place to relax and chat or just watch the waves roll in. Rooms are basic and clean with two double beds and private cold showers. There are 14 rooms, of which five are upstairs – better views, quieter, more expensive. Internet access and tour information are available.

***Cabinas Palmer*** (☎ 755-0243, e kpalmer@ racsa.co.cr) Singles/doubles US$15/20. This place is owned by some friendly locals. Most of the plain but clean rooms have hot showers. Rooms vary; ask to have a look.

***Cabinas Safari*** (☎ 755-0078, fax 755-0020) Singles/doubles US$15/20. Across the street from Cabinas Palmer, the six rooms here are consistently nicer and have private hot showers. Parking and money-exchange services are available. Next door, they also manage ***Cuartos Jabiru*** with seven simple rooms sharing baths for US$7/12 singles/doubles.

***Linda's Secret Garden*** (☎/fax 755-0327) Rooms US$18-30. This small, quiet Canadian-run lodge has two modern spacious rooms with private hot showers, leading out into a pretty garden. The smaller room will sleep up to three, and the larger sleeps up to four. An outdoor kitchen with complimentary tea and coffee is available, and there is secure parking.

***Cabinas Nirvana*** (☎ 755-0110, e nirvana99@racsa.co.cr) Doubles US$20-35. Out toward Playa Negra, this is a good budget choice with a variety of options. Built by a friendly Italian, all the wooden cabins are nice and have private hot showers, cross ventilation, and floor fans. There are two small cabins, two midsize ones (one with kitchenette), and a larger one sleeping four with a kitchenette. Though this place is tucked down a side road several hundred meters from the beach, coral juts up from the grassy lawn area.

***Centro Turístico Brigitte*** (☎/fax 755-0053, e brigittecahuita@hotmail.com, W www .brigittecahuita.com) Doubles US$15-25.

Small rooms are US$15; larger rooms with breakfast are US$25. The breakfast café is open to the public 7am to 10am.

***La Piscina Natural*** Doubles US$18. Farther out from town is this place, whose name means 'the natural pool' (named after a small inlet on the beach). Cabins are simple but adequate and have hot showers.

***Hotel National Park*** (☎/fax 755-0244, fax 755-0065) Doubles US$20-45. Almost at the entrance to Parque Nacional Cahuita, this place has 20 decent, clean rooms with private hot showers. The more expensive rooms are newer and have views, TV, and air-conditioning. A popular restaurant is attached (see Places to Eat, below).

***Cabinas Margarita*** (☎ 755-0205) Singles/ doubles US$15/20. The rooms here are clean and have electric showers.

***Cabinas Tito*** (☎ 755-0286) Singles/ doubles US$16/20. This friendly place has six pleasant rooms with cold showers and fans, some rooms have kitchenettes.

***Cabinas Arrecife Reef*** (☎/fax 755-0081) Singles/doubles with hot bath US$15/20. The rooms here are plain but have fans and electrically heated private showers, and the breezy, shaded porch has good sea views. There are 11 rooms, of which seven are considerably nicer and are good value for US$20.

**Mid-Range** Conveniently attached to a soda is ***Cabinas Jardín Tropical*** (☎ 755-0033) Cabins US$30, house US$50. This place rents two nice cabins with hot water, fans, refrigerators, and porch hammocks; there's also a larger house available.

***Cabinas Iguana*** (☎ 755-0005, fax 755-0054, e iguanas@racsa.co.cr) Doubles with shared bath US$17, cabins US$25-60. This place has three nice rooms with shared warm showers (often full of long-term guests). Several even nicer rooms and cabins with private hot bath, refrigerators and hot plates sleep two to six people. The staff will pick you up at the bus stop if you have reservations. There is a clean swimming pool, as well as a book exchange and sinks to do your laundry. Both Cabinas Jardín Tropical and Cabinas Iguana are quiet and out of the way.

***Kelly Creek Hotel & Restaurant*** (☎ 755-0007, e kellycr@racsa.co.cr, W www .2000.co.cr/hotelkellycreek) Doubles/triples

CARIBBEAN LOWLANDS

US$35/45. Right by the entrance to Parque Nacional Cahuita, this hotel offers attractive and spacious rooms with big, white-tiled hot showers. With only four rooms, each is on a corner and has slatted windows for excellent light and cross-ventilation. High ceilings keep the place cool, and it's a good deal. There's a fine restaurant here, too.

**Alby Lodge** (☎/fax 755-0031) Rooms US$30-50. Near Kelly Creek Hotel, this German-run place has pleasant grounds with attractive thatched wooden cabins built on stilts. All have hot showers, fans, mosquito nets, and a porch with a hammock. The high-roofed architecture helps keep the rooms cool.

**Bungalow Malu** (☎ 755-0114, 755-0006) US$45 double with breakfast. The Italian owner here offers three attractive boulder-and-wood bungalows, with another under construction. Each has a ceiling and a floor fan, refrigerator, and hot shower. A restaurant is attached.

**El Encanto B&B** (☎/fax 755-0113, e encanto@racsa.co.cr, w www.2000.co.cr/elencanto) Singles/doubles US$47/58. This hospitable place, run by charming French-Canadian artists Pierre and Patricia, is set in lovingly landscaped grounds, with statuettes and nooks reflecting the artistic and peaceful nature of the owners. An Asian-style pavilion is available for relaxing in hammocks or lounge chairs, and yoga classes are given here on the weekend; massages are also available. A meditation room provides a quiet environment from 5:30am to 6:30am, and again in the evening.

There are three comfortable and attractive wooden bungalows with hot water, ceiling fans, comfortable beds, and private patios. A separate house has three bedrooms, each with private bathroom, private patio, and sharing a fully equipped kitchen. The whole house can be rented for six people for US$145, or rooms are rented individually. Rates include a full breakfast with excellent home-baked bread. The open-sided breakfast room can be used for relaxation during the day; there is a refrigerator stocked with drinks on the honor system, and cable TV if you really need it. The owners can refer you to several good local guides.

**Chalet Hibiscus** (☎ 755-0021, fax 755-0015, e hibiscus@racsa.co.cr, w www.hotels.co.cr/hibiscus.html) Doubles US$40-50,

houses US$100-120. Set in attractive beachside gardens with flowering bushes and plants, this place is almost 2.5km northwest of the main bus stop in 'downtown' Cahuita – a good location if you're looking for peace and quiet. Three rustic-looking wooden rooms have private hot showers, table fans, and mosquito screens; rates vary depending on size. There are also two houses available, one with two bedrooms and one with three. Both have kitchens, dining areas, and patios, and they're both nice and airy. Amenities include a pool and a game room with pool table. Low-season discounts are offered, and English and German are spoken.

**Hotel Tropicana** (☎ 775-0106, e black steno@hotmail.com) Doubles US$25-35. In a quiet area even farther along the beach road, this is a simple lodge-style building set amid spacious, shady grounds. There's a wraparound wooden verandah upstairs and a kitchen (available to guests) downstairs. Some of the six rooms are wood floored, others are tiled; all have fans and private hot showers. The owners speak Italian and English.

**Atlántida Lodge** (☎ 755-0115, ☎/fax 755-0213, e atlantis@racsa.co.cr, w www.atlantida.co.cr) Singles/doubles US$53/66. Rates include full breakfast. This nice place, with owners and staff who are friendly and helpful, features about 30 rooms set in pleasant gardens. Rooms have fans and hot showers, and there's a swimming pool and an attractive thatched restaurant-bar. The lodge is near the soccer field, about 1km northwest of the central bus stop – if you have a reservation, the staff will pick you up. The hotel also arranges a private bus from San José several times a week – call for times. The one-way fare direct to the lodge is US$25 per person.

**Magellan Inn** (☎/fax 755-0035, e magellaninn@racsa.co.cr) Doubles US$75. Magellan Inn is almost 3km northwest of Cahuita, at the north end of Playa Negra, and far enough removed from the village to be a destination in itself. The inn is attractive, with Asian rugs on the wooden floors, and there is a small pool set in a pretty sunken garden, which is formed from an ancient coral reef. The inn has six carpeted rooms with fans, hot showers, comfortable queen-size beds, and private patios looking out onto the grounds. The rate includes breakfast.

Other meals are available in the inn's fine Creole Restaurant (see below).

## Places to Eat

*Miss Edith's* Dishes US$4-10. This long-established eatery has attracted the attention of many hungry travelers over the years. (As the local people get older and earn a place of respect in the community, they are called Miss or Mister, followed by their first name – hence, Miss Edith. You wouldn't refer to a young person in this way.) Miss Edith has been so successful creating mouthwatering Caribbean cuisine that the restaurant is no longer just a little local place on someone's front porch but also a popular tourist hangout. Meals are reasonably priced, with shrimp and lobster dishes starting at about US$10. Alcohol isn't served. Food is cooked to order and can take awhile, but it's worth the wait. Miss Edith herself often doesn't cook any more, but oversees her hardworking sisters and daughters.

*Restaurant El Palenque* Dishes US$3-5. Tasty vegetarian fare as well as fish and meat dishes are served here, cooked Caribbean Creole style (mildly spicy, sometimes with coconut or mango flavors). Casados are available, too.

*Cha Cha Cha!!* (☎ 394-4153) Main courses US$6-9. Open noon-10pm, closed Mon. In a corner verandah of an old, blue-painted clapboard house, this attractive eatery is unmistakably Caribbean. French-Canadian chef Bertrand and partner Julie offer 'cuisine del mundo.' Well-prepared dishes range from Jamaican jerked chicken to curried swordfish to Creole vegetarian; the house specialty is squid salad. The desserts are yummy and the music is New World and jazz played at conversational levels. This place is a hit.

*Roberto's* Dishes US$3-4. Next to the tour company and run by the same genial owner, this is a relaxed place serving good, simple, Caribbean-inflected meals. On the wall, the mission statement reads, 'Let's go fishing and later we'll cook the fish for you.'

*Soda Café Caribbean Flavor* On the other side of the park is this charming little café, which serves inexpensive local food.

*Pizzería El Cactus* (☎/fax 755-0276) Pizzas average US$7.50. Dishes US$8-12. Open for dinner only. On a side road northwest of downtown, this eatery serves pizzas (which will feed three people), pastas, and barbecue, seafood and meat dishes.

*Soda Pastry Shop* At the northwest end of town is this popular beachfront shop, which offers delicious fresh-baked bread, cakes, and pies, and has picnic tables by the shore – a good place for a snack while being cooled by ocean breezes.

*Restaurant Sobre Las Olas* (☎ 755-0109) Dinner dishes US$5.50-10. Open noon-10pm, closed Tues. Near the pastry shop, this place is traditionally good for a beachfront meal and has now been taken over by an excellent Italian chef. Meals include a variety of pastas and a selection of seafood (including octopus, which is hard to cook just right but he does it). There is also a small cheap menu of snacks and sandwiches for lunch and afternoon appetizers ('til 6pm). Choose to eat on a sea-view terrace or indoors.

For people staying out at the far end of Playa Negra, the *Restaurant Banana* sells good local food, and the *Creole Restaurant* at the Magellan Inn is reportedly excellent (Creole and French dishes, US$8 to US$10); call the hotel to see if reservations are required.

*Restaurant Cahuita National Park* Back in the heart of town, this restaurant, by the entrance to Parque Nacional Cahuita, is pricey but popular because of its location. The restaurant serves breakfast, lunch, and dinner in the high season, lunch and dinner only in the low season. The food is decent, and the place tends to be frequented by tourists who eat and drink at the outside tables.

*Restaurant Vista del Mar* Dishes US$3 and up. This place, across the street from Restaurant Cahuita National Park, is open all day and serves Chinese and seafood dishes.

*Kelly Creek Restaurant* Dishes US$8-10. Open 6:30pm 'til closing Thur-Tues. Right by the park entrance, this recommended place at the Kelly Creek Hotel specializes in paella (US$9 per person, two minimum) and other Spanish cuisine, authentically prepared by Spanish owners.

Between these last two restaurants is a little *snack hut* that is open erratically (Saturday and Sunday afternoon), selling delicious homemade empanadas (stuffed turnovers) for US50¢, and other snacks until they're gone. Local women sometimes set up shop and sell their homemade meals (US$2.50) and snacks direct from the cooking pot.

For breakfasts and other meals, nearby is the **Restaurant Sol y Mar** (attached to the cabinas of the same name)

**Relax** Dishes US$4-8. Closed Tues. This good Italian restaurant has inexpensive pastas and pricier meat and fish dishes.

**Restaurant Típico Cahuita** This place has a variety of pricey but decent fish dishes – budget travelers should order the casado.

### Entertainment

This can be summed up in one word: bars. The 'safest' bet is any one of the restaurants mentioned above, many of them away from the center of town.

**Cocos Bar** In the middle of town you'll find Cocos, where at night the back room pounds to the sounds of Caribbean disco or the occasional salsa night. Local 'Calypso King' and storyteller Walter Gavitt Ferguson (his music sounds a bit like a Caribbean talking-blues) no longer plays publicly, but sometimes he hangs out in the park across from Cocos. A tape of his original and traditional songs is available at Roberto Tours (see Activities & Organized Tours, earlier in the Cahuita section).

### Getting There & Away

Express buses leave from the Caribe terminal in San José at 6am, 10am, 1:30pm, 3:30pm, and 5pm. The fare is US$5 and the trip takes about four hours. Return buses leave from the central crossroads in Cahuita at 7am, 8am, 9:30am, 11:30am, and 4:30pm. Alternately, take a bus from San José to Puerto Limón and change there for service to Cahuita; there are seven buses daily between Limón and Cahuita. These buses go on to Puerto Viejo de Talamanca, and three of them also continue to Manzanillo. About four buses go to Bribri and Sixaola daily. You may have to catch these buses out on the highway, southwest of the bus crossroads in town; ask locally. For the Puerto Vargas entrance to Parque Nacional Cahuita, take any bus to Puerto Viejo de Talamanca, Manzanillo, or Sixaola.

Schedules are liable to change.

### PARQUE NACIONAL CAHUITA

This small park of 1067 hectares is one of the more frequently visited national parks

in Costa Rica. The reasons are simple: easy access and nearby hotels combined with attractive beaches, a coral reef, and coastal rainforest with many easily observed tropical species. Fortunately, Cahuita is still less visited than Manuel Antonio, on the Pacific coast.

The park is most often entered from the southeast end of Cahuita village, through the 'donate what you want' Kelly Creek entrance station. A steep increase of national park fees to US$15 several years ago (since reduced to US$6 or US$7) had the locals up in arms because they thought that travelers would refuse to fork out US$15 to go sit on the beach, and feared that visitors would go elsewhere instead. Accordingly, villagers closed down the park entrance booth and encouraged visitors to use the beach for free. This resulted in the then Minister of National Resources, René Castro, blaming the situation upon drug-taking budget travelers!

Currently, this station is open on a well-run 'donation only' basis. (Although locally known as Kelly Creek, some maps show the river at the entrance as Río Suárez.) Almost

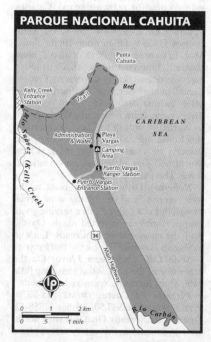

PARQUE NACIONAL CAHUITA

## Coral Reefs

The monkeys and other forest creatures are not the only wildlife attractions of Parque Nacional Cahuita. About 200m to 500m off Punta Cahuita is the largest living coral reef in Costa Rica (though very small compared to the huge barrier reef off Belize, for example). Corals are tiny, colonial, filter-feeding animals (cnidarians, or, more commonly, coelenterates) that deposit a calcium carbonate skeleton as a substrate for the living colony. These skeletons build up over millennia to form the corals we see. The outside layers of the corals are alive, but, because they are filter feeders, they rely on the circulation of clean water and nutrients over their surface.

Since the opening up of the Caribbean coastal regions in the last couple of decades, a lot of logging has taken place, and the consequent lack of trees on mountainous slopes has led to increased erosion. The loosened soil is washed into gullies, then streams and rivers, and eventually the sea. By the time the coral reef comes into the picture, the eroded soils are no more than minute mud particles – just the right size to clog up the filter-feeding cnidarians. The clogged animals die, and the living reef dies along with them.

After deforestation, the land is often given over to plantations of bananas or other fruit. These are sprayed with pesticides which, in turn, are washed out to sea and can cause damage to animals that need to pass relatively large quantities of water through their filtering apparatus in order to extract the nutrients they need.

The 1991 earthquake, which was centered near the Caribbean coast, also had a damaging effect on the reef. The shoreline was raised by over a meter, exposing and killing parts of the coral. Nevertheless, some of the reef has survived and remains the most important in Costa Rica.

It is important to note that the coral reef is not just a bunch of colorful rocks. It is a living habitat, just as a stream, lake, forest, or swamp is a living habitat. Coral reefs provide both a solid surface for animals such as sponges and anemones to grow on and a shelter for a vast community of fish and other organisms – octopi, crabs, algae, bryozoans, and a host of others. Some 35 species of coral have been identified in this reef, along with 140 species of mollusk (snails, chitons, shellfish, and octopi), 44 species of crustacean (lobsters, crabs, shrimps, and barnacles), 128 species of seaweed, and 123 species of fish. Many of these seemingly insignificant species represent important links in various food chains. Thus logging has the potential to cause much greater and unforeseen damage than simply destroying the rainforest.

On a more mundane level, the drier months in the highlands (from February to April), when less runoff occurs in the rivers and less silting occurs in the sea, are considered the best months for snorkeling and seeing the reef. Conditions are often cloudy at other times.

Visitors can reach the reef by swimming from Punta Cahuita, but this is not recommended. Snorkelers have been known to cut their feet walking on the coral (which also damages the living reef) and to get into other difficulties. It is best to hire a boat in Cahuita and snorkel from the boat.

immediately upon entering the park, the visitor sees a 2km-long white-sand beach stretching along a gently curving bay to the east. About the first 500m of beach have signs warning about unsafe swimming, but beyond that, waves are gentle and swimming is safe. (It is unwise to leave clothing unattended when you swim; take a friend. Mister Big J Tourist Service, near the entrance, stores valuables in individual security boxes for US$1 per day.)

A rocky headland known as Punta Cahuita separates this beach from the next one, Playa Vargas. At the end of Playa Vargas is the Puerto Vargas ranger station, which is about 7km from Kelly Creek. The two stations are linked by a trail that goes through the coastal jungle behind the beaches and Punta Cahuita. The trail ends at the southern tip of the reef, where it meets up with a paved road leading to the ranger station. At times, the trail follows the beach; at other times hikers are 100m or so away from the sand. A river must be forded near the end of the first beach, and the water can be thigh-deep at high tide. Animal and bird sightings are not uncommon, so keep your eyes wide open for coatis, raccoons, ibises, kingfishers, and other fauna. Snorkeling is an option at Punta Cahuita (see the boxed text 'Coral Reefs').

From the Puerto Vargas ranger station, a 1km road takes you out to the main coastal highway, where you'll find the Puerto Vargas entrance station.

### Information

The two park entrance stations are open daily 8am to 4pm. The Kelly Creek station accepts voluntary donations, while at the Puerto Vargas entrance you'll pay the US$6. No one stops you from entering the park on foot before or after these opening hours at Kelly Creek. At the Puerto Vargas area (where you can camp), a locked gate prevents vehicle entry outside of opening hours.

There is not much shade on the beaches, so remember to use sunscreen and a hat to avoid sunburn – and don't forget your sensitive feet after you take your shoes off. Also, carry plenty of drinking water and insect repellent.

### An Eerie Hike

I have a special memory of the trail behind the beaches of Parque Nacional Cahuita. I was hiking along it early one morning when I began to notice a distant moaning sound. It seemed as if the wind in the trees was becoming more forceful and I wondered whether a tropical storm was brewing. I decided to continue, and as I did, the noise became louder and eerier. This was unlike any wind I had heard – it sounded like a baby in pain.

I am not normally afraid of sounds, but the cries began sounding so eerie that I had to reason with myself that there was nothing to be apprehensive about. Finally, after much hesitant walking and frequent examinations of the forest through my binoculars, I found the culprit: a male howler monkey – the first I had ever seen. At the time, I knew only that the monkey was named for its vocalizations; I had no idea how weird and unsettling those cries could be. For more information on howler monkeys, see the Wildlife Guide at the back of this book.

### Places to Stay

**Camping** (US$2 per person) is permitted at Playa Vargas, less than 1km from the Puerto Vargas ranger station. There are outdoor showers and pit latrines at the administration center near the middle of the camping area. There is drinking water, and some sites have picnic tables. The area is rarely crowded; in fact, it is often empty, and people opt to camp close to the administration center for greater security. This is safe enough if you don't leave your gear unattended (this is important). Easter week and weekends tend to be more crowded, but the campground is rarely full. With a vehicle it's possible to drive as far as the campground via the Puerto Vargas ranger station.

### Getting There & Away

It's easy to enter the park by just walking in from central Cahuita village at the Kelly Creek entrance station. You could hike as described above and then bus back, or go as far as you want and return the way you came. Both are straightforward day trips for anyone in reasonably good shape. Alternatively, take a 6am Puerto Viejo de Talamanca bus (catch it at the central bus stop in Cahuita village) and ask to be let off at the Puerto Vargas park entrance road. A 1km walk takes you to the coast, and then you can walk the additional 7km back to Cahuita.

## PUERTO VIEJO DE TALAMANCA

This small village is known locally as Puerto Viejo – don't confuse it with Puerto Viejo de Sarapiquí. Here you'll find more influence from the local Bribri indigenous culture than in Cahuita. There is also more development, though mainly of an individual, low-key variety. The cabinas, bars, and craft stalls strung along the shoreline nicely sum up the feel of the village. As a whole, Puerto Viejo is more exposed to the sea than Cahuita, which encourages shoreside strolling (and partying). Also, the Puerto Viejo area has the best surfing on this coast, if not the whole country. If you're looking for peace and quiet rather than a lively beach village, head south toward Manzanillo, where there are many places to stay near stretches of empty shore.

Poor surfing conditions in September and October mean that these are the quietest months of the year (though snorkeling improves at this time).

## Information

**Tourist Offices** Puerto Viejo holds the headquarters of the Asociación Talamanqueña de Ecoturismo y Conservación (ATEC; ☎/fax 750-0191, 750-0398, ℮ atec mail@racsa.co.cr, Ⓦ www.greencoast.com/atec.htm). The office is open 7am to noon and 1pm to 9pm daily (with slight variations depending on staff scheduling). If you are interested in the local culture and environment, this is the place to come for information; the office also has a large flier board posting general tourist information, and the staff can field most questions. Internet access is available here.

ATEC is a nonprofit grassroots organization that began in the 1980s. Its purpose is to promote environmentally sensitive local tourism in a way that supports local people and enhances their communities while providing a meaningful and enjoyable experience for the traveler wishing to learn something about the region.

ATEC can provide you with information ranging from the problems caused by banana plantations to how to arrange a visit to a nearby indigenous reserve. ATEC is not a tour agency, but will arrange visits to local areas with local guides. Homestay opportunities with local people are currently rare, but possible. Trips can be geared toward the visitor's interests, be they natural history, birding (over 350 bird species have been recorded in the area; one group reported 120 species sighted on a two-day trip), indigenous and Afro-Caribbean cultures, environmental issues, adventure treks, snorkeling, or fishing. ATEC trains local guides to provide you with as much information as possible and they certainly do – if all your questions aren't satisfactorily answered, follow up at the ATEC office. Most trips involve hiking – ask about necessary levels of endurance. Hikes ranging from fairly easy to difficult are available. For the adventurous, information is available about a hiking route across the Continental Divide to Buenos Aires.

Although these trips aren't dirt cheap, they are a fair value. The idea is to charge the traveler less than the big tour companies, but to pay the guides more than they

---

### Books on Local Culture

Some of the older black and indigenous inhabitants of the area told their life stories to Paula Palmer, who collected this wealth of oral history, culture, and social anthropology in books that are sometimes available in San José or at ATEC in Puerto Viejo (see Books in the Facts for the Visitor chapter for specific titles).

The titles of these books include the phrases 'What happen' or 'Wa'apin man,' which are common forms of greeting among coastal Costa Ricans. The books are well worth reading. ATEC also has some interesting pamphlets about the area's history.

---

might make working for those companies. This avoids the middle person, giving more profits to local guides while saving the traveler some money.

A percentage of fees goes toward supporting community activities. Prices start at about US$15 per person for half-day trips, early-morning birding hikes, and nightwalks. All-day trips cost about US$25, and various overnight trips are available, priced depending on your food and lodging needs. Groups for outdoor activities are limited in size to six.

ATEC can arrange talks about a variety of local issues for around US$45 per group. Also, staff can arrange meals in local homes for various prices, depending on the meal required.

A useful website is Ⓦ www.puerto viejo.net, which provides links to about 20 area hotels, as well as restaurants, bars, tour agencies, house rentals, real estate sales, local pictures, and other information.

**Money** Many hotels and cabinas accept credit cards and payment in US dollars. The nearest bank is in Bribri (see that section, later in this chapter); try to bring as many colones as you'll need. At this writing, the best place to change money is still with 'El Chino,' the owner of Pulpería Manuel León, who charges 1% commission on cash and much more on traveler's checks. He may not always have large amounts of change available.

# PUERTO VIEJO DE TALAMANCA

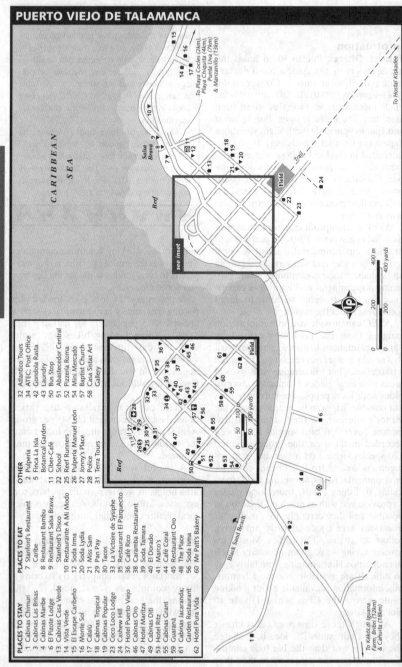

**PLACES TO STAY**
1   Cabinas Chimuri
3   Cabinas Las Brisas
4   Cabinas Maribe
6   El Pizote Lodge
13  Cabinas Casa Verde
14  Vista Verde
15  El Escape Caribeño
16  Monte Sol
17  Calalú
18  Cabinas Tropical
19  Cabinas Popular
23  Coco Loco Lodge
24  Cashew Hill
37  Hotel Puerto Viejo
46  Cabinas Oro
47  Hotel Maritza
49  Cabinas Diti
53  Hotel Ritz
55  Cabinas Grant
59  Guaraná
61  Cabinas Jacaranda;
    Garden Restaurant
62  Hotel Pura Vida

**PLACES TO EAT**
7   Stanford's Restaurant
    Caribe
8   Restaurant Bambu
9   Restaurant Salsa Brava;
    Stanford's Disco
10  Restaurante A Mi Modo
12  Soda Irma
20  Soda Lydia
21  Miss Sam
29  Pan Pay
30  Tacos
33  La Victoire de Sysiphe
35  Restaurant El Parquecito
36  Café Rico
38  Caramba Restaurant
39  Soda Tamara
40  El Dorado
41  Marco's
44  Café Coral
45  Restaurant Oro
48  The Place
56  Soda Isma
60  Mr Patt's Bakery

**OTHER**
2   Pulpería
5   Finca La Isla
    Botanical Garden
11  Ciber-Café
22  School
25  Reef Runners
27  Pulpería Manuel León
28  Jonny's Place
31  Terra Tours
32  Atlantico Tours
34  ATEC; Post Office
42  Gondola Rasta
43  Laundry
50  Bus Stop
51  Abastecedor Central
52  Pizzería Roma
54  Mini Mercado
57  Baptist Church
58  Casa Sistaz Art
    Gallery

**Telephone & Internet Access** There are several hundred phone lines in the area, but the phone book listings are notoriously inaccurate. The numbers listed in this section are those given out directly by businesses.

Public email and Internet access is available at ATEC and the Ciber Café. Also, inquire wherever you're staying.

## Indigenous Reserves

There are several reserves on the Caribbean slopes of the Cordillera de Talamanca, including the Reserva Indígena Cocles/KéköLdi, which comes down to the coast just east of Puerto Viejo. These reserves protect the land against commercial development in a variety of ways. Hunting is prohibited except to Indians hunting for food. Entrance to the reserves is limited to visitors with the necessary permits from the Reserve Associations – and these are difficult to obtain for the Talamanca reserves. ATEC is the most comprehensive source of information for those interested in going to the reserves.

The Talamanca Cabecar reserve is the most remote and difficult to visit. The Cabecar indigenous group is the most traditional and the least tolerant of visits from outsiders, while the Bribri people are more acculturated. Access to the reserves is generally on foot or on horseback.

## Finca La Isla Botanical Garden

To the west of town is the Finca La Isla Botanical Garden (✆/fax 750-0046, ℮ jarbot@racsa.co.cr, ⓦ www.greencoast .com/garden.htm; admission US$3; open 10am-3pm Fri-Mon), a working tropical farm where the owners have been growing local spices, tropical fruits, and ornamental plants for over a decade. Part of the farm is set aside as a botanical garden, which is also good for birding and wildlife observation (look for sloths and poison-arrow frogs). There is a picnic area. An informative guided tour (in English) costs US$8 (including admission, fruit tasting, and finishing with a glass of homemade juice), or you can buy a booklet for a self-guided tour for US$1.20.

## Samasati Retreat Center

Set on a lush hillside north of Puerto Viejo is Samasati Retreat Center (✆ 750-0315, fax 224-5032, ℮ samasati@racsa.co.cr, ⓦ www .samasati.com) Doubles US$111/172

without/with bath, including meals. This is a well-built, attractive complex with sweeping views of the coast – the village is just visible far below. German and English are spoken here, and daily programs of different meditation techniques are offered in its large open-air meditation/group room. There is a calendar of special events, and instruction is available in, among other things, yoga, bodywork, herbalism, and nutrition. Tasty vegetarian meals are served buffet-style on a wooden terrace with ocean views.

There are nine private bungalows with cool, wraparound screened walls, or you can stay in a guesthouse with five rooms sharing four bathrooms, all with hot showers. A yoga class (open to everyone) costs US$12, a meditation session is included in the daily rates, and a massage costs US$50. Packages and long-stay discounts are available, and tours of the area can be arranged. There is a sign for the retreat center about 1km north of the fork on the main highway where the road splits southeast to Puerto Viejo and west to Bribri. From here it's a 1km drive to the entrance and another 1.6km (4WD needed) to the center itself.

Staff will pick you up in Puerto Viejo if you have reservations.

## Water Sports

Dan Garcia, owner of the Hotel Puerto Viejo in the village, is a local surfing expert, and many surfers stay at his place (see Places to Stay, later in this section). He's a respected local board-maker who works out of his home; ask for him anywhere in town or at ATEC.

Surfers say surfing is best at the famous 'Salsa Brava,' outside the reef in front of Stanford's Restaurant Caribe. The reef here is shallow and sharp, so if you lose it, you're liable to smash yourself and your board on the reef; this wave is for experienced surfers only. If this doesn't appeal to you, try Playa Cocles, about 2km east of town (an area known as 'Beach Break,' after the restaurant there), where you'll find good and less-damaging breaks as well as some cabinas popular with surfers. Ask around for other places and up-to-date conditions.

The waves are generally best here from December to March, and there is a mini-season for surfing in June and July. From late March to May, and in September and October, the sea is at its calmest.

Generally, underwater visibility is best when the sea is calm; ie, when surfing is bad, snorkeling is good. The best snorkeling reefs are at Cahuita, Punta Uva, and by Manzanillo, which has the greatest variety of coral and fauna. Researchers are realizing something locals have known for years: that there is a small barrier reef off Manzanillo.

**Reef Runners** *(☎/fax 750-0480, 750-0099,* e *reefrun@racsa.co.cr)* offers all levels of diving. Introductory courses start at US$50 for three hours, and half-tank boat dives start at US$40. **Aquamor** (see Manzanillo, later in this chapter), which has helped coordinate reef research as well as compile data on nearby dolphin communities, also offers diving trips and courses, sea kayaking, and snorkeling.

The safest swimming around town is along Black Sand Beach, or in the natural sea pools in front of Pulpería Manuel León and Stanford's. Be cautious of currents at all beaches, particularly if the waves are high.

## Organized Tours
You'll find several cheery, somewhat raffish tour operators in the village.

**Atlantico Tours** *(☎ 750-0004, fax 750-0188)* Ed Oliver runs this company, which offers tours up and down the coast. Day trips to Refugio Nacional de Vida Silvestre Gandoca-Manzanillo and Parque Nacional Cahuita cost US$35, including lunch and guide; a two-day/one-night trip to Tortuguero costs US$55, not including accommodations. Rafting and surfing trips are also available, and you can rent snorkels, bikes, and surfboards for about US$8 per day.

**Gondola Rasta** *(☎ 750-0426, 750-0273, 750-0186)* Captain Marlon and Magnificent Marco of this company rent snorkeling and fishing equipment and can also take you out by boat. Other options include onboard reggae music, beach tours, and dolphin watches, with tour rates starting at US$30 per person. Look around for other small rental places.

**Terra Tours** *(☎ 750-0426)* has various boating tours, including a rafting option.

## South Caribbean Music Festival
The South Caribbean Music Festival features different performers appearing every week-end evening and offers music ranging from Caribbean and folk to classical and jazz. The festival has brought foreign and local performers together in an intimate setting near the beach and has become a great success. In putting it together, organizer Wanda Paterson (who is originally from Cahuita and lived in Paris and New York before settling again on the Caribbean) consulted with one of the original organizers of the long-standing Monteverde Music Festival.

Dates for the festival vary but are usually weekends in March and April (for about five weeks before Easter). Tickets cost US$5, and proceeds go to music programs for children on the southern Caribbean coast. For more information contact **Taller de Música** *(☎/fax 750-0062,* e *wolfbiss@ racsa.co.cr)*.

## Places to Stay
Puerto Viejo has developed much more rapidly than Cahuita in recent years, and there are many newish places in town, as well as along the road to Manzanillo. Keep your eye out for new places and competition-induced bargains. Places may fill up during the weekend in the surfing season and during Christmas and Easter holidays. Most of the rates given here are for a one-night stay during the high season. Bargain for long-term and low-season discounts.

Ask around about camping on hotel grounds, which is sometimes a possibility.

**Budget** Cold water is the norm in budget places, but the hot tropical weather makes this a minor inconvenience, perhaps even a blessing. Water pressure can be a problem in the cheaper places. The majority of hotels will provide either mosquito netting or fans (a breeze fanning the bed will help keep mosquitoes away). Check the facilities before getting a room. Solo travelers are often charged as much as much as two, so find a partner to economize.

Apart from the places listed below, local people may hang out a 'Rooms for Rent' sign and provide inexpensive accommodations. ATEC staff often know which local families are offering rooms.

The first two hotels listed here are recommended budget options. Both are on secluded hills that offer good birding and monkey sightings.

*Hostal Kiskadee* (☎ *750-0075*) Dorm beds less than US$10 per person. This place is a six- or seven-minute walk southeast of the soccer field. The path here is steep and is slippery after rain, so you should carry a flashlight if arriving after dark. Accommodations are provided in simple dormitory-style rooms.

*Cashew Hill* (☎ *750-0256*) Singles/doubles without bath US$10/15, with bath US$15/20. Closer to the soccer field, Cashew Hill has two simple cabins, each with a double and single bed, and also a larger room with a private bath. Rooms include kitchen privileges and a warm shared shower. You can check the surf down at Salsa Brava from the hilltop hammock area.

*Hotel Puerto Viejo* Rooms US$10 per person, doubles with bath US$16. With more than 30 double rooms, this is the biggest place in town. It is popular with surfers and budget travelers. There are bare, basic but reasonably clean upstairs rooms and a few downstairs rooms, which are not as good. There are also doubles with private cold showers.

*Hotel Ritz* (☎ *750-0176*) Singles without bath US$10, singles/doubles with bath US$15/20. This is an OK cheapie, reasonably clean, with single cubicles and cold baths.

*Cabinas Jacaranda* (☎ *750-0069*) Singles/doubles without bath US$15/20, doubles with hot bath US$27. This place has pleasant rooms (with shared cold showers), fans, and mosquito nets. It's a good value at the double rate.

*Cabinas Diti* (☎ *750-0311*) Singles/doubles with bath US$9/13. This place is OK; a bike-rental and souvenir-clothing store is attached.

*Hotel Pura Vida* (☎ *750-0002, fax 750-0296*) Singles/doubles without bath US$15/19, with bath US$25/30. This attractive and clean place has 10 decent rooms with fans. Those without bathrooms have sinks, and shared hot showers are down the hall. A kitchen is available for guest use, and there's parking and a pleasant garden to hang out in. German and English are spoken.

*Cabinas Grant* (☎ *758-2845, 750-0292*) Singles/doubles with bath US$16/23. This place has decent rooms with cold baths and fans and offers a locked parking area. The owners are helpful with local advice and operate a restaurant.

*Guaraná* (☎/*fax 750-0244,* ⓔ *info@ cabinasguarana.com,* Ⓦ *www.cabinas guarana.com*) Doubles/triples/quads US$28/39/48. This pleasant, Italian-owned place has 12 rooms with private hot showers, ceiling fans, writing desks, and patios or balconies with hammocks overlooking a garden. English, French, and Italian are spoken.

*Cabinas Popular* (☎ *750-0087*) Rooms US$10 per person. Rooms here have private cold showers.

*Cabinas Chimuri* (☎ *750-0119,* ⓔ *chimuribeach@racsa.co.cr,* Ⓦ *www.green coast.com/chimuri.htm*) Cabins US$35-50 a day, US$215-300 a week. Farther west, this place is owned by Mauricio Salazar and his European wife, Colocha, who know as much about the Bribri culture as anyone in Puerto Viejo. There are three cabins of different sizes, all with kitchenette, hot shower, refrigerator, and balcony. This is a nice place to stay for peace and quiet near the beach, though restaurants are not very close. Discounts are given for longer stays.

*Cabinas Maribe* (☎ *750-0182*) Doubles US$20. This place offers decent rooms with cold baths and fans.

Just east of the village are newer good budget choices, clustered at the end of a short side road that begins 250m east of Stanford's.

*Monte Sol* (☎/*fax 750-0098,* Ⓦ *www .montesol.net*) Doubles US$20. Monte Sol has simple, attractive rooms, some with imaginatively tiled bathrooms. The youthful German owners have added a bar and restaurant, and one of them, Birgit, also runs a hair salon here.

*Calalú* (☎ *750-0042*) Doubles without/with kitchen US$20/25 (US$5 additional people). This French-owned place has five well-built bungalows with hammock porches, some with a private kitchen. There is a Ping-Pong table, and a little butterfly garden (US$5, US$2.50 for guests) where you can eat breakfast. French, English, and German are spoken.

**Mid-Range** A choice of accommodations is available at *Hotel Maritza* (☎ *750-0003, fax 750-0313*) Doubles without/with bath US$15/24. The nicer cabins here have fans, private baths, and electric showers. There are also a few basic rooms with shared cold bath over the attached restaurant. This helpful hotel accepts credit cards and has a parking area.

*Cabinas Casa Verde* (☎ 750-0015, fax 750-0047, e cabinascasaverde@hotmail .com, w www.cabinascasaverde.com) Singles/doubles without bath US$24/26, with bath US$34/40. This friendly place is centrally located and has 14 pleasant rooms, most with private hot showers. All rooms are lightly painted in pastels with mural touches and have ceiling fans, mosquito nets, balconies, and hammocks. Some have refrigerators. The cabinas are set on tropically landscaped grounds. German and English are spoken by the Swiss/tico management. Bikes are available (US$4.50 a day), and breakfast is served daily except Monday.

*Cabinas Tropical* (☎/fax 750-0283, e rblancke@racsa.co.cr, w www.cabinas tropical.com) Singles/doubles US$20/25. At the southeast end of town, this place has six spotless rooms with large private hot showers, mosquito nets, and new beds. All rooms were totally renovated for 2002 and are a good value. The personable German owner, Rolf, is a biologist who has written and illustrated German-language guidebooks to the plants and fruits of Central America. He leads jungle hikes for birders from dawn until about 11am (US$30 per person, three minimum, breakfast provided.)

*Coco Loco Lodge* (☎/fax 750-0281, e cocoloco@racsa.co.cr, w www.cocoloco lodge.de) Singles/doubles with bath US$25/30. On the quiet edge of town, this place has five bungalows with hot water, set on spacious, pleasant grounds. Breakfast is available for US$5, and German and English are spoken.

*El Escape Caribeño* (☎/fax 750-0103, e escapec@racsa.co.cr, w www.green coast.com/escapec.htm) Doubles US$50-55 (US$10 additional people). About half a kilometer east of town, this recommended place is run by friendly Italians Gloria and Mauro, who treat guests like family. There are 14 varisized bungalows with fans, private hot baths, refrigerator bars, and porches with hammocks. Most sleep one to three people, a few sleep four, but one has seven beds in two bedrooms and is suitable for students or large families. One cabin has a kitchenette. Twelve cabins are set in a pretty garden that attracts many birds, while two are on the other side of the street facing the ocean and sleep four. They also have a nearby house to rent; ask about it. A rancho in the garden is available for breakfast (separate cost). Italian, English, French, and German are spoken.

*El Pizote Lodge* (☎ 750-0227, fax 750-0226; in San José ☎ 221-0986, fax 255-1527; e pizotelg@racsa.co.cr) Singles/doubles without baths US$34/50, bungalows with bath US$75. About 1km west of town on a quiet back road, this is a relatively comfortable place. The rooms are large and clean, and there are four shared bathrooms for eight rooms. There are also pleasant wooden bungalows with private baths that are more expensive. The lodge is set in a garden, and you can rent bicycles, horses, and snorkeling gear; boat and snorkeling tours are also available. Good meals are served in the rather pricey restaurant. Ask about big discounts in the low season. The owner also has some larger houses for rent.

## Places to Eat

Several small, locally owned places serve meals and snacks typical of the region – ask at ATEC for recommendations if you'd like to eat with a family or at a small local place. Some of these include the reasonably priced *Miss Sam*, *Soda Isma*, and *Soda Irma*, all run by women who are long-term residents of the area and will cook a good local meal for about US$3 or US$4. *Doña Juanita* cooks out of her house, which is shortly before the Cabinas Las Brisas as you enter Puerto Viejo. *Doña Guillerma* does the same a couple hundred meters away – ask locally for directions.

*Café Coral* Open 7am-noon Tues-Sun. This café serves breakfast and serves a variety of healthful items, such as yogurt and granola, homemade whole-wheat bread, and, of course, the tico specialty – *gallo pinto*. Eggs and pancakes are also served.

*Soda Tamara* (☎ 750-0148) Also popular for breakfasts and meals throughout the day is this friendly place – it has coconut bread, cakes, and casados.

*Soda Lydia* is another reasonably priced local soda. *Pan Pay* has strong coffee, croissants, and fresh pastries. *Restaurant El Parquecito* serves decent meals, and *Caramba Restaurant* serves Italian food.

*Restaurante A Mi Modo* (☎ 750-0257, fax 750-0204) Dishes US$6-12. Open 6pm-10pm Mon-Fri, noon-10pm or 11pm Sat & Sun. Meals here are more expensive than at Caramba, but better Italian food and wine are served here; the lasagne is recommended. Relaxing jazz is featured as background music.

*The Place* (☎ 750-0195) This is a recent recommended addition, with meals ranging from healthy breakfasts and veggie-burger lunches to kebab dinners, all reasonably priced; look for the chalkboard specials.

*Stanford's Restaurant Caribe* Dishes average U$5-8. This place is good for seafood, which ranges from US$3 to US$20 depending on how exotic a meal you order. There's a lively disco here on weekends.

*Café Rico* has cheap but good breakfasts.

The *Restaurant Bambú*, within sight of the wave action at Salsa Brava, serves fruit shakes and sandwiches, and becomes a popular bar in the evenings.

*Restaurant Salsa Brava* Dishes US$6-12. This place does candlelit seafood and steak dinners.

*Restaurant Oro* With its little open-air terrace, this is more a small restaurant than just a soda, and it serves good local food.

*Marco's* (☎ 750-0273) Marco's is a popular recent addition that serves good pizza and a variety of dinner entrées.

*Garden Restaurant* (☎ 750-0069) Dishes US$5.50-8. Open Thur-Tues. One of the best places in town is this warmly recommended place, whose Trinidadian chef, Vera, is a local legend. Caribbean, Asian, and vegetarian food is served. Try the Jamaican jerk chicken, chicken curry, or well-prepared red snapper. Desserts are also good. Vegetarian main courses begin at about US$5.50; others start at US$6.50 and go up from there – red snapper is US$8, for example. Service and preparation are a step or three above what you might expect in such a small, out-of-the-way town. The Garden, which is at the Cabinas Jacaranda, is often closed May-August.

*El Loco Natural* (☎ 750-0263) Closed Tues. This is an unusual combination of musical café, boutique, and crafts store – a great place to hang out and drink good coffee, with home-baked pastries, sandwiches, and light snacks. There is an upstairs balcony. Sometimes there is live music from 8pm to 10pm Thursday and Sunday. Hours vary depending on the season, but they are usually open 11am to 9pm when there are travelers in town.

*Tacos* Dishes US$3-5. This friendly bar-restaurant has an excellent small menu of tacos and hamburgers and is popular with local expats.

*La Victoire de Sysiphe* Main courses US$6-11. This open-fronted restaurant serves excellent French and international food prepared by the French owner-chef.

*El Dorado* Dishes US$3-6. This locally popular place serves meals ranging from burgers to Caribbean fish dinners. After eating, diners hang out playing pool and chatting.

## Entertainment

*Jonny's Place* This is the most happening dance club on weekends – some nights the sand and rocks around the shoreside tables are liberally decorated with lit candles, a lovely complement (or contrast) to the flashing lights in the disco.

*Stanford's Disco* There's also weekend dancing at this quieter spot; its shoreside attraction is the occasional bonfire and circle of chairs.

*Restaurant Bambú* This place has a popular bar and has good reggae nights (with DJ) on Monday and Friday.

*Pizzeria Roma* Musicians and music are often happening here.

## Shopping

*Sistaz Art Gallery* Sistaz sells local crafts ranging from tie-dyed T-shirts to splashily colorful paintings. Also see El Loco Natural, under Places to Eat.

## Getting There & Around

From San José, express buses leave at 6am, 10am, 1:30pm, and 3:30pm and cost about US$5 for the five-hour trip (the first morning bus may leave you at a crossroads 5km out of town; ask). Alternatively, go from Puerto Limón, where buses leave from a block north of the market seven times a day – again, check that they will go all the way into Puerto Viejo.

Buses from Puerto Viejo leave from the bus stop shown on the map. Buses usually start from somewhere else and are liable to be late going through Puerto Viejo. A recent schedule of departures from Puerto Viejo is below. Check with ATEC (see Information, earlier) for the latest schedule.

San José – US$5; 7:30am, 9am, 11am, 1:30pm (Fri & Sun only), 4pm

Bribri/Sixaola – US50¢/US$2.50; 6:15am, 8:15am, 9:15am, 5:15pm, 7:15pm

Bribri only – US50¢; 11:15am

Cahuita/Limón – US50¢/US$1.20; 5:30am, 6am, 9am, 1pm, 4pm, 4:30pm, 5:30pm

Manzanillo – US$1.20; 7am, 3:30pm, 7pm

Places renting bicycles tend to come and go, but there are usually several in operation. Look for signs, and shop around for bike quality and price – rust works fast on the coast. For horse rental, ask at ATEC.

## EAST OF PUERTO VIEJO DE TALAMANCA

A 13km road heads east from Puerto Viejo along the coast, past sandy, driftwood-strewn beaches and rocky points, through the small communities of Punta Uva and Manzanillo, through sections of the Reserva Indígena Cocles/KéköLdi, and ending up in the Refugio Nacional de Vida Silvestre Gandoca-Manzanillo.

The locals use horses and bicycles along this narrow road. Drive slowly; not only are there horses, bicycles, and small children to watch out for, but there are slick little one-lane bridges offering the unwary driver an intimate visit with the creek below.

This road more or less follows the shoreline, and a variety of places to stay and eat can be found along the way. Most have opened in the last 15 years; this area is experiencing a minor boom in tourism, and aside from what is listed here there are (and will be) other places along the way.

A number of people are buying land in this area, among them members of wealthy, influential Costa Rican families; not all of them are developing their property responsibly. The local people realize that the tourist industry is a double-edged sword and are trying to control its development to ensure that *talamanqueños* benefit fairly, and also that the environment is not irreparably damaged. They are hampered by a bureaucratic jungle that ensures that such apparently clear cut things as the borders of the KéköLdi

reserve and the Gandoca-Manzanillo refuge are poorly defined.

## Places to Stay & Eat

**Playa Cocles** Beginning 2km east of town, Playa Cocles has good surfing and is benefiting from the organization of a lifeguard system (a praiseworthy effort).

*El Tesoro* (☎/fax 750-0128, ⓦ *http:// puertoviejo.net/cabinaseltesoro.htm*) Rooms US$8-20 per person. This is the first place you come to after leaving Puerto Viejo, and it's a nice little place with several cabinas with private hot showers. The owners are energetic promoters of the area and offer free morning coffee, free email and phone service, and a communal kitchen; discounts and free taxis to town are available for longer stays. Four rooms have two bunk beds each, ceiling fans, and communal hot showers, while four others have private hot showers and sleep up to six. A balcony with hammocks invites relaxing.

*La Isla Inn* (☎ 750-0109) Doubles US$40. Next along, this place has a few spacious and clean rooms with hot water, fans, and sea views.

*Beach Break Restaurant* This place is slightly farther along and opposite one of the more popular surfing beaches.

*Cabinas & Soda Garibaldi* (☎ 750-0101) Doubles US$12. Many surfers stay at this place, which offers basic double guestrooms with private baths and sea views. Bicycles, snorkels, and surfboards are available for rent.

*Surf Point* Rooms US$25. Also popular with surfers, the rooms here are nicer than at Garibaldi.

*Cariblue* (☎ 750-0035, ☎/fax 750-0057, ⓔ *cariblue@racsa.co.cr*, ⓦ *www.cariblue .com*) Standard doubles US$64, bungalows US$75, house US$175. All rates include buffet breakfast. This complex, set in lovely gardens and built by a friendly young Italian surfer couple, is just before the Garibaldi. The nine standard cabins have high ceilings and insulated walls, and they're airy, quiet, and cool. A king or two queen-sized beds, ceiling fan, and hot showers are included. Four spacious hardwood bungalows with bathrooms (each with different mosaic tile) have a porch and hammock. The house has two bedrooms, two bathrooms, and a kitchen and will sleep up to seven. Breakfast is served in a lovely, thatched-roof rancho, which features a dart board. The rancho is also a recommended Italian dinner restaurant (US$5.50-14).

*La Costa de Papito* (☎/*fax 750-0080*, W *www.greencoast.com/papito.htm*) Doubles US$50. A little farther down the road is another attractive bungalow-style place on nice grounds, reflecting a mellow philosophy on life. Five large hardwood bungalows with two double beds, carved tables, porches, high ceilings, and fans all feature a nicely tiled hot shower; two smaller bungalows with one bed are US$44 for doubles. One extra-large bungalow is US$50 for doubles plus US$5 per person, and it will sleep seven. For an extra US$4, you can have a breakfast delivered to your porch – a nice way to start your day.

*Río Cocles Cabinas* (☎/*fax 750-0124*) Doubles US$30. This is the next place down the road and has nice doubles with private baths and hot showers.

This is a growing area, and there are several other places available, as well as houses where rooms are rented.

*Yaré Hotel & Restaurant* (☎ *750-0106, 233-0509*, W *www.hotelyare.com/Yare/Index .htm*) Doubles US$40-60, cabins US$90-100. Between Playa Cocles and Playa Chiquita, this is a bright and fanciful place with clean and pleasant rooms and family cabins, which can sleep up to four people. All rooms and cabins have private hot showers and fans, and covered walkways lead to a decent restaurant. The owner is both helpful and friendly. At night, the air is filled with great frog noises, which drift across the complex from the surrounding jungle.

*Casa Camarona* (☎ *283-6711, 750-0151, fax 222-6184, 750-0210*, e *camarona@ticonet .co.cr*, W *www.costaricabureau.com/casa camarona.htm*) Singles/doubles US$45/70, US$13 extra for air-conditioning. This modern and clean place by the beach has 18 rooms, half of them air-conditioned. Rooms have tiled hot-water bathrooms and private little patios. There's a restaurant-bar with TV, and an outdoor rancho has Ping-Pong and a dart board. A trail leads through a tree-filled garden to the beach.

*El Rinconcito Peruano* US$4-9. Closed Tues. Just beyond Casa Camarona is this little restaurant serving authentic Peruvian seafood; the ceviche is excellent.

*La Pecora Nera* (☎ *750-0490*) Main courses US$10-20. Closed Mon. This place is down a narrow, unpaved road leading from the Rinconcito Peruano to a large, open-sided building set on grassy grounds shaded by large trees. Run by dedicated and amicable Italian chefs Ilario and Andrea, the 'Black Sheep' is arguably the best Italian restaurant on this coast. No menu makes an appearance; the chef or a server will come to your table and discuss what you'd like to eat and make suggestions. Plates are freshly prepared to order, and washing your dinner down with some imported Italian wine and adding an appetizer and dessert will make it an expensive evening – but it's worth it.

**Playa Chiquita** It isn't exactly clear where Playa Cocles ends and Playa Chiquita begins; the names are applied loosely.

There are several places to stay along Playa Chiquita, a series of beaches about 4km to 7km east of Puerto Viejo. New places continue to open up along this bit of waterfront.

*Villas del Caribe* (☎ *750-0202; in San José* ☎ *233-2200, fax 221-2801;* e *info@villas caribe.net*, W *www.villascaribe.net*) Doubles US$92, discounts for drop-ins. This is the most luxurious place on this beach. Here you'll find a dozen nice beachfront apartments (all sleeping up to five people) with sea views, hot showers, full kitchens, and fans. Next door is a restaurant.

*Hotel La Caracola* (☎ *750-0248, fax 750-0135*) Doubles without/with kitchen US$50/60. This hotel, which is located near the beach, has simple, cheerfully painted rooms.

*Aguas Claras* (☎ *750-0180*) They have several pretty houses for rent by the week.

*Hotel Punta Cocles* (☎ *750-0338, fax 750-0036*, e *gandoca@racsa.co.cr*, W *www.punta cocles.com*) Doubles US$81. The entrance to this hotel is about 5km from Puerto Viejo, on the right. It is a modern hotel development, popular with tico families. The Punta Cocles has 60 comfortable air-conditioned bungalows with private hot showers, two double beds and private patios. It also has a swimming pool, spa, a playground for kids, a restaurant, bar, and local trails into the forest, though the grounds around the buildings themselves are bare. Guides and rental items (snorkels, surfboards, binoculars, horses, and bicycles) are available.

***Ranchita Blanca*** Doubles US$30. Also in the area is this clean little place, which has a few rooms (with private baths) and bicycles for rent.

***Kashá*** (☎ 750-0205, W *www.costarica hotelkasha.com*) Doubles US$40. Pleasant bungalows come with private hot showers and satellite TV; there is a restaurant and bar on the premises.

***Miraflores Lodge*** (☎ 750-0038, e *mira pam@racsa.co.cr*, W *www.mirafloreslodge .com*) Dorm bed US$10, doubles US$25-55 (US$10 additional people). A bit farther east is Miraflores Lodge. This small B&B-style lodge has a private trail leading 500m to the beach and offers about eight rooms in an attractive private home, as well as a variety of more basic budget options tucked away on the beautiful grounds.

Owner Pamela Carter has been living in the area since 1988 and has gradually financed the construction of the lodge by growing and selling exotic flowers. She is knowledgeable about local botany and wildlife and can organize trips to visit Bribri farming families or indigenous-medicine practitioners. A number of interesting healing and local-culture workshops are available. Breakfast includes seasonal fruits grown on the grounds; local people often stop by the restaurant for a morning snack and chat. The place is popular but small, so reservations are recommended.

There are half a dozen small restaurants within a few hundred meters, as well as a few small cabinas and houses advertising rooms for rent.

***Elena Brown's Soda & Restaurant*** Although no longer run by Elena (she rents it out) this is still a locally popular place to eat and drink; a TV has been added.

***Playa Chiquita Lodge*** (☎ 750-0408, ☎/fax 750-0062, e *info@playachiquita .com, www.playachiquitalodge.com*) Singles/ doubles/triples/quads with private bath US$30/40/50/60, including breakfast; house US$60/275 per night/week. On lush grounds, almost 6km from Puerto Viejo, this attractively thatched lodge is 200m from the beach – you can't see the ocean from the lodge because the owner, Wolf Bissinger, wanted to leave the intervening forest standing. Instead, a short but scenic jungle

hike leads to the beach. Bissinger's partner, Wanda Paterson, is active in local community issues and is the organizer of the South Caribbean Music Festival (see the Puerto Viejo de Talamanca section, earlier in this chapter), which was first held at the lodge. Rooms with overhead fans and private baths are simple but spacious and nicely designed. There is a good restaurant on the premises, open to the public. Full breakfasts cost US$6, lunches and dinners cost about US$8 to US$12. Local guided tours by boat or van can be arranged; massage is available for US$20 per hour. High-season room rates are given; discounts are available for groups, students, and low-season visitors. A fully equipped four-room house is available nearby.

***Shawandha Lodge*** (☎ 750-0018, fax 750-0037, e *shawandha@racsa.co.cr*, W *www .shawandhalodge.com*) Doubles US$105, including breakfast. Across the road from Playa Chiquita Lodge, this upscale lodge has 10 large, airy bungalows, all with fabulous bathroom mosaics – a feature that seems to represent a minor cultural movement along this stretch of coast. Each bathroom is equipped with a hair dryer. The French-Caribbean restaurant is a bit pricey, but it's elegant.

**Punta Uva** About 7km east of Puerto Viejo is the Punta Uva area, which offers several places to stay and eat. The protected curve on the western side of this lovely point offers tranquil swimming.

***Cabinas Selwyn*** Doubles without bath US$16, room with bath US$30. Near the beach is this long-standing place, which offers several basic rooms with shared bath, and another room that sleeps four people and has a private bath. Selvin is a member of the extensive Brown family, noted for their charm and unusual eyes (Selvin is from the one blue/one brown branch), which have attracted them both romantic and scientific attention. There is a locally popular ***restaurant-bar***, which is closed on Monday and Tuesday.

***Walaba Cabinas*** (☎ 750-0147) Rooms from US$10 per person. Back on the main road and 200m farther along is this reasonably cheap and popular place, offering both basic rooms and dormitories. The staff here will arrange house rentals.

*Viva* (☎ *750-0089*, e *puntauva@racsa .co.cr,* w *www.puntauva.net)* Houses US$400 per week for 2 people, US$75 extra people. Contact David and Jean Walter to rent one of these three beautiful, fully furnished houses, each with tiled hot-water shower, full kitchen, two bedrooms, and a wraparound verandah. Set in a semiformal garden with a croquet lawn (they'll lend you a mallet and balls), the secluded houses are a short walk from the beach.

## Getting There & Away

For information on accessing the beach areas east of Puerto Viejo de Talamanca, see Manzanillo, below.

## MANZANILLO

The school of Manzanillo, which marks the beginning of the village, is 12.5km from Puerto Viejo de Talamanca (Manzanillo village already existed when the Gandoca-Manzanillo wildlife refuge was established in 1985). The road continues for about one more kilometer and then peters out. From the end of the road, footpaths continue around the coast through the Gandoca-Manzanillo refuge. Costa Rica's Ministry of Natural Resources has an office here (in a lime-green wooden building a few hundred meters past the school), where information on the refuge is sometimes available.

## Water Sports

**Aquamor Talamanca Adventures** in Manzanillo (☎ 391-3417 cellular, ☎ 225-4049 pager, e aquamor@racsa.co.cr) offers scuba diving at prices ranging from US$30 for a one-tank beach dive to US$55 for a two-tank boat dive; rates include equipment and guide. PADI open-water certification courses cost US$300. Kayak rentals for sea and river trips cost US$5 per hour, snorkeling gear is US$12 per day, and various discounts are offered for all-day or overnight kayaking, diving, camping, and snorkeling adventures. The guides speak Spanish and English and are concerned about the environment, particularly the fragile coral reefs. Dolphin-watching tours by boat or kayak are available for US$25 to US$55.

## Places to Stay & Eat

*Maxi's Cabinas* Rooms US$15. You'll find this basic, seaside place near the bus stop in Manzanillo. There is a restaurant and a bar here, and even a disco on the weekends. Eating seafood here is a local tradition; craft stalls and picnickers gather on the beach outside of Maxi's.

*Cabinas Las Veraneras* (☎ *754-2298)* On the way into the village, by the *pulpería*, this inexpensive place has clean rooms.

*Pangea B&B* Rooms US$27 per person. This Italian-owned place has two pleasant rooms, as well as a beach house; leave messages with Aquamor (see Water Sports, above).

*Almonds and Corals Lodge Tent Camp* (in San José ☎ *272-2024, fax 272-2220,* e *almonds@racsa.co.cr,* w *www.almond sandcorals.com)* Singles/doubles US$65/80. This spot is on the outskirts of Manzanillo. The spacious, comfortable tents are on raised wooden platforms and contain single beds, mosquito nets, fans, lights, tables, and hammocks. A central lodge provides family style dining, and there are hot showers, toilet facilities, and a swimming pool. Guided hikes, snorkeling, bicycle rental, birding, and horseback riding are offered. The surrounding area is undeveloped and full of wildlife – insects and frogs call all night, and howler monkeys wake you at dawn. Meals here cost about US$8 each.

Several local women will prepare traditional Caribbean meals in their homes for travelers – ask around for details. For breakfast (and other meals), there is a little *soda* just inland past the Aquamor office.

## Getting There & Away

Buses leave Limón for Manzanillo at 6am, 2:30pm, and 6pm, passing through Cahuita and Puerto Viejo and arriving in Manzanillo about 2½ hours later. Return buses leave Manzanillo at 5am, 8:30am, and 5pm. There's also a daily 7am bus that goes direct to San José, plus a 1pm departure on Friday and Sunday.

For any of the destinations described above between Puerto Viejo and Manzanillo, simply ask the bus driver to let you off.

## REFUGIO NACIONAL DE VIDA SILVESTRE GANDOCA-MANZANILLO

This refuge lies on the coast around Manzanillo and extends southeast as far as the Panama border. It encompasses 5013 hectares of land plus 4436 hectares of sea. This is the only place in the country apart from Cahuita where there is a living coral reef. It lies about 200m offshore, so snorkeling is one of the refuge's attractions.

The land section has several different habitats, not least of which is farmland. The little village of Manzanillo is actually within the boundaries of the refuge, which also contains an area of rainforest and some of the most beautiful beaches on the Caribbean, unspoiled and protected by rocky headlands. Coconut palms form an attractive tropical backdrop. There is a coastal trail leading 5.5km from Manzanillo to Punta Mona. South of this trail is an unusual 400-hectare swamp containing holillo palms and sajo trees. One map shows a trail that leaves from just west of Manzanillo and skirts the southern edges of this swamp and continues to the small community of Gandoca, roughly 8km to 10km away. Experienced hikers could follow the Punta Mona trail, but a guide may be necessary for the trail to Gandoca; ask locally.

Beyond Punta Mona, protecting a natural oyster bank, is the only red mangrove swamp in Caribbean Costa Rica. In the nearby Río Gandoca estuary there is a spawning ground for Atlantic tarpon, and caimans and manatees have been sighted. The endangered Baird's tapir is also found in this wet and densely vegetated terrain.

Marine turtles, especially leatherbacks, have nested upon the beaches at the southeast end of the refuge. The leatherbacks nest from March to July, with a peak in April and May. Local conservation efforts are underway to protect these nesting grounds – the growth in the human population of the area has led to increased theft of turtle eggs to the point that the species is declining locally.

The Asociación Nacional de Asuntos Indígenas (ANAI), or National Association of Indigenous Affairs, is a grassroots organization that works with locals to protect the sea turtles. If you are interested in sea turtle conservation, you can volunteer to collect nesting and size data, patrol beaches, and move eggs that are in danger of being destroyed by high tides or predation. Volunteering involves long hours, no pay, hot and humid conditions, and a chance to help sea turtle conservation while seeing a remote part of Costa Rica. If this appeals to you, contact ANAI in San José (☎ 750-0020, 224-3570, 224-6090, fax 253-7524, e tortugas@racsa.co.cr) or write the organization for information at Apartado 170-2070, Sabanilla de Montes de Oca, San José, Costa Rica, or 1176 Bryson City Rd, Franklin, NC 28734, USA. If you can't volunteer, contributions are welcome – donations are tax-deductible in the USA for US taxpayers. ANAI is supported by The Nature Conservancy and US AID.

*Accommodations* for the volunteers range from camping to housing with local families; a minimum stay of seven days is required, and volunteers must contribute to the cost of meals and housing (from US$7 to US$30 per day, depending on how much comfort you want). The project runs from early March to late July each year, and there is a US$25 registration and training fee.

The variety of vegetation and the remote location of the refuge attract many tropical birds; sightings of the rare harpy eagle have been recorded here. Other birds to look for include the red-lored parrot, the red-capped manakin, and the chestnut-mandibled toucan, among hundreds of others. The birding here is considered very good. (I saw a flock of several hundred small parakeets come screaming overhead at dusk – quite a sight and quite a sound!)

The area is also known for incredible raptor migrations, with over a million individual birds flying overhead in the fall. ANAI also has a volunteer tracking program based in the Cocles/KéköLdi reserve, with accommodations in their Hone Creek office near Puerto Viejo. This project runs during migrations from March to June and August to December; registration is US$160 and accommodations are US$5 a day. For more information about the bird-conservation program, contact ANAI (see above, or send email to e anaicr@racsa.co.cr).

Finally, ANAI also has an agroforestry and crop experimentation project at nearby Finca Lomas, where volunteers can stay for US$90 a month, plus a one-time US$160 registration fee. Most volunteers stay one to four months.

## Information

Ask for Florentino Grenald, who lives in Manzanillo and used to serve as the reserve's administrator. He has a local bird list and can recommend guides.

A local boat captain, **Willie Burton**, will take you boating and snorkeling from Manzanillo. His house is the last one on the road through Manzanillo before you reach the trails leading to Punta Mona. If you have a car, you can leave it by his house while you go hiking. Horses and guides can also be hired locally.

ATEC in Puerto Viejo de Talamanca (see Information in that section, earlier in this chapter) offers a variety of tours into the refuge, including day and overnight trips on foot, horseback, or by boat.

### Places to Stay

*Camping* is permitted, but there are no organized facilities unless you are volunteering with ANAI (see above). Reportedly, camping on the beach is best, as there are fewer insects and more breezes. Most visitors take day hikes and stay in a hotel.

### Getting There & Away

The Gandoca-Manzanillo reserve is accessible from Manzanillo by trail or by boat.

### BRIBRI

You'll find this small village en route from Cahuita to Sixaola, on the Panama border, at the end of the paved (and badly potholed) coastal road. From Bribri, a 34km gravel road takes the traveler to the border.

Bribri is the center for the local indigenous communities in the Talamanca mountains, although there is not much to see here. Ask locally about a large waterfall near Volio, about 3km from Bribri.

The Ministry of Health operates a clinic in Bribri that serves both Puerto Viejo and the surrounding Indian communities. There is a Banco Nacional de Costa Rica here, also serving Puerto Viejo (about 12km away) and surrounding communities.

### Places to Stay & Eat

There are a couple of basic lodging options and some restaurants in Bribri. Accommodations tend to fill up on market days (Monday and Tuesday).

*Cabinas El Piculino* (☎ 751-0130) Doubles US$10-20. About 15 clean rooms offer private cold showers; some have TV and air-conditioning. A *soda* is attached.

*Bar Restaurant Los Mangos* (☎ 751-2253) Doubles US$10. Los Mangos is mainly a restaurant, but it will rent basic rooms on request. It is a few hundred meters out of town toward Puerto Viejo.

Buses sometimes stop for a meal or snack at the *Soda Restaurant Bribri*.

### Getting There & Away

Bribri is a regular stop for all buses to and from Sixaola. Buses leave from Bribri, heading through the communities of Chase and Bratsi (☎ 751-2175 public phone) to the village of Shiroles (☎ 751-2064 public phone), 17km away.

From Shiroles, horse and foot traffic continues on into the indigenous reserves. One village that can be reached is Amubri (☎ 751-2215 public phone), which reportedly has a mission with a place to stay. Ask at ATEC in Puerto Viejo about visiting these places.

Buses for other coastal towns stop outside the Soda Restaurant Bribri. If your bus is going to Puerto Viejo, ask if it is going into town or just as far as the *cruce* (crossroads).

### SIXAOLA

This is the end of the road as far as the Costa Rican Caribbean is concerned. Sixaola is the border town with Panama, but few foreign travelers cross the border here – most overlanders go via Paso Canoas on the Carretera Interamericana.

Sixaola is an unattractive little town, with nothing to recommend it except the border crossing itself, which is relaxed. Most of the town is strung along the main street. Remember, Panama's time is one hour ahead of Costa Rica's.

For details on crossing the border at this point, see the Getting There & Away chapter.

### Places to Stay & Eat

There are several basic restaurants and a few places to stay; ask around. Accommodations are generally unappealing, though they're OK for the unfastidious traveler looking for something different. It's best to get here as early as possible if going to or coming from Panama to avoid getting stuck here. There are better accommodations on the Panama side.

*Cabinas Sanchez* (☎ 754-2105) Doubles US$9. This place offers seven clean rooms with cold baths. There's no sign, so ask. Also try the very basic **Hotel Doris**. The **Pension Central** on the main street is pretty rough. The **Restaurant Hong Wing** is friendly and has a few basic rooms upstairs.

## Getting There & Away

Direct buses from San José leave from the Caribe terminal at 6am, 10am, 1:30pm, and 3:30pm, returning to San José at 5am, 7:30am, 9:30am, and 2:30pm (US$5.75, six hours). There are also a few buses a day to/from Puerto Limón via Cahuita and Puerto Viejo. A bus from San José to Changuinola, Panama (16km east of Sixaola), leaves the Hotel Cocorí near the Coca-Cola terminal at 10am.

Taxis with 4WD are available to visit local villages. You can reach Gandoca (within the Refugio Nacional de Vida Silvestre Gandoca-Manzanillo) from here. Taxis can also be hired for the journey to Almirante, Panama, for about US$20.

# Southern Costa Rica

The southbound Carretera Interamericana leaves San José to the east and skirts Cartago before heading truly south. The highway begins to climb steadily, reaching its highest point at over 3300m near the somberly named peak of Cerro de la Muerte (Death Mountain; 3491m). This area is about 100km south of San José and is often shrouded in mist. The next 30km stretch is a particularly dangerous section of highway. From the high point, the road drops steeply to San Isidro de El General at 702m. San Isidro is the first important town south of Cartago and is the main entry point for nearby Parque Nacional Chirripó, which contains Costa Rica's highest mountain, Cerro Chirripó (3820m), and others almost as high.

From San Isidro, the Interamericana continues southeast through mainly agricultural lowlands to the Panama border, a little over 200km away. There are no more big towns on this route, but several smaller ones are likely to be of interest to visitors wanting to see parts of Costa Rica that are not on the usual 'gringo trail.' From these towns, roads lead out to some of the more remote protected areas in the country, including the rarely visited and difficult-to-get-to Parque Internacional La Amistad and the Wilson Botanical Garden, arguably the best in the country.

Note that the yellow-topped, numbered posts along the Carretera Interamericana south of San José are kilometer markers and are referred to in the chapter text.

The magnificent wilderness of Parque Nacional Corcovado and the popular nearby Bahía Drake area in the Península de Osa are accessed from southern Costa Rica, but are covered in the separate Península de Osa & Golfo Dulce chapter. Some of Costa Rica's best surfing beaches are found at Pavones, in the far south, which is also covered in that chapter. Dominical, another well-known surfing beach often accessed through San Isidro, is covered in the Central Pacific Coast chapter.

## RUTA DE LOS SANTOS

The so-called Route of the Saints is a scenic backroads drive that leads from the Inter-

americana south of Cartago and winds back north to San José. It is named for the villages it passes through: San Pablo de León Cortés, San Marcos de Tarrazú, Santa María de Dota, San Cristóbal Sur, and several others named after saints. The towns themselves are not especially exciting, but the drive takes you through typical hilly farm country – coffee, cattle, and clouds. Narrow,

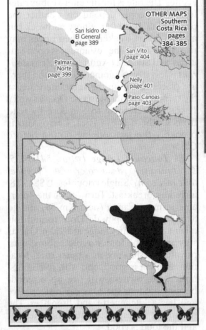

## Highlights

- Quetzal-watching in the San Gerardo de Dota area
- Strolling the extensive, well-planned grounds of Wilson Botanical Garden
- Making the challenging climb to Chirripó's summit, highest point in the country
- Soaking in the rustic hot springs near San Gerardo de Rivas
- Hiking in Parque Internacional La Amistad – only for the truly adventurous!

OTHER MAPS
Southern Costa Rica pages 384-385

San Isidro de El General page 389

San Vito page 404

Palmar Norte page 399

Neily page 401

Paso Canoas page 403

steep roads twist through a splendid landscape – green and inviting or dark and forbidding, depending on the weather.

## Places to Stay & Eat

Most visitors just drive through on a day trip, but some of the towns have inexpensive country hotels.

**Hotel Bar Restaurante Dota** (☎ 541-1026) Rooms with bath US$7 per person. This hotel is in Santa María de Dota.

In San Marcos de Tarrazú you can find the following three hotels: **Hotel Zacatecas** (☎ 546-6073), which has doubles with private hot baths for US$12 and larger rooms for US$20; the **Hotel Bar y Restaurante Continental** (☎/fax 546-6225), which charges US$13 for doubles but lacks hot water; and **Hotel Tarrazú** (☎ 546-6022), which charges US$18.

**Cerro Alto Hotel de Montaña** (☎ 382-2771 cellular, ☎/fax 551-5428, 571-1010) Cabins US$38. On the Interamericana, 3km north of the Empalme junction, this place has eight rustic but comfortable cabins, all of which sleep up to four people and have private hot showers, fireplaces, and kitchenettes. The rate is for the entire cabin; rates for fewer people depend on whether the place is full. It is often empty midweek but may fill up on weekends, when prices may rise accordingly. The restaurant is open Saturday and Sunday. (Another simple *restaurant* is less than a kilometer away, and there are places to eat on the Interamericana at the turnoff to Santa María de Dota as well.) If you are returning to San José by road from southern Costa Rica, Cerro Alto is probably the last lodging option before Cartago.

**El Toucanet Lodge** (☎/fax 541-1435, e toucanet@racsa.co.cr, w www.el toucanet.com) Singles/doubles US$45/58, including breakfast. Turn off of the Interamericana at Cañon (near Km 58) and go 8km south to Copey de Dota to find this quaint little country lodge at 1850m. Guests stay in one of four double cabins, with private hot showers, in a quiet rural location. Birding is good, and with five hours' notice, the owners will fire up a wood-burning outdoor spa. One cabin sleeps five and has a kitchenette and fireplaces. The restaurant is unpretentious and friendly, and the food is good.

# SOUTHERN COSTA RICA

## Getting There & Away

Most drivers take the Interamericana south to Empalme, a small gas station and *soda* stop almost 30km from Cartago. Shortly beyond there, a paved road turns west toward Santa María de Dota (about 10km away), San Marcos (7km farther), and San Pablo (4km farther). From here, a choice of paved roads takes you back to the Interamericana via San Cristóbal or winding north through San Gabriel and other villages to San José. A regular car can travel these roads, but available maps and road signs are poor – ask locals for directions.

Autotransportes Los Santos (☎ 223-1002) buses bound for Santa María de Dota leave from Avenida 16, Calles 19 & 21, in San José, several times a day. Some of these buses go via San Marcos de Tarrazú.

## GENESIS II

At about 2360m above sea level, this private nature reserve *(day-use fee US$10/5 adults/ students)* is possibly the highest in the country. Situated in the Cordillera de Talamanca, the reserve covers 38 hectares, almost all of which are virgin cloud forest (or, technically, tropical montane rainforest). This consists of evergreen and oak forest with epiphytic bromeliads, ferns, orchids, lichens, mosses, and other plants covering every available surface. A species of tree fern once generally thought to be extinct also grows here.

For seeing highland birds, butterflies, and plants, this is the place to stay. Some of the more spectacular birds include the resplendent quetzal, collared trogon, and emerald toucanet. An estimated 200 bird species inhabit this highland region, and identifying and classifying them is an ongoing project. Tropical red squirrels are often seen.

There are about 20km of trails within the reserve, of which 3.5km are well maintained; the rest are much wilder. The 'dry' season is from January to May, but it can rain at any time, so rainwear is essential. Mornings are usually clear – even during the rainy season. Average annual rainfall is 2300mm. The altitude makes for colder weather – bring warm clothes.

A new addition to Genesis II is 'Talamanca Treescape,' a canopy access system with a trail leading to a suspension bridge, two zip lines and three platforms. Visits are always done with a naturalist guide and are not the rushed affairs of some other canopy tours; nor do they have as many zip lines. The idea is education as much as adrenaline. Rates are US$40/35/30 for adults/students/ children under 12, including admission to the reserve. Add US$5 for a picnic lunch from one of the platforms. Guests staying at Genesis II get a US$10 discount.

## Volunteer Programs

The reserve runs a program for motivated volunteers over age 21, who help with trail construction and maintenance (the primary job) or on other jobs including repairing fences, producing brochures/maps, counting birds, and helping with reforestation, housework, gardening, and landscaping. Volunteers pay US$600 for four weeks of food and lodging (two work periods consisting of 10 six-hour days followed by four days off). Details and applications are available from the owners (see below).

## Places to Stay & Eat

*At the reserve (☎ 381-0739, ⓔ info@genesis -two.com, Ⓦ www.genesis-two.com)* Adult/ student rate US$85/50, including three meals and guided hike. There are five simple guest bedrooms (one with a double bed and four with two singles) in the main house, and two separate, basic cabins sleeping up to four people (usually student volunteers). All guests share the two hot-water showers and toilets in the main house. Electricity is available, but there is no TV. Tasty family style meals are prepared using fresh local produce, often right from the garden. The large balcony affords forest views.

The English-speaking, on-site owners, Steve and Paula Friedman, suggest a minimum stay of three days and recommend a week. Call them for further information or to make reservations. Guests staying four or more nights get complimentary laundry service and a free guided half-day trip to an alternate habitat. Guests staying a week or more receive a 10% discount and a full-day trip to an alternate habitat.

## Getting There & Away

The turnoff for Genesis II is at the Cañon church, just south of Km 58 on the Interamericana. Turn east and follow the rough road 4km to the refuge. You'll need 4WD. If traveling by bus, get off at the Cañon church; the owners will pick you up if you make arrangements with them, or you can walk. Roundtrip transportation from San José can also be arranged.

## MIRADOR DE QUETZALES

This farm and budget lodging option is also known as Finca del Eddie Serrano (☎/fax 381-8456, W www.exploringcostarica.com/mirador/quetzales.html). Rooms US$25/35 per person with shared/private shower. It's near Km 70 on the Interamericana (there is a sign), about 1km off the highway to the right (heading south). Quetzals are often seen from November to early April, and sometimes during other months. The farm has four simple rooms with bunk beds, and there are two shared hot showers. Eight *cabinas* with private bath include four doubles and two triples, which are in attractive wooden A-frame buildings with small heaters (the 2650m elevation means nights are cool), and two quintuple cabins, each with an upstairs room and suitable for families. The accommodations are rustic but clean and have good views. About 50m above the lodge, a lookout point gives glimpses of up to five volcanoes on a clear day. Rates includes dinner, breakfast, and a guided hike (one to two hours) to view quetzals. Day visitors can take a guided hike for US$6 per person.

## SAN GERARDO DE DOTA

This spread-out little farming community, on the western slopes of Cerro de la Muerte, is famous for excellent highland birding. Quetzals have been reported here regularly every April and May (during breeding season) but are often seen during the rest of the year as well. In fact, many people feel this is one of the best places in the country to see quetzals. The trout fishing in the Río Savegre is also good; the seasons are May and June for fly-fishing and December to March for lure-fishing.

### Places to Stay & Eat

*Trogon Lodge* (☎ 740-1051, fax 740-1052; in San José ☎ 223-2421, fax 222-5463; e trogon@grupomawamba.com, W www.grupomawamba.com) Singles/doubles US$45/65. Almost 7km from the Interamericana you pass the turnoff for Trogon Lodge, which is part of the Mawamba Group (see the Mawamba Lodge entry in the Tortuguero Area section in the Caribbean Lowlands chapter). This hotel has nicely landscaped grounds, a stocked trout-fishing pond (not much of a challenge to catch your own trout for dinner), and 16 rooms in attractive wooden cabins. Horse rental (US$10 per hour) is available. Rooms have hot baths and heaters. Full breakfast (US$7.50), lunch, and dinner (US$12) are offered.

*Cabinas El Quetzal* (☎ 740-1036) Rooms US$30 per person, including meals. This is a cheaper option, about 1km after the Trogon Lodge turnoff. Six rooms, with fireplaces and hot showers, sleep a total of 20 people.

Quetzals abound in San Gerardo de Dota

The staff here say that because they are lower in elevation than the Albergue de Montaña Savegre (see below), quetzals are seen nearby from December to March.

Opposite Cabinas El Quetzal is *Restaurant-Bar Los Lagos*, a nice little place.

*Albergue de Montaña Savegre* (*Cabinas Chacón;* ☎ *740-1028/9, fax 740-1027,* e *savegrehotel@racsa.co.cr,* w *www.savegre .co.cr*) Rooms US$75 per person, including home-cooked meals. Two kilometers beyond Restaurant-Bar Los Lagos is this well-known, long-established, and recommended place. The hotel is on the Chacón farm, which was carved out of the wilderness by Don Efraín Chacón in 1957 – an interesting story – and is still in the same family, overseen by the patriarch himself. The 400-hectare farm is now part orchard, part dairy ranch, and 250 hectares remain as virgin forest. The elevation here is about 2000m.

The owners are enthusiastic about their birds. They have a bird list and usually know where the quetzals are hanging out. Often, they'll set up telescopes on the property so guests can get a close look at nearby nests. The owners helped set up the Quetzal Education & Research Center in cooperation with US scientists. On the farm, there are trails of 4km and 8km and a hiking trail that leads to a waterfall. Half-day guided birding hikes are US$50 per group (maximum 10). More trips are available. Horseback rides with a bilingual guide cost US$10 per hour, and trout fishing is available near the hotel (in both the river at US$30 per half day with guide and tackle, or in a stocked pond). The 30 remodeled rooms have porches and hot showers. The restaurant-bar is popular with *ticos* on weekends.

### Getting There & Away

Buses to San Isidro de El General can drop you off at 'La Entrada a San Gerardo' (near Km 80), from where, if you have a reservation, the Chacóns at the Albergue will pick you up for US$12. Or you can walk – it's downhill. It's just over 9km to the Albergue and less to the other places.

You can drive down here (look for the entrance of the road to your right coming from San José); the road is very steep, though just passable to an ordinary car in good condition.

## CERRO DE LA MUERTE

The mountain overlooking the highest point on the Carretera Interamericana got its name before the road was built – but the steep, fog-shrouded highway in the area is known as one of the most dangerous in Costa Rica for accidents. During the rainy season, landslides may partially or completely block the road. On a dark and misty night, visibility can drop to a car length – frightening! Local wisdom advises never driving this section at night; if you do, take it slowly.

This area is the northernmost extent of the *páramo* – a highland shrub and tussock grass habitat more common in the Andes of Colombia, Ecuador, and Peru than in Costa Rica. Nevertheless, here it is – and you can drive through it. Birders here look for highland bird species such as the sooty robin, volcano junco, and two species of silky flycatchers. Costa Rica Expeditions and Horizontes will both arrange guided day and overnight birding excursions to this highland region, but all departures leave on request only (for contact information see the Getting Around chapter ).

When the weather is clear, the views can be very good, but drivers should concentrate on the very winding, steep, and narrow road.

*Hotel Georgina* (☎ *771-1299, 770-8043*) Rooms without/with bath US$6/10 per person. The friendly Hotel Georgina, about 5km beyond the highest point on the Interamericana, is where buses often stop for a meal and a break. Rates are less for groups or families. Simple meals are served, and there is good high-altitude birding nearby. Hot showers and electric blankets are offered – it's cold up here.

*Albergue de Montaña Tapantí* (☎/*fax 232-0436*) Doubles/triples/quads US$45/60/75. This is another place to stay along the highway, closer to San José and just north of Km 62 on the Interamericana. The 10 rooms have sitting areas or terraces or both; private bathrooms have hot water. Breakfast is about US$3, and other meals are US$6-8 for main courses.

## AVALON RESERVA PRIVADA

About 3.5km west of the Interamericana by way of the tiny community of División, just past Km 107, is the 170-hectare Avalon Reserva Privada (☎/*fax 770-1341,* e *avalon reserve@yahoo.com)*. Doubles without/with bath US$45/55. It's easy to miss the entrance to the dirt road; ask locally for directions. This is a private cloud forest reserve, home to high-altitude birds including quetzals, bellbirds, trogons, and toucans. There are hiking trails and good views of the mountains of southern Costa Rica. The hotel is under new management; travelers should call ahead for room availability and directions.

## SAN ISIDRO DE EL GENERAL

Some 136km from San José, San Isidro de El General (commonly known as simply San Isidro) is the most important town on the southern Interamericana. The town and its surrounding district are home to a population of about 45,000.

The Valle de El General is important for agriculture, as you can see as you descend from the bleak páramos of the Cerro de la Muerte through the increasingly lush farming country of the valley. San Isidro is the commercial center of the coffee fincas, cattle ranches, and plant nurseries that dot the mountain slopes. The town is also an important transport hub.

San Isidro is a bustling, pleasant, and fairly modern town. With the exception of a small museum, there really isn't much to see or do here, though its position as a gateway to other places makes it of interest to the traveler. San José, to the north, and Panama, to the southeast, are the most obvious nearby destinations. A road to the northeast leads to the village of San Gerardo de Rivas (see

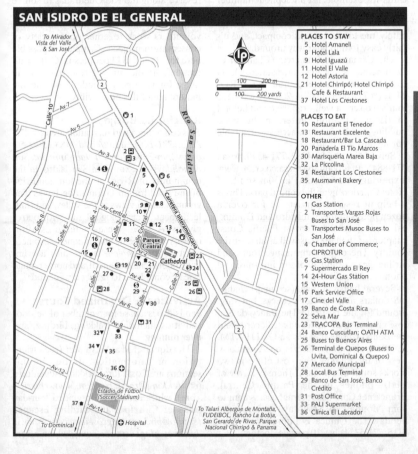

### SAN ISIDRO DE EL GENERAL

**PLACES TO STAY**
5 Hotel Amaneli
8 Hotel Lala
9 Hotel Iguazú
11 Hotel El Valle
12 Hotel Astoria
21 Hotel Chirripó; Hotel Chirripó Cafe & Restaurant
37 Hotel Los Crestones

**PLACES TO EAT**
10 Restaurant El Tenedor
13 Restaurant Excelente
18 Restaurant/Bar La Cascada
20 Panadería El Tío Marcos
30 Marisquería Marea Baja
32 La Piccolina
34 Restaurant Los Crestones
35 Musmanni Bakery

**OTHER**
1 Gas Station
2 Transportes Vargas Rojas Buses to San José
3 Transportes Musoc Buses to San José
4 Chamber of Commerce; CIPROTUR
6 Gas Station
7 Supermercado El Rey
14 24-Hour Gas Station
15 Western Union
16 Park Service Office
17 Cine del Valle
19 Banco de Costa Rica
22 Selva Mar
23 TRACOPA Bus Terminal
24 Banco Cuscutlan; OATH ATM
25 Buses to Buenos Aires
26 Terminal de Quepos (Buses to Uvita, Dominical & Quepos)
27 Mercado Municipal
28 Local Bus Terminal
29 Banco de San José; Banco Crédito
31 Post Office
33 PALI Supermarket
36 Clínica El Labrador

To Mirador Vista del Valle & San José

Río San Isidro

Carretera Interamericana

Parque Central

Cathedral

To Talari Albergue de Montaña, FUDEIBOL, Rancho La Botija, San Gerardo de Rivas, Parque Nacional Chirripó & Panama

Estadio de Fútbol (Soccer Stadium)

To Dominical

Hospital

SOUTHERN COSTA RICA

later in this chapter), where you'll find the ranger station for Parque Nacional Chirripó. To the southwest, another road leads to the Pacific coast and the beaches at Dominical; this road allows you to make a roundtrip from San José to Dominical and Parque Nacional Manuel Antonio without retracing your route. Other minor roads lead into quiet farming country. River-running trips on the nearby Ríos Chirripó and General, with overnight stops in San Isidro, can be arranged in San José (see Activities & Organized Tours, later in this section).

## Orientation & Information

Note that streets, though labeled on the map, are poorly signed. The locals tend not to know or use street names. Hotel business cards, for example, list a telephone number and either no address at all or something like, '100m northeast of the park.' Fortunately, the town center is compact, and it's fairly easy to find your way around.

The Cámara de Comercio (Chamber of Commerce; W www.costaricasur.co.cr), on Calle 4, Avenidas 1 & 3, houses CIPROTUR (☎ 771-6096, fax 771-2003, W www.eco tourism.co.cr), a well-organized and helpful tourist information center. In the same building, public Internet access is available during business hours.

Selva Mar (☎ 771-4582, 771-4579, ☎/fax 771-8841, e selvamar@racsa.co.cr, W www .exploringcostarica.com) is 50m south of Hotel Chirripó, near the central park. This is a helpful reservation service for over a dozen hotels in the San Isidro and Dominical areas (see the Central Pacific Coast chapter for the latter) as well as all over the country. The office can arrange tours and airline tickets, and it offers international phone and fax service.

Several banks in town (see map) change US dollars and traveler's checks, but shop around for the best rate. The Banco de San José gives cash advances on credit cards, and the Banco Cuscutalan has an OATH ATM. A Western Union office is on Avenida 4, west of the market. The post office is two blocks south of the park. There is a row of CHIP phones in the Parque Central. Brunc@net Café has Internet access 8am to 8pm Monday to Saturday, 9am to 5pm Sunday. The Clínica E Labrador (☎ 771-7115, 771-5354) has 10 private doctors.

There is a park service office (☎ 771-3155, fax 771-4836) on Calle 2, Avenidas 4 & 6, where you can make reservations for Parque Nacional Chirripó. It's open to take reservations 8am to noon weekdays and for information 1pm to 4pm as well. Information is also available here regarding Parque Internacional La Amistad, which, combined with Chirripó and a host of other protected areas, forms the UNESCO Reserva de la Biósfera La Amistad.

## FUDEIBOL Reserve

Seven kilometers northeast of San Isidro, FUDEIBOL, roughly an acronym for the Fundación para el Desarrollo del Centro Biológico Las Quebradas (☎/fax 771-4131; admission US$6), is a community-run reserve along the Río Quebradas (a source of drinking water for San Isidro). There are nature trails and views; local and foreign volunteers work together on a variety of conservation projects. Camping is possible here for about US$3 per person. Call for directions. At the time of research, a small lodge for visitors was under construction; inquire about this new facility.

## Rancho La Botija

This coffee finca and recreation area (☎ 771-2253, 771-1401; adult/child US$2.50/1.50; open 2pm-5pm Mon-Fri, 9am-5pm Sat, Sun & holidays) is 8km from San Isidro, in the community of Rivas, on the left-hand side of the road to San Gerardo de Rivas. The grounds afford views of the valley, and trails lead to an archaeological site with petroglyphs. A small museum features 19th-century implements and antiques. Also here are a working trapiche (sugar mill), a swimming pool, small restaurant, and horse rentals. Locals come here to relax on weekends.

## Activities & Organized Tours

San Isidro is a base for a number of outdoor activities, including **trekking**, **birding**, and **river running**.

Headquartered at Selva Mar (see Orientation & Information, earlier in this section) are **Costa Rica Trekking Adventures** (e trekking@racsa.co.cr, W www.chirripo .com), which specializes in guided four-day treks of Chirripó, and **Birding Escapes** (e info@birdwatchingcostarica.com, W www .birdwatchingcostarica.com), which offers packages and custom birding trips for all levels.

**Costa Rica Expeditions** and **Ríos Tropicales** have three- and four-day river-running trips on the Río Chirripó from mid-June to mid-December (see Organized Tours in the Getting Around chapter for contact information).This is mainly a Class IV river. Trips include roundtrip transportation from San José, all boating gear (including life vests), tents for camping by the side of the river, expert bilingual river guides, and all meals. Costs depend on the number of people; ask about joining other groups if your party has fewer than eight people.

Running the Río General is also possible, although none of the major river-running outfitters currently offer trips here on a regular basis. Ask around if you have a group and want to go – most likely something can be arranged.

## Special Events
The annual fair is held during the first week in February (occasionally it's held beginning at the end of January) and features agricultural, horticultural, and industrial shows and competitions.

San Isidro is the patron saint of farmers, who bring their stock into town to be blessed on the saint's feast day, May 15.

## Places to Stay
**San Isidro** There are plenty of cheap hotels in town; the fancier ones are on the outskirts.

*Hotel Lala* (☎ 771-0291) Rooms US$4.50 shared bath, US$6.50 cold private bath, for one or two people. The cheapest hotel in town is this rather poor place offering basic rooms, some with a double bed and private cold-water shower.

*Hotel Astoria* (☎ 771-0914) Singles/doubles without bath US$5/9, with bath US$6/10.This place, which has a parking lot, offers dozens of tiny, basic rooms with shared bath, and slightly better boxes with private cold showers. Half a dozen nicer doubles cost US$15 but are often full.

*Hotel Chirripó* (☎ 771-0529) Singles/doubles US$5/9, with bath US$8/14.This 40-room hotel is a good value, and some of the simple rooms have private hot showers. There's a decent restaurant and café on the premises (see Places to Eat, below) and a guarded parking area.

*Hotel Amaneli* (☎ 771-0352) Rooms with bath US$9 per person. This is a reasonable budget option. The 30 clean rooms with private hot showers and fans all sleep up to five people; try to avoid rooms facing the highway. A café here opens at 5am.

*Hotel Iguazú* (☎ 771-2571) Singles/doubles US$14/21. This place is clean and secure, and the 21 rooms come with private hot showers, TV, and fans.

*Hotel El Valle* (☎ 771-0246, fax 771-0220) Singles/doubles US$14/18. Most rooms have private hot showers, TVs and fans, and there is a parking area.

*Hotel Los Crestones* (☎ 770-1200, 770-1500, fax 771-6012, e hcrestonespz@hotmail.com) Singles/doubles US$25/40, air-conditioned doubles US$50, extra people US$10. This new, clean, 12-room hotel was the best in town at the time of research. Four rooms have air-conditioning, and all have hot showers, fans and cable TV. There is a parking area, and Internet access is available.

**Around San Isidro** *Hotel del Sur* (☎ 771-3033, fax 771-0527, e info@hoteldelsur.com, w www.hoteldelsur.com) Doubles US$40-70. Five kilometers south along the Interamericana, this is the best standard hotel. It has a swimming pool, tennis court, sauna, a nice restaurant and bar, a café, and mountain bike rentals. A small casino detracts somewhat from the pleasantly rural ambience. There are 55 rooms of five types and varying sizes, all with private baths, hot water, carpeting, and telephones. More expensive rooms also have air-conditioning, TV and minibars. Some sleep up to five.

*Mirador Vista del Valle* (☎ 771-6096, ☎/fax 384-4685, fax 771-2003) Doubles US$60. Overlooking San Isidro from 15km to the north on the Interamericana, this restaurant has a balcony with hummingbird feeders and great views. Behind the restaurant are a few cabinas, and rates include breakfast.

*Talari Albergue de Montaña* (☎/fax 771-0341, e talaripz@racsa.co.cr) Singles/doubles US$36/52, including breakfast.This recommended place is 7km northeast of San Isidro, en route to San Gerardo de Rivas and Parque Nacional Chirripó (just before the village of Rivas). Pilar and Jan, the friendly, multilingual tica/Dutch couple who own this place, will help organize hikes up Cerro Chirripó, arrange horseback tours, and provide local information. They also have a bird list; this is a good center for mid- to high-altitude birding. The 8-hectare property has a river running through it, a swimming pool, and a small restaurant and piano bar. (Jan is an accomplished pianist.) There are eight rooms with private hot showers, most with a fridge. Lunch (US$7.50) and dinner (US$10) are available on request. Low-season discounts are also available. The hotel is closed from September 15 to October 31.

## Places to Eat

There are many inexpensive *sodas* downtown and in the market/bus terminal area – this is the place for travelers watching their colones. However, none of the restaurants in town are expensive.

*Hotel Chirripó Cafe* Dishes US$2-4. Open from 6:30am for breakfast. This café is inexpensive and popular.

*Hotel Chirripó Restaurant* Dishes US$4-9. This restaurant has pleasant plaza views, but be aware that service can be slow.

*Panadería El Tío Marcos* On the same block as Chirripó Restaurant, this bakery has good pastries and other baked goods.

*Restaurant/Bar La Cascada* (☎ 771-6479) Dishes US$3.50-9. A block west of the Parque Central, this upstairs balcony restaurant is the trendiest place in a relatively sedate town. The food is mainly bar and tico food, and a younger clientele spends evenings here with beers and burgers, but you can get steak and seafood as well.

*Restaurant El Tenedor* (☎ 771-0881) Dishes US$1-7. Open 9am-11pm Tues-Sun. Next to Hotel Iguazú, this restaurant has a balcony overlooking a busy street and serves hamburgers for US$1 as well as other meals. Pizzas and Italian dishes are a specialty.

*La Piccolina* Meals US$5. Hours 11am-10pm, closed Tues. At the time of research, this was San Isidro's favored pizzeria.

*Restaurant Excelente* (☎ 771-8157) Dishes US$4-6. Chinese and tico food are indeed excellent here. It's on the northeast corner of the Parque Central.

*Restaurante Los Crestones* (☎ 777-1218) Dishes US$4.50-7.50. Open 11am-11pm daily. A barn of a place, this restaurant has a wide selection, specializing in seafood and also offering chicken and meat dishes.

For seafood, also try the *Marisquería Marea Baja*. For baked goods, there's a *Musmanni*.

## Getting There & Away

Buses from San José (US$3, three hours) depart from a terminal (☎ 222-2422, 771-0414, 223-0686) at Calle Central & Avenida 22, more or less hourly during the day.

The bus terminal/market complex in San Isidro opened in 1993, but most long-distance buses still leave from a variety of terminals and bus stops scattered throughout town (see the San Isidro map). The main bus terminal deals mostly with buses to nearby villages.

Buses to San José with Transportes Musoc (☎ 771-0414) or Transportes Vargas Rojas (☎ 771-0419) leave from Calle 2 & the Interamericana 13 times a day 5:30am to 4:30pm.

Buses to San Gerardo de Rivas (for Parque Nacional Chirripó) leave from the south side of the bus terminal at 5am and 2pm and take two hours.

Buses leave from the Terminal de Quepos (see map) for Quepos (on the Pacific coast) via Dominical at 7am and 1:30pm, and for Uvita via Dominical at 9am and 4pm. The fare to Quepos is US$2.50; tickets to the other places cost less. Buses leave here for Puerto Jiménez (☎ 771-2550) at 6:30am, 9am and 3pm. The five- to six-hour ride costs about US$4.

TRACOPA (☎ 771-0468), at Calle 3 & the Interamericana, has southbound routes. The ticket office is open 7am to 12:30pm and 1:30pm to 4pm Monday to Saturday; at other times, buy tickets on the bus. Buses originating in San Isidro for Palmar Norte, Río Claro, and Neily (US$3, four hours) leave at 4:45am, 7:30am, 12:30pm and 3pm. Buses to Paso Real, San Vito (US$2.75, 3½ hours), Sabalito, and Agua Buena leave at 5:30am and 2pm. These services may be changing, so check.

For Buenos Aires, buses leave about every two hours from 5am to 5pm from the small terminal at the east end of Avenida 2.

Alfaro buses from San José pass through San Isidro at approximately the following times for the following destinations – tickets are sold on a space-available basis. Ask locally to confirm the best time and place to wait for these buses. If they are full, take one of the buses originating in San Isidro and go to Palmar Norte for better connections to Sierpe and Ciudad Cortés, to Río Claro for connections to Golfito, and to Neily for Paso Canoas.

David (Panama) – 10am, 3pm

Golfito – 10am, 6pm

Palmar Norte – 7 times a day, 8am-9pm

Paso Canoas – 8am, 10:30am, 2pm, 4pm, 7:30pm, 9pm

San Vito – 9am, 11:30am, 2:45pm, 5:30pm

You can hire a 4WD taxi to San Gerardo de Rivas for US$16. A taxi to the Hotel del Sur costs about US$3.

## SAN GERARDO DE RIVAS
About 22km northeast of San Isidro, this small village is the entry point to Parque Nacional Chirripó. The elevation here is about 1350m; the climate is pleasant, and there are hiking and birding opportunities both around the village and in the park. (You can inquire for bilingual birding guides in the Selva Mar offices).

Everyone comes to climb the mountain! However, when you return, check out the **thermal hot springs** *(admission US$2; open 7am-6pm)*. Walk about 1km north of the ranger station on the road toward Herradura and you'll see a sign pointing right. Follow this trail about another 1km to a house, where the owner will charge you admission to hang out in the hot springs as long as you want. If you decide to stay overnight, they have a couple of cheap rooms and a small soda. Ease those aching muscles and enjoy the mountains for another day.

Over the last few years, foreigners have begun to buy land here. As more visitors come simply to enjoy the tranquillity and high-altitude beauty around the village, its character may begin to change. So far, foreign development has been private and discreet.

## Orientation & Information
The Chirripó ranger station is about 1km below the village on the road from San Isidro (see the Parque Nacional Chirripó section for hours of operation). Just above the ranger station, the road forks; take the right fork to San Gerardo (the left fork will take you almost 3km to the village of Herradura).

The village *pulpería* (☎ 771-1866), next to the Hotel y Restaurant Roca Dura Café (see below), has a public phone.

## Places to Stay & Eat
***Cabinas La Marín*** *(☎ 771-1866)* Rooms from US$8 per person. Just below the ranger station, this basic place has rooms with shared hot showers; at the time of writing it was adding rooms with private bath. It has a small restaurant.

***Cabinas El Bosque*** *(☎/fax 771-4129)* Rooms from US$7 per person. Across from the ranger station, this place has decent rooms and a restaurant-bar. Some rooms have private hot baths. There is some camping equipment for rent, and nonguests can store luggage for US$2 per day.

As you head up to the village from the ranger station, you pass a few more simple hotels. ***Cabinas & Soda El Descanso*** *(☎ 771-7962)* Rooms from US$6 per person. Owned by Francisco Elizondo and his family, all of whom are friendly and helpful, this is a good choice. Rooms are small but clean, with a shared electric shower. Decent meals are available on request.

***Cabinas Elimar*** Rooms US$15. Up the hill from Cabinas & Soda El Descanso, this place has four simple but spacious rooms (each with one double and one single bed) with private electric showers. The restaurant opens on request, and there is a trout pond.

***Hotel y Restaurant Roca Dura Café*** *(☎ 771-1866)* Camping US$4 per tent, rooms from US$6 per person. This hotel is in the center of San Gerardo. The campground, which has a cold shower, is behind the hotel, by the river, and has room for 25 tents. Eight small, basic, but clean rooms with a single or a double bed and shared hot showers are US$6 per person, while two rooms with private hot showers cost US$15 double. These two rooms are a good value; they're built into the mountain below the hotel, with one wall made of genuine *roca dura* (hard rock). The largest room costs US$20, has a single and a double bed, and is also built into the rock, with interesting architecture and a private stone shower. The hotel has a simple restaurant-bar with live music from 6pm to 8pm, attracting diners from other hotels. The village pulpería sells supplies next door. This is one of the most popular options for budget travelers and hikers. At the time of research, owner Luis Elizondo was planning to add some riverside cabinas. There is a parking area and a locker service (free for guests) to leave gear while hiking in the park.

*Albergue de Montaña El Pelicano* (☎ 382-3000, fax 771-0781, e *elizondo martinez@yahoo.com*) Rooms US$10-12 per person, including breakfast. About 200m below the ranger station, this place is owned by Rafael Elizondo, a late-blooming but prolific artist who grew up in the area and gradually began sculpting the shapes he saw suggested in the wood and stone around him. His carvings and rock arrangements dot the grounds, and his studio is always open for viewing – make sure you see his tree-stump busts and detailed all-wood motorcycle. None of it is for sale, but it's all worth seeing; this is a kind of anonymous, spirited creativity that makes you pleased to be human. The 10 attractive, simple rooms share four bathrooms (with heated showers) and a balcony overlooking the river valley.

*Uran Lodge* (☎ 388-2333, fax 771-8841) US$7 per person. Just a few minutes' walk below the trailhead, this lodge has 11 simple but spotless rooms with one or two beds and shared hot showers, and one large quadruple room with a private shower. It has a large good new restaurant (no beer or cigarettes), which is an ideal location to start a hike early in the morning; early breakfast is served on request.

*Vista al Cerro Lodge* (☎ 373-3365) US$6 per person. This simple and clean lodge is just 300m above the soccer field in San Gerardo. It offers shared hot showers, and breakfast is available from 3:30am if required by early hikers.

*Retreat Río Chirripó* (☎ 771-4582, fax 771-8841) Singles or doubles US$45, US$10 additional people, including breakfast. About 1.5km below the ranger station, in the community of Canaán, this was the most upscale lodge in the area at the time of writing. It has eight rustic cabins featuring balconies with river views and private bathrooms with hot water. There's also a restaurant, bar, and a warmed swimming pool. Yoga retreats take place here.

### Getting There & Away
Buses leave San Isidro at 5am and 2pm and take almost two hours to get to San Gerardo

de Rivas (there is another San Gerardo, so ask for San Gerardo de Rivas by its full name). Return buses leave at 7am and 4pm. The final stopping point and the departure points for return buses may vary depending on rain and road conditions; ask locally.

If you're driving, head south of San Isidro on the Interamericana, crossing the Río San Isidro at the south end of town. About 500m farther, cross the Río Jilguero and look for a steep turn up to the left, about 300m beyond the Jilguero. A small wooden sign with yellow lettering indicates the turnoff for the park; more visible above it is a large, red sign for the Universidad Nacional. If you are coming from the south, note that there are two entrances to this road, both most easily identified by the red university signs. If you cross the Río Jilguero, you've gone too far.

The ranger station is about 18km up this road, which is paved as far as Rivas. Beyond that it is steep and graveled, but still passable for ordinary cars.

## PARQUE NACIONAL CHIRRIPÓ
At 50,150 hectares, this is Costa Rica's principal mountain park and one of the country's largest protected areas. It holds three peaks over 3800m, including Cerro Chirripó (3820m), the highest mountain in the country. Of all the Central American countries, only Guatemala has higher mountains. Most of the park lies at over 2000m above sea level. There are hiking trails and a mountaintop lodge (see Places to Stay, later in this section) for people wishing to spend a few days trekking at high altitude. Travelers in tropical Central America are often delighted to find a park where they can get away from the heat for a while!

The park entrance at San Gerardo de Rivas is at 1350m, so the elevation gain to the top of Chirripó is about 2.5km straight up! An easy-to-follow trail leads all the way to the top, and no technical climbing is required. Almost all visitors use this trail to reach the summit, though alternatives are discussed below. Walking at the lower elevations is also rewarding, with excellent views and opportunities for good birding and butterfly observation.

The climb is a fascinating one because it takes you through constantly changing scenery, vegetation, and wildlife. After passing through the pastureland outside the park, the trail leads through tropical lower montane and then montane tropical cloud forests. These are essentially evergreen forests with heavy epiphytic growths in the trees, plus thick fern and bamboo understories. Emerging above the main canopy (25m to 30m high) are oak trees reaching 40m or even 50m in height.

These highland forests are home to such birds as the flame-throated warbler and buffy tuftedcheek, to name but two. Small brown frogs and lime-colored caterpillars thickly covered with stinging hairs make their way across the trail, and Baird's tapirs lurk in the thick vegetation (though you are much more likely to see squirrels than tapirs). Eventually, the trail climbs out of the rainforest and into the bare and windswept páramo of the mountaintops.

The Chirripó massif is part of the Cordillera de Talamanca, which continues to the northwest and southeast.

The eastern boundary of the national park coincides with the western boundary of the huge and largely inaccessible Parque Internacional La Amistad, so most of the mountains of the Talamanca range are protected. Chirripó and La Amistad, together with a number of biological and Indian reserves, make up the Reserva de la Biósfera La Amistad (see the Parque Internacional La Amistad section, later in this chapter).

## Information

The dry season (from late December to April) is the most popular time to visit the park. On weekends, and especially at Easter, the park is relatively crowded with Costa Rican hiking groups, and the Crestones Base Lodge may well be full. To protect the delicate páramo ecosystem, camping is not allowed anywhere. February and March are the driest months, though it may still rain at times. Note that the park is **closed in May**.

During the wet season there are fewer visitors. It rarely rains before 1pm, but it is worth remembering that as much as 7000mm of annual rainfall has been recorded in some areas of the park.

It can freeze at night, so warm clothes, rainwear and a good sleeping bag (available for rent) are necessary.

The ranger station outside of San Gerardo de Rivas is a good place to ask about weather conditions and to get an idea of how many people are in the park. Officially, you need to make a reservation with the central park office in San Isidro (☎ 771-5116, 771-3155, fax 771-4836) to stay in the lodge near the summit (see Places to Stay, later in this section). In reality, there are a lot of no-shows. It's best just to go to the ranger station near San Gerardo de Rivas and ask for a permit – it helps if you speak Spanish and check in immediately after arriving. Occasionally, travelers may find that the lodge is indeed full – but even then, if you can wait a day or two in the village, space will usually become available. The week before Easter and the Easter weekend are usually reserved well in advance, but there are rarely problems at other times.

In advance of your visit, you can contact the Chirripó ranger station through the park service office in San Isidro. Ranger station hours are 7:30am to 5pm daily (it is important to register the day before to be able to start early next day).

At the ranger station, you'll pay the US$15 park entrance fee for two days, plus US$10 for additional days, plus US$10 per night to stay in the lodge. Drivers can leave vehicles near the ranger station, and excess luggage can be locked up during your park stay at no extra charge.

Horses can be rented through a local association of porters – ask at hotels in the area or at the ranger station. You can ride a horse or just get one to carry your gear. The locals will not normally rent animals without a local guide to accompany you. Expect to pay about US$23 per day for a guide and a pack animal (30kg maximum weight in the dry season, 20kg in the wet), or US$31 for a riding horse and a guide. In the rainy season, the horses may stay home, depending on trail conditions, but the porters will carry up to 14kg for you for about US$20. It's a good idea to place everything in plastic bags inside your luggage or pack. When the luggage is sent with porters or horses up or down the mountain you will not be able to see your stuff until you get to the destination point, so make sure you have everything you need in your day pack.

Because of fire hazard (there was a major forest fire a few years ago), cigarette smoking is not permitted on the trail. There are designated smoking areas at the lodge.

See Places to Stay, below, for information on equipment rental.

**Maps** The maps available at the ranger station are fine for the main trails. Good topographical maps from the Instituto Geográfico Nacional de Costa Rica (IGN) are available in San José (see Planning in the Facts for the Visitor chapter for contact information); note that the hostel, shelters, and trails are not marked on these maps. Chirripó lies frustratingly at the corner of four separate 1:50,000-scale maps, so you need maps 3444 II San Isidro and 3544 III Durika to cover the area from the ranger station to the summit of Chirripó itself, and maps 3544 IV Fila Norte and 3444 I Cuerici to cover other peaks in the summit massif. Topographical maps are nice to have but not essential.

### Climbing Chirripó

From the ranger station it is a 16km climb to the Chirripó summit area. Allow seven to 14 hours to reach the lodge, depending on how fit and motivated you are. Anybody can show you the beginning of the trail, which is signed at approximately 2km intervals and easy to follow once you are on it. Remember to pack a flashlight in your day pack in case you are delayed.

The open-sided, insect-ridden *hut* at Llano Bonito, about halfway up, can provide shelter. However, this is intended for emergency use. Rangers recommend that hikers on day trips don't ascend beyond this point. Ask at the ranger station about sleeping here; this hut is a possible shelter for climbers who can't make it all the way to the

summit area in one day. Carry water on the trail, particularly during the dry season, when the only place to get water before reaching the lodge is at Llano Bonito.

From the lodge it is another 6km to the summit – allow at least two hours if you are fit, but carry a warm jacket, rain gear, water, snacks, and a flashlight just in case. A minimum of two days is needed to climb from the ranger station in San Gerardo de Rivas to the summit and back again; this gives you little time for resting or visiting the summit. Three days would be a better bet. If you don't return to San Gerardo by 4pm, you'll miss the last bus out.

Almost every visitor to the park climbs the main trail to Chirripó and returns the same way. Other nearby mountains can also be climbed via fairly obvious trails leading up from the lodge. These include Cerro Ventisqueros, at 3812m the second-highest peak in the country, and several other peaks over 3700m. Some maps show a couple of rarely used, unmaintained wilderness trails leading north and south out of the park; these trails are extremely difficult to find and are not recommended.

An alternative, rarely used route to Chirripó is to head north of the ranger station to the community of Herradura, 3km away. Guides can be hired here (about US$35 per day) to take you up a new trail entering the mountains from the west side. Porters can also be hired for US$20 per day, but you still require a local guide. Call the public phone at the pulpería in Herradura (☎ 771-1199) and ask for Fabio Badilla or Rodolfo Elizondo, who are active members of the guide association and speak some English. An overnight camp is necessary below Cerro Urán – the rangers will permit you to camp on this rarely used route. Also ask locally about other rarely used routes through the forest up to the mountain.

Apparently, there are a couple of places to stay beyond Herradura – ask locally. In Herradura, a lady named Mirna rents *rooms* near the river, and Rodolfo Elizondo can arrange accommodations, trout fishing, and horse rental. Both of them

can be contacted through the public phone. Rodolfo has a stocked trout pond where you can catch fish and have it cooked for you.

In San Isidro, contact Costa Rica Trekking Adventures (a branch of Selva Mar), which arranges guided and outfitted Chirripó climbs using both routes.

## Places to Stay

**Crestones Base Lodge** Dorm beds US$10 per person. This mountain hostel, which looks something like a monastery, is a thoughtfully designed stone building that sleeps up to 60 people. A solar panel powers electric lights from 6pm to 8pm. Showers are available but aren't heated, though the water is a little less frigid in the afternoon. At the time of research there were plans to heat showers and the building sometime in the future. Sleeping bags can be rented at the lodge for US$2; blankets are US$1. Camping stoves are US$1 a day, and camping-gas canisters are another US$2. These stoves can be used inside the lodge only. See Information, earlier in this section, for reservation information.

## Getting There & Around

See the San Gerardo de Rivas section, earlier in this chapter, for directions to get here. From opposite the ranger station, in front of Cabinas El Bosque, there is free transportation to the trailhead at 5am. Also, several hotels offer early-morning trailhead transportation for their guests.

## BUENOS AIRES

This small village is 64km southeast of San Isidro and 3km north of the Interamericana. It has a tree-filled plaza, a couple of banks, a gas station, a disco, and other services.

The village is in the center of an important pineapple-producing region. It is also an entry point for the rarely visited Parque Internacional La Amistad, as well as several Indian reserves to the north, and Reserva Indígena Boruca to the south. A road east of Buenos Aires goes through remote country and Indian reserves and eventually joins with the San Vito road at Jabillo. You probably won't see any other tourists in this area.

**Cabinas Violeta** Singles/doubles US$7.50/9. Ask at the Ferretería El Pueblo (☎ 730-0104), in the center of town at the corner of the park, for directions.

This is the best place to stay, offering a dozen simple but clean rooms.

Other cheap and basic places include **Cabinas Kanajaka** (☎ 730-0207), singles/doubles US$6/10, on the way into town from the highway, and **Cabinas Mary** (☎ 730-0187), US$7.50 per person, near the clinic. Both have private, warm showers.

To get here, take buses from San Isidro, or any bus that's heading south on the Interamericana, and ask to be let off at the turnoff for Buenos Aires. Buses to San Isidro leave about every hour from 5:30am to 5pm. There are also a few local buses to nearby towns. TRACOPA (☎ 730-0205), in the center, has a few buses a day to and from San José; these originate elsewhere and may be full when they come through.

## RESERVA BIOLÓGICA DURIKA

This 700-hectare private biological reserve is 17km north of Buenos Aires on the flanks of Cerro Durika in the Cordillera de Talamanca, and is within the Reserva de la Biósfera La Amistad. Within the Durika reserve is the **Finca Anael**, where a couple dozen people live in a more or less independent and sustainable manner. Community members are committed to local conservation. Most are ticos, but there are a few foreigners.

The reserve opened to tourism in 1992, and birding and hiking are the main activities. Day hikes, overnight tours and camping trips are offered to nearby waterfalls, the Cabecar Indian village of Ujarrás (where crafts such as string bags are sold), local farms, and to climb Cerro Durika (3280m) in Parque Internacional La Amistad. You can ride a horse if you prefer. Classes may be offered in yoga, vegetarian cooking, and meditation, among other things.

There are five **cabins** here of various sizes, sleeping two to eight people (US$35 per person). All have private bath and porches with mountain views. Rates include vegetarian meals, guided walks, and (for those staying more than one night) transport from Buenos Aires. There are discounts for groups, students, and long stays. If you have a sleeping bag, there is a basic hut where you can sleep for US$10 (student rate) including meals. Reservations and information are available from the Asociación Durika (☎ 730-0657, fax 730-1095, e *durika@racsa.co.cr)*. There is no phone at the Finca Anael, so you have to make phone reservations a week in advance by contacting the association; their phone connection isn't very reliable! They check their email about once a week. A trip to this reserve is for adventurous travelers.

## RESERVA INDÍGENA BORUCA

This reserve is centered around the village of Boruca, about 20km south of Buenos Aires. It is one of the few Indian reserves where visitors are welcome, perhaps because Boruca is only some 8km west of the Carretera Interamericana.

The Boruca indigenous group is known for its carvings, including balsa wood masks and decorated gourds. The women use pre-Columbian back-strap looms to weave cotton cloth and belts; these can sometimes be purchased from the locals. The people live a simple agricultural life in the surrounding hills.

If you are driving through the area on the Interamericana, you can stop at the community of Curré, where a small crafts cooperative store sells Boruca handicrafts.

### Special Events

The three-day Fiesta de los Diablitos (*diablitos* means 'little devils') is held in Boruca from December 31 to January 2. About 50 men wearing carved wooden devil masks and burlap costumes take the role of the Indians in their fight against the Spanish conquerors. The Spaniards, represented by a man in a bull costume, lose the battle. The Borucas may charge visitors a photography fee and require all photographers to wear a pass indicating they have paid.

Another festival, held during the second week of December, celebrates the Virgin of the Immaculate Conception (La Fiesta de los Negritos) with costumed dancing and traditional Indian music (played mainly on drums and bamboo flutes).

### Places to Stay

The village *pulpería* in Boruca has a few basic rooms for rent, but it isn't really set up for tourism. This option is for culturally sensitive travelers who can respect and appreciate the local lifestyle. Some local families may provide sleeping space for you in their houses.

### Getting There & Away

Buses (US$1.25, 1½ hours) leave the central market in Buenos Aires at 11:30am and 3:30pm daily, traveling to Boruca via a very poor dirt road. Drivers will find a better road that leaves the Interamericana about 3km south of Curré – look for the sign. The road is about 8km to Boruca; during the wet season you'll probably need 4WD.

## PALMAR NORTE & PALMAR SUR

These two places are basically the same town on different sides of the Río Grande de Térraba, which the Interamericana has been following for the last 40km (for those traveling southbound). Palmar is about 125km south of San Isidro and 95km northwest of the Panama border.

The town is the center of the banana-growing region of the Valle de Diquis, and it's also a transportation hub. You might find yourself staying here en route to Sierpe, Bahía Drake, and the Parque Nacional Corcovado region (see the Península de Osa & Golfo Dulce chapter).

The area has drawn the interest of archaeologists thanks to the discovery here of almost-perfect **stone spheres**, some up to 1.5m in diameter. The spheres were made by pre-Columbian Indians, but exactly who made them and how remains a mystery. Similar objects have been found on Isla del Caño (now a biological reserve). Ask in town if you want to see the spheres (*esferas de piedra*) – they are found in a variety of places, including backyards and banana plantations.

In Palmar Norte you'll find hotels, bus service, and a gas station; Palmar Sur has the airport. Banco Nacional (☎ 786-6263) and Banco Popular (☎ 786-7033) are on the Interamericana in Palmar Norte. Also on the Interamericana is *Osa Tours* (☎ 786-6534, 786-7825, fax 786-6335), which is both the local tourist information center and the place to arrange tours into the Península de Osa. To get from Palmar Norte to Palmar Sur, take the Interamericana southbound over the Río Grande de Térraba bridge, then take the first right beyond the bridge.

### Places to Stay & Eat

*Hotel Xenia* (☎ 786-6129) Rooms US$4.50 per person. This is one cheap and very basic

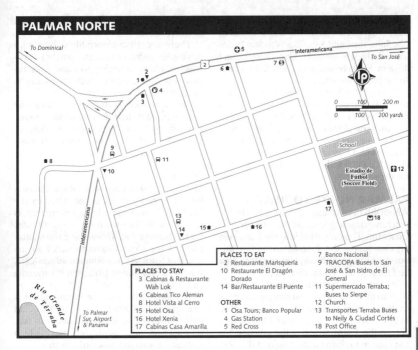

## PALMAR NORTE

To Dominical

Interamericana

To San José

School

Estadio de
Fútbol
(Soccer Field)

Interamericana

Río Grande
de Térraba

To Palmar
Sur, Airport
& Panama

**PLACES TO STAY**
3  Cabinas & Restaurante
   Wah Lok
6  Cabinas Tico Aleman
8  Hotel Vista al Cerro
15  Hotel Osa
16  Hotel Xenia
17  Cabinas Casa Amarilla

**PLACES TO EAT**
2  Restaurante Marisquería
10  Restaurante El Dragón
   Dorado
14  Bar/Restaurante El Puente

**OTHER**
1  Osa Tours; Banco Popular
4  Gas Station
5  Red Cross

7  Banco Nacional
9  TRACOPA Buses to San
   José & San Isidro de El
   General
11  Supermercado Terraba;
   Buses to Sierpe
12  Church
13  Transportes Terraba Buses
   to Neily & Ciudad Cortés
18  Post Office

option to try. Another equally basic place is
*Hotel Osa*.

*Cabinas Tico Aleman* (☎ 786-6232,
786-6235) Singles/doubles US$9/15, air-
conditioned doubles US$20. Just off the
Interamericana, this place has clean, airy
rooms with private baths and fans, and a
few air-conditioned doubles.

*Cabinas & Restaurante Wah Lok*
(☎ 786-6777) Singles/doubles US$7/11. Near
Cabinas Tico Aleman, this is a Chinese
restaurant with a few adjoining rooms, with
fans and showers, for rent.

*Cabinas Casa Amarilla* (☎ 786-6251)
Rooms US$4.50 per person, singles or
doubles US$16. This place has a private
parking lot and clean, secure rooms with
private baths and fans, as well as a few very
basic, cheaper rooms.

*Hotel Vista al Cerro* (☎ 786-7744, ☎/fax
786-6663) Singles/doubles US$15/21, air-
conditioned doubles US$24. This newer
place on the outskirts of town offers 20
rooms, five air-conditioned. All are clean and
have fans and basic, cold-water showers. A
restaurant has simple food, a TV and Internet access.

*Restaurante El Dragón Dorado* This is
one of the better of several inexpensive and
simple Chinese restaurants here.

*Bar/Restaurante El Puente* Popular with
locals, this place serves tico food.

*Restaurante Marisquería* Another locally
popular choice, this one serves good seafood.

## Getting There & Away

**Air** SANSA (☎ 786-6353) has daily flights
from San José (fare US$66/132 one-way/
roundtrip) and from Quepos. Travelair has
daily flights from San José for US$66/128.

These air schedules are prone to
change. Ask about flights to Golfito, Bahía
Drake, and Neily/Coto 47 with either or
both airlines.

The airport is in Palmar Sur. Taxis, which
charge US$3 to Palmar Norte or US$13 to
go to Sierpe, usually meet incoming flights.
The Palmar Norte-Sierpe bus heads through
Palmar Sur – you can board it if there's
space available.

**Bus** TRACOPA (☎ 786-6511) has buses to
San José (US$4.50, five hours) at 5:25am,
6:15am, 8:15am, 10am, 1pm, 2:30pm, and

4:45pm Monday to Saturday. On Sunday, buses depart at 6:15am, 8:15am, 10am, 12:15pm, 1pm, and 3pm. Buses to San Isidro leave daily at 8:30am, 11:30am, 2:30pm, and 4:30pm. Southbound buses sell tickets on a space-available basis only.

Transportes Terraba runs six buses daily to Neily between 6am and 4:50pm, and hourly buses to Ciudad Cortés.

Buses travel 14km to Sierpe from in front of the Supermercado Terraba at 5:45am, 7am, 9am, 11:30am, 2:30pm and 4:45pm (US50¢); a taxi will cost you about US$12.50 for the same trip.

## PALMAR NORTE TO NEILY

About 40km southeast of Palmar Norte, the Interamericana goes past the junction at Chacarita. The only road into the Península de Osa leaves the Interamericana at this point, heading southwest (see the Península de Osa & Golfo Dulce chapter).

About 15km beyond Chacarita, a signed road to the right of the Interamericana goes to the Esquinas Rainforest Lodge (see below). Driving an additional 14km brings you to **Río Claro**, which is the junction for the road to Golfito on the Golfo Dulce. Río Claro has a gas station, several restaurants, and a couple of places to stay.

*Hotel y Restaurant Papili* (☎ 789-9038) Doubles US$10. This hotel, which has six small but very clean rooms with private hot baths and fans, is the best place to stay in Río Claro. This is a better value than anywhere in Neily, which is 16km away. It also has a good restaurant and pizzeria. Nearby, the *Hotel Impala* is another clean choice.

## Esquinas Rainforest Lodge

In the village of Gamba, less than 6km south of the Interamericana, and above the Parque Nacional Piedras Blancas (formerly part of Parque Nacional Corcovado), is the Austrian-funded Esquinas Rainforest Lodge (☎ 775-0901, fax 775-0631, ⓔ esquinas@ racsa.co.cr, Ⓦ www.esquinaslodge.com, www .regenwald.at). Cabins US$95 per person, including three meals. This project embodies ecotourism in the truest sense. Most of the employees are from Gamba, and profits from the lodge go into community projects. The lodge is surrounded by 120 hectares of rainforest with trails. Bus, boat, horse, and foot tours are available into the nearby national park as well as other areas.

There are 10 comfortable cabins with private hot showers, fans, and porches. Facilities include a swimming pool and a restaurant with forest views. Multiday packages, including tours, are available.

The road from the Interamericana to the lodge is passable to ordinary cars year-round. From the lodge, a rough unpaved road continues 8km to Golfito; this route is also passable to normal cars most of the year.

## NEILY

This town, 17km northwest of the Panama border by road, is nicknamed 'Villa' by the locals. It is also sometimes referred to as Ciudad Neily. The town is the main center for the banana and African oil-palm plantations in the Coto Colorado valley to the south of town. At just 50m above sea level, it is a hot and humid place, but it's friendly and otherwise pleasant.

A road winds into the mountains that rise up north of Neily, leading about 30km to the attractive little town of San Vito (see that section, later in this chapter), which rests at a cooler elevation of 1000m.

Neily's main importance to the traveler is its role as a transport hub for southern Costa Rica. From here, roads and buses go to Panama and a host of small local agricultural settlements. Among these, the nearby towns of Golfito (see Northern Golfo Dulce Area in the Península de Osa & Golfo Dulce chapter) and San Vito are the most interesting.

### Orientation & Information

Be aware that this is a town where the residents generally don't use street names when giving directions; be prepared to rely on local landmarks instead.

There are a number of banks where you can change money; Banco Popular (☎ 783-3076) is usually the fastest. It has an ATM, changes traveler's checks, and is open 8am to 5pm weekdays, 8am to 11:30am Saturday. JJ Internet is open 9am to 9pm weekdays, 9am to 4pm Saturday. There is a hospital about 2km south of town on the Interamericana.

### Places to Stay

There are a number of hotels, all of which are fairly inexpensive.

*Pensión Elvira* (☎ 783-3057) US$4 per person. This basic but friendly place, which has a locked parking lot, is one of the cheapest.

Other equally cheap and basic places include the somewhat noisy *Hotel Villa* (☎ 783-5120) and *Cabinas Fontana* (☎ 783-3078), at US$6 per person.

*Hotel Musuco* (☎ 783-3048) Rooms US$5-6 per person. This clean and secure place offers small, basic rooms with shared showers or, for a little more, rooms with baths and fans. Other good possibilities, for about US$7 per person, are the *Cabinas Helga* (☎ 783-3146) and the plant-filled *Cabinas Heyleen* (☎ 783-3080), which is often full.

*Hotel El Rancho* (☎ 783-3060, 783-4210, ☎/fax 783-5435) Singles/doubles with fan US$8/12, with fan and TV US$12/18, with air-conditioning and TV US$18/24. Locally popular, this 52-room place has a spartan, holiday-camp feel. Decent, spacious though plain rooms have private cold baths, and there's a guarded parking lot.

*Hotel Andrea* (☎/fax 783-3784) Singles or doubles with fan US$22, with air-conditioning US$28. At the time of writing, this looked like the nicest place in town. It has 24 decent, cleanly tiled rooms, all with cold showers and TVs. Air-conditioned rooms are a little bigger. Ask about the three unadvertised rooms around back that are smaller and cheaper.

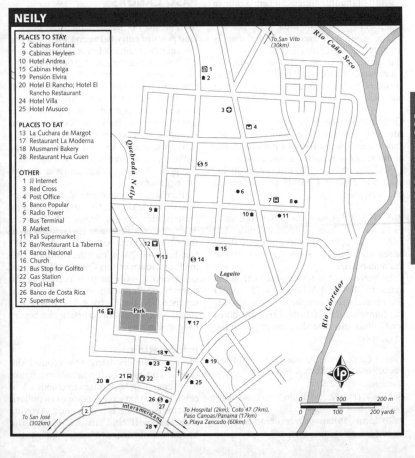

**NEILY**

PLACES TO STAY
2  Cabinas Fontana
9  Cabinas Heyleen
10  Hotel Andrea
15  Cabinas Helga
19  Pensión Elvira
20  Hotel El Rancho; Hotel El
    Rancho Restaurant
24  Hotel Villa
25  Hotel Musuco

PLACES TO EAT
13  La Cuchara de Margot
17  Restaurant La Moderna
18  Musmanni Bakery
28  Restaurant Hua Guen

OTHER
1  JJ Internet
3  Red Cross
4  Post Office
5  Banco Popular
6  Radio Tower
7  Bus Terminal
8  Market
11  Pali Supermarket
12  Bar/Restaurant La Taberna
14  Banco Nacional
16  Church
21  Bus Stop for Golfito
22  Gas Station
23  Pool Hall
26  Banco de Costa Rica
27  Supermarket

To San Vito
(30km)

Río Caño Seco

Quebrada Neily

Río Corredor

Laguito

Park

Interamericana

To San José
(302km)

To Hospital (2km), Coto 47 (7km),
Paso Canoas/Panama (17km)
& Playa Zancudo (60km)

0    100    200 m
0    100    200 yards

**SOUTHERN COSTA RICA**

## Places to Eat & Drink

The *Hotel El Rancho* has a noisy restaurant attached, where karaoke blares most evenings.

*Restaurant La Moderna* (☎ 783-3097) Dishes US$3-9. This pleasant place, offering a variety of meals ranging from hamburgers and pizza to chicken and fish, is the best in town. One side welcomes you with air-conditioning, though many locals prefer to eat at room temperature.

*La Cuchara de Margot* This place serves hamburgers and snacks and has a couple of outside tables. *Musmanni Bakery* serves the usual baked goods, as well as ice cream.

*Restaurant Hua Guen* (☎ 783-3041) US$2.50-6. Hours 10am-midnight daily. This reasonably priced Chinese restaurant is south of the Interamericana and features a nonsmoking, air-conditioned room as well as a room-temperature area.

The *pool hall* shown on the map is friendly but is surrounded by rough bars and uninviting for women. *Bar/Restaurant La Taberna*, where you'll find a young adult crowd of both men and women, is a better place to go for a drink.

## Getting There & Away

**Air** Coto 47 is about 7km southwest of Neily and is the closest airport to Panama. Some of the local buses pass near the airport.

SANSA (☎ 781-1275) offers daily flights from San José to Coto 47 for US$66/132 one-way/roundtrip.

**Bus** TRACOPA buses from San José leave six times a day from Calle 14, Avenidas 3 & 5. After stopping at Neily, most of these buses continue to Paso Canoas, at the Panama border.

In Neily, the bus terminal is next to the market. TRACOPA buses (☎ 783-3227) and several other companies leave here for the following destinations. Frequent buses for Golfito also pass the stop opposite the gas station:

Ciudad Cortés (near Palmar Norte) – 4:45am, 5am, 9am, noon, 2:30pm, 4:30pm, 5:45pm

Dominical – 6am, 2:30pm

Golfito – (US55¢, 1½ hours) 18 times daily between 6am & 7:30pm

Paso Canoas – 18 times daily between 6am & 6pm

Playa Zancudo – 9:30am, 2:15pm

Puerto Jiménez – (5–6 hours) 7am, 2pm

San Isidro – 7am, 10am, 1pm, 3pm

San José – (US$5.50, 7 hours) 4:30am *(directo)*, 5am, 8:30am, 11:30am, 1:45pm, 3:30pm

San Vito – (US$1.50, 2½ hours) 6am, 7:30 am, 9am, 1pm, 2pm, 4pm, 5:30pm via Agua Buena; 11am, 3pm via Cañas Gordas

Buses do run to other local communities, but these services may not operate in rainy weather or when road conditions are poor.

**Taxi** Taxis with 4WD are available to take you almost anywhere. The fare from Neily to Paso Canoas is about US$6; to Coto 47 it's about US$2.50. Taxis between Coto 47 and Paso Canoas cost about US$8.

## PASO CANOAS

This small town is on the Interamericana at the Panama border, making it the primary land point of entry between Costa Rica and Panama. A charmless border-crossing town, it is a popular destination for ticos who come on shopping trips to buy goods that are cheaper than in San José. This means hotels are often full of bargain hunters during weekends and holidays. Most of the shops and hotels are on the Costa Rican side. Paso Canoas is only worth visiting on your way across the border to/from Panama; there's nothing else of interest here, and the hotels are poor. Neily is 17km away and much more pleasant.

Travelers leaving Costa Rica should go directly to the Border Crossing Post to complete border crossing formalities. Travelers entering Costa Rica may also need to go to the Customs Post next to the TRACOPA Bus Terminal, 200m from the Border Crossing Post. However, this Customs Post is generally aimed more at ticos reentering the country or Panamanians rather than at tourists. See the Getting There & Away chapter for details on crossing the border to/from Panama.

## Information

Money changers hang out around the border and give better rates than banks for exchanging US dollars to colones. You can also convert excess colones to dollars, but this exchange is not as good. Arriving travelers will find an ATM near the border. Colones are accepted at the

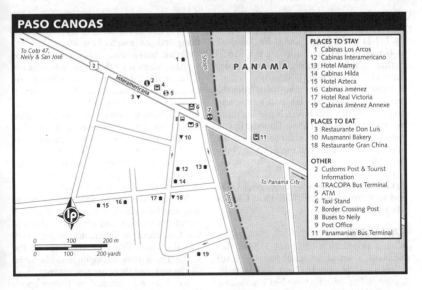

## PASO CANOAS

To Coto 47,
Neily & San José

PANAMA

Interamericana

To Panama City

Shops

Shops

0    100    200 m
0    100    200 yards

**PLACES TO STAY**
1   Cabinas Los Arcos
12  Cabinas Interamericano
13  Hotel Mamy
14  Cabinas Hilda
15  Hotel Azteca
16  Cabinas Jiménez
17  Hotel Real Victoria
19  Cabinas Jiménez Annexe

**PLACES TO EAT**
3   Restaurante Don Luis
10  Musmanni Bakery
18  Restaurante Gran China

**OTHER**
2   Customs Post & Tourist
    Information
4   TRACOPA Bus Terminal
5   ATM
6   Taxi Stand
7   Border Crossing Post
8   Buses to Neily
9   Post Office
11  Panamanian Bus Terminal

Panama border, but are difficult to get rid of farther into Panama. Other currencies are harder to deal with. Traveler's checks can be negotiated with persistence, but they're not as readily accepted as cash. The Panamanian currency is the balboa, which is on par with and interchangeable with US dollars.

### Places to Stay & Eat

The hotels in Paso Canoas aren't particularly good; there's really no reason to stay here unless you have to.

*Hotel Mamy* US$4.50 per person. This one is among the town's cheapest, but doesn't have much else to recommend it.

*Cabinas Interamericano* (☎ 732-2041) Singles/doubles US$7.50/12. This is a decent place in the town center, offering clean rooms with private baths and fans. One of the better restaurants in town is attached.

*Cabinas Hilda* (☎ 732-2873) Singles/doubles US$7.50/12; air-conditioned doubles US$19.50. This is also clean and adequate and has rooms with private baths.

*Hotel Real Victoria* (☎ 732-2486) Singles/doubles US$10.50/12; air-conditioned doubles US$19.50. This secure-looking place has 15 basic, air-conditioned rooms and 18 rooms with fans, all with cold-water showers. Amenities include a pool and large parking area.

*Cabinas Los Arcos* (☎ 732-1632) Rooms US$8 per person. This place is somewhat overpriced, offering scruffy rooms with private baths and fans. There is parking.

*Cabinas Jiménez* (☎ 732-2258) Singles/doubles US$9/12, with air-conditioning US$15/18. The 20 decent rooms here are clean and have TVs and private showers. There is an *annexe*, at a separate site, that is slightly cheaper.

*Hotel Azteca* (☎ 732-2217) US$9/12 with fan or US$15/24 with air-conditioning and TV. This good, clean, well-run hotel has 57 rooms and is among the town's best.

Dining options include a number of cheap *sodas*. For inexpensive Chinese food, the *Restaurante Gran China* seems better than most. *Restaurante Don Luis* serves a selection of tico fare. *Musmanni* has baked goods.

### Getting There & Away

**Air** The airport closest to the border is at Coto 47, near Neily (see the Neily section, earlier). There is a SANSA agent (☎ 732-2041) at the Cabinas Interamericano.

**Bus** From the TRACOPA terminal in San José, buses leave several times a day. Make reservations if you're traveling on Friday night, because the bus is usually full of weekend shoppers. The same applies to

SOUTHERN COSTA RICA

buses leaving Paso Canoas on Sunday. Direct buses leave the TRACOPA terminal (☎ 732-2119) in Paso Canoas for San José at 4am, 9am, and 1pm – the fare is US$6.50 for the eight-hour trip. Slightly slower buses leave at 7am and 3pm (US$5.40).

From a bus stop less than 100m from the border, buses to Neily leave at least every hour during daylight hours. Neily has more bus connections than Paso Canoas. If you just miss one and don't want to wait for the next, a taxi will take you the 17km to Neily for US$6.

**Taxi & Car** Taxis to Neily cost about US$6 and to Coto 47 about US$8. Paso Canoas has a gas station.

## SAN VITO

With a population of about 15,000, this pleasant town at 980m above sea level offers a respite from the heat of the nearby lowlands. The drive up from Neily is a scenic one, with superb views of the lowlands dropping away as you climb the steep and winding road up the coastal mountain range called Fila Costeña. Drivers should note

that the road is ear-poppingly steep, very narrow, and full of hairpin turns; you'll be using 2nd gear much of the way.

Some buses from Neily go via Cañas Gordas, which is on the Panama border but is not an official crossing point (though you can see Panama from here). There is reportedly a pensión here. The bus continues through Sabalito, where there's a gas station and a basic hotel, before reaching San Vito.

Other buses take the more direct route via Agua Buena, passing the Wilson Botanical Garden about 6km before reaching San Vito. Because it's paved all the way, this is the route that most drivers take.

You can also get to San Vito from San José via the Valle de Coto Brus – this is an incredibly scenic route with great views of the Cordillera de Talamanca to the north and the lower Fila Costeña range to the south. The narrow, swooping road is paved all the way, and there are few tourists.

San Vito was founded by Italian immigrants in the early 1950s, and you can occasionally hear Italian being spoken in the streets. Guaymí Indians, who are known to move undisturbed back and forth across the

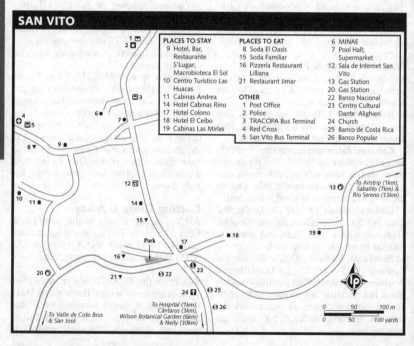

**SAN VITO**

| PLACES TO STAY | PLACES TO EAT | 6 MINAE |
|---|---|---|
| 9 Hotel, Bar, Restaurante S'Lugar; Macrobioteca El Sol | 8 Soda El Oasis | 7 Pool Hall; Supermarket |
| | 15 Soda Familiar | 12 Sala de Internet San Vito |
| | 16 Pizzería Restaurant Lilliana | 13 Gas Station |
| 10 Centro Turístico Las Huacas | 21 Restaurant Jimar | 20 Gas Station |
| 11 Cabinas Andrea | | 22 Banco Nacional |
| 14 Hotel Cabinas Rino | **OTHER** | 23 Centro Cultural Dante Alighieri |
| 17 Hotel Colono | 1 Post Office | 24 Church |
| 18 Hotel El Ceibo | 2 Police | 25 Banco de Costa Rica |
| 19 Cabinas Las Mirlas | 3 TRACOPA Bus Terminal | 26 Banco Popular |
| | 4 Red Cross | |
| | 5 San Vito Bus Terminal | |

To Airstrip (1km), Sabalito (7km) & Río Sereno (13km)

Park

To Valle de Coto Brus & San José

To Hospital (1km), Cántaros (3km), Wilson Botanical Garden (6km) & Neily (30km)

0    50    100 m
0    50    100 yards

border with Panama, sometimes come into town, barefoot and in traditional dress. San Vito is also a good base for visits to the splendid Wilson Botanical Garden and to infrequently visited Parque Internacional La Amistad.

## Information

The three banks in town will change money. The Centro Cultural Dante Alighieri has some information for tourists and historical displays on Italian immigration. The Sala de Internet is open 8am to 8pm Monday to Saturday. A MINAE national parks office (☎ 773-3955/6) is open 9am to 4pm weekdays.

There's a hospital 1km south of the town center.

## Places to Stay

*Wilson Botanical Garden* (see that section, later in this chapter) is the best place to stay in the San Vito area.

*Hotel Colono* (☎ 773-4543) Singles/doubles US$6/9. This is a basic but reasonably clean choice, with shared bathrooms.

*Cabinas Las Mirlas* (☎ 773-3714) Rooms US$7.50, cabins US$10.50, single or double. This is a clean, quiet, and pleasant place with private electric showers. Windows open onto an orchard. Go down the drive about 150m to the house on the right to ask about the eight slightly aging cabins, which are larger than the rooms.

*Hotel S'Lugar* (☎ 773-3173, 773-3535) Rooms US$6 per person. Rooms are basic, shabby and dark with private cold showers and are not a good value. The attached bar is locally popular, and food is available.

*Centro Turístico Las Huacas* (☎ 773-3115) Singles/doubles US$7/11. The rooms here, in the parking lot of a recreation center, are decent and have private electric showers (TV costs US$2 more).

*Hotel Cabinas Rino* (☎ 773-3071, 773-4030) Rooms US$7.50 per person. This small place has five clean rooms with private hot showers and TVs. Reception is available 24 hours, and there is a locked parking lot.

*Cabinas Andrea* (☎ 773-4712, 773-3165) Singles/doubles/triples US$13.50/19.50/22.50. Just two huge, clean upstairs rooms are offered here. Each has a TV and private hot shower. This is an excellent value.

*Hotel El Ceibo* (☎ 773-3025, fax 773-5025) Singles/doubles US$16.50/29. This renovated place is the best in town. Some of the 40 rooms boast little balconies with forest views, but others look out on the parking lot. Rooms vary in size and decor, but all have TV and private bath with hot water. There's a decent restaurant and bar.

## Places to Eat

*Pizzería Restaurant Lilliana* Sandwiches US$2, dishes average US$6. This place serves pizza along with Italian and local food.

*Hotel El Ceibo* The restaurant at this hotel has good Italian and other food.

*Soda El Oasis* Dishes US$1.50-2.50. Breakfast & lunch only. A bright, cheerful place, this soda makes good fruit drinks and has a special seating section for children.

*Soda Familiar* This soda has cheap meals and is locally popular.

*Macrobioteca El Sol* Under the Hotel S'Lugar, this is a macrobiotic health-food store.

*Restaurant Jirar* Dishes US$2-3. This cheap but recommended place, which has a small outdoor patio, serves burgers, casados and sandwiches.

## Shopping

*Cántaros* (☎ 773-3760) Open 9:30am-4pm Tues-Sat, 9:30am-1pm Sun. About 3km away, en route to Wilson Botanical Gardens, this is the best gift shop in southern Costa Rica. Housed in a great cabin built by early area pioneers and now restored, Cántaros stocks a small but carefully chosen selection of local and national crafts – no junk! Next to the gift shop is a children's library (mostly Spanish with some English books) and education area (puzzles, games, crayons). This great local resource is funded by the gift shop. Outside is a small park with a lake, trails and a viewpoint; admission is US80¢.

## Getting There & Away

**Air** You can charter light aircraft to/from the San Vito airstrip, 1km west of town. Otherwise, the nearest airports with scheduled services are at Coto 47 (near Neily) and Golfito (in the Península de Osa).

**Bus** There are two bus terminals. The TRACOPA terminal serves San José, and the San Vito terminal has other buses.

TRACOPA (☎ 773-3410) has a direct bus to San José at 5am and slower buses at 7:30am, 10am, and 3pm (US$6.50, about five to 6½ hours). There are also buses to San Isidro at 6:45am and 1:30pm. TRACOPA has buses from San José to San Vito at 5:45am, 8:15am, 11:30am, and 2:45pm, and from San Isidro to San Vito at 5:30am and 2pm.

Cepul (☎ 773-3848) has buses to many local destinations. Buses to Neily (US$1.50, 2½ hours) leave at 5:15am, 7am, 7:30am, 9am, noon, 2pm, and 5pm via Agua Buena (passing Wilson Botanical Gardens) and at 5:30am and 11am via Sabalito. These hours are subject to change.

For those wishing to reach Parque Internacional La Amistad, there are buses to Las Mellizas (US$1) at 9:30am, 2pm, and 5pm. Buses to Santa Elena leave at 8am, 10am, 2pm, 4pm, and 6pm. However, there are no park facilities at these places, though you could ask at the San Vito MINAE office to see if any have been added.

Other nearby destinations served include Río Sereno and Cañas Gordas on the Panama border, Los Reyes, Cotón, and Los Planes.

**Taxi** Call ☎ 773-3249, 773-3939 for taxis at any time.

## WILSON BOTANICAL GARDEN
About 6km south of San Vito is the small but truly world-class Wilson Botanical Garden (☎/fax 773-3665, e lcruces@hortus .ots.ac.cr; admission US$6; open 8am-5pm daily year-round).

Covering 12 hectares and surrounded by 254 hectares of natural forest, the garden was established by Robert and Catherine Wilson in 1963 and thereafter became internationally known for its collection. In 1973, the area came under the auspices of the Organization for Tropical Studies (OTS), and in 1983 it was incorporated into UNESCO's Reserva de la Biósfera La Amistad. Today, the well-maintained garden holds over 1000 genera of plants in about 200 families. Its celebrated palm collection is one of the largest in the world, with 700-plus species.

Wandering around the grounds is fun. The gardens are well laid out, and many of the plants are labeled, turning the walk into a learning adventure. There are many short trails (totaling 6km), each named for the plants found alongside it. Trails include the Bromeliad Walk, Heliconia Loop Trail, Tree Fern Hill Trail, Orchid Walk (with over 50 species), Fern Gully, and Bamboo Walk.

As part of the OTS, the gardens play a scientific role as a research center. Species threatened with extinction are preserved here for possible reforestation in the future. Conservation, sustainable development, horticulture, and agroecology are primary research topics, and scientific training and public education are also important roles of the facilities. Students and researchers stay here and use the greenhouse and laboratory.

## Information
The dry season is from January to March; during this time it is easier to get around the gardens. Nevertheless, the vegetation in the wet months is exuberant, with many epiphytic bromeliads, ferns, and orchids being sustained by the moisture in the air. Annual rainfall is about 4000mm, and the average high temperature is about 26°C. October and November are the wettest months.

Guided nature walks (in English) cost US$15/30 for a half/full day (US$10/20 for children under 12) for groups of four or less; ask about rates for larger groups. Reservations for guided hikes and visits, with lunch (US$8 more), must be made with the OTS in San José (☎ 240-6696, fax 240-6783, e reservas@cro.ots.ac.cr). For self-guided visits without lunch, no reservation is necessary – just show up. Fees go toward maintaining the gardens and research facilities.

For self-guided walking, a trail map is provided, and various booklets are available at low cost so visitors can learn about the collection. Selected Palms of Wilson Botanical Garden identifies palms along a walk that takes about 1½ hours. The grounds hold about 50 tree species, some of which are seen on a two-hour walk described in Selected Trees of Wilson Botanical Garden. A general overview is given in The Self-Guided Tour of the Natural History Trail. Smaller brochures and leaflets describe orchids, hummingbirds, and medicinal plants, and there is also a bird list of 330 species (birders can arrange to enter at dawn, before the official opening time). New publications are developed every year.

For visitors spending the night, the library is available for reference. Talks and slide shows are given on an erratic basis every few days for and by researchers and students; guests are welcome to attend.

The staff speaks English and Spanish.

## Places to Stay & Eat

Overnight guests can be accommodated if reservations are made in advance with the OTS in San José (see Information, above). Make reservations as far in advance as possible; otherwise, consider staying in San Vito. A one-night visit is not really enough to see what the gardens have to offer. Visitors with a serious interest in natural history are encouraged to spend three nights.

The 12 comfortable double cabins have telephones with modem hookups (obviously with the scientist and researcher in mind), private hot showers, and balconies with great views. There are also four older cabins, two with two bedrooms. These are mainly used by researchers, but may be available to travelers if everything else is full. Rates are US$61/100 for one/two people, or US$82/140 with three meals. Children under 12 sharing with adults pay US$25. Rates include entry to the gardens. There is a 20% discount from August to mid-December. Meals are an interesting, tasty affair, shared family style with scientists, graduate students, and other researchers working here.

## Getting There & Away

Buses between San Vito and Neily (and other destinations) pass the entrance to the gardens several times a day. Ask at the bus terminal about the right bus, because some buses to Neily take a different route. A taxi from San Vito to the gardens costs US$2 to US$3. From San Vito, it is a 6km mainly uphill walk to the gardens. A sign near the center of town claims it's 4km, but it's definitely 6km.

## PARQUE INTERNACIONAL LA AMISTAD

This huge 195,000-hectare park is by far the largest single protected area in Costa Rica. It is known as an international park because it continues across the border into Panama, where it is managed separately.

Combined with two adjoining national parks and a host of indigenous and biological reserves, La Amistad is part of a huge biological corridor protecting a great variety of tropical habitats, ranging from rainforest to páramo, and has thus attracted the attention of biologists, ecologists, and conservationists worldwide. In 1982, UNESCO declared La Amistad to be a Biosphere Reserve, and in 1983 it was given the status of a World Heritage Site.

Conservation International and other agencies continually work with Costa Rican authorities to implement a suitable management plan. This plan must preserve wildlife and habitat and develop resources, such as hydroelectricity, without disturbing the ecosystem or the traditional way of life of the Indian groups dwelling within the reserve.

La Amistad has the nation's largest population of Baird's tapirs, as well as giant anteaters, all six species of Neotropical cats – jaguar, puma (or mountain lion), margay, ocelot, oncilla (tiger cat), and jaguarundi – and many other, more common mammals. Over 500 bird species have been sighted (more than half of the total in Costa Rica); 49 of these species exist only within the biosphere reserve. In addition, 115 species of fish and 215 different reptile and amphibian species have been listed (an unconfirmed report puts this up at 263 species), and more are being added regularly. There are innumerable insect species. Nine of the nation's 12 Holdridge Life Zones are represented in the reserve.

### Time & Space

One of the treats offered by Costa Rica's astonishingly diverse landscape is the opportunity to change the season by changing your location. In the space of a few hours, you can travel from the dusty heat of Guanacaste to the cool 'eternal spring' of San José – or from the summery humidity of a coastal mangrove swamp to the crisp autumnal air of a highland forest. At high points on the Interamericana, it's cold enough to see your breath, and if you hike to the top of Chirripó, your water bottle can freeze – while far below, you might see the sunny beaches of the Caribbean and the Pacific.

– John Thompson

SOUTHERN COSTA RICA

The backbone of the reserve is the Cordillera de Talamanca, which not only includes the peaks of the Chirripó massif but has many mountains over 3000m in elevation. The thickly forested northern Caribbean slopes and southern Pacific slopes of the Talamancas are also protected in the park, but it is only on the Pacific side, on access roads outside of the actual park boundaries, that ranger stations are found.

Within the park, development is almost nonexistent, which means backpackers are limited to their own resources. Hiking through steep, thick, and wet rainforest is difficult and not recommended without a guide, except on the trails described below.

## Orientation & Information

Information is available at the MINAE office in San Vito (☎ 773-3955/6). Officially, as with other parks, admission costs US$6 per day and camping costs about US$2, but often there is nobody around to collect the fees; visitation is so low that it would cost more to collect fees than the income derived from the fees themselves.

Park headquarters is at **Estación Altamira**, near the Zona Protectora Las Tablas. This is the best-developed area of the park and has a ranger station, a small exhibit room covering the flora and fauna of the park, a camping area, showers and drinking water, electric light (!), and a lookout tower. There are several trails offering walks of up to six hours, some passing through primary forest and others sharing panoramic views or leading to tiny communities along the border of the park. The longest trail, the Valle del Silencio, leads to a camping area 20km from the ranger station.

Very few travelers visit the park.

## Places to Stay & Eat

Apart from *camping* near the Altamira ranger station or at the camping area at the end of the Valle del Silencio trail, there are two lodges.

*La Amistad Lodge* (☎ 773-3193, 770-8143, 200-5037 cellular) Rooms US$24 per person or US$64 with meals and guide service. When it opened in the early 1990s, this was the first tourist lodge in the area. It's about 3km by poor road with signs from the village of Las Mellizas (not near Altamira). You'll probably need 4WD for the last section, or you can ask to be picked up. This is a family-run place, and there are many kilometers of trails into the park as well as opportunities to see a pioneering ranch in action. Guides and horse rental are available. The owners strive to maintain a balance between organic agriculture and the natural environment, and they appear to have been successful so far. The birding is excellent.

There are 10 double rooms, some with shared facilities and others with private hot showers. They are rarely full, unless a group has reserved in advance. Family style meals are served, and electricity is available for most hours of the day (though you should bring a flashlight).

*Monte Amuo Lodge* (☎ 265-6149) Rooms US$75 per person. Set on 50 hectares of land bordering La Amistad, this is the other facility near the park. It's reached by driving northwest from San Vito on the scenic Valle de Coto Brus road. About 44km out of San Vito (and only 4km before the bridge over the Río Grande de Térraba at Paso Real), a signed road leads north to the community of Potrero Grande (5km) and continues into La Amistad. Monte Amuo Lodge is about 10km beyond Potrero Grande on signed but unpaved roads. You'll probably need 4WD beyond Potrero Grande. The rate includes accommodations in rustic cabins with private hot showers, all meals and guided hikes into the park. A conference room with panoramic views of the valley and mountains is available for groups. Electricity is available for part of the night (bring a flashlight).

Also see the Reserva Biológica Durika section, earlier in this chapter, for information about visits into La Amistad.

## Getting There & Away

Park rangers report that you can get a local bus to the Altamira station from Las Tablas (also known as Guacimo or Guacimal on maps and road signs); Las Tablas is accessible by taxi and bus from San Vito toward San José. At Las Tablas, there is a soda and pulpería where you can eat and wait. The buses to Altamira leave here at 1pm and 5pm.

Buses to Las Mellizas can get you close to La Amistad Lodge.

Taxis with 4WD can usually be hired from the nearest towns to get you to the park stations, but be prepared to do a bit of asking around before finding someone who knows the way. You could also try exploring the area in a rented 4WD vehicle. This is a trip only for adventurers with plenty of time.

# Península de Osa & Golfo Dulce

The large Península de Osa, second only to the Península de Nicoya in size, has the best remaining stands of Central America's Pacific coastal rainforest, preserved in Parque Nacional Corcovado. For many, this is the main reason to visit. Budget travelers backpack through the park, while those with more upscale budgets stay at a host of comfortable lodges and camps in various parts of the peninsula, using them as a base for guided natural history walks into the park.

Other noteworthy activities in this region include surfing in the Pavones area, where the waves are some of the best in the country, taking a snorkeling or dive trip to the very warm and clear waters of Reserva Biológica Isla del Caño (about 20km west of the peninsula), and going offshore fishing.

There are several ways to get onto the peninsula. One route is to take a boat from Sierpe to Bahía Drake, where there are several fine lodges. From here, you can walk or boat into Corcovado. It's also possible to fly into Bahía Drake or Carate, or charter flights into the national park. Another option is to go to the peninsula's biggest town, Puerto Jiménez, which is reached by air, bus, car, or boat from Golfito. From Puerto Jiménez, a rough road continues around the end of the peninsula to the southeast entrance of the national park. All these options are discussed in this chapter.

## Highlights

- Hiking Corcovado's rainforest
- Diving and snorkeling Isla del Caño
- Surfing the long left wave at Pavones
- Relaxing in one of the many excellent jungle lodges
- Bumping up your bird list with scores of new species
- Offshore fishing from Bahía Drake, Golfito, or Zancudo

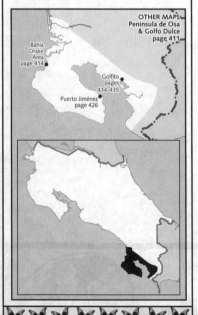

OTHER MAPS
Península de Osa
& Golfo Dulce
page 411

Bahía Drake Area
page 414

Golfito
pages
434-435

Puerto Jiménez
page 426

## To Corcovado via Bahía Drake

### SIERPE

This small village is on the Río Sierpe, almost 30km from the Pacific Ocean, yet it has about a 3m difference between high and low tides. Boats to Bahía Drake can be hired here, and most of the lodges around Bahía Drake will arrange boat pickup in Sierpe for guests who plan to use their accommodations.

Sonia Rojas at Pulpería Fenix (☎ 786-7311) knows boat operators and local hotels. Ask for advice here if you get stuck.

#### Places to Stay & Eat
**Sierpe** On the corner of a grassy square about three blocks from the dock is *Hotel Margarita* (☎ 786-7574) Rooms without bath US$3 per person, doubles with bath US$10. This hotel has five simple, very clean small rooms with private baths and 13 rooms with shared baths. The hotel will provide you with a towel.

# PENÍNSULA DE OSA & GOLFO DULCE

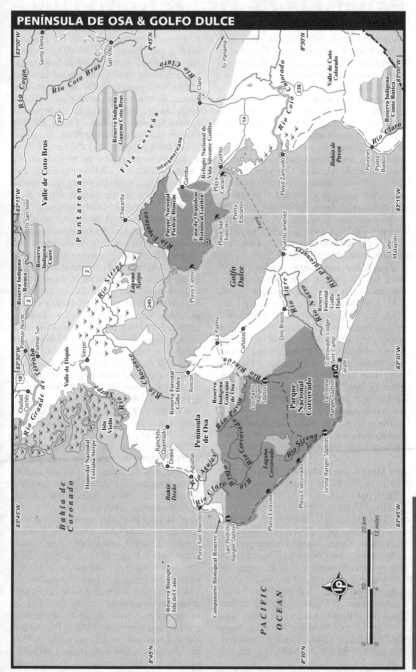

*Hotel Oleaje Sereno* (☎ 786-7580, fax 786-7111, ᴇ oleajesereno@racsa.co.cr, ᴡ www .oleajesereno.com) Singles/doubles US$25/35. A block from the dock, this place has 10 simple and clean air-conditioned rooms with private hot showers. The hotel has a restaurant.

*Estero Azul Lodge* (☎ 786-7422, ᴇ estero azul@hotmail.com, ᴡ www.samplecosta rica.com) Rooms US$65-105 per person with meals. This place is about 2km before you get to Sierpe. It has five wooden cabins, all with hardwood floors, tiled bathrooms, ceiling fans, and screened patios. Co-owner Patricia Kirk is an award-winning chef who promises guests will enjoy gourmet meals in the elegantly tropical dining room; free juice and coffee are available all day. The lodge arranges fishing, kayaking, scuba, and hiking trips. The grounds have river access and short walking trails.

*Eco Manglares Sierpe Lodge* (☎ 786-7414, fax 786-7441, ᴇ ciprotur@racsa.co.cr) Singles/doubles US$52/70, extra people US$11.50. Near Estero Azul Lodge, this place has five spacious, rustic cabins with private baths and hot water. The lodge is across the river and is reached by the narrowest of suspension bridges, which can accommodate a large car but not a bus. This lodge also has playground equipment and offers fishing, diving, and sightseeing tours. Meals are available for US$8/12/15 (breakfast/lunch/dinner).

The most popular restaurant is *Las Vegas Bar/Restaurant*, right next to the boat dock. There are also a few other cheap *sodas*.

**Río Sierpe Area** *Mapache Lodge* (☎ 786-6565, fax 786-6458) Singles/doubles: tents US$58/104, cabins US$70/128, rooms US$104/174, including three meals & transfer. This Italian-run lodge is a 30-minute boat ride from Sierpe in an isolated part of the Valle de Diquis. The 45-hectare property includes only two developed hectares; the rest is natural rainforest and mangroves. The lodge sponsors the Arborea Project, a conservation initiative dedicated to buying rainforest for protection and agricultural lands for reforestation. Adventurous local tours are offered, including kayaking, horseback riding, and hiking. Tours to Corcovado and other areas are available, as are fishing trips.

The lodge is nonsmoking and features a pool, exercise equipment, and an observation tower. Walking trails on the property offer good birding and wildlife watching. Accommodations are in either large, walk-in tents, rustic cabins with shared baths, or rooms with private baths in the owners' house. Contact them about all-inclusive tours ranging from three to 10 days, with various activities available. Italian, English, French, and Spanish are spoken.

*Sábalo Lodge* (☎ 770-1457, fax 771-5586, ᴇ info@sabalolodge.com, ᴡ www.sabalo lodge.com) Rooms US$55 per person. This small, rustic, solar-powered, family-run ecolodge can accommodate up to eight people in private screened rooms with clean shared bathrooms. A swimming hole and river are nearby, and the lodge has been recommended for wildlife observation and hiking. The friendly owners are certified Spanish teachers and can give personal language classes. Rates include three home-cooked meals, and it's US$48 for roundtrip boat transport from Sierpe (which can be shared). Various local tours can be arranged. Popular packages from San José include three nights at Sábalo Lodge, two nights at a lodge in San Josecito, all meals, roundtrip (land) transportation from San José, one guided tour in Corcovado, and horseback riding, for US$474. Other packages are available.

*Río Sierpe Lodge* (☎ 384-5595, fax 786-6291; in San José ☎ 253-2412, fax 283-7655; ᴇ vsftrip@racsa.co.cr) Singles/doubles US$80/130. Within 4km of the ocean and south of Isla Violín, this place is rustic, comfortable, and well run. Nature and birding tours, diving, and sportfishing are featured. There are 17 rooms with private solar-heated showers and six two-story rooms with sleeping lofts. The rooms are spacious; student discounts are available. Food is good and varied, and there's a recreation area with a large library of paperback books. Several trails around the lodge are suitable for birding and wildlife watching.

Room rates include meals, taxes, soft drinks, and road/river transfer from Palmar to the lodge. Optional full-day excursions (two-person minimum) include Parque Nacional Corcovado or Isla del Caño (US$55 per person), tidal-basin angling (US$80), and Pacific Ocean angling (US$225). Half-day trips to Isla Violín (good birding) cost US$25, and mangrove excursions (more birds) cost US$35. The lodge also does two-day overnight camping treks into the rainforest and through remote villages for US$65 per person or US$125 on horseback. These can be combined into excursion packages for naturalists or anglers – they go from three days/two nights to six days/five nights, and internal flights are included. There are substantial discounts for naturalist or student groups of eight or more – call the lodge for details.

Dive packages include boats, all gear, and a PADI- or NAUI-certified divemaster. You just need your swimwear, a mask, and a diver-certification card. Prices (including lodging, meals, and flights/transfers from San José) range from US$400 per person for three days/two nights to US$820 for six days/five nights with a six-person minimum; add about 50% if there are just two of you.

Fishing packages, also including everything from San José, cost about US$500 to US$1000 for three days/two nights to six days/five nights of tidal-basin fishing or US$600 to US$1200 for the same period of deep-sea fishing.

### Getting There & Away
**Air** Both scheduled flights and charters fly into Palmar Sur, 14km north of Sierpe (see the Southern Costa Rica chapter).

**Bus & Taxi** Buses depart Sierpe for Palmar Norte at 5:45am, 8am, 10am, 1pm, and 3pm. A taxi charges about US$12.50.

**Boat** If you haven't prearranged a boat pickup with a Bahía Drake or Río Sierpe lodge, ask around at the dock next to Las Vegas Bar or ask at the Pulpería Fenix. The going rate to Bahía Drake is about US$15 per person (four minimum). The trip takes about 90 minutes or more, depending on the size of the boat engine and the tides.

The trip to Bahía Drake is scenic and interesting: first along the river through rainforest, then through the mangrove estuary and on through the tidal currents and surf of the river mouth into the ocean. Keep your eyes open for monkeys, sloths, herons, macaws, parrots, kingfishers, ibises, and spoonbills along the river and dolphins, boobies, frigatebirds, and pelicans along the

coast. (Whales migrate through, especially in February and March.) The river mouth has a reputation for being dangerous, and in a small dugout it is. The larger boats with strong engines used by experienced operators going to the lodges don't have any problems, though it's pretty exciting riding the swells and avoiding the splashes.

## BAHÍA DRAKE
Simply called 'Drake' locally (pronounced 'DRA-cay' in Spanish), this area is rich in both 16th-century history and natural history. Sir Francis Drake himself supposedly visited the bay in March 1579 during his global circumnavigation in the *Golden Hind,* and there's a monument at Punta Agujitas to this effect. The bay is only a few kilometers north of Parque Nacional Corcovado, which can be visited from here, as can Reserva Biológica Isla del Caño. (Both Corcovado and Isla del Caño are described in this chapter.)

Agujitas is a small village on the bay with a *pulpería,* a public phone, a clinic, a school, and a couple of cheapish *cabinas*. You can visit Agujitas and pick up a cola or beer, watch kids coming home from school, and chat with the residents. Most people who visit tend to stay in their lodges, but locals enjoy talking with travelers, so stop by. A dance hall plays music on Saturday night.

Mosquitoes aren't much of a problem except in January – the first month of the drier season – when they hatch in standing pools of water. But they aren't so bad even then.

### Activities & Organized Tours
The variety of activities offered in this area will keep visitors busy for days, therefore the lodges in the area recommend a stay of at least three nights. Most of them offer the same tours and usually will set you up with another lodge if, for some reason, they can't provide you with your choice. Tours are generally priced competitively among the more expensive lodges, with cheaper tours offered by some of the budget accommodations. The latter will give discounts if you're part of a group, though the better lodges often have the best guides.

Probably the most popular tour is the day trip to Parque Nacional Corcovado. It includes a boat ride (almost one hour) to the north end of the park, a beach landing

PENÍNSULA DE OSA

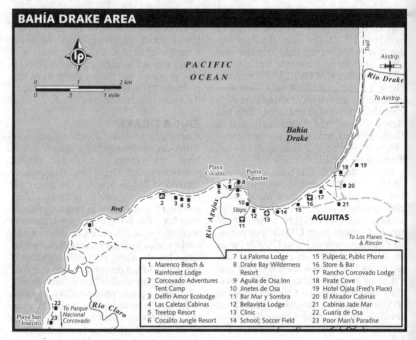

## BAHÍA DRAKE AREA

| | | |
|---|---|---|
| 1 Marenco Beach & Rainforest Lodge | 7 La Paloma Lodge | 15 Pulpería; Public Phone |
| 2 Corcovado Adventures Tent Camp | 8 Drake Bay Wilderness Resort | 16 Store & Bar |
| 3 Delfin Amor Ecolodge | 9 Aguila de Osa Inn | 17 Rancho Corcovado Lodge |
| 4 Las Caletas Cabinas | 10 Jinetes de Osa | 18 Pirate Cove |
| 5 Treetop Resort | 11 Bar Mar y Sombra | 19 Hotel Ojala (Fred's Place) |
| 6 Cocalito Jungle Resort | 12 Bellavista Lodge | 20 El Mirador Cabinas |
| | 13 Clinic | 21 Cabinas Jade Mar |
| | 14 School; Soccer Field | 22 Guaria de Osa |
| | | 23 Poor Man's Paradise |

(remove your shoes to keep them dry), and a hike. This can be short and easy or long and difficult – let the lodge know what you want. The tour costs about US$50 to US$75 plus a US$6 park fee, and it includes lunch. The main activities are birding, natural history interpretation, and swimming in rivers and at beaches. It's also possible to go as far as the Sirena ranger station for about US$100.

Reserva Biológica Isla del Caño has great **snorkeling** and can be visited for US$55 to US$80. **Scuba diving** is offered for beginners and experts. With advance reservation, beginners can take a PADI certification course (four days required). Certified divers can do two boat dives near Isla del Caño and other sites for approximately US$100 (gear is supplied). Advanced courses are also offered. The best lodges for dive trips are La Paloma Lodge, Jinetes de Osa, Drake Bay Wilderness Resort, and Aguila de Osa Inn (see Places to Stay & Eat, below).

Areas outside the national park and reserve can be visited with guided tours that are a little cheaper, and the birding is still good. You can **hike** up the Río Claro, visit waterfalls, or take a boat to Isla Violín or through mangroves on the Río Sierpe – the latter two are especially good for birding. **Horses** can be rented for about US$50 per day with a guide, less for shorter rides. You can hike up the Río Claro without a guide if you have wilderness skills – trails aren't signed. You can also hike around the lodge areas and along the beaches yourself.

Although the weather is hot, if you plan on riding a horse, bring a pair of long pants to protect your legs. Long pants are also a good idea for some hikes.

**Sportfishing** is available, starting at US$35 an hour in small boats and rising to about US$800 a day in a fully equipped 9m boat with a professional fishing guide. Up to four anglers can be accommodated in a boat. The best lodge for dedicated offshore anglers is Aguila de Osa, though all the lodges can easily arrange fishing.

**Canoes** for play on the river and **sea kayaks** for more serious trips can be borrowed or rented. Drake Bay Wilderness Resort has the best sea-kayaking tours. This is where Gulf Islands Kayaking (see the Getting There & Away chapter) does its tours.

**The Divine Dolphin** (☎ 775-1481, in the USA ☎ 305-443-0222, e info@divinedolphin .com, w www.divinedolphin.com) opened the Delfin Amor Ecolodge in 1999 (see the From Bahía Drake to Corcovado section, later in this chapter). Its **swimming-with-dolphin tours** are offered for people who want to interact directly with these animals and who are comfortable with swimming in the ocean several kilometers offshore. Guests of other lodges can take these tours. An all-day tour costs US$85 per person.

**Night Tours** (e eyeshine@racsa.co.cr, w www.thenighttour.com) are offered by the 'Bug Lady' – entomologist Tracie and her spotting partner Carlos. This 2½-hour tour (US$35) is one of the most fascinating excursions I've been on and I recommend it highly. Tracie knows more interesting facts about bugs than she's had hot dinners – and I don't mean boring scientific details. One of her fields of research is the military use of insects (really!), and her stories enthrall. Participants get to use night-vision scopes as an added bonus. Make reservations for the tour ahead of time; it's limited to six participants and it's often full.

And, of course, you can just hang out in a hammock and relax, surrounded by tropical scenery.

## Places to Stay & Eat

Reservations are recommended in the high season (mid-November to the end of April), especially in the top-end lodges. Discounts are offered in the low season. High-season prices are given below. (Also see accommodations described in the next section, From Bahía Drake to Corcovado). Some lodges close in September and/or October.

**Budget & Mid-Range** The cheapest places charge about US$35 per person per day, including three meals. Most are in or near the village. You can get a bed for about US$15 or US$20 if you cook for yourself. (There aren't any real restaurants outside the hotels.) A few places allow you to camp. If you can't get through on the phone, call the *pulpería* (☎ 771-2336) and leave a message.

**Cabinas Jade Mar** (☎ 384-6681 cellular, ☎ 661-4446 message, fax 786-6358, 786-7366) At this family-run place up a hill behind La

Bahía store, there are five double rooms, each with bath and fan; there's electricity from 6pm to 9pm. Marta Pérez Mendoza, the owner, arranges boat rides to/from Sierpe for US$15, as well as inexpensive local tours.

**El Mirador Cabinas** (☎ 387-9138 cellular, fax 735-5440) This friendly place, up a steep path at the north end of Bahía Drake, has seven rustic rooms with baths and double beds. All the rooms have superb views. There's no electricity, but candles are available. The owner is José Antonio Vargas Elizondo.

**Bellavista Lodge** Basic rooms with shared cold baths – this is the least attractive option.

**Rancho Corcovado Lodge** (in San José ☎ 241-0441) Campsites US$6, rooms US$40-45. This place has seven rooms with private baths. Each room sleeps from two to four people, and rates include meals. Campers can set up a tent and are permitted to use the lodge bathrooms.

**Jinetes de Osa** (☎/fax 385-9541, ☎ 233-3333 messages; in the USA ☎ 800-317-0333, 303-838-0969; e crventur@costaricadiving .com, w www.costaricadiving.com) US$65-80 per person, including meals. This PADI dive facility offers a certification course for about US$300 as well as two-tank dives at Isla del Caño for US$85. Beginners who don't want to be certified can try a 'resort course' for US$140, which includes two dives. All equipment is provided. The hotel has nine rooms. The four pricier and larger ones have fans, tiled baths (ocean themes), and hot showers. They share a balcony and have nice views. Three smaller rooms have private baths, and two share a bath. They also have fans and balcony views.

**Pirate Cove** (☎ 291-0324, 281-3260, 393-9449, ☎/fax 786-7845) Rooms US$55-70 per person including meals. Another PADI dive facility, Pirate Cove is also called 'Caño Divers.' They have four tiny cabins – basically a wooden screened box with a bed – that share bathrooms, and three larger cabins with balconies and private bath. There's no electricity here, but they're right on the beach.

**Hotel Ojala** (☎ 380-4763 cellular, e drake@racsa.co.cr, w www.hotelojala .com) Rooms $51 per person including three meals. This is a nice family house locally known as Fred's Place, after the US owner. It has four rooms, and good meals are served in the family dining room. It's a little bit out of the way, between the village and the airport. Fred is a locally known sportfishing enthusiast and can arrange a good angling trip for guests.

Away from the village, over the hill dominated by La Paloma Lodge (see below), a path leads to Playa Cocalito, a small beach. Most of the shoreline in the nearby area is rocky, and this little beach is the best bet for an ocean swim, though not at high tide.

***Cocalito Jungle Resort*** (☎ *in Canada 519-782-3978,* e *berrybend@aol.com)* Campsites US$7-10, rooms US$20-30 per person. Right behind Playa Cocalito is this small and rustic place with nine basic rooms sleeping two to four people. Three rooms have their own bathroom downstairs; the others have private in-room bathrooms with tiled floors and solar showers. There's a restaurant and beachside bar with somewhat erratic hours.

**Top End** Many of the top-end lodges offer multiday packages. Travelers should be aware that the last day usually consists of leaving in the morning and being in San José before lunch.

***Drake Bay Wilderness Resort*** (☎/fax *770-8012, in the USA* ☎ *561-371-3437,* e *emichaud@drakebay.com,* w *www.drake bay.com)* Standard 4-day/3-night package US$680 per person. This resort is run by an American/*tica* couple, Herb and Marleny, and is the longest established and most laid-back of the Bahía Drake lodges. The camp is on a low headland, so you can explore the tide pools or swim in the ocean (although the swimming is rocky and depends on the tide). You can borrow a canoe to go up the Río Agujas at high tide to explore the forest and look for birds and monkeys – or you can hang out in a hammock and wait for the monkeys to come to you. A small troop lives around the lodge and can often be seen swinging around the property. All the local tours are offered (see Activities & Organized Tours, above). In addition, mountain bikes are available, there's a trail to a small iguana and butterfly 'farm,' and tours are offered to Isla Violín, a remote and rarely visited area.

Most of the accommodations are in 19 comfortable cabins with fans and private

solar-heated tiled showers, and most have patios with ocean views. Most cabins are single or duplexes; one set of three cabins is suitable for families or small groups. Four slightly cheaper large walk-in tents with electricity and beds are available only in the drier months of January to April. Access to bathrooms (for tenters) is nearby, and free one-day laundry service is offered. A generator provides electricity, and phone and fax links are offered thanks to the radio-telephone. Tasty and ample buffet-style home-cooked meals are provided in the screened dining room just a few meters away from the Pacific Ocean. A nice bar by the beach offers complimentary snacks in the evening, and there's an ocean-fed pool nearby. In front of the pool is an oceanside 'mirador' built into a small rocky headland.

Visitors normally come on one of several tour packages that include flights from San José into the Bahía Drake airstrip, which is a short boat ride from the lodge (see Getting There & Away, later). The standard four-day/three-night package includes all meals and two guided tours (normally to Corcovado and to Isla del Caño, though others are available). Ask about specialized packages including kayaking, fishing, or diving (the lodge has a complete dive facility). Discounts are offered during the low season, or with full advance payment, or for families with children. This lodge is especially popular with family groups.

***La Paloma Lodge*** (☎ *239-2801,* ☎/fax *239-0954,* e *lapaloma@lapalomalodge .com,* w *www.lapalomalodge.com)* Standard 4-day/3-night package US$825, deluxe US$935, sunset deluxe US$995, per person, including air-transfer from San José. A five-minute walk up a hill above Bahía Drake brings you to this well-recommended lodge. La Paloma's hilltop location gives splendid views of the ocean and forest and catches whatever sea breezes may waft by. There are plenty of birds around; local species often nest on the grounds. English-speaking guides with biology training are on hand to help guests identify what they see.

The lodge has a compressor and dive shop with all equipment. They are justly proud of their 11m pontoon boat that makes fast time to Isla del Caño and is currently the most spacious and comfortable dive boat at Drake. In addition, the lodge has a small swimming pool with great ocean views – perfect for a cooling dip after a sweaty rainforest hike. One end is about 3m deep and is used for beginner's scuba-diving lessons (or just to practice, if you haven't dived for a while).

All the usual tours are available, and two are included in the standard four-day/three-night package. Low-season and Internet specials are available. Scuba diving costs an extra US$50 per person for a two-tank dive, if purchased with a package (US$110 otherwise). In addition, a massage therapist is available with a few hours' notice. Kayaks are available at no charge.

All the lodge buildings are elevated on stilts to take advantage of breeze and views. The dining room/bar has a spacious wraparound balcony that invites early-evening conversation while watching the sunset. There are four standard rooms and five deluxe ranchos; all have great sunset views, and one also has a superb sunrise view.

The four spacious standard rooms, each with a queen and single bed (another bed can be added on request), have plenty of closet space and great ventilation. The spotless, tiled private bathrooms have hot water and are designed with a shoulder-high wall so you can enjoy rainforest views while showering. Each room has a large private balcony with a hammock and with rainforest and ocean views. Beds are covered with huge mosquito nets, though there are rarely biting insects.

Five secluded, spacious, tiled-roof deluxe ranchos, each surrounded by exuberant vegetation and with a wide, wraparound balcony, can sleep two to five people on two levels – great for families. Each rancho has a private hot-water bathroom. Spending a night listening to the rain beating down on the roof is very romantic, and these ranchos are my favorite rooms in Drake.

Single occupancy is possible if there's room. Electric power is available at night. Excellent meals, with a choice of main entrée, are served at your table in the beautiful dining room/clubhouse with a high thatched roof. Because of the lodge's smaller size, service is more personalized than at the larger lodges, and guests soon get to know one another.

***Aguila de Osa Inn*** (☎ 296-2190, fax 232-7722, e *reserve@aguiladeosa.com*,

w *www.aguiladeosa.com*) Singles/doubles US$186/291, junior/master suite US$314/349 for 2 people. On the east side of the Río Agujas, this is considered the most upscale lodge in the area, specializing in sportfishing and scuba packages. There are 11 very nice rooms and two suites, all with attractive views, 24-hour electricity, fans, large tiled baths with hot water, and beautifully carved wooden doors. High-season room rates are given, and rates include tax and all three meals, served with elegant settings in an open-air restaurant. Deep-sea fishing is US$800 per day per boat, which will take four anglers. Inshore fishing is cheaper. Scuba diving costs US$110 for a two-tank dive. All the other usual local tours are available. This lodge tends to attract adults rather than families, and the bar stays open later (most other lodges wind down by about 9pm or 10pm, unless they have a partying group). Rooms are far enough away from the bar that its late hours don't preclude sleep.

***Drake Bay Rainforest Chalet*** (☎ 011-881-63-142-1536 satellite, US fax 334-281-3180, e *reservations@drakebayholiday.com*, w *www.drakebayholiday.com*) Packages US$760 for 4 days/3 nights to US$1150 for 7 days/6 nights, per person; US$100 extra nights, 2 adult minimum, children 50%. This luxurious house in the jungle features a decadent two-person spa-tub, satellite TV, and spacious modern accommodations with a fully stocked, mosaic-tiled, self-catering kitchen. A king-size bed with giant mosquito net makes for romantic nights, and two queen-size beds can be added on request. The chalet faces a river, a 10-minute walk from the beach. Packages include roundtrip transfer from San José, full-day guided tours of Corcovado and Isla del Caño, a Night Tour (see Activities & Organized Tours, earlier), and complimentary biologist guide service on local trails.

## Entertainment

***Aguila de Osa Inn*** This place stays open later than most lodge bars and has music; see above for details.

***Bar Mar y Sombra*** Up some steep stairs at the south end of Bahía Drake, this is a small, rustic hilltop bar with great views of the bay. Stop by for a beer, snack, and a game of pool.

There's also a dance hall, near the store, that sometimes has dances on weekends.

## Getting There & Away

Most travelers either fly into Bahía Drake or arrive by boat from Sierpe (see the Sierpe Getting There & Away section) after either flying to Palmar Sur or traveling by road. If you have a lodge reservation, the boat ride can be arranged for you. From the Bahía Drake airstrip, depending on water levels and sea conditions, you're transported to Bahía Drake either by boat (prepare to get your feet wet) or by jeep. It's a couple of hours faster than taking the scheduled SANSA or Travelair flights to Palmar Sur and continuing by taxi and boat.

A terrible 4WD road links Agujitas with Rancho Quemado (a tiny community to the east). This explains the few trucks and 4WDs seen in the village. Rancho Quemado can be reached on foot or by horseback; ask in Agujitas for the latest possibilities. From Rancho Quemado, a daily bus goes to Rincón, on the road to Puerto Jiménez.

Backpackers can hike to or from Parque Nacional Corcovado (see that section, later in this chapter). If you have a reservation at one of the lodges, they'll arrange to pick you up or drop you off in San Pedrillo, the closest ranger station to Bahía Drake. If you backpacked in, ask around in the Bahía Drake area for a boat to Sierpe.

## FROM BAHÍA DRAKE TO CORCOVADO

It's not difficult to hike from Bahía Drake to Corcovado along the coast. It takes four to seven hours to reach the San Pedrillo ranger station, and trails continue through the park from there. Dropping tides are always the best for coastal walks – high tides may cut you off or delay you. Ask locally about tide tables and conditions.

The route is usually easy to follow. Walk along the beach or, where a headland cuts you off, look inland for a trail over or around the headland, paralleling the coast. This route is hiked often, so if the trail appears to be overgrown, you're probably on the wrong one. Walk back a bit and try again.

## Places to Stay & Eat

Places to stay and eat along this section of coast can all be reached by boat from Sierpe

or Bahía Drake, or on foot. I describe them here in the order they're passed when hiking west and then south from Bahía Drake. *Camping* is possible, though there are no organized campgrounds.

*Treetop Resort* (☎ 387-5562, 380-8319, fax 786-7636; in the USA ☎ 310-450-1769, fax 310-396-8431; ⓔ info@drakebayresort.com, Ⓦ www.drakebayresort.com) Singles/doubles US$75/130, with three meals. Four screened cabins share a bathroom. Treetop is right next to the beach, and its youthful, friendly atmosphere is fostered by a laid-back Californian owner.

*Las Caletas Cabins* (☎ 381-4052 cellular, ☎ 233-3333 pager, ⓔ info@caletas.co.cr, Ⓦ www.caletas.co.cr) Doubles/triples/quads US$116/156/184, including 3 meals. Owned and operated by a friendly Swiss/tico family, this small three-room hotel has received several guest recommendations. Jolanda and David are warm hosts. Cabins are wooden and cozy, all with private tiled bathrooms and balconies with views. Two rooms are in the main house, and one private two-story cabin is a short walk above. Food is described as 'tico with a European flair.' All the usual tours can be arranged, and boat transfers from Sierpe are US$20 per person. German, English, and some Italian are spoken.

*Delfin Amor Ecolodge* (☎ 394-2632 cellular, fax 786-7636, ⓔ dolphins@costarica .net, Ⓦ www.divinedolphin.com/costarica dolphins.htm) Singles/doubles/triples/quads US$130/150/180/200, including 3 meals; packages available. About a 30-minute walk west from Bahía Drake, this small lodge provides dolphin-interaction trips (see Activities & Organized Tours under Bahía Drake, earlier in this chapter). There are five new cabins with bathroom (open late 2002). Cheaper cabins with shared bathroom may still be available – ask (note that rates are given for the new cabins). This is where all the local lodges send their clients for Dolphin Encounters, which cost US$95 per full day. All the other usual Drake tours are available. A nine-day/ eight-night package that includes pickup at San José's Juan Santamaría international airport, the first night in San José, air/boat roundtrip transportation to the lodge, three days of dolphin tours, a Corcovado park tour, an Isla del Caño tour, and a free day costs US$1450/2400 single/double. Recommended for dolphin lovers!

**Corcovado Adventures Tent Camp** (☎ 372-4877, e info@corcovado.com, w www.corcovado.com) Walk-in tents US$55 per person, including 3 meals. Less than an hour's walk from Drake brings you to this spot. There are 10 large tents, each set up on a wooden platform with a double and single bed, nightstand, and a plastic tarp roof to guarantee that it won't leak. There are five bathrooms and a dining room/bar with 24-hour solar power. The rate includes meals and free use of body boards and snorkeling gear. Waves suitable for body boards are a few minutes' walk away; Playa Josecito snorkeling is about a 1½-hour walk away. All the usual activities and tour options are available (at extra cost), and the staff can arrange boat transfers from Sierpe (US$15 per person, two people minimum). They plan to open a scuba facility.

**Marenco Beach & Rainforest Lodge** (☎ 258-1919, fax 255-1346; in the USA ☎ 800-278-6223, 305-908-4169; e info@ marencolodge.com, w www.marencolodge .com) 4-day/3-night packages US$528 per person. This place is 4km or 5km west of Bahía Drake and 5km or 6km north of Corcovado. Once a biological station, it's now a private Costa Rican–run tropical forest reserve set up to protect part of the rainforest. As such, the 500-hectare reserve is an important buffer zone around Parque Nacional Corcovado. The reserve is set on a bluff overlooking the Pacific and is a good place for trips to Corcovado, Isla del Caño, or simply into the forest surrounding the station. There are 4km of trails around Marenco, and many of the plant, bird, and other animal species seen in Corcovado can be found in the Marenco area. The Río Claro flows through the southern part of the reserve. All the usual excursions can be arranged here, though natural history is emphasized. If you want to scuba dive or fish, they can set you up with one of the Bahía Drake lodges. Whales are sometimes seen off the coast from June to September.

Accommodations are in rustic cabins and bungalows that are elevated enough to catch the breeze. Each room has a private bathroom and a verandah overlooking the Pacific Ocean. There are four bunks in some rooms, but double occupancy is the rule

except for student or discounted groups. A generator runs for a few hours in the evening. Meals are served family style in the dining room, where a few reference books are available. There are eight small cabins and 17 more spacious bungalows, and reservations are suggested during the 'dry' busy months of December to April. The wettest months are September and October, when the lodge may be almost empty.

Most people come on a package deal that includes two local tours and meals. Transportation costs extra, and the hotel will help you arrange bus, plane, or boat travel. Note that there is no dock at Marenco. Arriving guests transfer from launches to small boats that are anchored offshore – you'll almost certainly get your feet wet. Low-season discounts are considerable – doubles run US$45 to US$70 per night, depending on the room.

**Guaria de Osa** (w www.experientials .org) Packages US$1200 per week. New in 2002, this Asian-style lodge offers alternative programs involving yoga, ethnobotany, cultural exploration, spiritual study, shamanism, etc, as well as the usual tours of the area.

**Poor Man's Paradise** (☎ 384-7984 cellular; in San Isidro ☎ 771-4582, fax 771-8841; e selvamar@racsa.co.cr, w www.mypoor mansparadise.com) Campsites US$7 per person, rooms US$40-55 per person. Two or three kilometers south of Marenco is Playa San Josecito, one of the larger beach areas along this stretch of coast. Here you'll find Poor Man's Paradise, owned by Pincho Amaya, a well-known local sportfisher. Pincho's father homesteaded 160 hectares here in the 1960s, and the whole family is now involved in running the tourism operation. They're right on the beach, and it's about a 20-minute walk to a snorkeling area and about two hours to the Parque Nacional Corcovado border. Eight cabin tents (with mattress, linens, and shared bath) cost US$39 per person; two cabins with shared bath cost US$49 per person; and 11 cabins with private bath cost US$55 per person. Rates include home-cooked meals (fish, shrimp, and chicken are featured). This is a chance to hang out with a tico family. Backpackers can camp here and use the bathroom facilities. Meals cost US$7 for breakfast or lunch, and US$10 for dinner, though cheaper meals can be arranged if you stay for a few days. There's

PENÍNSULA DE OSA

electricity from dusk 'til 9pm. All the local tours can be arranged, and Pincho can take guests sportfishing at moderate rates (by sportfishing standards).

**Campanario Biological Reserve** (☎ 282-5898, fax 282-8750, e campanario@racsa .co.cr, w www.campanario.org) 4-day/3-night packages US$349 per person. This reserve has a biology field station, library, dorms with tiled showers, a kitchen/dining area, and five large covered platform tents, each sleeping two and with a separate private outdoor bath. The main lodge complex is behind a lawn on the beach and has good views. The reserve is about 100 hectares and climbs up to 155m above sea level behind the lodge. The basic package includes transportation from Sierpe, meals, a visit to Corcovado National Park, and a guided introductory hike into the reserve. All other excursions and activities can be arranged at extra cost; multiday excursions are available. See the website for details of longer visits, courses, and volunteer or research opportunities.

**Casa Corcovado Jungle Lodge** (☎ 256-3181, 256-8825, fax 256-7409, in the USA ☎ 888-896-6097, e corcovado@racsa.co.cr, w www.casacorcovado.com) 4-day/3-night packages, adults/children US$815/505. A couple of kilometers south of Playa San Josecito, right on the national park boundary, this comfortable place is recommended. This lodge is a steep 10-minute climb up from the beach (a tractor hauls up luggage and visitors), and trails from the property directly enter the national park (San Pedrillo ranger station is a 40-minute walk away). The lodge has 24-hour electricity from a hydroelectric and solar-power system, and it recycles. There are 14 bungalows, each screened all the way around for cross breezes and good views, and each has ceiling fans and spacious tiled bathrooms with hot showers. Bungalows have one to three beds. The standard package includes meals, transfer by airbus-boat from San José, a Corcovado tour, and an Isla del Caño tour. The restaurant-bar has forest views (bring binoculars to spot the many birds) and fresh meals. A short walk below the restaurant is a swimming pool. Halfway between the lodge and the beach is the Margarita Sunset Bar, with great sunset views.

## RESERVA BIOLÓGICA ISLA DEL CAÑO

This 326-hectare island is roughly 20km west of Bahía Drake. The reserve is of interest to snorkelers, divers, biologists, and archaeologists. About 5800 hectares of ocean are designated as part of the reserve.

**Snorkelers** will find incredibly warm water (almost body temperature!) and a good variety of marine life ranging from fish to sea cucumbers. The water is much clearer here than along the mainland coast (though not crystalline). Scuba-diving trips are arranged by the Bahía Drake area lodges – there are four dive sites with underwater rock formations, coral reefs, and abundant sea life. A tropical beach with an attractive rainforest backdrop provides sunbathing opportunities, and a trail leads inland, through an evergreen rainforest, to a ridge at about 110m above sea level.

Near the top, look for some of the rock spheres that were made by pre-Columbian indigenous people. Although these spheres have been found in several places in southern Costa Rica, archaeologists are still puzzling over their functions. Trees include milk trees (also called 'cow trees' after the drinkable white latex they exude), rubber trees, figs, and a variety of other tropical species. Birds include coastal and oceanic species as well as rainforest inhabitants, but wildlife is not as varied or prolific as on the mainland.

Camping is prohibited, and there are no facilities except a ranger station by the landing beach. The reserve is administered by Parque Nacional Corcovado. Admission costs US$6 per person for land visits and US$3.50 per person per day for scuba diving, which is mainly for divers with some experience. Most visitors arrive with tours arranged with any of the nearby lodges.

## PARQUE NACIONAL CORCOVADO

Part of the Area de Conservación Osa (Osa Conservation Area), this park has great biological diversity and has long attracted the attention of tropical ecologists who wish to study the intricate workings of the rainforest. The 42,469-hectare park is in the southwestern corner of the Península de Osa and protects at least eight distinct habitats. This assemblage is unique and the best remaining Pacific coastal rainforest in

Central America. Over 500 tree species have been identified here.

Because of its remoteness, the rainforest remained undisturbed until the 1960s, when logging began. The park was established in 1975, but a few years later gold miners moved into the park with detrimental effects. The miners were evicted in 1986, but some loggers and miners still continue to work clandestinely.

## Information

Park admission costs US$6 per person per visit. The park is administered by the Puerto Jiménez headquarters of the Area de Conservación Osa (☎ 735-5036, ☎/fax 735-5282, fax 735-5276), and there are several ranger stations; the main one is at Sirena (☎ 770-8222), near the coast in the middle of the park. There's also an airstrip at Sirena. Trails link Sirena with three other ranger stations that permit camping. With arrangements made a week in advance, the rangers will provide simple but filling meals (US$5 for breakfast, US$8 for lunch or dinner). Food and cooking fuel have to be packed in, and if you just show up, don't expect meals to be available.

*Camping* costs US$2 per person. Facilities consist of tent space, water, and latrines. Sirena provides a travelers' *shelter* for US$6 per person; you'll still need a sleeping bag and insect netting (or use your tent in the shelter). Make reservations in advance. The other ranger stations may have sleeping space available, but it's limited and you can't rely on it. Both La Leona and Los Patos can accommodate up to about 15 campers.

Reservations for meals at any ranger station or to sleep in the ranger stations must be made through the Puerto Jiménez office. Ask for Carlos Quintero and allow a few days for arrangements to be made. Self-sufficient backpackers can just show up and pay daily camping fees as they go. Camping is not officially permitted in areas other than at the ranger stations.

Because Corcovado has the best trail system of any rainforest park, it attracts a fair number of backpackers – sometimes as many as two dozen people may be camped at Sirena during the dry season, though there are fewer people at the other stations. During the wettest months (July to November), parts of the trail system or park may be closed; call the Puerto Jiménez office for current conditions.

## Wildlife Watching

The wildlife within the park is varied and prolific. Corcovado is home to Costa Rica's

### Visiting the Wilderness

Parque Nacional Corcovado holds some of the wildest yet most accessible rainforest in Costa Rica. This attracts all kinds of visitors, ranging from young backpackers going it alone for days to retired folks taking a guided day tour.

Corcovado may be accessible and may entice many visitors, but it's definitely a wilderness area, and travel there should not be taken lightly. A few years ago, a small guided group left Bahía Drake on a day trip to Corcovado. The guide became lost and what was supposed to be a day trip became a nightmare for the tourists, who envisioned spending a night without food or shelter in the rainforest. Fortunately, two group members were able to find their way to the coast (the guide stayed with the rest of the group) and alerted the park rangers, who rapidly raised a search party.

Late that night, the rangers found the group, scratched, shaken, and insect-bitten, but with no major injuries, and helped them back to the coast. Here, a boat took them back to their lodge and safety. The travelers were understandably quite upset. The park rangers, who work for a pittance and who receive no extra salary for carrying out nighttime rescues, are to be commended for their hard work.

I spoke to several Bahía Drake–area lodge managers and owners following this event. The general feeling was that there's no way to have a genuine wilderness experience without some possibility of discomfort, and it's impossible to guarantee that nothing will go wrong. 'There, but for the grace of God, go I,' said one lodge owner. This was an isolated incident.

The bottom line is that this is not Disney's Jungle World. This is the jungle. Even on a guided tour, you're taking a small risk. Live with it and enjoy.

largest population of the beautiful scarlet macaw. The park also protects many of the other important or endangered rainforest species: tapirs, five cat species, crocodiles, peccaries, giant anteaters, monkeys, and sloths. The rare harpy eagle, almost extinct in Costa Rica, may still breed in remote parts of Corcovado. Almost 400 bird species and about 140 mammal species have been seen here. However, it's only fair to say that most of the animals are very hard to see, national park or not, and staying in most of the lodges in the area will yield as good an opportunity for wildlife watching as you'll find in the park.

## Trails & Hiking

One of the most exciting aspects of Corcovado for visitors is that there are long-distance trails through the park leading to several ranger stations. At Corcovado, unlike many of Costa Rica's other lowland rainforest parks, backpackers can hike through the park. The trails are primitive and the hiking is hot, humid, and insect-ridden, but it can be done. For the traveler wanting to spend a few days hiking through

a lowland tropical rainforest, Corcovado is the best choice in Costa Rica.

It's safest to go in a small group. One reader claims that he hiked through the park alone and suffered several misadventures. First he was treed by a herd of 50 to 100 white-lipped peccaries that milled around underneath his tree clicking their teeth menacingly. Then he was robbed by a gang of youths who apparently were Panamanian poachers capturing scarlet macaws and endangered squirrel monkeys for illegal sale to zoos, collectors, and pet shops. After he had lost, among other things, his insect repellent, his trip ended uncomfortably with hundreds of itchy bug bites.

If, after reading his story, you still want to go, you'll have an easier time of it in the dry season (from January to April) rather than slogging around in calf-deep mud during the wet season. There are fewer bugs in the dry season, too. The largest herds of peccaries are on the Sirena to Los Patos trails, and if you climb about 2m off the ground, you'll avoid being bitten in the unlikely event of running into a herd.

## Parque Nacional Isla del Coco

This park occupies the entire Isla del Coco (Cocos Island), which is over 500km southwest of Costa Rica in the eastern Pacific. Despite its isolation, Cocos has been known since the early 16th century and was noted on a map drawn by Nicholas Dechiens as far back as 1541. It's extremely wet, with between 6000mm and 7000mm of annual rainfall, and thus attracted the attention of early sailors, pirates, and whalers, who frequently stopped for fresh water and coconuts. Legend has it that some of the early visitors buried a huge treasure here, but, despite hundreds of treasure-hunting expeditions, it has never been found. The heavy rainfall has enabled the island to support thick rainforest that soon covers all signs of digging.

Because of its isolation, Isla del Coco has evolved a unique ecosystem, earning it the protective status of national park. Over 70 species of animals (mainly insects) and 70 species of plants are endemic (occurring nowhere else in the world), and more remain to be discovered. Birders come to the island to see the colonies of seabirds, many of which nest on Cocos. Among the approximately 80 birds listed for the park are two species of frigatebird, three species of booby, four species of gull, and six species of storm petrel; more are expected to be added to the list. At least three of the birds are endemic: the Cocos Island cuckoo, Cocos Island finch, and Cocos Island flycatcher. (The Cocos Island finch is part of the group of endemic finches studied in the Galápagos Islands by Darwin; however, the Cocos species was not discovered until almost 60 years after Darwin's visit to the Galápagos.) There are two endemic lizard species. The marine life is also varied, with sea turtles, coral reefs, and tropical fish in abundance. Snorkeling and diving are excellent and are the main activities for visitors.

No people permanently live on the island, although unsuccessful attempts were made to colonize Cocos in the late 19th and early 20th centuries. After the departure of these people, feral populations of domestic animals began to create a problem, and today feral pigs are the greatest

You can hike in from the north, south, or east side of the park (see the Península de Osa & Golfo Dulce map) and exit a different way; thus you won't have to retrace your steps.

**San Pedrillo to Sirena** From the north, walk in along the coast from Bahía Drake and arrive at the San Pedrillo ranger station about a kilometer after entering the park. Allow a day to hike from Drake to San Pedrillo, or hire a boat. Most visitors to this area are on day trips from Bahía Drake lodges. From San Pedrillo, it's about a 10-hour hike to Sirena – check the tide tables or ask at the station. Most of the first few hours of hiking are through coastal rainforest; then the trail follows the beach – during the heat of the day and with a heavy pack, loose sand can slow you down. En route you'll pass the beautiful waterfall plunging onto the wild beach of Playa Llorona. A few hundred meters south of the waterfall, a small trail leads inland to a cascading river and a refreshing swimming hole. At this point, you'll have to ford the Río Llorona. At Playa Corcovado, two or three hours later, the Río Corcovado must also be crossed. And about a kilometer before reaching Sirena, you must ford the Río Sirena, which can be chest-deep in the rainy season – it's the largest river on the hike. Note that sharks and crocodiles have been reported near the mouth of this river, so cross as far up from the coast as you're able – see where local rangers and researchers go. The entire distance from San Pedrillo to Sirena is about 23km. This northern trail is the least frequently used one (though there are people hiking it most days during the high season).

**La Leona to Sirena** From the south, take air or land transportation to Carate, from where it's over an hour's hike to the ranger station at La Leona. From there, it's a six- to seven-hour hike to Sirena, but check that the tides are low – it's a beach hike with several rocky headlands to cross, and high tides can cut you off. If you look carefully, you can usually find trails going inland around the headlands. Often, these inland trails offer the best chances to see mammals, though jaguars

## Parque Nacional Isla del Coco

threat to the unique species native to the island. The pigs uproot vegetation, causing soil erosion that in turn contributes to sedimentation around the island's coasts and damage to the coral reefs surrounding the island. Feral rats, cats, and goats also contribute to the destruction of the natural habitat. Unregulated fishing and hunting pose further threats.

The Servicio de Parques Nacionales is aware of the problem, but lack of funding has made doing anything about it difficult. The island is rugged and heavily forested, with the highest point at Cerro Yglesias (634m). As a practical matter, how *can* you remove a large population of feral pigs from a thickly vegetated and hilly island that is 7.5km long and 4km wide?

### Information & Organized Tours

There's a park station, and permission is needed from the park service to visit it. (The dive operator that you use will arrange for the necessary permission.) There are some trails, but camping is not allowed. The few visitors who come stay on their boats; there's a US$35 daily per-person park fee.

In Costa Rica, the only outfitter specializing in dive trips to Cocos is **Undersea Hunter** (☎ 228-6535, 228-6613, fax 289-7334, in the USA ☎ 800-203-2120, e info@underseahunter.com, w www.underseahunter.com). It operates the 115-foot *Sea Hunter*, sleeping up to 18 passengers in eight cabins with private baths, and the slightly smaller *Undersea Hunter,* sleeping up to 14 passengers in six cabins, two with shared and four with private bath. The typical cost of a 10-day tour (including seven days of diving with three or four dives a day) is US$3095 per person from San José, plus US$35/day park fees. Longer trips are available.

The US-owned *Okeanos Aggressor* also does 11-day dive cruises. (See Organized Tours in the Getting There & Away chapter.) Note that these trips are for advanced, certified divers; beginners' lessons and basic certification are not offered.

have been seen loping along the beach. Keep your eyes open for paw prints. The entire distance from Carate to Sirena is about 16km, but parts of the hike are along the beach, where the heat and the loose, sandy footing make it heavy going, especially if you are carrying a big pack. Look for shady sections in the forest behind the beach.

**Los Patos to Sirena** From the east, take a bus to La Palma, from where it's about four hours along a rough road to Los Patos ranger station. The road is passable to 4WD vehicles, and you can hire a jeep-taxi. You might be able to hitch a ride in the dry season, but don't count on it, as vehicles are few. This trail/road crosses the river about 20 times in the last 6km before Los Patos. It's easy to miss the right turn shortly before the ranger station, but there are locals around who can advise you. Try to stick to the 4WD road and you'll find Los Patos more easily; there are other footpaths that gold miners made trying

### A Great Day at Corcovado

One day, hiking a trail south of Sirena with some friends, we stopped to look at one of the more common rainforest mammals, an agouti. With binoculars, we were all getting excellent looks at this reddish-brown rodent, which looks like an oversize rabbit with a squirrel-like face and an almost nonexistent tail. Suddenly, I saw a slight movement in the bushes behind the agouti and, through binoculars, I found myself staring at a small ocelot. I almost jumped out of my boots in excitement – a jungle cat in the wild! It took a long steady look at me and then melted into the undergrowth. No one else in my group saw it.

That same afternoon I saw all four species of Costa Rican monkeys, a white-nosed coati, and a good number of tropical birds, including trogons, scarlet macaws, a nesting common black hawk, a spectacled owl, and many others. The secret to seeing so much wildlife on one hike is to go in a small group (preferably with an experienced guide); to hike on a trail that has few visitors; to keep your eyes peeled; and, above all, to have a reasonable amount of good luck. Good luck to you!

### Biological Investigation

A biological station at Sirena houses scientists and students carrying out rainforest research. They get preference over travelers for accommodations. Ongoing research programs mean that some areas close to the station may be off-limits or that trees and sites might be marked with flags, tags, or other markers or equipment. Please avoid disturbing these sites if you come across them.

to avoid the ranger station! The birding along this road is reportedly good.

From Los Patos, a 6km trail leads to a small hill with a lookout point from which you can see Laguna Corcovado and a good portion of the park. This makes a good day hike if you want to spend two nights at Los Patos. Backpackers going in through Los Patos continue southwest to Sirena (about six hours). The trail undulates steeply through the hilly forest for two or three hours before finally flattening out near the swampy Laguna Corcovado.

If you hike out of the park through Los Patos, the rangers can help you call a jeep-taxi in the dry months to take you out at least part of the way.

Note that these are fairly conservative times. Fit hikers with light packs can probably move faster, though if you spend a lot of time birding or taking photos, you'll end up taking longer.

Check with rangers about changes in trail and river conditions.

### Getting There & Away

You can arrange with a Bahía Drake lodge for a boat ride to San Pedrillo or Playa Llorona in the northern part of the park; otherwise you'll have to walk.

Several buses a day depart from Puerto Jiménez to La Palma, for entrance via Los Patos.

From Puerto Jiménez, it's about 40km or 45km around the southern end of the Península de Osa as far as Carate (see the Carate section, later in this chapter). A truck or 4WD vehicle leaves Puerto Jiménez at 6am daily for US$7 per person. At other times you can hire a vehicle for US$60. The return to Puerto Jiménez from Carate departs around 8:30am.

Travelair flies from San José to Carate. You can also arrange to fly into Sirena by chartered aircraft from San José, Golfito, or Puerto Jiménez. (Allow about US$75 per person for a flight between Puerto Jiménez and Sirena.)

# To Corcovado via Puerto Jiménez

## FROM THE INTERAMERICANA TO PUERTO JIMÉNEZ

A 78km road links the Interamericana (at Chacarita) with Puerto Jiménez. The road is paved for 45km to the small town of **Rincón**, followed by 33km of gravel road to Puerto Jiménez. From Rincón, a very poor road goes to the coast at Bahía Drake. There's a daily bus from Rincón to Rancho Quemado, a community halfway between Rincón and Drake and unmarked on most maps. Beyond Rancho Quemado, the road is passable to high-clearance 4WD vehicles only in the dry season.

About 9km southeast of Rincón is the village of **La Palma**, from where a rough road goes to Los Patos ranger station. The women of La Palma run a tourist office of sorts, with homemade souvenirs and coffee available. There are restaurants, pulperías, and three inexpensive hotels here, all clustered around a right-angle turn in the main road.

About 12km beyond La Palma at **Cañazas** a turnoff leads 1.7km to the *Cañaza Lodge* (☎ 735-5062 messages only, fax 735-5045, @ yves_leheurteux@canaza.com, W www .canaza.com) Singles/doubles US$90/130 for 1-room bungalow, US$100/160 for 2-room bungalow, all including 3 meals & activities. This French-run, beachside resort consists of just six thatched bungalows, each with private cold shower, and a large thatched restaurant-bar-relaxation area – all set around a large garden and orchard. The lodge is closed from September through November. Guests can use a catamaran, sea canoe, snorkeling gear, and bicycles at no extra charge, and short horseback rides on the beach are also offered. Longer half-day guided rides are US$40, and scuba diving is US$75 including lunch. The food is tropical French, and evening cocktails and wine are included. Several readers have raved about this relaxing place.

Back on the main highway, about 4km beyond Cañazas on the left-hand side is *Jardín de las Aves Lodge* (☎ 735-5675 messages only, @ safariosa@hotmail.com, W www.safariosa.com) Campsites US$5 per person, singles/doubles US$35/45. Tucked into the jungle are two cabins, and three more are due to open by late 2002. One cabin is reached by a unique, covered-bridge; another has two floors. Both have private cold showers, though a shared hot shower is available. This place is suited to birding and natural history study, and to getting away from it all. Rates include breakfast, and kitchen facilities and other meals are available.

About 21km beyond La Palma and 4km before Puerto Jiménez, a turn to the right leads 8km to **Dos Brazos**, a gold-mining and farming village. *Bosque del Río Tigre* (☎ 735-5725 messages only, fax 735-5045, in the USA ☎ 888-875-9453, @ info@osaadventures .com, W www.osaadventures.com) Rooms US$79 per person, including meals; children under 12 US$45. A couple of kilometers beyond Dos Brazos lies this small, private sanctuary and lodge. Run by naturalists Elizabeth Jones and Abraham Gallo, the lodge has four rustic rooms with forest views and shared clean bathrooms, and one cabin with a private bath. Solar-powered fans are in the rooms. You can arrange moderately priced horseback rides or hikes to the national park, take gold-panning excursions, or go kayaking. Birding is excellent. A *colectivo* taxi (driven by Antonio Garbanzo) leaves from the Super 96 store in Puerto Jiménez at 11am and 4pm daily; it leaves Dos Brazos at 7am and 1:30pm. If you're driving, 4WD is recommended, as a river must be crossed just before the lodge.

## PUERTO JIMÉNEZ

With about 6100 inhabitants, Puerto Jiménez is the only town of any size on the Península de Osa. Until the 1960s, the peninsula was one of the most remote parts of Costa Rica, with exuberant rainforests and a great variety of plants and animals. Then logging began here, and later gold was discovered, creating a minor gold rush and increased settlement. In the face of this, Parque Nacional Corcovado was created in 1975. Logging and gold mining go on around it, but within the park's boundaries, valuable, unique rainforest habitats are preserved.

The gold rush and logging industry, along with accompanying colonization, made Puerto Jiménez a fairly important little town. And because access is now relatively straightforward, there's a burgeoning tourist industry. Ticos like to come to Puerto Jiménez for its slightly frontier atmosphere and for the pleasant beaches nearby. Foreigners tend to come because this is the entry town to the famous Parque Nacional Corcovado, which has an administration and information office here. It's a pleasant town

and still remote enough that you can see parrots and macaws flying around.

## Information

Doña Isabel, the Travelair agent (☎ 735-5062, 735-5722, fax 735-5043, ⓔ osatropi@racsa.co.cr) is a good source of local travel information and handles hotel and transportation arrangements of all kinds. She has a radio to call lodges in both the peninsula and Golfito areas. The folks listed under Organized Tours, below, are also excellent information sources.

Osa Natural (☎/fax 735-5440, ⓔ osa natur@racsa.co.cr, ⓦ www.osanatural .com) is a local tourism office that offers Internet access (US$3 per hour). Staff can make Corcovado reservations for you with

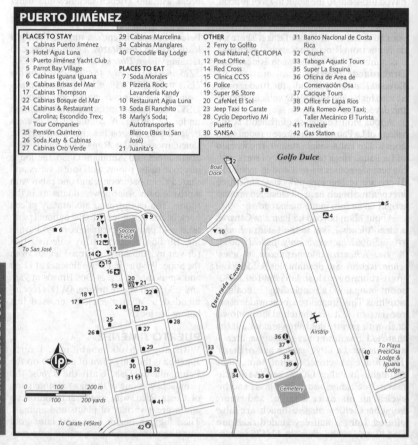

## PUERTO JIMÉNEZ

**PLACES TO STAY**
1 Cabinas Puerto Jiménez
3 Hotel Agua Luna
4 Puerto Jiménez Yacht Club
5 Parrot Bay Village
6 Cabinas Iguana Iguana
9 Cabinas Brisas del Mar
17 Cabinas Thompson
22 Cabinas Bosque del Mar
24 Cabinas & Restaurant Carolina; Escondido Trex; Tour Companies
25 Pensión Quintero
26 Soda Katy & Cabinas
27 Cabinas Oro Verde

29 Cabinas Marcelina
34 Cabinas Manglares
40 Crocodile Bay Lodge

**PLACES TO EAT**
7 Soda Morales
8 Pizzería Rock; Lavandería Kandy
10 Restaurant Agua Luna
13 Soda El Ranchito
18 Marly's Soda; Autotransportes Blanco (Bus to San José)
21 Juanita's

**OTHER**
2 Ferry to Golfito
11 Osa Natural; CECROPIA
12 Post Office
14 Red Cross
15 Clínica CCSS
16 Police
19 Super 96 Store
20 CafeNet El Sol
23 Jeep Taxi to Carate
28 Cyclo Deportivo Mi Puerto
30 SANSA

31 Banco Nacional de Costa Rica
32 Church
33 Taboga Aquatic Tours
35 Super La Esquina
36 Oficina de Area de Conservación Osa
37 Cacique Tours
38 Office for Lapa Ríos
39 Alfa Romeo Aero Taxi; Taller Mecánico El Turista
41 Travelair
42 Gas Station

15 days' advance notice. Hours are 8am to 8pm in the high season. Internet access and tourism information are also available at Cafenet El Sol – they claim to be open 24 hours but have been known to close. Ciclo Deportivo Mi Puerto rents bikes – they're well-used so check them out before you rent.

The Oficina de Area de Conservación Osa (☎ 735-5036, 735-5580, fax 735-5276) has information about Corcovado, Isla del Caño, Parque Nacional Marino Ballena (see the Central Pacific Coast chapter), and Golfito parks and reserves. Hours are 8am to noon and 1pm to 4pm Monday to Thursday, 8am to noon Friday, though phones are sometimes answered on weekends. They have up-to-date information on Corcovado.

The Banco Nacional de Costa Rica (☎ 735-5020) changes US dollars. Emergency medical treatment can be obtained at the Clínica CCSS, or call the Red Cross (☎ 735-5109).

## Organized Tours

*Escondido Trex* (☎/fax 735-5210, e osatrex@racsa.co.cr, w www.escondidotrex.com) has an office in the Restaurant Carolina. They do half-day to 10-day tours, primarily kayaking for all levels of experience, but also other trips. There are several other tour agencies on the same block.

Personable naturalist Andy Pruter runs *Everyday Adventures* (☎/fax 735-5138, e everyday@racsa.co.cr), specializing in sea kayaking and rainforest treks in the Osa area, including hikes with a climb up a hollow strangler fig tree. Both day and overnight adventures are available. Ask for him at the Restaurant Carolina or Travelair office. Rates are negotiable depending on group size, etc, but figure on about US$40 a half day or US$110 to US$160 a day for multiday trips, including accommodations and meals.

Tours can also be arranged with *Osa Natural* (see Information, above) and *Osa Aventura* (☎/fax 735-5431), which specializes in adventure treks of up to 10 days on the Península de Osa. *Taboga Aquatic Tours* (☎ 735-5265, fax 735-5121) is run by local fisher Marco Loaiciga, who has been recommended for fishing and snorkeling trips as well as boat sightseeing. *Cacique Tours* (☎ 735-5564, fax 735-5045, 735-5530,

e agualu@racsa.co.cr), run by Oscar Cortes (who speaks a little English), specializes in Corcovado and birding tours. *Aventuras Tropicales* (☎ 735-5195, fax 735-5692, e kayak@racsa.co.cr) does kayaking and other adventure tours.

## Places to Stay

**Budget** During Easter week, many hotels are full. On dry-season weekends, hotel choices can be limited. Call ahead to make reservations, or arrive midweek. Rates below are for the dry high season; the usual discounts apply for the wet low season.

*Puerto Jiménez Yacht Club* You can camp inexpensively on the grass at this place, which has a basic bathroom but no lockers.

*Pensión Quintero* (☎ 735-5087) Rooms US$4 per person. This place has clean rooms, some without windows or fans, though table fans are provided on request. Shared bathroom facilities are rustic.

*Cabinas Thompson* (☎ 735-5140) Rooms US$5 per person. Basic but adequate rooms with private cold baths are offered here. Also try the similarly priced *Soda Katy y Cabinas*.

*Cabinas Puerto Jiménez* (☎ 735-5090) Rooms with bath US$7.50 per person. Clean, good-value rooms with fans are available here.

*Cabinas Oro Verde* (☎ 735-5241) Rooms with bath US$7.50 per person. This place has good rooms with private baths and fans.

*Cabinas Bosque del Mar* (☎/fax 735-5681, fax 735-5621) Rooms from US$8 per person. Excellent value and popular, Bosque del Mar has rooms with fans and private hot showers. A soda and TV room are attached. A couple of air-conditioned doubles are US$30.

*Cabinas Marcelina* (☎ 735-5007, fax 735-5045, e osanatur@racsa.co.cr) Singles/doubles/triples US$12/16/20. This friendly place was remodeled in 2002 and offers six clean rooms with fans and private cold showers. There's parking and a small lawn.

*Restaurant y Cabinas Carolina* (☎ 735-5185) Doubles US$13.50-20. This place offers seven clean rooms, two of which are air-conditioned. All have private cold showers and fans.

*Cabinas Brisas del Mar* (☎ 735-5028, fax 735-5012) Standard rooms US$9 per person, deluxe doubles US$40. There are 10 clean standard rooms with fans and private cold showers. Some sleep up to four people. Four air-conditioned rooms feature private hot showers and attractive furniture. There's a TV room with videos; a bar, restaurant, and deck with views are planned.

*Cabinas Iguana Iguana (☎ 735-5158)* Rooms from US$10 per person. The basic rooms here are being upgraded. There's a pool and a very good restaurant.

**Mid-Range & Top End** Away from the town center is *Cabinas Manglares (☎ 735-5002, fax 735-5605, e manglarestin@costarricense.cr)* Singles/doubles US$16/28, air-conditioned doubles US$35. Behind the hotel are a small café and a mangrove area where you can look for frogs, etc. Eight rooms have fans and private baths; two are air-conditioned.

*Hotel Agua Luna (☎/fax 735-5393, e agualu@racsa.co.cr)* Singles/doubles US$40/55. Near the boat dock, this hotel has six clean, reasonably large air-conditioned rooms, each with two beds, a large tiled hot-water bathroom, cable TV, telephone, and minifridge.

*Parrot Bay Village (☎ 735-5180, 735-5748, fax 735-5568, e mail@parrotbayvillage.com, w www.parrotbayvillage.com)* Singles/doubles/triples/quads US$105/128/151/175, add US$11.50 for air-con. A strong focus here is fishing, and three boats are available (a 6m Mako for two anglers at US$500 a day and two 9m Sea-Vees for four anglers at US$600 a day). Experienced captains all speak English. Other tours are offered as well. Close to the beach are seven separate spacious cabins with wraparound screens and attractively carved wooden doors. All have fans and hot showers, and hardwood details abound. Three cabins have two floors and are suitable for families. In addition, their 'casa cabina' sleeps six and rents for US$215. The cabins loosely surround an open-air restaurant-bar that serves good meals. A volleyball net and kayaks are available for guests. Behind the cabins are mangroves and an egret rookery, with most of the nesting activity taking place in May and June.

*Crocodile Bay Lodge (☎ 735-5617, fax 735-5712, e info@crocodilebay.com, w www.crocodilebay.com)* Fishing package: standard 3-6 days US$2195-3295 per person, deluxe 3-6 days US$2895-4595. Designed for upscale anglers, this large, new, modern complex features two dozen luxurious, white-tiled air-conditioned suites, some with Jacuzzi tubs. Rates include transfers from San José, first and last nights' lodging in San José, fishing, and meals. Non-anglers pay US$1235 to US$1545. Discounts for three or four people in a room/boat are offered.

Several lodges have opened on Playa Preciosa/Playa Platanares, about 5km east of the airstrip.

*Playa PreciOsa Lodge (☎ 735-5062, fax 735-5043, w www.playa-preciosa-lodge.de)* Doubles with bath US$50. This place is popular with German-speaking tourists, though English is also spoken. There are four simple circular thatched bungalows, each with a loft, fan, and balcony with hammocks. Beds have mosquito netting, though bugs don't seem to be a problem. Complimentary tea and coffee are served all day. Simple meals are available at extra cost and are either served family style or barbecued on the beach.

*Iguana Lodge (☎ 735-5205, fax 735-5043, e info@iguanalodge.com, w www.iguanalodge.com)* Singles/doubles US$151/210, including 3 meals. This alluring place has the most architecturally memorable cabins in the area. Four beautifully airy, two-story hardwood cabins provide guests with huge decks, comfortable beds, and lovely hot-water bathrooms, some semi-outdoors. Meals are high-end gourmet served in a down-home atmosphere within a huge thatched rancho where guests relax with board games and beer. The American owners have children, and families are welcome.

*Pearl of the Osa (w www.thepearlof theosa.com)* Doubles US$65-87, including breakfast. Near to and owned by Iguana Lodge, this beachside place has eight simpler rooms for folks who can't afford the Iguana. Rates depend on views and windows (middle rooms with jungle views to corner rooms with ocean views). Meals are available.

Also see South of Puerto Jiménez, below.

## Places to Eat & Drink

*Restaurant Carolina* Dishes US$3-8. This reasonably priced and centrally located restaurant is perhaps the town's best-known and most popular restaurant and meeting spot. Cheaper places nearby include *Soda Katy*, *Soda El Ranchito*, *Soda Morales*, and *Marly's Soda*, by the main bus stop; all are OK.

*Restaurant Agua Luna* (☎ 735-5033) Dishes US$4-6. This restaurant offers reasonable Chinese food and a river view from the back porch.

*Pizzería Rock* This establishment serves pizzas and has take-out.

*Juanita's* Meals average US$6. This popular place serves Mexican fare and is a good place to hang out with a beer and new friends.

There are several other locally popular bars on the main street near Restaurant Carolina.

## Shopping

If you're stocking up on picnic items, one of the best general stores is *Super La Esquina*, near the airstrip. The *Super 96 Store*, on the main drag, also has supplies.

## Getting There & Away

**Air** SANSA (☎ 735-5017) and Travelair have daily flights from San José. The Travelair agent (see Information, earlier) is helpful with transportation arrangements. Both offices are closed on Sunday.

Alfa Romeo Aero Taxi (☎ 735-5178, fax 735-5112) has charter flights to local destinations like Carate, Sirena, Golfito, and other places. Three-seater aircraft can be chartered into Corcovado for about US$180; five-seaters cost US$220. A five-seater charter to San José costs about US$480.

**Bus** Autotransportes Blanco has buses at 5am and 11am daily via San Isidro (US$4.50) to San José (US$7, nine hours), although the 5am bus might not run in the rainy season. Buses to San Isidro also run at 4am and 1pm. Next to the departure point, Marly's Soda sells tickets from 7am to 11am daily and 1pm to 5pm Monday to Saturday. Buy tickets in advance, especially for the 5am departure. In San José, buses leave at 6am and noon from Calle 12 & Avenida 9.

There are also buses at 5am and 2pm daily for Neily (US$3, four to six hours). The San José and Neily buses take you the 23km to La Palma, the eastern exit/entry point for Parque Nacional Corcovado.

**Truck & Taxi** To go to Carate, south of Puerto Jiménez at the southern end of Corcovado, take a jeep/truck that leaves at 6am daily. There may be more departures in the dry season; some departures may be canceled in the wet. The fare is US$6 to US$7 per person. At other times, you can hire a truck or 4WD taxi for about US$50 or US$60.

**Car** Drivers will find Taller Mecánico El Turista (☎ 735-5060, 735-5161) next to the Alfa Romeo Aero Taxi office. This is the best mechanic in the area.

**Boat** The passenger ferry to Golfito leaves at 6am daily, takes 1½ hours, and costs US$3.

## SOUTH OF PUERTO JIMÉNEZ

It's 45km by dirt road around the tip of the Península de Osa to the end of the road at Carate near Parque Nacional Corcovado. The road is drivable in a 2WD vehicle all the way during the dry season, though there are some pretty rough stretches where you'll need to drive very carefully unless you have high clearance. In the wet season, 4WD is needed. All places in this section can be reached by taxi from Puerto Jiménez, or the scheduled jeep/truck to Carate can drop you off at the entrance roads.

About 16km from Puerto Jiménez is the *Buena Esperanza Bar*, where you can get a cold drink or snack. A kilometer beyond, on the left and slightly set back from the road, is a white cement gate (locally called 'El Portón Blanco') that leads into a hilly area above the coast, with dirt roads accessing several small *lodges* and *houses* for rent; ask at Travelair in Puerto Jiménez about others that may be available beyond those listed below.

### El Portón Blanco Area

*Casa Bambú* (*in the USA* ☎ 512-263-1650, fax 512-263-7553, e casabambu@earth link.net) Doubles US$95, US$35 additional people. This rustic two-story wooden house is set back 100m from the beach. Each of its three bedrooms has a double bed, indoor bathroom and open-air shower, kitchen, dining room, covered porch, and solar-powered fans. There is a three-night minimum stay, with discounts for larger groups and children. Meals are available at lodges within walking distance, and maid service is offered.

**Encanta La Vida** (☎/fax 735-5678; in the USA ☎ 805-969-4270, fax 805-969-0238; ☒ info@encantalavida.com, ☒ www.encanta lavida.com) Rooms US$75 per person, including 3 meals. This is a 2½-story house (the top story is a lookout tower) with four bedrooms (two with private baths) and nearby beach access; kayaks are available. There's a two-day minimum. Three new private cabinas have been added – call for rates.

**Hacienda Bahía Esmeralda** (☎ 381-8521 cellular, fax 735-5045, ☒ pandulce@racsa .co.cr) Rooms US$120 per person, including 3 meals. This place has two large rooms in the main lodge and three comfortably appointed cabins, all with private bath and fans. High-season rates are listed, and discounts for weeklong stays are offered.

## Lapa Rios

A few hundred meters beyond El Portón Blanco, on the right side of the road, is the fabulous wilderness resort of Lapa Rios (in Puerto Jiménez ☎ 735-5130, fax 735-5179, ☒ info@laparios.com, ☒ www .laparios.com). Singles/doubles US$320/420. In a 400-hectare private nature reserve that's 80% virgin forest, Lapa Rios has a commitment to conserve and protect the surrounding rainforest; it developed a program for training locals to work at the lodge and built a new school. The excellent local guides include an indigenous shaman who knows medicinal plants and talks about the ancient spiritual value of the rainforest, and some natural history guides who can educate guests about their surroundings.

The main activities are hiking the extensive trail system and observing nature. Most of the trails are steep and not recommended for people with walking limitations, though a 3km path on the property gives easy access to the rainforest.

A medium-difficulty trail system near the lodge offers scenic looks at a waterfall and a huge strangler fig, as well as good birding. Longer, more difficult trails require guides (US$20 to US$40 depending on length) and include a hike to the border of the Corcovado park, a wild and difficult trek to a 30m waterfall, a night walk (by flashlight), and other options.

A beach about 500m from the lodge offers tide pools, surfing, swimming, and snorkeling opportunities. Body boards can be rented. Horse rental starts at US$30 per half day (two people minimum). A guided boat tour to Casa de Orquídeas botanical garden (US$40 per person) or a guided natural history cruise up the Río Esquinas estuary and through the mangroves (US$300 per boat for up to four people) can be arranged, as can excursions to Corcovado or fishing trips (about US$850 per day for four anglers). A massage therapist is also available.

The impressive lodge has a pool, restaurant, bar, reading room, and wonderful views. Particularly memorable is the soaring thatched roof of the restaurant, which towers, cathedral-like, over diners. A long spiral staircase climbs three stories to an observation deck near the rooftop. Fourteen spacious and attractive wooden bungalows are scattered over the site, and some of them are a long climb up or down a steep path (with stairs) that would be difficult to access if you have a mobility problem. Each has a large bathroom (two sinks!) and hot water, electricity, a fan, two queen-size beds with mosquito nets (more for a romantic display than necessity), large screened view windows, and an ample deck. The listed high-season rates include all three meals.

A transfer from Puerto Jiménez costs US$20 roundtrip. It's a 19km drive from Puerto Jiménez airport.

## Bosque del Cabo

South of Lapa Rios, the road continues through the Cabo Matapalo area, the peninsula's southernmost cape. There are stands of virgin forest interspersed with cattle ranches and great ocean views.

Two kilometers beyond Lapa Rios, a signed turn to the left leads 2km farther to the recommended wilderness lodge, Bosque del Cabo (☎ 381-4847 cellular, in Puerto Jiménez ☎/fax 735-5206, ☒ phil@bosquedel cabo.com, ☒ www.bosquedelcabo.com). Singles/doubles US$165/250, deluxe units US$175/270, both including 3 meals; 2-/3-bedroom houses US$250/325. The lodge is set on 140 hectares, half of it virgin forest. There are nine rustic, attractive thatched-roof bungalows set on a bluff with ocean views (whales pass by from December to

March), comfortable beds, and sun-warmed showers. The showers are outside each bungalow and, while completely private, give the impression of bathing in the forest. (The flush toilet is inside.) The bungalows are spaced apart for privacy, and two of them have fantastic ocean views from private patios. Five deluxe units are slightly larger and have solar power and decks or porches; four standard cabins are romantically lit by candles. There's electricity in the main lodge, where good food is served family style. A swimming pool is naturally filled by a spring and emptied for cleaning every 10 days. It's a 15-minute hike down to the beach.

Birding in the area is excellent, and hikes can be taken (alone or with a naturalist guide) through the forest, to the ocean, to nearby rivers, and to a waterfall. Large flocks of scarlet macaws are commonly seen. Horseback riding (US$35 per person), tide-pool exploration, and swimming are all options.

The two houses have two or three bedrooms. Each house has a private hot bath, full kitchen, and hydroelectric energy that powers the fridge, blender, and microwave. The houses are rented for a three-day minimum, and meals are not included; rates are for up to four or six people.

## CARATE

This is the beginning of the road if you're departing from Corcovado, or the end of the road if you're arriving at the park from Puerto Jiménez. There's an airstrip and a pulpería. If you're driving, you can leave your car here (US$4.50 a night) and hike to the tent camp (less than an hour) or La Leona ranger station (1½ hours).

### Places to Stay & Eat

Apart from the airstrip and pulpería, there's no village as such, but there are small lodges nearby. Note that communication is often through Puerto Jiménez; a fax, telephone message, or email may not be picked up for several days, so be patient.

The *pulpería* has very basic singles/doubles with cold showers for US$15/25. Ask about camping here. Meals are available.

*Playa Carate Jungle Camp* (☎ 735-5211, fax 735-5049, e leegott@aol.com) Campsites with/without your own tent US$5/10 per person, rooms US$20 per person, including meals. This rustic camp is a couple of kilometers before the airstrip (coming from Puerto Jiménez). There are six large, screened, but simple cabins with shared showers and electricity 'til 9pm.

*Lookout Inn* (☎/fax 735-5431, in the USA ☎ 815-941-4803, e info@lookout-inn.com, w www.lookout-inn.com) Singles/doubles US$99/178, including meals. A little closer to the airstrip, this inn has six lovely rooms with handcarved wooden doors and private hot showers. The small lodge has an observation deck with pretty coastal and rainforest views (the beach is a short walk away), a swimming pool, and a hot tub. It also has a walk-in wine cellar and homemade tropical fruit wines, which are proudly served. Guided and on-your-own hikes are available, and kayaking, fishing, and horseback riding can be arranged.

Just beyond the airstrip and behind the pulpería, the Río Carate comes steeply out of the rainforested coastal hills.

*Luna Lodge* (☎ 380-5036 cellular, in the USA ☎ 888-409-8448, e information@lunalodge.com, w www.lunalodge.com) Tents/cabins US$75/125 per person, including meals. A steep road (4WD needed) goes about 2km up the river valley to this place, with a design that blends into the surrounding rainforest. The hillside location gives superb forest views reaching distantly to the ocean, and the high-roofed, open-sided restaurant takes full advantage of them. Each of the seven spacious and comfortable hardwood cabins has a huge private garden bath and a personal patio. Five secluded tents have two single beds each. The new Wellness Center is a 144-sq-m roofed open area designed for classes and activities including yoga, tai chi, rolfing, massage therapy, meditation, aromatherapy, guided relaxation, other holistic experiences – or just sitting and absorbing the views. Contact the lodge for class information. Meals include plenty of organically grown food from the lodge garden, which features no less than 19 different types of salad greens among a host of other tropical herbs, fruits, spices, and vegetables. Guests are welcome to wander through and chat with the resident gardener to learn about tropical organic-gardening techniques (and sample the results). Waterfall hikes are offered to guests, and other tours and activities are available at extra charge.

PENÍNSULA DE OSA

## CORCOVADO LODGE TENT CAMP

Just 500m from the southern border of Parque Nacional Corcovado, 1.7km west of Carate along the beach, is the comfortable Corcovado Lodge Tent Camp. Tents only US$30 per person, singles/doubles with 2 meals US$57/96, with 3 meals US$75/133; packages available.

Owned and operated by Costa Rica Expeditions (see Organized Tours in the Getting Around chapter), it makes an excellent base from which to explore Corcovado in reasonable comfort, or serves as a restful spot for those who have hiked through the national park. A great feature here is an exciting canopy platform that can be accessed for day and overnight trips.

A sandy beach fronts the camp. A steep trail leads to the rainforest 100m away, where a 160-hectare private preserve is available for hiking and wildlife observation. The lodge is low impact, with 20 walk-in tents, two bathhouses (with eight individual showers, toilets, and washbasins), a dining room, and a bar/lounge area. A small generator provides electricity to the dining room and bathhouses only – a flashlight is needed in the tents. Each tent is 3m square, high enough to stand up in, pitched on a platform, and contains a canopied deck and two beds with linens. All sides are screened to allow maximum ventilation. Food is served family style and is excellent and plentiful.

This is a chance to camp in the wilderness in relative comfort. 'Relative' means that you should think of the possibility of high humidity and temperatures reaching from 30°C to 40°C, as well as biting insects during the day.

A tent with no meals is available; otherwise, rates include breakfast and dinner (the meals are all-you-can-eat, so this is certainly a good budget option if you bring some lunch snacks). For a little more, you get all three meals. Coffee and purified water are available all day, and a bar serves soft drinks and alcohol. Meals cost US$13 for breakfast, US$18 for lunch, and US$21 for dinner. While reservations are encouraged, if you just show up you can eat or sleep if space is available.

Various tours and activities are offered. You can take the 3km hike through the rainforest behind the lodge – there are good views and lots of birds and monkeys – or you can hike along the beach into the park. These hikes are self-guided and free. Half-day guided hikes to more remote areas in the park cost US$25 plus US$6 park fee per person. Horses can be rented. Sunset horseback rides (3½ hours) cost US$35.

The canopy platform (moved every few years) is currently halfway up a 60m-tall guapinol tree (Hymenaea courbaril). It's within the private reserve, about a 30-minute hike up from the lodge. Access to the platform is by a rope and pulley system. Basically, you sit in a seat that's winched up to the platform by hand, a slow ride that gives you plenty of time to enjoy the changing views of the different levels of the forest. All visitors wear a hard hat and a body harness attached to a separate belay as a safety backup. The operators of both winch and belay are fully trained; safety is assured. Once you arrive, you're secured to a rope that allows free movement around the platform in safety.

Visitors normally take a half-day tour to the canopy. It lasts about four to five hours and allows at least two hours on the platform. Guides are not only trained in platform safety but are well-versed in ecology and wildlife spotting and identification. Visitors need to be patient; animals can take an hour or two to appear. The cost is US$69 per person (two people minimum, six maximum). Overnight canopy stays for US$125 per person (two maximum) offer the chance to sleep on foam pads in a tent pitched on the platform, accompanied by a guide. This is a popular option – book ahead!

Most guests arrive on a package trip that includes roundtrip flights from San José to Carate, luggage transfer by horse cart from Carate to the lodge (you hike in), meals, tours, and a local canopy guide. One of the most popular packages is for three days and two nights, with a canopy platform tour and preserve hiking. These cost US$569 per person (three people minimum) and have fixed departures several times a week. Note that the third day is a travel day, returning to San José about lunchtime. Additional nights can be added at US$67 per person, including meals. Too expensive? Take a bus to Puerto Jiménez, a shared taxi to Carate, and make reservations for the nights you want to stay.

Many other options are available from Costa Rica Expeditions in San José, which is in radio communication with the tent camp. You can also choose to be accompanied by a trained bilingual naturalist guide throughout your trip; this is considerably more expensive but worth it for an in-depth learning experience.

# Northern Golfo Dulce Area

## GOLFITO

Golfito is named after a tiny gulf that emerges into the much larger Golfo Dulce, a large Pacific Ocean gulf just west of Panama. It's the most important port in the far southern part of Costa Rica, although its maritime importance has declined greatly in recent years. From 1938 to 1985 Golfito was the center of a major banana-growing region, and for many years it was the headquarters of the United Fruit Company. However, a combination of declining foreign markets, rising Costa Rican export taxes, worker unrest, and banana diseases led to the closing of the United Fruit complex in 1985. Some of the plantations have since been turned to African palm-oil production, but this didn't alleviate the high unemployment and economic loss caused by United Fruit's departure.

In the late 1980s, a small tourism industry began in the area, and it has since blossomed. The town is pleasantly situated, and visitors often stop by for a day or two en route to somewhere else. There are good **surfing** and **swimming beaches** nearby (though none in Golfito itself – Playa Cacao, across the little gulf, is the closest). The town is surrounded by the steep hills of the Refugio Nacional de Fauna Silvestre Golfito, which create a splendid rainforest backdrop and have good birding opportunities. There are a couple of good fishing/boating marinas. Boats and light planes cross the Golfo Dulce to the Península de Osa, where Parque Nacional Corcovado is found. A growing number and good variety of hotels, as well as a number of interesting jungle lodges, have been pioneered by adventurous expats. The Golfito area has a distinct sense of community, and businesses are often referred to by their owners' names.

In an attempt to boost the region's economy, Costa Rica built a duty-free facility in the northern part of Golfito. 'Duty-free' is a misnomer, because items for sale here are still heavily taxed and do not offer significant savings for foreign tourists. Nevertheless, the taxes here are substantially lower than elsewhere in Costa Rica, which lures ticos from all over the country into visiting Golfito on shopping sprees for microwave ovens and TV sets. In order to do so, however, they must spend at least 24 hours in Golfito, which puts hotel rooms at a premium on weekends, especially near holidays.

Golfito is still, superficially, two towns strung out along a coastal road with a backdrop of steep, thickly forested hills. The southern part of town is where you find most of the bars and businesses – this sector feels pleasantly decrepit in the way tropical seaports tend to be, but without the usual hustle and danger. Warner Brothers chose this site to film *Chico Mendes,* the true story of a Brazilian rubber tapper's efforts to preserve the rainforest. One of the few remnants of the movie set is an old steam locomotive that still graces the park.

The northern part of town was the old United Fruit Company headquarters, and it retains a languid, tropical air with its large, well-ventilated homes with verandahs and attractively landscaped surroundings. Several of these houses now offer inexpensive accommodations. The airport and duty-free zone are also at this end.

The port is a well-protected one, and a few foreign yachts on oceanic or coastal cruises are usually anchored here, as well as the occasional freighter looming above the local taxi boats and fishing launches.

### Information

Land Sea Tours (☎/fax 775-1614, ℮ landsea@racsa.co.cr), on the shoreline at Km 2, is a good source of local information, as well as the place to book plane tickets and tours. They also have the best book-exchange selection in town. Katie Duncan, who keeps all these services in motion, is a knowledgeable and enthusiastic advocate of the Golfito area; if she can't connect you with what you're looking for, she'll know who can. Ask her ahead of time to set up an itinerary for you using lodging, transportation, and tours at various budgets.

# GOLFITO

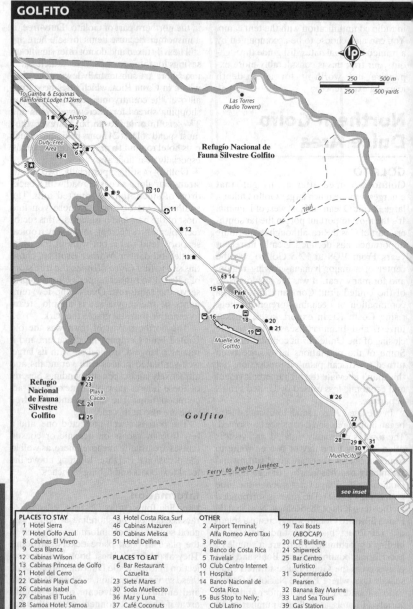

To Gamba & Esquinas
Rainforest Lodge (12km)

Las Torres
(Radio Towers)

Duty-Free
Area

Airstrip

Refugío Nacional de
Fauna Silvestre Golfito

Trail

Park

Muelle de
Golfito

Refugío
Nacional
de Fauna
Silvestre
Golfito

Playa
Cacao

*Golfito*

see inset

*Ferry to Puerto Jiménez*

Muellecito

0   250   500 m
0   250   500 yards

**PLACES TO STAY**
1   Hotel Sierra
7   Hotel Golfo Azul
8   Cabinas El Vivero
9   Casa Blanca
12  Cabinas Wilson
13  Cabinas Princesa de Golfo
21  Hotel del Cerro
22  Cabinas Playa Cacao
26  Cabinas Isabel
27  Cabinas El Tucán
28  Samoa Hotel; Samoa
    Restaurant
29  Hotel/Restaurant Uno
34  Las Gaviotas Hotel
35  Hotel El Gran Ceibo
38  Hotel Golfito

43  Hotel Costa Rica Surf
46  Cabinas Mazuren
50  Cabinas Melissa
51  Hotel Delfina

**PLACES TO EAT**
6   Bar Restaurant
    Cazuelita
23  Siete Mares
30  Soda Muellecito
36  Mar y Luna
37  Café Coconuts
40  Restaurant Hong Kong
41  Musmanni Bakery;
    Latitud 8 Bar
42  La Cubana
47  La Eurekita

**OTHER**
2   Airport Terminal;
    Alfa Romeo Aero Taxi
3   Police
4   Banco de Costa Rica
5   Travelair
10  Club Centro Internet
11  Hospital
14  Banco Nacional de
    Costa Rica
15  Bus Stop to Neily;
    Club Latino
16  Boats to Playa Cacao
17  CONSUCOOP
    Supermarket
18  TRACOPA Bus
    Terminal

19  Taxi Boats
    (ABOCAP)
20  ICE Building
24  Shipwreck
25  Bar Centro
    Turistico
31  Supermercado
    Pearsen
32  Banana Bay Marina
33  Land Sea Tours
39  Gas Station
44  Doctor's Office
45  Post Office
48  Church
49  Railway
    Locomotive

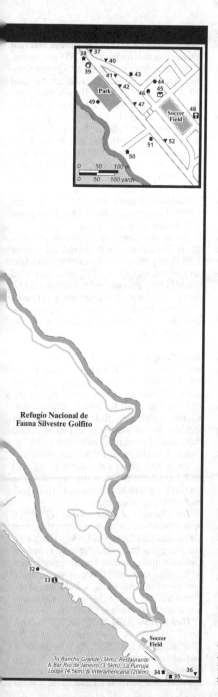

Refugio Nacional de
Fauna Silvestre Golfito

To Rancho Grande (3km), Restaurante
& Bar Rio de Janeiro (3.5km), La Purruja
Lodge (4.5km) & Interamericana (20km)

Arriving sailors will find the port captain (☎/fax 775-0487) and immigration authorities (☎ 775-0423) opposite the Muelle de Golfito, also known as the Muelle Bananero (Banana Company Dock). Hours are 7:30am to 11am and 12:30pm to 4pm weekdays.

Many places around Golfito communicate with one another by VHF radio. If you need to reach someone by VHF from Golfito, ask at Land Sea Tours, Las Gaviotas Hotel, or one of the marinas to borrow their VHF. Alternatively, call Doña Isabel, the Travelair agent in Puerto Jiménez (☎ 735-5062, fax 735-5043), who can put you in radio contact with anywhere in the area. (You should remember that she doesn't work on Sunday.)

Another good source of information is Dave Corella at Café Coconuts, where there's a public bulletin board. Odette López, at the Travelair office, is also helpful. There are plenty of other local 'experts.'

Internet access is available at Club Centro Internet from 1pm to 8pm Tuesday to Sunday for about US$3 an hour. Café Coconuts also has Internet access.

A couple of banks (see map) will change US dollars and traveler's checks. The gas station (locally called La Bomba) changes US dollars as well. Mail from abroad can take weeks to reach Golfito, but the post office does have a public fax facility. Laundry service is available next to the Hotel Delfina in the southern part of town. Emergency medical attention can be obtained at the Hospital de Golfito (☎ 775-0011). A recommended local physician is Dr Guillermo Torres Álvarez (see 'doctor's office' on the Golfito map), open 9am to noon and 5pm to 8pm Monday to Friday.

## Sportfishing & Boating
Sportfishing is a highlight of the Golfo Dulce area, with popular operators leaving both from here and from the more southern Playa Zancudo (see Playa Zancudo under Southern Golfo Dulce Area, later in this chapter). You can fish year-round, but the best season for the sought-after Pacific sailfish in the Golfito area is November to May.

**Banana Bay Marina** (☎ 775-0838, e bb marina@hotmail.com, w www.bananabay marina.com), run by Bruce Blevins, has a floating dock marina with a full range of services accommodating up to 155 foreign

PENÍNSULA DE OSA

yachts. Charters can be arranged; a full day of fishing on 6m to 17m boats, all-inclusive, costs US$500 to US$1200.

**Land Sea Tours** (see the Information section, earlier) has a boat dock for foreign sailors; they provide 'boat-sitting' for sailors wanting to visit inland Costa Rica. They also arrange fishing charters and **sea kayak** rentals; several of the lodges around the bay also offer kayaks.

## Places to Stay

**Budget** One of the cheapest places in the country is **Hotel/Restaurant Uno** (☎ 775-0061) Rooms US$1.50 per person. Rooms are basic boxes without fans. Most rooms lack a window, but if all you need is a bed….

**Cabinas Mazuren** (☎ 775-0058) Rooms US$6 per person. This better budget choice is small but welcoming. It's a house with a hodgepodge of seven clean rooms, all different and with private bath and fans.

**Hotel Delfina** (☎ 775-0043) Rooms US$3 per person, rooms with bath US$6 per person. This place has 17 rooms (many don't have windows) that have table fans and share five bathrooms. Also available are seven better rooms with private baths and fans.

**Cabinas Isabel** (☎ 775-1774) Rooms US$6 per person. The decent rooms here are in an attractive old house; the staff says they can make tour arrangements.

**Cabinas Melissa** (☎ 775-0443) Rooms US$6 per person. Behind the Delfina, Cabinas Melissa overlooks the water and offers four clean, quiet rooms with bath.

**Hotel Golfito** (☎ 775-0047) Rooms US$9-12. Another reasonable choice on the waterfront, the Golfito rents eight rooms with private baths and fans, and six rooms with air-conditioning.

**Cabinas El Tucán** (☎ 775-0553) Rooms US$6-15 per person. This is two hotels side by side, both with private cold showers. El Tucán 1 is older, with smaller rooms with fans and some with TV. The new El Tucán 2 boasts cable TV and air-conditioning, and some rooms sleep six or even 10 people – a bargain for group discounts. There's parking.

**Hotel Costa Rica Surf** (☎/fax 775-0034) Most rooms US$9 per person. This dark, rambling old hotel has 27 rooms, many of which either lack windows or have only a sky-light. There are private cold bathrooms and

fans. Three rooms have air-conditioning and hot showers for US$15 per person, and four tiny singles share a bath for US$6 per person.

In the quieter north end are several families that take guests in their homes. **Cabinas El Vivero** (☎ 775-0217) Rooms US$6 per person. This is run by the friendly and interesting Beatham family, who also grow and sell ornamental plants; hence the name. Rooms are airy with fans and shared baths.

**Casa Blanca** (☎ 775-0124) Rooms US$9. Across the street from Cabinas El Vivero, this family-run place has rooms with fans and private baths.

**Cabinas Wilson** (☎ 775-0795) Rooms US$9. To the south, the rooms here come with fans and private baths.

**Hotel del Cerro** (☎ 775-0006, fax 775-0551) Dormitories with shared bath about US$6 per person, singles/doubles with fans and private baths US$12/15, air-conditioned doubles with phones and hot water US$24. South of the park, this place has great views of the bay. It offers a variety of clean rooms, and there are plenty of bathrooms for the shared-bath rooms.

**Mid-Range** The local Golfito bus terminates outside of **Hotel El Gran Ceibo** (☎ 775-0403, W www.soldeosa.com/gran ceibo) Rooms & cabins US$25-35. At the entrance to Golfito about 3km or 4km southeast of town, this hotel has 15 decent modern rooms with fans and private cold bath, and 12 air-conditioned cabins with hot water. All have cable TV and can sleep four or six people. There's also a swimming pool and a restaurant-bar on the premises. The owner, Capt Ray Smith, arranges river, gulf, and offshore fishing trips.

**La Purruja Lodge** (☎/fax 775-1054, e info@purruja.com, W www.purruja.com) Campsites US$2, doubles US$20. This Swiss-run place is southeast of the town center on Golfito's main road. It has five nice cabins with ceiling fans and private showers. Meals, transportation into Golfito, and tours of the Península de Osa (including a unique one down the Río Claro) are available.

**Hotel Golfo Azul** (☎ 775-0871, 775-0004, fax 775-1849, e golfazul@racsa.co.cr) Doubles/quads US$25/35. Right in the north end of town, this clean hotel has 20 large rooms with air-conditioning and private cold showers. A few rooms have cable TV for

US$2 more. A restaurant serves breakfast on request, and a parking area is available.

**Hotel Sierra** (☎ 775-0666, 775-0336, fax 775-0506, ✉ hotelsierra@racsa.co.cr) Singles/doubles US$48/52. In the far north of town, convenient to the airport (which results in high room rates), this modern hotel features a restaurant, two pools, and 72 air-conditioned rooms with hot showers and cable TV.

**Las Gaviotas Hotel** (☎ 775-0062, fax 775-0544, ✉ gaviotas@racsa.co.cr) Doubles: standard US$42, deluxe US$54, bungalows US$84. Almost opposite the Hotel El Gran Ceibo, right on the coast, this place is well known and recommended. It's set in a tropical garden and has an excellent restaurant-bar (meals US$5 to US$10, plus cheaper snacks), two pools, and a boat dock from which you can watch the *gaviotas* (gulls). The 21 spacious air-conditioned rooms come with ceiling fans, cable TV, small patios, and hot water in clean, white-tiled bathrooms. Seven of these rooms are larger and feature a minifridge. Three bungalows have two bedrooms, two bathrooms, and a kitchenette overlooking the ocean.

**Samoa Hotel** (☎ 775-0233, 775-0264, fax 775-0573, ✉ samoasur@racsa.co.cr) RV sites US$8 per vehicle, rooms US$50. This large, pyramid-roofed building is north of the center – you can't miss it. It has both hotel and restaurant facilities, and there are plans to add 40 more rooms and a marina for 2003/4. Currently, there are 14 clean, spacious air-conditioned rooms, each with two queen-size beds, a fan, TV, telephone, and hot water; each room sleeps up to four people. The hotel's RV campground is a popular stop for RV vehicles from North America. The charge per vehicle includes use of showers and the restaurant. There's 24-hour guarded parking. The staff will arrange any local tour you want. Apart from their restaurant, they have a bar with a pool table, darts, and foosball that are in much better condition than most games in Costa Rica. They have a darts club on Monday and Wednesday night, when you can try beating some of the local champions. They're very good! There's also a book exchange, gift shop, and a shell museum (open to the public).

## Places to Eat
Budget travelers will find several restaurants where the meals start at US$2 to US$3.

**Hotel/Restaurant Uno** This place has been around for decades and serves decent Chinese food.

**Café Coconuts** (☎ 775-0518) Open 6:30am-8pm in high season. This café is owned by the friendly Dave Corella and provides Internet access. It's very popular with local gringos and ticos and is a good place for swapping information and meeting people, especially in the morning. A good *casado* costs US$4, and the fruit drinks are large and fresh.

**Soda Muellecito** This place, by the Muellecito (Little Dock), is popular for early breakfasts.

**La Eurekita** (☎ 775-1616) Good fruit juices, as well as slightly pricey but good tico dishes, are sold at this breezy open-air restaurant.

**La Cubana** Casados US$3. This place is almost next door to La Eurekita and is the latest and most long-lasting incarnation of a restaurant that has gone through several name changes.

**Restaurant Hong Kong** Dishes US$3-8. Decent Chinese and tico food is served here in the center of town.

**Samoa Restaurant** Sandwiches US$2.50, meals US$5-12. Open 24 hrs. Heading north, you'll pass this eatery in the Samoa Hotel (see Places to Stay). Meals include fish dishes (US$5), steaks (US$8), and large pizzas (US$12). There's good food and good ambience here.

**Bar Restaurant Cazuelita** (☎ 775-0921) Dishes US$3-6. In the northern zone, this place has decent Chinese meals.

Also in the northern zone are a number of cheap sodas near the duty-free area, across from the school, and near the TRACOPA bus office.

**Las Gaviotas Hotel** Open 6am-10pm. The restaurant here serves a variety of pricier food – it's locally popular.

**Mar y Luna** (☎ 775-0192) Dishes US$3-6. This waterfront restaurant serves mainly seafood and is recommended for excellent food and amiable service.

**Rancho Grande** Dishes US$5-12. Open 7am-10pm. Almost 3km farther out of town, this rustic, thatched-roof place serves country-style tico food cooked over a wood stove. Margarita, the tica owner, is one of Golfito's established characters. It's worth the trip out here.

PENÍNSULA DE OSA

*Restaurante & Bar Río de Janeiro* (☎ 775-0509) Dishes US$2-12. Almost a kilometer farther out of town, this nice roadside bar has a dart board. Its small but changing menu ranges from cheap cheeseburgers to US$12 steaks. You have to ask them what they have – there's no written menu.

*Reserva Titi* (☎ 775-0165) Singles/doubles US$25/35. Also called the 'Monkey Reserve,' this place is in La Mora, 8km southeast of Golfito. There's lots of wildlife here. There are two, two-story cabins with fans, kitchenettes, and insect screens.

## Entertainment

In an old port town like Golfito, beer, conversation, and darts have a flavor hard to find anywhere else. Try any of the popular bar-restaurants mentioned above.

*Latitud 8 Bar* In the center of town, this place is popular with ex-pats, especially North Americans, and has US sports TV.

*Club Latino* At the north end of town, this place has dancing, especially on weekends, and is popular with ticos.

## Shopping

Assuming you're not in town to load up on booze or microwaves at the duty-free area, you can find a small but high-quality selection of crafts at *Land Sea Tours* and quite a good gift shop at the *Samoa Hotel*.

## Getting There & Away

**Air** SANSA (☎ 775-0303) and Travelair (☎/fax 775-0210) fly out of San José every day. Some flights stop at Palmar Sur or Puerto Jiménez, or elsewhere, on demand. Odette López, the Travelair agent, is very helpful and knowledgeable. Alfa Romeo Aero Taxi (☎ 775-1515) has light aircraft (three and five passengers) for charter flights to Puerto Jiménez, Parque Nacional Corcovado, and other areas. Land Sea Tours is helpful with charters.

The airport is almost 4km north of the town center.

**Bus** TRACOPA has buses at 7am and 3pm daily from San José to Golfito (eight hours). The buses leave from Calle 14, Avenidas 3 & 5. Return buses from Golfito (☎ 775-0365) leave at 5am (express) and 1:30pm daily. Fares are US$7 to San José and US$5 to San Isidro. TRACOPA's office hours in

Golfito are 7:30am to 11:30am and 2pm to 4:30pm Monday to Saturday, 7:30am to 11:30am on Sunday and holidays.

Buses for Neily leave every hour from the bus stop outside the Club Latino, near the park at the north end of town; as they pass through town, they'll pick up additional passengers for the one-hour trip. Buses for the surfing area of Pavones and for the beach at Playa Zancudo leave from the Muellecito. Departures depend on the weather, the condition of the road, and the condition of the bus – ask locally. Services may be interrupted during the rainy season – it's a poor road. During the dry season, the bus leaves at 10am and 3pm for Pavones (three hours) and at 2pm for Zancudo (three hours), with a transfer at the Río Coto Colorado. The bus might not run after heavy rains.

**Boat** There are two main boat docks for passenger services (apart from the various marinas). The Muellecito is the main dock in the southern part of town, and boat drivers here will bargain. An association of taxi boats operates from another dock opposite the ICE building near the north end of Golfito; the taxis here have set prices but can be more expensive than from the Muellecito.

The daily passenger ferry (☎ 735-5017) to Puerto Jiménez leaves at 11:30am from the Muellecito (US$3, 1½ hours). One report claims that there are not enough life jackets aboard for all the passengers. A passenger boat from the Muellecito to Playa Zancudo leaves at around 4:30am and noon on some days and costs about US$2 per person; it returns at 6am and 1pm. The boat is captained by Miguel 'Macarela' Esquivel (☎ 775-1116). Arena Alta Sportfishing (☎ 766-0115, e arenaalta@aol.com) has boats from Zancudo to Hotel Samoa most days (see the Playa Zancudo section, below) and is competing with Macarela; it's unclear who leaves on which days, so ask. Local boat operators may profess ignorance of these services, because they would prefer to take you yourselves!

The Asociación de Boteros (ABOCAP; ☎ 775-0357) has boat taxis, from the dock opposite the ICE building, for eight or more passengers. They have services to Playa Zancudo at various prices, depending on the size and speed of the boat and whom you talk to (average cost is about US$25 per boat). Other destinations (Pavones, Puerto Jiménez, Punta Encanto, Rainbow Adventures, Casa de Orquídeas, and others) can also be reached but cost more; these journeys are more exposed to weather, and conditions may affect prices. Most of the lodges can pick you up.

Boats to nearby Playa Cacao are slightly cheaper from a point on the other side of the Muelle de Golfito, because it's the closest point to that beach (described below), but the ride from the Muellecito is a cheap way to get a look across the bay. The fare is US$3 minimum or US$1 per person.

### Getting Around
City buses go up and down the main road of Golfito for about US20¢ per ride.

Colectivo taxis go up and down the main road from the airport down to Las Gaviotas Hotel. Just flag one down if it has a seat. The set fare is US75¢, with group discounts.

A private taxi from downtown to the airport costs about US$2.

### PLAYA CACAO
This beach is opposite Golfito, and the view of the bay, port, and surrounding rainforest is worth the short boat ride out here. As for swimming, although it's cleaner than the polluted waters just off the town, the water isn't pristine. This is not the Golfo Dulce proper, and though efforts have been made to clean up trash, you're still near a dock visited by freighters.

### Places to Stay & Eat
*Cabinas Playa Cacao* (e *isabel@racsa .co.cr*) Doubles US$30. This place has six spacious cabins with high thatched roofs and tiled floors. Each cabin has a private bath, fan, microwave, and fridge; some have kitchenettes. It's next to the beach, and with Golfito across the water, this is a tranquil spot from which to enjoy the old port. It was temporarily closed in 2002.

There are reportedly places to *camp*, some *beach houses* for rent, and a couple of basic *cabinas*.

*Bar Centro Turístico* (☎ 391-8236; ask, in Spanish, for Juan) Doubles US$10.50. There are just a few rooms here, but more are planned. At any rate, you can certainly down a couple of beers in the shoreside bar. The pulpería is a good source of information.

*Siete Mares* Dishes US$4-8. Open 7am-9pm. This place is good for inexpensive breakfasts, lunches, and dinners. It specializes in local dishes and seafood.

### Getting There & Away
The five-minute boat ride from Golfito costs US$1 per person for a group of three or more people (or US$3 total for one or two people). You can also get there by walking or driving along a dirt road west and then south from the airport – about 6km total from the airport. (This road is drivable most of the time.)

## REFUGIO NACIONAL DE FAUNA SILVESTRE GOLFITO
This small (2810-hectare) refuge was originally created to protect the Golfito watershed. It encompasses most of the steep hills surrounding the town, and while the refuge has succeeded in keeping Golfito's water clean and flowing, it has also had the side effect of conserving a number of rare and interesting plant species. These include a species of *Caryodaphnopsis*, which is an Asian genus otherwise unknown in Central America, and *Zamia*, which are cycads. Cycads are called 'living fossils' and are among the most primitive of plants. They were abundant before the time of the dinosaurs, but relatively few species are now extant. *Zamia* are known for the huge, cone-like inflorescences that emerge from the center of the plant, which looks rather like a dwarf palm.

Other species of interest include many heliconias, orchids, tree ferns, and tropical trees including copal, the kapok tree, the butternut tree, and the cow tree.

The vegetation attracts a variety of birds such as parrots, toucans, tanagers, trogons, and hummingbirds. Although the scarlet macaw has been recorded here, poaching in this area has made it rare. Peccaries, pacas, raccoons, coatis, and monkeys are among the mammals that have been sighted here.

### Information
The refuge administration is in the Oficina de Area de Conservación Osa in Puerto Jiménez (see that section, earlier). Camping is permitted in the refuge, but there are no facilities – most people stay in Golfito.

Rainfall is very high: October, the wettest month, receives over 700mm. January to mid-April is normally a dry time.

## Getting There & Away

About 2km south of the center of Golfito, before you come to Las Gaviotas Hotel, a gravel road heads inland, past a soccer field, and winds its way up to some radio towers (Las Torres), 7km away and 486m above sea level. This is a good access road to the refuge (most of the road actually goes through the middle of the preserve). You could take a taxi up first thing in the morning and hike down, birding as you go. A few trails lead from the road down to the town, but there's so little traffic on the road itself that you'll probably see more from the cleared road than from the overgrown trails.

Another way is to take the poor dirt road to Gamba and the Esquinas Rainforest Lodge (see the Southern Costa Rica chapter). This road leaves from a couple of kilometers northwest of the duty-free area and crosses through part of the refuge. You'll probably need 4WD. A local bus goes to the beginning of this dirt road – ask for the bus that goes to the road for Gamba or Esquinas. From where the bus leaves you, it's about 10km to Gamba, so you could walk and bird-watch.

Finally, a very steep hiking trail leaves from almost opposite the Samoa Hotel. A somewhat strenuous hike (allow about two hours) will bring you out on the road to the radio towers, mentioned previously. The trail is in fairly good shape, but easier to find in Golfito than at the top. Once you reach the radio tower road, return the way you came or, for a less knee-straining descent, head down along the road.

## NORTH ALONG THE GOLFO DULCE

Boat taxis can take you out of Golfito and up along the northeast coast of the Golfo Dulce, past remote beaches and headlands interspersed with several jungle lodges. The backdrop to the coastline is mainly virgin rainforest protected by the new Parque Nacional Piedras Blancas. It can be visited from the coastal lodges, although this park has no facilities and only limited trails.

Note that some of the following places are difficult to contact directly; you may have to call a local agent and ask for a radio link, or leave a message.

## Playa San Josecito

A few kilometers north of Punta Encanto, secluded Playa San Josecito has a couple of places to stay.

*Golfo Dulce Lodge* (☎ 383-4839 cellular, fax 775-0573, @ info@golfodulcelodge.com, 🅦 www.golfodulcelodge.com) Singles/doubles US$115/190, or US$130/210 including meals. This Swiss-owned place is set back 250m from the rocky beach on the edge of a 275-hectare property, much of which is rainforest. The owners are informative about local flora and fauna and support a nearby wildcat rehabilitation project. They have five individual wooden cabins, each with a large verandah, and three cheaper adjoining rooms with smaller verandahs. All have private bathrooms with sun-warmed showers. There's a small, chlorine-free pool. A minimum two-night stay is required, and various packages and excursions are available. Add US$20 per person for roundtrip boat transfers from either Golfito or Puerto Jiménez.

*Dolphin Quest* (☎ 775-1742, fax 775-0373, @ dolphinquest@email.com, 🅦 www.dolphinquestcostarica.com) Singles/doubles including meals: campsites US$35/60 (plus US$7 tent rental), bunkhouse $50/70, cabins US$50/90, house US$60/100. Here's a jungle lodge with a relaxed family atmosphere. It offers access to an interesting community and as much privacy as a mile of beach and 700 acres of mountainous rainforest can offer. Owner Ray first bought property on the beach over 15 years ago and has been slowly developing since then; both of his sons were born here. Three round, thatched-roof cabins sleeping two and a larger house sleeping up to seven are spread out around 2 hectares of landscaped grounds. Bunkhouse accommodations and camping are also options. Meals are served communally in an open-air pavilion near the shore, and the food is good; many ingredients are grown organically on the property. Various activities are available, including horseback rides (US$12.50 per hour), kayaking (free for experienced kayakers), motorboat excursions (US$25 per hour for a group), a butterfly garden (US$5), snorkeling, scuba diving, dolphin tours, and plenty of hiking. Access to the trails is free after an introductory tour outlining the beauties and dangers of the forest, which costs US$10. A red macaw release program run by Zoo Ave (see the Central Valley & Surrounding Highlands chapter) is hosted here, and Casa de Orquídeas (see below) is a short walk down the beach.

Other options include massage, a work-exchange program for skilled people who want to stay awhile (accommodations in the bunkhouse), a small library, and local pickup soccer games.

## Casa de Orquídeas

This private botanical garden is a veritable Eden *(Radio Channel 68; tours at 8:30am Sat-Thur; admission & tour US$5)*. Surrounded by primary rainforest, the garden has been lovingly collected and tended by Ron and Trudy MacAllister, who have homesteaded in this remote region since the 1970s. They first planted fruit trees simply to survive and soon became interested in plants. Self-taught botanists, they've amassed a wonderful collection of tropical fruit trees, bromeliads, cycads, palms, heliconias, ornamental plants, and over 100 varieties of orchids, after which their garden is named.

The gardens are open for guided tours at 8:30am as the early hours avoid the wilting heat of the midday sun. Guided tours last about two hours and are fascinating and fun – touching, smelling, feeling, and tasting is encouraged. One seasonal highlight is chewing on the pulp surrounding a 'magic seed' whose effect is to make lemons taste sweet instead of sour; another is the smell of vanilla. You might also see bats hanging out in a 'tent' made from a huge leaf, insects trapped in bromeliad pools, or torch ginger in glorious flower – available treats vary according to season.

Casa de Orquídeas is at the west end of Playa San Josecito and can be reached from the lodges on that beach by foot. Otherwise, it's accessible only by boat. Transport and tours can be arranged with all the area's lodges, or through Zancudo Boat Tours (☎/fax 776-0012) or Land Sea Tours (☎/fax 775-1614, e landsea@racsa.co.cr).

## Rainbow Adventures

This private 400-hectare preserve is bordered by Parque Nacional Piedras Blancas, at the far northeast corner of Golfo Dulce. It's reached by a scenic 45-minute boat ride from Golfito to Playa Cativo. One of the attractions of the trip is 'shooting the rock,' where the boat hurtles through a narrow gap between a rocky islet and the coast. At the preserve, you can walk, swim, or snorkel along the 1.5km-long Playa Cativo or wander into the nearby forest. Howler monkeys and olingos (see the Raccoon Family in the Wildlife Guide in this book) can be seen just a few meters away from the lodge.

*Rainbow Adventures Lodge (no lodge phone; in the USA ☎ 800-565-0722, 503-690-7750, fax 503-690-7735, e info@rainbowcostarica.com, w www.rainbowcostarica.com)* Singles/doubles US$235/335, penthouse US$250/355, cabins US$275/375, additional adults/children 4-10 yrs US$75/60. The all-wood, wide-balconied, rustic appearance of the lodge belies the elegance within – handmade furniture, silk rugs, turn-of-the-20th-century antiques, and fresh flowers make this a special place in the wilderness. The first level is the dining room, lounge, library, and relaxation area, and the remaining two levels hold guestrooms. The private rooms are partially exposed to the outside to allow unimpeded views of the rainforest, the beach, and the gulf. Each bed is equipped with a fine-mesh mosquito net that can be raised or lowered as desired. It's almost like camping in the jungle, but with all comforts, including a private hot shower, comfortable beds, and balconies. A hydroelectric system on the property provides power, there are electric hair dryers in the bathrooms, and there's a laundry.

There are also two attractive, spacious wooden cabins, each with one large bedroom and one small bedroom, a private bathroom, and a spacious verandah. The cabins' large bedrooms can be partitioned off into two minibedrooms suitable for parents with children, though they'd be tight for adult couples. Outside is a chemical-free swimming pool filled with spring water.

All prices include meals (buffet-style – local fish, vegetarian, dairy-free, etc, options are available on request), beer and wine with meals, nonalcoholic drinks, snacks, transportation from and to the Golfito airport, a short tour of the nearby jungle, and use of snorkeling gear and jungle boots (although it's always wise to bring your own to ensure the best fit).

Boats are available for US$45 per hour per boat (up to four passengers) for fishing or tours. Kayak rental costs US$10 for three hours. Guided jungle tours cost US$6 per hour per person.

The owner has a collection of 8000 natural history publications (in English), which, he says, is the largest private natural history library in Latin America. It's air-conditioned, and guests are welcome to relax and read.

### Cabinas Caña Blanca

Cabinas Caña Blanca (☎ 383-5707 voicemail, fax 735-5043, ⓔ canablan@racsa.co.cr, ⓦ www.soldeosa.com/canablanca) Cabins from US$125 per person. A couple of kilometers north of Playa Cativo and Rainbow Adventures is a small beach with three well-designed, breezy, comfortable hardwood cabins. Each cabin has a spacious verandah and private hot outdoor showers with forest views. Guests have access to 10km of rainforest trails that have excellent birding and a waterfall. Rates are based on double occupancy and a three-night minimum. Included are transport from the Golfito or Puerto Jiménez airports, three daily gourmet meals, hors d'oeuvres and rum cocktails, wine with dinner, and use of kayaks and snorkels. Other tours can be arranged on request.

# Southern Golfo Dulce Area

## PLAYA ZANCUDO

This beach, on the south side of the mouth of the Río Coto Colorado, about 15km south of Golfito, is a popular destination for locals, who claim that the 6km-long, dark-sand beach has the best swimming in the area. The surf is gentle, and at night the quiet water sometimes sparkles with bioluminescence, tiny phosphorescent marine plants and plankton that light up if you sweep a hand through the water – the effect is like underwater fireflies, which is especially fabulous on a starry night. At the far south end, the waves get big enough for surfing; views all along the beach and out across the bay are beautiful. The beach gets

mildly busy during the dry season when there may be weekend dances, but it's quiet at other times. Many visitors end up hanging out here for a week or more.

There are mangroves in the area around the river mouth that offer wildlife-watching possibilities, even on the boat-taxi ride from Golfito. Look for crocodiles, monkeys, and birds.

### Information

Several hotels offer Internet access for their guests. Coloso del Mar and Arena Alta Sportfishing have public Internet access for US$1 for 12 minutes. The largest store is the Super Bellavista, opposite Cabinas Tío Froylan. There's a public phone here.

### Activities

The best **sportfishing** is from December to May for sailfish, though you can catch something almost any month. Sportfishing can be arranged at **Roy's Zancudo Lodge** (see Places to Stay & Eat, below). Captain Bob Baker's **Golfito Sportfishing** (☎ 776-0007, ⓔ info@costaricafishing.com, ⓦ www.costaricafishing.com) is based in Playa Zancudo; he offers offshore fishing packages for three to seven days for US$2165 to US$4235 for one person, US$3530 to US$7050 for two people, including flights from San José, overnights in Playa Zancudo cabins with hot water, English-speaking skippers and everything else. Dar Randall's **Arena Alta Sportfishing** (☎ 766-0115, ⓔ arenaalta@aol.com) is another option that also arranges boating excursions and has four comfortable new cabins for rent. Their rates for three to seven days of fishing, all-inclusive, are US$3290 to US$6480 for one person, and US$3500 to US$7950 for two people.

**Zancudo Boat Tours** (☎/fax 776-0012, ⓔ loscocos@loscocos.com) Run by knowledgeable Susan and Andrew of Cabinas Los Cocos, they have three- to four-hour boat tours for about US$40 per person (two people minimum). One goes up the river estuary and mangroves behind Zancudo for wildlife watching and some local history. Another goes to Casa de Orquídeas. They have kayaks for rent. A popular kayaking tour is to go by boat up the river and then float back – about four hours.

**Horseback riding** is available, with the best horses at Zancudo Beach Club (see below).

**Surfing lessons** are available from Billy (☎ 776-0014) or just ask at any hotel. Billy charges US$20 per hour for private lessons and rents boards for US$15 a day.

## Places to Stay & Eat

Cabins, restaurants, and other businesses are strung out along 5km of beach. There are few single rooms, and on a busy weekend single travelers may get stuck paying the double rate. At quieter times you should bargain for a single rate. Most hotels have a restaurant attached.

*Bar/Cabinas Suzy* (☎ 776-0107) Rooms with shared bath US$6 per person. This is one of the cheapest places. There are seven rooms sleeping two to five people. The locally popular bar has a pool table.

*Restaurant & Cabinas Tranquilo* ('Maria's Place'; ☎ 776-0131) This similarly priced place is popular with European budget travelers. One traveler reports that Maria, at the simple and inexpensive restaurant, is the best cook in town.

*Cabinas Tío Froylan* (☎ 776-0101/2/3) Rooms US$7.50 per person. This place is friendly and popular with vacationing tico groups and families. There are 20 basic concrete rooms with up to four or five beds, cold shower, and fan. They're improved by a shady patio, a garden, beach access, and an attached restaurant with a pool table.

*Rancho Coquito* (☎ 776-0128, 776-0136) Rooms with bath US$6. This place is a concrete block row of 16 rather stuffy rooms painted an unappetizing institutional green. The windowless rooms are alleviated somewhat by ceiling fans and a private cold shower. A soda serves good inexpensive meals.

*Cabinas La Palmera de Oro* (☎ 776-0121, fax 776-0134) Doubles US$48, US$10 additional people up to 6. A couple minutes' walk south of the dock, on the inland side of the road, this place has eight simple, tiled, modern cabins, each with air-conditioning, a minifridge, TV, and telephone. There's a small pool, bar, and restaurant. These cabinas are OK but overpriced.

*Cabinas Los Cocos* (☎/fax 776-0012, e loscocos@loscocos.com, w www.loscocos .com) Cabins US$58-64, houses US$200/450 per week/month. This beachfront place is about a kilometer south of the public dock and is also the home of the boat-taxi/tour

service Zancudo Boat Tours, owned by Susan and Andrew. Both are artists, and Andrew's sculptures, some of which showcase his wry sense of humor, decorate the grounds. Two cabins used to be banana company homes in Palmar and were transported in pieces to Zancudo, reassembled and completely refurbished. These sleep three. Two larger thatched-roof cabins sleeping four are a little more expensive. All are attractively designed, have private baths, kitchenettes, hot water, fridges, fans, body boards, porches with hammocks, and a faithful clientele that rents them out by the week for a 10% discount. Each cabin is quite private, with beach access and an outdoor shower to wash off the sand. There are also two large rustic houses that rent by the week or month.

*Cabinas Sol y Mar* (☎ 776-0014, fax 776-0015, e solymar@zancudo.com, w www .zancudo.com) Campsites US$2 per person (six maximum), singles US$34-38, doubles US$39-43. Just south of Los Cocos, this is a popular place, and owners Rick and Lori are a good source of local information. They have four nice cabins with stone-pebbled private baths, hot water, and fans. Next door is their recommended *restaurant*, which serves good food for reasonable prices in a relaxed atmosphere. Prices are about US$3 for breakfast or lunch and average US$6 for dinner. They also have a nice bar. Horseshoes and volleyball attract locals and guests on weekends. Fishing and other excursions can be arranged. They have a rental house for US$700 a month – book well in advance.

*Coloso del Mar* (☎/fax 776-0050, e info@ coloso-del-mar.com, w www.coloso-del -mar.com) Doubles US$40. South of Sol y Mar, this place has four airy, clean wooden cabins with hot showers close to the beach. There's a recommended restaurant (though it's not always open) and public Internet access. The owners speak Dutch, English, and German.

*Latitud 8* (☎ 776-0168, e ty@8-above -the-equator.com, w www.latitude8lodge .com) Doubles US$50, US$10 extra for aircon. Two spacious, well-furnished cabins are available, both with kitchenette, fridge, huge showers, and barbecue pits outside. Next door, *Cindy's Cabin* (☎ 776-0151, e cyndy kasket@yahoo.com) is US$45 a night and has a full kitchen.

***Zancudo Beach Club*** (☎ *776-0087, fax 776-0052,* ℮ *zbc@costarica.net,* Ⓦ *www .zancudobeachclub.com)* Doubles US$58, villas US$76. About another kilometer south (and near the entrance of the beach if you're driving in), this place is run by Gary and Debbie, former New Englanders realizing their dream of beach life. It has four attractive, spacious wooden cabinas, each with cool tiled floors, big showers, a fridge, coffeemaker, ceiling fans, and a patio. The surf is bigger at this end of the beach, so ask about currents before going swimming. The international restaurant with a view is excellent; so are the mixed drinks. Lunches average US$6, dinners are in the US$10 to US$15 range and nightly specials vary from Tex-Mex to Asian. Saturday and Sunday pizza nights draw the local crowds. They have a dozen horses in a farm at La Virgen, 7km away, and arrange 6am rides over the hills, down to the beach and back to the hotel for a full breakfast at 10am (US$50 per person).

***Roy's Zancudo Lodge*** (☎ *776-0008, fax 776-0011,* ℮ *rroig@golfito.net,* Ⓦ *www.roys zancudolodge.com)* Rooms US$110 per person including meals, no fishing; all-inclusive 3- to 6-day fishing packages US$2525-4265 for 1 person, US$4300-6500 for 2 people. This is one of the oldest places to stay at Zancudo; its faithful clientele consists especially of anglers. The lodge has over 50 world records for fishing. Rooms are air-conditioned, with private hot baths, fans, and telephones; some also have kitchenettes. There's a pool, hot tub, pool table, bar, and restaurant, and reputable owner Roy Ventura has a fleet of 10, 7.5m center-console fishing boats with 200hp motors. The lodge is closed mid-September to mid-November for maintenance.

***Macondo*** (☎ *776-0157)* Dishes US$5-9. The pleasant balcony of this Italian restaurant, which serves espressos and cappuccinos, overlooks a garden. They recently added a pool and six cabins with fans and private hot showers for US$18/24 singles/doubles.

***Iguana Verde*** (☎ *390-4824 cellular)* Dishes average US$6.50. With an Italian chef, this is another excellent Italian restaurant. They recently opened three cabins for US$30/doubles.

***La Puerta Negra*** Dishes average US$7. Dinner only, closed Mon. And again – an Italian chef and excellent food. They have

an outdoor dining patio and serve imported Italian wine.

***Soda Katherine*** Dishes US$2-4. This small, typical, open-air soda has just five tables, but they're often full of locals and savvy visitors enjoying fruit juices, *gallo pintos,* and casados.

## Getting There & Around

Boat or bus from Golfito is the usual way to get here. It's also possible to drive to Golfito by taking the road south of Río Claro for about 10km and turning left at the Rodeo Bar, then following the road another 10km to the Río Coto Colorado ferry, which carries three vehicles (US$1 per car) and runs all day except during the lowest tides. From there, 30km of dirt roads bring you to Zancudo. There are few signs, but at two major road intersections take a right. Cars are OK during dry weather, but 4WD is needed in the wet season.

**Bus** Daily buses leave Golfito for Zancudo at 2pm; it's also possible to get buses from Neily (5:30am and 2pm) and Paso Canoas (2pm). From Zancudo, the bus for Golfito leaves El Coquito at 5am and takes about three hours, with a ferry transfer at the Río Coto Colorado. Service may be suspended or hours changed in the wet season; ask locally.

Arena Alta Sportfishing rents golf carts for US$65 a day for getting around Zancudo. Otherwise, ask around for bicycle rental (about US$7 per day) or do as the locals do – walk or hitch.

**Boat** Public boats leave for Golfito for about US$2 per person. Departure hours were daily at 6am and 1pm but now are erratic since Arena Alta Sportfishing started a service in 2002 at 8am on Tuesday, Thursday, and Friday for US$6/9 one-way/roundtrip, or charters for about US$40. Ask locally. The boat dock is near the north end of the beach on the inland, estuary side. It can be a kilometer or more from where you're staying.

Zancudo Boat Tours (☎/fax 776-0012) charges US$12.50 per person to Golfito (two-passenger minimum). The boat can pick you up in Golfito by advance arrangement and can drop you close to where you're staying.

## PAVONES

About 15km south of Zancudo is the Bahía de Pavón, which is said to have some of the best surfing on the Pacific side of Central America. The name Pavones is used locally to refer to the area comprising both Playa Río Claro de Pavones and, 5km southeast, Punta Banco. There's little to do except hang out and surf, which doesn't seem to pose any kind of problem for visitors.

The beach at Pavones is rockier and rougher than at Punta Banco, which is sandier and has fewer surfers. The best season is from April to October, when the waves are at their biggest and the famous long left can reportedly give a three-minute ride. Legend has it that the wave passes so close to the Esquina del Mar Cantina that you could toss beers to surfers as they come by on their boards. (Camera, anyone?) This is definitely not the beach to bring your small children to for a gentle paddle. Note that the best season coincides with the rainy months.

### Information

Run by the helpful Candyce Speck, Arte Nativo (☎ 383-6939, e tomello@racsa.co.cr), next to the Esquina del Mar restaurant in the 'center' on the beach, has public fax and email service and sells local art and Indian crafts. It's open 1pm to 5pm Monday to Saturday. Note that phone lines are poor and there is no bank.

Evergreen sells and repairs surfboards.

### Places to Stay & Eat

There are several basic places to stay and eat stretched out along a few kilometers of beach.

*Esquina del Mar Cantina* Rooms US$8 per person. This popular, central place has three breezy upstairs rooms. You're lulled to sleep by the sounds of the surf – and the bar below. The bar owner has six rooms across the street that are quieter; bathrooms are shared.

*Hotel Maureen* Rooms US$6 per person. Seven clean rooms, some with a balcony, are otherwise quite basic and share showers. Others to look for in this price range are *Cabina La Plaza*, with just one double room next to a soda, *Cabinas Mendoza* by the soccer field, and *Carol's Cabinas*. All these are close to one another in the 'center' and there are other places nearby.

*Cabinas La Ponderosa* (☎ 384-7430 to leave a message, in the USA ☎ 954-771-9166, w www.cabinaslaponderosa.com) Rooms without/with 3 meals US$30/45 per person, US$5 for air-con. This is a nice, small place to stay near the south end of the beach, 3km or 4km from the center. Five clean rooms have huge screened windows, electricity, air-conditioning, fans, and private hot baths. The owners, brothers Brian and Marshall and partner Angela, surf every day but will arrange a horseback ride or a spot of fishing for a change of pace. There's a dining room and lounge with Ping-Pong and satellite TV/VCR with videos to watch. Surfers hang out here for weeks and get discounted long-stay rates.

*Cabinas Mira Olas* (☎ 393-7742 cellular, e miraolas@hotmail.com checked weekly) Doubles US$28-35 per night, US$140-186 per week, US$8 additional people. Set inland on an 11-acre farm full of wildlife and fruit trees by the Río Claro, this is a good choice for those more interested in nature than surfing. Two high-ceilinged cabins have kitchens, private baths, and porch hammocks; a smaller, more rustic cabin is a little cheaper. The friendly English-speaking owners arrange horseback rides into the Guaymi Indian Reservation and other excursions.

*Casa Siempre Domingo* (☎ 775-0932, fax 775-0373, w www.casa-domingo.com) Rooms US$50, including breakfast. This luxurious private home on a hill above Pavones has fabulous cathedral-like high ceilings and a huge deck with gulf views. The three big rooms sleep four; rates given are for one or two people. Other meals are available on request. There's a TV in the family room.

*Rancho Burica* (e info@ranchoburica .com, w www.ranchoburica.com) Rooms without bath US$4-12. Near the end of the road in Punta Banco, this friendly Dutch-run place has a variety of pleasant rooms sleeping up to 20 people. Some have decks with ocean views; none have private bath. An attractive bathing option is the nearby waterfall. Snorkeling, surfing, and horseback rides are equally regarded options here. A lookout point is a five-minute hike away.

*Camping* on the beach is possible, but watch your stuff. Thefts from tents have been reported. Don't leave your campsite unattended.

## Getting There & Away

The daily bus leaves Rancho Burica for Golfito at 5am and will pick you up along the way as it passes La Ponderosa and Esquina del Mar. It returns from Golfito at 3pm. A 4WD taxi will charge about US$50 from Golfito. You can drive here (see the Playa Zancudo section, earlier). About halfway between the ferry and Zancudo, a signed turnoff goes left to Pavones.

Local boat captain Walter Jiménez can take you to Zancudo, Golfito, Península de Osa, and other destinations. It's about US$100 to Golfito in a boat that takes four passengers.

## TISKITA JUNGLE LODGE

This is a private biological reserve and experimental fruit farm on 160 hectares of land at Punta Banco, about 30km due south of Golfito, 6km south of Pavones, and 10km from the Panama border. About 100 hectares are virgin rainforest. Tiskita also has a coastline with tide pools and beaches suitable for swimming.

The lodge is run by Peter Aspinall, who has an orchard with over 100 varieties of tropical fruits from all over the world. He plans to ship the most suitable of these fruits to San José and abroad. Meanwhile, guests are able to sample dozens of seasonal exotic fruits and fruit drinks during their visit to the lodge.

There are trails in the surrounding rainforest, which contains waterfalls and freshwater pools suitable for swimming. The tide pools have a variety of marine life such as chitons, nudibranchs, bristle and feather worms, starfish, sea urchins, anemones, tunicates, crabs, and many shells. Ask for booklets describing the rainforest trail, the tide pools, and the land crabs, and for a butterfly list.

Birders will find that the combination of rainforest, fruit farm, and coastline produces a long list of birds. About 300 species have been recorded here, depending on who's counting. The fruit farm is particularly attractive to frugivorous (fruit-eating) birds such as parrots and toucans, which can be more easily observed in the orchard than the rainforest. Nature trails into the forest help the birder see the more reticent species, and a local checklist is available. This includes such exotic-sounding birds as yellow-billed cotingas, fiery-billed aracaris, green honeycreepers, and lattice-tailed trogons, to name a few. Monkeys, sloths, agoutis, coatis, and other mammals are often seen. Of course, insects and plants abound.

The lodge runs Fundación Tiskita, a non-profit organization involved with arranging medical care in the nearby community of Punta Banco. It also financially supports local research and conservation efforts to protect marine turtles.

*Jungle Lodge* Singles/doubles/triples US$145/240/315, US$60 for children under 12. Accommodations are in 16 rooms with private baths and Pacific Ocean views. The rooms are in eight rustic cabins of one, two, three, or four rooms each.

The private baths are on the outside of the cabins, allowing rainforest views as you shower – an invigorating way to start the day. A lodge with a small library serves as an informal relaxation area, and a dining room serves home-cooked food. There's a refreshing swimming pool with ocean views.

Reservations are essential, because the lodge is sometimes full of birding groups and the like. Make reservations with Tiskita's San José office (☎ 296-8125, fax 296-8133, @ info@tiskita-lodge.co.cr, w www .tiskita-lodge.co.cr). Daily rates include accommodations, meals, and guided walks with a naturalist. Many people come on package tours that can include flights from either Golfito or Puerto Jiménez to Tiskita's private airstrip.

Various other tours are available. An interesting one is flying from the private Tiskita airstrip to Sirena in Parque Nacional Corcovado, spending about four hours hiking with a local guide, and returning by air. This costs US$150 per person, two minimum. Body boards, snorkeling gear, and horse rental are also available.

The lodge is closed from approximately mid-September to mid-October.

## Getting There & Away

It is possible to drive to the lodge with a 4WD vehicle (or, with care, a car in the dry season), but many people opt to fly to the nearby private airstrip that's a five-minute walk from the lodge. Getting there yourself is rather difficult but can be done by public transport or your own vehicle. Ask the Aspinalls for directions.

# Central Pacific Coast

Costa Rica's major Pacific coastal town is Puntarenas, about 110km west of San José by paved highway. This has traditionally been the town that highlanders descend to when they want to spend a few days by the ocean, but there are now many other popular vacation spots on the Pacific coast south of Puntarenas. These include swimming and surfing beach resorts, sportfishing towns, well-developed and almost undeveloped beaches, a biological reserve, a national marine park, and the famous coastal national park at Manuel Antonio.

Generally, the Pacific coast is better developed for tourism than the Caribbean coast, and if you are looking for some luxury, it's easy to find here. You can also find deserted beaches, wildlife, and small coastal villages.

There are marked wet and dry seasons along the Pacific coast. The rains begin in April, and you can expect a lot of precipitation from May to November. This eases in December, and the dry season continues for the next four months.

The dry months coincide with Costa Rican school vacations in January and February and the biggest holiday of the year, Easter. So the dry season is the high season; wherever you travel on the Pacific coast, you should expect a lot of visitors and make sure you have hotel reservations on weekends for the better hotels.

Many beach hotels are booked weeks or months in advance for Easter week. If you travel during the low (wet) season, you'll see fewer visitors and have little difficulty booking into hotels.

It's worth asking about low-season discounts, which range from 10% to 40% or even 50%. (Prices given throughout this chapter are high-season rates.)

Average temperatures on the coast, year-round, are about 22°C minimum and about 32°C maximum. The dry season is generally a little hotter than the wet.

## PUNTARENAS

This city of about 50,000 inhabitants is the capital of the province of Puntarenas, which stretches along the Pacific coast from Golfo de Nicoya to the Panama border.

During the 19th century, in the days before easy access to the Caribbean coast, Puntarenas was Costa Rica's major port. Goods such as coffee were hauled by ox cart from the highlands down the Pacific slope to Puntarenas, and then they were shipped around the Horn to Europe – a long trip!

## Highlights

- Observing monkeys, motmots, morphos, and manzanillos at Manuel Antonio
- Climbing the canopy at Hacienda Barú
- Tanning on an empty beach – try Matapalo or Esterillos or Uvita
- Watching for scarlet macaws and crocodiles at Carara
- Surfing at Jacó and Playa Hermosa, or surfing lessons at Dominical
- Riding a horse through forested hillsides and ending up on a beach at sunset

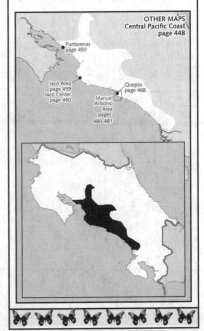

OTHER MAPS
Central Pacific Coast
page 448

Puntarenas
page 450

Jacó Area
page 459
Jacó Center
page 460

Quepos
page 468

Manuel
Antonio
Area
pages
480-481

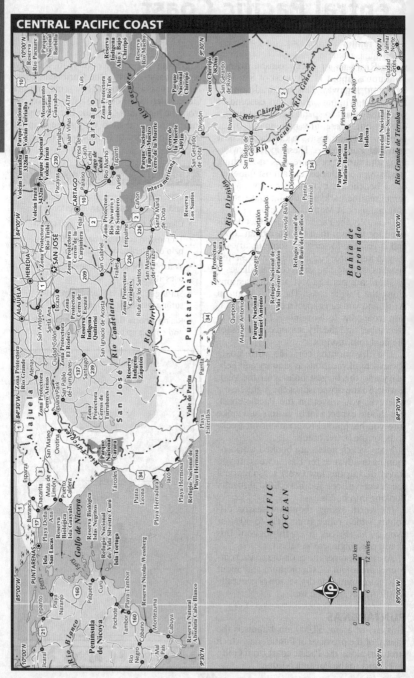

After the railway to Puerto Limón was built, Puntarenas became less significant but remained the most important port on the Pacific side of the country. This changed in 1981 when a new port was opened at Caldera, about 18km southeast of Puntarenas by road. This facility has become the major Pacific port.

Despite the loss of shipping, Puntarenas remains a bustling town during the dry season, when tourists arrive to catch ferries to Península de Nicoya. During the wet months, however, the city is much quieter.

There are plenty of sandy beaches, but, unfortunately, the water is polluted. Puntarenas has cleaned up its act somewhat, and the last kilometer of the south side of the point is now OK for swimming. The beaches themselves are regularly cleaned and the views across the Golfo de Nicoya are nice. You can stroll along the beach or the aptly named Paseo de los Turistas beach road, stretching along the southern coast of town. Cruise ships make day visits to the eastern end of this beach road, and a variety of souvenir stalls and beach *sodas* are there to greet passengers.

Although the town remains somewhat popular with Costa Rican holidaymakers, foreigners tend to look for a destination where they can swim without worrying about pollution. There are plenty of possibilities in the towns and beaches south of Puntarenas, and many people go there and avoid Puntarenas completely.

The locals have a reputation for friendliness. Hang out on the beachfront with the *tico* tourists, and check out the busy comings and goings during the season. Walk by the church – perhaps the most attractive building in Puntarenas. Some people even like to come during the wet season, when it's quiet and fresh with daily rain showers. It's the closest coastal town to San José for a quick getaway, although there are plenty of better beaches elsewhere. The main reason most people spend time here, however, is to wait for a ferry to the Península de Nicoya.

## Orientation

The geographical setting of the town is an intriguing one. Puntarenas literally means a 'sandy point' or sand spit. The city is on the end of a sandy peninsula that is almost 8km long but only 600m wide at its widest point

(downtown) and less than 100m wide in several other parts. The city has 60 *calles* running north to south but only five *avenidas* running west to east at its widest point. Driving into town with the waters of the Pacific lapping up on either side of the road is a memorable experience. Make sure you leave or arrive in daylight hours to see this.

With such a long, narrow street configuration, you are never more than a few minutes' walk away from the coast.

## Information

The Casa de Cultura (☎ 661-1394) has some tourist information. Right outside on the north side are some Internet cafés charging US$2 per hour.

Various banks in the center (shown on the Puntarenas map) change money.

Emergency medical attention is available from the Hospital Monseñor Sanabria (☎ 663-0033), 8km east of town.

## Things to See & Do

The **Casa de Cultura** has an art gallery and occasional cultural events. Behind it is the **Museo Histórico Marino** (☎ 661-5036, 256-4139, Ⓦ *www.museocostarica.com; admission free; open 9:45am-noon & 1pm-5:15pm Tues-Sun*). This museum describes the history of Puntarenas through audiovisual presentations, old photos, and artifacts. A block away, the city **church** is one of the town's most attractive buildings. A walk along the Paseo de los Turistas is pleasant, and you might take a swim in La Punta Municipal Pool at the very tip of the point (currently closed for renovation).

Opened April 27, 2002, the **Puntarenas Marine Park** features an aquarium (*adult/ student/child 11 and under US$7/4/1.50; open 8am-4pm daily*) that showcases manta rays and other creatures from the Pacific. The park is where the train station used to be, and there are plans to add a railway museum and marina and to enlarge the aquarium. There's a snack bar, gift shop, and information center.

Although most cruise ships dock at Caldera for servicing and to unload passengers for land tours, cruise ships do make day visits to a dock at the east end of the Paseo de los Turistas. A large modern building (which houses the Bancredito – see the Puntarenas map), near the beach, will be

# PUNTARENAS

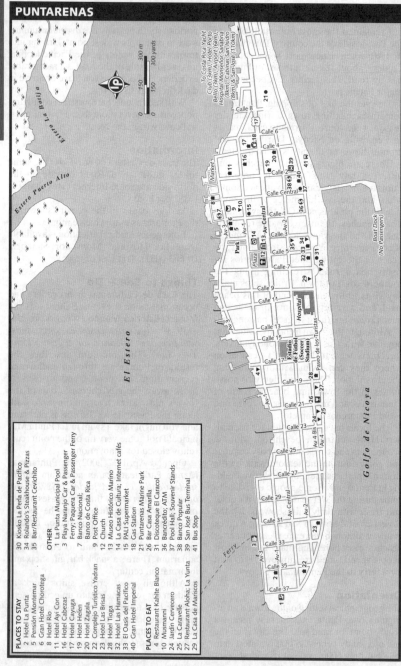

0   150   300 m
0   150   300 yards

*Estero La Botija*

*Estero Puerto Alto*

*El Estero*

*Golfo de Nicoya*

To Costa Rica Yacht
Club (3km); Hotel Porto
Bello (3km); Hotel Porto
Hospital Monseñor Sanabria
(8km); Cabinas San Isidro
(8km); & San José (110km)

Market

*Park*

Plaza

Estadio
de Fútbol
(Soccer
Stadium)

Hospital

Paseo de los Turistas

Boat Dock
(No Passengers)

Ferry

**PLACES TO STAY**
2   Hotel La Punta
5   Pensión Montemar
6   Gran Hotel Chorotega
8   Hotel Río
11  Hotel Ayi Con
16  Hotel Cabezas
17  Hotel Cayuga
19  Hotel Helen
20  Hotel Zagala
22  Complejo Turístico Yadran
23  Hotel Las Brisas
28  Hotel Tioga
32  Hotel Las Hamacas
33  El Oasis del Pacífico
40  Gran Hotel Imperial

**PLACES TO EAT**
4   Restaurant Kahite Blanco
10  Musmanni
24  Jardín Cervecero
25  La Caravelle
27  Restaurant Aloha; La Yunta
29  La Casa de Mariscos

30  Kiosko La Perla de Pacifico
34  Rolando's Steakhouse & Pizzas
35  Bar/Restaurant Cevichito

**OTHER**
1   La Punta Municipal Pool
3   Playa Naranjo Car & Passenger
    Ferry; Paquera Car & Passenger Ferry
7   Banco Nacional;
    Banco de Costa Rica
9   Post Office
12  Church
13  Museo Histórico Marino
14  La Casa de Cultura; Internet cafés
15  PALI Supermarket
18  Gas Station
21  Puntarenas Marine Park
26  Bar Casa Amarilla
31  Discoteque El Caracol
36  Bancrédito; ATM
37  Pool Hall; Souvenir Stands
38  Banco Popular
39  San José Bus Terminal
41  Bus Stop

home to an indoor shopping and dining area. The existing souvenir stalls and beach sodas have a festive air, but the new air-conditioned complex will likely provide a more upscale retreat from the heat.

## Activities & Organized Tours

Several tour companies can take you via boat to visit local beaches and the islands described under Islands Near Bahía Gigante in the Península de Nicoya chapter. Many of these tours are booked in San José. **Coonatramar** (☎ *661-9011, 661-1069,* W *www .coonatramar.com)* does tours around the estuaries and mangroves of Puntarenas and to nearby islands. Fares range from US$6 to US$15 per person with a minimum of five to eight people, depending on the tour. Fred Wagner at **Casa Alberta** (☎/*fax 663-0107)* in Roble (10km east of town) offers fishing trips for about US$200 per day, as well as cheaper local sightseeing cruises.

## Special Events

Apart from the usual tico holidays, Puntarenas celebrates the Fiesta de La Virgen del Mar (Fiesta of the Virgin of the Sea) on the Saturday closest to July 16. This parade is fairly typical, except that the gaily decorated floats really do float! Fishing boats and elegant yachts are beautifully bedecked with lights, flags, and all manner of fanciful embellishments as they sail around the harbor. There are also boat races, a carnival, and plenty of food, drink, and dancing.

## Places to Stay

**Budget** Make sure your room has a decent fan; without one you'll be very hot and, during the wet months, likely to be bitten by mosquitoes.

**Hotel Helen** (☎ *661-2159, Calle 2, Avenidas Central & 2)* Doubles without bath US$9, singles/doubles with bath US$9/15. This place is basic with very small rooms, but it's clean and a good budget choice.

**Hotel Río** (☎ *661-0331, Calle Central & Avenida 3)* Rooms US$5.50/8 per person without/with bath. This basic and rather noisy place is next to the water and market area, which is a little rough, but the hotel is safe and the management is friendly. Rooms have fans.

**Pensión Montemar** (☎ *661-2771, Avenida 3, Calles 1 & 3).* Rooms US$6 per person.

This place is adequately clean and secure, but otherwise very basic.

**Hotel Cabezas** (☎ *661-1045, Avenida 1, Calles 2 & 4)* Rooms US$9/12 per person without/with private showers. The rooms in this basic but friendly place are clean and have fans – this is a good choice in this price range. Parking in a locked lot costs US$3.

**Hotel Ayi Con** (☎ *661-0164, 661-1477, Calle 2, Avenidas 1 & 3)* Rooms without/with bath US$7.50/10.50 per person, singles/doubles with air-con US$15/27. This hotel has rather basic and dark but clean rooms. All rooms have fans.

**Hotel Zagala** (☎ *661-1319, Avenida 2 & Calle 4)* Singles/doubles without bath US$9/12. This basic old family-run place is clean and secure. It has nice rooms with fans, but showers are shared.

**Gran Hotel Imperial** (☎ *661-0579, 661-0600, Paseo de los Turistas, Calles Central & 2)* Rooms without/with bath US$10/14 per person. This is a large old wooden hotel, near the bus stations. The place has atmosphere. The rickety upstairs rooms have balconies, some with ocean views, but bathrooms are shared. Darker downstairs rooms have private bathrooms and fans.

**Gran Hotel Chorotega** (☎ *661-0998, Avenida 3 & Calle 1)* Rooms without bath US$9 per person, singles/doubles with bath US$13/25. This old motel-like place has clean rooms, most with private baths and fans.

**Mid-Range** Overpriced but literally cool is **Hotel Cayuga** (☎ *661-0344, Calle 4, Avenidas Central & 1)* Singles/doubles US$30/40. The hotel has very efficient air-con, which is a relief in the hot temperatures. The rooms have private cold showers, TVs, and telephones and are uninspiring but clean. The desk staff is perfunctory. The restaurant attached to the hotel is quite good – although not very cheap. A locked parking lot is behind the hotel.

**Hotel Las Hamacas** (☎/*fax 661-0398, Paseo de los Turistas, Calles 5 & 7)* Singles/doubles US$30/39 with fan, doubles with air-con US$45. Popular with younger ticos, this place has a pool, kiddie pool, restaurant, disco, and bar, but it's noisy if your room is close to the revelries. Basic older rooms with private cold baths and fans come with free dance music all night. Again, somewhat overpriced.

*El Oasis del Pacífico* (☎ 661-0209, *Paseo de los Turistas, Calles 3 & 5*) Singles/doubles US$24/30, doubles with air-con US$39. This place has a pool, disco, restaurant, bar, and parking and is popular with tico families on vacation. The simple rooms have private hot showers.

*Hotel La Punta* (☎/*fax 661-1900, 661-0696, Avenida 1 & Calle 35*) Singles/doubles with fan US$22/31, with air-con US$39/46. At the far-western point of town near the car ferry terminal, you'll find this decent little hotel. There's a pleasant bar, small pool, and restaurant, and all the rooms have hot water, fans, and balconies.

*Hotel Las Brisas* (☎ 661-4040, *fax 661-2120,* ⓔ *hbrisas@racsa.co.cr, Paseo de los Turistas & Calle 31*) Singles/doubles US$55/65. Near the west end of Puntarenas, this is a quiet, clean, pleasant hotel with a good restaurant and small pool. All rooms have air-con, TVs, private baths, and hot water.

*Hotel Tioga* (☎ 661-0271, *fax 661-0127,* ⓔ *tiogacr@racsa.co.cr,* ⓦ *www.hoteltioga.com, Paseo de los Turistas, Calles 17 & 19*) Singles US$65-85, doubles US$80-99. Opened in 1959, this is the 'grand dame' of the downtown hotels. There are 46 rooms, but as it's often full, call ahead. All rooms have air-con and private baths, most with hot water. The more expensive rooms have balconies with a sea view; cheaper ones are inside around the pool. The beach is right outside and guests can borrow a beach umbrella. Rates include breakfast in the upstairs dining room with ocean view.

*Costa Rica Yacht Club* (☎ 661-0784, *fax 661-2518,* ⓔ *cryacht@racsa.co.cr, Calle 74*) Singles/doubles with fan US$30/45, with air-con & TV US$50/70. Some 3km east of downtown, this place is near the north end of Calle 74 in the suburb of Cocal, at the narrowest portion of the peninsula. The club caters to members of both local and foreign yacht clubs as well as the public. There's a decent restaurant-bar and a pool, and rooms are spartan but spotless. Standard rooms have fans, and superior rooms come with air-con, but it's sometimes hard to get in – the place is often full of yachties.

*Hotel Porto Bello* (☎ 661-1322, *fax 661-0036*) Singles/doubles US$40/55. Near the Yacht Club, this place is set on pleasant grounds (though the entrance from the road is run-down) and has rooms with air-con,

TVs, and patios. The restaurant overlooks the estuary.

*Complejo Turístico Yadran* (☎ 661-2662, *fax 661-1944,* ⓔ *yadran@racsa.co.cr,* ⓦ *www.puntarenas.com/yadran, Paseo de los Turistas & Calle 35*) Doubles US$80, suites US$100. At the end of town near the point of the sand spit, this place has two restaurants, a bar, casino, disco, and children's and adults' pools. Comfortable rooms come with all the usual facilities plus TVs and phones. Tours and fishing can be arranged.

## Places to Eat

Eating in Puntarenas (at least in the cheaper places) tends to be a little more expensive than in other parts of Costa Rica. Many restaurants are along the Paseo de los Turistas and tend to be tourist-oriented and a little pricey – but not outrageously so. The cheapest food for the impecunious is in the sodas around the market area. This area is also inhabited by sailors, drunks, and prostitutes, but it seems raffish rather than dangerous – during the day, at least. There are also several inexpensive Chinese restaurants within a block or two of the intersection of Calle Central and Avenida Central.

There's a row of fairly cheap *sodas* on the beach by the Paseo de los Turistas, Calles Central & 3. They are good for outdoor people watching and serve snacks and non-alcoholic drinks; one specializes in huge fruit salads (you'll see people eating them).

*La Casa de Mariscos* This is a popular and friendly place on the Paseo de los Turistas where most seafood entrées cost US$5 (though jumbo shrimp costs US$10).

Other good places where a fish meal costs under US$5 are *Kiosko La Perla de Pacífico* and *Bar/Restaurant Cevichito*.

*Rolando's Steakhouse & Pizzas* Dishes US$6-12. True to its name, this place serves steaks and pizzas (and seafood, too) in a slightly 'Wild West' setting.

Just west of the Hotel Tioga and Calle 19 are several international restaurants to choose from. Most have meals in the US$5 to US$10 range – more for shrimp and lobster, less for a snack.

*Restaurant Aloha* (☎ 661-0773) Meals US$6-14. This is one of the better places in town and has a varied menu. Next door, *La Yunta* is a good bet for seafood; main dishes average US$6.

*La Caravelle* Dishes US$8-10. Open Wed-Sun. Halfway down the next block from Restaurant Aloha, this popular French restaurant with some outdoor dining is often crowded.

*Jardín Cervecero* Just beyond La Caravelle, this is a German-style bar and restaurant. Apart from beer, it has a variety of snacks and light meals.

*Bar Casa Amarilla* This place is good for snacks by the beach.

*Restaurant Kahite Blanco* (☎ 661-2093, *Avenida 1 & Calle 17*) Dishes US$4-9. On the north side of town, this is a rambling restaurant popular with the locals. It serves good seafood (more than US$9 for jumbo shrimp and lobster) and generous *bocas* (appetizers). There's music and dancing on weekends.

Most of the better hotels have decent restaurants. Ones that have been recommended are at the hotels *Porto Bello* and *Las Brisas*.

## Entertainment

Look for plays and concerts presented at the *Casa de Cultura* during the high season (from December to late March/early April).

There are several dancing spots. On Paseo de los Turistas near Calle 7 is the *Discoteque El Caracol*. Several of the hotels have dancing some nights.

## Getting There & Away

Note that passenger train services to San José were discontinued in 1991.

**Bus** The trip from San José takes less than two hours and costs about US$2.50. Buses leave frequently from Calle 16, Avenidas 10 & 12 – there may be a wait during holiday weekends. From Puntarenas, buses for San José leave frequently from the terminal on Calle 2, just north of the Paseo de los Turistas. The first bus leaves at 4:30am and the last at about 7pm. This terminal is being rebuilt and may provide more services in the future.

Across the Paseo from the San José bus terminal is a covered bus stop right by the ocean, from where buses leave to many nearby destinations. There are 15 buses daily to Miramar (near the Refugio Silvestre de Peñas Blancas) and buses inland to Esparza every hour or so. Buses to Liberia

leave at 4:40am, 5:30am, 7:30am, 9:30am, 11am, 12:30pm, and 3pm.

Other buses include the 11:45am and 4:30pm departures for Tilarán, a bus to Guácimal at 1pm, and a bus to Santa Elena (near Monteverde) at 2:15pm. Buses to Quepos (which could drop you at Jacó) leave at 5am, 11am, 2:30pm, and 4:30pm. (The 11am bus may be canceled in the wet season.)

Buses serving the communities on the coast north of Puntarenas include a 1pm bus to Pitahaya, a 12:15pm bus to Chomes, and buses to Costa de Pajaro at 5:50am, 10:45am, 1:15pm, and 4:30pm.

Buses for the port of Caldera (also going past Playa Doña Ana and Mata de Limón) leave from the market about every hour and head out of town along Avenida Central.

**Boat** There are various ferries, carrying cars and passengers, that leave from the dock at the northwest end of town – drivers arriving for the ferry will find several signs. The ferries go to either Paquera or Playa Naranjo on the Península de Nicoya. Travelers wanting to go to popular beaches at the south end of the peninsula (including Montezuma and Mal País) should catch the Paquera ferry to get bus connections. Travelers heading to the rest of the peninsula should catch a ferry to Playa Naranjo to connect with buses going to Nicoya. Drivers should follow suit, because the road between Paquera and Playa Naranjo is extremely rough.

Ferries to Paquera are operated by Ferry Peninsular (☎ 641-0515) and Ferry Tambor (☎ 661-2084). Passengers going to the Hotel Playa Tambor have preference on the Ferry Tambor, otherwise it is first-come, first-served, and lines can be very long on weekends. Daily except Friday and Sunday, Peninsular ferries leave at 8:15am, 2pm, and 8:15pm, while Tambor ferries leave at 5am, 12:30pm, and 5pm. On Friday, Peninsular ferries depart at 6am, 10am, 2pm, and 8:15pm; Tambor departs at 4am, 8am, 12:30pm, and 5pm. On Sunday, Peninsular departures are at 8:45am, 1pm, 5pm, and 10pm; Tambor departures are at 5am, noon, 4pm, and 8pm. Fares are about US$12 for cars with driver, US$2.50 for motorcycles, US60¢ for bicycles. Passengers are US$1.25, US60¢ for children. The Tambor ferry has an air-conditioned passenger lounge that costs an extra US$2.50. The trip takes about 90 minutes.

Ferries to Playa Naranjo are operated by Contranamar (☎ 661-1069) and leave daily at 3:15am, 7am, 10:50am, 2:50pm, and 7pm. The trip takes an hour and fares are about the same as to Paquera.

## Getting Around

Buses marked 'Ferry' run up Avenida Central and go to the ferry terminal, 1.5km from downtown. The taxi fare from the San José bus terminal in Puntarenas to the ferry terminal is about US$2.

## IGUANA PARK

Also known as 'Jungle Park,' this park *(adult/child or student with ID US$10/6; open 8am-4pm daily)* is a nonprofit project of the Fundación Pro Iguana Verde (☎ 240-6712, fax 235-2007, ⓔ iguverde@racsa.co.cr), which protects the endangered green iguana through breeding and release programs. The green iguana is endangered in part because it's good to eat and has been severely overhunted. The foundation has developed breeding programs that not only have returned over 100,000 individuals into the wild, but also provide income for breeders who 'farm' the iguana for food.

The foundation also has projects to monitor and protect tropical birds, including the scarlet macaw. Habitat protection and local education are key features. There's a training center where students and biologists from all over Latin America can learn more about both resident and migratory birds. The park has a visitor center where you can see exhibits and videos to learn more about the project, and a restaurant where you can sample iguana meat (tastes like chicken!). A souvenir store sells iguana-leather products. It seems odd that to protect the iguana, it has to be farmed for food and leather, but this is the best way to stop poaching and overhunting.

The 400-hectare park is set in a tropical forest 14km east of Orotina. There are 4km of trails in an area of transitional forest between the dry tropical forest of the northern lowlands and the tropical rainforest of the south. In the park's primary forest, The Canopy Tour (see Organized Tours in the Getting Around chapter) has set up canopy platforms that are accessed by cables. Visitors are guided from tree to tree using the cables, traversing high above the forest floor.

Entrance fees at Iguana Park go toward supporting the foundation and tours are available. **The Canopy Tour** *(☎/fax 257-5149, 256-7626, ⓔ canopy@canopytour.com; adult/student/child US$45/35/25)* takes about four hours, including hiking to the access point. Two daily tours are offered. The Canopy Tour organizes a complete package from San José, Jacó, or Puntarenas for US$75/65/55, including the guided tour, lunch, and roundtrip transportation from your hotel. Jungle Park admission is extra. If you want to drive to the park yourself and take a canopy tour, a reservation is recommended; the guides may take the day off if there are no reservations.

Getting there is a little tricky, as there aren't any public buses (other than those run by The Canopy Tour). From just south of Orotina, look for a road to the east signed 'Coopebaro, Puriscal.' This road goes over a wooden suspension bridge to the park, and there are signs, though not many. It's about 9km, and half the road is paved. Call the Fundación or The Canopy Tour for up-to-date directions.

## FROM PUNTARENAS TO PARQUE NACIONAL CARARA

About 13km away from downtown Puntarenas, **Playa Doña Ana** is the first clean beach. There are actually two beaches a few hundred meters away from each other: Boca Barranca and Doña Ana. Surfing is good at both beaches, especially Boca Barranca. The Doña Ana beach has been developed for tourism – there's a sign on the Costanera Sur (coastal highway) south of Puntarenas that reads 'Paradero Turístico Doña Ana.' At the beach entrance is a parking lot (US60¢). Day-use fees for the beach are US$1.50 for adults, half that for children, and the beach is open 8am to 5pm. There are snack bars, picnic shelters, and changing areas, and the swimming is good.

*Hotel Río Mar* *(☎ 663-0158)* Rooms with fan/air-con US$25/35. This friendly place is on the east side of the Costanera Sur, a half kilometer north of Playa Doña Ana. Rooms have private baths and there's a restaurant and bar.

**Mata de Limón** is an old beach resort that has long been popular with locals from Puntarenas, as well as with highlanders. It's near the port of Caldera, and the buses from Puntarenas to Caldera will get you to Mata de Limón. The turnoff is 5.5km south of Playa Doña Ana.

The village is situated around a mangrove lagoon that is good for birding (especially at low tide), though not very good for swimming. It's divided in two by a river, with the lagoon and most facilities on the south side. Aside from the occasional Jet Ski buzzing by, this is a sleepy little place with a few simple cabins and restaurants catering to the weekend tico beachgoers.

The major port on the Pacific coast is **Puerto Caldera**, which you pass soon after leaving Mata de Limón. There's nothing to do here apart from looking at the ships – there's no town.

## PARQUE NACIONAL CARARA

This 5242-hectare park is at the mouth of the Río Tárcoles, by road around 50km southeast of Puntarenas, or about 90km west of San José via the Orotina highway. The park is surrounded by pasture and agricultural land and forms an oasis for wildlife in a large surrounding area. It's the northernmost tropical wet forest on the Pacific coast, in the transition zone to the tropical dry forests farther north, and five Holdridge Life Zones occur within the park. (See Ecology & Environment in the Facts about Costa Rica chapter for an explanation of life zones.) There are also archaeological remains that you can see only with a guide – but they are not very exciting ruins.

If you're driving from Puntarenas or San José, pull over to the left immediately after crossing the Río Tárcoles bridge, also known as the **Crocodile Bridge**. Basking crocodiles are often seen along the muddy banks below the bridge. Binoculars help a great deal. A variety of water birds may also be seen – herons, spoonbills, storks, and anhingas.

*A warning:* Armed robbery has been reported in this area. Sometimes a park ranger or policeman is on duty; there's a police post. Otherwise, use caution. Robbers sometimes dress like affluent locals, complete with binoculars – and a gun!

Some 600m farther south on the left-hand side is a locked gate leading to the Laguna

Meandrica trail. Another 2km brings you to the Carara administration building/ranger station, which is open 7am to 4pm. There are bathrooms, picnic tables, and a short nature trail. You can get information here and pay the US$6 fee to enter the reserve. Trail maps are available for US$1. English- and Spanish-speaking guides can be hired for US$15 per person (two minimum) for a two-hour hike. About 1km farther south are two loop trails. The first, Sendero Las Araceas, is 1.2km long and can be combined with Sendero Quebrada Bonita (another 1.5km).

Visitors are advised that cars parked at the trails have been broken into. There may be guards on duty, but drivers are advised to park their cars in the parking lot at the Carara ranger station and walk along the Costanera Sur for 2km north or 1km south. Go in a group and don't carry unnecessary valuables. Alternately, park by Restaurante Ecológico Los Cocodrilos (see below).

A variety of forest birds inhabit the reserve but can be difficult to see without an experienced guide. The most exciting bird for many visitors to see, especially in June or July, is the brilliantly patterned scarlet macaw. Other birds to watch for include guans, trogons, toucans, motmots, and many other forest species. Monkeys, squirrels,

### Slothful Habits

Sloths live in trees for most of their lives. They are fastidious with their toilet habits, always climbing down from their trees to deposit their weekly bowel movement on the ground. Biologists don't know why they do this; one hypothesis is that by defecating at the base of a particular tree, the sloth provides a fertilizer that increases the quality of the leaves of that tree, thus improving the sloth's diet.

sloths, and agoutis are among the more common mammals present.

The dry season from December to April is the easiest time to go – though the animals are still there in the wet months! March and April are the driest months. Rainfall is almost 3000mm annually, which is less than in the rainforests farther south. It's fairly hot, with average temperatures of 25°C to 28°C – but it's cooler within the rainforest. Make sure you have insect repellent. An umbrella is important in the wet season and occasionally needed in the dry months.

### Organized Tours

If you are not experienced at watching for wildlife in the rainforest, you will have difficulty seeing much. Going on a tour with a guide is expensive but worthwhile if you want to see a reasonable number of species. Guides who visit several times a week will know where the wildlife is. Most tour companies have day tours to Carara from San José for about US$75 to US$100 per person. (For further information, see Organized Tours in the Getting Around chapter.) It takes about 2½ hours to drive down from San José.

### Places to Stay & Eat

Camping is not allowed, and there's nowhere to stay in the park, so most people come on day trips.

*Restaurante Ecológico Los Cocodrilos* (☎ 428-8005, 428-9009) Doubles US$18. This is the nearest place to stay and eat and is on the north side of the Río Tárcoles bridge. It offers basic, clean roadside cabins, but most travelers just stop at the restaurant. Otherwise, the nearest hotels and restaurants are at Tárcoles, 2km or 3km south of the park, or at Jacó, 22km south. Several readers have recommended staying in Tárcoles and walking up to the park early in the morning before tours begin to arrive.

### Getting There & Away

There are no buses to Carara, but you can get off any bus bound for Jacó, Quepos, or Parque Nacional Manuel Antonio. This may be a bit problematic on weekends, when buses are full, so go midweek if you are relying on a bus ride. This budget option has pleased some travelers, though others complain that they 'didn't see anything' in the

park, which is why it can be worth going on a guided trip.

Many of the more remote parts of the Pacific coast are best visited by car.

## TÁRCOLES AREA

Two kilometers south of the Carara ranger station is the Tárcoles turnoff to the right (west) and the Hotel Villa Lapas turnoff to the left. To get to Tárcoles, turn right and drive for a kilometer, then go right at the T-junction to the village, with cabins and a beach. To reach the mudflats of the Río Tárcoles, continue past the village for 2km or 3km; this is a prime area for birders looking for shorebirds, particularly at low tide.

### Waterfall

A 5km dirt road past the Hotel Villa Lapas (see Places to Stay & Eat, below) leads to a waterfall variously called El Manantial de Agua Viva (Spring of Living Water) or simply La Catarata, meaning 'Waterfall' (☎ 637-0346, fax 236-1506; admission US$10; open 8am-3pm Dec 15-Apr 15). It's about 200m high, and to see it in its full glory, you need to clamber down a steep trail (45 minutes) and then climb back out (90 minutes). It'll probably take you longer (four hours average) if you examine the black-and-green poison-arrow frogs on the trail, watch the many birds above, and stop

at various lookout points. The trail and falls are in virgin rainforest. At the bottom of the falls, the river continues through a series of natural swimming holes. A camping area and outhouse are available at the bottom.

The waterfall is on private property owned by Daniel Bedard, who cut the trail a few years ago, reportedly in seven months, working 60-hour weeks with five other men. The trail is officially open the dates listed above. It's also open in the wet season (when the waterfall is at its fullest) when conditions and weather permit. Call for information in wet months.

Several kilometers up the road beyond Bedard's trailhead, the Complejo Ecológico Catarata has reportedly bulldozed a trail that gives you a view of the top of the falls.

### Crocodile Tours
Signs in the Río Tárcoles area advertise crocodile tours during which visitors can get close to crocs on pontoon boats and watch the guide feed the animals. Ask around about these events.

### Places to Stay & Eat
This place can be almost deserted midweek in the wet season. Finding a restaurant can be problematic at that time.

**Cabinas Carara** (☎ 637-0178) Doubles US$38-54. Situated in the village, this place has decent rooms with showers. The rates vary depending on whether you want fans, views, or air-con. It has a small pool. Another possibility is the small, simple, family-run **Cabinas Mar y Luna**.

**Hotel Villa Lapas** (☎ 222-5191, 637-0232, fax 222-3450, 637-0227, e info@villalapas.com, w www.villalapas.com) Rooms US$90. This hotel is half a kilometer inland from the Tárcoles turnoff. The hotel has a small pool; its pleasant gardens are surrounded by hillside and forest with good birding along trails that wind up the Río Tarcolitos in a private reserve. There's a butterfly garden (US$3), a pool table, and a minigolf course. The restaurant opens at 7am and is open to the public all day. The 47 rooms are clean, spacious, and airy, with fans and private hot showers.

**Tarcol Lodge** (☎ 430-0400, ☎/fax 267-7138, e johnerb@racsa.co.cr) Rooms US$99 per person, including meals. This lodge is on the south bank of the Río Tárcoles, at the northwest end of the village. At low tide, a huge expanse of mudflats attracts thousands of shorebirds during migration, and hundreds at other times. At high tide, the mudflats disappear, and the river comes up close to the lodge on three sides. Definitely bring binoculars.

The lodge is run by the Erb family, the same folks who have the Rancho Naturalista near Turrialba (see the Central Valley & the Surrounding Highlands chapter). The focus is similar, with birding and nature tours, rustic but comfortable lodging, and good food. The birding is special – a three-day visit will usually yield at least 150 species, and over 400 are recorded on the lodge list. The owners are friendly, fun, and good birders. This place is highly recommended for birders.

The lodge is small and rustic – four double rooms sharing two bathrooms (larger groups can be accommodated in a nearby house). All rooms have fans, and the bathrooms have hot water. The rate includes a free guided tour if you stay three nights or more. Resident naturalists assist with birding around the lodge during your visit. Longer stays cost US$650 per person per week, including two guided tours, meals, and lodging. Bottled drinks cost extra. Tours are led by naturalist guides and visit either two different trails in Carara or the estuary at high tide (by boat), either at night or during the day. Weeks can also be split between the Tarcol Lodge and Rancho Naturalista. Transportation from San José can be arranged for an extra US$60 each way.

**Chalets Paradise** (☎ 637-0168) Doubles US$36. Just over 3km south of the Tárcoles turnoff, this place offers decent double rooms, some with kitchenettes. Its Swiss-style tin roofs (built by the original Swiss owner, who left long ago) have a certain oddball charm. There's a pool.

## PUNTA LEONA AREA
This tiny headland is about halfway between Tárcoles and Jacó. There are a couple of upscale places to stay with super views.

### Activities
US-based **JD's Watersports** (☎/fax 256-6391, e jdwater@racsa.co.cr; see Organized Tours in the Getting There & Away chapter for US contacts) operates a complete water-sports center here and offers sportfishing (US$195

per person per day, four to six anglers), scuba diving (two-tank boat dives US$80, beginners' resort course US$100), very popular half-day jungle river cruises (US$55), sunset cruises (US$38), and rentals of ocean kayaks or sailboards (US$12 per hour), Sunfish sailboats (US$25 per hour), body boards or snorkeling gear (US$16.50 per day), and scuba gear (US$35 per day). Boat charters to various destinations are available. The company can also arrange complete packages including all meals and your choice of accommodations.

### Places to Stay & Eat

*Hotel Punta Leona* (☎ 231-3131, fax 232-0791, e info@hotelpuntaleona.com, w www.hotelpuntaleona.com) Doubles US$90-105, suites & apartments US$160-280. About 6km south of Tárcoles and 11km north of Jacó, a guarded gate lets guests onto the 4km dirt road to this place, surrounded by the rainforest. This is a 300-hectare cliff-top resort with beach access and 108 rooms and 73 apartments, all with TVs and air-con. There are three pools, four restaurants, tennis, horseback riding, and children's activities. Double rooms vary in kind, size, and price. The apartments, which have kitchens and two bedrooms, sleep up to six. A reader points out that some apartments have air-conditioned bedrooms, but lack air-con in the kitchen and bathroom, which are therefore very hot. The usual weekly and low-season discounts apply.

*Hotel Villa Caletas* (☎ 637-0606, fax 637-0404, e caletas@racsa.co.cr, w www.hotelvilla caletas.com) Rooms, villas & suites US$160-390. This luxurious place is 3km south of the Punta Leona entry and 8km north of the Jacó turnoff from the Costanera. A steep 1km paved road leads to the beautiful hotel, decorated with art and antiques. There are stunning views, one of those marvelous pools that appear to drop off at the horizon, and a French-influenced restaurant. The hotel sometimes hosts classical music recitals in a small open-air amphitheater, from which you can watch the sun go down behind the Península de Nicoya. It's about 1km down a steep trail to the beach. There are 35 units of eight different types and prices dotted around the steep and forested property; each has a private view balcony, cable TV, telephone, minibar and coffeemaker. À la carte

meals cost about US$25 for lunch or dinner, US$11 for breakfast. Although tours and activities can be arranged, many guests just do nothing more strenuous than relax, with an occasional dip in the pool.

### PLAYA HERRADURA

The Herradura turnoff is on the Costanera Sur 3.5km north of the turnoff to Jacó. A paved road leads 3km west to Playa Herradura – a quiet, sheltered, palm-fringed, black-sand beach. Until the mid 1990s, this was a rural beach, popular mainly with campers. Now it's home to a marina, hotel, and a condominium complex that is one of the largest new tourism developments in the country.

A few hundred meters before the beach on the main road is a *campground* with showers and basic facilities, charging about US$4.50 per person.

*Cabinas Herradura* (☎ 643-3181) Singles/doubles US$26/36, US$6 per additional person, up to six. This place facing the beach has simple, spacious cabins with air-con and kitchens; rates may go up on dry-season weekends.

*Cabinas del Río* (☎ 643-3275) Singles/doubles US$15/21, US$5 per additional person. About half a kilometer from the beach, this German-owned place has cabins of varying comfort and size spread out around a tiny creek. It costs slightly more for the two cabins with kitchens.

*Los Sueños Marriott Beach and Golf Resort* (☎ 630-9000, fax 630-9090, e information@lossuenosresort.com, w www.lossuenosresort.com) Doubles US$200-300. This US$40 million hotel and condominium project at the north end of the bay features a 250-slip marina, golf course, tennis courts, an enormous swimming pool, shopping center, casino, sportfishing, and all the activities and amenities a resort can offer. Hills above the bay have been bulldozed to make way for million-dollar homes. On the plus side, most of the land that the resort is being built on was a cattle ranch, not rainforest, and the builders seem to be obeying the environmental laws that do exist – a refreshing change from the situation at Tambor in Nicoya. Although a resort that advertises 'eco-golf' is kidding itself somewhat, careful steps are being taken to keep pollution produced by the complex within legal limits.

On the beach are a couple of simple *restaurants*.

## JACÓ AREA

Jacó is the first developed beach town on the Pacific coast as you head south. It's a large, pretty beach, and its proximity to San José makes it popular and, by Costa Rican standards, crowded – though it will seem relatively quiet to many visitors who may be used to shoulder-to-shoulder sunbathing on their own crowded beaches. Jacó has something of a reputation as a 'party beach' – especially during the dry season – but it's pretty sedate compared to some North American party beaches, like Daytona Beach in Florida. Nevertheless, it's popular with young people and vacation-package

visitors. Swimming is possible, though you should be careful of rip currents (people drown each year) and avoid the areas nearest the estuaries, which are polluted.

The turnoff from the Costanera Sur for Jacó is just 3.5km beyond Herradura. Playa Jacó is about 2km off the Costanera. The beach itself is about 3km long, and hotels and restaurants line the road running behind it. Development has been fast in Jacó – perhaps too fast. The crowded center of Jacó can get somewhat trashed at the end of a busy weekend, although the fringes are quieter and cleaner. However, hoteliers and tourist-industry personnel are making successful efforts to keep the beach clean. Though there are many quieter and less crowded places elsewhere, Jacó continues

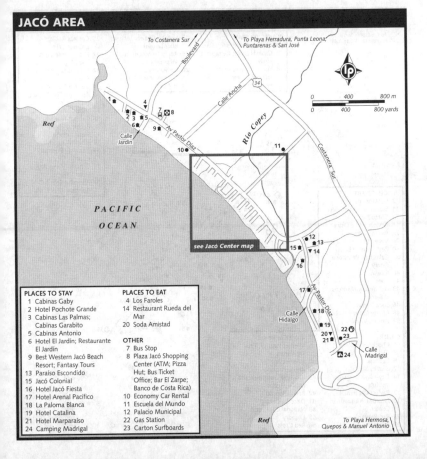

**JACÓ AREA**

*To Costanera Sur*

*To Playa Herradura, Punta Leona, Puntarenas & San José*

*Reef*

*PACIFIC OCEAN*

*Río Copey*

*Costanera Sur*

*Av Pastor Díaz*

*Calle Jardín*

*Calle Ancha*

*Boulevard*

see Jacó Center map

0   400   800 m
0   400   800 yards

*Reef*

*Calle Hidalgo*

*Av Pastor Díaz*

*Calle Madrigal*

*To Playa Hermosa, Quepos & Manuel Antonio*

| PLACES TO STAY | PLACES TO EAT |
|---|---|
| 1 Cabinas Gaby | 4 Los Faroles |
| 2 Hotel Pochote Grande | 14 Restaurant Rueda del |
| 3 Cabinas Las Palmas; | Mar |
| Cabinas Garabito | 20 Soda Amistad |
| 5 Cabinas Antonio | |
| 6 Hotel El Jardín; Restaurante | **OTHER** |
| El Jardín | 7 Bus Stop |
| 9 Best Western Jacó Beach | 8 Plaza Jacó Shopping |
| Resort; Fantasy Tours | Center (ATM; Pizza |
| 13 Paraíso Escondido | Hut; Bus Ticket |
| 15 Jacó Colonial | Office; Bar El Zarpe; |
| 16 Hotel Jacó Fiesta | Banco de Costa Rica) |
| 17 Hotel Arenal Pacífico | 10 Economy Car Rental |
| 18 La Paloma Blanca | 11 Escuela del Mundo |
| 19 Hotel Catalina | 12 Palacio Municipal |
| 21 Hotel Marparaíso | 22 Gas Station |
| 24 Camping Madrigal | 23 Carton Surfboards |

to grow and draw tourists who want to hang out in a busy beach town.

## Information & Orientation

In an effort to make foreign visitors feel more at home, the town has placed signs with street names on most streets. These names are shown on the map – however, the locals continue using the traditional landmark system.

There's no unbiased tourist information office, although several tour offices will give information. Three banks change money, and the Banco de Costa Rica has a Visa ATM. A couple of Internet places are shown on the map; they charge about US$3 an hour. The Red Cross (☎ 643-3090) can help with medical emergencies.

## Surfing

Jacó is called the surfing capital of Costa Rica – not so much because it has the best waves, but for several other reasons. The waves in the Jacó area tend to be a little more consistent than elsewhere. Although the rainy season is considered the best for Pacific coast surfing, this area has some decent possibilities even in the dry months. Jacó is quickly and easily reached from the capital and provides a huge infrastructure of hotels, restaurants, and surf shops, and it's a central place to get information about surfing conditions anywhere in the country.

Surfers will find a number of places in the center of town competing to rent boards and provide information. At the north end, Chuck's Surf Shop has been around a while.

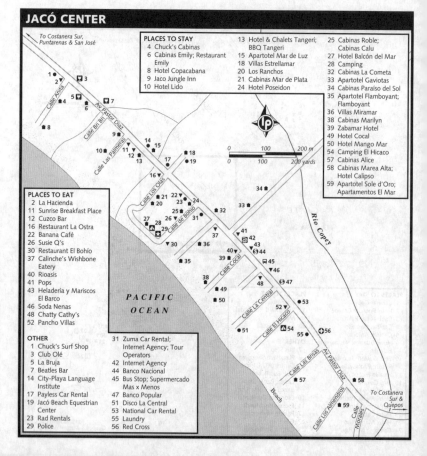

### JACÓ CENTER

To Costanera Sur,
Puntarenas & San José

**PLACES TO STAY**
4 Chuck's Cabinas
6 Cabinas Emily; Restaurant Emily
8 Hotel Copacabana
9 Jaco Jungle Inn
10 Hotel Lido
13 Hotel & Chalets Tangerí; BBQ Tangerí
15 Apartotel Mar de Luz
18 Villas Estrellamar
20 Los Ranchos
21 Cabinas Mar de Plata
24 Hotel Poseidon
25 Cabinas Roble; Cabinas Calu
27 Hotel Balcón del Mar
28 Camping
32 Cabinas La Cometa
33 Apartotel Gaviotas
34 Cabinas Paraíso del Sol
35 Apartotel Flamboyant; Flamboyant
36 Villas Miramar
38 Cabinas Marilyn
39 Zabamar Hotel
49 Hotel Cocal
50 Hotel Mango Mar
54 Camping El Hicaco
57 Cabinas Alice
58 Cabinas Marea Alta; Hotel Calipso
59 Apartotel Sole d'Oro; Apartamentos El Mar

**PLACES TO EAT**
2 La Hacienda
11 Sunrise Breakfast Place
12 Cuzco Bar
16 Restaurant La Ostra
22 Banana Café
26 Susie Q's
30 Restaurant El Bohío
37 Calinche's Wishbone Eatery
40 Rioasis
41 Pops
43 Heladería y Mariscos El Barco
46 Soda Nenas
48 Chatty Cathy's
52 Pancho Villas

**OTHER**
1 Chuck's Surf Shop
3 Club Olé
5 La Bruja
7 Beatles Bar
14 City-Playa Language Institute
17 Payless Car Rental
19 Jacó Beach Equestrian Center
23 Rad Rentals
29 Police
31 Zuma Car Rental; Internet Agency; Tour Operators
42 Internet Agency
44 Banco Nacional
45 Bus Stop; Supermercado Mas x Menos
47 Banco Popular
51 Disco La Central
53 National Car Rental
55 Laundry
56 Red Cross

PACIFIC OCEAN

Rio Copey

To Costanera Sur & Quepos

0    100    200 m
0    100    200 yards

At the south end, Carton Surfboards makes custom boards. Signs for surf lessons abound – look at the notice board at the Restaurant El Bohío, for example.

The beach at **Playa Hermosa** begins about 5km south of Jacó and has its own small cluster of hotels and restaurants. This beach stretches for about 10km and has a strong break that draws expert surfers; there's an annual contest here in August.

## Other Activities & Organized Tours

Several places advertise **bike rentals**. These usually cost about US$2 an hour or US$6.50 a day. Mopeds and small scooters cost from US$35 to US$50 a day (many places ask for a cash or credit card deposit of about US$200); look for signs in the center. One place is **Rad Rentals** (☎ 643-1310), which also rents body boards and surfboards (US$2 per hour, US$7 per day). There are several car rental agencies, and though rates are a little higher than in San José, they are convenient.

The main tour company is **Fantasy Tours** in the Best Western Jacó Beach lobby. The **Jacó Beach Equestrian Center** (☎ 643-1569) offers horseback tours starting at US$25. **Diana's Trail Rides** (☎ 643-3808) in Playa Hermosa offers one- to three-hour rides for US$25 to US$45. Riders can visit forest, hilltops, waterfalls, and beaches.

## Language Courses

The *City-Playa Language Institute* (☎/fax 645-2123) offers inexpensive courses in Spanish. Ask about group rates. *Escuela del Mundo* (e delmundo@racsa.co.cr, w www.spanish-language.org/school_world.htm) offers programs in Spanish, or Spanish combined with ecology, culture, art, and surfing, and attracts young adult students.

## Places to Stay – Jacó Area

Reservations are recommended during the December to April dry season and definitely required during the Christmas–New Year period, during Easter week, and on most weekends. There are plenty of places to stay, but travelers on a shoestring budget will not find many good deals, especially if they're looking for single rooms. Camping is an option, as is staying in cabins that sleep six.

Low-season discounts are available in most hotels, as are surfers' discounts – the latter probably because surfers tend to stay for days or even weeks. If you plan on a lengthy stay (surfer or not), ask for a discount. The rates given here are full high-season rates, but discounts could be as great as 40% to 50% if you're staying for several nights in the low season, especially in the mid- and higher-priced places where good deals can be made. Although singles/doubles rates are given here, many hotels have larger rooms where budget travelers can economize as a group.

Playa Jacó is a large resort, and not every hotel can be shown in this book. Also, many places have rooms of varying ages and quality. If you are planning on spending a few days, it definitely pays to shop around.

During the rainy season, there are reports of water problems in hotels, because heavy rains can cause landslides and damage water pipes.

**Camping** A friendly place is in the center of town is *Camping El Hicaco* (☎ 643-3004) Campsites US$3 per person. It has picnic tables, bathrooms, and a lock-up for your gear. Don't leave valuables in your tent. The campsites are sandy rather than grassy, which may reduce the number of insects you'll encounter.

*Camping Madrigal* Campsites US$2 per person. South of the center, this place is grassier and has a bar-restaurant next door. There's another camping area next to the police station.

**Budget** In the center of town is *Cabinas Mar de Plata* (☎ 643-3580) Doubles US$18. The basic rooms here have private cold baths.

*Cabinas Roble* (☎ 643-3558) Singles/doubles US$15/20. This is clean and a decent value for rooms with showers.

*Hotel Calipso* (☎ 643-3208, fax 643-3728) Doubles US$20-30. At the south end of downtown, the basic double rooms here have fans and shared cold baths. There are some better cabins with private baths and TV for US$30.

*Cabinas Marea Alta* (☎ 643-3554) Doubles US$25. Next door to Hotel Calipso, this place has fairly basic cabins with private cold showers and refrigerators.

*Cabinas Emily* (☎ 643-3513) Cabins US$22. This basic place is popular with and recommended by shoestringers and has a good local restaurant next door.

***Chuck's Cabinas*** *(☎/fax 643-3328,* e *chucks@racsa.co.cr)* Rooms without bath US$7 per person, doubles/triples/quads with bath US$25/30/35. Near Cabinas Emily, this place provides a few simple rooms with high-powered fans and shared showers, and a larger room with a private bathroom. Chuck also runs a surf shop, has lived in the area for years, and is bursting with information about surfing in Costa Rica; ask about his Bro Deal and Ultra Bro Deal.

***Cabinas Garabito*** *(☎ 643-3321)* Singles without bath US$10, doubles with cold bath US$25. This place is at the north end of town.

***Cabinas La Cometa*** *(☎ 643-3615)* Doubles without/with bath US$22/32. This friendly place is run by French-Canadians and popular with international travelers. There are four clean rooms that have fans and shared cold showers, and three rooms with private hot showers.

***Cabinas Calu*** *(☎ 643-1107)* Doubles US$24. Next door to the less-expensive Cabinas Roble, this friendly place has gotten good reviews from several readers for good-size, clean rooms that have private showers and fans.

***Cabinas Marilyn*** *(☎ 643-3215)* Doubles US$18-25. The large bare rooms here have private baths, and some of the more expensive have fridges.

***Cabinas Antonio*** *(☎ 643-3043)* Doubles US$27. At the north end of town, this place is also OK, with private hot showers and a restaurant next door.

***Hotel Lido*** *(☎ 643-3171)* Rooms US$20 per person. Rooms here have kitchenettes, fans, and cold water, and there's also a pool here.

**Mid-Range** Rooms are set in pleasant gardens at ***Cabinas Las Palmas*** *(☎ 643-3005, fax 643-3512)* Singles/doubles US$23/27, units with fan/air-con US$40/60. Older rooms have cold water and fans. Newer units have hot water and kitchenettes.

***Jacó Colonial*** *(☎ 643-3727)* Doubles US$32. At the south end of town, this is an old mock-Spanish-colonial-style hotel with about a dozen decent rooms with fans and hot water.

***Los Ranchos*** *(☎/fax 643-3070)* Doubles without/with kitchens US$30/40, bungalows

US$65. This place is very popular with English-speaking visitors and attracts many repeat clients. It has a pool, pleasant garden, small paperback library, and friendly staff offering information on local tours and surfing. Rooms are quiet and all have fans and private baths with hot water. The upstairs rooms are smaller, while larger downstairs rooms have kitchenettes and are more expensive. Bungalows sleep up to five.

***Apartamentos El Mar*** *(☎ 643-3165, fax 272-2280)* Doubles US$33, apartments US$55. The good-size apartments here are clean and have hot water, kitchenettes, and fans. They can sleep up to five people – a good deal. A few cheaper doubles are also available. There's a small pool.

***Cabinas Alice*** *(☎ 643-3061)* Doubles US$35. Here you'll find decent, clean rooms with private cold baths and fans. The restaurant has been recommended, the beach is just steps away, and there's a pool. A few units have kitchenettes for another US$10.

***Apartotel Mar de Luz*** *(☎/fax 643-3259,* e *mardeluz@racsa.co.cr)* Doubles/quads US$45/60. This recommended place has attractive, air-conditioned rooms with patios, kitchens, and hot water, and larger rooms for four. There's a pool. Management speaks Spanish, English, German, and Dutch and is friendly, knowledgeable, and informative.

***Zabamar Hotel*** *(☎/fax 643-3174)* Singles/doubles with fan US$30/45, with air-con US$45/60. The clean, pleasant rooms here each have their own bath with hot water. There's a pool and a small, reasonably priced breakfast/snack bar.

***Cabinas Gaby*** *(☎ 643-3080, fax 441-5922)* Doubles with air-con US$40, cabins with fan US$55. At the far north end of town, this place has pleasant rooms with kitchenettes, hot water, and a choice of fans or air-con. There's a small pool and a shady garden. A cabin with fans sleeps five.

***Hotel El Jardín*** *(☎ 643-3050)* Singles/doubles US$25/40. Also at the north end of town, this friendly, Belgian-owned place is known for its French restaurant. Rooms are simple but clean and have hot water and fans. There's a pool.

***Jacó Jungle Inn*** *(☎ 643-1631, fax 643-1664)* Doubles with bath US$40. This friendly place has plain, clean rooms. The inn has a pool, Jacuzzi, and Tarzan/Jane bathrooms by its small poolside bar.

*Apartotel Sole d'Oro* (☎ 643-3172, fax 643-3441) Doubles with fan/air-con US$50/70. Rooms here are clean, modern, and spacious, with kitchenettes, cold water, and fans or air-con. Rooms sleep three or four, and there's a pool and Jacuzzi.

*Apartotel Gaviotas* (☎ 643-3092, fax 643-3054) Rooms US$40-80. Here you'll find 12 spacious and modern apartments with kitchenettes, refrigerators, sitting areas, fans, and hot water. They sleep five. There's a fine pool, a bar, and a TV room. It's a few hundred meters' walk to the beach – if you can put up with that, you'll find this to be a great deal in the rainy season, when rates as low as US$30 have been reported.

*Apartotel Flamboyant* (☎ 643-3146, 643-1068) Singles/doubles US$50/55. Just steps from the beach, this place has eight clean and pleasant studio rooms. All have fans, hot showers, kitchenettes, and little patios, and they're a good value. Amenities include a good restaurant, a barbecue area, and a pool.

*Cabinas Paraíso del Sol* (☎ 643-3250, fax 643-3137, e parsolcr@racsa.co.cr) Doubles US$45, larger rooms US$65. Nice clean rooms are equipped with fans or air-con, kitchenettes, and hot water. There's a small pool and a bar with cable TV, Ping-Pong, and surf videos.

*Villas Miramar* (☎ 643-3003, fax 643-3617, e villasmiramar@racsa.co.cr) Doubles US$60. This is a good place with large rooms, kitchenettes, refrigerators, hot water, fans, and a pool. It's set in a pleasant and quiet garden with picnic/barbecue areas. Recommended.

*Villas Estrellamar* (☎ 643-3102, fax 643-3453) Doubles with fan/air-con US$54/65. This place has a nice pool and pleasant gardens. There are about 20 good rooms with cable TVs, hot water, and kitchens. Rates drop to a bargain half-price in the low season.

*Hotel Marparaíso* (☎ 643-3277, e mar hotel@racsa.co.cr) Rooms US$72. This is an older hotel that has had a recent face-lift. There are two pools, a game room, and a restaurant. Rooms sleep up to six; some have air-con.

*Hotel Balcón del Mar* (☎/fax 643-3251, e balcon@racsa.co.cr) Doubles US$60. This beachfront place has a pool and rooms with private balconies and ocean views. Some rooms are air-conditioned, and all have hot water and refrigerators. There's a good restaurant.

*Apartotel Mango Mar* (☎/fax 643-3670) Doubles US$60. Also on the beach, this a good place with a dozen nice air-conditioned rooms with kitchenettes, hot water, and balconies overlooking the pool and Jacuzzi. It also has two larger apartments.

*La Paloma Blanca* (☎ 643-1893, fax 643-1892, e iwann@mailcity.com) Doubles US$45-75; house US$120/500 per night/month. In the south end of town and facing the beach, this is a nice B&B in a former duplex home. There's an upstairs room with private bath (US$45), a ground floor suite with a full kitchen and patio (US$60), and an upstairs room with a canopy bed and ocean-view verandah (US$75). There's a pool, and discounts are available for longer stays; the house can also be rented as a whole. The owners are from the USA.

*Hotel Catalina* (☎ 643-3217, fax 643-3544, e info@hotelcatalina.net, w www .hotelcatalina.net) Triples US$50. Facing the same stretch of beach, here you'll find 15 housekeeping units, all with kitchenettes, hot water, and fans. Each unit has a small balcony or patio, and there's a small pool. Four units have air-con (US$65). This place is good for families.

*Hotel & Chalets Tangerí* (☎ 643-3001, fax 643-3636) Doubles US$71. Here you'll find air-conditioned rooms with TVs and fridges. It also has some spacious chalets with three bedrooms and kitchens – they'll sleep up to eight for about US$140. There's a pool, and the grounds behind the hotel stretch down to the beach.

*Hotel Poseidon* (☎ 643-1642, e info@ hotel-poseidon.com, w www.hotel-poseidon .com) Doubles with fans US$80, with air-con US$115. This modern place has un-complicated, attractive rooms with hot-water baths. There's an elegant open-air restaurant, a pool, bar, Jacuzzi, and private parking. French, Spanish, English, and German are spoken.

**Top End** There are 44 pleasant air-conditioned rooms with hot water at *Hotel Cocal* (☎ 643-3067, fax 643-3082, e cocalcr@ racsa.co.cr) Doubles US$90 with breakfast. It also has two pools, a small casino, a good restaurant with ocean views, and a bar. The hotel brochures point out that the town disco is close by, which is an advantage or disadvantage depending on your point of view. Local tours are arranged.

**Hotel Copacabana** (☎ 643-1005, ☎/fax 643-3131, e hotcopa@racsa.co.cr, w www .hotelcopacabana.com) Doubles with fan/ air-con US$65/85, suites US$100-165. This Canadian-run hotel is near the beach. The owners will help arrange car rentals and tours to nearby national parks. There's a pool, restaurant, and sports bar with satellite TV and pool table. Standard rooms have fans and hot showers, and the air-conditioned suites with kitchenettes and private balconies sleep up to four people.

**Best Western Jacó Beach Resort** (☎ 643-1000, fax 643-3246, e jaco@bestwestern .co.cr, w www.bestwestern.co.cr/bwjaco.html) Rooms US$115. This is the biggest hotel in Jacó, featuring well over 100 rooms, and many Canadian charter groups stay here. It's a full-service beach resort, with bicycle, surfboard, kayak, boat, and car rentals. It has a restaurant, disco, casino, swimming pools, and sunbathing areas. All rooms are air-conditioned and have hot water.

**Hotel Jacó Fiesta** (☎ 643-3147, fax 643-3148, e jacofies@racsa.co.cr) Doubles/quads US$105/133. This is the other big resort hotel in town. It's slightly smaller but still has four pools, a casino, disco, tennis court, and various tours and rentals. The somewhat faded rooms have air-con and refrigerators, and they're often full with charter groups.

## Places to Stay – Playa Hermosa

About 4km south from Jacó on the Costanera are a few hotels offering good access to the surfing at Playa Hermosa.

**Cabinas Vista Hermosa** (☎ 643-3422) Doubles US$30. Beachfront cabins have kitchens and some can sleep up to eight. There's a restaurant, bar, and pool.

**Cabinas Las Olas** (☎/fax 643-3687, e lasolas@racsa.co.cr, w www.cabinaslas olas.com) Doubles US$40-65, larger rooms US$20 per person. The nice bungalows here have kitchens, fans, and hot water. Some larger rooms sleep up to seven. It has a pool and restaurant, and staff will give advice on, and arrange transportation to, the best local surfing and snorkeling spots.

**Safari Surf** (☎/fax 643-3508) Doubles US$30. Next door to Cabinas Las Olas, this place offers movies and laundry service.

**Cabinas Rancho Grande** (☎ 643-3529) Rooms with bath US$10 per person. Run by a friendly couple from Florida, this place has cane-paneled rooms, including a cute A-frame room on the top floor. Some rooms sleep up to seven and share a communal kitchen.

Just north of the cabins are several more upscale options. **Terraza del Pacífico** (☎ 643-3222, fax 643-3424, e terraza@racsa.co.cr) Rooms US$85. This place has modern, spacious rooms with ocean views, air-con, TVs, and hot water. The hotel has children's and adults' pools, a bar, and a good Italian restaurant. The listed rate is good for up to three people.

**Villa Hermosa Hotel** (☎ 643-3373, fax 643-3506, e taycole@racsa.co.cr, w www .surf-hermosa.com) Doubles/triples/up to 5 US$35/45/55. This smaller place offers rooms with air-con and kitchenettes. There's a garden-shaded pool.

**Hotel Fuego del Sol** (☎ 643-3737, fax 643-3736, e fuegos@costarica.net, w www .fuegodelsol.com) Doubles US$85. Nearby, this is a small resortlike complex that includes a pool, bar, and gym. The eighteen rooms come with air-con, hot water coffeemakers, and telephones. Tours, beach parties, and transportation to surfing spots can be arranged.

## Places to Eat

Plenty of restaurants busily cater to the crowds in the dry season but may falter a bit in the rainy months. New ones open (and close) every year. A stroll through Jacó in the high season can result in an assault of billboards advertising the 'best' places to eat. Shoestring travelers will find that the set menus at the sodas and restaurants frequented by locals are the best deals for budget meals.

**Soda Nenas** Set meals US$3-5. In the center, this place has good casados.

**Soda Amistad** Meals US$1.50-3. Open 7am-9pm Tues-Sat, 7am-2pm Sun. At the far south end, this cheap soda attracts mainly locals and has both good service and good meals. A bargain!

**Restaurant Emily** Open all day. Next to the cheap Cabinas Emily, this place has great local food at reasonable prices.

**La Hacienda** (☎ 643-3191) Meals US$3 and up. This place serves sandwiches and burgers for around US$3, while the steaks and seafood begin at US$5

There are a number of pizzerias, most with wood-burning ovens; try the popular *Rioasis*, in the central part of town.

*Calinche's Wishbone Eatery* Meals US$5-10. Overseen by the charming Calinche, this is a good pizza choice and has a spacious, shady patio. Pita sandwiches, stuffed potatoes, and grilled seafood are also specialties.

*Sunrise Breakfast Place* (☎ 643-3361) Meals US$4-7. This serves generous, North American–style breakfasts, as does the Canadian-run (and reader-recommended) *Chatty Cathy's*, which is a good deal for both breakfast and lunch. Note that Chatty Cathy's is in a 2nd-floor location, up a set of stairs, and is closed weekends; the restaurant below it sells overpriced breakfasts.

*Banana Café* Meals US$2-10. This is good for 'natural' breakfasts, sold all day, as well as snacks, sandwiches and a variety of meals.

*Restaurant El Jardín* (☎ 643-3050) Meals average US$5. Mainly tico and some international food is served here.

*Restaurant El Bohío* Meals average US$4-8. This place is quite good and has a sea view. It's open for breakfast and serves dinners (shrimp or lobster at US$18).

*Cuzco Bar* (☎ 643-3771) Meals average US$7. This place sells authentic Peruvian-style seafood.

*Susie Q's* Dishes US$6-9. Open 6pm-9pm, closed Mon. Decent ribs and barbecue dinners can be had here.

*Restaurant La Ostra* Meals US$6-10. This is a good midpriced seafood place.

*Los Faroles* (☎ 643-3167) is also currently popular for seafood and meat dinners.

*Restaurant Rueda del Mar* Meals US$5-10. This big barn of a place at the south end serves tico and international food and is popular with tour groups.

*Heladería y Mariscos El Barco* Meals average US$7.50. An unusual combination – one side of this restaurant serves ice creams and shakes, while the other does good seafood. Between the two of them, they do a brisk business.

*Pancho Villas* (☎ 643-3571) Meals average US$8. This place serves Mexican food, but I think the steaks and international food are better (I live an hour's drive

from Mexico, so I'm picky about Mexican food). It's very popular and gets crowded late on Saturday, when the bar upstairs can get rowdy.

The best hotels have decent restaurants open to the public.

## Entertainment

There are several dance clubs. Note that the ones in the center are very loud on Friday and Saturday night and are not places to go if you want to talk. Any hotel within two or three blocks is within reach of the booming music, so if this is a problem for you, find a hotel farther away. In this fast-changing town, it's definitely worth asking and walking around to find the latest hot spots. Several hotels have a disco and/or casino.

*Disco La Central* (☎ 643-3076) This hip place for foreign travelers is in the middle of town. It has had a recent reputation for drug-related troubles.

*Bar El Zarpe* (☎ 643-3473) Inside the Plaza Jacó in the north end of town, this is an air-conditioned bar with a mix of travelers and locals. There's a dart board, sports bar with satellite TV, and Californian and Mexican food.

*La Bruja* Closer to the center, this is a quieter place.

*Beatles Bar* The Fab Four set the tone for this famous bar, which was extremely popular in San José for years. Now it has moved down to the coast where they hope to do equally well with their seven TVs, pool table, and, of course, rock and roll.

*Club Ole* This is a very loud but mellow bar.

*Pancho Villas* If you're still going after 2am, this restaurant is a popular place to meet and eat.

## Getting There & Away

**Bus** Direct buses from the Coca-Cola terminal in San José leave at 7:30am, 10:30am, and 3:30pm daily. The journey takes about 2½ to three hours and costs about US$2. Buses between either San José or Puntarenas and Quepos could drop you off at the entrance to Jacó. Buses tend to be full on weekends, when extra buses may run, but get to the terminal early if possible.

Buses leave Jacó for San José at 5am, 11am, and 3pm daily. Departures for Puntarenas are daily at 6am, 9am, noon, and 4:30pm; and for Quepos at 6am, noon, 3:30pm, and 5:30pm. It's best to inquire locally, especially for Puntarenas and Quepos departures, which are the most subject to change. You can phone for bus information in Jacó (☎ 643-3135) at the bus ticket office in Plaza Jacó. Most buses stop at or leave from here, but ask about other stops. Most hotels know the current timetable.

The Gray Line bus stop and office is in the Best Western hotel.

**Taxi** Taxi 30-30 (☎ 643-3030) will get you anywhere – for a price.

## JACÓ TO QUEPOS

The paved Costanera continues southeast from Jacó to Quepos, 65km away. The road parallels the Pacific coastline but comes down to it only a few times. The route has a few good beaches (some with good surf), which are rather off the beaten track and most easily visited by car, though you could get off buses going to Quepos or Manuel Antonio and walk down to the beach.

**Esterillos Oeste, Esterillos Centro**, and **Esterillos Este** are about 22km, 25km, and 30km southeast of Jacó, respectively; all are a couple of kilometers off the Costanera. Between them, the Playa Esterillos stretches for several deserted kilometers, and there are several surfing areas. The Esterillos area is undiscovered and little visited; there are a few cheap and basic *cabinas* and camping areas that are used by surfers for off-the-beaten-path relaxation.

*Auberge du Pélican* (☎/fax 779-9236, e aubergepelican@racsa.co.cr) Doubles US$30-40. This French Canadian–run place has been recommended by readers. There are 12 simple, attractive rooms, most with private baths. Two rooms are wheelchair-accessible. All have fans and are very clean. There's hot water, a pool, and a restaurant, and boat tours can be arranged. There's a small runway near the hotel, and air transport from San José is available for US$200 in a plane seating five.

*Fleur de Lys* (☎ 779-9117, ☎/fax 779-9141, e business@racsa.co.cr) Doubles US$60. Another nice little place, also French Canadian, this place has 10 cabins of various sizes, all with hot showers and fans. There's a restaurant.

Infrequently visited beaches beyond Esterillos include Playa Bejuco (good surfing) and Playa Palma, both reached by short side roads from the Costanera. *Hotel El Delfín* (☎ 779-9246, ☎/fax 770-8308) Doubles US$45. At Playa Bejuco, this sleepy little hotel has rooms with private baths (hot water) and balconies with sea views. Some rooms are air-conditioned, and there's a beachfront restaurant and pool.

**Parrita**, a bustling little banana town on the river of the same name, 40km from Jacó, has a couple of basic hotels, many restaurants and sodas, two gas stations and two banks. *Beso del Viento B&B* (☎ 779-9674, fax 779-9675, e bdviento@racsa.co.cr, w www.besodelviento.com) Doubles US$70, extra people up to six US$11.50 each. At the east end of Parrita, you'll see a sign for this place, which has been recommended by at least one reader. All four apartments have private tiled hot baths, kitchens, and fans. There's a pool, and the uncrowded beach is nearby. Kayaks, bikes, and horses can be rented. French and English are spoken.

After Parrita, the coastal road is now well inland and continues so until Quepos. The road has been paved all the way, although some sections have bad potholes, and there are several rickety one-way bridges to watch out for. African oil-palm plantations stretch for several kilometers before Quepos is reached, and little identical-looking plantation villages are regularly passed. Ten kilometers east of the easternmost gas station in Parrita is the village of Pocares (not marked on any maps), where a side road turns inland to the Rainmaker project (see the boxed text). In 15 more kilometers you'll come to the bridge at the northern entrance of Quepos.

## QUEPOS

This town gets its name from the Quepoa Indian tribe, a subgroup of the Borucas, who inhabited the area at the time of the conquest. The Quepoa people's numbers declined because of diseases brought by the Europeans, warfare with other Indian groups, and because they were sold as slaves. By the end of the 19th century, no pure-blooded Quepoa were left, and the area began to be colonized by farmers from the highlands.

## Rainmaker

Rainmaker, an exciting and unique project, lets visitors walk through the rainforest canopy on a series of suspension bridges attached to the largest trees in the forest. Fabulous! There are aerial walkways like this in the Peruvian Amazon and in Asia, but this was the first in Central America.

Reaching the suspension bridges is almost as interesting as going up into the canopy. From the parking lot/orientation area, visitors walk up a magical rainforest canyon with a pristine stream tumbling down the rocks. To avoid damaging the delicately beautiful canyon bottom, a wooden boardwalk and series of bridges were built along the canyon floor, crossing the stream a number of times and giving lovely views of cascades and waterfalls. After about half a kilometer, the base of the walkway is reached, and visitors climb up several hundred steps to a tree platform, from which the first of six suspension bridges spans the treetops to another platform. The longest span is about 90m, and the total walkway is about 250m long. At the highest point, you are some 20 stories above the forest floor.

In addition to the canyon boardwalk and aerial walkway, there are short interpretive trails that enable the visitor to identify some of the local plants, and some long and strenuous trails into the heart of the 2000-hectare preserve that Rainmaker encompasses.

Currently, visits with professional naturalist guides leave hotels in Manuel Antonio and Quepos daily except Sunday; reservations can be made at most hotels or by calling their office (see Quepos map; ☎ 375-7700, fax 288-0155, ℮ reservations@rainmaker-costarica.com, ⓦ www.rainmaker -costarica.com). Tours, including a light tropical breakfast, cost US$45 per person.

Visitors should come with realistic expectations. This is not a zoo, and you are unlikely to spot large numbers of mammals, though you'll see plenty of birds, plants, and insects. Binoculars are invaluable for watching the birds. Bring sun protection and water.

Rainmaker is reached by turning inland at the large water tower on the Costanera at the north end of the village of Pocares (10km east of Parrita or 15km west of Quepos). From the turnoff, it is 6km or 7km to the parking area.

Quepos first came to prominence as a banana-exporting port. Its importance has declined appreciably in recent decades because of disease that has severely reduced banana crops. African oil-palms (which stretch away in dizzying rows in the fields around Quepos) have replaced bananas as the major local crop. Processed into oils used in cosmetics, machine oils, and cooking fat, the finished product is much less bulky than bananas.

Consequently, Quepos has not been able to recover as a major shipping port. Instead, it has become important as a sportfishing center and as the nearest town to Parque Nacional Manuel Antonio, which is only 7km away and one of the most-visited national parks in Costa Rica. There are regularly scheduled flights and buses from San José, and Quepos has gradually developed a new economic niche for itself as a year-round tourism destination, with tour companies, bars, and cafés rounding out the attractions.

## Orientation & Information

The town of Quepos is the gateway to Parque Nacional Manuel Antonio – you have to go through the town to reach the park. There are plenty of hotels and services both in Quepos (described here) and all the way along the road to the park (described in the next section).

Banco Nacional de Costa Rica (☎ 777-0113) changes US dollars and traveler's checks and is extremely air-conditioned – a cool wait. Banco Popular (☎ 777-0344) allows cash withdrawals on Visa cards and has an ATM; it has chairs to wait in and a TV often showing cartoons. Banco de Costa Rica also has a branch and ATM here; its TV favors sports.

Lynch Tourist Service (☎ 777-0161, 777-1170, fax 777-1571, ℮ lyntur@racsa.co.cr, ⓦ www.lynchtravel.com) will change US dollars and specializes in making all local arrangements you need, and reserves places elsewhere in the country and sells international air tickets. The old information center

# QUEPOS

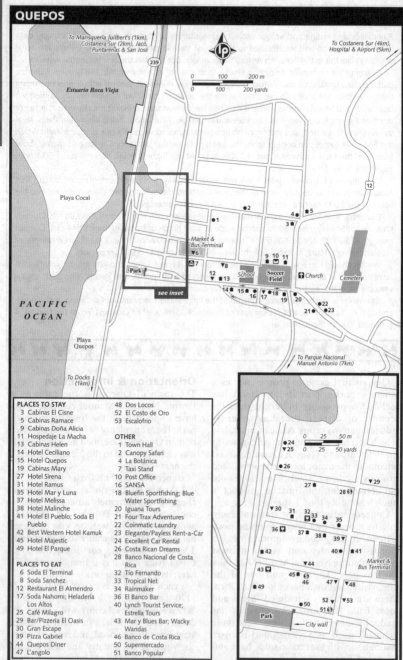

**PLACES TO STAY**
3 Cabinas El Cisne
5 Cabinas Ramace
9 Cabinas Doña Alicia
11 Hospedaje La Macha
13 Cabinas Helen
14 Hotel Ceciliano
15 Hotel Quepos
19 Cabinas Mary
27 Hotel Sirena
31 Hotel Ramus
35 Hotel Mar y Luna
37 Hotel Melissa
38 Hotel Malinche
41 Hotel El Pueblo; Soda El
   Pueblo
42 Best Western Hotel Kamuk
45 Hotel Majestic
49 Hotel El Parque

**PLACES TO EAT**
6 Soda El Terminal
8 Soda Sanchez
12 Restaurant El Almendro
17 Soda Nahomi; Heladería
   Los Altos
25 Café Milagro
29 Bar/Pizzeria El Oasis
30 Gran Escape
39 Pizza Gabriel
44 Quepos Diner
47 L'angolo

48 Dos Locos
52 El Costo de Oro
53 Escalofrio

**OTHER**
1 Town Hall
2 Canopy Safari
4 La Botánica
7 Taxi Stand
10 Post Office
16 SANSA
18 Bluefin Sportfishing; Blue
   Water Sportfishing
20 Iguana Tours
21 Four Trax Adventures
22 Coinmatic Laundry
23 Elegante/Payless Rent-a-Car
24 Excellent Car Rental
26 Costa Rican Dreams
28 Banco Nacional de Costa
   Rica
32 Tio Fernando
33 Tropical Net
34 Rainmaker
36 El Banco Bar
40 Lynch Tourist Service;
   Estrella Tours
43 Mar y Blues Bar; Wacky
   Wandas
46 Banco de Costa Rica
50 Supermercado
51 Banco Popular

t La Buena Nota has moved to the Manuel Antonio road (see Information in the Manuel Antonio section, later in this chapter). Information is also available in the free English-language monthly magazine *Quepolandia*, which is found in many of the town's businesses.

Internet access is available at an increasing number of places in the center; Tropical Net (☎ 777-2436, 777-2460) is a good one, open 8:30am 'til whenever they close at night. Sandwiches are available.

The Hospital Dr Max Teran V (☎ 777-0922, ☎/fax 777-1398, fax 777-0020) provides emergency medical care for the Quepos/Manuel Antonio area. It's on the Costanera Sur en route to the airport. However, this hospital doesn't have a trauma center and seriously injured patients are evacuated to San José. A locally recommended physician is Dr Serrano (☎ 777-0808, 387-5595 cellular), who speaks some English. The Red Cross is at ☎ 777-0118.

Coinmatic Laundry is open 8am to noon and 1pm to 5pm, Monday to Saturday. Self-service is US$4.50 to wash and dry a 5kg load, or they'll do it for US$5.50.

**Dangers & Annoyances** The town's large number of easily spotted tourists has attracted thieves. In response, the Costa Rican authorities have greatly increased police presence in the area, but travelers should be careful to always lock hotel rooms and never leave cars unattended, except in guarded parking areas. Local kids will volunteer to watch your car for you in many places for a small fee. The area is far from dangerous, but the laid-back tropical beach atmosphere should not lull you into a false sense of security.

Note that the beaches in Quepos are not recommended for swimming because of pollution. Go over the hill to Manuel Antonio instead.

**Sportfishing**
Sportfishing is big in the Quepos area. Offshore fishing is best from December to April, and sailfish are the big thing, though marlin, dorado, wahoo, amberjack, and yellowfin tuna are also caught. You can fish inshore year-round; mackerel, jack, and roosterfish are the main attractions. Places chartering sportfishing boats may take you

out sightseeing, snorkeling, or diving if they don't have any anglers.

A boat for a full day of fishing can cost from US$450 to US$1200, depending on the size and speed of the boat, the experience of the skipper, and whether lunch, drinks, fishing gear, and bait are included. Most boats can take three anglers, and a few can take six. In the December-to-April season, many boats are reserved well in advance. Individuals looking to join up with a group of anglers can, if they call around, find a spot on a boat for about US$150.

A good place to find out what's going on is the Gran Escape bar and restaurant, which is locally regarded as an anglers' hangout. Because fishing is so expensive, this is a good place to come if you are looking to split costs with a fishing partner. If you prefer to talk directly with the charters, call the following:

Bluefin Sportfishing Charters (☎ 777-1676, 777-0674, e bluefin@racsa.co.cr, w www.bluefin sportfishing.com)

Blue Water Sportfishing (☎ 777-1596)

Costa Rican Dreams (Richard and Nancy Bebo; ☎/fax 777-0593)

High Tec Fishing (☎ 777-3465, 388-6617 cellular)

Luna Tours (in Hotel Kamuk; ☎/fax 777-0725)

**Organized Tours**
**Iguana Tours** *(☎/fax 777-1262, e info@ iguanatours.com, w www.iguanatours.com)* arranges park tours and one-day river-rafting, sea-kayaking, and dolphin-watching trips. It also books Ríos Tropicales river trips (see Organized Tours in the Getting Around chapter). **Estrella Tours** *(☎/fax 777-1286)* specializes in bike tours and rentals, horseback riding, and sea kayaking, but arranges a variety of other tours as well. Steve Wofford of **Planet Dolphin** *(☎ 777-1647, e dolphncr@racsa.co.cr, w www .planetdolphin.com)* is a good contact for dolphin-watching tours, which start at US$65 for four hours, including snacks and snorkeling. Look around for other little tour and rental companies – they're there. **Four Trax Adventures** *(☎ 777-1829)* has guided four-hour tours on ATVs for US$95 per person. **Brisas del Nara** *(☎ 779-1235, fax 779-1049, e brisasnara@racsa .co.cr, w www.tourbrisasnara.com)* has been locally recommended for horse tours.

The farm is in Londres, about a 20-minute drive inland.

## Places to Stay

Hotels tend to be full on weekends in the dry season. They are cheaper here than closer towards Manuel Antonio. You can get substantial wet-season discounts; rates listed are high-season weekend rates. More and more hotels accept credit cards, but those that do often add a 7% surcharge.

**Budget** Rooms are basic boxes with fans at *Hotel Majestic* Rooms US$4 per person. This is the cheapest place in town. Several shoestring travelers have told me it's OK.

*Hospedaje La Macha* (☎ 777-0216) Rooms without bath US$7.50 per person, doubles with bath US$18. This simple and clean place has rooms with fans.

*Cabinas Doña Alicia* (☎ 777-0419) Doubles without bath US$8, rooms with bath US$9 (one double bed) & US$15 (two beds). The rooms here are clean.

*Cabinas Mary* (☎ 777-0128) Singles/doubles US$9/15. The clean, acceptable rooms here have private baths; so do those at *Hotel El Parque* (☎ 777-0063) and *Hotel Quepos* (☎ 777-0274).

*Hotel Ramus* (☎ 777-0245) Doubles US$18. Also known as 'Hector's place,' this hotel is a little dark but is central and has character. Rooms have baths.

*Hotel Mar y Luna* (☎ 777-0394) Doubles US$16. Near the Ramus, this one is friendly and festooned with plants, but it has rather small rooms.

*Hotel Melissa* (☎ 777-0025) Rooms US$9 per person. This place has a balcony to read on and clean rooms. Travelers have recommended it.

*Hotel El Pueblo* (☎ 777-1003) Doubles without/with air-con US$20/35. This hotel's location, right next to the bus station, is a minor convenience in a town this small. The 24-hour bar-restaurant downstairs is fun and noisy and brings a lot of traffic through the hotel (ie, lock your doors and windows). Rooms have fans and private baths; two rooms have air-con and TVs.

On the start of the road to the Costanera Sur, *Cabinas El Cisne* (☎ 777-0719) and *Cabinas Ramace* (☎ 777-0590) each offer parking and rooms with private hot baths and fridges for about US$20 double.

*Cabinas Helen* (☎ 777-0504) Rooms US$20. This friendly place has decent rooms with private baths, refrigerators, fans, and hot water. Rooms sleep up to three people

**Mid-Range** *Hotel Malinche* (☎ 777-0093) Singles/doubles with cold bath & fan US$14/20, doubles with air-con, hot bath & TV US$45. This is a good choice for various budgets. It has older rooms with private cold showers and fans for a fair price. For a bit more, newer and nicer rooms have private hot showers and air-con. Several readers have reported much lower prices outside the high season.

*Hotel Ceciliano* (☎/fax 777-0192) Doubles US$25. These clean rooms all have private baths, fans, and hot water.

**Top End** Breakfast is included at *Hotel Sirena* (☎ 777-0528, fax 777-0165) Doubles US$55. Here you'll get modern air-conditioned rooms, private hot showers, a restaurant, and pool. The hotel arranges horse tours and sportfishing.

*Best Western Hotel Kamuk* (☎ 777-0379, fax 777-0258, ⓔ info@kamuk.co.cr, ⓦ www .kamuk.co.cr) Standard rooms US$65, balcony rooms US$75-95. This is the most upscale hotel in downtown Quepos. All rooms have air-con, hot water, and phones. Amenities include a bar, 3rd-floor restaurant (with good sunset views), coffee shop, pool, and casino. There are standard rooms and better rooms, with balcony and ocean view, which vary in price depending on the size of the room. Rates include breakfast.

## Places to Eat

Cheap snacks and casados are available at the market and near the bus station. The following have meals for US$2-3. *Soda El Terminal*, at the bus terminal, has cheerful staff and is recommended. *Soda El Pueblo*, under the hotel of that name, is open 24 hours. *El Costa de Oro* is a good value and locally popular. *Soda Sanchez* is another budget option. *Soda Nahomi* is at the east end of town on the way out to Manuel Antonio beach.

*Restaurant El Almendro* Dishes US$2.50-6. Open 24 hrs. This tico place has a wide selection and plenty of tables; while quiet during the day, it does a busy trade late at night when it might be all that's open.

Just west of the market is *Pizza Gabriel*, with good individual pizzas for US$3 to US$5.

*Café Milagro (☎/fax 777-1707)* Open 6am-10pm daily. This establishment recently opened another café on the Manuel Antonio road. It serves great cappuccino, espresso, and baked treats and is a nice place to relax and read. Newspapers and magazines in English are available.

*Quepos Diner* Dishes US$3-7. This American-style diner serves breakfast, lunch, and dinner.

*Escalofrio (☎ 777-0833)* Ice cream US$1.50, meals US$3-6. Open 2:30 pm 'til whenever; closed Mon. This place is said to have the best ice cream in the area; it offers 20 flavors and a spacious seating area. It also serves espresso, cappuccino, spaghetti, and Italian food.

*Heladería Los Altos* Desserts US$1-2.50. From a scoop to a sundae, you'll find a good selection of ice creams here.

*Gran Escape (☎/fax 777-0395)* Dishes US$4-12. Open 6am-11pm daily. This place is popular with sportfishing visitors ('You hook 'em, we cook 'em,' says the sign) and other tourists and is one of the more lively bars. It serves tasty and varied midpriced food that's a good value.

*Dos Locos (☎ 777-1526)* Dishes US$4-14. Open 7am-11pm Mon-Sat, 11am-10pm Sun. This is a very popular and recommended Mexican-food eatery. It has live bands (mainly rock and blues) some nights.

*Bar/Pizzería El Oasis* Dishes US$5-9. Open 5:30pm-11:30pm, closed Wed. This place serves authentic and recommended Italian food.

*L'Angolo* Dishes US$3 and up. This excellent Italian deli has sandwiches and other treats to go and has a tiny, recommended café. Three indoor tables are air-conditioned, and a couple outdoor tables are usually available. This place is a good choice for picnic lunches.

*Marisquería Juilbert's* Dishes US$3-10. This place is about 1km north of town, and many locals say it has the best seafood.

## Entertainment

Popular places for a beer include the outdoor *Mar y Blues Bar* for good music, and the air-conditioned *Wacky Wanda's (☎ 777-2574)* next door. Both have food and are popular

with anglers. *El Banco Bar (☎/fax 777-0478)* is good for music and satellite sports TV, *Gran Escape Bar* is where to go to swap fishing stories, and *Tío Fernando* is a nice choice for a quiet drink. The *Hotel Kamuk* has a casino.

## Shopping

*Café Milagro* This café sells roasted coffee to go, as well as fine cigars and other assorted souvenirs.

*La Botánica (☎ 777-1223)* Organically cultivated herbs, spices, and teas, which make good gifts, are sold here. The street west of the SANSA office has several souvenir and clothing shops.

## Getting There & Away

**Air** Lynch Tourist Service (☎ 777-0161, 777-1170, fax 777-1571, e lyntur@racsa.co.cr) is the Travelair agent and sells all airline tickets. The SANSA agent (☎ 777-0683) is near the soccer field. The San José-Quepos flight takes 20 minutes, and schedules change often. Between them, the airlines will have several flights a day from San José, with some continuing on to Palmar Sur or elsewhere south of Quepos.

Make reservations and pay for your ticket well in advance to ensure a confirmed space. Reconfirm your flight as often as you can. Flights are often full, with a waiting list.

It's also possible to charter light planes to Quepos through Lynch Tourist Service, which will also arrange airport transfers for US$3 from anywhere in the Quepos-Manuel Antonio area. The airport is 5km from Quepos.

**Bus** Buses leave San José several times a day from the Coca-Cola terminal. Direct express buses leave for Manuel Antonio (US$5, 3½ hours) at 6am, 9:30am, noon, and 6pm, and regular services to Quepos (five hours) leave at 7am, 10am, 2pm, and 4pm. You can also get here from Puntarenas, Jacó, San Isidro, and Dominical.

The ticket office (☎ 777-0263) in the Quepos bus terminal is open 7am to 11am and 1pm to 5pm Monday to Saturday, 7am to 1pm Sunday. There are regular services to San José at 5am, 8am, 2pm, and 4pm daily (US$3). Direct buses leave four times a day (US$5) from Manuel Antonio (see below) and pick up passengers in Quepos before continuing directly to San José. In the high season, bus tickets to San José are bought days in advance – buy a ticket as early as you can.

Buses to Puntarenas (US$2.75, 3½ hours) via Jacó (US$1.50, two hours) leave at 4:30am, 7:30am, 10:30am, and 3pm. There are 11 daily buses to Parrita and six to Jacó. Buses leave for San Isidro (via Dominical) at 5am and 1:30pm. Buses go to Dominical and on to Uvita at 9:30am and 4pm and to various local communities in the agricultural country surrounding Quepos.

Buses for Manuel Antonio leave about 15 times a day between about 5am and 9:30pm, returning from Manuel Antonio as soon as they arrive. There are many more buses in the dry season than in the wet season. The 20-minute trip costs less than US50¢.

**Boat** Planet Dolphin (☎ 777-1647) operates water-taxi services to anywhere you need to go on the coast. It also advertises dolphin-watching and snorkeling cruises. The boats depart from the Quepos dock.

**Taxi** Quepos Taxi (☎ 777-0425, 777-0734) will take you to Manuel Antonio for about US$5.

### Getting Around
Elegante/Payless Rent-a-Car (☎ 777-0115) has an office in Quepos, though it's best to arrange car rentals in advance in San José to guarantee getting a car. Elegante will deliver your car to the airport by advance arrangement. Also try Alamo (☎ 777-3344) and Excellent (777-3052) car rentals.

## QUEPOS TO MANUEL ANTONIO
From the port of Quepos, the road swings inland for 7km before reaching the beaches of Manuel Antonio village and the national park. The road goes over a series of hills with picturesque views of the ocean. Along this road, every hilltop vista has been commandeered by a hotel that lists 'ocean views' as a major attraction. Certainly, these views are often magnificent. Some of these hotels are so pleasant and comfortable that for some, spending the whole day there's an attractive alternative to visiting the nearby national park.

This is perhaps the most publicized stretch of coast in Costa Rica. Visitors might be expecting pristine nature, but the Manuel Antonio area has been discovered by the masses and is no longer the unspoiled gem that it was as recently as the 1980s. The proliferation of hotels in an area where the sewage system is primitive at best has led to serious threats of pollution to the once pristine beaches. The famous national park can be overwhelmed by visitors, and hotel prices tend to average much higher here than in the rest of the country.

Note that the road is steep, winding, and very narrow. There are almost no places to pull over in the event of an emergency. Drive and walk with extreme care.

### Information
See La Buena Nota in the Manuel Antonio Information section, later in this chapter, for a good source of tourist information.

At this writing, there are three Internet cafés along the road: the Cantina Internet Café, opposite the Costa Verde hotel; TicoNet, in the Centro Comercial Si Como No; and the Internet in the El Dorado Mojado hotel. Many hotels have Internet access for their guests.

Super Jenny is the best grocery and sundries store on this stretch of road.

### Things to See & Do
Massage is available in the better hotels. A recommended spa is the **Sea Glass Spa** near the Villas Nicolas; they pamper clients with papaya body polishes, hot-stone massages, coconut body scrubs, and other tropical therapies. Reservations are essential and your hotel will arrange this.

*Equus Stables (☎ 777-0001)* has horse rental.

### Language Courses
*Escuela de Idiomas D'Amore (☎/fax 777-1143, 777-0233, in the USA ☎ 323-912-0600,* e *damore@racsa.co.cr,* w *www.escuela damore.com)* This school has received enthusiastic reader recommendations and offers Spanish immersion courses at all levels. Classes are small, and local homestays can be arranged. Rates are comparable to those at schools in San José. The school is about 3.5km south of Quepos.

*Centro de Idiomas del Pacífico (☎ 777-0805, ☎/fax 777-0010,* e *info@cipacifico .com,* w *www.cipacifico.com)* This school advertises personalized Spanish tutorials; the proprietors are personable and the school seems well run. The staff can offer a variety of housing options, and they make it easy to arrive and settle in.

## Places to Stay

The hotels below are listed in the order that they are passed as you travel from Quepos to Manuel Antonio. Most are top-end hotels, but there are a few mid-range options as well. Quoted rates include tax for the high and dry season (December to Easter).

Substantial discounts (around 40% is not unusual) are available in the wet season, euphemistically called the 'green season.' Getting reservations is a must for weekends and sometimes midweek in the dry months.

Many of these hotels (even the most expensive ones) will not accept credit cards or personal checks, so you need cash or traveler's checks. Ask about this when making reservations. When credit cards are accepted, a 7% surcharge may be added. Most of the places are small and intimate – these are not big beachside resorts.

**Cabinas Pedro Miguel** (☎ 777-0035, fax 777-0279) Doubles US$30, cabins US$60. This place is up the hill out of Quepos, a short way out of town on the right. It has fairly basic rooms with baths, plus cabins that sleep three to five people, with kitchenettes. The place is family-run and friendly, and meals are available.

**Hotel Plinio** (☎ 777-0055, fax 777-0558, e plinio@racsa.co.cr) Doubles US$70, suites from US$128. Here you'll find air-conditioned rooms and suites, some on two levels. There's hot water, the rooms are attractive, and there are plenty of nooks for hammocks and relaxing. Breakfast is included, and both the restaurant and hotel are recommended. The grounds boast two pools and several kilometers of trails into the forest. There's a 17m-high lookout tower along the trails. The restaurant and tower are open to the public, and the staff is friendly.

**Mimo's Hotel** (☎/fax 777-0054, e h mimos@racsa.co.cr, w www.hotelmimos .com) Doubles US$75-90 with breakfast. Mimo's has spacious rooms (with fans or air-con), kitchenettes, cable TV, hot water, and a pool.

**Hotel Mono Azul** (☎ 777-1548, ☎/fax 777-1954, e monoazul@racsa.co.cr, w www

.monoazul.com) Standard singles/doubles/triples/quads US$53/58/63/70. Deluxe rooms add US$11.50. This well-recommended place is friendly, comfortable, and a good value. The Mono Azul ('Blue Monkey') is home to 'Kids Saving the Rainforest' (KSTR), started by two local schoolchildren who were concerned about the endangered *mono titi* (Central American squirrel monkey). Many of these monkeys were run over on the narrow road to the national park, or electrocuted on the electric wires while crossing the roads, so the KSTR purchased and erected seven monkey bridges across the road (you can see them, often in use, as you drive to the park). The hotel also has a sloth rehabilitation program, nursing baby sloths that have been abandoned on injured. Ten percent of the hotel receipts are donated to the KSTR. Guests can use an environmental research library (which also has children's and spiritual books), photograph baby sloths, buy souvenirs from the KSTR art gallery, and generally feel good about learning more about the rainforest.

The hotel has 20 rooms; the standard rooms have private hot showers and ceiling fans, and the deluxe rooms also have air-con and a patio. For an extra US$5, you can add a TV to your room. There are two pools, sunning decks, a game room with cable TV, a small gym, Internet access, and an excellent restaurant open 6am to 10pm. The menu features both tico and American food (the owners are from the USA), and folks from other hotels come to eat here – always a good sign. They always have a vegetarian selection and also have pizza, for take out or delivery. Local tours and activities can be arranged. And finally, co-owner Jennifer Rice is a minister and is happy to plan a wedding for you and then make it official.

**Hotel California** (☎ 777-1234, ☎/fax 777-1062, e hotelcal@racsa.co.cr, w www.hotel -california.com) Standard/deluxe rooms US$111/133. Look for a driveway to the left to find this quiet hotel, which is well set back from the road and has 10km of hiking trails into rainforest surrounding the property. The trails lead to waterfalls and an observation tower. The 22 rooms, completely renovated in 2001, are cool, spacious and comfortable. They all feature hardwood floors, light walls with attractive wall hangings, air-con, cable TV, telephone, minibar, and a large bathroom with hot shower. The deluxe rooms are slightly larger and have a private terrace with lovely sea views. There's a striking pool with a waterfall, next to which is the hotel restaurant, offering the same sea view and good food. Their breakfasts are especially scrumptious and can be delivered to your room.

*Hotel Villa Teca* (☎ 777-1117) Rooms US$75. On the other side of the main road from Hotel California, another driveway leads to this place, which has 40 air-conditioned rooms with balconies. Rates include breakfast.

*Hotel Las Tres Banderas* (☎ 777-1284, 777-1521, fax 777-1478, e banderas@racsa .co.cr, w www.hotel-tres-banderas.com/costa -rica) Singles/doubles US$64/70, suites US$110 (up to four people). About 2.5km south of Quepos, this recommended place is owned by a couple of friendly Polish-born guys who are US citizens and live in Costa Rica – hence 'Tres Banderas,' or three flags. There's an attractively landscaped pool with a waterfall, sun terrace, balcony overlooking the pool, and a huge Jacuzzi. Alongside is a nice wooden bar named Pod Papugami after a popular Polish song (that translates to 'Beneath the Parrots'). Eleven spotless rooms and three suites have air-con, large bathrooms, hot water, cable TVs, elegant furnishings (including a writing desk – something that's missing in many Costa Rican hotels), and private balconies. Each suite also has a bathtub, microwave, and fridge. There's a private dining room where meals can be prepared on request for guests.

*La Colina* (☎ 777-0231, e lacolina@ racsa.co.cr, w www.lacolina.com) Rooms/ suites US$57/94, including breakfast. Just down the road from Tres Banderas, this is a friendly place built by a young couple from Colorado; it's related to the La Colina in Monteverde. They have a small but popular public restaurant, a pool with swim-up bar, and live music on some weekends. There are five small but clean and attractive air-conditioned rooms with hot water and fans, and five air-conditioned suites with cable TV and small private terraces with good sea views. One suite without air-con is US$10 cheaper. The included breakfasts are big and good, and readers have liked this place.

*Hotel Flor Blanca* (☎ 777-0032, ☎/fax 777-1633) Doubles with fan/air-con US$39/49.

This place has simple, clean rooms with private bath and fridge; while they aren't special, they do offer a good value for the area.

*Tulemar Bungalows* (☎ 777-1325, fax 777-1579, e tulemar@racsa.co.cr, w www.tulemar .com) Bungalows US$272, including breakfast. This luxurious place has 14 modern, air-conditioned octagonal bungalows that sleep up to four people. Each has huge picture windows with great views of forest and ocean, and the bungalows are well separated for privacy. They all have bedrooms with two queen-size beds, sitting rooms with two fold-out queen-size beds, well-equipped kitchenettes, telephones, TVs, VCRs, and hair dryers. There's a splendid infinity-edge pool with a snack bar, or you can hike a 15-minute private trail through forest to the beach, where kayaks and snorkeling gear are available free to guests.

*Hotel Divisimar* (☎ 777-0371, fax 777-0525,) Doubles US$65-85, suite US$100, US$15 additional person. This hotel has a pool, whirlpool, and restaurant set in a pleasant garden. There are a dozen standard rooms, another 12 superior rooms, and a master suite. All units are air-conditioned and have plenty of hot water. The hotel is popular with affluent ticos as well as with foreign tourists. Horseback, sea kayak, and fishing tours are available.

Just beyond the Divisimar, a side road heads to the next three places, which are among the region's most exclusive.

*Hotel La Mariposa* (☎ 777-0355, 777-0456, fax 777-0050, e mariposa@racsa.co.cr, w www.lamariposa.com) Rooms US$151-175, villas & suites US$227. This internationally acclaimed hotel was the area's first luxury hotel, and it has grown from its original 10 luxurious private villas into a complex of about 40 units, many with splendid views. Murals, flowers, hammocks, and balconies are here for the enjoyment of the guests, and there are three pools and an expensive restaurant. Staff will arrange all the usual activities.

. *Makanda by the Sea* (☎ 777-0442, fax 777-1032, e makanda@racsa.co.cr, w www .makanda.com) Studios US$232, villas US$309-350 single or double (US$29 additional person). About 1km down a very steep gravel road, this place is memorable for peaceful luxury and attentive, helpful staff. There are nine contemporary studios and villas in a rainforest setting, with good chances of seeing monkeys during your stay. There's a beautiful infinity pool and Jacuzzi with a superb view. Villa 1 (the largest) has a vista that may take your breath away – the entire wall is open to the rainforest and the ocean. The unit has a full kitchen, dining area, king-size bed, balcony, hammock, and large bathroom with hot shower.

Several of the units can be interconnected to create personalized accommodations. Each one has a king-size bed, kitchenette, and bathroom. Some have a balcony and small Japanese garden; others have a terrace and air-con. There are also large individual villas similar in amenities and price to Villa 1, one with two bedrooms, another with a large Japanese garden, and a third in the forest near the pool. Children under 16 years are not allowed, and prepaid reservations are required (credit cards accepted). All rates include continental breakfast delivered to your room, and poolside lunch and dinner are available at extra cost in the high season (and possibly in other months). The restaurant is small and exclusive – reservations are required.

*El Parador* (☎ 777-1411, fax 777-1437, in the USA ☎ 800-648-1136, e parador@racsa .co.cr, w www.hotelparador.com) Doubles: standard US$200, deluxe US$230, premium US$287, junior suites US$350; extra person US$30. Breakfast included. About a kilometer down the steep unpaved road is this exclusive place, perhaps Manuel Antonio's most opulent hotel. It resembles a Spanish fortress on a hill overlooking the ocean, and may put you in mind of a James Bond movie. The formerly forested hilltop was dynamited away to build the 68-room, 10-suite hotel complete with private helicopter landing pad, two Jacuzzis, infinity swimming pool with swim-up bar, sauna, tennis court, and minigolf course. Inside are large conference rooms, a wine cellar and tasting room, dining rooms, a small fitness center, art gallery, and a library.

This is a place for security-conscious VIPs; the armed guards at the gatehouse wouldn't let me in without an escort. Inside the hotel, the lavish elegance is somewhat overpowering. A wall of photographs shows hotel owners and staff with the presidents and leaders of dozens of countries, including the USA. A priceless collection of 17th- and 18th-century European art, suits of Spanish armor, rare antique model boats, castle doors and gates from England, Italy and Spain – it's all a bit much!

Some guidebooks have gushed about how wonderful this place is. It may be right for some high-powered folks, but others may not feel comfortable. All rooms have a private terrace or balcony, cable TVs, telephones, air-con, hot water, and minibars. There are standard rooms; deluxe rooms with larger bathrooms and tubs; premium rooms with exceptional views; nine suites with whirlpool baths, sitting rooms, and coffeemakers; and a three-room presidential suite (US$780).

*El Dorado Mojado* (☎ 777-0368, fax 777-1248, e dorplaya@racsa.co.cr, w www .doradomojado.com) Rooms US$69-87, villas US$105. Back on the main Quepos-to-Manuel Antonio road, this place has four pleasant and spacious rooms with air-con and hot water and four villas with kitchens. There's a pool and an Internet café.

*Villas El Parque* (☎ 777-0096, fax 777-0538, e vparque@racsa.co.cr) Suites US$70-160. Just beyond El Dorado Mojado, this place has a variety of differently sized and appointed suites, some with kitchens.

*Villas Nicolas* (☎ 777-0481, fax 777-0451, e nicolas@racsa.co.cr, w www.villasnicolas .com) Doubles US$75-116. There are about 20 rooms with varying views and facilities. Some of them are gorgeous, and all are nicely decorated and have hot water, fans, and a balcony. There's a pool and Jacuzzi; the restaurant is open in the high season. The cheapest rooms lack ocean views, and some bigger rooms have hammocks and views (US$95) and kitchens (US$116).

*Si Como No* (☎ 777-0777, fax 777-1093, in the USA ☎ 800-237-8201, e sicomono@ racas.co.cr, w www.sicomono.com) Doubles: standard US$186, superior US$203, deluxe US$226, deluxe suites US$261 (US$29 additional person), honeymoon suites US$290. This fabulous, architecturally arresting hotel has been gently eased into the environment with minimal disturbance. The cathedral-like atrium lobby was built around existing trees, and few full-grown trees were cut during the construction of this 58-room hotel. If you can get past the stained-glass windows, viewing deck, and soothing atmosphere of the atrium, you'll find two lovely pools (one with a toboggan slide for kids; one for adults only; both with swim-up bars), a solar-heated Jacuzzi, and the delightful Rico Tico outdoor bar and grill with a varied US-style bar menu. For more upscale dining there's the Claro Que Si! Seafood restaurant with main courses in the US$10-20 range. There are trees everywhere, and birds and monkeys treat the property as if it were theirs, which, owner Jim Damalas insists, it is. He built the hotel to incorporate the rainforest, and it is one of the best places to stay in the area. In 1996, Si Como No won the grand prize out of a field of 60 contestants in Costa Rica's Biennial of Architecture competition, organized by the College of Architecture every two years.

Another amenity is the laser theater with a state-of-the-art sound system, where nature videos and Hollywood films are shown (and which can be used for conferences and presentations). This is free to guests and people dining in one of the restaurants. Rooms are insulated for comfort and conservation and use energy-efficient air-conditioners and fans, water is recycled into the landscaping system, and solar-heating panels are used. Everything has been done right! There's no sacrifice in comfort, however. Most rooms have a private balcony (a few have picture windows) with unobstructed views of forest below and ocean beyond, as well as queen- or king-size beds and spacious hot-water bathrooms. Standard rooms are spacious, superior suites have wet bars or kitchens and there are larger deluxe suites, some with memorably attractive stained-glass windows. Standard features in all units include minibars, hair dryers, telephones, alarm clocks, reading lamps, irons, coffeemakers and air-con. The rate includes breakfast, and children under 12 stay free. Four honeymoon suites have a private Jacuzzi.

Across the street is the hotel's Finas Naturales private rainforest preserve and butterfly garden (W www.butterflygardens .co.cr), perhaps one of the most impressive butterfly gardens in the country. Built with a huge wraparound spiral entranceway, visitors walk along at butterfly level while enjoying a gentle rainforest experience. About three dozen species of butterflies are bred here. The garden has a sound-and-image show at night and is surrounded by nature trails. Guided visits cost US$15; the night presentation is US$40.

*La Plantación* (☎ 777-1332, 777-1115, fax 777-0432, in the USA & Canada ☎ 800-477-7829, e costarica@bigrubys.com, W www .bigrubys.com) Doubles: standard US$162, deluxe US$186-197. Rates include full breakfast and cocktail hour. This exclusive hotel caters mainly to gay men, though lesbians are welcome. The 24 lovely rooms are cool, light, and spacious with large bathrooms, fans, air-conditioning, cable TV and VCR, and big mosquito nets over the king-size beds. Nine rooms are standard; the larger deluxe rooms have patios looking out over the attractively landscaped gardens with free-form pool. Two deluxe rooms have sea views and share a private pool with an apartment that rents for US$340 per night. The restaurant offers a choice of indoor and outdoor dining, and a bar with pool table is attached. Entrance to the hotel is through a private guarded gate, ensuring a relaxing and comfortable retreat for guests. Staff will help with tour arrangements.

*Hotel Casitas Eclipse* (☎/fax 777-0408, 777-1738, e eclipsehcr@racsa.co.cr, W www .casitaseclipse.com) Rooms and suites US$130-200; house US$320. This pure white building is unmistakable, comprising a good restaurant, three swimming pools, and nine attractive split-level houses on the property. The bottom floor of each air-conditioned house is a spacious junior suite with queen-size and single beds, bathroom with hot water, living room, kitchen, and patio. The upper floor is a standard room with queen-size bed, bathroom, and terrace. These have a separate entrance and are the same rate for single or double occupancy. A staircase (with lockable door) combines the two and, voilà (the owners *are* French), you have a house sleeping up to five. If you're adding up, you'll see there's a discount for renting both units. There are also seven unconnected rooms and suites. There's an excellent Italian restaurant on the premises.

*Costa Verde* (☎ 777-0584, 777-0187, fax 777-0560, e costaver@racsa.co.cr, W www .costaverde.net) Rooms & apartments US$92-150. This is the sister hotel of the Costa Verde Inn in Escazú. It has a pool with ocean views, a bar, and restaurant, and the helpful staff will arrange local tours and activities. Attractive rooms all have fans, kitchenettes, private hot showers, and balconies with forest or ocean views (the latter are the most expensive). There are small 'efficiency rooms' and larger 'studio apartments.' Some of these have whirlpool baths and air-con.

*Hotel Karahé* (☎ 777-0170, 777-0152, fax 777-1075, e karahe@ns.goldnet.co.cr, w www .karahe.com) Doubles US$90-125. On the final hill before you reach Manuel Antonio, you'll find this place. You could easily walk to the national park entrance from here in about 20 leisurely minutes. There's a pool, spa, restaurant, and three levels of rooms. The oldest cabins have superb views and are reached by climbing a flight of steep stairs (not for people with ambulatory problems). All have hot water and air-con. Rates depend mainly on views, and include breakfast.

A few minutes' walk farther, the beach level is reached; there are more accommodations along here and in Manuel Antonio village (all of them cheaper); see the next Places to Stay section in this chapter.

**Guesthouses** If you want to stay for at least a week or more, it's possible to rent a fully equipped house and cater for yourself. The owner of La Buena Nota (see the Manuel Antonio section, below) has two houses and two, two-bedroom apartments near the Hotel La Mariposa, and knows about others. Houses are generally comfortable and come fully equipped, and you can expect to pay between US$350 and US$700 a week.

## Places to Eat
Many hotels mentioned above have good restaurants open to the public; the following are particularly recommended, though most hotel restaurants in this area are good. If you aren't staying in the hotel, call ahead at the numbers listed above to make a reservation in the high season.

*Hotel Plinio* This very popular hotel serves reasonably priced Italian and German food. The affordable *Gato Negro* in the Hotel Casitas Eclipse specializes in Italian food. The poolside *Rico Tico Bar 'n Grill*, at Si Como No, is low-key and atmospheric. *Hotel Mono Azul* has an excellent menu and pizza take-out and delivery service to anywhere in Manuel Antonio if you want to eat in your room.

There are several good nonhotel restaurants, referred to in the order that they are passed as you head south of Quepos. Some may have reduced hours in the rainy season or may open on their 'off' days in the height of the dry season.

*Restaurant Barba Roja* (☎ 777-0331) Dishes US$3-8. Open for breakfast, lunch, and dinner Tues-Sun year-round, plus dinner on Mon in the high season. Here you can eat well-prepared North American food (hamburgers, sandwiches, Mexican dishes, steak, and seafood), and there's a great view. Fish dinners cost around US$8, hamburgers start at US$3, and the 'margarita sunsets' are good while the sun goes down. There's both inside and outside dining. This recommended place is a good value.

*Bar Restaurante Karola's* (☎ 777-1557) Dishes US$5-15. Open 11am-11pm Thur-Tues. This place is right next to Barba Roja and is also recommended. It serves Mexican plates, steaks, excellent ribs, and seafood in an attractive garden setting. The jumbo shrimp is a little more expensive than the average range. The macadamia nut pie has been recommended.

*Restaurant Mar Luna* Dishes US$5-10. This new place attracted an instant local following. Reviews have been consistently good for the tico/international menu.

*Jungle Room* (☎ 777-1645) Dishes US$4-10. Open 5pm-10pm daily. This place features salads, Italian dishes, snacks, meat, and seafood. It becomes a disco and bar after 10pm, so you can eat first and dance the calories off later.

*El Avión* (☎ 777-3378) El Avión means 'Airplane,' and that's exactly what it is. Perched incongruously on the edge of a cliff, this ex-military cargo plane grabs your attention. The food here is less of an attention-grabber – basic bar food – but it's an interesting place to sit with a beer and burger. The restaurant is mainly outside the plane, to enjoy the view, though you can enter the plane if you want.

*Café Milagro* This café has the same great cappuccino, espresso, baked treats, and tranquil atmosphere you can find in the Quepos outlet. In addition, they serve a full breakfast here. Walking here from the beach for an afternoon coffee, then hopping on the bus back to Quepos, makes a nice outing for budget travelers looking for a way to enjoy the luxuries of the hill.

Also see below in Manuel Antonio village and above in Quepos for other suggestions.

## Getting There & Away

Many visitors get to Quepos by private or rented car, which enables them to drive the few kilometers to Manuel Antonio. Drive carefully on this narrow, steep, and winding road. Others rely on the Quepos taxi service or the frequent Quepos-Manuel Antonio bus service (for more on these options, see the Quepos section, earlier), or walk or hitchhike down to the park.

## MANUEL ANTONIO

The small village at the entrance to the national park has a number of less-expensive hotels and restaurants and is popular with younger international travelers. The usual advice regarding hotel reservations during the high season applies here – the village is packed during Easter week, and few rooms are available on weekends. The usual comments about poorly regulated development and subsequent pollution and litter also apply – the government periodically tries to control development, but this has not been entirely effective. In an effort to protect the nation's coasts, a law was passed in the late 1970s making all of Costa Rica's beaches national and public property and closed to any kind of construction within 50m of the high-tide mark. It remains unclear what to do with those hotels and restaurants that are in violation of the law but were built before it was passed.

There's a good beach (Playa Espadilla), but swimmers are warned to beware of rip currents. There are some lifeguards working on this beach (but not at the others in the area). Reportedly, there's a nude bathing beach frequented by gay men just beyond the far west end of Playa Espadilla. The town is generally safe, but swimmers should never leave belongings unattended on the beach here, or on the national-park beaches. Make sure your hotel room is securely locked when you are out, even briefly.

## Information

La Buena Nota (☎ 777-1002, fax 777-1946, e buenanota@racsa.co.cr) is a gift shop that has for years functioned as an informal (and

relatively unbiased) information center in the Manuel Antonio area. Still under Anita Myketuk's management, it's in a spacious air-conditioned building just north of the Cabinas Piscis, at the north end of Manuel Antonio village. It provides assistance and information to travelers (in English) and also sells maps, guidebooks (including this one), new and used books in English, US newspapers, beach supplies, surfboard wax, sundries, and souvenirs galore, including T-shirts hand-painted by local artists and Costa Rican jewelry.

Tucan Tours, in the village near Playa Espadilla, offers Internet access.

## Activities & Organized Tours

**Marlboro Horse Stables** (☎ 777-1108), opposite the Cabinas Piscis, rents horses for US$30 for two or three hours. Body boards are rented at **La Buena Nota** (see above). Surfboards, body boards, and kayaks are rented all along the beach at Playa Espadilla. The Restaurant Mar y Sombra also rents chairs and umbrellas.

Tucan Tours offers some tours and equipment rentals.

Also see Information in the Quepos to Manuel Antonio section, earlier in this chapter.

## Places to Stay

**Budget** The cheapest place to stay is *Costa Linda* (☎ 777-0304) Rooms US$7.50-10 per person. It's reasonably clean, has shared cold showers, and is popular with shoestringers. Rooms with private showers may be available.

*Cabinas Irarosa* Singles/doubles US$14/20. Here you'll find simple but clean rooms with fans and private cold baths.

*Cabinas ANEP* (☎ 777-0565) Doubles US$21 with bath. This place may be hard to get into – ANEP is the Asociación Nacional de Empleados Públicos, so the cabinas may be full of tico workers taking a beach vacation.

*Cabinas Ramírez* Doubles/triples US$25/30. This place has about 18 rooms with private cold baths and fans. There's direct access to the beach. Rooms on the ocean side are OK, but the ones on the street side are dark and dank. In high season, it may be difficult to get cheaper single rates, but in low season it charges US$7.50 per person. The nearby disco in the Restaurant Mar y Sombra may preclude sleep.

**Cabinas Piscis** (☎ 777-0046) Doubles US$30-35. There are 12 fairly basic but clean double rooms with private cold baths. All rooms have fans, and the staff is friendly. One large room (US$65) sleeps five with air-conditioning.

**Mid-Range** Rates vary depending on the size and whether you want air-con at **Hotel Vela Bar** (☎ 777-0413, fax 777-1071, e vela bar@maqbeach.com, w www.velabar.com) Doubles US$35-70. Hotel Vela has 10 pleasant rooms with private baths and fans. The owners are pleasant and run a popular restaurant.

**Hotel Manuel Antonio** (☎ 777-1237) Doubles US$58-75. Newly rebuilt since the last edition, the cheapest rooms now have a private hot shower and fan; better rooms have air-con and cable TV. It's also close to the beach.

**Hotel del Mar** (☎/fax 777-0543) Rooms with fan/air-con US$45/55. On nice grounds, the spacious rooms are OK and have private cold showers.

**Cabinas Los Almendros** (☎/fax 777-0225, 777-5137) Doubles or triples with fan US$50, with air-con US$60. This place, managed by the friendly Doña Emilia, has large, quiet, pleasant rooms with hot water baths. There's a pool, and a decent restaurant is attached.

**Hotel Playa Espadilla** (☎ 777-0416, ☎/fax 777-0903, e hotel@espadilla.com, w www .espadilla.com) Rooms US$80-123 for up to 4 people, with kitchenette US$95-135. This new hotel is near the park entrance and has 16 air-conditioned rooms with cable TV and phone; four of these include a kitchenette. The grounds are still a little bare, but a rainy season should fill out the landscaping, and there's a pool with swim-up bar and a bar with a pool table. Trails behind the hotel lead into a small private forested area.

**Hotel Villabosque** (☎ 777-0463, fax 777-0401) Doubles US$95. This attractive place has nice air-conditioned rooms with fans, balconies, and hot water. There are 16 rooms, a pool, a restaurant, and guided tours into the national park.

### Places to Eat
**Vela Bar** Dishes US$6-12. This is the best and priciest restaurant in Manuel Antonio.

It serves a variety of meals, including a few vegetarian plates. The slightly cheaper restaurant at **Hotel Villabosque** and the steakhouse in **Cabinas Los Almendros** are also good.

**Restaurant Mar y Sombra** Dishes US$3-6. This is also popular and serves seafood. It has casados and chicken and pasta plates for about US$3 and fish dinners for twice that. Nearby is a quieter **beach restaurant** with inexpensive seafood meals and a pleasant terrace. There are good sunset views at both places. A number of other cheap **sodas** and **roadside stands** can be found in the beach area.

### Entertainment
**Restaurant Mar y Sombra** The disco at this place gets down on weekends and, in the busy season, on midweek nights as well.

### Getting There & Away
All flights to Manuel Antonio go to Quepos.

Also see the Quepos section for bus information. Buses leaving Manuel Antonio for San José will pick you up in front of your hotel if you are on the road to flag them down, or from the Quepos bus terminal, after which there are no stops. Buy tickets in advance if possible, particularly on weekends, when they sell out days ahead. Try calling the ticket office in Quepos (☎ 777-0263) for bus reservations in Manuel Antonio.

Buses for destinations other than San José leave from Quepos.

### PARQUE NACIONAL MANUEL ANTONIO
This park was enlarged by about 1000 hectares in 2000. Nevertheless, at 1625 hectares, Manuel Antonio is the second-smallest park in the national park system, but it's also one of the most popular. This is because of its beautiful forest-backed tropical beaches, dramatic rocky headlands with ocean and island views, prolific wildlife, and maintained trail network.

Fortunately, Manuel Antonio was declared a national park back in 1972, thus preserving it from hotel development. The many hotels in the area north of the park, however, have made this gem the focus of much visitation. Clearly, large numbers of people in such a small area tend to detract

CENTRAL PACIFIC COAST

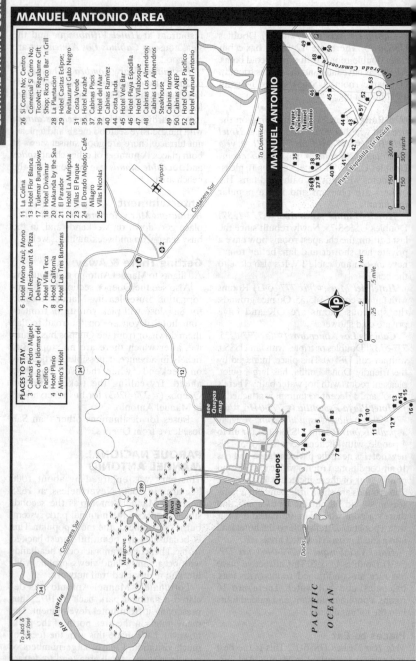

# MANUEL ANTONIO AREA

PLACES TO STAY

3  Cabinas Pedro Miguel;
   Centro de Idiomas del
   Pacifico
4  Hotel Plinio
5  Mimo's Hotel

6  Hotel Mono Azul; Mono
   Azul Restaurant & Pizza
   Delivery
7  Hotel Villa Teca
8  Hotel California
10 Hotel Las Tres Banderas

11 La Colina
13 Hotel Flor Blanca
17 Tulemar Bungalows
18 Hotel Divisimar
20 Makanda by the Sea
21 El Parador
22 Hotel La Mariposa
23 Villas El Parque
24 El Dorado Mojado; Café
   Milagro
25 Villas Nicolas

26 Si Como No; Centro
   Comercial Si Como No;
   TicoNet; Regalame Gift
   Shop; Rico Tico Bar 'n Grill
28 La Plantacion
29 Hotel Casitas Eclipse;
   Restaurant Gato Negro
31 Costa Verde
35 Hotel Karahé
37 Cabinas Piscis
39 Hotel del Mar
40 Cabinas Ramirez
44 Costa Linda
45 Hotel Vela Bar
46 Hotel Playa Espadilla
47 Hotel Villabosque
48 Cabinas Los Almendros;
   Cabinas Los Almendros
   Steakhouse
49 Cabinas Irarosa
50 Cabinas ANEP
52 Hotel Ola de Pacifico
53 Hotel Manuel Antonio

MANUEL ANTONIO

Parque
Nacional
Manuel
Antonio

Quebrada Camaronera

Playa Espadilla (1st Beach)

0        150      300 m
0        150      300 yards

To Dominical

Airport

Costanera Sur

To Jacó &
San José

Costanera Sur

Río Naranjo

Río Paquita

Mangrove

Estuario
Boca Vieja

Quepos

see
Quepos
map

Docks

PACIFIC
OCEAN

0        .5       1 km
0   .25   .5          1 mile

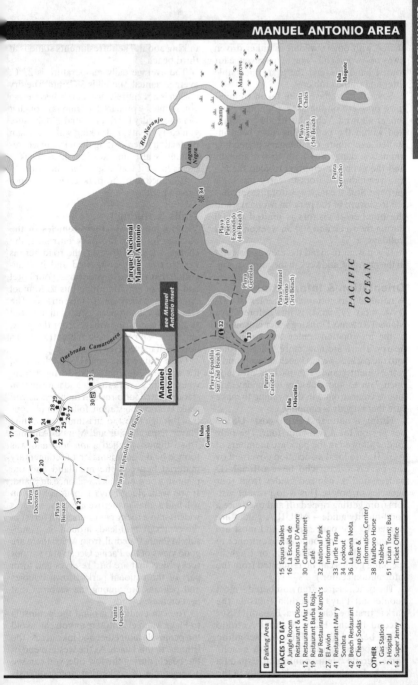

**MANUEL ANTONIO AREA**

**PLACES TO EAT**
9  Jungle Room
   Restaurant & Disco
12  Restaurante Mar Luna
19  Restaurante Barba Roja;
    Bar Restaurante Karola's
27  El Avión
41  Restaurant Mar y
    Sombra
42  Beach Restaurant
43  Cheap Sodas

**OTHER**
1  Gas Station
2  Hospital
14  Super Jenny
15  Equus Stables
16  La Escuela de
    Idiomas D'Amore
30  Cantina Internet
    Café
32  National Park
    Information
33  Turtle Trap
34  Lookout
36  La Buena Nota
    (Store &
    Information Center)
38  Marlboro Horse
    Stables
51  Tucan Tours; Bus
    Ticket Office

☐ Parking Area

from the experience of visiting the park. Idyllic and romantic beaches have to be shared with others, wildlife is either driven away or – worse still – taught to scavenge for tourist handouts, and there are inevitable litter and traffic problems.

Several steps have been taken to minimize pressure on the park. Camping is no longer allowed. Vehicular traffic is prohibited within the park. Signs have been installed explaining the dangers of feeding animals – dangerous both to the animals and the people attempting to feed them – and reminding visitors to carry out their garbage. Still, the heavy visitor pressure has led to closure of the park on Mondays, and the number of visitors is limited to 600 during the week and 800 on weekends and holidays.

If you want to avoid the crowds, go early in the morning, midweek in the rainy season.

## Orientation & Information

A national park information center (☎ 777-0644, ☎/fax 777-0654) is just before Playa Manuel Antonio. Drinking water is available at the information center, and toilets are nearby. There are now more toilets farther into the park, as well as beach showers and a refreshment stand. The park is officially open 7am to 4pm Tuesday to Sunday, and guards come around in the evening to make sure that nobody is camping.

Hiring a naturalist guide costs US$20 per person for a two-hour tour. The only guides allowed in the park are members of AGUILA (a local association governed by the park service) who have official ID badges, and recognized guides from tour agencies or hotels. This is to prevent visitors from getting ripped off and to ensure a good-quality guide – AGUILA guides are trained by the park service and most are bilingual. They are found at the entrance to the park. (French-, German-, or English-speaking guides can be requested from the information center.)

The beaches are often numbered – most people call Playa Espadilla (outside the park) 'first beach,' Playa Espadilla Sur 'second beach,' Playa Manuel Antonio 'third beach,' Playa Puerto Escondido 'fourth beach,' and Playita 'fifth beach.' Some people begin counting at Espadilla Sur, which is the first beach actually in the

park, so it can be a bit confusing trying to figure out which beach people may be talking about. The refreshments stand is at third beach.

The average daily temperature is 27°C; average annual rainfall is 3875mm. The dry season is not entirely dry, merely less wet, so you should be prepared for rain (although it can also be dry for days on end). Make sure you carry plenty of drinking water and sun protection when visiting the park. Insect repellent is also an excellent idea. Pack a picnic lunch if you're spending the day.

Entrance into the park costs US$6 per person per day.

## Trails & Hiking

Visitors must leave their vehicles in the parking lot near the park entrance; the charge is US$3. However, the road here is very narrow and congested and it's suggested that you leave your car at your hotel and take an early morning bus to Manuel Antonio and then walk to the entrance. The Quebrada Camaronera estuary divides the southern end of the village from the park, and there's no bridge, so the entrance has now been moved (see map).

Once you've paid your US$6 admission, it's about a 30-minute hike to the beach, where there's a park ranger and information station; watch for birds and monkeys as you walk. West of the station, follow an obvious trail through forest to an isthmus separating Playas Espadilla Sur and Manuel Antonio. This isthmus is called a *tombolo* and was formed by the accumulation of sedimentary material between the mainland and the peninsula beyond, which was once an island. If you walk along Playa Espadilla Sur, you will find a small mangrove area. The isthmus widens into a rocky peninsula, with forest in the center. A trail leads around the peninsula to Punta Catedral, from which there are good views of the Pacific Ocean and various rocky islets that are bird reserves and form part of the national park. Brown boobies and pelicans are among the seabirds that nest on these islands.

You can continue around the peninsula to Playa Manuel Antonio, or you can avoid the peninsula altogether and hike across the isthmus to this beach. At the western end of the beach, during the low tide, you can see a semicircle of rocks that archaeologists

ROBERTO SONCIN GEROMETTA

Kayaking down the Isla Damas estuary in Parque Nacional Manuel Antonio

believe were arranged by pre-Columbian Indians to function as a turtle trap. The beach itself is an attractive one of white sand and is popular for bathing. It's protected and safer than the Playas Espadilla.

Beyond Playa Manuel Antonio, the trail divides. The lower trail is steep and slippery during the wet months and leads to the quiet and aptly named Playa Puerto Escondido (Hidden Port Beach). This beach can be more or less completely covered by high tides, so don't get cut off. The upper trail climbs to a view point on a bluff overlooking Puerto Escondido and Punta Serrucho beyond – a nice vista. Reportedly, rangers limit the number of hikers on this trail to 45.

## Wildlife Watching

Monkeys abound in the park, and it's difficult to spend a day walking around without seeing some. White-faced monkeys are the most commonly seen, but the rarer (and locally endangered) squirrel monkeys are also present and howler monkeys may be seen. Sloths, agoutis, peccaries, armadillos, coatis, and raccoons are also seen quite regularly. Over 350 species of bird are reported in the park and surrounding area, and a variety of lizards, snakes, iguanas, and other animals may be observed. All the trails within the park are good for wildlife watching – ask the rangers where the most interesting recent sightings have occurred. Some trails may

limit the number of hikers to minimize disturbance of the animals. There's a small coral reef off Playa Manuel Antonio, but the water is rather cloudy and the visibility limited. Despite this, snorkelers can see a variety of fish, as well as marine creatures like crabs, corals, sponges, sea snails, and many others.

Immediately inland from the beaches is an evergreen littoral forest. This contains many different species of trees, bushes, and other plants. A common tree to watch out for is the manzanillo *(Hippomane mancinella)*. Manzanillo means 'little apple' in Spanish – this tree has poisonous fruits that look like little crab apples. The sap exuded by the bark and leaves is also toxic, and it causes the skin to itch and burn, so give the manzanillo a wide berth. Warning signs are prominently displayed by examples of this tree near the park entrance.

## MANUEL ANTONIO TO DOMINICAL

To continue farther south along the coast from Manuel Antonio, you have to backtrack to Quepos and from there head 4km inland to the Costanera Sur. It's 44km from Quepos to the next village of any size, Dominical. The road is bone-shaking gravel, easily passable in the dry season but requiring care to negotiate with an ordinary car in the wet. Residents of this area have long complained to the government that the

Costanera Sur should be paved. The government promised to pave and improve this road some time ago, though it has yet to happen. Maybe it'll be paved by the time you get there, though don't bet your last colón on it.

The drive is through kilometer after kilometer of African oil-palm plantations, with identical-looking settlements along the way. These are minor centers for the palm-oil extracting process. Each settlement has a grassy village square, institutional-looking housing, a store, church, and bar.

**Matapalo** offers a mainly unvisited stretch of beach with long vistas and safe swimming (ie, not a surfing beach). In the tiny village, on the main highway, the sign for the *Express Deli del Pacífico* announces that Matapalo is 'Center of the World but the World Doesn't Know It!' This is where the turnoff from the main road to the beach is.

*El Oasis Americano Cabinas* Singles/doubles US$10/15. You'll find this place near the beach, and it has a bar, restaurant, English-speaking owners, and basic cabins.

*El Coquito del Pacífico (☎/fax 384-7220, e el-coquito@gmx.net, w www.elcoquito .com)* Singles/doubles US$49/55, US$10 additional person. This place, about 1km toward the ocean from the main road, has eight spacious cabins, most with three beds, in a pretty, shady spot right next to the beach. It has a pool, restaurant, and bar and can arrange horseback rides. The Austrian/German owners speak English.

*The Jungle House (☎/fax 777-2748, e info@junglehouse.com, w www.jungle house.com)* Cabins US$65 per person, including full breakfast & welcome cocktail. This American-owned place is the epitome of relaxation, with five cabins close to the beach. Each comes with a kitchenette and a sitting area. The owner, Charlie, volunteers at the local school and is an all-around nice guy.

*La Puedra Buena* Almost next door to The Jungle Place, this Swiss-run restaurant offers the best food in the area – a kind of gourmet tico-Swiss blend. There's also a bar.

*Camping* on the beach is a possibility and there are probably other cabins in the area, which is still isolated and spread out; this is an area that is sure to see more development. Buses between Quepos and Dominical can drop you in the village; from there it's a couple of kilometers to the beach.

South of Matapalo, about a kilometer before reaching the Río Barú, is the private nature reserve at Hacienda Barú. A bridge crosses the Río Barú, and immediately beyond is the village of Dominical on the southeast side of the river mouth. From the west side of the bridge, a steep but paved road climbs 34km inland to San Isidro de El General. Therefore, if you can negotiate the somewhat rough Quepos-to-Dominical road, a roundtrip from San José to Quepos, Dominical, San Isidro de El General, and back to San José is quite possible and, indeed, makes a good excursion for a few days.

The road south of Dominical continues through Uvita and reconnects with the Interamericana just southeast of Ciudad Cortés.

## HACIENDA BARÚ

This private nature reserve covers only 336 hectares but manages to pack a large number of species into its small area. This is because its location on the steep coastal hills encompasses a variety of habitat, including 3km of beach, 16 hectares of mangroves, 1km of the Río Barú, pasture and plantations, and lowland and hilly rainforest up to 320m above sea level. About 80 hectares are undisturbed primary rainforest, 50 hectares is rainforest that was selectively logged almost two decades ago and then left, and 25 hectares are secondary forest growing on abandoned pastures. There are tree-growing areas, fruit orchards, cocoa plantations, open pasture, and brushy areas. In addition, the reserve contains several pre-Columbian cemetery sites and petroglyphs.

The Hacienda Barú bird list is well over 330 species and growing; the mammal list is 56 species (including 23 bats); the amphibian and reptile list is 49 species, and there are many frogs, toads, and snakes yet to be identified; and the plant list is far from complete with over 100 trees and 75 orchid species. An impressive list!

The owners, Jack and Diane Ewing, have lived and raised their family here since 1970. They are a delightful couple with a fund of stories to tell and information to dispense. They have always been active in pushing for environmentally responsible legislation in Costa Rica and are currently focusing their energy on the creation of biological corridors – stretches of undisturbed land connecting different habitats within Costa Rica and throughout Central America. Buying land is a key part of these projects and if you're interested in contributing you should definitely contact Jack – his fascination with the rainforest is infectious and his dedication to preserving it inspiring.

When the Ewings first arrived in the area, transportation was mostly by horseback – now the road goes by and tourism is increasing. Nevertheless, Barú still has a remote feel to it. The Ewings have worked hard at preserving the area and are active in encouraging and helping their neighbors to do likewise; they want to be ready to properly handle the inevitable growth in tourism, which has already begun.

In 1992, they were joined by Steve Stroud, who has worked hard to make the reserve a great place to visit. He has been instrumental in developing ecologically sensitive tours and building a superb rainforest canopy platform, which for many people is the highlight of their visit. Their newest venture is the 'Flight of the Toucan' canopy tour, which is described below.

## Information

Obtain information and make reservations for tours or accommodations with the Hacienda Barú (☎ 787-0003, fax 787-0004, e hacbaru@racsa.co.cr, w www.hacienda baru.com).

The Ewings' El Ceibo gas station, 1.7km north of the hacienda, is the only one for a good way in any direction. Groceries, fishing gear, tide tables, and other useful sundries are available, and there are clean toilets.

Near the junction of the road from San Isidro and the coastal highway, at the south end of the Hacienda property between it and the village of Dominical, an information center is being built. This will have information about the Hacienda and the surrounding area.

## Activities & Organized Tours

Three interpretive trails and a new wooden birding tower are open to the public. Trail fees are US$3 per person (60% goes to the government, the rest is for trail maintenance). For an extra US$3 per group, you can hire a local schoolkid who knows the trails and has been taught to spot the birds and animals of interest to hikers. An interpretive booklet is also available for US$3. If

you want to go in at (or before!) dawn, you can either pay the night before or as you leave. There's no charge for guests of Hacienda Barú or for people who pay for one of the tours listed below.

There are several **guided tours** offered at Hacienda Barú. These include a 2½-hour lowland **birding walk** (US$20); a 5½-hour **rainforest hike**, including lunch (US$35); a combination of the preceding two hikes (US$40); a **mangrove and beach hike** (US$20); and an **overnight** stay in the rainforest or on the beach with meals and comfortable camping (US$60). These prices are for one person, and there's a two-person minimum. A maximum of eight people at a time are allowed in the rainforest so that you don't meet other hikers. **Horseback rides** (US$25 for two hours, US$5 each additional hour) are also available. A **kayak tour** through the mangrove estuary costs US$35. These tour prices include knowledgeable native guides. Jim Zook (a very knowledgeable English-speaking naturalist and ornithologist), Jack Ewing, or another of the English-speaking naturalists will accompany any tour for an additional US$50 per day. One day's advance notice is usually needed.

An exciting activity is a rope ascent into the canopy. There's a **canopy platform** about 32m above the ground, built in a tree that is reached after a 15-minute hike through the forest. Each participant is given a safety helmet, attached to a climbing harness, and winched up by rope to the platform. About 45 minutes is spent on the platform, accompanied by a guide who will point out things of interest. The ocean is visible in the distance, but the chance of wildlife observation is more exciting than seeing the ocean. I saw a pair of toucans mating and a sloth on a branch just below the platform, totally oblivious of my presence. Great! On the way down, you can control the pace of descent and spend about 10 minutes hanging, suspended like a spider spinning on a cord, in the middle layers of the canopy. The tour costs US$35 per person with a maximum of three allowed on the platform at a time. No climbing experience is needed – everything is done for you.

If you feel like even more adventure, you can climb into the canopy by a rope hanging from a tree. No platforms, just rope climbing about 35m up into the canopy, accompanied by an experienced climber and naturalist guide. No experience is needed, but this is more strenuous than being winched to a platform, so you need to be in good shape. Two trees are usually climbed, and the cost is US$45 per person.

The **Flight of the Toucan** canopy tour has eight cables with spans ranging from 20m to 91m. There are 15 different take-off and landing platforms, some on the ground and some in trees. The cables go from ridge to ridge, so you go through and over the canopy, seeing it with different perspectives. Education is an important part of these tours – you aren't just shuttled through as quickly as possible for an adrenaline rush (though that's there, of course!). The English-speaking naturalist guides try to explain as much about what you are seeing as possible and answer your questions about the rainforest. This tour costs US$30.

These tours and activities are open to the public; you don't have to stay here.

**Volunteering** is a possibility in August and September, when help is needed to gather olive ridley turtle eggs for a turtle-nursery project. You may not get to see the turtles laying, but the chance to be of use in a fascinating and beautiful environment makes this a worthwhile experience. Ask about other volunteering possibilities.

### Places to Stay & Eat
*Cabins* Doubles US$70, US$11.50 additional person. There are six simple but spacious two- and three-bedroom cabins available; each has a kitchenette, refrigerator, fans in every room, a hot shower, sitting room, and insect screens. Continental breakfast is included, and lunch (US$7.50) and dinner (US$8.50) are available in the restaurant.

### Getting There & Away
The Quepos-Dominical-San Isidro bus stops outside the hacienda entrance. The San Isidro-Dominical-Uvita bus will drop you at the Río Barú bridge, 2km from the hacienda office.

## DOMINICAL
This little coastal village is 1.2km south of Hacienda Barú. The Dominical beach is a long one and has a reputation for strong rip currents – exercise extra caution. Despite this, the surfing is good, so a number of surfers hang out here. A small but popular language school in the village means that visitors making extended stays are not all surfers. A small ecotourism industry is developing, and local operators, led by the owners of the Hacienda Barú, are banding together in an effort to promote the area without spoiling it. Apart from surfing, attractions include rainforest hiking and camping, wildlife observation, horseback riding, fishing, and visits to the nearby Parque Nacional Marino Ballena. Slowly, Dominical is being discovered, and the little town can get full on weekends, both with tico and foreign visitors.

### Orientation & Information
The main Costanera highway bypasses Dominical; the entrance to the village is immediately past the Río Barú bridge. There's a main road through the village, where many of the services mentioned are found, and a parallel road along the beach.

Selva Mar (☎ 771-4582, 771-4579, ☎/fax 771-8841, ⓔ selvamar@racsa.co.cr, Ⓦ www .exploringcostarica.com) is a booking agent and tour operator with offices in San Isidro. It communicates with several remote lodges and businesses in the Dominical-Uvita area by radiotelephone. The staff can arrange car rental, horseback rides, boat trips, diving, and fishing.

The telephone system reached town in 1996 and is expanding. Internet access is available above the San Clemente Bar & Grill, and at Internet Dominical next to the DiuWak hotel and restaurant. The local police can be reached on ☎ 787-0011.

### Dangers & Annoyances
This is a surfing area, and the waves, currents, and riptides are very strong. Many people have drowned off the local beaches, including an American man on his honeymoon in late 2001. Locals say that over a dozen people drowned in the area in 2001. Since these deaths, signs and lifeguards have been installed. Follow the instructions on the signs, swim on beaches with lifeguards on them, and read the section on Ocean Hazards in the Facts for the Visitor chapter.

### Centro Turístico
### Cataratas Nauyaca
About 10km away on the road to San Isidro, just before the village of Platanillo, an en-

trance to the right leads into this tourism center (☎ 787-0198, 771-3187, fax 771-2003, ⓔ ciprotur@racsa.co.cr, ⓦ www.ecotourism.co.cr/nauyacawaterfalls/index.html). There's no vehicle access to the area – you can hire horses for a guided ride to two waterfalls, 20m and 45m high, that plunge into a deep swimming hole. With a day's notice, a tour can be arranged, including guided horseback rides, swimming in the pool under the falls, and country meals with a local family. Tours leave about 8am or 9am and take six to seven hours. The cost is about US$40 per person. A campground with dressing rooms and toilets is available.

## Activities & Courses

Although known for **surfing**, the area is also good for **horseback rides** to waterfalls in the hills above the coast. The Hacienda Barú and several hotels can arrange horseback rides, or just ask around – Dominical is a very small place.

**Green Iguana Surf Camp** (☎ 787-0192, ⓔ admin@greeniguanasurfcamp.com, ⓦ www.greeniguanasurfcamp.com), run by experienced surfers Jason and Karla Butler, offers surfing lessons and seven- to 10-day surfing camps. Spanish lessons are also available. They provide accommodations for a variety of budgets.

In the former Albergue Willdale is the new **Adventure Spanish School** (☎ 787-0023, ⓦ www.adventurespanishschool.com). Family stays can be arranged.

## Places to Stay

*Antorchas Camping* (☎ 787-0307, 380-2755 cellular) Campsites US$3 per person, rooms US$9/12 singles/doubles. Just a few meters from the beach, this place provides lockers and showers. If you don't have a tent, they'll rent you one for less than US$1 per night. There are six basic rooms sharing cold showers. For an extra fee of US$3 per stay, basic kitchen privileges are available.

*Pyramis Camping* (no phone) This is another place advertising camping near the beach.

*Cabinas Coco* (☎ 787-0235) Doubles US$12, with bath US$27. This basic but clean place is on the main street. The rooms with bath will sleep four (US$36). Showers are cold. Note that the accompanying bar and Thrusters disco across the

street may keep you up late, especially on weekend nights.

*Sundancer Cabinas* (☎ 787-0189) Doubles US$21. Close to Cabinas Coco, here are eight quieter but basic rooms in a pleasant family home. Showers are shared but hot, and there are kitchen privileges and a swimming pool.

*Posada del Sol* (☎/fax 787-0085) Singles/doubles US$20/25. This quiet and friendly place on the main street has clean rooms with fans and hot water.

*Cabinas Villa Dominical* (☎ 787-0030, 771-0621) Singles/doubles US$25/30. Near the Adventure Spanish School, this place has 10 simple, bare rooms with hot water and fans.

*Tortilla Flats* (☎ 787-0033) Rooms with bath/air-con US$35/50. Closer to the beach, all rooms here have private baths and fans; some have air-con.

*DiuWak* (☎ 787-0087, fax 787-0089, ⓔ diuwak@racsa.co.cr, ⓦ www.diuwak.com) Doubles with fan/air-con US$40/50. On a road to the beach, DiuWak has eight clean, spacious rooms with fans and hot water, and eight bright, nicely tiled air-conditioned units with kitchenettes and refrigerators. It has a restaurant, bar, Jacuzzi, minimarket, and public Internet access.

*Cabinas San Clemente* (☎ 787-0055, 787-0026) This attractive place, associated with the bar and grill, has some air-conditioned rooms on the beach in the same price range as DiuWak.

*Hotel Río Lindo* (☎/fax 787-0028, ⓔ rio lindo@racsa.co.cr, ⓦ www.dominical.net/hotelriolindo) Doubles with fan US$53

---

### Surfer Cool

Surfing – a sport that demands strength, skill, and daring, and has the side benefits of a great tan and ocean-buffed physique – is undeniably cool. Unfortunately, this leads some surfers to treat nonsurfers at the beach like caddies that have crashed the country-club bar. If you're a surfer, try not to be so stodgy! If you're a nonsurfer, it can help to think of surfers as dolphins – graceful, inexplicable creatures known on occasion to be friendly to mere humans.

– John Thompson

(US$5 additional person), with air-con US$70 (US$11.50 additional person). This hotel is near the entrance to Dominical. It has five clean, attractive, spacious rooms with private baths and five more with air-con. There's hot water in the evenings, and it has a pool, Jacuzzi, and pool bar.

*Costa Paraíso Lodge* (☎/fax 787-0025) Doubles US$65, apartments US$90-107, US$10 additional person. This attractive, tranquil, and comfortable place is about 2km south of Dominical. Two double rooms in the main house include breakfast in the rates. The two fully equipped apartments have fans, kitchens, living rooms, and porches overlooking the ocean.

*Hotel y Restaurante Roca Verde* (☎ 787-0036, fax 787-0013, ⓦ www.hotelroca verde.com) Doubles US$87. Overlooking a smaller beach about 1km south of the village, this hotel has undergone a big renovation. It offers 12 air-conditioned, tropical-theme rooms with pretty murals and hot showers, a spacious and recommended restaurant-bar (main courses US$4 to US$14), and a pool. On Saturday there's dancing 'til 2am, and on Sunday there's a poolside barbecue complete with a live mariachi band; both are popular local events.

*Hotel Villas Río Mar* (☎ 787-0246, fax 787-0054, ⓔ riomar@racsa.co.cr, ⓦ www .villasriomar.com) Singles/doubles US$80/100. Just beyond the entrance into town, a sign points under the bridge to this hotel – about 800m from the village. It has thatched bungalows with 40 spacious rooms, each with fan, wet bar, minifridge, private hot shower, and private patio. There's a pool, Jacuzzi, tennis court, restaurant, and bar. The hotel can arrange local tours and has mountain bikes for rent.

### Places to Eat

There are several inexpensive sodas in Dominical, of which the best are the *Soda Laura* and friendly *Soda Nanyoa*, both on the main road. They open by about 6:30am for breakfast and serve casados for about US$2.50.

*San Clemente Bar & Grill* Dishes US$3-9. This popular place, also on the main road, has good, big breakfasts and US-style bar food the rest of the day (Tex-Mex and pizza are among the favorites). Its satellite TV shows sports programs and surfing videos.

*Thrusters Bar* Just off the main road toward the beach (by the ICE office and a surf shop), this eatery makes pizzas.

*La Capanna* (☎ 787-0072) Dishes US$5-13. Near the entrance to town, this hot spot is known for fabulous Italian food, though rumors are that it might close soon.

*Restaurante Roca Verde* Dishes US$4-14. About 1km south of town, this restaurant in the hotel of that name is fun and popular. The international menu is cooked to order, and you can enjoy a beer at the bar or play a game of pool while you wait in this relaxed restaurant.

On the main Costanera highway, there's a small shopping plaza with a *deli*. Also, see Cabinas Punta Dominical, in the Southeast of Dominical section, below, for another suggestion.

### Entertainment

The two village hot spots are the *San Clemente* and the larger *Thrusters*; both have pool tables and loud music. *Hotel y Restaurante Roca Verde* has music on weekends.

### Getting There & Away

The bus stop in Dominical is by the San Clemente Bar & Grill. It has schedules as well as ticket information.

Buses for Quepos leave at 5:45am, 8:15am, 1pm, and 3pm; for San Isidro at 6:45am, 7am, 11:15am, 2:45pm, and 3:30pm; and for Uvita at 4:30am and 10am.

In addition, buses from San José to Uvita pass through Dominical at about 10:30am and 9pm. Buses from Uvita to Quepos and San José pass through Dominical at about 6am and 2pm. It's well worth asking locally about all these schedules; some may change now that the road has been paved.

## SOUTHEAST OF DOMINICAL

The road continues southeast of Dominical about 18km to Uvita and then on to Palmar. This was once a hellish road, but after paving in 2002 it became the best road on the coast. Don't get lulled into a sense of false security – the wide stretches of smooth new tarmac have a couple of speed bumps in them at inopportune and unmarked places, and the late 2002 rainy season may produce some surprisingly large potholes for 2003.

There are occasional glimpses of the ocean but, for the most part, the road is a little way inland. The improvement of the road has heated up real estate business in the area, though most new buyers are private owners rather than big entrepreneurs or hotel groups – so far. The beaches are too rough to draw big resort developers, and home and small hotel owners tend to hide their buildings inside acres of forested land.

There are several interesting places to stay south of Dominical, off the road to Uvita. You can contact some of them via Selva Mar (see Orientation & Information in the Dominical section, above).

## Places to Stay & Eat

*Cabinas Bellavista* Doubles US$53, cabins US$75, US$6 additional person. Just over 2km south of the Hotel y Restaurante Roca Verde in Dominical, along the gravel road to Uvita, a sign points to a road to the left for these cabinas. Owned by longtime resident Woody Dyer, who has a wealth of stories about his many years in the area, this remote lodge is in a revamped farmhouse 500m above sea level. A balcony gives superb ocean views, and there's rainforest and a waterfall nearby. Accommodations are rustic but clean; tiled solar-heated hot showers are available in each room. There are four rooms in the main building; two cabins sleep four and six, respectively, and have kitchens. Tasty home-cooked meals cost about US$15 per day. A guesthouse for up to eight people has a private bathroom and a kitchen. Rainforest/waterfall hiking or horseback tours with lunch and local guide cost US$40 per person. Bring extra batteries for your flashlight.

This place is difficult to get to. You need 4WD to get up their road, which is locally called the Escaleras (Staircase). If you don't have 4WD, Woody will pick you up in Dominical for US$10. (You might struggle up there with a car in the dry season.) However, it's only about 7km or 8km from Dominical, so the hardy could hike up.

*Villas Escaleras Inn* (W www.villas -escaleras.com) Villas: 2/3/4 bedrooms US$240/280/320. About another kilometer up the Escaleras road, this place offers two luxurious private houses each with gorgeous views, a pool, and full kitchen. Each bedroom has a queen bed, and there are two futons in the living room, so the four-bedroom option could sleep up to 10 people. Maid service, coffee supplies, and a wrap-around balcony with telescope come with the villas, and surfboards and body boards can be borrowed. Local tours are also arranged, and there are discounts for longer stays.

*Finca Brian y Milena* (☎ 396-6206) Cabins without/with bath US$36/50 per person. Also on the Escaleras road, this is a small, isolated, working farm surrounded by rainforest. It has a screened cabin (sleeping up to six) with a bathroom. The rate includes all meals and a short hiking tour. There's a heated rock pool to soak in. There's also the aptly named Birdhouse Cabin, which sleeps two and shares the bathroom with the main house. Discounts are given for longer stays, and the staff can arrange a variety of hiking trips to visit rainforest waterfalls and eat with local campesino families. If you don't have 4WD, you can either hike from the main highway (1½ hours) or ride a horse (about US$10 to US$14 in Dominical) to get here.

*Pacific Edge* (☎ 381-4369, e pacificedge@ pocketmail.com) Singles/doubles US$47/58, quad bungalow US$116. Eventually, the Escaleras road drops back down to the Costanera but, before it does, you pass this friendly place. It's actually easier to get here by avoiding the first Escaleras entrance to Bellavista and taking the second entrance, where a sign indicates Pacific Edge one steep kilometer up from the Costanera. Four cabins are perched on a knife-edge ridge about 200m above sea level. The rainforest drops off all around and the views are stunning. The cabins are spacious and take advantage of their location with view balconies on the edge of the ridge (don't fall off!). Each has a solar-heated shower and kitchenette, and there's also a restaurant-bar. It's US$5 extra for use of the kitchenettes. Long-term rentals are cheaper. One larger bungalow has a full kitchen and sleeps four. Meals cost US$5 for breakfast, US$6 for lunch. Dinner, on request, costs US$12 to US$16.

*Cabinas Punta Dominical* (☎ 787-0016, 787-0034, ☎/fax 787-0240, e punta dominical@racsa.co.cr) Doubles US$58, US$6 additional person. Meals US$6-16. This place is 3.5km south of Dominical and then to the right on a dirt road to the beach. Situated high on a rocky headland named, appropriately enough, Punta Dominical, the cabins are isolated and attractive, yet retain a modicum of comfort. There are four pleasant cabins with fans, private baths with electric showers, and porches to hang a hammock. Each cabin will sleep up to six people. Reservations are recommended, especially on weekends. The cabins overlook a rocky beach; there's a sandy beach nearby, and boat trips can be arranged. The *restaurant* on the premises is widely regarded as one of the best in the area and is open to the public 7am to 9:30pm daily. The view while you dine is superb – come before sunset! The menu specializes in seafood, but the pastas and steaks are superb as well. Recommended.

*Las Casitas de Puertocito* (☎ 393-4327 cellular, fax 743-8150, ✉ lascasitas@pocket mail.com, ⓦ www.lascasitashotel.com) Doubles US$45-55, US$18 additional person, breakfast included. A couple of kilometers farther is this place with five bi-level rustic thatched cabins with private hot showers, fans, patios, and upstairs sleeping decks. It has a pool, small bar, a recommended Italian restaurant, and nearby beach access. The surroundings are lushly forested, and there are ocean views. Adriano, the owner, speaks Italian, English, and French. Guests can rent horses and arrange hiking, snorkeling, diving, and boat trips.

## UVITA

This tiny village is 17km south of Dominical and is the nearest community to Parque Nacional Marino Ballena. There's no real center as such – it's just a loose straggle of farms and houses on both sides of the highway, with a couple of stores, sodas, and places to stay. There are several entrances from the highway, and the beaches are locally referred to as Playa Uvita and, to the south, Playa Bahía Uvita. Both are popular with ticos looking for a place to swim – this is not a surfing area. At low tide you can walk out along Punta Uvita. People are friendly and will show you where to go. Several places to stay in this area can also be contacted through Selva Mar (see Orientation & Information in the Dominical section, earlier in this chapter).

### Reserva Biológica Oro Verde

This private reserve is on the farm of the friendly Duarte family, who have home-

steaded the area for over three decades. About two-thirds of their 150-hectare property is rainforest. They operate tours to see the forest, waterfalls, and wildlife, and give you a look at traditional Costa Rican life. Horse rental starts at US$5 per hour, and hikes with a Spanish-speaking local guide cost US$15 per person for three to four hours. It's about 3.5km inland from Uvita along a signed rough road. As you drive up, look over your shoulder for great views of Parque Nacional Marino Ballena.

### Rancho La Merced

Opposite the turnoff to Oro Verde is Rancho La Merced, a working cattle ranch, more than half of which has been left as protected forest. It has recently been designated as a 346-hectare national wildlife refuge. Horseback tours are offered, including 'Cowboy for a Day,' where you ride with the local cowboys and help on the ranch. They'll show you what to do if this is your first time, dude. A three- to five-hour tour costs US$20, total, for three or more people, or US$30 per person for one or two people. They also offer a variety of other tours on horseback and on foot, with the chance to spot wildlife in various habitats. You can lodge on the ranch in *Cabina El Kurukuzungo* or *The Old Farm House* for US$55 per person including meals and a tour. The cabin has two bedrooms (shared bathroom), a living room, and a kitchen; it sleeps a maximum of six people. The house has five bedrooms (shared bathroom), a kitchen, and porch; it sleeps a maximum of 10 people. Electricity is available by generator from 6pm to 9pm.

### Places to Stay & Eat

You can *camp* on the beach; at the base of Punta Uvita is a soda that will guard your goods for a small fee. Apart from the tourism projects above, Uvita has a few other low-key options; some can be contacted through Selva Mar. Those below are listed roughly north to south.

*Cabinas Los Laureles* (☎ 743-8008, 771-7648) Singles/doubles/triples US$18/25/30. The main entrance to Uvita leads inland, east of the highway, where you'll find this place, which has eight cabins with bathrooms. It can arrange horseback tours. You'll find the cabins a few hundred meters to the left of the *abastecedor* (general store); there's a sign.

*Cascada Verde (no phone)* Various accommodations US$4-12 per person. About 2km inland and uphill from Uvita (a taxi will cost US$2), the Cascada Verde is an alternative lodging dedicated to permaculture and holistic living. Food is vegetarian, and massages, chakra healing, reflexology, Reiki, etc are all among the activities. Meditating by the beautiful waterfall, two minutes' walk away, is a highlight of any stay. Accommodations include tents, hammocks, mattresses, dorm rooms, and some private rooms for two or three people. All bathrooms are shared and one has a hot shower. German and English are spoken. Guests can volunteer to work for discounts on board and lodging.

*Cabinas Hegalva (☎ 382-5780 messages)* Campsites US$3, rooms US$10 per person. Near Playa Bahía Uvita, this is a friendly place. It's run by Doña Cecilia, who cooks great food. The rooms have shared baths, and rates include breakfast, but for campers and nonguests breakfast costs about US$2. Also in this area are *Cabinas Betty*, by a soda of the same name, and *Cabinas María Jesus*, both basic rural places charging about US$5 per person.

*Villas Bejuco (☎ 771-0965)* Doubles US$44. Villas Bejuco is 2km south of the bridge over the Río Uvita, just inland off the Costanera and only a few hundred meters from the ocean. It has six large, clean cabins with huge screened windows for cross ventilation, private hot baths, and patios.

*Hotel El Chaman (☎ 787-0090, fax 771-7771, e domini@racsa.co.cr)* Doubles US$16-28. Near Villas Bejuco you'll see a big sign for this place, which is on the beach and has about a dozen simple cabins. Some have private hot showers, and some smaller ones share showers. There's a restaurant and a pool. The friendly owner arranges adventurous horse tours – four days and three nights cost US$148 per person.

*La Colonia* Doubles/triples US$14.50/18. A few spacious cabins with private baths make up this place on the road leading from the Costanera to El Chaman.

### Getting There & Away
When the road opened to ordinary traffic in 1996, the frequency of buses increased. Now that the road is fully and beautifully paved

(as of 2002) there may well be more buses, so ask locally about these forthcoming changes. Now there are a couple of buses daily to and from San José, leaving the capital at 5am and 3pm and returning at 5am and 1pm. Buses to San Isidro de El General, which pass through Dominical, leave at 6am and 2pm, returning to Uvita at 9am and 4pm. Three buses a day travel the road to Ciudad Cortés and on to Palmar; ask locally for times, and whether departures are from the village or the highway.

## PARQUE NACIONAL MARINO BALLENA
This national marine park was created in 1990 to protect coral and rock reefs in 5375 hectares of ocean around Isla Ballena, south of Uvita. The island has nesting colonies of magnificent frigatebirds, blue-footed boobies, and other seabirds, as well as many green iguanas and basilisk lizards. Humpback whales migrate through the area and may be sighted from December to March. The Spanish word for whale is *ballena* – this gives the name to the vaguely whale-shaped island as well as to the park. Both common and bottle-nosed dolphins are found here year-round, and there's a good variety of other marine life.

From Punta Uvita heading southeast, the park includes 13km of sandy and rocky beaches, mangrove swamps, river mouths, and rocky headlands – a total of 110 land hectares. The sandy beaches are the nesting sites of olive ridley and hawksbill turtles during the rainy months of May to November, with peak laying occurring in September and October. All six kinds of Costa Rica's mangroves occur within the park: two species of black mangrove, red, tea, white, and (the rarest) buttonwood.

The ranger station is in the community of Bahía, the seaside extension of Uvita. The rangers told me that you can hire boats from Bahía to Isla Ballena for about US$15 to US$20 per hour; landing on the island and snorkeling are permitted. From the ranger station you can walk out onto Punta Uvita and snorkel. This is best on an ebb/low tide (especially when the tides are not extreme). High and extreme tides make the water turbid.

Although there's a ranger station, the park remains undeveloped, though this may change. The official park authorities have been overshadowed somewhat by 'ASOPARQUE,' which is the 'Association for the Development of the Ballena Marine National Park – Working Together for the Park' (☎ 771-4582, fax 771-8841). There's now a staffed entrance station where a US$6 per person fee is charged and visitor information is available. You can camp near here, but there's little or no water and there are no bathroom facilities yet.

## SOUTHEAST OF UVITA

Beyond Uvita, the newly paved road follows the coast as far as Palmar almost 40km away. This road, previously a major challenge even with high-clearance 4WD, was passable to ordinary vehicles for the first time in 1996. There are several remote beaches along here that are becoming discovered as hotels begin opening their doors to visitors who are traveling the Costanera all the way through. This route, which provides an alternative to the Interamericana and had been planned for years, is now a reality. Drivers now have the choice of traveling south along coastal roads or inland through the mountains along the Interamericana. About four daily buses currently traveling this stretch of road can drop you near any of the places described below. Telephone links here are poor; be patient when leaving messages, faxes and emails.

*La Cusinga* (Finca Tres Hermanas; ☎/fax 771-2465, **W** www.lacusingalodge.com) Cabins US$79 per person including three meals and trail guide. About 5km south of Uvita is a new rainforest lodge with beach views. This rustic place features a small stream that provides hydroelectricity for the lodge, a farm growing organic crops, five cabins with two to four beds, and two dorms sleeping eight. Each unit has a private hot shower. Food served is 'rural tico' and includes fish, vegetarian options, and chicken, but no beef. Boat trips to the national park, hiking on several kilometers of trails, birding, snorkeling, surfing, and other activities are offered in this attractive rural lodge.

About 7km south of Uvita is **Playa Bahía Ballena**, which is within the marine boundaries of the park. There's no village here but there are a number of small places to stay along the road, all of them near the beach.

*Cabinas Punta Uvita* (☎ 771-2311) Rooms without bath US$4.50 per person, doubles with bath US$13. This place has pleasant grounds, a few rooms with shared baths, and a double with private bath. You can camp here, and horse rental is available.

*Cabinas Flamingo* (☎ 771-8078, 787-7921, fax 787-0116, **e** vidaverde@racsa.co.cr) Cabins US$30. This place has a restaurant-bar and some large cabins sleeping up to six. Baths are cold, but surfing, kayaking and horseback riding are all available.

*Villa Leonor* (☎ 225-8151, 280-6284 for reservations) Cabins US$20. Villa Leonor has an attractive garden and is near a particularly lovely part of the beach, and apparently a cavern and waterfall are nearby. A few rustic cabins with solar-heated water sleep up to six. Meals are available.

About 10km beyond Uvita is **Playa Piñuela**, at the far southeastern corner of the Ballena national park, followed 1.5km later by **Playa Ventanas** just outside the park. At the south end of this beach is **Mystic Dive Center** (☎ 788-8351, 788-8636, **e** info@mysticdivecenter.com, **W** www.mysticdivecenter.com), which offers local scuba diving and snorkeling trips. Their Canadian-run dive shop is staffed by well-trained divemasters, some of whom are divemaster instructors, so all levels of diving can be accommodated. Ballena National Park and Isla del Caño are among the destinations featured.

About 14km south of Uvita is **Playa Tortuga** (also called Turtle Beach by expats or Ojochal by locals), where several hotels and restaurants are found. Look for the signs on the roadway and follow them. The hotel restaurants are open to the public. Ask locally about Ojochal Internet Café, which serves coffee and has public Internet access.

*Balcón de Uvita* Meals average US$8. Open 11am-9pm Thur-Sun. The current open hours may expand as word gets out of the excellent Asian cuisine, especially Thai food, served at this restaurant with a view.

*Gringo Mike's Pizza* Until recently located in Dominical, this garrulous New Yorker has moved to Ojochal and does great pizza and sandwiches, New York deli style. Ask about the B&B (called La Posada) that he and his wife are opening near the beach.

*Lookout at Turtle Beach* (formerly Paraíso del Pacífico; ☎ 378-7473, message only, **e** info@hotelcostarica.com, **W** www

*.hotelcostarica.com)* Doubles US$74. This place is on a hill overlooking Playa Tortuga. It has 12 bright and colorful rooms with hot showers, fans, and private balconies. There's a pool and an excellent international restaurant, and all local tours are arranged. The enthusiastic new Californian owners completely renovated the hotel for 2002.

*Hotel Villas Gaia (☎/fax 256-9996, 282-5333, 382-8240 cellular, e hvgaia@racsa.co.cr, w www.villasgaia.com)* Doubles US$70. Along the road is this Dutch-run place. Set in tranquil forested grounds are 12 wooden cabins decorated with tropical colors; each has a private terrace, hot water, and ceiling fans. A brief walk leads to a spacious restaurant and hilltop pool. Tours of all kinds (including ultralight flights) can be arranged.

*Villas El Bosque (☎ 398-2112 cellular, fax 786-6358, e villaselbosque@yahoo.com, w www.villaselbosque.com)* Doubles US$53, including breakfast, cabins US$300 per week. This friendly little place has three spotless rooms with hot showers, patios and ocean views and two cabins with kitchens and hot showers.

*El Perezoso (in the USA fax 435-518-8923; e elperezosocr@yahoo.com, w www.el perezoso.net)* Doubles US$46-58. Just south and inland is this charming, hilltop place

with great views, a small pool, and pleasant rooms in a small vine-covered villa. British owner Roger is anxious to help out and will pick guests up at the Palmar airport by arrangement. There are seven rooms, all with fans, some with private baths, some with balcony views. Baths have hot water. A small restaurant and bar are on the premises.

*Rancho Soluna (☎/fax 788-8351, 778-8210)* Campsites US$5-7 per person, singles/doubles US$26/34. Just past an office for Ventana del Pacífico realty, you'll see signs for this low-key place on attractive grounds. It has a small bar-restaurant and a pool table on an open-air patio with a thatched roof and mosquito netting. A few simple rooms have private bath. Some cabins have kitchenettes and are available by the week. You can camp and use the facilities, or sleep in another net-protected patio.

Look around for other places to eat, drink, and camp.

The paved road continues for about 15km to the turnoff to the small town of Ciudad Cortés, which is now 4km off the coastal highway and has a forgotten air about it. Three kilometers beyond the turnoff, you reach the Interamericana at Palmar Norte (see the Southern Costa Rica chapter).

# Language

Although Spanish is the most widely spoken language in Costa Rica, travelers to the region will occasionally encounter a mix of other European tongues, indigenous languages and colorful dialects. This chapter addresses such variations only briefly, mainly discussing the type of Spanish that is understood more or less throughout the country.

Every visitor to Costa Rica should attempt to learn some Spanish, the basic elements of which are easily acquired (perhaps more so for speakers of English and Romance languages). A month-long language course taken before departure can go a long way toward facilitating communication and comfort on the road. Language courses are also available in San José and some other towns. Even if classes are impractical, you should make the effort to learn a few basic phrases and pleasantries. Do not hesitate to practice your new skills – in general, Latin Americans meet attempts to communicate in the vernacular, however halting, with enthusiasm and appreciation.

## Latin American Spanish

The Spanish of the Americas comes in a bewildering array of varieties. Depending on the areas in which you travel, consonants may be glossed over, vowels squashed into each other, and syllables and even words dropped entirely. Slang and regional vocabulary, much of it derived from indigenous languages, can further add to your bewilderment.

Throughout Latin America, the Spanish language is referred to as *castellano* more often than *español*. Unlike in Spain, the plural of the familiar *tú* form is *ustedes* rather than *vosotros;* the latter term will sound quaint and archaic in the Americas. In addition, the letters 'c' and 'z' are never lisped in Latin America; attempts to do so could well provoke amusement or even contempt.

## Spanish in Costa Rica

The following colloquialisms and slang *(tiquismos)* are frequently heard and are for the most part used only in Costa Rica.

| | | | |
|---|---|---|---|
| *¡Adios!* | Hi! (used when passing a friend in the street, or anyone in remote rural areas; also means 'farewell,' but only when leaving for a long time) | *mi amor* | my love (used as a familiar form of address by both men and women) |
| *bomba* | gas station | *pulpería* | corner grocery store |
| *Buena nota.* | OK/Excellent. (literally 'good note') | *¡Pura vida!* | Super! (literally 'pure life,' also an expression of approval or even a greeting) |
| *chapulines* | a gang, usually of young thieves | *sabanero* | cowboy, especially one from Guanacaste Province |
| *chunche* | thing (can refer to almost anything) | *Salado.* | Too bad/Tough luck. |
| *cien metros* | one city block | *soda* | café or lunch counter |
| *¿Hay campo?* | Is there space? (on a bus) | *¡Tuanis!* | Cool! |
| *machita* | blonde woman (slang) | *¡Upe!* | Is anybody home? (used mainly in rural areas at people's houses, instead of knocking) |
| *mae* | buddy (pronounced 'ma' as in 'mat' followed with a quick 'eh'; mainly used by boys and young men) | *vos* | you (informal, same as *tú*) |

## Other Languages

Travelers will find English is often spoken in the better hotels and travel agencies, and some other European languages are encountered in hotels run by Europeans. On the Caribbean

494

coast, many of the locals speak some English, albeit with a local Creole dialect. A few thousand people speak indigenous languages, but these are rarely encountered by travelers.

## Phrasebooks & Dictionaries
Lonely Planet's *Costa Rica Spanish phrasebook,* by Thomas Kohnstamm, will be extremely helpful during your trip. If you're traveling outside of Costa Rica, LP's *Latin American Spanish phrasebook,* by Anna Cody, is another worthwhile addition to your backpack. An exceptionally useful resource is the *University of Chicago Spanish-English, English-Spanish Dictionary* – its small size, light weight, and thorough entries make it ideal for travel. It also makes a great gift for any newfound friends upon your departure.

## Pronunciation
The pronunciation of written Spanish is, in theory, consistently phonetic. Once you are aware of the basic rules, they should cause little difficulty. Speak slowly to avoid getting tongue-tied until you become confident of your ability. Of course, the best way to familiarize yourself with the pronunciation of the area you're traveling in is to chat with locals, keeping an ear out for regional variations.

Traditionally, there were three Spanish letters that did not exist in English: 'ch,' 'll,' and 'ñ.' These followed 'c,' 'l,' and 'n' respectively in the alphabet, and had their own corresponding sections in the dictionary. However, in the mid-1990s, Spain's Academia Real de la Lengua Española abolished 'ch' and 'll' as separate letters; hence, newer Spanish dictionaries list them in their English alphabetical order. The practice varies from region to region, so look for a 'ch' section in the phone book if you can't find 'Chávez' under 'c.'

**Vowels** Spanish vowels are generally consistent and have close English equivalents:

| | |
|---|---|
| **a** is like the 'a' in 'father' | **o** is like the 'o' in 'note' |
| **e** is somewhere between the 'e' in 'met' and the 'ey' in 'hey' | **u** is like the 'oo' in 'boot'; it is silent after 'q' and in the pairings 'gue' and 'gui,' unless it's carrying a dieresis ('ü,' as in *güero*) |
| **i** is like the 'ee' in 'feet' | |

**Consonants** Spanish consonants generally resemble their English equivalents. The following are the major differences in consonants.

**b** resembles the English 'b,' but is a softer sound produced by holding the lips nearly together. When beginning a word or when preceded by 'm' or 'n,' it's pronounced like the 'b' in 'book' *(bomba, embajada).* The Spanish 'v' is pronounced almost identically; for clarification, Spanish speakers refer to 'b' as 'b larga' and to 'v' as 'b corta.'

**c** is like the 's' in 'see' before 'e' and 'i'; otherwise, it's like the English 'k.'

**d** is produced with the tongue up against the front teeth, almost like the 'th' in 'feather'; after 'l' and 'n,' it's pronounced like the English 'd' in 'dog.'

**g** before 'e' and 'i' acts as a more guttural English 'h'; otherwise, it's like the 'g' in 'go.'

**h** is invariably silent; if your name begins with this letter, listen carefully when immigration officials summon you to pick up your passport.

**j** acts as a more guttural English 'h.'

**ll** acts as a Spanish 'y,' although it is never a vowel; see Semiconsonant, later.

**ñ** is like the 'ny' in 'canyon.'

**r** is produced with the tongue touching the palate and flapping down, almost like the 'tt' of 'butter.' At the beginning of a word or following 'l,' 'n,' or 's,' it is rolled strongly.

**rr** is a very strongly rolled 'r.'

**t** resembles the English 't,' but without the puff of air.

**v** is pronounced like the Spanish 'b.'

**x** is generally pronounced like the 'x' in 'taxi' except for a few words in which it acts as the Spanish 'j' (as in 'México').

**z** is like the 's' in 'his.'

**Semiconsonant** The Spanish **y** is a semiconsonant; it's pronounced as the Spanish 'i' when it stands alone or appears at the end of a word. Normally, 'y' is pronounced like the 'y' in 'yesterday.'

**Diphthongs** Diphthongs are combinations of two vowels that form a single syllable. In Spanish, the formation of a diphthong depends on combinations of the two 'weak vowels,' 'i' and 'u,' or one weak and one of the three 'strong' vowels, 'a,' 'e,' and 'o.' Two strong vowels form separate syllables.

An example of two weak vowels forming a diphthong is the word *viuda* (widow; pronounced **vyu**-tha). The initial syllable of 'Guatemala' is a combination of weak and strong vowels. In contrast, the verb *caer* (to fall) has two syllables (pronounced ca-**er**). Other examples include the following:

| | | | |
|---|---|---|---|
| **ai** | as in 'hide' | **ie** | as in 'yes' |
| **au** | as in 'how' | **oi** | as in 'boy' |
| **ei** | as in 'hay' | **ua** | as in 'wash' |
| **ia** | as in 'yard' | **ue** | as in 'well' (unless preceded by 'q' or 'g') |

**Stress** Stress is extremely important as it can change the meaning of words. In general, words ending in vowels or the letters 'n' or 's' have stress on the next-to-last syllable, while those with other endings have stress on the last syllable. Thus *vaca* (cow) and *caballos* (horses) are both stressed on their penultimate syllables, while *catedral* (cathedral) is stressed on its last syllable.

To indicate departures from these general rules, Spanish employs the acute accent, which can occur anywhere in a word. If there is an accented syllable, stress is always on that syllable. Thus *sótano* (basement), 'América' and 'Panamá' have the first, second, and third syllable stressed, respectively. When words are written in capital letters, the accent is often omitted, but the stress still falls where the accent would be.

## Basic Grammar

Although even colloquial Spanish comprises a multitude of tenses and moods, learning enough grammar to enable basic conversation is not particularly difficult. In general, Spanish word order in sentences resembles that of English.

**Nouns & Pronouns** Nouns in Spanish are masculine or feminine. In general, nouns ending in 'o,' 'e,' or 'ma' are masculine, while those ending in 'a,' 'ión,' or 'dad' are feminine. Of course, there are scores of exceptions to this rule: both *día* (day) and *mapa* (map) are masculine, while *mano* (hand) is feminine. To pluralize a noun, add 's' if it ends in an unaccented vowel – eg, *libro* (book) becomes *libros* – and 'es' if it ends in a consonant or accented vowel – eg, *rey* (king) becomes *reyes*. Fortunately for speakers of English, there is no declension of nouns as in Latin.

The personal pronouns are *yo* (I), *tú*, or *vos* (you, informal), *usted* (you, formal; abbreviated Ud), *el/ella* (he/she), *nosotros/nosotras* (we), *ustedes* (you, plural; abbreviated Uds), and *ellos/ellas* (they). Note that to use the feminine plurals *nosotras* and *ellas*, the group referred to must be entirely composed of females; the presence of even one male calls for the masculine pronoun. In common speech, the personal pronoun may be omitted when it is the subject of a sentence if the subject's identity is made clear by the verb ending: *estoy aquí* rather than *yo estoy aquí* (both mean 'I am here').

The possessive pronouns are *mi* (my), *tu* (your, informal), *nuestro* (our), and *su* (his/her/their/your, formal; singular and plural). As in English, possessive pronouns precede the noun they modify; however, they must agree in number and gender with that noun – not with the possessor. Thus we get *nuestro hombre* (our man), *nuestra mujer* (our woman), *nuestros novios* (our boyfriends), and *nuestras novias* (our girlfriends). *Mi*, *tu*, and *su* do not change with gender, but add an 's' for plural nouns: *mis libros* means 'my books.'

The demonstrative pronouns are *este* (this) and *ese* (that). Gender and number also affect demonstrative pronouns:

| | | | |
|---|---|---|---|
| *este libro* | this book | *ese chico* | that boy |
| *estos cuadernos* | these notebooks | *esos muchachos* | those guys |
| *esta carta* | this letter | *esa chica* | that girl |
| *estas tijeras* | these scissors | *esas muchachas* | those gals |

**Articles, Adjectives & Adverbs** The definite articles ('the' in English) are *el, la, los,* and *las*. These four forms correspond to the four possible combinations of gender and number. Similarly, the indefinite articles ('a,' 'an,' and 'some') are *un, una, unos,* and *unas*. In Spanish, the definite article is used more extensively than in English, while the indefinite article is utilized less. As in English, the articles precede the nouns they modify, eg, *el papel* (the paper), *unas frutas* (some fruits).

In contrast, adjectives in Spanish usually follow the noun they modify. Those ending in 'o' agree with the noun in gender and number (thus *alto* means 'tall,' while *mujeres altas* means 'tall women'); those ending in other letters merely agree in number. To form a comparative, add *más* (more) or *menos* (less) before the adjective. For superlatives, add the *más* or *menos* as well as *lo, la, los,* or *las* (depending on gender and number). For example, *pequeño* is 'small,' *más pequeño* 'smaller,' and *lo más pequeño* 'the smallest.'

Adverbs can often be formed from adjectives by adding the suffix *-mente*. If the adjective ends in an 'o,' convert it to an 'a' before affixing the ending. Thus *actual* (current) becomes *actualmente* (currently) and *rápido* (rapid) becomes *rápidamente*.

**Verbs** Spanish has three main categories of verbs: those ending in 'ar,' such as *hablar* (to speak); those ending in 'er,' such as *comer* (to eat); and those ending in 'ir,' such as *reir* (to laugh). Verbs are conjugated by retaining the verb's stem and altering the ending depending on subject, tense, and mood. While most verbs follow a complicated yet predictable pattern of conjugation, there are scores of 'irregular' verbs, often the most commonly used, that must be memorized. For a more detailed explanation of verb conjugation, refer to Lonely Planet's *Costa Rica Spanish phrasebook*.

## Greetings & Civilities

In public behavior, Latin Americans are often cordial yet polite and expect others to reciprocate. Never, for example, address a stranger without extending a greeting such as *buenos días* or *buenas tardes*. The usage of the informal second-person singular *tú* and *vos* differs from country to country; when in doubt, use the more formal *usted*. You must *always* use *usted* when addressing the police or persons with considerable power.

| | | | |
|---|---|---|---|
| Hello. | *Hola.* | You're welcome./ | *De nada./* |
| Good morning/day. | *Buenos días.* | It's a pleasure. | *Con mucho gusto.* |
| Good afternoon. | *Buenas tardes.* | Excuse me. (when | |
| Good evening/night. | *Buenas noches.* | passing someone) | *Permiso.* |
| | | Excuse me. | *Discúlpeme* or *Perdón.* |
| (The above three are often shortened to | | I'm sorry. | *Lo siento.* |
| *Buenos* or *Buenas*.) | | What is your | |
| | | name? | *¿Cómo se llama usted?* |
| Goodbye. | | My name is … | *Me llamo …* |
| *Adiós* or *Hasta luego,* but also see | | A pleasure | |
| 'Spanish in Costa Rica,' earlier. | | (to meet you). | *Mucho gusto.* |
| Please. | *Por favor.* | | |
| Thank you. | *Gracias.* | | |

LANGUAGE

## Words & Phrases

| | | | |
|---|---|---|---|
| yes | *sí* | I don't understand. | *No entiendo.* |
| no | *no* | I don't speak much Spanish. | |
| and | *y* | | *No hablo mucho castellano.* |
| to/at | *a* | Is/are there …? | *¿Hay …?* |
| for | *por, para* | I would like … | *Me gustaría … or* |
| of/from | *de/desde* | | *Quisiera* |
| in/on | *en* | Where? | *¿Dónde?* |
| with | *con* | Where is/are …? | *¿Dónde está/están …?* |
| without | *sin* | When? | *¿Cuándo?* |
| before | *antes* | What? | |
| after | *después de* | | *¿Qué?* (use *¿Cómo?* to ask someone to |
| soon | *pronto* | | repeat something) |
| already | *ya* | Which (ones)? | *¿Cuál(es)?* |
| now | *ahora* | Who? | *¿Quién?* |
| right away | *ahorita, en seguida* | Why? | *¿Por qué?* |
| here | *aquí* | How? | *¿Cómo?* |
| there | *allí* or *allá* | How much? | *¿Cuánto?* |
| I understand. | *Entiendo.* | How many? | *¿Cuántos?* |

## Emergencies

| | | | |
|---|---|---|---|
| Help! | *¡Socorro!* or *¡Auxilio!* | I've been robbed. | *Me han robado.* |
| Help me! | *¡Ayúdenme!* | They took my … | *Se me llevaron …* |
| Thief! | *¡Ladrón!* | money | *el dinero* |
| Fire! | *¡Fuego!* | passport | *el pasaporte* |
| police | *policía* | bag | *la bolsa* |
| doctor | *doctor* | Leave me alone! | *¡Déjeme!* |
| hospital | *hospital* | Go away! | *¡Váyase!* |

## Getting Around

| | | | |
|---|---|---|---|
| plane | *avión* | first/last/next | *primero/último/próximo* |
| train | *tren* | one-way/roundtrip | *ida/ida y vuelta* |
| bus | *bus, autobús* | left luggage | *guardería de equipaje* |
| small bus | *colectivo, buseta, microbus* | tourist office | *oficina de turismo* |
| ship | *barco, buque* | | |
| car | *auto* or *carro* | I would like a ticket to … | |
| taxi | *taxi* | | *Quiero un boleto/pasaje a …* |
| truck | *camión* | What's the fare to …? | |
| pickup | *camioneta* | | *¿Cuánto cuesta el pasaje a …?* |
| bicycle | *bicicleta* | When does the next plane/bus leave for …? | |
| motorcycle | *motocicleta* | | *¿Cuándo sale el próximo avión/bus* |
| hitchhike | *hacer dedo* or *pedir un* ride | | *para …?* |
| airport | *aeropuerto* | Are there student discounts? | |
| train station | *estación de ferrocarril* | | *¿Hay descuentos estudiantiles?/¿Hay* |
| bus terminal | *terminal de buses* | | *rebajas para estudiantes?* |

**Traffic Signs** Keep in mind that traffic signs will invariably be in Spanish and may not be accompanied by internationally recognized symbols. Pay especially close attention to signs reading *Peligro* (Danger), *Cede el Paso* (Yield, or Give way; especially prevalent on one-lane bridges), and *Hundimiento* (Dip; often a euphemistic term for axle-breaking sinkhole). Disregarding these warnings could result in disaster.

The following phrases are frequently seen on traffic signs:

| | | | |
|---|---|---|---|
| *Adelante* | Ahead | *Hundimiento* | Dip |
| *Alto* | Stop | *Mantenga Su Derecha* | Keep to the right |
| *Cede el Paso* | Yield/Give way | *No Adelantar/Rebase* | No passing |
| *Curva Peligrosa* | Dangerous curve | *No Estacionar* | No parking |
| *Derrumbes en la Vía* | Landslides or Rockfalls (in the road) | *No Hay Paso* | No entrance |
| | | *Peligro* | Danger |
| | | *Trabajos en la Vía* | Construction/ Roadwork |
| *Despacio* | Slow | | |
| *Desvío* | Detour | *Tránsito Entrando* | Entering traffic |

## Accommodations

| | | | |
|---|---|---|---|
| hotel | *hotel, pensión, residencial, hospedaje* | cheaper | *más económico/ barato* |
| single room | *habitación sencilla* | the bill | *la cuenta* |
| double room | *habitación doble/ matrimonial* | What does it cost? | *¿Cuánto cuesta?* |
| | | May I see it? | *¿Puedo verlo?* |
| per night | *por noche* | I don't like it. | *No me gusta.* |
| full board | *pensión completa* | Can you give me a deal? | |
| shared bath | *baño compartido* | | *¿Me puede hacer precio?/¿Me puede hacer promoción?/¿Me puede rebajar?* |
| private bath | *baño privado* | | |
| too expensive | *demasiado caro* | | |

## Toilets

The most common word for 'toilet' is *baño*, but *servicios sanitarios* or just *servicios* (services) is a frequent alternative. Men's toilets will usually be signaled by *hombres, caballeros,* or *varones*. Women's toilets will say *señoras* or *damas*.

## Eating & Drinking

| | | | |
|---|---|---|---|
| I (don't) eat/drink … | *(No) como/tomo …* | juice | *jugo* |
| I'm a vegetarian. | *Soy vegetariano/a.* | vegetables | *vegetales* or *legumbres* |
| water | *agua* | fish | *pescado* |
| purified water | *agua purificada* | seafood | *mariscos* |
| bread | *pan* | coffee | *café* |
| meat | *carne* | tea | *té* |
| cheese | *queso* | beer | *cerveza* |
| eggs | *huevos* | alcohol | *alcohol* |
| milk | *leche* | | |

## Post & Communications

| | | | |
|---|---|---|---|
| post office | *correo* | phone call | *llamada (telefónica)* |
| letter | *carta* | collect call | *llamada por cobrar* |
| parcel | *paquete* | public telephone | *teléfono público* |
| postcard | *postal* | local call | *llamada local* |
| airmail | *correo aéreo* | long-distance call | *llamada de larga distancia* |
| registered mail | *correo certificado* | | |
| stamps | *estampillas* | person to person | *persona a persona* |
| | | email | *correo electrónico* |

## Geographical Expressions

The expressions below are among the most common you will encounter in Spanish-language maps and guides.

| | | | |
|---|---|---|---|
| *avenida* | avenue | *estancia, granja,* | |
| *bahía* | bay | *rancho* | ranch |
| *calle* | street | *estero* | marsh, estuary |
| *camino* | road | *lago* | lake |
| *campo, finca,* | | *montaña* | mountain |
| *hacienda* | farm | *parque nacional* | national park |
| *carretera, camino,* | | *paso* | pass |
| *ruta* | highway | *puente* | bridge |
| *cascada, salto* | waterfall | *río* | river |
| *cerro* | hill or mount | *seno* | sound |
| *cordillera* | mountain range | *valle* | valley |

## Countries

The list below includes some of the countries whose names are spelled differently in English and Spanish.

| | | | |
|---|---|---|---|
| Canada | *Canadá* | Spain | *España* |
| Denmark | *Dinamarca* | Sweden | *Suecia* |
| England | *Inglaterra* | Switzerland | *Suiza* |
| France | *Francia* | United States | *Estados Unidos* |
| Germany | *Alemania* | Wales | *Gales* |
| Great Britain | *Gran Bretaña* | | |
| Ireland | *Irlanda* | I am from… | |
| Italy | *Italia* | *Soy de…* | |
| Japan | *Japón* | Where are you from? | |
| Netherlands | *Países Bajos* | *¿De dónde viene usted?* | |
| New Zealand | *Nueva Zelandia* | Where do you live? | |
| Scotland | *Escocia* | *¿Dónde vive usted?* | |

## Numbers

| | | | | | |
|---|---|---|---|---|---|
| 1 | *uno* | 19 | *diecinueve* | 110 | *ciento diez* |
| 2 | *dos* | 20 | *veinte* | 200 | *doscientos* |
| 3 | *tres* | 21 | *veintiuno* | 300 | *trescientos* |
| 4 | *cuatro* | 22 | *veintidós* | 400 | *cuatrocientos* |
| 5 | *cinco* | 23 | *veintitrés* | 500 | *quinientos* |
| 6 | *seis* | 24 | *veinticuatro* | 600 | *seiscientos* |
| 7 | *siete* | 30 | *treinta* | 700 | *setecientos* |
| 8 | *ocho* | 31 | *treinta y uno* | 800 | *ochocientos* |
| 9 | *nueve* | 32 | *treinta y dos* | 900 | *novecientos* |
| 10 | *diez* | 33 | *treinta y tres* | 1000 | *mil* |
| 11 | *once* | 40 | *cuarenta* | 1100 | *mil cien* |
| 12 | *doce* | 50 | *cincuenta* | 1200 | *mil doscientos* |
| 13 | *trece* | 60 | *sesenta* | 2000 | *dos mil* |
| 14 | *catorce* | 70 | *setenta* | 10,000 | *diez mil* |
| 15 | *quince* | 80 | *ochenta* | 50,000 | *cincuenta mil* |
| 16 | *dieciséis* | 90 | *noventa* | 100,000 | *cien mil* |
| 17 | *diecisiete* | 100 | *cien* | 1,000,000 | *un millón* |
| 18 | *dieciocho* | 101 | *ciento uno* | 2,000,000 | *dos millones* |
| | | 102 | *ciento dos* | 1,000,000,000 | *un billón* |

## Ordinal Numbers

As with other adjectives, ordinals must agree in gender and number with the noun they modify. Ordinal numbers are often abbreviated using a numeral and a superscript 'o' or 'a' in street names, addresses, and so forth: Calle 1ª, 2º piso (1st Street, 2nd floor).

| | | | |
|---|---|---|---|
| 1st | *primero/a* | 8th | *octavo/a* |
| 2nd | *segundo/a* | 9th | *noveno/a* |
| 3rd | *tercero/a* | 10th | *décimo/a* |
| 4th | *cuarto/a* | 11th | *undécimo/a* |
| 5th | *quinto/a* | 12th | *duodécimo/a* |
| 6th | *sexto/a* | 20th | *vigésimo/a* |
| 7th | *séptimo/a* | | |

## Days of the Week

| | | | |
|---|---|---|---|
| Monday | *lunes* | Friday | *viernes* |
| Tuesday | *martes* | Saturday | *sábado* |
| Wednesday | *miércoles* | Sunday | *domingo* |
| Thursday | *jueves* | | |

## Time

Eight o'clock is *las ocho,* while 8:30 is *las ocho y treinta* (eight and thirty) or *las ocho y media* (eight and a half). However, 7:45 is *las ocho menos quince* (eight minus fifteen) or *las ocho menos cuarto* (eight minus one quarter).

Times are modified by morning *(de la mañana)* or afternoon *(de la tarde)* instead of am or pm. Use of the 24-hour clock, or military time, is also common, especially with transportation schedules.

What time is it?
   *¿Qué hora es? or ¿Qué horas son?*
It's one o'clock.
   *Es la una.*

It's two/three, etc, o'clock.
   *Son las dos/tres,* etc.
At three o'clock…
   *A las tres…*

# Glossary

For traffic signs and related terms in Spanish, refer to the boxed text 'Traffic Signs' in the Getting Around chapter. Spanish equivalents for common food and drink terms are provided in the Facts for the Visitor chapter.

**almuerzo ejecutivo** – inexpensive set lunch menu; special of the day (literally 'business lunch')
**alquiler de automóviles** – car rental
**apartado** – PO Box

**boca** – appetizer, often served with drinks in a bar

**campesino** – peasant; person who works in agriculture
**carretas** – colorfully painted wooden ox carts, now a form of folk art
**casado** – a set bargain meal, normally rice, black beans, a small salad, a cooked vegetable and either chicken, fish, meat, or cheese
**catedral** – cathedral
**colectivos** – buses, minivans, or cars operating as shared taxis
**colón** (plural: **colones**) – Costa Rican unit of currency
**cordillera** – mountain range
**corriente** – long-distance bus with many stops
**costarricense** – Costa Rican (see also *tico*)

**directo** – long-distance bus with few stops

**fauna silvestre** – wildlife
**finca** – farm or plantation
**frontera** – border
**fútbol** – soccer

**guapote** – large fish caught for sport, equivalent to rainbow bass

**Holdridge Life Zones** – A classification system developed in the 1960s by US botanist LR Holdridge, whereby climate, latitude, and altitude are used to define 116 distinct natural environmental zones, each with a particular type of vegetation

**ICE** – Instituto Costarricense de Electricidad; Costa Rican utilities (phone and electricity) company
**ICT** – Instituto Costarricense de Turismo; Costa Rican tourism institute, which provides tourist information
**iglesia** – church
**IGN** – Instituto Geográfico Nacional; National Geographic Institute, which publishes topographic maps of Costa Rica
**invierno** – winter; the wet season in Costa Rica

**josefino** – resident of San José

**kilometraje** – distance in kilometers; 'mileage'

**lavandería** – laundry facility, usually offering dry-cleaning services
**llanuras** – tropical plains

**maize** – corn
**malecón** – pier, sea wall, or waterfront promenade
**marías** – local name for taxi meters
**mercado** – market
**meseta central** – central plateau; central valley
**mestizo** – person of mixed descent, usually Spanish and Indian
**migración (Oficina de Migración)** – immigration (Immigration Office)
**MINAE** – Ministerio de Ambiente y Energía; Ministry of Environment and Energy, in charge of the national park system
**muelle** – dock
**museo** – museum

**normal** – long-distance bus with many stops

**OTS** – Organization for Tropical Studies

**parada** - bus stop
**páramo** – habitat characterized by highland shrub and tussock grass; common to the Andes of Colombia, Ecuador, and Peru, as well as parts of Costa Rica
**parque** – park
**playa** – beach

**PLN** – Partido de Liberación Nacional; National Liberation Party
**puerto** – port
**pulpería** – corner grocery store
**PUSC** – Partido Unidad Social Cristiana; Social Christian Unity Party

**sendero natural** – nature trail
**soda** – lunch counter; inexpensive eatery

**tico/a** – what Costa Ricans call themselves

**UNESCO** – United Nations Educational, Scientific, and Cultural Organization
**USGS** – US Geological Survey

**verano** – summer; the dry season in Costa Rica
**vivero** – plant nursery

# COSTA RICAN WILDLIFE GUIDE

Costa Rica's wildlife is incredibly diverse. This guide is a reasonably comprehensive overview of the most interesting animals and those that are most often seen by observant visitors. For detailed information, see the books listed in the Facts for the Visitor chapter. Also refer to Flora & Fauna in the Facts about Costa Rica chapter for an overview of the country's wildlife and habitats.

The mammals and birds are described in the taxonomic order found in wildlife guidebooks, based on evolutionary history: the most ancient come first and the most recently evolved come last. Spanish names (which vary region to region) and scientific names (which change occasionally with new research) are included.

## Mammals

### Opossums

Opossums are the American representatives of the marsupials, which have one of the strangest methods of mammalian reproduction. Newborns, which look like tiny embryos, crawl from the birth canal through the mother's fur into a pouch containing the teats. Here, the young latch onto a nipple and complete most of their development.

The first marsupial seen in Europe was an opossum, brought home by the Spanish explorer Pinzón in the 16th century. Male opossums have a forked penis, and early naturalists thought that the animals copulated through the nose and the mother then blew the embryo into the pouch! Gestation is 12 days, followed by two months in the pouch.

Nine of approximately 70 opossum species are found in Costa Rica. The most frequently seen is the **common opossum** (zorro pelón; *Didelphis marsupialis*). Resembling overgrown, long-legged rats, they reach almost a meter in length, of which the tail is almost half. Adults weigh 0.6 to 1.8kg, although there have been reports of some reaching 5kg! Males are larger than females. The back and legs are blackish brown or gray and the head and underparts light brown or yellowish, with much variation in color due to the coarse, two-layered fur.

They are mainly nocturnal, often seen foraging for anything edible along watercourses and in garbage dumps. Distribution is nationwide, but normally below 1500m. They are both terrestrial and arboreal and, when cornered, will hiss and attempt to bite, rather than pretending to lie dead, as North American opossums do.

A smaller species seen quite often is the **gray four-eyed opossum** *(Philander opossum)*, found in rainforest regions and recognized by a black face mask with large white spots over the eyes, and a grayer, smoother appearance than the previous species. The water opossum *(Chironectes minimus)* is locally common on some rivers and has a light/dark-gray-striped pattern on its back.

### Anteaters

Anteaters, members of the New World order Edentata (Latin for 'untoothed'), are unique among land mammals in that they lack teeth and use a long, sticky tongue to slurp up ants and termites. Their eyesight is poor, but strong; their heavily clawed forelegs rip open ant nests; and they use a well-developed sense of smell to detect their prey.

All four species of anteater are restricted to Central and South America, and three are recorded in Costa Rica. The largest of those is the locally rare **giant anteater** *(Myrmecophaga tridactyla)*,

**Anteater**

which reaches a length of almost 2m in size and has a tongue that protrudes an astonishing 60cm up to 150 times a minute!

Much more common is the **lesser anteater** (or northern tamandua; oso mielero; *Tamandua mexicana*), with a distinctive golden-tan and black pattern. Its length is 0.93 to 1.45m and it weighs 4 to 8kg. It too has a prodigious tongue, up to 40cm long, covered with microscopic backward-pointing spines to direct food into its mouth. Graced with a prehensile tail, it is a good tree climber and forages both on and above the ground. The tamandua is nocturnal and diurnal, and is seen, with luck, in most forests below 2000m. Though relatively common, it is, unfortunately, seen more often as roadkill than in the wild. If disturbed, it rears up on its hind legs and slashes wildly with strong front claws – an intimidating and potentially severe defense.

The last Costa Rican species is the 40cm-long **silky anteater** (tapacara; *Cyclopes didactylus*). Nocturnal and arboreal, it eats about 6000 ants per night. By day, it curls up in a tight ball and is hard to see.

## Sloths

Though related to anteaters, sloths are not true edentates as they have a few rudimentary teeth. They also share skeletal characteristics such as extra joint surfaces between the vertebrae (hence a new sub-order, the Xenarthra, from the Greek 'strange joint'). All five species are found only in the Neotropics; the two Costa Rican species are the **brown-throated three-toed sloth** (perezoso de tres dedos; *Bradypus variegatus*) and the **Hoffman's two-toed sloth** (perezoso de dos dedos; *Choloepus hoffmanni*).

The diurnal three-toed sloth is often sighted, whereas the nocturnal two-toed sloth is less often seen. Both are 50 to 75cm in length with stumpy tails. The three-toed is grayish brown with a distinctive gray-and-white mask on the face; the two-toed is generally a tan color. Sloths often hang motionless from branches or slowly progress upside down along a branch toward leaves, which are their primary food. Digestion of the tough food takes several days and sloths defecate about once

ALFREDO MAIQUEZ

**Brown-throated three-toed sloth**

a week (see the 'Slothful Habits' boxed text in the Central Pacific Coast chapter).

They are infrequently sighted on the ground, where their gait is clearly uncomfortable. They are sexually mature at three years and females then have a baby most years. The baby is carried on the mother's chest for 5½ months, feeding on milk for a few weeks but soon taught to eat leaves. The relationship between mother and offspring is close but not deep during this period – the youngster stays on or perishes. A baby that falls off its mother is ignored.

Some favorite leaves are from the Cecropia tree (although others are also eaten). These are common trees on riverbanks in the rainforest; this is the best place to spot sloths in the wild.

## Armadillos

Armadillos, armored with bony plates, look very different from their relatives, the anteaters and sloths. Few animal orders have such unlikely looking related members as the edentates.

The armadillos are the only edentates that have migrated as far north as the southern USA. Of about 20 species, two are seen in Costa Rica. The best known is the **nine-banded armadillo** (cusuco; *Dasypus novemcinctus*), which lives in the USA and Central and South America.

**Nine-banded armadillo**

Despite the name, there can be seven to 10 plates (bands). They are 65cm to 1m in length, of which about one-third is the tail, and weight is 3 to 7kg. Babies are identical quadruplets arising from a single egg.

Mainly nocturnal, they are noisy foragers, blindly crashing around well-drained rainforest slopes. Their eyesight is poor and they have been known to walk into stationary observers! They have few vocalizations, but their snuffling and crashing are sometimes heard in the forest at night. With their primitive teeth, they are limited to a diet of mainly insects, and occasionally fruit, fungi, carrion, and other material. Their burrows dug into the ground are often seen on rainforest hikes.

## Bats
Of the more than 200 Costa Rican mammal species, 50% are bats. Many lowland open areas have small bats swooping around at dusk, catching insects. Larger bats eat fish, fruit, or small animals, and others drink flower nectar or animal blood.

During the day bats roost in hollow trees (local naturalist guides know where to look) or under wooden roofs. I saw several **white-lined sac-winged bats** (murciélago de saco; *Saccopteryx bilineata*) in buildings in Parque Nacional Santa Rosa. These small social bats roost in colonies of five to 50 individuals and have dark fur with two long wavy white lines on the back.

One of the largest bats is the **fishing bulldog bat** (murciélago pescador; *Noctilio leporinus*), which has a 60cm wingspan. Most of this is skin and bones, so adults weigh under 90g – big as bats go. They fish in both salt and fresh water, and the Tortuguero canals are ideal for watching them grab large insects and small fish with their sharply clawed enlarged feet. You can tell them apart from other bats that are drinking by watching their feet dip into the water.

Another large bat, the **Jamaican fruit bat** (murciélago frutero; *Artibeus jamaicensis*), feeds on fruits of large trees, especially figs, which they grab on the wing and take to a feeding roost for consumption. They have 40cm wingspans and weigh 50g; there are several smaller species of fruit bat. These bats won't feed during the brightest full-moon nights for fear of owls.

All three species of **vampire bats** (vampiros) are restricted to the Neotropics (not Transylvania!) and are found in Costa Rica, where the most common is *Desmodus rotundus*. Unusual among bats, vampires are agile on the ground and can hop, run, and crawl toward their prey, which consists of birds and mammals, though cattle are preferred. Razor-sharp incisors make a small cut on the prey, and the flowing blood is licked up, not sucked. Anticoagulants in the bats' saliva ensure the blood flows freely during the meal. The process doesn't cause much harm to cattle, but there is potential danger of bat-borne diseases, especially rabies, which kill the prey (but not the bat).

Because of local misconceptions that all bats are vampires, they may be indiscriminately killed. However, their usefulness in controlling insects and pollinating flowers far outweighs their potential damage.

Most people think of bats as being black, but a variety of browns, grays, yellows, and reds also exists. Two uncommon Costa Rican species are white: the tiny **Honduran white bat** *(Ectophylla alba)* of the Caribbean slopes, and the larger **ghost bat** *(Diclidirus virgo)*, seen in the Península de Osa.

## Monkeys

Costa Rica has four monkey species, all members of the family Cebidae. These are the tropical mammals most likely to be seen and enjoyed by travelers. I once saw all four in one day in Parque Nacional Corcovado.

**Central American Squirrel Monkey** (mono tití; *Saimiri oerstedii*). Weighing under 1kg, these are the smallest, rarest, and most endangered Costa Rican monkeys. Over half of their 63 to 68cm length is a non-prehensile tail. The back and legs are a golden brown, the tail is olive brown with a black tuft at the tip, the chest is light colored, the neck, ears, and areas around the eyes are white, and the cap and muzzle are black. They travel in small to medium-size groups during the day, squealing or chirping noisily and leaping and crashing through vegetation in search of insects and fruit in the middle and lower levels of lowland forests. They exist only in isolated areas of the south Pacific coastal rainforests. Manuel Antonio and Corcovado National Parks (especially around Sirena) are good places to see them.

Central American squirrel monkey

**White-Faced Capuchin Monkey** (mono cara blanca; *Cebus capucinus*). These small and inquisitive monkeys are the easiest to observe in the wild. Like the squirrel monkeys, capuchins travel through the forest in groups searching for fruit and insects; they are sometimes seen with squirrel monkeys. Unlike squirrel monkeys, however, they have prehensile tails and forage at all forest levels, occasionally descending to the ground where crops such as corn and even oysters are part of their diet. Their thorough foraging, carefully searching through leaves and litter,

White-faced capuchin monkey

peeling off bark, and generally prying into everything, makes them enjoyable to watch.

These capuchins are black, with a whitish face, throat, and chest. The tail is typically carried with the tip coiled, a feature seen when viewed in silhouette. Ranging in length from 70cm to 1m, of which just over half is tail, they weigh between 1.5 and 3.9kg, with males larger than females. They are widespread in both wet and tropical dry forests on both sides of the country. The dry forests of Parque Nacional Santa Rosa and Reserva Cabo Blanco are two excellent places to view them during the dry season, when few leaves obscure the view. They are seen in most national parks with lowland and mid-elevation forests.

**Central American Spider Monkey** (mono colorado; *Ateles geoffroyi*). The spider monkeys are named for their long and thin legs, arms, and tail, which enable them to pursue an arboreal existence. They brachiate (swing from arm to arm) through the canopy and can hang supported just by their prehensile tail while using their long limbs to pick fruit. They rarely descend to the ground, and require large tracts of unbroken forest. Logging, hunting (their flesh is eaten), and other disturbances have made them endangered. Recovery is slow because reproductive rates are low, with a 7½-month pregnancy resulting in a single infant about every three years.

The baby rides on the mother's chest for its first two months and then moves onto the mother's back, where it stays for another month before venturing off on brief trips. It returns frequently to the mother to ride or nurse until it's almost a year old.

Spider monkeys are 1 to 1.5m long, with the tail accounting for 60% of that. They weigh 7 to 9kg. Their color varies from dark brown through reddish brown to gray. They often forage during the day in varisized groups high in the canopy and are also seen resting

RALPH LEE HOPKINS

**Central American spider monkey**

quietly on high branches. Vocalizations include screams, grunts, barks, and whinnies. When they spot people, a characteristic response is to scream or growl and jump up and down while rattling branches and even hurling vegetation down on the viewers. They favor large tracts of wet forest, as found in some of the larger parks, especially Tortuguero.

**Mantled Howler Monkey** (mono congo; *Alouatta palliata*). These large monkeys are often heard before being seen. The loud vocalizations of male howlers can carry for over 1km even in dense rainforest. They howl (or roar or grunt), especially at dawn and dusk, and at other times in response to intruders. Air is passed through a specialized, hollow, and much enlarged hyoid bone in the throat, producing the strange and resonant call. The hyoid bone contributes to the typically thick-necked appearance of the males.

Howlers live in small groups of about a dozen individuals, and the male calls keep the groups spaced out so they don't compete for food, consisting mainly of leaves, supplemented by fruit and flowers. Howlers travel less than other monkeys, preferring instead to maintain separated home ranges of about 10 hectares per group. Therefore howlers have survived better than other species in the face of fragmentation of the forest.

**Howler monkey**

Howlers are stocky, with wide shoulders, large heads and necks (especially in the males), and relatively small hindparts. Their prehensile tail is often carried coiled. They are black, with the exception of their sides and back, where long hairs can give them a golden brown or buff-colored mantle. They weigh 5 to 8kg and are 1 to 1.25m in length, of which just over half is tail. They browse and rest in the canopy, making it hard to spot them from the ground. Good places to see them are hilly forests where you look out over the treetops.

## Dog Family

Costa Rica has two canine species, the **coyote** (*Canis latrans*) and the **gray fox** (zorro gris; *Urocyon cinereoargenteus*). The brownish gray coyote (also found in North America) is omnivorous. In Costa Rica it prefers the drier forests and open areas of Guanacaste, although it is found in other regions. Active at any time, it is seen in parks such as Santa Rosa, where its trademark nighttime howling and yapping are heard. It is also common in Monteverde. The gray fox is grayer, much smaller, and more nocturnal. Both species avoid the rainforest.

## Raccoon Family

This family, the Procyonidae, has six members in Costa Rica, most of which are quite common. Along with dogs, weasels, and cats, they are classified as carnivores, though many procyonids eat fruit. The classification is based on dental characteristics, not diet.

The **northern raccoon** (mapache; *Procyon loctor*) is the species found in North America. In Costa Rica, they favor water and are commonly found along both coasts as well as near lowland rivers and marshes, where they are often seen at night. When disturbed, they may

Northern raccoon

climb trees. Their most distinctive feature is a white face with a black mask giving a bandit-like appearance. The rest of the body is gray and the tail is gray with black rings. Costa Rican raccoons are smaller than their northern counterparts, measuring under 1m in length, of which one-third is tail, and weighing about 5kg.

The similar-looking **crab-eating raccoon** (*Procyon cancrivorous*) is also nocturnal but limited to the Pacific coast. This raccoon has blackish (not gray) fur on the front of its legs and the fur on top of its neck grows forward, toward the head, rather than smoothly away as in most animals.

White-nosed coati

The **white-nosed coati** (pizote; *Nasua narica*) is the most diurnal and frequently seen procyonid. They are brownish and longer, but slimmer and lighter, than raccoons. Their most distinctive features are a long, mobile, upturned whitish snout with which they snuffle around on the forest floor looking for insects, fruit, and small animals, and a long, faintly ringed tail held straight up in the air when foraging. Although they feed on the ground, they are agile climbers and sleep and copulate in trees. They are found countrywide in all types of forest up to 3000m.

The **kinkajou** (martilla; *Potus flavus*) is a cuddly procyonid that lacks the facial markings and ringed tail of its cousins. It is an attractive reddish brown color and is hunted both for food and the pet trade. Nocturnal and mainly arboreal, it jumps from tree to tree searching for fruits (especially figs), which comprise most of its diet.

An animal heard jumping around trees at night is most probably a kinkajou, almost a meter in length, or it might be the smaller and rarer **olingo** *(Bassaricyon gabbi),* which has similar habits. Both have sneezing calls and a two-toned yelp and travel singly or in small groups. The kinkajou has a prehensile tail, which it often curls lightly around tree branches as it travels. The olingo is more gray and has a bushier, faintly ringed tail. Both prefer primary humid forests, but only the kinkajou is found also in secondary forests, tropical dry forests, and even gardens and orchards.

Similar to the previous two species is the **cacomistle** (cacomistle or olingo; *Bassariscus sumichrasti*); locals don't necessarily differentiate among them. The cacomistle is similar to the ring-tailed cat

Kinkajou

of North America, having a very bushy white tail with black rings and white spectacles around the eyes. Its ears are more pointed than those of the olingo and it is slimmer and lighter, but otherwise it has a similar body shape and habits. It is more common in highland than lowland forests.

## Weasel Family

These tough little carnivores are known for their bite, which is very strong for their size, and their smell – skunks are in the weasel family. Seven members of this family (the Mustelidae) are found in Costa Rica, and some are quite common.

Skunks are perhaps the most obvious. They are widespread but nocturnal, and smelled as often as seen. Their disgusting odor is known to most people in the Americas, and visitors from other continents will be surprised at how bad a skunk can smell! The 'scent' is produced by anal glands and is sprayed at predators (unsurprisingly, skunks tend to get left alone). There are three species in Costa Rica: the **striped hog-nosed skunk** (zorro hediondo; *Conepatus semistriatus*), the **spotted skunk** *(Spilogale putorius),* and the **hooded skunk** *(Mephitis macroura).* Despite their smell, they look attractive. The hog-nosed is black with a broad white stripe along its back and a bushy white tail. It is 50 to 75cm in length and widespread throughout the country. The smaller and less common spotted skunk is black with white blotches. The hooded skunk is the least common. All are terrestrial.

The **southern river otter** (perro de agua; *Lutra longicaudis*) is the only Costa Rican otter. It lives in and by fast-moving lowland rivers, but is infrequently seen. It is a rich brown color with whitish undersides and has the streamlined shape of an aquatic weasel. The **tayra** (tolumuco; *Eira barbara*) is similarly shaped but is blackish brown, with a tan head, and is terrestrial and arboreal. It can reach over a meter in length (the tail is about 40cm) and is found in forests up to 2000m. If you see what looks like an otter running around the forest, it's probably a tayra.

Southern river otter

The **grison** (grisón; *Galictis vittata*) is a large weasel with distinctive coloration. The body, tail, and crown of the head are light gray and the legs, chest, and lower face are black. A white band across the forehead, ears, and sides of the neck gives the head a black/white/gray tricolor. The tail is shorter than that of most weasels. It is found in the lowland rainforests but is uncommon. The smallest Costa Rican weasel is the **long-tailed weasel** (comadreja; *Mustela frenata*), a nervous brown animal with a pale belly that is reportedly common but rarely seen.

Grison

## Cat Family

It is every wildlife watcher's dream to see a **jaguar** (tigre, jaguar; *Felis onca*) in the wild. However, they are rare, often silent, and well camouflaged, so the chance of seeing one is remote. This big cat (males occasionally reach over 150kg) is the largest Central American carnivore. They have large territories and you may see their prints or droppings in large lowland parks with extensive forest like Corcovado. Occasionally you may hear them roaring – a sound more like a series of deep coughs. There's no mistaking this 2m-long yellow cat with black spots in rosettes and a whitish belly. Good luck seeing one.

Jaguar

There are five other Costa Rican felids. The **ocelot** (manigordo; *Felis pardalis*) is also yellow but the spotting is variable, often merging into lines. It is a little over a meter in length and the tail is shorter than the hind leg. The most common of the Costa Rican cats, it is shy and rarely seen. It adapts well to a variety of terrain, wet and dry, forested and open, and has been recorded in most of the larger national parks. Smaller still, the **yellow margay** (tigrillo or caucel; *Felis wiedii*) has more distinctive spots and a tail longer than the hind leg, which helps distinguish it from the ocelot. The margay, the size of a large house cat, is rare and endangered (as are all the Central American cats). It lives in forests, particularly near rivers, and has been recorded as high as 3000m. Even smaller and rarer is the similar-looking **oncilla** *(Felis tigrina)*, which has been recorded in various habitats up to over 3000m. It is hard to differentiate the smaller spotted cats in the field, as you only get a brief glimpse of them, if you are lucky.

Ocelot

Two cats are unspotted. The **puma** (or mountain lion; león; *Felis concolor*) is almost as large as the jaguar but is a uniform brown (the shade varies from area to area and among individuals), with paler underparts, a white throat and muzzle, and a dark tip to the tail. Like all the cats, they are active both day and night, are fairly widespread but rarely seen, and are endangered. The smaller **jaguarundi** (león breñero; *Felis yagouaroundi*) is darker brown (much variation), with an elongated slim body, long tail, and rather short legs.

LUKE HUNTER

Puma

## Peccaries

Known as javelinas in the USA, these animals are related to and look like pigs. The most widespread is the **collared peccary** (saíno; *Tayassu tajacu*), which ranges from the southwestern USA to Argentina in a wide variety of habitats. It is about 80cm long, weighs around 20kg, and has coarse gray hair with a light collar from its shoulders forward to the lower jaw. The larger **white-lipped peccary** (chancho de monte; *Tayassu pecari)* is darker and lacks the collar but has a whitish area on the lower chin.

Both species move around in varisized groups; numbers of over 300 are reported for the white-lipped, but considerably fewer for the collared peccary. The latter is more commonly seen

TOM BOYDEN

White-lipped peccary

but is quieter and shyer. The white-lipped peccaries are noisy and rather aggressive with their audible tooth gnashing and clicking – quite frightening if you hear 300 animals performing this way! Corcovado rangers warn visitors to be prepared to climb a tree if they are charged, though this rarely happens. Peccaries leave pungent, churned-up mud wallows, which can be seen (and smelled) in Corcovado.

## Deer

The **white-tailed deer** (venado; *Odocoileus virginianus*) is well known to North Americans. The Costa Rican variety is smaller. They are gray to red with a straight back, white belly, and white markings on the throat, eyes, ears, and muzzle. When running, the tail is lifted, revealing the conspicuous white underside. The males have branched antlers, except for the yearlings, which have single prongs.

The smaller, shyer, and less common **red brocket deer** (cabro de monte; *Mazama americana*) is reddish (including the belly), with a slightly humped back and no facial markings. The tail is white below and is also raised in alarm. The male antlers are single prongs at all ages. These deer are more likely to be seen in rainforests, while white-tailed deer are fairly common in drier areas such as Guanacaste.

Baird's tapir

## Tapirs

The only Central American tapir is **Baird's tapir** (danta; *Tapirus bairdii*), endangered because of hunting and logging. Weighing 150 to 300kg, it is the region's largest land mammal. Tapirs are among the world's most ancient large mammals; 20-million-year-old fossils have been found. Their closest relatives are horses and rhinos.

They are stocky, rather short-legged, stumpy-tailed animals that are more agile than they appear. They can run as fast as a person and are adept at climbing steep riverbanks. The skin is grayish and covered with sparse, coarse, blackish hairs. Young tapirs are reddish with white spots or stripes. The upper lip is elongated into a mobile snout like a small trunk, which is used in feeding.

Their favored habitat is waterside forests and they have been most frequently reported on riverbanks in Corcovado, usually singly and occasionally in small groups. Their eyesight is poor but their senses of smell and hearing are excellent. They will run off when they detect people, probably the result of associating humans with hunting. Kayakers silently gliding up coastal rivers in Corcovado have been able to get good looks at these animals, but hikers have had less luck.

## Rodents

Some large rodents are among the most commonly seen rainforest mammals, including the **Central American agouti** (guatusa; *Dasyprocta punctata*) and the **paca** (tepezcuintle; *Agouti paca*), which are relatives of the guinea pig.

The agouti is diurnal and terrestrial and found in forests from the coast up to 2000m. It looks like an oversize cross between a rabbit and a squirrel, with a barely visible tail and short ears. The color is a variable brownish gray. A chunky, brownish, apparently tailless mammal of about 4kg and 50 to 60cm in length running on the forest floor is probably an agouti.

Central American agouti

TOM BOYDEN

TOM BOYDEN

**Paca**

The closely related paca looks similar, except it has white stripy marks on its sides and is twice the size of an agouti. It is common but seen less often because it is nocturnal. It has been much hunted for food and suggestions have been made that pacas might be 'farmed.' They can remain underwater for some minutes, a behavior that has helped them survive hunting. They have been reported in suburban gardens in Costa Rican cities.

LUKE HUNTER

**Variegated squirrel**

There are five squirrel species. The **red-tailed squirrel** (ardilla roja; *Sciurus granatensis*) is grayish with a red belly and red tail, and is quite common. More abundant is the **variegated squirrel** (chiza; *Sciurus variegatoides*), which has various forms. The most frequently seen are mainly whitish with a black back or reddish with a black back and a black-and-white tail with red markings below. The other squirrels are less likely to be seen and are usually smaller and live at high altitudes.

Biologists can't agree what to call the Costa Rican **porcupine** (puerco espín; *Coendou mexicanus*), so various names refer to one species, easily identified by its spiny coat. Generally blackish with a lighter head and belly, it is roughly 40cm long plus a 25cm tail. It is arboreal and mainly nocturnal. During the day it may rest on a branch or den inside a hollow tree; local guides may know about favored sleeping places. A Monteverde guide reports seeing one about every fourth night when leading flashlight nightwalks in the preserve.

Some 40 species of rats, mice, spiny rats, pocket mice, and pocket gophers are of interest to ecologists, agriculturists, and other specialists.

## Rabbits

Three species of rabbits are found in Costa Rica. The **eastern cottontail** (conejo cola blanca; *Sylvilagus floridensis*) is familiar to North American visitors. It is a small (about 40cm) brown rabbit with a little brown-and-white tail like a ball of cotton wool. It is widespread at most elevations except inside rainforests, where it is replaced by the **forest rabbit** (conejo de bosque; *Sylvilagus brasiliensis*), which looks similar, except the tail is brown and even tinier. Cottontails are found on the rainforest edge, but not inside it. A third species, *Sylvilagus dicei*, is reported in some highland areas.

## Marine Mammals

There aren't many of these. In a few rivers, estuaries, and coastal areas (especially around Tortuguero) you may glimpse the endangered **West Indian manatee** (manatí; *Trichechus manatus*), a large marine mammal (up to 4m and 600kg, though usually smaller) that feeds on aquatic vegetation. There are no seals or sea lions, so a manatee is easy to recognize.

Out at sea, dolphins and whales might briefly be seen as they break the water's surface. Off the coast of the Península de Osa and Parque Nacional Marino Ballena, migrating whales, especially the **humpback whale** (ballena; *Megaptera novaeanglia*), may be seen from December to March. The **common dolphin** (delfín; *Delphinus delphis*) and **bottle-nosed dolphin** *(Tursiops truncatus)* live in these waters year-round.

West Indian manatee

# Birds

From a newly hatched chick to an adult, a bird goes through several plumage changes or molts, sometimes over a period of years in the cases of larger birds. Juveniles often look nothing like their parents. Descriptions below are for adult birds, unless specified.

## Tinamous

There are five Costa Rican tinamous, chunky, almost tailless birds considered the most primitive (or ancient) of the nation's avifauna, which is why they are at the beginning of bird guidebooks. They feed on the forest floor, and fly with alarmingly loud wing beats only when disturbed. Their beautiful songs, a series of tremulous and often deep whistles, are often heard in the forest.

## Seabirds

Among the most spectacular seabirds is the **magnificent frigatebird** (rabihorcado magno; *Fregata magnificens*), a large, elegant, streamlined black seabird with a long forked tail that gives it the nickname tijereta or 'scissor tail.' They make an acrobatic living by aerial piracy, often harassing small birds into dropping or regurgitating their catch and then swooping to catch their stolen meal in mid-air. This is partly because frigatebirds do not have waterproof feathers and so cannot enter the water to catch prey. They are, however, able to catch fish on the surface by snatching them up with their hooked beaks. With a wingspan of over 2m and a weight of only 1.5kg, the birds have the largest wingspan to weight ratio of any bird and are magnificent fliers.

Magnificent frigatebird

Frigatebirds are found along both coasts but are more common on the Pacific. The males have red throat pouches, which normally look like little skin flaps but are inflated to balloon size when courting and nesting. Unfortunately, nesting in Costa Rica is limited to a few islands off the Pacific coast, so you are unlikely to see this.

The **brown pelican** (pelícano; *Pelecanus occidentalis*) is unmistakable with its large size and huge pouched bill. They have wide fingered wings and are good gliders. They are often seen flying in a squadron-like formation, flapping and gliding in unison as if performing in an elegant aerial ballet.

A pelican feeds by shallow plunge-diving and scooping up as much as 10 liters of water in its distensible pouch. The water rapidly drains out through the bill and the trapped fish are swallowed. It sounds straightforward, but it isn't. Although parents raise broods of two or three chicks, many of the fledged young are unable to learn the scoop-fishing technique quickly enough and starve to death as a result.

Pelicans are found along both coasts but are more common on the Pacific, especially in the Golfo de Nicoya, where some islands provide them with breeding grounds.

Other seabirds are more likely to be seen farther offshore, perhaps on a trip to Isla del Caño biological reserve. These include shearwaters, petrels, storm-petrels, boobies, phalaropes, and jaegers.

**Brown pelicans**

ALFREDO MAIQUEZ

## Cormorants & Anhingas

The **olivaceous cormorant** (cormorán; *Palacrocorax olivaceus*) and its relative, the **anhinga** (pato aguja; *Anhinga anhinga*), are large blackish waterbirds with long necks and short tails. Both are common in the Tortuguero, Palo Verde, and Caño Negro areas but can be found in other lowland regions. Like frigatebirds, to which they are related, these birds do not have waterproof feathers, yet they are both good swimmers and divers and catch fish underwater. When their plumage becomes waterlogged, they climb onto perches and stand with their wings stretched wide to dry in the sun – this is when they are commonly seen.

Anhingas have longer necks and tails than cormorants, and silvery streaks on their backs and wings. Female anhingas have a buff-colored head and neck. Cormorants are generally black, though juveniles are a light gray below. Anhingas are able to sink almost below the water's surface, leaving just the lengthy neck, slim head, and long, sharp bill above the water, giving them the descriptive nickname of 'snake bird.'

DAVID TIPLING

**Anhinga**

## Herons & Relatives

Herons, wading birds with long legs and necks, are in the same family as egrets and bitterns. Along with storks and ibises, they are in the order Ciconiiformes, which has about 25 representatives in Costa Rica. The best places to see many of these are the Palo Verde and Caño Negro areas and northwestern Costa Rica.

The most commonly seen is the **cattle egret** (garcilla bueyera; *Bubulcus ibis*), which was first recorded in Costa Rica in 1954. Since then, the population of this white heron has exploded dramatically and it is seen countrywide up to about 2000m. It is distinguished from other white herons by its stockier appearance and terrestrial feeding habits (often in pastures), whereas most herons feed in water. In the breeding season, buff-colored head plumes, chest, and back are distinctive.

During non-breeding, you can tell the white herons apart by the colors of their legs and bills. The cattle egret has blackish legs and a yellow bill. The larger

**Cattle egret**

**snowy egret** (garceta nivosa; *Egretta thula*) has black legs with bright yellow feet ('golden slippers') and a black bill with yellow facial skin. The immature **little blue heron** (garceta azul; *Egretta caerula*) is white with yellowish legs, a gray bill with a black tip, and gray wing tips. (The adult little blue heron is bluish gray with a purplish head and neck.) The **great egret** (garceta grande; *Casmeroidus albus*) is by far the largest white heron, standing over a meter tall, with a very long neck, black legs, and yellow bill. All these are quite common.

Of the non-white herons, the most abundant is the **green-backed heron** (garcilla verde; *Butorides striatus*), which, at an average length of 43cm, is the smallest heron. A greenish back, maroon neck, white stripe down the front of its throat and chest, black cap, and bright yellow eyes and legs make this quite a colorful bird when seen in sunlight, which is not often. They prefer to forage stealthily, singly or in pairs, in the dense vegetation at the side of most bodies of water and are often seen on boat trips. When disturbed, they squawk and fly to another bush, where they typically pump their tail.

Larger species include the **boat-billed heron** (pico cuchara; *Cochlearius cochlearius*), a stocky, mainly gray heron with a black cap and crest and distinctively large and wide bill. The **yellow-crowned night heron** (martinete cabecipinto; *Nyctanassa violacea*) is common in coastal areas and has an unmistakable black-and-white head with a yellow crown. Despite its name, it's mainly active by day.

**Roseate spoonbill**

Tiger-herons are large brownish herons with fine horizontal barring on most of their plumage and bright yellow legs. The most common of three such Costa Rican species is the **bare-throated tiger-heron** (garza-tigre cuellinuda; *Tigrisoma mexicanum*), with a bare yellow throat.

The descriptively named **roseate spoonbill** (espátula rosada; *Ajaia ajaja*) is the only large pink bird in Costa Rica and is most often seen in the Palo Verde and Caño Negro areas. It has a white head and a distinctive spoon-shaped bill. Unlike most birds, which feed by sight, spoonbills, ibises, and many storks feed by touch. The spoonbill swings its open bill around, submerged underwater, stirring up the bottom with its feet, until it feels a small fish, frog, or crustacean and then snaps the bill shut.

Three ibis species, related to spoonbills, have long and down-curved bills, which probe the bottoms of swamps, streams, and ponds. The **white ibis** (ibis blanco; *Eudocimus albus*) is the most often seen, especially in the northwest and Nicoya areas. It is white with black wing tips (seen in flight) and has a bright red bill and legs, which separate it from the **green ibis** (ibis verde; *Mesembrinibis cayennensis*), which is blackish green and more common on the Caribbean coast.

**White ibis**

The **wood stork** (cigueñón; *Mycteria americana*) is a large white bird, over a meter tall, with a very heavy bill and bare, blackish head. The flight feathers are black, which gives it a distinctive white-and-black pattern in flight. The rarer **jabiru** *(Jabiru mycteria)* is a much larger white stork with a black head, bill, and neck and a red band at the base of the neck.

## Ducks

Of the 15 duck species recorded in Costa Rica, most are uncommon to rare, or winter migrants from North America. As in other Neotropical countries, ducks and geese are under-represented bird families.

The most common is the **black-bellied whistling-duck** (pijije común; *Dendrocygna autumnalis*), which favors the Pacific lowlands. It stands rather than swims and has a rusty-brown body with a black belly, whitish wing stripe, reddish feet and bill, and gray-brown face. Also seen fairly often is the **Muscovy duck** (pato real; *Cairina moschata*), which is a large Neotropical duck with a glossy greenish-black body and white wing patches. The most common winter migrant is the **blue-winged teal** (cerceta aliazul; *Anas discors*).

**Muscovy duck**

## Vultures

These large black birds are often seen hovering ominously in the sky, searching for carrion, which is their main source of food. In common with most vultures, their heads are bare, and the color of the skin on their heads is the best way to identify them.

The **turkey vulture** (zopilote cabecirrojo; *Cathartes aura*) and the **black vulture** (zopilote negro; *Coragyps atratus*) are both common countrywide below 2000m and occasionally higher. The turkey vulture soars with V-shaped wings and has gray primary feathers, giving the wings a two-toned appearance from below, and has a red head. The black vulture has flatter, broader wings with a whitish patch at the base of the primaries, and a black head. (Young turkey vultures also have blackish heads.) Turkey vultures soar fairly low and can detect carrion by scent, while black vultures soar higher and look for carcasses visually, which is why the latter are more common over open areas and near towns, while the turkey vultures are seen over forests. The black vultures watch for other vultures descending to food, and when both species are present at a carcass, the stockier, heavier black vultures will force the turkey vultures away unless there is an excess of meat.

The **lesser yellow-headed vulture** (zopilote cabecigualdo; *Cathartes burrovianus*) looks like a small turkey vulture with a yellow head but is much less common. The **king vulture** (zopilote rey; *Sarcoramphus papa*) is the largest vulture and is easily identified by its off-white body and legs, black primary wing feathers and tail, and a wattled head colored black with various shades of orange-yellow. It is most frequently seen in Corcovado, though it lives almost countrywide in small numbers.

King vulture

## Birds of Prey

These include hawks, eagles, kites, falcons, caracaras, and the osprey, all of which hunt for food and are collectively called raptors. About 50 species have been recorded in Costa Rica, and many are hard to tell apart because of similar plumage and flight. Being hunters, they rely on stealth and speed, which makes them hard to observe closely; identification is difficult without binoculars. Raptors are, however, common throughout the country. Among the most frequently seen and easily identified are the following.

The **osprey** (águila pescadora; *Pandion haliaetus*) is one of the few birds found on every inhabited continent. Its prey is unusual for raptors: the Spanish name 'fishing eagle' describes it perfectly. The osprey fishes by plunging into salt or fresh water, feet first, and grabbing the

Osprey

slippery fish. The feet are adapted for the purpose with long, sharp claws and horny spines beneath the toes. The plumage is distinctive – almost completely white below and brown above, with a white head striped black through the eyes. The white underside camouflages it against the sky (so fish can't see it easily) and the dark upperside camouflages it against the water (so predators can't see it). It is found in lowlands along both coasts and in the Caño Negro area.

A long, deeply forked, black tail distinguishes the **American swallow-tailed kite** (elanio ti-jereta; *Elanoides forficatus*) from other raptors. It has a white head and underparts, black back, and black-and-white wings. It feeds on the wing, plucking insects out of the air or grabbing

**Black-shouldered kite**

small lizards from branches, and is normally seen flying gracefully in areas with some humid forests (but not in the drier northwest). The **black-shouldered kite** (elanio coliblanco; *Elanus caerulus*) is a small, white hawk with black shoulders and a light gray back and primary feathers. The feet are yellow and the yellow bill is tipped black. This bird was first reported in Costa Rica in 1958 but has now become common in open agricultural areas and grasslands.

The **black-chested hawk** (gavilán pechinegro; *Leucopternis princeps*) is a hawk with very broad wings found in mid-elevation humid forests, from 400m (usually higher) to 2500m. Its plumage is mainly black with a white band in its tail, and fine black barring in the white belly and under-wings, giving it a light gray appearance from a distance. The distinct contrast between the black chest and light

belly is a good field mark. It is an acrobatic flier and hunts mainly inside the forest. In the lowlands on both coasts, the **common black hawk** (gavilán cangrejero; *Buteogallus anthracinus*) is often seen near water, where it feeds on crabs and other coastal animals. It is quite large and all black except for a white band in the tail, yellow feet, and a yellow base of the bill.

The **white hawk** (gavilán blanco; *Leucopternis albicollis*) is almost all white except for a black band in the tail and black markings at the ends of the wings. Hawks have very broad wings and short, wide tails, while kites have long, slim tails and slim wings that are bent back. This distinguishes the white hawk from the fairly similarly colored black-shouldered kite.

The most common resident hawk is the **roadside hawk** (gavilán chapulinero; *Buteo magnirostris*), which perches on trees and posts in open areas waiting for small mammals, reptiles, or large insects to pass below. Because perches in open areas tend to follow roads or tracks, the bird is well named. It is a small hawk with a grayish head and chest merging into a brown-gray back and a pale belly barred with rusty brown. The tail is widely banded in light and dark gray. The throat

**Roadside hawk**

is whitish and the feet, eyes, and base of bill are yellow. It prefers the lowlands and is more common on Pacific slopes. The most frequently seen hawk from late September to May is the migrant **broad-winged hawk** (gavilán aludo; *Buteo platypterus*), which also likes to pounce on its prey from a low perch, often at the forest edge. It looks rather like a browner, larger version of the roadside hawk, but it has a more distinctly white throat.

Apart from hunting small rodents, reptiles, and amphibians, the **crested caracara** (caracara cargahuesos; *Polyborus plancus*) also eats carrion and is often seen feeding on roadkill, rather like a vulture. Its plumage, however, quickly separates it from the vultures. It has a black body and wings, with a white face and neck merging to a black-and-white barred chest and upper back. The tail is barred and tipped with black as well. The front of its face is red, the cap is black, and the legs are yellow. The distinctive **yellow-headed caracara** (caracara cabecigualdo; *Milvago chimachima*) has a buff body and head with a dark brown back. In flight, the underside of the wings is buff with black primaries and a large, pale 'window' at the end of the wings. Although not recorded in Costa Rica until 1973, it is

Crested caracara

now quite common on the Pacific slope, especially the Corcovado area.

The **laughing falcon** (guaco; *Herpetotheres cachinnans*) looks like a large, slightly paler, yellow-headed caracara with a broad black stripe through the eye and a striped black and pale-buff tail. It is fairly common in the lowlands. Its calls are loud and varied, with the most frequently heard being a hollow 'wah-co' (the pronunciation of its Spanish name) repeated many times, especially at dusk, when it sounds rather eerie. It perches high and searches for snakes.

The **harpy eagle** (águila arpía; *Harpia harpyja*), a spectacular meter-long eagle, was, until recently, widespread in Costa Rica's primary forests but has become almost extinct because of deforestation. It flies strongly and acrobatically through the forest canopy, snatching sloths and monkeys while on the wing! A few reportedly survive in the Corcovado area.

## Game Birds

Costa Rica has 13 species of the order Galliformes, descriptively called chickenlike birds, which look and taste a bit like domestic fowl. They are hunted, which makes them rare in populated areas, though they are seen in remote areas and in some national parks. They include guans, chacalacas, curassows, and various members of the pheasant family.

Harpy eagle

One of the more common game birds is the **black guan** (pava negra; *Chamaepetes unicolor*), a 65cm-long glossy black bird with a long tail. It has bare blue facial skin and red legs. Look for it walking along branches in forests above 1000m, such as in Monteverde, where it isn't much hunted and is seen fairly often.

## Rails & Relatives

These birds, members of the order Gruiformes, are represented by 18 species in Costa Rica. Most live on or near water, swamps, or marshes. They are poor fliers and prefer swimming or running. Many rails and crakes are furtive inhabitants of waterside grasses or rushes and, in most cases, are difficult to see even if they are present. Exceptions include the **gray-necked wood-rail** (rascón cuelligrís; *Aramides cajanea*), a large rail (38cm tall) with an olive back and tail; gray head, neck, and upper breast; chestnut lower breast; black belly and thighs; red legs and eyes; and yellow bill – quite a palette! It forages with its short tail pumping, walking over muddy vegetated ground, probing the mud and leaf layer in search of frogs and fruits. It can be found near water below 1400m throughout the country.

Purple gallinule

In the water, you may see the **purple gallinule** (gallareta morada; *Porphyrula martinica*), a colorful and more common version of the **common gallinule** or **moorhen** (gallareta frentirroja; *Gallinula chloropus*), which is familiar in North America, Eurasia, and Africa. The purple gallinule is violet-purple on the front, neck, and head, bronzy green on the back, and white under the tail. It has bright yellow legs, a red bill with a yellow tip, and a light blue frontal shield on its forehead. It is seen on many ponds below 1500m and is more frequently seen in Costa Rica than the common gallinule. The **American coot** (focha Americana; *Fulica americana*) is a dark gray to black waterbird with a white bill and frontal shield and white marks under the tail. This migrant is common from October to April.

The male **sungrebe** (pato cantil; *Heliornis fulica*) has the remarkable ability to carry its young suspended in a fold of skin under its wings. With a chick under each wing it can swim or even fly. This secretive and shy bird can be seen in several slowly flowing lowland rivers, including the canals of Tortuguero, which is one of the best places to look. It is a mainly brown waterbird with a wide tail tipped in white but has bold and distinctive black-and-white striping on the neck and head, and a red bill, which make identification easy.

The **sunbittern** (garza del sol; *Eurypyga helias*) is a long-legged waterbird with a long bill and slim neck. The head is black with white stripes, the neck and breast brown with fine

Sungrebe

black lines, the back brown with wider black lines, the belly and throat creamy, the tail gray with two black-brown bands, the bill and legs orange, and the wings gray with large white spots. Its most distinctive feature is the sunburst pattern in a combination of browns, white, and black on its upper wings when it flies. It is an unusual bird, placed in its own family, the Eurypygidae, and high on the 'must see' list of many birders. It lives by rivers in forests in the foothills of the Caribbean and south Pacific slopes but is diminishing in numbers because of deforestation.

## Shorebirds & Gulls

Costa Rica has about 70 species of shorebirds and gulls, in the diverse order Charadriiformes. Almost all are known to North American visitors. Some, such as the familiar **herring gull** (gaviota argéntea; *Larus argentatus*) are Holarctic (found in all northern continents). Many are winter migrants to Costa Rica and few are seen in summer.

The most common gull is the **laughing gull** (gaviota reidora; *Larus atricilla*), which is a widespread and abundant migrant (September to November and April to mid-May) but is also present in large numbers year-round, especially on the Pacific coast.

The most widespread shorebird is the **spotted sandpiper** (andarríos maculado; *Actitis macularia*), found along inland lakes and rivers up to 1850m as well as on both coasts. It is often seen from August to May but rarely in the summer. It is small, brown above and white below, with a faint white eye stripe and yellowish legs. Its most distinctive feature is its teetering back and forth while walking and foraging.

Herring gull

It is usually seen singly. The most abundant shorebird is the **western sandpiper** (correlimos occidental; *Calidris mauri*), which is grayish-brown above with fine streaks and white below. This bird is seen in flocks of hundreds along both coasts, but especially the Pacific, from August to April. Also common is the **sanderling** (playero arenero; *Calidris alba*), especially from mid-August to October and mid-March to early May. Fewer birds are seen in winter and almost none in summer. This shorebird is found in small flocks on both coasts and is paler than other similar shorebirds. It runs up and down the surf line with a distinctive gait like a clockwork toy.

A favorite of many visitors is the **northern jacana** (jacana centroamericana; *Jacana spinosa*), which has extremely long, thin toes that enable it to walk on top of aquatic plants, earning it the nickname 'lily-trotter.' They are common on many lowland lakes and waterways. At first glance, their brown bodies, black necks and heads, and yellow bill and frontal shield seem rather nondescript, but when disturbed the birds stretch their wings to reveal startling yellow flight feathers. This may serve to momentarily confuse would-be predators and makes them easy for us to identify. The female is polyandrous, mating with up to four males within her territory. The males do most of the nest building and incubation – whether the female manages to lay the right eggs in each father's nest remains in doubt.

Northern jacana

## Pigeons & Doves

These birds, in the order Columbiformes, are represented by 25 species in Costa Rica. Some are familiar to North Americans, while others are specialties of the tropics. They are unusual among birds because the parents secrete 'pigeon milk' in the crop (part of the esophagus), and this is the chicks' only food during their first days. The milk is similar in constitution to mammalian milk but is thicker and also is produced by both sexes. The milk is regurgitated from the crop and the young eat it from the parent's mouth. After a few days, solid food is also regurgitated and mixed with the milk in increasing amounts. By the time the chicks fledge (about two weeks in small birds and over a month in large ones), milk is only a small portion of the regurgitated mixture.

The largest species is the 35cm-long **band-tailed pigeon** (paloma collareja; *Columba fasciata*), so called because of the dark gray band in its pale gray tail, but better identified by a white crescent on the back of its neck and a yellow bill. It is frequently seen in flocks in the mountains above 900m.

There are several small ground-doves, of which the most common is the **ruddy ground-dove** (tortolita colorada; *Columbina talpacoti*). The male is reddish, distinguishing it from other ground-doves. It has a pale gray head and almost white throat. It prefers open habitat and is often seen in agricultural country and along roads below 1400m on both slopes. As the name implies, these birds spend much of the time on the ground, foraging for seeds, berries, and possibly insects and other small invertebrates.

Pigeons and doves generally have cooing calls. One of the most distinctive is that of the **short-billed pigeon** (paloma piquicorta; *Columba nigrirostris*), which sounds like 'cu-COO cu-COO,' accented on the second and fourth notes, and is frequently heard from the middle and upper layers of humid forests up to about 1400m.

## Parrots

These are truly tropical birds, found throughout the tropics anywhere there are trees and extending into the subtropics. Of about 330 species in the world, 16 are recorded from Costa Rica. All have a short but very powerful bill with a pronounced hook that is used to open buds and flowers in search of nuts and seeds, which are their main food.

The most spectacular Costa Rican parrot is the **scarlet macaw** (lapa roja; *Ara macao*), unmistakable with its large size (84cm long), bright red body, blue-and-yellow wings, long red tail, and white face. Macaws mate for life (as is generally true of all parrots) and are often seen flying overhead, in pairs or small flocks, calling raucously to one another. Recorded as common in 1900, they have suffered devastating reductions in numbers because of deforestation and poaching for the pet trade. Now, it is rare to see these birds outside of Carara and Corcovado.

Scarlet macaw

Costa Rica's other macaw is the **great green macaw** (lapa verde; *Ara ambigua*), which is similar in size and shape to the scarlet macaw but is mainly green and blue, with some red on top of its tail. This macaw is found on the Caribbean side.

The remaining parrots are much smaller and mainly green. The largest of them (38cm) is the **mealy parrot** (loro verde; *Amazona farinosa*). In common with other Amazona parrots, it has a stumpy tail and flies with quick flaps of its short, broad wings, usually in raucously calling flocks. Parakeets, of which there are six species, are also small and green but have long tails. Telling the individual parrots and parakeets apart is not easy because they all are green and usually glimpsed flying. Look for small orange, red, blue, white, and yellow markings on the head and wings, which are best observed when the bird is at rest. For example, the **orange-fronted parakeet** (perico frentinaranja; *Aratinga canicularis*) has an orange forehead, bluish crown, and yellowish white eye ring, is yellowish green below, and has some blue flight feathers – but in flight, it seems generally green.

JOHN ELK III

**Great green macaw**

## Cuckoos

European cuckoos lay their eggs in the nest of another species and then let another bird raise their young, a behavior known as brood parasitism. Only two of Costa Rica's 11 species of cuckoos practice this. Most of the cuckoos are slim, long-tailed birds, skulking stealthily through vegetation rather than flying.

The most common is the **squirrel cuckoo** (cuco ardilla; *Piaya cayana*), which is 46cm long, with the boldly black-and-white-striped tail taking up about half that length. The rest of the body is mainly rufous brown, with a gray belly and yellow bill and eye ring. It is hard to mistake this combination for any other bird. It is found creeping along branches and jumping rather than flying to the next branch – hence the descriptor 'squirrel' in its name. It inhabits woodlands and forests countrywide up to 2400m.

There are two heavy-billed, floppy-tailed, all-black cuckoos called

DAVID M WATSON

**Squirrel cuckoo**

LUKE HUNTER

Groove-billed ani

anis. The **groove-billed ani** (garrapatero piquiestrado; *Crotophaga sulcirostris*) is 30cm long and commonly found in small flocks in hedges, fields, grasslands, marshes, and watersides throughout the country up to about 2300m, except in the south Pacific region. Their flight is weak and wobbly and they call 'tee-ho' frequently, giving them their local nickname, *tijo*. In the south Pacific, they are replaced by the slightly larger but otherwise similar-looking **smooth-billed ani** (garrapatero piquisilo; *Crotophaga ani*).

## Owls

Costa Rica has 17 owl species. As elsewhere, they are nocturnal hunters and are more often heard than seen. They have various hooting, drumming, screeching, and other slightly eerie calls, mainly heard at night or at dawn and dusk.

One species of owl that will occasionally hunt during the day is the widely distributed **spectacled owl** (buho de anteojos; *Pulsatrix perspicillata*). It's one of the larger owls, 48cm in length with conspicuous white markings around the eyes, forming spectacles. Others are generally smaller, but all have the typical owl appearance.

Spectacled owl

## Nightjars & Relatives

About a dozen of these mainly nocturnal birds are found in Costa Rica. At dusk they may be mistaken for bats; look for white bars at the ends of the wings to distinguish them. The most abundant is the **common pauraque** (cuyeo; *Nyctidromus albicollis*). You might catch sight of one by car headlights at night. During the day, they roost quietly on branches and flat areas. (I once saw a nightjar sitting in the middle of a hiking trail and it refused to budge even when I stood next to it.) They are camouflaged with a mottled brown, black, and gray, often with a white throat and usually with long bristles around the beak to help them catch insects at night.

Potoos are nightjars found only in the Neotropics. They have a unique camouflage during the day: Instead of sitting horizontally, as most birds do, they adopt a vertical posture and often perch on an exposed tree stump, looking very much like an elongation of it. Your guide gets an extra tip for spotting one. At night, their calls are among the eeriest in the forest. The two Costa Rican species are the **great potoo** (nictibio grande; *Nyctibius grandis*) and the **common potoo** (nictibio común; *Nyctibius griseus*).

## Swifts
These birds are among the best fliers in the avian world. Their streamlined bodies and long, thin, swept-back wings enable them to spend most waking hours in the air, with their small but wide bills agape to catch insects. They can briefly sleep and even copulate on the wing. Their short legs are poorly developed and they never land on the ground because they would have difficulty taking off. Instead, they have strong feet, and perch and

Common pauraque

nest on vertical cliffs and buildings from which they can easily glide off.

Costa Rica has 11 species, all mainly dark gray or black, some with white or brown markings. The largest and most common countrywide is the **white-collared swift** (vencejón collarejo; *Streptoprocne zonaris*), which is 22cm long and has a slim white collar and a square or slightly notched tail. The 13cm-long **lesser swallow-tailed swift** (macua; *Panyptila cayennensis*) also has a white collar, which extends over the chin and upper breast. It has a deeply forked tail and is found below 800m on the Caribbean and up to 1000m on the south Pacific slope.

## Hummingbirds
The world's 330 species of hummingbirds live exclusively in the Americas, predominantly in the tropics. Over 50 species have been recorded in Costa Rica, and their beauty is matched by extravagant names. For many visitors these birds are the most delightful to observe.

Hummingbirds can beat their wings up to 80 times a second, thus producing the typical hum for which they are named. This exceptionally rapid beat, combined with the ability to rotate the whole wing, enables them to hover in place when feeding on nectar (their preferred food), or even to fly backward – unique traits in birds. The energy needed to keep these tiny birds flying is high, and species living in the mountains have evolved an amazing strategy to survive a cold night: They go into a state of torpor, like a nightly hibernation, by lowering their body temperature between 17°C and 28°C depending on the species, thus lowering their metabolism drastically.

Apart from nectar, hummingbirds eat small insects for protein. They are generally quite pugnacious, and many will defend individual feeding territories, driving off any other bird that tries to feed. The males of some species gather together in a lek, a communal displaying area, where they attract females. After mating, however, males play little or no part in nesting or chick rearing.

The often dazzling iridescent colors of hummingbirds are caused by microscopic structures on the end of the feathers. These appear black in certain angles of light but, at other angles, refraction and interference cause the plumage to flash brilliantly. A shining green is the normal color of most hummingbirds, further decorated by brief fiery splashes of red, yellow, purple, or blue, usually in the head and upper breast area. Some have specially modified gorgets, or feathers sticking out from the throat. Normally, the males are the brightest.

Their small size (many under 10cm), speedy flight, tendency to be metallic green (or black in some lights), and lack of conspicuous coloration in the females make it difficult to tell the hummingbirds apart. With a little practice, however, some species become quickly recognizable. The **long-tailed hermit** (ermitaño colilargo; *Phaethornis superciliosus*) is common in forests of the Caribbean and south Pacific slopes below 1000m. Hikers often notice a sudden 'Zzzip!' as a 15cm-long hummer comes very close and inspects them before zipping off again. This inquisitive bird is probably the long-tailed hermit, identified by its brownish plumage, very long white central tail feathers extending about 3cm beyond the rest of the tail, and a long down-curved bill. If the bird is smaller (9cm) and has short white central tail feathers, it's the **little hermit** (ermitaño enano; *Phaethornis longuemares*). In mid-elevation forests, 600 to 2000m on both slopes, the long-tailed hermit is replaced by the similar-sized **green hermit** (ermitaño verde; *Phaethornis guy*), which is mainly green but has the distinctive elongated white central tail feathers of the hermits.

Other commonly seen lowland hummers include the **white-necked jacobin** (jacobino nuquiblanco; *Florisuga mellivora*), which breeds in the Caribbean and south Pacific lowlands from January to June. From September to December they are rarely seen, but nobody is sure where they disappear to! Their range is Mexico to the Amazon. The male has a blue head and throat with a white collar on the back of its neck and a white belly and outer tail feathers. The females sometimes look like the males but are quite variable; some lose their blue head and white collar and have instead a scaled blue breast. Females, when discovered on the nest, will often flutter off gently like moths, in an attempt to hoodwink predators.

The **violet sabrewing** (ala de sable violáceo; *Campylopterus hemileucurus*) is the largest Costa Rican hummingbird (15cm long) and has a striking violet body and head, with dark green wings and back and white feathers on the outside of the tail. It is found in mid-elevations and is commonly seen at Monteverde. In fact, Monteverde is the single best place in the country to see hummingbirds, though many are attracted to feeders. Also abundant here is the **green violet-ear** (colibrí orejivioláceo verde; *Colibri thalassinus*), a 10cm-long, almost all-green

Violet sabrewing

hummer with a violet eye patch and a blackish band near the end of the tail. A highland species found only in the cloud forests of Costa Rica (including Monteverde) and into northern Panama is the **fiery-throated hummingbird** (colibrí garganta de fuego; *Panterpe insignis*). This very pugnacious shimmering green hummer with a blue tail has an amazingly brilliant blue cap and orange-and-yellow throat when viewed in good light.

## Trogons

These are 40 species of very colorful, medium-size, upright-perching, long-tailed birds that inhabit the tropics worldwide. Ten species are found in Costa Rica, and the most famous is undoubtedly the **resplendent quetzal** (quetzal; *Pharomachrus mocinno*), perhaps one of the most dazzling and culturally important birds of Central America. It had great ceremonial significance to the Aztecs and the Mayas and is now the national bird and symbol of Guatemala. It is extremely difficult to keep in captivity, where it usually dies quickly, which is perhaps why it became a symbol of liberty to Central Americans during the colonial period.

RALPH LEE HOPKINS

**Resplendent quetzal**

The male lives up to its name with glittering green plumage set off by a crimson belly, and white tail feathers contrasting with bright green tail coverts stream over 60cm beyond the bird's body. The head feathers stick out in a spiky green helmet through which the yellow bill peeks coyly. The male tries to impress the duller-colored female by almost vertical display flights during which the long tail coverts flutter sensuously. A glimpse of this bird is the highlight of many birders' trips. The quetzal (pronounced 'ket-SAL') is fairly common from 1300 to 3000m in forested or partially forested areas. Locals will usually know where to find one; good places to look are Monteverde and various areas in southern Costa Rica. The March to June breeding season is the easiest time to see the birds. At other times, they are less active and quite wary, in common with all the trogons.

The other nine species of Costa Rican trogons are boldly colored – green and red, blue and red, blue and yellow, and green and yellow are typical combinations for the body, usually with a black-and-white or gray tail. Although they are not uncommon, they sit quietly, motionless on mid-level branches in the forest and, despite their bright colors, are hard to spot. Their calls, which vary from gruff barks to clear whistled notes, are the best way to locate them. This is when a good local bird guide can be invaluable.

## Kingfishers

Of the world's 90 species of kingfishers, only six live in the Americas. All six are found in Costa Rica. They are often seen by travelers along rivers. The most common species are the ringed and the green kingfishers. The **ringed kingfisher** (martín pescador collarejo; *Ceryle torquata*) is 41cm long and one of the largest kingfishers in the world. The name derives from the white ring around the collar. The rest of the bird is a slaty blue-gray with rufous breast and belly. The less common **belted kingfisher** (martín pescador norteño; *Ceryle alcyon*) is similar but much smaller and has white underparts. Smaller still, the 18cm-long **green kingfisher** (martín pescador verde; *Chloroceryle americana*) is dark green above and

Belted kingfisher

Green kingfisher

white below. The male has a rufous breast band and both sexes have a white collar and white spots on the tail and wings. The similar **Amazon kingfisher** (martín pescador Amazónico; *Chloroceryle amazonica*) is 29cm long and has less spotting on the wings and tail. The other kingfishers are uncommon.

Amazon kingfisher

## Motmots

These birds, related to the kingfishers, are found only in the Neotropics, and Costa Rica has six of the nine known species. They are colorful birds characterized by an unmistakable long racquet-tail (with barbs missing along part of the feather shaft, leaving a tennis-racquet appearance). The most frequently seen are the **blue-crowned motmot** (momoto común; *Momotus momata*) and the **turquoise-browed motmot** (momoto cejileste; *Eumomota superciliosa*). The first has a bright blue crown with black at the very top and a black face, and is otherwise mainly green with brownish underparts. The other has broad turquoise eyebrows, rufous back and belly, a black face, and a large black spot on its chest, and is otherwise green. It has the longest bare area in the 'handles' of its racquets.

**Blue-crowned motmot**

## Toucans

The 42 species of toucans are Neotropical birds, and six of them are found in Costa Rica. Their best-known feature is their huge bills, which are very light because they are almost hollow, supported internally by thin cross struts. The purpose of these greatly oversized beaks is unknown. Toucans prefer to stay at treetop level and nest in holes in trees. With a little luck, you can see all six species.

The largest is the 56cm-long **chestnut-mandibled toucan** (dios tedé; *Ramphastos swainsonii*), often heard loudly calling with a shrill 'DiOS teDAY teDAY' as it perches high in Caribbean and south Pacific wet forests to about 1800m. It is mainly black with a yellow face and chest and red under the tail, and has a bicolored bill, yellow above and chestnut below. The slightly smaller **keel-billed toucan** (tucan pico iris; *Ramphastos sulfuratus*) is similarly plumaged, but the bill is multicolored. It inhabits the Caribbean slope and the Guanacaste area but not the south Pacific.

**Chestnut-mandibled toucan**

Smaller and slimmer are the **collared aracari** (tucancillo collarejo; *Pteroglossus torquatus*) and the **fiery-billed aracari** (tucancillo piquianaranjado; *Pteroglossus frantzii*), about 42cm long. Both have dark olive-green back, wings and tail, black head and chest, and a bright yellow belly with a red-and-black band. The collared's bill is pale yellowish above and black below, while the fiery-billed's is bright orange above. The easiest way to separate the aracaris is by range – the collared is found on the Caribbean side and in the Guanacaste area, while the fiery-billed is found in the south Pacific.

**Keel-billed toucan**

**Collared aracari**

The smaller **yellow-eared toucanet** (tucancillo orejiamarillo; *Selenidera spectabilis*) is the only local toucan with an all-black belly. It is found mainly in the Caribbean lowlands. The smallest is the **emerald toucanet** (tucancillo verde; *Aulacorhynchus prasinus*), which has a green body and lives in the highlands from 800 to 3000m.

## Woodpeckers & Relatives

Woodpeckers and their relatives, along with the toucans, are members of the order Piciformes. They share the characteristics of nesting in tree holes and having the first and fourth toe pointing backward and the second and third pointing forward (a zygodactyl foot).

The 16 Costa Rican woodpeckers vary in size, from the 9cm-long **olivaceous piculet** (carpenterito oliváceo; *Picumnus olivaceus*) to the 37cm-long **pale-billed woodpecker** (carpintero picoplata; *Campephilus guatemalensis*). They are frequently heard drumming on resonant branches before they are seen. The drumming is sometimes done for communication, and at other times to excavate a hole for nesting or to dislodge insects, which are the main food.

Relatives include jacamars, barbets, puffbirds, and nunbirds. The male **red-headed barbet** (barbudo cabecirrojo; *Eubucco bourcierii*) is striking with its bright red head and chest, yellow bill, green back, and yellow belly. It forages in trees at mid-elevations. The **white-fronted nunbird** (monja frentiblanca; *Monasa morphoes*) is an upright-perching black bird of the Caribbean lowlands. It is immediately identified by its bright red bill with white feathers at the base.

## Passerines

This order, the Passeriformes, is also called 'perching birds' because all members have a foot with three toes pointed forward and one long toe pointing backward, making a claw suitable for perching on twigs. The passerines also share other anatomical features as well as a unique type of sperm. This is the largest, most recently evolved, and most taxonomically confusing order of birds, and ornithologists are constantly changing the names and relationships of the species, sometimes splitting one species into two or more, sometimes lumping two to make one, and sometimes moving them into a different family.

About half of Costa Rica's birds are passerines, including, among others, the families of flycatchers (78 species), antbirds (30 species), wrens (22 species), ovenbirds (18 species), woodcreepers (16 species), and the huge catchall Emberizidae family, which includes the warblers (52 species, including many North American migrants), tanagers (50 species), blackbirds (20 species), and a confusing array of over 50 sparrows, finches, and grosbeaks. Some, like the woodcreepers, are so similar to one another that ornithologists cannot reliably identify them unless they catch the birds. Others, like some tanagers and cotingas, are so extravagantly and uniquely plumaged that identification is very easy. It is some of the latter that I discuss here.

Tanagers are fairly small but often very colorful birds that mainly live in the Neotropics. The most abundant, and one of the country's most common birds, is the **blue-gray tanager** (tangara azuleja; *Thraupis episcopus*). Its head and body are a pale blue gray that

Blue-gray tanager

becomes brighter blue on the wings and tail. It prefers open, humid areas and is seen up to 2300m everywhere except the dry northwest and deep inside the forest. The male **scarlet-rumped tanager** (tangara lomiescarlata; *Ramphocelus passerinii*) is jet black with a bright scarlet rump and lower back, a flashy and unmistakable combination. This bird is common in the Caribbean and southern Pacific slopes. The females, which travel with the males, are a varied mixture of olive, orange, and gray and look like a different species. Both, however, have a silvery bill.

Costa Rican cotingas flaunt their colors. Two are shining white and two others are a brilliant blue and purple. The white ones are the **snowy cotinga** (cotinga nivosa; *Carpodectes nitidus*),

Scarlet-rumped tanager

found on the Caribbean slope, and the *yellow-billed cotinga* (cotinga piquia-marillo; *Carpodectes antoniae*), found on the south Pacific slope. In both cases, the female is a pale gray. The blue ones, both with a purple throat and belly, are uncommon though unmistakable if seen. The **lovely cotinga** *(Cotinga amablis)* is found on the Caribbean and the **turquoise cotinga** *(Cotinga ridgwayi)* is in the south Pacific lowlands. One of the strangest cotingas is the **three-wattled bellbird** (pájaro campano; *Procnias tricaruncu-lata)*; see the boxed text 'A Hike on the Sendero Bosque Nuboso' in the Northwestern Costa Rica chapter.

The 46cm-long **white-throated magpie jay** (urraca; *Calocitta formosa*) is blue above and white below and on the face, with a very long tail and a crest of forward-curling, black-tipped feathers. It is often seen in the drier

TOM BOYDEN

**Three-wattled bellbird**

TOM BOYDEN

**White-throated magpie jay**

northwest slopes and the Península de Nicoya. The slightly smaller **brown jay** (piapia; *Cyanocorax morio*) is mainly brown with creamy outer tail feathers and belly. It is found in deforested areas. Jays are noisy birds with harsh calls.

The colonial **Montezuma oropendola** (oropéndola de Moctezuma; *Psarocolius Montezuma*) weaves a large sacklike nest, sometimes over a meter in length. Colonies of these nests are often seen hanging from branches of tall trees in open areas of the Caribbean lowlands. It has a chestnut-colored body, black head and neck, and golden-yellow outer tail feathers that are conspicuous in flight. The dark bill is orange-tipped and there is a bluish patch on the face. The less-common **chestnut-headed oropendola** *(Psarocolius wagleri)* builds similar nests and has yellow tail feathers, but is black with a chestnut head and pale yellow bill. Both are found mainly on the Caribbean slope and occasionally elsewhere. Their calls are varied, loud, gurgling, and at times mechanical sounding.

# Reptiles

Over half of the 200-plus species of reptiles found in Costa Rica are **snakes**. Though much talked about, they are seldom seen. Most are well camouflaged or slither into the undergrowth when people approach, and few travelers catch sight of one.

More frequently seen reptiles include the common **Ameiva lizards**, which have a white stripe running down their backs. Also common, the bright **green basilisk lizard** *(Basiliscus basiliscus)* is seen on or near water. The males are noted for the huge crests running the length of their head, body, and tail, which give them the appearance of small dinosaurs almost a meter in length. Nicknamed Jesus Christ lizards, they can literally run across water when disturbed. They do this on their greatly elongated and webbed hind feet, and the behavior is more common in young, light individuals.

The **green iguana** *(Iguana iguana)* and blackish **ctenosaur** (garrobo; *Ctenosaura similis*) are large iguanid lizards that are often seen, despite being hunted for food. Ctenosaurs are found in the dry lands of the northwest, while iguanas are also found in wetter regions.

Larger reptiles in coastal national parks such as Tortuguero on the Caribbean or Santa Rosa and Las Baulas on the Pacific include turtles, crocodiles, and caimans. There are 14 species of turtles, some marine and others freshwater or terrestrial. The freshwater ones are often seen sunning in a row on top of a log; as a boat approaches, they quietly slip off, one by one.

Green iguana

Marine turtles climb up sandy beaches to lay their eggs – a spectacular sight. The largest is the **leatherback turtle** (baula; *Dermochelys coriacea*), which has a carapace (shell) up to 1.6m long and an average weight of 360kg, though 500kg individuals have been recorded. Watching this giant come lumbering out of the sea is a memorable experience (see the Península de Nicoya chapter). The **olive ridley** (Lora; *Lepidochelys olivacea*) is much smaller (average 40kg) but practices synchronous nesting when tens of thousands of females may emerge from the sea on a single night – another unforgettable sight (see the Northwestern Costa Rica and Península de Nicoya chapters). The most studied is the **green turtle** (tortuga; *Chelonia mydas*), found on the Caribbean coast (see the Parque Nacional Tortuguero section in the Caribbean Lowlands chapter).

Green turtle

The **spectacled caiman** *(Caiman crocodilus)* and the **American crocodile** *(Crocodylus acutus)* are both confusingly called 'lagarto' by locals. Caimans average about 1m in length and are the most commonly seen, especially in the Tortuguero and Caño Negro areas. The much larger crocodile is often seen near the Carara reserve on the Pacific.

Spectacled caiman

# Amphibians

The approximately 150 species of amphibians include the tiny and colorful **poison-arrow frogs**, in the family Dendrobatidae. Some are bright red with black legs, others red with blue legs, and still others are bright green with black markings. Several species have skin glands exuding toxins that can cause paralysis and death in many animals, including humans. Dendrobatids have been used by Latin American forest Indians to provide a poison in which to dip the tips of their hunting arrows. The toxins are effective when introduced into the bloodstream (as with arrows) but don't have much effect when a frog is casually touched.

Two of the brightly colored, sometimes poisonous, poison-arrow frogs

The so-called **marine toad** (sapo grande; *Bufo marinus*) is actually found both on the coast and inland up to a height of 2000m. Frequently seen in the evenings around human habitations in rural areas, its size makes it unmistakable. It is the largest Neotropical lowland toad and specimens reaching 20cm long and weighing up to 1.2kg have been recorded – that's one big toad!

Marine toad

# Insects

Over 35,000 species of insects have been recorded in Costa Rica, and many thousands remain undiscovered. Butterflies are abundant. One source claims that Costa Rica has 10% of all the world's butterfly species, and another reports that over 3000 species of butterflies and moths are recorded from Parque Nacional Santa Rosa alone.

The most dazzling butterfly is the **morpho** *(Morpho peleides)*. With a 15cm wingspan and electric-blue upper wings, it lazily flaps and glides along tropical rivers and through openings in the rainforest in a shimmering display. When it lands, however, the wings close and only the brown underwings are visible, an instantaneous change from outrageous display to modest camouflage.

TOM BOYDEN

**Morpho butterfly**

Camouflage plays an important part in the lives of many insects. Some resting butterflies look exactly like green or brown leaves, while others look like the scaly bark of the tree on which they are resting. Caterpillars are often masters of disguise. One species is capable of constricting certain muscles to make itself look like the head of a viper, other species mimic twigs, and yet another species looks so much like a bird dropping that it rarely gets attacked by unwitting predators.

There are many hundreds of ant species in tropical forests. **Leaf-cutter ants** *(Atta spp)* are often seen marching in columns along the forest floor, carrying pieces of leaves like little parasols above their heads. The leaf segments are taken into an underground colony and there allowed to decay into mulch. The ants tend their mulch gardens carefully, allowing a certain species of fungus to grow there. Parts of the fungus are then used to feed the colony, which can be several million ants.

Other insects are so tiny as to be barely visible, yet their lifestyles are no less esoteric. The **hummingbird flower mite** *(Rhinoseius colwelli)* is barely half a millimeter in length and lives in flowers. When the flowers are visited by hummingbirds, the mites scuttle up into the birds' nostrils and use this novel form of air transport to disperse themselves to other plants. Smaller still are mites that live on the proboscis of the morpho butterflies. From the tiniest mite to the largest butterfly, insects form an incredibly diverse part of the country's wildlife.

# Thanks

Many thanks to the readers of earlier editions who wrote to us with helpful hints, advice and information:

Craig L Abrams, Jean Vincent Accoce, Dawn M Adams, Rudolf M Ahr, Alex Aiken, Marco Akermann, Philip Alford, Christina Alksnis, Ron Alldridge, Brett Allen, Ian Allen, Lesli Allison, Michael L Altman, Danny Alvarez Uribe, Katherine Amheiter, Y Amorelli, M Amsler, Paul Anderson, George Anelay, Marc Anthony Meyer, Giuseppe Anzalone, Marcus von Appen, Emanuela Appetiti, Annie Appleyard, Mariamalia Araya, Leah Archer, Joey Archibald, Yoar Aren, David Arguello, Ronald Ariesen, Jorge Artavia, Rafael Artavia, Jonathan Ashdown, Bill Athineos, Irene Atting, Mayra E August, Jason Aulepe, Jorg Ausfelt, Nathan Axel, Jeremy Bachmann, Peter Baciewicz, Sandra Backlund, Moti Bahadur Tailor, John and Molly Bailey, Tristan Baird, David Bamford, Thorn Barn, Cliff Barnes, Kai Bartels, Gary Bartolacci, José Tomas Batalla, Brett Batty, James and Jody Bavis, Tony and Anastasija Bayliss, Andrew Beadles, Bill Beard, Nadine Beard, Sharon Beaudoin, Franz Becker, Stuart Behrens, Gill and Racheli Bejerano, Mariska Belyea, George Bement, Paula Bennett, Mike Benveniste, Pamela Berghegen, Edward Berkovich, Edith Bernard, Jacques Bertrand, Abel and TWP Beyene, Wayne and Marge Bigelow, Tracy Blahy, N Blankendal, Paula Blanski, Joel Bleskacek, Brian Blunden, John Boal, Herold Boertjens, Jan Bohuslav, Eliza G Bonner, Phillip Boorman, Rutger Boot, Gregory Borferding, Dirk Kapteyn den Boumeester, Kathy Boutis, Michael Bowen, Gregoire Boyen, Jaymie Boyum, Wim Braakhuis, Adrian Bracho, Matthew Braham, Annemarie Breeve, Dirk Bremecke, Shaun Brennand, Karel Brevet, Sarah Brodie, John Brown, James and Kristen Browne, Ariel Brunner, Ann Bugeda, T Burdine, Steve Burger, Jane-Lauren Burn, Carolyn Burnett, Nancy Burnett, Marlene Burvenich, Jurgen Busink, Karla Butler, RCB Butler, Jamie Buttle, Karel Caals, Diana Cafazzo, Jeff Caldwell, Eva Calvo, Teri Campbell, Giorgio Carletto, Thierry Carquet, Devon Carr, Jana Carter, Martin Carter, Michel Cavelier, Gonzalo Chacon, Ingeborg Chandler, VM Charlesworth, Laurence and Jean-Pierre Charton-Le Solleu, Robert Chatenever, Jeannie Choi, Daniel Christen, Robyn Christie, Alan Chung, Ulrika Claesson, John Clark, Brian Clifton, Rachel Cohen, Joy Coker, Ralph Combs, Frank and Fran Conn, Jay Connerley, Jean-Paul Connock, Louise and Michael Connolly, Meghan Connolly, Rouy Constable, David Cook, Ron Cook, Karen Cooper, Kyla Copp, Laura Cordero, Greg Cornell, Mike Cotterill, Bryce Coulter, Christina Cox, Frank Crawford, Jim Crawford, Earl Crews, Mike Crimmins, Julia Crislip, Tom Croom, Christopher J Cross, Russ and Barb Crum, Antonio Cuco, Glenn Culbreth, Pete Curtice, Janet Cutlip, Julian Dalby, Elizabeth Dames, Walker Daves, Steven Davey, Becky Davis, Belle Davis, Joe Davis, Sue Davis, Robert Davison, Heather Day, Michael Day, Simone de Haan, Andrea de K, Daniel De Ugarte, Matthijs de Zwaan, David DeFranza, Peter Deixelberger, Peter and Renata Deixelberger, Mirta Del Frari, Maria del Pilar Costa, Kirsten Delegard, Mark Dellar, Lyle Demery, Willem-Henri den Hartog, Luc Deschacht, Joni Diamond, Sylvie Didierlaurent, Katharine Dillon, Katherine Dobson, Eshed Doni, Lea Donovan, DeVona Dors, Charlie Drozdyk, Tim Drummond, Ernest P Dubois, Lee Dubs, Waltraud Duerst, Ilse Duijvestein, Jean-Marc Dumont, Noreen Duncan, Amanda Dunham, Stephanie Duparc, Marc Dyer, Tim Eastling, Richard W Easton, Richard Eaton, Gerhard Eckert, Carey Edmeades, Brian Eggleston, Diane Eisold, David Elmore, Maury Englander, Ines Erhard, Christina Eriksson, Jimena Esteve, Kathy and Brent Evjen, Tim Oliver Eynck, Carrie Faber, Adrian Farmer, Delia Fasiolo, Ted R Feldpausch, Amy Ferguson, Dr Ronald Fernandez, Jordi Fernandez, Mariluz Fernandez Pérez, Daniel Fey, Pierre and Karen Filipowicz, David Filliard, Maarten Fischer, Leah Fisher, Heather Fleming, Tom Fletcher, Camilla Fossum, Pam Foster, Heidi Frankl, Bettina Freihofer, Jonathan French, Richard French, Mark Friedman, Max Friedman, Victoria E Fritz, Stephanie Frohman, John B Frost, Sarah Fullerton, Brian Furness, Denis Gagnon, Michelle Gagnon, Christophe Gaillard, Ryan Gamlin, A Gammage, Ellen Garber, Christer Garbis, Matt Garceau, Rita Garczynski, Terry Gardner, Irene E Gashu, Dirk Geeraerts, Virginie and Frédérik Geldhof, Anna Genet, Cynthia Gerrie, Joke Gesel, Jill Gibson, Bryan Gieszl, José Luis Fernandez Gil, Gilbert Gimm, Duncan Gittins, Jack Glass, Tracy Gluckman, Carl Ulrich Gminder, Bing Goei, Maria Goepfert-Maguire, Michael Golden, Samantha Goldstein, Christian Goltz, Steven Jon Gonzales, Elizabeth Gonzalez, Louisa Goode, Greg Gordon, Matthew Gore, Adam R Goss, Stuart Graham, Michel Grant, Clair Graves, Elizabeth Grier, Dianne

Grimmer, Hans Grob, Rokus Groeneveld, José Groothuis, Allan Groves, Angela Leon Guerrero, Fredrik Gustafsson, Cesar Gutierrez, Edwarda Gutkowski, Joanne Haase, Rosene Haigh, Mary Haller, Brian Hallmark, Casey Halloran, Ralph Hammelbacher, Mark and Anoeska Hardeman, Tom Harman, Melanie Harper, Langdon W Harris, Susanne Hartung, Alison Heath, Robert Heerekop, Stefan Hegnauer, Freddie Heitman, Caroline Helbig, Steven Hemsley, Joseph L Henley, Patrick Hennessey, Janne Brunt Henriksen, Elli Herczeg, Jolanda Hess, Phyllis Hicks, Calvin Hill, Edward Hill, Sue Hill, Christine Hillenbrand, Tom, Janet, Colleen and Liam Hilliard, Joe Hlebica, Tom Ho, Shai Hod, Jim Hogan, Rebecca Hogue, Arjan Hollemans, Dorsey Holoppa, Stefan Holtel, Anouk Holthuizen, Brandon Holton, Justine and David Horton, Monty Horton, Alex Horvath, Adrian Hoskins, Coquille Houshour, Angeline van Hout, Ron Howard, Nick and Sue Howes, Pat Hoyman, Teri Hudson, Derek Hughey, Polly Hunt, David Hunter, Tim Hurley, Andy Hurst, Nathan Hutto, Stailee Hyduck, Marc Iffenecker, Beryl Jackson, Anna Parry Jacobs, Karin Jacobsson, Jenny Jaffe, Roger Jaggli, Bonnie Jakubos, Richard James, Maggie Jamieson, Gerbert Jansen, Carole G Jean, Jennifer Jensen, Ryan Joffe, Kean Johal, Altron W Johnson, Sandy Johnson, Scott Johnson, Emily Jones, Melanie Jones, Jerven Jongkind, Laura Joseph, Marc Julien, Sara Junker, Garneyr Jurgen, Stefan Kalchmair, Astrid, Van and Manfred Kalkeren-Scheeve, Stuart Kanchuger, Bjorn Karlsson, Nik Katsourides, Janathan Katz, Eiichi Kawabata, Helen Kay, Gerald Keating, Kyle Keegan, Dave Keeney, Felix Keller, John Keller, Terence Kemp, Chantal Kenens, Beverly Kennedy, Ralf Kettner, Patricia Kim, Guillermo Kimenez Chacon, Tristan Kincaid, Ray and Lisa King, Nicole Kinson, Jennifer Kitson, Katie Klemsen, Heidi Klose, Deanna L Kluepfel, Page Klug, Jos Koeleman, Anke Kohn, Michael Koll, Elly Kommer, Katerina Komselis, John Korte, Stephanie Krook, Christine Krulj, Jeff Krum, Keri Krupp, Roman Kucbel, Deanna Kuhn, Ueli Kuhni, Bob Kurkijian, Lyn La Cava, Annemarie Lagerman, Richard Laing, Sally Laird, Jasmine Lallier, Martin Lammerding, Catherine Lampe, Todd Lang, Johan Langenaeken, Gunhild Ross Lauritsen, Inger Marie Laursen, Gayle Lazoration, Veronique Leblanc, Nancy Lebo, Stegan Lechner, Susanne Leckband, Karen Lee, Wilbert and Gwen Lee, Laura Lee Hartshorn, George Lefrevre, Henriette Leifert, Hetty and Yvo Leijnse, Damon Lenski, Elizabeth Leon, Martin Lessard, Uri Levin, Navah Levine, Robert Levy, Shara Levy, Mark Lewis, Wayne Lewis, Florence J Licata, Steve Lidgey, Andreas Lindberg, Tom Linhart, Steven M

Link, Dave Lloyd, Travis Lloyd, Liam Loftus, Ana Lombardo, Christian Loncle, Matt Long, Erin Longley, Daryl Loth, Panos Loupasis, Veronica Luca, Thomas and Jackie Luijkx, Janet Lutz, Tamara Lyons, Silvie M, William E Macauley, Jane MacBeth, Barbara MacGregor, Therese M Macintyre, Steve and Demi Mackintosh, Janet MacLeod, Matthias Mahr, Dominic Mailhot, Solveig Maisan, Gabriella Malnati, Kerlai Man, Nick Manesis, Robert Manley, Linda Manoll, Ole Markussen, Ofer Marom, Xenia Marotto, Michael Marquardt, Ian Marsh, Kevin Martin, Lara Martinez, Rafael R Martinez, Vicky and Rob Martinez, Anne Masorti, Ruth Masterson, Nancy Matson, Mike Maurice, Emilio Mayorga, Paola Mazzali, Maria Mazzone, Georgiana McCall, Bruce McCartney, Wendy McClellan, Frank McComb, Robert McCorkindale, Jennifer McCready, Tricia McDonald, Dan McDougall, James Brown, Matt McKean, Byrne and Heidi McKenna, Sarah McKinnon, Holli McVean, Chris Mead, Jens Meier, Manfred Melchinger, Malene Melgaaard, Sue Mellen, Hannah Mermelstein, John and Lisa Merrill, Jon Messner, Assaf Metuki, Michael Metzger, Alain Meyer, Alexandra and Beverly Meyer, Corinna Meyer, Julia Meyer, Rodger Meyers, Juliet Michelle, Adrian Miller, Andrew Miller, Aubree Miller, David Miller, Fred and Melissa Miller, Terence Mills, Michael Minozzi, Barry Misenheimer, Charles Mittman, David Mogensen, Dennis Mogerman, George Molander, Jason M Moll, Heidi and Alvaro Monge, Jamie Monk, Charles Montange, Kathryn Mooney, Margarita Mooney, Arthur Moore, Bob Morris, Dale Morris, Daniel Morris, J Mortarott, Amy Motti, Judy Moy, Julie Mucci, Joseph Mulligan, Peter Mumby, Anke Munderloh, Catherine Munier, Keith Mustard, Walter Naaf, Shannon Nally, Miguel Naranjo, Roger Nash, Frekrik Naumann, Stan Needle, Silvian Nees, Jan Nelis, Joan Neuheimen, Camille Ng, Bruno Nicholson, Ole Kruse Nielsen, Silvian Nies, Klaas Nijs, Emilie Nolet, Adrian Nordenborg, Vern Noren, Kate Norgrove, Alan Nunns, Ruth Nussbaumer, Kevin O'Brien, Kathleen O'Hara, Justin Oliver, Irene Oliveri, Inger Olsen, David Olson, Wayne Olson, Guus Otten, Lisotte Ottingen, Phillip Owen, Kristen Page, Robert Page, Monique Paquette, David Parbery, Mor Parnass, Lisa Parsons, Sandra van der Pas, Erin Pass, Donald Patterson, Gary W Paukert, RH Payne, Kim Pearson, M Peis, Carlos Pelejero, Deborah Pencharz, Jamie Penk, Luis Pereira, Steve Pete, Darren Peterson, Severine Peudupin, Michael Pfeiffer, Regina Phelps, Eric Philippouci, F Phillips, Janice Pickering, Donna Pinner, Mick Pirie, E Pling, Andrea Plomp, Snapper Poche, Nava and Hans

Polman, Kristin Porter, James Pospychala, Oren Postrel, Susan Pot, Richard and Ann Powell, Gina and Sylvian Pradervand-Angulo, Molly Prindiville, Max Prokopy, Annabella Proudlock, Peter Proudlock, Dennis Rabun, Bjoern Rackoll, Sage Radachowsky, Marc Raez, Bill and Stefanie Raitt, Bruce Ramsay, Ian Ramsay, Jim Randall, Thorsten Rasche, Paul Raushenbush, Jeremy and Johanna Ray, Jean Reagan, Andrew Redfern, JD Reed, John Reeve, Sanne Reijs, Kevin Reilly, Jurgen Reinking, John Richards, Suzanne Richards, Carolyn Rieger, Frank M Riethdorf, Kyle Robbins, Paul Roberts, Chris P Robinson, Jackie Robson, Jacquie Rodgers, Vincent Roering, Jan Rohde, Trish Rohrer, Megan Romano, Melanie Ronai, Margot Ros, Renee Rose, Pat and Marvin Rosen, Phyllis Rosenberg, Lisa Ross, Marc Roth, R Roth, Rose Rothe, Marie-Jacques Rouleau, Richard P Rubinstein, Mike Rudolph, Nico Ruijter, Karen and Michael Russell, Lucie Russell, Kristi Russo, Bernadette Ryan, Andrew Rymes, Matthew Salganik, Annalyn Saludares, Per Samuelsson, Armando Sanchez, Michele Sanna, Jim Satterly, Bill Schaap, Judy Scheig, Xavier and Kristina Scheurer, Micheal Schiesser, Inid Schiller, Judie Schinz, Susanna Schlette, Emil and Liliana Schmid, Michael Schmid, Petra Schmitz, Michael Schnitzler, Lioba Schoen, Leonie Schreve, Joke Schrijvershof, Adelina Schutt, Johannes Schwartlander, Jon-Bernard Schwartz, Martin Schweinberger, Steve Scofield, Gary W Scott, Robert Scott, Wendy Scott, Rick Scull, Diane Scully, Tatjana Sczerba, Angel Sebastian, Jana Seelbach, Jane Segleau, Maggie Sennish, Emil Sernbo, Tracey Seslen, W Shane Turner, Algy Sharman, Jeff Shaw, S Shea, Georgia Shebay, Carla Sher, Debbie Sherman, Randi and Jeff Shields, James Shiffer, Volker Siegel, Arleen Sierra, Bente Sig Nielsen, Christopher Silke, Mike Simmonds, Daniel Simons, Dean Simonsen, Bonnie Simpson, Jessica Sinha, Florian Sinnegger, Ander Smith, Matthew Smith, Megan Smith, Pauline Smith, Wayne Smits, Marc Sokol, Shari Solomon, Tuija Sonkkila, Paivi Sonninen, George Sosnowski, Annette Spates, Dara Spatz, Matthew Sperry, Ren Spinnler, Wietske Spoelstra, Greg Spycia, Scott Stacey, Maria and Robert Staeheli, Grant Stafford, Monti Staton, Karin Steinkamp, Scot Stennis, Julien Stern, Maarten Stoffels, Meghan Storey, Joleen Stran, Emma Stratton, Josh Stratton, Oliver and Elly Strauss, Doris Strube, Therese Stukel, Ed Styffe, Joanna Sullivan, Bob Summa, Amanda Sumpter, Kerry Suson, Martin Suter, Malmoe Sweden, Nancy Taylor, Jonas Tegenfeldt, Pierre-Leon Tetreault, Sarah Thayer, Christian Thivierge, Gerry Thompson, Lisa Thompson, Richard Thompson, Sherwood and Lois Thompson, Antonia Thomson, Jacob Thyssen, Peter Timmermans, Raffaele Tola, Lynn Tomita, Pere Torrodellas, David Townsend, Mari Toyohara, Fram W Trager, Nghia Tran, Anne Tremblay, Lydia Trimmings, KJ Troy, D Turner, John Turner, Karen Turner, Susan Twombly, Ilona Unterhalt, Marcy Upchurch, Julie Urbanek, Nicole van Beeck, Jenny Van Belle, Marjolein van de Paverd, Xander Van der Burgt, Rick Van der Kamp, Inez van der Linden, Anje C Van der Naald, Vanessa Van Eeden, Jeffrey van Fleet, Daniel van Grootheest, Ine van Ham, Erik and Margo van Roekel, Joop van Staalduinen, Guy Vancraybex, Sara Vazquez, Bauke Van Der Veen, Larry Vega, Pilar Velasco, Harry Ven Belle, Eddy Veraghtert, Anthony Verebes, Anne Vial, Joerg Viereck, Susan Viner, Ivonne Vlies, Hans and Silvia Voellmin, Axel Vogt, Lynn Vogt, Annette von Apiegel, Herman Von Harten, Jared W, NC Walker, Sheila Walker, Marc Wallace, Allan Wallach, Mike Walls, Heidi Wampfler, Catherine Wareing, Gunnar Wass, Murray Watt, Colin Way, Sarah Weber, Nurit Weiner, Allan Weisbard, Kristin Wendorf, Stella Wenger, Karl W Werther, Mark Westerfield, Pieter Westra, Meghan Wheaton, Gary and Paula Wheeler, Mitch Wheeler, Geoff and Melanie Whitehead, Jonathan Wickens, Jennifer Widom, Zita O'Rourke Wigger, Jennifer Wilkinson, Patrick William-Powlett, John Williams, Marica Williston, Judy Wilson, Lucia Wilson, Tristram Winfield, Melanie Winskie, Mary Winston, Joanna Wisniewska, Nicole Wittig, Meredith Witucki, Martin Woerner, Monica Wojtaszewski, Judi Wolford, James M Wolken, Linda Wood, Wendy Wood, Suzanna and Andi Woodley, Leah Woods, Paul Wotherspoon, Paula Yeadon, Rosemary Yeldham, Be Yeo, David Young, Marilyn Young, Rodger Young, Nitzan Yudan, Justin Zaman, Angelo Zaragovia, Gary Zendell, Tim Zijderveld and Joel Zwanziger

# Lonely Planet Guides by Region

**L** onely Planet Is known worldwide for publishing practical, reliable and no-nonsense travel information in our guides and on our Web site. The Lonely Planet list covers just about every accessible part of the world. Currently there are 16 series: Travel guides, Shoestring guides, Condensed guides, Phrasebooks, Read This First, Healthy Travel, Walking guides, Cycling guides, Watching Wildlife guides, Pisces Diving & Snorkeling guides, City Maps, Road Atlases, Out to Eat, World Food, Journeys travel literature and Pictorials.

**AFRICA** Africa on a shoestring • Botswana • Cairo • Cairo City Map • Cape Town • Cape Town City Map • East Africa • Egypt • Egyptian Arabic phrasebook • Ethiopia, Eritrea & Djibouti • Ethiopian Amharic phrasebook • The Gambia & Senegal • Healthy Travel Africa • Kenya • Malawi • Morocco • Moroccan Arabic phrasebook • Mozambique • Namibia • Read This First: Africa • South Africa, Lesotho & Swaziland • Southern Africa • Southern Africa Road Atlas • Swahili phrasebook • Tanzania, Zanzibar & Pemba • Trekking in East Africa • Tunisia • Watching Wildlife East Africa • Watching Wildlife Southern Africa • West Africa • World Food Morocco • Zambia • Zimbabwe, Botswana & Namibia
**Travel Literature:** Mali Blues: Traveling to an African Beat • The Rainbird: A Central African Journey • Songs to an African Sunset: A Zimbabwean Story

**AUSTRALIA & THE PACIFIC** Aboriginal Australia & the Torres Strait Islands • Auckland • Australia • Australian phrasebook • Australia Road Atlas • Cycling Australia • Cycling New Zealand • Fiji • Fijian phrasebook • Healthy Travel Australia, NZ and the Pacific • Islands of Australia's Great Barrier Reef • Melbourne • Melbourne City Map • Micronesia • New Caledonia • New South Wales • New Zealand • Northern Territory • Outback Australia • Out to Eat – Melbourne • Out to Eat – Sydney • Papua New Guinea • Pidgin phrasebook • Queensland • Rarotonga & the Cook Islands • Samoa • Solomon Islands • South Australia • South Pacific • South Pacific phrasebook • Sydney • Sydney City Map • Sydney Condensed • Tahiti & French Polynesia • Tasmania • Tonga • Tramping in New Zealand • Vanuatu • Victoria • Walking in Australia • Watching Wildlife Australia • Western Australia
**Travel Literature:** Islands in the Clouds: Travel in the Highlands of New Guinea • Kiwi Tracks: A New Zealand Journey • Sean & David's Long Drive

**CENTRAL AMERICA & THE CARIBBEAN** Bahamas, Turks & Caicos • Baja California • Belize, Guatemala & Yucatán • Bermuda • Central America on a shoestring • Costa Rica • Costa Rica Spanish phrasebook • Cuba • Cycling Cuba • Dominican Republic & Haiti • Eastern Caribbean • Guatemala • Havana • Healthy Travel Central & South America • Jamaica • Mexico • Mexico City • Panama • Puerto Rico • Read This First: Central & South America • Virgin Islands • World Food Caribbean • World Food Mexico • Yucatán
**Travel Literature:** Green Dreams: Travels in Central America

**EUROPE** Amsterdam • Amsterdam City Map • Amsterdam Condensed • Andalucía • Athens • Austria • Baltic States phrasebook • Barcelona • Barcelona City Map • Belgium & Luxembourg • Berlin • Berlin City Map • Britain • British phrasebook • Brussels, Bruges & Antwerp • Brussels City Map • Budapest • Budapest City Map • Canary Islands • Catalunya & the Costa Brava • Central Europe • Central Europe phrasebook • Copenhagen • Corfu & the Ionians • Corsica • Crete • Crete Condensed • Croatia • Cycling Britain • Cycling France • Cyprus • Czech & Slovak Republics • Czech phrasebook • Denmark • Dublin • Dublin City Map • Dublin Condensed • Eastern Europe • Eastern Europe phrasebook • Edinburgh • Edinburgh City Map • England • Estonia, Latvia & Lithuania • Europe on a shoestring • Europe phrasebook • Finland • Florence • Florence City Map • France • Frankfurt City Map • Frankfurt Condensed • French phrasebook • Georgia, Armenia & Azerbaijan • Germany • German phrasebook • Greece • Greek Islands • Greek phrasebook • Hungary • Iceland, Greenland & the Faroe Islands • Ireland • Italian phrasebook • Italy • Kraków • Lisbon • The Loire • London • London City Map • London Condensed • Madrid • Madrid City Map • Malta • Mediterranean Europe • Milan, Turin & Genoa • Moscow • Munich • Netherlands • Normandy • Norway • Out to Eat – London • Out to Eat – Paris • Paris • Paris City Map • Paris Condensed • Poland • Polish phrasebook • Portugal • Portuguese phrasebook • Prague • Prague City Map • Provence & the Côte d'Azur • Read This First: Europe • Rhodes & the Dodecanese • Romania & Moldova • Rome • Rome City Map • Rome Condensed • Russia, Ukraine & Belarus • Russian phrasebook • Scandinavian & Baltic Europe • Scandinavian phrasebook • Scotland • Sicily • Slovenia • South-West France • Spain • Spanish phrasebook • Stockholm • St Petersburg • St Petersburg City Map • Sweden • Switzerland • Tuscany • Ukrainian phrasebook • Venice • Vienna • Wales • Walking in Britain • Walking in France • Walking in Ireland • Walking in Italy • Walking in Scotland • Walking in Spain • Walking in Switzerland • Western Europe • World Food France • World Food Greece • World Food Ireland • World Food Italy • World Food Spain **Travel Literature:** After Yugoslavia • Love and War in the Apennines • The Olive Grove: Travels in Greece • On the Shores of the Mediterranean • Round Ireland in Low Gear • A Small Place in Italy

# Lonely Planet Mail Order

Lonely Planet products are distributed worldwide. They are also available by mail order from Lonely Planet, so if you have difficulty finding a title, please write to us. North and South American residents should write to 150 Linden St, Oakland, CA 94607, USA; European and African residents should write to 10a Spring Place, London NW5 3BH, UK; and residents of other countries to Locked Bag 1, Footscray, Victoria 3011, Australia.

**INDIAN SUBCONTINENT & THE INDIAN OCEAN** Bangladesh • Bengali phrasebook • Bhutan • Delhi • Goa • Healthy Travel Asia & India • Hindi & Urdu phrasebook • India • India & Bangladesh City Map • Indian Himalaya • Karakoram Highway • Kathmandu City Map • Kerala • Madagascar • Maldives • Mauritius, Réunion & Seychelles • Mumbai (Bombay) • Nepal • Nepali phrasebook • North India • Pakistan • Rajasthan • Read This First: Asia & India • South India • Sri Lanka • Sri Lanka phrasebook • Tibet • Tibetan phrasebook • Trekking in the Indian Himalaya • Trekking in the Karakoram & Hindukush • Trekking in the Nepal Himalaya • World Food India **Travel Literature:** The Age of Kali: Indian Travels and Encounters • Hello Goodnight: A Life of Goa • In Rajasthan • Maverick in Madagascar • A Season in Heaven: True Tales from the Road to Kathmandu • Shopping for Buddhas • A Short Walk in the Hindu Kush • Slowly Down the Ganges

**MIDDLE EAST & CENTRAL ASIA** Bahrain, Kuwait & Qatar • Central Asia • Central Asia phrasebook • Dubai • Farsi (Persian) phrasebook • Hebrew phrasebook • Iran • Israel & the Palestinian Territories • Istanbul • Istanbul City Map • Istanbul to Cairo • Istanbul to Kathmandu • Jerusalem • Jerusalem City Map • Jordan • Lebanon • Middle East • Oman & the United Arab Emirates • Syria • Turkey • Turkish phrasebook • World Food Turkey • Yemen **Travel Literature:** Black on Black: Iran Revisited • Breaking Ranks: Turbulent Travels in the Promised Land • The Gates of Damascus • Kingdom of the Film Stars: Journey into Jordan

**NORTH AMERICA** Alaska • Boston • Boston City Map • Boston Condensed • British Columbia • California & Nevada • California Condensed • Canada • Chicago • Chicago City Map • Chicago Condensed • Florida • Georgia & the Carolinas • Great Lakes • Hawaii • Hiking in Alaska • Hiking in the USA • Honolulu & Oahu City Map • Las Vegas • Los Angeles • Los Angeles City Map • Louisiana & the Deep South • Miami • Miami City Map • Montréal • New England • New Orleans • New Orleans City Map • New York City • New York City City Map • New York City Condensed • New York, New Jersey & Pennsylvania • Oahu • Out to Eat – San Francisco • Pacific Northwest • Rocky Mountains • San Diego & Tijuana • San Francisco • San Francisco City Map • Seattle • Seattle City Map • Southwest • Texas • Toronto • USA • USA phrasebook • Vancouver • Vancouver City Map • Virginia & the Capital Region • Washington, DC • Washington, DC City Map • World Food New Orleans **Travel Literature**: Caught Inside: A Surfer's Year on the California Coast • Drive Thru America

**NORTH-EAST ASIA** Beijing • Beijing City Map • Cantonese phrasebook • China • Hiking in Japan • Hong Kong & Macau • Hong Kong City Map • Hong Kong Condensed • Japan • Japanese phrasebook • Korea • Korean phrasebook • Kyoto • Mandarin phrasebook • Mongolia • Mongolian phrasebook • Seoul • Shanghai • South-West China • Taiwan • Tokyo • World Food Hong Kong • World Food Japan **Travel Literature:** In Xanadu: A Quest • Lost Japan

**SOUTH AMERICA** Argentina, Uruguay & Paraguay • Bolivia • Brazil • Brazilian phrasebook • Buenos Aires • Buenos Aires City Map • Chile & Easter Island • Colombia • Ecuador & the Galápagos Islands • Healthy Travel Central & South America • Latin American Spanish phrasebook • Peru • Quechua phrasebook • Read This First: Central & South America • Rio de Janeiro • Rio de Janeiro City Map • Santiago de Chile • South America on a shoestring • Trekking in the Patagonian Andes • Venezuela **Travel Literature:** Full Circle: A South American Journey

**SOUTH-EAST ASIA** Bali & Lombok • Bangkok • Bangkok City Map • Burmese phrasebook • Cambodia • Cycling Vietnam, Laos & Cambodia • East Timor phrasebook • Hanoi • Healthy Travel Asia & India • Hill Tribes phrasebook • Ho Chi Minh City (Saigon) • Indonesia • Indonesian phrasebook • Indonesia's Eastern Islands • Java • Lao phrasebook • Laos • Malay phrasebook • Malaysia, Singapore & Brunei • Myanmar (Burma) • Philippines • Pilipino (Tagalog) phrasebook • Read This First: Asia & India • Singapore • Singapore City Map • South-East Asia on a shoestring • South-East Asia phrasebook • Thailand • Thailand's Islands & Beaches • Thailand, Vietnam, Laos & Cambodia Road Atlas • Thai phrasebook • Vietnam • Vietnamese phrasebook • World Food Indonesia • World Food Thailand • World Food Vietnam

**ALSO AVAILABLE:** Antarctica • The Arctic • The Blue Man: Tales of Travel, Love and Coffee • Brief Encounters: Stories of Love, Sex & Travel • Buddhist Stupas in Asia: The Shape of Perfection • Chasing Rickshaws • The Last Grain Race • Lonely Planet…On the Edge: Adventurous Escapades from Around the World • Lonely Planet Unpacked • Lonely Planet Unpacked Again • Not the Only Planet: Science Fiction Travel Stories • Ports of Call: A Journey by Sea • Sacred India • Travel Photography: A Guide to Taking Better Pictures • Travel with Children • Tuvalu: Portrait of an Island Nation

# LONELY PLANET

You already know that Lonely Planet produces more than this one guidebook, but you might not be aware of the other products we have on this region. Here is a selection of titles which you may want to check out as well:

**Panama**
ISBN 1 86450 307 6
US$16.99 • UK£10.99

**Diving & Snorkeling Cocos Island**
ISBN 1 55992 092 0
US$14.95 • UK£7.99

**Healthy Travel Central & South America**
ISBN 1 86450 053 0
US$5.95 • UK£3.99

**Central America on a shoestring**
ISBN 1 86450 186 3
US$21.99 • UK£13.99

**Watching Wildlife Central America**
ISBN 1 86450 034 4
US$24.99 • UK£13.99

**Costa Rica Spanish phrasebook**
ISBN 1 86450 105 7
US$7.99 • UK£4.50

**Available wherever books are sold.**

# Index

## Abbreviations

Nic – Nicaragua
Pan – Panama
PN – Parque Nacional

PNM – Parque Nacional
   Marino
RB – Reserva Biológica
RI – Reserva Indígena

RNFS – Refugio Nacional de
   Fauna Silvestre
RNVS – Refugio Nacional de
   Vida Silvestre

## TEXT

### A

accidents 57, 88, 90
accommodations 65–7.
   *See also individual*
   *locations*
   B&Bs 66
   camping 65–6
   homestays 67, 116
   hostels 36, 65–6
   hotels 66–7
   reservations 115–6
activities 58–65. *See also*
   *individual activities*
agouti 424, 515
Aguas Zarcas 321
AIDS 49–50
air travel
   airlines 72, 84, 141–2
   airports 45, 72, 141,
   146
   domestic 84–5, **85**
   international 72–6
Alajuela 152–6, **153**
alcoholic drinks 69–70
Alma Ata 327
altitude sickness 50
Ameiva lizard 537
amphibians 200, 201,
   539
anhinga 518
anis 528
anteaters 505–6
ants, leaf-cutter 540
aquarium 449
aracaris 534
Araya, Rolando 14–5
archaeological sites
   Alma Ata 327
   Ciudad Cutris 321

Guayabo 188–9
Arenal (village) 252
Arenal (volcano) 15, 203,
   243, 250–2
Arenal Botanical Gardens
   252–3
Arias, Oscar 14, 294
armadillos 506–7
art galleries 140–1, 200–1,
   256
arts 27–8. *See also* crafts
Asociación Nacional de
   Asuntos Indígenas (ANAI)
   380
astronomy 301
ATEC 369
Atenas 157–8
ATMs 38
Avalon Reserva Privada
   388–9
Avellana, Playa 281–2
Aviarios del Caribe 359

### B

B&Bs. *See* accommodations
Bagaces 222
Bahía Ballena, Playa 492
Bahía Drake 413–8, **414**
Bahía Gigante 300
Bahía Junquillal, RNVS
   236–7
Bahía Potrero 272–3
Bahía Salinas 240–1
Bajos de Chilamate 321
Ballena, PNM 491–2
ballooning, hot-air 65
banana paper 28, 71
bananas 25, 322, 333
banks 38
barbet, red-headed
   534
Barra del Colorado 352–7,
   **353**
Barra Honda, PN 288–99

bars 136–8
Barva (town) 170
Barva (volcano) 175–6
Basílica de Nuestra Señora de
   los Angeles 177–8
basilisk lizard 537
basketball 70
bathrooms 45, 67
bats 235, 507–8
   fishing bulldog 507
   ghost 508
   Honduran white 508
   Jamaican fruit 507
   vampire 51, 507–8
   white-lined sac-winged
   507
beaches. *See* playas
bees 224
Bellavista Fortress 109
bellbird, three-wattled 21–2,
   214, 536
bicycling 63, 91
   rentals 148
   tours 93–4
Biesanz, Barry 28, 140
Bijagua 220–1
biodiversity 19, 20, 171
biological reserves 22,
   **23**
   Bosque Nuboso
     Monteverde 212–5
   Durika 397–8
   Hitoy Cerere 359–60
   Isla del Caño 420
   Isla Pájaros 197
   Lomas de Barbudal
     223–4
   Nosara 290, 291
   Oro Verde 490
birding 21–2
   Caribbean lowlands 346,
     380
   central Pacific Coast 483,
     485

**Bold** indicates maps.

Central Valley 189, 190
Golfo Dulce 446
Isla del Coco 422
northern lowlands 316,
    320, 321, 325, 329,
    330
northwestern Costa Rica
    201–2, 214, 216,
    222–3, 224, 230, 235
Península de Nicoya 300–1
southern Costa Rica 386,
    387, 390, 406, 407
birds. See also individual
    species
    books 43
    cormorants & anhingas
        518
    cuckoos 527–8
    ducks 520
    extinction 21
    game 523
    herons & relatives 519–20
    hummingbirds 529–31
    kingfishers 532
    motmots 533
    nightjars & relatives 528–9
    owls 528
    parrots 526–7
    passerines 534–6
    pigeons & doves 526
    of prey 521–3
    rails & relatives 524–5
    seabirds 517–8
    shorebirds & gulls 525
    swifts 529
    tinamous 517
    toucans 533–4
    trogons 531
    vultures 521
    woodpeckers & relatives
        534
blacks
    discrimination against
        28–9, 56
    history 14, 26, 28, 357
    population 26, 332, 357
    religion 30
boats 91–2, 354, 355, 435–6.
    See also cruises; sailing
Bonita, Playa 339, 341–2
books 42–4, 369. See also
    literature
bookstores 106
border crossings 77–80
    Nicaragua 77–9

Panama 79–80
Boruca, RI 398
Borucas (people) 26, 398
Bosque del Cabo 430–1
Bosque Nuboso Monteverde,
    RB 212–5
botanical gardens. See
    gardens
bowling 112
Brasilito, Playa 270–1
Braulio Carrillo, PN 173–6
Bribri (people) 19, 26, 30, 43,
    332, 369, 371
Bribri (village) 381
Buenos Aires 397
bullfighting 70
bungee jumping 65
buses 142–6
    domestic 86–7, 142–3
    international 77
    local 92
business hours 57
butterflies 43, 540
    Butterfly Farm 157
    Butterfly Garden 200
    La Paz Waterfall Gardens
        165–7
    morpho 540
    Selva Verde 325
    Spirogyra Jardín de
        Mariposas 110

## C

Cabécares 19, 26, 30, 332,
    371
Cabinas Caña Blanca 442
Cabo Blanco, Reserva Natural
    Absoluta 310
Cabuya 309–10
Cacao Biological Station
    237–8
Cacao, Playa 439
cacomistle 511
Café Britt Finca 170–1
cafés 130
Cahuita (village) 360–6, 361
Cahuita, PN 366–8, 366
caimans 537, 538
Calderón Fournier, Rafael
    Angel 14
Calderón Guardia, Rafael
    Angel 13
camping. See accommoda-
    tions
Cañas 217–20, 218

Cañazas 425
Caño Negro, RNVS 316–8
canoeing 348, 414
canopy tours 64, 94, 174–5,
    202–3, 269, 386, 432,
    454, 467, 485–6
capuchin monkey, white-
    faced 508
caracaras 523
Carara, PN 455–6
Carate 431
Carazo, Rodrigo 161
Cariari Country Club 112
Caribbean Conservation
    Corporation (CCC)
    347–8
Caribbean lowlands 332–82,
    334–5
carretas 28, 71, 160
Carretera Interamericana 88,
    193, 196, 383, 425
Carrillo, Playa 297–8
cars
    accidents 57, 88, 90
    driver's license 36
    driving to Costa Rica
        76–80
    ferries 91, 217, 289, 299,
        453–4
    insurance 36, 77, 89
    renting 89–90, 147
    road guides 42
    road rules 87–9
Cartago 12, 177–9, 178
Casa de Orquídeas 441
casinos 139–40
Catarata de La Fortuna
    243–4
Catarata la Paz 165–7
Catholicism 30
CATIE 188
Cattleya skinneri 20, 21
caving 288, 314
central Pacific coast 447–93,
    448
Central Valley 149–92, 150–1
Centro Neotrópico Sarapiquís
    326–7
Centro Turístico Cataratas
    Nauyaca 486–7
Cerro de la Muerte 388
Cerro Tortuguero 348
charter flights 85
cheese 200
chiggers 48

children
    activities for 109, 111
    traveling with 54
Chiquita, Playa 377–8
Chirripó, PN 50, 394–7
cholera 47
Chorotegas 11, 26, 28, 284
churches, historic 177–8
cinemas 138
Ciudad Cutris 321
Ciudad Neily. See Neily
Ciudad Quesada (San Carlos)
    241–3
climate 16, 17
climbing 50, 175–6, 348,
    396–7
clothing
    appropriate 30, 52
    laundry 45
    packing 34
cloud forests. See tropical
    forests
clubs 136–8
coati, white-nosed 511
Cóbano 303
Coca-Cola bus terminal 103,
    **102**
Cocles, Playa 376–7
Cocos Island 422–3
coffee
    cafés 130
    exports 25
    history 13, 25
    shopping 70
    tours 170–1
Colonia Virgen del Socorro
    321
Columbus, Christopher 12,
    339
Conchal, Playa 271
Conselvatur 358–9
conservation 9, 17–20, 22,
    171, 212–3, 349
consulates 36–7
coot, American 524
coral reefs 367
Corcovado Lodge Tent Camp
    432–3
Corcovado, PN 420–5
Cordillera Central 15, 149
Cordillera de Guanacaste 15,
    193

Cordillera de Talamanca 15,
    16, 149, 408
Cordillera de Tilarán 15, 193
cormorant 518
Coronado 177
Coronado, Juan Vásquez de
    12
Corrales, José Miguel 14
corruption 88
Costa Flores 336
costs 39–40
COTERC 349
cotingas
    lovely 536
    snowy 535–6
    three-wattled bellbird
        21–2, 214, 536
    turquoise 536
courier flights 73
coyote 510
crafts 28, 70–1, 159–60, 284
credit cards 38–9
crime 39, 55, 67, 107–8, 358
Crocodile Bridge 455
crocodiles 455, 457, 537,
    538
cruises 80–1, 94
ctenosaur 537
cuckoos 527–8
currency 37
Curú, RNVS 302
customs 37
cycads 439
cycling. See bicycling

**D**

dance classes 113
dance clubs 136–8
debit cards 38–9
deer 515
deforestation 17–9, 20
democracy 13–5
dengue fever 47
diarrhea 46
disabled travelers 53–4, 73
diving 62, 82
    Caribbean lowlands 372,
        379
    central Pacific Coast 492
    Península de Nicoya 263,
        264, 268, 276
    Península de Osa 414,
        420
documents 35–6
dogs 51, 315

dolphins 415, 418–9, 491,
    517
Dominical 486–8
Doña Ana, Playa 454
Dos Brazos 425
dove, ruddy ground 526
Drake Bay 413–8, **414**
drinks 69–70
driving. See cars
drugs 57, 358
ducks 520
Durika, RB 397–8
dysentery 46

**E**

eagle, harpy 21, 380, 422,
    523
EARTH 336
earthquakes 56, 289
Ecolodge San Luis &
    Biological Station 216
ecology 16–17. See also
    environmental issues
Ecomuseo de las Minas de
    Abangares 217
economy 25–6
ecotourism 18, 19–20, 289,
    326–7. See also birding;
    nature tours; wildlife
    watching
    books 43
    responsible 33
education 26–7, 204–5. See
    also language courses
egrets 519
El Gavilán 328
El Manatial de Agua Viva
    456–7
El Portón Blanco 429–30
electricity 45
email 41–2
embassies 36–7
emergencies 56
    driving accidents 90
    medical 51
employment 65
endangered species 21
entertainment 70, 136–40
environmental issues 17–20,
    201, 268, 303, 322,
    367
Escalante, Geovanny 28
Escazú 101, 125–7, 135–6,
    **104–5**
Espadilla, Playa 478

Esquinas Rainforest Lodge 400
Estación Altamira 408
Estación Biológica La Selva 329–30
Esterillos area 466
etiquette 28–30
exchange rates 37–8
exports 25

**F**

falcon, laughing 523
farms, organic 203, 358
fauna. *See* wildlife
fax 41
fer-de-lance 49
Ferdinand, King 12
Fernández, Juan Mora 13
ferries 91, 217, 289, 299, 453–4
festivals 27, 205, 372
fiction 44
field guides 43
Figueres Ferrer, José (Don Pepe) 13, 14
Figueres, José María 14
Filadelfia 270
films 138
Finca Anael 397
Finca del Eddie Serrano 387
Finca Ecológica 202
Finca La Isla Botanical Garden 371
finch, Cocos Island 422
first-aid kit 46
Fischel, Astrid 51
fishing 59–60
    Caribbean lowlands 343–4, 354–7
    central Pacific Coast 469
    Golfo Dulce 435–6, 442
    northern lowlands 321
    northwestern Costa Rica 252
    Península de Nicoya 263, 275, 305
    Península de Osa 414
    tours 82, 94
Flamingo, Playa 271–2
flora. *See* plants
food 46, 67–9
Fortuna 243–50, **244**
fox, gray 510
freighters 81
frigatebirds 517–8

frogs
    disappearance of 201
    poison-arrow 320, 539
FUDEIBOL Reserve 390
furniture 70, 160
fútbol. *See* soccer

**G**

gallinules 524
gambling 139–40
Gandoca-Manzanillo, RNVS 379–81
gardens
    Arenal Botanical Gardens 252–3
    Butterfly Garden 200
    Casa de Orquídeas 441
    Centro Neotrópico Sarapiquís 327
    Finca La Isla Botanical Garden 371
    Jardín Botánico Las Cusingas 333, 335
    La Paz Waterfall Gardens 165–7
    Lankester Gardens 181
    Selva Verde 325
    Spirogyra Jardín de Mariposas 110
    Wilson Botanical Garden 406–7
Garrón, Victoria 51
gays & lesbians
    attitudes toward 52–3
    meeting places 53, 138, 478
    organizations 53
    tourism 29, 53
Genesis II 386–7
geography 15–6
geology 16
global warming 19
golf 112
Golfito (town) 433–9, **434–5**
Golfito, RNFS 439–40
Golfo Dulce 433–46, **411**
González Dávila, Gil 12, 286
government 24–5
Grande, Playa 280
Grecia 159
greetings 30
grison 512
ground-dove, ruddy 526
Guabito (Pan) 80
Guácimo 336

Guaitil 284
guan, black 523
guanacaste 235
Guanacaste, PN 237–9
Guápiles 333, 335–6
Guatuso (people) 315
Guatuso (town) 314–5
Guayabo (village) 221
Guayabo, Monumento Nacional 11, 188–9
Guayami 26
guidebooks 42–3
gulls 525

**H**

Hacienda Barú 484–6
harpy eagle 21, 380, 422, 523
hawks 522–3
health issues 45–51
    first-aid kit 46
    medical problems 46–51
    treatment 50, 51
    vaccinations 46
    water & food 46
heat, effects of 50
hepatitis 46
Heredia 167–70, **168**
hermits 530
Hermosa, Playa 267–8, 462, 464
herons 519–20
Herradura, Playa 458–9
highlights 32
hiking & backpacking 62–3
    books 43
    Caribbean lowlands 348
    central Pacific Coast 482–3, 485
    Central Valley 175–6
    northern lowlands 325, 329–30
    northwestern Costa Rica 201–2, 214–5, 230–1
    Península de Nicoya 310
    Península de Osa 414, 421, 422–4
    safety 56, 421
    southern Costa Rica 390, 394–7
    tours 93
history 11–5
hitchhiking 91
Hitoy Cerere, RB 359–60
HIV 49–50

holidays 57–8
homestays. *See* accommodations
Horquetas 322
horseback riding 63–4
    central Pacific Coast 485, 487
    Golfo Dulce 442
    northwestern Costa Rica 203, 204, 212
    Península de Nicoya 304
    Península de Osa 414
hostels. *See* accommodations
hot springs 182, 220, 221, 230–1, 393
hotels. *See* accommodations
houseboats 355
howler monkey 368, 509–10
Huetares 26
hummingbirds 201, 529–31
    fiery-throated 164, 531
    flower mite 540
    green violet-ear 530–1
    hermits 530
    violet sabrewing 530
    white-necked jacobin 530
humpback whale 517
Hurricane Mitch 15
hydrobiking 348

**I**

ibis 520
iguana, green 454, 537
Iguana Park 454
immunizations 46
INBio 19, 171
independence 12–3
indigenous peoples 26, 29, 30, 141
    Borucas 26, 398
    Bribri 19, 26, 30, 43, 332, 369, 371
    Cabécares 19, 26, 30, 332, 371
    Chorotegas 11, 26, 28, 284
    Guatuso 314, 315
    Guaymi 26
    Huetares 26
    Malekus 26
    Quepoa 466
    Térrabas 26

indigenous reserves 22, 26, **23**
    Boruca 398
    Cocles/KéköLdi 371
    Guatuso 314
    Talamanca Cabecar 371
insects
    museums 110, 326
    problems with 47–8
    species of 540
    tour 415
Instituto Clodomiro Picado 177
Instituto Nacional de Biodiversidad (INBio) 19, 171
insurance
    car 36, 77, 89
    travel 35–6, 46
Interamericana. *See* Carretera Interamericana
International Arts Festival 27
international transfers 39
Internet
    access 41–2
    resources 42
Irazú 179–81
Isla Catalina 263, 264, 272
Isla Damas 483
Isla del Caño, RB 420
Isla del Coco, PN 422–3
Isla Gitana 300
Isla Guayabo 300
Isla Pájaros, RB 197
Isla San Lucas 300, 301
Isla Tortuga 300
Isla Uvita 339
Islas Negritos 300
Islita 298–9

**J**

jabiru 520
jacana, northern 525
Jacó 459–66, **459, 460**
jacobin, white-necked 530
jade 108–9
jaguar 513
jaguarundi 514
Janzen, Daniel H 233
Jardín Botánico Las Cusingas 333, 335
Jardines de la Catarata La Paz 165–7
jays 536
Jicaral 299
Juan Castro Blanco, PN 163

Juan Santamaría International Airport 72, 141
Junquillal, Playa 282–4
Juntas 217

**K**

kayaking 64–5, 93, 263, 348, 379, 414, 436, 483, 485. *See also* river running
kingfishers 532
kinkajou 511
kites 522

**L**

La Amistad, Parque Internacional 407–9
La Casona 234–5
La Cruz 239–40
La Danta Selvaje 335
La Fortuna de San Carlos 243–50, **244**
La Garita 158
La Laguna del Lagarto Lodge 320
La Palma 425
La Quinta de Sarapiquí Lodge 326
La Selva 329–30
La Tigra 161
La Virgen 321, 327, 328
Lago de Cachí 181
Laguna de Arenal 63, 252–7
Laguna Fraijanes 163
Laguna Hule 321
language courses 30–1, 65
    Dominical 487
    Heredia 167, 169
    Jacó 461
    Orosi 183
    Quepos 472–3
    San José 113–4
languages
    indigenous 30
    Spanish 30–1
Lankester Gardens 181
Lapa Ríos 430
Las Baulas de Guanacaste, PNM 280–1
Las Pumas 219
*Latin American Travel Advisor* 54
laundry 45
legal matters 56–7
leishmaniasis 47
Lepanto 299

lesbians. *See* gays & lesbians
Liberia 17, 224–9, **225**
lice 48
life zones 17–8
literature 27. *See also* books
Little Theater Group 27
lizards 537
llanuras 311
Lomas de Barbudal, RB 223–4
Los Angeles Cloud Forest Reserve 161–2
Los Chiles 78–9, 318–20
Lucky Bug Gallery 256

## M

macaws
  great green 320, 527
  scarlet 422, 455, 526
machismo 51–2
magazines 44
mail 40
Mal País 308–9
malaria 47
Malekus 26
mammals 43, 505–17. *See also individual species*
manatee, West Indian 517
mangroves 280, 485, 491
Manuel Antonio (area) 472–84, **480–1**
Manuel Antonio (village) 478–9
Manuel Antonio, PN 479, 482–3
Manzanillo 379
manzanillo 483
maps 33–4, 42
margay 513
Maritza Biological Station 237
massage 275, 290, 371, 472
Mata de Limón 455
Matapalo 484
measurements 45
meditation 371
Mercado Central 111
Meseta Central. *See* Central Valley
MINAE 22
mining 217
Mirador de Quetzales 387
Miravalles 221–2
mite, hummingbird flower 540

Moin 342–3
money 37–40
monkeys 483, 508–10
  howler 368, 509–10
  spider 509
  squirrel 508
  white-faced capuchin 508
Monte de la Cruz 171, 172
Monteverde 197–212, **198–9**
  accommodations 205–10
  entertainment 211
  restaurants 210–1
  transportation 211–2
Monteverde Music Festival 27, 205
Montezuma 303–8, **304**
moorhen 524
Mora, Juan Rafael 13
Moravia 176
morpho butterfly 540
mosquitoes 47, 48
motmots 533
motorcycles
  accidents 90
  renting 90, 147
  road rules 87–9
mountain biking. *See* bicycling
mountain lion 514
movies 138
Muelle de San Carlos 313–4
Mundo de la Tortuga 281
museums
  Centro Neotrópico Sarapiquís 327
  Ecomuseo de las Minas de Abangares 217
  Museo de Arte Costarricense 109
  Museo de Arte y Diseño Contemporáneo 109
  Museo de Ciencias Naturales 109–10
  Museo de Criminología 110
  Museo de Cultura Popular 170–1
  Museo de Insectos 110
  Museo de Jade 11, 108–9
  Museo de los Niños 109
  Museo de Oro Precolombino 11, 109
  Museo de San Ramón 161
  Museo Joyas del Trópico Húmedo 326

Museo Juan Santamaría 152, 154
Museo Nacional 109
Museo Postal, Telegráfico y Filatélico de Costa Rica 110
Museo Zoomarino 167
music
  festivals 27, 205, 372
  live 136
  National Symphony Orchestra 27

## N

Naranjo, Carmen 27
Naranjo, Playa 299–300
national marine parks 22, **23**
  Ballena 491–2
  Las Baulas de Guanacaste 280–1
national parks 22–4, 43, **23**
  Barra Honda 288–99
  Braulio Carrillo 173–6
  Cahuita 366–8, **366**
  Carara 455–6
  Chirripó 50, 394–7
  Corcovado 420–5
  Guanacaste 237–9
  Isla del Coco 422–3
  Juan Castro Blanco 163
  Manuel Antonio 479, 482–3
  Palo Verde 222–3
  Rincón de la Vieja 229–33
  Santa Rosa 233–6
  Tapantí-Macizo Cerro de la Muerte 184
  Tortuguero 344–6
  Turrialba 189–90
  Volcán Arenal 250–2
  Volcán Irazú 179–81
  Volcán Poás 163–5
  Volcán Tenorio 220
National Symphony Orchestra 27
national wildlife refuges 22, **23**
  Bahía Junquillal 236–7
  Barra del Colorado 352–7, **353**
  Caño Negro 316–8
  Curú 302
  Gandoca-Manzanillo 379–81
  Golfito 439–40

Ostional 293–4
Peñas Blancas 196–7
native peoples. See indigenous peoples
nature tours 81–2, 93, 355
Negra, Playa 281–2, 360
Neily 400–2, **401**
newspapers 44
Nicaragua
  boats to 324, 354
  border crossings 77–9
  buses to 143–4
  entry requirements 78
Nicoya 286–8, **286**
Nicuesa, Diego de 12
nightjars 528–9
northern lowlands 311–31, **312**
northwestern Costa Rica 193–258, **194–5**
Nosara, Playa 290–3
Nosara, RB 290, 291
Nuevo Arenal. See Arenal (village)
nunbird, white-fronted 534

**O**

ocelot 424, 513
Ocotal, Playa 268–9
Odio, Elizabeth 51
Ojo de Agua 156–7
olingo 511
oncilla 513
opossums 505
orchids 20, 43, 181
Oro Verde, RB 490
oropendolas 189, 536
Orosi 182–3
osprey 521–2
Ostional, RNFS 293–4
otter, southern river 512
owl, spectacled 528
ox carts. See carretas

**P**

paca 515–6
Pacheco, Abel 14–5, 25
packing 34
Pacuare Nature Reserve 344
Palmar Norte 398–400, **399**
Palmar Sur 398–400
Palmares 161

Palo Verde, PN 222–3
Pan de Azúcar, Playa 273
Panama
  border crossings 79–80
  buses to 144
  entry requirements 79
Panamá, Playa 268
Papagayo Project 268
Paquera 301–2
Paraíso 181, 282
parakeet, orange-fronted 527
Parismina 343–4
Parque Internacional La Amistad 407–9
Parque La Sabana 112
Parque Purisil 183
Parque Viborana 188
Parque Zoológico Simón Bolívar 110
parques nacionales. See national parks
Parrita 466
parrots 526–7
  great green macaw 320, 527
  mealy 527
  scarlet macaw 422, 455, 526
Paso Canoas 79–80, 402–4, **403**
passerines 534–6
passports 35
pauraque, common 528, 529
Pavones 445–6
Pecas Figueres, Cecilia Facio 28
peccaries 514
pelicans 300, 518
Peñas Blancas (border post) 77–8, 241
Peñas Blancas, RNFS 196–7
Península de Nicoya 259–310, **260–1**
Península de Osa 410–33, **411**
Penon, Margarita 14, 51
phones 40–1
photography 44–5
Picado, Teodoro 13
pickpockets 39
piculet, olivaceous 534
pigeons 526
Piñuela, Playa 492
Pitilla Biological Station 238
planning 32–4

plants 20. See also gardens; individual species
playas (beaches)
  Avellana 281–2
  Bahía Ballena 492
  Bahía Potrero 272
  Bonita 339, 341–2
  Brasilito 270–1
  Cacao 439
  Carrillo 297–8
  Chiquita 377–8
  Cocles 376–7
  Conchal 271
  del Coco 262–7, **262**
  Doña Ana 454
  Espadilla 478
  Flamingo 271–2
  Grande 280
  Hermosa 267–8, 462, 464
  Herradura 458–9
  Junquillal 282–4
  Naranjo 299–300
  Negra 281–2, 360
  Nosara 290–3
  Ocotal 268–9
  Pan de Azúcar 273
  Panamá 268
  Piñuela 492
  Pochote 302–3
  Sámara 294–7, **295**
  San Josecito 440–1
  Tamarindo 274–80, **274**
  Tambor 302–3
  Tortuga 492
  Ventanas 492
  Zancudo 442–4
Poás 163–5
Pochote, Playa 302–3
poison-arrow frogs 539
police 55, 88
politics 10, 14–5, 24–5, 43
Poll, Claudia 64
population 26
porcupine 516
Portete 341–2
postal services 40
potoos 529
pottery 11, 28, 71, 284
pre-Columbian cultures 11–2, 188–9, 321, 398, 420
prostitution 29, 49
provinces 24, **24**
Proyecto Nacaome 289
Puerto Caldero 455
Puerto Jiménez 425–9, **426**

Puerto Limón 17, 337–41, **338, 342**
Puerto Viejo de Sarapiquí 321, 323–5, **323**
Puerto Viejo de Talamanca 368–76, **370**
puma 514
Punta Leona 457–8
Punta Uva 378–9
Puntarenas 17, 447, 449–54, **450**
Puntarenas Marine Park 449

### Q

Quakers 29, 197, 205, 212
Quepoa 466
Quepos 466–72, **468**
quetzal, resplendent 184, 214, 387, 388, 531

### R

rabbits 516
rabies 51
raccoons 510
racism 28–9, 56
radio 44
rafting. See river running
rail, gray-necked wood  524
Rainbow Adventures 441–2
Rainforest Aerial Tram 174–5
rainforests. See tropical forests
Rainmaker 467
Ranarium 200
Rancho La Botija 390
Rancho La Merced 490
Rancho Leona 327–8
Rancho Naturalista 190–1
Rancho Redondo 177
raptors 380, 521–3
Rara Avis 330–1
Red Cross 51, 90
Refugio de Vida Silvestre Cipanci 219
religion 30
reptiles 537–8
Reserva Natural Absoluta Cabo Blanco 310
Reserva Santa Elena 215–6
Reserva Sendero Tranquilo 202
restaurants 67–9. See also individual locations
retirement 42
Rincón 425

Rincón de la Vieja, PN 229–33
Río Celeste 220
Río Chirripó 391
Río Claro 400
Río Corobicí 218–9
Río Estrella 359
Río Frío 322
Río Macho 182
Río Orosi valley 181–2
Río Pacuare 191–2
Río Palomo 182
Río Peñas Blancas 245
Río Reventazón 184–5
Río San Juan 325, 352, 354
Río Sarapiquí 321–2, 324
Río Sereno (Pan) 80
Río Sierpe 410, 412–3
Río Toro 245
riptides 55–6
river running 60, 62
    books 43
    Río Chirripó 391
    Río Corobicí 218–9
    Río Pacuare 191–2
    Río Peñas Blancas 245
    Río Reventazón 184–5
    Río Sarapiquí 321–2
    Río Toro 245
    safety 58–9
    tours 93
rodents 515–6
Rodríguez, Miguel Angel 14, 25
Ruta de los Santos (Route of the Saints) 383–4, 386

### S

sabaneros 226
sabrewing, violet 530
Sacramento 171
safety issues. See also health issues
    adventure activities 58–9
    canopy tours 58–9, 64
    crime 39, 55, 67, 107–8, 358
    earthquakes 56
    hiking 56, 421
    swimming 55–6
sailing 263, 276
Salsa Brava 371
Sámara, Playa 294–7, **295**
Samasati Retreat Center 371
San Carlos 241–3

San Gerardo de Dota 387–8
San Gerardo de Rivas 393–4
San Isidro de Coronado 177
San Isidro de El General 389–93, **389**
San José 96–148, 104–5, **97–102**
    accommodations 115–28
    activities 112
    climate 17
    entertainment 136–40
    highlights 96
    language courses 113–4
    organized tours 114–5
    restaurants 128–36
    shopping 140–1
    sports 140
    transportation 141–8
San José de la Montaña 171, 172
San Josecito, Playa 440–1
San Juan del Norte (Nic) 354
San Miguel 321
San Pedro de Barva 171
San Rafael de Guatuso 314–5
San Ramón 161
San Vicente de Moravia 176
San Vito 404–6, **404**
sand flies 47
sanderling 525
sandpipers 525
SANSA 84–5, 141–2
Santa Bárbara 171, 172
Santa Cruz 284–5
Santa Elena (village) 197–212, **198–9**
    accommodations 205–10
    entertainment 211
    restaurants 210–1
    transportation 211–2
Santa Elena, Reserva 215–6
Santa Rosa, PN 233–6
Santamaría, Juan 13, 152, 154
Santo Domingo de Heredia 172–3
Sarapiquí Ecolodge 330
Sarchí 159–61
scorpions 48
scuba diving. See diving
Selva Verde 325–6
Sendero Bosque Nuboso 214–5
Sendero Tranquilo, Reserva 202

senior travelers 54
Serpentario 109
Serpentarium 200
sex tourism 29, 53
sexually transmitted diseases 49
shopping 70–1, 140–1
showers 67
Sí a Paz 318
Sierpe 410, 412–3
SINAC 22
Siquirres 336–7
Sirena 423–4
Sixaola 80, 381–2
skunks 511–2
Sky Walk 202
sloths 324, 339, 359, 455, 506
smoking 30
snakes
   bites 48–9
   places to see 109, 159, 177, 188, 200
   species of 537
snorkeling 62
   Caribbean lowlands 367, 372, 379
   Península de Nicoya 263, 269, 304
   Península de Osa 414, 420
soccer 15, 70, 156
soil erosion 17
Solís, Ottón 14–5
South American Explorers (SAE) 54
South Caribbean Music Festival 27, 372
southern Costa Rica 383–409, **384–5**
Spanish. See languages
Spanish conquest 12
special events 57–8
spelunking. See caving
spider monkey 509
spiders 48
Spirogyra Jardín de Mariposas 110
spoonbill, roseate 519–20
sports 70. See also soccer
squirrel monkey 508
squirrels 516
STDs 49

stone spheres 11–2, 398, 420
storks 520
street addresses 103, 186
students 72
sunbittern 325, 524–5
sunburn 50
sungrebe 524
surfing 60, **61**
   attitude 487
   Caribbean lowlands 371–2
   central Pacific Coast 460–1, 487
   Golfo Dulce 433, 443, 445
   northwestern Costa Rica 236
   Península de Nicoya 263, 274, 275, 290
   tours 82
swifts 529
swimming 55–6, 64, 112, 433. See also playas (beaches)

**T**

Tamarindo, Playa 274–80, **274**
Tambor, Playa 302–3
tanagers 535
Tapantí-Macizo Cerro de la Muerte, PN 184
tapir, Baird's 407, 515
Tárcoles 456–7
taxes 40, 67
taxis 90–1, 92, 147–8
tayra 512
teal, blue-winged 520
Teatro Nacional 27, 110–1, 138
telephones 40–1
television 44
Tempisque ferry 217, 289
tennis 112
Tenorio, PN 220
Terrabas 26
theater 27, 110–1, 138–9
tickets
   buying airline 72–4
   onward 35
Tilarán 257–8
time zone 45
tinamous 517
Tinoco, Federico 13
tipping 40
Tirimbina Rainforest Center 327

Tiskita Jungle Lodge 446
Toad Hall 254
toads
   disappearance of 201
   golden 201
   marine 539
toilets 45, 67
topes 226
Tortuga, Playa 492
Tortuguero (village) 346–52, **347**
Tortuguero, PN 344–6
toucans 533–4
tourism. See also ecotourism
   growth in 18, 25
   healthcare 50
   responsible 33, 205
   sex 29, 53
tourist offices 34–5
tours, organized 81–3, 92–5. See also individual activities
traffic signs 87
trains 87, 333
transportation
   air travel 72–6, 84–5
   bicycles 91
   boats 80–1, 91–2
   buses 77, 86–7, 92, 142–6
   cars 76–80, 87–90
   hitchhiking 91
   motorcycles 87–90
   taxis 90–1, 92
   trains 87
travel insurance 35–6, 46
Travelair 84–5, 141–2
traveler's checks 38
Trejos, José Juaquin 14
Trejos, Juan José 14
trekking. See hiking & backpacking
Trinidad Lodge 328–9
trogons 531
tropical forests. See also individual parks & reserves
   books 43
   canopy tours 64, 94, 174–5, 202–3, 269, 386, 432, 454, 467, 485–6
   destruction of 17–9, 20
   importance of 17–8
   plants in 20
Turrialba (town) 185–8, **185**
Turrialba, PN 189–90

turtles
  green 293, 344, 345–6,
    538
  leatherback 280, 293,
    346, 380, 538
  olive ridley 235, 293, 486,
    538
  protecting 293, 346, 380
  watching 235, 280–1,
    293–4, 345–6
TV 44

## U

Ujarrás 181
Ulate, Otilio 13
Upala 315–6
Uvita 490–1

## V

vaccinations 46
Valle de la Estrella 359
vampire bats 51, 507–8
Venado 254
Ventanas, Playa 492
video 44–5
violet-ear, green 530–1
visas 35
volcanoes 15
  Arenal 15, 203, 243,
    250–2
  Barva 175–6
  Irazú 179–81
  Miravalles 221–2
  Poás 163–5

Rincón de la Vieja 229–33
Tenorio 220
Turrialba 189–90
volunteer opportunities 65,
  344, 347–8, 349, 380,
  386, 486
vultures 521

## W

Walker, William 13, 111, 233
water 46
water parks 157
waterfalls
  Catarata de La Fortuna
    243–4
  Catarata La Paz 165–7
  Cataratas Nauyaca 486–7
  El Manatial de Agua Viva
    456–7
water-skiing 263
weasels 512
websites 42
weights 45
whales 517
wildlife 505–40. See also
  biological reserves;
  national wildlife refuges;
  individual species
  amphibians 539
  birds 517–36
  endangered species 21
  field guides 43
  insects 540
  mammals 505–17

number of species 20–1
  reptiles 537–8
wildlife watching 21–2, 59
  Caribbean lowlands 346
  central Pacific Coast 483
  northern lowlands 319
  northwestern Costa Rica
    216, 230, 235–6
  Península de Nicoya 310
  Península de Osa 421–2,
    424
Wilson Botanical Garden
  406–7
windsurfing 63, 240, 253
women
  attitudes toward 51–2
  clothing for 52
  organizations for 52
wooden bowls 28
woodpeckers 534
work 65
World of Snakes 159

## Y

yoga 275, 290, 371
Yoko Hot Springs 221

## Z

Zancudo, Playa 442–4
Zarcero 162–3
zoos
  Parque Zoológico Simón
    Bolívar 110
  Zoo Ave 158

Bold indicates maps.

# Boxed Text

Banana Trains 333
Bananas 322
Biological Investigation 424
Bird Extinction 21
Blowing, Blowing & Blowing... 28
Books on Local Culture 369
Clamor in Tambor 303
Claudia Poll's Gold 64
Communicating with Costa Rica 41
Coral Reefs 367
Costa Rican Street Addresses 103
COTERC 349
Crossing Borders 79
Dance Schools 113
Dogs 315
Drinkers Beware 69
Driving Accidents 90
The Earthquake 289
Ecotourism 18
An Eerie Hike 368
Gambling Tico-Style 139
A Great Day at Corcovado 424
Guaitil 284
Healthcare Tourism 50
A Hike on the Sendero
   Bosque Nuboso 214
INBio 171
Indigenous Art 141
Insect Repellent 48

Kids' Stuff 111
Kissing Parks 107
Massage & Yoga 275
National Holidays 58
Pacuare Nature Reserve 344
Parque Nacional Isla del Coco 422–3
Police Corruption 88
Prostitution 29
The Quakers of Monteverde 197
Rainforest Aerial Tram 174–5
Rainmaker 467
Research at Santa Rosa 233
Responsible Tourism 33, 205
The Sabanero 226
Sailing to Nicaragua 324
Scuba Diving 264
Sí a Paz 318
Sleeping in a Houseboat 355
Slothful Habits 455
Surfer Cool 487
A Terrific Tumor 51
Time & Space 407
To Ride or Not to Ride? 204
Traffic Signs 87
Visiting the Wilderness 421
Warning 73
Where Am I? 186
Who Has Seen the Golden Toad? 201
World-Class Windsurfing 253

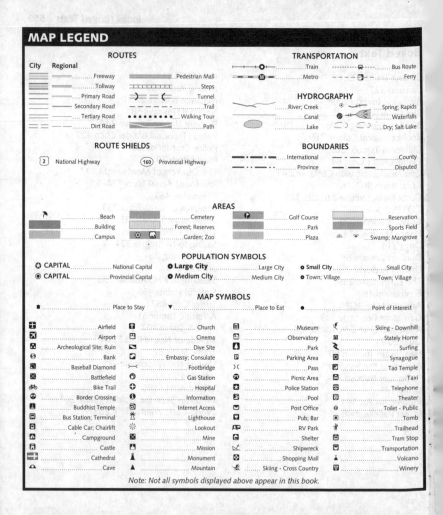

# MAP LEGEND

## ROUTES

| City | Regional | |
|---|---|---|
| | Freeway | Pedestrian Mall |
| | Tollway | Steps |
| | Primary Road | Tunnel |
| | Secondary Road | Trail |
| | Tertiary Road | Walking Tour |
| | Dirt Road | Path |

## ROUTE SHIELDS

2 National Highway    160 Provincial Highway

## TRANSPORTATION

Train ............... Bus Route
Metro ............... Ferry

## HYDROGRAPHY

River; Creek ............... Spring; Rapids
Canal ............... Waterfalls
Lake ............... Dry; Salt Lake

## BOUNDARIES

International ............... County
Province ............... Disputed

## AREAS

| | | |
|---|---|---|
| Beach | Cemetery | Golf Course | Reservation |
| Building | Forest; Reserves | Park | Sports Field |
| Campus | Garden; Zoo | Plaza | Swamp; Mangrove |

## POPULATION SYMBOLS

| | | | |
|---|---|---|---|
| ○ CAPITAL | National Capital | ● Large City | Large City |
| ◉ CAPITAL | Provincial Capital | ● Medium City | Medium City |
| | | ● Small City | Small City |
| | | ● Town; Village | Town; Village |

## MAP SYMBOLS

● Place to Stay          ▼ Place to Eat          ● Point of Interest

| | | | |
|---|---|---|---|
| Airfield | Church | Museum | Skiing - Downhill |
| Airport | Cinema | Observatory | Stately Home |
| Archeological Site; Ruin | Dive Site | Park | Surfing |
| Bank | Embassy; Consulate | Parking Area | Synagogue |
| Baseball Diamond | Footbridge | Pass | Tao Temple |
| Battlefield | Gas Station | Picnic Area | Taxi |
| Bike Trail | Hospital | Police Station | Telephone |
| Border Crossing | Information | Pool | Theater |
| Buddhist Temple | Internet Access | Post Office | Toilet - Public |
| Bus Station; Terminal | Lighthouse | Pub; Bar | Tomb |
| Cable Car; Chairlift | Lookout | RV Park | Trailhead |
| Campground | Mine | Shelter | Tram Stop |
| Castle | Mission | Shipwreck | Transportation |
| Cathedral | Monument | Shopping Mall | Volcano |
| Cave | Mountain | Skiing - Cross Country | Winery |

*Note: Not all symbols displayed above appear in this book.*

# LONELY PLANET OFFICES

## Australia
Locked Bag 1, Footscray, Victoria 3011
☎ 03 8379 8000  fax 03 8379 8111
email talk2us@lonelyplanet.com.au

## USA
150 Linden Street, Oakland, CA 94607
☎ 510 893 8555, TOLL FREE 800 275 8555
fax 510 893 8572
email info@lonelyplanet.com

## UK
10a Spring Place, London NW5 3BH
☎ 020 7428 4800 fax 020 7428 4828
email go@lonelyplanet.co.uk

## France
1 rue du Dahomey, 75011 Paris
☎ 01 55 25 33 00 fax 01 55 25 33 01
email bip@lonelyplanet.fr
www.lonelyplanet.fr

**World Wide Web: www.lonelyplanet.com** *or* **AOL keyword: lp**
**Lonely Planet Images: lpi@lonelyplanet.com.au**